Modern American Poetry
Modern British Poetry

EDITED BY *Louis Untermeyer*

NEW YORK • BURLINGAME

Printed in the United States of America

Library of Congress Catalog Card Number: 62-12185

YAS
STO

2-5-65

MODERN AMERICAN POETRY
and
MODERN BRITISH POETRY

Combined New and Enlarged Edition

COMBINED NEW AND ENLARGED EDITION

HARCOURT, BRACE & WORLD, INC.

NEW AND ENLARGED EDITION

Modern American Poetry

EDITED BY *Louis Untermeyer*

HARCOURT, BRACE & WORLD, INC.
NEW YORK • BURLINGAME

Printed in the United States of America

Library of Congress Catalog Card Number: 62-12183

LIST OF COPYRIGHTS

Vincent Millay, "Wild Swans," copyright 1920, 1948, by Edna St. Vincent Millay, from *Second April,* published by Harper & Brothers. "I Shall Go Back," "What Lips My Lips Have Kissed," "Pity Me Not," "Euclid Alone," copyright 1920, 1948, by Edna St. Vincent Millay, "Departure," copyright 1919, 1947, by Edna St. Vincent Millay, from *The Harp-Weaver and Other Poems,* published by Harper & Brothers. "Sonnet to Gath," and "Justice Denied in Massachusetts," copyright 1927, by Edna St. Vincent Millay, "On Hearing a Symphony," and "The Cameo," copyright 1928, by Edna St. Vincent Millay, from *The Buck in the Snow,* published by Harper & Brothers. "Oh, Sleep Forever in the Latmian Cave" from *Fatal Interview,* published by Harper & Brothers, copyright 1931, by Edna St. Vincent Millay. "The Return" and "See Where Capella with Her Golden Kids" from *Wine from These Grapes,* copyright 1934, by Edna St. Vincent Millay.

CITY LIGHTS BOOKS for quotation from Allen Ginsberg from *Howl and Other Poems,* copyright 1956, 1959, by Allen Ginsberg with the permission of City Lights Books.

CURTIS BROWN, LTD. for the poems from *The Bad Parent's Garden of Verse,* by Ogden Nash.

COWARD-MCCANN, INC. for the selections from *Compass Rose* by Elizabeth J. Coatsworth.

JOHN DAY COMPANY for the selections from *High Falcon* by Léonie Adams.

DIAL PRESS for the selections from *Observations* by Marianne Moore, copyright, 1924; and for "The Death of the Ball Turret Gunner" from *Little Friend,* by Randall Jarrell, copyright, 1945, by Dial Press, Inc.

DODD, MEAD & COMPANY for the selections from *Golden Fleece* by William Rose Benét, copyright 1935.

DOUBLEDAY & COMPANY, INC. for the selections from *Man Possessed* and *Moons of Grandeur,* by William Rose Benét, *The Man with the Hoe* and *Lincoln and Other Poems* by Edwin Markham, *Tiger Joy* and *John Brown's Body* by Stephen Vincent Benét, *Leaves of Grass* (Inclusive and Authorized Edition) by Walt Whitman, and "Ajanta" from *Beast in View* by Muriel Rukeyser, copyright 1944, by Muriel Rukeyser. "Elegy for Jane," "Four for Sir John Davies," and "The Waking," copyright 1950, 1952, 1953, by Theodore Roethke, from *The Waking* by Theodore Roethke, and "I Knew a Woman," copyright 1954, by Theodore Roethke, from *Words for the Wind (The Collected Verse of Theodore Roethke: 1958).* Reprinted by permission of Doubleday & Company, Inc.

RICHARD EBERHART for "Rainscapes, Hydrangeas, Roses and Singing Birds" and "A New England Bachelor" copyright 1960, 1961, by Richard Eberhart.

FABER AND FABER, LTD. for "Journey of the Magi" from *The Ariel Poems* by T. S. Eliot, with the permission of T. S. Eliot.

FARRAR, STRAUS & CUDAHY, INC. for "Waking in the Blue" and "Skunk Hour" from *Life Studies* by Robert Lowell, copyright 1956, 1959, by Robert Lowell. Used by permission of the publishers Farrar, Straus & Cudahy, Inc.

FOUR SEAS COMPANY for the selections from *The Charnel Rose* by Conrad Aiken, *The Jig of Forslin* by Conrad Aiken, and *The House of Dust* by Conrad Aiken, and *Sour Grapes* by William Carlos Williams.

HARCOURT, BRACE & WORLD, INC. for the selections from *American Poetry: A Miscellany: 1920, 1922; American Poetry: A Miscellany: 1925-1927; The Book of the American Negro; Collected Poems* by E. E. Cummings, copyright, 1923, 1925, 1931, 1935, 1938, by E. E. Cummings; *Behind Dark Spaces* by Melville Cane; *Poems: 1930-1940* by Horace Gregory, copyright, 1941; *Land of the Free* by Archibald MacLeish, copyright, 1938; *The Noise That Time Makes* and *Six Sides to a Man* by Merrill Moore; *Smoke and Steel,* copyright, 1920, by Carl Sandburg; *Slabs of the Sunburnt West* by Carl Sandburg, copyright, 1922; *Good Morning, America* by Carl Sandburg, copyright, 1928; *The People, Yes* by Carl Sandburg, copyright 1936; *Complete Poems* by Carl Sandburg, copyright, 1950; *Food and Drink* and *Selected Poems and Parodies* by Louis Untermeyer, copyright, 1935; *Losses* by Randall Jarrell, copyright, 1948, by Harcourt, Brace and Company, Inc.; *Selected Poems 1923-1943* by Robert Penn Warren, copyright, 1944, by Harcourt, Brace and Company, Inc.; *Lord Weary's Castle,* copyright, 1944, 1946, by Robert Lowell; *Stranger at Coney Island,* copyright, 1944, 1945, 1946, 1947, 1948, by Kenneth Fearing; *Collected Poems 1909-1935* by T. S. Eliot, copyright, 1936, by Harcourt, Brace and Company, Inc., *Four Quartets* by T. S. Eliot, copyright, 1943, by T. S. Eliot. "Advice to a Prophet," copyright, 1959, by Richard Wilbur, reprinted from *Advice to a Prophet and Other Poems* by Richard Wilbur, first published in *The New Yorker;* "In the Smoking-Car," copyright, 1960, by Richard Wilbur, reprinted from *Advice to a Prophet and Other Poems* by Richard Wilbur, first published in *The New Yorker;* "After the Last Bulletins," copyright, 1953, by *The New Yorker Magazine,* and "Love Calls Us to the Things of This World," © 1956 by Richard Wilbur, from *Things of This World* by Richard Wilbur; "Bell Speech" from *The Beautiful Changes and Other Poems,* copyright, 1947, by Richard Wilbur; "A World Without Objects Is a Sensible Emptiness" from *Ceremony and Other Poems,* copyright, 1948, 1949, 1950, by Richard Wilbur. "Falling Asleep Over the Aeneid" from *The Mills of the Kavanaughs,* copyright, 1946, 1947, 1948, 1950, 1951, by Robert Lowell. "anyone lived in a pretty how town," copyright, 1940, by E. E. Cummings, reprinted from *Poems 1923-1954* by E. E. Cummings; "what if a much of a which of a wind," copyright, 1944, by E. E. Cummings, reprinted from *Poems 1923-1954* by E. E. Cummings. "The Magnet," "In An Iridescent Time," "Vernal Equinox," from *In an Iridescent Time,* copyright, 1953, 1957, 1958, by Ruth Stone. These poems reprinted by permission of Harcourt, Brace & World, Inc.

HARPER & BROTHERS for the selections from *Copper Sun* and *Color* by Countee Cullen, *Renascence* (copyright 1917) by Edna St. Vincent Millay, *A Few Figs from Thistles* (copyright 1922) by Edna St.

Vincent Millay, *The Buck in the Snow* (copyright 1928) by Edna St. Vincent Millay, *Fatal Interview* (copyright 1931) by Edna St. Vincent Millay, and *Wine from These Grapes* (copyright 1934) by Edna St. Vincent Millay.

HARVARD ADVOCATE for "Asides on the Oboe," by Wallace Stevens.

HOLT, RINEHART & WINSTON, INC. for the selections from *A Boy's Will* (copyright 1915) by Robert Frost; *North of Boston* (copyright 1915) by Robert Frost; *Mountain Interval* (copyright 1916) by Robert Frost; *New Hampshire* (copyright 1923) by Robert Frost; *West-Running Brook* (copyright 1928) by Robert Frost; *A Further Range* (copyright 1936) by Robert Frost; *A Witness Tree* (copyright 1942) by Robert Frost; *Steeple Bush* (copyright 1947) by Robert Frost; *Complete Poems of Robert Frost: 1949* (copyright 1949). "Directive" and "Acquainted with the Night" from *Complete Poems of Robert Frost,* copyright 1930, 1949 by Holt, Rinehart & Winston, Inc. These poems reprinted by permission of the publishers. The selections from *Chicago Poems,* copyright, 1916, by Carl Sandburg, and *Cornhuskers,* copyright, 1918, by Carl Sandburg, reprinted by permission of Carl Sandburg and the publishers, Holt, Rinehart & Winston, Inc.

HOUGHTON MIFFLIN COMPANY for the selections from *The Shoes That Danced* by Anna Hempstead Branch, *Sea Gardens* by H. D., *Preludes and Symphonies* by John Gould Fletcher, *Sword Blades and Poppy Seed* (copyright 1914) by Amy Lowell, *What's O'Clock* (copyright 1925) by Amy Lowell, *Selected Poems by Amy Lowell* (copyright 1922, 1925, 1926, and 1927), *Streets in the Moon* (copyright 1926) by Archibald MacLeish, *New Found Land* (copyright 1930) by Archibald MacLeish, *Poems: 1924-1933* (copyright 1933) by Archibald MacLeish, *Panic* (copyright 1935) by Archibald MacLeish, and the quotations from *Some Imagist Poets,* and *North & South* (copyright 1946) by Elizabeth Bishop. "You, Dr. Martin," "Funnel," and "Some Foreign Letters" from *To Bedlam and Part Way Back* by Anne Sexton, copyright © by Anne Sexton. These poems used by permission of and by special arrangement with the publishers.

BARBARA HOWES for "On Galveston Beach" copyright 1960, 1961 by Barbara Howes.

ALFRED A. KNOPF, INC. for the selections from *Punch: The Immortal Liar* (copyright 1921) by Conrad Aiken; *A Letter to Robert Frost* (copyright 1937) by Robert Hillyer; *Pattern of a Day* (copyright 1940) by Robert Hillyer; *The Collected Verse of Robert Hillyer* (copyright 1933); *Fine Clothes to the Jew* (copyright 1927) by Langston Hughes; *Lustra* (copyright 1917) by Ezra Pound; *Chills and Fever* (copyright 1924) by John Crowe Ransom; *Two Gentlemen in Bonds* (copyright 1927) by John Crowe Ransom; *Harmonium* (copyright 1923) by Wallace Stevens; *Parts of a World* (copyright 1942) by Wallace Stevens; *Transport to Summer* (copyright 1942-1947) by Wallace Stevens; *Travelling Standing Still* (copyright 1922, 1928) by Genevieve Taggard; *Nets to Catch the Wind* (copyright 1921) by Elinor Wylie; *Black Armour* (copyright 1923) by Elinor Wylie; *Trivial Breath* (copyright 1928) by Elinor Wylie; *Angels and Earthly Creatures* (copyright 1929) by Elinor Wylie; and *Collected Poems of Elinor Wylie* (copyright 1932). "Ten Days Leave," "Song," and "Heart's Needle (Child of my winter, born)" from *Heart's Needle* by William Snodgrass, copyright 1956, 1957, 1959 by William Snodgrass. "Song" was first published in *The New Yorker.* These poems reprinted by permission of and by special arrangement with the publisher.

LITTLE, BROWN & COMPANY for the selections from *The Poems of Emily Dickinson: Centenary Edition* (copyright 1930) edited by Martha Dickinson Bianchi and Alfred Leete Hampson; *Unpublished Poems of Emily Dickinson* (copyright 1935) edited by Martha Dickinson Bianchi and Alfred Leete Hampson; from *The Face Is Familiar* by Ogden Nash, copyright, 1931, 1940, by Ogden Nash; *Many Long Years Ago* by Ogden Nash, copyright, 1933 by Ogden Nash and *I'm a Stranger Here Myself* by Ogden Nash, copyright 1938 by Ogden Nash. "The Science of the Night" copyright © 1953 by Stanley Kunitz, "End of Summer" copyright © 1953 by Stanley Kunitz, "The Thief" copyright © 1956 by Stanley Kunitz, "When the Light Falls" copyright © 1958 by Stanley Kunitz, from *Selected Poems by Stanley Kunitz.* Reprinted by permission of the publishers. For "American Primitive," Copyright 1953, by William Jay Smith; "Plain Talk," Copyright, ©, 1957 by William Jay Smith; "A Pavane for the Nursery," Copyright 1954, by William Jay Smith, from *Poems: 1947-1957,* by William Jay Smith. Reprinted by permission of the publishers.

LIVERIGHT PUBLISHING CORPORATION for the selections from *White Buildings* by Hart Crane, copyright 1926, by Boni & Liveright, Inc., and *Collected Poems of Hart Crane,* copyright 1933, by Liveright, Inc.; *Collected Poems of H. D.,* copyright 1925, by Boni & Liveright, Inc.; *Personae* by Ezra Pound, copyright 1926. "The Broken Tower" and "At Melville's Tomb" from *Collected Poems of Hart Crane.* By permission of Liveright, Publishers, © 1961, Liveright Publishing Corporation.

THE MACMILLAN COMPANY for the selections from *The Chinese Nightingale* (copyright 1917) by Vachel Lindsay; *Collected Poems* (copyright 1913, 1923) by Vachel Lindsay; *Spoon River Anthology* (copyright 1914, 1915, and 1916) by Edgar Lee Masters; *Songs and Satires* (copyright 1916) by Edgar Lee Masters; *The Man Against the Sky* (copyright 1916) by Edwin Arlington Robinson; *Collected Poems of Edwin Arlington Robinson* (copyright 1896, 1934 by Edwin Arlington Robinson, copyright 1921, 1935, and 1937 by The Macmillan Company); *Dionysus in Doubt* (copyright 1925) by Edwin Arlington Robinson; *Rivers to the Sea* (copyright 1915) by Sara Teasdale; *Love Songs* (copyright 1907, 1917) by Sara Teasdale; *Flame and Shadow* (copyright 1920) by Sara Teasdale; *Dark of the Moon* (copyright 1926) by Sara Teasdale; *Steep Ascent* (copyright 1927) by Jean Starr Untermeyer; *Cold Morning Sky* (copyright 1937) by Marya Zaturenska; *The Listening Landscape* (copyright 1941) by Marya Zaturenska; *The Golden Mirror* (copyright 1944) by Marya Zaturenska; *Selected Poems* (copyright 1935) by Marianne Moore; *What Are Years* (copyright 1941) by Marianne Moore; and *Nevertheless* (copyright 1944) by Marianne Moore. "The Second Coming" from *The Collected Poems of W. B. Yeats: Definitive Edition,* copyright 1924 by The

Macmillan Company, renewed 1952 by Bertha Georgie Yeats. "Byzantium" and "A Dialogue of Self and Soul" from *The Collected Poems of W. B. Yeats: Definitive Edition,* copyright 1933 by The Macmillan Company. These poems used by permission of the publishers.

Edwin Markham and Virgil Markham for the selections from *The Man with the Hoe and Other Poems; Poems; The Shoes of Happiness and Other Poems;* and *New Poems,* published by Doubleday, Doran & Company and copyright by the late Edwin Markham, with whose permission, by special arrangement, the poems are reprinted.

Robert M. McBride & Company for the selections from *Those Not Elect* (copyright 1925) by Léonie Adams, and *Body of This Death* (copyright 1923) by Louise Bogan.

Vassar Miller for "Judas" copyright 1960, 1961 by Vassar Miller.

William Morris Agency, Inc. for "Pursuit" from *Selected Poems 1923-1943* by Robert Penn Warren. Copyright 1944 by Robert Penn Warren.

New Directions for selections from *First Will & Testament* by Kenneth Patchen; *In Dreams Begin Responsibilities* by Delmore Schwartz; *The Complete Collected Poems: 1906-1938 of William Carlos Williams; The Broken Span* by William Carlos Williams; and *The Poems of Ezra Pound.* "Canto I," "Canto II," and "Hugh Selwyn Mauberley" from *Selected Poems of Ezra Pound.* Copyright 1926, 1934, 1937, 1940, 1948, 1949, 1956 by Ezra Pound, © 1957 by Ezra Pound. "To a Military Rifle," "John Sutter," and "Time and the Garden" from *The Giant Weapon* by Yvor Winters. Copyright 1944 by New Directions. These poems reprinted by permission of the publisher, New Directions.

The New Yorker "Little Exercise at 4 A.M." by Elizabeth Bishop, copyright 1946 The F-R Pub. Corp.; "The Escape" by Mark Van Doren, copyright 1930 The F-R Pub. Corp.; "Nightmare Number Three" and "1935" by Stephen Vincent Benét, copyright 1935 The F-R Pub. Corp.; "The Postman's Bell Is Answered Everywhere" and "This Is the Place to Wait" by Horace Gregory, copyright 1941 The F-R Pub. Corp.; "The Rhinoceros" and "Song to Be Sung by the Fathers of Six-Month-Old Female Children" by Ogden Nash; "The People vs. the People," "Portrait," "American Rhapsody," "Reading, Forecasts, Personal Guidance" by Kenneth Fearing.

Oxford University Press, Inc. for "The Groundhog," "The Horse Chestnut Tree," and "Seals, Terns, Time" from *Collected Poems 1930-1960* © 1960 by Richard Eberhart. Reprinted by permission of Oxford University Press, Inc.

Random House for the selections from *Collected Poems* (copyright 1940) by Kenneth Fearing; *The Selected Poetry of Robinson Jeffers* (copyright 1927, 1928, 1938, by Robinson Jeffers; copyright 1933, 1935, 1937, by Random House, Inc.); *The Double Axe* (copyright 1948) by Robinson Jeffers; *Act Five* (copyright 1948) by Archibald MacLeish. *Person, Place and Thing,* copyright 1942, by Karl Jay Shapiro; *V-Letter and Other Poems,* copyright 1944, by Karl Shapiro. Reprinted by permission of Random House, Inc. "When the Century Dragged" from *Promises: Poems 1954-1956* by Robert Penn Warren, copyright © 1957 by Robert Penn Warren. Reprinted by permission of Random House, Inc.

Norman Remington Company for the selections from *Spicewood* and *Wild Cherry* by Lizette Woodworth Reese.

Theodore Roethke for "Meditation at Oyster River," which originally appeared in *The New Yorker,* "In a Dark Time," and "Light Listened" copyright, 1960, 1961, by Theodore Roethke.

Charles Scribner's Sons for the selections from *Selected Poems* (copyright 1918, 1929) by Conrad Aiken; *Preludes for Memnon* (copyright 1931) by Conrad Aiken; *Dark Summer* (copyright 1929) by Louise Bogan; *Poems and New Poems* (copyright 1941) by Louise Bogan; *The Crows* (copyright 1934) by David McCord; *The Children of the Night* (copyright 1897), and *The Town Down the River* (copyright 1910, by Charles Scribner's Sons, 1938 by Ruth Nivison) by Edwin Arlington Robinson; *Poems: 1928-1931* (copyright 1932) by Allen Tate; *Dust and Light* (copyright 1919) and *The Black Panther* (copyright 1922) by John Hall Wheelock; and *Terror and Decorum* (copyright 1948) by Peter Viereck. "The Swimmers" by Allen Tate, first published in *The Hudson Review,* copyright 1953 by Allen Tate. Reprinted with the permission of Charles Scribner's Sons from *Poems* (1960) by Allen Tate. "The House in the Green Well," which originally appeared in *The New Yorker,* from *The Gardener and Other Poems* © 1961 by John Hall Wheelock. Reprinted by permission of and by special arrangement with the publishers, Charles Scribner's Sons.

Anne Sexton for "The Truth the Dead Know" and "In the Deep Museum," copyright 1960-1961 by Anne Sexton.

William Sloane Associates, Inc. for the selections from *The Dispossessed* (copyright 1948) by John Berryman.

William Jay Smith for "The Lovers" and "The Tempest," copyright 1961 by William Jay Smith.

W. D. Snodgrass for "Lying Awake," "In the Men's Room" and "Mementos," copyright 1960, 1961 by W. D. Snodgrass.

F. A. Stokes Company for the selections from *War Is Kind* by Stephen Crane.

Alan Swallow for "Montana Pastoral," "Coffee," and "Three Epigrams" by J. V. Cunningham, reprinted from his volume *The Exclusions of a Rhyme* by permission of the publisher, Alan Swallow. Copyright 1942, 1947, 1960 by J. V. Cunningham.

The Viking Press for *God's Trombones* by James Weldon Johnson, copyright 1927 by The Viking Press, Inc.; *Growing Pains* by Jean Starr Untermeyer, copyright 1918 by B. W. Huebsch, 1946 by Jean Starr Untermeyer; *Dreams Out of Darkness* by Jean Starr Untermeyer, copyright 1921 by B. W. Huebsch,

Inc., 1949 by Jean Starr Untermeyer; *Love and Need* by Jean Starr Untermeyer, copyright 1940 by Jean Starr Untermeyer, "Trinity Place," copyright 1937 by Phyllis McGinley; "Intimations of Mortality," copyright 1950 by Phyllis McGinley; "The Day After Sunday," originally printed in *The New Yorker,* copyright 1952 by Phyllis McGinley; "The Theology of Jonathan Edwards," copyright © 1957 by Phyllis McGinley. These poems from *Times Three* (1960) published by The Viking Press, Inc. and reprinted by permission of the publisher, The Viking Press, Inc. "Ship of Death" from *Last Poems* by D. H. Lawrence. Copyright 1933 by Frieda Lawrence, reprinted by permission of The Viking Press, Inc.

Wesleyan University Press for "Portrait of the Boy as Artist," © 1956 by Barbara Howes; "Death of a Vermont Farm Woman," © 1959 by Barbara Howes; "The Triumph of Death," © 1955 by Barbara Howes; and "On a Bougainvillæa Vine at the Summer Palace," originally printed in *The New Yorker,* © 1954 by Barbara Howes: these poems reprinted from *Light and Dark* (1959), by Barbara Howes, by permission of Wesleyan University Press. Also for "Without Ceremony," © 1958 by Vassar Miller; "Bout with Burning," "Christmas Mourning," and "Defense Rests," all © 1960 by Vassar Miller: these poems reprinted from *Wage War on Silence* (1960), by Vassar Miller, by permission of Wesleyan University Press.

Wyckoff & Gelber for the selections from *Hawaiian Hilltop* by Genevieve Taggard.

The Yale University Press for the selections from *Young Adventure* by Stephen Vincent Benét; *The Burglar of the Zodiac* by William Rose Benét; *Permit Me Voyage* by James Agee; and *Theory of Flight* by Muriel Rukeyser.

Foreword to the New and Enlarged Edition

◆§ By the middle of the twentieth century mankind found itself facing a choice between adjustment and annihilation. Distance shrank as jet planes streaked across continents faster than the speed of sound, and the peoples of the world realized that they had never been both so meaningfully and so dangerously close together. It was a time to choose either mutual understanding or mutual destruction.

The unprecedented technological progress, the vastly increased knowledge of the physical universe, the enormous changes in man's ways of living caused startling reactions in all thoughtful persons as individuals and as artists. Confronted by an intolerably militant world, many expressed themselves in a hopeless defeatism; most, however, struggled to regard themselves and the warring systems with the steady hope of a regenerated life. Poetry, being essentially an act of faith, continued to voice its belief in creative renewal.

This collection reflects not only the range and direction of modern American poetry but also its rich and even conflicting diversities. It aims to present a panorama in which the outstanding figures assume proper prominence but in which lesser personalities are not lost.

It is here that debate begins and choice is likely to be arbitrary. Never before have so many poets distinguished themselves in America; never before has even the lesser verse been on such a level of competence. Following the appearance of *Poetry: A Magazine of Verse* in 1912, more than one hundred magazines devoted themselves to the printing and appraisal of verse. Almost every major city had its Poetry Society feverishly competing for prizes; every county had its local laureate. A rough calculation indicates that, in the years covering the "renascence" of American poetry, no fewer than four thousand poets had volumes of their poetry offered for public sale. But, though an array of four thousand poets in any one period may be sufficiently imposing, this number gives no idea of the armies of writers who have whipped up their emotions, girded up their lines, and fought for the crucial adjective. It is safe to say that for every poet fortunate enough to emerge from the struggle with a volume or two to his credit, there were ten (the number is probably nearer fifty) who were not so victorious and had to content themselves with publication in magazines, trade journals, and the poetry corner of the local newspaper.

Selection of the fifteen or twenty "leading" poets for an anthology is not so difficult. Almost everyone will agree on the poets whose appearance is imperative in a collection of this type. It is when one goes further and attempts to suggest the flux and fecundity of the period, or presumes to indicate the shape of things to come, that differences of opinion are sure to arise. Controversy and even enmity are likely to follow. In the end every editor is driven back upon that mixture of preference, prejudice, and intuition known as personal taste—and it is only rarely that he can escape the limitations imposed by his temperament and training.

That inescapable personal factor explains the method of editing as well as the manner of selection. That a poem has appeared in various compilations is no proof that it is a good poem. Nor (in spite of those opposed to anthologies) is such publication anything against it. A good poem remains a good poem, no matter how often it is reprinted. On the other hand, it should be admitted that where there has been a choice between a much-quoted poem and one which has not been handed on from one anthologist to another, the editor has—where both poems seemed equally worthy—favored the less familiar example.

This eighth edition of *Modern American Poetry,* like its predecessors, does not pretend to be a complete history of the period. No collection, no matter how large or how inclusive, can be. Though this anthology indicates the range of contemporary native poetry, many poets have been omitted from these pages. The editor regrets the cruel stringency of space, and apologizes to those (many of them his friends) whom it was impossible to include. The table of contents, with its emphasis on the more important poets, must speak for itself. Some of the poets included have been hailed as pioneers; some have provoked controversy and have changed the direction of contemporary art; some have maintained their quiet utterance with no regard whatsoever to warring movements. Nevertheless, each has established his individuality by a unique command of his medium and a strongly pronounced personal idiom.

The biographical and critical paragraphs have not only been brought up-to-date but sharply re-examined. The volume, as before, begins with Walt Whitman, with whom modern American poetry may be said to have begun, but it now includes a larger proportion of those writers in whose poetry the present is significantly expressed.

One thing remains to be said. Although the notes as well as the number of poems selected make the editor's preference obvious, it should be added that he has attempted to make each poet's group rounded and representative. To accomplish this, not only the early but the most recent writing of the contemporaries appears here—some of it for the first time between covers. The editor is greatly indebted to most of the living poets, not only for invaluable data, but for their collaborative assistance; many of the following pages embody their choice of their own poems as well as the editor's preferences.

Contents

Robert Frost (Cont.)

MODERN AMERICAN POETRY

New and Enlarged Edition

Preface

☙ The word "modern" is such a shifting and relative term that it escapes final definition. Yet it is generally conceded that, with the advent of Mark Twain, Herman Melville, and Walt Whitman, American literature became modern as well as American. In the history of poetry the line may be drawn with some certainty. The publication of *Leaves of Grass* and the Civil War symbolized the close of one era and the beginning of another. It is with these events that the beginnings of modern American poetry may be defined.

AFTERMATH OF THE CIVIL WAR

The Civil War inspired volumes of indignant, military, religious, and patriotic verse without adding more than four or five memorable pieces to the anthologies; the conflict produced a vast quantity of poems but practically no important poetry. Its end marked the end of an epoch, political, social, and literary. The arts declined; the New England group began to disintegrate. The poets had overstrained and outsung themselves; it was a time of surrender and swan-songs. Unable to respond to the new forces of political nationalism and industrial reconstruction, the Brahmins (that famous group of intellectuals who had dominated literary America) withdrew into their libraries. Such poets as Longfellow, Bryant, Taylor, turned their eyes away from the native scene, rhapsodized endlessly about Europe, echoed the "parlor poetry" of England, or left creative writing altogether and occupied themselves with translations. "They had been borne into an era in which they had not part," writes Fred Lewis Pattee (*A History of American Literature Since 1870*), "and they contented themselves with reëchoings of the old music." For them poetry ceased to be a reflection of actuality, "an extension of experience." Within a period of six years, from 1867 to 1872, there appeared Longfellow's *Divina Commedia,* C. E. Norton's *Vita Nuova,* T. W. Parsons' *Inferno,* William Cullen Bryant's *Iliad* and *Odyssey,* and Bayard Taylor's *Faust.*

Suddenly the break came. America developed a national consciousness; the West discovered itself, and the East discovered the West. Grudgingly at first, the aristocratic leaders made way for a new expression; crude, jangling, vigorously democratic. The old order was changing with a vengeance. All the preceding writers—poets like Emerson, Lowell, Longfellow, Holmes—were not only products of the New England colleges, but typically "Boston gentlemen of the early Renaissance." To them the new men must have seemed like a regiment recruited from the ranks of vulgarity. Walt Whitman, Mark Twain, Bret Harte, John Hay, Joaquin Miller, Joel Chandler Harris, James Whitcomb Riley—these were men who had graduated from the farm, the frontier, the mine, the pilothouse, the printer's shop! For a while, the movement seemed of little consequence; the impact of Whitman and the Westerners was averted.

The poets of the transition, with a deliberate art, ignored the surge of a spontaneous national expression. They were even successful in holding it back. But it was gathering force.

THE "POST-MORTEM" PERIOD

The nineteenth century, up to its last quarter, had been a period of new vistas and revolts: a period of protest and iconoclasm—the era of Shelley and Byron, the prophets of "liberty, equality and fraternity." It left no immediate heirs. In England, its successors by default were the lesser Victorians. In America, the intensity of men like Emerson and Whittier gave way to the pale romanticism and polite banter of the transition, or what might be called the "post-mortem," poets. "Much of our poetry," Thoreau wrote, "has the very best manners, but no character." These interim lyrists were frankly the singers of an indefinite reaction, reminiscently digging among the bones of a long-dead past. They burrowed and borrowed, half archeologists, half artisans, impelled not so much by the need of creation as recreation. They did not write poetry, they echoed it.

From 1866 to 1880 the United States was in a chaotic and frankly materialistic condition; it was full of political scandals, panics, frauds, malfeasance in high places. The moral fiber was flabby; the country was apathetic, corrupt and contented. As in all such periods of national unconcern, the artists turned from life altogether, preoccupying themselves with the by-products of art: with method and technique, with elaborate and artificial conceits, with facile ideas rather than fundamental ideals.

Bayard Taylor, Thomas Buchanan Read, Richard Henry Stoddard, Paul Hamilton Hayne, Thomas Bailey Aldrich—all of these authors, in an effort to escape a reality they could not express and did not even wish to understand, fled to a more congenial realm of fantasy. They took the easiest routes to a prim and academic Arcadia, to a cloying and devitalized Orient, to a mildly sensuous, "reconstructed" Greece. Their verse, confessing its own defeat, was cluttered with silk divans, Astrakhans, Vesuvian Bays, burning deserts, Assyrian temples, Spanish cloths of gold. Originality was as far from their thoughts as thinking itself; they followed wherever Keats, Shelley (in his lesser lyrics) and Tennyson seemed to lead them. However, not being explorers themselves, they ventured no further than their predecessors, but remained politely in the rear, repeating dulcetly what they had learned from their greater guides—pronouncing it with little variety but with a sentimental unction. In their desperate preoccupation with lures and legends overseas, they were not, except for the accident of birth, American at all; all of them owed much more to old England than to New England.

WALT WHITMAN

Whitman, who was to influence future generations so profoundly in Europe as well as in America, had already appeared. The third edition of that stupendous volume, *Leaves of Grass,* had been printed in 1860. Almost immediately after, the publisher failed and the book passed out of public notice. But private scrutiny was keen. In 1865 a petty official discovered that Whitman was the author of the "notorious" *Leaves of Grass* and, in spite of Whitman's sacrifice in nursing hundreds of wounded soldiers, in spite of his many past services and his present poverty, the offending poet was dismissed from his clerkship in the Department of the Interior at Washington, D. C. Other reverses followed rapidly. But Whitman, broken in health and cheated by his exploiters, lived to see not only a seventh edition of his work published in 1881, but a complete collection printed in his seventy-third year (1892) in which the twelve poems of the experimental first edition had grown to nearly four hundred.

The influence of Whitman can scarcely be overestimated. It has touched every shore of letters, quickened every current of contemporary art. And yet, as late as 1900, Barrett Wendell in his *Literary History of America* could speak of Whitman's "eccentric insolence of phrase and temper," and, perturbed by the poet's increasing vogue across the Atlantic (Whitman had been hailed by men as eminent as Swinburne, Symonds, Rossetti), he was led to write such a preposterous sentence as "In temperament and style he was an exotic member of that sterile brotherhood which eagerly greeted him abroad."

Such a judgment would be impossible today. Whitman has been acclaimed by a great and growing public. He has been hailed as prophet, as pioneer, as rebel, as fiery humanist not only in America, but in England and throughout Europe. The whole scheme of *Leaves of Grass* is inclusive rather than exclusive; its form is elemental, dynamic, free.

Nor was it only in the relatively minor matter of form that Whitman became a poetic emancipator. He led the way toward a wider aspect of democracy; he took his readers out of fusty, lamp-lit libraries into the coarse sunlight and the buoyant air. He was, as Burroughs wrote, preëminently the poet of vista; his work had the power "to open doors and windows, to let down bars rather than to put them up, to dissolve forms, to escape narrow boundaries, to plant the reader on a hill rather than in a corner." He could do this because, first of all, he believed implicitly in life—in its physical as well as its spiritual manifestations; he sought to grasp existence as a whole, not rejecting the things that, to other minds, had seemed trivial or tawdry. The cosmic and the commonplace were synonymous to him; he declared he was part of elemental, primitive things and constantly identified himself with them. He transmuted, by the intensity of his emotion, material which had been hitherto regarded as too unpoetic for poetry. His long poem "Song of Myself" is a magnificent example. Here his "barbaric yawp," sounded "over the roofs of the world," is softened, time and again, to express a lyric ecstasy and naïf wonder.

I believe a leaf of grass is no less than the journeywork of the stars,
And the pismire is equally perfect, and a grain of sand, and the egg of the wren,
And the tree-toad is a chef-d'œuvre for the highest,
And the running blackberry would adorn the parlors of heaven,
And the narrowest hinge in my hand puts to scorn all machinery,
And the cow crunching with depress'd head surpasses any statue,
And a mouse is miracle enough to stagger sextillions of infidels!

It is this large naturalism, this affection for all that is homely and of the soil, that sets Whitman apart from his fellow craftsmen as our first distinctively American poet. This blend of familiarity and grandeur, this racy but religious mysticism animates all his work. It swings with tremendous vigor through "Crossing Brooklyn Ferry"; it sharpens the sturdy rhythms (and occasional rhymes) of the "Song of the Broad-Ax"; it beats sonorously through "Drum-Taps"; it whispers immortally through the "Memories of President Lincoln" (particularly that magnificent threnody "When Lilacs Last in the Dooryard Bloom'd"); it quickens the "Song of the Open Road" with what Tennyson called "the glory of going on," and lifts with a biblical solemnity "Out of the Cradle Endlessly Rocking."

Whitman did not scorn the past; no one was quicker than he to see its wealth and glories. But most of the older flowerings belonged to their own era; they were foreign to his country—transplanted, they did not flourish on this soil. What was original with many transatlantic poets was being merely aped by facile and unoriginal bards in these States; they seemed bent on transforming poetry into a pedant's stroll through Bulfinch's *Age of Fable.* Concerned only with the myths of other and older countries, they were blind to the living legends of their own. In his "Song of the Exposition" Whitman wrote not only his own *credo,* but uttered the manifesto of the new generation —especially in these lines:

Come, Muse, migrate from Greece and Ionia,
Cross out please those immensely overpaid accounts,
That matter of Troy and Achilles' wrath, and Aeneas', Odysseus' wanderings,
Placard "Removed" and "To Let" on the rocks of your snowy Parnassus, . . .
For know a better, fresher, busier sphere, a wide, untried domain awaits, demands
you.

The final estimate of Whitman's work is yet to be written. Whitman's universality—and his inconsistencies—have defeated his commentators. To the craftsmen, Whitman's chief contribution was his form; hailing him as the father of the free verse movement, they placed their emphasis on his flexible sonority, his orchestral *timbre,* his tidal rhythms, his piling up of details into a symphonic structure. To the philosophers, he was the first of modern prophets; a rhapsodic mystic with a magnificently vulgar sense of democracy. To the psychologist, he was the most revealing of autobiographers; "whoever touches this book, touches a man," he wrote. To the lay reader, he was a protagonist of "the divine average"; celebrating himself—hearty, gross, noble, "sane and sensual to the core"—he celebrated humanity.

But it is Whitman's spirit, not his technique nor his subject-matter, which assures him permanence. It is the broad and resistless affirmation—Whitman's favorite term "democracy" is too special a word for it—which quickens everything he wrote and which so profoundly affected the spirit (not the letter) of subsequent writing. It is the spirit synthesized in the poem to a common prostitute: "Not till the sun excludes you do I exclude you." It is the quick recognition of the commonplace, the glorification of the unnoticed in a pismire and a grain of sand.

What the extent of this spirit is no one has determined. It is gross and sensual and, at the same time, tender and mystical; it calls for "life coarse and rank," yet it lifts appetite beyond life and death; it is as explosive as a teamster's oath and as grave as the Psalms which influenced it. Its ecstasy, even its exhibitionism, though flushed with a raw and rowdy exuberance, is filled with a calm "mortis'd in granite." It is, possibly, a too all-embracing love which intensifies whatever it touches, an over-vigorous optimism compared to which even Browning's seems anemic. But its indiscriminate acceptance is the very core of its faith, enclosing good and evil, beauty and ugliness in the mystic's circle of complete affirmation.

EMILY DICKINSON

Contemporary with Whitman, though, as far as the records show, utterly unaware of him, that strange phenomenon, Emily Dickinson, lived and wrote in near secrecy. Only seven of her seventeen hundred poems were printed during her lifetime; she care nothing for a public, less for publicity. It was not until forty years after her death that she was recognized as one of the most original of American poets and, in some ways, the most remarkable woman poet since Sappho. Her centenary, occurring in the same year as Christina Rossetti's, was signaled by salvos of appreciation and the inevitable comparisons with the Englishwoman born five days earlier than her Amherst contemporary. Both poets were born in 1830; both were strongly influenced by their fathers. Both were, in spite of every difference, puritan "beyond the blood." Both made "the great abnegation"—Christina because she could not face marriage, Emily because, it is assumed, the man she loved was married and she could face misery without him better than social tragedy with him. Here the personal similarities end. The poetic likenesses are more remote. True, both poets are linked by language, but even that tie cannot hold the two together long. They, themselves, would have been the first to repudiate the bond. Emily Dickinson would have been impatient with the round rhetoric of Christina Rossetti; much that the American wrote would have seemed reprehensible and, oftener than not, incomprehensible to the Englishwoman. As Christina grew older, her verse grew thinner and more repetitive; moments of vision were expanded into ever-lengthening sententiousness. After Emily weathered the crisis, her verse grew continually tighter, her divinations condensed until the few lines became telegraphic and these telegrams seemed not only self-addressed but written in code. Not that Christina lacked divination; in the magnificent "From House to Home," in several of the austere sonnets, and in some fifteen lyrics she attained sheer illumination. What is more difficult, she communicated it. At her infrequent highest, Christina Rossetti breathed a clearer, calmer air than "the nun of Amherst." Hers was a cloistral faith, secure above time and a troubling universe. Rumor to the contrary, there was nothing nun-like about Emily Dickinson. If the episodes of her childhood (*vide* the *Life and Letters*) were not sufficient to prove it, the poetry is; the freedom of her spirit manifests itself in the audacity of her images, the wild leap of her epithets, the candor which extends from irreverent mischief to divine challenge. Sometimes elliptical, sometimes so concentrated as to be cryptic, hers is a poetry of continual surprise where metaphors turned to epigrams, epigrams to compact dramas, a poetry where playfulness and passion merged and were sublimated in pure thought.

Could anyone have failed to recognize this revelation at the outset? One supposes a few tense quatrains, a dozen syllables must have been sufficient to reveal the definiteness of her genius. "The authorities" disdained or forgot her. As late as 1914 *The New International Encyclopaedia* dismissed her life and work in ten lines, concluding "In thought her introspective lyrics are striking but are deficient in form." *The Encyclopaedia Britannica* seemed even less aware of her existence until 1926; the thirteenth edition contained only a mention, a cross-reference by way of comparison; her name did not appear in the Index. Yet her *Poems* (*First Series*) had appeared as early as 1890 and two subsequent collections had been published before 1896. In these volumes—as well as in *The Single Hound* (1915) and *Further Poems,* an amazing set of "newly discovered" verses published in 1929—Emily Dickinson anticipated not only her avowed disciples but a score of poets unaware of her influence. Quaintly, without propaganda, she fashioned her imagist etchings fifty years before Imagism became a slogan; her experiments in "slant" or "suspended" rhyme were far more radical than those of any exponent of assonance; her ungrammatical directness was more spontaneous than the painful dislocations of "the new primitives."

The evidence of this anticipating modernity is everywhere. Emily would have been the last to claim anything, particularly the claim of being a forerunner, yet "Death's large democratic fingers" might well have prompted E. E. Cummings. MacLeish's *"Ars Poetica"* startles us by its abstraction:

> Poetry should not mean
> But be—

and Emily, sometime in the '70s, concludes:

> Beauty is not caused,
> It is.

Hodgson tells us "God loves an idle rainbow no less than laboring seas" and that "Reason has moons, but moons not hers lie mirrored on the sea, confounding her astronomers but, Oh, delighting me." And Emily (who knows how many years earlier?) was saying:

> The rainbow never tells me
> That gust and storm are by,
> Yet she is more convincing
> Than all philosophy.

Not that she despised philosophy. On the contrary, in the midst of her cakes and puddings and ice-creams, the family breadmaker (for Emily gloried in her housewifery) would turn to consider Bishop Berkeley. Intricately but with a final clarity, she expressed herself on the paradox of discipline:

Experience is the angled road
Preferred against the mind
By paradox, the mind itself
Presuming it to lead
Quite opposite. How complicate
The discipline of man,
Compelling him to choose himself
His pre-appointed plan.

Thus, and continuously, Emily would jot down the notes for her uncoordinated autobiography. Not until 1955—almost a century after the poems were composed—when Thomas H. Johnson collated a three-volume edition, did the complete poet emerge, and an order was established in which the differing versions of many of her lines and the mischief of her editors were resolved. In 1891, one of them (Mabel Loomis Todd) wrote: "To what further rigorous pruning her verses would have been subjected had she published them herself, we cannot know. They should be regarded in many cases as merely the first strong and suggestive sketches of an artist, intended to be embodied at some time in the finished picture." Her manner of writing made it equally hazardous for her editors, some of whom erred by too much editing, some by a too literal following of spacing, punctuation and obvious mistakes. "In most of her poems, particularly the later ones, everything by way of punctuation was discarded, except numerous dashes; and all important words began with capitals."

Thus Emily Dickinson became a puzzle. Biographers supplied fresh confusions and misleading clues in a mistaken zeal for detection. As in life, the poet escaped them all. Much of her problem remains in the realm of the mysterious. She was like no other poet; her very "roughnesses" were individual. Time and again she skipped the expected rhyme, twisted the easy phrase, and put her indubitable mark on every line she wrote. Wholly underivative, her poetry was unique; her influence, negligible at first, is now incalculable.

THE AWAKENING OF THE WEST

By 1875 the public had been surfeited with sugared conceits and fine-spun delicacies. For almost twelve years, Whitman had stormed at the squeamish overrefinements of the period, but comparatively few had listened. Yet an instinctive distaste for the prevailing affectations had been growing, and when the West began to express itself in the raw accents of Mark Twain and Bret Harte, the people turned to them with enthusiasm and no little relief. Mark Twain, a frustrated prose Whitman, revealed the romantic Mississippi and the vast mid-West; Bret Harte, beginning a new American fiction in 1868, ushered in the wild humor and wilder poetry of California. It is still a question whether Bret Harte or John Hay first discovered the literary importance of Pike County narratives. Twain was positive that Hay was the pioneer; documentary evidence points to Harte. But it is indisputable that Harte developed—and even overdeveloped—the possibilities of his backgrounds, whereas Hay, after a few brilliant ballads, reverted to his early poetic ideals and turned to the production of studied, polished, and undistinguished verse. Lacking the gusto of Mark Twain or even the native accuracy of Hay, Bret Harte perfected a terse, dramatic idiom. Less exuberant than his compeers, he became more skillful in making his situations "effective"; he popularized dialects, sharpening his outlines and intensifying the edges of his prose. Harte's was an influence that found its echo in the Hoosier stories of Edward Eggleston and made so vivid an impress on nineteenth-century literature.

To the loose swagger of the West, two other men added their diverse contributions. Edward Rowland Sill, cut short just as his work was gaining headway and strength, brought to it a gentle radicalism, a calm and cultured honesty; Joaquin Miller, rushing to the other extreme, theatricalized and exaggerated all he touched. He shouted platitudes at the top of his voice. His lines boomed with the pomposity of a brass band; floods, fires, hurricanes, extravagantly blazing sunsets, Amazonian women, the thunder of a herd of buffaloes—all were unmercifully piled upon each other. And yet, even in its most blatant *fortissimo,* Miller's poetry occasionally captured the grandeur of his surroundings, the spread of the Sierras, the lavish energy of the Western world.

Now that the leadership of letters had passed from the East, all parts of the country began to try their voices. The West continued to hold its rugged supremacy; the tradition of Harte and Hay was followed (softened and sentimentalized) by Eugene Field and James Whitcomb Riley. In the South, Irwin Russell was pioneering in negro dialect (1875), Sidney Lanier fashioned his intricate harmonies (1879), and Madison Cawein began to create his tropical and overluxuriant lyrics. A few years later the first phase of the American renascence had passed.

REACTION AND REVOLT IN THE '90S

The reaction set in at the beginning of the last decade of the nineteenth century. The passionate urge had spent itself, and in its place there remained nothing but imitation and gesticulation, the dumb-show of poetry. The poetasters wrote verse that was precise, scholarly, and patently echoed their literary loves. "In 1890," writes Percy H. Boynton, "the poetry-reading world was chiefly conscious of the passing of its leading singers for the last half-century. It was a period when they were recalling Emerson's 'Terminus' and Longfellow's 'Ultima Thule,' Whittier's 'A Lifetime,' Tennyson's 'Crossing the Bar,' and Browning's 'Asolando.'" . . . The poetry of this period (whether it is the fine-chiseled verse of John B. Tabb or the ornate delicacy of Richard Watson Gilder) reflects a kind of moribund resignation; it is dead because it detached itself from the actual world. But those who regarded poetry chiefly as a not too energetic indoor-exercise were not to rule unchallenged. Restlessness was in the air and revolt openly declared itself with the publication of *Songs from Vagabondia* (1894), *More Songs from Vagabondia* (1896) and *Last Songs from Vagabondia* (1900). No one could have been more surprised at the tremendous popularity of these care-free celebrations (the first of the three collections went through seven rapid editions) than the young authors, Richard

Hovey and Bliss Carman. For theirs was a revolt without a program, a headlong flight to escape—what? In the very first poem, Hovey voices their manifesto:

> Off with the fetters
> That chafe and restrain!
> Off with the chain!
> Here Art and Letters,
> Music and Wine
> And Myrtle and Wanda,
> The winsome witches,
> Blithely combine.
> Here is Golconda,
> Here are the Indies,
> Here we are free—
> Free as the wind is,
> Free as the sea,
> Free!

Free for what? one asks doggedly. Hovey does not answer directly, but with unflagging buoyancy, whipped up by scorn for the smug ones, he continues:

> I tell you that we,
> While you are smirking
> And lying and shirking
> Life's duty of duties,
> Honest sincerity,
> We are in verity
> Free!
> Free to rejoice
> In blisses and beauties!
> Free as the voice
> Of the wind as it passes!
> Free . . . *etc.*

Free, one concludes, to escape and dwell with Music and Wine, Myrtle and Wanda, Art and Letters. Free, in short, to follow, with a more athletic energy, the same ideals as the parlor-poets they gibed so relentlessly. But the new insurgence triumphed. It was the heartiness, the gypsy jollity, the rush of high spirits that conquered. Readers of the *Vagabondia* books were swept along by their speed faster than by their philosophy.

The enthusiastic acceptance of these new apostles of outdoor vigor was, however, not as much of an accident as it seemed. On one side (the world of art) the public was wearied by barren meditations set to tinkling music; on the other (the world of action) it was faced by a staggering growth of materialism which it feared. Hovey, Carman and their imitators offered a swift way out. But it was neither an effectual nor a permanent escape. The war with Spain, the industrial turmoil, the growth of social consciousness and new ideas of responsibility made America look for fresh valuations. Hovey began to go deeper into himself and his age; in the mid-West, William Vaughn Moody grappled with the problems of his times only to have his work cut short by death in 1910. But these two were exceptions. In the main, it was another interval—two decades of appraisal and expectancy, of pause and preparation.

INTERIM—1890-1912

This interval of about twenty years was notable for its effort to treat the spirit of the times with a cheerful evasiveness, a humorous unconcern. Its most representative craftsmen were, with four exceptions, the writers of light verse. These four exceptions were Richard Hovey, Bliss Carman, William Vaughn Moody and Edwin Markham.

Moody's power was the greatest, although it never reached its potentialities. In "An Ode in Time of Hesitation," he protested against turning the "new-world victories into gain" and painted American idealism on an idealistic canvas. In "The Quarry" he celebrated America's part in preventing the breaking up of China by the empires of Europe, an act accomplished by John Hay, poet and diplomat. In "On a Soldier Fallen in the Philippines," a dirge wrenched from the depths of his nature, Moody cried out against our own imperialists. It was the fulfillment of this earlier poem which found its climax in the lengthy Ode, with such lines as:

> Was it for this our fathers kept the law?
> This crown shall crown their struggle and their ruth?
> Are we the eagle nation Milton saw
> Mewing its mighty youth? . . .
> . . . O ye who lead
> Take heed!
> Blindness we may forgive, but baseness we will smite.

Early in 1899, the name of Edwin Markham flashed across the land when, out of San Francisco, rose the challenge of "The Man with the Hoe." This poem, which was once ecstatically called "the battle-cry of the next thousand years" (Joaquin Miller declared it contained "the whole Yosemite—the thunder, the might, the majesty"), caught up the passion for social justice that was waiting to be intensified in poetry. Markham summed up and spiritualized the unrest that was in the air; in the figure of one man with a hoe, he drew a picture of men in the mines, men in the sweatshop, men working without joy, without hope. To social consciousness he added social conscience. In a ringing if rhetorical blank verse, Markham crystallized the expression of outrage, the heated ferment of the period.

Inspiring as these examples were, they did not generate others of their kind; the field lay fallow for more than a decade. The lull was pronounced, the gathering storm remained inaudible.

RENASCENCE—1913

Suddenly the "new" poetry burst upon the country with unexpected vigor and extraordinary variety. Moody and Markham were its immediate forerunners; Whitman its spiritual godfather. October, 1912, saw the first issue of

Poetry: A Magazine of Verse, a monthly that was to introduce the work of hitherto unknown poets, schools, and "movements." The magazine came at the very moment of the breaking of the storm. Flashes and rumblings had already been troubling the literary heavens; a few months later came the deluge! For four years the skies continued to discharge such strange and divergent phenomena as Ezra Pound's *Canzoni* and *Ripostes* (1912), Vachel Lindsay's *General William Booth Enters into Heaven* (1913), James Oppenheim's *Songs for the New Age* (1914), the first anthology of *The Imagists* (1914), *Challenge* (1914), Amy Lowell's *Sword Blades and Poppy Seed* (1914), Lindsay's *The Congo and Other Poems* (1914), Robert Frost's *North of Boston* (1914), Edgar Lee Masters' *Spoon River Anthology* (1915), John Gould Fletcher's *Irradiations* (1915), Conrad Aiken's *Turns and Movies* (1916), Edwin Arlington Robinson's *The Man Against the Sky* (1916), Carl Sandburg's *Chicago Poems* (1916). By 1917, the "new" poetry was ranked as "America's first national art"; its success was sweeping, its sales unprecedented. People who never before had read verse, turned to it and found they could not only read but relish it. They discovered that for the enjoyment of poetry it was no longer necessary to have at their elbows a dictionary of rare words and classical references; they were not required to be acquainted with Latin legendry and the minor love-affairs of the Greek divinities. Life was their glossary, not literature. The new work spoke to them in their own language. And it did more: it spoke to them of what they rarely had heard expressed; it was not only closer to their soil but nearer to their souls.

EDWIN ARLINGTON ROBINSON

One reason why the new poetry achieved so sudden a success was its freedom from the traditionally stilted "poetic diction." Revolting strongly against the assumption that poetry must have a vocabulary of its own, the poets of the new era spoke in the oldest and most stirring tongue; they used a language that was the language not of the poetasters but of the people. In the tones of ordinary speech they rediscovered the strength, the dignity, the vital core of the commonplace.

Edwin Arlington Robinson had already been employing the sharp epithet, the direct and clarifying utterance which was to become part of our present technique. As early as 1897, in *The Children of the Night,* Robinson anticipated the brief characterizations and etched outlines of Masters' *Spoon River Anthology;* he stressed the psychological element with unerring artistry and sureness of touch. His sympathetic studies of men whose lives were, from a worldly standpoint, failures were a sharp reaction to the current high valuation on financial achievements, ruthless efficiency, and success at any cost. Ahead of his period, he had to wait until 1916, when a public prepared for him by the awakened interest in native poetry discovered *The Man Against the Sky* (1916) and the richness of Robinson at the same time. After that, his audience increased steadily. His Arthurian legends replaced Tennyson's, *Tristram* (1927), achieving a greater response than most successful novels. *Cavender's House* (1929), although a difficult and lengthy monologue, solidified his position; the Pulitzer Prize for Poetry was thrice awarded to him; and there was no longer any doubt as to the importance of his contribution to American literature. Death in 1935 found him at the peak of fame.

EDGAR LEE MASTERS

Frost and Masters were the bright particular planets of 1915, although the star of the latter waned while the light of the former grew in magnitude. Yet Masters' most famous book ranks as a landmark. In it, Masters synthesized the small towns of the mid-West with a background unmistakably local and with implications that are universal. This amazing volume, in its curiosity and comprehensiveness, laid open a broad cross-section of whole communities. Beneath its surface tales and dramas, its condensation of grocery-store gossip, *Spoon River Anthology* was a great part of America in microcosm; it prepared the way for Sinclair Lewis' *Main Street* and the critical fiction of small-town life.

The success of the volume was sensational. In a few months, it went into edition after edition. Perhaps most readers passed over the larger issues (Masters' revelation of the sordid cheats and hypocrisies, his arraignment of dirty politics and dirtier chicanery) intent on seeing their neighbors pitilessly exposed. Yet had Masters dwelt only on the drab disillusion of the village, had he (as he was constantly in danger of doing) overemphasized the morbid and sensual episodes, he would have left only a spectacular and poorly balanced work. But the book ascends to a definite exaltation and ends on a plane of half-victorious idealism. Indigenous to its roots, it is stark, unflinching, unforgettable.

ROBERT FROST

The same year that brought forth *Spoon River Anthology* saw the American edition of Frost's *North of Boston*. It was evident at once that the true poet of New England had arrived. Unlike his predecessors, Frost was never a poetic provincial—never parochial in the sense of America still being a literary parish of England. Frost was as native as the lonely farmhouses, the dusty blueberries, the isolated people, the dried-up brooks and mountain intervals that he described. Loving, above everything else, the beauty of the Fact, he shared, with Robinson and Masters, the determination to tell not merely the actual but the factual truth. But Frost, a less disillusioned though a more saddened poet, wore his rue and his realism with a difference. Where Robinson was definite, Frost diverged, going roundabout and, in his speculative wandering, covering a wider territory of thought. Where Masters was violent and hotly scornful, Frost was reticent and quietly sympathetic. Again where Masters, viewing the mêlée above the struggle, wrote *about* his characters, Frost was *of* his people. Where Robinson, in his more racy and reminiscent moods, often reflected New England, Frost *was* New England.

North of Boston was well described by the poet's own subtitle: "a book of people." In it one not only sees a countryside of people living out the intricate pattern of their lives, one catches them thinking out loud, one can hear the very tones of their voices. Here we have speech so arranged and translated that the speaker is heard on the printed page; any reader will be led by the kind and color of these words into reproducing the changing accents in which they are supposed to be uttered. It is this insistence that "all poetry is the reproduction of the tones of actual speech" which gives these poems, as well as the later lyrics, a quickly communicated emotional appeal. It endows them with the deepest power of which words are capable—the power to transmit significant sounds. These sounds, let in from the vernacular, are full of a robust, creative energy; they are compacted of the blood and bones of the people they speak for.

But Frost was by no means the dark naturalist that many suspected. Behind the mask of "grimness" which many critics fastened upon him, there is a continual elfin pucker; a whimsical smile, a half-disclosed raillery glints beneath his most somber monologues. The later *New Hampshire* (1923) and *West-Running Brook* (1928) proved his "other side"; Frost's lyrics are no less personal for being philosophical. Now it is obvious how Vergilian a spirit animated a passionate Puritan; his *Collected Poems* (1930) reveals him as one of the three great pastoral poets of all time. Nor is his greatness due to his self-limited choice of material; Frost's concrete facts are symbols of spiritual values. Through his very reticence as well as through his revelation one hears much more than the voice of New England.

CARL SANDBURG

The great mid-West, that vast region of steel mills and slaughter-houses, of cornfields and prairies, of crowded cities and empty skies, spoke through Carl Sandburg. In Sandburg, industrial America found its voice: *Chicago Poems* (1916), *Cornhuskers* (1918), *Smoke and Steel* (1920) and *Good Morning, America* (1928) vibrate with the immense purring of dynamos, the rhythms of threshing arms, the gossip and laughter of construction gangs, the gigantic and tireless energy of the machine. Frankly indebted to Whitman, Sandburg's poems are less sweeping but more varied; musically his lines mark an advance. He sounds the extremes of the gamut; there are few poems in our language more violent than "To a Contemporary Bunkshooter," few lyrics as hushed and tender as "Cool Tombs."

Like Frost, Sandburg was true to things. But *Frost* was content with the inexhaustible fact and its spiritual implications; he never hoped to drain it all. Sandburg also fed on the fact, but it did not satisfy him. He had strange hungers; he hunted eagerly for the question behind, the answer beyond. The actual scene, to him, was a point of vivid and abrupt departure. Reality, far from being the earth on which he dwelt, was, for Sandburg, the ground he touched before rising; realism acted merely as a springboard from which this poet dove into a romantic mysticism. His later work, in fact, was almost too full of gnomic gestures.

When *Chicago Poems* first appeared, it was received with a disfavor ranging from hesitant patronization to the scornful jeers of the academicians. Sandburg was accused of verbal anarchy; of a failure to distinguish prose matter from poetic material; of uncouthness, vulgarity, assaults on the English language and a score of other crimes. In the face of those who even in *Good Morning, America* (1928) still see only a coarseness and distorted veritism in Sandburg, it cannot be said too often that he is brutal only when dealing with brutal things; that his "vulgarity" springs from love of life as a whole, not from affection for a drab or decorative part of it; that his bitterest invectives are the result of a disgust of shams. The strength of his hatred is exceeded by the challenge of his love.

THE IMAGISTS AND AMY LOWELL

Sandburg established himself as the most daring user of American words—rude words ranging from the racy metaphors of the soil to the slang of the street. But long before this, the possibilities of a new vocabulary were being tested. As early as 1865, Whitman was saying, "We must have new words, new potentialities of speech—an American range of self-expression. . . . The new times, the new people need a tongue according, yes, and what is more, they will have such a tongue—will not be satisfied until it is evolved."

It is curious to think that one of the most effective agents to fulfill Whitman's prophecy and free modern poetry from an affected diction was that little band of preoccupied specialists, the Imagists. They were, for all their preciosity and occasional extravagances, liberators in the sense that their programs, pronouncements, and propaganda compell their most dogged adversaries to acknowledge the integrity of their aims. Their restatement of old truths was one of the things which helped the new poetry out of a bog of rhetorical rubbish.

Ezra Pound was the first to gather the insurgents into a definite group. During the winter of 1913, he collected a number of poems illustrating the Imagist point of view, conceiving Imagism as a discriminating term like "lyricism," and had them printed in a volume: *Des Imagistes* (1914). A little later Pound withdrew from the clan. The rather queerly assorted group began to disintegrate, and Amy Lowell, then in England, brought some of the younger members together in three yearly anthologies (*Some Imagist Poets*) which appeared in 1915, 1916 and 1917. There were, in Miss Lowell's new grouping, three Englishmen (D. H. Lawrence, Richard Aldington, F. S. Flint), three Americans (H. D., John Gould Fletcher, Amy Lowell), and their creed summed up in six statements,[1] was as follows:

1. To use the language of common speech, but to employ always the *exact* word, not the merely decorative word.
2. To create new rhythms—as the expression of new moods. We do not insist upon "free-verse" as the only method of writing poetry. . . . We do believe that the individuality of a poet may often be better expressed in free verse than in conventional forms.
3. To allow absolute freedom in the choice of subject.
4. To present an image (hence the name: "Imagist"). We are not a school of

[1] The stern injunction to "use no word which does not contribute to the presentation"—a Spartan injunction originating with Pound—was soon forgotten by Miss Lowell's "Amygists."

painters, but we believe that poetry should render particulars exactly and not deal in vague generalities, however magnificent and sonorous.

5. To produce poetry that is hard and clear, never blurred or indefinite.
6. Finally, most of us believe that concentration is the very essence of poetry.

It does not seem possible that these six obvious and almost platitudinous principles (which, incidentally, the Imagists often neglected in their poetry) could have evoked the storm of argument, fury, and downright vilification that broke as soon as the militant Miss Lowell began to champion them. Far from being revolutionary, these principles were not new; they were not even thought so by their sponsors. The Imagists themselves realized that they were restating ideals which had fallen into desuetude, and declared, "They are the essentials of all great poetry, indeed of all great literature." And yet many conservative critics, joined by the one hundred per cent reactionaries, rushed wildly to combat these "heresies"! They forgot that, in trying to protect the future from such lawlessness as "using the exact word," from "freedom in the choice of subject," from the importance of "concentration," they were actually attacking the highest traditions of their enshrined past.

The fracas succeeded in doing more good than the work of the Imagists themselves. H. D. removed herself from controversies and took up her residence in Switzerland, perfecting her delicate and exquisitely finished designs. John Gould Fletcher, a more restless expatriate, returned to America and continued to strengthen his gift through shifting his standards; his later and richer work was in complete opposition to the early pronouncements. Miss Lowell was left to carry on the battle single-handed, to defend the theories which, in practice, she was beginning to violate brilliantly. A most energetic and unflagging experimenter, the late Miss Lowell was amazing in her versatility. She wielded a controversial cudgel with one hand and, with the other, wrote Chaucerian stanzas, polyphonic prose, monologs in New England dialect, irregular *vers libre,* conservative couplets, myths from the Peruvian, translations from the French, echoes from the Japanese, re-creations of Indian folk-lore!

The work of the Imagists was done. Its members began to develop themselves by themselves. They had helped to swell the tide of realistic and romantic naturalism—a tide of which their contribution was merely one wave, a breaker that carried its impact far inshore.

THE FREE VERSE FURORE

One of the tenets of the Imagists (the belief that the individuality of a poet may often be expressed better in free verse than in conventional forms) spread further than all the other articles of their faith. The ease of its fulfillment more than its apparent truth led hundreds who were not, in any sense, Imagist poets to adopt *vers libre* as their medium. The result was an inundation of footless—and often headless—writing; the little which was incisive and original was lost in heavy floods of merely loquacious "shredded prose." For fully ten years there was produced an incalculable quantity of tiresome exhibitionism. Most of this verse was frankly bad. But so, the defenders of *vers libre* objected, are most sonnets. The fact, however, remains that the original exponents of free verse began to look with distrust on the dubious achievements of their camp-followers. H. D.'s chiseled lines, Amy Lowell's enameled pictures, Edgar Lee Masters' brusque epitaphs remain unusual examples of their genre. Other writers gave this amorphous medium a certain definiteness: John Gould Fletcher based his symphonic effects on free sweep and cadence instead of meter; Maxwell Bodenheim forced unions of unhappy nouns and pitiless adjectives without benefit of rhyme; Alfred Kreymborg accomplished a type of staccato whimsy in which no particular beat was perceptible. But the poets themselves, partly because of the wish to change, partly to show that they were not bound by a theory, began to turn back to orthodox patterns.

Amy Lowell's last work was largely in formal verse; her later rhymes and ballads relied greatly on the steady pace of iambics. Bodenheim and Fletcher employed more symmetrical structures; Masters returned to the blank verse of his youth. H. D., who was the one perfect Imagist, the surest artisan in unrhymed cadence, achieved delicate effects in interwoven rhyme. And Kreymborg, who surpassed them all in metrical eccentricities, whose lines were so brittle and elusive that melodic comments (performed by the poet on his mandolute) were required to fill out the elisions, finally turned to the creation of straightforward sonnets and simple couplets. Only Carl Sandburg was faithful to his experiments; he remained the most consistent as well as the most colorful user of free verse. In his fidelity to the loose rhythms, whether employed for thumbnail impressions or extended apostrophes, he was practically alone.

To what can we attribute the return of the prodigal *vers libertine?* To a reversion to orthodox type? Or a revulsion from mere novelty of expression? It seems more likely that, having passed through various phases of experimentation, these poets, like all other workers, desired to crystallize their idiom in some lasting shape. The chief fault with free verse was that it yielded too easily, and what the creator enjoys is the feel of a firm medium, a half-forbidding, half-pliant form. No real artist has failed to want—and work with—"the resisting mass."

FOLK-RHYTHMS AND THE NEGRO

In a country that has not been mellowed by antiquity, that has not possessed songs for its peasantry or traditions for its singers, one cannot look for a wealth of folk-stuff. In the United States folk-poetry followed the path of the pioneer. At first these homely songs were mere adaptations and localized versions of English ballads and border minstrelsy, of which Cecil Sharp's *Folk Songs of the Appalachian Highlands* and the *Lonesone Tunes* recovered in the Kentucky mountains by Howard Brockway and Loraine Wyman are excellent examples. But a more definitely native spirit found expression in various sections of these States. In the West (during the Seventies) Bret Harte and John Hay celebrated, in their own accents, the rough miners, ranchers, steamboat pilots, the supposed descendants of the emigrants from Pike County,

Missouri. In the Middle West the desire for local color and music led to the popularity of James Whitcomb Riley's Hoosier ballads and the spirited jingles of Eugene Field. In the South the inspiration of the negro spirituals and ante bellum songs was utilized to good effect by Irwin Russell, Joel Chandler Harris and, later, by Paul Laurence Dunbar.

The Indian, a more ancient primitive, has remained as difficult to adopt poetically as he has been to assimilate ethnically. Nevertheless, in spite of the fact that the white and red races are worlds apart in sentiment, philosophy, and attitude to life, many gallant attempts were made to bring the spirit of the Indian into our literature. Natalie Curtis Burlin did excellent pioneering work in *The Indians' Book;* Mary Austin, in spite of a far-fetched theory and dubious conclusions, made an extended study of the matter in *The American Rhythm;* and *The Path on the Rainbow,* edited by George W. Cronyn in 1918, proved to be the best general collection on the subject available to the public. Among the individual workers in the field, other than those mentioned, praise was given to Constance Lindsay Skinner, Alice Corbin Henderson, and Witter Bynner.

Since the days of Dunbar, the Negro has made great strides in self-expression. American music—"classical" as well as popular—benefited from the strong insistence of African drums and the syncopated shuffling of the feet of slaves. Jazz itself became glorified; the intelligentsia claimed it as their own! In sociology the Negro, through men like W. E. Burghardt DuBois, Benjamin Brawley, Walter White, turned to be his own analyst. In poetry the results were mixed and uneven. But it became apparent that the Negro was beginning to free himself, not only from a sentimentality designed to please the whites, but from an attitude which was not so much race-conscious as self-conscious. He established his identity at the same time as his poetic integrity.

Beginning in about 1922, the Negro, so long despised as a creator, became a literary fashion. Several volumes of the stirring Spirituals were followed by collections of his secular songs, "blues," "mellows," work-ballads, etc. His ante bellum chants swept over post-war America and Europe; his primitive rhythms affected the most sophisticated of modern composers. James Weldon Johnson's pioneer anthology, *American Negro Poetry* (1922), was followed by Countee Cullen's *Caroling Dusk* (1927) and C. V. Calverton's *An Anthology of American Negro Literature* (1929). Appraisal set in almost simultaneously; a dozen tomes bristling with energy and research appeared, one of them (*American Negro Folk-Songs* by Newman I. White) containing over eight hundred songs divided into thirteen groups. These imposingly annotated collections, added to the more original work, made interest assume the proportions of a Revival. The Negro himself became suddenly articulate; his novels, essays, poems—many of them of unsuspected high caliber—were published everywhere. James Weldon Johnson, after a long career as propagandist, leapt into prominence with *God's Trombones,* seven negro sermons in verse; Claude McKay expressed a stern if over-violent spirit in verse and prose; Countee Cullen, Langston Hughes and Jean Toomer ranged from dulcet lyrics to hot "blues" and savage protests. *The Poetry of the Negro* (1949), a rich collection and a definitive book of reference, was edited by Langston Hughes and Arna Bontemps.

Meanwhile, scholars all over America were ransacking backwood and byway. South Carolina ballads, songs of Maine lumberjacks, ballads of men who worked in the woods of Wisconsin, songs of the "shanty-boy" of Michigan and Minnesota, original and derived folk-tunes of the South, cowboy songs from the West—into every State the recorders went, hot on the trail of the vanishing folk-idiom. The poets were not far behind. The tradition of Harte and Hay was carried on by such interpreters as Harry Herbert Knibbs and Edwin Ford Piper. The Kentucky Mountain region was interpreted by Elizabeth Madox Roberts and Roy Helton. The "white South" found expression through John Crowe Ransom, Allen Tate, Donald Davidson, Merrill Moore and Robert Penn Warren. A group of Oregon poets—Oluf Olsen, H. L. Davis, H. M. Corning—emerged in the late 1920s. But, of all who absorbed and approximated the spirit of folk-poetry, none made more striking or more indubitably American contributions than Vachel Lindsay of Springfield, Illinois.

LINDSAY AND OPPENHEIM

Lindsay was essentially a people's poet. He did not hesitate to express himself in terms of the lowest common denominator; his fingers seemed alternately on his pen and the public pulse. Living near enough to the South to appreciate the Negroes' qualities without wishing to theatricalize them, Lindsay was tremendously influenced by the colorful suggestions, the fantastic superstitions, the revivalistic gusto, the half-savage Christianity and, above all, by the curiously syncopated music that once characterized the black man in America. In "The Congo," "John Brown" and the less extended "Simon Legree," the words roll with the solemnity of an exhortation, dance with a grotesque fervor, or snap, crackle, and leap with all the humorous rhythms of a piece of "ragtime." Lindsay caught the burly color and boisterous music of camp-meetings, minstrel shows, revival jubilees. He was an itinerant evangelist preaching the Gospel through a saxophone.

And Lindsay did more. He carried his democratic determinations further than any of his *confrères*. Dreaming of a great communal Art, he insisted that all villages should be centers of beauty, all citizens, artists. At heart a missionary even more than a minstrel, Lindsay often lost himself in his own doctrines. Worse, he frequently cheapened himself and caricatured his own gift by pandering to the vaudeville instinct, putting a noisy "punch" into everything, regardless of taste, artistry, or a sense of proportion. He was most impressive when purely fantastic (as in "The Ghosts of the Buffaloes," the shorter fancies, the series of metaphorical poems about the moon) or when a greater theme and a finer restraint unite (as in "The Eagle That Is Forgotten") to create a preaching that does not cease to be poetry.

Something of the same blend of prophet and poet was found in the work of James Oppenheim. Oppenheim, a throwback to the ancient Hebrew singers, rolled the music of the Psalms through his lines; his poetry, with its obvious reminders of Whitman, was biblical in its inflection, Oriental in its heat. It carried to the Western world the color of the East, adding the gift of prophecy to purpose. In books like *War and Laughter* and *Songs for the New Age* the race of god-breakers and god-makers spoke with a new voice; here, with analytic intensity, the old iconoclasm and still older worship were united.

ELIOT AND HIS INFLUENCE

Two strongly opposed tendencies influenced all American poetry after 1915. The one was a use of the colloquial speech popularized by Sandburg, Lindsay, and Masters and heightened by Frost; the other was a striking departure from both the consistent conversational tone and the traditional "poetic" language to which such poets as E. A. Robinson and Edna St. Vincent Millay remained loyal. The abrupt break in idiom was brought about by T. S. Eliot, who brought it from France. Eliot, borrowing the method from Laforgue, Valéry, and Rimbaud, used the technique of the Symbolist school with such skill that he soon had a host of imitators on both sides of the Atlantic. Some were unable, some unwilling to follow Eliot's inner difficulties and despairs, but all were fascinated by his technical devices, and only a few were uninfluenced by them. The formula was, roughly, this: To reveal man in his complex relation to the universe the poet must show him not only concerned with the immensities but with the trivialities of daily life, with a sense of the past continually interrupting the present, and with swiftly contradictory moods disputing dream and action. This was, obviously, a difficult if not impossible program to achieve in any one poem or even a set of poems. It was, however, attempted and suggested by a variety of effects: by a rapid leaping from image to image with a minimum of "explanatory" metaphors; by a liberal use of discords, juxtaposing tense images and prosy statements, following lyrical passages with deliberate banalities; by the continual play of free association, in which one idea prompted a chain of others, accomplishing an emotional (or literary) progress, often gaining a new series of overtones, often sacrificing all continuity—Ezra Pound's *Cantos,* Crane's *The Bridge,* and Eliot's *The Waste Land* being the most famous examples of the mood "mixing memory and desire."

The method had its distinct advantages; it enlarged the gamut of poetic devices and permitted a greater sensitivity of expression. But it was abused by many and even its champions were aware of its limitations. "The substitution of emotional for logical sequence," wrote C. Day Lewis in *A Hope for Poetry,* "may finally be classed as one of the manifestations of the general distrust of logic and dethroning of reason brought about by the Great War." Such a poem as *The Waste Land,* though it helped shape a subtler poetic speech, made one aware of "the nervous exhaustion, the exaggerated self-consciousness, the pathetic gropings after the fragments of a shattered faith. . . . But in so doing it enlarged our conception of the field of poetic activity; as Eliot himself said, 'the essential advantage for a poet is not to have a beautiful world with which to deal; it is to be able to see beneath both beauty and ugliness; to see the boredom, and the horror, and the glory.' "

The earlier *Prufrock* and *Sweeney* series accomplished the purpose in an acrid light verse; Eliot's later ironies emphasized, with new bitterness, the hollowness of a life without purpose and without faith. Far from celebrating the feeble, Eliot satirized the futilitarians:

We are the hollow men
We are the stuffed men
Leaning together
Headpiece filled with straw. Alas!
Our dried voices, when
We whisper together
Are quiet and meaningless
As wind in dry grass
Or rats' feet over broken glass
In our dry cellar

Shape without form, shade without color,
Paralyzed force, gesture without motion—

But most of those so strongly influenced by Eliot—and by Eliot's influences—captured nothing except his (and Jules Laforgue's) idiom. His abrupt allusiveness, his style at once coarse and subtle, his emotional acuteness, could be imitated but not captured; his unacknowledged disciples merely parodied the trick of disassociation, the erudition without Eliot's wisdom, the gesture without (if I may misquote) emotion. The results were inevitable: sterile intellectualism at one extreme, infantile barbarism at the other.

However, to condemn an entire group because of the failures is unjust. The younger poets (1920-1930), sometimes condemned as "a lost generation," matured in a period which afforded them no security nor dignity nor any semblance of peace. Being sensitive, even over-sensitive recorders, they reflected the doubt, the very discontinuity of the times. Little wonder theirs was a "literature of nerves," little wonder their symbols were uncertain, their allusions private, and their work often obscure to the point of unintelligibility. The clearest of them maintained their individuality, though they demonstrated their limited heritage; even the more prominent acknowledged the influence of Eliot. As in England, where Stephen Spender, W. H. Auden, and C. Day Lewis were affected by Eliot's technique, though not by his philosophy, so Eliot's experiments may be traced in the work of Archibald MacLeish, Conrad Aiken, Horace Gregory, and the entire Nashville group.

THE NEW BARBARISM

The common reader, confronted by the extremely "modernist" poet, was unsure whether to claim his rights as reader, or turn altogether from what seemed a communication that communicated nothing more intelligible than the author's wish to be let alone. Robert Graves and Laura Riding in *A Survey of Modernist Poetry* (1927) summarized the situation: "The bond between the Victorian poet and his reader was at least an agreement between them of a common, though not an original, sentiment. The meaning of a poem was understood between them beforehand from the very title, and the persuasion of the word-music was intended to keep the poem vibrating in the memory long after it had been read. . . . The modernist poet does not have to issue a program declaring his intentions toward the reader or to issue an announcement of tactics. . . . The important part of poetry is now not the personality of the poet as embodied in a poem, but the personality of the poem itself; that is, its quality of independence from both the reader and the poet, once the poet has separated it from his personality by making it complete—a new and self-explanatory creature."

Sometimes these "self-explanatory creatures" explained; sometimes they did not. Often they exhibited nothing more specific than self-conscious snobbery. But the best of them, oppressed by the dead hand of the past, were effective in their revolt; they destroyed that semi-comatose condition which so often attends the reading of poetry and (being a criticism of bad poetry as well as of the reader) revealed new wit, new vitality, new signals of beauty beneath the surface oddities. Thus E. E. Cummings, a lyrical poet in spite of his eccentricities, wrote: "To create is first of all to destroy . . . There is and can be no such thing as authentic art until the *bons trucs* (whereby we are taught to see and imitate on canvas and in stone and by words this so-called world) are entirely and thoroughly and perfectly annihilated by that vast and painful process of unthinking which may result in a minute bit of purely personal feeling. Which minute bit is art."

Thus we had the phenomenon of Gertrude Stein "destroying" the English language, attempting to create a speech in which words had only tonal and abstract values, and James Joyce, in his later work, breaking up and reconstructing syllables until they resembled a colorful game of anagrams. Between a literature of obscure scholasticism and experiments in "the vast and painful process of unthinking," the younger writers evolved a phase if not a philosophy of their own. Malcolm Cowley, expressing this for them, summarized it: "We ourselves have found that most of our philosophical difficulties can be solved not by philosophy itself, but by living on, by changing one's angle of approach, and often simply by changing one's place. The war, which carried many of our generation into strange countries, had a partly intellectual, partly emotional effect that is generally disregarded. It destroyed our sense of dull security and taught us to live from day to day. It gave us a thirst for action and adventure. It presented us with violent contrasts, with very simple tragedies, and so led us back toward the old themes of love and death."

PROLETARIAN POETS AND MACLEISH

Much was written concerning an imminent proletarian school of poetry, but no one expressed in verse what such novelists as Robert Cantwell, Albert Halper, and James T. Farrell expressed in prose. *The New Masses* printed a quantity of proletarian free verse, but, of all the contributors to the group, Kenneth Fearing alone combined slang and a staccato rhetoric (not quite successfully) to satirize the cheap heroics and blatant miseries, the five-and-ten cent lives and tabloid minds of the industrial centers and a decaying system. Horace Gregory sounded the depths of social dissatisfaction with a subtlety that delighted the artists, but failed to move the masses. Langston Hughes concerned himself with the plight of the black workers. Clifford Odets seemed the most promising poet of revolt, but Odets' work was in the theater, where

Awake and Sing, Till the Day I Die, and *Waiting for Lefty* voiced the passion and poetry of the inarticulate. Lola Ridge remained the most intense as well as the most integrated of the revolutionaries, yet her work in *Firehead* and *Dance of Fire* was traditional in pattern, the peak of the latter volume being a sequence of mystical sonnets.

Much also had been expected from those who celebrated a "machine age poetry." In 1929 Hart Crane wrote, "Unless poetry can absorb the machine, i.e., *acclimatize* it as naturally and casually as trees, cattle, galleons, castles, and all other human associations of the past, then poetry has failed of its full contemporary function." This sentiment was echoed by many, but few Americans carried out the process of assimilating or "acclimatizing" the machine. Three young English poets—W. H. Auden, Stephen Spender, and C. Day Lewis—went further to justify Crane than any poet in this country. Crane himself almost accomplished it in *The Bridge,* but this ambitious poem failed in the end, partly because it lacked a culminating effect, partly because Crane was unable to solidify his mood and his material. MacKnight Black, hoping to communicate the spirit of Diesel engines and piston-rings in his *Machinery* and *Thrust at the Sky,* attempted unsuccessfully to unite new subject-matter and an old poetic vocabulary, merely romanticizing the mechanical objects. Others considered the wish to "express" the machine ill-advised and futile. For one thing, they maintained, the machine has been always with us without winning our affections; today it is no closer to man's emotions—and the stuff of poetry—than it was in the first days of the loom, the mill, the cotton-gin. For another, the machine has no fixed character; it changes too rapidly to become part of man's deeper experience.

It was a poet of the aristocratic tradition whose later work—particularly in *Frescoes for Mr. Rockefeller's City* and in *Panic*—symbolized the impasse of the current social system and its tragic consequences. This poet who made the deepest impression since the advent of Frost and Eliot was Archibald MacLeish. MacLeish took the Symbolist manner further and broke new ground; he adapted the Eliot-Laforgue technique, as well as the form of Pound's *Cantos* and Perse's *Anabase,* and extended it. He began tentatively enough with *The Pot of Earth,* enlarged the gamut in *Streets in the Moon,* and declared himself fully in *New Found Land* and *Conquistador,* an epic in little. Adding several devices of his own—notably a skillful interior rhyme and a suspended *terza rima*—MacLeish perfected a verse which is both firm and delicate, sinewy yet supple. His unusually flexible line was used with genuine, not theatrical, eloquence in the drama *J. B.,* produced in 1959, an effort which explored the modern relevance of Job's situation, and which was another example of the attempt to revive poetic drama.

THE NASHVILLE GROUP

In a preceding section mention was made of the spirit animating the new South. Apart from the short-lived Carolina local color school and the work of the previously considered Negro poets, the most important group centered about Vanderbilt University in Nashville, Tennessee. It originated in a body of teachers and students known as "The Fugitives," after their magazine which was published from April, 1922, to December, 1925. It was never explained what the fugitives were fleeing to escape, and it soon became apparent that there were differences of taste and temperament among the members. But a sense of their backgrounds, a sympathy beyond an ear for quaint localisms, bound them together. This unannounced expression of unity—a union of old dreams and new issues—was to develop into a controversy centering about Agrarianism, but it began with poetry and it was on poetry that the group maintained itself.

John Crowe Ransom was the stimulator if not the founder of the school. He guided its fortunes and, for a while, dictated (unconsciously perhaps) its program and style. That style was a curious fusion of the pedantic and the metaphysical, a fusion which even he, in his later poetry, failed to lift above a cryptic overelaboration. At his best—and no less than a dozen poems represent him at that enviable height—Ransom has a finesse and a flavor unlike any other poet; he is master of an urbane grace and a mockery which masks a teasing tenderness. His vocabulary and his highly original technique equip him to sound the depths with a light and almost nonchalant touch; there are times when he even accomplishes an integration of the sublime and the ridiculous.

Donald Davidson's style is less metaphysical and more emotional than Ranson's; his poems, particularly *The Tall Men,* reveal his concern with things rather than with abstractions. Originally influenced by Ransom and Eliot, Davidson found himself in his recreations and reveries of the War Between the States and, though he spent much of his energies teaching and reviewing, his longer poems have an almost epic breadth.

Allen Tate was the most unpredictable and belligerent of the group. Ten years younger than Ransom and five years younger than Davidson, his energy was astonishing. He turned from poetry to biography, from biography to criticism, from criticism to controversy, from controversy back to poetry. Everything he did was achieved with distinction and despatch, everything except his poetry. His poetry continually called for revision—at least so it seemed to its author—and before he was forty Tate had published several versions of the same poems. Robert Penn Warren, born in 1905, the youngest of the group, is also the most fiery. Strong feeling forces itself through the simplest of his poems; pictorial verses, whose effect would ordinarily be merely visual, are surcharged with a plain-spoken force which seldom fails to communicate its excitement. Even the metaphysical conceit (a favorite device of "The Fugitives") achieves an unexpected intensity in his image-crowded lines. Merrill Moore, 1903-1957, was the most fecund of the group, probably the most prolific of American poets. Before he was thirty he had composed so many sonnets—a rough calculation approximated the number at twenty thousand—that he had to resort to short-hand to get them down between his labors as instructor and psychiatrist. His poetry has both the charm and the handicap of improvisation; it suffers from its speed and the author's inability to review his errors or revise a single unfortunate phrase. But Moore's fluency results in many startling effects. Moreover, he has a particularly Southern humor—half grave, half grotesque—and he can make beauty out of banality, confronting the reader with wildness wrung from conversational small change.

The outstanding excellence of the Nashville group was its free use of the discord—juxtaposing the traditionally poetic and the common colloquial—and the establishment of a sharp-edged diction. In thought as well as technique it emphasized intelligence; it insisted on adult poetry as against the plethora of pretty, thoughtless, and immature verse written by adults. Its chief defect was a too frequent retreat into a remote classicism; with its metaphysical predilections the poetry sometimes became recondite and even incomprehensible. The stock of subjects grew low and, as John Gould Fletcher concluded in an otherwise sympathetic consideration of the school, "the 'Southern type' of poem tends to become distorted, fragmentary, obscure the more the poets speculate on the *intellectual* content as opposed to the emotional, or *sensible,* content of their subject matter." But the best of this poetry rose above its limitations and cleared a direction of its own.

RANGE AND DIVERSITY: STEVENS TO JEFFERS

After the First World War, groups divided, quarreled, and split apart; many tendencies were in the air at one time. The difficult and re-creative "process of unthinking" often degenerated into mere thoughtlessness, a tendency glorified by the "Super-realists" and the editors of *transition.* Opposed to this the "classicism" of Eliot pointed in a contrary direction. Joined to a cool scholasticism, orderliness came to offset the loose writing and looser thinking of the free verse plethora. Founded on a definite esthetic intellectual rather than emotional, much of the new work achieved a shapeliness in which thought restrained sentiment, in which conception and perception were skillfully balanced.

Language was being tested in a dozen different directions; where one poet tightened the forms, another loosened them. A new semi-cavalier grace warred with forthright declarations. Wallace Stevens, departing from a depiction of things—actually disputing the "thinginess" of literature—perfected an orchidaceous flowering of words from words, achieving a type of witty suggestion new to the period. The euphuistic distortions of Maxwell Bodenheim and the over-luxuriant figures of E. E. Cummings grew in the same lustrum as the austere, later lyrics of Sara Teasdale and the emotional directness of Edna St. Vincent Millay.

Of the younger men Horace Gregory and James Agee contributed striking work. Widely different though their poems were they had two characteristics in common: a combination of "high seriousness" and irony, and the ability to employ images straight from contemporary life.

An unprecedented vigor of language was brought into American poetry about 1926 by Robinson Jeffers. Jeffers successfully experimented with a peculiarly long line, whose strength matched the dark power of its author's philosophy. His technique derived from Whitman's, but his attitude was the antithesis of that over-emphatic affirmer's, and his images attained a strange pessimistic splendor. "The creatures of Jeffers's imagination," wrote Horace Gregory in *The New Mythology,* "strive, love, and die within a nightmare that is becoming known as the American consciousness, which is a poetic distortion of the American scene. They are manifestations of a civilization that seems childishly innocent and harmlessly insane." Never had the range of American verse been so extensive, and Jeffers strenuously helped to extend it.

THE NEW LYRICISTS

The lyric note was bound to be affected. It, too, fluctuated to express the shift from convention to revolt, from decision to doubt, from a fixed form to an almost dissolving line. Conrad Aiken developed a peculiarly wavering music which, if often vague and repetitive, was capable of haunting effects, both in the early lyrics and the later somber preludes. David McCord alternated easily from the meditative to the whimsically mocking. Stephen Vincent Benét and William Rose Benét, brothers in blood and balladry, plundered modernity and antiquity for their fancies; the former, taking the Civil War for a background in *John Brown's Body,* constructed a many-voiced lyric of epic proportions. John Hall Wheelock luxuriated in leaping if somewhat determined affirmations. George Dillon, a singer in water-color, composed delicately patterned interrogations. The short lyrics of Robert Frost grew consistently in strength and suggestiveness.

The work of the women ranged from the outspoken to the involved. Two distinct influences governed many of them: Emily Dickinson and Lizette Woodworth Reese. The epigrammatic condensations of the former affected an entire generation with increasing force. The firm speech and sparse imagery of the latter won many away from the lush and cloying love-songs of the type enshrined in 1842 by Rufus W. Griswold in his waxworks *Gems from American Female Poets.* Edna St. Vincent Millay, in the later sonnets no less than in the early "Renascence," deepened an already impassioned note, increasing the admiration as well as the size of her audience. Sara Teasdale intensified a simple but flexible melodic line. Genevieve Taggard and Jean Starr Untermeyer lifted the ordinary round of woman's everyday into the extraordinary and, not seldom, into the ecstatic.

Others, refining their poetry of a too thickly human passion, turned to an elliptical metaphysics. The "mechanism of sensibility" brought them back to Crashaw, Vaughan, Webster, and Donne. One caught the overtones of the late Elizabethans in the accents of Louise Bogan, Léonie Adams, Hazel Hall, Elinor Wylie, among others. Elinor Wylie acknowledged the relationship implicitly, the title of her first volume (*Nets to Catch the Wind*) being taken from a poem by Webster, the title of her last (*Angels and Earthly Creatures*) from a sermon by Donne. But these poets did not depend too much on intellectual virtuosity and involuted images; their sensibility was their own. Less prodigal (and, it may be added, less passionate) than Donne and his followers, they reflected something of his order and his fiercely conceived beauty through temperaments essentially modern and feminine. Elinor Wylie, never "confusing the spiritual and the sensual either through false fear or false reverence," began with verbal brilliance and ended by celebrating the radiance of spirit and "the pure and valiant mind." Léonie Adams, a more withdrawn metaphysician, yielded her secret only to those who were already poets, though even the unlettered could sense the music and far-reaching implications. Tracing the swift mutability of time, and in particular these times, Louise Bogan, Marya Zaturenska, and Muriel Rukeyser outlined a poetry which was both sensuous and cerebral, intricately designed but deeply impassioned.

CRISIS AND DEPRESSION: 1929

Social as well as financial values crashed in October, 1929, but the blow did not immediately register on the poetry of the period. A few years later it became evident that a crisis had occurred in literature as well as in finance and government. The poets turned, tentatively enough, to a consideration of economic and social problems; some of them deserted poetry altogether. It is noteworthy that whereas the five years from 1913 to 1918 produced a dozen or more poets of national importance, not more than three or four new poets of any significance appeared between 1930 and 1940.

Poetry was affected by the general paralysis, unable to express the crisis except by negation. Yet, no matter what the conditions, man cannot remain inarticulate for long; there were signs that the younger poets, deeply affected by the breakdown, were grappling with the situation. It was not long before they attempted to express the universal bewilderment, doubtfully, even desperately. Theirs was a difficult task. Values were distorted, standards questioned, the traditional responses deadened. But the basic feelings, disbalanced and temporarily stunned, could not remain paralyzed.

The aftermath of the depression took the form of an increasingly critical examination of contemporary life, a frank and unflattering appraisal of men and motives. The questioning habit grew. At its best it attained the vigor of a challenge; at its worst it assumed a worn disillusion. Too often the loss of an integrating faith was reflected in a philosophy of formlessness, and complacent optimism was exchanged for complacent despair.

The style shifted to match the changing tempo, increasing speed and violence. The manner alternated from brusque to bitter; the tone was pungent rather than poignant; the attack was spasmodic, nervously staccato. The romanticized "personal attitude" was regarded with suspicion. The tensions of the false peace and the premonitions of war prompted a literature of nervous foreboding. Writers were torn by the contradictory claims of a planned economy and a planless do-nothingism. The result was a contradiction of outer form and inner confusion. Much of the poetry of the early thirties is not only the record of a vast nightmare, but an attempt to analyze it.

DIVISION IN THE THIRTIES

The decade following the crisis of 1929 revealed the growing importance of such highly idiomatic poets as William Carlos Williams, Hart Crane, and Horace Gregory, as well as the promise of Kenneth Fearing, Kenneth Patchen, and Delmore Schwartz. It also disclosed two sharply divided tendencies. Division was marked in subject matter and vocabulary; it was emphasized by the writers' divergent attitudes to the reader. On the one hand, the work of the younger poets addressed itself to the common man; influenced by the music-hall, the movies, and the radio, it attempted to be persuasive and "popular." The tone was easy-going, pseudo-jocular, masking grimness in a false gaiety. An excellent example is Harry Brown's "The Ambulant Blues," which begins:

> Went into a skyscraper, asked for love,
> They said I'd better try the floor up above,
> Thanked them politely and climbed the stair,
> But I didn't find anything but thin, thin air.
> Turned me around and went away,
> And heard them whispering, "He didn't stay."
> But there was no use in standing around
> To wait for a wound.

On the other hand, many of the youngest writers assumed a solemnly detached air and addressed themselves not to the common man but to the exceptional man, the scholar, the wit. It was no accident that the original Nashville "Fugitives" (see page 25) were teachers, and their descendants, the scattered "Neo-Fugitives" (Randall Jarrell, W. R. Moses, George Marion O'Donnell) were pupils who became professors. Their highly stylized manner was deceptive, adroitly elaborate and yet remote; sometimes it was so clever that it outwitted its subject. More often than not it was vague in is references, allusive in a pedantic way, as in W. R. Moses' "Old Triton's Wreathed Horn," which concludes:

> One x may represent commodities
> Largely diverse, so one thing be the same;
> Restraint, imposed by hunger or by will,
> Ones waves of thoughts and starlings. What's a piece,
> By part of it we represent: the tame
> Thoughts I may drop, be pennoned by the game
> Of black, bird-waves in grey, mid-winter seas.

At one extreme the writing of the thirties tended to grow polemical and flatly "proletarian." At the other extreme it became hypersensitive, obscure, and abstractly "patrician."

SYSTEMATIC CONFUSION: SURREALISM

The advance-guard experimenters of the late thirties, unlike their immediate predecessors, were uninterested in political issues, indifferent to a world of revolutionary change. They were not ignorant of war and revolution, but they were determined to evade and, if possible, to avoid the issues. Concerned almost wholly with the "need of self-expression," they became defenders of a repudiated position. Theirs was a retreat to the crumbling ivory tower, a championship of the almost forgotten "Art for Art's sake," an elaborate if topsy-turvy estheticism.

The inevitable result of the evasion of ordinary experience was a plunge into fantasy; the fear of reality was answered by surrealism. Surrealism was the "justification" of failure to deal with the actual and difficult world; it was the ultimate escape, the denial of logic, the triumph of unmeaning. In surrealism irresponsibility was glorified; cause and effect were casually reversed; the image, liberated from all restraint, flew off into orgies of free association. In 1940 such magazines as *Diogenes* and *Experimental Review* and collections like *New Directions* devoted much of their space to examples and examination of non-logical writing, purposeful incongruity, and "uncensored dictations from the unconscious."

Although surrealism made a point of ridiculing all formulas, it did not disdain a program of its own. The pronouncements were not troubled by consistency. A leading protagonist of surrealism, Nicola Calas, wrote, "To *responsibility* the surrealists oppose *revelation*." And Salvador Dali, painter and theorist, asked: "May not one succeed in systematizing confusion, and so assist the total discrediting of the world of reality?"

Such attempts to "discredit the world of reality" by "systematizing confusion" had already begun in Europe early in the twentieth century. But the effort "to reduce and finally dispose of the contradictions between dream and waking, between the 'real' and the 'unreal'" had its American protagonists. One of them, Charles Henri Ford, began a poem lightly entitled "He Cut His Finger on Eternity" with these lines:

> What grouchy war-tanks intend to shred
> or crouch the road's middle to stop my copy?
> I'll ride roughshod as an anniversary
> down the great coiled gap of your ear.

Oscar Williams, a poet of energetic if wanton metaphors, opened his poem "Mister I" with this kaleidoscopic verse:

> He climbed up the walls of the well into the forbidden nest
> And caught the ambushed bird by the scruff of its great voice:
> Meadows full of insects trundled off under a bushel of abstraction;
> Ingots of rodent drummed at his conscience armored in action.

Richard Eberhart, who never subscribed to the surrealist doctrine, surpassed many of the official adherents in triumphs of discontinuity. When he was most persuasive Eberhart was most obscure. For example:

> In prisons of established craze
> Hear the sane tread without noise
> Whose songs no iron walls will raze
> Though hearts are as of girls and boys.
>
> By the waters burning clear
> Where sheds of men are only seen,
> Accept eloquent time, and revere
> The silence of the great machine.

In spite of providing a few entertaining adventures in verbal anarchy, the surrealist movement remained a cult for the eccentric and an exhibit of the curious. Only the extremists welcomed the dissolution of form, the desirability of automatic responses, and the "law of incongruity." The voluble escapists hailed surrealism as a rebelliously esthetic adventure, a gleeful revolt against morality as well as reality, against logic, order, and the bugbear of good taste.

THE BEAT GENERATION

In the 1950s a group originating in San Francisco rode high on waves of publicity. An extension of what was once "the new barbarism," the members of the clan classed themselves as "The Holy Barbarians" or "Beatniks." Scorning the shibboleths of the day, they erupted in poems which combined amorality, surrealism, hedonism, jazz, fragments of Zen philosophy, marijuana sessions, casual obscenities, and a program of general irresponsibility. Their technique was derived from the blunt statements of William Carlos Williams and the kaleidoscopic effects of Ezra Pound, whose influence on contemporary American poetry had become as varied as it was pervasive. Their reaction against the apathy of the average citizen in a world bent upon self-destruction, their contempt for the compromises of respectability, and their rejection of organized society expressed itself in outcries by Jack Kerouac, Lawrence Ferlinghetti, Gregory Corso, Peter Orlovsky, Philip Lamantia, Michael McClure, and Allen Ginsberg, whose "Howl" was one of the key-poems of the group. It begins:

I saw the best minds of my generation destroyed by madness, starving hysterical naked,
dragging themselves through the negro streets at dawn looking for an angry fix,
angelheaded hipsters burning for the ancient heavenly connection to the starry dynamo in the machinery of night,
who poverty and tatters and hollow-eyed and high sat up smoking in the supernatural darkness of cold-water flats floating across the tops of cities contemplating jazz,
who bared their brains to Heaven under the El and saw Mohammedan angels staggering on tenement roofs illuminated,
who passed through universities with radiant cool eyes hallucinating Arkansas and Blake-light tragedy among the scholars of war,
who were expelled from the academies for crazy & publishing obscene odes on the windows of the skull,
who cowered in unshaven rooms in underwear, burning their money in wastebaskets and listening to the Terror through the wall . . .

Such exacerbated poetry was only incidentally a revulsion from the romantic attitude. Primarily it was a revolt in which words were used as an act of revenge, a resentment directed against a conformist culture which the Beats felt had been arbitrarily imposed upon them. The Angry Young Men who congregated in coffee houses and night clubs declaiming their poetry to the beat of jazz instruments were sounding what Ginsberg called "mad mouthfuls of language" to register their exasperation. If their expostulations had a plethora of verbal violence and no reformist intent, if they wrote in a welter of fragments, it was because they were trying to reflect the welter itself, the shattering effect of a shaken society upon its people. Their subjects, and seemingly they themselves, were propelled by forces of which they were fearfully aware, forces that affected them with dread as much as loathing. Too disillusioned to hope for a better order of things, they gave themselves up to consuming hates and the distortions of a nightmare world. It was their pain rather than their poetry which affected the reader.

THE NEO-STYLISTS

Opposed to the cult of disorganization, other poets of the 1950s heightened the reader's response to "the boredom, and the horror, but also to the glory." With a sense of responsibility to form as well as to substance, they placed emphasis on skill, meaning, and style. It was not merely a matter of technique, for as Pierre Francastel wrote in *Peinture et Société,* "technique alone is powerless to account for the appearance of a new style; a new style means the appearance of a new attitude of man toward the world."

The new attitude, embodied in a new style, was actually a return to the old standards: clarity, precision, and formalism. Sometimes fastidiousness went so far that elegance took the place of eloquence, and the poet concerned himself with the dissection of minutiae instead of an amplified vision. Writing as though they were afraid of uncontrolled emotion, some took pleasure in craftsmanship and overintellectualized their poems into flat and often toneless statements without urgency or any strong feeling.

However, such poets as Karl Shapiro, Elizabeth Bishop, Stanley Kunitz, Randall Jarrell, Theodore Roethke, Robert Lowell, Peter Viereck, Richard Wilbur, W. D. Snodgrass, Anne Sexton, and Ruth Stone composed poems which, while formal, were rich in imagination, strictly disciplined but never discarding passion and the magic which lifts poetry above the most painstaking and thoughtful verse.

The poet's dilemma was the ever-recurring problem: he had to create order in the midst of disorder. Often overwhelmed by the deep cleavages of his time and the sense of impending chaos, he retreated into private experience and personal symbolism. Here he often brought forth a mandarin art. But more hopefully there were continual compensating efforts to fit the broken pieces into a larger pattern, to avoid willful obscurity and direct the turbulent stream of the unconscious into channels of communication.

This volume purports to show the fluctuations of taste, the claims of both tradition and experiment, the constant play between convention and revolt. It is not held that every poem in this collection is a great poem. It is maintained, however, that the selection from each poet achieves a union of the known and the unknown, the combination of the familiar and the surprising which is the essence and power of poetry.

L. U.

Walt Whitman

⇝§ Walt (originally Walter) Whitman was born at West Hills, near Huntington, Long Island, May 31, 1819. His mother's people were hard-working Dutch Quakers, his maternal grandfather having been a Long Island horse-breeder. On his father's side he was descended from English Puritans who had farmed American soil for a century and a half.

Whitman's father was a less successful agrarian than his ancestors and, since he was a better carpenter than farmer, the elder Whitman moved his family to the then provincial suburb of Brooklyn. Here the country child grew into the town boy, was lifted up for a moment by Lafayette when the hero revisited America, was equally fascinated by his father's wood-smelling shop and the city streets, received his first sight of the "million-footed" city which was to become his beloved Mannahatta, learned at least the rudiments of the three R's, and left school before his teens. At eleven he was already at work as an errand-boy. At twelve he became a "printer's devil." By the time he was fourteen he had learned the various fonts and began to set type in the composing-room of *The Long Island Star*. At seventeen, taking up residence in the more profitable metropolis, he was well on the road to being an itinerant printer-journalist. But New York was no Golconda for an uneducated, self-conscious youth and, after a few months, Whitman went back to Long Island, his "fish-shaped Paumanok."

There he remained until his twenty-second year, living with his numerous relations, intermittently teaching school, delivering papers, contributing "pieces" to *The Long Island Democrat.* In 1841 Whitman returned to Brooklyn and New York, writing sentimental fillers, novelettes, rhetorical and flabby verses, hack-work editorials for journals now forgotten. In 1842 he wrote a temperance tract, *Franklin Evans, or The Inebriate,* a mixture of campaign material and fourth-rate Dickens, a volume which Whitman later claimed was written for cash in three days. Blossoming out in frock coat and high hat, debonair, his beard smartly trimmed, Whitman at twenty-three was editor of *The Daily Aurora.* In the capacity of reporter-about town, he promenaded lower Broadway, spent much time in the theaters, cultivated the opera, flirted impartially with street-corner politics and the *haut monde.* He was still Walter Whitman, when, at the age of twenty-seven, he joined the *Brooklyn Eagle.*

Various biographers—Emory Holloway, in particular—have ferreted out Whitman's sketches and editorials of this period and, while there are occasional suggestions of the poet to come, most of them betray him as a fluent, even a prolific, journalist and nothing more. The style is alternately chatty and highfalutin; the ideas are undistinguished. At the end of two years, either because of his politics or his unsatisfactory articles, Whitman suddenly lost his editorial position and, with equal abruptness, received an offer from a stranger who was about to start an independent paper in New Orleans. Thereupon he left New York early in 1848 to become a special writer on the staff of the daily *Crescent.*

Whitman's few months in the South have led to much speculation. Emory Holloway concludes that New Orleans was the background for the poet's first love-affair and implies that his inamorata was one of the *demimonde,* probably a quadroon beauty. But this is sheer guess-work, barely supported by Whitman's later poetry where the wish often substitutes for the action. This much is evident: He and his younger brother Jeff enjoyed the more languorous tempo of the Creole culture; the "Paris of America" made him less priggish; his quickened perceptions took in the whole alphabet of sights and sounds, "not missing a letter from A to Izzard." His literary style, however, had not improved and, after three months, he was dismissed from the *Crescent,* possibly because of his careless, even puerile writing.

Returning to New York, Whitman immediately plunged into editing another paper. His failures as a journalist had not yet convinced him he was mistaking his career and in his thirtieth year he was in charge of the Brooklyn *Freeman.* This free-soil journal soon shifted its political course; Whitman was not agile enough to turn with it; and in September, 1849, he withdrew, "taking his flag with him." As a free-lance, he wrote for the New York *Evening Post* and the *Advertiser,* his contributions being chiefly articles—and badly over-written ones—on music. He "took up" art, gushed about Donizetti's "Favorita," became a metropolitan Bohemian. Meanwhile, finding he could not live by the pen alone, he helped his father and brothers build houses in Brooklyn. Meanwhile, also, he began to write the book which was to be his life-work.

It was at this time that Walter Whitman, the dandified journalist, disappeared and the Walt Whitman of tradition suddenly emerged. He was, one suspects, not unconscious of the tradition and, from the outset, used every means to foster it.

Whitman was now thirty-one; an entirely different apparition from the man who, in his late twenties, frequented the more fashionable lobbies. The once trim beard, streaked with premature gray, was now worn loose and prophetic; the well-tailored coat and spruce cane were discarded in favor of rough workman's clothes, high boots, a large felt hat and a red shirt with the collar nonchalantly—or carefully—opened wide enough to show red flannel underneath. He prepared several lectures on the democracy of art and delivered one at the Brooklyn Art Union in 1851, but found lecturing too tame. He consorted with ferry-men, bus-drivers and other "powerful, uneducated persons." The legend persists that, when one of the drivers was ill, Whitman took his route and drove the omnibus, shouting passages of Shakespeare up and down Broadway. Another legend—repeated by Holloway as a fact—pictures Whitman reading Epictetus to one of the boatmen and, afterwards, "cramming his own volume into the pocket of the sailor's monkey-jacket." These are Homeric gestures and one would like to believe them uncalculated. But even the most confirmed Whitman-worshiper must have his doubts. Subsequent actions add to the admirer's misgivings.

The first edition of *Leaves of Grass* was published in 1855. This epochal volume made its initial appearance as a poorly printed pamphlet of twelve poems brought out anonymously and bearing, instead of a signature, a portrait of the author with one hand in his pocket, one on his hip, the characteristic open shirt and a slouch hat rakishly tilted. One of the first copies of the pamphlet was sent to Ralph Waldo

Emerson, which—considering Whitman's indebtedness in spirit if not in form—was no more than proper. Within a fortnight, Emerson, overlooking the questionable taste of the frontispiece, and with something of the master's gratification on being hailed by an unknown but fervent disciple, wrote the famous letter of July 21, 1855, in which he hailed the young writer, concluding, "I give you joy of your free and brave thought. I have great joy in it. . . . I find the courage of treatment which so delights us, and which large perception only can inspire. I greet you at the beginning of a great career."

But Emerson's lavish praise (which Whitman, without waiting for permission, blazoned on the cover of his second edition) was not loud enough. Nor, was Whitman, despite the convictions contained in the lengthy prose preface, confident enough of his work; he sought to force public approval. In direct opposition to Emersonian standards and the spiritual ideals implied in his foreword, Whitman set about to cause a controversy, to inflame opinion by inflating himself. The task—considering the howls which greeted *Leaves of Grass*—was not difficult. It was—so defenders have insisted—the day of the anonymous review and "self-puffery" was not uncommon. But Whitman's offenses in this regard (and there were many of them) are inexcusable in view of the principles he professed. Two months after the first printing of *Leaves of Grass,* he caused one of a series of anonymous articles to be printed in the Brooklyn *Times* (September 29, 1855). In it—and the idiom is unmistakable—he wrote: "Very devilish to some, and very divine to some, will appear the poet of these new poems, these *Leaves of Grass:* an attempt, as they are, of a naïve, masculine, affectionate, contemplative, sensual, imperious person to cast into literature not only his own grit and arrogance, but his own flesh and form, undraped, regardless of models, regardless of modesty or law." There was much more in the same self-laudatory vein, stressing Whitman's unkempt virility, his firm attachment for loungers and the "free rasping talk of men," his refusal to associate with literary people or (forgetting his lecture programs) to appear on platforms, his lusty physiology "corroborating a rugged phrenology," not even forgetting to mention the fact that he "is always dressed freshly and clean in strong clothes—neck open, shirt-collar flat and broad." Other anonymous salutations announced that the author was "a fine brute," "the most masculine of beings," "one of the roughs, large, proud affectionate, eating, drinking and breeding."

It requires little psychology to analyze what is so obvious an over-compensation. In these anonymous tributes to himself, Whitman revealed far more than he intended. None but a blinded devotee can fail to suspect a softness beneath the bluster; a psychic impotence poorly shielded by all the talk about fine brutishness, drinking and breeding, flingng his arms right and left, "drawing men and women to his close embrace, loving the clasp of their hands, the touch of their necks and breasts." The poet protests his maleness too vociferously.

Meanwhile, the second edition of *Leaves of Grass,* containing thirty-two instead of the original twelve poems (as well as the press notices written by himself) appeared in 1856. In the third edition (1860) the number of poems leaped to one hundred and fifty-seven. Then the Civil War made all other controversies negligible.

Whitman did not go to war, although his married brother George was one of the first to enlist. Holloway implies an idealistic motive; Harvey O'Higgins charges a cowardly Narcissism. In any case, Whitman refused to join the conflict and, only when George was reported missing, did he see at first hand what he had begun to sketch in "Drum-Taps." Finding his brother wounded in a camp on the Rappahannock, Whitman nursed him and remained in Washington, serving in the hospitals. He acted not only as wound-dresser but as good angel—"a bearded fairy godmother"—for the disabled men; he wrote their letters, brought them tobacco and ice-cream, read tales and poems, made life livelier and death easier for the sufferers. These ministrations, so freely given, gave him much in return: an intimacy with life in the raw which, for all his assertions, he had never seen so closely. No longer a spectator, he was a participant, and purgation as well as passion are manifest in the series of war-echoes, "Drum-Taps," and the uplifted "Memories of President Lincoln" with its immortal elegy "When Lilacs Last in the Dooryard Bloom'd." The end of the Civil War defined a new spirit in Whitman: the man and his poetry became one.

In 1864, through the pressure of friends, a minor clerkship in the Indian Bureau of the Interior Department was found for Whitman. But, though he was promoted, he did not hold the position long. His chief, Secretary James Harlan, once a Methodist preacher, had heard rumors of his subordinate's "immorality." Without stopping to consider the ethics of the situation, Harlan purloined Whitman's private copy of *Leaves of Grass* after closing-time, and fell afoul of the "Children of Adam" section. Nothing more was needed to prove the truth of the rumors and, without an hour's notice, Whitman was dismissed. A few friends rushed to his defense but Harlan, a sincere bigot, stuck to his resolve. William Douglas O'Connor, an Abolitionist author who was one of Whitman's staunchest admirers, issued a pamphlet not merely defending but glorifying Whitman, coining, for his title, the phrase "The Good Gray Poet"—a sobriquet which has outlasted all of O'Connor's works.

Affairs were at a low ebb. As a person, Whitman was stranded with no livelihood and little influence; as a poet he was repudiated by all but a small coterie at home and abroad. Eight years later, and seventeen years after the first edition of *Leaves of Grass* (in January, 1872), Whitman complained to Dowden, who had praised him unreservedly in England, "If you write again for publication about my books . . . I think it would be proper and even essential to include the important facts (for facts they are) that the *Leaves of Grass* and their author are contemptuously ignored by the recognized literary organs here in the United States, rejected by the publishing houses, the author turned out of a government clerkship and deprived of his means of support . . . solely on account of having written the book."

Transferred to the office of the Attorney General after his dismissal, Whitman remained there until 1873 when, on the night of February twenty-second, he was struck by paralysis. Whitman's mother, lying ill in his brother George's house, was spared the news of his attack. She died the following May and Whitman somehow rallied sufficiently to be at her bedside. For months after he could not use his limbs and—let the psychoanalysts make what they will of it—it is doubtful if he ever recovered from the effect of her death. Two years later, while arranging his prose writings for publication, he confided, "I occupy myself . . . still enveloped in thoughts of my dear Mother, the most perfect and magnetic character, the rarest combination of practical, moral and spiritual, and the least selfish, of all and any I have ever known—and by me O so much the most deeply loved."

At fifty-five Whitman was almost completely incapacitated. He did not suffer the daily agonies of Heine on his mattress grave, but confinement in Camden, where his mother had died and where his brother lived, was grueling enough. His solitude was alleviated by letters from abroad and the beginnings of recognition at home. Although he got out of doors a little, he could not walk any distance, and Edward Carpenter, John Burroughs, Richard Maurice Bucke (later one of Whitman's executors) and others made pilgrimages to his room in Mickle Street, near the railroad yards. There were intervals when his health improved sufficiently to permit small visits to New York and Boston, but by 1877, he was enfeebled and, in spite of friends, poverty-stricken. He was reduced to peddling his books from a basket in the streets of Philadelphia and Camden, and, although his brother George offered him a special place in the house he was building in Burlington, New Jersey, Whitman chose to stay where he was.

Whitman grew old with dignity and not without honor. In June, 1888, after a longer drive than usual, Whitman took cold. A new and more severe paralytic shock followed. For a time Whitman lost the power of speech. In 1890 he bought ground for his grave and planned an appropriately massive tomb. The following March he was wheeled over to Philadelphia—a move that meant much discomfort and actual suffering—to deliver a tribute to Lincoln. He was failing, but not rapidly. In 1891 a birthday dinner tendered by friends was served in his own rooms, a festive occasion, to judge from his own letter, at which Whitman drank champagne, speaking "a few words of honor and reverence for our Emerson, Bryant, Longfellow—dead—and then for Whittier and Tennyson, the boss of us all." That December Whitman contracted pneumonia "with complications" and knew he would not recover. Aided by Horace Traubel, the young Jewish Quaker who became the Boswell of his later days, he prefaced a final "deathbed edition" of *Leaves of Grass*. Death came toward the end of his seventy-third year, on March 26, 1892.

Analysis of Whitman's poetry is the more difficult because it presents a paradox—a paradox of which Whitman was not unaware. He knew his "barbaric yawp" was untranslatable, unconforming, impossible to transfix with a phrase or a theory. "I depart as air . . . If you want me again look for me under your boot-soles." The same contradictions which marked his personality are evident in his rhapsodies. *Leaves of Grass* sets out to be the manifesto of the ordinary man, "the divine average," yet it is doubtful if the ordinary man understands its rhetoric or, understanding, responds to it. No great common audience has rallied to Whitman's philosophy, no army of poets has followed his form. Few of the "powerful uneducated persons" for whom Whitman believed his book would be a "democratic Gospel" can appreciate, and fewer still can admire, his extraordinary mixture of self-adulation and impotence, abnormality and mysticism. The same contradictions which mark his personality are evident in his style. His work aims toward a simplification of speech—an American language experiment—yet its homeliness is not always racy. Sometimes it is mere flat statement, sometimes it is a grotesque combination of the colloquial and the grandiose. Sometimes, indeed, it is corrupted by linguistic bad taste and polyglot phrasing as naïvely absurd as "the tangl'd long deferr'd éclaircissement of human life" . . . "See my cantabile—you Libertad!" "Exalté . . . the mighty earth-eidólon" . . . "These from me, O Democracy, to serve you, ma femme!" "No dainty dolce affetuoso I!"

Only Whitman's lack of ease and certainty in rhyme made him sacrifice its counterpoint for the looser cadence. Nor was his form as revolutionary as it seemed. Heine's "North Sea" cycles had been composed in "free," unrhymed rhythms and the sonorous strophes of the Old Testament were Whitman's avowed model. Whitman was the first to object to the charge that his work had "the freedom of formlessness." He did not even admit its irregularity. In one of the unsigned reviews of *Leaves of Grass* he explained, "His rhythm and *uniformity* he will conceal in the roots of his verses, not to be seen of themselves, but to break forth loosely as lilacs on a bush or take shapes compact as the shapes of melons." None can deny the music in this poetry which is capable of the widest orchestral effects. It is a music accomplished in a dozen ways—by the Hebraic "balance" brought to perfection in Job and the Psalms, by the long and extraordinarily flexible line suddenly whipped taut, by repetitions at the beginnings of lines and reiterations within the lines, by following his recitatives with a soaring aria. Thus, in the midst of the elaborate piling up in "Song of Myself" there are such sheer lyrical outbursts as the passages beginning "Press close, bare-bosomed night," "Smile, O voluptuous cool-breath'd earth," "The last scud of the day holds back for me," "A child said 'What is the grass?' " . . . "No counting of syllables," wrote Anne Gilchrist, "will reveal the mechanism of this music." But the music is there, now rising in gathering choirs of brasses, now falling to the rumor of a flute.

Mass and magnitude are the result. And rightly, for mass was the material. Unlike the cameo-cutting Aldrich and the polished Stedman, both of whom belittled him, Whitman was no lapidary. His aim was not to remodel or brighten a few high facets of existence; he sought to embody a universe in the rough. For him no aspect of life was trivial; every common, superficial cover was a cavern of rich and inexhaustible depths. A leaf of grass, with its tendrils twined about the core of earth, was no less than the journey-work of the stars; the cow, "crunching with depressed head," put Phidias to shame; the roadside running blackberry, seen with the eye of vision, was "fit to adorn the parlors of heaven." Nothing was mean; nothing was rejected. Whitman had read Blake, Dante, Shakespeare, Shelley; besides knowing his Bible, he was acquainted with the sacred books of the East and their reëxpression in Emerson. His transcendentalism was not a new thing; but the fusion of identity and impersonality, the union of the ego-driven self and the impartially moving universe was newly synthesized in his rhapsodies. His aim was inclusive—the lack of exclusiveness may be Whitman's chief defect—for though he celebrated the person in all his separateness, he added "the word democratic, the word *En-masse*." All was included in "the procreant urge of the world." Opposites merge into one: the unseen is proved by the seen; all goes onward and outward, nothing collapses. Light and dark, good and evil, body and soul do not merely emphasize but complete each other.

Whitman's insistence that the body was holy in all its manifestations caused a great deal of contemporary misunderstanding and developed into mysterious whisperings. His early commentators—Burroughs (whose estimates were dictated by Whitman), Carpenter, Bucke, Traubel—magnified his maleness, insisted too much on his normality, and generally misinterpreted him. As late as 1926 Emory Holloway made no effort to resolve the contradictions and, apart from an obscure hint or two, scarcely suggested that there was a split between Whitman's pronouncements and his nature. The split was actually a gulf. Whitman's preoccupation with the details of clothes—he was as fastidious about the way a workman's shirt should be worn as he once was about the set of a high hat—his rôle as nurse during the Civil War, his pathetic insistence that he was the father of six children, none of which ever appeared, and his avoidance of women make it clear that this "fine brute," this "most masculine of beings," was really an invert. Whitman's brother told Traubel that "Walt never fell in love. . . . He did not seem to affect the girls," and even Edward Carpenter concluded "there can be no doubt that his intimacies with men were much more numerous than with women." Not the least of his inconsistencies is Whitman's delusion that an "adhesive" love, the love of "comrades," was the basis on which a broader democracy would be built.

Whitman's "all-inclusive love" springs not only from his own pathological eccentricities, but from an undefined Pantheism. His very eagerness to express the whole cosmos often results in a chaotic pouring forth of prophecy and claptrap. For this reason Whitman should be read, not as one reads a book of lyrics, weighing and appraising individual stanzas, but as one reads an epic, letting the movement, the swelling volume, carry the lines along. It is only in the rare instances that we stop to remark the particularities—the extraordinarily graphic description of an old-time sea-fight in "Song of Myself," or images as breath-taking as "the indolent, sinking sun, burning, expanding the air" and "The hands of the sisters Death and Night incessantly softly wash again, and ever again, this soil'd world" and "Out of the cradle endlessly rocking; out of the mocking bird's throat, the musical shuttle . . ."

Here, framed in firm syllables, are large convictions, strong wants. Tenderness, not pretty sentiment, rises to new heights in the Lincoln elegies, in "Out of the Cradle Endlessly Rocking," in the superbly quiet "On the Beach at Night." There is, it is true, a degree of affectation here—affectation of nationalism and simplicity (referring to Six-month rather than to May, to Mannahatta rather than to New York); affectation of hybrid terms ("Me imperturbe!" "Camerado!" "I exposé," "Deliriate, thus preluding," "Allons! from all formules!" "How plenteous! how spiritual! how *résumé!*" etc.); affectations, always, of too insistent a strength. It is also true that we read Whitman in youth—as we read Swinburne—for intoxication, uncritically, contemptuous of reservations which maturity compels.

The contradictions resist complete synthesis. It is impossible to analyze Whitman's final significance to American social and cultural development; we can only record the greatness of his contribution. His windy optimism remains an emotional rather than a rational influence. His whole-heartedness, his large yea-saying, coming at a time of cautious skepticism, hesitancy and insecurity, is Whitman's gift not only to his period but to posterity.

Whitman's inconsistency, especially his paradox of democracy, continues to baffle the literary historians. In 1930, in the third volume of his monumental *Main Currents in American Thought* (the uncompleted volume entitled *The Beginnings of Critical Realism in America*) the late Vernon L. Parrington concludes that Whitman is the complete embodiment of Enlightenment—"the poet and prophet of a democracy that the America of the Gilded Age was daily betraying." Yet Parrington himself, though he sees Whitman as "the most deeply religious soul that American literature knows," sees also Whitman's failure as a prophet. "The great hopes on which he [Whitman] fed have been belied by after events—so his critics say; as the great hopes of the Enlightenment have been belied. Certainly in this welter of today, with science become the drab and slut of war and industrialism, with sterile money-slaves instead of men, Whitman's expansive hopes seem grotesque enough. Democracy may indeed be only a euphemism for the rulership of fools."

Yet the paradox must be grasped—or, at least, admitted—if one is to understand Whitman at all. Somehow the contradictions are resolved; somehow the prophet, the pamphleteer, and the poet achieve a unity if only through an intensification of the inner life: a liberal humanism. That Whitman was self-confounded is fairly obvious; he seems to have confused an ideal culture founded on quality with a merely quantitative conception of life. But his faith, romantic as it was resurgent, triumphed over his contradictions, actually imposed a sort of harmony upon them.

Thus Whitman rises above his defects. The reader forgets the lesser flaws, the lumbering failures. The illumined phrases burn clear; the pictures, once etched upon the imagination, are there to stay. Above all, the *effect* remains, an effect not reducible to phrases; a sense of released power, irresistible and benevolent, immense in affirmation. Beyond what Symonds called "delicate and evanescent moods of sensibility" is the communication of amplitudes. It expands the air.

Such poetry, whatever its lapses, has the stuff of permanence. It will persist not only because of its rebellious and compelling power, but because the poet has transcended his material. The personal contact is achieved, as Whitman knew it would be. "Who touches this book touches a man." Lascelles Abercrombie, a poet of an entirely different persuasion, said that Whitman created "out of the wealth of his experience that vividly personal figure which is surely one of the few supremely great things in modern poetry—the figure of himself." But his work was larger than the man. Whitman was not dilating his value when he claimed to contain multitudes. His book projects and creates them in a sphere nobler than our own. Employing words, he harnessed elements.

I HEAR AMERICA SINGING

I hear America singing, the varied carols I hear,
Those of mechanics, each one singing his as it should be blithe and strong,
The carpenter singing his as he measures his plank or beam,
The mason singing his as he makes ready for work, or leaves off work,
The boatman singing what belongs to him in his boat, the deckhand singing on the steamboat deck,
The shoemaker singing as he sits on his bench, the hatter singing as he stands,
The wood-cutter's song, the plowboy's on his way in the morning, or at noon intermission or at sundown,
The delicious singing of the mother, or of the young wife at work, or of the girl sewing or washing,
Each singing what belongs to him or her and to none else,
The day what belongs to the day—at night the party of young fellows, robust, friendly,
Singing with open mouths their strong melodious songs.

THE MUSE IN THE NEW WORLD

(*from "Song of the Exposition"*)

Come, Muse, migrate from Greece and Ionia,
Cross out please those immensely overpaid accounts,
That matter of Troy and Achilles' wrath, and Aeneas', Odysseus' wanderings,
Placard "Removed" and "To Let" on the rocks of your snowy Parnassus,
Repeat at Jerusalem, place the notice high on Jaffa's gate and on Mount Moriah,
The same on the walls of your German, French and Spanish castles, and Italian collections,
For know a better, fresher, busier sphere, a wide, untried domain awaits, demands you.

Responsive to our summons,
Or rather to her long-nurs'd inclination,
Join'd with an irresistible, natural gravitation,
She comes! I hear the rustling of her gown,
I scent the odor of her breath's delicious fragrance,
I mark her step divine, her curious eyes a-turning, rolling,
Upon this very scene.
I say I see, my friends, if you do not, the illustrious émigré, (having it is true in her day, although the same, changed, journey'd considerable,)
Making directly for this rendezvous, vigorously clearing a path for herself, striding through the confusion,
By thud of machinery and shrill steam-whistle undismay'd,
Bluff'd not a bit by drain-pipe, gasometers, artificial fertilizers;
Smiling and pleas'd with palpable intent to stay,
She's here, install'd amid the kitchen-ware!

RECORDERS AGES HENCE

Recorders ages hence,
Come, I will take you down underneath this impassive exterior, I will tell you what to say of me,
Publish my name and hang up my picture as that of the tenderest lover,
The friend the lover's portrait, of whom his friend his lover was fondest,
Who was not proud of his songs, but of the measureless ocean of love within him, and freely pour'd it forth,
Who often walk'd lonesome walks thinking of his dear friends, his lovers,
Who pensive away from one he lov'd often lay sleepless and dissatisfied at night,
Who knew too well the sick, sick dread lest the one he lov'd might secretly be indifferent to him,
Whose happiest days were far away through fields, in woods, on hills, he and another wandering hand in hand, they twain apart from other men,
Who oft as he saunter'd the streets curv'd with his arm the shoulder of his friend, while the arm of his friend rested upon him also.

THE COMMONPLACE

The commonplace I sing;
How cheap is health! how cheap nobility!
Abstinence, no falsehood, no gluttony, lust;
The open air I sing, freedom, toleration,
(Take here the mainest lesson—less from books—less from the schools,)
The common day and night—the common earth and waters,
Your farm—your work, trade, occupation,
The democratic wisdom underneath, like solid ground for all.

A NOISELESS PATIENT SPIDER

A noiseless patient spider,
I mark'd where on a little promontory it stood isolated,
Mark'd how to explore the vacant vast surrounding,
It launch'd forth filament, filament, filament, out of itself.
Ever unreeling them, ever tirelessly speeding them.

And you O my soul where you stand,
Surrounded, detached, in measureless oceans of space,
Ceaselessly musing, venturing, throwing, seeking the spheres to connect them.
Till the bridge you will need be form'd, till the ductile anchor hold,
Till the gossamer thread you fling catch somewhere, O my soul.

TO A COMMON PROSTITUTE

Be composed—be at ease with me—I am Walt Whitman, liberal and lusty as Nature,
Not till the sun excludes you do I exclude you,
Not till the waters refuse to glisten for you and the leaves to rustle for you, do my words refuse to glisten and rustle for you.
My girl I appoint with you an appointment, and I charge you that you make preparation to be worthy to meet me,
And I charge you that you be patient and perfect till I come.

Till then I salute you with a significant look that you do not forget me.

WHEN I HEARD THE LEARN'D ASTRONOMER

When I heard the learn'd astronomer,
When the proofs, the figures, were ranged in columns before me,
When I was shown the charts and diagrams, to add, divide, and measure them,
When I sitting heard the astronomer where he lectured with much applause in the lecture-room,
How soon unaccountable I became tired and sick,
Till rising and gliding out I wander'd off by myself,
In the mystical moist night-air, and from time to time,
Look'd up in perfect silence at the stars.

RECONCILIATION

Word over all, beautiful as the sky,
Beautiful that war and all its deeds of carnage must in time be utterly lost,
That the hands of the sisters Death and Night incessantly softly wash again, and
    ever again, this soil'd world;
For my enemy is dead, a man divine as myself is dead,
I look where he lies white-faced and still in the coffin—I draw near,
Bend down and touch lightly with my lips the white face in the coffin.

I HEAR IT WAS CHARGED AGAINST ME

I hear it was charged against me that I sought to destroy institutions,
But really I am neither for or against institutions,
(What indeed have I in common with them? or what with the destruction of them?)
Only I will establish in the Mannahatta and in every city of these States inland and
    seaboard,
And in the fields and woods, and above every keel little or large that dents the water,
Without edifices or rules or trustees or any argument,
The institution of the dear love of comrades.

MANNAHATTA

I was asking for something specific and perfect for my city,
Whereupon lo! upsprang the aboriginal name.

Now I see what there is in a name, a word, liquid, sane, unruly, musical, self-
    sufficient,
I see that the word of my city is that word from of old,
Because I see that word nested in nests of water-bays, superb,
Rich, hemm'd thick all around with sailships and steamships, an island sixteen
    miles long, solid-founded,
Numberless crowded streets, high growths of iron, slender, strong, light, splendidly
    uprising toward clear skies,
Tides swift and ample, well-loved by me, toward sundown,
The flowing sea-currents, the little islands, larger adjoining islands, the heights, the
    villas,
The countless masts, the white shore-steamers, the lighters, the ferry-boats, the black
    sea-steamers well model'd,
The down-town streets, the jobbers' houses of business, the houses of business of the
    ship-merchants and money-brokers, the river-streets,
Immigrants arriving, fifteen thousand in a week,
The carts hauling goods, the manly race of drivers of horses, the brown-faced sailors,
The summer air, the bright sun shining, and the sailing clouds aloft,
The winter snows, the sleigh-bells, the broken ice in the river, passing along up or
    down with the flood-tide or ebb-tide,
The mechanics of the city, the masters, well-form'd, beautiful-faced, looking you
    straight in the eyes,
Trottoirs throng'd, vehicles, Broadway, the women, the shops and shows,

A million people—manners free and superb—open voices—hospitality—the most courageous and friendly young men,
City of hurried and sparkling waters! city of spires and masts!
City nested in bays! my city!

....

SONG OF MYSELF

1

I celebrate myself, and sing myself,
And what I assume you shall assume,
For every atom belonging to me as good belongs to you.

I loafe and invite my soul,
I lean and loafe at my ease observing a spear of summer grass.

My tongue, every atom of my blood, form'd from this soil, this air,
Born here of parents born here from parents the same, and their parents the same,
I, now thirty-seven years old in perfect health begin,
Hoping to cease not till death.
Creeds and schools in abeyance,
Retiring back a while sufficed at what they are, but never forgotten,
I harbor for good or bad, I permit to speak at every hazard,
Nature without check with original energy.

2

Houses and rooms are full of perfumes, the shelves are crowded with perfumes,
I breathe the fragrance myself and know it and like it,
The distillation would intoxicate me also, but I shall not let it.

The atmosphere is not a perfume, it has no taste of the distillation, it is odorless,
It is for my mouth forever, I am in love with it,
I will go to the bank by the wood and become undisguised and naked,
I am mad for it to be in contact with me.

The smoke of my own breath,
Echoes, ripples, buzz'd whispers, love-root, silk-thread, crotch and vine,
My respiration and inspiration, the beating of my heart, the passing of blood and air through my lungs,
The sniff of green leaves and dry leaves, and of the shore and dark-color'd sea-rocks, and of hay in the barn,
The sound of the belch'd words of my voice loos'd to the eddies of the wind,
A few light kisses, a few embraces, a reaching around of arms,
The play of shine and shade on the trees as the supple boughs wag,
The delight alone or in the rush of the streets, or along the fields and hill-sides,
The feeling of health, the full-noon trill, the song of me rising from bed and meeting the sun.
Have you reckon'd a thousand acres much? have you reckon'd the earth much?
Have you practic'd so long to learn to read?
Have you felt so proud to get at the meaning of poems?

Stop this day and night with me and you shall possess the origin of all poems,
You shall possess the good of the earth and sun, (there are millions of suns left,)
You shall no longer take things at second or third hand, nor look through the eyes of the dead, nor feed on the specters in books,
You shall not look through my eyes either, nor take things from me,
You shall listen to all sides and filter them from your self.

3

I have heard what the talkers were talking, the talk of the beginning and the end,
But I do not talk of the beginning or the end.

There was never any more inception than there is now,
Nor any more youth or age than there is now,
And will never be any more perfection than there is now,
Nor any more heaven or hell than there is now.

Urge and urge and urge,
Always the procreant urge of the world.
Out of the dimness opposite equals advance, always substance and increase, always sex,
Always a knit of identity, always distinction, always a breed of life.

To elaborate is no avail, learn'd and unlearn'd feel that it is so.

Sure as the most certain sure, plumb in the uprights, well center-tied, braced in the beams,
Stout as a horse, affectionate, haughty, electrical,
I and this mystery here we stand.
Clear and sweet is my soul, and clear and sweet is all that is not my soul.

Lack one lacks both, and the unseen is proved by the seen,
Till that becomes unseen and receives proof in its turn.

Showing the best and dividing it from the worst age vexes age,
Knowing the perfect fitness and equanimity of things, while they discuss I am silent, and go bathe and admire myself.

Welcome is every organ and attribute of me, and of any man hearty and clean,
Not an inch nor a particle of an inch is vile, and none shall be less familiar than the rest.

I am satisfied—I see, dance, laugh, sing;
As the hugging and loving bed-fellow sleeps at my side through the night, and withdraws at the peep of the day with stealthy tread,
Leaving me baskets cover'd with white towels swelling the house with their plenty,
Shall I postpone my acceptation and realization and scream at my eyes,
That they turn from gazing after and down the road,
And forthwith cipher and show to me a cent,
Exactly the value of one and exactly the value of two, and which is ahead?

4

Trippers and askers surround me,
People I meet, the effect upon me of my early life or the ward and city I live in, or the nation,
The latest dates, discoveries, inventions, societies, authors old and new,
My dinner, dress, associates, looks, compliments, dues,
The real or fancied indifference of some man or woman I love,
The sickness of one of my folks or of myself, or ill-doing or loss or lack of money, or depressions or exaltations,
Battles, the horrors of fratricidal war, the fever of doubtful news, the fitful events;
These come to me days and nights and go from me again,
But they are not the Me myself.

Apart from the pulling and hauling stands what I am,
Stands amused, complacent, compassionating, idle, unitary,
Looks down, is erect, or bends an arm on an impalpable certain rest,
Looking with side-curved head curious what will come next,
Both in and out of the game and watching and wondering at it.

Backward I see in my own days where I sweated through fog with linguists and contenders,
I have no mockings or arguments, I witness and wait.

5

I believe in you my soul, the other I am must not abase itself to you,
And you must not be abased to the other.

Loafe with me on the grass, loose the stop from your throat,
Not words, not music or rhyme I want, not custom or lecture, not even the best.
Only the lull I like, the hum of your valvèd voice.

✣

Swiftly arose and spread around me the peace and knowledge that pass all the argument of the earth,
And I know that the hand of God is the promise of my own,
And I know that the spirit of God is the brother of my own,
And that all the men ever born are also my brothers, and the women my sisters and lovers,
And that a kelson of the creation is love,
And limitless are leaves stiff or drooping in the fields,
And brown ants in the little wells beneath them,
And mossy scabs of the worm fence, heap'd stones, elder, mullein and poke-weed.

6

A child said, *What is the grass?* fetching it to me with full hands;
How could I answer the child? I do not know what it is any more than he.

I guess it must be the flag of my disposition, out of hopeful green stuff woven.

Or I guess it is the handkerchief of the Lord,
A scented gift and remembrancer designedly dropt,
Bearing the owner's name someway in the corner, that we may see and remark, and
say *Whose?*

Or I guess the grass is itself a child, the produced babe of the vegetation.
Or I guess it is a uniform hieroglyphic,
And it means, Sprouting alike in broad zones and narrow zones,
Growing among black folks as among white,
Kanuck, Tuckahoe, Congressman, Cuff, I give them the same, I receive them the
same.

And now it seems to me the beautiful uncut hair of graves,

Tenderly will I use you curling grass,
It may be you transpire from the breasts of young men,
It may be if I had known them I would have loved them,
It may be you are from old people, or from offspring taken soon out of their mothers'
laps,
And here you are the mothers' laps.

This grass is very dark to be from the white heads of old mothers,
Darker than the colorless beards of old men,
Dark to come from under the faint red roofs of mouths.
O I perceive after all so many uttering tongues,
And I perceive they do not come from the roofs of mouths for nothing.
I wish I could translate the hints about the dead young men and women,
And the hints about old men and mothers, and the offspring taken soon out of their
laps.

What do you think has become of the young and old men?
And what do you think has become of the women and children?

They are alive and well somewhere,
The smallest sprout shows there is really no death,
And if ever there was it led forward life, and does not wait at the end to arrest it,
And ceas'd the moment life appear'd.

All goes onward and outward, nothing collapses,
And to die is different from what anyone supposed, and luckier.

7

Has anyone supposed it lucky to be born?
I hasten to inform him or her it is just as lucky to die, and I know it.

I pass death with the dying and birth with the new-wash'd babe, and am not
contain'd between my hat and boots,
And peruse manifold objects, no two alike and every one good,
The earth good and the stars good, and their adjuncts all good.

I am not an earth nor an adjunct of an earth,
I am the mate and companion of people, all just as immortal and fathomless as myself,
(They do not know how immortal, but I know.)
Every kind for itself and its own, for me mine male and female,
For me those that have been boys and that love women,
For me the man that is proud and feels how it stings to be slighted,
For me the sweet-heart and the old maid, for me mothers and the mothers of mothers,
For me lips that have smiled, eyes that have shed tears,
For me children and the begetters of children.

Undrape! you are not guilty to me, nor stale nor discarded,
I see through the broadcloth and gingham whether or no,
And am around, tenacious, acquisitive, tireless, and cannot be shaken away.

8

The little one sleeps in its cradle,
I lift the gauze and look a long time, and silently brush away flies with my hand.

The youngster and the red-faced girl turn aside up the bushy hill,
I peeringly view them from the top.

The suicide sprawls on the bloody floor of the bedroom,
I witness the corpse with its dabbled hair, I note where the pistol has fallen.

The blab of the pave, tires of carts, sluff of boot-soles, talk of the promenaders,
The heavy omnibus, the driver with his interrogating thumb, the clank of the shod horses on the granite floor,
The snow-sleighs, clinking, shouted jokes, pelts of snow-balls,
The hurrahs for popular favorites, the fury of rous'd mobs,
The flap of the curtain'd litter, a sick man inside borne to the hospital,
The meeting of enemies, the sudden oath, the blows and fall,
The excited crowd, the policeman with his star quickly working his passage to the center of the crowd,
The impassive stones that receive and return so many echoes,
What groans of over-fed or half-starv'd who fall sunstruck or in fits,
What exclamations of women taken suddenly who hurry home and give birth to babes,
What living and buried speech is always vibrating here, what howls restrain'd by decorum,
Arrests of criminals, slights, adulterous offers made, acceptances, rejections with convex lips,
I mind them or the show or resonance of them—I come and I depart.

9

The big doors of the country barn stand open and ready,
The dried grass of the harvest-time loads the slow-drawn wagon,
The clear light plays on the brown gray and green intertinged,
The armfuls are pack'd to the sagging mow.

I am there, I help, I came stretch'd atop of the load,
I felt its soft jolts, one leg reclined on the other,
I jumped from the cross-beams and seize the clover and timothy,
And roll head over heels and tangle my hair full of wisps.

10

Alone far in the wilds and mountains I hunt,
Wandering amazed at my own lightness and glee,
In the late afternoon choosing a safe spot to pass the night,
Kindling a fire and broiling the fresh-kill'd game,
Falling asleep on the gather'd leaves with my dog and gun by my side.

The Yankee clipper is under her sky-sails, she cuts the sparkle and scud,
My eyes settle the land, I bend at her prow or shout joyously from the deck.

The boatmen and clam-diggers arose early and stopt for me,
I tuck'd my trowser-ends in my boots and went and had a good time;
You should have been with us that day round the chowder-kettle.

I saw the marriage of the trapper in the open air in the far west, the bride was a red girl,
Her father and his friends sat near cross-legged and dumbly smoking, they had moccasins to their feet and large thick blankets hanging from their shoulders,
On a bank lounged the trapper, he was drest mostly in skins, his luxuriant beard and curls protected his neck, he held his bride by the hand,
She had long eyelashes, her head was bare, her coarse straight locks descended upon her voluptuous limbs and reach'd to her feet.

The runaway slave came to my house and stopt outside,
I heard his motions crackling the twigs of the woodpile,
Through the swung half-door of the kitchen I saw him limpsy and weak,
And went where he sat on a log and led him in and assured him,
And brought water and fill'd a tub for his sweated body and bruis'd feet,
And gave him a room that enter'd from my own, and give him some coarse clean clothes,
And remember perfectly well his revolving eyes and his awkwardness,
And remember putting plasters on the galls of his neck and ankles;
He staid with me a week before he was recuperated and pass'd north,
I had him sit next me at table, my fire-lock lean'd in the corner.

11

Twenty-eight young men bathe by the shore.
Twenty-eight young men and all so friendly;
Twenty-eight years of womanly life and all so lonesome.
She owns the fine house by the rise of the bank,
She hides handsome and richly drest aft the blinds of the window.

Which of the young men does she like the best?
Ah the homeliest of them is beautiful to her.

Where are you off to, lady? for I see you,
You splash in the water there, yet stay stock still in your room.

Dancing and laughing along the beach came the twenty-ninth bather,
The rest did not see her, but she saw them and loved them.

The beards of the young men glisten'd with wet, it ran from their long hair,
Little streams pass'd all over their bodies.

An unseen hand also pass'd over their bodies,
It descended tremblingly from their temples and ribs.

The young men float on their backs, their white bellies bulge to the sun, they do not ask who seizes fast to them,
They do not know who puffs and declines with pendant and bending arch,
They do not think whom they souse with spray.

14

The wild gander leads his flock through the cool night,
Ya-honk he says, and sounds it down to me like an invitation,
The pert may suppose it meaningless, but I listening close,
Find its purpose and place up there toward the wintry sky.

The sharp-hoof'd moose of the north, the cat on the house-sill, the chickadee, the prairie-dog,
The litter of the grunting sow as they tug at her teats,
The brood of the turkey-hen and she with her half-spread wings,
I see in them and myself the same old law.

The press of my foot to the earth springs a hundred affections,
They scorn the best I can do to relate them.

I am enamour'd of growing out-doors,
Of men that live among cattle or taste of the ocean or woods,
Of the builders and steerers of ships and the wielders of axes and mauls, and the drivers of horses,
I can eat and sleep with them week in and week out.

What is commonest, cheapest, nearest, easiest, is Me,
Me going in for my chances, spending for vast returns,
Adorning myself to bestow myself on the first that will take me,
Not asking the sky to come down to my good will,
Scattering it freely forever.

15

The pure contralto sings in the organ loft,
The carpenter dresses his plank, the tongue of his foreplane whistles its wild ascending lisp,
The married and unmarried children ride home to their Thanksgiving dinner,
The pilot seizes the king-pin, he heaves down with a strong arm,
The mate stands braced in the whale-boat, lance and harpoon are ready,

The duck-shooter walks by silent and cautious stretches,
The deacons are ordain'd with cross'd hands at the altar,
The spinning-girl retreats and advances to the hum of the big wheel,
The farmer stops by the bars as he walks on a First-day loaf and looks at the oats and rye,
The lunatic is carried at last to the asylum a confirm'd case,
(He will never sleep any more as he did in the cot in his mother's bedroom;)
The jour printer with gray head and gaunt jaws works at his case,
He turns his quid of tobacco while his eyes blur with the manuscript;
The malform'd limbs are tied to the surgeon's table,
What is removed drops horribly in a pail;
The quadroon girl is sold at the auction-stand, the drunkard nods by the barroom stove,
The machinist rolls up his sleeves, the policeman travels his beat, the gate-keeper marks who pass,
The young fellow drives the express-wagon, (I love him, though I do not know him;)
The half-breed straps on his light boots to compete in the race,
The western turkey-shooting draws old and young, some lean on their rifles, some sit on logs,
Out from the crowd steps the marksman, takes his position, levels his piece;
The groups of newly-come immigrants cover the wharf or levee,
As the woolly-pates hoe in the sugar-field, the overseer views them from his saddle,
The bugle calls in the ball-room, the gentlemen run for their partners, the dancers bow to each other,
The youth lies awake in the cedar-roof'd garret and harks to the musical rain,
The Wolverine sets traps on the creek that helps fill the Huron,
The squaw wrapt in her yellow-hemm'd cloth is offering moccasins and bead-bags for sale,
The connoisseur peers along the exhibition-gallery with half-shut eyes bent sideways,
As the deck-hands make fast the steamboat the plank is thrown for the shore-going passengers,
The young sister holds out the skein while the elder sister winds it off in a ball, and stops now and then for the knots,
The one-year wife is recovering and happy having a week ago borne her first child,
The clean-hair'd Yankee girl works with her sewing machine or in the factory or mill,
The paving-man leans on his two-handed rammer, the reporter's lead flies swiftly over the note-book, the sign-painter is lettering with blue and gold,
The canal boy trots on the tow-path, the book-keeper counts at his desk, the shoe-maker waxes his thread,
The conductor beats time for the band and all the performers follow him,
The child is baptized, the convert is making his first profession,
The regatta is spread on the bay, the race is begun, (how the white sails sparkle!)
The drover watching his drove sings out to them that would stray,
The peddler sweats with his pack on his back, (the purchaser higgling about the odd cent;)
The bride unrumples her white dress, the minute-hand of the clock moves slowly,
The opium-eater reclines with rigid head and just-open'd lips,
The prostitute draggles her shawl, her bonnet bobs on her tipsy and pimpled neck,

The crowd laugh at her blackguard oaths, the men jeer and wink to each other,
(Miserable! I do not laugh at your oaths nor jeer you;)
The President holding a cabinet council is surrounded by the great Secretaries,
On the piazza walk three matrons stately and friendly with twined arms,
The crew of the fish-smack pack repeated layers of halibut in the hold,
Coon-seekers go through the regions of the Red river or through those drain'd by the Tennessee, or through those of the Arkansas,
Torches shine in the dark that hangs on the Chattahooche or Altamahaw,
Patriarchs sit at supper with sons and grandsons and great grandsons around them,
In walls of adobie, in canvas tents, rest hunters and trappers after their day's sport
The city sleeps and the country sleeps,
The living sleep for their time, the dead sleep for their time,
The old husband sleeps by his wife and the young husband sleeps by his wife;
And these tend inward to me, and I tend outward to them,
And such as it is to be of these more or less I am,
And of these one and all I weave the song of myself.

18

With music strong I come, with my cornets and my drums,
I play not marches for accepted victors only, I play marches for conquer'd and slain persons.

Have you heard that it was good to gain the day?
I also say it is good to fall, battles are lost in the same spirit in which they are won.

I beat and pound for the dead,
I blow through my embouchures my loudest and gayest for them.

Vivas to those who have fail'd!
And to those whose war-vessels sank in the sea!
And to those themselves who sank in the sea!
And to all generals that lost engagements, and all overcome heroes!
And the numberless unknown heroes equal to the greatest heroes known!

19

This is the meal equally set, this the meat for natural hunger,
It is for the wicked just the same as the righteous, I make appointments with all,
I will not have a single person slighted or left away,
The kept-woman, sponger, thief, are hereby invited,
There shall be no difference between them and the rest.

This is the press of a bashful hand, this the float and odor of hair,
This the touch of my lips to yours, this the murmur of yearning,
This the far-off depth and height reflecting my own face,
This the thoughtful merge of myself, and the outlet again.
Do you guess I have some intricate purpose?
Well I have, for the Fourth-month showers have, and the mica on the side of the rock has.

Do you take it I would astonish?
Does the daylight astonish? does the early redstart twittering through the woods?
Do I astonish more than they?

This hour I tell things in confidence,
I might not tell everybody, but I will tell you.

20

Who goes there? hankering, gross, mystical, nude;
How is it I extract strength from the beef I eat?

What is a man anyhow? what am I? what are you?

All I mark as my own you shall offset it with your own,
Else it were time lost listening to me.

I do not snivel that snivel the world over,
That months are vacuums and the ground but wallow and filth.

Whimpering and truckling fold with powders for invalids, conformity goes to the fourth-remov'd,
I wear my hat as I please indoors or out.

Why should I pray? why should I venerate and be ceremonious?

Having pried through the strata, analyzed to a hair, counsel'd with doctors and calculated close,
I find no sweeter fat than sticks to my own bones.

In all people I see myself, none more and not one a barleycorn less,
And the good or bad I say of myself I say of them.
I know I am solid and sound,
To me the converging objects of the universe perpetually flow,
All are written to me, and I must get what the writing means.

I know I am deathless,
I know this orbit of mine cannot be swept by a carpenter's compass,
I know I shall not pass like a child's carlacue cut with a burnt stick at night.

I know I am august,
I do not trouble my spirit to vindicate itself or be understood,
I see that the elementary laws never apologize,
(I reckon I behave no prouder than the level I plant my house by, after all.)

I exist as I am, that is enough,
If no other in the world be aware I sit content,
And if each and all be aware I sit content.

One world is aware and by far the largest to me, and that is myself,
And whether I come to my own today or in ten thousand or ten million years,
I can cheerfully take it now, or with equal cheerfulness I can wait.

My foothold is tenon'd and mortis'd in granite,
I laugh at what you call dissolution,
And I know the amplitude of time.

21

I am the poet of the Body and I am the poet of the Soul,
The pleasures of heaven are with me and the pains of hell are with me,
The first I graft and increase upon myself, the latter I translate into a new tongue,
I am the poet of the woman the same as the man,
And I say it is as great to be a woman as to be a man,
And I say there is nothing greater than the mother of men.

I chant the chant of dilation or pride,
We have had ducking and deprecating about enough,
I show that size is only development.

Have you outstript the rest? are you the President?
It is a trifle, they will more than arrive there every one, and still pass on.

I am he that walks with the tender and growing night,
I call to the earth and sea half-held by the night.

Press close bare-bosom'd night—press close magnetic nourishing night!
Night of south winds—night of the large few stars!
Still nodding night—mad naked summer night.

Smile O voluptuous cool-breath'd earth!
Earth of the slumbering and liquid trees!
Earth of departed sunset—earth of the mountains misty-topt!
Earth of the vitreous pour of the full moon just tinged with blue!
Earth of shine and dark mottling the tide of the river!
Earth of the limpid gray of clouds brighter and clearer for my sake!
Far-swooping elbow'd earth—rich apple-blossom'd earth!
Smile, for your lover comes.

Prodigal, you have given me love—therefore I to you give love!
O unspeakable passionate love.

22

You sea! I resign myself to you also—I guess what you mean,
I behold from the beach your crooked inviting fingers,
I believe you refuse to go back without feeling of me,
We must have a turn together, I undress, hurry me out of sight of the land,
Cushion me soft, rock me in billowy drowse,
Dash me with amorous wet, I can repay you.

Sea of stretch'd ground-swells,
Sea breathing broad and convulsive breaths,
Sea of the brine of life and of unshovel'd yet always-ready graves,
Howler and scooper of storms, capricious and dainty sea,
I am integral with you, I too am of one phase and of all phases.

Partaker of influx and efflux I, extoller of hate and conciliation,
Extoller of amies [1] and those that sleep in each other's arms,

[1] Friends, as distinguished from lovers.

I am he attesting sympathy,
(Shall I make my list of things in the house and skip the house that supports them?)

I am not the poet of goodness only, I do not decline to be the poet of wickedness also.

What blurt is this about virtue and about vice?
Evil propels me and reform of evil propels me, I stand indifferent,
My gait is no fault-finder's or rejecter's gait,
I moisten the roots of all that has grown.

Did you fear some scrofula out of the unflagging pregnancy?
Did you guess the celestial laws are yet to be work'd over and rectified?

I find one side a balance and the antipodal side a balance,
Soft doctrine as steady help as stable doctrine,
Thoughts and deeds of the present our rouse and early start.

This minute that comes to me over the past decillions,
There is no better than it and now.

What behaved well in the past or behaves well today is not such a wonder,
The wonder is always and always how there can be a mean man or an infidel.

25

Dazzling and tremendous how quick the sunrise would kill me,
If I could not now and always send sun-rise out of me.

We also ascend dazzling and tremendous as the sun,
We found our own O my soul in the calm and cool of the daybreak.

My voice goes after what my eyes cannot reach,
With the twirl of my tongue I encompass worlds and volumes of worlds.

Speech is the twin of my vision, it is unequal to measure itself,
It provokes me forever, it says sarcastically,
Walt you contain enough, why don't you let it out then?

Come now I will not be tantalized, you conceive too much of articulation,
Do you not know O speech how the buds beneath you are folded?
Waiting in gloom, protected by frost,
The dirt receding before my prophetical screams,
I underlying causes to balance them at last,
My knowledge my live parts, it keeping tally with the meaning of all things,
Happiness, (which whoever hears me let him or her set out in search of this day.)

My final merit I refuse you, I refuse putting from me what I really am,
Encompass worlds, but never try to encompass me,
I crowd your sleekest and best by simply looking toward you.

Writing and talking do not prove me,
I carry the plenum of proof and every thing else in my face,
With the hush of my lips I wholly confound the skeptic.

30

All truths wait in all things,
They neither hasten their own delivery nor resist it,
They do not need the obstetric forceps of the surgeon,
The insignificant is as big to me as any,
(What is less or more than a touch?)

Logic and sermons never convince,
The damp of the night drives deeper into my soul.

(Only what proves itself to every man and woman is so,
Only what nobody denies is so.)

A minute and a drop of me settle my brain,
I believe the soggy clods shall become lovers and lamps,
And a compend of compends is the meat of a man or woman,
And a summit and flower there is the feeling they have for each other,
And they are to branch boundlessly out of that lesson until it becomes omnific,
And until one and all shall delight us, and we them.

31

I believe a leaf of grass is no less than the journeywork of the stars,
And the pismire is equally perfect, and a grain of sand, and the egg of the wren,
And the tree-toad is a chef-d'œuvre for the highest,
And the running blackberry would adorn the parlors of heaven,
And the narrowest hinge in my hand puts to scorn all machinery,
And the cow crunching with depress'd head surpasses any statue,
And a mouse is miracle enough to stagger sextillions of infidels.

I find I incorporate gneiss, coal, long-threaded moss, fruits, grains, esculent roots,
And am stucco'd with quadrupeds and birds all over,
And have distanced what is behind me for good reasons,
But call any thing back again when I desire it.

In vain the speeding or shyness,
In vain the plutonic rocks send their old heat against my approach,
In vain the mastodon retreats beneath its own powder'd bones,
In vain objects stand leagues off and assume manifold shapes,
In vain the ocean settling in hollows and the great monsters lying low,
In vain the buzzard houses herself with the sky,
In vain the snake slides through the creepers and logs,
In vain the elk takes to the inner passes of the woods,
In vain the razor-bill'd auk sails far north to Labrador,
I follow quickly, I ascend to the nest in the fissure of the cliff.

32

I think I could turn and live with animals, they are so placid and self-contain'd,
I stand and look at them long and long.

They do not sweat and whine about their condition,
They do not lie awake in the dark and weep for their sins,

They do not make me sick discussing their duty to God,
Not one is dissatisfied, not one is demented with the mania of owning things,
Not one kneels to another, nor to his kind that lived thousands of years ago,
Not one is respectable or unhappy over the whole earth.

So they show their relations to me and I accept them,
They bring me tokens of myself, they evince them plainly in their possession.

I wonder where they get those tokens,
Did I pass that way huge times ago and negligently drop them?

Myself moving forward then and now and forever,
Gathering and showing more always and with velocity,
Infinite and omnigenous, and the like of these among them,
Not too exclusive toward the reachers of my remembrancers,
Picking out here one that I love, and now go with him on brotherly terms.

A gigantic beauty of a stallion, fresh and responsive to my caresses,
Head high in the forehead, wide between the ears,
Limbs glossy and supple, tail dusting the ground,
Eyes full of sparkling wickedness, ears finely cut, flexibly moving.
His nostrils dilate as my heels embrace him,
His well-built limbs tremble with pleasure as we race around and return.

I but use you a minute, then I resign you, stallion,
Why do I need your paces when I myself out-gallop them?
Even as I stand or sit passing faster than you.

35

Would you hear of an old-time sea-fight?
Would you learn who won by the light of the moon and stars?
List to the yarn, as my grandmother's father the sailor told it to me.

Our foe was no skulk in his ship I tell you, (said he,)
His was the surly English pluck, and there is no tougher or truer, and never was, and never will be;
Along the lower'd eve he came horribly raking us.

We closed with him, the yards entangled, the cannon touch'd,
My captain lash'd fast with his own hands.

We had receiv'd some eighteen pound shots under the water,
On our lower-gun-deck two large pieces had burst at the first fire, killing all around and blowing up overhead.

Fighting at sun-down, fighting at dark,
Ten o'clock at night, the full moon well up, our leaks on the gain, and five feet of water reported,
The master-at-arms loosing the prisoners confined in the afterhold to give them a chance for themselves.
The transit to and from the magazine is now stopt by the sentinels,
They see so many strange faces they do not know whom to trust.

Our frigate takes fire,
The other asks if we demand quarter?
If our colors are struck and the fighting done?

Now I laugh content, for I hear the voice of my little captain,
We have not struck, he composedly cries, *we have just begun our part of the fighting.*

Only three guns are in use,
One is directed by the captain himself against the enemy's mainmast,
Two well serv'd with grape and canister silence his musketry and clear his decks.

The tops alone second the fire of this little battery, especially the main-top,
They hold out bravely during the whole of the action.

Not a moment's cease.
The leaks gain fast on the pumps, the fire eats toward the powder-magazine.

One of the pumps has been shot away, it is generally thought we are sinking.

Serene stands the little captain,
He is not hurried, his voice is neither high nor low,
His eyes give more light to us than our battle-lanterns.

Toward twelve there in the beams of the moon they surrender to us.

36

Stretch'd and still lies the midnight,
Two great hulls motionless on the breast of the darkness,
Our vessel riddled and slowly sinking, preparations to pass to the one we have conquer'd.
The captain on the quarter-deck coldly giving his orders through a countenance white as a sheet,
Near by the corpse of the child that serv'd in the cabin,
The dead face of an old salt with long white hair and carefully curl'd whiskers,
The flames spite of all that can be done flickering aloft and below,
The husky voices of the two or three officers yet fit for duty,
Formless stacks of bodies and bodies by themselves, dabs of flesh upon the masts and spars,
Cut of cordage, dangle of rigging, slight shock of the soothe of waves,
Black and impassive guns, litter of powder-parcels, strong scent,
A few large stars overhead, silent and mournful shining.
Delicate sniffs of sea-breeze, smells of sedgy grass and fields by the shore, death-messages given in charge to survivors,
The hiss of the surgeon's knife, the gnawing teeth of his saw,
Wheeze, cluck, swash of falling blood, short wild scream, and long, dull, tapering groan,
These so, these irretrievable.

37

You laggards there on guard! look to your arms!
In at the conquer'd doors they crowd! I am possess'd!
Embody all presences outlaw'd or suffering,

See myself in prison shaped like another man,
And feel the dull intermitted pain.

For me the keepers of convicts shoulder their carbines and keep watch,
It is I let out in the morning and barr'd at night.
Not a mutineer walks handcuff'd to jail but I am handcuff'd to him and walk by his side,
(I am less the jolly one there, and more the silent one with sweat on my twitching lips.)

Not a youngster is taken for larceny but I go up too, and am tried and sentenced.

Not a cholera patient lies at the last gasp but I also lie at the last gasp,
My face is ash-color'd, my sinews gnarl, away from me people retreat.

Askers embody themselves in me and I am embodied in them,
I project my hat, sit shame-faced, and beg.

38

Enough! enough! enough!
Somehow I have been stunn'd. Stand back!
Give me a little time beyond my cuff'd head, slumbers, dreams, gaping,
I discover myself on the verge of a usual mistake.

That I could forget the mockers and insults!
That I could forget the trickling tears and the blows of the bludgeons and hammers!
That I could look with a separate look on my own crucifixion and bloody crowning!

I remember now,
I resume the overstaid fraction,
The grave of rock multiplies what has been confided to it, or to any graves,
Corpses rise, gashes heal, fastenings roll from me.

I troop forth replenish'd with supreme power, one of an average unending procession,
Inland and sea-coast we go, and pass all boundary lines,
Our swift ordinances on their way over the whole earth,
The blossoms we wear in our hats the growth of thousands of years.

40

Flaunt of the sunshine I need not your bask—lie over!
You light surfaces only, I force surfaces and depths also.

Earth! you seem to look for something at my hands,
Say, old top-knot, what do you want?

Behold, I do not give lectures or a little charity,
When I give I give myself.

You there, impotent, loose in the knees,
Open your scarf'd chops till I blow grit within you

Spread your palms and lift the flaps of your pockets,
I am not to be denied, I compel, I have stores plenty and to spare,
And any thing I have I bestow.

I do not ask who you are, that is not important to me,
You can do nothing and be nothing but what I will infold you.

To cotton-field drudge or cleaner of privies I lean,
On his right cheek I put the family kiss,
And in my soul I swear I never will deny him.

To anyone dying, thither I speed and twist the knob of the door,
Turn the bed-clothes toward the foot of the bed,
Let the physician and the priest go home.

I seize the descending man and raise him with resistless will,
O despairer, here is my neck,
By God, you shall not go down! hang your whole weight upon me.

44

It is time to explain myself—let us stand up.

What is known I strip away,
I launch all men and women forward with me into the Unknown.

The clock indicates the moment—but what does eternity indicate?

We have thus far exhausted trillions of winters and summers,
There are trillions ahead, and trillions ahead of them.

Rise after rise bow the phantoms behind me,
Afar down I see the huge first Nothing, I know I was even there,
I waited unseen and always, and slept through the lethargic mist,
And took my time, and took no hurt from the fetid carbon.

Long I was hugg'd close—long and long.
Immense have been the preparations for me,
Faithful and friendly the arms that have help'd me.

Cycles ferried my cradle, rowing and rowing like cheerful boatmen,
For room to me stars kept aside in their own rings,
They sent influences to look after what was to hold me.

Before I was born out of my mother generations guided me,
My embryo has never been torpid, nothing could overlay it.

For it the nebula cohered to an orb,
The long slow strata piled to rest it on,
Vast vegetables gave it sustenance,
Monstrous sauroids transported it in their mouths and deposited it with care.

All forces have been steadily employ'd to complete and delight me,
Now on this spot I stand with my robust soul.

48

I have said that the soul is not more than the body,
And I have said that the body is not more than the soul,
And nothing, not God, is greater to one than one's self is,
And whoever walks a furlong without sympathy walks to his own funeral drest in his shroud,
And I or you pocketless of a dime may purchase the pick of the earth,
And to glance with an eye or show a bean in its pod confounds the learning of all times,
And there is no trade or employment but the young man following it may become a hero,
And there is no object so soft but it makes a hub for the wheel'd universe,
And I say to any man or woman, Let your soul stand cool and composed before a million universes.

And I say to mankind, Be not curious about God,
For I who am curious about each am not curious about God,
(No array of terms can say how much I am at peace about God and about death.)

I hear and behold God in every object, yet understand God not in the least,
Nor do I understand who there can be more wonderful than myself.

Why should I wish to see God better than this day?
I see something of God each hour of the twenty-four, and each moment then,
In the faces of men and women I see God, and in my own face in the glass,
I find letters from God dropt in the street, and every one is sign'd by God's name,
And I leave them where they are, for I know that wheresoe'er I go,
Others will punctually come for ever and ever.

49

And as to you Death, and you bitter hug of mortality, it is idle to try to alarm me.

To his work without flinching the accoucheur comes,
I see the elder-hand pressing receiving supporting,
I recline by the sills of the exquisite flexible doors,
And mark the outlet, and mark the relief and escape.
And as to you Corpse I think you are good manure, but that does not offend me,
I smell the white roses sweet-scented and growing,
I reach to the leafy lips, I reach to the polish'd breasts of melons.

And as to you Life I reckon you are the leavings of many deaths,
(No doubt I have died myself ten thousand times before.)

I hear you whispering there O stars of heaven,
O suns—O grass of graves—O perpetual transfers and promotions,
If you do not say any thing how can I say any thing?

Of the turbid pool that lies in the autumn forest,
Of the moon that descends the steeps of the soughing twilight,
Toss, sparkles of day and dusk—toss on the black stems that decay in the muck,
Toss to the moaning gibberish of the dry limbs.

I ascend from the moon, I ascend from the night,
I perceive that the ghastly glimmer is noonday sunbeams reflected,
And debouch to the steady and central from the offspring great or small.

50

There is that in me—I do not know what it is—but I know it is in me.

Wrench'd and sweaty—calm and cool then my body becomes,
I sleep—I sleep long.

I do not know it—it is without name—it is a word unsaid,
It is not in any dictionary, utterance, symbol.

Something it swings on more than the earth I swing on,
To it the creation is the friend whose embracing awakes me.
Perhaps I might tell more. Outlines! I plead for my brothers and sisters.
Do you see O my brothers and sisters?
It is not chaos or death—it is form, union, plan—it is eternal life—it is Happiness.

51

The past and present wilt—I have fill'd them, emptied them,
And proceed to fill my next fold of the future.

Listener up there! what have you to confide to me?
Look in my face while I snuff the sidle of evening,
(Talk honestly, no one else hears you, and I stay only a minute longer.)

Do I contradict myself?
Very well then I contradict myself,
(I am large, I contain multitudes.)

I concentrate toward them that are nigh, I wait on the door-slab.

Who has done his day's work? who will soonest be through with his supper?
Who wishes to walk with me?

Will you speak before I am gone? will you prove already too late?

52

The spotted hawk swoops by and accuses me, he complains of my gab and my
loitering.

I too am not a bit tamed, I too am untranslatable,
I sound my barbaric yawp over the roofs of the world.

The last scud of day holds back for me,
It flings my likeness after the rest and true as any on the shadow'd wilds,
It coaxes me to the vapor and the dusk.
I depart as air, I shake my white locks at the runaway sun,
I effuse my flesh in eddies, and drift it in lazy jags.

I bequeath myself to the dirt to grow from the grass I love,
If you want me again look for me under your boot-soles.

You will hardly know who I am or what I mean,
But I shall be good health to you nevertheless,
And filter and fiber your blood.

Failing to fetch me at first keep encouraged,
Missing me one place search another,
I stop somewhere waiting for you.

SONG OF THE OPEN ROAD

(*Condensed*)

Afoot and light-hearted I take to the open road,
Healthy, free, the world before me,
The long brown path before me leading wherever I choose.

Henceforth I ask not good-fortune, I myself am good-fortune,
Henceforth I whimper no more, postpone no more, need nothing,
Done with indoor complaints, libraries, querulous criticisms,
Strong and content I travel the open road.

The earth, that is sufficient,
I do not want the constellations any nearer,
I know they are very well where they are,
I know they suffice for those who belong to them

(Still here I carry my old delicious burdens,
I carry them, men and women, I carry them with me wherever I go,
I swear it is impossible for me to get rid of them,
I am fill'd with them, and I will fill them in return.)

You road I enter upon and look around, I believe you are not all that is here,
I believe that much unseen is also here.
Here the profound lesson of reception, nor preference nor denial,
The black with his woolly head, the felon, the diseas'd, the illiterate person, are not denied;
The birth, the hasting after the physician, the beggar's tramp, the drunkard's stagger, the laughing party of mechanics,
The escaped youth, the rich person's carriage, the fop, the eloping couple,
The early market-man, the hearse, the moving of furniture into the town, the return back from the town,

They pass, I also pass, any thing passes, none can be interdicted,
None but are accepted, none but shall be dear to me.

You air that serves me with breath to speak!
You objects that call from diffusion my meanings and give them shape!
You light that wraps me and all things in delicate equable showers!
You paths worn in the irregular hollows by the roadsides!
I believe you are latent with unseen existences, you are so dear to me.

I inhale great draughts of space,
The east and the west are mine, and the north and the south are mine.

I am larger, better than I thought,
I did not know I held so much goodness.

All seems beautiful to me,
I can repeat over to men and women, You have done such good to me I would do the same to you,
I will recruit for myself and you as I go,
I will scatter myself among men and women as I go,
I will toss a new gladness and roughness among them,
Whoever denies me it shall not trouble me,
Whoever accepts me he or she shall be blessed and shall bless me.

Allons! whoever you are come travel with me!
Traveling with me you find what never tires.

The earth never tires,
The earth is rude, silent, incomprehensible at first, Nature is rude and incomprehensible at first,
Be not discouraged, keep on, there are divine things well envelop'd,
I swear to you there are divine things more beautiful than words can tell.

Allons! we must not stop here,
However sweet these laid-up stores, however convenient this dwelling we cannot remain here,
However shelter'd this port and however calm these waters we must not anchor here,
However welcome the hospitality that surrounds us we are permitted to receive it but a little while.

Allons! the inducements shall be greater,
We will sail pathless and wild seas,
We will go where winds blow, waves dash, and the Yankee clipper speeds by under full sail.

Allons! with power, liberty, the earth, the elements,
Health, defiance, gayety, self-esteem, curiosity;
Allons! from all formules!
From your formules, O bat-eyed and materialistic priests.

Allons! through struggles and wars!
The goal that was named cannot be countermanded.

Have the past struggles succeeded?
What has succeeded? yourself? your nation? Nature?
Now understand me well—it is provided in the essence of things that from any fruition of success, no matter what, shall come forth something to make a greater struggle necessary.

My call is the call of battle, I nourish active rebellion,
He going with me must go well arm'd,
He going with me goes often with spare diet, poverty, angry enemies, desertions.

Allons! the road is before us!
It is safe—I have tried it—my own feet have tried it well—be not detain'd!
Let the paper remain on the desk unwritten, and the book on the shelf unopen'd!
Let the tools remain in the workshop! let the money remain unearn'd!
Let the school stand! mind not the cry of the teacher!
Let the preacher preach in his pulpit! let the lawyer plead in the court, and the judge expound the law.

Camerado, I give you my hand!
I give you my love more precious than money,
I give you myself before preaching or law;
Will you give me yourself? will you come travel with me?
Shall we stick by each other as long as we live?

THE BROAD-AX

(*from "Song of the Broad-Ax"*)

Weapon shapely, naked, wan,
Head from the mother's bowels drawn,
Wooded flesh and metal bone, limb only one and lip only one,
Gray-blue leaf by red-heat grown, helve produced from a little seed sown,
Resting the grass amid and upon,
To be lean'd and to lean on.

ON THE BEACH AT NIGHT

On the beach at night,
Stands a child with her father,
Watching the east, the autumn sky.

Up through the darkness,
While ravening clouds, the burial clouds, in black masses spreading,
Lower sullen and fast athwart and down the sky,
Amid a transparent clear belt of ether yet left in the east,
Ascends large and calm the lord-star Jupiter,
And nigh at hand, only a very little above,
Swim the delicate sisters the Pleiades.

From the beach the child holding the hand of her father,
Those burial clouds that lower victorious soon to devour all,
Watching, silently weeps.

Weep not, child,
Weep not, my darling,
With these kisses let me remove your tears,
The ravening clouds shall not long be victorious;
They shall not long possess the sky, they devour the stars only in apparition,
Jupiter shall emerge, be patient, watch again another night, the Pleiades shall
emerge,
They are immortal, all those stars both silvery and golden shall shine out again,
The great stars and the little ones shall shine out again, they endure,
The vast immortal suns and the long-enduring pensive moons shall again shine.

Then dearest child mournest thou only for Jupiter?
Considerest thou alone the burial of the stars?

Something there is,
(With my lips soothing thee, adding I whisper,
I give thee the first suggestion, the problem and indirection,)
Something there is more immortal even than the stars,
(Many the burials, many the days and nights, passing away,)
Something that shall endure longer even than lustrous Jupiter,
Longer than sun or any revolving satellite,
Or the radiant sisters the Pleiades.

OUT OF THE CRADLE ENDLESSLY ROCKING

Out of the cradle endlessly rocking,
Out of the mocking-bird's throat, the musical shuttle,
Out of the Ninth-month midnight,
Over the sterile sands and the fields beyond where the child leaving his bed wan-
der'd alone, bareheaded, barefoot,
Down from the shower'd halo,
Up from the mystic play of shadows twining and twisting as if they were alive,
Out from the patches of briers and blackberries,
From the memories of the bird that chanted to me,
From your memories sad brother, from the fitful risings and fallings I heard,
From under that yellow half-moon late-risen and swollen as if with tears,
From those beginning notes of yearning and love there in the mist,
From the thousand responses of my heart never to cease,
From the myriad thence-arous'd words,
From the word stronger and more delicious than any,
From such as now they start the scene revisiting,
As a flock, twittering, rising, or overhead passing,
Borne hither, ere all eludes me, hurriedly,
A man, yet by these tears a little boy again,
Throwing myself on the sand, confronting the waves,
I, chanter of pains and joys, uniter of here and hereafter,
Taking all hints to use them, but swiftly leaping beyond them,
A reminiscence sing.

Once Paumanok,
When the lilac-scent was in the air and Fifth-month grass was growing,
Up this seashore in some briers,
Two feather'd guests from Alabama, two together,
And their nest, and four light-green eggs spotted with brown,
And every day the he-bird to and fro near at hand,
And every day the she-bird crouch'd on her nest, silent, with bright eyes,
And every day I, a curious boy, never too close, never disturbing them,
Cautiously peering, absorbing, translating.

Shine! shine! shine!
Pour down your warmth, great sun!
While we bask, we two together,

Two together!
Winds blow south, or winds blow north,
Day come white, or night come black,
Home, or rivers and mountains from home,
Singing all time, minding no time,
While we two keep together.

Till of a sudden,
May-be kill'd, unknown to her mate,
One forenoon the she-bird crouch'd not on the nest,
Nor return'd that afternoon, nor the next,
Nor ever appear'd again.

And thenceforward all summer in the sound of the sea,
And at night under the full of the moon in calmer weather,
Over the hoarse surging of the sea,
Or flitting from brier to brier by day,
I saw, I heard at intervals the remaining one, the he-bird,
The solitary guest from Alabama.

Blow! blow! blow!
Blow up sea-winds along Paumanok's shore;
I wait and I wait till you blow my mate to me.

Yes, when the stars glisten'd,
All night long on the prong of a moss-scallop'd stake,
Down almost amid the slapping waves,
Sat the lone singer wonderful causing tears.

He call'd on his mate,
He pour'd forth the meanings which I of all men know.

Yes my brother I know,
The rest might not, but I have treasur'd every note,
For more than once dimly down to the beach gliding,
Silent, avoiding the moonbeams, blending myself with the shadows,
Recalling now the obscure shapes, the echoes, the sounds and sights after their sorts.

The white arms out in the breakers tirelessly tossing,
I, with bare feet, a child, the wind wafting my hair,
Listen'd long and long.

Listen'd to keep, to sing, now translating the notes,
Following you my brother.

Soothe! soothe! soothe!
Close on its wave soothes the wave behind,
And again another behind embracing and lapping, every one close,
But my love soothes not me, not me.
Low hangs the moon, it rose late,
It is lagging—O I think it is heavy with love, with love.

O madly the sea pushes upon the land,
With love, with love.

O night! do I not see my love fluttering out among the breakers?
What is that little black thing I see there in the white?

Loud! loud! loud!
Loud I call to you, my love!
High and clear I shoot my voice over the waves,
Surely you must know who is here, is here,
You must know who I am, my love.

Low-hanging moon!
What is that dusky spot in your brown yellow?
O it is the shape, the shape of my mate!
O moon do not keep her from me any longer.

Land! land! O land!
Whichever way I turn, O I think you could give me my mate back again if you only would,
For I am almost sure I see her dimly whichever way I look.

O rising stars!
Perhaps the one I want so much will rise, will rise with some of you.

O throat! O trembling throat!
Sound clearer through the atmosphere!
Pierce the woods, the earth,
Somewhere listening to catch you must be the one I want.

Shake out carols!
Solitary here, the night's carols!
Carols of lonesome love! death's carols!
Carols under that lagging, yellow, waning moon!
O under that moon where she droops almost down into the sea!
O reckless despairing carols.

But soft! sink low!
Soft, let me just murmur,
And do you wait a moment you husky-nois'd sea,
For somewhere I believe I heard my mate responding to me,
So faint, I must be still, be still to listen,
But not altogether still, for then she might not come immediately to me.

Hither my love!
Here I am! here!
With this just-sustain'd note I announce myself to you,
This gentle call is for you my love, for you.

Do not be decoy'd elsewhere,
That is the whistle of the wind, it is not my voice,
That is the fluttering, the fluttering of the spray,
Those are the shadows of leaves.
O darkness! O in vain!
O I am very sick and sorrowful.

O brown halo in the sky near the moon, drooping upon the sea!
O troubled reflection in the sea!
O throat! O throbbing heart!
And I singing uselessly, uselessly all the night.

O past! O happy life! O songs of joy!
In the air, in the woods, over fields,
Loved! loved! loved! loved! loved!
But my mate no more, no more with me!
We two together no more.

The aria sinking,
All else continuing, the stars shining,
The winds blowing, the notes of the bird continuous echoing,
With angry moans the fierce old mother incessantly moaning,
On the sands of Paumanok's shore gray and rustling,
The yellow half-moon enlarged, sagging down, drooping, the face of the sea almost
touching,
The boy ecstatic, with his bare feet the waves, with his hair the atmosphere dallying,
The love in the heart long pent, now loose, now at last tumultuously bursting,
The aria's meaning, the ears, the soul, swiftly depositing,
The strange tears down the cheeks coursing,
The colloquy there, the trio, each uttering,
The undertone, the savage old mother incessantly crying,
To the boy's soul's questions sullenly timing, some drown'd secret hissing,
To the outsetting bard.

Demon or bird! (said the boy's soul,)
Is it indeed toward your mate you sing? or is it really to me?
For I, that was a child, my tongue's use sleeping, now I have heard you,

Now in a moment I know what I am for, I awake,
And already a thousand singers, a thousand songs, clearer, louder and more sorrowful than yours,
A thousand warbling echoes have started to life within me, never to die.

O you singer solitary, singing by yourself, projecting me,
O solitary me listening, never more shall I cease perpetuating you,
Never more shall I escape, never more the reverberations,
Never more the cries of unsatisfied love be absent from me,
Never again leave me to be the peaceful child I was before what there in the night,
By the sea under the yellow and sagging moon,
The messenger there arous'd, the fire, the sweet hell within,
The unknown want, the destiny of me.

O give me the clue! (it lurks in the night here somewhere,)
O if I am to have so much, let me have more!

A word then, (for I will conquer it,)
The word final, superior to all,
Subtle, sent up—what is it?—I listen;
Are you whispering it, and have been all the time, you sea-waves?
Is that it from your liquid rims and wet sands?

Whereto answering, the sea,
Delaying not, hurrying not,
Whisper'd me through the night, and very plainly before daybreak,
Lisp'd to me the low and delicious word death,
And again death, death, death, death,
Hissing melodious, neither like the bird nor like my arous'd child's heart,
But edging near as privately for me rustling at my feet,
Creeping thence steadily up to my ears and laving me softly all over,
Death, death, death, death, death.

Which I do not forget,
But fuse the song of my dusky demon and brother,
That he sang to me in the moonlight on Paumonok's gray beach,
With the thousand responsive songs at random,
My own songs awaked from that hour,
And with them the key, the word up from the waves,
The word of the sweetest song and all songs,
That strong and delicious word which, creeping to my feet,
(Or like some old crone rocking the cradle, swathed in sweet garments, bending aside,)
The sea whisper'd me.

FACING WEST FROM CALIFORNIA'S SHORES

Facing west from California's shores,
Inquiring, tireless, seeking what is yet unfound,
I, a child, very old, over waves, towards the house of maternity, the land of migrations, look afar,

Look off the shores of my Western sea, the circle almost circled;
For starting westward from Hindustan, from the vales of Kashmere,
From Asia, from the north, from the God, the sage, and the hero,
From the south, from the flowery peninsulas and the spice islands,
Long having wander'd since, round the earth having wander'd,
Now I face home again, very pleas'd and joyous,
(But where is what I started for so long ago?
And why is it yet unfound?)

WHEN LILACS LAST IN THE DOORYARD BLOOM'D[1]

1

When lilacs last in the dooryard bloom'd,
And the great star early droop'd in the western sky in the night,
I mourn'd, and yet shall mourn with ever-returning spring.

Ever-returning spring, trinity sure to me you bring,
Lilac blooming perennial and drooping star in the west,
And thought of him I love.

2

O powerful western fallen star!
O shades of night—O moody, tearful night!
O great star disappear'd—O the black murk that hides the star!
O cruel hands that hold me powerless—O helpless soul of me!
O harsh surrounding cloud that will not free my soul.

3

In the dooryard fronting an old farm-house near the whitewash'd palings,
Stands the lilac-bush tall-growing with heart-shaped leaves of rich green,
With many a pointed blossom rising delicate, with the perfume strong I love,
With every leaf a miracle—and from this bush in the dooryard,
With delicate-color'd blossoms and heart-shaped leaves of rich green,
A sprig with its flower I break.

4

In the swamp in secluded recesses,
A shy and hidden bird is warbling a song.

Solitary the thrush,
The hermit withdrawn to himself, avoiding the settlements,
Sings by himself a song.

Song of the bleeding throat,
Death's outlet song of life, (for well dear brother I know,
If thou wast not granted to sing thou would'st surely die.)

5

Over the breast of the spring, the land, amid cities,
Amid lanes and through old woods, where lately the violets peep'd from the ground,
 spotting the gray débris,

[1] This, one of the noblest elegies in the language, and the rhymed stanzas that follow on the same theme, are part of a group which Whitman entitled "Memories of President Lincoln."

Amid the grass in the fields each side of the lanes, passing the endless grass,
Passing the yellow-spear'd wheat, every grain from its shroud in the dark-brown fields uprisen,
Passing the apple-tree blows of white and pink in the orchards,
Carrying a corpse to where it shall rest in the grave,
Night and day journeys a coffin.

6

Coffin that passes through lanes and streets,
Through day and night with the great cloud darkening the land,
With the pomp of the inloop'd flags with the cities draped in black,
With the show of the States themselves as of crape-veil'd women standing,
With processions long and winding and the flambeaus of the night,
With the countless torches lit, with the silent sea of faces and the unbared heads,
With the waiting depot, the arriving coffin, and the somber faces,
With dirges through the night, with the thousand voices rising strong and solemn,
With all the mournful voices of the dirges pour'd around the coffin,
The dim-lit churches and the shuddering organs—where amid these you journey,
With the tolling tolling bells' perpetual clang,
Here, coffin that slowly passes,
I give you my sprig of lilac.

7

(Nor for you, for one alone,
Blossoms and branches green to coffins all I bring,
For fresh as the morning, thus would I chant a song for you O sane and sacred death.

All over bouquets of roses,
O death, I cover you over with roses and early lilies,
But mostly and now the lilac that blooms the first,
Copious I break, I break the sprigs from the bushes,
With loaded arms I come, pouring for you,
For you and the coffins all of you O death.)

8

O western orb sailing the heaven,
Now I know what you must have meant as a month since I walk'd,
As I walk'd in silence the transparent shadowy night,
As I saw you had something to tell as you bent to me night after night,
As you droop'd from the sky low down as if to my side, (while the other stars all look'd on,)
As we wander'd together the solemn night, (for something I know not what kept me from sleep,)
As the night advanced, and I saw on the rim of the west how full you were of woe,
As I stood on the rising ground in the breeze in the cool transparent night,
As I watch'd where you pass'd and was lost in the netherward black of the night,
As my soul in its trouble dissatisfied sank, as where you sad orb,
Concluded, dropt in the night, and was gone.

9

Sing on there in the swamp,
O singer bashful and tender, I hear your notes, I hear your call,
I hear, I come presently, I understand you,

But a moment I linger, for the lustrous star has detain'd me,
The star my departing comrade holds and detains me.

10

O how shall I warble myself for the dead one there I loved?
And how shall I deck my song for the large sweet soul that has gone?
And what shall my perfume be for the grave of him I love?

Sea-winds blown from east and west,
Blown from the Eastern sea and blown from the Western sea, till there on the prairies meeting,
These and with these and the breath of my chant,
I'll perfume the grave of him I love.

11

O what shall I hang on the chamber walls?
And what shall the pictures be that I hang on the walls,
To adorn the burial-house of him I love?
Pictures of growing spring and farms and homes,
With the Fourth-month eve at sundown, and the gray smoke lucid and bright,
With floods of the yellow gold of the gorgeous, indolent, sinking sun, burning, expanding the air,
With the fresh sweet herbage under foot, and the pale green leaves of the trees prolific,
In the distance the flowing glaze, the breast of the river, with a wind-dapple here and there,
With ranging hills on the banks, with many a line against the sky, and shadows,
And the city at hand, with dwellings so dense, and stacks of chimneys,
And all the scenes of life and the workshops, and the workmen homeward returning.

12

Lo, body and soul—this land,
My own Manhattan with spires, and the sparkling and hurrying tides, and the ships,
The varied and ample land, the South and the North in the light, Ohio's shores and flashing Missouri,
And ever the far-spreading prairies cover'd with grass and corn.

Lo, the most excellent sun so calm and haughty,
The violet and purple morn with just-felt breezes,
The gentle soft-born measureless light,
The miracle spreading bathing all, the fulfill'd noon,
The coming eve delicious, the welcome night and the stars,
Over my cities shining all, enveloping man and land.

13

Sing on, sing on you gray-brown bird,
Sing from the swamps, the recesses, pour your chant from the bushes,
Limitless out of the dusk, out of the cedars and pines.
Sing on dearest brother, warble your reedy song,
Loud human song, with voice of uttermost woe.

O liquid and free and tender!
O wild and loose to my soul—O wondrous singer!
You only I hear—yet the star holds me, (but will soon depart,)
Yet the lilac with mastering odor holds me.

14

Now while I sat in the day and look'd forth,
In the close of the day with its light and the fields of spring, and the farmers preparing their crops,
In the large unconscious scenery of my land with its lakes and forests,
In the heavenly aerial beauty, (after the perturb'd winds and the storms,)
Under the arching heavens of the afternoon swift passing, and the voices of children and women,
The many-moving sea-tides, and I saw the ships how they sail'd,
And the summer approaching with richness, and the fields all busy with labor,
And the infinite separate houses, how they all went on, each with its meals and minutia of daily usages,
And the streets how their throbbings throbb'd, and the cities pent—lo, then and there,
Falling upon them all and among them all, enveloping me with the rest,
Appear'd the cloud, appear'd the long black trail,
And I knew death, its thought, and the sacred knowledge of death.

Then with the knowledge of death as walking one side of me,
And the thought of death close-walking the other side of me,
And I in the middle as with companions, and as holding the hands of companions,
I fled forth to the hiding receiving night that talks not,
Down to the shores of the water, the path by the swamp in the dimness,
To the solemn shadowy cedars and ghostly pines so still.

And the singer so shy to the rest receiv'd me,
The gray-brown bird I know receiv'd us comrades three,
And he sang the carol of death, and a verse for him I love.

From deep secluded recesses,
From the fragrant cedars and the ghostly pines so still,
Came the carol of the bird.

And the charm of the carol rapt me
As I held as if by their hands my comrades in the night,
And the voice of my spirit tallied the song of the bird.

Come lovely and soothing death,
Undulate round the world, serenely arriving, arriving,
In the day, in the night, to all, to each,
Sooner or later delicate death.

Prais'd be the fathomless universe,
For life and joy, and for objects and knowledge curious,
And for love, sweet love—but praise! praise! praise!
For the sure-enwinding arms of cool-enfolding death.

Dark mother always gliding near with soft feet,
Have none chanted for thee a chant of fullest welcome?
Then I chant it for thee, I glorify thee above all,
I bring thee a song that when thou must indeed come, come unfalteringly.

Approach strong deliveress,
When it is so, when thou hast taken them I joyously sing the dead,
Lost in the loving floating ocean of thee,
Laved in the flood of thy bliss O death.

From me to thee glad serenades,
Dances for thee I propose saluting thee, adornments and feastings for thee,
And the sights of the open landscape and the high-spread sky are fitting,
And life and the fields, and the huge and thoughtful night.

The night in silence under many a star,
The ocean shore and the husky whispering wave whose voice I know,
And the soul turning to thee O vast and well-veil'd death,
And the body gratefully nestling close to thee.

Over the tree-tops I float thee a song,
Over the rising and sinking waves, over the myriad fields and the prairies wide,
Over the dense-pack'd cities all and the teeming wharves and ways,
I float this carol wtih joy, with joy to thee O death.

15

To the tally of my soul,
Loud and strong kept up the gray-brown bird,
With pure deliberate notes spreading filling the night.

Loud in the pines and cedars dim,
Clear in the freshness moist and the swamp-perfume,
And I with my comrades there in the night.

While my sight that was bound in my eyes unclosed,
As to long panoramas of visions.

And I saw askant the armies,
I saw as in noiseless dreams hundreds of battle-flags,
Borne through the smoke of the battles and pierc'd with missiles I saw them,
And carried hither and yon through the smoke, and torn and bloody,
And at last but a few shreds left on the staffs, (and all in silence,)
And the staffs all splinter'd and broken.

I saw battle-corpses, myriads of them,
And the white skeletons of young men, I saw them,
I saw the débris and débris of all the slain soldiers of the war,
But I saw they were not as was thought,
They themselves were fully at rest, they suffer'd not,
The living remain'd and suffer'd, the mother suffer'd,
And the wife and the child and the musing comrade suffer'd,
And the armies that remain'd suffer'd.

16

Passing the visions, passing the night,
Passing, unloosing the hold of my comrades' hands,

Passing the song of the hermit bird and the tallying song of my soul,
Victorious song, death's outlet song, yet varying ever-altering song,
As low and wailing, yet clear the notes, rising and falling, flooding the night,
Sadly sinking and fainting, as warning and warning, and yet again bursting with joy,
Covering the earth and filling the spread of the heaven,
As that powerful psalm in the night I heard from recesses,
Passing, I leave thee lilac with heart-shaped leaves,
I leave thee there in the dooryard, blooming, returning with spring.

I cease from my song for thee,
From my gaze on thee in the west, fronting the west, communing with thee,
O comrade lustrous with silver face in the night.

Yet each to keep and all, retrievements out of the night,
The song, the wondrous chant of the gray-brown bird,
And the tallying chant, the echo arous'd in my soul,
With the lustrous and drooping star with the countenance full of woe,
With the holders holding my hand nearing the call of the bird,
Comrades mine and I in the midst, and their memory ever to keep, for the dead I loved so well,
For the sweetest, wisest soul of all my days and lands—and this for his dear sake,
Lilac and star and bird twined with the chant of my soul,
There in the fragrant pines and the cedars dusk and dim.

O CAPTAIN! MY CAPTAIN!

O Captain! my Captain! our fearful trip is done,
The ship has weather'd every rack, the prize we sought is won,
The port is near, the bells I hear, the people all exulting,
While follow eyes the steady keel, the vessel grim and daring;
But O heart! heart! heart!
O the bleeding drops of red,
Where on the deck my Captain lies,
Fallen cold and dead.

O Captain! my Captain! rise up and hear the bells;
Rise up—for you the flag is flung—for you the bugle trills,
For you bouquets and ribbon'd wreaths—for you the shores a-crowding,
For you they call, the swaying mass, their eager faces turning;
Here Captain! dear father!
The arm beneath your head!
It is some dream that on the deck,
You've fallen cold and dead.

My Captain does not answer, his lips are pale and still,
My father does not feel my arm, he has no pulse nor will,
The ship is anchor'd safe and sound, its voyage closed and done,
From fearful trip the victor ship comes in with object won;
Exult O shores, and ring O bells!
But I with mournful tread,
Walk the deck my Captain lies,
Fallen cold and dead.

DIRGE FOR TWO VETERANS

The last sunbeam
Lightly falls from the finished Sabbath,
On the pavement here, and there beyond it is looking,
Down a new-made double grave,

Lo, the moon ascending,
Up from the east the silvery round moon,
Beautiful over the house-tops ghastly, phantom moon,
Immense and silent moon.

I see a sad procession,
And I hear the sound of coming full-key'd bugles,
All the channels of the city streets they're flooding,
As with voices and with tears.

I hear the great drums pounding,
And the small drums steady whirring,
And every blow of the great convulsive drums,
Strikes me through and through.

For the son is brought with the father,
(On the foremost ranks of the fierce assault they fell,
Two veterans son and father dropt together,
And the double grave awaits them).

Now nearer blow the bugles,
And the drums strike more convulsive,
And the daylight o'er the pavement quite has faded,
And the strong dead-march enwraps me.

In the eastern sky up-buoying,
The sorrowful vast phantom moves illumin'd,
('Tis some mother's large transparent face,
In heaven brighter growing).

O strong dead-march, you please me!
O moon immense with your silvery face, you soothe me!
O my soldiers twain! O my veterans passing to burial!
What I have I also give you.

The moon gives you light,
And the bugles and the drums give you music,
And my heart, O my soldiers, my veterans,
My heart gives you love.

COME UP FROM THE FIELDS, FATHER

Come up from the fields, father, here's a letter from our Pete,
And come to the front door, mother, here's a letter from thy dear son.

Lo, 'tis autumn,
Lo, where the trees, deeper green, yellower and redder,
Cool and sweeten Ohio's villages with leaves fluttering in the moderate wind,
Where apples ripe in the orchards hang and grapes on the trellis'd vines,
(Smell you the smell of the grapes on the vines?
Smell you the buckwheat where the bees were lately buzzing?)
Above all, lo, the sky so calm, so transparent after the rain, and with wondrous clouds,
Below too, all calm, all vital and beautiful, and the farm prospers well.

Down in the fields all prospers well,
But now from the fields come, father, come at the daughter's call,
And come to the entry, mother, to the front door come right away.

Fast as she can she hurries, something ominous, her steps trembling,
She does not tarry to smooth her hair nor adjust her cap.

Open the envelope quickly,
O this is not our son's writing, yet his name is sign'd,
O a strange hand writes for our dear son, O stricken mother's soul!
All swims before her eyes, flashes with black, she catches the main words only,
Sentences broken, *gunshot wound in the breast, cavalry skirmish, taken to hospital,*
At present low, but will soon be better.

Ah, now the single figure to me,
Amid all teeming and wealthy Ohio with all its cities and farms,
Sickly white in the face and dull in the head, very faint,
By the jamb of a door leans.

Grieve not so, dear mother (the just-grown daughter speaks through her sobs,
The little sisters huddle around speechless and dismay'd),
See, dearest mother, the letter says Pete will soon be better.

Alas, poor boy, he will never be better (nor maybe needs to be better, that brave and simple soul),
While they stand at home at the door he is dead already,
The only son is dead.

But the mother needs to be better,
She with thin form presently drest in black,
By day her meals untouch'd, then at night fitfully sleeping, often waking,
In the midnight waking, weeping, longing with one deep longing,
O that she might withdraw unnoticed, silent from life escape and withdraw,
To follow, to seek, to be with her dear dead son.

VIGIL STRANGE I KEPT ON THE FIELD ONE NIGHT

Vigil strange I kept on the field one night;
When you, my son and my comrade, dropt at my side that day,
One look I but gave which your dear eyes return'd with a look I shall never forget,
One touch of your hand to mine, O boy, reach'd up as you lay on the ground,

Then onward I sped in the battle, the even-contested battle,
Till late in the night reliev'd to the place at last again I made my way,
Found you in death so cold, dear comrade, found your body, son of responding kisses (never again on earth responding),
Bared your face in the starlight, curious the scene, cool blew the moderate night-wind,
Long there and then in vigil I stood, dimly around me the battle-field spreading,
Vigil wondrous and vigil sweet there in the fragrant silent night,
But not a tear fell, not even a long-drawn sigh, long, long I gazed,
Then on the earth partially reclining sat by your side leaning my chin in my hands,
Passing sweet hours, immortal and mystic hours with you, dearest comrade—not a tear, not a word,
Vigil of silence, love and death, vigil for you, my son and my soldier,
As onward silently stars aloft, eastward new ones upward stole,
Vigil final for you, brave boy (I could not save you, swift was your death,
I faithfully loved you and cared for you living, I think we shall surely meet again),
Till at latest lingering of the night, indeed just as the dawn appear'd,
My comrade I wrapt in his blanket, envelop'd well his form,
Folded the blanket well, tucking it carefully over head and carefully under feet,
And there and then and bathed by the rising sun, my son in his grave, in his rude-dug grave I deposited,
Ending my vigil strange with that, vigil of night and battlefield dim,
Vigil for boy of responding kisses (never again on earth responding),
Vigil for comrade swiftly slain, vigil I never forget, how as day brighten'd,
I rose from the chill ground and folded my soldier well in his blanket,
And buried him where he fell.

THE POET

(From "By Blue Ontario's Shore")

I listened to the Phantom by Ontario's shore,
I heard the voice arising demanding bards,
By them all native and grand, by them alone can these States be fused into the compact organism of a Nation.

To hold men together by paper and seal or by compulsion is no account,
That only holds men together which aggregates all in a living principle, as the hold of the limbs of the body or the fibres of plants.

Of all races and eras these States with veins full of poetical stuff most need poets, and are to have the greatest, and use them the greatest,
Their Presidents shall not be their common referee so much as their poets shall.

(Soul of love and tongue of fire!
Eye to pierce the deepest deeps and sweep the world!
Ah, Mother, prolific and full in all besides, yet how long barren, barren?)

* * *

10

Of these States the poet is the equable man,
Not in him but off from him things are grotesque, eccentric, fail of their full returns,
Nothing out of its place is good, nothing in its place is bad,
He bestows on every object or quality its fit proportion, neither more nor less,
He is the arbiter of the diverse, he is the key,
He is the equaliser of his age and land,
He supplies what wants supplying, he checks what wants checking,
In peace out of him speaks the spirit of peace, large, rich, thrifty, building populous towns, encouraging agriculture, arts, commerce, lighting the study of man, the soul, health, immortality, government,
In war he is the best backer of the war, he fetches artillery as good as the engineer's, he can make every word he speaks draw blood,
The years straying toward infidelity he withholds by his steady faith,
He is no arguer, he is judgment (Nature accepts him absolutely),
He judges not as the judge judges but as the sun falling round a helpless thing,
As he sees the farthest he has the most faith,
His thoughts are the hymns of the praise of things,
In the dispute on God and eternity he is silent,
He sees eternity less like a play with a prologue and denouement,
He sees eternity in men and women, he does not see men and women as dreams or dots.

For the great Idea, the idea of perfect and free individuals,
For that, the bard walks in advance, leader of leaders,
The attitude of him cheers up slaves and horrifies foreign despots.
Without extinction is Liberty, without retrograde is Equality,
They live in the feelings of young men and the best women,
(Not for nothing have the indomitable heads of the earth been always ready to fall for Liberty).

11

For the great Idea,
That, O my brethren, that is the mission of poets.

Songs of stern defiance ever ready,
Songs of the rapid arming and the march,
The flag of peace quick-folded, and instead the flag we know,
Warlike flag of the great Idea.

(Angry cloth I saw there leaping!
I stand again in leaden rain your flapping folds saluting,
I sing you over all, flying beckoning through the fight—O the hard-contested fight!

The cannons ope their rosy-flashing muzzles—the hurtled balls scream,
The battle-front forms amid the smoke—the volleys pour incessant from the line,
Hark, the ringing word *Charge!*—now the tussle and the furious maddening yells,
Now the corpses tumble curl'd upon the ground,
Cold, cold in death, for precious life of you,
Angry cloth I saw there leaping.)

12

Are you he who would assume a place to teach or be a poet here in the States?
The place is august, the terms obdurate.

Who would assume to teach here may well prepare himself body and mind,
He may well survey, ponder, arm, fortify, harden, make lithe himself,
He shall surely be question'd beforehand by me with many and stern questions.

Who are you indeed who would talk or sing to America?
Have you studied out the land, its idioms and men?
Have you learn'd the physiology, phrenology, politics, geography, pride, freedom, friendship of the land? its substratums and objects?
Have you consider'd the organic compact of the first day of the first year of Independence, sign'd by the Commissioners, ratified by the States, and read by Washington at the head of the army?
Have you possess'd yourself of the Federal Constitution?
Do you see who have left all feudal processes and poems behind them, and assumed the poems and processes of Democracy?
Are you faithful to things? do you teach what the land and sea, the bodies of men, womanhood, amativeness, heroic angers, teach?
Have you sped through fleeting customs, popularities?
Can you hold your hand against all seductions, follies, whirls, fierce contentions? are you very strong? are you really of the whole People?
Are you not of some coterie? some school or mere religion?
Are you done with reviews and criticisms of life? animating now to life itself?
Have you vivified yourself from the maternity of these States?
Have you too the old ever-fresh forbearance and impartiality?
Do you hold the like love for those hardening to maturity? for the last-born? little and big? and for the errant?

What is this you bring my America?
Is it uniform with my country?
Is it not something that has been better told or done before?
Have you not imported this or the spirit of it in some ship?
Is it not a mere tale? a rhyme? a prettiness?—is the good old cause in it?
Has it not dangled long at the heels of the poets, politicians, literats, of enemies' lands?
Does it not assume that what is notoriously gone is still here?
Does it answer universal needs? will it improve manners?
Does it sound with trumpet-voice the proud victory of the Union in that secession war?
Can your performance face the open fields and the seaside?
Will it absorb into me as I absorb food, air, to appear again in my strength, gait, face?
Have real employments contributed to it? original makers, not mere amanuenses?
Does it meet modern discoveries, calibres, facts, face to face?
What does it mean to American persons, progresses, cities? Chicago, Kanada, Arkansas?
Does it see behind the apparent custodians the real custodians standing, menacing, silent, the mechanics, Manhattanese, Western men, Southerners, significant alike in their apathy and in the promptness of their love?

Does it see what finally befalls, and has always finally befallen, each temporiser, patcher, outsider, partialist, alarmist, infidel, who has ever ask'd anything of America?
What mocking and scornful negligence?
The track strew'd with the dust of skeletons,
By the roadside others disdainfully toss'd.

13

Rhymes and rhymers pass away, poems distill'd from poems pass away,
The swarms of reflectors and the polite pass, and leave ashes,
Admirers, importers, obedient persons, make but the soil of literature,
America justifies itself, give it time, no disguise can deceive it or conceal from it, it is impassive enough,
Only toward the likes of itself will it advance to meet them,
If its poets appear it will in due time advance to meet them, there is no fear of mistake,
(The proof of a poet shall be sternly deferr'd till his country absorbs him as affectionately as he has absorb'd it).

He masters whose spirit masters, he tastes sweetest who results sweetest in the long run,
The blood of the brawn beloved of time is unconstraint;
In the need of songs, philosophy, an appropriate native grand-opera, shipcraft, any craft.
He or she is greatest who contributes the greatest original practical example.

Already a nonchalant breed, silently emerging, appears on the streets,
People's lips salute only doers, lovers, satisfiers, positive knowers,
There will shortly be no more priests, I say their work is done,
Death is without emergencies here, but life is perpetual emergencies here,
Are your body, days, manners, superb? After death you shall be superb,
Justice, health, self-esteem, clear the way with irresistible power;
How dare you place anything before a man?

14

Fall behind me States!
A man before all—myself, typical, before all.

Give me the pay I have served for,
Give me to sing the songs of the great Idea, take all the rest,
I have loved the earth, sun, animals, I have despised riches,
I have given alms to every one that ask'd, stood up for the stupid and crazy, devoted my income and labor to others,
Hated tyrants, argued not concerning God, had patience and indulgence toward the people, taken off my hat to nothing known or unknown,
Gone freely with powerful uneducated persons and with the young, and with the mothers of families,
Read these leaves to myself in the open air, tried them by trees, stars, rivers,
Dismiss'd whatever insulted my own soul or defiled my body,
Claim'd nothing to myself which I have not carefully claim'd for others on the same terms,

Sped to the camps, and comrades found and accepted from every State,
(Upon this breast has many a dying soldier lean'd to breathe his last,
This arm, this hand, this voice, have nourish'd, rais'd, restored,
To life recalling many a prostrate form);
I am willing to wait to be understood by the growth of the taste of myself,
Rejecting none, permitting all.

(Say, O Mother, have I not to your thought been faithful?
Have I not through life kept you and yours before me?)

15

I swear I begin to see the meaning of these things,
It is not the earth, it is not America who is so great,
It is I who am great or to be great, it is You up there, or any one,
It is to walk rapidly through civilisations, governments, theories,
Through poems, pageants, shows, to form individuals.

Underneath all, individuals,
I swear nothing is good to me now that ignores individuals,
The American compact is altogether with individuals,
The only government is that which makes minute of individuals,
The whole theory of the universe is directed unerringly to one single individual—
namely to You.

(Mother! with subtle sense severe, with the naked sword in your hand,
I saw you at last refuse to treat but directly with individuals.)

16

Underneath all, Nativity,
I swear I will stand by my own nativity, pious or impious so be it;
I swear I am charm'd with nothing except nativity,
Men, women, cities, nations, are only beautiful from nativity.

Underneath all is the Expression of love for men and women,
(I swear I have seen enough of mean and impotent modes of expressing love for
men and women,
After this day I take my own modes of expressing love for men and women).

I swear I will have each quality of my race in myself,
(Talk as you like, he only suits these States whose manners favor the audacity
and sublime turbulence of the States).

Underneath the lessons of things, spirits, Nature, governments, ownerships, I swear
I perceive other lessons,
Underneath all to me is myself, to you yourself (the same monotonous old song).

17

O I see flashing that this America is only you and me,
Its power, weapons, testimony, are you and me,
Its crimes, lies, thefts, defections, are you and me,
Its Congress is you and me, the officers, capitols, armies, ships, are you and me,
Its endless gestations of new States are you and me,

The war (that war so bloody and grim, the war I will henceforth forget), was you and me,
Natural and artificial are you and me,
Freedom, language, poems, employments, are you and me,
Past, present, future, are you and me.

I dare not shirk any part of myself,
Not any part of America good or bad,
Not to build for that which builds for mankind,
Not to balance ranks, complexions, creeds, and the sexes,
Not to justify science nor the march of equality,
Nor to feed the arrogant blood of the brawn belov'd of time.

I am for those that have never been master'd,
For men and women whose tempers have never been master'd,
For those whom laws, theories, conventions, can never master.

I am for those who walk abreast with the whole earth,
Who inaugurate one to inaugurate all.

I will not be outfaced by irrational things,
I will penetrate what it is in them that is scarcastic upon me,
I will make cities and civilisations defer to me,
This is what I have learnt from America—it is the amount, and it I teach again.

GIVE ME THE SPLENDID SILENT SUN

Give me the splendid silent sun with all his beams full-dazzling,
Give me juicy autumnal fruit ripe and red from the orchard,
Give me a field where the unmowed grass grows,
Give me an arbor, give me the trellised grape,
Give me fresh corn and wheat, give me serene-moving animals teaching content,
Give me nights perfectly quiet as on high plateaus west of the Mississippi, and I looking up at the stars,
Give me odorous at sunrise a garden of beautiful flowers where I can walk undisturbed,
Give me for marriage a sweet-breathed woman of whom I should never tire,
Give me a perfect child, give me, away aside from the noise of the world, a rural domestic life,
Give me to warble spontaneous songs recluse by myself, for my own ears only,
Give me solitude, give me Nature, give me again O Nature your primal sanities!
These demanding to have them, (tired with ceaseless excitement, and racked by the war-strife)
These to procure incessantly asking, rising in cries from my heart.
While yet incessantly asking still I adhere to my city,
Day upon day and year upon year, O city, walking your streets,
Where you hold me enchained a certain time refusing to give me up,
Yet giving to make me glutted, enriched of soul, you give me forever faces;
(O I see what I sought to escape, confronting, reversing my cries,
I see my own soul trampling down what it asked for.)

Keep your splendid silent sun,
Keep your woods, O Nature, and the quiet places by the woods,
Keep your fields of clover and timothy, and your cornfields and orchards,
Keep the blossoming buckwheat fields where the Ninth-month bees hum;
Give me faces and streets—give me these phantoms incessant and endless along the trottoirs!
Give me interminable eyes—give me women—give me comrades and lovers by the thousand!
Let me see new ones every day—let me hold new ones by the hand every day!
Give me such shows—give me the streets of Manhattan!
Give me Broadway, with the soldiers marching—give me the sound of the trumpets and drums!
(The soldiers in companies or regiments—some starting away flushed and reckless,
Some, their time up, returning with thinned ranks, young, yet very old, worn, marching, noticing nothing;)
Give me the shores and wharves heavy-fringed with black ships!
O such for me! O an intense life, full of repletion and varied!
The life of the theatre, bar-room, huge hotel, for me!
The saloon of the steamer! The crowded excursion for me! The torchlight procession!
The dense brigade bound for the war, with high-piled military wagons following;
People, endless, streaming, with strong voices, passions, pageants,
Manhattan streets with their powerful throbs, with beating drums as now,
The endless and noisy chorus, the rustle and clank of muskets (even the sight of the wounded),
Manhattan crowds, with their turbulent musical chorus!
Manhattan faces and eyes forever for me.

TO A LOCOMOTIVE IN WINTER

Thee for my recitative,
Thee in the driving storm even as now, the snow, the winter-day declining,
Thee in thy panoply, thy measur'd dual throbbing and thy beat convulsive,
Thy black cylindric body, golden brass and silvery steel,
Thy ponderous side-bars, parallel and connecting rods, gyrating, shuttling at thy sides,
Thy metrical, now swelling pant and roar, now tapering in the distance,
Thy great protruding head-light fix'd in front,
Thy long, pale, floating vapor-pennants, tinged with delicate purple,
The dense and murky clouds out-belching from thy smokestack,
Thy knitted frame, thy springs and valves, the tremulous twinkle of thy wheels,
Thy train of cars behind, obedient, merrily following,
Through gale or calm, now swift, now slack, yet steadily careering;
Type of the modern—emblem of motion and power—pulse of the continent
For once come serve the Muse and merge in verse, even as here I see thee,
With storm and buffeting gusts of wind and falling snow,
By day thy warning ringing bell to sound its notes,
By night thy silent signal lamps to swing.

Fierce-throated beauty!
Roll through my chant with all thy lawless music, thy swinging lamps at night,

Thy madly-whistled laughter, echoing, rumbling like an earthquake, rousing all,
Law of thyself complete, thine own track firmly holding,
(No sweetness debonair of tearful harp or glib piano thine,)
Thy trills of shrieks by rocks and hills return'd,
Launch'd o'er the prairies wide, across the lakes,
To the free skies unpent and glad and strong.

THIS COMPOST

1

Something startles me where I thought I was safest,
I withdraw from the still woods I loved,
I will not go now on the pastures to walk,
I will not strip the clothes from my body to meet my lover the sea,
I will not touch my flesh to the earth as to other flesh to renew me.

O how can it be that the ground itself does not sicken?
How can you be alive you growths of spring?
How can you furnish health you blood of herbs, roots, orchards, grain?
Are they not continually putting distemper'd corpses within you?
Is not every continent work'd over and over with sour dead?

Where have you disposed of their carcasses?
Those drunkards and gluttons of so many generations?
Where have you drawn off all the foul liquid and meat?
I do not see any of it upon you to-day, or perhaps I am deceiv'd,
I will run a furrow with my plough, I will press my spade through the sod and turn it up underneath,
I am sure I shall expose some of the foul meat.

2

Behold this compost! behold it well!
Perhaps every mite has once form'd part of a sick person—yet behold!
The grass of spring covers the prairies,
The bean bursts noiselessly through the mould in the garden,
The delicate spear of the onion pierces upward,
The apple-buds cluster together on the apple-branches,
The resurrection of the wheat appears with pale visage out of its graves,
The tinge awakes over the willow-tree and the mulberry-tree,
The he-birds carol mornings and evenings while the she-birds sit on their nests,
The young of poultry break through the hatch'd eggs,
The new-born of animals appear, the calf is dropt from the cow, the colt from the mare,
Out of its little hill faithfully rise the potato's dark green leaves,
Out of its hill rises the yellow maize-stalk, the lilacs bloom in the dooryards,
The summer growth is innocent and disdainful above all those strata of sour dead.

What chemistry!
That the winds are really not infectious,
That this is no cheat, this transparent green-wash of the sea which is so amorous after me,
That it is safe to allow it to lick my naked body all over with its tongues,

That it will not endanger me with the fevers that have deposited themselves in it,
That all is clean forever and forever,
That the cool drink from the well tastes so good,
That blackberries are so flavorous and juicy,
That the fruits of the apple-orchard and the orange-orchard, that melons, grapes, peaches, plums, will none of them poison me,
That when I recline on the grass I do not catch any disease,
Though probably every spear of grass rises out of what was once a catching disease.

Now I am terrified at the Earth, it is that calm and patient,
It grows such sweet things out of such corruptions,
It turns harmless and stainless on its axis, with such endless successions of diseas'd corpses,
It distills such exquisite winds out of such infused fetor,
It renews with such unwitting looks its prodigal, annual, sumptuous crops,
It gives such divine materials to men, and accepts such leavings from them at last.

AFTER THE SUPPER AND TALK

After the supper and talk—after the day is done,
As a friend from friends his final withdrawal prolonging,
Good-bye and Good-bye with emotional lips repeating,
(So hard for his hand to release those hands—no more will they meet,
No more for communion of sorrow and joy, of old and young,
A far-stretching journey awaits him, to return no more,)
Shunning, postponing severance—seeking to ward off the last word ever so little,
E'en at the exit-door turning—charges superfluous calling back—e'en as he descends the steps,
Something to eke out a minute additional—shadows of nightfall deepening,
Farewells, messages lessening—dimmer the forthgoer's visage and form,
Soon to be lost for aye in the darkness—loth, O so loth to depart!
Garrulous to the very last.

THE LAST INVOCATION

At the last, tenderly,
From the walls of the powerful fortress'd house,
From the clasp of the knitted locks, from the keep of the well-closed doors,
Let me be wafted.

Let me glide noiselessly forth;
With the key of softness unlock the locks—with a whisper,
Set ope the doors O soul.

Tenderly—be not impatient,
(Strong is your hold O mortal flesh.
Strong is your hold O love.)

THE UNTOLD WANT

The untold want by life and land ne'er granted,
Now voyager sail thou forth to seek and find.

JOY, SHIPMATE, JOY

Joy, shipmate, joy!
(Pleas'd to my soul at death I cry,)
Our life is closed, our life begins,
The long, long anchorage we leave,
The ship is clear at last, she leaps!
She swiftly courses from the shore,
Joy, shipmate, joy.

Emily Dickinson

⸎ Emily (Elizabeth [1]) Dickinson was born in Amherst, Massachusetts, December 10, 1830. Her life was, except for a circumstance which has caused much speculation and a controversy among her biographers, bare of outward event. She died in the house in which she was born; after she was twenty-six she rarely left it. Her childhood had the ordinary uneventful events common to other children in Amherst which at that time was so remote that, only a few years before, her mother's dower had been brought to the town by a team of oxen. Her family was not quite like other families; it was a distillation of all that was New England, a synthesis and refinement of its reticence and high thinking. A contemporary, Samuel G. Ward, commented shrewdly, "We came to this country to think our own thoughts with nobody to hinder. We conversed with our own souls till we lost the art of communicating with other people. . . . It was awfully high but awfully lonesome. . . . If the gift of articulateness was not denied, you had Channing, Emerson, Hawthorne, a stupendous example, and many others. Mostly, it was denied, and became a family fate. This is where Emily Dickinson comes in. She was the articulate inarticulate."

Emily Dickinson's father, Edward Dickinson, was a lawyer who was nominated for the office of Lieutenant Governor (which he declined) and one of the town's most influential men. Emily adored him. In the *Life and Letters of Emily Dickinson* Martha Dickinson Bianchi, Emily's niece, quotes her as saying, "If father is asleep on the sofa the house is full." At sixteen she formed a close friendship with a girl who visited Amherst and later married her brother Austin (the "sister Sue" of *The Single Hound*) and who disputed with Lavinia the belated honor of being Emily's confidante. At seventeen Emily entered South Hadley Female Seminary, disliked it intensely, grew homesick, rebelled at the extremities of its Puritanism and, on one occasion, packed her bags and took the stage home. From eighteen to twenty-three she was, according to her first biographer, "a social creature in the highest sense."

When she was twenty-three she spent some weeks in Washington with her father who was in Congress for two terms. On the return to Amherst Emily visited in Philadelphia and met the Reverend Charles Wadsworth—a meeting which, according to one of her biographers, determined not only the course of her life but the

[1] Often given as "Norcross," which was not her middle name, but her sister Lavinia's.

character of her poetry. As late as 1929 Mme. Bianchi (Sue's daughter) wrote, "Even now, after the many slow years she has been removed from us in the body, her spirit hinders the baring of that chapter which has been so universally misunderstood." Nothing could have done more to further the misunderstanding; it provoked speculation, inspired the very gossip it purported to evade, and placed the emphasis on a puzzle rather than on the poetry.

But this was part of a posthumous wrangle from which Emily Dickinson was mercifully spared. The known facts are these: After 1856 she immured herself in the family mansion. She was rarely seen even in the house except as a figure vanishing ghostily down a corridor; she loved music, but refused to come in the parlor where it was played, and remained seated, out of view, in the hall. She developed certain idiosyncrasies: was an indefatigable letter-writer but had a congenital prejudice against addressing her notes and got others to do this for her; invariably dressed in white, but refused to be "fitted," her sister performing this task for her; sent perennial roots and cookies with cryptic lines to neighbors and even to children, and became, in short, the village oddity. She died of Bright's disease, May 15, 1886, in her fifty-sixth year.

Thus the flat physical data of the woman. The poet made her appearance only after her death. During her lifetime seven of her poems had been published—through no desire of her own. She never cared to see her emotions in print; "she habitually concealed her mind, like her person, from all but a very few friends," wrote Higginson. Even more deeply than Heine she might have cried, *"Aus meinen grossen Schmerzen mach ich die kleinen Lieder"*—and these brief, almost telegraphic revelations tucked away in boxes and hidden in bureau drawers have outlasted the more pretentious writing of a century. After Emily's death her executors were amazed at the amount of material which she had left. More than twelve hundred poems were unearthed; many more remained hidden for years. "Sister Sue" had written a tribute to Emily in the town paper, but it was upon Lavinia that the burden fell. Lavinia assumed it. She knew her limitations, but she knew, or at least surmised, the greatness of which she was guardian. She called upon her friends Mabel Loomis Todd and Thomas Wentworth Higginson. Mrs. Todd began to copy the poems, and not only to copy but to edit them, for Emily usually appended a list of alternative words, and it was Mrs. Todd who had to decide which word should appear as Emily's choice. In November, 1890, the first volume of the *Poems of Emily Dickinson* appeared with an introduction by Thomas Wentworth Higginson. It has been supposed that these spontaneous illuminations, so different from the politely prepared verse of the day, fell on barren ground. The opposite is true. Though there were many scoffers and parodists, critics were not slow to see the essential quality—a Blake-like purity combined with a most un-Puritan pertness—readers responded, and six editions were printed in as many weeks. A year later *Poems of Emily Dickinson—Second Series* (1891) appeared, again edited by Mabel Loomis Todd and Thomas Wentworth Higginson. In 1893 the first *Letters of Emily Dickinson* was edited by Mrs. Todd, incorporated by Mme. Bianchi in her later volume, and revised and enlarged in 1931, the original two volumes being an invaluable mine of source material. In 1896 Mrs. Todd alone was responsible for *Poems—Third Series.*

The public taste changed; for thirty years little was heard of Emily Dickinson; her *Letters* went out of print, the publishers thought so little of them that they did not even renew the copyright. The "authorities" contained only slighting references to her or none at all. The *Britannica,* as late as 1926, failed to mention her name except as a cross-reference. In 1955 and 1958, however, through Thomas H. Johnson's scrupulous editions of her complete *Poems* (3 vols.) and *Letters* (3 vols.), the texts were finally given as they were originally written.

In 1914 Mme. Bianchi prepared a further volume, *The Single Hound,* but, though the reception was cordial, it was by no means overwhelming. An occasional article appeared, showing the poet's "lack of control" or, beneath a cover of condescension, ridiculing her "hit-or-miss grammar, sterile rhythms, and appalling rhymes." A devotee here and there defended the quaint charm of her use of assonance and half-rhyming vowels. Her audience grew, but gradually. Suddenly, in 1924, Emily Dickinson became a figure of international importance. Almost forty years after her death her name became a poetic shibboleth when in one year there were published Martha Dickinson Bianchi's *The Life and Letters of Emily Dickinson,* the first collected *Complete Poems* (a misnomer as it turned out to be), and the first English compilation, *Selected Poems of Emily Dickinson,* edited with a penetrating preface by Conrad Aiken.

The enthusiasm attending the triple appearance was unprecedented. Martin Armstrong, the English poet, said, "Mr. Aiken calls Emily Dickinson's poetry 'perhaps the finest by a woman in the English language.' I quarrel only with his 'perhaps.' " Nor were other plaudits less vociferous. "A feminine Blake," "an epigrammatic Walt Whitman," "a New England mystic," were a few of the characterizations fastened upon her. Other appraisals sought to "interpret" her involved but seldom obscure verses in the light of the "mystery" of her life. But "The Amherst Nun" would have repudiated the amateur psychoanalyst as vigorously as she, whose verses and letters brim with mischievous fancy, would have laughed at their epithets.

In 1929 there was published another generous collection of "undiscovered" or "withheld" poems, *Further Poems of Emily Dickinson,* edited by Martha Dickinson Bianchi and Alfred Leete Hampson. There were one hundred and seventy-six hitherto unpublished pieces, and their clear beauty as well as mysterious appearance, all too vaguely explained, caused something of a furore. The excitement increased in 1930, the centenary of Emily Dickinson's birth. A new volume, *Unpublished Poems by Emily Dickinson,* appeared toward the end of 1935.

Three widely differing biographies were published in the year of Emily Dickinson's centenary. The mysterious event which caused her to keep herself immured was variously detailed and disputed. *Emily Dickinson: The Human Background* (1930) by Josephine Pollitt identified the man who prompted the love poems and her proud withdrawal from the world as Edward Hunt, husband of the author, Helen Hunt (Jackson), one of Emily Dickinson's few close friends. This theory was used as the basis of a drama, *Brittle Heaven,* by Frederick J. Pohl and Vincent York (1934). A more theatrical but less literary work than this was Susan Glaspell's *Alison's House,* a play, based on the posthumous publication of the poems, which won the Pulitzer Prize for the drama in 1931. Another play, *Eastward in Eden* by Dorothy Gardner, produced in 1947, revolved about Emily's frustrated love for Dr. Charles Wadsworth. *The Life and Mind of Emily Dickinson* (1930) by the poet, Genevieve Taggard, discovered a secret lover in George Gould of Amherst College, and disclosed a romance which this biographer maintains was shattered by Emily's patriarchal and harshly possessive father. MacGregor Jenkins' *Emily Dickinson: Friend and Neighbor* (1930) added nothing but confusing childhood memories. The confusion was increased by Martha Dickinson Bianchi, Emily's niece, the only daughter of Austin Dickinson. In *Emily Dickinson Face to Face* (1932) Mrs. Bianchi told a vague story of an abortive love affair with an anonymous married clergyman, of Emily's refusal to destroy another woman's happiness, her sudden flight home, the pursuit of her nameless lover, of a melodramatic scene in Amherst, and Emily's final abnegation.

It remained for George Frisbie Whicher to establish the facts in *This Was a Poet: Emily Dickinson* (1938). In his critical biography Whicher cut through the obscurities of speculation. He rescued Emily Dickinson from the Freudian father-complex and disposed of the incongruous lovers once and for all. In the chapter "Rowing in Eden" Whicher told the whole story of Emily Dickinson's meeting with the Reverend Charles Wadsworth, of her admiration for his preaching, and her growing infatuation with the man. His letters of spiritual counsel were translated by Emily into symbols of an agonizing and almost unbearable intimacy. She brooded upon them until she thought herself dedicated to him. Her love poems say it over and over with unalterable insistence.

For more than half a century after her death, and from time to time, hitherto unpublished poems were unearthed. In 1945 two important books were published by Millicent Todd Bingham, daughter of Mabel Loomis Todd, Emily Dickinson's first editor. One, *Ancestors' Brocades,* presented a bitterly controversial picture of the Dickinson background, an account of the poet's literary "debut" and the drama which followed it, culminating in a feud among the editors, dark recriminations, and a family law suit. The other, *Bolts of Melody,* contained more than 650 poems, many of which appeared for the first time and were ranked among the poet's richest and most characteristic work.

The two new volumes re-emphasized the compressed power of Emily Dickinson's achievement and her admirers' claim that she was among the world's original geniuses. Added to the now familiar lines the newly published poems stressed the extraordinary union of intellectual reticence and emotional flamboyance. They were a rebuke to the sprawling rhetoric of her contemporaries and a strict example to her followers. Although most of the books about Emily Dickinson are accounts of the embattled family, the poet ignored the gossip and continued to put down her tart and provocative images on the backs of newspaper clippings, on margins of newspapers, on brown paper bags and, more economically and more often, on the insides of envelopes. "My wars," she wrote, "are laid away in books."

A French translation (*Choix de Poèmes,* 1945) by Felix Ansermoz-Dubois carried an introduction which called attention to the poet's intoxication with words. "She hesitated before them, filling her margins with variants, was tormented to see them ever go forth on their far missions." The seal of genius, that unmistakable insignia, is on everything she wrote. Here is that unmistakable idiom, playful yet profound; here are the rapid ascent of images and the sudden swoop of immensities, the keen epithet that cuts to the deepest layer of consciousness, and the paradox on whose point innumerable angels dance. She is Blake one moment, Vaughan the next, then Jonathan Edwards, and herself all the time. Emotion, idea, and words are not marshaled in their usual order; they spring simultaneously, inevitably, one including the other. Here is the effect—never the affectation—of emotion and its enveloping phrase.

More fully than her biographers Emily Dickson told the secret of her love, her first rebellious impulse, her inner denial, her resignation, her assured waiting for reunion in Eternity. There is little to add except meaningless names and irrelevant street numbers.

I took one draught of life,
I'll tell you what I paid,
Precisely an existence—
The market-price, they said.

They weighed me dust by dust,
They balanced film with film,
Then handed me my being's worth—
A single dram of Heaven.

The poetry of Emily Dickinson courts criticism and evades it. Occasional essays, such as Allen Tate's in *On the Limits of Poetry* and F. O. Matthiessen's "The Problem of the Private Poet," emphasized both her extraordinary diction and her unconscious but omnipresent discipline. That her verses were sometimes erratic, half-done, and thrown off in the heat of creation is self-evident. But, in the great majority of her poems the leap of thought is so daring, the idea so provocative, that passages which, in a smaller spirit, would be merely pretty or audacious conceits become snatches of revelation. Is it a flippancy or an anguished cry when, robbed by Life, she stands "a beggar before the door of God," and confronts Him with "Burglar, banker, father!" Is it anything less than Olympian satire when, asking God to accept "the supreme iniquity," she declares:

We apologize to Thee
For Thine own duplicity.

Beauty, Love, Justice—these were no abstractions to her, but entities, weights and measures, which the architect had failed to use perfectly. She sought the Builder not to commend but to question Him. Emily argued, upbraided, accused Creation; she recognized an angel only when she wrestled with him. Paradox was her native element.

Her gnomic imagery was tremendous in implication, and her range is far greater than a first reading reveals. Although the poet often indulged herself by retreating into a style cryptic and wayward, her tiny quatrains are lavish with huge ideas and almost overpowering figures. She speaks of music as "the silver strife"; she sees the railway train "lap the miles and lick the valleys up"; she speaks ironically of splitting the lark to find the music "bulb after bulb in silver rolled"; she pictures the thunder crumbling "like a stuff" while the lightning "skipped like mice"; she glimpses evening as "the house-wife in the west" sweeping the sunset "with many colored brooms"; she asks "who laid the rainbow piers." Pondering on the power of words, she meditates:

> Could mortal lip divine
> The undeveloped freight
> Of a delivered syllable,
> 'Twould crumble with the weight.

Her lightest phrases bear the accent of finality. Without striving to be clever she achieves one startling epigram after another; no poet ever existed with a more aphoristic mind. "Denial is the only fact received by the denied." "At leisure is the soul that gets a staggering blow." "Renunciation is the choosing against itself." "Longing is like the seed that wrestles in the ground."

Her letters, sometimes marred with affectations, have an unpredictable way of turning about their subject; they combine the impish with the mystical; they announce tremendous things in an offhand tone of voice. Few definitions of poetry give us the sense of poetry as sharply as her informal:

"If I read a book and it makes my whole body so cold no fire can ever warm me, I know it is poetry. If I feel physically as if the top of my head were taken off, I know this is poetry. These are the only ways I know it."

Are there no reservations? In the midst of her telegraphic concisions—all sparks and flashes—does one never miss the long line, the sustained breath? She lived in metaphor, and the terse luxuriance of her figures—the impulse to point every adjective—has had an unhappy effect on most of her admirers, an effect of pretty artifice. Worse still is her habit of acting coy among the immensities. She is overfond of playing the spoiled, "old-fashioned, naughty child"—a little girl who sits in the lap of Deity and tweaks His beard and asks God coyly to lift her over the stile, an imperious child for whose success guns should be fired at sea, for a glimpse of whom saints should run to windows and seraphs swing their snowy hats. The impulse to pirouette before the mirror of her soul has already had its result in hundreds of young "female poets" (Griswold's phrase) who, lacking their model's intensities, have succeeded only in being verbally arresting and "cute."

A critical appraisal does not have to be a condemnatory one, but it must steer a course between the early ridicule and the present unreserved adulation. The undoubted charm does not necessarily extend to errors in grammar, nor does the taut, uncanny rightness of her epithets disguise her frequent failure to differentiate between inspiration and whim. Can one, need one, applaud all the eccentricities, the familiarities, the pertnesses. Banter may be refreshing, but is archness with God always delightful? And what is one to say of that more reprehensible spinsterly failing, archness to children?

And yet it is a tough and poetry-resisting soul which does not eventually succumb to her rhetoric, irregularities and all. Her vivacity covers self-consciousness and carries off her contradictions. Her swift condensations—surpassed by no writer of any age—win the most reluctant. One gasps at the way she packs huge ideas into an explosive quatrain (a living poet has called her verse "uncombusted meteors") fascinated by an utterance so paradoxical, so seemingly naïve, so actually metaphysical. She may annoy us with her self-indulgent waywardness, but illumination is never far off;

out of a smooth, even sentimental sky, comes a crackling telegram from God and, tucked in a phrase, the "imperial thunderbolt that scalps your naked soul."

The obvious defects and quaint irregularities have been accepted; they even have a charm of their own. The brilliance of her imaginery blinds us to her overfrequent coyness and the overstressed self-pity which could allow the poet to call herself "Empress of Calvary." The consistency of her imperfections is, in itself, a kind of perfection. Her personal magic—a kind of super-observation—lives in such phrases as a dog's "belated feet, like intermittent plush," a humming bird whose flight is "a route of evanescence, a resonance of emerald," an engine "neighing like Boanerges," a mushroom whose whole career "is shorter than a snake's delay," the wind "tapping like a tired man."

What else, then, matters? Whatever the provocation, all that remains is the poetry. The much-sought but still unknown inspirer of the love poems may have been Wadsworth or Gould or Hunt—or Legion—but it is not he who is immortalized in her book; it is Emily. Though there are evocations of the vanished lover, we are never made to see him, hear him, realize his being, whereas we have (in the same poems) a complete projection of Emily, her heart, soul, and housekeeping, her books, birds, and influences, her bodily postures, tricks of thought, even her way of crossing the room and reading a letter.

Denied a public, even of one, Emily perfected her imperfections in secret. Lacking the partner, she played her game with herself. Yet, when all the biographies are considered, the most successful game was the one she played on the world: a solitary recluse who had the world in her garden; an escapist who summoned infinity with the trick of a forefinger. It is doubtful if, in spite of her isolation, there was ever a less lonely woman. She who contained a universe did not need the world.

I TASTE A LIQUOR NEVER BREWED

I taste a liquor never brewed,
From tankards scooped in pearl;
Not all the vats upon the Rhine
Yield such an alcohol!

Inebriate of air am I,
And debauchee of dew,
Reeling, through endless summer days,
From inns of molten blue.

When landlords turn the drunken bee
Out of the foxglove's door,
When butterflies renounce their drams,
I shall but drink the more!

Till seraphs swing their snowy hats,
And saints to windows run,
To see the little tippler
Leaning against the sun!

A BIRD CAME DOWN THE WALK

A bird came down the walk:
He did not know I saw;
He bit an angle-worm in halves
And ate the fellow, raw.

And then he drank a dew
From a convenient grass,
And then hopped sidewise to the wall
To let a beetle pass.

He glanced with rapid eyes
That hurried all abroad,—
They looked like frightened beads, I thought
He stirred his velvet head

Like one in danger; cautious,
I offered him a crumb,
And he unrolled his feathers
And rowed him softer home

Than oars divide the ocean,
Too silver for a seam,
Or butterflies, off banks of noon,
Leap, plashless, as they swim.

ELYSIUM IS AS FAR

Elysium is as far as to
The very nearest room,
If in that room a friend await
Felicity or doom.

What fortitude the soul contains,
That it can so endure
The accent of a coming foot,
The opening of a door.

I NEVER SAW A MOOR

I never saw a moor,
I never saw the sea;
Yet know I how the heather looks,
And what a wave must be.

I never spoke with God,
Nor visited in Heaven;
Yet certain am I of the spot
As if the chart were given.

I NEVER LOST AS MUCH

I never lost as much but twice,
And that was in the sod;
Twice have I stood a beggar
Before the door of God!

Angels, twice descending,
Reimbursed my store.
Burglar! banker! father!
I am poor once more!

INDIAN SUMMER

These are the days when birds come back,
A very few, a bird or two,
To take a backward look.

These are the days when skies resume
The old, old sophistries of June,—
A blue and gold mistake.

Oh, fraud that cannot cheat the bee,
Almost thy plausibility
Induces my belief,

Till ranks of seeds their witness bear,
And softly through the altered air
Hurries a timid leaf!

Oh, sacrament of summer days,
Oh, last communion in the haze,
Permit a child to join,

Thy sacred emblems to partake,
Thy consecrated bread to break,
Taste thine immortal wine!

I DIED FOR BEAUTY

I died for beauty, but was scarce
Adjusted in the tomb,
When one who died for truth was lain
In an adjoining room.

He questioned softly why I failed?
"For beauty," I replied.
"And I for truth,—the two are one;
We brethren are," he said.

And so, as kinsmen met a night,
We talked between the rooms,
Until the moss had reached our lips
And covered up our names.

THE SKY IS LOW

The sky is low, the clouds are mean,
A traveling flake of snow
Across a barn or through a rut
Debates if it will go.

A narrow wind complains all day
How someone treated him.
Nature, like us, is sometimes caught
Without her diadem.

MYSTERIES

The murmur of a bee
A witchcraft yieldeth me.
If any ask me why,
'Twere easier to die
Than tell.

The red upon the hill
Taketh away my will;
If anybody sneer,
Take care, for God is here,
That's all.

The breaking of the day
Addeth to my degree;
If any ask me how,
Artist, who drew me so,
Must tell!

I LIKE TO SEE IT LAP THE MILES

I like to see it lap the miles,
And lick the valleys up,
And stop to feed itself at tanks;
And then, prodigious, step

Around a pile of mountains,
And, supercilious, peer
In shanties by the sides of roads;
And then a quarry pare

To fit its sides, and crawl between,
Complaining all the while
In horrid, hooting stanza;
Then chase itself down hill

And neigh like Boanerges;
Then, punctual as a star,
Stop—docile and omnipotent—
At its own stable door.

THE SOUL SELECTS

The soul selects her own society,
Then shuts the door;
On her divine majority
Obtrude no more.

Unmoved, she notes the chariots pausing
At her low gate;
Unmoved, an emperor is kneeling
Upon her mat.

I've known her from an ample nation
Choose one;
Then close the valves of her attention
Like stone.

MY LIFE CLOSED TWICE BEFORE ITS CLOSE

My life closed twice before its close;
It yet remains to see
If Immortality unveil
A third event to me,

So huge, so hopeless to conceive,
As these that twice befell.
Parting is all we know of heaven,
And all we need of hell.

THE HEART ASKS PLEASURE FIRST

The heart asks pleasure first;
And then, excuse from pain;
And then, those little anodynes
That deaden suffering;

And then, to go to sleep;
And then, if it should be
The will of its Inquisitor,
The liberty to die.

I CANNOT LIVE WITH YOU

I cannot live with you.
It would be life,
And life is over there
Behind the shelf

The sexton keeps the key to,
Putting up
Our life, his porcelain,
Like a cup

Discarded of the housewife,
Quaint or broken;
A newer Sèvres pleases,
Old ones crack.

I could not die with you,
For one must wait
To shut the other's gaze down,
You could not.

And I, could I stand by
And see you freeze,
Without my right of frost,
Death's privilege?

Nor could I rise with you,
Because your face
Would put out Jesus',
That new grace

Grow plain and foreign
On my homesick eye,
Except that you, than he
Shone closer by.

They'd judge us—how?
For you served Heaven, you know,
Or sought to;
I could not,

Because you saturated sight,
And I had no more eyes
For sordid excellence
As Paradise.

And were you lost, I would be,
Though my name
Rang loudest
On the heavenly fame.

And were you saved,
And I condemned to be
Where you were not,
That self were hell to me.

So we must keep apart,
You there, I here,
With just the door ajar
That oceans are,
And prayer,
And that pale sustenance,
Despair!

OF COURSE I PRAYED

Of course I prayed—
And did God care?
He cared as much as
On the air
A bird had stamped her foot
And cried "Give me!"

My reason, life,
I had not had, but for yourself.
'Twere better charity
To leave me in the atom's tomb,
Merry and nought and gay and numb,
Than this smart misery.

THERE IS NO FRIGATE LIKE A BOOK

There is no frigate like a book
  To take us lands away,
Nor any coursers like a page
  Of prancing poetry.
This travel may the poorest take
  Without oppress of toll;
How frugal is the chariot
  That bears the human soul!

I HAD BEEN HUNGRY ALL THE YEARS

I had been hungry all the years;
My noon had come to dine;
I, trembling, drew the table near,
And touched the curious wine.

'Twas this on tables I had seen,
When turning, hungry, lone,
I looked in windows, for the wealth
I could not hope to own.

I did not know the ample bread;
'Twas so unlike the crumb
The birds and I had often shared
In Nature's dining-room.

The plenty hurt me, 'twas so new,—
Myself felt ill and odd,
As berry of a mountain bush
Transplanted to the road.

Nor was I hungry; so I found
That hunger was a way
Of persons outside windows,
The entering takes away.

I HEARD A FLY BUZZ WHEN I DIED

I heard a fly buzz when I died;
The stillness round my form
Was like the stillness in the air
Between the heaves of storm.

The eyes beside had wrung them dry,
And breaths were gathering sure
For that last onset, when the king
Be witnessed in his power.

I willed my keepsakes, signed away
What portion of me I
Could make assignable,—and then
There interposed a fly,

With blue, uncertain, stumbling buzz,
Between the light and me;
And then the windows failed, and then
I could not see to see.

THERE'S A CERTAIN SLANT OF LIGHT

There's a certain slant of light,
On winter afternoons,
That oppresses, like the weight
Of cathedral tunes.

Heavenly hurt it gives us;
We can find no scar,
But internal difference
Where the meanings are.

None may teach it anything,
'Tis the seal, despair,—
An imperial affliction
Sent us of the air.

When it comes, the landscape listens,
Shadows hold their breath;
When it goes, 'tis like the distance
On the look of death.

I MEASURE EVERY GRIEF I MEET

I measure every grief I meet
With analytic eyes;
I wonder if it weighs like mine,
Or has an easier size.

I wonder if they bore it long,
Or did it just begin?
I could not tell the date of mine,
It feels so old a pain.

I wonder if it hurts to live,
And if they have to try,
And whether, could they choose between
They would not rather die.

I wonder if when years have piled—
Some thousands—on the harm
Of early hurt, if such a lapse
Could give them any balm;

Or would they go on aching still
Through centuries of nerve,
Enlightened to a larger pain
By contrast with the love.

The grieved are many, I am told;
The reason deeper lies,—
Death is but one and comes but once,
And only nails the eyes.

There's grief of want, and grief of cold,
A sort they call "despair";
There's banishment from native eyes,
In sight of native air.

And though I may not guess the kind
Correctly, yet to me
A piercing comfort it affords
In passing Calvary,

To note the fashions of the cross,
Of those that stand alone,
Still fascinated to presume
That some are like my own.

THE BRAIN IS WIDER THAN THE SKY

The brain is wider than the sky,
For, put them side by side,

The one the other will include
With ease, and you beside.

The brain is deeper than the sea,
For, hold them, blue to blue,
The one the other will absorb,
As sponges, buckets do.

The brain is just the weight of God,
For, lift them, pound for pound,
And they will differ, if they do,
As syllable from sound.

BRING ME THE SUNSET IN A CUP

Bring me the sunset in a cup,
Reckon the morning's flagons up,
And say how many dew;
Tell me how far the morning leaps,
Tell me what time the weaver sleeps
Who spun the breadths of blue!

Write me how many notes there be
In the new robin's ecstasy
Among astonished boughs;
How many trips the tortoise makes,
How many cups the bee partakes,—
The debauchee of dews!

Also, who laid the rainbow's piers,
Also, who leads the docile spheres
By withes of supple blue?
Whose fingers string the stalactite,
Who counts the wampum of the night,
To see that none is due?

Who built this little Alban house
And shut the windows down so close
My spirit cannot see?
Who'll let me out some gala day,
With implements to fly away,
Passing pomposity?

THE TINT I CANNOT TAKE IS BEST

The tint I cannot take is best,
The color too remote
That I could show it in bazaar
A guinea at a sight—

The fine impalpable array
That swaggers on the eye
Like Cleopatra's company
Repeated in the sky—

The moments of dominion
That happen on the Soul
And leave it with a discontent
Too exquisite to tell—

The eager look on landscapes
As if they just repressed
Some secret that was pushing,
Like chariots, in the breast—

The pleading of the Summer,
That other prank of snow
That covers mystery with tulle
For fear the squirrels know—

Their graspless manners mock us,
Until the cheated eye
Shuts arrogantly in the grave,
Another way to see.

I DREADED THAT FIRST ROBIN SO

I dreaded that first robin so,
But he is mastered now,
And I'm accustomed to him grown,—
He hurts a little, though.

I thought if I could only live
Till that first shout got by,
Not all pianos in the woods
Had power to mangle me.

I dared not meet the daffodils,
For fear their yellow gown
Would pierce me with a fashion
So foreign to my own.

I wished the grass would hurry,
So when 'twas time to see,
He'd be too tall, the tallest one
Could stretch to look at me.

I could not bear the bees should come,
I wished they'd stay away
In those dim countries where they go:
What word had they for me?

They're here, though; not a creature failed,
No blossom stayed away
In gentle deference to me,
The Queen of Calvary.

Each one salutes me as he goes,
And I my childish plumes
Lift, in bereaved acknowledgment
Of their unthinking drums.

AFTER GREAT PAIN A FORMAL FEELING COMES

After great pain a formal feeling comes—
The nerves sit ceremonious like tombs;
The stiff heart questions—was it He that bore?
And yesterday—or centuries before?

The feet mechanical go round
A wooden way,
Of ground or air of Ought,
Regardless grown;
A quartz contentment like a stone.

This is the hour of lead
Remembered if outlived
As freezing persons recollect
The snow—
First chill, then stupor, then
The letting go.

A CEMETERY

This quiet Dust was Gentlemen and Ladies,
And Lads and Girls;
Was laughter and ability and sighing,
And frocks and curls.

This passive place a Summer's nimble mansion,
Where Bloom and Bees
Fulfilled their Oriental Circuit,
Then ceased like these.

AMPLE MAKE THIS BED

Ample make this bed,
Make this bed with awe;
In it wait till judgment break
Excellent and fair.

Be its mattress straight,
Be its pillow round;
Let no sunrise' yellow noise
Interrupt this ground.

ALTHOUGH I PUT AWAY HIS LIFE

Although I put away his life,
An ornament too grand
For forehead low as mine to wear,
This might have been the hand

That sowed the flowers he preferred,
Or smoothed a homely pain,
Or pushed a pebble from his path,
Or played his chosen tune

On lute the least, the latest,
But just his ear could know
That whatsoe'er delighted it
I never would let go.

The foot to bear his errand
A little boot I know
Would leap abroad like antelope
With just the grant to do.

His weariest commandment
A sweeter to obey
Than "Hide and Seek," or skip to flutes,
Or all day chase the bee.

Your servant, Sir, will weary,
The surgeon will not come,
The world will have its own to do,
The dust will vex your fame.

The cold will force your tightest door
Some February day,
But say my apron bring the sticks
To make your cottage gay,

That I may take that promise
To Paradise with me—
To teach the angels avarice
Your kiss first taught to me!

THE WORLD FEELS DUSTY

The world feels dusty
When we stop to die;
We want the dew then,
Honors taste dry.

Flags vex a dying face,
But the least fan
Stirred by a friend's hand
Cools like the rain.

Mine be the ministry
When thy thirst comes,
Dews of thyself to fetch
And holy balms.

LIGHTLY STEPPED A YELLOW STAR

Lightly stepped a yellow star
To its lofty place,
Loosed the Moon her silver hat
From her lustral face.
All of evening softly lit
As an astral hall—
"Father," I observed to Heaven,
"You are punctual!"

GO NOT TOO NEAR A HOUSE OF ROSE

Go not too near a house of rose,
The depredation of a breeze
Or inundation of a dew
Alarm its walls away;
Nor try to tie the butterfly;
Nor climb the bars of ecstasy.
In insecurity to lie
Is joy's insuring quality.

I RECKON, WHEN I COUNT AT ALL

I reckon, when I count at all,
First Poets—then the Sun—
Then Summer—then the Heaven of God—
And then the list is done.
But looking back—the first so seems
To comprehend the whole—
The others look a needless show,
So I write Poets—All.
Their summer lasts a solid year,
They can afford a sun
The East would deem extravagant,
And if the final Heaven
Be beautiful as they disclose
To those who trust in them,
It is too difficult a grace
To justify the dream.

BECAUSE THAT YOU ARE GOING

Because that you are going
And never coming back
And I, however absolute
May overlook your track

Because that Death is final,
However first it be
This instant be suspended
Above Mortality.

Significance that each has lived
The other to detect
Discovery not God himself
Could now annihilate.

Eternity, Presumption
The instant I perceive
That you, who were existence
Yourself forgot to live.

The "Life that is" will then have been
A thing I never knew,
As Paradise fictitious
Until the Realm of you.

The "Life that is to be," to me
A Residence too plain
Unless in my Redeemer's Face
I recognize your own.

Of Immortality who doubts
He may exchange with me
Curtailed by your obscuring Face
Of Everything but He.

Of Heaven and Hell I also yield
The Right to reprehend
To whoso would commute this Face
For his less priceless Friend.

If "God is Love" as he admits
We think that he must be
Because he is a "jealous God"
He tells as certainly.

If "all is possible with him"
As he besides concedes,
He will refund as finally
Our confiscated Gods.

WHAT SOFT, CHERUBIC CREATURES

What soft, cherubic creatures
These gentlewomen are!
One would as soon assault a plush
Or violate a star.

Such dimity convictions,
A horror so refined
Of freckled human nature,
Of Deity ashamed,—

It's such a common glory,
A fisherman's degree!
Redemption, brittle lady,
Be so ashamed of thee.

BECAUSE I COULD NOT STOP FOR DEATH

Because I could not stop for Death,
He kindly stopped for me;
The carriage held but just ourselves
And Immortality.

We slowly drove, he knew no haste,
And I had put away
My labor, and my leisure too,
For his civility.

We passed the school where children played,
Their lessons scarcely done;
We passed the fields of gazing grain,
We passed the setting sun.

We paused before a house that seemed
A swelling on the ground;
The roof was scarcely visible,
The cornice but a mound.

Since then 'tis centuries; but each
Feels shorter than the day
I first surmised the horses' heads
Were toward eternity.

THE MOUNTAINS GROW UNNOTICED

The mountains grow unnoticed,
Their purple figures rise
Without attempt, exhaustion,
Assistance or applause.

In their eternal faces
The sun with broad delight
Looks long—and last—and golden
For fellowship at night.

TRUTH IS AS OLD AS GOD

Truth is as old as God,
His twin identity—
And will endure as long as He,
A co-eternity,
And perish on the day
That He is borne away
From mansion of the universe,
A lifeless Deity.

THE RETURN

Though I get home how late, how late!
So I get home, 't will compensate.
Better will be the ecstasy
That they have done expecting me,
When, night descending, dumb and dark,
They hear my unexpected knock.
Transporting must the moment be,
Brewed from decades of agony!

To think just how the fire will burn,
Just how long-cheated eyes will turn
To wonder what myself will say,
And what itself will say to me,
Beguiles the centuries of way!

SUCCESS IS COUNTED SWEETEST

Success is counted sweetest
By those who ne'er succeed.
To comprehend a nectar
Requires sorest need.

Not one of all the purple host
Who took the flag to-day
Can tell the definition,
So clear, of victory,

As he, defeated, dying,
On whose forbidden ear
The distant strains of triumph
Burst, agonized and clear.

THE LONELY HOUSE

I know some lonely houses off the road
A robber'd like the look of,—
Wooden barred,
And windows hanging low,
Inviting to
A portico,
Where two could creep:
One hand the tools,
The other peep
To make sure all's asleep.
Old-fashioned eyes,
Not easy to surprise!

How orderly the kitchen'd look by night,
With just a clock,—
But they could gag the tick,
And mice won't bark;
And so the walls don't tell,
None will.

A pair of spectacles ajar just stir—
An almanac's aware.
Was it the mat winked,
Or a nervous star?
The moon slides down the stair
To see who's there.

There's plunder,—where?
Tankard, or spoon,
Earring, or stone,
A watch, some ancient brooch
To match the grandmamma,
Staid sleeping there.

Day rattles, too,
Stealth's slow;
The sun has got as far
As the third sycamore.
Screams chanticleer,

"Who's there?"
And echoes, trains away,
Sneer—"Where?"
While the old couple, just astir,
Fancy the sunrise left the door ajar!

PAIN HAS AN ELEMENT OF BLANK

Pain has an element of blank;
It cannot recollect
When it began, or if there were
A day when it was not.

It has no future but itself,
Its infinite realms contain
Its past, enlightened to perceive
New periods of pain.

RENUNCIATION

There came a day at summer's full
Entirely for me;
I thought that such were for the saints,
Where revelations be.

The sun, as common, went abroad,
The flowers, accustomed, blew,
As if no soul the solstice passed
That maketh all things new.

The time was scarce profaned by speech;
The symbol of a word
Was needless, as at sacrament
The wardrobe of our Lord.

Each was to each the sealed church,
Permitted to commune this time,
Lest we too awkward show
At supper of the Lamb.

The hours slid fast, as hours will,
Clutched tight by greedy hands;
So faces on two decks look back,
Bound to opposing lands.

And so, when all the time had failed,
Without external sound,
Each bound the other's crucifix,
We gave no other bond.

Sufficient troth that we shall rise—
Deposed, at length, the grave—
To that new marriage, justified
Through Calvaries of Love!

SOME KEEP THE SABBATH GOING TO CHURCH

Some keep the Sabbath going to church;
I keep it staying at home,
With a bobolink for a chorister,
And an orchard for a dome.

Some keep the Sabbath in surplice;
I just wear my wings,
And instead of tolling the bell for church
Our little sexton sings.

God preaches,—a noted clergyman,—
And the sermon is never long;
So instead of getting to heaven at last,
I'm going all along!

PURPLE CLOVER

There is a flower that bees prefer,
And butterflies desire;
To gain the purple democrat
The humming-birds aspire.

And whatsoever insect pass,
A honey bears away
Proportioned to his several dearth
And her capacity.

Her face is rounder than the moon,
And ruddier than the gown
Of orchis in the pasture,
Or rhododendron worn.

THE BEE

Like trains of cars on tracks of plush
I hear the level bee:
A jar across the flowers goes,
Their velvet masonry

Withstands until the sweet assault
Their chivalry consumes,
While he, victorious, tilts away
To vanquish other blooms.

His feet are shod with gauze,
His helmet is of gold;
His breast, a single onyx
With chrysoprase, inlaid.

His labor is a chant,
His idleness a tune;
Oh, for a bee's experience
Of clovers and of noon!

HOPE IS THE THING WITH FEATHERS

Hope is the thing with feathers
That perches in the soul,
And sings the tune without the words,
And never stops at all,

And sweetest in the gale is heard;
And sore must be the storm
Γhat could abash the little bird
Γhat kept so many warm.

've heard it in the chillest land,
\nd on the strangest sea;
'et, never, in extremity,
t asked a crumb of me.

HE WIND TAPPED LIKE A TIRED MAN

'he wind tapped like a tired man,
nd like a host, "Come in,"
boldly answered; entered then
ly residence within

rapid, footless guest,
o offer whom a chair
'ere as impossible as hand
sofa to the air.

o bone had he to bind him,
is speech was like the push
numerous humming-birds at once
om a superior bush.

s countenance a billow
s fingers, as he passed,

Let go a music, as of tunes
Blown tremulous in glass.

He visited, still flitting,
Then, like a timid man,
Again he tapped—'twas flurridly—
And I became alone.

AT HALF-PAST THREE A SINGLE BIRD

At half-past three a single bird
Unto a silent sky
Propounded but a single term
Of cautious melody.

At half-past four, experiment
Had subjugated test,
And lo! her silver principle
Supplanted all the rest.

At half-past seven, element
Nor implement was seen,
And place was where the presence was,
Circumference between.

CALLED BACK

Just lost when I was saved!
Just felt the world go by!
Just girt me for the onset with eternity,
When breath blew back,
And on the other side
I heard recede the disappointed tide!

Therefore, as one returned, I feel,
Odd secrets of the line to tell!
Some sailor, skirting foreign shores,
Some pale reporter from the awful doors
Before the seal!

Next time, to stay!
Next time, the things to see
By ear unheard,
Unscrutinized by eye.

Next time, to tarry,
While the ages steal,—
Slow tramp the centuries,
And the cycles wheel.

Edwin Markham

☙ Edwin Markham was born in Oregon City, Oregon, April 23, 1852, the youngest son of pioneer parents. His father died before he reached his fifth year and in 1857 he was taken by his mother to a wild valley in the Suisun Hills in central California. Here he grew to young manhood: farming, broncho-riding, laboring on a cattle ranch, educating himself in the primitive country schools. At eighteen he determined to be a teacher and entered the State Normal School at San José.

Since childhood, Markham had been writing verses of no extraordinary merit, one of his earliest pieces being a Byronic echo (*A Dream of Chaos*) full of the high-sounding fustian of the period. Several years before he uttered his famous challenge, Markham was writing poems of protest, insurrectionary in theme but conventional in effect. Suddenly, in 1899, a sense of outrage at the inequality of human struggle voiced itself in the sonorous poem, "The Man with the Hoe." Inspired by Millet's painting, Markham made the bowed, broken French peasant a symbol of the poverty-stricken toiler in all lands—his was a protest not against toil but the exploitation of labor. "The Yeoman is the landed and well-to-do farmer," says Markham, "you need shed no tears for him. But here in the Millet picture is his opposite—the Hoeman; the landless workman of the world."

The success of the poem upon its appearance in the San Francisco *Examiner* (January 15, 1899) was instantaneous. The lines appeared in every part of the globe; they were quoted and copied in every walk of life, in the literary and the labor world. The same year of its publication, it was incorporated in Markham's first volume, *The Man with the Hoe and Other Poems* (1899). Two years later, his almost equally well known poem was published. The same passion that fired Markham to champion the great common workers equipped him to write of the great Commoner in *Lincoln, and Other Poems* (1901). His later volumes are a descent, melodious but scarcely remarkable. They have the rhetoric without the resonance of the forerunners. Never reaching the heights, there are, nevertheless, moments of dignity in *The Shoes of Happiness* (1914), *The Gates of Paradise* (1920), and *New Poems: Eighty Songs at Eighty* (1932), published with a nice appropriateness on the poet's eightieth birthday. Many of the quatrains are memorable epigrams.

Markham came East in 1901 and made his home on Staten Island, New York, until death in his eighty-eighth year. His life spanned the continent; born near one ocean, he died facing the other on March 7, 1940.

OUTWITTED

He drew a circle that shut me out—
Heretic, rebel, a thing to flout.
But Love and I had the wit to win:
We drew a circle that took him in!

THE MAN WITH THE HOE[1]

(*Written after seeing Millet's world-famous painting*)

Bowed by the weight of centuries he leans
Upon his hoe and gazes on the ground,
The emptiness of ages in his face,
And on his back the burden of the world.
Who made him dead to rapture and despair,
A thing that grieves not and that never hopes,
Stolid and stunned, a brother to the ox?
Who loosened and let down this brutal jaw?
Whose was the hand that slanted back this brow?
Whose breath blew out the light within this brain?

Is this the Thing the Lord God made and gave
To have dominion over sea and land;
To trace the stars and search the heavens for power;
To feel the passion of Eternity?
Is this the dream He dreamed who shaped the suns
And marked their ways upon the ancient deep?
Down all the caverns of Hell to their last gulf
There is no shape more terrible than this—
More tongued with censure of the world's blind greed—
More filled with signs and portents for the soul—
More packt with danger to the universe.

What gulfs between him and the seraphim!
Slave of the wheel of labor, what to him
Are Plato and the swing of Pleiades?
What the long reaches of the peaks of song,
The rift of dawn, the reddening of the rose?
Through this dread shape the suffering ages look;
Time's tragedy is in that aching stoop;
Through this dread shape humanity betrayed,
Plundered, profaned, and disinherited,
Cries protest to the Judges of the World,
A protest that is also prophecy.

O masters, lords and rulers in all lands,
Is this the handiwork you give to God,
This monstrous thing distorted and soul-quenched?
How will you ever straighten up this shape;
Touch it again with immortality;
Give back the upward looking and the light;
Rebuild in it the music and the dream;
Make right the immemorial infamies,
Perfidious wrongs, immedicable woes?

O masters, lords and rulers in all lands,
How will the Future reckon with this man?

[1] Revised version, 1920. Copyright by Edwin Markham.

How answer his brute question in that hour
When whirlwinds of rebellion shake all shores?
How will it be with kingdoms and with kings—
With those who shaped him to the thing he is—
When this dumb terror shall rise to judge the world,
After the silence of the centuries?

THE AVENGERS

The laws are the secret avengers,
And they rule above all lands;
They come on wool-soft sandals,
But they strike with iron hands.

PREPAREDNESS

For all your days prepare,
And meet them ever alike:
When you are the anvil, bear—
When you are the hammer, strike.

LINCOLN, THE MAN OF THE PEOPLE

When the Norn Mother saw the Whirlwind Hour
Greatening and darkening as it hurried on,
She left the Heaven of Heroes and came down
To make a man to meet the mortal need.
She took the tried clay of the common road—
Clay warm yet with the genial heat of earth,
Dasht through it all a strain of prophecy;
Tempered the heap with thrill of human tears;
Then mixt a laughter with the serious stuff.
Into the shape she breathed a flame to light
That tender, tragic, ever-changing face;
And laid on him a sense of the Mystic Powers,
Moving—all husht—behind the mortal veil.
Here was a man to hold against the world,
A man to match the mountains and the sea.

The color of the ground was in him, the red earth;
The smack and tang of elemental things:
The rectitude and patience of the cliff;
The good-will of the rain that loves all leaves;
The friendly welcome of the wayside well;
The courage of the bird that dares the sea;
The gladness of the wind that shakes the corn;
The pity of the snow that hides all scars;
The secrecy of streams that make their way
Under the mountain to the rifted rock;
The tolerance and equity of light
That gives as freely to the shrinking flower
As to the great oak flaring to the wind—
To the grave's low hill as to the Matterhorn
That shoulders out the sky. Sprung from the West,
He drank the valorous youth of a new world.
The strength of virgin forests braced his mind,
The hush of spacious prairies stilled his soul.

His words were oaks in acorns; and his thoughts
Were roots that firmly gript the granite truth.

Up from log cabin to the Capitol,
One fire was on his spirit, one resolve—
To send the keen ax to the root of wrong,
Clearing a free way for the feet of God,
The eyes of conscience testing every stroke,
To make his deed the measure of a man.
He built the rail-pile as he built the State,
Pouring his splendid strength through every blow:
The grip that swung the ax in Illinois
Was on the pen that set a people free.

So came the Captain with the mighty heart.
And when the judgment thunders split the house,
Wrenching the rafters from their ancient rest,
He held the ridgepole up, and spiked again
The rafters of the Home. He held his place—
Held the long purpose like a growing tree—
Held on through blame and faltered not at praise.
And when he fell in whirlwind, he went down
As when a lordly cedar, green with boughs,
Goes down with a great shout upon the hills,
And leaves a lonesome place against the sky.

Lizette Woodworth Reese

Lizette Woodworth Reese was born January 9, 1856, in Waverly, Baltimore County, Maryland, of mixed English and German stock. After receiving an education chiefly in private schools she taught English at the Western High School in Baltimore, where she lived. After many years of service, she retired in 1921. In 1923, the alumni of the High School where she had taught for a score of years, together with the teachers and pupils, presented the school with a bronze tablet inscribed with her poem, "Tears," one of the most famous sonnets written by an American.

At first glance, Miss Reese's work seems merely a continuation of the traditional strain; some of her critics decried her poetry as being English rather than American. But it was natural that her verse should sound a note which has been the dominant one in English pastoral poetry from Wordsworth to Housman. Nor was Miss Reese's inheritance alone responsible for this. The country around Baltimore, every tree and path of which Miss Reese knew intimately, was settled by the English and had the shape and color of counties like Sussex and Buckinghamshire.

Miss Reese's first book, *A Branch of May* (1887), had an undercurrent of intensity beneath its quiet contours. Few of its readers in the Nineties would have dreamed that this straightforward undidactic speech would pave the way for the direct songs of Sara Teasdale and Edna St. Vincent Millay. In a period of sugared sentiment and lace valentine lyrics, Miss Reese's crisp lines were a generation ahead of the times and were consequently appreciated only for their pictorial if somewhat prim felicities. *A Handful of Lavender* (1891), *A Quiet Road* (1896), and *A Wayside Lute* (1909) established an artistry which, for all its seemingly old-fashioned elegance, is as spontaneous as it is skillful. Here are no verbal tricks, no false postures; here is a simple record which is, somehow, never banal. "This poetry of hers," writes Mary Colum, "will persist, not because the author was cleverer or more original than other writers, but because in some way her nerves were more subtle in response to the kinds of life and experiences that came her way."

From 1909 to 1920 there was a silence. During these ten years, Miss Reese wrote little, and published less. Suddenly her work appeared again, more concise than ever. *Spicewood* was published in 1920; *Wild Cherry* in 1923; a generous *Selected Poems* in 1926; *Little Henrietta* in 1927, the poet's seventy-second year; *A Victorian Village,* her reminiscences of a changing world, in 1929.

White April (1930) and *Pastures* (1933), published in the poet's seventy-eighth year, are as fresh as anything she wrote in her youth. The limitations are obvious, but they are the limitations which marked her from the beginning: a preoccupation with the surprise of spring, the inevitable changes of love, the unchanging heart of nature. Individual poems make romance out of the commonplace, juxtaposing the minute with the momentous, and, while the poems lack singularity, the verve is unmistakable.

These volumes, like the earlier ones, reveal the qualities which influenced a generation of women poets. In her late seventies, writing like a young girl, the poet sings of lilacs in Old York Lane, of thorn trees and blackberry rain, of Judas-blossoms and daffodils, of spring ecstasy and lost love, of a dead lady in her garden, and Mary at the manger. But there is always something personal, always something which makes the very repetitions take on a light which is fresh and clear. At least a dozen of her brief songs and lyrical sonnets have found a niche in American literature. Hers is a singing that is not dependent on a fashion.

Lizette Reese died, after a brief illness, a few weeks before her eightieth birthday, December 17, 1935.

TEARS

When I consider Life and its few years—
A wisp of fog betwixt us and the sun;
A call to battle, and the battle done
Ere the last echo dies within our ears;
A rose choked in the grass; an hour of fears;
The gusts that past a darkening shore do beat;
The burst of music down an unlistening street,—
I wonder at the idleness of tears.

Ye old, old dead, and ye of yesternight,
Chieftains, and bards, and keepers of the sheep,
By every cup of sorrow that you had,
Loose me from tears, and make me see aright
How each hath back what once he stayed to weep.
Homer his sight, David his little lad!

SPICEWOOD

The spicewood burns along the gray, spent sky,
In moist unchimneyed places, in a wind,
That whips it all before, and all behind,
Into one thick, rude flame, now low, now high.
It is the first, the homeliest thing of all—
At sight of it, that lad that by it fares,
Whistles afresh his foolish, town-caught airs—
A thing so honey-colored and so tall!

It is as though the young Year, ere he pass
To the white riot of the cherry tree,
Would fain accustom us, or here, or there,
To his new sudden ways with bough and grass,
So starts with what is humble, plain to see,
And all familiar as a cup, a chair.

SPRING ECSTASY

Oh, let me run and hide,
Let me run straight to God;
The weather is so mad with white
From sky down to the clod!

If but one thing were so,
Lilac, or thorn out there,
It would not be, indeed,
So hard to bear.

The weather has gone mad with white;
The cloud, the highway touch.
White lilac is enough;
White thorn too much!

OWNERSHIP

Love not a loveliness too much,
For it may turn and clutch you so,
That you be less than any serf,
And at its nodding go.

Be master; otherwise you grow
Too small, too humble, like to one
Long dispossessed, who stares through tears
At his lost house across the sun.

Wild carrot in an old field here,
Or steeple choked with music there,
Possess, as part of what is yours;
Thus prove yourself the heir.

Your barony is sky and land,
From morning's start to the night's close
Bend to your need Orion's hounds,
Or the small fagot of a rose.

A PURITAN LADY

Wild Carthage held her, Rome,
Sidon. She stared to tears
Tall, golden Helen, wearying
Behind the Trojan spears.

Towered Antwerp knew her well;
She wore her quiet gown
In some hushed house in Oxford grass,
Or lane in Salem town.

Humble and high in one,
Cool, certain, different,
She lasts; scarce saint, yet half a child,
As hard, as innocent.

What grave, long afternoons,
What caged airs round her blown,
Stripped her of humor, left her bare
As cloud, or wayside stone?

Made her as clear a thing,
In this slack world as plain
As a white flower on a grave,
Or sleet sharp at a pane?

A FLOWER OF MULLEIN

I am too near, too clear a thing for you,
A flower of mullein in a crack of wall,
The villagers half-see, or not at all;
Part of the weather, like the wind or dew.
You love to pluck the different, and find
Stuff for your joy in cloudy loveliness;
You love to fumble at a door, and guess
At some strange happening that may wait behind.
Yet life is full of tricks, and it is plain,
That men drift back to some worn field or roof,
To grip at comfort in a room, a stair;
To warm themselves at some flower down a lane:
You, too, may long, grown tired of the aloof,
For the sweet surety of the common air.

Edwin Arlington Robinson

Edwin Arlington Robinson was born December 22, 1869, in the village of Head Tide, Maine. When he was still a child, the Robinson family moved to the near-by town of Gardiner, which figures in Robinson's poetry as "Tilbury Town." In 1891 he entered Harvard College, but left in 1893. A little collection of verse (*The Torrent and the Night Before*) was privately printed in 1896 and the following year much of it was incorporated with other work in *The Children of the Night* (1897), a first volume which contains some of Robinson's most quoted verse.

In New York, unable to support himself by writing, Robinson struggled against drink and other difficulties. Five years passed before *Captain Craig* (1902) was published. This narrative, recalling Browning's method, increased Robinson's audience, and his work was brought to the attention of Theodore Roosevelt (then President of the United States), who became interested in the half-starved poet trying to earn a living as a time-checker in the New York Subway. In 1904, President Roosevelt offered him a clerkship in the New York Custom House. Robinson held this position from 1905 to 1910, leaving it the same year which marked the appearance of his volume, *The Town Down the River*. Robinson's three books, up to this time, showed his clean, firmly drawn quality, but, in spite of their excellences, they seem little more than a succession of preludes for the dynamic volume that was to establish him in the first rank of American poets. *The Man Against the Sky,* in many ways Robinson's fullest and most penetrating work, appeared in 1916. This was followed by *The Three Taverns* (1920), a less arresting but equally concentrated, many voiced collection of poems.

In all these books there is manifest a searching for the light beyond illusion. But Robinson's transcendentalism is no mere emotional escape; his temper subjects the slightest phrase to critical analysis, his intuitions are supported—or scrutinized—by a vigorous intellectuality. Purely as a psychological portrait painter, Robinson has given American literature an entire gallery of memorable figures: Richard Cory, who "glittered when he walked," gnawing his dark heart while he fluttered pulses with his apparent good fortune; Miniver Cheevy, frustrate dreamer, sighing "for what was not"; Aaron Stark, the miser with eyes "like little dollars in the dark"; the nameless mother in "The Gift of God," transmuting her mediocrity of a son into a shining demigod; Bewick Finzer, the wreck of wealth, coming for his pittance, "familiar as an old mistake, and futile as regret," Luke Havergal, Cliff Klingenhagen, Reuben Bright, Annandale, the tippling Mr. Flood—they persist in the mind more vividly than most living people. Such sympathetic illuminations reveal Robinson's sensitive power, especially in his projection of the apparent failures of life. Indeed, much of Robinson's work seems a protest, a criticism by implication, of that type of standardized success which so much of the world worships. Frustration and defeat are like an organ-point heard below the varying music of his verse; failure is almost glorified in his pages.

Technically, Robinson is as precise as he is dextrous. He is, in company with Frost, a master of the slowly diminished ending. But he is capable of cadences as rich as that which ends "The Gift of God," as pungent as the climax of "Calvary," as brilliantly fanciful as the sestet of his sonnet, "The Sheaves," as muted but sustained as the finale of "Eros Turannos" which might have been composed by a more controlled Swinburne.

There is never a false image or a blurred line in any of these verses which, while adhering to the strictest models and executed according to traditional forms, are always fresh and surprising. It is interesting to observe how the smoothness of his rhymes, playing against the hard outlines of his verse, emphasizes the epigrammatic strength of poems like "The Gift of God," that magnificent modern ballad, "John Gorham," "For a Dead Lady," and "The Master," one of the finest evocations of Lincoln which is, at the same time, a bitter commentary on the commercialism of the times and the "shopman's test of age and worth."

Robinson's blank verse is scarcely less individual. It is astringent, personal, packed with the instant. In "Ben Jonson Entertains a Man from Stratford" we have the clearest and most human portrait of Shakespeare ever attempted; the lines run as fluently as good conversation, as inevitably as a perfect melody. In his reanimations of the Arthurian legends, *Merlin* (1917), *Launcelot* (1920), *Tristam* (1927), Robinson, shaming the tea-table idyls of Tennyson, had colored the tale with somber reflections of the collapse of old orders and the darkness of an age in ashes.

Avon's Harvest, which the author considered "a dime novel in verse," a study of a fear-haunted, hate-driven man, appeared in 1921. In the same year the Macmillan Company issued his *Collected Poems,* which received the Pulitzer Prize for 1921 and which was enlarged in 1929. Subsequent volumes strengthened his admirers' convictions and disproved any fears that Robinson might have "written himself out." *Roman Bartholow* (1923) is a single poem of almost two hundred pages; a dramatic and introspective narrative in blank verse. *The Man Who Died Twice* (1924), which was awarded the Pulitzer Prize for that year, is likewise one long poem: a tale which is a cross between a grotesque recital and inspired metaphysics. Curiously enough, the mixture is one of Robinson's greatest triumphs; none of his portraits, either miniatures or full-length canvases, has given us a profounder insight of a tortured soul than this of Fernando Nash, "the king who lost his crown before he had it."

Dionysus in Doubt (1925) begins and ends with a caustic arraignment of our mechanistic civilization, and is primarily a scornful and carefully premeditated condemnation of the Eighteenth Amendment, an attack which never descends to polemics or political diatribe. Robinson's ironic accents lift every phrase above the argumentative matter; the darkest of his doubts are illumined by "the salvage of a smile." Besides two other longish poems, this volume includes eighteen sonnets which again display Robinson's supremacy in the form. Time and again, he packs huge scenes into fourteen lines; if sonnets can assume the proportion of dramatic narratives, Robinson's have achieved the almost impossible feat.

Possibly the fact that Robinson had already won the Pulitzer Prize twice, possibly the increasing interest of his work may have accounted for his increased audience. Not even his most enthusiastic admirers awaited the reception accorded to *Tristram* (1927). Adopted by the most prominent book-club as its "book-of-the-month," awarded unstinted praise and the Pulitzer Prize for the third time, it outsold most "best-selling" novels. This was something of a phenomenon, for *Tristram* was not only a single poem of over forty thousand words, it was Robinson's most intricate and knotted work. But it was no mere problem in involution; Robinson, as though reacting against the charge of Puritanism, abandoned himself to a drama passionate and headlong.

Cavender's House (1929) was scarcely less esteemed. Formerly regarded as a poet's poet, the later volumes established Robinson in popular favor, no matter from what epoch he chose his theme. *Tristram* was medieval, *Cavender's House* was modern. Like *Avon's Harvest* and *Roman Bartholow,* the latter was melodrama glorified, but sharper and tenser than its predecessors. Both renewed the inevitable—and false—comparisons. Robinson's manner was likened to Browning's, his matter (particularly in the Arthurian tales) to Tennyson's. The comparison to Browning, though superficial and inaccurate, is at least comprehensible. The author of *Merlin,* like the author of *Sordello,* delights in subtly psychological portraiture, in the half-withheld inner drama, in the shift of suspensions and nuances of tension. But where Browning is forthright, Robinson is tangential; where Browning is lavish with imagery and flaring interjections, Robinson is sparse in metaphor and so economic with words that almost every phrase seems twisted and wrung of everything except its essential meaning. But the principal dissimilarity lies in their *Weltanschauung;* here they are diametrically opposed. Where Browning regards the universe compact of sweetness and light, Robinson observes a scheme whose chief components are bitterness and blight; the realm where "God's in his heaven, all's right with the world" becomes (as in the significantly entitled *The Man Against the Sky*) a place where

> He may go forward like a stoic Roman
> Where pangs and terrors in his pathway lie—
> Or, seizing the swift logic of a woman,
> Curse God and die.

Although Robinson was accused of holding consistently a negative attitude toward life, his poetry reveals a restless, uncertain, but persistent search for moral values. This quest—and questioning—of ultimates runs through his work as it ran through an age no longer satisfied with arid skepticism. It is significant that the same year which disclosed Eliot turning to a faith beyond intellect showed Robinson driving past reason to find

. . . There must be God; or if not God, a purpose and a law.

The conclusion of his sonnet to Crabbe might well be applied to him:

Whether or not we read him, we can feel
From time to time the vigor of his name
Against us like a finger for the shame
And emptiness of what our souls reveal
In books that are as altars where we kneel
To consecrate the flicker, not the flame.

After 1928 Robinson's poetry tended to become repetitious and prolix. Writing for an income and fearing the future, he felt it incumbent upon him to write an annual volume. Each year for seven years, until the very month of his death, he planned and issued a narrative poem in which personal as well as physical fatigue was increasingly evident. *The Glory of the Nightingales* (1930) is a melancholy tragedy which suffers from dryness of thought and atrophy of emotion. *Matthias at the Door* (1931) is another gloomy study which exhibits the author's narrowing limitations—the dark, deliberate idiom spoken indiscriminately by all the characters, the lack of life in any of the *dramatis personae* who function only as disembodied intellects in a state of continually painful thought, and a sense of hopeless defeatism. *Nicodemus* (1932) attempts to revive earlier spirits, but the summoned Annandale, Ponce de Leon, and Toussaint L'Ouverture are little more than garrulous ghosts. *Talifer* (1933) is far better, the happiest and most teasing of Robinson's longer poems, an unexpected blend of wisdom and wicked irony. *Amaranth* (1934) is another nightmare narrative of deluded failures and dream-ridden mediocrities. Unfortunately the poem, for all its dramatic possibilities, is wholly without drama, and it is difficult to tell whether Robinson is sympathizing with his lost shadows or satirizing them. The theme of frustration is continued in the posthumous *King Jasper* (1935) which was introduced with a shrewd analysis of "new ways of being new" by Robert Frost; unfortunately *King Jasper* is an involved and dubious allegory.

Subsequent to 1911 Robinson lived most of his summers at Peterborough, New Hampshire, at the MacDowell Colony, of which he was the unofficial but acknowledged presiding genius. He divided his winters between New York and Boston until ill health forced him to forego travel of any sort. His last winter in Boston was full of suffering, chiefly due to a growth in the pancreas, and when he was taken to the New York Hospital he was in a pitifully weakened condition. It was impossible to operate successfully and he died there April 6, 1935.

Upon his death there were the inevitable belated tributes to an unhappy poet and a lonely man. The most eloquent of them was Robinson Jeffers' spontaneous response. "I cannot speak of E. A. Robinson's work," wrote Jeffers. "Better critics than I have praised its qualities, and will again. Let me notice instead the debt we owe him for the qualities of his life; for the dignity with which he wore his fame, for the example of his reticence and steady concentration, for the single-mindedness with which he followed his own sense of direction, unbewildered and undiverted. . . . We are grateful that he was not what they call 'a good showman,' but gave himself to his work, not to his audience, and would have preferred complete failure to any success with the least taint of charlatanry." A biography by Hermann Hagedorn (1938), another by Emery Neff (1948), and a volume of letters (1940) explored Robinson's anxieties, but failed to analyze the reason for his distrust and desperate loneliness.

It has been said that Robinson's pessimism alienated part of his audience. But Robinson always took pains to refute this charge, not only in his private protests—in his letters and conversations—but in his poems. He denied that life was merely a material phenomenon. In the sonnet "Credo" he implied his faith; he said it explicitly when he maintained that humanity might be unaware of its destiny and unsure of its divinity, but it could not surrender its belief: "The world is not a 'prison-house' but a kind of spiritual kindergarten, where millions of bewildered infants are trying to spell God with the wrong blocks."

EXIT

For what we owe to other days,
Before we poisoned him with praise,
May we who shrank to find him weak
Remember that he cannot speak.

For envy that we may recall,
And for our faith before the fall,
May we who are alive be slow
To tell what we shall never know.

For penance he would not confess,
And for the fateful emptiness
Of early triumph undermined,
May we now venture to be kind.

CREDO

I cannot find my way: there is no star
In all the shrouded heavens anywhere;
And there is not a whisper in the air
Of any living voice but one so far
That I can hear it only as a bar
Of lost, imperial music, played when fair
And angel fingers wove, and unaware,
Dead leaves to garlands where no roses are.

No, there is not a glimmer, nor a call,
For one that welcomes, welcomes when he fears,
The black and awful chaos of the night;
For through it all—above, beyond it all—
I know the far-sent message of the years,
I feel the coming glory of the Light!

JAMES WETHERELL

We never half believed the stuff
They told about James Wetherell;
We always liked him well enough,
And always tried to use him well;
But now some things have come to light,
And James has vanished from our view.—
There isn't very much to write,
There isn't very much to do.

MINIVER CHEEVY

Miniver Cheevy, child of scorn,
Grew lean while he assailed the seasons;
He wept that he was ever born,
And he had reasons.

Miniver loved the days of old
When swords were bright and steeds were prancing:
The vision of a warrior bold
Would set him dancing.

Miniver sighed for what was not,
And dreamed, and rested from his labors;
He dreamed of Thebes and Camelot,
And Priam's neighbors.

Miniver mourned the ripe renown
That made so many a name so fragrant;
He mourned Romance, now on the town,
And Art, a vagrant.

Miniver loved the Medici,
Albeit he had never seen one;
He would have sinned incessantly
Could he have been one.

Miniver cursed the commonplace
And eyed a khaki suit with loathing;
He missed the medieval grace
Of iron clothing.

Miniver scorned the gold he sought,
But sore annoyed was he without it;
Miniver thought, and thought, and thought,
And thought about it.

Miniver Cheevy, born too late,
Scratched his head and kept on thinking;
Miniver coughed, and called it fate,
And kept on drinking.

CLIFF KLINGENHAGEN

Cliff Klingenhagen had me in to dine
With him one day; and after soup and meat,
And all the other things there were to eat,
Cliff took two glasses and filled one with wine
And one with wormwood. Then, without a sign
For me to choose at all, he took the draught
Of bitterness himself, and lightly quaffed
It off, and said the other one was mine.

And when I asked him what the deuce he meant
By doing that, he only looked at me
And grinned, and said it was a way of his.
And though I know the fellow, I have spent
Long time a-wondering when I shall be
As happy as Cliff Klingenhagen is.

THE HOUSE ON THE HILL

They are all gone away,
The House is shut and still,
There is nothing more to say.

Through broken walls and gray
The winds blow bleak and shrill;
They are all gone away.

Nor is there one today
To speak them good or ill:
There is nothing more to say.

Why is it then we stray
Around that sunken sill?
They are all gone away,

And our poor fancy-play
For them is wasted skill:
There is nothing more to say.

There is ruin and decay
In the House on the Hill:
They are all gone away,
There is nothing more to say.

AN OLD STORY

Strange that I did not know him then,
That friend of mine.
I did not even show him then
One friendly sign;

But cursed him for the ways he had
To make me see
My envy of the praise he had
For praising me.

I would have rid the earth of him
Once, in my pride.
I never knew the worth of him
Until he died.

RICHARD CORY

Whenever Richard Cory went down town,
We people on the pavement looked at him:
He was a gentleman from sole to crown,
Clean favored, and imperially slim.

And he was always quietly arrayed,
And he was always human when he talked;
But still he fluttered pulses when he said,
"Good-morning," and he glittered when he walked.

And he was rich—yes, richer than a king—
And admirably schooled in every grace:
In fine, we thought that he was everything
To make us wish that we were in his place.

So on we worked, and waited for the light,
And went without the meat, and cursed the bread;
And Richard Cory, one calm summer night,
Went home and put a bullet through his head.

BEWICK FINZER

Time was when his half million drew
The breath of six per cent;
But soon the worm of what-was-not
Fed hard on his content;
And something crumbled in his brain
When his half million went.

Time passed, and filled along with his
The place of many more;
Time came, and hardly one of us
Had credence to restore,
From what appeared one day, the man
Whom we had known before.

The broken voice, the withered neck,
The coat worn out with care,

The cleanliness of indigence,
The brilliance of despair,
The fond imponderable dreams
Of affluence,—all were there.

Poor Finzer, with his dreams and schemes,
Fares hard now in the race,
With heart and eye that have a task
When he looks in the face

Of one who might so easily
Have been in Finzer's place.

He comes unfailing for the loan
We give and then forget;
He comes, and probably for years
Will he be coming yet,—
Familiar as an old mistake,
And futile as regret.

REUBEN BRIGHT

Because he was a butcher and thereby
Did earn an honest living (and did right)
I would not have you think that Reuben Bright
Was any more a brute than you or I;
For when they told him that his wife must die,
He stared at them and shook with grief and fright,
And cried like a great baby half that night,
And made the women cry to see him cry.

And after she was dead, and he had paid
The singers and the sexton and the rest,
He packed a lot of things that she had made
Most mournfully away in an old chest
Of hers, and put some chopped-up cedar boughs
In with them, and tore down the slaughter-house.

FOR A DEAD LADY

No more with overflowing light
Shall fill the eyes that now are faded,
Nor shall another's fringe with night
Their woman-hidden world as they did.
No more shall quiver down the days
The flowing wonder of her ways,
Whereof no language may requite
The shifting and the many-shaded.

The grace, divine, definitive,
Clings only as a faint forestalling;
The laugh that love could not forgive
Is hushed, and answers to no calling;
The forehead and the little ears
Have gone where Saturn keeps the years;
The breast where roses could not live
Has done with rising and with falling.

The beauty, shattered by the laws
That have creation in their keeping,
No longer trembles at applause,
Or over children that are sleeping;
And we who delve in beauty's lore
Know all that we have known before
Of what inexorable cause
Makes Time so vicious in his reaping.

CALVARY

Friendless and faint, with martyred steps and slow,
Faint for the flesh, but for the spirit free,
Stung by the mob that came to see the show,
The Master toiled along to Calvary;
We gibed him, as he went, with houndish glee,
Till his dimmed eyes for us did overflow;

We cursed his vengeless hands thrice wretchedly,—
And this was nineteen hundred years ago.
But after nineteen hundred years the shame
Still clings, and we have not made good the loss
That outraged faith has entered in his name.
Ah, when shall come love's courage to be strong!
Tell me, O Lord—tell me, O Lord, how long
Are we to keep Christ writhing on the cross!

VICKERY'S MOUNTAIN

Blue in the west the mountain stands,
And through the long twilight
Vickery sits with folded hands,
And Vickery's eyes are bright.

Bright, for he knows what no man else
On earth as yet may know:
There's a golden word that he never tells,
And a gift that he will not show.

He dreams of honor and wealth and fame,
He smiles, and well he may;
For to Vickery once a sick man came
Who did not go away.

The day before the day to be,
"Vickery," said the guest,
"You know as you live what's left of me—
And you shall know the rest.

"You know as you live that I have come
To what we call the end.
No doubt you have found me troublesome,
But you've also found a friend;

"For we shall give and you shall take
The gold that is in view;
The mountain there and I shall make
A golden man of you.

"And you shall leave a friend behind
Who neither frets nor feels;
And you shall move among your kind
With hundreds at your heels.

"Now this I have written here
Tells all that need be told;
So, Vickery, take the way that's clear,
And be a man of gold."

Vickery turned his eyes again
To the far mountain-side,
And wept a tear for worthy men
Defeated and defied.

Since then a crafty score of years
Have come; and they have gone;
But Vickery counts no lost arrears:
He lingers and lives on.

Blue in the west the mountain stands,
Familiar as a face,
Blue, but Vickery knows what sands
Are golden at its base.

He dreams and lives upon the day
When he shall walk with kings.
Vickery smiles—and well he may:
The life-caged linnet sings.

Vickery thinks the time will come
To go for what is his;
But hovering, unseen hands at home
Will hold him where he is.

There's a golden word that he never tells
And a gift that he will not show.
All to be given to someone else—
And Vickery shall not know.

TOO MUCH COFFEE

Together in infinite shade
They defy the invincible dawn:
The Measure that never was made,
The Line that never was drawn.

THE MASTER

(*Lincoln. Supposed to have been written not long after the Civil War*)

A flying word from here and there
Had sown the name at which we sneered,
But soon the name was everywhere,
To be reviled and then revered:

A presence to be loved and feared,
We cannot hide it, or deny
That we, the gentlemen who jeered,
May be forgotten by and by.

He came when days were perilous
And hearts of men were sore beguiled;
And having made his note of us,
He pondered and was reconciled.
Was ever master yet so mild
As he, and so untamable?
We doubted, even when he smiled,
Not knowing what he knew so well.

He knew that undeceiving fate
Would shame us whom he served unsought;
He knew that he must wince and wait—
The jest of those for whom he fought;
He knew devoutly what he thought
Of us and of our ridicule;
He knew that we must all be taught
Like little children in a school.

We gave a glamour to the task
That he encountered and saw through,
But little of us did he ask,
And little did we ever do.
And what appears if we review
The season when we railed and chaffed?
It is the face of one who knew
That we were learning while we laughed.

The face that in our vision feels
Again the venom that we flung,
Transfigured to the world reveals
The vigilance to which we clung.
Shrewd, hallowed, harassed, and among
The mysteries that are untold,
The face we see was never young,
Nor could it ever have been old.

For he, to whom we had applied
Our shopman's test of age and worth,
Was elemental when he died,
As he was ancient at his birth:
The saddest among kings of earth,
Bowed with a galling crown, this man
Met rancor with a cryptic mirth,
Laconic—and Olympian.

The love, the grandeur, and the fame
Are bounded by the world alone;
The calm, the smoldering, and the flame
Of awful patience were his own:
With him they are forever flown
Past all our fond self-shadowings,
Wherewith we cumber the Unknown
As with inept Icarian wings.

For we were not as other men:
'Twas ours to soar and his to see.
But we are coming down again,
And we shall come down pleasantly;
Nor shall we longer disagree
On what it is to be sublime,
But flourish in our perigee
And have one Titan at a time.

MR. FLOOD'S PARTY

Old Eben Flood, climbing alone one night
Over the hill between the town below
And the forsaken upland hermitage
That held as much as he should ever know
On earth again of home, paused warily.
The road was his with not a native near;
And Eben, having leisure, said aloud,
For no man else in Tilbury Town to hear:

"Well, Mr. Flood, we have the harvest moon
Again, and we may not have many more;
The bird is on the wing, the poet says,
And you and I have said it here before.
Drink to the bird." He raised up to the light
The jug that he had gone so far to fill,

And answered huskily: "Well, Mr. Flood,
Since you propose it, I believe I will."

Alone, as if enduring to the end
A valiant armor of scarred hopes outworn,
He stood there in the middle of the road
Like Roland's ghost winding a silent horn.
Below him, in the town among the trees,
Where friends of other days had honored him,
A phantom salutation of the dead
Rang thinly till old Eben's eyes were dim.

Then, as a mother lays her sleeping child
Down tenderly, fearing it may awake,
He set the jug down slowly at his feet
With trembling care, knowing that most things break;
And only when assured that on firm earth
It stood, as the uncertain lives of men
Assuredly did not, he paced away,
And with his hand extended paused again:

"Well, Mr. Flood, we have not met like this
In a long time; and many a change has come
To both of us, I fear, since last it was
We had a drop together. Welcome home!"
Convivially returning with himself,
Again he raised the jug up to the light;
And with an acquiescent quaver said:
"Well, Mr. Flood, if you insist, I might.

"Only a very little, Mr. Flood—
For auld lang syne. No more, sir; that will do."
So, for the time, apparently it did,
And Eben evidently thought so too;
For soon amid the silver loneliness
Of night he lifted up his voice and sang,
Secure, with only two moons listening,
Until the whole harmonious landscape rang—

"For auld lang syne." The weary throat gave out,
The last word wavered; and the song being done,
He raised again the jug regretfully
And shook his head, and was again alone.
There was not much that was ahead of him,
And there was nothing in the town below—
Where strangers would have shut the many doors
That many friends had opened long ago.

GEORGE CRABBE

Give him the darkest inch your shelf allows,
Hide him in lonely garrets, if you will,—

But his hard, human pulse is throbbing still
With the sure strength that fearless truth endows.
In spite of all fine science disavows,
Of his plain excellence and stubborn skill
There yet remains what fashion cannot kill,
Though years have thinned the laurel from his brows.

Whether or not we read him, we can feel
From time to time the vigor of his name
Against us like a finger for the shame
And emptiness of what our souls reveal
In books that are as altars where we kneel
To consecrate the flicker, not the flame.

LUKE HAVERGAL

Go to the western gate, Luke Havergal,
There where the vines cling crimson on the wall,
And in the twilight wait for what will come.
The leaves will whisper there of her, and some,
Like flying words, will strike you as they fall;
But go, and if you listen, she will call.
Go to the western gate, Luke Havergal—
Luke Havergal.

No, there is not a dawn in eastern skies
To rift the fiery night that's in your eyes;
But there, where western glooms are gathering,
The dark will end the dark, if anything:
God slays himself with every leaf that flies,
And hell is more than half of paradise.
No, there is not a dawn in eastern skies—
In eastern skies.

Out of a grave I come to tell you this,
Out of a grave I come to quench the kiss
That flames upon your forehead with a glow
That blinds you to the way that you must go.
Yes, there is yet one way to where she is,
Bitter, but one that faith may never miss.
Out of a grave I come to tell you this—
To tell you this.

There is the western gate, Luke Havergal,
There are the crimson leaves upon the wall.
Go, for the winds are tearing them away,—
Nor think to riddle the dead words they say,
Nor any more to feel them as they fall;
But go, and if you trust her she will call.
There is the western gate, Luke Havergal—
Luke Havergal.

JOHN GORHAM

"Tell me what you're doing over here, John Gorham,
Sighing hard and seeming to be sorry when you're not;
Make me laugh or let me go now, for long faces in the moonlight
Are a sign for me to say again a word that you forgot."—

"I'm over here to tell you what the moon already
May have said or maybe shouted ever since a year ago;
I'm over here to tell you what you are, Jane Wayland,
And to make you rather sorry, I should say, for being so."—

"Tell me what you're saying to me now, John Gorham,
Or you'll never see as much of me as ribbons any more;
I'll vanish in as many ways as I have toes and fingers,
And you'll not follow far for one where flocks have been before."—

"I'm sorry now you never saw the flocks, Jane Wayland,
But you're the one to make of them as many as you need.
And then about the vanishing: It's I who mean to vanish;
And when I'm here no longer you'll be done with me indeed."—

"That's a way to tell me what I am, John Gorham!
How am I to know myself until I make you smile?
Try to look as if the moon were making faces at you,
And a little more as if you meant to stay a little while."—

"You are what it is that over rose-blown gardens
Makes a pretty flutter for a season in the sun;
You are what it is that with a mouse, Jane Wayland,
Catches him and lets him go and eats him up for fun."—

"Sure I never took you for a mouse, John Gorham;
All you say is easy, but so far from being true,
That I wish you wouldn't ever be again the one to think so;
For it isn't cats and butterflies that I would be to you."—

"All your little animals are in one picture—
One I've had before me since a year ago tonight;
And the picture where they live will be of you, Jane Wayland,
Till you find a way to kill them or to keep them out of sight."—

"Won't you ever see me as I am, John Gorham,
Leaving out the foolishness and all I never meant?
Somewhere in me there's a woman, if you know the way to find her.
Will you like me any better if I prove it and repent?"—

"I doubt if I shall ever have the time, Jane Wayland;
And I dare say all this moonlight lying round us might as well
Fall for nothing on the shards of broken urns that are forgotten,
As on two that have no longer much of anything to tell."

HOW ANNANDALE WENT OUT

"They called it Annandale—and I was there
To flourish, to find words, and to attend:
Liar, physician, hypocrite, and friend,
I watched him; and the sight was not so fair
As one or two that I had seen elsewhere:
An apparatus not for me to mend—
A wreck, with hell between him and the end,
Remained of Annandale; and I was there.

"I knew the ruin as I knew the man;
So put the two together, if you can,
Remembering the worst you know of me.
Now view yourself as I was, on the spot,
With a slight kind of engine. Do you see?
Like this . . . You wouldn't hang me? I thought not."

THE FIELD OF GLORY

War shook the land where Levi dwelt,
And fired the dismal wrath he felt,
That such a doom was ever wrought
As his, to toil while others fought;
To toil, to dream—and still to dream,
With one day barren as another;
To consummate, as it would seem,
The dry despair of his old mother.

Far off one afternoon began
The sound of man destroying man;
And Levi, sick with nameless rage,
Condemned again his heritage,
And sighed for scars that might have come,
And would, if once he could have sundered
Those harsh, inhering claims of home
That held him while he cursed and wondered.

Another day, and then there came,
Rough, bloody, ribald, hungry, lame,
But yet themselves, to Levi's door,
Two remnants of the day before.
They laughed at him and what he sought;
They jeered him and his painful acre;
But Levi knew that they had fought,
And left their manners to their Maker.

That night, for the grim widow's ears,
With hopes that hid themselves in fears,
He told of arms, and fiery deeds,
Whereat one leaps the while he reads,
And said he'd be no more a clown,
While others drew the breath of battle.
The mother looked him up and down,
And laughed—a scant laugh with a rattle.

She told him what she found to tell,
And Levi listened, and heard well
Some admonitions of a voice
That left him no cause to rejoice.—
He sought a friend, and found the stars,
And prayed aloud that they should aid him;
But they said not a word of wars,
Or of a reason why God made him.

And who's of this or that estate
We do not wholly calculate,
When baffling shades that shift and cling
Are not without their glimmering;
When even Levi, tired of faith,
Beloved of none, forgot by many,
Dismissed as an inferior wraith,
Reborn may be as great as any.

THE CLERKS

I did not think that I should find them there
When I came back again; but there they stood,
As in the days they dreamed of when young blood
Was in their cheeks and women called them fair.
Be sure they met me with an ancient air,—
And yes, there was a shop-worn brotherhood
About them; but the men were just as good,
And just as human as they ever were.

And you that ache so much to be sublime,
And you that feed yourselves with your descent,
What comes of all your visions and your fears?
Poets and kings are but the clerks of Time,
Tiering the same dull webs of discontent
Clipping the same sad alnage of the years.

THE DARK HILLS

Dark hills at evening in the west,
Where sunset hovers like a sound
Of golden horns that sang to rest
Old bones of warriors under ground,
Far now from all the bannered ways
Where flash the legions of the sun,
You fade—as if the last of days
Were fading and all wars were done.

EROS TURANNOS

She fears him, and will always ask
  What fated her to choose him;
She meets in his engaging mask
  All reasons to refuse him;
But what she meets and what she fears
Are less than are the downward years,
Drawn slowly to the foamless weirs
  Of age, were she to lose him.

Between a blurred sagacity
  That once had power to sound him,
And Love, that will not let him be
  The Judas that she found him,
Her pride assuages her almost,
As if it were alone the cost.
He sees that he will not be lost,
  And waits and looks around him.

A sense of ocean and old trees
  Envelopes and allures him;
Tradition, touching all he sees,
  Beguiles and reassures him;
And all her doubts of what he says
Are dimmed with what she knows of days—
Till even prejudice delays
  And fades, and she secures him.

The falling leaf inaugurates
  The reign of her confusion;
The pounding wave reverberates
  The dirge of her illusion;
And home, where passion lived and died,
Becomes a place where she can hide,
While all the town and harbor-side
  Vibrate with her seclusion.

We tell you, tapping on our brows,
  The story as it should be,
As if the story of a house
  Were told, or ever could be;
We'll have no kindly veil between
Her visions and those we have seen,—
As if we guessed what hers have been,
  Or what they are or would be.

Meanwhile we do no harm; for they
  That with a god have striven,
Not hearing much of what we say,
  Take what the god has given;
Though like waves breaking it may be,
Or like a changed familiar tree,
Or like a stairway to the sea
  Where down the blind are driven.

THE SHEAVES

Where long the shadows of the wind had rolled,
Green wheat was yielding to the change assigned;
And as by some vast magic undivined
The world was turning slowly into gold.
Like nothing that was ever bought or sold
It waited there, the body and the mind;
And with a mighty meaning of a kind
That tells the more the more it is not told.

So in a land where all days are not fair,
Fair days went on till on another day
A thousand golden sheaves were lying there,
Shining and still, but not for long to stay—
As if a thousand girls with golden hair
Might rise from where they slept and go away.

BEN JONSON ENTERTAINS A MAN FROM STRATFORD

You are a friend then, as I make it out,
Of our man Shakespeare, who alone of us
Will put an ass's head in Fairyland
As he would add a shilling to more shillings,
All most harmonious—and out of his
Miraculous inviolable increase
Fills Ilion, Rome, or any town you like
Of olden time with timeless Englishmen;
And I must wonder what you think of him—
All you down there where your small Avon flows
By Stratford, and where you're an Alderman.
Some, for a guess, would have him riding back
To be a farrier there, or say a dyer;
Or maybe one of your adept surveyors;
Or like enough the wizard of all tanners.
Not you—no fear of that; for I discern
In you a kindling of the flame that saves—
The nimble element, the true caloric;
I see it, and was told of it, moreover,
By our discriminate friend himself, no other.
Had you been one of the sad average,
As he would have it—meaning, as I take it,
The sinew and the solvent of our Island,
You'd not be buying beer for this Terpander's
Approved and estimated friend Ben Jonson;
He'd never foist it as a part of his
Contingent entertainment of a townsman
While he goes off rehearsing, as he must,
If he shall ever be the Duke of Stratford.
And my words are no shadow on your town—

Far from it; for one town's like another
As all are unlike London. Oh, he knows it—
And there's the Stratford in him; he denies it,
And there's the Shakespeare in him. So, God help him!

I tell him he needs Greek; but neither God
Nor Greek will help him. Nothing will help that man.
You see the fates have given him so much,
He must have all or perish—or look out
Of London, where he sees too many lords.
They're part of half what ails him: I suppose
There's nothing fouler down among the demons
Than what it is he feels when he remembers
The dust and sweat and ointment of his calling
With his lords looking on and laughing at him.
King as he is, he can't be king *de facto,*
And that's as well, because he wouldn't like it;
He'd frame a lower rating of men then
Than he has now; and after that would come
An abdication or an apoplexy.
He can't be king, not even king of Stratford—
Though half the world, if not the whole of it,
May crown him with a crown that fits no king
Save Lord Apollo's homesick emissary:
Not there on Avon, or on any stream
Where Naiads and their white arms are no more
Shall he find home again. It's all too bad.
But there's a comfort, for he'll have that House—
The best you ever saw; and he'll be there
Anon, as you're an Alderman. Good God!
He makes me lie awake o' nights and laugh,

And you have known him from his origin,
You tell me; and a most uncommon urchin
He must have been to the few seeing ones—
A trifle terrifying, I dare say,
Discovering a world with his man's eyes,
Quite as another lad might see some finches,
If he looked hard and had an eye for Nature.
But this one had his eyes and their foretelling,
And he had you to fare with, and what else?
He must have had a father and a mother—
In fact I've heard him say so—and a dog,
As a boy should, I venture; and the dog,
Most likely, was the only man who knew him.
A dog, for all I know, is what he needs
As much as anything right here today,
To counsel him about his disillusions,
Old aches, and parturitions of what's coming—
A dog of orders, an emeritus,
To wag his tail at him when he comes home,

And then to put his paws up on his knees
And say, "For God's sake, what's it all about?"

I don't know whether he needs a dog or not—
Or what he needs. I tell him he needs Greek;
I'll talk of rules and Aristotle with him,
And if his tongue's at home he'll say to that,
"I have your word that Aristotle knows,
And you mine that I don't know Aristotle."
He's all at odds with all the unities,
And what's yet worse it doesn't seem to matter;
He treads along through Time's old wilderness
As if the tramp of all the centuries
Had left no roads—and there are none, for him;
He doesn't see them, even with those eyes—
And that's a pity, or I say it is.
Accordingly we have him as we have him—
Going his way, the way that he goes best,
A pleasant animal with no great noise
Or nonsense anywhere to set him off—
Save only divers and inclement devils
Have made of late his heart their dwelling-place.
A flame half ready to fly out sometimes
At some annoyance may be fanned up in him,
But soon it falls, and when it falls goes out;
He knows how little room there is in there
For crude and futile animosities,
And how much for the joy of being whole,
And how much for long sorrow and old pain.
On our side there are some who may be given
To grow old wondering what he thinks of us
And some above us, who are, in his eyes,
Above himself—and that's quite right and English.
Yet here we smile, or disappoint the gods
Who made it so; the gods have always eyes
To see men scratch; and they see one down here
Who itches, manor-bitten, to the bone,
Albeit he knows himself—yes, yes, he knows—
The lord of more than England and of more
Than all the seas of England in all time
Shall ever wash. D'ye wonder that I laugh?
He sees me, and he doesn't seem to care;
And why the devil should he? I can't tell you.
I'll meet him out alone of a bright Sunday,
Trim, rather spruce, and quite the gentleman.
"What, ho, my lord!" say I. He doesn't hear me;
Wherefore I have to pause and look at him.
He's not enormous, but one looks at him.
A little on the round if you insist,
For now, God save the mark, he's growing old;
He's five and forty, and to hear him talk

These days you'd call him eighty; then you'd add
More years to that. He's old enough to be
The father of a world, and so he is.
"Ben, you're a scholar, what's the time of day?"
Says he; and there shines out of him again
An aged light that has no age or station—
The mystery that's his—a mischievous
Half-mad serenity that laughs at fame
For being won so easy, and at friends
Who laugh at him for what he wants the most,
And for his dukedom down in Warwickshire:—
By which you see we're all a little jealous. . . .
Poor Greene! I fear the color of his name
Was even as that of his ascending soul;
And he was one where there are many others—
Some scrivening to the end against their fate,
Their puppets all in ink and all to die there;
And some with hands that once would shade an eye
That scanned Euripides and Aeschylus
Will reach by this time for a pot-house mop
To slush their first and last of royalties.
Poor devils! and they all play to his hand;
For so it was in Athens and old Rome.
But that's not here or there; I've wandered off.
Greene does it, or I'm careful. Where's that boy?

Yes, he'll go back to Stratford. And we'll miss him?
Dear sir, there'll be no London here without him.
We'll all be riding, one of these fine days,
Down there to see him—and his wife won't like us;
And then we'll think of what he never said
Of women—which, if taken all in all
With what he did say, would buy many horses.
Though nowadays he's not so much for women.
"So few of them," he says, "are worth the guessing."
But there's a worm at work when he says that,
And while he says it one feels in the air
A deal of circumambient hocus-pocus.
They've had him dancing till his toes were tender,
And he can feel 'em now, come chilly rains.
There's no long cry for going into it,
However, and we don't know much about it.
But you in Stratford, like most here in London,
Have more now in the *Sonnets* than you paid for;
He's put one there with all her poison on,
To make a singing fiction of a shadow
That's in his life a fact, and always will be.
But she's no care of ours, though Time, I fear,
Will have a more reverberant ado
About her than about another one
Who seems to have decoyed him, married him,

And sent him scuttling on his way to London—
With much already learned, and more to learn,
And more to follow. Lord! how I see him now,
Pretending, maybe trying, to be like us.
Whatever he may have meant, we never had him;
He failed us, or escaped, or what you will—
And there was that about him (God knows what—
We'd flayed another had he tried it on us)
That made as many of us as had wits
More fond of all his easy distances
Than one another's noise and clap-your-shoulder.
But think you not, my friend, he'd never talk!
Talk? He was eldritch at it; and we listened—
Thereby acquiring much we knew before
About ourselves, and hitherto had held
Irrelevant, or not prime to the purpose.
And there were some, of course, and there be now,
Disordered and reduced amazedly
To resignation by the mystic seal
Of young finality the gods had laid
On everything that made him a young demon;
And one or two shot looks at him already
As he had been their executioner;
And once or twice he was, not knowing it—
Or knowing, being sorry for poor clay
And saying nothing . . . Yet, for all his engines,
You'll meet a thousand of an afternoon
Who strut and sun themselves and see around 'em
A world made out of more that has a reason
Than his, I swear, that he sees here today;
Though he may scarcely give a Fool an exit
But we mark how he sees in everything
A law that, given that we flout it once too often,
Brings fire and iron down on our naked heads.
To me it looks as if the power that made him,
For fear of giving all things to one creature,
Left out the first—faith, innocence, illusion,
Whatever 'tis that keeps us out o' Bedlam—
And thereby, for his too consuming vision,
Empowered him out of nature; though to see him,
You'd never guess what's going on inside him.
He'll break out some day like a keg of ale
With too much independent frenzy in it;
And all for cellaring what he knows won't keep,
And what he'd best forget—but that he can't.
You'll have it, and have more than I'm foretelling;
And there'll be such a roaring at the Globe
As never stunned the bleeding gladiators.
He'll have to change the color of its hair
A bit, for now he calls it Cleopatra.
Black hair would never do for Cleopatra.

But you and I are not yet two old women,
And you're a man of office. What he does
Is more to you than how it is he does it—
And that's what the Lord God has never told him.
They work together, and the Devil helps 'em;
They do it of a morning, or if not,
They do it of a night; in which event
He's peevish of a morning. He seems old;
He's not the proper stomach or the sleep—
And they're two sovran agents to conserve him
Against the fiery art that has no mercy
But what's in that prodigious grand new House.
I gather something happening in his boyhood
Fulfilled him with a boy's determination
To make all Stratford 'ware of him. Well, well,
I hope at last he'll have his joy of it,
And all his pigs and sheep and bellowing beeves,
And frogs and owls and unicorns, moreover,
Be less than hell to his attendant ears.
Oh, past a doubt we'll all go down to see him.

He may be wise. With London two days off,
Down there some wind of heaven may yet revive him,
But there's no quickening breath from anywhere
Shall make of him again the young poised faun
From Warwickshire, who'd made, it seems, already
A legend of himself before I came
To blink before the last of his first lightning.
Whatever there be, there'll be no more of that;
The coming on of his old monster Time
Has made him a still man; and he has dreams
Were fair to think on once, and all found hollow.
He knows how much of what men paint themselves
Would blister in the light of what they are;
He sees how much of what was great now shares
An eminence transformed and ordinary;
He knows too much of what the world has hushed
In others, to be loud now for himself;
He knows now at what height low enemies
May reach his heart, and high friends let him fall;
But what not even such as he may know
Bedevils him the worst: his lark may sing
At heaven's gate how he will, and for as long
As joy may listen, but *he* sees no gate,
Save one whereat the spent clay waits a little
Before the churchyard has it, and the worm.

Not long ago, late in an afternoon,
I came on him unseen down Lambeth way,
And on my life I was afear'd of him:
He gloomed and mumbled like a soul from Tophet,

His hands behind him and his head bent solemn.
"What is it now," said I, "another woman?"
That made him sorry for me, and he smiled.
"No, Ben," he mused; "it's Nothing. It's all Nothing.
We come, we go; and when we're done, we're done;
Spiders and flies—we're mostly one or t'other—
We come, we go; and when we're done, we're done."
"By God, you sing that song as if you knew it!"
Said I, by way of cheering him; "what ails ye?"
"I think I must have come down here to think,"
Says he to that, and pulls his little beard;
"Your fly will serve as well as anybody,
And what's his hour? He flies, and flies, and flies,
And in his fly's mind has a brave appearance;
And then your spider gets him in her net,
And eats him out, and hangs him up to dry.
That's Nature, the kind mother of us all.
And then your slattern housemaid swings her broom,
And where's your spider? And that's Nature, also.
It's Nature, and it's Nothing. It's all Nothing.
It's all a world where bugs and emperors
Go singularly back to the same dust,
Each in his time; and the old, ordered stars
That sang together, Ben, will sing the same
Old stave tomorrow."

When he talks like that,
There's nothing for a human man to do
But lead him to some grateful nook like this
Where we be now, and there to make him drink.
He'll drink, for love of me, and then be sick;
A sad sign always in a man of parts,
And always very ominous. The great
Should be as large in liquor as in love—
And our great friend is not so large in either:
One disaffects him, and the other fails him;
Whatso he drinks that has an antic in it,
He's wondering what's to pay in his insides;
And while his eyes are on the Cyprian
He's fribbling all the time with that damned House.
We laugh here at his thrift, but after all
It may be thrift that saves him from the devil:
God gave it, anyhow—and we'll suppose
He knew the compound of His handiwork.
Today the clouds are with him, but anon
He'll out of 'em enough to shake the tree
Of life itself and bring down fruit unheard-of—
And, throwing in the bruised and whole together,
Prepare a wine to make us drunk with wonder;
And if he live, there'll be a sunset spell

Thrown over him as over a glassed lake
That yesterday was all a black wild water.

God send he live to give us, if no more,
What now's a-rampage in him, and exhibit,
With a decent half-allegiance to the ages
An earnest of at least a casual eye
Turned once on what he owes to Gutenberg,
And to the fealty of more centuries
Than are as yet a picture in our vision.
"There's time enough—I'll do it when I'm old,
And we're immortal men," he says to that;
And then he says to me, "Ben, what's 'immortal'?
Think you by any force of ordination
It may be nothing of a sort more noisy
Than a small oblivion of component ashes
That of a dream-addicted world was once
A moving atomy much like your friend here?"
Nothing will help that man. To make him laugh
I said then he was a mad mountebank—
And by the Lord I nearer made him cry.
I could have eat an eft then, on my knees,
Tails, claws, and all of him; for I had stung
The king of men, who had no sting for me,
And I had hurt him in his memories;
And I say now, as I shall say again,
I love the man this side idolatry.
He'll do it when he's old, he says. I wonder.
He may not be so ancient as all that.
For such as he the thing that is to do
Will do itself—but there's a reckoning;
The sessions that are now too much his own,
The roiling inward of a still outside,
The churning out of all those blood-fed lines,
The nights of many schemes and little sleep,
The full brain hammered hot with too much thinking,
The vexed heart over-worn with too much aching—
This weary jangling of conjoined affairs
Made out of elements that have no end,
And all confused at once, I understand,
Is not what makes a man to live forever.
O, no, not now! He'll not be going now:
There'll be time yet for God knows what explosions
Before he goes. He'll stay awhile. Just wait:
Just wait a year or two for Cleopatra,
For she's to be a balsam and a comfort;
And that's not all a jape of mine now, either.
For granted once the old way of Apollo
Sings in a man, he may then, if he's able,
Strike unafraid whatever strings he will
Upon the last and wildest of new lyres;
Nor out of his new magic, though it hymn

The shrieks of dungeoned hell, shall he create
A madness or a gloom to shut quite out
A cleaving daylight, and a last great calm
Triumphant over shipwreck and all storms.
He might have given Aristotle creeps,
But surely would have given him his *katharsis.*
He'll not be going yet. There's too much yet
Unsung within the man. But when he goes,
I'd stake ye coin o' the realm his only care
For a phantom world he sounded and found wanting
Will be a portion here, a portion there,
Of this or that thing or some other thing
That has a patent and intrinsical
Equivalence in those egregious shillings.
And yet he knows, God help him! Tell me, now,
If ever there was anything let loose
On earth by gods or devils heretofore
Like this mad, careful, proud, indifferent Shakespeare!
Where was it, if it ever was? By heaven,
'Twas never yet in Rhodes or Pergamon—
In Thebes or Nineveh, a thing like this!
No thing like this was ever out of England;
And that he knows. I wonder if he cares.
Perhaps he does. . . . O Lord, that House in Stratford!

NEW ENGLAND

Here where the wind is always north-north-east
And children learn to walk on frozen toes,
Wonder begets an envy of all those
Who boil elsewhere with such a lyric yeast
Of love that you will hear them at a feast
Where demons would appeal for some repose,
Still clamoring where the chalice overflows
And crying wildest who have drunk the least.

Passion is here a soilure of the wits,
We're told, and Love a cross for them to bear;
Joy shivers in the corner where she knits
And Conscience always has the rocking-chair,
Cheerful as when she tortured into fits
The first cat that was ever killed by Care.

THE GIFT OF GOD

Blessed with a joy that only she
Of all alive shall ever know,
She wears a proud humility
For what it was that willed it so,—
That her degree should be so great
Among the favored of the Lord
That she may scarcely bear the weight
Of her bewildering reward.

As one apart, immune, alone,
Or featured for the shining ones,
And like to none that she has known
Of other women's other sons,—

The firm fruition of her need,
He shines anointed; and he blurs
Her vision, till it seems indeed
A sacrilege to call him hers.

She fears a little for so much
Of what is best, and hardly dares
To think of him as one to touch
With aches, indignities, and cares;
She sees him rather at the goal,
Still shining; and her dream foretells
The proper shining of a soul
Where nothing ordinary dwells.

Perchance a canvass of the town
Would find him far from flags and shouts,
And leave him only the renown
Of many smiles and many doubts;
Perchance the crude and common tongue
Would havoc strangely with his worth;
But she, with innocence unwrung,
Would read his name around the earth.

And others, knowing how this youth
Would shine, if love could make him great,
When caught and tortured for the truth
Would only writhe and hesitate;
While she, arranging for his days
What centuries could not fulfill,
Transmutes him with her faith and praise,
And has him shining where she will.

She crowns him with her gratefulness,
And says again that life is good;
And should the gift of God be less
In him than in her motherhood,
His fame, though vague, will not be small,
As upward through her dream he fares,
Half clouded with a crimson fall
Of roses thrown on marble stairs.

THE PRODIGAL SON

You are not merry, brother. Why not laugh,
As I do, and acclaim the fatted calf?
For, unless ways are changing here at home,
You might not have it if I had not come.
And were I not a thing for you and me
To execrate in anguish, you would be
As indigent a stranger to surprise,
I fear, as I was once, and as unwise.
Brother, believe as I do it is best
For you that I'm again in the old nest—
Draggled, I grant you, but your brother still,
Full of good wine, good viands, and good will.
You will thank God, some day, that I returned,
And may be singing for what you have learned,
Some other day; and one day you may find
Yourself a little nearer to mankind.
And having hated me till you are tired,
You will begin to see, as if inspired,
It was fate's way of educating us.
Remembering then when you were venomous,
You will be glad enough that I am gone,
But you will know more of what's going on;
For you will see more of what makes it go,
And in more ways than are for you to know.
We are so different when we are dead,
That you, alive, may weep for what you said;
And I, the ghost of one you could not save,
May find you planting lentils on my grave.

THE PITY OF THE LEAVES

Vengeful across the cold November moors,
Loud with ancestral shame there came the bleak
Sad wind that shrieked, and answered with a shriek,
Reverberant through lonely corridors.
The old man heard it; and he heard, perforce,
Words out of lips that were no more to speak—
Words of the past that shook the old man's cheek
Like dead, remembered footsteps on old floors.

And then there were the leaves that plagued him so!
The brown, thin leaves that on the stones outside
Skipped with a freezing whisper. Now and then
They stopped, and stayed there—just to let him know
How dead they were; but if the old man cried,
They fluttered off like withered souls of men.

AARON STARK

Withal a meagre man was Aaron Stark—
Cursed and unkempt, shrewd, shrivelled, and morose.
A miser was he, with a miser's nose,
And eyes like little dollars in the dark.
His thin, pinched mouth was nothing but a mark;
And when he spoke there came like sullen blows
Through scattered fangs a few snarled words and close,
As if a cur were chary of its bark.

Glad for the murmur of his hard renown,
Year after year he shambled through the town—
A loveless exile moving with a staff;
And oftentimes there crept into his ears
A sound of alien pity, touched with tears—
And then (and only then) did Aaron laugh.

UNCLE ANANIAS

His words were magic and his heart was true,
  And everywhere he wandered he was blessed.
Out of all ancient men my childhood knew
  I choose him and I mark him for the best.
Of all authoritative liars, too,
  I crown him loveliest.

How fondly I remember the delight
  That always glorified him in the spring;
The joyous courage and the benedight
  Profusion of his faith in everything!

He was a good old man, and it was right
  That he should have his fling.

And often, underneath the apple-trees,
  When we surprised him in the summer-time,
With what superb magnificence and ease
  He sinned enough to make the day sublime!
And if he liked us there about his knees,
  Truly it was no crime.

All summer long we loved him for the same
  Perennial inspiration of his lies;
And when the russet wealth of autumn came,
  There flew but fairer visions to our eyes—
Multiple, tropical, winged with a feathery flame,
  Like birds of paradise.

So to the sheltered end of many a year
  He charmed the seasons out with pageantry
Wearing upon his forehead, with no fear,
  The laurel of approved iniquity.
And every child who knew him, far or near,
  Did love him faithfully.

KARMA

Christmas was in the air and all was well
With him, but for a few confusing flaws
In divers of God's images. Because
A friend of his would neither buy nor sell,
Was he to answer for the axe that fell?
He pondered; and the reason for it was,
Partly, a slowly freezing Santa Claus
Upon the corner, with his beard and bell.

Acknowledging an improvident surprise,
He magnified a fancy that he wished
The friend whom he had wrecked were here again.
Not sure of that, he found a compromise;
And from the fullness of his heart he fished
A dime for Jesus who had died for man.

Edgar Lee Masters

⁂ Edgar Lee Masters was born at Garnett, Kansas, August 23, 1869, of Puritan and pioneering stock. When he was still a boy, the family moved to Illinois, where, after desultory schooling, he studied law in his father's office at Lewiston. For a year he practiced with his father and then went to Chicago, where be became a successful attorney. Before going to Chicago, Masters had composed a quantity of rhymed verse in traditional forms on traditional themes; by the time he was twenty-four he had written about four hundred poems, the result of wide reading and the influence of Poe, Keats, Shelley, and Swinburne.

Masters' first volume of poems, published in his twenty-ninth year, was modestly entitled (perhaps with an implied bow to Omar Khayyám) *A Book of Verses*. With even greater modesty his second volume, *The Blood of the Prophets* (1905), was signed with a pseudonym, "Dexter Wallis." For the third book, *Songs and Sonnets* (1910), Masters adopted another pseudonym composed, this time, of the names of two Elizabethan dramatists: "Webster Ford." Meanwhile, under his own name, the author had published several plays—*Maximilian* (1902), *Althea* (1907), *The Trifler* (1908), *The Leaves of the Tree* (1909), *Eileen* (1910), *The Locket* (1910)—and a set of essays, *The New Star Chamber* (1904).

Although industry is evident in the number and variety of these volumes, there is little to indicate the vigor and driving honesty which propelled the succeeding work. Masters himself felt uncertain of his future, crippled by his environment. "I feel that no poet in English or American history had a harder life than mine was in the beginning at Lewiston," he wrote in his autobiography, *Across Spoon River* (1936), "among a people whose flesh and whose vibrations were better calculated to poison, to pervert, and even to kill a sensitive nature."

Masters left Lewiston for Chicago and became the partner of a famous criminal lawyer. Eight years later, his partner defaulted, professional and political enemies combined against him, and he plunged into the excited Chicago literary "movement" of 1912.

In 1914, Masters, at the suggestion of his friend, William Marion Reedy, turned from his preoccupation with classic subjects and began to draw upon the life he knew from those concise records which made him famous. Taking as his model *The Greek Anthology,* which Reedy had pressed upon him, Masters evolved *Spoon River Anthology,* that astonishing assemblage of over two hundred self-inscribed epitaphs, in which the dead of a Middle Western town are supposed to have written the truth about themselves. Through these frank revelations, many of them interrelated, the village is re-created; it lives again with all its intrigues, hypocrisies, feuds, martyrdoms and occasional exaltations. The monotony of existence in a drab township, the defeat of ideals, the struggle toward higher goals are synthesized in these crowded pages. All moods and all manner of voices are heard here—even Masters', who explains the selection of his form through "Petit, the Poet."

The success of the volume was extraordinary. With every new attack (and its frankness continued to make fresh enemies) its readers increased. It was imitated, parodied, reviled as "a piece of yellow journalism"; it was hailed as "an American

Comédie Humaine." Finally, after the storm of controversy, it has taken its place as a landmark in American literature.

With *Spoon River Anthology* Masters arrived—and left. He went back to his first rhetorical style, resurrecting many of his earlier trifles, reprinting dull echoes of Tennyson, imitations of Shelley, archaic paraphrases in the manner of Swinburne. Yet, though none of Masters' subsequent volumes can be compared to his masterpiece, all of them contain passages of the same straightforwardness and the stubborn searching that intensified his best-known characterizations.

Songs and Satires (1916) includes the startling "All Life in a Life" and the gravely moving "Silence." *The Great Valley* (1917) is packed with echoes and a growing dependence on Browning. In *Toward the Gulf* (1918), the Browning influence predominates. *Starved Rock* (1919), *Domesday Book* (1920) and *The New Spoon River* (1924) are queerly assembled mixtures of good, bad, and derivative verse. These volumes prepared us for the novels which, in their mixture of sharp concept and dull writing, were as uneven as his verse. *The Fate of the Jury* (1929) is a continuation of *Domesday Book* with its mechanics suggested by *The Ring and the Book*, large in outline, feeble in detail. *Godbey* (1931) is a dramatic poem containing six thousand lines of rhymed verse with a few sharply projected ideas, an occasionally vivid scene, and literally thousands of pedestrian couplets given over to debate and diatribe. *Invisible Landscapes* (1935) contains several ambitious poems devoted to varying manifestations of Nature, but they are impressive chiefly in length. One has only to compare Masters' "Hymn to Earth" with Elinor Wylie's poem of the same title to realize the difference between clairvoyance and dullness.

Between 1935 and 1938 Masters was more prolific than ever. In less than three years he published a long autobiography, a novel, three biographies, three books of poems—eight volumes of declining merit. One of them, *The New World* (1937), was a quasi-epic which attempted to synthesize history and philosophy, law and literature, *Poems of People* (1936) was the best of the six; it marked a return to Masters' power of characterization plus a wider range than he had ever accomplished. The manner was equally varied, alternating from the gracefully lyrical "Week-End by the Sea" to the deeply etched "Widows," which contrasts the women living in "forsakeness and listless ease" with their menial sisters.

More People (1939) again reveals Masters as a grim historian of American life, lonely and bitter, but frequently turning the minutiae of history into poetry. The prairie section where Masters was born and where he grew up is spread out in the indigenous *Illinois Poems* (1941), in which the poet demonstrates his early environment and his late nostalgia. In spite of his repetitions and rhetoric, Masters' work is a continual if irritable quest for some key to the mystery of truth and the mastery of life. And there is always that milestone, the original *Spoon River Anthology*.

In 1930 Masters had moved East. He died in Philadelphia, March 5, 1950.

WEEK-END BY THE SEA

I

Far off the sea is gray and still as the sky,
Great waves roar to the shore like conch shells water-groined.

With a flapping coat I step, brace back as the wind drags by;
No ship as far as the seam where the sea and the sky are joined.

I am watched from the hotel, I think. Who faces the cold?
Why does he walk alone? 'Tis a bitter day.
But I trade dreams with the sea, for the sea is old,
And knows the dreams of a heart whose dreams are gray.

Two apple trees alone in the waste on a sandy ledge,
Grappled and woven together with sprouts in a blackened mesh,
They are dead almost at the roots, but nourish the sedge;
They are dead and at truce, like souls of outlived flesh.

I have startled a gull to flight. I thought him a wave:
White of his wings seemed foam, breast hued like the sand-hued roll.
When a part of the sea takes wing you would think that the grave
Of dead days might release to the heights a soul.

II

I slept as the day was ending: scarlet and gilt
Behind the Japan screen of shrubs and trees.
I awoke to the scabbard of night and the starry hilt
Of the sunken sun, to the old unease.

Sleeping, a void in my heart is awake;
Waking, there is the moon and the wind's moan.
I would I were as the sea that can break
Over the rocks, indifferent and alone.

III

I have climbed to the little burial plot of the lost
In wrecks at sea. West of me lies the town.
Below are the apple trees, pulling each other down.
Children are romping to school, ruddy from frost.

How the wind grieves around these weedy wisps,
And shakes them like a dog, sniffing from patch to patch.
I try the battered gate, lift up the latch,
And enter where the grass like a thistle lisps.

Lost at sea! Nothing thought out or planned!
What need? Thought enough in a moment that battles a wave!
What words tell more? And where is the hand to 'grave
Words that tell so much for the lost on land?

WIDOWS

For twenty years and more surviving after
Their husbands have been hidden away,
Gray, old, thin, or obese, day after day
Pillowed in luxury, waking with quavering laughter
From the drowsiness of midday food,
They sit, fingering long strands of crystals,
Reading a little in a waking mood;

Or waiting for the postman with epistles,
Or for telephones, or callers coming to tea.
Bonds, stocks, are theirs; or pensions it may be,
Since the long-dead husband, under-salaried,
Helped to subdue some barbarous isle;
Now that he lies with the half-forgotten dead,
His widow draws an honorarium,
To prop her prestige yet a little while.
The public treasury is rich, and feels
The drain but little; yet it is a sum
Which would relieve the anxious mind whose zeals
For thought and progress dread the time to come.

In the hives of all the cities, high above
The smoke and noise, where the air is pure,
Are numberless widows, comfortable and secure,
Protected by the watchman and God's love;
Saved by the Church, and by the lawyer served,
And by the actor, dancer, novelist amused.
Some practise poetry; some, who are younger nerved,
Dabble in sculpture; but all are used
To win the attention of celebrities
At dinners, or at the opera, to imbibe
The high vitality of purchased devotees.
But when not modeling, or scribbling verse,
Nor drinking tea, nor tottering forth to dine,
They sit concocting some new bribe
To life for soul relief; they count what's in their purse;
They stare at the window half asleep from wine
Or poppy juice; they wait the luncheon hour;
They visit with their maids; or they receive
The heads of research schools, the which they dower,
Or magazines, the better to achieve
A place in memory or a present power;
Or out of social bitterness they dictate
The policies of journals, and compel
Adherence to their husbands' inveterate
Violence, like souls that brood in hell.
From rents and funds, prescriptions, old mortmains
They gather with fingers brown from moldy spots
Exhaustless gold, with which they feed the veins
Of palsied privilege, and they foil the plots
Of living generations against the dying brains.

The hives of all the cities are full of these
Widows, who in a complexity of combs
Live in forsakeness and listless ease:
All is deserted about them in such homes.
Long has the rain fallen, and the snow been piled
On the man under the trees outdoors;
Even the bones in granite domiciled
Have fallen apart—but still the widow sits

By the window resting above the city's floors.
The drone, the gadfly, or the hornet flits
About her lifeless hive; and she may gasp
Beholding at times the black bees of the rites
Of dead men, drag a fallen bee or wasp
To the outdoors of rain or starry nights.
And then she shudders, knowing the time is soon
When the chauffeur of the ebon car will call
To take her from the city where the moon
Will eye the loneliness of hills; and all
Her crystal necklaces and possessions will be strewn;
And all the rentals of her lands,
And dividends will re-assume with wings
New shapes before the same insatiate hands.

And in the city there are numberless women,
Widows grown old and lame, who scrub, or wait
On entrance doors, or cook; whose lonely fate
Is part of the city's pageant, part of the human
Necessity, victims of profligate
Or unprevisioned life! They have no spoil,
No dividends, and no power of subsidy
Over the world of care and poverty;
They have but patience and a little room,
Patience and the withered hands of toil.

PETIT, THE POET

Seeds in a dry pod, tick, tick, tick,
Tick, tick, tick, like mites in a quarrel—
Faint iambics that the full breeze wakens—
But the pine tree makes a symphony thereof.
Triolets, villanelles, rondels, rondeaus.
Ballades by the score with the same old thought:
The snows and the roses of yesterday are vanished;
And what is love but a rose that fades?
Life all around me here in the village:
Tragedy, comedy, valor and truth,
Courage, constancy, heroism, failure—
All in the loom, and, oh, what patterns!
Woodlands, meadows, streams and rivers—
Blind to all of it all my life long.
Triolets, villanelles, rondels, rondeaus,
Seeds in a dry pod, tick, tick, tick,
Tick, tick, tick, what little iambics,
While Homer and Whitman roared in the pines!

LUCINDA MATLOCK

I went to the dances at Chandlerville,
And played snap-out at Winchester.
One time we changed partners.

Driving home in the moonlight of middle June,
And then I found Davis.
We were married and lived together for seventy years,
Enjoying, working, raising the twelve children,
Eight of whom we lost
Ere I had reached the age of sixty.
I spun, I wove, I kept the house, I nursed the sick,
I made the garden, and for holiday
Rambled over the fields where sang the larks,
And by Spoon River gathering many a shell,
And many a flower and medicinal weed—
Shouting to the wooded hills, singing to the green valleys.
At ninety-six I had lived enough, that is all,
And passed to a sweet repose.
What is this I hear of sorrow and weariness,
Anger, discontent and drooping hopes?
Degenerate sons and daughters,
Life is too strong for you—
It takes life to love Life.

ANNE RUTLEDGE

Out of me unworthy and unknown
The vibrations of deathless music:
"With malice toward none, with charity for all."
Out of me the forgiveness of millions toward millions,
And the beneficent face of a nation
Shining with justice and truth.
I am Anne Rutledge who sleep beneath these weeds,
Beloved in life of Abraham Lincoln,
Wedded to him, not through union,
But through separation.
Bloom forever, O Republic,
From the dust of my bosom!

SILENCE

I have known the silence of the stars and of the sea,
And the silence of the city when it pauses,
And the silence of a man and a maid,
And the silence for which music alone finds the word,
And the silence of the woods before the winds of spring begin,
And the silence of the sick
When their eyes roam about the room.
And I ask: For the depths
Of what use is language?
A beast of the field moans a few times
When death takes its young.
And we are voiceless in the presence of realities—
We cannot speak.

A curious boy asks an old soldier
Sitting in front of the grocery store,
"How did you lose your leg?"
And the old soldier is struck with silence,
Or his mind flies away
Because he cannot concentrate it on Gettysburg.
It comes back jocosely
And he says, "A bear bit it off."
And the boy wonders, while the old soldier
Dumbly, feebly lives over
The flashes of guns, the thunder of cannon,
The shrieks of the slain,
And himself lying on the ground,
And the hospital surgeons, the knives,
And the long days in bed.
But if he could describe it all
He would be an artist.
But if he were an artist there would be deeper wounds
Which he could not describe.

There is the silence of a great hatred,
And the silence of a great love,
And the silence of a deep peace of mind,
And the silence of an embittered friendship,
There is the silence of a spiritual crisis,
Through which your soul, exquisitely tortured,
Comes with visions not to be uttered
Into a realm of higher life.
And the silence of the gods who understand each other without speech,
There is the silence of defeat.
There is the silence of those unjustly punished;
And the silence of the dying whose hand
Suddenly grips yours.
There is the silence between father and son,
When the father cannot explain his life,
Even though he be misunderstood for it.

There is the silence that comes between husband and wife.
There is the silence of those who have failed;
And the vast silence that covers
Broken nations and vanquished leaders.
There is the silence of Lincoln,
Thinking of the poverty of his youth.
And the silence of Napoleon
After Waterloo.
And the silence of Jeanne d'Arc
Saying amid the flames, "Blessèd Jesus"—
Revealing in two words all sorrow, all hope.
And there is the silence of age,
Too full of wisdom for the tongue to utter it
In words intelligible to those who have not lived
The great range of life.

And there is the silence of the dead.
If we who are in life cannot speak
Of profound experiences,
Why do you marvel that the dead
Do not tell you of death?
Their silence shall be interpreted
As we approach them.

Stephen Crane

⤙§ Stephen Crane, whose literary career was one of the most meteoric in American letters, was born in Newark, New Jersey, November 1, 1871. After taking a partial course at Lafayette College, he entered journalism at sixteen and, until the time of his death, was a reporter and writer of newspaper sketches. When he died prematurely, at the age of thirty, he had ten printed volumes to his credit, two more announced for publication, and two others which were appearing serially.

Crane's most famous novel, *The Red Badge of Courage* (1895), was a *tour de force,* written when he was twenty-two years old. What is even more astonishing is the fact that this detailed description of blood and battlefields was written by a civilian far from the scene of conflict. *The Atlantic Monthly* pronounced it "great enough to set a new fashion in literature"; H. G. Wells, speaking of its influence in England, said Crane was "the first expression of the opening mind of a new period . . . a record of intensity beyond all precedent."

Crane's other books, although less powerful than *The Red Badge of Courage,* are scarcely less vivid. *The Open Boat* (1898) and *The Monster* (1899) are full of an intuitive wisdom and a passionate sensitivity that caused Wells to exclaim, "The man who can call these 'brilliant fragments' would reproach Rodin for not 'completing' his fragments."

At various periods in Crane's brief career, he experimented in verse, seeking to find new effects in unrhymed lines, a new acuteness of symbol and vision. The results were embodied in two volumes of unusual poetry—*The Black Riders* (1895) and *War Is Kind* (1899), lines that strangely anticipated the Imagists and the elliptical free verse that followed fifteen years later. Acidulous and biting, these concisions were unappreciated in his day; Crane's suggestive verse has not yet received its due in an age which employs its very technique. But it was forty years before Emily Dickinson won her rightful audience, and a quarter of a century passed before a publisher risked a *Complete Works of Stephen Crane.* It was not until 1930 that a *Collected Poems* appeared.

Besides novels, short stories and poems, Crane was writing, at the time of his death, descriptions of the world's great battles for *Lippincott's Magazine;* his droll *Whilomville Stories* for boys were appearing in *Harper's Monthly,* and he was beginning a series of similar stories for girls. It is more than probable that this feverish energy of production aggravated the illness that caused Crane's death. He died of tuberculosis in the German Black Forest, June 5, 1900.

I SAW A MAN

I saw a man pursuing the horizon;
Round and round they sped.
I was disturbed at this;
I accosted the man.
"It is futile," I said,
"You can never—"
"You lie," he cried,
And ran on.

THE WAYFARER

The wayfarer,
Perceiving the pathway to truth,
Was struck with astonishment.
It was thickly grown with weeds.
"Ha," he said,
"I see that no one has passed here
In a long time."
Later he saw that each weed
Was a singular knife.
"Well," he mumbled at last,
"Doubtless there are other roads."

HYMN

A slant of sun on dull brown walls,
A forgotten sky of bashful blue.

Toward God a mighty hymn,
A song of collisions and cries,
Rumbling wheels, hoof-beats, bells,
Welcomes, farewells, love-calls, final moans,
Voices of joy, idiocy, warning, despair,
The unknown appeals of brutes,
The chanting of flowers,
The screams of cut trees,
The senseless babble of hens and wise men—
A cluttered incoherency that says to the stars:
"O God, save us!"

THE BLADES OF GRASS

In Heaven,
Some little blades of grass
Stood before God.
"What did you do?"
Then all save one of the little blades
Began eagerly to relate
The merits of their lives.
This one stayed a small way behind,
Ashamed.

Presently, God said,
"And what did you do?"
The little blade answered, "Oh, my Lord,
Memory is bitter to me,
For, if I did good deeds,
I know not of them."
Then God, in all his splendor,
Arose from his throne.
"Oh, best little blade of grass!" he said.

THE BOOK OF WISDOM

I met a seer.
He held in his hands
The book of wisdom.
"Sir," I addressed him,
"Let me read."
"Child—" he began.
"Sir," I said.
"Think not that I am a child,
For already I know much
Of that which you hold;
Aye, much."

He smiled.
Then he opened the book
And held it before me.
Strange that I should have grown so suddenly blind.

THE CANDID MAN

Forth went the candid man
And spoke freely to the wind—
When he looked about him he was in a far strange country.

Forth went the candid man
And spoke freely to the stars—
Yellow light tore sight from his eyes.

"My good fool," said a learned bystander,
"Your operations are mad."

"You are too candid," cried the candid man.
And when his stick left the head of the learned bystander
It was two sticks.

THE HEART

In the desert
I saw a creature, naked, bestial,
Who, squatting upon the ground,
Held his heart in his hands,
And ate of it.
I said, "Is it good, friend?"
"It is bitter—bitter," he answered;
"But I like it
Because it is bitter,
And because it is my heart."

THERE WAS A MAN

There was a man with a tongue of wood
Who essayed to sing,
And in truth it was lamentable.
But there was one who heard
The clip-clapper of this tongue of wood
And knew what the man
Wished to sing,
And with that the singer was content.

A LEARNED MAN

A learned man came to me once.
He said, "I know the way—come."
And I was overjoyed at this.
Together we hastened.
Soon, too soon, were we
Where my eyes were useless,
And I knew not the ways of my feet.
I clung to the hand of my friend;
But at last he cried, "I am lost."

A YOUTH

A youth in apparel that glittered
Went to walk in a grim forest.
There he met an assassin
Attired all in garb of old days;
He, scowling through the thickets,
And dagger poised quivering,
Rushed upon the youth.
"Sir," said the latter,
"I am enchanted, believe me,
To die, thus,
In this mediæval fashion,
According to the best legends;
Ah, what joy!"
Then took he the wound, smiling,
And died, content.

James Weldon Johnson

☙ James Weldon Johnson was born in Jacksonville, Florida, June 17, 1871. He was educated at Atlanta University and at Columbia University, where he received his A.M. He was principal of the colored high school in Jacksonville, was admitted to the Florida bar in 1897, and in 1901 removed to New York City, where he collaborated with his brother J. Rosamond Johnson in writing for vaudeville and the light opera stage. He served seven years as United States Consul in Venezuela and Nicaragua, became secretary of the National Association for Advancement of Colored People, and occupied the chair of Creative Literature at Fisk University. His version of the libretto of *Goyescas* was produced at the Metropolitan Opera House in 1915. His death came suddenly and tragically; his automobile was struck by a railroad train near Wiscasset, Maine, June 26, 1938.

His first book of verse *Fifty Years and Other Poems* (1918) contains much that is meretricious and facile; but, half buried in the midst of clichés, there is not only the humor but the stern pathos characteristic of the Negro as singer. This quality was pronounced in *God's Trombones* (1927), Johnson's richest book of poems. The volume consists of seven Negro sermons in verse, done after the manner of the old Negro plantation sermons. In these poems the folk-stuff is used much as a composer might use folk-themes in writing a larger musical composition. "The Creation" and "Go Down, Death," in particular are large in conception; sonorous, strongly rhythmical free verse, reflecting the unctuous periods, the uninhibited imagery of the plantation preacher. They and, in a lesser degree, the other poems in *God's Trombones,* are a rambling mixture of Biblical and tropical figures, but always an artistically governed expression.

Saint Peter Relates an Incident of the Resurrection Day (privately distributed in 1930 and re-issued, with other poems, for general circulation in 1935) is a stirring expression in which irony masks a sense of outrage. Johnson was at work on the manuscript of a book when he picked up a newspaper and read that the government was sending to France a contingent of Gold Star mothers whose soldier sons were buried there, but that the Negro Gold Star mothers would not be allowed to sail on the ship with the white mothers. He threw the manuscript he was writing aside and did not take it up until he had finished the long satirical poem.

Among Johnson's other work are the novel *The Autobiography of an Ex-Colored Man* (1912, republished in 1927), *Black Manhattan* (1930), the story of the Negro in New York, and the eloquent autobiography *Along This Way* (1933). He also collaborated with his brother in the two collections of American Negro Spirituals in 1925 and 1926 and edited *The Book of American Negro Poetry.*

THE CREATION

(A Negro Sermon)

And God stepped out on space,
And He looked around and said,
"I'm lonely—
I'll make me a world."

And far as the eye of God could see
Darkness covered everything,
Blacker than a hundred midnights
Down in a cypress swamp.

Then God smiled,
And the light broke,
And the darkness rolled up on one side,
And the light stood shining on the other,
And God said, *"That's good!"*

Then God reached out and took the light in His hands,
And God rolled the light around in His hands,
Until He made the sun;
And He set that sun a-blazing in the heavens.
And the light that was left from making the sun
God gathered up in a shining ball
And flung against the darkness,
Spangling the night with the moon and stars.
Then down between
The darkness and the light
He hurled the world;
And God said, *"That's good!"*

Then God himself stepped down—
And the sun was on His right hand,
And the moon was on His left;
The stars were clustered about His head,
And the earth was under His feet.
And God walked, and where He trod
His footsteps hollowed the valleys out
And bulged the mountains up.

Then He stopped and looked and saw
That the earth was hot and barren.
So God stepped over to the edge of the world
And He spat out the seven seas;
He batted His eyes, and the lightnings flashed;
He clapped His hands, and the thunders rolled;
And the waters above the earth came down,
The cooling waters came down.

Then the green grass sprouted,
And the little red flowers blossomed,
The pine-tree pointed his finger to the sky,
And the oak spread out his arms;
The lakes cuddled down in the hollows of the ground,
And the rivers ran down to the sea;
And God smiled again,
And the rainbow appeared,
And curled itself around His shoulder.

Then God raised His arm and He waved His hand
Over the sea and over the land,
And He said, *"Bring forth! Bring forth!"*
And quicker than God could drop His hand,
Fishes and fowls
And beast and birds
Swam the rivers and the seas,
Roamed the forests and the woods,
And split the air with their wings,
And God said, *"That's good!"*

Then God walked around
And God looked around
On all that He had made.
He looked at His sun,
And He looked at His moon,
And He looked at His little stars;
He looked on His world
With all its living things,
And God said, *"I'm lonely still."*

Then God sat down
On the side of a hill where He could think;
By a deep, wide river He sat down;
With His head in His hands,
God thought and thought,
Till He thought, *"I'll make me a man!"*

Up from the bed of the river
God scooped the clay;
And by the bank of the river
He kneeled Him down;
And there the great God Almighty,
Who lit the sun and fixed it in the sky,
Who flung the stars to the most far corner of the night,
Who rounded the earth in the middle of His hand—
This Great God,
Like a mammy bending over her baby,
Kneeled down in the dust
Toiling over a lump of clay
Till He shaped it in His own image;
Then into it He blew the breath of life,
And man became a living soul.
Amen. Amen.

Anna Hempstead Branch

Anna Hempstead Branch was born at New London, Connecticut. She was graduated from Smith College in 1897 and devoted herself to literature and social service, mostly in New York. She died in her home September 8, 1937.

Her two chief volumes, *The Shoes That Danced* (1905) and *Rose of the Wind* (1910), reveal the lyrist, but they show a singer who is less fanciful than philosophic. A typical poem is "The Monk in the Kitchen," which is a celebration of cleanness that gives order an almost mystical nobility and recalls George Herbert.

Although nothing she has ever written has attained the popularity of her shorter works, "Nimrod" has an epic sweep, a large movement which, within the greater curve, contains moments of exalted imagery. The deeply religious feeling implicit governs the author as person no less than as poet, for Miss Branch had given a great part of her life to settlement work at Christadora House on New York's East Side. "To a Dog" is more direct than is Miss Branch's wont; "The Monk in the Kitchen" is no less straightforward, though its metaphysics make it seem less forthright.

THE MONK IN THE KITCHEN

I

Order is a lovely thing;
On disarray it lays its wing,
Teaching simplicity to sing.
It has a meek and lowly grace,
Quiet as a nun's face.
Lo—I will have thee in this place!
Tranquil well of deep delight,
All things that shine through thee appear
As stones through water, sweetly clear.
Thou clarity,
That with angelic charity
Revealest beauty where thou art,
Spread thyself like a clean pool.
Then all the things that in thee are,
Shall seem more spiritual and fair,
Reflection from serener air—
Sunken shapes of many a star
In the high heavens set afar.

II

Yet stolid, homely, visible things,
Above you all brood glorious wings
Of your deep entities, set high,
Like slow moons in a hidden sky.
But you, their likenesses, are spent
Upon another element.
Truly ye are but seemings—
The shadowy cast-off gleamings
Of bright solidities. Ye seem
Soft as water, vague as dream;
Image, cast in a shifting stream.

III

What are ye?
I know not.
Brazen pan and iron pot,
Yellow brick and gray flagstone
That my feet have trod upon—
Ye seem to me
Vessels of bright mystery
For ye do bear a shape, and so
Though ye were made by man, I know
An inner Spirit also made,
And ye his breathings have obeyed.

IV

Shape, the strong and awful Spirit,
Laid his ancient hand on you.
He waste chaos doth inherit;
He can alter and subdue.
Verily, he doth lift up
Matter, like a sacred cup.
Into deep substance he reached, and lo
Where ye were not, ye were; and so
Out of useless nothing, ye
Groaned and laughed and came to be,
And I use you, as I can,

Wonderful uses, made for man,
Iron pot and brazen pan.

V

What are ye?
I know not;
Nor what I really do
When I move and govern you.
There is no small work unto God.
He required of us greatness;
Of his least creature
A high angelic nature,
Stature superb and bright completeness.
He sets to us no humble duty.
Each act that he would have us do
Is haloed round with strangest beauty;
Terrific deeds and cosmic tasks
Of his plainest child he asks.
When I polish the brazen pan
I hear a creature laugh afar
In the gardens of a star,
And from his burning presence run
Flaming wheels of many a sun.
Whoever makes a thing more bright,
He is an angel of all light.
When I cleanse this earthen floor
My spirit leaps to see
Bright garments trailing over it,
A cleanness made by me.
Purger of all men's thoughts and ways,
With labor do I sound Thy praise,
My work is done for Thee.
Whoever makes a thing more bright,
He is an angel of all light.
Therefore let me spread abroad
The beautiful cleanness of my God.

VI

One time in the cool of dawn
Angels came and worked with me.
The air was soft with many a wing.
They laughed amid my solitude
And cast bright looks on everything.
Sweetly of me did they ask
That they might do my common task.
And all were beautiful—but one
With garments whiter than the sun
Had such a face
Of deep, remembered grace;
That when I saw I cried—"Thou art
The great Blood-Brother of my heart.
Where have I seen thee?"—And he said,
"When we were dancing round God's throne,
How often thou art there.
Beauties from thy hands have flown
Like white doves wheeling in mid-air.
Nay—thy soul remembers not?
Work on, and cleanse thy iron pot."

VII

What are we? I know not.

Amy Lowell

Amy Lowell was born in Brookline, Massachusetts, February 9, 1874, of a long line of quoted publicists and poets; the first colonist (a Percival Lowell) arrived in Newburyport in 1637. James Russell Lowell was a cousin of her grandfather; Abbott Lawrence, her mother's father, was minister to England; Percival Lowell, the astronomer who charted the conjectural canals on Mars, was a brother; and Abbott Lawrence Lowell, her other brother, was president of Harvard University.

Miss Lowell obtained her early education through private tuition and travel abroad. It was not until 1902, when she was twenty-eight years old, that she definitely determined to be a poet. For eight years she served a rigorous apprenticeship, reading the classics of all schools, studying the technique of verse. In 1910 her first poem was printed in *The Atlantic Monthly;* two years later her first book appeared.

This volume, *A Dome of Many-colored Glass* (1912), was a strangely unpromising first book. Subject and treatment were conventional; the influence of Keats and

Tennyson was evident; the tone was soft and sentimental, without a trace of personality. It was a queer prologue to the vivid *Sword Blades and Poppy Seed* (1914), which marked not only an extraordinary advance but a new individuality. This second volume contained many poems written in the usual forms, a score of pictorial pieces illustrating Miss Lowell's identification with the Imagists, and, possibly most important from a technical standpoint, the first appearance in English of "polyphonic prose." Of this extremely flexible form, Miss Lowell, in an essay on John Gould Fletcher, wrote, " 'Polyphonic' means 'many-voiced,' and the form is so-called because it makes use of the 'voices' of poetry, namely: meter, *vers libre,* assonance, alliteration, rhyme and return. It employs every form of rhythm, even prose rhythm at times." By this time Miss Lowell had "captured" the Imagist movement from Ezra Pound, had reorganized it, and, by her belligerent championing of *vers libre,* freedom of choice of subject, and other seeming innovations, had made poetry a fighting word.

It was because of her experiments in form and technique that Miss Lowell first attracted attention and is still best known. But, beneath a preoccupation with theories and novelty of utterance, there was the skilled story-teller, who revivified history with creative excitement. *Men, Women and Ghosts* (1916) brims with this contagious vitality; it is richer in variety than its predecessors, swifter in movement. It is, in common with all of Miss Lowell's work, best in its portrayal of colors and sounds, of physical perceptions rather than the reactions of inner experience. She is, preeminently, the poet of the external world; her visual effects are as "hard and clear" as the most uncompromising Imagist could desire. The colors with which her works are studded seem like bits of bright enamel; every leaf and flower has a lacquered brilliance. To compensate for the lack of the spirit's warmth, Miss Lowell feverishly agitates all she touches; nothing remains quiescent. Whether she writes about a fruit shop, or a flower-garden, or a string quartet, or a Japanese print—everything flashes, leaps, startles, and burns with dynamic, almost savage, speed. Motion too often takes the place of emotion.

In *Can Grande's Castle* (1918) Miss Lowell achieves a broader line; the teller of stories, the bizarre decorator, and the experimenter finally fuse. The poems in this volume are only four in number—four polyphonic prose-poems of unusual length, extraordinarily varied in their sense of amplitude and time. *Pictures of the Floating World* (1919) which followed is, in many ways, Miss Lowell's most personal revelation. Although there are pages devoted to the merely dazzling and grotesque, most of the poems are in a quieter key.

Legends (1921) is closely related to *Can Grande's Castle;* eleven stories are placed against seven different backgrounds. The first poem must be rated among Miss Lowell's most dazzling achievements: a *tour de force* with colors as strange and metallic as the scene it pictures. The next years were devoted to her Keats researches.

Besides Miss Lowell's original poetry, she undertook many studies in foreign literatures; she made the English versions of the poems translated from the Chinese by Florence Ayscough in the vivid *Fir-Flower Tablets* (1921). She also wrote two volumes of critical essays: *Six French Poets* (1915) and *Tendencies in Modern American Poetry* (1917), valuable aids to the student of contemporary literature. Two years after its publication she acknowledged the authorship of the anonymous *A Critical Fable* (1922), a modern sequel to James Russell Lowell's *A Fable for Critics.*

Her monumental *John Keats,* an exhaustive biography and analysis of the poet in two volumes, appeared early in 1925.

For years Miss Lowell had been suffering from ill health; she had been operated upon several times, but her general condition, as well as her continual desire to work, nullified the effects of the operations. In April, 1925, her condition became worse; she was forced to cancel a projected lecture trip through England and to cease all work. She died as the result of a paralytic stroke on May 12, 1925. Her death occasioned nation-wide tributes; the very journals which had ridiculed her during her life were loud in praise: it was agreed that hers was one of the most daring and picturesque figures in contemporary literature. Like all pioneers, she was the target of scorn and hostility; but, unlike most innovators, she lived to see her experiments rise from the limbo of ridicule to a definite place in their period.

Three posthumous volumes appeared at yearly intervals immediately after her death: *What's O'Clock* (1925) which was awarded the Pulitzer Prize for that year, *East Wind* (1926), and *Ballads for Sale* (1927). The first was arranged by the poet herself and includes such poems as "Meeting-House Hill" and "Lilacs" which are tart and native; the second is a set of dialect and highly overdramatized New England narratives; the third is a miscellaneous collection.

A comprehensive biography of the poet as storm center was published in 1935 by S. Foster Damon.

MEETING-HOUSE HILL

I must be mad, or very tired,
When the curve of a blue bay beyond a railroad track
Is shrill and sweet to me like the sudden springing of a tune,
And the sight of a white church above thin trees in a city square
Amazes my eyes as though it were the Parthenon.
Clear, reticent, superbly final,
With the pillars of its portico refined to a cautious elegance,
It dominates the weak trees,
And the shot of its spire
Is cool and candid,
Rising into an unresisting sky.

Strange meeting-house
Pausing a moment upon a squalid hill-top.
I watch the spire sweeping the sky,
I am dizzy with the movement of the sky;
I might be watching a mast
With its royals set full
Straining before a two-reef breeze.
I might be sighting a tea-clipper,
Tacking into the blue bay,
Just back from Canton
With her hold full of green and blue porcelain
And a Chinese coolie leaning over the rail
Gazing at the white spire
With dull, sea-spent eyes.

A LADY

You are beautiful and faded,
Like an old opera tune
Played upon a harpsichord;
Or like the sun-flooded silks
Of an eighteenth-century boudoir.
In your eyes
Smolder the fallen roses of outlived minutes,
And the perfume of your soul
Is vague and suffusing,
With the pungence of sealed spice-jars.
Your half-tones delight me,
And I grow mad with gazing
At your blent colors.

My vigor is a new minted penny,
Which I cast at your feet.
Gather it up from the dust
That its sparkle may amuse you.

SOLITAIRE

When night drifts along the streets of the city,
And sifts down between the uneven roofs,
My mind begins to peek and peer.
It plays at ball in odd, blue Chinese gardens,
And shakes wrought dice-cups in Pagan temples
Amid the broken flutings of white pillars.
It dances with purple and yellow crocuses in its hair,
And its feet shine as they flutter over drenched grasses.
How light and laughing my mind is,
When all good folk have put out their bedroom candles,
And the city is still.

PATTERNS

I walk down the garden-paths,
And all the daffodils
Are blowing, and the bright blue squills.
I walk down the patterned garden-paths
In my stiff, brocaded gown.
With my powdered hair and jeweled fan,
I too am a rare
Pattern. As I wander down
The garden-paths.

My dress is richly figured,
And the train
Makes a pink and silver stain
On the gravel, and the thrift

Of the borders.
Just a plate of current fashion,
Tripping by in high-heeled, ribboned shoes.
Not a softness anywhere about me,
Only whalebone and brocade.
And I sink on a seat in the shade
Of a lime tree. For my passion
Wars against the stiff brocade.
The daffodils and squills
Flutter in the breeze
As they please.
And I weep;
For the lime-tree is in blossom
And one small flower has dropped upon my bosom.

And the plashing of waterdrops
In the marble fountain
Comes down the garden-paths.
The dripping never stops.
Underneath my stiffened gown
Is the softness of a woman bathing in a marble basin,
A basin in the midst of hedges grown
So thick, she cannot see her lover hiding,
But she guesses he is near,
And the sliding of the water
Seems the stroking of a dear
Hand upon her.
What is Summer in a fine brocaded gown!
I should like to see it lying in a heap upon the ground.
All the pink and silver crumpled up on the ground.

I would be the pink and silver as I ran along the paths,
And he would stumble after,
Bewildered by my laughter.
I should see the sun flashing from his sword-hilt and the buckles on his shoes
I would choose
To lead him in a maze along the patterned paths,
A bright and laughing maze for my heavy-booted lover.
Till he caught me in the shade,
And the buttons of his waistcoat bruised my body as he clasped me,
Aching, melting, unafraid.
With the shadows of the leaves and the sundrops,
And the plopping of the waterdrops,
All about us in the open afternoon—
I am very like to swoon
With the weight of this brocade,
For the sun sifts through the shade.

Underneath the fallen blossom
In my bosom
Is a letter I have hid.
It was brought to me this morning by a rider from the Duke.

"Madam, we regret to inform you that Lord Hartwell
Died in action Thursday se'nnight."
As I read it in the white, morning sunlight,
The letters squirmed like snakes.
"Any answer, Madam," said my footman.
"No," I told him.
"See that the messenger takes some refreshment.
No, no answer."
And walked into the garden,
Up and down the patterned paths,
In my stiff, correct brocade.
The blue and yellow flowers stood up proudly in the sun,
Each one.
I stood upright too,
Held rigid to the pattern
By the stiffness of my gown;
Up and down I walked,
Up and down.

In a month he would have been my husband.
In a month, here, underneath this lime,
We would have broke the pattern;
He for me, and I for him,
He as Colonel, I as Lady,
On this shady seat.
He had a whim
That sunlight carried blessing.
And I answered, "It shall be as you have said."
Now he is dead.

In Summer and in Winter I shall walk
Up and down
The patterned garden-paths
In my stiff, brocaded gown.
The squills and daffodils
Will give place to pillared roses, and to asters, and to snow.
I shall go
Up and down
In my gown.
Gorgeously arrayed,
Boned and stayed.
And the softness of my body will be guarded from embrace
By each button, hook, and lace.
For the man who should loose me is dead,
Fighting with the Duke in Flanders,
In a pattern called a war.
Christ! What are patterns for?

WIND AND SILVER

Greatly shining,
The Autumn moon floats in the thin sky;
And the fish-ponds shake their backs and flash their dragon scales
As she passes over them.

NIGHT CLOUDS

The white mares of the moon rush along the sky
Beating their golden hoofs upon the glass Heavens;
The white mares of the moon are all standing on their hind legs
Pawing at the green porcelain doors of the remote Heavens.
Fly, mares!
Strain your utmost,
Scatter the milky dust of stars,
Or the tiger sun will leap upon you and destroy you
With one lick of his vermilion tongue.

FREE FANTASIA ON JAPANESE THEMES

All the afternoon there has been a chirping of birds,
And the sun lies warm and still on the western sides of swollen branches,
There is no wind;
Even the little twigs at the ends of the branches do not move,
And the needles of the pines are solid
Bands of inarticulated blackness
Against the blue-white sky,
Still, but alert;
And my heart is still and alert,
Passive with sunshine,
Avid of adventure.

I would experience new emotions,
Submit to strange enchantments,
Bend to influences
Bizarre, exotic,
Fresh with burgeoning.
I would climb a sacred mountain
Struggle with other pilgrims up a steep path through pine-trees,
Above to the smooth, treeless slopes,
And prostrate myself before a painted shrine,
Beating my hands upon the hot earth,
Quieting my eyes upon the distant sparkle
Of the faint spring sea.

I would recline upon a balcony
In purple curving folds of silk,
And my dress should be silvered with a pattern
Of butterflies and swallows,
And the black band of my *obi*
Should flash with gold circular threads,

And glitter when I moved.
I would lean against the railing
While you sang to me of wars
Past and to come—
Sang, and played the samisen.
Perhaps I would beat a little hand drum
In time to your singing;
Perhaps I would only watch the play of light
Upon the hilt of your two swords.

I would sit in a covered boat,
Rocking slowly to the narrow waves of a river,
While above us, an arc of moving lanterns,
Curved a bridge,
A hiss of gold
Blooming out of darkness,
Rockets exploded,
And died in a soft dripping of colored stars.
We would float between the high trestles,
And drift away from other boats,
Until the rockets flared soundless,
And their falling stars hung silent in the sky,
Like wistaria clusters above the ancient entrance of a temple.

I would anything
Rather than this cold paper;
With outside, the quiet sun on the sides of burgeoning branches,
And inside, only my books.

A DECADE

When you came, you were like red wine and honey,
And the taste of you burnt my mouth with its sweetness.
Now you are like morning bread,
Smooth and pleasant.
I hardly taste you at all, for I know your savor;
But I am completely nourished.

LILACS

Lilacs,
False blue,
White,
Purple,
Color of lilac,
Your great puffs of flowers
Are everywhere in this my New England.
Among your heart-shaped leaves
Orange orioles hop like music-box birds and sing
Their little weak soft songs;
In the crooks of your branches
The bright eyes of song sparrows sitting on spotted eggs
Peer restlessly through the light and shadow
Of all Springs.

Lilacs in dooryards
Holding quiet conversations with an early moon;
Lilacs watching a deserted house
Settling sideways into the grass of an old road;
Lilacs, wind-beaten, staggering under a lopsided shock of bloom
Above a cellar dug into a hill.
You are everywhere.
You were everywhere.
You tapped the window when the preacher preached his sermon,
And ran along the road beside the boy going to school.
You stood by pasture-bars to give the cows good milking,
You persuaded the housewife that her dish-pan was of silver
And her husband an image of pure gold.
You flaunted the fragrance of your blossoms
Through the wide doors of Custom Houses—
You, and sandalwood, and tea,
Charging the noses of quill-driving clerks
When a ship was in from China.
You called to them: "Goose-quill men, goose-quill men,
May is a month for flitting,"
Until they writhed on their high stools
And wrote poetry on their letter-sheets behind the propped-up ledgers.
Paradoxical New England clerks,
Writing inventories in ledgers, reading the "Song of Solomon" at night,
So many verses before bedtime,
Because it was the Bible.
The dead fed you
Amid the slant stones of graveyards.
Pale ghosts who planted you
Came in the night time
And let their thin hair blow through your clustered stems.
You are of the green sea,
And of the stone hills which reach a long distance.
You are of elm-shaded streets with little shops where they sell kites and marbles,
You are of great parks where everyone walks and nobody is at home.
You cover the blind sides of greenhouses
And lean over the top to say a hurry-word through the glass
To your friends, the grapes, inside.

Lilacs,
False blue,
White,
Purple,
Color of lilac,
You have forgotten your Eastern origin,
The veiled women with eyes like panthers,
The swollen, aggressive turbans of jeweled Pashas.
Now you are a very decent flower,
A reticent flower,
A curiously clear-cut, candid flower,
Standing beside clean doorways,

Friendly to a house-cat and a pair of spectacles,
Making poetry out of a bit of moonlight
And a hundred or two sharp blossoms.

Maine knows you,
Has for years and years;
New Hampshire knows you,
And Massachusetts
And Vermont.
Cape Cod starts you along the beaches to Rhode Island;
Connecticut takes you from a river to the sea.
You are brighter than apples,
Sweeter than tulips,
You are the great flood of our souls
Bursting above the leaf-shapes of our hearts,
You are the smell of all Summers,
The love of wives and children,
The recollection of the gardens of little children,
You are State Houses and Charters
And the familiar treading of the foot to and fro on a road it knows.
May is lilac here in New England,
May is a thrush singing "Sun up!" on a tip-top ash-tree,
May is white clouds behind pine-trees
Puffed out and marching upon a blue sky.
May is a green as no other,
May is much sun through small leaves,
May is soft earth,
And apple-blossoms,
And windows open to a South wind.
May is a full light wind of lilac
From Canada to Narragansett Bay.

Lilacs,
False blue,
White,
Purple,
Color of lilac,
Heart-leaves of lilac all over New England,
Roots of lilac under all the soil of New England,
Lilac in me because I am New England,
Because my roots are in it,
Because my leaves are of it,
Because my flowers are for it,
Because it is my country
And I speak to it of itself
And sing of it with my own voice
Since certainly it is mine.

THE TAXI

When I go away from you
The world beats dead
Like a slackened drum.
I call out for you against the jutted stars
And shout into the ridges of the wind.
Streets coming fast,
One after the other,
Wedge you away from me,
And the lamps of the city prick my eyes
So that I can no longer see your face.
Why should I leave you,
To wound myself upon the sharp edges of the night?

Robert Frost

◈ Although known as the chief interpreter of New England, Robert (Lee) Frost was born in San Francisco, California, March 26, 1874. His father, born in New Hampshire, taught school, edited a paper, entered politics, and moved to San Francisco where his "copperhead" sympathy with the South led him to christen his son Robert Lee. Frost's mother, after the death of her husband, supported herself and her children by teaching school; bringing the family back East to the towns and hills where, for eight generations, his forefathers had lived and where, much later, Frost was to uphold the tradition by lecturing, accepting an "idle professorship" ("being a sort of poetic radiator") at Amherst, and buying farms in Vermont. After graduating from the high school at Lawrence, Massachusetts in 1892, Frost entered Dartmouth College, where he remained only a few months. The routine of study was too much for him and he decided to earn his living. He became a bobbin-boy in one of the mills at Lawrence. He had already begun to write poetry; a few of his verses had appeared in *The Independent.* But the strange, soil-flavored quality which even then distinguished his lines was not relished by the editors, and the very magazines to which he sent poems that today are famous rejected his verse with unanimity. For twenty years Frost continued to write his highly characteristic work in spite of the discouraging apathy, and for twenty years the poet remained completely unknown.

In 1897, two years after his marriage, Frost moved his family to Cambridge, Massachusetts, entering Harvard in a final determination to achieve culture. This time he followed the curriculum for two years, but at the end of that dry period he stopped trying to learn and started to teach. (Curiously enough, though Frost made light of and even ridiculed his scholarship, his marks in Greek and the classical studies were always exceptionally high.) For three years he followed the family tradition and taught school in New England; he also made shoes, edited a weekly paper, and in 1900 became a farmer at Derry, New Hampshire. During the next eleven years Frost labored to wrest a living from stubborn hills with scant success. Loneliness claimed him for its own; the rocks refused to give him a living; the literary world continued to remain oblivious of his existence. Frost sought a change of environment and, after a few years' teaching at Derry and Plymouth, New Hampshire, sold his farm and, with his wife and four children, sailed for England in September, 1912.

For the first time in his life, Frost moved in a literary world. Groups merged, dissolved and separated overnight; controversy and creation were in the air. A friendship was established with the poets Abercrombie, Brooke and Gibson, a close intimacy with Edward Thomas. Here Frost wrote most of his longer narratives, took his lyrics to a publisher with few hopes, went back to the suburban town of Beaconsfield and turned to other matters. A few months later *A Boy's Will* (1913) was published and Frost was recognized at once as one of the authentic voices of modern poetry.

A Boy's Will is seemingly subjective; in spite of certain reminiscences of Browning it is no set of derivations. In *A Boy's Will* Frost is not yet completely in possession of his own idiom; but the *timbre* is recognizably his. No one but Frost could have written "Reluctance" or "The Tuft of Flowers." Wholly lyrical, this volume, lacking the concentrated emotion of his subsequent works, is a significant introduction to the following book, which became an international classic. Early in 1914, Frost leased a small place in Gloucestershire; in the spring of the same year, *North of Boston* (1914), one of the most intensely American books ever printed, was published in England. (See Preface.) This is, as he has called it, a "book of people." And it is more than that—it is a book of backgrounds as living and dramatic as the people they overshadow. Frost vivifies a stone wall, an empty cottage, a grindstone, a mountain, a forgotten wood-pile left

> To warm the frozen swamp as best it could
> With the slow, smokeless burning of decay.

North of Boston, like its successor, contains much of the finest poetry of our time. Rich in its actualities, richer in its spiritual values, every line moves with the double force of observation and implication. The very first poem in the book illustrates this power of character and symbolism. Although Frost is not arguing for anything in particular, one senses here something more than the enemies of walls. In "Mending Wall," we see two elemental and opposed forces. "Something there is that doesn't love a wall," insists the rebellious spirit; "Good fences make good neighbors," doggedly replies the literal-minded lover of tradition. Here, beneath the whimsical turns and pungency of expression, we have the essence of nationalism versus the internationalist: the struggle, though the poet would be the last to prod the point, between blind obedience to custom and questioning iconoclasm.

So with all of Frost's characters. Like the worn-out incompetent in "The Death of the Hired Man" (one of the finest *genre* pictures of our time), or the autobiographical country boy climbing "black branches up a snow-white trunk toward heaven" in "Birches," or the positive, tight-lipped old lady in "The Black Cottage," or the headlong but laconic Brown of "Brown's Descent," his people are always amplified through the poet's circumlocutory but precise psychology. They remain close to their soil, Frost's monologs and dramatic idyls, written in a conversational blank verse, establish the connection between the vernacular and the language of literature; they remain rooted in realism. But Frost is never a photographic realist. "There are," he once said, "two types of realist—the one who offers a good deal of dirt with his potato to show that it is a real one; and the one who is satisfied with the potato brushed clean. I'm inclined to be the second kind. . . . To me, the thing that art does for life is to clean it, to strip it to form."

In March, 1915, Frost came back to America—to a hill outside of Franconia, New Hampshire. *North of Boston* had been reprinted in the United States and its author, who had left the country an unknown writer, returned to find himself famous. Honors were awarded to him; within ten years one university after another conferred degrees upon him who was unwilling to graduate from any of them; he became "professor in residence" at Amherst. His lectures (actually glorified philosophic speculations) were notable, although he permitted only one of them, *Education by Poetry* (1930), which Frost called "a meditative monologue," to be reduced to print.

Mountain Interval, containing some of Frost's most characteristic poems ("Birches," and "An Old Man's Winter Night" are typical), appeared in 1916. The idiom is the same as in the earlier volumes, but the notes are more varied, the lyrics intensified, the assurance is stronger. The subtle variations of the tones of speech find their sympathetic reporter here; the lines disclose delicate shades of emphasis in the way they present an entire scene by giving only a significant detail. Altogether natural, yet fanciful no less than realistic, this poetry escapes labels, "but," Frost once said, with a suspicion of a twinkle, "if I must be classified as a poet, I might be called a Synecdochist; for I prefer the synecdoche in poetry—that figure of speech in which we use a part for the whole."

New Hampshire (1923), which was awarded the Pulitzer Prize for the best volume of poetry published in 1923, synthesizes Frost's qualities: it combines the stark unity of *North of Boston* and the diffused geniality of *Mountain Interval.* If one thing predominates, it is a feeling of quiet classicism; the poet has lowered his voice but not the strength of his convictions. To say, as was said, that Frost gives us a poetry "without the delight of the senses, without the glow of warm feeling" is—particularly when faced with *New Hampshire*—to utter an absurdity. Frost, in spite of a superficial underemphasis, does not hesitate to declare his close affection. Such poems as "Two Look at Two," with its tremendous wave of love, "To Earthward," with its unreserved intensity, even the brilliantly condensed "Fire and Ice," with its candidly registered passion—all these brim with a physical radiance, with the very delight and pain of the senses. Nor is the fanciful by-play, the sly banter so characteristic of this poet, absent from the volume. Who but Frost could put so whimsical an accent in the farewell to an orchard entitled "Good-by and Keep Cold"; who but he could summon, with so few strokes, the frightened colt "with one forefoot on the wall, the other curled at his breast" in "The Runaway"? The very scheme of *New Hampshire* is an extended whimsicality: he offers the contents of the volume as a series of explanatory notes (and grace notes) to the title poem, which is supposed to be the book's *raison d'être*. The long poems (the "notes") rank with the narrative monologs in *North of Boston;* the "grace notes" contain not merely Frost's finest lines but some of the most haunting lyrics ever written by an American. Such a poem as "Stopping by Woods on a Snowy Evening" once in the mind of a reader will never leave it. Had Frost written nothing but these thirty "grace notes" his place in poetry would be assured. A revised *Selected Poems* (revised in 1928 and 1935) and a rearranged *Collected Poems* (1930) which again won the Pulitzer Prize, confirmed the conclusions; the unpretentious bucolics had become contemporary classics.

It has been said that Frost's work suffers from an exclusiveness, and even his most ardent admirers would be willing to admit that his is not an indiscriminately inclusive passion like Whitman's. But Frost loves what he loves with a fierce attachment, a tenderness fixed beyond a more easily transferred regard. His devotion to the intimacies of earth is, even more than Wordsworth's, rich, almost inordinate in its fidelity; what his emotion (or his poetry) may lack in windy range, is trebly compensated for by its untroubled depths.

This is more true than ever of *West-Running Brook* (1928) which was hailed with loud—and misleading—enthusiasm. No contemporary poet received more praise than Frost, and none was more praised for the wrong attributes. As late as 1928, most of the critics were surprised that the writer identified with the long monologs in *North of Boston* should turn to lyrics, forgetting that Frost's first volume (written in the 1890's and published twenty years later) was wholly and insistently lyrical. One reviewer, echoing the false platitude concerning New England bleakness, applauded Frost's almost colorless reticence, his "preference for black and white." Another made the discovery that "where he was formerly content to limn a landscape . . . here the emphasis is primarily the poet's emotion." A more understanding consideration of Frost's poetry would have instructed the critics. They would have seen that no volumes have ever been less black and white, no poetry so delicately shaded. The so-called inhibitions disappear upon rereading. Frost's poems are only superficially reticent; actually they are profound and personal revelations. Frost has never been "content to limn a landscape." He cannot suggest a character or a countryside without informing the subject with his own philosophy, a philosophy whose bantering accents cannot hide a moral earnestness. Beyond the fact ("the dearest dream that labor knows"), beyond the tone of voice, which is—at least technically—the poet's first concern, there is that ardent and unifying emotion which is Frost's peculiar quality and his essential spirit. Nothing could prove it more fully than the title-poem with its seemingly casual but actually cosmic philosophy. Such poetry, with its genius for suggestive understatement, establishes Frost among the first of contemporary writers and places him with the very best of American poets past or present. It is not the technique nor even the thought, but the essence which finally convinces; the reader is fortified by Frost's serenity, strengthened by his strength.

West-Running Brook is a reflection and restatement of all that has gone before. The autobiographical references are a little more outspoken; Amy Lowell's assertion that "there is no poem which has San Francisco as a background nor which seems to owe its inception to the author's early life" is answered again and again by poems which are packed with long memories. There is outspoken recognition of cruelty, of general loneliness—the loneliness of all humanity—and a poignant expression of personal isolation. It speaks through the sadness of "Bereft" and "Once by the Pacific," through the recollective somberness of "Acquainted with the Night" and the frightening summoning of evil in "The Lovely Shall Be Choosers."

The poetry published between Frost's fiftieth and sixtieth years grew in intensity and intimacy. The tone was deeper as well as darker; the communication more expansive. The poet still maintained his rôle of half-earnest synecdochist. He reaffirmed his conviction: "All that an artist needs is samples." This employment of the part for the whole sharpens the ruminating accents of "Tree at My Window," fastens the epigrammatic irony of "The Peaceful Shepherd," quickens the somber power of "Bereft" and "Once by the Pacific," points the teasing play of "The Bear."

A Further Range (1936) reveals the renewed play of the serious mind. It is emphasized by the self-disclosing "A Leaf-Trader" and "Desert Places" and "Two Tramps in Mud-Time," the last being one of the most persuasive poems of the period. In the later poems Frost is more than ever a "revisionist"; he uses his power to revise stereotypes of thought as well as clichés of expression. If it were not for the journalistic connotations one might add the term "humorist" to the roll-call of "classicist," "realist," and "revisionist." His style, so seemingly casual and yet so inimitable, so colloquial and so elevated, has a way of uniting opposites. It is a remarkable prestidigitation in which fact becomes fantasy, and the fancy is more convincing than the fact. Inner seriousness and outer humor continually shift their centers of gravity—and levity—until it must be plain that Frost's banter is as full of serious implications as his somber speculations, that his playfulness is even more profound than his profundity. *A Further Range* won the Pulitzer Prize in 1937.

A new and comprehensive *Complete Poems* (1949) reveals the greater scope and increasing depth of the poet's gift. Published in Frost's seventy-fifth year, much of the poetry seems younger than ever. Retaining the tart accent of his forefathers, and sometimes recording what might be called New England's heritage of chronic adversity, Frost sounds a new tenderness and pathos. The combination of youthful vigor and aging sapience is manifest in *A Witness Tree* (1942), the fourth of Frost's books to win a Pulitzer Prize; *Steeple Bush* (1947); *A Masque of Reason* (1945); and *A Masque of Mercy* (1947). The first two are collections of lyrics, some of which are as stern and sinewy as anything the poet ever wrote; *Steeple Bush* is particularly salted with wit and peppered with satire. The sadness of age is sounded in the later works, yet there is neither despair nor despondency. It is sometimes, as in such poems as "Directive," moody and almost anguished, but the darkening moments are offset by shafts of light, as in "Happiness Makes Up in Height for What It Lacks in Length," "Come In," the quietly patriotic "The Gift Outright," and "Choose Something Like a Star," which the poet put toward the end of his book as "an afterword." At eighty-five Frost continued to write homespun monologs and lyrics that were even more nimble than those he had written half a century before.

To his *Collected Poems* Frost furnished a preface entitled "The Figure a Poem Makes," a piece of prose as characteristic as his poetry. In it he wrote: "A poem begins in delight and ends in wisdom." This is the secret of Frost's popularity, the reason why those who create poetry and those who seldom read it turn to Frost with equal pleasure. They are charmed as well as challenged. They are happy not only because they have learned something new but have experienced something old, something which "begins in delight and ends in wisdom."

THE PASTURE

I'm going out to clean the pasture spring;
I'll only stop to rake the leaves away
(And wait to watch the water clear, I may):
I shan't be gone long.—You come too.

I'm going out to fetch the little calf
That's standing by the mother. It's so young,
It totters when she licks it with her tongue.
I shan't be gone long.—You come too.

THE ONSET

Always the same when on a fated night
At last the gathered snow lets down as white
As may be in dark woods, and with a song
It shall not make again all winter long—
Of hissing on the yet uncovered ground—
I almost stumble looking up and round,
As one, who, overtaken by the end,
Gives up his errand and lets death descend
Upon him where he is, with nothing done
To evil, no important triumph won
More than if life had never been begun.

Yet all the precedent is on my side:
I know that winter-death has never tried
The earth but it has failed; the snow may heap
In long storms an undrifted four feet deep
As measured against maple, birch or oak,
It cannot check the Peeper's silver croak;
And I shall see the snow all go down hill
In water of a slender April rill
That flashes tail through last year's withered brake
And dead weed like a disappearing snake.
Nothing will be left white but here a birch
And there a clump of houses with a church.

THE TUFT OF FLOWERS

I went to turn the grass once after one
Who mowed it in the dew before the sun.

The dew was gone that made his blade so keen
Before I came to view the leveled scene.

I looked for him behind an isle of trees;
I listened for his whetstone on the breeze.

But he had gone his way, the grass all mown,
And I must be, as he had been,—alone,

"As all must be," I said within my heart,
"Whether they work together or apart."

But as I said it, swift there passed me by
On noiseless wing a bewildered butterfly,

Seeking with memories grown dim over night
Some resting flower of yesterday's delight.

And once I marked his flight go round and round,
As where some flower lay withering on the ground.

And then he flew as far as eye could see,
And then on tremulous wing came back to me.

I thought of questions that have no reply,
And would have turned to toss the grass to dry;

But he turned first, and led my eye to look
At a tall tuft of flowers beside a brook,

A leaping tongue of bloom the scythe had spared
Beside a reedy brook the scythe had bared.

I left my place to know them by their name,
Finding them butterfly-weed when I came.

The mower in the dew had loved them thus,
By leaving them to flourish, not for us,

Nor yet to draw one thought of ours to him,
But from sheer morning gladness at the brim.

The butterfly and I had lit upon,
Nevertheless, a message from the dawn,

That made me hear the wakening birds around,
And hear his long scythe whispering to the ground,

And feel a spirit kindred to my own;
So that henceforth I worked no more alone;

But glad with him, I worked as with his aid,
And weary, sought at noon with him the shade;

And dreaming, as it were, held brotherly speech
With one whose thought I had not hoped to reach.

"Men work together," I told him from the heart,
"Whether they work together or apart."

RELUCTANCE

Out through the fields and the woods
  And over the walls I have wended;
I have climbed the hills of view
  And looked at the world, and descended;
I have come by the highway home,
  And lo, it is ended.

The leaves are all dead on the ground,
  Save those that the oak is keeping
To ravel them one by one
  And let them go scraping and creeping
Out over the crusted snow,
  When others are sleeping.

And the dead leaves lie huddled and still,
  No longer blown hither and thither;
The last lone aster is gone;
  The flowers of the witch-hazel wither;
The heart is still aching to seek,
  But the feet question "Whither?"

Ah, when to the heart of man
  Was it ever less than a treason
To go with the drift of things,
  To yield with a grace to reason,
And bow and accept the end
  Of a love or a season?

MENDING WALL

Something there is that doesn't love a wall,
That sends the frozen-ground-swell under it,
And spills the upper bowlders in the sun;
And makes gaps even two can pass abreast.
The work of hunters is another thing:
I have come after them and made repair
Where they have left not one stone on a stone,
But they would have the rabbit out of hiding,
To please the yelping dogs. The gaps I mean,
No one has seen them made or heard them made,
But at spring mending-time we find them there.
I let my neighbor know beyond the hill;
And on a day we meet to walk the line
And set the wall between us once again.
We keep the wall between us as we go.
To each the bowlders that have fallen to each.
And some are loaves and some so nearly balls
We have to use a spell to make them balance:
"Stay where you are until our backs are turned!"

We wear our fingers rough with handling them.
Oh, just another kind of outdoor game,
One on a side. It comes to little more:
There where it is we do not need the wall:
He is all pine and I am apple-orchard.
My apple trees will never get across
And eat the cones under his pines, I tell him.
He only says, "Good fences make good neighbors."
Spring is the mischief in me, and I wonder
If I could put a notion in his head:
"*Why* do they make good neighbors? Isn't it
Where there are cows? But here there are no cows.
Before I built a wall I'd ask to know
What I was walling in or walling out,
And to whom I was like to give offense.
Something there is that doesn't love a wall,
That wants it down!" I could say "elves" to him,
But it's not elves exactly, and I'd rather
He said it for himself. I see him there,
Bringing a stone grasped firmly by the top
In each hand, like an old-stone savage armed.
He moves in darkness, as it seems to me,
Not of woods only and the shade of trees.
He will not go behind his father's saying,
And he likes having thought of it so well
He says again, "Good fences make good neighbors."

THE COW IN APPLE-TIME

Something inspires the only cow of late
To make no more of a wall than an open gate,
And think no more of wall-builders than fools.
Her face is flecked with pomace and she drools
A cider sirup. Having tasted fruit,
She scorns a pasture withering to the root.
She runs from tree to tree where lie and sweeten
The windfalls spiked with stubble and worm-eaten.
She leaves them bitten when she has to fly.
She bellows on a knoll against the sky .
Her udder shrivels and the milk goes dry.

THE DEATH OF THE HIRED MAN

Mary sat musing on the lamp-flame at the table
Waiting for Warren. When she heard his step,
She ran on tip-toe down the darkened passage
To meet him in the doorway with the news
And put him on his guard. "Silas is back."
She pushed him outward with her through the door
And shut it after her. "Be kind," she said.

She took the market things from Warren's arms
And set them on the porch, then drew him down
To sit beside her on the wooden steps.
"When was I ever anything but kind to him?
But I'll not have the fellow back," he said.
"I told him so last haying, didn't I?
'If he left then,' I said, 'that ended it.'
What good is he? Who else will harbor him
At his age for the little he can do?
What help he is there's no depending on.
Off he goes always when I need him most.
'He thinks he ought to earn a little pay,
Enough at least to buy tobacco with,
So he won't have to beg and be beholden.'
'All right,' I say, 'I can't afford to pay
Any fixed wages, though I wish I could.'
'Someone else can.' 'Then someone else will have to.'
I shouldn't mind his bettering himself
If that was what it was. You can be certain,
When he begins like that, there's someone at him
Trying to coax him off with pocket-money,—
In haying time, when any help is scarce.
In winter he comes back to us. I'm done."

"Sh! not so loud: he'll hear you," Mary said.

"I want him to: he'll have to soon or late."

"He's worn out. He's asleep beside the stove.
When I came up from Rowe's I found him here,
Huddled against the barn-door fast asleep,
A miserable sight, and frightening, too—
You needn't smile—I didn't recognize him—
I wasn't looking for him—and he's changed.
Wait till you see."

"Where did you say he'd been?"

"He didn't say. I dragged him to the house,
And gave him tea and tried to make him smoke.
I tried to make him talk about his travels,
Nothing would do: he just kept nodding off."

"What did he say? Did he say anything?"

"But little."

"Anything? Mary, confess
He said he'd come to ditch the meadow for me."

"Warren!"

"But did he? I just want to know."

"Of course he did. What would you have him say?
Surely you wouldn't grudge the poor old man
Some humble way to save his self-respect.
He added, if you really care to know,
He meant to clear the upper pasture, too.
That sounds like something you have heard before?
Warren, I wish you could have heard the way
He jumbled everything. I stopped to look
Two or three times—he made me feel so queer—
To see if he was talking in his sleep.
He ran on Harold Wilson—you remember—
The boy you had in haying four years since.
He's finished school, and teaching in his college.
Silas declares you'll have to get him back.
He says they two will make a team for work:
Between them they will lay this farm as smooth!
The way he mixed that in with other things.
He thinks young Wilson a likely lad, though daft
On education—you know how they fought
All through July under the blazing sun,
Silas up on the cart to build the load,
Harold along beside to pitch it on."

"Yes, I took care to keep well out of earshot."

"Well, those days trouble Silas like a dream.
You wouldn't think they would. How some things linger!
Harold's young college boy's assurance piqued him.
After so many years he still keeps finding
Good arguments he sees he might have used.
I sympathize. I know just how it feels
To think of the right thing to say too late.
Harold's associated in his mind with Latin.
He asked me what I thought of Harold's saying
He studied Latin like the violin
Because he liked it—that an argument!
He said he couldn't make the boy believe
He could find water with a hazel prong—
Which showed how much good school had ever done him.
He wanted to go over that. But most of all
He thinks if he could have another chance
To teach him how to build a load of hay—"

"I know, that's Silas' one accomplishment.
He bundles every forkful in its place,
And tags and numbers it for future reference,
So he can find and easily dislodge it
In the unloading. Silas does that well.
He takes it out in bunches like birds' nests.

You never see him standing on the hay
He's trying to lift, straining to lift himself."

"He thinks if he could teach him that, he'd be
Some good perhaps to someone in the world.
He hates to see a boy the fool of books.
Poor Silas, so concerned for other folk,
And nothing to look backward to with pride,
And nothing to look forward to with hope,
So now and never any different."

Part of a moon was falling down the west,
Dragging the whole sky with it to the hills.
Its light poured softly in her lap. She saw
And spread her apron to it. She put out her hand
Among the harp-like morning-glory strings,
Taut with the dew from garden bed to eaves,
As if she played unheard some tenderness
That wrought on him beside her in the night.
"Warren," she said, "he has come home to die:
You needn't be afraid he'll leave you this time."

"Home," he mocked gently.

"Yes, what else but home?
It all depends on what you mean by home.
Of course he's nothing to us, any more
Than was the hound that came a stranger to us
Out of the woods, worn out upon the trail."

"Home is the place where, when you have to go there,
They have to take you in."

"I should have called it
Something you somehow haven't to deserve."

Warren leaned out and took a step or two,
Picked up a little stick, and brought it back
And broke it in his hand and tossed it by.
"Silas has better claim on us, you think,
Than on his brother? Thirteen little miles
As the road winds would bring him to his door.
Silas has walked that far no doubt today.
Why didn't he go there? His brother's rich,
A somebody—director in the bank."

"He never told us that."

"We know it though."

"I think his brother ought to help, of course.
I'll see to that if there is need. He ought of right

To take him in, and might be willing to—
He may be better than appearances.
But have some pity on Silas. Do you think
If he'd had any pride in claiming kin
Or anything he looked for from his brother,
He'd keep so still about him all this time?"

"I wonder what's between them."

"I can tell you.
Silas is what he is—we wouldn't mind him—
But just the kind that kinsfolk can't abide.
He never did a thing so very bad.
He don't know why he isn't quite as good
As anyone. Worthless though he is,
He won't be made ashamed to please his brother."

"I can't think Si ever hurt anyone."

"No, but he hurt my heart the way he lay
And rolled his old head on that sharp-edged chair-back
He wouldn't let me put him on the lounge.
You must go in and see what you can do.
I made the bed up for him there tonight.
You'll be surprised at him—how much he's broken.
His working days are done; I'm sure of it."

"I'd not be in a hurry to say that."

"I haven't been. Go, look, see for yourself.
But, Warren, please remember how it is:
He's come to help you ditch the meadow.
He has a plan. You mustn't laugh at him.
He may not speak of it, and then he may.
I'll sit and see if that small sailing cloud
Will hit or miss the moon."

It hit the moon.
Then there were three there, making a dim row,
The moon, the little silver cloud, and she.

Warren returned—too soon, it seemed to her,
Slipped to her side, caught up her hand and waited.

"Warren?" she questioned.

"Dead," was all he answered.

AFTER APPLE-PICKING

My long two-pointed ladder's sticking through a tree
Toward heaven still,
And there's a barrel that I didn't fill
Beside it, and there may be two or three
Apples I didn't pick upon some bough.
But I am done with apple-picking now.
Essence of winter sleep is on the night,
The scent of apples: I am drowsing off.
I cannot rub the strangeness from my sight
I got from looking through a pane of glass
I skimmed this morning from the drinking trough
And held against the world of hoary grass.
It melted, and I let it fall and break.
But I was well
Upon my way to sleep before it fell,
And I could tell
What form my dreaming was about to take.
Magnified apples appear and disappear,
Stem-end and blossom-end,
And every fleck of russet showing clear.
My instep arch not only keeps the ache,
It keeps the pressure of a ladder-round.
I feel the ladder sway as the boughs bend.
And I keep hearing from the cellar bin
The rumbling sound
Of load on load of apples coming in.
For I have had too much
Of apple-picking: I am overtired
Of the great harvest I myself desired.
There were ten thousand thousand fruit to touch,
Cherish in hand, lift down, and not let fall.
For all
That struck the earth,
No matter if not bruised or spiked with stubble,
Went surely to the cider-apple heap
As of no worth.
One can see what will trouble
This sleep of mine, whatever sleep it is.
Were he not gone,
The woodchuck could say whether it's like his
Long sleep, as I describe its coming on,
Or just some human sleep.

AN OLD MAN'S WINTER NIGHT

All out of doors looked darkly in at him
Through the thin frost, almost in separate stars,
That gathers on the pane in empty rooms.
What kept his eyes from giving back the gaze

Was the lamp tilted near them in his hand.
What kept him from remembering what it was
That brought him to that creaking room was age.
He stood with barrels round him—at a loss.
And having scared the cellar under him
In clomping there, he scared it once again
In clomping off; and scared the outer night,
Which has its sounds, familiar, like the roar
Of trees and crack of branches, common things,
But nothing so like beating on a box.
A light he was to no one but himself
Where now he sat, concerned with he knew what;
A quiet light, and then not even that.
He consigned to the moon, such as she was,
So late-arising, to the broken moon
As better than the sun in any case
For such a charge, his snow upon the roof,
His icicles along the wall to keep;
And slept. The log that shifted with a jolt
Once in the stove, disturbed him and he shifted,
And eased his heavy breathing, but still slept.
One aged man—one man—can't fill a house,
A farm, a countryside, or if he can,
It's thus he does it of a winter night.

BIRCHES

When I see birches bend to left and right
Across the line of straighter darker trees,
I like to think some boy's been swinging them.
But swinging doesn't bend them down to stay.
Ice-storms do that. Often you must have seen them
Loaded with ice a sunny winter morning
After a rain. They click upon themselves
As the breeze rises, and turn many-colored
As the stir cracks and crazes their enamel.
Soon the sun's warmth makes them shed crystal shells
Shattering and avalanching on the snow-crust—
Such heaps of broken glass to sweep away
You'd think the inner dome of heaven had fallen.
They are dragged to the withered bracken by the load,
And they seem not to break; though once they are bowed
So low for long, they never right themselves:
You may see their trunks arching in the woods
Years afterwards, trailing their leaves on the ground
Like girls on hands and knees that throw their hair
Before them over their heads to dry in the sun.
But I was going to say when Truth broke in
With all her matter-of-fact about the ice-storm
I should prefer to have some boy bend them
As he went out and in to fetch the cows—

Some boy too far from town to learn baseball,
Whose only play was what he found himself,
Summer or winter, and could play alone.
One by one he subdued his father's trees
By riding them down over and over again
Until he took the stiffness out of them,
And not one but hung limp, not one was left
For him to conquer. He learned all there was
To learn about not launching out too soon
And so not carrying the tree away
Clear to the ground. He always kept his poise
To the top branches, climbing carefully
With the same pains you use to fill a cup
Up to the brim, and even above the brim.
Then he flung outward, feet first, with a swish,
Kicking his way down through the air to the ground.

So was I once myself a swinger of birches;
And so I dream of going back to be.
It's when I'm weary of considerations,
And life is too much like a pathless wood
Where your face burns and tickles with the cobwebs
Broken across it, and one eye is weeping
From a twig's having lashed across it open.
I'd like to get away from earth awhile
And then come back to it and begin over.
May no fate willfully misunderstand me
And half grant what I wish and snatch me away
Not to return. Earth's the right place for love:
I don't know where it's likely to go better.
I'd like to go by climbing a birch tree,
And climb black branches up a snow-white trunk
Toward heaven, till the tree could bear no more,
But dipped its top and set me down again.
That would be good both going and coming back.
One could do worse than be a swinger of birches.

BROWN'S DESCENT

OR, THE WILLY-NILLY SLIDE

Brown lived at such a lofty farm
That everyone for miles could see
His lantern when he did his chores
In winter after half-past three.

And many must have seen him make
His wild descent from there one night,
'Cross lots, 'cross walls, 'cross everything,
Describing rings of lantern light.

Between the house and barn the gale
Got him by something he had on
And blew him out on the icy crust
That cased the world, and he was gone

Walls were all buried, trees were few:
He saw no stay unless he stove
A hole in somewhere with his heel.
But though repeatedly he strove

And stamped and said things to himself,
And sometimes something seemed to yiel
He gained no foothold, but pursued
His journey down from field to field.

Sometimes he came with arms outspread
Like wings revolving in the scene
Upon his longer axis, and
With no small dignity of mien.

Faster or slower as he chanced,
Sitting or standing as he chose,
According as he feared to risk
His neck, or thought to spare his clothes,

He never let the lantern drop.
And some exclaimed who saw afar
The figure he described with it,
"I wonder what those signals are

"Brown makes at such an hour of night!
He's celebrating something strange.
I wonder if he's sold his farm,
Or been made Master of the Grange."

He reeled, he lurched, he bobbed, he checked;
He fell and made the lantern rattle
(But saved the light from going out).
So half-way down he fought the battle

Incredulous of his own bad luck.
And then becoming reconciled
To everything, he gave it up
And came down like a coasting child.

"Well—I—be—" that was all he said,
As standing in the river road,
He looked back up the slippery slope
(Two miles it was) to his abode.

Sometimes as an authority
On motor-cars, I'm asked if I
Should say our stock was petered out,
And this is my sincere reply:

Yankees are what they always were.
Don't think Brown ever gave up hope
Of getting home again because
He couldn't climb that slippery slope;

Or even thought of standing there
Until the January thaw
Should take the polish off the crust.
He bowed with grace to natural law,

And then went round it on his feet,
After the manner of our stock;
Not much concerned for those to whom,
At that particular time o'clock,

It must have looked as if the course
He steered was really straight away
From that which he was headed for—
Not much concerned for them, I say,

But now he snapped his eyes three times;
Then shook his lantern, saying, "Ile's
'Bout out!" and took the long way home
By road, a matter of several miles.

THE RUNAWAY

Once when the snow of the year was beginning to fall,
We stopped by a mountain pasture to say, "Whose colt?"
A little Morgan had one forefoot on the wall,
The other curled at his breast. He dipped his head
And snorted to us. And then he had to bolt.
We heard the miniature thunder where he fled,
And we saw him, or thought we saw him, dim and gray,
Like a shadow against the curtain of falling flakes.
"I think the little fellow's afraid of the snow.
He isn't winter-broken. It isn't play
With the little fellow at all. He's running away.
I doubt if even his mother could tell him, 'Sakes,
It's only weather.' He'd think she didn't know!
Where is his mother? He can't be out alone."
And now he comes again with a clatter of stone
And mounts the wall again with whited eyes

And all his tail that isn't hair up straight.
He shudders his coat as if to throw off flies.
"Whoever it is that leaves him out so late,
When other creatures have gone to stall and bin,
Ought to be told to come and take him in."

TO EARTHWARD

Love at the lips was touch
As sweet as I could bear;
And once that seemed too much;
I lived on air

That crossed me from sweet things,
The flow of—was it musk
From hidden grapevine springs
Down hill at dusk?

I had the swirl and ache
From sprays of honeysuckle
That when they're gathered shake
Dew on the knuckle.

I craved strong sweets, but those
Seemed strong when I was young;
The petal of the rose
It was that stung.

Now no joy but lacks salt
That is not dashed with pain
And weariness and fault;
I crave the stain
Of tears, the aftermark
Of almost too much love,
The sweet of bitter bark
And burning clove.

When stiff and sore and scarred
I take away my hand
From leaning on it hard
In grass and sand,

The hurt is not enough:
I long for weight and strength
To feel the earth as rough
To all my length.

FIRE AND ICE

Some say the world will end in fire,
Some say in ice.
From what I've tasted of desire
I hold with those who favor fire.
But if it had to perish twice,
I think I know enough of hate
To say that for destruction ice
Is also great
And would suffice.

TWO LOOK AT TWO

Love and forgetting might have carried them
A little further up the mountain side
With night so near, but not much further up.
They must have halted soon in any case
With thoughts of the path back, how rough it was
With rock and washout, and unsafe in darkness;
When they were halted by a tumbled wall
With barbed-wire binding. They stood facing this,
Spending what onward impulse they still had
In one last look the way they must not go,
On up the failing path, where, if a stone
Or earthslide moved at night, it moved itself;
No footstep moved it. "This is all," they sighed,
"Good-night to woods." But not so; there was more.
A doe from round a spruce stood looking at them
Across the wall as near the wall as they.

She saw them in their field, they her in hers.
The difficulty of seeing what stood still,
Like some up-ended bowlder split in two,
Was in her clouded eyes: they saw no fear there.
She seemed to think that two thus they were safe.
Then, as if they were something that, though strange,
She could not trouble her mind with too long,
She sighed and passed unscared along the wall.
"*This,* then, is all. What more is there to ask?"
But no, not yet. A snort to bid them wait.
A buck from round the spruce stood looking at them
Across the wall, as near the wall as they.
This was an antlered buck of lusty nostril.
Not the same doe come back into her place.
He viewed them quizzically with jerks of head,
As if to ask, "Why don't you make some motion?
Or give some sign of life? Because you can't.
I doubt if you're as living as you look."
Thus till he had them almost feeling dared
To stretch a proffering hand—and a spell-breaking.
Then he too passed unscared along the wall.
Two had seen two, whichever side you spoke from.
"This *must* be all." It was all. Still they stood,
A great wave from it going over them,
As if the earth in one unlooked-for favor
Had made them certain earth returned their love.

A SKY PAIR

CANIS MAJOR

The Great Overdog,
That heavenly beast
With a star in one eye,
Gives a leap in the East.

He dances upright
All the way to the West,
And never once drops
On his forefeet to rest.

I'm a poor Underdog;
But tonight I will bark,
With the Great Overdog
That romps through the dark.

THE PEACEFUL SHEPHERD

If heaven were to do again,
And on the pasture bars
I leaned to line the figures in
Between the dotted stars,

I should be tempted to forget,
I think, the Crown of Rule,
The Scales of Trade, the Cross of Faith,
As hardly worth renewal.

For these have governed in our lives,
And see how men have warred!
The Cross, the Crown, the Scales, may all
As well have been the Sword.

BEREFT

Where had I heard this wind before
Change like this to a deeper roar?
What would it take my standing there for,
Holding open a restive door,
Looking down hill to a frothy shore?
Summer was past and day was past.
Somber clouds on the West were massed.
Out in the porch's sagging floor
Leaves got up in a coil and hissed,
Blindly struck at my knee and missed.
Something sinister in the tone

Told me my secret must be known:
Word I was in the house alone
Somehow must have gotten abroad;
Word I was in my life alone;
Word I had no one left but God.

TREE AT MY WINDOW

Tree at my window, window tree,
My sash is lowered when night comes on;
But let there never be curtain drawn
Between you and me.

Vague dream-head lifted out of the ground,
And thing next most diffuse to cloud,
Not all your light tongues talking aloud
Could be profound.

But, tree, I have seen you taken and tossed,
And if you have seen me when I slept,
You have seen me when I was taken and
swept
And all but lost.

That day she put our heads together,
Fate had her imagination about her,
Your head so much concerned with outer,
Mine with inner, weather.

WEST-RUNNING BROOK

"Fred, where is north?"
"North? North is there, my love.
The brook runs west."
"West-running Brook then call it."
(West-running Brook men call it to this day.)
"What does it think it's doing running west
When all the other country brooks flow east
To reach the ocean? It must be the brook
Can trust itself to go by contraries
The way I can with you—and you with me—
Because we're—we're—I don't know what we are.
What are we?"
"Young or new?"
"We must be something
We've said we two. Let's change that to we three.
As you and I are married to each other,
We'll both be married to the brook. We'll build
Our bridge across it, and the bridge shall be
Our arm thrown over it asleep beside it.
Look, look, it's waving to us with a wave
To let us know it hears me."
"Why, my dear,
That wave's been standing off this jut of shore—"
(The black stream, catching on a sunken rock,
Flung backward on itself in one white wave,
And the white water rode the black forever,
Not gaining but not losing, like a bird
While feathers from the struggle of whose breast
Flecked the dark stream and flecked the darker pool
Below the point, and were at last driven wrinkled
In a white scarf against the far shore alders.)
"That wave's been standing off this jut of shore

Ever since rivers, I was going to say,
Were made in heaven. It wasn't waved to us."

"It wasn't, yet it was. If not to you
It was to me—in an annunciation."

"Oh, if you take it off to lady-land,
As 'twere the country of the Amazons
We men must see you to the confines of
And leave you there, ourselves forbid to enter,—
It is your brook! I have no more to say."

"Yes, you have, too. Go on. You thought of something."

"Speaking of contraries, see how the brook
In that white wave runs counter to itself.
It is from that in water we were from
Long, long before we were from any creature.
Here we, in our impatience of the steps,
Get back to the beginning of beginnings,
The stream of everything that runs away.
Some say existence like a Pirouot
And Pirouette, forever in one place,
Stands still and dances, but it runs away,
It seriously, sadly, runs away
To fill the abyss' void with emptiness.
It flows beside us in this water brook,
But it flows over us. It flows between us
To separate us for a panic moment.
It flows between us, over us, and *with* us.
And it is time, strength, tone, light, life and love
And even substance lapsing unsubstantial;
The universal cataract of death
That spends to nothingness—and unresisted,
Save by some strange resistance in itself,
Not just a swerving, but a throwing back,
As if regret were in it and were sacred.
It has this throwing backward on itself
So that the fall of most of it is always
Raising a little, sending up a little.
Our life runs down in sending up the clock.
The brook runs down in sending up our life.
The sun runs down in sending up the brook.
And there is something sending up the sun.
It is this backward motion toward the source,
Against the stream, that most we see ourselves in,
The tribute of the current to the source.
It is from this in nature we are from.
It is most us."

"Today will be the day

You said so."
"No, today will be the day
You said the brook was called West-running Brook."

"Today will be the day of what we both said."

ONCE BY THE PACIFIC

The shattered water made a misty din,
Great waves looked over others coming in,
And thought of doing something to the shore
That water never did to land before.
The clouds were low and hairy in the skies
Like locks blown forward in the gleam of eyes.
You could not tell, and yet it looked as if
The sand was lucky in being backed by cliff,
The cliff in being backed by continent.
It looked as if a night of dark intent
Was coming, and not only a night, an age.
Someone had better be prepared for rage.
There would be more than ocean water broken
Before God's last *Put out the light* was spoken.

THE BEAR

The bear puts both arms around the tree above her
And draws it down as if it were a lover
And its choke-cherries lips to kiss good-by,
Then lets it snap back upright in the sky.
Her next step rocks a bowlder on the wall
(She's making her cross-country in the fall.)
Her great weight creaks the barbed-wire in its staples
As she flings over and off down through the maples,
Leaving on one wire tooth a lock of hair.
Such is the uncaged progress of the bear.
The world has room to make a bear feel free;
The universe seems cramped to you and me.
Man acts more like a poor bear in a cage
That all day fights a nervous inward rage,
His mood rejecting all his mind suggests.
He paces back and forth and never rests
The toe-nail click and shuffle of his feet,
The telescope at one end of his beat,
And at the other end the microscope,
Two instruments of nearly equal hope,
And in conjunction giving quite a spread.
Or if he rests from scientific tread,
'Tis only to sit back and sway his head
Through ninety odd degrees of arc, it seems,
Between two metaphysical extremes.

He sits back on his fundamental butt
With lifted snout and eyes (if any) shut,
(He almost looks religious but he's not),
And back and forth he sways from cheek to cheek,
At one extreme agreeing with one Greek,
At the other agreeing with another Greek
Which may be thought, but only so to speak.
A baggy figure, equally pathetic
When sedentary and when peripatetic.

SAND DUNES

Sea waves are green and wet,
But up from where they die
Rise others vaster yet,
And those are brown and dry.

They are the sea made land
To come at the fisher town,
And bury in solid sand
The men she could not drown.

She may know cove and cape,
But she does not know mankind
If by any change of shape
She hopes to cut off mind.

Men left her a ship to sink;
They can leave her a hut as well,
And be but more free to think
For the one more cast-off shell.

THE LOVELY SHALL BE CHOOSERS 53

The Voice said, "Hurl her down!"

The Voices, "How far down?"

"Seven levels of the world."

"How much time have we?"

"Take twenty years.
She would refuse love safe with wealth and honor.
The Lovely shall be choosers, shall they?
Then let them choose!"

"Then we shall let her choose?"

"Yes, let her choose.
Take up the task beyond her choosing."

Invisible hands crowded on her shoulder
In readiness to weigh upon her.

But she stood straight still,
In broad round ear-rings, gold and jet with pearls,
And broad round suchlike brooch,
Her cheeks high colored,
Proud and the pride of friends.

The Voice asked, "You can let her choose?"

"Yes, we can let her and still triumph."

"Do it by joys. And leave her always blameless.
Be her first joy her wedding,
That though a wedding,
Is yet—well, something *they* know, he and she.
And after that her next joy
That though she grieves, her grief is secret:
Those friends know nothing of her grief to make it shameful.
Her third joy that though now they cannot help but know,
They move in pleasure too far off
To think much or much care.
Give her a child at either knee for fourth joy
To tell once and once only, for them never to forget,
How once she walked in brightness,
And make them see in the winter firelight.
But give her friends, for them she dares not tell
For their foregone incredulousness.
And be her next joy this:
Her never having deigned to tell them.
Make her among the humblest even
Seem to them less than they are.
Hopeless of being known for what she has been,
Failing of being loved for what she is,
Give her the comfort of her sixth of knowing
She fails from strangeness to a way of life
She came to from too high too late to learn.
Then send some *one* with eye to see
And wonder at her where she is
And words to wonder in her hearing how she came there.
But without time to stay and hear her story.
Be her last joy her heart's going out to this one
So that she almost speaks.

You know them—seven in all."

"Trust us," the Voices said.

THE EGG AND THE MACHINE

He gave the solid rail a hateful kick.
From far away there came an answering tick;
And then another tick. He knew the code:
His hate had roused an engine up the road.

He wished when he had had the track alone
He had attacked it with a club or stone
And bent some rail wide open like a switch
So as to wreck the engine in the ditch.
Too late, though, now to throw it down the bank;
Its click was rising to a nearer clank.
Here it came breasting like a horse in skirts.
(He stood well back for fear of scalding squirts.)
Then for a moment there was only size,
Confusion, and a roar that drowned the cries
He raised against the gods in the machine.
Then once again the sand-bank lay serene.
The traveler's eye picked up a turtle trail,
Between the dotted feet a streak of tail,
And followed it to where he made out vague,
But certain signs of buried turtle egg;
And probing with one finger not too rough,
He found suspicious sand, and sure enough
The pocket of a little turtle mine.
If there was one egg in it, there were nine,
Torpedo-like, with shell of gritty leather
All packed in sand to wait the trump together.
"You'd better not disturb me any more,"
He told the distance. "I am armed for war.
The next machine that has the power to pass
Will get this plasm in its goggle glass."

STOPPING BY WOODS ON A SNOWY EVENING

Whose woods these are I think I know.
His house is in the village though;
He will not see me stopping here
To watch his woods fill up with snow.

My little horse must think it queer
To stop without a farmhouse near
etween the woods and frozen lake
The darkest evening of the year.

He gives his harness bells a shake
To ask if there is some mistake.
The only other sound's the sweep
f easy wind and downy flake.

The woods are lovely, dark and deep,
ut I have promises to keep,
nd miles to go before I sleep,
nd miles to go before I sleep.

NOTHING GOLD CAN STAY

Nature's first green is gold,
Her hardest hue to hold.
Her early leaf's a flower;
But only so an hour.
Then leaf sudsides to leaf.
So Eden sank to grief,
So dawn goes down to day.
Nothing gold can stay.

THE ROAD NOT TAKEN

Two roads diverged in a yellow wood,
And sorry I could not travel both
And be one traveler, long I stood
And looked down one as far as I could
To where it bent in the undergrowth;

Then took the other, as just as fair,
And having perhaps the better claim,
Because it was grassy and wanted wear;
Though as for that the passing there
Had worn them really about the same,

And both that morning equally lay
In leaves no step had trodden black.
Oh, I kept the first for another day!
Yet knowing how way leads on to way,
I doubted if I should ever come back.

I shall be telling this with a sigh
Somewhere ages and ages hence:
Two roads diverged in a wood, and I—
I took the one less traveled by,
And that has made all the difference.

A LEAF-TREADER

I have been treading on leaves all day until I am autumn-tired.
God knows all the color and form of leaves I have trodden on and mired.
Perhaps I have put forth too much strength and been too fierce from fear.
I have safely trodden under foot the leaves of another year.

All summer long they were overhead more lifted up than I;
To come to their final place in earth they had to pass me by.
All summer long I thought I heard them threatening under their breath,
And when they came it seemed with a will to carry me with them to death.

They spoke to the fugitive in my heart as if it were leaves to leaf;
They tapped at my eyelids and touched by lips with an invitation to grief.
But it was no reason I had to go because they had to go.
Now up, my knee, to keep on top of another year of snow.

LOST IN HEAVEN

The clouds, the source of rain, one stormy night
Offered an opening to the source of dew,
Which I accepted with impatient sight,
Looking for my old sky-marks in the blue.

But stars were scarce in that part of the sky,
And no two were of the same constellation—
No one was bright enough to identify.
So 'twas with not ungrateful consternation,

Seeing myself well lost once more, I sighed,
"Where, where in heaven am I? But don't tell me,"
I warned the clouds, "by opening me wide!
Let's let my heavenly lostness overwhelm me."

DESERT PLACES

Snow falling and night falling fast, oh, fast
In a field I looked into going past,
And the ground almost covered smooth in snow,
But a few weeds and stubble showing last.

The woods around it have it—it is theirs.
All animals are smothered in their lairs.
I am too absent-spirited to count:
The loneliness includes me unawares.

And lonely as it is, that loneliness
Will be more lonely ere it will be less,
A blanker whiteness of benighted snow,
With no expression—nothing to express.

They cannot scare me with their empty spaces
Between stars—on stars void of human races.
I have it in me so much nearer home
To scare myself with my own desert places.

TWO TRAMPS IN MUD-TIME

Out of the mud two strangers came
And caught me splitting wood in the yard.
And one of them put me off my aim
By hailing cheerily "Hit them hard!"
knew pretty well why he dropped behind
And let the other go on a way.
knew pretty well what he had in mind:
He wanted to take my job for pay.

Good blocks of beech it was I split,
As large around as the chopping-block;
And every piece I squarely hit
Fell splinterless as a cloven rock.
The blows that a life of self-control
Spares to strike for the common good
That day, giving a loose to my soul,
spent on the unimportant wood.

The sun was warm but the wind was chill.
ou know how it is with an April day:
When the sun is out and the wind is still,
ou're one month on in the middle of May.
ut if you so much as dare to speak,
cloud comes over the sunlit arch,
wind comes off a frozen peak,
nd you're two months back in the middle of March.

bluebird comes tenderly up to alight
nd fronts the wind to unruffle a plume,
is song so pitched as not to excite
single flower as yet to bloom.
is snowing a flake: and he half knew
inter was only playing possum.
xcept in color he isn't blue,
ut he wouldn't advise a thing to blossom.

e water for which we may have to look
summertime with a witching-wand,
every wheelrut's now a brook,
In every print of a hoof a pond.
Be glad of water, but don't forget
The lurking frost in the earth beneath
That will steal forth after the sun is set
And show on the water its crystal teeth.

The time when most I loved my task
These two must make me love it more
By coming with what they came to ask.
You'd think I never had felt before
The weight of an ax head poised aloft,
The grip on earth of outspread feet,
The life of muscles rocking soft
And smooth and moist in vernal heat.

Out of the woods two hulking tramps
(From sleeping God knows where last night
But not long since in the lumber camps).
They thought all chopping was theirs of right.
Men of the woods and lumber-jacks,
They judged me by their appropriate tool.
Except as a fellow handled an ax,
They had no way of knowing a fool.

Nothing on either side was said.
They knew they had but to stay their stay
And all their logic would fill my head:
As that I had no right to play
With what was another man's work for gain.
My right might be love but theirs was need
And where the two exist in twain
Theirs was the better right—agreed.

But yield who will to their separation,
My object in life is to unite
My avocation and my vocation
As my two eyes make one in sight
Only where love and need are one,
And the work is play for mortal stakes,
Is the deed ever really done
For Heaven and the future's sakes.

DEPARTMENTAL

OR, MY ANT JERRY

An ant on the table-cloth
Ran into a dormant moth
Of many times her size.
He showed not the least surprise.
His business wasn't with such.
He gave it scarcely a touch,
And was off on his duty run.
Yet if he encountered one
Of the hive's enquiry squad
Whose work is to find out God
And the nature of time and space,
He would put him onto the case.
Ants are a curious race;
One crossing with hurried tread
The body of one of their dead
Isn't given a moment's arrest—
Seems not even impressed.
But he no doubt reports to any
With whom he crosses antennae,
And they no doubt report
To the higher up at court.
Then word goes forth in Formic:
"Death's come to Jerry McCormic,
Our selfless forager Jerry.
Will the special Janizary
Whose office it is to bury
The dead of the commissary
Go bring him home to his people
Lay him in state on a sepal.
Wrap him for shoud in a petal.
Embalm him with ichor of nettle.
This is the word of your Queen."
And presently on the scene
Appears a solemn mortician;
And taking formal position
With feelers calmly atwiddle,
Seizes the dead by the middle,
And heaving him high in air,
Carries him out of there.
No one stands round to stare.
It is nobody else's affair.

It couldn't be called ungentle.
But how thoroughly departmental.

A CONSIDERABLE SPECK

A speck that would have been beneath my sight
On any but a paper sheet so white
Set off across what I had written there,
And I had idly poised my pen in air
To stop it with a period of ink,
When something strange about it made me think
This was no dust speck by my breathing blown,
But unmistakably a living mite
With inclinations it could call its own.
It paused as with suspicion of my pen,
And then came racing wildly on again
To where my manuscript was not yet dry,
Then pause again and either drank or smelt—
With horror, for again it turned to fly.
Plainly with an intelligence I dealt.
It seemed too tiny to have room for feet,
Yet must have had a set of them complete
To express how much it didn't want to die.
It ran with terror and with cunning crept.
It faltered! I could see it hesitate—
Then in the middle of the open sheet
Cower down in desperation to accept
Whatever I accorded it of fate.
I have none of the tenderer-than-thou

Political collectivistic love
With which the modern world is being swept—
But this poor microscopic item now!
Since it was nothing I knew evil of
I let it lie there till I hope it slept.
I have a mind myself, and recognize
Mind where I meet with it in any guise.
No one can know how glad I am to find
On any sheet the least display of mind.

HAPPINESS MAKES UP IN HEIGHT FOR WHAT IT LACKS IN LENGTH

Oh stormy, stormy world,
The days you were not swirled
Around with mist and cloud,
Or wrapped as in a shroud,
And the sun's brilliant ball
Was not in part or all
Obscured from mortal view,
Were days so very few
I can but wonder whence
I get the lasting sense
Of so much warmth and light.
If my mistrust is right
It may be altogether
From one day's perfect weather
When starting clear at dawn
The day went clearly on
To finish clear at eve.
I verily believe
My fair impression may
Be all from that one day
No shadow crossed but ours,
As through the blazing flowers
We went from house to wood
For change of solitude.

COME IN

As I came to the edge of the woods,
Thrush music—hark!
Now if it was dusk outside,
Inside it was dark.

Too dark in the woods for a bird
By sleight of wing
To better its perch for the night,
Though it still could sing.

The last of the light of the sun
That had died in the west
Still lived for one song more
In a thrush's breast.

Far in the pillared dark
Thrush music went—
Almost like a call to come in.
To the dark and lament.

But no, I was out for stars:
I would not come in.
I meant not even if asked;
And I hadn't been.

FROM PLANE TO PLANE

Neither of them was better than the other.
They both were hired. And though Pike had the advantage
Of having hoed and mowed for fifty years,
Dick had of being fresh and full of college.
So if they fought about equality
It was on an equality they fought.

"Your trouble is not sticking to the subject,"
Pike said with temper. And Dick longed to say,

"Your trouble is bucolic lack of logic,"
But all he did say was, "What *is* the subject?"
"It's whether these professions really work.
Now take the Doctor—"

They were giving corn
A final going over with the hoe
Before they turned from everything to hay.
The wavy upflung pennons of the corn
Were loose all round their legs—you couldn't say
How many thousand of them in an acre.
Every time Dick or Pike looked up the Doctor
With one foot on the dashboard of his buggy
Was still in sight like someone to depend on.
Nowhere but on the Bradford Interval
By the Connecticut could anyone
Have stayed in sight so long as an example.

"Taking his own sweet time as if to show
He don't mind having lost a case," Pike said,
And when he caught Dick looking once too often,
"Hoeing's too much like work for Dick," he added,
"Dick wishes he could swap jobs with the Doctor.
Let's holler and ask him if he won't prescribe
For all humanity a complete rest
From all this wagery. But what's the use
Of asking any sympathy from him.
That class of people don't know what work is—
More than they know what courage is that claim
The moral kind's as brave as facing bullets."

Dick told him to be fairer to the Doctor:
"He looks to me like going home successful,
Full of success, with that foot on the dashboard,
As a small self-conferred reward of virtue.
I get you when you hoe out to the river
Then pick your hoe up, maybe shoulder it,
And take your walk of recreation back
To curry favor with the dirt some more.
Isn't it pretty much the same idea?
You said yourself you weren't avoiding work.
You'd bet you got more work done in a day,
Or at least in a lifetime, by that method."

"I wouldn't hoe both ways for anybody!"

"And right you are. You do the way we do
In reading, don't you, Bill?—at every line-end
Pick up our eyes and carry them back idle
Across the page to where we started from.
The other way of reading, back and forth,
Known as boustrophedon was found too awkward."

Pike grunted rather grimly with misgiving
At being thus expounded to himself
And made of by a boy; then having reached
The river bank, quit work defiantly,
As if he didn't care who understood him
And started his march back again discoursing:
"A man has got to keep his extrication.
The important thing is not to get bogged down
In what he has to do to earn a living.
What's more, I hate to keep afflicting weeds.
I like to give my enemies a truce."

"Be careful how you use your influence.
If I decided to become a doctor,
You'd be to blame for furnishing the reasons."

"I thought you meant to be an Indian Chief—
You said the second coming of Tecumseh.
Remember how you envied General Sherman.
William Tecumseh Sherman. Why Tecumseh?
(He tried to imitate Dick's tone of voice.)
You wished your middle name had been Tecumseh."

"I think I'll change my mind."

"You're saying that
To bother me by siding with the Doctor.
You've got no social conscience, as they say,
Or you'd feel differently about the classes.
You can't claim you're a social visionary."

"I'm saying it to argue his idea's
The same as your idea, only more so—
And I suspect it may be more and more so
The further up the scale of work you go.
You could do worse than boost me up to see."

"It isn't just the same and some day, schoolboy,
I'll show you why it isn't—not today.
Today I want to talk about the sun.
May as expected was a disappointment,
And June was not much better, cold and rainy.
The sun then had his longest day in heaven,
But no one from the feeling would have guessed
His presence was particularly there.
He only stayed to set the summer on fire,
Then fled for fear of getting stuck in lava
In case the rocks should melt and run again.
Everyone has to keep his extrication."

"That's what the Doctor's doing, keeping his.
That's what I have to do in school, keep mine
From knowing more than I know how to think with.

You see it in yourself and in the sun.
Yet you refuse to see it in the Doctor."

"All right, let's harmonize about the Doctor.
He may be some good in a manner of speaking.
I own he does look busy when the sun
Is in the sign of Sickness in the winter
And everybody's being sick for Christmas.
Then's when his Morgan lights out throwing snowballs
Behind her at the dashboard of his pung."

"But Cygnus isn't in the Zodiac,"
Dick longed to say, but wasn't sure enough
Of his astronomy. (He'd have to take
A half course in it next year.) And besides,
Why give the controversy a relapse?

They were both bent on scuffling up
Alluvium so pure that when a blade
To their surprise rang once on stone all day
Each tried to be the first at getting in
A superstitious cry for farmers' luck—
A rivalry that made them both feel kinder.
And so to let Pike seem to have the palm
With grace and not too formal a surrender
Dick said, "You've been a lesson in work-wisdom
To work with, Bill. But you won't have my thanks.
I like to think the sun's like you in that—
Since you bring up the subject of the sun.
(This would be my interpretation of him.)
He bestows summer on us and escapes
Before our realizing what we have
To thank him for. He doesn't want our thanks.
He likes to turn his back on gratitude
And avoid being worshipped as a god.
Our worship was a thing he had too much of
In the old days in Persia and Peru.
Shall I go on, or have I said enough—
To convey my respect for your position?

"I guess so," Pike said, innocent of Milton.
"That's where I reckon Santa Claus comes in—
To be our parents' pseudonymity
In Christmas giving, so they can escape
The thanks and let him catch it as a scapegoat.
And even he, you'll notice, dodges off
Up chimney to avoid the worst of it.
We all know his address, Mt. Hecla, Iceland.
So anyone can write to him that has to,
Though they do say he doesn't open letters.

A Santa Claus was needed. And there *is* one."

"So I have heard and do in part believe,"
Dick said to old Pike, innocent of Shakespeare.

CHOOSE SOMETHING LIKE A STAR

O Star (the fairest one in sight),
We grant your loftiness the right
To some obscurity of cloud—
It will not do to say of night,
Since dark is what brings out your light.
Some mystery becomes the proud.
But to be wholly taciturn
In your reserve is not allowed.
Say something to us we can learn
By heart and when alone repeat.
Say something! And it says "I burn."
But say with what degree of heat.
Talk Fahrenheit, talk Centigrade.
Use language we can comprehend.
Tell us what elements you blend.
It gives us strangely little aid,
But does tell something in the end.
And steadfast as Keats' Eremite,
Not even stooping from its sphere,
It asks a little of us here.
It asks of us a certain height,
So when at times the mob is swayed
To carry praise or blame too far,
We may choose something like a star
To stay our minds on and be staid.

THE GIFT OUTRIGHT

The land was ours before we were the land's.
She was our land more than a hundred years
Before we were her people. She was ours
In Massachusetts, in Virginia;
But we were England's, still colonials,
Possessing what we still were unpossessed by,
Possessed by what we now no more possessed.
Something we were withholding made us weak
Until we found out that it was ourselves
We were withholding from our land of living,
And forthwith found salvation in surrender.
Such as we were we gave ourselves outright
(The deed of gift was many deeds of war)
To the land vaguely realizing westward,
But still unstoried, artless, unenhanced,
Such as she was, such as she would become.

DIRECTIVE

Back out of all this now too much for us,
Back in a time made simple by the loss
Of detail, burned, dissolved, and broken off
Like graveyard marble sculpture in the weather,
There is a house that is no more a house
Upon a farm that is no more a farm
And in a town that is no more a town.
The road there, if you'll let a guide direct you
Who only has at heart your getting lost,
May seem as if it should have been a quarry—
Great monolithic knees the former town
Long since gave up pretense of keeping covered.
And there's a story in a book about it:
Besides the wear of iron wagon wheels
The ledges show lines ruled southeast northwest,
The chisel work of an enormous Glacier
That braced his feet against the Arctic Pole.
You must not mind a certain coolness from him
Still said to haunt this side of Panther Mountain.
Nor need you mind the serial ordeal
Of being watched from forty cellar holes
As if by eye pairs out of forty firkins.
As for the woods' excitement over you
That sends light rustle rushes to their leaves,
Charge that to upstart inexperience.
Where were they all not twenty years ago?
They think too much of having shaded out
A few old pecker-fretted apple trees.
Make yourself up a cheering song of how
Someone's road home from work this once was,
Who may be just ahead of you on foot
Or creaking with a buggy load of grain.

The height of the adventure is the height
Of country where two village cultures faded
Into each other. Both of them are lost.
And if you're lost enough to find yourself
By now, pull in your ladder road behind you
And put a sign up CLOSED to all but me.
Then make yourself at home. The only field
Now left's no bigger than a harness gall.
First there's the children's house of make-believe,
Some shattered dishes underneath a pine,
The playthings in the playhouse of the children.
Weep for what little things could make them glad.
Then for the house that is no more a house,
But only a belilaced cellar hole,
Now slowly closing like a dent in dough.
This was no playhouse but a house in earnest.
Your destination and your destiny's
A brook that was the water of the house,
Cold as a spring as yet so near its source,
Too lofty and original to rage.
(We know the valley streams that when aroused
Will leave their tatters hung on barb and thorn.)
I have kept hidden in the instep arch
Of an old cedar at the waterside
A broken drinking goblet like the Grail
Under a spell so the wrong ones can't find it,
So can't get saved, as Saint Mark says they mustn't.
(I stole the goblet from the children's playhouse.)
Here are your waters and your watering place.
Drink and be whole again beyond confusion.

ACQUAINTED WITH THE NIGHT

I have been one acquainted with the night.
I have walked out in rain—and back in rain.
I have outwalked the furthest city light.

I have looked down the saddest city lane.
I have passed by the watchman on his beat
And dropped my eyes, unwilling to explain.

I have stood still and stopped the sound of feet
When far away an interrupted cry
Came over houses from another street,

But not to call me back or say good-bye;
And further still at an unearthly height,
One luminary clock against the sky

Proclaimed the time was neither wrong nor right
I have been one acquainted with the night

Carl Sandburg

Carl (August) Sandburg was born of Swedish stock at Galesburg, Illinois, January 6, 1878. His schooling was haphazard; at thirteen he went to work on a milk wagon. During the next six years he was, in rapid succession, porter in a barber shop, scene-shifter in a cheap theater, truck-handler in a brickyard, turner-apprentice in a pottery, dish-washer in Denver and Omaha hotels, harvest hand in Kansas wheatfields. These tasks equipped him, as no amount of learning could have done, to be the laureate of industrial America. When war with Spain was declared in 1898, Sandburg, avid for fresh adventure, enlisted in Company C, Sixth Illinois Volunteers.

On his return from the campaign in Puerto Rico, Sandburg entered Lombard College in Galesburg and, for the first time, began to think in terms of literature. After leaving college, where he had been captain of the basket-ball team as well as editor-in-chief of the college paper, Sandburg became a salesman, advertising manager, and journalist.

Meanwhile the newspaperman was struggling to keep the poet alive. Until he was thirty-six years old Sandburg was unknown to the literary world. In 1914, a group of his poems appeared in *Poetry: A Magazine of Verse;* during the same year one of the group (the now famous "Chicago") was awarded the Levinson prize of two hundred dollars. A little more than a year later his first real book was published, and Sandburg's stature was apparent to all who cared to look.

Chicago Poems (1916) is full of ferment; it seethes with loose energy. If Frost is an intellectual aristocrat, Sandburg might be termed an emotional democrat. Sandburg's speech is simple and powerful; he uses slang as freely as his predecessors used the now archaic tongue of their times. Never has the American vulgate been used with such artistry and effect. Immediately cries of protest were heard: Sandburg was coarse and brutal; his work ugly and distorted; his language unrefined, unfit for poetry. His detractors forgot that Sandburg was brutal only to condemn brutality; that beneath his toughness, he was one of the tenderest of living poets; that, when he used colloquialisms and a richly metaphorical slang, he was searching for new poetic values in "limber, lasting, fierce words"—unconsciously answering Whitman who asked, "Do you suppose the liberties and brawn of These States have to do only with delicate lady-words? With gloved gentleman-words?"

Cornhuskers (1918) is another step forward; it is as sweeping as its forerunner and more sensitive. The gain in power and restraint is evident in the very first poem, a wide-swept vision of the prairie. Here is something of the surge of a Norse saga; *Cornhuskers* is keen with a salty vigor, a sympathy for all that is splendid and terrible in Nature. But the raw violence is restrained to the point of half-withheld mysticism. There are, in this volume, dozens of those delicate perceptions of beauty that must astonish those who think that Sandburg can write only a big-fisted, roughneck sort of poetry. As Sandburg has sounded some of the most *fortissimo* notes in modern poetry, he has also breathed some of its softest phrases. "Cool Tombs," one of the most poignant lyrics of our times, moves with a low music; "Grass" whispers as quietly as the earlier "Fog" steals in on stealthy, cat feet.

Smoke and Steel (1920) is the synthesis of its predecessors. In this collection, Sandburg has fused mood, accent and image. Whether the poet evokes the spirit of a jazz-band or, having had the radiance (the "flash crimson"), prays to touch life at its other extreme, this volume is not so vociferous as it is assured. Smoke-belching chimneys are here, quarries and great bowlders of iron-ribbed rock; here are titanic visions: the dreams of men and machinery. And silence is here—the silence of sleeping tenements and sun-soaked cornfields.

Slabs of the Sunburnt West (1923) is a fresh fusing: here in quick succession are the sardonic invectives of "And So Today," the rhapsody of "The Windy City" (an amplification of the early "Chicago"), and the panoramic title-poem. Although the book's chief exhibit is the amplitude of its longer poems, there are a few brevities (such as "Upstream") which have the vigor of a jubilant cry. Sandburg is still tempted to talk at the top of his voice, to bang the table and hurl his loudest epithets into the teeth of his opponents. But often he goes to the other extreme; he is likely to leave his material soft and loose instead of solidifying his emotions. There are times when the poet seems unsure whether or not he can furnish more than a clue to the half-realized wisps of his imagination. But though his meaning may not always be clear, there is no mistaking the power of his feeling nor the curious cadences of his music.

Good Morning, America (1928) is characteristically Sandburg at his best and worst. There are passages which are hopelessly enigmatic, passages which are only inflations of commonplace ideas. On the other hand, there are pages which are remarkable experiments in suspension, pages sensitive with a beauty delicately perceived. The thirty-eight "Tentative (First Model) Definitions of Poetry" with which the volume is prefaced are footnotes as well as prologues to his work in general, and the purely descriptive pieces are among his finest. Incidentally, the volume shows how far Sandburg has gone in critical esteem since the time when his *Chicago Poems* was openly derided, the title poem of *Good Morning, America* having been read as a Phi Beta Kappa poem at Harvard. Here, too, one is impressed by Sandburg's hatred of war; Sandburg was one of the first American poets to express the growing protests in "A.E.F." and other poems.

Besides his poetry, Sandburg has written three volumes of imaginative and, if one can conceive of such a thing, humorously mystical tales for children: *Rootabaga Stories* (1922), *Rootabaga Pigeons* (1923), and *Potato Face* (1930), the last being—so the poet and publisher insist—tales for adults of all ages. A collection of the Rootabaga stories was illustrated by Peggy Bacon in 1929. Eight years were spent traveling and studying documents for his vitalized *Abraham Lincoln: The Prairie Years* (1926), and assembling material for his collection of native folk-tunes *The American Songbag* (1927), a massive and revealing folio of words, music, and accompaniments to two hundred and eighty songs, more than one hundred of them never in print until Sandburg's ear and notebook gathered them from pioneer grandmothers, work-gangs, railroad men, hoboes, convicts, cowboys, mountain people and others who sing "because they must."

At fifty-eight the biographer, folklorist, and poet were merged in *The People, Yes* (1936), a synthesis of the collector's energy and the creator's imagination. The book is a carryall of folkstuff, catch phrases, tall tales, gossip, and history. Never, except in Whitman, has the common man been so apostrophized; never has there been a greater tribute to the people's shrewd skepticism and stubborn optimism, their patience and their power. Here are "the human reserves," misled and misunderstood, bewildered and betrayed, but stronger and wiser than they know. "The Long Shadow of Lincoln," which had not previously appeared in any volume, was the Phi Beta Kappa poem at William and Mary College, Williamsburg, in 1944.

In his early sixties Sandburg published the long-awaited "sequel" to *Abraham Lincoln: The Prairie Years.* It was called *Abraham Lincoln: The War Years* (1939) and was awarded the Pulitzer Prize for the best historical work of the year. The completed biography ran to six volumes and constituted a most extensive and penetrating interpretation of Lincoln and his times.

At seventy Sandburg made a spectacular debut as a writer of fiction. His first novel, *Remembrance Rock* (1948), was a book of more than one thousand pages. It was called a saga, a panorama, a prose epic; the author confessed he hoped to weave "the mystery of the American Dream with the costly toil and bloody struggles that have gone to keep alive and carry farther than Dream." Book One starts with the Pilgrims in seventeenth-century England; Book Two occupies itself with the Revolution; Book Three takes the story westward and through the Civil War.

Always the Young Strangers, a long nostalgic autobiographical memoir, published when Sandburg was seventy-five, was followed four years later by *The Sandburg Range,* a comprehensive selection of his prose and poetry.

Sandburg spent most of his life in his native Middle West, chiefly in Illinois and Michigan—his Galesburg, Illinois, birthplace became a shrine to the son of an immigrant Swedish blacksmith. In his sixties, he moved South, to a two hundred and forty acre farm in the Smokies, a place to ruminate and roam with his grandchildren. He had come a long way from the proletarian poet of the Windy City. Unable to rusticate completely, however, Sandburg made trips north, undertook sporadic forays into politics, toured the country with his guitar, and continued to discover fresh material for his ever-growing collection of Lincolniana.

TEN DEFINITIONS OF POETRY

1 Poetry is a projection across silence of cadences arranged to break the silence with definite intentions of echoes, syllables, wave lengths.
2 Poetry is the journal of a sea animal living on land, wanting to fly the air.
3 Poetry is a series of explanations of life, fading off into horizons too swift for explanations.
4 Poetry is a search for syllables to shoot at the barriers of the unknown and the unknowable.
5 Poetry is a theorem of a yellow-silk handkerchief knotted with riddles, sealed in a balloon tied to the tail of a kite flying in a white wind against a blue sky in spring.
6 Poetry is the silence and speech between a wet struggling root of a flower and a sunlit blossom of that flower.
7 Poetry is the harnessing of the paradox of earth cradling life and then entombing it.
8 Poetry is a phantom script telling how rainbows are made and why they go away.
9 Poetry is the synthesis of hyacinths and biscuits.
10 Poetry is the opening and closing of a door, leaving those who look through to guess about what is seen during a moment.

CHICAGO

Hog Butcher for the World,
Tool Maker, Stacker of Wheat,
Player with Railroads and the Nation's Freight Handler;
Stormy, husky, brawling,
City of the Big Shoulders:
They tell me you are wicked and I believe them, for I have seen your painted women under the gas lamps luring the farm boys.
And they tell me you are crooked and I answer: Yes, it is true I have seen the gunman kill and go free to kill again.
And they tell me you are brutal and my reply is: On the faces of women and children I have seen the marks of wanton hunger.
And having answered so I turn once more to those who sneer at this my city, and I give them back the sneer and say to them:
Come and show me another city with lifted head singing so proud to be alive and coarse and strong and cunning.

Flinging magnetic curses amid the toil of piling job on job, here is a tall bold slugger set vivid against the little soft cities;
Fierce as a dog with tongue lapping for action, cunning as a savage pitted against the wilderness,
Bareheaded,
Shoveling,
Wrecking,
Planning,
Building, breaking, rebuilding.
Under the smoke, dust all over his mouth, laughing with white teeth,
Under the terrible burden of destiny laughing as a young man laughs,
Laughing even as an ignorant fighter laughs who has never lost a battle,
Bragging and laughing that under his wrist is the pulse, and under his ribs the heart of the people,
Laughing!
Laughing the stormy, husky, brawling laughter of Youth, half-naked, sweating, proud to be Hog Butcher, Tool Maker, Stacker of Wheat, Player with Railroads and Freight Handler to the Nation.

FOG

The fog comes
on little cat feet.
It sits looking
over harbor and city
on silent haunches
and then moves on.

GRASS

Pile the bodies high at Austerlitz and Waterloo.
Shovel them under and let me work—
I am the grass; I cover all.

And pile them high at Gettysburg
And pile them high at Ypres and Verdun.
Shovel them under and let me work.
Two years, ten years, and passengers ask the conductor:
What place is this?
Where are we now?

I am the grass.
Let me work.

COOL TOMBS

When Abraham Lincoln was shoveled into the tombs, he forgot the copperheads and the assassin . . . in the dust, in the cool tombs.
And Ulysses Grant lost all thought of con men and Wall Street, cash and collateral turned ashes . . . in the dust, in the cool tombs.

Pocahontas' body, lovely as a poplar, sweet as a red haw in November or a pawpaw in May, did she wonder? does she remember? . . . in the dust, in the cool tombs?

Take any streetful of people buying clothes and groceries, cheering a hero or throwing confetti and blowing tin horns . . . tell me if the lovers are losers . . . tell me if any get more than the lovers . . . in the dust . . . in the cool tombs.

NOCTURNE IN A DESERTED BRICKYARD

Stuff of the moon
Runs on the lapping sand
Out to the longest shadows.
Under the curving willows,
And round the creep of the wave line,
Fluxions of yellow and dusk on the waters
Make a wide dreaming pansy of an old pond in the night.

LIMITED

I am riding on a limited express, one of the crack trains of the nation.
Hurtling across the prairie into blue haze and dark air go fifteen all-steel coaches holding a thousand people.
(All the coaches shall be scrap and rust and all the men and women laughing in the diners and sleepers shall pass to ashes.)
I ask a man in the smoker where he is going and he answers: "Omaha."

FOUR PRELUDES ON PLAYTHINGS OF THE WIND

"The Past Is a Bucket of Ashes."

1

The woman named Tomorrow
sits with a hairpin in her teeth
and takes her time
and does her hair the way she wants it
and fastens at last the last braid and coil
and puts the hairpin where it belongs
and turns and drawls: Well, what of it?
My grandmother, Yesterday, is gone
What of it? Let the dead be dead.

2

The doors were cedar
and the panel strips of gold
and the girls were golden girls
and the panels read and the girls chanted:
We are the greatest city,
and the greatest nation:
nothing like us ever was.

The doors are twisted on broken hinges,
Sheets of rain swish through on the wind
        where the golden girls ran and the panels read:
        We are the greatest city,
        the greatest nation,
        nothing like us ever was.

3

It has happened before.
Strong men put up a city and got
    a nation together,
And paid singers to sing and women
    to warble: We are the greatest city,
        the greatest nation,
        nothing like us ever was.

And while the singers sang
and the strong men listened
and paid the singers well,
    there were rats and lizards who listened
    . . . and the only listeners left now
    . . . are . . . the rats . . . and the lizards.
    And there are black crows
    crying, "Caw, caw,"
    bringing mud and sticks
    building a nest
    over the words carved
    on the doors where the panels were cedar
    and the strips on the panels were gold
    and the golden girls came singing:
        We are the greatest city,
        the greatest nation:
        nothing like us ever was.

The only singers now are crows crying, "Caw, caw,"
And the sheets of rain whine in the wind and doorways.
And the only listeners now are . . . the rats . . . and the lizards.

4

The feet of the rats
scribble on the doorsills;
the hieroglyphs of the rat footprints
chatter the pedigrees of the rats
and babble of the blood
and gabble of the breed
of the grandfathers and the great-grandfathers
of the rats.

And the wind shifts
and the dust on a doorsill shifts
and even the writing of the rat footprints
tells us nothing, nothing at all

about the greatest city, the greatest nation
where the strong men listened
and the women warbled: Nothing like us ever was.

A. E. F.

There will be a rusty gun on the wall, sweetheart,
The rifle grooves curling with flakes of rust.
A spider will make a silver string nest in the darkest, warmest corner of it.
The trigger and the range-finder, they too will be rusty.
And no hands will polish the gun, and it will hang on the wall.
Forefingers and thumbs will point absently and casually toward it.
It will be spoken among half-forgotten, wished-to-be-forgotten things.
They will tell the spider: Go on, you're doing good work.

PRAYERS OF STEEL

Lay me on an anvil, O God.
Beat me and hammer me into a crowbar.
Let me pry loose old walls;
Let me lift and loosen old foundations.

Lay me on an anvil, O God.
Beat me and hammer me into a steel spike.
Drive me into the girders that hold a skyscraper together.
Take red-hot rivets and fasten me into the central girders.
Let me be the great nail holding a skyscraper through blue nights into white stars.

JAZZ FANTASIA

Drum on your drums, batter on your banjos, sob on the long cool winding saxophones. Go to it, O jazzmen.

Sling your knuckles on the bottoms of the happy tin pans, let your trombones ooze, and go husha-husha-hush with the slippery sandpaper.

Moan like an autumn wind high in the lonesome treetops, moan soft like you wanted somebody terrible, cry like a racing car slipping away from a motorcycle-cop, bang-bang! you jazzmen, bang altogether drums, traps, banjos, horns, tin cans—make two people fight on the top of a stairway and scratch each other's eyes in a clinch tumbling down the stairs.

Can the rough stuff . . . Now a Mississippi steamboat pushes up the night river with a hoo-hoo-hoo-oo . . . and the green lanterns calling to the high soft stars . . . a red moon rides on the humps of the low river hills. . . . Go to it, O jazzmen.

BLUE ISLAND INTERSECTION

Six street-ends come together here.
They feed people and wagons into the center.

In and out all day horses with thoughts of nose-bags,
Men with shovels, women with baskets and baby buggies.
Six ends of streets and no sleep for them all day.
The people and wagons come and go, out and in.
Triangles of banks and drug stores watch.
The policemen whistle, the trolley cars bump:
Wheels, wheels, feet, feet, all day.

In the false dawn where the chickens blink
And the east shakes a lazy baby toe at tomorrow,
And the east fixes a pink half-eye this way,
In the time when only one milk wagon crosses
These three streets, these six street-ends
It is the sleep time and they rest.
The triangle banks and drug stores rest.
The policeman is gone, his star and gun sleep.
The owl car blutters along in a sleep-walk.

FROM "SMOKE AND STEEL"

Smoke of the fields in spring is one,
Smoke of the leaves in autumn another.
Smoke of a steel-mill roof or a battleship funnel,
They all go up in a line with a smokestack,
Or they twist . . . in the slow twist . . . of the wind.

If the north wind comes they run to the south.
If the west wind comes they run to the east.
        By this sign
        all smokes
        know each other.
Smoke of the fields in spring and leaves in autumn,
Smoke of the finished steel, chilled and blue,
By the oath of work they swear: "I know you."

Hunted and hissed from the center
Deep down long ago when God made us over,
Deep down are the cinders we came from—
You and I and our heads of smoke.

✣

Some of the smokes God dropped on the job
Cross on the sky and count our years
And sing in the secrets of our numbers;
Sing their dawns and sing their evenings,
Sing an old log-fire song:
        You may put the damper up,
        You may put the damper down,
        The smoke goes up the chimney just the same.

Smoke of a city sunset skyline,
Smoke of a country dusk horizon—
        They cross on the sky and count our years.

✣

Smoke of a brick-red dust
        Winds on a spiral
        Out of the stacks
For a hidden and glimpsing moon.
This, said the bar-iron shed to the blooming mill,
This is the slang of coal and steel.
The day-gang hands it to the night-gang,
The night-gang hands it back.

Stammer at the slang of this—
Let us understand half of it.
        In the rolling mills and sheet mills,
        In the harr and boom of the blast fires,
        The smoke changes its shadow
        And men change their shadow;
        A nigger, a wop, a bohunk changes.

        A bar of steel—it is only
Smoke at the heart of it, smoke and the blood of a man.
A runner of fire ran in it, ran out, ran somewhere else,
And left smoke and the blood of a man
And the finished steel, chilled and blue.

So fire runs in, runs out, runs somewhere else again,
And the bar of steel is a gun, a wheel, a nail, a shovel,
A rudder under the sea, a steering-gear in the sky;
And always dark in the heart and through it,
        Smoke and the blood of a man.
Pittsburgh, Youngstown, Gary, they make their steel with men.

In the blood of men and the ink of chimneys
The smoke nights write their oaths:
Smoke into steel and blood into steel;
Homestead, Braddock, Birmingham, they make their steel with men.
Smoke and blood is the mix of steel. . . .

LOSERS

If I should pass the tomb of Jonah
I would stop there and sit for a while;
Because I was swallowed one time deep in the dark
And came out alive after all.

If I pass the burial spot of Nero
I shall say to the wind, "Well, well!"—

I who have fiddled in a world on fire,
I who have done so many stunts not worth the doing.

I am looking for the grave of Sinbad, too.
I want to shake his ghost-hand and say,
"Neither of us died very early, did we?"

And the last sleeping-place of Nebuchadnezzar—
When I arrive there I shall tell the wind:
"You ate grass; I have eaten crow—
Who is better off now or next year?"

Jack Cade, John Brown, Jesse James,
There too I could sit down and stop for a while.
I think I could tell their headstones:
"God, let me remember all good losers."

I could ask people to throw ashes on their heads
In the name of that sergeant at Belleau Woods
Walking into the drumfires, calling his men,
"Come on, you . . . Do you want to live forever?"

WIND SONG

Long ago I learned how to sleep,
In an old apple orchard where the wind swept by counting its money and throwing it away,
In a wind-gaunt orchard where the limbs forked out and listened or never listened at all,
In a passel of trees where the branches trapped the wind into whistling, "Who, who are you?"
I slept with my head in an elbow on a summer afternoon and there I took a sleep lesson.
There I went away saying: I know why they sleep, I know how they trap the tricky winds.
Long ago I learned how to listen to the singing wind and how to forget and how to hear the deep whine,
Slapping and lapsing under the day blue and the night stars:
Who, who are you?

Who can ever forget
listening to the wind go by
counting its money
and throwing it away?

PRIMER LESSON

Look out how you use proud words.
When you let proud words go, it is not easy to call them back.
They wear long boots, hard boots; they walk off proud; they can't hear you calling—
Look out how you use proud words.

BROKEN-FACE GARGOYLES

All I can give you is broken-face gargoyles.
It is too early to sing and dance at funerals,
Though I can whisper to you I am looking for an undertaker humming a lullaby and throwing his feet in a swift and mystic buck-and-wing, now you see it and now you don't.

Fish to swim a pool in your garden flashing a speckled silver,
A basket of wine-saps filling your room with flame-dark for your eyes and the tang of valley orchards for your nose,
Such a beautiful pail of fish, such a beautiful peck of apples, I cannot bring you now.
It is too early and I am not footloose yet.

I shall come in the night when I come with a hammer and saw.
I shall come near your window, where you look out when your eyes open in the morning,
And there I shall slam together bird-houses and bird-baths for wing-loose wrens and hummers to live in, birds with yellow wing tips to blur and buzz soft all summer.

So I shall make little fool homes with doors, always open doors for all and each to run away when they want to.
I shall come just like that even though now it is early and I am not yet footloose,
Even though I am still looking for an undertaker with a raw, wind-bitten face and a dance in his feet.
I make a date with you (put it down) for six o'clock in the evening a thousand years from now.

All I can give you now is broken-face gargoyles.
All I can give you now is a double gorilla head with two fish mouths and four eagle eyes hooked on a street wall, spouting water and looking two ways to the ends of the street for the new people, the young strangers, coming, coming, always coming.

It is early.
I shall yet be footloose.

FLASH CRIMSON

I shall cry God to give me a broken foot.

I shall ask for a scar and a slashed nose.

I shall take the last and the worst.

I shall be eaten by gray creepers in a bunkhouse where no runners of the sun come and no dogs live.

And yet—of all "and yets" this is the bronze strongest—

I shall keep one thing better than all else; there is the blue steel of a great star of early evening in it; it lives longer than a broken foot or any scar.

The broken foot goes to a hole dug with a shovel or the bone of a nose may whiten on a hilltop—and yet—"and yet"—

There is one crimson pinch of ashes left after all; and none of the shifting winds that whip the grass and none of the pounding rains that beat the dust know how to touch or find the flash of this crimson.

I cry to God to give me a broken foot, a scar, or a lousy death.

I who have seen the flash of this crimson, I ask God for the last and worst.

EARLY LYNCHING

Two Christs were at Golgotha.
One took the vinegar, another looked on.
One was on the cross, another in the mob.
One had the nails in his hands, another the stiff fingers holding a hammer driving nails.
There were many more Christs at Golgotha, many more thief pals, many many more in the mob howling the Judean equivalent of "Kill Him! Kill Him!"
The Christ they killed, the Christ they didn't kill, those were the two at Golgotha.

Pity, pity, the bones of these broken ankles.
Pity, pity, the slimp of these broken wrists
The mother's arms are strong to the last.
She holds him and counts the heart drips.

The smell of the slums was on him,
Wrongs of the slums lit his eyes.
Songs of the slums wove in his voice
The haters of the slums hated his slum heart.

The leaves of a mountain tree,
Leaves with a spinning star shook in them,
Rocks with a song of water, water, over them,
Hawks with an eye for death any time, any time,
The smell and the sway of these were on his sleeves, were in his nortrils, his words.

The slum man they killed, the mountain man lives on.

PRECIOUS MOMENTS

Bright vocabularies are transient as rainbows.
Speech requires blood and air to make it.
Before the word comes off the end of the tongue,
While the diaphragms of flesh negotiate the word,
In the moment of doom when the word forms
It is born, alive, registering an imprint—

Afterward it is a mummy, a dry fact, done and gone,
The warning holds yet: Speak now or forever hold your peace.
Ecce homo had meanings: Behold the man! Look at him!
Dying he lives and speaks!

MOIST MOON PEOPLE

The moon is able to command the valley tonight.
The green mist shall go a-roaming, the white river shall go a-roaming.
Yet the moon shall be commanding, the moon shall take a high stand on the sky.

When the cats crept up the gullies,
And the goats fed at the rim a-laughing,
When the spiders swept their rooms in the burr oaks,
And the katydids first searched for this year's accordions,
And the crickets began a-looking for last year's concertinas—

I was there, I saw that hour, I know God had grand intentions about it.
If not, why did the moon command the valley, the green mist and white river go a-roaming, and the moon by itself take so high a stand on the sky?

If God and I alone saw it, the show was worth putting on,
Yet I remember others were there, Amos and Priscilla, Axel and Hulda, Hank and Jo, Big Charley and Little Morningstar.
They were all there; the clock ticks spoke with castanet clicks.

BUNDLES

I have thought of beaches, fields,
Tears, laughter.

I have thought of homes put up—
And blown away.

I have thought of meetings and for
Every meeting a good-by.

I have thought of stars going alone,
Orioles in pairs, sunsets in blundering
Wistful deaths.

I have wanted to let go and cross over
To a next star, a last star.

I have asked to be left a few tears
And some laughter.

UPSTREAM

The strong men keep coming on,
They go down shot, hanged, sick, broken.

They live on fighting, singing, lucky as plungers.
The strong mothers pulling them on . . .
The strong mothers pulling them from a dark sea, a great prairie, a long mountain.
Call hallelujah, call amen, call deep thanks.
The strong men keep coming on.

SUNSETS

There are sunsets who whisper a good-by.
It is a short dusk and a way for stars.
Prairie and sea rim they go level and even,
And the sleep is easy.

There are sunsets who dance good-by.
They fling scarves half to the arc,
To the arc then and over the arc.
Ribbons at the ears, sashes at the hips,
Dancing, dancing good-by. And here sleep
Tosses a little with dreams.

ELEPHANTS ARE DIFFERENT TO DIFFERENT PEOPLE

Wilson and Pilcer and Snack stood before the zoo elephant.

Wilson said, "What is its name? Is it from Asia or Africa? Who feeds it? Is it a he or a she? How old is it? Do they have twins? How much does it cost to feed? How much does it weigh? If it dies how much will another one cost? If it dies what will they use the bones, the fat, and the hide for? What use is it besides to look at?"

Pilcer didn't have any questions; he was murmuring to himself, "It's a house by itself, walls and windows, the ears came from tall cornfields, by God; the architect of those legs was a workman, by God; he stands like a bridge out across deep water; the face is sad and the eyes are kind; I know elephants are good to babies."

Snack looked up and down and at last said to himself, "He's a tough son-of-a-gun outside and I'll bet he's got a strong heart, I'll bet he's strong as a copper-riveted boiler inside."

They didn't put up any arguments.
They didn't throw anything in each other's faces.
Three men saw the elephant three ways
And let it go at that.
They didn't spoil a sunny Sunday afternoon;
"Sunday comes only once a week," they told each other.

FOR YOU

The peace of great doors be for you.
Wait at the knobs, at the panel oblongs;
Wait for the great hinges.

The peace of great churches be for you,
Where the players of loft pipe-organs
Practice old lovely fragments, alone.

The peace of great books be for you,
Stains of pressed clover leaves on pages,
Bleach of the light of years held in leather.

The peace of great prairies be for you.
Listen among windplayers in cornfields,
The wind learning over its oldest music.

The peace of great seas be for you.
Wait on a hook of land, a rock footing
For you, wait in the salt wash.

The peace of great mountains be for you,
The sleep and the eyesight of eagles,
Sheet mist shadows and the long look across

The peace of great hearts be for you,
Valves of the blood of the sun,
Pumps of the strongest wants we cry.

The peace of great silhouettes be for you,
Shadow dancers alive in your blood now,
Alive and crying, "Let us out, let us out."

The peace of great changes be for you.
Whispers, oh beginners in the hills.
Tumble, oh cubs—tomorrow belongs to you.

The peace of great loves be for you.
Rain, soak these roots; wind, shatter the dry rot.
Bars of sunlight, grips of the earth; hug these.

The peace of great ghosts be for you,
Phantoms of night-gray eyes, ready to go
To the fog-star dumps, to the fire-white doors.

Yes, the peace of great phantoms be for you,
Phantom iron men, mothers of bronze,
Keepers of the lean clean breeds.

THEY HAVE YARNS

(from "The People, Yes")

They have yarns
Of a skyscraper so tall they had to put hinges
On the two top stories so to let the moon go by,
Of one corn crop in Missouri when the roots
Went so deep and drew off so much water
The Mississippi riverbed that year was dry,
Of pancakes so thin they had only one side,
Of "a fog so thick we shingled the barn and six feet out on the fog,"
Of Pecos Pete straddling a cyclone in Texas and riding it to the west coast where "it rained out under him,"
Of the man who drove a swarm of bees across the Rocky Mountains and the Desert "and didn't lose a bee,"
Of a mountain railroad curve where the engineer in his cab can touch the caboose and spit in the conductor's eye,
Of the boy who climbed a cornstalk growing so fast he would have starved to death if they hadn't shot biscuits up to him,
Of the old man's whiskers: "When the wind was with him his whiskers arrived a day before he did."
Of the hen laying a square egg and cackling, "Ouch!" and of hens laying eggs with the dates printed on them,
Of the ship captain's shadow: it froze to the deck one cold winter night,
Of mutineers on that same ship put to chipping rust with rubber hammers,
Of the sheep counter who was fast and accurate: "I just count their feet and divide by four,"
Of the man so tall he must climb a ladder to shave himself,
Of the runt so teeny-weeny it takes two men and a boy to see him,
Of mosquitoes: one can kill a dog, two of them a man,
Of a cyclone that sucked cookstoves out of the kitchen, up the chimney flue, and on to the next town,
Of the same cyclone picking up wagon-tracks in Nebraska and dropping them over in the Dakotas,
Of the hook-and-eye snake unlocking itself into forty pieces, each piece two inches long, then in nine seconds flat snapping itself together again,
Of the watch swallowed by the cow—when they butchered her a year later the watch was running and had the correct time,
Of horned snakes, hoop snakes that roll themselves where they want to go, and rattlesnakes carrying bells instead of rattles on their tails,
Of the herd of cattle in California getting lost in a giant redwood tree that had hollowed out,

Of the man who killed a snake by putting its tail in its mouth so it swallowed itself,
Of railroad trains whizzing along so fast they reach the station before the whistle,
Of pigs so thin the farmer had to tie knots in their tails to keep them from crawling through the cracks in their pens,
Of Paul Bunyan's big blue ox, Babe, measuring between the eyes forty-two ax-handles and a plug of Star tobacco exactly,
Of John Henry's hammer and the curve of its swing and his singing of it as "a rainbow round my shoulder."

"Do tell!"
"I want to know!"
"You don't say so!"
"For the land's sake!"
"Gosh all fish-hooks!"
"Tell me some more.
I don't believe a word you say
but I love to listen
to your sweet harmonica
to your chin-music.
Your fish stories hang together
when they're just a pack of lies:
you ought to have a leather medal:
you ought to have a statue
carved of butter: you deserve
a large bouquet of turnips."

"Yessir," the traveler drawled,
"Away out there in the petrified forest
everything goes on the same as usual.
The petrified birds sit in their petrified nests
and hatch their petrified young from petrified eggs."

A high pressure salesman jumped off the Brooklyn Bridge and was saved by a policeman. But it didn't take him long to sell the idea to the policeman. So together they jumped off the bridge.

One of the oil men in heaven started a rumor of a gusher down in hell. All the other oil men left in a hurry for hell. As he gets to thinking about the rumor he had started he says to himself there might be something in it after all. So he leaves for hell in a hurry.

"The number 42 will win this raffle, that's my number." And when he won they asked him whether he guessed the number or had a system. He said he had a system, "I took up the old family album and there on page 7 was my grandfather and grandmother both on page 7. I said to myself this is easy for 7 times 7 is the number that will win and 7 times 7 is 42."

Once a shipwrecked sailor caught hold of a stateroom door and floated for hours till friendly hands from out of the darkness threw him a rope. And he called across the night, "What country is this?" and hearing voices answer, "New Jersey,' he took a fresh hold on the floating stateroom door and called back half-wearily, "I guess I'll float a little farther."

An Ohio man bundled up the tin roof of a summer kitchen and sent it to a motor car maker with a complaint of his car not giving service. In three weeks a new car arrived for him and a letter: "We regret delay in shipment but your car was received in a very bad order."

A Dakota cousin of this Ohio man sent six years of tin can accumulations to the same works, asking them to overhaul his car. Two weeks later came a rebuilt car, five old tin cans, and a letter: "We are also forwarding you five parts not necessary in our new model."

Thus fantasies heard at filling stations in the midwest. Another relates to a Missouri mule who took aim with his heels at an automobile rattling by. The car turned a somersault, lit next a fence, ran right along through a cornfield till it came to a gate, moved onto the road and went on its way as though nothing had happened. The mule heehawed with desolation, "What's the use?"

Another tells of a farmer and his family stalled on a railroad crossing, how they jumped out in time to see a limited express knock it into flinders, the farmer calling, "Well, I always did say that car was no shucks in a real pinch."

When the Masonic Temple in Chicago was the tallest building in the United States west of New York, two men who would cheat the eyes out of you if you gave 'em a chance, took an Iowa farmer to the top of the building and asked him, "How is this for high?" They told him that for $25 they would go down in the basement and turn the building around on its turn-table for him while he stood on the roof and saw how this seventh wonder of the world worked. He handed them $25. They went. He waited. They never came back.

This is told in Chicago as a folk tale, the same as the legend of Mrs. O'Leary's cow kicking over the barn lamp that started the Chicago fire, when the Georgia visitor, Robert Toombs, telegraphed an Atlanta crony, "Chicago is on fire, the whole city burning down, God be praised!"

Nor is the prize sleeper Rip Van Winkle and his scolding wife forgotten, nor the headless horseman scooting through Sleepy Hollow

Nor the sunken treasure-ships in coves and harbors, the hideouts of gold and silver sought by Coronado, nor the Flying Dutchman round the Cape doomed to nevermore pound his ear nor ever again take a snooze for himself.

Nor the sailor's caretaker Mother Carey seeing to it that every seafaring man in the afterworld has a seabird to bring him news of ships and women, an albatross for the admiral, a gull for the deckhand

Nor the sailor with a sweetheart in every port of the world, nor the ships that set out with flying colors and all the promises you could ask, the ships never heard of again

Nor Jim Liverpool, the riverman who could jump across any river and back without touching land he was that quick on his feet

Nor Mike Fink along the Ohio and the Mississippi, half wild horse and half cockeyed alligator, the rest of him snags and snapping turtle. "I can out-run, out jump, out-shoot, out-brag, out-drink, and out-fight, rough and tumble, no holts barred, any man on both sides of the river from Pittsburgh to New Orleans and back again to St. Louis. My trigger finger itches and I want to go redhot. War, famine and bloodshed puts flesh on my bones, and hardship's my daily bread."

Nor the man so lean he threw no shadow: six rattlesnakes struck at him at one time and every one missed him.

THE PEOPLE WILL LIVE ON

(from "The People, Yes")

The people will live on.
The learning and blundering people will live on.
They will be tricked and sold and again sold
And go back to the nourishing earth for rootholds,
The people so peculiar in renewal and comback,
You can't laugh off their capacity to take it.
The mammoth rests between his cyclonic dramas.

The people so often sleepy, weary, enigmatic,
is a vast huddle with many units saying:
"I earn my living.
I make enough to get by
and it takes all my time.
If I had more time
I could do more for myself
and maybe for others.
I could read and study
and talk things over
and find out about things.
It takes time.
I wish I had the time."

The people is a tragic and comic two-face:
hero and hoodlum: phantom and gorilla twist-
ing to moan with a gargoyle mouth: "They
buy me and sell me . . . it's a game . . .
sometime I'll break loose . . ."

Once having marched
Over the margins of animal necessity,
Over the grim line of sheer subsistence
Then man came
To the deeper rituals of his bones,
To the lights lighter than any bones,
To the time for thinking things over,
To the dance, the song, the story,
Or the hours given over to dreaming,
Once having so marched.

Between the finite limitations of the five senses
and the endless yearnings of man for the beyond
the people hold to the humdrum bidding of work and food
while reaching out when it comes their way
for lights beyond the prison of the five senses,
for keepsakes lasting beyond any hunger or death.
This reaching is alive.
The panderers and liars have violated and smutted it.
Yet this reaching is alive yet
for lights and keepsakes.

The people know the salt of the sea
and the strength of the winds
lashing the corners of the earth.
The people take the earth
as a tomb of rest and a cradle of hope.
Who else speaks for the Family of Man?
They are in tune and step
with constellations of universal law.

The people is a polychrome,
a spectrum and a prism
held in a moving monolith,
a console organ of changing themes,
a clavilux of color poems
wherein the sea offers fog
and the fog moves off in rain
and the labrador sunset shortens
to a nocturne of clear stars
serene over the shot spray
of northern lights.

The steel mill sky is alive.
The fire breaks white and zigzag
shot on a gun-metal gloaming.
Man is a long time coming.
Man will yet win.
Brother may yet line up with brother:

This old anvil laughs at many broken hammers.
There are men who can't be bought.
The fireborn are at home in fire.
The stars make no noise.
You can't hinder the wind from blowing.
Time is a great teacher.
Who can live without hope?
In the darkness with a great bundle of grief
the people march.
In the night, and overhead a shovel of stars for
keeps, the people march:
"Where to? what next?"

Vachel Lindsay

⤳§ (Nicholas) Vachel Lindsay was born in Springfield, Illinois, November 10, 1879. His home for many years was next door to the executive mansion of the State of Illinois; from the window where Lindsay did most of his writing, he saw governors come and go, including the martyred John P. Altgeld, whom he has celebrated in one of his finest poems. He graduated from the Springfield High School, attended Hiram College (1897-1900), studied at the Art Institute at Chicago (1900-03) and at the New York School of Art (1904). After two years of lecturing and settlement work, he took the first of his long tramps, walking through Florida, Georgia, and the Carolinas, preaching "the gospel of beauty," and formulating his unique plans for a communal art. During the following five years, Lindsay made several of these trips, traveling as a combination missionary and minstrel. Like a true revivalist, he attempted to wake a response to beauty, distributing a little pamphlet entitled "Rhymes to Be Traded for Bread."

Lindsay began to create more poetry to reach the public—all of his verse was written in his rôle of apostle. He was, primarily, a rhyming John the Baptist singing to convert the heathen, to stimulate and encourage the half-hearted dreams that hide and are smothered in sordid villages and townships. But the great audiences he was endeavoring to reach did not hear him, even though his collection *General William Booth Enters Into Heaven* (1913) struck many a loud and racy note.

Lindsay broadened his effects, developed the chant, and, the following year, published his *The Congo and Other Poems* (1914), an infectious blend of rhyme, religion, and rag-time. In the title-poem and, in a lesser degree, the three companion chants, Lindsay struck his most powerful—and most popular—vein. When intoned in Lindsay's resonant baritone, it gave people that primitive joy in syncopated sound that is at the very base of song. In these experiments in breaking down the barriers between poetry and music, Lindsay (obviously infected by the echolalia of Poe's "Bells") tried to create what he called a "Higher Vaudeville" imagination, carrying the form back to the old Greek precedent where every line was half-spoken, half-sung. Gestures and stage directions, even chanted responses, were added.

Lindsay's innovation succeeded at once. The novelty, the speed, the clatter, forced the attention of people who had never paid the slightest heed to the poet's quieter verses. Men heard the *sounds* of hurtling America in these lines even when they were deaf to its spirit. They failed to see that, beneath the noise of "The Kallyope Yell" and "The Santa Fé Trail," Lindsay was partly an admirer, partly an ironical critic of the shrieking energy of these states. By his effort to win the enemy over, Lindsay had persuaded the proverbially tired business man to listen at last. But, in overstressing the vaudeville features, there arose the danger of Lindsay the poet being lost in Lindsay the entertainer. The sympathetic celebration of Negro spirits and psychology (seen at their best in "The Congo," "John Brown" and "Simon Legree") degenerated into the crude buffooneries of "The Daniel Jazz" and "The Blacksmith's Serenade." The three bracketed poems, and a few others, are certain of a place in the history of American poetry.

Lindsay's earnestness, keyed up by an exuberant fancy, saved him. *The Chinese*

Nightingale (1917) begins with the most whimsical extended rhymes Lindsay ever devised. This title-poem, with its air of free improvisation, is his finest piece of sheer texture. And if the subsequent *The Golden Whales of California* (1920) is less distinctive, it is principally because the author had written too much and too speedily to be self-critical. It is his peculiar appraisal of loveliness, the rollicking high spirits joined to a stubborn evangelism, that makes Lindsay so representative a product of his environment.

Collected Poems (1923) is a complete and almost cruel exhibit of Lindsay's best and worst. Inflated stanzas alternate with some of the most charming children's poetry of the times; the set of fanciful Moon Poems would be enough to keep Lindsay's name alive. That Lindsay had lost whatever faculty of self-appraisal he may have possessed is evidenced by page after page of crudities; verses are propelled by nothing more than physical energy whipping up a trivial idea. What mars so much of this writing is Lindsay's attempt to give every wisp of fancy a cosmic or at least a national significance. Thus that intoxicating chant "The Ghosts of the Buffaloes" appears in the later edition with an unfortunate appendage, an irrelevant hortatory appeal beginning, "Would I might rouse the Lincoln in you all!" But, in spite of the fact that the poet suffered from a complex of undiscriminating patriotism, a curious hero-worship which makes him link Woodrow Wilson with Socrates, his very catholicity was representative of a great part of his country. Johnny Appleseed and John L. Sullivan, Daniel Boone and William Jennings Bryan, Andrew Jackson and P. T. Barnum—such figures were the symbols of his motley America. They were not merely heroes but demi-gods. They typified the incongruous blend of high idealism and childish fantasy, of beauty and ballyhoo which made America resemble (to Lindsay) a County Fair—

> every soul resident
> In the earth's one circus tent.

It was a combination that made the United States "the golden dream" created by pioneers and baseball players, Presidents and movie-queens. Nuances of thought or expression were forgotten; exuberance, uncontrolled by taste or reason, triumphed. *Going-to-the-Sun* (1923), *Going-to-the-Stars* (1926), and *The Candle in the Cabin* (1927), illustrated with Lindsay's characteristic and flowery drawings, contain some charming and almost girlish verses, but followed each other in too rapid succession and betray Lindsay's uncritical loquacity. His prose is far better than the later verse. *The Litany of Washington Street* (1929), described as "a kind of Washington's birthday, Lincoln's birthday, Whitman's birthday, Jefferson's birthday book," is a set of Fourth of July orations on an idealized Main Street stretching from Connecticut to Calcutta.

Much of Lindsay will die; he will not live as either a prophet or a politician. But the vitality which impels the best of his galloping meters will persist; his innocent wildness of imagination, outlasting his naïve programs, will charm even those to whom his declamations are no longer a novelty. His gospel is no less original for being preached through a saxophone.

Besides his original poetry, Lindsay had embodied his experiences and meditations on the road in two prose volumes, *A Handy Guide for Beggars* (1916) and *Adventures While Preaching the Gospel of Beauty* (1914), as well as an enthusiastic study of the "silent drama," *The Art of the Moving Picture* (1915). A curious document, half rhapsody, half visionary novel, entitled *The Golden Book of Springfield,* appeared in 1920.

Lindsay traded on his surplus energy. Some of it went into private games, such as the establishment of each individual's "personal hieroglyphics," some into grandiose but futile schemes, most into lecturing. For more than twenty years he ranged the country, exciting his audiences and exhausting himself. After fifty the strain was too much for him. He collapsed at the beginning of his fifty-third year just as he should have been turning to the larger works he had so often discussed with friends. The fear of poverty overcame him; his exuberance vanished; he was plagued with self-doubt. He felt that he was being neglected, even persecuted; he convinced himself he was a failure. The high-spirited "broncho that would not be broken" was broken at last. He committed suicide on the night of December 5, 1931.

THE CONGO

(*A Study of the Negro Race*)

I. Their Basic Savagery

Fat black bucks in a wine-barrel room,
Barrel-house kings, with feet unstable,
Sagged and reeled and pounded on the table,
Pounded on the table,
Beat an empty barrel with the handle of a broom,
Hard as they were able,
Boom, boom, Boom,
With a silk umbrella and the handle of a broom,
Boomlay, boomlay, boomlay, Boom.

A deep rolling bass.

Then I had religion, Then I had a vision.
I could not turn from their revel in derision.
Then I saw the Congo, creeping through the black,
Cutting through the jungle with a golden track.

More deliberate. Solemnly chanted.

Then along that riverbank
A thousand miles
Tattooed cannibals danced in files;
Then I heard the boom of the blood-lust song
And a thigh-bone beating on a tin-pan gong.
And "Blood" screamed the whistles and the fifes of the warriors,
"Blood" screamed the skull-faced, lean witch-doctors,
"Whirl ye the deadly voo-doo rattle,
Harry the uplands,
Steal all the cattle,
Rattle-rattle, rattle-rattle,
Bing!
Boomlay, boomlay, boomlay, Boom,"
A roaring, epic, rag-time tune
From the mouth of the Congo
To the Mountains of the Moon.

A rapidly piling climax of speed and racket.

With a philosophic pause.

Death is an Elephant,
Torch-eyed and horrible,
Foam-flanked and terrible.
BOOM, steal the pygmies,
BOOM, kill the Arabs,
BOOM, kill the white men,
Hoo, Hoo, Hoo.
Listen to the yell of Leopold's ghost
Burning in Hell for his hand-maimed host.
Hear how the demons chuckle and yell
Cutting his hands off, down in Hell.
Listen to the creepy proclamation,
Blown through the lairs of the forest-nation,
Blown past the white-ants' hill of clay,
Blown past the marsh where the butterflies play:—
"Be careful what you do,
Or Mumbo-Jumbo, God of the Congo,
And all of the other
Gods of the Congo,
Mumbo-Jumbo will hoo-doo you,
Mumbo-Jumbo will hoo-doo you,
Mumbo-Jumbo will hoo-doo you."

Shrilly and with a heavily accented meter.

Like the wind in the chimney.

All the o sounds very golden. Heavy accents very heavy. Light accents very light. Last line whispered.

II. THEIR IRREPRESSIBLE HIGH SPIRITS

Wild crap-shooters with a whoop and a call
Danced the juba in their gambling-hall
And laughed fit to kill, and shook the town,
And guyed the policemen and laughed them down
With a boomlay, boomlay, boomlay, BOOM. . . .
THEN I SAW THE CONGO, CREEPING THROUGH THE BLACK,
CUTTING THROUGH THE JUNGLE WITH A GOLDEN TRACK.
A negro fairyland swung into view,
A minstrel river
Where dreams come true.
The ebony palace soared on high
Through the blossoming trees to the evening sky,
The inlaid porches and casements shone
With gold and ivory and elephant-bone.
And the black crowd laughed till their sides were sore
At the baboon butler in the agate door,
And the well-known tunes of the parrot band
That trilled on the bushes of that magic land.
A troupe of skull-faced witch-men came
Through the agate doorway in suits of flame,
Yes, long-tailed coats with a gold-leaf crust
And hats that were covered with diamond-dust.
And the crowd in the court gave a whoop and a call
And danced the juba from wall to wall.
But the witch-men suddenly stilled the throng
With a stern cold glare, and a stern old song:—
"Mumbo-Jumbo will hoo-doo you." . . .

Rather shrill and high.

Read exactly as in first section.

Lay emphasis on the delicate ideas. Keep as light-footed as possible.

With pomposity.

With a great deliberation and ghostliness.

Just then from the doorway, as fat as shotes,
Came the cake-walk princes in their long red coats,
Shoes with a patent leather shine,
And tall silk hats that were red as wine.
And they pranced with their butterfly partners there,
Coal-black maidens with pearls in their hair,
Knee-skirts trimmed with the jessamine sweet,
And bells on their ankles and little black feet.
And the couples railed at the chant and the frown
Of the witch-men lean, and laughed them down.
(O rare was the revel, and well worth while
That made those glowering witch-men smile).

With overwhelming assurance, good cheer, and pomp.

With growing speed and sharply marked dance-rhythm.

The cake-walk royalty then began
To walk for a cake that was tall as a man
To the tune of "Boomlay, boomlay, Boom,"
While the witch-men laughed, with a sinister air,
And sang with the scalawags prancing there:—
"Walk with care, walk with care,
Or Mumbo-Jumbo, God of the Congo,
And all of the other
Gods of the Congo,
Mumbo-Jumbo will hoo-doo you.
Beware, beware, walk with care,
Boomlay, boomlay, boomlay, boom.
Boomlay, boomlay, boomlay, boom.
Boomlay, boomlay, boomlay, boom.
Boomlay, boomlay, boomlay,
Boom."
O rare was the revel, and well worth while
That made those glowering witch-men smile.

With a touch of negro dialect, and as rapidly as possible toward the end.

Slow philosophic calm.

III. The Hope of Their Religion

A good old negro in the slums of the town
Preached at a sister for her velvet gown.
Howled at a brother for his low-down ways,
His prowling, guzzling, sneak-thief days.
Beat on the Bible till he wore it out,
Starting the jubilee revival shout.
And some had visions, as they stood on chairs,
And sang of Jacob, and the golden stairs.
And they all repented, a thousand strong,
From their stupor and savagery and sin and wrong
And slammed their hymn books till they shook the room
With "Glory, glory, glory,"
And "Boom, boom, Boom."
THEN I SAW THE CONGO, CREEPING THROUGH THE BLACK,
CUTTING THROUGH THE JUNGLE WITH A GOLDEN TRACK.
And the gray sky opened like a new-rent veil
And showed the Apostles with their coats of mail,
In bright white steel they were seated round

Heavy bass. With a literal imitation of camp-meeting racket, and trance.

Exactly as in the first section.

And their fire-eyes watched where the Congo wound.
And the twelve Apostles, from their thrones on high,
Thrilled all the forest with their heavenly cry:—
"Mumbo-Jumbo will die in the jungle;
Never again will he hoo-doo you,
Never again will he hoo-doo you."

Sung to the tune of "Hark, ten thousand harps and voices."

Then along that river, a thousand miles
The vine-snared trees fell down in files.
Pioneer angels cleared the way
For a Congo paradise, for babes at play,
For sacred capitals, for temples clean.
Gone were the skull-faced witch-men lean.
There, where the wild ghost-gods had wailed
A million boats of the angels sailed
With oars of silver, and prows of blue
And silken pennants that the sun shone through.
'Twas a land transfigured, 'twas a new creation.
Oh, a singing wind swept the negro nation
And on through the backwoods clearing flew:—
"Mumbo-Jumbo is dead in the jungle.
Never again will he hoo-doo you.
Never again will he hoo-doo you."

With growing deliberation and joy.

In a rather high key—as delicately as possible.

To the tune of "Hark, ten thousand harps and voices."

Redeemed were the forests, the beasts and the men,
And only the vulture dared again
By the far, lone mountains of the moon
To cry, in the silence, the Congo tune:—
"Mumbo-Jumbo will hoo-doo you,
Mumbo . . . Jumbo . . . will . . . hoo-doo . . . you."

Dying off into a penetrating, terrified whisper.

TO A GOLDEN-HAIRED GIRL IN A LOUISIANA TOWN

You are a sunrise,
If a star should rise instead of the sun.
You are a moonrise,
If a star should come in the place of the moon.
You are the Spring,
If a face should bloom instead of an apple-bough.
You are my love,
If your heart is as kind
As your young eyes now.

GENERAL WILLIAM BOOTH ENTERS INTO HEAVEN

(To be sung to the tune of "The Blood of the Lamb" with indicated instruments)

I

(*Bass drum beaten loudly.*)
Booth led boldly with his big bass drum—
(Are you washed in the blood of the Lamb?)
The Saints smiled gravely and they said: "He's come."

(Are you washed in the blood of the Lamb?)
Walking lepers followed, rank on rank,
Lurching bravos from the ditches dank,
Drabs from the alleyways and drug fiends pale—
Minds still passion-ridden, soul-powers frail:—
Vermin-eaten saints with moldy breath,
Unwashed legions with the ways of Death—
(Are you washed in the blood of the Lamb?)

(*Banjos.*)
Every slum had sent its half-a-score
The round world over. (Booth had groaned for more.)
Every banner that the wide world flies
Bloomed with glory and transcendent dyes.
Big-voiced lasses made their banjos bang,
Tranced, fanatical they shrieked and sang:—
"Are you washed in the blood of the Lamb?"
Hallelujah! It was queer to see
Bull-necked convicts with that land make free.
Loons with trumpets blowed a blare, blare, blare
On, on upward thro' the golden air!
(Are you washed in the blood of the Lamb?)

II

(*Bass drum slower and softer.*)
Booth died blind and still by faith he trod,
Eyes still dazzled by the ways of God.
Booth led boldly, and he looked the chief,
Eagle countenance in sharp relief,
Beard a-flying, air of high command
Unabated in that holy land.

(*Sweet flute music.*)
Jesus came from out the court-house door,
Stretched his hands above the passing poor.
Booth saw not, but led his queer ones there
Round and round the mighty court-house square.
Yet in an instant all that blear review
Marched on spotless, clad in raiment new.
The lame were straightened, withered limbs uncurled
And blind eyes opened on a new, sweet world.

(*Bass drum louder.*)
Drabs and vixens in a flash made whole!
Gone was the weasel-head, the snout, the jowl!
Sages and sibyls now, and athletes clean,
Rulers of empires, and of forests green!

(*Grand chorus of all instruments. Tambourines to the foreground.*)
The hosts were sandaled, and their wings were fire!
(Are you washed in the blood of the Lamb?)
But their noise played havoc with the angel-choir

(Are you washed in the blood of the Lamb?)
Oh, shout Salvation! It was good to see
Kings and Princes by the Lamb set free.
The banjos rattled and the tambourines
Jing-jing-jingled in the hands of Queens.

(Reverently sung, no instruments.)
And when Booth halted by the curb for prayer
He saw his Master thro' the flag-filled air.
Christ came gently with a robe and crown
For Booth the soldier, while the throng knelt down.
He saw King Jesus. They were face to face,
And he knelt a-weeping in that holy place.
Are you washed in the blood of the Lamb?

THE EAGLE THAT IS FORGOTTEN

(John P. Altgeld. Born December 30, 1847; died March 12, 1902)

Sleep softly . . . eagle forgotten . . . under the stone.
Time has its way with you there, and the clay has its own.
"We have buried him now," thought your foes, and in secret rejoiced.
They made a brave show of their mourning, their hatred unvoiced,
They had snarled at you, barked at you, foamed at you, day after day,
Now you were ended. They praised you, . . . and laid you away.

The others that mourned you in silence and terror and truth,
The widow bereft of her pittance, the boy without youth,
The mocked and the scorned and the wounded, the lame and the poor
That should have remembered forever, . . . remember no more.

Where are those lovers of yours, on what name do they call
The lost, that in armies wept over your funeral pall?
They call on the names of a hundred high-valiant ones,
A hundred white eagles have risen, the sons of your sons,
The zeal in their wings is a zeal that your dreaming began
The valor that wore out your soul in the service of man.

Sleep softly, . . . eagle forgotten, . . . under the stone,
Time has its way with you there, and the clay has its own.
Sleep on, O brave-hearted, O wise man, that kindled the flame—
To live in mankind is far more than to live in a name,
To live in mankind, far, far more . . . than to live in a name.

THE GHOSTS OF THE BUFFALOES

Last night at black midnight I woke with a cry,
The windows were shaking, there was thunder on high,
The floor was atremble, the door was ajar,
White fires, crimson fires, shone from afar.

I rushed to the dooryard. The city was gone.
My home was a hut without orchard or lawn.
It was mud-smear and logs near a whispering stream,
Nothing else built by man could I see in my dream . . .

Then . . .
Ghost-kings came headlong, row upon row,
Gods of the Indians, torches aglow.
They mounted the bear and the elk and the deer,
And eagles gigantic, agèd and sere,
They rode long-horn cattle, they cried "A-la-la."
They lifted the knife, the bow, and the spear,
They lifted ghost-torches from dead fires below,
The midnight made grand with the cry "A-la-la."
The midnight made grand with a red-god charge,
A red-god show,
A red-god show,
"A-la-la, a-la-la, a-la-la, a-la-la."

With bodies like bronze, and terrible eyes
Came the rank and the file, with catamount cries,
Gibbering, yipping, with hollow-skull clacks,
Riding white bronchos with skeleton backs,
Scalp-hunters, beaded and spangled and bad,
Naked and lustful and foaming and mad,
Flashing primeval demoniac scorn,
Blood-thirst and pomp amid darkness reborn,
Power and glory that sleep in the grass
While the winds and the snows and the great rains pass.
They crossed the gray river, thousands abreast,
They rode out in infinite lines to the west,
Tide upon tide of strange fury and foam,
Spirits and wraiths, the blue was their home,
The sky was their goal where the star-flags are furled,
And on past those far golden splendors they whirled.
They burned to dim meteors, lost in the deep,
And I turned in dazed wonder, thinking of sleep.

And the wind crept by
Alone, unkempt, unsatisfied,
The wind cried and cried—
Muttered of massacres long past,
Buffaloes in shambles vast . . .
An owl said, "Hark, what is a-wing?"
I heard a cricket caroling,
I heard a cricket caroling,
I heard a cricket caroling.

Then . . .
Snuffing the lightning that crashed from on high
Rose royal old buffaloes, row upon row.
The lords of the prairie came galloping by.

And I cried in my heart "A-la-la, a-la-la.
A red-god show,
A red-god show,
A-la-la, a-la-la, a-la-la."
Buffaloes, buffaloes, thousands abreast,
A scourge and amazement, they swept to the west.
With black bobbing noses, with red rolling tongues,
Coughing forth steam from their leather-wrapped lungs,
Cows with their calves, bulls big and vain,
Goring the laggards, shaking the mane,
Stamping flint feet, flashing moon eyes,
Pompous and owlish, shaggy and wise.

Like sea-cliffs and caves resounded their ranks
With shoulders like waves, and undulant flanks.
Tide upon tide of strange fury and foam,
Spirits and wraiths, the blue was their home,
The sky was their goal where the star-flags are furled,
And on past those far golden splendors they whirled.
They burned to dim meteors, lost in the deep,
And I turned in dazed wonder, thinking of sleep.

I heard a cricket's cymbals play,
A scarecrow lightly flapped his rags,
And a pan that hung by his shoulder rang,
Rattled and thumped in a listless way,
And now the wind in the chimney sang,
The wind in the chimney,
The wind in the chimney,
The wind in the chimney,
Seemed to say:—
"Dream, boy, dream,
If you anywise can.
To dream is the work
Of beast or man.
Life is the west-going dream-storm's breath,
Life is a dream, the sigh of the skies,
The breath of the stars, that nod on their pillows
With their golden hair mussed over their eyes."
The locust played on his musical wing,
Sang to his mate of love's delight.
I heard the whippoorwill's soft fret.
I heard a cricket caroling,
I heard a cricket caroling,
I heard a cricket say: "Good-night, good-night,
Good-night, good-night, . . . good-night."

THE TRAVELER

The moon's a devil jester
Who makes himself too free.

The rascal is not always
Where he appears to be.
Sometimes he is in my heart—
Sometimes he is in the sea;
Then tides are in my heart,
And tides are in the sea.

O traveler, abiding not
Where he pretends to be!

A NEGRO SERMON:—SIMON LEGREE

Legree's big house was white and green.
His cotton-fields were the best to be seen.
He had strong horses and opulent cattle,
And bloodhounds bold, with chains that would rattle.
His garret was full of curious things:
Books of magic, bags of gold,
And rabbits' feet on long twine strings,
But he went down to the Devil.

Legree, he sported a brass-buttoned coat,
A snake-skin necktie, a blood-red shirt.
Legree, he had a beard like a goat,
And a thick hairy neck, and eyes like dirt.
His puffed-out cheeks were fish-belly white,
He had great long teeth, and an appetite.
He ate raw meat, 'most every meal,
And rolled his eyes till the cat would squeal.
His fist was an enormous size
To mash poor niggers that told him lies:
He was surely a witch-man in disguise.
But he went down to the Devil.

He wore hip-boots, and would wade all day
To capture his slaves that had fled away.
But he went down to the Devil.
He beat poor Uncle Tom to death
Who prayed for Legree with his last breath.
Then Uncle Tom to Eva flew,
To the high sanctoriums bright and new;
And Simon Legree stared up beneath,
And cracked his heels, and ground his teeth:
And went down to the Devil.
He crossed the yard in the storm and gloom;
He went into his grand front room.
He said, "I killed him, and I don't care."
He kicked a hound, he gave a swear;
He tightened his belt, he took a lamp,
Went down cellar to the webs and damp.

There in the middle of the moldy floor
He heaved up a slab; he found a door—
And went down to the Devil.

His lamp blew out, but his eyes burned bright.
Simon Legree stepped down all night—
Down, down to the Devil.
Simon Legree he reached the place,
He saw one half of the human race,
He saw the Devil on a wide green throne,
Gnawing the meat from a big ham-bone,
And he said to Mister Devil:
"I see that you have much to eat—
A red ham-bone is surely sweet.
I see that you have lion's feet;
I see your frame is fat and fine,
I see you drink your poison wine—
Blood and burning turpentine."

And the Devil said to Simon Legree:
"I like your style, so wicked and free.
Come sit and share my throne with me,
And let us bark and revel."
And there they sit and gnash their teeth,
And each one wears a hop-vine wreath.
They are matching pennies and shooting craps,
They are playing poker and taking naps.
And old Legree is fat and fine:
He eats the fire, he drinks the wine—
Blood and burning turpentine—
Down, down with the Devil;
Down, down with the Devil;
Down, down with the Devil.

JOHN BROWN

(To be sung by a leader and chorus, the leader
nging the body of the poem, while the chorus in-
rrupts with the question)

ve been to Palestine.
What did you see in Palestine?
saw the ark of Noah—
was made of pitch and pine.
saw old Father Noah
sleep beneath his vine.
saw Shem, Ham and Japhet
anding in a line.
aw the tower of Babel
the gorgeous sunrise shine—
a weeping willow tree
side the Dead Sea.

I've been to Palestine.
What did you see in Palestine?
I saw abominations
And Gadarene swine.
I saw the sinful Canaanites
Upon the shewbread dine,
And spoil the temple vessels
And drink the temple wine.
I saw Lot's wife, a pillar of salt
Standing in the brine—
By a weeping willow tree
Beside the Dead Sea.

I've been to Palestine.
What did you see in Palestine?
Cedars on Mount Lebanon,
Gold in Ophir's mine,

And a wicked generation
Seeking for a sign,
And Baal's howling worshipers
Their god with leaves entwine.
And . . .
I saw the war-horse ramping
And shake his forelock fine—
By a weeping willow tree
Beside the Dead Sea.

I've been to Palestine.
What did you see in Palestine?
Old John Brown.
Old John Brown.
I saw his gracious wife
Dressed in a homespun gown.
I saw his seven sons
Before his feet bow down.
And he marched with his seven sons,
His wagons and goods and guns,
To his campfire by the sea,
By the waves of Galilee.

I've been to Palestine.
What did you see in Palestine?
I saw the harp and psalt'ry
Played for Old John Brown.
I heard the ram's horn blow,
Blow for Old John Brown.
I saw the Bulls of Bashan—
They cheered for Old John Brown.
I saw the big Behemoth—
He cheered for Old John Brown.
I saw the big Leviathan—
He cheered for Old John Brown.
I saw the Angel Gabriel
Great power to him assign.
I saw him fight the Canaanites
And set God's Israel free.
I saw him when the war was done
In his rustic chair recline—
By his campfire by the sea
By the waves of Galilee.

I've been to Palestine.
What did you see in Palestine?
Old John Brown.
Old John Brown.
And there he sits
To judge the world.
His hunting-dogs
At his feet are curled.
His eyes half-closed,
But John Brown sees
The ends of the earth,
The Day of Doom.
And his shot-gun lies
Across his knees—
Old John Brown,
Old John Brown.

THE DOVE OF NEW SNOW

I give you a house of snow,
I give you the flag of the wind above it,
I give you snow-bushes
In a long row,
I give you a snow-dove,
And ask you
To love it.

The snow-dove flies in
At the snow-house window,
He is a ghost
And he casts no shadow.
His cry is the cry of love
From the meadow,
The meadow of snow where he walked in a glow,
The glittering, angelic meadow.

THE FLOWER-FED BUFFALOES

The flower-fed buffaloes of the spring
In the days of long ago,
Ranged where the locomotives sing
And the prairie flowers lie low;
The tossing, blooming, perfumed grass
Is swept away by wheat,
Wheels and wheels and wheels spin by
In the spring that still is sweet.
But the flower-fed buffaloes of the spring
Left us long ago.
They gore no more, they bellow no more,
They trundle around the hills no more:—
With the Blackfeet lying low,
With the Pawnees lying low.

ABRAHAM LINCOLN WALKS AT MIDNIGHT

(*In Springfield, Illinois*)

It is portentous, and a thing of state
That here at midnight, in our little town
A mourning figure walks, and will not rest,
Near the old court-house pacing up and down,

Or by his homestead, or in shadowed yards
He lingers where his children used to play,
Or through the market, on the well-worn stones
He stalks until the dawn-stars burn away.

A bronzed, lank man! His suit of ancient black,
A famous high top-hat and plain worn shawl
Make him the quaint great figure that men love,
The prairie-lawyer, master of us all.

He cannot sleep upon his hillside now.
He is among us:—as in times before!
And we who toss and lie awake for long,
Breathe deep, and start, to see him pass the door.

His head is bowed. He thinks of men and kings.
Yea, when the sick world cries, how can he sleep?
Too many peasants fight, they know not why;
Too many homesteads in black terror weep.

The sins of all the war-lords burn his heart.
He sees the dreadnaughts scouring every main.
He carries on his shawl-wrapped shoulders now
The bitterness, the folly and the pain.

He cannot rest until a spirit-dawn
Shall come;—the shining hope of Europe free:
A league of sober folk, the workers' earth,
Bringing long peace to Cornland, Alp and Sea.

It breaks his heart that kings must murder still,
That all his hours of travail here for men
Seem yet in vain. And who will bring white peace
That he may sleep upon his hill again?

THE CHINESE NIGHTINGALE

"How, how," he said. "Friend Chang," I said,
"San Francisco sleeps as the dead—

Ended license, lust and play:
Why do you iron the night away?
Your big clock speaks with a deadly sound,
With a tick and a wail till dawn comes round,
While the monster shadows glower and creep,
What can be better for man than sleep?"

"I will tell you a secret," Chang replied;
"My breast with vision is satisfied,
And I see green trees and fluttering wings,
And my deathless bird from Shanghai sings."
Then he lit five firecrackers in a pan,
"Pop, pop," said the firecrackers, "cra-cra-crack."
He lit a joss stick long and black.
Then the proud gray joss in the corner stirred;
On his wrist appeared a gray small bird,
And this was the song of the gray small bird:
"Where is the princess, loved forever,
Who made Chang first of the kings of men?"

And the joss in the corner stirred again;
And the carved dog, curled in his arms, awoke,
Barked forth a smoke-cloud that whirled and broke.
It piled in a maze round the ironing-place,
And there on the snowy table wide
Stood a Chinese lady of high degree,
With a scornful, witching, tea-rose face. . . .
Yet she put away all form and pride,
And laid her glimmering veil aside
With a childlike smile for Chang and me.

The walls fell back, night was aflower,
The table gleamed in a moonlit bower,
While Chang, with a countenance carved of stone,
Ironed and ironed, all alone.
And thus she sang to the busy man Chang:
"Have you forgotten . . .
Deep in the ages, long, long ago,
I was your sweetheart, there on the sand—
Storm-worn beach of the Chinese land?
We sold our grain in the peacock town—
Built on the edge of the sea-sands brown—
Built on the edge of the sea-sands brown. . . .
When all the world was drinking blood
From the skulls of men and bulls
And all the world had swords and clubs of stone,
We drank our tea in China beneath the sacred spice-trees,
And heard the curled waves of the harbor moan.
And this gray bird, in Love's first spring,
With a bright-bronze breast and a bronze-brown wing,
Captured the world with his caroling.

Do you remember, ages after,
At last the world we were born to own?
You were the heir of the yellow throne—
The world was the field of the Chinese man
And we were the pride of the Sons of Han?
We copied deep books and we carved in jade,
And wove blue silks in the mulberry shade. . . ."

"I remember, I remember
That Spring came on forever,
That Spring came on forever,"
Said the Chinese nightingale.

My heart was filled with marvel and dream,
Though I saw the western street-lamps gleam,
Though dawn was bringing the western day,
Though Chang was a laundryman ironing away.
Mingled there with the streets and alleys,
The railroad-yard and the clock-tower bright,
Demon clouds crossed ancient valleys;
Across wide lotus-ponds of light
I marked a giant firefly's flight.

And the lady, rosy-red,
Flourished her fan, her shimmering fan,
Stretched her hand toward Chang, and said:
"Do you remember,
Ages after,
Our palace of heart-red stone?
Do you remember
The little doll-faced children
With their lanterns full of moon-fire,
That came from all the empire
Honoring the throne?—
The loveliest fête and carnival
Our world had ever known?
The sages sat about us
With their heads bowed in their beards,
With proper meditation on the sight.
Confucius was not born;
We lived in those great days
Confucius later said were lived aright. . . .
And this gray bird, on that day of spring,
With a bright-bronze breast and a bronze-brown wing,
Captured the world with his caroling.
Late at night his tune was spent.
Peasants,
Sages,
Children,
Homeward went,
And then the bronze bird sang for you and me.

We walked alone. Our hearts were high and free.
I had a silvery name, I had a silvery name,
I had a silvery name—do you remember
The name you cried beside the tumbling sea?"

Chang turned not to the lady slim—
He bent to his work, ironing away;
But she was arch, and knowing and glowing,
For the bird on his shoulder spoke for him.

"Darling . . . darling . . . darling . . . darling . . ."
Said the Chinese nightingale.

The great gray joss on the rustic shelf,
Rakish and shrewd, with his collar awry,
Sang impolitely, as though by himself,
Drowning with his bellowing the nightingale's cry:
"Back through a hundred, hundred years
Hear the waves as they climb the piers,
Hear the howl of the silver seas,
Hear the thunder.
Hear the gongs of holy China
How the waves and tunes combine
In a rhythmic clashing wonder,
Incantation old and fine:
  'Dragons, dragons, Chinese dragons,
  Red firecrackers, and green firecrackers
  And dragons, dragons, Chinese dragons.' "

Then the lady, rosy-red,
Turned to her lover Chang and said:
"Dare you forget that turquoise dawn
When we stood in our mist-hung velvet lawn,
And worked a spell this great joss taught
Till a God of the Dragons was charmed and caught?
From the flag high over our palace home
He flew to our feet in rainbow-foam—
A king of beauty and tempest and thunder
Panting to tear our sorrows asunder.
A dragon of fair adventure and wonder.
We mounted the back of that royal slave
With thoughts of desire that were noble and grave.
We swam down the shore to the dragon-mountains,
We whirled to the peaks and the fiery fountains.
To our secret ivory house we were borne.
We looked down the wonderful wind-filled regions
Where the dragons darted in glimmering legions.
Right by my breast the nightingale sang;
The old rhymes rang in the sunlit mist
That we this hour regain—
Song-fire for the brain.

When my hands and my hair and my feet you kissed,
When you cried for your heart's new pain,
What was my name in the dragon-mist,
In the rings of the rainbowed rain?"

"Sorrow and love, glory and love,"
Sang the Chinese nightingale,
"Sorrow and love, glory and love,"
Said the Chinese nightingale.

And now the joss broke in with his song:
"Dying ember, bird of Chang,
Soul of Chang, do you remember?—
Ere you returned to the shining harbor
There were pirates by ten thousand
Descended on the town
In vessels mountain-high and red and brown,
Moon-ships that climbed the storms and cut the skies.
On their prows were painted terrible bright eyes.
But I was then a wizard and a scholar and a priest;
I stood upon the sand;
With lifted hand I looked upon them
And sunk their vessels with my wizard eyes,
And the stately lacquer-gate made safe again.
Deep, deep below the bay, the seaweed and the spray,
Embalmed in amber every pirate lies,
Embalmed in amber every pirate lies."

Then this did the noble lady say:
"Bird, do you dream of our home-coming day
When you flew like a courier on before
From the dragon-peak to our palace-door,
And we drove the steed in your singing path—
The ramping dragon of laughter and wrath:
And found our city all aglow,
And knighted this joss that decked it so?
There were golden fishes in the purple river
And silver fishes and rainbow fishes.
There were golden junks in the laughing river,
And silver junks and rainbow junks:
There were golden lilies by the bay and river,
And silver lilies and tiger-lilies,
And tinkling wind-bells in the gardens of the town
By the black-laquer gate
Where walked in state
The kind king Chang
And his sweetheart mate. . . .
With his flag-born dragon
And his crown of pearl . . . and . . . jade,
And his nightingale reigning in the mulberry shade,
And sailors and soldiers on the sea-sands brown,
And priests who bowed them down to your song—

By the city called Han, the peacock town,
By the city called Han, the nightingale town,
The nightingale town."

Then sang the bird, so strangely gay,
Fluttering, fluttering, ghostly and gray,
A vague, unraveling, final tune,
Like a long unwinding silk cocoon;
Sang as though for the soul of him
Who ironed away in that bower dim:—
"I have forgotten
Your dragons great,
Merry and mad and friendly and bold.
Dim is your proud lost palace-gate.
I vaguely know
There were heroes of old,
Troubles more than the heart could hold,
There were wolves in the woods
Yet lambs in the fold,
Nests in the top of the almond tree. . . .
The evergreen tree . . . and the mulberry tree. . . .
Life and hurry and joy forgotten,
Years and years I but half-remember . . .
Man is a torch, then ashes soon,
May and June, then dead December,
Dead December, then again June.
Who shall end my dream's confusion?
Life is a loom, weaving illusion. . . .
I remember, I remember
There were ghostly veils and laces. . . .
In the shadowy bowery places. . . .
With lovers' ardent faces
Bending to one another,
Speaking each his part.
They infinitely echo
In the red cave of my heart.
'Sweetheart, sweetheart, sweetheart,'
They said to one another.
They spoke, I think, of perils past.
They spoke, I think, of peace at last
One thing I remember:
Spring came on forever,
Spring came on forever,"
Said the Chinese nightingale.

WHY I VOTED THE SOCIALIST TICKET

I am unjust, but I can strive for justice.
My life's unkind, but I can vote for kindness.
I, the unloving, say life should be lovely.
I that am blind, cry out against my blindness.

Man is a curious brute—he pets his fancies—
Fighting mankind, to win sweet luxury.
So he will be, tho' law be clear as crystal,
Tho' all men plan to live in harmony.

Come, let us vote against our human nature,
Crying to God in all the polling places
To heal our everlasting sinfulness
And make us sages with transfigured faces.

Melville Cane

⚜ Melville Cane was born April 15, 1879, at Plattsburg, New York. He was educated at Columbia Grammar School, received his A.B. at Columbia in 1900, LL.B. in 1903. At Columbia he was editor-in-chief of the Literary Monthly. He engaged in the practice of law, specializing in the law of copyright and the theater.

After an interval of twenty years, he turned to poetry and published *January Garden* (1926), the antithesis of the light verse of Cane's youth; it is sensitive and unequivocally serious.

Cane's *Behind Dark Spaces* (1930) is less impressionistic, but what it loses in suggestion it gains in sharpness. Mixing "pure" and "suspended" rhyme, his tone-color has grown richer. *Poems, New and Selected* (1938) and the aptly named *A Wider Arc* (1947) emphasize Cane's nimble virtuosity and grace. *And Pastures New* (1956) is a selected volume. *Bullet-Hunting and Other New Poems* (1960) continues the poet's lively work.

TREE IN DECEMBER

Frost has sealed
The still December field.
Over fern and furrow,
Over the quickening
Within each meadowy acre,
Frost, invisibly thorough,
Spreads its thickening
Stiffening lacquer.

Above the field, beneath a sky
Heavy with snow stirring to fly,
A tree stands alone,
Bare of fruit, leaves gone
Bleak as stone.

Once, on a similar glazed
Field, on a similar tree,
Dead as the eye could see,
The first man, dazed
In the first December, grimly gazed,
Never having seen
The miracle of recurring green,
The shining spectacle of rebirth
Rising out of frozen earth.

Snow fell and all about
Covered earth, and him with doubt.
More chill grew the air
And his mute despair.

Leaves that April had uncurled
Now were blown dust in the world,
Apples mellowing sweet and sound
Now were icy rot in the ground;
Roses August sunned in bloom
Now were less than lost perfume.

Had he seen the final hour
Of fruit and leaf and flower?
Had the last bird taken wing,
Nevermore to sing?
Never to fly in the light of another spring?

The man trembled with cold, with dread,
Thinking of all things dead
And his own earthen bed.

Trembling, he grew aware
Of a new quiet in the air;
Snow had ceased;
A ray came faintly through;
The wavering slit of blue
Vaguely increased.

Trembling, the first man gazed
At the glazed
And glittering tree,
Dead as the eye could see.

Whence came the sight
To read the sign aright?
The hint,—
The glad intimation, flashing:
"Wintry rains
Are blood in the veins;
Under snows and binding sleets
Locked roots live, a heart still beats"?

From what impalpable breath
Issued the faith,
The inner cry: "This is not death"?

DAWN HAS YET TO RIPPLE IN

What is this that I have heard?
Scurrying rat or stirring bird?
Scratching in the wall of sleep?
Twitching on the eaves of sleep?
I can hear it working close
Through a space along the house,
Through a space obscure and thin.
Night is swiftly running out,
Dawn has yet to ripple in,
Dawn has yet to clear the doubt,
Rat within or bird without.

HYMN TO NIGHT

Now it grows dark.
Red goes
Out of the rose;
Out of the lawn
Green's withdrawn;
Each buttercup now yields
Its gold from blurring fields;
Larkspur and sky surrender
Blue wonder.

We were dark within, we relied
For our strength on the nourishing sun;
Now it is under and gone.
Now, as the light grows duller,
We, who had flourished on color,
Stand, in the ever-deepening shade,
Bereft, dismayed.

We were dark within, it was death
We saw, we had never seen
Within the dark, we had never known
The spark, the vital breath.
If only we had known
That black is neither loss nor lack
But holds the essential seed
Of mortal hope and need!

Now sheltering dusk,
Shepherd of color and light for dawns unending,
Tends the holy task.

Praise be to black, the benign,
No longer malign,
Prolonger of days!
Praise the preserver of shine,
The keeper of blaze!

Praise Night,
Forever praise
Savior Night,
Who surely stays
The arm of time,
Who guards the flame,
Who hoards the light.

Praised be the Night.

Wallace Stevens

☙ Wallace Stevens was born in Reading, Pennsylvania, October 2, 1879. A student at Harvard University and New York Law School, he was admitted to the Bar in 1904 and engaged in the general practice of law in New York City. In 1916 he became associated with the Hartford Accident and Indemnity Company, of which he became vice-president in 1934. He died suddenly, after an operation, August 2, 1955.

A poet of peculiar reticence, he kept himself from book publication for a long and rigorous time. Although many of his poems appeared as early as 1913, he was so self-critical that he refused to publish a volume until 1923 when the first edition of *Harmonium* appeared. The most casual reading of this volume discloses that Stevens is a stylist of unusual delicacy. Even the least sympathetic reader must be struck by the poet's hypersensitive and ingenious imagination. It is a curiously ambiguous world which Stevens paints: a world of merging half-lights, of finicking shadows, of disembodied emotions. Even this last word is an exaggeration, for emotion itself seems absent from the clear and often fiercely colored segments of the poet's designs.

Considered as a painter, Stevens is one of the most original impressionists of the times. He is fond of little blocks of color, verbal mosaics in which syllables are used as pigments. Little related to any human struggle, the content of *Harmonium* progresses toward a sort of "absolute" poetry which, depending on tone rather than on passion, aims to flower in an air of pure estheticism. His very titles—which deliberately add to the reader's confusion by having little or no connection with most of the poems—betray this quality: "Hymn from a Watermelon Pavilion," "The Paltry Nude Starts on a Spring Voyage," "Frogs Eat Butterflies, Snakes Eat Frogs, Hogs Eat Snakes, Men Eat Hogs." Such poems have much for the eye, something for the ear, but they are too fantastic and dandified for common understanding.

> Chieftain Iffucan of Azcan in caftan
> Of tan with henna hackles, halt!

Thus Stevens begins his "Bantam in Pine-Woods" and his pleasure in playing with sounds must be evident to the most perplexed reader. Like William Carlos Williams, to whose *Collected Poems* Stevens furnished an introduction, Stevens is interested in things chiefly from their "unreal" aspect. He is, nevertheless, romantic. A romantic poet nowadays, says Stevens, "happens to be one who still dwells in an ivory tower, but who insists that life there would be intolerable except for the fact that one has, from the top, such an exceptional view of the public dump and the advertising signs. . . . He is the hermit who dwells alone with the sun and moon, and insists on taking a rotten newspaper." That is why Stevens can write of "The Worms at Heaven's Gate" with no disrespect to Shakespeare, make a study in esthetics of the contents of a cab, and entitle a poem on death ("the finale of seem") "The Emperor of Ice-Cream."

"Sunday Morning" and "Sea Surface Full of Clouds" are blends of disintegrated fantasy and fictitious reality. These poems are highly selective in choice of allusions, inner harmonies, and special luxuriance of sound. They burst into strange bloom; they foliate in a region where the esthetic impulse encroaches on the reasoning intellect. "Thirteen Ways of Looking at a Blackbird" and "Domination of Black" have a delicacy of design which suggests the Chinese; "Peter Quince at the Clavier" and the exquisite "To the One of Fictive Music" (Stevens' most obviously musical moment) reveal a distinction which places "this auditor of insects, this lutanist of fleas" as one who has perfected a kind of poetry which is a remarkable, if strangely hermetic, art.

After a twelve years' silence Stevens published *Ideas of Order* (1935) in a limited edition. The format of the book and its private publication emphasizes the limitation as well as the elegance of the contents. Here, as in *Harmonium,* Stevens seldom writes poetry about the *Ding an sich,* but almost always about the overtones which the thing creates in his mind. Here the candid surface breaks into cryptic epigrams, and the scenes are recorded in a deft but elusive phrase. Often enough a poem refuses to yield its meaning, but "Academic Discourse at Havana" and "The Idea of Order at Key West" surrender themselves in an almost pure music.

The Man with the Blue Guitar (1937), with a bow to Picasso, places its emphasis on man as artist and on the complicated relations between art and life. It is a far cry from the delight in luxuriance for its own sake which Stevens once called "the essential gaudiness of poetry." There is little mischievous playing with the sound of words, as in the much-quoted line (from "The Emperor of Ice-Cream") which had the "roller of big cigars" whip

In kitchen cups concupiscent curds.

There is, instead, an increasing concern with the problem of a society in chaos and the difficult "idea of order." Stevens has sacrified some of the barbaric piling up of effects; his work is no longer a pageant of colors, sounds, and smells. The riotousness has been replaced by a grave awareness of the plight of man. Without losing the wit and delicacy of what Allen Tate has characterized as "floating images," Stevens has gained compassion. A new preoccupation with man's bewilderment and despair strengthens Stevens' later work.

Parts of a World (1942) and *Transport to Summer* (1947) enlarge Stevens' position as a poet. The esthete has become an essayist, although he remains poet-philosopher of "the ultimate elegance." A section in "Esthétique Du Mal" begins:

The greatest poverty is not to live
In a physical world, to feel that one's desire
Is too difficult to tell from despair. Perhaps,
After death, the non-physical people, in paradise,
Itself non-physical, may, by chance, observe
The green corn gleaming and experience
The minor of what we feel.

As always there is opulence, a sensory delight, in everything which Stevens touches. The opening of the early "Sunday Morning" has the flat but brilliant colors of a Matisse, especially one of that master's odalisque series. The later poetry is no less lush even when it is less spectacular. In "Thirteen Ways of Looking at a Blackbird" Stevens wrote:

I do not know which to prefer,
The beauty of inflections
Or the beauty of innuendoes.

It is apparent that Stevens concerns himself more and more with "the beauty of innuendoes" than with "the beauty of inflections"; his lines, sliding from one dissolving metaphor to another, are built on ambiguities that fall into indefinite and shifting designs. Much of his later writing is devoted to poems about poetry and the poetic process. *Three Academic Pieces* (1948) is almost wholly concerned with the subject of metaphor, to the multiple meanings seen by the imagination, and the profuse ingenuities which permit the artist to escape the limitations of ordinary existence. In an essay, *From Poe to Valéry* (1948) T. S. Eliot wrote: "There is, first, the doctrine, elicited from Poe by Baudelaire, 'A poem should have nothing in view but itself'; second the notion that the composition of a poem should be as conscious and deliberate as possible, that the poet should observe himself in the act of composition—and this, in a mind as sceptical as Valéry's, leads to the conclusion, so paradoxically inconsistent with the other, that the act of composition is more interesting than the poem which results from it." Much of this is true of Stevens. But Stevens would maintain that the poet's role is to lead men out of their sordid world into the world of the imagination, "the supreme fiction," that escape is not evasion but entrance into a wider and richer sphere than the "violent order" which is our disorder.

At seventy-five Stevens published his *Collected Poems,* including a new section, "The Rock." Two years after his death there appeared *Opus Posthumous,* which, besides poems, contained three plays and miscellaneous prose. *The Necessary Angel* (1951) preserves the best of Stevens' essays.

Critics differed widely concerning Stevens' importance as philosopher, designer, and creator. Some commentators maintained that Stevens was obsessed with nuances, superficial shades of color, infinitesimal gradations. Others declared that Stevens had added new dimensions to American poetry. "Stevens' poetry," wrote Morton Dauwen Zabel, "is distinguished by a mastery of two qualities in which he remains largely unrivalled among his contemporaries—the richness of its imagery and the sustained authority of his rhetoric. . . . No recent poet has surpassed the effects of verbal luxuriance in his works; they describe an inexhaustible festival of the senses." "More than for almost any other contemporary American poet," argued Theodore Spencer, "words have for Stevens a magic; they are means for incantation." Comparing Stevens to Spenser, Milton, and Shakespeare, Delmore Schwartz concluded "Confronted by the need of conclusion or summary, one is impressed by how much more there is always to say about Stevens. No matter what aspect one begins, one has a sense of inexhaustible richness of significance and connection."

In spite of the growing chorus of praise there were many who continued to object that Stevens' poetry was without drama and, though characters were occasionally introduced, without human beings. Yet Stevens had the last word with the conviction that a work of art is primarily a work of art, a moment arrested out of chaos, and that "Poetry is the subject of the poem."

ANECDOTE OF THE JAR

I placed a jar in Tennessee,
And round it was, upon a hill.
It made the slovenly wilderness
Surround that hill.

The wilderness rose up to it,
And sprawled around, no longer wild.
The jar was round upon the ground
And tall and of a port in air.

It took dominion everywhere.
The jar was gray and bare.
It did not give of bird or bush,
Like nothing else in Tennessee.

PETER QUINCE AT THE CLAVIER

I

Just as my fingers on these keys
Make music, so the self-same sounds
On my spirit make a music, too.

Music is feeling, then, not sound;
And thus it is that what I feel,
Here in this room, desiring you,

Thinking of your blue-shadowed silk,
Is music. It is like the strain
Waked in the elders by Susanna:

Of a green evening, clear and warm,
She bathed in her still garden, while
The red-eyed elders, watching, felt

The bases of their beings throb
In witching chords, and their thin blood
Pulse pizzicati of Hosanna.

II

In the green water, clear and warm,
Susanna lay,
She searched
The touch of springs,
And found
Concealed imaginings.
She sighed,
For so much melody.

Upon the bank, she stood
In the cool
Of spent emotions,
She felt, among the leaves,
The dew
Of old devotions.

She walked upon the grass,
Still quavering.
The winds were like her maids
On timid feet,
Fetching her woven scarves,
Yet wavering.

A breath upon her hand
Muted the night.
She turned—
A cymbal crashed,
And roaring horns.

III

Soon, with a noise like tambourines,
Came her attendant Byzantines.

They wondered why Susanna cried
Against the elders by her side;

And as they whispered, the refrain
Was like a willow swept by rain.

Anon, their lamps' uplifted flame
Revealed Susanna and her shame.

And then, the simpering Byzantines
Fled with a noise like tambourines.

IV

Beauty is momentary in the mind—
The fitful tracing of a portal;
But in the flesh it is immortal.

The body dies; the body's beauty lives.
So evenings die, in their green going,
A wave, interminably flowing.
So gardens die, their meek breath scenting
The cowl of Winter, done repenting.
So maidens die, to the auroral
Celebration of a maiden's choral.

Susanna's music touched the bawdy strings
Of those white elders; but, escaping,
Left only Death's ironic scraping.
Now, in its immortality, it plays
On the clear viol of her memory,
And makes a constant sacrament of praise.

TO THE ONE OF FICTIVE MUSIC

Sister and mother and diviner love,
And of the sisterhood of the living dead
Most near, most clear, and of the clearest bloom,
And of the fragrant mothers the most dear
And queen, and of diviner love the day
And flame and summer and sweet fire, no thread
Of cloudy silver sprinkles in your gown
Its venom of renown, and on your head
No crown is simpler than the simple hair.

Now, of the music summoned by the birth
That separates us from the wind and sea,
Yet leaves us in them, until earth becomes,
By being so much of the things we are,
Gross effigy and simulacrum, none
Gives motion to perfection more serene
Than yours, out of our imperfections wrought,
Most rare, or ever of more kindred air
In the laborious weaving that you wear.

For so retentive of themselves are men
That music is intensest which proclaims
The near, the clear, and vaunts the clearest bloom,
And of all vigils musing the obscure,
That apprehends the most which sees and names,
As in your name, an image that is sure,
Among the arrant spices of the sun,
O bough and bush and scented vine, in whom
We give ourselves our likest issuance.

Yet not too like, yet not so like to be
Too near, too clear, saving a little to endow
Our feigning with the strange unlike, whence springs
The difference that heavenly pity brings.
For this, musician, in your girdle fixed
Bear other perfumes. On your pale head wear
A band entwining, set with fatal stones.
Unreal, give back to us what once you gave:
The imagination that we spurned and crave.

SUNDAY MORNING

I

Complacencies of the peignoir, and late
Coffee and oranges in a sunny chair,
And the green freedom of a cockatoo
Upon a rug mingle to dissipate
The holy hush of ancient sacrifice.
She dreams a little, and she feels the dark
Encroachment of that old catastrophe,
As a calm darkens among water-lights.
The pungent oranges and bright, green wings
Seem things in some procession of the dead,
Winding across wide water, without sound.
The day is like wide water, without sound.
Stilled for the passing of her dreaming feet
Over the seas, to silent Palestine,
Dominion of the blood and sepulchre.

II

Why should she give her bounty to the dead?
What is divinity if it can come
Only in silent shadows and in dreams?
Shall she not find in comforts of the sun,
In pungent fruit and bright, green wings, or else
In any balm or beauty of the earth,
Things to be cherished like the thought of heaven?
Divinity must live within herself:
Passions of rain, or moods in falling snow;
Grievings in loneliness, or unsubdued
Elations when the forest blooms; gusty
Emotions on wet roads on autumn nights;
All pleasures and all pains, remembering
The bough of summer and the winter branch.
These are the measures destined for her soul.

III

Jove in the clouds had his inhuman birth.
No mother suckled him, no sweet land gave
Large-mannered motions to his mythy mind.
He moved among us, as a muttering king,
Magnificent, would move among his hinds,
Until our blood, commingling, virginal,
With heaven, brought such requital to desire
The very hinds discerned it, in a star
Shall our blood fail? Or shall it come to be
The blood of paradise? And shall the earth
Seem all of paradise that we shall know?
The sky will be much friendlier then than now,
A part of labor and a part of pain,
And next in glory to enduring love,
Not this dividing and indifferent blue.

IV

She says, "I am content when wakened birds,
Before they fly, test the reality
Of misty fields, by their sweet questionings;
But when the birds are gone, and their warm fields
Return no more, where, then, is paradise?"
There is not any haunt of prophecy,
Nor any old chimera of the grave,
Neither the golden underground, nor isle
Melodious, where spirits gat them home,
Nor visionary south, nor cloudy palm
Remote on heaven's hill, that has endured
As April's green endures; or will endure
Like her remembrance of awakened birds,
Or her desire for June and evening, tipped
By the consummation of the swallow's wings.

V

She says, "But in contentment I still feel
The need of some imperishable bliss."
Death is the mother of beauty; hence from her,
Alone, shall come fulfilment to our dreams
And our desires. Although she strews the leaves
Of sure obliteration on our paths,
The path sick sorrow took, the many paths
Where triumph rang its brassy phrase, or love
Whispered a little out of tenderness,
She makes the willow shiver in the sun
For maidens who were wont to sit and gaze
Upon the grass, relinquished to their feet.
She causes boys to pile new plums and pears
On disregarded plate. The maidens taste
And stray impassioned in the littering leaves.

VI

Is there no change of death in paradise?
Does ripe fruit never fall? Or do the boughs
Hang always heavy in that perfect sky,
Unchanging, yet so like our perishing earth,
With rivers like our own that seek for seas
They never find, the same receding shores
That never touch with inarticulate pang?
Why set the pear upon those river-banks
Or spice the shores with odors of the plum?
Alas, that they should wear our colors there,
The silken weavings of our afternoons,
And pick the strings of our insipid lutes!
Death is the mother of beauty, mystical,
Within whose burning bosom we devise
Our earthly mothers waiting, sleeplessly.

VII

Supple and turbulent, a ring of men
Shall chant in orgy on a summer morn
Their boisterous devotion to the sun,
Not as a god, but as a god might be,
Naked among them, like a savage source.
Their chant shall be a chant of paradise,
Out of their blood, returning to the sky;
And in their chant shall enter, voice by voice,
The windy lake wherein their lord delights,
The trees, like serafim, and echoing hills,
That choir among themselves long afterward.
They shall know well the heavenly fellowship
Of men that perish and of summer morn.
And whence they came and whither they shall go
The dew upon their feet shall manifest.

VIII

She hears, upon that water without sound,
A voice that cries, "The tomb in Palestine
Is not the porch of spirits lingering.
It is the grave of Jesus, where he lay."
We live in an old chaos of the sun,
Or old dependency of day and night,
Or island solitude, unsponsored, free,
Of that wide water, inescapable.
Deer walk upon our mountains, and the quail
Whistle about us their spontaneous cries;
Sweet berries ripen in the wilderness;
And, in the isolation of the sky,
At evening, casual flocks of pigeons make
Ambiguous undulations as they sink,
Downward to darkness, on extended wings.

DOMINATION OF BLACK

At night, by the fire,
The colors of the bushes
And of the fallen leaves,
Repeating themselves,
Turned in the room,
Like the leaves themselves
Turning in the wind.
Yes: but the color of the heavy hemlocks
Came striding.
And I remembered the cry of the peacocks.

The colors of their tails
Were like the leaves themselves
Turning in the wind,
In the twilight wind.

They swept over the room,
Just as they flew from the boughs of the hemlocks
Down to the ground.
I heard them cry—the peacocks.
Was it a cry against the twilight
Or against the leaves themselves
Turning in the wind,
Turning as the flames
Turned in the fire,
Turning as the tails of the peacocks
Turned in the loud fire,
Loud as the hemlocks
Full of the cry of the peacocks?
Or was it a cry against the hemlocks?

Out of the window,
I saw how the planets gathered
Like the leaves themselves
Turning in the wind.
I saw how the night came,
Came striding like the color of the heavy hemlocks.
I felt afraid.
And I remembered the cry of the peacocks.

SEA SURFACE FULL OF CLOUDS

I

In that November off Tehuantepec,
The slopping of the sea grew still one night
And in the morning summer hued the deck

And made one think of rosy chocolate
And gilt umbrellas. Paradisal green
Gave suavity to the perplexed machine

Of ocean, which like limpid water lay.
Who, then, in that ambrosial latitude
Out of the light evolved the moving blooms,

Who, then, evolved the sea-blooms from the clouds
Diffusing balm in that Pacific calm?
C'était mon enfant, mon bijou, mon âme.

The sea-clouds whitened far below the calm
And moved, as blooms move, in the swimming green
And in its watery radiance, while the hue

Of heaven in an antique reflection rolled
Round those flotillas. And sometimes the sea
Poured brilliant iris on the glistening blue.

II

In that November off Tehuantepec
The slopping of the sea grew still one night.
At breakfast jelly yellow streaked the deck

And made one think of chop-house chocolate
And sham umbrellas. And a sham-like green
Capped summer-seeming on the tense machine

Of ocean, which in sinister flatness lay.
Who, then, beheld the rising of the clouds
That strode submerged in that malevolent sheen,

Who saw the mortal massives of the blooms
Of water moving on the water-floor?
C'était mon frère du ciel, ma vie, mon or.

The gongs rang loudly as the windy blooms
Hoo-hooed it in the darkened ocean-blooms.
The gongs grew still. And then blue heaven spread

Its crystalline pendentives on the sea
And the macabre of the water-glooms.
In an enormous undulation fled.

III

In that November off Tehuantepec,
The slopping of the sea grew still one night,
And a pale silver patterned on the deck

Made one think of porcelain chocolate
And pied umbrellas. An uncertain green,
Piano-polished, held the tranced machine

Of ocean, as a prelude holds and holds.
Who, seeing silver petals of white blooms
Unfolding in the water, feeling sure

Of the milk within the saltiest spurge, heard, then,
The sea unfolding in the sunken clouds?
Oh! C'était mon extase et mon amour.

So deeply sunken were they that the shrouds,
The shrouding shadows, made the petals black
Until the rolling heaven made them blue,

A blue beyond the rainy hyacinth.
And smiting the crevasses of the leaves
Deluged the ocean with a sapphire hue.

IV

In that November off Tehuantepec
The night-long slopping of the sea grew still.
A mallow morning dozed upon the deck

And made one think of musky chocolate
And frail umbrellas. A too-fluent green
Suggested malice in the dry machine

Of ocean, pondering dank stratagem.
Who then beheld the figures of the clouds,
Like blooms secluded in the thick marine?

Like blooms? Like damasks that were shaken off
From the loosed girdles in the spangling must.
C'était ma foi, la nonchalance divine.

The nakedness would rise and suddenly turn
Salt masks of beard and mouths of bellowing,
Would— But more suddenly the heaven rolled

Its bluest sea-clouds in the thinking green
And the nakedness became the broadest blooms,
Mile-mallows that a mallow sun cajoled.

V

In that November off Tehuantepec
Night stilled the slopping of the sea. The day
Came, bowing and voluble, upon the deck,

Good clown. . . . One thought of Chinese chocolate
And large umbrellas. And a motley green
Followed the drift of the obese machine

Of ocean, perfected in indolence.
What pistache one, ingenious and droll,
Beheld the sovereign clouds as jugglery

And the sea as turquoise-turbaned Sambo, neat
At tossing saucers—cloudy-conjuring sea?
C'était mon esprit bâtard, l'ignominie.

The sovereign clouds came clustering. The conch
Of loyal conjuration trumped. The wind
Of green blooms turning crisped the motley hue

To clearing opalescence. Then the sea
And heaven rolled as one and from the two
Came fresh transfigurings of freshest blue.

ANNUAL GAIETY

In the morning in the blue snow
The catholic sun, its majesty,
Pinks and pinks the ice-hard melanchole.

Wherefore those prayers to the moon?
Or is it that alligators lie
Along the edges of your eye
Basking in desert Florida?

Père Guzz, in heaven, thumb your lyre
And chant the January fire
And joy of snow and snow.

HOMUNCULUS ET LA BELLE ÉTOILE

In the sea, Biscayne, there prinks
The young emerald, evening star,
Good light for drunkards, poets, widows,
And ladies soon to be married.

By this light the salty fishes
Arch in the sea like tree-branches,
Going in many directions
Up and down.

This light conducts
The thoughts of drunkards, the feelings
Of widows and trembling ladies,
The movements of fishes.

How pleasant an existence it is
That this emerald charms philosophers,
Until they become thoughlessly willing
To bathe their hearts in later moonlight,

Knowing that they can bring back thought
In the night that is still to be silent,
Reflecting this thing and that,
Before they sleep!

It is better that, as scholars,
They should think hard in the dark cuffs
Of voluminous cloaks,
And shave their heads and bodies.

It might well be that their mistress
Is no gaunt fugitive phantom.
She might, after all, be a wanton,
Abundantly beautiful, eager,

Fecund,
From whose being by starlight, on sea-coast,
The innermost good of their seeking
Might come in the simplest of speech.

It is a good light, then, for those
That know the ultimate Plato,
Tranquilizing with this jewel
The torments of confusion.

TWO FIGURES IN DENSE VIOLET LIGHT

I had as lief be embraced by the porter at the hotel
As to get no more from the moonlight
Than your moist hand.

Be the voice of night and Florida in my ear.
Use dusky words and dusky images.
Darken your speech.

Speak, even, as if I did not hear you speaking,
But spoke for you perfectly in my thoughts,
Conceiving words,

As the night conceives the sea-sounds in silence,
And out of their droning sibilants makes
A serenade.

Say, puerile, that the buzzards crouch on the ridge-pole
And sleep with one eye watching the stars fall
Below Key West.

Say that the palms are clear in a total blue,
Are clear and are obscure; that it is night;
That the moon shines.

GALLANT CHÂTEAU

Is it bad to have come here
And to have found the bed empty?

One might have found tragic hair,
Bitter eyes, hands hostile and cold.

There might have been a light on a book
Lighting a pitiless verse or two.

There might have been the immense solitude
Of the wind upon the curtains.

Pitiless verse? A few words tuned
And tuned and tuned and tuned.

It is good. The bed is empty,
The curtains are stiff and prim and still.

THE IDEA OF ORDER AT KEY WEST

She sang beyond the genius of the sea.
The water never formed to mind or voice,
Like a body wholly body, fluttering
Its empty sleeves; and yet its mimic motion
Made constant cry, caused constantly a cry,
That was not ours although we understood,
Inhuman, of the veritable ocean.

The sea was not a mask. No more was she.
The song and water were not medleyed sound,
Even if what she sang was what she heard,
Since what she sang she uttered word by word.
It may be that in all her phrases stirred
The grinding water and the gasping wind;
But it was she and not the sea we heard.

For she was the maker of the song she sang.
The ever-hooded, tragic-gestured sea
Was merely a place by which she walked to sing.
Whose spirit is this? we said, because we knew
It was the spirit that we sought and knew
That we should ask this often as she sang.

If it was only the dark voice of the sea
That rose, or even colored by many waves;
If it was only the outer voice of sky
And cloud, of the sunken coral water-walled,
However clear, it would have been deep air,
The heaving speech of air, a summer sound
Repeated in a summer without end
And sound alone. But it was more than that,
More even than her voice, and ours, among
The meaningless plungings of water and the wind,
Theatrical distances, bronze shadows heaped
On high horizons, mountainous atmospheres
Of sky and sea.

It was her voice that made
The sky acutest at its vanishing.
She measured to the hour its solitude.
She was the single artificer of the world
In which she sang. And when she sang, the sea,
Whatever self it had, became the self
That was her song, for she was maker. Then we,
As we beheld her striding there alone,
Knew that there never was a world for her
Except the one she sang and, singing, made.

Ramon Fernandez, tell me, if you know,
Why, when the singing ended and we turned
Toward the town, tell why the glassy lights,
The lights in the fishing boats at anchor there,
As the night descended, tilting in the air,
Mastered the night and portioned out the sea,
Fixing emblazoned zones and fiery poles,
Arranging, deepening, enchanting night.

Oh! Blessed rage for order, pale Ramon,
The maker's rage to order words of the sea,
Words of the fragrant portals, dimly-starred,
And of ourselves and of our origins,
In ghostlier demarcations, keener sounds.

BOUQUET OF BELLE SCAVOIR

It is she alone that matters.
She made it. It is easy to say
The figures of speech, as why she chose
This dark, particular rose.

Everything in it is herself.
Yet the freshness of the leaves, the burn
Of the colors, are tinsel changes,
Out of the changes of both light and dew.

How often had he walked
Beneath summer and the sky
To receive her shadow into his mind . . .
Miserable that it was not she.

The sky is too blue, the earth too wide.
The thought of her takes her away
The form of her in something else
Is not enough.

The reflection of her here, and then there,
Is another shadow, another evasion,

Another denial. If she is everywhere,
She is nowhere, to him.

But this she has made. If it is
Another image, it is one she has made.
It is she that he wants, to look at directly,
Someone before him to see and to know.

ASIDES ON THE OBOE

The prologues are over. It is question, now,
Of final belief. So, say that final belief
Must be in a fiction. It is time to choose.

That obsolete fiction of the wide river in
An empty land; the gods that Boucher killed;
And the metal heroes that time granulates—
The philosophers' man alone still walks in dew,
Still by the sea-side mutters milky lines
Concerning an immaculate imagery.
If you say on the hautboy man is not enough
Can never stand as god, is ever wrong
In the end, however naked, tall, there is still
The impossible possible philosophers' man,
The man who has had the time to think enough,
The central man, the human globe, responsive
As a mirror with a voice, the man of glass,
Who in a million diamonds sums us up.

2

He is the transparence of the place in which
He is, and in his poems we find peace.
He sets this peddler's pie and cries in summer,
The glass man, cold and numbered, dewily cries,
"Thou art not August unless I make thee so."
Clandestine steps upon imagined stairs
Climb through the night, because his cuckoos call.

One year, death and war prevented the jasmine scent
And the jasmine islands were bloody martyrdoms.
How was it then with the central man? Did we
Find peace? We found the sum of men. We found,
If we found the central evil, the central good.
We buried the fallen without jasmine crowns.
There was nothing he did not suffer, no; nor we.

It was not as if the jasmine ever returned.
But we and the diamond globe at last were one.
We had always been partly one. It was as we came
To see him, that we were wholly one, as we heard
Him chanting for those buried in their blood,
In the forests that had been jasmine, that we knew
The glass man, without external reference.

THE GLASS OF WATER

That the glass would melt in heat,
That the water would freeze in cold,
Shows that this object is merely a state,
One of many, between two poles. So,
In the metaphysical, there are these poles.

Here in the centre stands the glass. Light
Is the lion that comes down to drink. There
And in that state, the glass is a pool.
Ruddy are his eyes and ruddy are his claws
When light comes down to wet his frothy jaws

And in the water winding weeds move round.
And there and in another state—the refractions,
The *metaphysica,* the plastic parts of poems
Crash in the mind— But, fat Jocundus, worrying
About what stands here in the center, not in the glass,

But in the centre of our lives, this time, this day,
It is a state, this spring among the politicians
Playing cards. In a village of the indigenes,
One would have still to discover. Among the dogs and dung,
One would continue to contend with one's ideas.

THE SENSE OF THE SLEIGHT-OF-HAND MAN

One's grand flights, one's Sunday baths,
One's tootings at the weddings of the soul
Occur as they occur. So bluish clouds
Occurred above the empty house and the leaves
Of the rhododendrons rattled their gold,
As if someone lived there. Such floods of white
Came bursting from the clouds. So the wind
Threw its contorted strength around the sky.

Could you have said the bluejay suddenly
Would swoop to earth? It is a wheel, the rays
Around the sun. The wheel survives the myths.
The fire eye in the clouds survives the gods.

To think of a dove with an eye of grenadine
And pines that are cornets, so it occurs,
And a little island full of geese and stars:
It may be that the ignorant man, alone,
Has any chance to mate his life with life
That is the sensual, pearly spouse, the life
That is fluent in even the wintriest bronze.

THE MOTIVE FOR METAPHOR

You like it under the trees in autumn,
Because everything is half dead.
The wind moves like a cripple among the leaves
And repeats words without meaning.

In the same way, you were happy in spring,
With the half colors of quarter-things,
The slightly brighter sky, the melting clouds,
The single bird, the obscure moon—

The obscure moon lighting an obscure world
Of things that would never be quite expressed,
Where you yourself were never quite yourself
And did not want nor have to be,

Desiring the exhilarations of changes:
The motive for metaphor, shrinking from
The weight of primary noon,
The A B C of being,

The ruddy temper, the hammer
Of red and blue, the hard sound—
Steel against intimation—the sharp flash,
The vital, arrogant, fatal, dominant X.

William Carlos Williams

William Carlos Williams was born September 17, 1883, in Rutherford, New Jersey, where he has lived and practiced medicine ever since. His father, William George Williams, was born in Birmingham, England; his father's mother's name was, curiously enough, Emily Dickinson. His mother, Raquel Ellen Rose Hoheb, was born in Mayaguez, Puerto Rico. Her mother, a Basque named Meline Hurrard, was born in Martinique; her father, Solomon Hoheb, of Dutch-Spanish-Jewish descent, was born in St. Thomas. This liberal mixture of bloods made Williams a complete melting-pot in himself; there are those who claim that the mingled strains fused logically into some of the most definitely American writing of the period.

Williams was educated at Horace Mann High School, New York, at Château de Lancy, near Geneva, Switzerland, and at the University of Pennsylvania, from which he graduated in medicine in 1906. There followed two years of interneship in New York and a year of graduate study in pediatrics in Leipzig. In his twenty-third year he published the traditionally imitative first volume, *Poems* (1909), which was followed by *The Tempers* (1913), published in London and bearing the influence of Pound and his fellow-imagists. *Al Que Quiere* (1917) strikes a more decisive experimental note; from the mocking directions for a funeral which Williams has entitled "Tract" to the extended suite called "January Morning" Williams achieves a purposeful distortion which intensifies his objects in sharp detail. *Kora in Hell* (1921) and *Sour Grapes* (1922) pay increasing attention to the "pure" value of physical things. *Spring and All* (1923) was followed by *The Descent of Winter* in which Williams alternated between exact description and an attempt to record the wavering outlines of the unconscious. At one moment Williams declared he was "sick of rime," but, almost immediately after, he concluded: "And we thought to escape rime / by imitation of the senseless / unarrangement of wild things—the stupidest rime of all." Those who have been quick to accuse Williams of disorganization have not examined the strong color and delicate movement of such poems as "Metric Figure," "Dawn," "Queen-Ann's-Lace," "Daisy," and the remarkable "Poem" beginning "By the road to the contagious hospital."

When the first *Collected Poems* appeared in 1934 Wallace Stevens wrote in the Preface: "The man has spent his life in rejecting the accepted sense of things. His passion for the anti-poetic is a blood passion and not a passion for the ink-pot. Something of the unreal is necessary to fecundate the real; something of the sentimental is necessary to fecundate the anti-poetic. . . . One might run through these pages and point out how often the essential poetry is the result of the conjunction of the unreal and the real, the sentimental and the anti-poetic, the constant interaction of two opposites." A few years later, in "A Note on Poetry," Williams replied to those who had attacked his poems for being bare in outline and violent in idiom. "The American writer," Williams began, "uses a language . . . which has been modified by time and the accidents of place to acquire a character differing greatly from that of present-day English. For the appreciation of American poetry it is necessary that the reader accept this language difference from the beginning."

The Complete Collected Poems: 1906-1938 reveals with what increasing strength Williams has developed in the idiom of the United States. Although his lines rarely descend to slang, they are full of the conversational speech of the country; they express the brusque nervous tension, the vigor and rhetoric of American life. Even when they are purposely unadorned and non-melodic they intensify some common object with pointed detail and confident, if clipped, emotion. "Emotion," says Williams, "clusters about common things, the pathetic often stimulates the imagination to new patterns—but the job of the poet is to use language effectively, his own language, the only language which is to him authentic. In my own work it has always sufficed that the object of my attention be presented without further comment." Actually Williams' gamut is much greater than he implies. With characteristic growth he freed himself from Pound and the pretty escapism of the Imagists; some of the richest and most individualized free verse of the period can be found in "Flowers by the Sea," "The Poor," "The Yachts," and "These." Again and again Williams proves that everything in the world is the poet's material, and that the most tawdry objects have their use and beauty "if the imagination can lighten them."

The scope and quality of his work justify Williams' theory. His poems have grown simpler and more austere; his compositions are stricter in form; the colors are flat but fresh. This is evident even in the thirty-page pamphlet, *The Broken Span* (1941), which ranges from the early objective poetry of sheer sensation to a deep concern with the ordinary aspects of everyday life.

Williams' attempts to intensify the fact and give fresh perspectives to the word (and to the world) are given new emphasis in *Paterson* (*Books I-V,* 1946-1958), a rich "personal epic." As in Eliot's *The Waste Land,* Williams paints a picture of life in disintegration and brings it into focus by his juxtaposition of the exquisite and the crass. He continues to insist on the object not only as a visual thing but as a symbol. The early imagist-objectivist joins with the pioneering observer: "No ideas but in things." Sensitive without being sensuous, the thoughtful commentator and the lyric improviser present everything with sharp and usually unadorned immediacy. Williams' *Autobiography* appeared in his sixty-eighth year; *The Desert Music and Other Poems* three years later. By this time Williams was the recipient of various prizes and distinguished awards.

Several prose works, notably the essays *In the American Grain* (1925), and the novels *A Voyage to Pagany* (1928), *White Mule* (1937), and *In the Money* (1940), mingle history and reappraisal, reportorial accuracy and creative imagination.

METRIC FIGURE

There is a bird in the poplars—
It is the sun!
The leaves are little yellow fish
Swimming in the river;
The bird skims above them—
Day is on his wings.
Phoenix!
It is he that is making
The great gleam among the poplars.
It is his singing
Outshines the noise
Of leaves clashing in the wind.

LOVE SONG

Sweep the house clean,
hang fresh curtains
in the windows
put on a new dress
and come with me!

The elm is scattering
its little loaves
of sweet smells
from a white sky!

Who shall hear of us
in the time to come?
Let him say there was
a burst of fragrance
from black branches.

DAWN

Ecstatic bird songs pound
the hollow vastness of the sky
with metallic clinkings—
beating color up into it
at a far edge,—beating it, beating it
with rising, triumphant ardor,—
stirring it into warmth,
quickening in it a spreading change,—
bursting wildly against it as
dividing the horizon, a heavy sun
lifts himself—is lifted—
bit by bit above the edge
of things,—runs free at last
out into the open—! lumbering
glorified in full release upward—
songs cease.

POEM

By the road to the contagious hospital,
under the surge of the blue
mottled clouds driven from the
northeast—cold wind. Beyond, the
waste of broad, muddy fields,
brown with dried weeds, standing and fallen,

patches of standing water,
the scattering of tall trees.

All along the road the reddish,
purplish, forked, upstanding, twiggy
stuff of brushes and small trees
with dead, brown leaves under them
leafless vines—

Lifeless in appearance, sluggish,
dazed spring approaches—

They enter the new world naked,
cold, uncertain of all
save that they enter. All about them
the cold, familiar wind—

Now the grass, tomorrow
the stiff curl of wild-carrot leaf.

One by one objects are defined—
It quickens: clarity, outline of leaf,

But now the stark dignity of
entrance— Still, the profound change
has come upon them; rooted, they
grip down and begin to awaken.

JANUARY

Again I reply to the triple winds
running chromatic fifths of derision
outside my window:
Play louder.
You will not succeed. I am
bound more to my sentences
the more you batter at me
to follow you.
And the wind,
as before, fingers perfectly
its derisive music.

QUEEN-ANN'S-LACE

Her body is not so white as
anemone petals nor so smooth—nor
so remote a thing. It is a field
of the wild carrot taking
the field by force; the grass
does not raise above it.
Here is no question of whiteness,
white as can be, with a purple mole
at the center of each flower.
Each flower is a hand's span
of her whiteness. Wherever
his hand has lain there is
a tiny purple blemish. Each part

is a blossom under his touch
to which the fibers of her being
stem one by one, each to its end,
until the whole field is a
white desire, empty, a single stem,
a cluster, flower by flower,
a pious wish to whiteness gone over—
or nothing.

DAISY

The dayseye hugging the earth
in August, ha! Spring is
gone down in purple,
weeds stand high in the corn,
the rainbeaten furrow
is clotted with sorrel
and crabgrass, the
oranch is black under
the heavy mass of the leaves—
The sun is upon a
slender green stem
ribbed lengthwise.
He lies on his back—
t is a woman also—
ie regards his former
najesty and
ound the yellow center,
plit and creviced and done into
ninute flowerheads, he sends out
iis twenty rays—a little
nd the wind is among them
o grow cool there!

One turns the thing over
n his hand and looks
t it from the rear: brownedged,
reen and pointed scales
rmor his yellow.
But turn and turn,
he crisp petals remain
rief, translucent, greenfastened,
barely touching at the edges:
blades of limpid seashell.

ON GAY WALLPAPER

The green-blue ground
is ruled with silver lines
to say the sun is shining

And on this mural sea
of grass or dreams lie flowers
or baskets of desires

Heaven knows what they are
between cerulean shapes
laid regularly round

Mat roses and tridentate
leaves of gold
threes, threes and threes

Three roses and three stems
the basket floating
standing in the horns of blue

Repeated to the ceiling
to the windows
where the day

Blows in
the scalloped curtains to
the sound of rain.

TRACT

I will teach you my townspeople
how to perform a funeral—
for you have it over a troop
of artists—
unless one should scour the world—
you have the ground sense necessary.

See! the hearse leads.
I begin with a design for a hearse.
For Christ's sake not black—
nor white either—and not polished!
Let it be weathered—like a farm wagon—
with gilt wheels (this could be
applied fresh at small expense)
or no wheels at all:
a rough dray to drag over the ground.

Knock the glass out!
My God—glass, my townspeople!
For what purpose? Is it for the dead
to look out or for us to see
how well he is housed or to see
the flowers or the lack of them—
or what?
To keep the rain and snow from him?
He will have a heavier rain soon:
pebbles and dirt and what not.
Let there be no glass—
and no upholstery! phew!
and no little brass rollers
and small easy wheels on the bottom—
my townspeople what are you thinking of!

A rough plain hearse then
with gilt wheels and no top at all.
On this the coffin lies
by its own weight.

No wreaths please—
especially no hot-house flowers.
Some common memento is better,
something he prized and is known by:
his old clothes—a few books perhaps—
God knows what! You realize
how we are about these things,
my townspeople—
something will be found—anything—
even flowers if he had come to that.
So much for the hearse.

For heaven's sake though see to the driver!
Take off the silk hat! In fact
that's no place at all for him
up there unceremoniously
dragging our friend out to his own dignity!
Bring him down—bring him down!
Low and inconspicuous! I'd not have him ride
on the wagon at all—damn him—

the undertaker's understrapper!
Let him hold the reins
and walk at the side
and inconspicuously too!

Then briefly as to yourselves:
Walk behind—as they do in France,
seventh class, or if you ride
Hell take curtains! Go with some show
of inconvenience; sit openly—
to the weather as to grief.
Or do you think you can shut grief in?
What—from us? We who have perhaps
nothing to lose? Share with us
share with us—it will be money
in your pockets.
Go now
I think you are ready.

SMELL

Oh strong ridged and deeply hollowed
nose of mine! what will you not be smelling?
What tactless asses we are, you and I, boney nose,
always indiscriminate, always unashamed,
and now it is the souring flowers of the bedraggled
poplars: a festering pulp on the wet earth
beneath them. With what deep thirst
we quicken our desires
to that rank odor of a passing springtime!
Can you not be decent? Can you not reserve your ardors
for something less unlovely? What girl will care
for us, do you think, if we continue in these ways?
Must you taste everything? Must you know everything?
Must you have a part in everything?

A GOODNIGHT

Go to sleep—though of course you will not—
to tideless waves thundering slantwise against
strong embankments, rattle and swish of spray
dashed thirty feet high, caught by the lake wind,
scattered and strewn broadcast in over the steady
car rails! Sleep, sleep! Gulls' cries in a wind-gust
broken by the wind; calculating wings set above
the field of waves breaking.
Go to sleep to the lunge between foam-crests,
refuse churned in the recoil. Food! Food!
Offal! Offal! that holds them in the air, wave-white
for the one purpose, feather upon feather, the wild

chill in their eyes, the hoarseness in their voices—
sleep, sleep . . .

Gentlefooted crowds are treading out your lullaby.
Their arms nudge, they brush shoulders,
hitch this way, then that, mass and surge at the crossings—
lullaby, lullaby! The wild-fowl police whistles,
the enraged roar of the traffic, machine shrieks:
it is all to put you to sleep,
to soften your limbs in relaxed postures,
and that your head slip sidewise, and your hair loosen
and fall over your eyes and over your mouth,
brushing your lips wistfully that you may dream,
sleep and dream—

A black fungus springs out about lonely church doors—
sleep, sleep. The Night, coming down upon
the wet boulevard, would start you awake with his
message, to have in at your window. Pay no
heed to him. He storms at your sill with
cooings, with gesticulations, curses!
You will not let him in. He would keep you from sleeping.
He would have you sit under your desk lamp
brooding, pondering; he would have you
slide out the drawer, take up the ornamented dagger
and handle it. It is late, it is nineteen-nineteen—
go to sleep, his cries are a lullaby;
his jabbering is a sleep-well-my-baby; he is
a crackbrained messenger.

The maid waking you in the morning
when you are up and dressing,
the rustle of your clothes as you raise them—
it is the same tune.
At table the cold, greenish, split grapefruit, its juice
on the tongue, the clink of the spoon in
your coffee, the toast odors say it over and over.

The open street-door lets in the breath of
the morning wind from over the lake.
The bus coming to a halt grinds from its sullen brakes—
lullaby, lullaby. The crackle of a newspaper,
the movement of the troubled coat beside you—
sleep, sleep, sleep, sleep . . .
It is the sting of snow, the burning liquor of
the moonlight, the rush of rain in the gutters packed
with dead leaves: go to sleep, go to sleep.
And the night passes—and never passes—

THE RED WHEELBARROW

so much depends
upon

a red wheel
barrow

glazed with rain
water

beside the white
chickens

FLOWERS BY THE SEA

When over the flowery, sharp pasture's
edge, unseen, the salt ocean

lifts its form—chicory and daisies
tide, released, seem hardly flowers alone

but color and the movement—or the shape
perhaps—of restlessness, whereas

the sea is circled and sways
peacefully upon its plantlike stem

THE POOR

t's the anarchy of poverty
lelights me, the old
vellow wooden house indented
mong the new brick tenements

)r a cast iron balcony
vith panels showing oak branches
n full leaf. It fits
he dress of the children

eflecting every stage and
ustom of necessity—
himneys, roofs, fences of
vood and metal in an unfenced

ge and enclosing next to
othing at all: the old man
a sweater and soft black
at who sweeps the sidewalk—

is own ten feet of it—
a wind that fitfully
rning his corner has
verwhelmed the entire city

THESE

are the desolate, dark weeks
when nature in its barrenness
equals the stupidity of man.

The year plunges into night
and the heart plunges
lower than night

to an empty, windswept place
without sun, stars or moon
but a peculiar light as of thought

that spins a dark fire—
whirling upon itself until,
in the cold, it kindles

to make a man aware of nothing
that he knows, not loneliness
itself— Not a ghost but

would be embraced—emptiness,
despair— (They
whine and whistle) among

the flashes and booms of war;
houses of whose rooms
the cold is greater than can be thought,

the people gone that we loved,
the beds lying empty, the couches
damp, the chairs unused—

Hide it away somewhere
out of the mind, let it get roots
and grow, unrelated to jealous

ears and eyes—for itself.
In this mine they come to dig—all.
Is this the counterfoil to sweetest

music? The source of poetry that
seeing the clock stopped, says,
The clock has stopped

that ticked yesterday so well?
and hears the sound of lakewater
splashing—that is now stone.

ILLEGITIMATE THINGS

Water still flows—
The thrush still sings

though in
the skirts of the sky

at the bottom of
the distance

huddle . . .
. . . echoing cannon!

Whose silence revives
valley after

valley to peace
as poems still conserve

the language
of old ecstasies.

THE YACHTS

contend in a sea which the land partly encloses
shielding them from the too heavy blows
of an ungoverned ocean which when it chooses

tortures the biggest hulls, the best man knows
to pit against its beating, and sinks them pitilessly.
Mothlike in mists, scintillant in the minute

brilliance of cloudless days, with broad bellying sails
they glide to the wind tossing green water
from their sharp prows while over them the crew crawls

ant-like, solicitously grooming them, releasing,
making fast as they turn, lean far over and having
caught the wind again, side by side, head for the mark.

In a well guarded arena of open water surrounded by
lesser and greater craft which, sycophant, lumbering
and flittering follow them, they appear youthful, rare

as the light of a happy eye, live with the grace
of all that in the mind is fleckless, free and
naturally to be desired. Now the sea which holds them

is moody, lapping their glossy sides, as if feeling
for some slightest flaw but fails completely.
Today no race. Then the wind comes again. The yachts

move, jockeying for a start, the signal is set and they
are off. Now the waves strike at them but they are too
well made, they slip through, though they take in canvas.

Arms with hands grasping seek to clutch at the prows.
Bodies thrown recklessly in the way are cut aside.
It is a sea of faces about them in agony, in despair

until the horror of the race dawns staggering the mind,
the whole sea become an entanglement of watery bodies
lost to the world bearing what they cannot hold. Broken,

beaten, desolate, reaching from the dead to be taken up
they cry out, failing, failing! their cries rising
in waves still as the skillful yachts pass over.

THE YELLOW SEASON

The black, long-tailed
one then, unexpectedly, another
glide easily on a curtain
of yellow leaves, upward—

The season wakens! loveliness
chirping and barking stands
among the branches, its
narrow-clawed toes and furry
hands moving in the leaves—

Round white eyes dotted with
jet live still, alert—in
all gentleness! unabated
beyond the crackle
of death's stinking certainty.

Sara Teasdale

Sara Teasdale was born August 8, 1884, in St. Louis, Missouri, and educated there. After leaving school she traveled in Europe and the Near East. She was fascinated and frightened by the poet Vachel Lindsay who courted her with overwhelming exuberance. In 1914 she married Ernst Filsinger and, two years later, moved with him to New York. But she was essentially the solitary spirit pictured in her poem on page 266, and the marriage was not successful. After her divorce, she lived in seclusion, and ill health emphasized her unhappiness. She was found drowned in the bath of her New York apartment, January 28, 1933.

Her first book was a slight volume, *Sonnets to Duse* (1907), which gave little promise of the lyricism to follow. *Helen of Troy and Other Poems* (1911) contains hints of that delicate craftsmanship which this poet brought to such finesse. The six opening monologues are written in a blank verse as musical as many of her lyrics. At times her quatrains suffer from too conscious a cleverness; the dexterity with which Miss Teasdale turns a phrase or twists her last line is frequently too obtrusive to be unreservedly enjoyable. Moreover, they seem written in a mood of predetermined and too picturesque romance, the mood of languishing roses, silken balconies, moonlight on guitars, and unemotional kisses for unreal Colins.

Rivers to the Sea (1915) emphasizes a new skill and a greater restraint. The volume contains at least a dozen unforgettable snatches, lyrics in which the words seem to fall into place without art or effort. Seldom employing metaphor or striking imagery, almost bare of ornament, these poems have the touch of folk-song. Theirs is an artlessness that is something more than art.

Love Songs (1917) is a collection of Miss Teasdale's previous melodies for the *viola d'amore* together with several in which the turns are no longer obviously unexpected. Maturity is evident in the poet's rejection of many of her facile stanzas and her choice of firmer material.

Flame and Shadow (1920; revised edition, published in England, in 1924) is the ripest of her books. Here the emotion is fuller and deeper; an almost mystic radiance plays from these verses. Technically, also, this volume marks Miss Teasdale's greatest advance. The words are chosen with a keener sense of their actual as well as their musical values; the rhythms are more subtle and varied; the line moves with a greater naturalness. Beneath the symbolism of poems like "Water-Lilies," "The Long Hill," and "Let It Be Forgotten," one is conscious of a finer artistry, a more flexible speech that is all the lovelier for its slight (and logical) irregularities.

After *Flame and Shadow* Miss Teasdale's theme became somewhat autumnal. Though never funereal, the songs are preoccupied with the coming of age, the gathering of night, the mutability of things. *Dark of the Moon* (1926) is more thoughtful than any other previous verse. It is, as the title indicates, even more somber. If the movement is slower it is a no less delicate music that moves under the surface rhythms. "Wisdom," "The Solitary," "The Flight" may not be the most popular poems that Miss Teasdale has written, but they must be numbered among her best. Hers is a disillusion without cynicism; her proud acceptance of life's darker aspects adds new dignity to the old lyricism.

Strange Victory (1933) is Sara Teasdale's posthumous memorial to a world she never quite despised yet never wholly trusted. The poems are sad yet not sentimental. Though death overshadows the book there is never the querulous cry of frustration nor the melodrama of dying. As in the later lyrics the lines are direct, the emotion unwhipped; the beauty is in the restraint, the careful selection, the compression into the essential spirit, into a last serenity. It is an irony that as her admirers grew less voluble her work increased in value.

Besides her own books, Miss Teasdale had compiled an anthology, *The Answering Voice* (1917), comprising one hundred love lyrics by women, and a collection for children, *Rainbow Gold* (1922). Her *Collected Poems* appeared in 1937.

NIGHT SONG AT AMALFI

I asked the heaven of stars
  What I should give my love—
It answered me with silence,
  Silence above.

I asked the darkened sea
  Down where the fishermen go—
It answered me with silence,
  Silence below.

Oh, I could give him weeping,
  Or I could give him song—
But how can I give silence
  My whole life long?

SPRING NIGHT

The park is filled with night and fog,
  The veils are drawn about the world.
The drowsy lights along the paths
  Are dim and pearled.

Gold and gleaming the empty streets,
  Gold and gleaming the misty lake,
The mirrored lights like sunken swords,
  Glimmer and shake.

Oh, is it not enough to be
Here with this beauty over me?
My throat should ache with praise, and I
Should kneel in joy beneath the sky.
O beauty, are you not enough?
Why am I crying after love
With youth, a singing voice, and eyes
To take earth's wonder with surprise?

Why have I put off my pride,
Why am I unsatisfied,—
I, for whom the pensive night
Binds her cloudy hair with light,—
I, for whom all beauty burns
Like incense in a million urns?
O beauty, are you not enough?
Why am I crying after love?

I SHALL NOT CARE

When I am dead and over me bright April
   Shakes out her rain-drenched hair,
Though you should lean above me broken-hearted,
   I shall not care.

I shall have peace, as leafy trees are peaceful
   When rain bends down the bough;
And I shall be more silent and cold-hearted
   Than you are now.

THE LONG HILL

I must have passed the crest a while ago
   And now I am going down—
Strange to have crossed the crest and not to know,
   But the brambles were always catching the hem of my gown.

All the morning I thought how proud I should be
   To stand there straight as a queen,
Wrapped in the wind and the sun with the world under me—
   But the air was dull, there was little I could have seen.

It was nearly level along the beaten track
   And the brambles caught in my gown—
But it's no use now to think of turning back,
   The rest of the way will be only going down.

WATER-LILIES

If you have forgotten water-lilies floating
   On a dark lake among mountains in the afternoon shade,
If you have forgotten their wet, sleepy fragrance,
   Then you can return and not be afraid.

But if you remember, then turn away forever
   To the plains and the prairies where pools are far apart,
There you will not come at dusk on closing water-lilies,
   And the shadow of mountains will not fall on your heart.

LET IT BE FORGOTTEN

Let it be forgotten, as a flower is forgotten,
Forgotten as a fire that once was singing gold,
Let it be forgotten for ever and ever,
Time is a kind friend, he will make us old.

If anyone asks, say it was forgotten
Long and long ago,
As a flower, as a fire, as a hushed footfall
In a long-forgotten snow.

WISDOM

It was a night of early spring,
The winter-sleep was scarcely broken;
Around us shadows and the wind
Listened for what was never spoken.

Though half a score of years are gone,
Spring comes as sharply now as then—
But if we had it all to do
It would be done the same again.

It was a spring that never came;
But we have lived enough to know
That what we never have, remains;
It is the things we have that go.

THE SOLITARY

My heart has grown rich with the passing of years,
I have less need now than when I was young
To share myself with every comer,
Or shape my thoughts into words with my tongue.

It is one to me that they come or go
If I have myself and the drive of my will,
And strength to climb on a summer night
And watch the stars swarm over the hill.

Let them think I love them more than I do,
Let them think I care, though I go alone,
If it lifts their pride, what is it to me,
Who am self-complete as a flower or a stone?

THE CRYSTAL GAZER

I shall gather myself into myself again,
I shall take my scattered selves and make them one,
I shall fuse them into a polished crystal ball
Where I can see the moon and the flashing sun.

I shall sit like a sibyl, hour after hour intent,
Watching the future come and the present go—
And the little shifting pictures of people rushing
In tiny self-importance to and fro.

APPRAISAL

Never think she loves him wholly,
Never believe her love is blind,
All his faults are locked securely
In a closet of her mind;
All his indecisions folded
Like old flags that time has faded,
Limp and streaked with rain,
And his cautiousness like garments
Frayed and thin, with many a stain—
Let them be, oh, let them be,
There is treasure to outweigh them,
His proud will that sharply stirred,
Climbs as surely as the tide,
Senses strained too taut to sleep,
Gentleness to beast and bird,
Humor flickering hushed and wide
As the moon on moving water,
And a tenderness too deep
To be gathered in a word.

ON THE SOUTH DOWNS

Over the downs there were birds flying,
Far off glittered the sea,
And toward the north the weald of Sussex
Lay like a kingdom under me.

I was happier than the larks
That nest on the downs and sing to the sky—
Over the downs the birds flying
Were not so happy as I.

It was not you, though you were near,
Though you were good to hear and see;
It was not earth, it was not heaven,
It was myself that sang in me.

AUGUST NIGHT

On a midsummer night, on a night that was eerie with stars,
In a wood too deep for a single star to look through,
You led down a path whose turnings you knew in the darkness,
But the scent of the dew-dripping cedars was all that I knew.

I drank of the darkness, I was fed with the honey of fragrance,
I was glad of my life, the drawing of breath was sweet;
I heard your voice, you said, "Look down, see the glow-worm!"
It was there before me, a small star white at my feet.

We watched while it brightened as though it were breathed on and burning,
This tiny creature moving over earth's floor—
"*'L'amor che move il sole e l'altre stelle,'*"
You said, and no more.

Elizabeth Madox Roberts

☙ Elizabeth Madox Roberts was born in 1885, at Perryville, near Springfield, Kentucky, and attended the University of Chicago, where she received her Ph.B. in 1921. Except when obliged to travel for health or warmth, she lived in the Salt River country of Kentucky, twenty-eight miles from Harrodsburg, old Fort Harrod, the first settlement in the state. Suffering from anemia she died March 13, 1941.

As an undergraduate she won the local Fiske Prize with a group of poems which later appeared in *Poetry: A Magazine of Verse.* An amplification of these verses appeared as *Under the Tree* (1922) and critics were quick to recognize the unusually fresh accents in this first volume. *Under the Tree* spoke directly to the young, for it was written, not so much for children, but as a sensitive child might write. The observation is precise, the reflections are candidly clear, the humor delicate, never simpering or archly beribboned. Here is a simplicity which is straightforward without being shrill or mincing. The verse is graceful where grace commands the gesture, but Miss Roberts' unforced *naïveté* allows her to be gauche whenever awkwardness is natural.

After this volume Miss Roberts returned to her native state, and spent much of her time studying the archaic English speech still spoken in the remote parts of Kentucky. "Orpheus," although written later than her first book, is a highly interesting use of her early idiom, localizing as well as vitalizing the old myth. "Stranger" is more definitely indigenous; it has something of the flavor of the *Lonesome Tunes* collected by Howard Brockway and Loraine Wyman. Concerning this poem, Miss Roberts writes, "In these verses I have used material from the old ballads—or suggestions from them, material which may be found abundantly in Kentucky, together with modern syncopation and a refrain designed to call up banjo notes." These, as well as the earlier ingenuous poems, are curiously wrought out of material which is both tender and tough, illusive and yet plain. They have, wrote Paul Goodman, "a combination of impulsive feeling, somewhat indeterminate of its object —longing, the sense of being haunted—with an objective and even minute picture of agricultural activity."

In 1925 Miss Roberts turned to the prose for which she has been so widely celebrated. *The Time of Man* (1926), one of the most moving novels of the period, is an epic of the Appalachians in which every chapter has the effect of a poem. *My Heart and My Flesh* (1927), a darker and more difficult exploration, discloses less local and more universal regions of the spirit. *Jingling in the Wind* (1928) is a less successful experiment, a light farce which tries but fails to be a satire on industrial civilization. All three are characterized by a lyrical charm and an inscrutability which set Miss Roberts apart from the competent writers of easy fiction.

The Great Meadow (1930) is an exploration of the material uncovered in her first novel. Placed in the Kentucky meadow-lands against the heroic backgrounds of early American history, it is a pioneering panorama. Native to the least grass-blade, it is much more than a narrative of the soil; it is a widening saga of the men and women who imposed themselves and their pattern on the unshaped wilderness.

Thus *The Great Meadow* acts both as the preparation for and the rich completion of *The Time of Man*. A novel *He Sent Forth a Raven* (1935) combines her early individual diction with the later restrained mysticism, a combination that is curiously lilting and intense.

THE SKY

I saw a shadow on the ground
And heard a bluejay going by;
A shadow went across the ground,
And I looked up and saw the sky.

It hung up on the poplar tree,
But while I looked it did not stay;
It gave a tiny sort of jerk
And moved a little bit away.

And farther on and farther on
It moved and never seemed to stop.
I think it must be tied with chains
And something pulls it from the top.

It never has come down again,
And every time I look to see,
The sky is always slipping back
And getting far away from me.

CHRISTMAS MORNING

Bethlehem were here today,
r this were very long ago,
here wouldn't be a winter time
or any cold or snow.

l run out through the garden gate,
nd down along the pasture walk;
nd off beside the cattle barns
l hear a kind of gentle talk.

l move the heavy iron chain
nd pull away the wooden pin;
l push the door a little bit
nd tiptoe very softly in.

ne pigeons and the yellow hens
nd all the cows would stand away;
neir eyes would open wide to see
lady in the manger hay,
this were very long ago
nd Bethlehem were here today.

nd Mother held my hand and smiled—
nean the lady would—and she
Would take the woolly blankets off
Her little boy so I could see.

His shut-up eyes would be asleep,
And he would look just like our John,
And he would be all crumpled too,
And have a pinkish color on.

I'd watch his breath go in and out.
His little clothes would all be white.
I'd slip my finger in his hand
To feel how he could hold it tight.

And she would smile and say, "Take care,"
The mother, Mary, would, "Take care";
And I would kiss his little hand
And touch his hair.

While Mary put the blankets back
The gentle talk would soon begin.
And when I'd tiptoe softly out
I'd meet the wise men going in.

ORPHEUS

He could sing sweetly on a string.
He'd make the music curve around;
He'd make it tremble through the woods
And all the trees would leave the ground.

The tunes would walk on steps of air,
For in his hand a wire would sing;
The songs would fly like wild quick geese—
He could play sweetly on a string.

✣

If Orpheus would come today,
Our trees would lean far out to hear,
And they would stretch limb after limb;
Then the ellum trees would leave the ground
And the sycamores would follow him.

And the poplar tree and the locust tree
And the coffeeberry tree would come
And all the rows of osage thorns,
And then the little twisted plum.

He'd lead them off across the hill.
They'd flow like water toward his feet.
He'd walk through fields and turn in roads;
He'd bring them down our street.

And he'd go by the blacksmith shop,
And one would say, "Now who are these?—
I wonder who that fellow is,
And where he's going with the trees!"

"To the sawmill, likely," one would say,
"Oh, yes, the sawmill, I should think."
And then he'd cut the horse's hoof
And hammers would go *clink* and *clink*.

✣

He could play sweetly on a wire.
And he would lean down near his lyre
To hear its songs unfold and wind,
And it would reach up toward his ear
To hear the music in his mind.

And when the road turned by the kiln,
Then Orpheus would happen to see
The little plum and the sycamore
And the poplar tree and the chinaberry tree,

And all the rows of osage thorns—
When he happened once to look—
He'd see them coming after him . . .
Three birches, and he'd see the oak.

And he would lead them back again.
He'd bring each one to its own ground.
He'd bring each to its growing-place
And set them back with sound and sound.

He'd fit them in with whispered chords,
And tap them down with humming words.

STRANGER

When Polly lived back in the old deep woods,
Sing, sing, sing and howdy, howdy-o!
Nobody ever went by her door,
Tum a-tum tum and danky, danky-o!

Valentine worked all day in the brush,
He grubbed out stumps and he chopped with his ax,
He chopped a clear road up out of the branch;
Their wheels made all the tracks.
And all they could see out doors were the trees,
And all the night they could hear the wolves go;
But one cold time when the dark came on
A man's voice said, "Hello, there, hello!"

He stood away by the black oak tree
When they opened the door in the halfway light;
He stood away by the buttonwood stump,
And Valentine said, "Won't you stay all night?"

He sat by the fire and warmed his bones.
He had something hidden down deep in a sack,
And Polly watched close while she baked her pones;
He felt of it once when she turned her back—
Polly had a fear of his sack.

Nobody lived this way or there,
And the night came down and the woods came dark,
A thin man sat by the fire that night,
And the cabin pane was one red spark.

He took the something out of his sack,
When the candle dimmed and the logs fell low,
It was something dark, as Polly could see,
Sing, sing, sing and howdy, howdy-o!

He held it up against his chest,
And the logs came bright with a fresh new glow,
And it was a fiddle that was on his breast,
Tum tum-a tum and danky, danky-o!

He played one tune and one tune more;
He played five tunes all in a long row.
The logs never heard any songs before.
Sing, sing, sing and howdy, howdy-o!

The tunes lay down like drowsy cats;
They tumbled over rocks where the waterfalls go;
They twinkled in the sun like little June gnats;
Tum a-tum tum and danky dee-o!

The stumps stood back in Valentine's mind;
The wolves went back so Polly couldn't see;
She forgot how they howled and forgot how they whined.
Tum tum a-tum and danky-dee!

The tunes flew by like wild quick geese,
Sing, sing, sing and howdy howdy-o!
And Polly said, "That's a right good piece."
Tum tum tum and danky danky-o!
Tum a-tum tum and danky dee-o!

Elinor Wylie

☙ Elinor (Hoyt) Wylie was born September 7, 1885, in Somerville, New Jersey, but she was, as she often protested, of pure Pennsylvania stock. The family was a literary one and it was soon evident that Elinor, the first born, was a prodigy. The facts of her life, if not the inner conflicts and personal sufferings, have been recorded by Nancy Hoyt, her younger sister, in *Elinor Wylie: The Portrait of an Unknown Woman* (1935), and, though the biography might have been fuller and franker without diminishing the poet's stature, it is invaluable source material. On both sides Elinor Wylie traced her ancestry back through old American families. A grandfather was Governor of Pennsylvania; her father, at the age of thirty-six, was Assistant Attorney-General under McKinley, later Solicitor General during Theodore Roosevelt's administration.

Elinor Hoyt's youth was spent in Washington, D. C. At eighteen she attended a life class at the Corcoran Museum of Art, composing poems in secret, and wavering between painting and writing as a possible career. Shortly after her "coming-out party" there was a youthful romance and, disappointed because it was inconclusive, Elinor "rushed off and, without the knowledge of her parents, became engaged to a nice-looking and well-born young suitor with a bad temper," Philip Hichborn, son of an admiral. A son was born of the union, but the marriage was an unhappy one. Three years after, when scarcely twenty-four, she eloped with Horace Wylie, unable to obtain a divorce, disrupting the social circles in which she had conducted herself so primly. Elinor and Horace Wylie lived in England, where they were married some years later, until the World War forced them to return to America. It was in England that her first work was published, a tiny book of forty-three pages entitled *Incidental Numbers* (1912), privately printed and unsigned. It is a tentative collection and Elinor was so sensitive about its "incredible immaturity" that she pleaded with the few who knew of its existence never to refer to it until after her death. But she had no reason to be ashamed of it. ("I think the juvenilia superior to the rest," she wrote to the editor many years later.) Much of it is manifestly immature, since most of it was written in her early twenties and the rest was the product of her teens. Yet her characteristic touch—the firm thought matched by the firmly molded line—is already suggested, especially in such poems as "The Knight Fallen on Evil Days," anticipating the later beautifully knit sonnets, and "Pegasus Lost," a strangely ironic fantasy written at seventeen.

She returned to America in the summer of 1916, and lived in Boston and in Mount Desert, Maine. Her poems began to appear in the magazines; she moved to Washington, where she met various friends of her brother Henry, including William Rose Benét. In 1921 her first "real" volume, *Nets to Catch the Wind,* appeared. Three years later she was a famous person, the author of two volumes of poems and an extraordinary first novel (*Jennifer Lorn*), married to William Rose Benét, and part of the literary life of New York.

Nets to Catch the Wind impresses immediately because of its brilliance. The brilliance is one which, at first, seems to sparkle without burning. In several of the poems the author achieves a frigid ecstasy; emotion is not absent from her lines, but too frequently it seems a passion frozen at its source. It is the brilliance of moonlight coruscating on a plain of ice. But if Mrs. Wylie seldom allows her verses to grow agitated, she never permits them to remain dull. As a technician, she is always admirable; in "August" the sense of heat is conveyed by tropic luxuriance and contrast; in "The Eagle and the Mole" she lifts didacticism to a proud level. Her auditory effects are scarcely less remarkable; never has snow-silence been so remarkably projected as in "Velvet Shoes," perhaps the whitest poem ever written.

Black Armour (1923) exhibits Mrs. Wylie's keenness against a mellower background. The beauty evoked in this volume no longer has "the hard heart of a child." The intellect has grown more fiery, the mood has grown warmer, and the craftsmanship is more dazzling than ever. This devotee of severe elegance has perfected an accent which is clipped and patrician; she varies the perfect modulation with rhymes that are delightfully acrid and unique departures which never fail of success. Mrs. Wylie, it is evident from the very titles of her volumes, had read the metaphysicians; Donne, Webster, and Eliot found a voice in her lines. She felt

> "behind a carnal mesh,
> The clean bones crying in the flesh."

Possibly the most obvious and arresting feature of her work is the variety of her gifts. She reached from the nimble dexterity of a rondo like "Peregrine" to the introspective poignance of "Self Portrait," from the fanciful "Escape" to the grave mockery of "Let No Charitable Hope." But a greater unfoldment was to come.

Trivial Breath (1928) is the work of a poet in transition. At times the craftsman is uppermost; at times the creative genius. A preoccupation with her material obscures the half-uttered wisdom. Many of the verses, steeped in literature, pay homage to the letter; a smaller number, less absorbed in shaping an immaculate phrase, do reverence to the spirit. Mrs. Wylie recognized the danger of her own exquisiteness, of a style where elegance was too often a richly embroidered cloak draped upon a neat triviality. In "Minotaur" she admonished herself:

> Go study to disdain
> The frail, the overfine
> That tapers to a line
> Knotted about the brain.

Her distrust of the "overfine" deepened; she became more influenced by the fiery spirit of Shelley; her prose grew less mannered and more searching; her poetry attained a new richness. While in England during the summer of 1928 she wrote, with almost breathless haste but with calm certainty, the verses which compose her posthumous volume. In the autumn she returned to America; suffering from high blood pressure and partial paralysis, she began to arrange her final work. The day before she died she decided on the order of the poems, affixed the motto from Donne, and got the manuscript ready for the printer. She died December 16, 1928.

Angels and Earthly Creatures (1929) is the sublimation of all her gifts. Here are the cunningly poised and polished syllables, here are the old concerns with freezing silvers, frail china, and pearly monotones, but here is a quality which lifts them high above themselves. Still indebted to the Jacobean metaphysicians, the poet transcends her influences and develops a highly personal mysticism. To say that her emotion is governed and disciplined is not to say that *Angels and Earthly Creatures* suffers from a lack of emotion. On the contrary, the sequence of nineteen sonnets has the spontaneity of a passionate improvisation, of something close to abandonment. The other poems share this intensity. "This Corruptible" is both visionary and philosophic; "O Virtuous Light" deals with that piercing clarity, the intuition which disturbs the senses, threatens reason and, "begotten of itself," unreconciled to ordinary experience, is "not a light by which to live." The other poems are scarcely less uplifted, finding their summit in "Hymn to Earth," which is possibly the deepest of her poems and one which is certain to endure. It was, as it happened, a clear premonition; it remains a noble valedictory. She could go no further. She had perfected her technique; without discarding her idiom, her spirit reached toward a final expression.

A sumptuous *Collected Poems of Elinor Wylie* was published in 1932, containing, with the exception of the booklet issued in England, her four books of poems as well as a section of forty-eight poems hitherto uncollected. Some of the posthumous verse had never seen print; others published in magazines—notably "Golden Bough" and "The Pebble"—may be ranked among the poet's ripest utterances. "The Pebble" is significant not only as a fine piece of craftsmanship but as a revealing bit of spiritual autobiography.

Though more mannered than her verse, her prose was scarcely less accomplished. *Jennifer Lorn* (1923), subtitled "A Sedate Extravaganza," *The Venetian Glass Nephew* (1925), and *The Orphan Angel* (1926) adroitly juggle a harlequin style, even when it is least appropriate to the matter. *Mr. Hodge and Mr. Hazard* is a somewhat more serious and ironic allegory. Differing widely from each other in plot, ranging from macabre artifice to an apocryphal legend of Shelley *redivivus* in America, the manipulation of these novels is always deft and the iridescent phrasing is the product of an unusually "jeweled" brain. An omnibus volume *Collected Prose of Elinor Wylie* (1933) includes the four novels besides ten uncollected short stories and essays introduced by William Rose Benét in the section "Fugitive Prose." Although one must admire the fine-spun filigree of *Jennifer Lorn* and the delicate diablerie of *The Venetian Glass Nephew,* even the height of her prose cannot match the peaks attained by such poems as "This Corruptible," "Hymn to Earth" and "O Virtuous Light."

For it was as a poet that Elinor Wylie was most at home in the world, and it is as a poet that she will be remembered. Whether she spins a web of words to catch an elusive whimsicality, or satirizes herself, or plunges from the fragmentary to the profound, every line bears her authentic stamp. The intellectual versatility is eventually reënforced by spiritual strength, insuring permanence to work which "preserves a shape utterly its own."

THE EAGLE AND THE MOLE

Avoid the reeking herd,
Shun the polluted flock,
Live like that stoic bird,
The eagle of the rock.

The huddled warmth of crowds
Begets and fosters hate;
He keeps, above the clouds,
His cliff inviolate.

When flocks are folded warm,
And herds to shelter run,
He sails above the storm,
He stares into the sun.

If in the eagle's track
Your sinews cannot leap,
Avoid the lathered pack,
Turn from the steaming sheep.

If you would keep your soul
From spotted sight or sound,
Live like the velvet mole;
Go burrow underground.

And there hold intercourse
With roots of trees and stones,
With rivers at their source,
And disembodied bones.

THE KNIGHT FALLEN ON EVIL DAYS

God send the Devil is a gentleman,
Else had I none amongst mine enemies!
O what uncouth and cruel times are these
In which the unlettered Boor and Artisan,
The snarling Priest and smirking Lawyer can
Spit filthy enmity at whom they please—
At one, returned from spilling overseas
The Princely blood of foes Olympian.

Apothecaries curse me, who of late
Was cursed by Kings for slaughtering French lords!
Friendless and loverless is my estate,
Yet God be praised that Hell at least affords
An adversary worthy of my hate,
With whom the Angels deigned to measure swords!

PEGASUS LOST

And there I found a gray and ancient ass,
With dull glazed stare, and stubborn wrinkled smile,
Sardonic, mocking my wide-eyed amaze.
A clumsy hulking form in that white place
At odds with the small stable, cleanly, Greek,
The marble manger and the golden oats.
With loathing hands I felt the ass's side,
Solidly real and hairy to the touch.
Then knew I that I dreamed not, but saw truth;
And knowing, wished I still might hope I dreamed.
The door stood wide, I went into the air.
The day was blue and filled with rushing wind,
A day to ride high in the heavens and taste
The glory of the gods who tread the stars.
Up in the mighty purity I saw
A flashing shape that gladly sprang aloft—
My little Pegasus, like a far white bird
Seeking sun-regions, never to return.
Silently then I turned my steps about,
Entered the stable, saddled the slow ass;
Then on its back I journeyed dustily
Between sun-wilted hedgerows into town.

MADMAN'S SONG

Better to see your cheek grown hollow,
Better to see your temple worn,
Than to forget to follow, follow,
After the sound of a silver horn.

Better to bind your brow with willow
And follow, follow until you die,
Than to sleep with your head on a golden pillow,
Nor lift it up when the hunt goes by.

Better to see your cheek grown sallow
And your hair grown gray, so soon, so soon,
Than to forget to hallo, hallo,
After the milk-white hounds of the moon.

SANCTUARY

This is the bricklayer; hear the thud
Of his heavy load dumped down on stone.
His lustrous bricks are brighter than blood,
His smoking mortar whiter than bone.

Set each sharp-edged, fire-bitten brick
Straight by the plumb-line's shivering length;
Make my marvelous wall so thick
Dead nor living may shake its strength.

Full as a crystal cup with drink
Is my cell with dreams, and quiet, and cool. . . .
Stop, old man! You must leave a chink;
How can I breathe? *You can't, you fool!*

VELVET SHOES

Let us walk in the white snow
  In a soundless space;
With footsteps quiet and slow,
  At a tranquil pace,
  Under veils of white lace.

I shall go shod in silk,
  And you in wool,
White as a white cow's milk,
  More beautiful
  Than the breast of a gull.

We shall walk through the still town
  In a windless peace;
We shall step upon white down,
  Upon silver fleece,
  Upon softer than these.

We shall walk in velvet shoes:
  Wherever we go
Silence will fall like dews
  On white silence below.
  We shall walk in the snow.

ESCAPE

When foxes eat the last gold grape,
And the last white antelope is killed,
I shall stop fighting and escape
Into a little house I'll build.

But first I'll shrink to fairy size,
With a whisper no one understands,
Making blind moons of all your eyes,
And muddy roads of all your hands.

And you may grope for me in vain
In hollows under the mangrove root,
Or where, in apple-scented rain,
The silver wasp-nests hang like fruit.

GOLDEN BOUGH

These lovely groves of fountain-trees that shake
  A burning spray against autumnal cool,
Descend again in molten drops to make
  The rutted path a river and a pool.

They rise in silence, fall in quietude,
  Lie still as looking-glass to every sense;
Only their lion-color in the wood
  Roars to miraculous heat and turbulence.

AUGUST

Why should this Negro insolently stride
Down the red noonday on such noiseless feet?
Piled in his barrow, tawnier than wheat,
Lie heaps of smoldering daisies, somber-eyed,
Their copper petals shriveled up with pride,
Hot with a superfluity of heat,
Like a great brazier borne along the street
By captive leopards, black and burning pied.

Are there no water-lilies, smooth as cream,
With long stems dripping crystal? Are there none
Like those white lilies, luminous and cool,
Plucked from some hemlock-darkened northern stream
By fair-haired swimmers, diving where the sun
Scarce warms the surface of the deepest pool?

PURITAN SONNET

Down to the Puritan marrow of my bones
There's something in this richness that I hate.
I love the look, austere, immaculate,
Of landscapes drawn in pearly monotones.
There's something in my very blood that owns
Bare hills, cold silver on a sky of slate,
A thread of water, churned to milky spate
Streaming through slanted pastures fenced with stones.

I love those skies, thin blue or snowy gray,
Those fields sparse-planted, rendering meager sheaves;
That spring, briefer than apple-blossom's breath,
Summer, so much too beautiful to stay,
Swift autumn, like a bonfire of leaves,
And sleepy winter, like the sleep of death.

NEBUCHADNEZZAR

My body is weary to death of my mischievous brain;
I am weary forever and ever of being brave;
Therefore I crouch on my knees while the cool white rain
Curves the clover over my head like a wave.

The stem and the frosty seed of the grass are ripe;
I have devoured their strength; I have drunk them deep;
And the dandelion is gall in a thin green pipe;
But the clover is honey and sun and the smell of sleep.

LET NO CHARITABLE HOPE

Now let no charitable hope
Confuse my mind with images
Of eagle and of antelope;
I am in nature none of these.

I was, being human, born alone;
I am, being woman, hard beset;
I live by squeezing from a stone
The little nourishment I get.

In masks outrageous and austere
The years go by in single file;
But none has merited my fear,
And none has quite escaped my smile.

CONFESSION OF FAITH

I lack the braver mind
That dares to find
The lover friend, and kind.

I fear him to the bone;
I lie alone
By the beloved one,

And, breathless for suspense,
Erect defense
Against love's violence

Whose silences portend
A bloody end
For lover never friend.

But, in default of faith,
In futile breath,
I dream no ill of Death.

"DESOLATION IS A DELICATE THING"

Sorrow lay upon my breast more heavily than winter clay
Lying ponderable upon the unmoving bosom of the dead;
Yet it was dissolved like a thin snowfall; it was softly withered away;
Presently like a single drop of dew it had trembled and fled.

This sorrow, which seemed heavier than a shovelful of loam,
Was gone like water, like a web of delicate frost;
It was silent and vanishing like smoke; it was scattered like foam;
Though my mind should desire to preserve it, nevertheless it is lost.

This sorrow was not like sorrow; it was shining and brief;
Even as I waked and was aware of its going, it was past and gone;
It was not earth; it was no more than a light leaf,
Or a snowflake in spring, which perishes upon stone.

This sorrow was small and vulnerable and short-lived;
It was neither earth nor stone; it was silver snow
Fallen from heaven, perhaps; it has not survived
An hour of the sun; it is sad it should be so.

This sorrow, which I believed a gravestone over my heart,
Is gone like a cloud; it eluded me as I woke;
Its crystal dust is suddenly broken and blown apart;
It was not my heart; it was this poor sorrow alone which broke.

PETER AND JOHN

Twelve good friends
Walked under the leaves
Binding the ends
Of the barley sheaves.

Peter and John
Lay down to sleep
Pillowed upon
A haymaker's heap.

John and Peter
Lay down to dream.
The air was sweeter
Than honey and cream.

Peter was bred
In the salty cold.
His hair was red
And his eyes were gold.

John had a mouth
Like a wing bent down.
His brow was smooth
And his eyes were brown.

Peter to slumber
Sank like a stone,
Of all their number
The bravest one.

John more slowly
Composed himself,
Young and holy
Among the Twelve.

John as he slept
Cried out in grief,
Turned and wept
On the golden leaf:

"Peter, Peter,
Stretch me your hand
Across the glitter
Of the harvest land!

"Peter, Peter
Give me a sign!
This was a bitter
Dream of mine,—

"Bitter as aloes
It parched my tongue.
Upon the gallows
My life was hung.

"Sharp it seemed
As a bloody sword.
Peter, I dreamed
I was Christ the Lord!"

Peter turned
To holy Saint John:
His body burned
In the falling sun.

In the falling sun
He burned like flame:
"John, Saint John,
I have dreamed the same!

"My bones were hung
On an elder tree;
Bells were rung
Over Galilee.

"A silver penny
Sealed each of my eyes.
Many and many
A cock crew thrice."

When Peter's word
Was spoken and done,
"Were you Christ the Lord
In your dream?" said John.

"No," said the other,
"That I was not.
I was our brother
Iscariot."

FULL MOON

My bands of silk and miniver
Momently grew heavier;
The black gauze was beggarly thin;
The ermine muffled mouth and chin;
I could not suck the moonlight in.

Harlequin in lozenges
Of love and hate, I walked in these
Striped and ragged rigmaroles;
Along the pavement my footsoles
Trod warily on living coals.

Shouldering the thoughts I loathed,
In their corrupt disguises clothed,
Mortality I could not tear
From my ribs, to leave them bare
Ivory in silver air.

There I walked and there I raged;
The spiritual savage caged
Within my skeleton, raged afresh
To feel, behind a carnal mesh,
The clean bones crying in the flesh.

EPITAPH

For this she starred her eyes with salt
And scooped her temples thin,
Until her face shone pure of fault
From the forehead to the chin.

In coldest crucible of pain
Her shrinking flesh was fired
And smoothed into a finer grain
To make it more desired.

Pain left her lips more clear than glass
It colored and cooled her hand.
She lay a field of scented grass
Yielded as pasture land.

For this her loveliness was curved
And carved as silver is:
For this she was brave: but she deserved
A better grave than this.

BIRTHDAY SONNET

Take home Thy prodigal child, O Lord of Hosts!
Protect the sacred from the secular danger;
Advise her, that Thou never needst avenge her;
Marry her mind neither to man's nor ghost's
Nor holier domination's, if the costs
Of such commingling should transport or change her;
Defend her from familiar and stranger,
And earth's and air's contagions and rusts.

Instruct her strictly to preserve Thy gift
And alter not its grain in atom sort;
Angels may wed her to their ultimate hurt
And men embrace a specter in a shift
So that no drop of the pure spirit fall
Into the dust: defend Thy prodigal.

O VIRTUOUS LIGHT

A private madness has prevailed
Over the pure and valiant mind;
The instrument of reason failed
And the star-gazing eyes struck blind.

Sudden excess of light has wrought
Confusion in the secret place
Where the slow miracles of thought
Take shape through patience into grace.

Mysterious as steel and flint
The birth of this destructive spark
Whose inward growth has power to print
Strange suns upon the natural dark.

O break the walls of sense in half
And make the spirit fugitive!
This light begotten of itself
Is not a light by which to live!

The fire of farthing tallow dips
Dispels the menace of the skies
So it illuminate the lips
And enter the discerning eyes.

O virtuous light, if thou be man's
Or matter of the meteor stone,
Prevail against this radiance
Which is engendered of its own!

THE PEBBLE

If any have a stone to shy,
Let him be David and not I;
The lovely shepherd, brave and vain,
Who has a maggot in the brain,
Which, since the brain is bold and pliant,
Takes the proportions of a giant.
Alas, my legendary fate!
Who sometimes rage, but never hate.
Long, long before the pebble flieth
I see a virtue in Goliath;
Yea, in the Philistine his face,
A touching majesty and grace;
Then like the lights of evening shine
The features of the Philistine
Until my spirit faints to see
The beauty of my enemy.
If any have a stone to fling
Let him be a shepherd-king,
Who is himself so beautiful
He may detest the gross and dull
With holy rage and heavenly pride
To make a pebble sanctified
And feather its course with wings of scorn.
But, from the day that I was born
Until like corn I bow to the sickle,
I am in hatred false and fickle.
I am most cruel to anyone
Who hates me with devotion;
I will not freeze, I will not burn;
I make his heart a poor return
For all the passion that he spends
In swearing we shall never be friends;
For all the pains his passion spent
In hatred I am impotent;
The sad perversity of my mind
Sees in him my kin and kind.
Alas, my shameful heritage,
False in hate and fickle in rage!
Alas, to lack the power to loathe!
I like them each; I love them both;
Philistine and shepherd-king
They strike the pebble from my sling;
My heart grows cold, my spirit grows faint;
Behold, a hero and a saint
Where appeared, a moment since,
A giant and a heathen prince;
And I am bound and given over
To be no better than a lover,
Alas, who strove as a holy rebel!
They have broke my sling and stole my
pebble:
If any have a stone to throw
It is not I, ever or now.

SONNET FROM "ONE PERSON"

I hereby swear that to uphold your house
I would lay my bones in quick destroying lime
Or turn my flesh to timber for all time;
Cut down my womanhood; lop off the boughs

Of that perpetual ecstasy that grows
From the heart's core; condemn it as a crime
If it be broader than a beam, or climb
Above the stature that your roof allows.

I am not the hearthstone nor the cornerstone
Within this noble fabric you have builded;
Not by my beauty was its cornice gilded;
Not on my courage were its arches thrown:
My lord, adjudge my strength, and set me where
I bear a little more than I can bear.

THIS CORRUPTIBLE

The body, long oppressed
And pierced, then prayed for rest
(Being but apprenticed to the other Powers);
And kneeling in that place
Implored the thrust of grace
Which makes the dust lie level with the flowers.

Then did that fellowship
Of three, the Body strip;
Beheld his wounds, and none among them mortal;
The Mind severe and cool;
The Heart still half a fool;
The fine-spun Soul, a beam of sun can startle.

These three, a thousand years
Had made adventurers
Amid all villainies the earth can offer,
Applied them to resolve
From the universal gulph
What pangs the poor material flesh may suffer.

"This is a pretty pass;
To hear the growing grass
Complain; the clay cry out to be translated;
Will not this grosser stuff
Receive reward enough
If stabled after laboring, and baited?"

Thus spoke the Mind in scorn.
The Heart, which had outworn
The Body, and was weary of its fashion,
Preferring to be dressed
In skin of bird or beast,
Replied more softly, in a feigned compassion.

"Anatomy most strange
Crying to chop and change;

Inferior copy of a higher image;
While I, the noble guest,
Sick of your second-best
Sigh for embroidered archangelic plumage:

"For shame, thou fustian cloak!"
And then the Spirit spoke;
Within the void it swung securely tethered
By strings composed of cloud;
It spoke both low and loud
Above a storm no lesser star had weathered.

"O lodging for the night!
O house of my delight!
O lovely hovel builded for my pleasure!
Dear tenement of clay
Endure another day
As coffin sweetly fitted to my measure.

"Take Heart and call to Mind
Although we are unkind;
Although we steal your shelter, strength, and clothing;
'Tis you who shall escape
In some enchanting shape
Or be dissolved to elemental nothing.

"You, the unlucky slave,
Are the lily on the grave;
The wave that runs above the bones a-whitening;
You are the new-mown grass;
And the wheaten bread of the Mass;
And the fabric of the rain, and the lightning.

"If one of us elect
To leave the poor suspect
Imperfect bosom of the earth our parent;
And from the world avert
The Spirit of the Heart
Upon a further and essential errand;

"His chain he cannot slough
Nor cast his substance off;
He bears himself upon his flying shoulder;
The Heart, infirm and dull;
The Mind, in any skull;
Are captive still, and wearier and colder.

" 'Tis you who are the ghost,
Disintegrated, lost;
The burden shed; the dead who need not bear it;
O grain of God in power,
Endure another hour!
It is but for an hour," said the Spirit.

HYMN TO EARTH

Farewell, incomparable element,
Whence man arose, where he shall not return;
And hail, imperfect urn
Of his last ashes, and his firstborn fruit;
Farewell, the long pursuit,
And all the adventures of his discontent;
The voyages which sent
His heart averse from home:
Metal of clay, permit him that he come
To thy slow-burning fire as to a hearth;
Accept him as a particle of earth.

Fire, being divided from the other three,
It lives removed, or secret at the core;
Most subtle of the four,
When air flies not, nor water flows,
It disembodied goes,
Being light, elixir of the first decree,
More volatile than he;
With strength and power to pass
Through space, where never his least atom was:
He has no part in it, save as his eyes
Have drawn its emanation from the skies.

A wingless creature heavier than air,
He is rejected of its quintessence;
Coming and going hence,
In the twin minutes of his birth and death,
He may inhale as breath,
As breath relinquish heaven's atmosphere,
Yet in it have no share,
Nor can survive therein
Where its outer edge is filtered pure and thin:
It doth but lend its crystal to his lungs
For his early crying, and his final songs.

The element of water has denied
Its child; it is no more his element;
It never will relent;
Its silver harvests are more sparsely given
Than the rewards of heaven,
And he shall drink cold comfort at its side:
The water is too wide:
The seamew and the gull
Feather a nest made soft and pitiful
Upon its foam; he has not any part
In the long swell of sorrow at its heart.

Hail and farewell, beloved element,
Whence he departed, and his parent once;
See where thy spirit runs
Which for so long hath had the moon to wife;
Shall this support his life
Until the arches of the waves be bent
And grow shallow and spent?
Wisely it cast him forth
With his dead weight of burdens nothing worth,
Leaving him, for the universal years,
A little seawater to make his tears.

Hail, element of earth, receive thy own,
And cherish, at thy charitable breast,
This man, this mongrel beast:
He plows the sand, and, at his hardest need,
He sows himself for seed;
He plows the furrow, and in this lies down
Before the corn is grown;
Between the apple bloom
And the ripe apple is sufficient room
In time, and matter, to consume his love
And make him parcel of a cypress grove.

Receive him as thy lover for an hour
Who will not weary, by a longer stay,
The kind embrace of clay;
Even within thine arms he is dispersed
To nothing, as at first;
The air flings downward from its four-quartered tower
Him whom the flames devour;
At the full tide, at the flood,
The sea is mingled with his salty blood:
The traveler dust, although the dust be vile,
Sleeps as thy lover for a little while.

Ezra Pound

☙ One of the most controversial figures of the period and unquestionably the most belligerent expatriate of his generation, Ezra (Loomis) Pound was born at Hailey, Idaho, October 30, 1885. A precocious reader, he entered the University of Pennsylvania at the age of fifteen. At sixteen, unbeknown to the faculty, he began studying comparative literature; before he was seventeen (in 1902) he enrolled as special student "to avoid irrelevant subjects." He continued the process at Hamilton College (1903-5) and from 1905 to 1907 was "Instructor with professorial functions" at the University of Pennsylvania. His next move brought him to

Crawfordsville, Indiana—" 'the Athens of the West,' a town with literary traditions, Lew Wallace having died there." Pound was dismissed from Wabash College after four months—"all accusations," he says, "having been ultimately refuted save that of being 'the Latin Quarter type.' "

Though a born educator, actually burning to teach, Pound was compelled to seek less academic circles. In 1908 he landed in Gibraltar with eighty dollars and lived on the interest for some time. The same year found him for the first time in Italy, which was to become his future home. *A Lume Spento* (1908) was printed in Venice. A few months later he was established in London, where he lived until 1920. Convinced of the aridity of England, he crossed over to Paris, from which, after four years, he moved to Rapallo, Italy, where he lived until the Second World War.

Shortly after Pound's arrival in London he published *Personae* (1909), a work which, though small, contains some of his most arresting verse.

Although the young American was a total stranger to the English literary world, his book made a definite impression on critics of all shades and tastes. Edward Thomas, one of the most cautious appraisers, wrote, "The beauty of it is the beauty of passion, sincerity and intensity, not of beautiful words and images and suggestions. . . . The thought dominates the words and is greater than they are." Another critic (Scott James) placed the chief emphasis on Pound's metrical innovations, saying, "At first the whole thing may seem to be mere madness and rhetoric, a vain exhibition of force and passion without beauty. But as we read on, these curious meters seem to have a law and order of their own."

Exultations (1909) was printed in the autumn of the same year that saw the appearance of *Personae*. It was received with even greater cordiality; a new force and freedom were manifest in such poems as "Sestina: Altaforte," "Ballad of the Goodly Fere," and the stark "Ballad for Gloom." Both books were republished in a single volume, with other poems, as *Personae,* in 1926.

In these books there is evident Pound's erudition—a familiarity with medieval literature, Provençal singers, Troubadour ballads—an erudition which, later, was to degenerate into pedantry. Too often Pound seemed to become theory-logged, to sink himself in an intellectual Sargasso Sea, to be more the archeologist than the artist. *Canzoni* (1911) and *Ripostes* (1912) contain much that is sharp and living; they also contain the germs of desiccation and decay. Pound began to scatter his talents; to start movements which he quickly discarded for new ones; to spend himself in poetic propaganda for the Vorticists and others; to give more and more time to translation (*The Sonnets of Guido Cavalcanti* appeared in 1912) and arrangements from the Chinese (*Cathay,* paraphrased from the notes of Ernest Fenollosa, was issued in 1915); to lay the chief stress on technique, shades of color, verbal *nuances*. The result was a confusion of the creative faculties and a disturbance of emotion. In the later books, Pound seemed to suffer from a decadence which appraises the values in life chiefly as esthetic values.

Lustra appeared in 1916. In this collection, as in the preceding volumes, Pound struggled with his influences; accents of Swinburne, Browning, Lionel Johnson, and Yeats mingled with those of the Provençal poets. From his immediate predecessors Pound learned the value of "verse as speech" while, as Eliot has pointed out, from the more antiquarian studies Pound was learning the importance of "speech as song." It was not until *Hugh Selwyn Mauberley* (1920) and the *Cantos* that Pound integrated his own inflection, form, and philosophy.

Mauberley is a thinly disguised autobiographical account of the artist-esthete in an anti-cultural society. The conflict of the hard-pressed creator and the contemptuous philistine is accentuated by contrasts of tone and occasional portraits of the period, circa 1910-1920. ("M. Verog" is the minor Victorian poet Victor Plarr; "Mr. Nixon" is the novelist Arnold Bennett.) It is also, wrote T. S. Eliot in his introduction to Pound's *Selected Poems,* "a document of an epoch . . . and it is, in the best sense of Arnold's worn phrase, a 'criticism of life.' "

The *Cantos* are more difficult of comprehension. Nine volumes of them appeared between 1925 and 1959, concluding with *Canto 109.* (One of the volumes, *The Pisan Cantos,* so called because it was composed when Pound was imprisoned near Pisa in 1945, was awarded the Bollingen Prize and stirred up violent contention.) Only a scholar versed in many cultures and languages can follow the mixture of allusions interrupted by private digressions, jokes, imprecations, myths, ideograms, a preoccupation with usury, and Pound's obsession that he is the only clear thinker in a muddled world.

Chaotic though the *Cantos* appear, their design is formal. When Pound began his monumental project he conceived it in terms of an elaborate fugue. As the work enlarged, he abandoned the likeness to Bach and thought of it in terms of Dante and referred to it as a Human Comedy. The Greek, Renaissance, and First World War episodes are the *Inferno;* the history of money and banking represents the *Purgatorio;* a climactic finale, unwritten, suggests the *Paradiso.* Rarely in literature has there been such a voluminous, eccentric, and apocalyptic monologue. "It is all fragmentary," wrote Allen Tate. "Every canto begins with a bit of heroic antiquity, some myth, or classical quotation, or a lovely piece of lyrical description in a grand style. It invariably breaks down. It trails off into a piece of contemporary satire, or a flat narrative of the rascality of some Italian prince. This is the special quality of Pound's form, the essence of his talk, the direction of these magnificent conversations."

Critical opinion of the *Cantos* was sharply divided. To most readers the work was a masterpiece of obfuscation, a jig-saw puzzle with the important pieces missing. "About the poems," wrote Edward Fitzgerald, "there hangs a dismal mist of unresolved confusion. Through that mist we can see fact, but fact historically stated, enlivened in no way by either a creative or a critical process." Some found it a garble of literature and nothing else, composed of scraps from newspapers, oddments from documents difficult of access, and the minor classics, all piled upon each other without an original idea or an experience outside of print. To others it was a modern Gospel. "One of the three great works of poetry of our time," wrote Allan Tate. Ford Madox Ford's enthusiasm was even less guarded. "The first words you have to say about the *Cantos,*" said Ford, "is: Their extraordinary beauty . . . They form an unparalleled history of a world seen from those shores which are the home of our civilization." John Crowe Ransom's estimate was more temperate. He concluded, "Mr. Pound, in his capacity of guide to literature, never wearies of telling us about the troubadour songs of Provence, which he reveres. He lays down the law that, the further the poem goes from its original character of song, the more dubious is its estate. But what if we apply that canon to the *Cantos?* The result is that we find ourselves sometimes admiring in Mr. Pound's poetry an effect of brilliance and nearly always missing the effect of poetry."

Whatever differences arose concerning the finality of Pound's performance, none could dispute the power of his influence. The accent of the *Cantos* can be traced through Eliot's *The Waste Land,* Hart Crane's *The Bridge,* and MacLeish's longer poems, particularly his *Conquistador.* Moreover, any attempt to do justice to Pound must take account of the chronology of his work in relation to others. He invented the term "Imagism" and organized the Imagist school long before the ensuing period of exploitation. He published *Cathay* in 1915, and rendered *Certain Noble Plays of Japan from the Fenollosa Manuscripts,* anticipating the flood of Chinese and Japanese translations that, soon after, inundated the country. He "placed" Tagore as literary artist, not as messiah, and saw the Bengalese poet become a cult. He fought for the musician George Antheil; wrote a study of Gaudier Brzeska, when that sculptor was unknown; created a controversy by his Provençal paraphrases, expanded his Italian studies into *The Poems of Guido Cavalcanti.*

Besides his poetry Pound wrote, translated, and edited more than fourteen volumes of prose, the most characteristic being *A B C of Reading* (1934), an exposition of a critical method; *Make it New* (1935), which is a deceptive title since all but one of the essays appeared in *Pavannes and Divisions* (1918) and *Instigations* (1920). In his argumentative introduction to *The Oxford Book of Modern Verse* Yeats maintained that, although Ezra Pound had more style than any contemporary poet, his style was constantly broken and "twisted into nothing by its direct opposite: nervous obsession, nightmare, stammering confusion." Conceding Pound's influence, Yeats concluded that Pound was "a brilliant improvisator translating at sight from an unknown Greek masterpiece." The "confusion" grew into madness.

During the Second World War Pound, who had made his home in Italy, became an active supporter of Fascism. Beginning in 1941 he broadcast diatribes against the American system, attacks on Roosevelt, anti-Semitic slurs—all of which were indicated in the later *Cantos*—and acted as a paid propagandist who, twice a week, gave aid and comfort to the enemy and counseled fascist officials in operations against the United States. The inspired *enfant terrible* had become the public traitor. In May, 1945, he was taken prisoner and indicted for treason; the indictment charged nineteen overt acts. Brought to Washington, Pound escaped trial when four psychiatrists testified that the poet was of unsound mind; one of them diagnosed Pound as a "paranoid psychopathic personality." After a court hearing on February 14, 1946, Pound was committed to St. Elizabeth's Hospital as an insane person. Twelve years later he was released and returned to Italy.

As a major poet Pound is too wrong-headed, too arrogant and too special to attract a wide audience. Yvor Winters has written of him critically as a "barbarian on the loose in a museum," but a barbarian with "a rich if disordered memory." As a political thinker Pound was not only ineffectual but absurd; as a person he was intermittently unbalanced. But his literary importance should not be belittled. He was a pioneer in new forms, a champion of new poets. He fought complacency wherever he encountered it; he experimented in a speech which he made his own and transmitted to others. The feeling of isolation, the sense of being an expatriate self-separated from his audience, may explain Pound's eccentricities and obsessions, his bitter blasts and irresponsible nose-thumbings, his crackpot theories of economics, and his treasonable activities. There remains the gifted translator, the poet, the maker, who was also the creative critic and one of the great originators of his day.

SALUTATION

O Generation of the thoroughly smug
and thoroughly uncomfortable,
I have seen fishermen picnicking in the sun,
I have seen them with untidy families,
I have seen their smiles full of teeth
and heard ungainly laughter.
And I am happier than you are,
And they were happier than I am;
And the fish swim in the lake
and do not even own clothing.

THE GARDEN

En robe de parade.
SAMAIN

Like a skein of loose silk blown against a wall
She walks by the railing of a path in Kensington Gardens,
And she is dying piece-meal
of a sort of emotional anaemia.

And round about there is a rabble
Of the filthy, sturdy, unkillable infants of the very poor.
They shall inherit the earth.

In her is the end of breeding.
Her boredom is exquisite and excessive.
She would like some one to speak to her,
And is almost afraid that I
will commit that indiscretion.

SESTINA: ALTAFORTE

Loquitur: En *Bertrans de Born.*
Dante Alighieri put this man in hell for that he was a stirrer up of strife. Eccovi! Judge ye!
Have I dug him up again?
The scene is at his castle, Altaforte. "Papiols" is his jongleur.
"The Leopard," the device of Richard Cœur de Lion.

Damn it all! all this our South stinks peace.
You whoreson dog, Papiols, come! Let's to music!

I have no life save when the swords clash.
But ah! When I see the standards gold, vair, purple, opposing
And the broad fields beneath them turn crimson,
Then howl I my heart nigh mad with rejoicing.

In hot summer have I great rejoicing
When the tempests kill the earth's foul peace,
And the lightnings from black heav'n flash crimson,
And the fierce thunders roar me their music
And the winds shriek through the clouds mad, opposing,
And through all the riven skies God's swords clash.

Hell grant soon we hear again the swords clash!
And the shrill neighs of destriers in battle rejoicing,
Spiked breast to spiked breast opposing!
Better one hour's stour than a year's peace
With fat boards, bawds, wine and frail music!
Bah! there's no wine like the blood's crimson!

And I love to see the sun rise blood-crimson.
And I watch his spears through the dark clash
And it fills all my heart with rejoicing
And pries wide my mouth with fast music
When I see him so scorn and defy peace,
His lone might 'gainst all darkness opposing.

The man who fears war and squats opposing
My words for stour, hath no blood of crimson
But is fit only to rot in womanish peace
Far from where worth's won and the swords clash
For the death of such sluts I go rejoicing;
Yea, I fill all the air with my music.

Papiols, Papiols, to the music!
There's no sound like to swords swords opposing,
No cry like the battle's rejoicing
When our elbows and swords drip the crimson
And our charges 'gainst "The Leopard's" rush clash.
May God damn for ever all who cry "Peace!"

And let the music of the swords make them crimson!
Hell grant soon we hear again the swords clash!
Hell blot black for alway the thought "Peace"!

THE RIVER-MERCHANT'S WIFE: A LETTER

(*After Rihaku*)

While my hair was still cut straight across my forehead
I played about the front gate, pulling flowers.

You came by on bamboo stilts, playing horse,
You walked about my seat, playing with blue plums.
And we went on living in the village of Chokan:
Two small people, without dislike or suspicion.

At fourteen I married My Lord you.
I never laughed, being bashful.
Lowering my head, I looked at the wall.
Called to, a thousand times, I never looked back.

At fifteen I stopped scowling,
I desired my dust to be mingled with yours
Forever and forever and forever.
Why should I climb the lookout?

At sixteen you departed,
You went into far Ku-to-yen, by the river of swirling eddies,
And you have been gone five months.
The monkeys make sorrowful noise overhead.
You dragged your feet when you went out.
By the gate now, the moss is grown, the different mosses,
Too deep to clear them away!
The leaves fall early this autumn, in wind.
The paired butterflies are already yellow with August
Over the grass in the West garden;
They hurt me. I grow older.
If you are coming down through the narrows of the river Kiang,
Please let me know beforehand,
And I will come out to meet you
    As far as Cho-fu-sa.

AN IMMORALITY

Sing we for love and idleness,
Naught else is worth the having.
Though I have been in many a land,
There is naught else in living.

And I would rather have my sweet,
Though rose-leaves die of grieving,

Than do high deeds in Hungary
To pass all men's believing.

A VIRGINAL

No, No! Go from me. I have left her lately.
I will not spoil my sheath with lesser brightness,

For my surrounding air has a new lightness;
Slight are her arms, yet they have bound me straitly
And left me cloaked as with a gauze of ether;
As with sweet leaves; as with a subtle clearness.
Oh, I have picked up magic in her nearness
To sheathe me half in half the things that sheathe her.

No, no! Go from me. I have still the flavor,
Soft as spring wind that's come from birchen bowers.
Green come the shoots, aye April in the branches,
As winter's wound with her sleight hand she staunches,
Hath of the trees a likeness of the savor:
As white their bark, so white this lady's hours.

BALLAD FOR GLOOM

For God, our God is a gallant foe
That playeth behind the veil.

I have loved my God as a child at heart
That seeketh deep bosoms for rest,
I have loved my God as a maid to man—
But lo, this thing is best:

To love your God as a gallant foe that plays behind the veil;
To meet your God as the night winds meet beyond Arcturus' pale.

I have played with God for a woman,
I have staked with my God for truth,
I have lost to my God as a man, clear-eyed—
His dice be not of ruth.

For I am made as a naked blade,
But hear ye this thing in sooth:

Who loseth to God as man to man
Shall win at the turn of the game.
I have drawn my blade where the lightnings meet
But the ending is the same:
Who loseth to God as the sword blades lose
Shall win at the end of the game.

For God, our God is a gallant foe that playeth behind the veil.
Whom God deigns not to overthrow hath need of triple mail.

GREEK EPIGRAM

Day and night are never weary,
Nor yet is God of creating

For day and night their torch-bearers
The aube and the crepuscule.

So, when I weary of praising the dawn and the sunset,
Let me be no more counted among the immortals;
But number me amid the wearying ones,
Let me be a man as the herd,
And as the slave that is given in barter.

BALLAD OF THE GOODLY FERE[1]

Simon Zelotes speaketh it somewhile after the Crucifixion)

Ia' we lost the goodliest fere o' all
'or the priests and the gallows tree?
ye, lover he was of brawny men,
)' ships and the open sea.

Vhen they came wi' a host to take Our Man
Iis smile was good to see,
First let these go!" quo' our Goodly Fere,
Or I'll see ye damned," says he.

ye, he sent us out through the crossed high spears,
nd the scorn of his laugh rang free,
Why took ye not me when I walked about
lone in the town?" says he.

h we drank his "Hale" in the good red wine
/hen we last made company,
'o capon priest was the Goodly Fere
ut a man o' men was he.

ha' seen him drive a hundred men
'i' a bundle o' cords swung free,
/hen they took the high and holy house
or their pawn and treasury.

hey'll no get him a' in a book I think
hough they write it cunningly;
o mouse of the scrolls was the Goodly Fere
ut aye loved the open sea.

If they think they ha' snared our Goodly Fere
They are fools to the last degree.
"I'll go to the feast," quo' our Goodly Fere,
"Though I go to the gallows tree."

"Ye ha' seen me heal the lame and the blind,
And wake the dead," says he,
"Ye shall see one thing to master all:
'Tis how a brave man dies on the tree."

A son of God was the Goodly Fere
That bade us his brothers be.
I ha' seen him cow a thousand men.
I ha' seen him upon the tree.

He cried no cry when they drave the nails
And the blood gushed hot and free,
The hounds of the crimson sky gave tongue
But never a cry cried he.

I ha' seen him cow a thousand men
On the hills o' Galilee,
They whined as he walked out calm between,
Wi' his eyes like the gray o' the sea.

Like the sea that brooks no voyaging
With the winds unleashed and free,
Like the sea that he cowed at Gennesaret
Wi' twey words spoke' suddenly.

A master of men was the Goodly Fere,
A mate of the wind and sea,
If they think they ha' slain our Goodly Fere
They are fools eternally.

[1] Fere = Mate, Companion.

I ha' seen him eat o' the honey-comb
Sin' they nailed him to the tree.

A GIRL

The tree has entered my hands,
The sap has ascended my arms,
The tree has grown in my breast
Downward,
The branches grow out of me, like arms.

Tree you are,
Moss you are,
You are violets with wind above them.
A child—so high—you are;
And all this is folly to the world.

IN A STATION OF THE METRO

The apparition of these faces in the crowd;
Petals on a wet, black bough.

DANCE FIGURE

(For the Marriage in Cana of Galilee)

Dark eyed,
O woman of my dreams,
Ivory sandaled,
There is none like thee among the dancers,
None with swift feet.

I have not found thee in the tents,
In the broken darkness.
I have not found thee at the well-head
Among the women with pitchers.
Thine arms are as a young sapling under the bark;
Thy face as a river with lights.

White as an almond are thy shoulders;
As new almonds stripped from the husk.
They guard thee not with eunuchs;
Not with bars of copper.

Gilt turquoise and silver are in the place of thy rest.
A brown robe with threads of gold woven in patterns hast thou gathered about thee,
O Nathat-Ikanaie, "Tree-at-the-river."

As a rillet among the sedge are thy hands upon me;
Thy fingers a frosted stream.

Thy maidens are white like pebbles;
Their music about thee!

There is none like thee among the dancers;
None with swift feet.

ΔΩΡΙΑ

Be in me as the eternal moods
of the bleak wind, and not
As transient things are—
gayety of flowers.

Have me in the strong loneliness
  of sunless cliffs
And of gray waters.
  Let the gods speak softly of us
In days hereafter,
  the shadowy flowers of Orcus
Remember thee.

SILET

When I behold how black, immortal ink
Drips from my deathless pen—ah, well-away!
Why should we stop at all for what I think?
There is enough in what I chance to say.

It is enough that we once came together;
What is the use of setting it to rime?
When it is autumn do we get spring weather,
Or gather may of harsh northwindish time?

It is enough that we once came together;
What if the wind have turned against the rain?
It is enough that we once came together;
Time has seen this, and will not turn again.

And who are we, who know that last intent,
To plague tomorrow with a testament!

PORTRAIT D'UNE FEMME

Your mind and you are our Sargasso Sea,
London has swept about you this score years
And bright ships left you this or that in fee:
Ideas, old gossip, oddments of all things,
Strange spars of knowledge and dimmed wares of price.
Great minds have sought you—lacking someone else.
You have been second always. Tragical?
No. You preferred it to the usual thing:
One dull man, dulling and uxorious,
One average mind—with one thought less, each year.
Oh, you are patient. I have seen you sit
Hours, where something might have floated up.
And now you pay one. Yes, you richly pay.
You are a person of some interest, one comes to you
And takes strange gain away:
Trophies fished up; some curious suggestion;
Fact that leads nowhere; and a tale for two,
Pregnant with mandrakes, or with something else
That might prove useful and yet never proves,
That never fits a corner or shows use,

Or finds its hour upon the loom of days:
The tarnished, gaudy, wonderful old work;
Idols, and ambergris and rare inlays.
These are your riches, your great store; and yet
For all this sea-hoard of deciduous things,
Strange woods half sodden, and new brighter stuff:
In the slow float of differing light and deep,
No! there is nothing! In the whole and all,
Nothing that's quite your own.
Yet this is you.

THE RETURN

See, they return; ah see the tentative
Movements, and the slow feet,
The trouble in the pace and the
uncertain
Wavering!

See, they return, one, and by one,
With fear, as half-awakened;
As if the snow should hesitate
And murmur in the wind,
and half turn back;
These were the "Wing'd-with-Awe,"
Inviolable.

Gods of the wingèd shoe!
With them the silver hounds,
sniffing the trace of air!

Haie! Haie!
These were the swift to harry;
These were the keen-scented;
These were the souls of blood.

Slow on the leash,
pallid the leash-men!

ENVOI

Go, dumb-born book,
Tell her that sang me once that song of
Lawes:
Hadst thou but song
As thou hast subjects known,
Then were there cause in thee that should
condone
Even my faults that heavy upon me lie,
And build her glories their longevity.

Tell her that sheds
Such treasure in the air,
Recking naught else but that her graces give
Life to the moment,
I would bid them live
As roses might, in magic amber laid,
Red overwrought with orange and all made
One substance and one color
Braving time.

Tell her that goes
With song upon her lips
But sings not out the song, nor knows
The maker of it, some other mouth,
May be as fair as hers,
Might, in new ages, gain her worshipers,
When our two dusts with Waller's shall be
laid,
Siftings on siftings in oblivion,
Till change hath broken down
All things save Beauty alone.

THE REST

O helpless few in my country,
O remnant enslaved!

Artists broken against her,
Astray, lost in the villages,
Mistrusted, spoken-against,

Lovers of beauty, starved,
Thwarted with systems,
Helpless against the control;

You who cannot wear yourselves out
By persisting to successes,
You who can only speak,
Who cannot steel yourselves into reiteration

You of the finer sense,
Broken against false knowledge,
You who can know at first hand,
Hated, shut in, mistrusted:

Take thought:
I have weathered the storm,
I have beaten out my exile.

ITÉ

Go, my songs, seek your praise from the young and from the intolerant,
Move among the lovers of perfection alone.
Seek ever to stand in the hard Sophoclean light
And take your wounds from it gladly.

CANTO I

And then went down to the ship,
Set keel to breakers, forth on the godly sea, and
We set up mast and sail on that swart ship,
Bore sheep aboard her, and our bodies also
Heavy with weeping, and winds from sternward
Bore us out onward with bellying canvas,
Circe's this craft, the trim-coifed goddess.
Then sat we amidships, wind jamming the tiller,
Thus with stretched sail, we went over sea till day's end.
Sun to his slumber, shadows o'er all the ocean,
Came we then to the bounds of deepest water,
To the Kimmerian lands, and peopled cities
Covered with close-webbed mist, unpierced ever
With glitter of sun-ray
Nor with stars stretched, nor looking back from heaven
Swartest night stretched over wretched men there.
The ocean flowing backward, came we then to the place
Aforesaid by Circe.
Here did they rites, Perimedes and Eurylochus,
And drawing sword from my hip
I dug the ell-square pitkin;
Poured we libations unto each the dead,
First mead and then sweet wine, water mixed with white flour.
Then prayed I many a prayer to the sickly death's-heads;
As set in Ithaca, sterile bulls of the best
For sacrifice, heaping the pyre with goods,
A sheep to Tiresias only, black and a bell-sheep.
Dark blood flowed in the fosse,
Souls out of Erebus, cadaverous dead, of brides
Of youths and of the old who had borne much;
Souls stained with recent tears, girls tender,
Men many, mauled with bronze lance heads,
Battle spoil, bearing yet dreary arms,
These many crowded about me; with shouting,
Pallor upon me, cried to my men for more beasts;
Slaughtered the herds, sheep slain of bronze;

Poured ointment, cried to the gods,
To Pluto the strong, and praised Prosperine;
Unsheathed the narrow sword,
I sat to keep off the impetuous impotent dead,
Till I should hear Tiresias.
But first Elpenor came, our friend Elpenor,
Unburied, cast on the wide earth,
Limbs that we left in the house of Circe,
Unwept, unwrapped in sepulcher, since toils urged other.
Pitiful spirit. And I cried in hurried speech:
"Elpenor, how art thou come to this dark coast?
"Cam'st thou afoot, outstripping seamen?"
                    And he in heavy speech:
"Ill fate and abundant wine. I slept in Circe's ingle.
"Going down the long ladder unguarded,
"I fell against the buttress,
"Shattered the nape-nerve, the soul sought Avernus.
"But thou, O King, I bid remember me, unwept, unburied,
"Heap up mine arms, be tomb by sea-board, and inscribed:
"*'A man of no fortune and with a name to come.'*
"And set my oar up, that I swung mid fellows."

And Anticlea came, whom I beat off, and then Tiresias Theban,
Holding his golden wand, knew me, and spoke first:
"A second time? why? man of ill star,
"Facing the sunless dead and this joyless region?
"Stand from the fosse, leave me my bloody bever
"For soothsay."
                    And I stepped back,
And he strong with the blood, said then: "Odysseus
"Shalt return through spiteful Neptune, over dark seas,
"Lose all companions." And then Anticlea came.
Lie quiet Divus. I mean that is Andreas Divus,
In officina Wecheli, 1538, out of Homer.
And he sailed, by Sirens and thence outward and away
And unto Circe.
                    Venerandam,
In the Cretan's phrase, with the golden crown, Aphrodite,
Cypri munimenta sortita est, mirthful, oricalchi, with golden
Girdles and breast bands, thou with dark eyelids
Bearing the golden bough of Argicida.

CANTO II

Hang it all, Robert Browning,
there can be but the one "Sordello."
But Sordello, and my Sordello?
Lo Sordels si fo di Mantovana.
So-shu churned in the sea.
Seal sports in the spray-whited circles of cliff-wash,
Sleek head, daughter of Lir, eyes of Picasso
Under black fur-hood, lithe daughter of Ocean;

And the wave runs in the beach-groove:
"Eleanor, ἑλέναυς and ἑλέπτολις!"
                    And poor old Homer blind, blind, as a bat,
Ear, ear for the sea-surge, murmur of old men's voices:
"Let her go back to the ships,
"Back among Grecian faces, lest evil come on our own,
"Evil and further evil, and a curse cursed on our children,
"Moves, yes she moves like a goddess
"And has the face of a god and the voice of Schoeney's daughters,
"And doom goes with her in walking,
"Let her go back to the ships, back among Grecian voices."
And by the beach-run, Tyro,
                    Twisted arms of the sea-god,
Lithe sinews of water, gripping her, cross-hold,
And the blue-gray glass of the wave tents them,
Glare azure of water, cold-welter, close cover.
Quiet sun-tawny sand-stretch,
The gulls broad out their wings, nipping between the splay feathers;
Snipe come for their bath, bend out their wing-joints,
Spread wet wings to the sun-film,
And by Scios, to left of the Naxos passage,
Naviform rock overgrown, algæ cling to its edge,
There is a wine-red glow in the shallows, a tin flash in the sun-dazzle.

The ship landed in Scios, men wanting spring-water,
And by the rock-pool a young boy loggy with vine-must,
                    "To Naxos? Yes, we'll take you to Naxos,
Cum' along lad." "Not that way!"
"Aye, that way is Naxos."
                    And I said: "It's a straight ship."
And an ex-convict out of Italy knocked me into the fore-stays,
(He was wanted for manslaugher in Tuscany)
                    And the whole twenty against me,
Mad for a little slave money.
                    And they took her out of Scios
And off her course . . .
                    And the boy came to, again, with the racket
And looked out over the bows, and to eastward, and to the Naxos passage.
God-sleight then, god-sleight:
                    Ship stock fast in sea-swirl,
Ivy upon the oars, King Pentheus, grapes with no seed but sea-foam,
Ivy in scupper-hole.
Aye, I, Acœtes, stood there, and the god stood by me,
Water cutting under the keel,
Sea-break from stern forrards, wake running off from the bow,
And where was gunwhale, there now was vine-trunk,
And tenthril where cordage had been, grape-leaves on the rowlocks,
Heavy vine on the oarshafts,
And, out of nothing, a breathing, hot breath on my ankles,
Beasts like shadows in glass, a furred tail upon nothingness.
Lynx-purr, and heathery smell of beasts, where tar smell had been,
Sniff and pad-foot of beasts, eye-glitter out of black air.

The sky overshot, dry, with no tempest,
Sniff and pad-foot of beasts, fur brushing my knee-skin,
Rustle of airy sheaths, dry forms in the *æther*.
And the ship like a keel in ship-yard, slung like an ox in smith's sling,
Ribs stuck fast in the ways, grape-cluster over pin-rack, void air taking pelt.
Lifeless air become sinewed, feline leisure of panthers,
Leopards sniffing the grape shoots by scupper-hole,
Crouched panthers by fore-hatch,
And the sea blue-deep about us, green-ruddy in shadows,
And Lyæus: "From now, Acœtes, my altars,
Fearing no bondage, fearing no cat of the wood,
Safe with my lynxes, feeding grapes to my leopards,
Olibanum is my incense, the vines grow in my homage."

The black-swell now smooth in the rudder-chains,
Black snout of a porpoise where Lycabs had been,
Fish-scales on the oarsmen.
            And I worship.
I have seen what I have seen.
            When they brought the boy I said:
"He has a god in him, though I do not know which god."
And they kicked me into the fore-stays.
I have seen what I have seen:
            Medon's face like the face of a dory,
Arms shrunk into fins. And you, Pentheus,
Had as well listen to Tiresias, and to Cadmus, or your luck will go out of you.
Fish-scales over groin muscles, lynx-purr amid sea . . .
And of a later year, pale in the wine-red algæ,
If you will lean over the rock, the coral face under wave-tinge,
Rose-paleness under water-shift,
            Ileuthyeria, fair Dafne of sea-bords,
The swimmer's arms turned to branches,
Who will say in what year, fleeing what band of tritons,
The smooth brows, seen, and half seen, now ivory stillness.

And So-shu churned in the sea, So-shu also, using the long moon for a churn-
    stick . . .
Lithe turning of water, sinews of Poseidon,
Black azure and hyaline, glass wave over Tyro,
Close cover, unstillness, bright welter of wave-cords,
Then quiet water, quiet in the buff sands,
Sea-fowl stretching wing-joints, splashing in rock-hollows and sand-hollows
In the wave-runs by the half-dune;
Glass-glint of wave in the tide-rips against sunlight, pallor of Hesperus,
Grey peak of the wave, wave, colour of grape's pulp,

Olive grey in the near, far, smoke grey of the rock-slide,
Salmon-pink wings of the fish-hawk cast grey shadows in water,
The tower like a one-eyed great goose cranes up out of the olive-grove,
And we have heard the fauns chiding Proteus in the smell of hay under the olive-
    trees,
And the frogs singing against the fauns in the half-light.
And . . .

HUGH SELWYN MAUBERLEY

E. P. Ode pour l'élection de son sépulchre

For three years, out of key with his time,
He strove to resuscitate the dead art
Of poetry; to maintain "the sublime"
In the old sense. Wrong from the start—

No, hardly, but seeing he had been born
In a half savage country, out of date;
Bent resolutely on wringing lilies from the
  acorn;
Capaneus; trout for factitious bait;

Ἴδμεν γάρ τοι πάνθ', ὅσ' ἐνὶ Τροίῃ
Caught in the unstopped ear;
Giving the rocks small lee-way
The chopped seas held him, therefore, that
  year.

His true Penelope was Flaubert,
He fished by obstinate isles;
Observed the elegance of Circe's hair
Rather than the mottoes on sun-dials.

Unaffected by "the march of events,"
He passed from men's memory in *l'an
  trentiesme*
De son eage; the case presents
No adjunct to the Muses' diadem.

II

The age demanded an image
Of its accelerated grimace,
Something for the modern stage,
Not, at any rate, an Attic grace;

Not, not certainly, the obscure reveries
Of the inward gaze;
Better mendacities
Than the classics in paraphrase!

The "age demanded" chiefly a mould in
  plaster,
Made with no loss of time,
A prose kinema, not, not assuredly, alabaster
Or the "sculpture" of rhyme.

III

The tea-rose tea-gown, etc.
Supplants the mousseline of Cos,
The pianola "replaces"
Sappho's barbitos.

Christ follows Dionysus,
Phallic and ambrosial
Made way for macerations;
Caliban casts out Ariel.

All things are a flowing,
Sage Heracleitus says;
But a tawdry cheapness
Shall outlast our days.

Even the Christian beauty
Defects—after Samothrace;
We see τὸ καλὸν
Decreed in the market place.

Faun's flesh is not to us,
Nor the saint's vision.
We have the press for wafer;
Franchise for circumcision.

All men, in law, are equals.
Free of Pisistratus,
We choose a knave or an eunuch
To rule over us.

O bright Apollo,
  τίν' ἄνδρα, τίν' ἥρωα, τίνα θεὸν,
What god, man, or hero
Shall I place a tin wreath upon!

IV

These fought in any case,
and some believing,
        pro domo, in any case . . .

Some quick to arm,
some for adventure,
some from fear of weakness,
some from fear of censure,
some for love of slaughter, in imagination,
learning later . . .
some in fear, learning love of slaughter;
Died some, pro patria,
        non "dulce" non "et decor" . . .
walked eye-deep in hell
believing in old men's lies, then unbelieving
came home, home to a lie,
home to many deceits,

home to old lies and new infamy;
usury age-old and age-thick
and liars in public places.

Daring as never before, wastage as never
  before.
Young blood and high blood,
fair cheeks, and fine bodies;

fortitude as never before

frankness as never before,
disillusions as never told in the old days,
hysterias, trench confessions,
laughter out of dead bellies.

V

There died a myriad,
And of the best, among them,
For an old bitch gone in the teeth,
For a botched civilization,

Charm, smiling at the good mouth,
Quick eyes gone under earth's lid,

For two gross of broken statues,
For a few thousand battered books.

YEUX GLAUQUES

Gladstone was still respected,
When John Ruskin produced
"King's Treasuries"; Swinburne
And Rossetti still abused.

Fœtid Buchanan lifted up his voice
When that faun's head of hers
Became a pastime for
Painters and adulterers.

The Burne-Jones cartons
Have preserved her eyes;
Still, at the Tate, they teach
Cophetua to rhapsodize;

Thin like brook-water,
With a vacant gaze.
The English Rubaiyat was still-born
In those days.

The thin, clear gaze, the same
Still darts out faunlike from the half-ruin'd
  face,
Questing and passive. . . .
"Ah, poor Jenny's case" . . .

Bewildered that a world
Shows no surprise
At her last maquero's
Adulteries.

"SIENA MI FE'; DISFECEMI MAREMMA"

Among the pickled fœtuses and bottled bones,
Engaged in perfecting the catalogue,
I found the last scion of the
Senatorial families of Strasbourg, Monsieur Verog.

For two hours he talked of Gallifet;
Of Dowson; of the Rhymers' Club;
Told me how Johnson (Lionel) died
By falling from a high stool in a pub . . .

But showed no trace of alcohol
At the autopsy, privately performed—
Tissue preserved—the pure mind
Arose toward Newman as the whiskey warmed.

Dowson found harlots cheaper than hotels;
Headlam for uplift; Image impartially imbued
With raptures for Bacchus, Terpsichore and the Church.
So spoke the author of "The Dorian Mood,"

M. Verog, out of step with the decade,
Detached from his contemporaries,
Neglected by the young,
Because of these reveries.

BRENNBAUM

The skylike limpid eyes,
The circular infant's face,
The stiffness from spats to collar
Never relaxing into grace;

The heavy memories of Horeb, Sinai and the forty years,
Showed only when the daylight fell
Level across the face
Of Brennbaum "The Impeccable."

MR. NIXON

In the cream gilded cabin of his steam yacht
Mr. Nixon advised me kindly, to advance with fewer
Dangers of delay. "Consider
"Carefully the reviewer.

"I was as poor as you are;
"When I began I got, of course,
"Advance on royalties, fifty at first," said Mr. Nixon,
"Follow me, and take a column,
"Even if you have to work free.

"Butter reviewers. From fifty to three hundred
"I rose in eighteen months;
"The hardest nut I had to crack
"Was Dr. Dundas.

"I never mentioned a man but with the view
"Of selling my own works.
"The tip's a good one, as for literature
"It gives no man a sinecure.
"And no one knows, at sight, a masterpiece.
"And give up verse, my boy,
"There's nothing in it."

✣

Likewise a friend of Bloughram's once advised me:
Don't kick against the pricks,
Accept opinion. The "Nineties" tried your game
And died, there's nothing in it.

X

Beneath the sagging roof
The stylist has taken shelter,
Unpaid, uncelebrated,
At last from the world's welter

Nature receives him;
With a placid and uneducated mistress
He exercises his talents
And the soil meets his distress.

The haven from sophistications and contentions
Leaks through its thatch;
He offers succulent cooking;
The door has a creaking latch.

Louis Untermeyer

☙ Louis Untermeyer was born October 1, 1885, in New York City, where he was raised and miseducated. Unable to comprehend the elements of geometry, he failed to graduate from high school and entered his father's manufacturing jewelry business at seventeen. At thirty-eight he went abroad, lived in Europe for two years and, upon his return, devoted himself to writing and lecturing. In his early forties he retired to a large farm and half a mountain of sugar maples in the Adirondacks, but the Second World War brought him back to New York, where he served as editor of the Office of War Information and the Armed Services Editions.

By the time he had reached his seventies he had conducted seminars at various colleges where he was "poet in residence," had lectured in every state of the union, and had written, edited, and translated some seventy volumes of prose and poetry. His early work, influenced by Horace, Heine, and Housman, is derivative, although his vision (according to the Boston *Transcript*) "is a social vision, his spirit a passionately energized command of the forces of justice." Many critics found the volumes which followed—*These Times* (1917), *The New Adam* (1920), and *Roast Leviathan* (1923)—too exuberant, but Edwin Muir wrote: "On every subject he treats he gives opulent measure, an opulence within the reach of nobody in contemporary verse but himself." *Burning Bush* (1928) and *Food and Drink* (1932) are quieter, masking serious emotions in a casual tone of voice. The best of these volumes, as well as the choice of his four books of parodies, was assembled in *Selected Poems and Parodies* (1935) and *Long Feud* (1962).

His interest in German backgrounds was manifest in *Poems of Heinrich Heine* (1917); an adaptation of Ernst Toller's *Masse Mensch* (*Man and the Masses*), produced by the Theatre Guild in 1923; *Blue Rhine-Black Forest,* an informal guide and day-book; and an analytical biography *Heinrich Heine: Paradox and Poet* (1937), accompanied by a volume containing 500 translations of the German poet's lyrics. He also made a new translation of Rostand's *Cyrano de Bergerac* for The Limited Editions Club and The Heritage Press, for whom he also prepared *The Wonderful Adventures of Paul Bunyan,* and a series, issued in de luxe editions, of the classic American poets.

Of his fiction he favors *Moses* (1928), a combination of historical reconstruction and poetic fantasy, but most of his stories have been written for a younger audience: *The Fat of the Cat* (1928), a free rendering of Gottfried Keller's Swiss tales; *The Donkey of God* (1932), which won the Italian Enit Award for a book on Italy written by a non-Italian, and *The Last Pirate* (1934), in which the author presumed to do for Gilbert and Sullivan what the Lambs had done for Shakespeare.

A book of essays, *The New Era in American Poetry* (1919), was amplified and shaped into a more balanced set of twenty subdivided chapters as *American Poetry Since 1900* (1923). The critical anthologies *Modern American Poetry* and *Modern British Poetry* were revised and enlarged several times since their original publication in 1919 and 1920, and used as textbooks in the universities. A companion volume, *American Poetry from the Beginning to Whitman* (1931), attempted a comprehensive and drastic reappraisal of native poetry from 1620 to 1880.

Besides these critical compilations the editor prepared several anthologies with a minimum of prefatory or interpretive matter: *The Book of Living Verse* (1932), the widest in scope, ranging from the thirteenth century to the twentieth; *Yesterday and Today* (1927), a comparative collection of the present and the immediate past; *This Singing World* (1923), a selection of modern verse for a not too elderly audience; *This Singing World for Younger Readers* (1926); *Rainbow in the Sky* (1935); and *Stars to Steer By* (1941). These volumes were widely adopted in high schools and colleges, as was *The Forms of Poetry* (1926), a "pocket dictionary of verse."

New Songs for New Voices (1928), a collaboration with David and Clara Mannes, wedded modern music to modern poetry and gave the editor the opportunity to make his first (and last) public appearance as composer. *Poetry: Its Appreciation and Enjoyment* (1934), written with Carter Davidson, is a cross between a treatise and a textbook. His standing as critic was enhanced by *Play in Poetry* (1937), a set of commentaries delivered as lectures for the Henry Ward Beecher Foundation at Amherst. *From Another World* (1939) is not so much an autobiography as a set of autobiographical reminiscences which give a multiple picture of a period.

As he grew older he cared more for the work of his colleagues than for his own poetry. His pleasure in discovery and reappraisal went into such collections as *A Treasury of Great Poems* (1942, amplified in 1955), *A Treasury of Laughter* (1946), *The New England Poets* (1948), *The Inner Sanctum Poetry and Prose of Walt Whitman* (1949), *The Magic Circle* (1952), *Makers of the Modern World* (1955), which was translated into several languages, *A Treasury of Ribaldry* (1956), *Lives of the Poets* (1959), *The Britannica Library of Great American Writing* (two volumes, 1960), and various paperback anthologies. In 1961 he was appointed Consultant in Poetry at the Library of Congress.

PRAYER

God, though this life is but a wraith,
  Although we know not what we use,
Although we grope with little faith,
  Give me the heart to fight—and lose.

Ever insurgent let me be,
  Make me more daring than devout;
From sleek contentment keep me free,
  And fill me with a buoyant doubt.

Open my eyes to visions girt
  With beauty, and with wonder lit—
But let me always see the dirt,
  And all that spawn and die in it.

Open my ears to music; let
  Me thrill with Spring's first flutes and drums—
But never let me dare forget
  The bitter ballads of the slums.

From compromise and things half-done,
  Keep me, with stern and stubborn pride.
And when, at last, the fight is won,
  God, keep me still unsatisfied.

CALIBAN IN THE COAL MINES

God, we don't like to complain;
  We know that the mine is no lark.
But—there's the pools from the rain;
  But—there's the cold and the dark.

God, You don't know what it is—
  You, in Your well-lighted sky—
Watching the meteors whizz;
  Warm, with a sun always by.

God, if You had but the moon
  Stuck in Your cap for a lamp,
Even You'd tire of it soon,
  Down in the dark and the damp.

Nothing but blackness above
  And nothing that moves but the cars . . .
God, if You wish for our love,
  Fling us a handful of stars!

THE DARK CHAMBER

The brain forgets, but the blood will remember.
  There, when the play of sense is over,
The last, low spark in the darkest chamber
  Will hold all there is of love and lover.

The war of words, the life-long quarrel
  Of self against self will resolve into nothing;
Less than the chain of berry-red coral
  Crying against the dead black of her clothing.

What has the brain that it hopes to last longer?
  The blood will take from forgotten violence,
The groping, the break of her voice in anger.
  There will be left only color and silence.

These will remain, these will go searching
  Your veins for life when the flame of life smolders:
The night that you two saw the mountains marching
  Up against dawn with the stars on their shoulders—

The jetting poplars' arrested fountains
  As you drew her under them, easing her pain—
The notes, not the words, of a half-finished sentence—
  The music, the silence. . . . These will remain.

LONG FEUD

Where, without bloodshed, can there be
A more relentless enmity
Than the long feud fought silently

Between man and the growing grass.
Man's the aggressor, for he has
Weapons to humble and harass

The impudent spears that charge upon
His sacred privacy of lawn.
He mows them down, and they are gone

Only to lie in wait, although
He builds above and digs below
Where never a root would dare to go.

His are the triumphs till the day
There's no more grass to cut away
And, weary of labor, weary of play,

Having exhausted every whim,
He stretches out each conquering limb.
And then the small grass covers him.

PORTRAIT OF A MACHINE

What nudity is beautiful as this
Obedient monster purring at its toil;
These naked iron muscles dripping oil
And the sure-fingered rods that never miss.
This long and shining flank of metal is
Magic that greasy labor cannot spoil;
While this vast engine that could rend the soil
Conceals its fury with a gentle hiss.

It does not vent its loathing, does not turn
Upon its makers with destroying hate.
It bears a deeper malice; throbs to earn
Its master's bread and lives to see this great
Lord of the earth, who rules but cannot learn,
Become the slave of what his slaves create.

TO A VINE-CLAD TELEGRAPH POLE

You should be done with blossoming by now.
Yet here are leaves closer than any bough
That welcomes ivy. True, you were a tree
And stood with others in a marching line,
Less regular than this, of spruce and pine
And boasted branches rather than a trunk.
This is your final winter, all arms shrunk
To one cross-bar bearing, haphazardly,
Four rusty strands. You cannot hope to feel
The electric sap run through those veins of steel.

The birds know this; the birds have hoodwinked you,
Crowding about you as they used to do.
The rainy robins huddled on your wire
And those black birds with shoulders dipped in fire
Have made you dream these vines; these tendrils are
A last despair in green, familiar
To derelicts of earth as well as sea.
Do not believe them, there is mockery
In their cool little jets of song. They know
What everyone but you learned long ago:
The stream of stories humming through your head
Is not your own. You dream. But you are dead.

FROM "FOOD AND DRINK"

Why has our poetry eschewed
The rapture and response of food?
What hymns are sung, what prayers are said
For home-made miracles of bread?
Since what we love has always found
Expression in enduring sound,
Music and verse should be competing
To match the transient joy of eating.
There should be present in our songs
As many tastes as there are tongues;
There should be humbly celebrated
One passion that is never sated . . .
Earth's fat and fiber, root and leaf,
Become quick pleasure and slow grief.
So, until man abjures the meats
Terrestrial and impermanent sweets,
Growing beyond the thing he eats,
Let us be thankful for the good
Beauty and benison of food;
Let us join chiming vowel with vowel
To rhapsodize fish, flesh, and fowl;
And let us thank God in our songs
There are as many tastes as tongues!

LAST WORDS BEFORE WINTER

All my sheep
Gather in a heap,
For I spy the woolly, woolly wolf.

Farewell, my flocks,
Farewell. But let me find you
Safe in your stall and barn and box
With your winter's tale behind you.

Farewell, my cattle (both).
I leave you just as loath
As though you were a hundred head,
Instead
Of two-and-a-half.
(Two cows and a calf.)

Farewell, my apple-trees;
You have learned what it is to freeze,
With the drift on your knees.
But, oh, beware
Those first kind days, the snare
Of the too promising air,
The cost
Of over-sudden trust—
And then the killing frost.

Farewell, belovéd acres;
I leave you in the hands
Of one whose earliest enterprise was lands:
Your Maker's.

Yard, hutch, and house, farewell.
It is for you to tell
How you withstood the great white wolf, whose fell
Is softer than a lambkin's, but whose breath
Is death.
Farewell, hoof, claw, and wing,
Finned, furred, and feathered thing,
Till Spring—

All my sheep
Gather in a heap,
For I spy the woolly, woolly wolf.

MOTHER GOOSE UP-TO-DATE

JOHN MASEFIELD

Relates the Story of Tom, Tom, the Piper's Son

Thomas, the vagrant piper's son,
Was fourteen when he took to fun;
He was the sixth of a bewilderin'
Family of eleven children.
Mary, the first of all the lot,
Was married to a drunken sot;
And Clement, second on the list,
Fell off the roof and was never missed.
Susan and little Goldilocks
Were carried off by the chicken-pox;
And Franky went—though I can't recall
Whatever happened to him at all.
Thomas was next—and he's still alive,
The only one of them all to thrive.
The rest just petered out somehow—
At least, nobody hears of them now.

Now Tom, as I said when I'd begun,
Was fourteen when he took to fun.
Wine was the stuff he loved to swim in;
He lied, and fought, and went with women,
He scattered oaths, as one flings bounties,
The dirtiest dog in seven counties.

One morning when the sun was high
And larks were cleaving the blue sky,
Singing as though their hearts would break
With April's keen and happy ache,
Thomas went walking, rather warm,

Beside old Gaffer Hubbard's farm.
He saw that wintry days were over
And bees were out among the clover.
Earth stretched its legs out in the sun;
Now that the spring was well begun,
Heaven itself grew bland and fat.
So Thomas loafed a while and spat,
And thought about his many follies—
Yonder the gang was tipping trollies.
The sight made Tom's red blood run quicker
Than whiskey, beer or any liquor.
"By cripes," he said, "that's what I need;
'Twill make a man of me indeed.
Why should I be a roaring slob
When there's Salvation in a job!"
He started up—when lo, behind him,
As though it sought to maim and blind him,
A savage pig sprang straight against him.
At first Tom kicked and fought and fenced him,
And then he fell. But as they rolled
Tom took a tight and desperate hold
And thought the bloody fight was over.
"Here is one pig that's *not* in clover—
Tonight I'll have you in my cupboard!"
Who should come up but Gaffer Hubbard.
"Leggo that pig."
"What for?" says Tom.
"It's mine, you thief! you vagrant scum!"
"It ain't."
"It is."
"Clear out!"
"We'll see."
"I'll fix 'ee!"
"Better let me be."

With that the farmer turned again
And called out half a dozen men.
Up they came running. "Here," said he,
"Here is a pig belongs to me—
But ye can have it all for eating
If ye will give this tramp a beating."
"Hurroo!" they shouted in high feather,
And jumped on Thomas all together.
So the pig was eat, and Tom was beat;
And Tom went roaring down the street!

WALTER DE LA MARE

Tells the Listener About Jack and Jill

Up to the top of the haunted turf
They climbed on the moonlit hill.

Not a leaf rustled in the underbrush;
The listening air was still,

And only the noise of the water pail
As it struck on a jutting stone,
Clattered and jarred against the silence
As the two trod on alone.

Up to the moonlit peak they went;
And, though not a word would they say,
Their thoughts outnumbered a poet's love-songs
In the first green weeks of May.

The stealthy shadows crept closer;
They clutched at the hem of Jill's gown;
And there at the very top she stumbled,
And Jack came shuddering down.

Their cries rang out against the stillness,
Pitiful and high and thin.
And the echoes edged back still further
As the silence gathered them in.

EDNA ST. VINCENT MILLAY

Exhorts Little Boy Blue

From that last acre on oblivion's heap
Come, lad tricked out in bold and trumpery blue;
Come, blow your idle horn, and send the few
Notes with no name against the night. Here sheep
Trample the fetid meadow; here cows creep,
Raising their eyes wherever one or two
Crushing the corn, pause to admire the view;
Come, doubtful dreamer, spurn ignoble sleep.

I tell you this, Boy Blue, lift up your horn
Against the world's deliberate apathy,
Or what we held so dear will be the scorn
Of casual rats and roaches; life will be
A town not worth the taking, a spent call.
Grimly I tell you this. And this is all.

ARCHIBALD MAC LEISH

Suspends the Five Little Pigs

. . . So
Went this little pig from the mainland to the market:
Autumn it was: and a salt wind flowing:

And the rotten grain left on the stalk for no harvest:
And the going rough: the bread wormy: the smoke turned sour:
And the towns a jungle of dogs let loose in a rubble of garbage:

And this little pig stayed home: and this one devoured
Roast upon roast of beef and drank the milk of the aloe:
Rinsing his mouth with the melons: drowsing

In a grove of clean sun interwoven with swallows:
And the earth kind to the bone with rain's fragrance:
And the moon stroking the breast and the hand grown callous:

And this little pig had none—not for love nor the paying—
Dust in his corded throat: and the knife above it:
And the quick slit under the jaw: and he took it bravely:

And this little pig—the littlest and the loveliest—
Gallic in breed to the impudent turn of his tail
Cried, "Oui! Oui! Oui!" all the way home . . .
. . . and the hovering
Gale from the . . .
north . . .
the sun-bright names . . .
Gone from the page . . .
and the blazing . . .
lives
Hazy . . .
the days passing . . .
the faces
Blurred or erased . . .
and the five . . .
the hunted five
A word . . .
a child's rhyme . . .
in that country. . . .

EDGAR A. GUEST

Syndicates the Old Woman Who Lived in a Shoe

It takes a heap o' children to make a home that's true,
And home can be a palace grand, or just a plain, old shoe;
But if it has a mother dear, and a good old dad or two,
Why, that's the sort of good old home for good old me and you.

Of all the institutions this side the Vale o' Rest
Howe'er it be, it seems to me a good old mother's best;
And fathers are a blessing, too, they give the place a tone;
In fact each child should try and have some parents of its own.

The food can be quite simple; just a sop of milk and bread
Are plenty when the kiddies know it's time to go to bed.
And every little sleepy-head will dream about the day
When he can go to work because a Man's Work is his Play.

And, oh, how sweet his life will seem, with nought to make him cross;
And he will never watch the clock and always mind the boss.
And when he thinks (as may occur), this thought will please him best:
That ninety million think the same—including *Eddie Guest.*

John Gould Fletcher

⸎ John Gould Fletcher was born at Little Rock, Arkansas, January 3, 1886. He was educated at Harvard (1903-7) and, after spending several years in Massachusetts, moved to England, where he lived for fifteen years. In 1933 he returned to America, to the family home in Little Rock.

In 1913 Fletcher published five books of poems which he has referred to as "his literary wild oats," five small collections of experimental and faintly interesting verse. In 1914, shortly after the publication of his *Fire and Wine* (one of the early quintet), Fletcher joined the Imagists. With H. D. and Amy Lowell he became one of the leaders of this interesting movement and his contributions were among the outstanding features of the three anthologies which furnish so illuminating a record of the esthetics of the period. Coincident with the first appearance of *Some Imagist Poets,* Fletcher discarded his previous style and emerged as a decidedly less conservative and far more arresting poet with *Irradiations—Sand and Spray* (1915). This volume is full of an extraordinary fancy; imagination riots through it, though it is sometimes a bloodless and bodiless imagination. It is crowded—even overcrowded—with shifting subtleties; a brilliant, haphazard series of improvisations.

In the following book, *Goblins and Pagodas* (1916), Fletcher carries his unrelated harmonies much further. Color dominates him; the ambitious set of eleven "color symphonies" is an elaborate design in which tone and thought are summoned by color-associations, sometimes closely related, sometimes far-fetched. "It contains," says Conrad Aiken in his appreciative chapter on Fletcher in *Scepticisms,* "little of the emotion which relates to the daily life of men and women. . . . It is a sort of absolute poetry, a poetry of detached waver and brilliance, a beautiful flowering of language alone—a parthenogenesis, as if language were fertilized by itself rather than by thought or feeling. Remove the magic of phrase and sound and there is nothing left: no thread of continuity, no thought, no story, no emotion. But the magic of phrase and sound is powerful, and it takes one into a fantastic world."

In 1917 Fletcher again began to change in spirit as well as style. Emotion declared itself with surprising candor. After having appeared in the three Imagist anthologies, he sought for depths rather than surfaces; his "Lincoln" accomplished a closer relation to humanity. A moving mysticism speaks from *The Tree of Life* (1918); the more obviously native *Granite and Breakers* (1921) and *Parables* (1925) contain a prophetic note new to this poet. Though less arresting than the ones by which he is best known, the later poems reach depths which the preceding verses never attained. Although the unconscious often dictates Fletcher's fantasies, a calm music dominates them. A grave, subdued lyricism moves through *The Black Rock* (1928) and *Branches of Adam* (1926), in which the philosophy is akin to Nietzsche's while the motto might well be Blake's "How is it we have walked through fire, and yet are not consumed?" Never a popular poet, Fletcher gains—and suffers—from his original and fluctuating power. He is the poet held in a state of flux.

XXIV Elegies (1935) is a work which took Fletcher twenty years to write; the poems, one for each hour of the twenty-four, having been composed between 1914 and 1934. The dignified tone and depth of feeling are communicated throughout.

There are, as there would be in a work of this character, many tedious passages, and an American poet in the twentieth century might have spared himself an elegy on "Tristan in Brittany" and an "Elegy on Tintern Abbey." He atones for these lapses by an inflection which uses the grand manner but restrains the rhetoric. *South Star* (1941) combines experience and legend; much of it is regional in theme. *The Burning Mountain* (1946) contains twenty-four long poems, odes, and symphonies. *Life Is My Song* is Fletcher's autobiography as far as 1937; his *Selected Poems* won the Pulitzer Prize in 1939. Fletcher died by drowning on May 10, 1950.

Fletcher ranks high as a translator from the French; he made the English versions of *The Dance over Fire and Water* (by Elie Faure) in 1926 and *The Reveries of a Solitary* (by J. J. Rousseau) in 1927. *The Two Frontiers* (1930) is prophetic historical essay regarding the parallels and contrasts of America and Russia.

FROM "IRRADIATIONS"

I

Over the roof-tops race the shadows of clouds;
Like horses the shadows of clouds charge down the street.

Whirlpools of purple and gold,
Winds from the mountains of cinnabar,
Lacquered mandarin moments, palanquins swaying and balancing
Amid vermilion pavilions, against the jade balustrades,
Glint of the glittering wings of dragon-flies in the light:
Silver filaments, golden flakes settling downwards,
Rippling, quivering flutters, repulse and surrender,
The sun broidered upon the rain,
The rain rustling with the sun.

Over the roof-tops race the shadows of clouds;
Like horses the shadows of clouds charge down the street.

II

Flickering of incessant rain
On flashing pavements:
Sudden scurry of umbrellas:
Bending, recurved blossoms of the storm.

The winds come clanging and clattering
From long white highroads whipping in ribbons up summits:
They strew upon the city gusty wafts of apple-blossom,
And the rustling of innumerable translucent leaves.

Uneven tinkling, the lazy rain
Dripping from the eaves.

III

The trees, like great jade elephants,
Chained, stamp and shake 'neath the gadflies of the breeze;
The trees lunge and plunge, unruly elephants:
The clouds are their crimson howdah-canopies,

The sunlight glints like the golden robe of a Shah.
Would I were tossed on the wrinkled backs of those trees.

IV

O seeded grass, you army of little men
Crawling up the long slope with quivering, quick blades of steel:
You who storm millions of graves, tiny green tentacles of Earth,
Interlace yourselves tightly over my heart,
And do not let me go:
For I would lie here forever and watch with one eye
The pilgrimaging ants in your dull, savage jungles,
The while with the other I see the stiff lines of the slope
Break in mid-air, a wave surprisingly arrested,—
And above them, wavering, dancing, bodiless, colorless, unreal,
The long thin lazy fingers of the heat.

V

The morning is clean and blue and the wind blows up the clouds:
Now my thoughts gathered from afar
Once again in their patched armor, with rusty plumes and blunted swords,
Move out to war.

Smoking our morning pipes we shall ride two and two
Through the woods,
For our old cause keeps us together,
And our hatred is so precious not death or defeat can break it.

God willing, we shall this day meet that old enemy
Who has given us so many a good beating.
Thank God we have a cause worth fighting for,
And a cause worth losing and a good song to sing.

GREEN SYMPHONY

I

The glittering leaves of the rhododendrons
Balance and vibrate in the cool air;
While in the sky above them
White clouds chase each other.

Like scampering rabbits,
Flashes of sunlight sweep the lawn;
They fling in passing
Patterns of shadow,
Golden and green.

With long cascades of laughter,
The mating birds dart and swoop to the turf:
'Mid their mad trillings
Glints the gay sun behind the trees.

Down there are deep blue lakes:
Orange blossom droops in the water.
In the tower of the winds
All the bells are set adrift:
Jingling
For the dawn.

Thin fluttering streamers
Of breeze lash through the swaying boughs,
Palely expectant
The earth receives the slanting rain.

The glittering leaves of the rhododendron
Are shaken like blue-green blades of grass,
Flickering, cracking, falling:
Splintering in a million fragments.

The wind runs laughing up the slope
Stripping off handfuls of wet green leaves,
To fling in people's faces.
Wallowing on the daisy-powdered turf,
Clutching at the sunlight,
Cavorting in the shadow.

Like baroque pearls,
Like cloudy emeralds,
The clouds and the trees clash together;
Whirling and swirling,
In the tumult
Of the spring,
And the wind.

II

The trees splash the sky with their fingers,
A restless green rout of stars.

With whirling movement
They swing their boughs
About their stems:
Planes on planes of light and shadow
Pass among them,
Opening fanlike to fall.

The trees are like a sea;
Tossing,
Trembling,
Roaring,
Wallowing,
Darting their long green flickering fronds up at the sky,
Spotted with white blossom-spray.

The trees are roofs:
Hollow caverns of cool blue shadow,
Solemn arches
In the afternoons.
The whole vast horizon
In terrace beyond terrace,
Pinnacle above pinnacle,
Lifts to the sky
Serrated ranks of green on green.

They caress the roofs with their fingers,
They sprawl about the river to look into it;
Up the hill they come
Gesticulating challenge:
They cower together
In dark valleys;
They yearn out over the fields.

Enameled domes
Tumble upon the grass,
Crashing in ruin,
Quiet at last.

The trees lash the sky with their leaves,
Uneasily shaking their dark green manes.

III

Far let the voices of the mad wild birds be calling me,
I will abide in this forest of pines.

When the wind blows
Battling through the forest,
I hear it distantly,
The crash of a perpetual sea.

When the rain falls,
I watch the silver spears slanting downwards
From pale river-pools of sky,
Enclosed in dark fronds.

When the sun shines,
I weave together distant branches till they enclose mighty circles,
I sway to the movement of hooded summits,
I swim leisurely in deep blue seas of air.

I hug the smooth bark of stately red pillars
And with cones carefully scattered
I mark the progression of dark dial-shadows
Flung diagonally downwards through the afternoon.

This turf is not like turf:
It is a smooth dry carpet of velvet,
Embroidered with brown patterns of needles and cones.
These trees are not like trees:
They are innumerable feathery pagoda-umbrellas,
Stiffly ungracious to the wind,
Teetering on red-lacquered stems.

In the evening I listen to the winds' lisping,
While the conflagrations of the sunset flicker and clash behind me,
Flamboyant crenellations of glory amid the charred ebony boles.

In the night the fiery nightingales
Shall clash and trill through the silence:
Like the voices of mermaids crying
From the sea.

Long ago has the moon whelmed this uncompleted temple.
Stars swim like gold fish far above the black arches.

Far let the timid feet of dawn fly to catch me:
I will abide in this forest of pines:
For I have unveiled naked beauty,
And the things that she whispered to me in the darkness,
Are buried deep in my heart.

Now let the black tops of the pine-trees break like a spent wave,
Against the gray sky:
These are tombs and temples and altars sun-kindled for me.

LONDON NIGHTFALL

I saw the shapes that stood upon the clouds:
And they were tiger-breasted, shot with light,
And all of them, lifting long trumpets together,
Blew over the city, for the night to come.
Down in the street, we floundered in the mud;
Above, in endless files, gold angels came
And stood upon the clouds, and blew their horns
For night.

Like a wet petal crumpled,
Twilight fell soddenly on the weary city;
The 'buses lurched and groaned,
The shops put up their doors.

But skywards, far aloft,
The angels, vanishing, waved broad plumes of gold,
Summoning spirits from a thousand hills
To pour the thick night out upon the earth.

THE SKATERS

Black swallows swooping or gliding
In a flurry of entangled loops and curves;
The skaters skim over the frozen river.
And the grinding click of their skates as they impinge upon the surface,
Is like the brushing together of thin wing-tips of silver.

LINCOLN

I

Like a gaunt, scraggly pine
Which lifts its head above the mournful sandhills;
And patiently, through dull years of bitter silence,
Untended and uncared for, begins to grow.

Ungainly, laboring, huge,
The wind of the north has twisted and gnarled its branches;
Yet in the heat of midsummer days, when thunder-clouds ring the horizon,
A nation of men shall rest beneath its shade.

And it shall protect them all,
Hold everyone safe there, watching aloof in silence;
Until at last one mad stray bolt from the zenith
Shall strike it in an instant down to earth.

II

There was a darkness in this man; an immense and hollow darkness,
Of which we may not speak, nor share with him, nor enter;
A darkness through which strong roots stretched downwards into the earth
Towards old things;
Towards the herdman-kings who walked the earth and spoke with God,
Towards the wanderers who sought for they knew not what, and found their goal
at last;
Towards the men who waited, only waited patiently when all seemed lost,
Many bitter winters of defeat;
Down to the granite of patience
These roots swept, knotted fibrous roots, prying, piercing, seeking,
And drew from the living rock and the living waters about it
The red sap to carry upwards to the sun.

Not proud, but humble,
Only to serve and pass on, to endure to the end through service;
For the ax is laid at the root of the trees, and all that bring not forth good fruit
Shall be cut down on the day to come and cast into the fire.

III

There is silence abroad in the land today,
And in the hearts of men, a deep and anxious silence;
And, because we are still at last, those bronze lips slowly open,
Those hollow and weary eyes take on a gleam of light.

Slowly a patient, firm-syllabled voice cuts through the endless silence
Like laboring oxen that drag a plow through the chaos of rude clay-fields:
"I went forward as the light goes forward in early spring,
But there were also many things which I left behind.

"Tombs that were quiet;
One, of a mother, whose brief light went out in the darkness,
One, of a loved one, the snow on whose grave is long falling,
One, only of a child, but it was mine.

"Have you forgot your graves? Go, question them in anguish,
Listen long to their unstirred lips. From your hostages to silence,
Learn there is no life without death, no dawn without sun-setting,
No victory but to Him who has given all."

IV

The clamor of cannon dies down, the furnace-mouth of the battle is silent.
The midwinter sun dips and descends, the earth takes on afresh its bright colors.
But he whom we mocked and obeyed not, he whom we scorned and mistrusted,
He has descended, like a god, to his rest.

Over the uproar of cities,
Over the million intricate threads of life wavering and crossing,
In the midst of problems we know not, tangling, perplexing, ensnaring,
Rises one white tomb alone.
Beam over it, stars.
Wrap it round, stripes—stripes red for the pain that he bore for you—
Enfold it forever, O flag, rent, soiled, but repaired through your anguish;
Long as you keep him there safe, the nations shall bow to your law.

Strew over him flowers:
Blue forget-me-nots from the north, and the bright pink arbutus
From the east, and from the west rich orange blossoms,
But from the heart of the land take the passion-flower;

Rayed, violet, dim,
With the nails that pierced, the cross that he bore and the circlet,
And beside it there lay also one lonely snow-white magnolia,
Bitter for remembrance of the healing which has passed.

A REBEL

Tie a bandage over his eyes,
And at his feet
Let rifles drearily patter
Their death-prayers of defeat.

Throw a blanket over his body,
It need no longer stir;
Truth will but stand the stronger
For all who died for her.

Now he has broken through
To his own secret place;
Which, if we dared to do,
We would have no power left to look on that dead face.

BEFORE OLYMPUS

Across the sky run streaks of white light, aching;
Across the earth the chattering grass is sprawling;
Across the sea roll troubled gleams awaking,
Across the steeps dark broken shapes are crawling.

We have been scourged with youth, a rod in pickle
To cut the hide from our own hearts. We know
The tree of life is also cursed. We heed
The silent laughter of gray gods of time.

We do not seek the lithe and brittle music
Of swords and flame. We have no more desire
For glory or contempt. The moment flies
Past us, and shouting carries its echo on.

The clank of wheels and pumps, the screech of levers
No longer now afflicts our inmost bearing;
The old wise nightingales have longer ears,
They sing the blooming of wild immortelles.

And through the desolation of great cities
As in a madhouse we go peering where
Black butterflies flit about a carcass. Words
Gallop about the sky. The earth broods like a stone.

Heaven is a blank news-sheet fixed and trembling
Between the knees of God. The grass runs crawling.
The waves of the sea their laughter are dissembling,
But who will reap them when our scythes are falling?

William Rose Benét

⁂ William Rose Benét was born at Fort Hamilton, New York Harbor, February 2, 1886. He was educated at Albany Academy and graduated from Yale in 1907. After various experiences as freelance writer, publisher's reader, magazine editor, and second lieutenant in the U. S. Air Service, Benét became Associate Editor of the New York Post's *Literary Review* in 1920. He resigned in 1924 to become one of the founders and editors of *The Saturday Review of Literature.*

The outstanding feature of Benét's verse is its extraordinary versatility; an Oriental imagination runs through his pages. Like the title-poem of his first volume, *Merchants from Cathay* (1913), Benét's volumes vibrate with a vigorous music; they are full of the sonorous stuff that one rolls out crossing wintry fields or tramping a road alone. But Benét's charm is not confined to the lift and swing of rollicking choruses. *The Falconer of God* (1914), *The Great White Wall* (1916) and *The Burglar of the Zodiac* (1918) contain decorations bold as they are brilliant; they ring with a strange and spicy music evoked from seemingly casual words. His scope is wide, although he is most at home in fancies which glow with a half-lurid, half-humorous reflection of the grotesque. There are times indeed when Benét seems to be forcing his ingenuity. The poet frequently lets his fantastic Pegasus run away with him, and what started out to be a gallop among the stars ends in a scraping of shins on the pavement. But he is saved by an acrobatic dexterity even when his energy betrays him. *Perpetual Light* (1919), a memorial to his first wife, is, naturally, a more subdued collection.

Moons of Grandeur (1920) represents an appreciable development of Benét's whimsical gift; a combination of Eastern phantasy and Western vigor. Even more arresting are those poems which appeared subsequent to this volume. A firmer line, a cooler condensation may be found in *Man Possessed* (1927), a selection of the best of the previous volumes with many new poems. "Whale" is a particularly brilliant example; "The Horse Thief" is one of the most fanciful and one of the most popular of American ballads; "Jesse James" rocks with high spirits and the true balladist's gusto; "Inscription for a Mirror in a Deserted Dwelling," written during the life of his second wife, Elinor Wylie, reflects the poet who wrote it and the poet to whom it was written, while "Sagacity" is a tribute to her memory. *Golden Fleece* (1935) is a more critical selection of Benét's poems with the addition of several new verses. *The Stairway to Surprise* (1947) discloses the enthusiasms of one who is often too high-spirited to be critical. Besides his verse, Benét is the author of two novels and several tales for children, and the editor (with Henry Seidel Canby and John Drinkwater) of *Twentieth Century Poetry* (1929). *The Dust Which Is God* (1941) is a portrait in which the autobiographical element is lightly disguised. It was awarded the Pulitzer Prize for poetry in 1942. Benét died May 4, 1950.

MERCHANTS FROM CATHAY

How that They came.

Their heels slapped their bumping mules; their fat chaps glowed.
  Glory unto Mary, each seemed to wear a crown!
Like sunset their robes were on the wide, white road:
  So we saw those mad merchants come dusting into town!

Of their Beasts,

Two paunchy beasts they rode on and two they drove before.
  May the Saints all help us, the tiger-stripes they had!
And the panniers upon them swelled full of stuffs and ore!
  The square buzzed and jostled at a sight so mad.

And their Boast,

They bawled in their beards, and their turbans they wried.
  They stopped by the stalls with curvetting and clatter.
As bronze as the bracken their necks and faces dyed—
  And a stave they sat singing, to tell us of the matter.

With its Burthen

"For your silks, to Sugarmago! For your dyes, to Isfahan!
Weird fruits from the Isle o' Lamaree.
But for magic merchandise,
For treasure-trove and spice,
Here's a catch and a carol to the great, grand Chan,
The King of all the Kings across the sea!

And Chorus.

"Here's a catch and a carol to the great, grand Chan;
For we won through the deserts to his sunset barbican;
And the mountains of his palace no Titan's reach may span
Where he wields his seignorie!

A first Stave Fearsome,

"Red-as-blood skins of panthers, so bright against the sun
On the walls of the halls where his pillared state is set
They daze with a blaze no man may look upon.
And with conduits of beverage those floors run wet.

And a second Right hard To stomach

"His wives stiff with riches, they sit before him there.
Bird and beast at his feast make song and clapping cheer.
And jugglers and enchanters, all walking on the air,
Make fall eclipse and thunder—make moons and suns appear!

And a third, Which is a Laughable Thing.

"Once the Chan, by his enemies sore-prest, and sorely spent,
Lay, so they say, in a thicket 'neath a tree
Where the howl of an owl vexed his foes from their intent:
Then that fowl for a holy bird of reverence made he!

We gape to Hear them end,

"A catch and a carol to the great, grand Chan!
Pastmasters of disasters, our desert caravan
Won through all peril to his sunset barbican,
Where he wields his seignorie!
And crowns he gave us! We end where we began:
A catch and a carol to the great, grand Chan!
The King of all the Kings across the sea!"

And are in Terror,

Those mad, antic Merchants! . . . Their stripèd beasts did beat
The market-square suddenly with hooves of beaten gold!
The ground yawned gaping and flamed beneath our feet!
They plunged to Pits Abysmal with their wealth untold!

And dread it is Devil's Work!

And some say the Chan himself in anger dealt the stroke—
For sharing of his secrets with silly, common folk:
But Holy, Blessed Mary, preserve us as you may
Lest once more those mad Merchants come chanting from Cathay!

NIGHT

Let the night keep
What the night takes,
Sighs buried deep,
Ancient heart-aches,
Groans of the lover,
Tears of the lost;
Let day discover not
All the night cost!

Let the night keep
Love's burning bliss,
Drowned in deep sleep
Whisper and kiss,

Thoughts like white flowers
In hedges of May;
Let such deep hours not
Fade with the day!

Monarch is night
Of all eldest things,
Pain and affright,
Rapturous wings;
Night the crown, night the sword
Lifted to smite.
Kneel to your overlord,
Children of night!

THE FAWN IN THE SNOW

The brown-dappled fawn
Bereft of the doe
Shivers in blue shadow
Of the glaring snow,

His whole world bright
As a jewel, and hard,
Diamond white,
Turquoise barred.

The trees are black,
Their needles gold,
Their boughs crack
In the keen cold.

The brown-dappled fawn
Bereft of the doe
Trembles and shudders
At the bright snow.

The air whets
The warm throat,
The frost frets
At the smooth coat.

Brown agate eyes
Opened round
Agonize
At the cold ground,

At the cold heaven
Enameled pale,
At the earth shriven
By the snowy gale,

At magic glitter
Burning to blind,
At beauty bitter
As an almond rind.

Fawn, fawn,
Seek for your south,
For kind dawn
With her cool mouth,

For green sod
With gold and blue
Dappled, as God
Has dappled you, . . .

The shivering fawn
Paws at the snow.
South and dawn
Lie below;

Richness and mirth,
Dearth forgiven,
A happy earth,
A warm heaven.

The sleet streams;
The snow flies;
The fawn dreams
With wide brown eyes.

WHALE

Rain, with a silver flail;
Sun, with a golden ball;
Ocean, wherein the whale
Swims minnow-small;

I heard the whale rejoice
And cynic sharks attend;
He cried with a purple voice,
"The Lord is my Friend!"

"With flanged and battering tail,
With huge and dark baleen,
He said, 'Let there be Whale
In the Cold and Green!'

"He gave me a water-spout,
A side like a harbor wall;
The Lord from cloud looked out
And planned it all.

With glittering crown atilt
  He leaned on a glittering rail;
He said, 'Where Sky, is split,
  Let there be Whale.'

"Tier upon tier of wings
  Blushed and blanched and bowed;
Phalanxed fiery things
  Cried in the cloud;

"Million-eyed was the mirk
  At the plan not understood;
But the Lord looked on His work
  And saw it was good.

"He gave me marvelous girth
  For the curve of back and breast,
And a tiny eye of mirth
  To hide His jest.

"He made me a floating hill,
  A plunging deep-sea mine.
This was the Lord's will;
  The Lord is Divine.

"I magnify His name
  In earthquake and eclipse,
In weltering molten flame
  And wrecks of ships,

"In waves that lick the moon;
  I, the plow of the sea!
I am the Lord's boon;
  The Lord made me!"

The sharks barked from beneath,
  As the whale rollicked and roared,
"Yes, and our grinning teeth,
  Was it not the Lord?"

Then questions pattered like hail
  From fishes large and small.
"The Lord is mighty," said Whale,
  "The Lord made all!

"His is a mammoth jest
  Life may never betray;
He has laid it up in His breast
  Till Judgment Day;

"But high when combers foam
  And tower their last of all,
My power shall haul you home
  Through Heaven wall.

"A trumpet then in the gates,
  To the ramps a thundering drum,
I shall lead you where He waits
  For His Whale to come.

"Where His cloudy seat is placed
  On high in an empty dome,
I shall trail the Ocean abased
  In chains of foam,

"Unwieldy, squattering dread.
  Where the blazing cohorts stand
At last I shall lift my head
  As it feels His hand.

"Then wings with a million eyes
  Before mine eyes shall quail:
'Look you, all Paradise,
  I was His Whale!' "

I heard the Whale rejoice,
  As he splayed the waves to a fan:
"And the Lord shall say with His Voice,
  'Leviathan!'
"The Lord shall say with His Tongue,
  'Now let all Heaven give hail
To my Jest when I was young,
  To my very Whale.' "

Then the Whale careered in the Sea,
  He floundered with flailing tail;
Flourished and rollicked he,
  "Aha! Mine Empery!
For the Lord said, 'Let Whale Be!'
  And there Was Whale!"

THE HORSE THIEF

There he moved, cropping the grass at the purple canyon's lip.
  His mane was mixed with the moonlight that silvered his snow-white side,
For the moon sailed out of a cloud with the wake of a spectral ship.
  I crouched and I crawled on my belly, my lariat coil looped wide.

Dimly and dark the mesas broke on the starry sky.
  A pall covered every color of their gorgeous glory at noon.
I smelt the yucca and mesquite, and stifled my heart's quick cry,
  And wormed and crawled on my belly to where he moved against the moon!

Some Moorish barb was that mustang's sire. His lines were beyond all wonder.
  From the prick of his ears to the flow of his tail he ached in my throat and eyes.
Steel and velvet grace! As the prophet says, God had "clothed his neck with thunder."
  Oh, marvelous with the drifting cloud he drifted across the skies!

And then I was near at hand—crouched and balanced, and cast the coil;
  And the moon was smothered in cloud, and the rope through my hands with a rip!
But somehow I gripped and clung, with the blood in my brain a-boil,—
  With a turn round the rugged tree-stump there on the purple canyon's lip.

Right into the stars he reared aloft, his red eye rolling and raging.
  He whirled and sunfished and lashed, and rocked the earth to thunder and flame.
He squealed like a regular devil horse. I was haggard and spent and aging—
  Roped clean, but almost storming clear, his fury too fierce to tame.

And I cursed myself for a tenderfoot moon-dazzled to play the part,
  But I was doubly desperate then, with the posse pulled out from town,
Or I'd never have tried it. I only knew I must get a mount and a start.
  The filly had snapped her foreleg short. I had had to shoot her down.

So there he struggled and strangled, and I snubbed him around the tree.
  Nearer, a little nearer—hoofs planted, and lolling tongue—
Till a sudden slack pitched me backward. He reared right on top of me.
  Mother of God—that moment! He missed me . . . and up I swung.

Somehow, gone daft completely and clawing a bunch of his mane,
  As he stumbled and tripped in the lariat, there I was—up and astride
And cursing for seven counties! And the mustang? *Just insane!*
  Crack-bang! went the rope; we cannoned off the tree—then—gods, that ride!

A rocket—that's all, a rocket! I dug with my teeth and nails.
  Why, we never hit even the high spots (though I hardly remember things),
But I heard a monstrous booming like a thunder of flapping sails
  When he spread—well, *call* me a liar!—when he spread those wings, those wings!

So white that my eyes were blinded, thick-feathered and wide unfurled,
  They beat the air into billows. We sailed, and the earth was gone.
Canyon and desert and mesa withered below, with the world.
  And then I knew that mustang; for I—was Bellerophon!

Yes, glad as the Greek, and mounted on a horse of the elder gods,
  With never a magic bridle or a fountain-mirror nigh!
My chaps and spurs and holster must have looked it? What's the odds?
  I'd a leg over lightning and thunder, careering across the sky!

And forever streaming before me, fanning my forehead cool,
  Flowed a mane of molten silver; and just before my thighs
(As I gripped his velvet-muscled ribs, while I cursed myself for a fool),
  The steady pulse of those pinions—their wonderful fall and rise!

The bandanna I bought in Bowie blew loose and whipped from my neck.
  My shirt was stuck to my shoulders and ribboning out behind.
The stars were dancing, wheeling and glancing, dipping with smirk and beck.
  The clouds were flowing, dusking and glowing. We rode a roaring wind.

We soared through the silver starlight to knock at the planets' gates.
  New shimmering constellations came whirling into our ken.
Red stars and green and golden swung out of the void that waits
  For man's great last adventure. The Signs took shape—and then

I knew the lines of that Centaur the moment I saw him come!
  The musical box of the heavens all round us rolled to a tune
That tinkled and chimed and trilled with silver sounds that struck you dumb,
  As if some archangel were grinding out the music of the moon.

Melody-drunk on the Milky Way, as we swept and soared hilarious,
  Full in our pathway, sudden he stood—the Centaur of the Stars,
Flashing from head and hoofs and breast! I knew him for Sagittarius.
  He reared, and bent and drew his bow. He crouched as a boxer spars.

Flung back on his haunches, weird he loomed—then leapt—and the dim void lightened.
  Old White Wings shied and swerved aside, and fled from the splendor-shod.
Through a flashing welter of worlds we charged. I knew why my horse was frightened.
  He *had* two faces—a dog's and a man's—that Babylonian god!

Also, he followed us real as fear. Ping! went an arrow past.
  My broncho buck-jumped, humping high. We plunged . . . I guess that's all!
I lay on the purple canyon's lip, when I opened my eyes at last—
  Stiff and sore and my head like a drum, but I broke no bones in the fall.

So you know—and now you may string me up. Such was the way you caught me.
  Thank you for letting me tell it straight, though you never could greatly care.
For I took a horse that wasn't mine! . . . But there's one the heavens brought me,
  And I'll hang right happy, because I know he is waiting for me up there.

From creamy muzzle to cannon-bone, by God, he's a peerless wonder!
  He is steel and velvet and furnace-fire, and death's supremest prize,
And never again shall be roped on earth that neck that is "clothed with thunder. . . ."
  String me up, Dave! Go dig my grave! *I rode him across the skies!*

BRAZEN TONGUE

Quick in spite I said unkind
Words that should have struck me blind.
Flatly on my eardrums rung
The raucous echoes of my tongue.

Burnished bees in an iron hive
Seemed my wits, and scarce alive
I sat with elbows on my knees
Sick with silence like disease.

Slowly through the solid floor
I sank, till there was nothing more
Than a grease-spot of me there
Shadowed by the upright chair.

O last night I lay awake
Parrying darkness for your sake,
Like an armory glittered bright
The lilied hours of our delight!

O this morning I intended
All the virtues this has ended,
Golden as a new-coined planet!
Now I wither into granite.

Tongue, you are a tongue of fire,
Shriveling like a white-hot wire,
Blackening like a dragon's breath
Flower-fluttering fields with death.

Tongue, you are a tongue of brass
In the jawbone of an ass,
Slaying what was most divine,—
Not the reeking Philistine.

So, she dug me from my quarry;
Came and said that she was sorry;
Sprinkled me with words like myrrh;
So I sat and stared at her;

And so I climbed the burning mountain
And sit beside the lava fountain,
And, white with ashes, wonder why
In the devil I am I.

JESSE JAMES

(*A Design in Red and Yellow for a Nickel Library*)

Jesse James was a two-gun man,
(*Roll on, Missouri!*)
Strong-arm chief of an outlaw clan,
(*From Kansas to Illinois!*)
He twirled an old Colt forty-five;
(*Roll on, Missouri!*)
They never took Jesse James alive.
(*Roll, Missouri, roll!*)

Jesse James was King of the Wes';
(*Cataracts in the Missouri!*)
He'd a di'mon' heart in his lef' breas';
(*Brown Missouri rolls!*)
He'd a fire in his heart no hurt could stifle;
(*Thunder, Missouri!*)
Lion eyes an' a Winchester rifle.
(*Missouri, roll down!*)

Jesse James rode a pinto hawse;
Come at night to a water-cawse;
Tetched with the rowel that pinto's flank;
She sprung the torrent from bank to bank.

Jesse rode through a sleepin' town;
Looked the moonlit street both up an' down;

Crack-crack-crack, the street ran flames
An' a great voice cried, "I'm Jesse James!"

Hawse, an' afoot they're after Jess!
    (*Roll on, Missouri!*)
Spurrin' an' spurrin'—but he's gone Wes'.
    (*Brown Missouri rolls!*)
He was ten foot tall when he stood in his boots;
    (*Lightnin' like the Missouri!*)
More'n a match fer sich galoots.
    (*Roll, Missouri, roll!*)

Jesse James rode outa the sage;
Roun' the rocks come the swayin' stage;
Straddlin' the road a giant stan's
An' a great voice bellers, "Throw up yer han's!"

Jesse raked in the di'mon' rings,
The big gold watches an' the yuther things;
Jesse divvied 'em then an' thar
With a cryin' child had lost her mar.

They're creepin'; they're crawlin'; they're stalkin' Jess;
    (*Roll on, Missouri!*)
They's a rumor he's gone much further Wes';
    (*Roll, Missouri, roll!*)
They's word of a cayuse hitched to the bars
    (*Ruddy clouds on Missouri!*)
Of a golden sunset that busts into stars.
    (*Missouri, roll down!*)

Jesse James rode hell fer leather;
He was a hawse an' a man together;
In a cave in a mountain high up in air
He lived with a rattlesnake, a wolf, an' a bear.

Jesse's heart was as sof' as a woman;
Fer guts an' stren'th he was sooper-human;
He could put six shots through a woodpecker's eye
And take in one swaller a gallon o' rye.

They sought him here an' they sought him there,
    (*Roll on, Missouri!*)
But he strides by night through the ways of the air;
    (*Brown Missouri rolls!*)
They say he was took an' they say he is dead,
    (*Thunder, Missouri!*)
But he ain't—he's a sunset overhead!
    (*Missouri down to the sea!*)

Jesse James was a Hercules.
When he went through the woods he tore up the trees.
When he went on the plains he smoked the groun'
An' the hull lan' shuddered fer miles aroun'.

Jesse James wore a red bandanner
That waved on the breeze like the Star Spangled Banner;
In seven states he cut up dadoes.
He's gone with the buffler an' the desperadoes.

Yes, Jesse James was a two-gun man
(*Roll on, Missouri!*)
The same as when this song began;
(*From Kansas to Illinois!*)
An' when you see a sunset bust into flames
(*Lightnin' like the Missouri!*)
Or a thunderstorm blaze—that's Jesse James!
(*Hear that Missouri roll!*)

ETERNAL MASCULINE

Neither will I put myself forward as others may do,
Neither, if you wish me to flatter, will I flatter you;
I will look at you grimly, and so you will know I am true.

Neither when all do agree and lout low and salute,
And you are beguiled by the tree and devout for the fruit,
Will I seem to be aught but the following eyes of a brute.

I will stand to one side and sip of my hellebore wine,
I will snarl and deride the antics and airs of the swine;
You will glance in your pride, but I will deny you a sign.

I will squint at the moon and be peaceful because I am dead,
I will whistle a tune and be glad of the harshness I said.
O you will come soon, when the stars are a mist overhead!

You will come, with eyes fierce; you will act a defiant surprise.
Quick lightings will pierce to our hearts from the pain in our eyes,
Standing strained and averse, with the trembling of love that defies.

And then I will know, by the heartbreaking turn of your head,
My madness brought low in a hell that is spared to the dead.
The upas will grow from the poisonous words that I said;

From under its shade out to where like a statue you stand,
Without wish to evade, I will reach, I will cry with my hand,
With my spirit dismayed, with my eyes and my mouth full of sand. . . .

NSCRIPTION FOR A MIRROR IN A DESERTED DWELLING

Set silver cone to tulip flame!
The mantel mirror floats with night
Reflecting still green watery light.
The sconces glimmer. If she came
Like silence through the shadowy wall
Where walls are wading in the moon
The dark would tremble back to June.
So faintly now the moonbeams fall,
So soft this silence, that the verge
Of speech is reached. Remote and pale
As through some faint viridian veil
The lovely lineaments emerge,
The clearly amber eyes, the tint
Of pearl and faintest rose, the hair

To lacquered light, a silken snare
Of devious bronze, the tiny dint
With which her maker mocked the years
Beneath her lip imprinting praise.
Dim flower of desecrating days,
The old reflection, strange with tears,
Is gazing out upon the gloom,
Is widening eyes to find the light
In reminiscence, in the night
Of this foregone, forgotten room.

And you, the watcher, with your eyes
As wide as hers in dark distress,
Who never knew her loveliness
But guess through glass her shadowy guise,
For you around the glass I trace
This secret writing, that will burn
Like witch-fire should her shade return
To haunt you with that wistful face.

At least no gesturing figures pass;
Here is no tragic immanence
Of all the scenes of small events
That pantomimed before the glass.
No bliss, no passion, no despair,
No other actor lingers now;
The moonlight on a lifted brow
Is all,—the eyes so wide aware
Of clouds that pass with stars, and suns,
Of mystery that pales the cheek,
Of all the heart could never speak,
Of joy and pain so vivid once,
That ceased with music and the lights,
Dimming to darkness and repose. . . .
Lean then and kiss that ghostly rose
That was her face, this night of nights,—
And know the vision fled indeed,
The mirror's surface smooth and cold,
The words unbreathed, the tale untold,
The past unpiteous to your need!

SAGACITY

We knew so much; when her beautiful eyes could lighten,
Her beautiful laughter follow our phrase;
Or the gaze go hard with pain, the lips tighten,
On the bitterer days.
Oh, ours was all knowing then, all generous displaying.
Such wisdom we had to show!
And now there is merely silence, silence, silence saying
All we did not know.

Jean Starr Untermeyer

Jean Starr was born at Zanesville, Ohio, May 13, 1886, and educated at the Putnam Seminary in the city of her birth. At sixteen she came to New York City, pursuing special studies at Columbia and married Louis Untermeyer in 1907. Except for sojourns abroad, she lived in New York before and after her divorce.

Growing Pains (1918) is a thin book of thirty-four poems, the result of eight years' slow and critical creation. This highly selective process did much to bring the volume up to an unusual level; a severity of standards maintains the poet on an austere plane. Acutely self-analytical, there is a stern, uncompromising relentlessness toward her introspections. A sharp color sense, a surprising whimsicality, a translation of the ordinary in terms of the unexplored illumine such poems as "Sinfonia Domestica" and the much-quoted "Autumn," a celebration of domesticity which might be described as a housekeeper's paean. In the last named Mrs. Untermeyer has reproduced her early environment with bright pungency; "Verhaeren's Flemish *genre* pictures are no better," writes Amy Lowell. Several of her purely pictorial poems establish a swift kinship between the most romantic and most prosaic objects. "High Tide," in one extended metaphor, turns the mere fact of a physical law into an arresting fancy. *Dreams Out of Darkness* (1921) is a ripening of this author's power with a richer musical undercurrent. An increase of melody is manifest on every page, possibly most striking in the unrhymed lyrics. Amy Lowell declared, "This is the very heart of a woman, naked and serious, beautiful and unashamed."

Her training as a musician (she made her début as a *Liedersinger* in Vienna and London in 1924) added to her equipment as translator of the "official" life of *Franz Schubert* by Oscar Bie in 1928. *Steep Ascent* (1927) marks a spiritual as well as poetic climax. The dominant note, as might have been foreseen, is ethical, but there is no reliance on mere religiosity. "What is most remarkable about Jean Starr Untermeyer," wrote Edmund Wilson, "is the peculiar shading and force of her style. I believe that hers is classically Hebraic. She has always seemed to me one of the few writers who have successfully preserved in a modern language something of the authentic austerity of Jewish literature."

The poems in *Wingèd Child* (1936) have a new serenity, even a sly humor; they do not proceed, as did many of the others, from struggle, but from assurance. The early *vers libriste* gives way to the later formalist, even the "dissonant" rhymes of "Dew on a Dusty Heart" being cast in a sonnet. *Love and Need* (1940) assembles the four preceding volumes with the addition of twenty-one deeply thoughtful poems.

After the publication of her collected poems, Mrs. Untermeyer spent much of her time on a translation of Hermann Broch's *The Death of Virgil* (1945), a work which combines the novel and lyric poetry, history, philosophy, and stream-of-consciousness. Stephan Zweig said that the book, beyond the life and death of a poet, "reflects the problems of all ages."

HIGH TIDE

I edged back against the night.
The sea growled assault on the wave-bitten shore.
And the breakers,
Like young and impatient hounds,
Sprang with rough joy on the shrinking sand.
Sprang—but were drawn back slowly
With a long, relentless pull,
Whimpering, into the dark.

Then I saw who held them captive;
And I saw how they were bound
With a broad and quivering leash of light,
Held by the moon,
As, calm and unsmiling,
She walked the deep fields of the sky.

AUTUMN

(To My Mother)

How memory cuts away the years,
And how clean the picture comes
Of autumn days, brisk and busy;
Charged with keen sunshine.
And you, stirred with activity,
The spirit of those energetic days.

There was our back-yard,
So plain and stripped of green,
With even the weeds carefully pulled away
From the crooked red bricks that made the walk,
And the earth on either side so black.

Autumn and dead leaves burning in the sharp air.
And winter comforts coming in like a pageant.
I shall not forget them:—
Great jars pompous with the raw green of pickles,
Standing in a solemn row across the back of the porch,
Exhaling the pungent dill;
And in the very center of the yard,
You, tending the great catsup kettle of gleaming copper,
Where fat, red tomatoes bobbed up and down
Like jolly monks in a drunken dance.
And there were bland banks of cabbages that came by the wagon-load,
Soon to be cut into delicate ribbons
Only to be crushed by the heavy, wooden stompers.
Such feathery whiteness—to come to kraut!
And after, there were grapes that hid their brightness under a gray dust,
Then gushed thrilling, purple blood over the fire;
And enameled crab-apples that tricked with their fragrance
But were bitter to taste.
And there were spicy plums and ill-shaped quinces,
And long string beans floating in pans of clear water
Like slim, green fishes.
And there was fish itself,
Salted, silver herring from the city. . . .

And you moved among these mysteries,
Absorbed and smiling and sure;
Stirring, tasting, measuring,
With the precision of a ritual.
I like to think of you in your years of power—
You, now so shaken and so powerless—
High priestess of your home.

SINFONIA DOMESTICA

When the white wave of a glory that is hardly I
  Breaks through my mind and washes it clean,
I know at last the meaning of my ecstasy,
  And know at last my wish and what it can mean.

To have sped out of life that night—to have vanished
  Not as a vision, but as something touched, yet grown
Radiant as the moonlight, circling my naked shoulder;
  Wrapped in a dream of beauty, longed for, but never known.

For how with our daily converse, even the sweet sharing
  Of thoughts, of food, of home, of common life,
How shall I be that glory, that last desire
  For which men struggle? Is Romance in a wife?

Must I bend a heart that is bowed to breaking
  With a frustration, inevitable and slow,
And bank my flame to a low hearth fire, believing
  You will come for warmth and life to its tempered glow?

Shall I mold my hope anew, to one of service,
  And tell my uneasy soul, "Behold, this is good"?
And meet you (if we do meet), even at Heaven's threshold,
  With ewer and basin, with clothing and with food?

COUNTRY OF NO LACK

A lilac ribbon is unbound,
A band of gradual rose untied,
And lo, the glowing book of day
Is opened on the mountainside.

What curves salute, what colors sound
From this so-rich-illumined scroll,
For whose perusal one need pay
Only a just delight as toll.

The brook's clean silver set in stones
Is balanced by the silver sheen
Of clean-stripped logs, which in a field
Seem floating down a river of green.

Furze are not flowers, but the tones
Of sunlight that a bird has sung,
And broken purples but the yield
Of hoarded twilights, meadow-flung.

Against a heaven's faithful blue,
A fadeless forest lifts its pines,
From shadows deepening into black
A slim and shadowy road inclines.

Upon the printed air, how true
Stand lizard, lake and leaf, page-still.
Here in the country of no lack,
What care can move, what grief can chill?

DEW ON A DUSTY HEART

If come into this world again I must
And take unto myself another form,
Oh, let it be unblemished by a mist
Of imperfections or the line infirm.
And let it shapen to a secret wish
Untouched, untinctured, even by a dram
Of earthiness; nor let the fretted wash
Of passion fray the fine-immaculate dream.

Oh, let me come back as a melody
New as the air it takes, no taint of ill
To halt such lovely flying as birds do
Going from infinite nought to infinite all.
Giving to dusty hearts that lag at even
The dewy rest they dream of and call heaven.

FALSE ENCHANTMENT

Crossing there under the trees with leaden pace,
Set upon those whom Saturn has in pawn,
Reading a book and brooding with shut face
Now on a Sunday near the croquet lawn,
The woman set apart and doubly lost
Walks in her legend, which is hanging down
About her stately limbs like a heavy gown—
A fabled figure from a page embossed.

She reads the word and she has lived the life,
Isolde was less desolate than she,
Mourned by the shepherd with his lonely fife,
Fulfilled in death with Tristan by the sea.
She does not hear the mallet strike the ball,
Nor how the motor-car frets at the gate;
Weighing her irksome years against her fate
She waits with impatient heart a certain call.

And since she cannot die, it must be love
Will come to tear her from this memory-mesh,
And find the elements she is fashioned of,
Permit her to evaporate from the flesh
Desire that balks at change. The moon at crescent
Is younger than herself, though casual eye
Sees her stream-linear as a plane on sky.
How shall she be un-mythed into the present?

Her will that argues to accept her lot
Is outdebated by her clamoring blood
That will not check its race, or cool, or clot,
Or shelter in a pool its heedless flood.
Her will says: "Let me rest awhile and keep
This body in chaste readiness for death."
The blood with each revolving of the breath
Cries: "Who will come to kiss me from this sleep?"

H. D.

Hilda Doolittle was born September 10, 1886, at Bethlehem, Pennsylvania. When she was still a child, her father became Director of the Flower Observatory and the family moved to a suburb in the outskirts of Philadelphia. Hilda Doolittle attended a private school in West Philadelphia; entered Bryn Mawr College in 1904; and went abroad, for what was intended to be a short sojourn, in 1911. After a visit to Italy and France she came to London, joined Ezra Pound, and helped to organize the Imagists. She married one of the original group, Richard Aldington, the English poet and novelist, whom she later divorced. Her work (signed "H. D.") began to appear in a few magazines and its unusual quality was recognized at once. Remaining for a while in London, she became one of the leaders of the movement, creating through a chiseled verse her flawless evocations of Greek poetry and sculpture. In 1920 she made a long-deferred visit to America, settling on the Californian coast, returning the following year to England. After 1921 H. D. lived in Switzerland on the shore of Lake Geneva. She died September 27, 1961, in Zurich.

Her first collection, *Sea Garden,* appeared in 1916; an interval of five years elapsed before the publication of her second volume, *Hymen,* which was printed simultaneously in England and America in 1921. These volumes showed H. D. as the most important of her group. She was the only one who steadfastly held to the letter as well as the spirit of its *credo.* She was, in fact, the only true Imagist. Her poems are like a set of Tanagra figurines. Here, at first glance, the effect is chilling—beauty seems held in a frozen gesture. But it is in this very fixation of light, color and emotion that she achieves intensity. What at first seemed static becomes fluent; the arrested moment glows with a quivering tension.

Observe the poem entitled "Heat." Here, in the fewest possible words, is something beyond the description of heat—here is the effect of it. In these lines one feels the weight and solidity of a midsummer afternoon. So in "The Islands" a propulsion of feeling hurries forward the syllables balancing on light and dark vowels, and what might have been only a list of antique names becomes an outcry. Her efforts to draw the contemporary world are less happy. H. D. is best in her reflections of clear-cut loveliness in a quietly pagan world; in most of her moods, she seems less a modern writer than an inspired anachronism.

Heliodora and Other Poems appeared in 1924. So much had already been written concerning the form of H. D.'s poetry that it was no longer necessary to expatiate on the unique features of her metric. Even those least impressed by the program of the Imagists readily conceded her exquisite if oversubtle flavor, the stripped purity of her line, the precision of her epithets. But the most apparent feature of *Heliodora*—even more noticeable than its beauties of form—is its intensity. A freely declared passion radiates from lines which are at once ecstatic and austere. Even the most casual reading must convince one that this poet is not, as she first seemed to us, a Greek statue faintly flushed with life, a delightful but detached relic of another world. This is a woman responsive to color and pain, aroused by loveliness, shocked by betrayal, affected by all those manifestations which are too old to be timely, too fresh to be "antique."

Practically all of H. D.'s previous volumes were assembled in *Collected Poems* (1925) which contains not only her original work but the spirited translations from the Odyssey and her flexible expansions of fragmentary phrases of Sappho. A play, *Hippolytus Temporizes,* appeared in 1927. In the later works it is interesting to trace the tightening of form, the approximation of more regular structure, even the introduction of half-candid, half-concealed rhyme.

Red Roses for Bronze (1932) stresses the note of personal emotion, the emotion of love once requited but now unreturned. The poetry is more weighted than before, less dependent on decorations. *The Walls Do Not Fall* (1944), *Tribute to the*

Angels (1945), and *The Flowering of the Rod* (1946) form a war trilogy. The idiom, especially in the last, is clipped, colloquial, and sharply effective.

H. D.'s prose is somewhat more derivative, bearing overtones of Gertrude Stein, but it rises above its influences. *Palimpsest* (1926) and *Hedylus* (1928) embody a poet's prose, the former a triptych of interrelated tragedies, actual and intuitive.

OREAD

Whirl up, sea—
Whirl your pointed pines.
Splash your great pines
On our rocks.
Hurl your green over us—
Cover us with your pools of fir.

PEAR TREE

Silver dust
lifted from the earth,
higher than my arms reach,
you have mounted.
O silver,
higher than my arms reach
you front us with great mass;
no flower ever opened
so staunch a white leaf,
no flower ever parted silver
from such rare silver;
O white pear,
your flower-tufts,
thick on the branch,
bring summer and ripe fruits
in their purple hearts.

HEAT

O wind, rend open the heat,
cut apart the heat,
rend it to tatters.

Fruit cannot drop
through this thick air—
fruit cannot fall into heat
that presses up and blunts
the points of pears
and rounds the grapes.

Cut through the heat—
plow through it,
turning it on either side
of your path.

ORCHARD

I saw the first pear
as it fell—
the honey-seeking, golden-banded,
the yellow swarm,
was not more fleet than I,
(spare us from loveliness!)
and I fell prostrate,
crying:
you have flayed us with your blossoms,
spare us the beauty
of fruit-trees!

The honey-seeking
paused not;
the air thundered their song,
and I alone was prostrate.

O rough-hewn
god of the orchard,
I bring you an offering—
do you, alone unbeautiful,
son of the god,
spare us from loveliness:

these fallen hazel-nuts,
stripped late of their green sheaths,
grapes, red-purple,
their berries
dripping with wine;
pomegranates already broken,
and shrunken figs,
and quinces untouched,
I bring you as offering.

SONG

You are as gold
as the half-ripe grain
that merges to gold again,
as white as the white rain
that beats through
the half-opened flowers
of the great flower tufts
thick on the black limbs
of an Illyrian apple bough.
Can honey distill such fragrance
as your bright hair—
for your face is as fair as rain;
yet as rain that lies clear
on white honey-comb
lends radiance to the white wax,
so your hair on your brow
casts light for a shadow.

FROM "LET ZEUS RECORD"

Stars wheel in purple, yours is not so rare
as Hesperus, nor yet so great a star
as bright Aldebaran or Sirius,
nor yet the stained and brilliant one of War;

stars turn in purple, glorious to the sight;
yours is not gracious as the Pleiads are,
nor as Orion's sapphires, luminous;

yet disenchanted, cold, imperious face,
when all the others, blighted, reel and fall,
your star, steel-set, keeps lone and frigid tryst
to freighted ships baffled in wind and blast.

LAIS

Let her who walks in Paphos
take the glass,
let Paphos take the mirror
and the work of frosted fruit,
gold apples set
with silver apple-leaf,
white leaf of silver
wrought with vein of gilt.

Let Paphos lift the mirror;
let her look
into the polished center of the disk.
Let Paphos take the mirror:
did she press
flowerlet of flame-flower
to the lustrous white
of the white forehead?
Did the dark veins beat
a deeper purple
than the wine-deep tint
of the dark flower?

Did she deck black hair,
one evening, with the winter-white

flower of the winter-berry?
Did she look (reft of her lover)
at a face gone white
under the chaplet
of white virgin-breath?

Lais, exultant, tyrannizing Greece,
Lais who kept her lovers in the porch,
lover on lover waiting
(but to creep
where the robe brushed the threshold
where still sleeps Lais),
so she creeps, Lais,
to lay her mirror at the feet
of her who reigns in Paphos.

Lais has left her mirror,
for she sees no longer in its depth
the Lais' self
that laughed exultant,
tyrannizing Greece.

Lais has left her mirror,
for she weeps no longer,
finding in its depth
a face, but other
than dark flame and white
feature of perfect marble.

Lais has left her mirror
(so one wrote)
to her who reigns in Paphos;
Lais who laughed a tyrant over Greece,
Lais who turned the lovers from the porch,
that swarm for whom now
Lais has no use;
Lais is now no lover of the glass,
seeing no more the face as once it was,
wishing to see that face and finding this.

FROM "HALCYON"

("*Bird—loved of sea-men*")

I'm not here,
everything's vague, blurred everywhere,
than you are blown
into a room;

the sea comes where a carpet
laid red and purple,
and where the edge showed marble
there is sea-weed;

sedge breaks the wall
where the couch stands,
the hands of strange people,
twisting tassel and fringe

of rich cloth, become clear;
I understand the people,
they aren't hateful but dear;
over all

a shrill wind, clear sky;
O why, why, why
am I fretful, insecure,
why am I vague, unsure

until you are blown,
unexpected, small, quaint, unnoticeable,
a gray gull
into a room.

SONGS FROM CYPRUS

I

Gather for festival
bright weed and purple shell;
make on the holy sand
pattern as one might make
who tread with rose-red heel
a measure
pleasureful;

such as those songs we made
in rose and myrtle shade
where rose and myrtle fell
(shell-petal or rose-shell)
on just such holy sand;
ah, the song
musical;

give me white rose and red;
find me in citron glade
citron of precious weight,
spread gold before her feet,
ah, weave the citron flower;
hail, goddess
beautiful.

II

Where is the nightingale,
in what myrrh-wood and dim?
ah, let the night come black,
for we would conjure back
all that enchanted him,
all that enchanted him.

Where is the bird of fire?
in what packed hedge of rose?
in what roofed ledge of flower?
no other creature knows
what magic lurks within,
what magic lurks within.

Bird, bird, bird, bird, we cry,
hear, pity us in pain;
hearts break in the sunlight,
hearts break in daylight rain,
only night heals again,
only night heals again.

HOLY SATYR

Most holy Satyr,
like a goat,
with horns and hooves
to match thy coat
of russet brown,
I make leaf-circlets
and a crown of honey-flowers
for thy throat;
where the amber petals
drip to ivory,
I cut and slip
each stiffened petal
in the rift
of carven petal;
honey horn
has wed the bright
virgin petal of the white
flower cluster: lip to lip
let them whisper,
let them lilt, quivering.

Most holy Satyr,
like a goat,
hear this our song,
accept our leaves,
love-offering,
return our hymn,
like echo fling
a sweet song,
answering note for note.

THE ISLANDS

I

What are the islands to me,
what is Greece,
what is Rhodes, Samos, Chios,
what is Paros facing west,
what is Crete?

What is Samothrace,
rising like a ship,
what is Imbros rending the storm-waves
with its breast?

What is Naxos, Paros, Milos,
what the circle about Lycia,
what the Cyclades'
white necklace?

What is Greece—
Sparta, rising like a rock,
Thebes, Athens,
what is Corinth?

What is Euboia
with its island violets,
what is Euboia, spread with grass,
set with swift shoals,
what is Crete?

What are the islands to me,
what is Greece?

II

What can love of land give to me
that you have not—
what do the tall Spartans know,
and gentler Attic folk?

What has Sparta and her women
more than this?

What are the islands to me
if you are lost—
what is Naxos, Tinos, Andros,

and Delos, the clasp
of the white necklace?

III

What can love of land give to me
that you have not,
what can love of strife break in me
that you have not?

Though Sparta enter Athens,
Thebes wrack Sparta,
each changes as water,
salt, rising to wreak terror
and falling back.

IV

"What has love of land given to you
that I have not?"

I have questioned Tyrians
where they sat
on the black ships,
weighted with rich stuffs;
I have asked the Greeks
from the white ships,
and Greeks from ships whose hulks
lay on the wet sand, scarlet
with great beaks.
I have asked bright Tyrians
and tall Greeks—
"what has love of land given you?"
And they answered—"peace."

V

But Beauty is set apart,
beauty is cast by the sea,
a barren rock,
beauty is set about
with wrecks of ships,
upon our coast, death keeps
the shallows—death waits
clutching toward us
from the deeps.

Beauty is set apart;
the winds that slash its beach,
swirl the coarse sand
upward toward the rocks.

Beauty is set apart
from the islands
and from Greece.

VI

In my garden
the winds have beaten
the ripe lilies;
in my garden, the salt
has wilted the first flakes
of young narcissus,
and the lesser hyacinth,
and the salt has crept
under the leaves of the white hyacinth.

In my garden,
even the wind-flowers lie flat,
broken by the wind at last.

VII

What are the islands to me
if you are lost,
what is Paros to me
if your eyes draw back,
what is Milos
if you take fright of beauty,
terrible, tortuous, isolated,
a barren rock?

What is Rhodes, Crete,
what is Paros facing west,
what, white Imbros?

What are the islands to me
if you hesitate,
what is Greece if you draw back
from the terror
and cold splendor of song
and its bleak sacrifice?

HELEN

All Greece hates
the still eyes in the white face,
the luster as of olives
where she stands,
and the white hands.

All Greece reviles
the wan face when she smiles,
hating it deeper still
when it grows wan and white,
remembering past enchantments
and past ills.

Greece sees unmoved,
God's daughter, born of love,

the beauty of cool feet
and slenderest knees,
could love indeed the maid,
only if she were laid,
white ash amid funereal cypresses.

LETHE

Nor skin nor hide nor fleece
Shall cover you,
Nor curtain of crimson nor fine
Shelter of cedar-wood be over you,
Nor the fir-tree
Nor the pine.

Nor sight of whin nor gorse
Nor river-yew,
Nor fragrance of flowering bush,
Nor wailing of reed-bird to waken you.
Nor of linnet
Nor of thrush.

Nor word nor touch nor sight
Of lover, you
Shall long through the night but for this:
The roll of the full tide to cover you
Without question,
Without kiss.

John Hall Wheelock

☙ John Hall Wheelock was born at Far Rockaway, Long Island, in 1886. He was graduated from Harvard, finished his studies at the Universities of Göttingen and Berlin, 1908-10, and, as a publisher, lived in New York.

Wheelock's first book is unreservedly exuberant: *The Human Fantasy* (1911) sings with the voice of youth—youth vibrantly, even vociferously, in love with existence. Rhapsodic and obviously influenced by Whitman and Henley, these lines beat bravely; headlong ecstasy rises from pages whose refrain is "Splendid it is to live and glorious to die." *The Beloved Adventure* (1912) is less powerful, but scarcely less passionate. Lyric after lyric moves by its athletic affirmation.

Wheelock's subsequent volumes are less individualized. *Love and Liberation* (1913) and *Dust and Light* (1919) are long dilutions of the earlier strain. The music is still here, but most of the vigor has gone. Wheelock has allowed himself to be exploited by his own fluency and the result is lyrical monotony. Yet vast stretches of two hundred and thirty unvaried love-songs cannot bury a dozen vivid poems which lie, half-concealed, in a waste of verbiage.

The Black Panther (1922) furnishes additional proof that though Wheelock's star may have waned it did not die. In this volume the poet's gift assumes greater dignity; the flashing athleticism has matured into a steady fervor. With the exception of a few innocuous songs, there is revealed a graver music than Wheelock has accomplished. In the longer poems, most effectively in "Earth," he expresses the paradox of conflict and consent: the philosophy of the single Consciousness which reconciles terror and tenderness, murder and laughter, dawn and destruction—"Life, the dreadful, the magnificent."

Poems Old and New (1956) is a critical winnowing of Wheelock's preceding six volumes, including *The Bright Doom* (1927). The later work, particularly the meditative poetry in *The Gardener and Other Poems* (1961), reveals a richer content accompanied by a music deeper and graver than anything Wheelock had heretofore attempted.

SUNDAY EVENING IN THE COMMON

Look—on the topmost branches of the world
The blossoms of the myriad stars are thick;
Over the huddled rows of stone and brick,
A few, sad wisps of empty smoke are curled
Like ghosts, languid and sick.

One breathless moment now the city's moaning
Fades, and the endless streets seem vague and dim;
There is no sound around the whole world's rim,
Save in the distance a small band is droning
Some desolate old hymn.

Van Wyck, how often have we been together
When this same moment made all mysteries clear;
—The infinite stars that brood above us here,
And the gray city in the soft June weather,
So tawdry and so dear!

TRIUMPH OF LOVE

I shake my hair in the wind of morning
For the joy within me that knows no bounds,
I echo backward the vibrant beauty
Wherewith heaven's hollow lute resounds.

I shed my song on the feet of all men,
On the feet of all shed out like wine,
On the whole and the hurt I shed my bounty,
The beauty within me that is not mine.

Turn not away from my song, nor scorn me,
Who bear the secret that holds the sky
And the stars together, but know within me
There speaks another more wise than I.

Nor spurn me here from your heart, to hate me.
Yet hate me here if you will—not so
Myself you hate, but the Love within me
That loves you, whether you would or no.

Here love returns with love to the lover,
And beauty unto the heart thereof,
And hatred unto the heart of the hater,
Whether he would or no, with love!

NIRVANA

Sleep on, I lie at heaven's high oriels,
  Over the stars that murmur as they go
  Lighting your lattice-window far below;
And every star some of the glory spells
  Whereof I know.

I have forgotten you long, long ago,
  Like the sweet silver singing of thin bells
Vanished, or music fading faint and low.
  Sleep on, I lie at heaven's high oriels,
Who loved you so.

LOVE AND LIBERATION

Lift your arms to the stars
And give an immortal shout;
Not all the veils of darkness
Can put your beauty out!

You are armed with love, with love,
Nor all the powers of Fate
Can touch you with a spear,
Nor all the hands of hate.

What of good and evil,
Hell and Heaven above—
Trample them with love!
Ride over them with love!

EARTH

Grasshopper, your fairy song
And my poem alike belong
To the dark and silent earth
From which all poetry has birth.
All we say and all we sing
Is but as the murmuring
Of that drowsy heart of hers
When from her deep dream she stirs:
If we sorrow, or rejoice,
You and I are but her voice.

Deftly does the dust express
In mind her hidden loveliness,
And from her cool silence stream
The cricket's cry and Dante's dream;
For the earth that breeds the trees
Breeds cities too, and symphonies.
Equally her beauty flows
Into a savior, or a rose—
Looks down in dream, and from above
Smiles at herself in Jesus' love.
Christ's love and Homer's art
Are but the workings of her heart;
Through Leonardo's hand she seeks
Herself, and through Beethoven speaks
In holy thunderings around
The awful message of the ground.

The serene and humble mold
Does in herself all selves enfold—
Kingdoms, destinies, and creeds,
Great dreams, and dauntless deeds,
Science that metes the firmament,
The high, inflexible intent
Of one for many sacrificed—
Plato's brain, the heart of Christ;
All love, all legend, and all lore
Are in the dust forevermore.

Even as the growing grass,
Up from the soil religions pass,
And the field that bears the rye
Bears parables and prophecy.
Out of the earth the poem grows
Like the lily, or the rose;
And all man is, or yet may be,
Is but herself in agony
Toiling up the steep ascent
Toward the complete accomplishment
When all dust shall be, the whole
Universe, one conscious soul.
Yea, the quiet and cool sod
Bears in her breast the dream of God.

If you would know what earth is, scan
The intricate, proud heart of man,
Which is the earth articulate,
And learn how holy and how great,
How limitless and how profound
Is the nature of the ground—
How without terror or demur
We may entrust ourselves to her
When we are wearied out and lay
Our faces in the common clay.

For she is pity, she is love,
All wisdom, she, all thoughts that move
About her everlasting breast
Till she gathers them to rest:
All tenderness of all the ages,
Seraphic secrets of the sages,

Vision and hope of all the seers,
All prayer, all anguish, and all tears
Are but the dust that from her dream
Awakes, and knows herself supreme—
Are but earth, when she reveals
All that her secret heart conceals
Down in the dark and silent loam,
Which is ourselves, asleep, at home.
Yea, and this, my poem, too,
Is part of her as dust and dew,
Wherein herself she doth declare
Through my lips, and say her prayer.

THIS QUIET DUST

Here in my curving hands I cup
This quiet dust; I lift it up.
Here is the mother of all thought;
Of this the shining heavens are wrought,
The laughing lips, the feet that rove,
The face, the body, that you love:
Mere dust, no more, yet nothing less,
And this has suffered consciousness,
Passion, and terror, this again
Shall suffer passion, death, and pain.

For, as all flesh must die, so all,
Now dust, shall live. 'Tis natural;
Yet hardly do I understand—
Here in the hollow of my hand
A bit of God Himself I keep,
Between two vigils fallen asleep.

THE HOUSE IN THE GREEN WELL

You came to it through wild country, there the sea's voice
Has sounded always. Rampant meadow and thicket
Bordered it on three sides. The approaches were
By a winding road under tall elms, or circuitous
Woodland paths that led to a slight incline;
From this the house flowed upward as if earth, thrusting
Great trunks of trees up round it, had thrust up
The house itself, in springtime and in summer
Girdled by walls of green. The fresh loam,
Cool from long sleep, flowed up through bole and branches
And out, through branches into green leaves. Just so
The cool silence of that country flowed
Into green sounds—old oceanic echoes,
Whispers and suspirations of the sea,
Broken at times by surf-bruit, bellowing
Of blind sea-mouths—flowed also into green songs
Hidden among green leaves. The silence there
Had a certain thing to say, could not be said
By harp or oboe, flute or violoncello,
Or by the lesser strings! it could not be said
By the human voice; but in sea-sounds you heard it
Perhaps, or in the water-dripping jargon
Of summer birds: endless reiteration
Of chat or vireo, the woodcock's call,
Chirrup and squeegee, larrup, squirt and trill
Of liquid syrinxes—bright drops of song
Spangling the silence. Also, you could compare it,
This silence, to a great rock that the sea's steady

Lament steadily wore away, the acute
Chisel of the thrush's song cut into it,
Cut out small chips of silence, while the clouds,
Those nuns of heaven, paced heaven's corridors,
Robed in Dominican white, the spaces between them,
As they made forward in that grave procession,
Were ceremonial. On Heaven above the green well
At the bottom of which the house appeared to be lying
Could be likened, if you preferred, to a huge lens
Focusing the sun's light: the eye of day
Opened and closed again as the cloudy shutter
Shrank or expanded; the shadow patterns sharpened,
Faltered, or stayed, or swayed as the wind's hand
Trembled the leaves. All day long, in the house
Shifting of light and cloud shed light or gloom
Along the passages where the blowing arras
Lifted and settled; the polished surfaces
Of highboy, bureau and hanging mirror darkened
Or brightened as the slant light strengthened or dimmed
From windows opening on the green well of trees;
And into this at night the stars looked down,
Or one star, riding in some deep rift of cloud,
Would stare steadily. The wall of green surrounding
The house allowed no view of the outer world,
But in mid-autumn, when the leaves had fallen
And boughs were sere, in the month of wasps, when the numbed
Spider starved in his web, when the torpid hornet
Crawled upon casement and curtain, and friendly fires
Kindled on every hearth—suddenly, by chance,
From an upstairs window you might glimpse far off,
Between bare branches, the cold steel-blue of the sea.

Roy Helton

Roy (Addison) Helton was born at Washington, D. C., in 1886 and graduated from the University of Pennsylvania in 1908. He studied art—and found he was color-blind. He spent two years at inventions—and found he had no business sense. He became a schoolmaster, a novelist, and a poet.

Outcasts in Beulah Land (1918) and *Lonesome Water* (1930), like the fanciful prose of *The Early Adventures of Peacham Grew* (1925), disclose Helton's intimate understanding of the backgrounds of folksy and primitive lore. "Old Christmas Morning" is a Kentucky mountain dialogue in which Helton introduces an element seldom encountered in sophisticated modern verse. Told with the directness of an ancient ballad, it is a drama of Twelfthnight which unfolds a ghost story, a tale whose surprises are heightened by the skillful use of suspension and suggestiveness.

OLD CHRISTMAS MORNING

(A Kentucky Mountain Ballad)

"Where are you coming from, Lomey Carter,
  So airly over the snow?
And what's them pretties you got in your hand,
  And where you aiming to go?

"Step in, Honey: Old Christmas morning
  I ain't got nothing much;
Maybe a bite of sweetness and corn bread,
  A little ham meat and such.

"But come in, Honey! Sally Anne Barton's
  Hungering after your face.
Wait till I light my candle up:
  Set down! There's your old place.

"Now where you been so airly this morning?"

  "Graveyard, Sally Anne.
Up by the trace in the salt lick meadows
  Where Taulbe kilt my man."

"Taulbe ain't to home this morning . . .
  I can't scratch up a light:
Dampness gets on the heads of the matches;
  But I'll blow up the embers bright."

"Needn't trouble. I won't be stopping:
  Going a long ways still."

"You didn't see nothing, Lomey Carter,
  Up on the graveyard hill?"

"What should I see there, Sally Anne Barton?"

  "Well, sperits do walk last night."

"There were an elder bush a-blooming
  While the moon still give some light."

"Yes, elder bushes, they bloom, Old Christmas,
  And critters kneel down in their straw.
Anything else up in the graveyard?"

  "One thing more I saw:
I saw my man with his head all bleeding
  Where Taulbe's shot went through."

"What did he say?"

"He stooped and kissed me."

"What did he say to you?"

"Said, Lord Jesus forguv your Taulbe;
But he told me another word;
He said it soft when he stooped and kissed me.
That were the last I heard."

"Taulbe ain't to home this morning."

"I know that, Sally Anne,
For I kilt him, coming down through the meadow
Where Taulbe kilt my man.

"I met him upon the meadow trace
When the moon were fainting fast,
And I had my dead man's rifle gun
And kilt him as he come past."

"But I heard two shots."

" 'Twas his was second:
He shot me 'fore he died:
You'll find us at daybreak, Sally Anne Barton:
I'm laying there dead at his side."

LONESOME WATER

Drank lonesome water:
Warn't but a tad then
Up in a laurel thick
Digging for sang;
Came on a place where
The stones were hollow,
Something below them
Tinkled and rang.

Dug whar I heard it
Drippling below me:
Should a knowed better,
Should a been wise;
Leant down and drank it,
Clutching and gripping
The over hung cliv
With the ferns in my eyes.

Tasted of heart leaf
And that smells the sweetest,
Pawpaw and spice bush
And wild brier rose;
Must a been counting
The heels of the spruce pines,
And neighboring round
Whar angelica grows.

I'd drunk lonesome water,
I knowed in a minute:
Never larnt nothing
From then till today:
Nothing worth larning
Nothing worth knowing,
I'm bound to the hills
And I can't get away.

Mean sort of dried up old
Ground-hoggy fellow,
Laying out cold here
Watching the sky;
Pore as a hipporwill,
Bent like a grass blade;
Counting up stars
Till they count too high.

I know whar the gray foxes
Uses up yander:
Know what will cure you
Of tisic and chills,
But I never been way from here,
Never got going;
I've drunk lonesome water.
I'm bound to the hills.

Marianne Moore

⁂ Marianne Moore was born in St. Louis, Missouri, November 15, 1887. She received her B.A. from Bryn Mawr College in 1909; taught stenography at the United States Indian school at Carlisle, Pennsylvania, from 1911 to 1915; was an assistant in the Hudson Park Branch of the New York Public Library, and editor of *The Dial* from 1925 to its demise in 1929.

It was not until 1921 that a few of her friends "pirated" her work; without her coöperation, *Poems* was published in that year by *The Egoist Press.* Three years later she received the Dial Award of two thousand dollars for "distinguished service to American letters." *Observations* (1924), including the early poems as well as some new ones, appeared at the same time.

Miss Moore's work is frankly puzzling, not only to the disinterested reader, but to the student of modern poetry. Although her early verses present no difficulties, her more characteristic lines seem to erect a barrier of jagged clauses, barbed quotations and suspicious barriers between herself and her audience. It has been said that Miss Moore's writing is "objectivist," and the title, *Observations,* suggests that she has, as she herself has said, "an exaggerated tendency to visualize." Her versification is equally strange. Lacking music and verbal sensuousness, its origins seem to be prose. Moreover, she makes a pattern not by flexible measures, but by strict syllables. The results are often rigid and tend to dryness. But she is so sensitive "a literalist of the imagination" and her prosody is so unique that she has expanded the gamut of poetry.

Selected Poems (1935), with a laudatory introduction by T. S. Eliot, and *What Are Years?* (1941) emphasize the distinction of Miss Moore's talents. Mathematically precise, many of the poems are problems which the author poses but never fails to solve, a kind of witty and ironic geometry. Largely concerned with oddities, queer animals, inanimate rococo objects, and disjointed phrases, her poems are triumphs of sensibility—"imaginary gardens with real toads in them." Their fastidiousness is sometimes a fault. "Lacking resonance, belonging to an outlook that has to break things into small pieces to see them," wrote Clement Greenberg, "Miss Moore makes only esthetic discriminations; otherwise everything seems to exist on the same single plane. It is a kind of esthetic pantheism." But Greenberg, conceding that Miss Moore's poetry delights even when it irritates, concludes that her exact quality "is that of felicity in the purest and most difficult sense." Variations on trivial themes are embellished with baroque structures and heightened with curiously embedded quotations. Her images are unforgettable. The lizard is a "nervous naked sword on little feet"; the elephant is "black earth preceded by a tendril"; the snake has "hypodermic teeth"; the pangolin is an armored animal whose overlapping scales have "spruce-cone regularity," he is a "near artichoke," a "night miniature artist-engineer."

Regarding the charge that she makes too frequent use of quotations, Miss Moore appended "A Note on the Notes" to *What Are Years?,* stating that in everything she has written since the early *Observations* there are lines "in which the chief interest is borrowed, and since I have not been able to outgrow this hybrid method of composition, acknowledgments seem only honest." Like Eliot, Miss Moore has made the borrowings her own, although, unlike Eliot, she scrupulously puts her quotations between inverted commas. Paradoxically enough, no poet owes more to more sources than Miss Moore, and yet no author is more original.

Nevertheless (1944) consists of only six poems, yet one of them, "In Distrust of Merits," is one of the most compassionate expressions prompted by war. *Collected Poems* (1951) received the three most coveted honors: the National Book Award, the Bollingen Prize, and the Pulitzer Prize.

Like a Bulwark (1957) and *O To Be a Dragon* (1959) contain more of her characteristically analyzed memories, quaintly angled reflections of a mind which is distinctive, precise, and quietly persuasive.

A TALISMAN

Under a splintered mast,
torn from the ship and cast
near her hull,

a stumbling shepherd found,
embedded in the ground,
a sea-gull

of lapis lazuli,
a scarab of the sea,
with wings spread—

curling its coral feet,
parting its beak to greet
men long dead.

THAT HARP YOU PLAY SO WELL

O David, if I had
Your power, I should be glad—
In harping, with the sling,
In patient reasoning!

Blake, Homer, Job, and you,
Have made old wine-skins new.
Your energies have wrought
Stout continents of thought.

But, David, if the heart
Be brass, what boots the art
Of exorcising wrong,
Of harping to a song?

The scepter and the ring
And every royal thing
Will fail. Grief's lustiness
Must cure the harp's distress.

TO A STEAM ROLLER

The illustration
is nothing to you without the application.
You lack half wit. You crush all the particles down
into close conformity, and then walk back and forth on them.

Sparkling chips of rock
are crushed down to the level of the parent block.
Were not "impersonal judgment in esthetic
matters, a metaphysical impossibility," you

might fairly achieve
it. As for butterflies, I can hardly conceive
of one's attending upon you; but to question
the congruence of the complement is vain, if it exists.

ENGLAND

with its baby rivers and little towns, each with its abbey or its cathedral;
with voices—one voice perhaps, echoing through the transept—the
criterion of suitability and convenience: and Italy with its equal
shores—contriving an epicureanism from which the grossness has been

extracted: and Greece with its goats and its gourds, the nest of modified illusions:
and France, the "chrysalis of the nocturnal butterfly" in
whose products, mystery of construction diverts one from what was originally one's
object—substance at the core: and the East with its snails, its emotional

shorthand and jade cockroaches, its rock crystal and its imperturbability,
all of museum quality: and America where there
is the little old ramshackle victoria in the south, where cigars are smoked on the
street in the north; where there are no proof readers, no silkworms, no digressions;

the wild man's land; grass-less, links-less, language-less country—in which letters
are written
not in Spanish, not in Greek, not in Latin, not in shorthand,
but in plain American which cats and dogs can read! The letter "a" in psalm and
calm when
pronounced with the sound of "a" in candle, is very noticeable but

why should continents of misapprehension have to be accounted for by the
fact? Does it follow that because there are poisonous toadstools
which resemble mushrooms, both are dangerous? In the case of mettlesomeness
which may be
mistaken for appetite, of heat which may appear to be haste, no con-

clusions may be drawn. To have misapprehended the matter, is to have confessed
that one has not looked far enough. The sublimated wisdom
of China, Egyptian discernment, the cataclysmic torrent of emotion compressed
in the verbs of the Hebrew language, the books of the man who is able

to say, "I envy nobody but him and him only, who catches more fish than
I do,"—the flower and fruit of all that noted superi-
ority—should one not have stumbled upon it in America, must one imagine
that it is not there? It has never been confined to one locality.

THE FISH

Wade
through black jade
Of the crow-blue mussel shells, one
keeps
adjusting the ash heaps;
opening and shutting itself like

an
injured fan.

The baracles which encrust the
side
of the wave, cannot hide
there for the submerged shafts of the

sun,
split like spun
glass, move themselves with spotlight swift-
ness
into the crevices—
in and out, illuminating

the
turquoise sea
of bodies. The water drives a
wedge
of iron through the iron edge
of the cliff, whereupon the stars,

pink
rice grains, ink
bespattered jelly-fish, crabs like
green
lilies and submarine
toadstools, slide each on the other.

All
external
marks of abuse are present on
this
defiant edifice—
all the physical features of

ac-
cident—lack
of cornice, dynamite grooves, burns
and
hatchet strokes, these things stand
out on it; the chasm side is

dead.
Repeated
evidence has proved that it can
live
on what cannot revive
its youth. The sea grows old in it.

POETRY

I, too, dislike it: there are things that are important beyond all this fiddle.
Reading it, however, with a perfect contempt for it, one discovers in
it, after all, a place for the genuine.

Hands that can grasp, eyes
that can dilate, hair that can rise
if it must, these things are important not because a

high-sounding interpretation can be put upon them but because they are
useful. When they become so derivative as to become unintelligible,
the same thing may be said for all of us, that we
do not admire what
we cannot understand: the bat
holding on upside down or in quest of something to

eat, elephants pushing, a wild horse taking a roll, a tireless wolf under
a tree, the immovable critic twitching his skin like a horse that feels a flea, the base-
ball fan, the statistician—
nor is it valid
to discriminate against 'business documents and

school-books'; all these phenomena are important. One must make a distinction
however: when dragged into prominence by half poets, the result is not poetry,
nor till the poets among us can be
'literalists of
the imagination'—above
insolence and triviality and can present

for inspection, imaginary gardens with real toads in them, shall we have
it. In the meantime, if you demand on the one hand,
the raw material of poetry in
all its rawness and
that which is on the other hand
genuine, then you are interested in poetry.

WHAT ARE YEARS?

What is our innocence,
what is our guilt? All are
naked, none is safe. And whence
is courage: the unanswered question,
the resolute doubt—
dumbly calling, deafly listening—that
in misfortune, even death,
encourages others
and in its defeat, stirs

the soul to be strong? He
sees deep and is glad, who
accedes to mortality
and in his imprisonment, rises
upon himself as
the sea in a chasm, struggling to be
free and unable to be,

in its surrendering
finds its continuing.

So he who strongly feels,
behaves. The very bird,
grown taller as he sings, steels
his form straight up. Though he is captive,
his mighty singing
says, satisfaction is a lowly
thing, how pure a thing is joy.
This is mortality,
this is eternity.

THE MIND IS AN ENCHANTING THING

is an enchanted thing
like the glaze on a
katydid-wing
subdivided by sun
till the nettings are legion.
Like Gieseking playing Scarlatti;

like the apteryx-awl
as a beak, or the
kiwi's rain-shawl
of haired feathers, the mind
feeling its way as though blind,
walks along with its eyes on the ground.

It has memory's ear
that can hear without
having to hear.
Like the gyroscope's fall,
truly unequivocal
because trued by regnant certainty,

it is a power of
strong enchantment. It
is like the dove-
neck animated by
sun; it is memory's eye;
it's conscientious inconsistency.

It tears off the veil; tears
the temptation, the
mist the heart wears,
from its eyes,—if the heart
has a face; it takes apart
dejection. It's fire in the dove-neck's

iridescence; in the
inconsistencies
of Scarlatti.

Unconfusion submits
its confusion to proof; it's
not a Herod's oath that cannot change.

IN DISTRUST OF MERITS

Strengthened to live, strengthened to die for
medals and positioned victories?
They're fighting, fighting, fighting the blind
man who thinks he sees,—
who cannot see that the enslaver is
enslaved; the hater, harmed. O shining O
firm star, O tumultuous
ocean lashed till small things go
as they will, the mountainous
wave makes us who look, know

depth. Lost at sea before they fought! O
star of David, star of Bethlehem,
O black imperial lion
of the Lord—emblem
of a risen world—be joined at last, be
joined. There is hate's crown beneath which all is
death; there's love's without which none
is king; the blessed deeds bless
the halo. As contagion
of sickness makes sickness,

contagion of trust can make trust. They're
fighting in deserts and caves, one by
one, in battalions and squadrons;
they're fighting that I
may yet recover from the disease, *my*
self; some have it lightly, some will die. "Man's
wolf to man?" And we devour
ourselves? The enemy could not
have made a greater breach in our
defenses. One pilot-

ing a blind man can escape him, but
Job disheartened by false comfort knew,
that nothing is so defeating
as a blind man who
can see. O alive who are dead, who are
proud not to see, O small dust of the earth
that walks so arrogantly,
trust begets power and faith is
an affectionate thing. We
vow, we make this promise

to the fighting—it's a promise—"We'll
never hate black, white, red, yellow, Jew,

Gentile, Untouchable." We are
  not competent to
make our vows. With set jaw they are fighting,
fighting, fighting,—some we love whom we know,
    some we love but know not—that
      hearts may feel and not be numb.
    It cures me; or am I what
      I can't believe in? Some

in snow, some on crags, some in quicksands,
  little by little, much by much, they
are fighting fighting fighting that where
  there was death there may
be life. "When a man is prey to anger,
he is moved by outside things; when he holds
    his ground in patience patience
      patience, that is action or
    beauty," the soldier's defense
      and hardest armor for

the fight. The world's an orphan's home. Shall
  we never have peace without sorrow?
without pleas of the dying for
  help that won't come? O
quiet form upon the dust, I cannot
look and yet I must. If these great patient
    dyings—all these agonies
      and woundbearings and blood shed—
    can teach us how to live, these
      dyings were not wasted.

Hate-hardened heart, O heart of iron,
  iron is iron till it is rust.
There never was a war that was
  not inward; I must
fight till I have conquered in myself what
causes war, but I would not believe it.
    I inwardly did nothing.
      O Iscariotlike crime!
    Beauty is everlasting
      and dust is for a time.

AT REST IN THE BLAST

Like a bulwark against fate,
    By the thrust of the blast
  Lead-saluted;
  Saluted by lead?
As though flying
    Old Glory full mast.

Pent by power that holds it fast—
    A paradox. . . . Hard-pressed,
  You take the blame
  And are inviolate—
  Down-cast but not cast

Down. Some would bind by promises,
    But not the tempest-tossed—
  Borne by the might
  Of the storm to a height,
From destruction—
    At rest in the blast.

Robinson Jeffers

⁂ Robinson Jeffers' condensed autobiography runs as follows: "Born in Pittsburgh in 1887; my parents carried me about Europe a good deal. Of the first visit I remember three things—a pocketful of snails loosed on the walls of a kindergarten in Zürich, paintings of Keats and Shelley hanging side by side somewhere in London, and Arthur's Seat, the hill about Edinburgh. When I was fifteen I was brought home. Next year my family moved to California and I graduated at eighteen from Occidental College, Los Angeles. After that, desultory years at the University of Southern California, University of Zürich, Medical School in Los Angeles, University of Washington, but with faint interest. I wasn't deeply interested in anything but poetry. I married Una Call Kuster in 1913. We were going to England in the autumn of 1914. But the August news turned us to this village of Carmel instead; and when the stagecoach topped the hill from Monterey, and we looked down through pines and sea-fogs on Carmel Bay, it was evident that we had come without knowing it to our inevitable place." There, on the ocean's edge, Jeffers has lived ever since, identifying himself with the Californian rocks and headlands. He died there in January, 1962.

Flagons and Apples (1912) was Jeffers' undistinguished first volume; it was followed by *Californians* (1916), a scarcely more original book. In 1925 *Tamar and Other Poems* was brought out by a small printer and caused an overnight sensation. It was reprinted the following year, with the addition of new work, as *Roan Stallion, Tamar and Other Poems* (1926). This, it was evident at once, was masculine poetry, stark, even terrible in its intensities. Whatever defects this verse has—and it must be confessed that Jeffers piles on his catastrophes with little humor and less restraint—there is no denying its elemental power. He combines two almost contrary types of strength: the impetuous American and the stoic Greek.

The Women at Point Sur (1927) shows how easily Jeffers can swing the long line, how suddenly his phrases soar from the tawdry into the terrible, how boldly he can lift a language which, in the hands of most poets, would be nothing more than wild rhetoric.

Cawdor (1928) again reveals Jeffers turning away from gentle themes to almost unbearable ones. The long poem is a continuation of the bewilderment announced in the preceding volumes. Jeffers himself says, "I think of *Cawdor* as making a third with *Tamar* and *The Women at Point Sur;* but as if in Tamar human affairs had been seen looking westward against the ocean; in *Point Sur* looking upward, minimized to ridicule against the stars; in *Cawdor* looking eastward, against the earth, reclaiming a little dignity from that association. . . . Where not only generations but races drizzle away so fast, one wonders the more urgently what it is for, and whether this beautiful earth is amused or sorry at the procession of her possessors." There are also a number of shorter poems, not actually subversive but, continues Jeffers, "the mere common sense of our predicament as passionate bits of earth and water." . . . The setting of *Cawdor* is monstrous, the symbols excessive, the speech of his characters unreal; yet the backgrounds are not much more tragic than Jeffers' own weird Carmel coast and his people move in an atmosphere larger if more forbidding than reality. As in his other work, exaggerations of lust and violence outdo each other; but these, which in a lesser man would be absurd, are compelling because of the sheer force behind them and the malefic universe they imply.

This force is not only inherent in Jeffers' extraordinary language, but in his demonic search for ultimates. He disdains the illusions by which man makes life endurable: love, nature, the mind—these are all self-destructive and useless. Quiet is empty denial and peace a forlorn hope. Death seems the one freedom, "the huge gift," but annihilation itself, he realizes, is impossible. There is left only despair—and this is the cry beneath Jeffers' strength. The longing for oblivion explains his wild dreams, bloodshot landscapes, inhuman crimes, incests, brutalities, nightmare-struggles where life "drinks her defeat and devours her famine for food."

Thus he celebrates "the charm of the dark," enlarges on passions turned inward and men "all matted in one mesh"; he sings a frustrated *Dies Irae* to unresponding Nothingness. Therefore the things he loves best are rocks, black cypresses, depths of ocean, granite mountains—things that have their being without ambition, without hope, without consciousness.

But negation alone cannot explain the poet's dark persuasiveness. To Jeffers consciousness is the great curse of mankind; unconsciousness is the desirable state of nature. That man can never know such unconsciousness is what compels Jeffers' anguish and dictates his most impassioned lines. Impassioned they are, whatever one may think of the philosophy that prompts them, and an examination of Jeffers' utterance discloses a strange phenomenon: This poet preaches the gospel of Nothingness with an exuberant liveliness. He mourns, with inconsistent vigor, "the broken balance, the hopeless prostration of the earth under men's hands." His Jesus (in *Dear Judas*) is only an extension of the fanatically possessive Barclay (in *The Women at Point Sur*); even mystical passion becomes a high-pitched turbulence and love a last despair.

Thus Jeffers is in danger of emotional abandonment. His dramas are too often conditioned not by the exigencies of the situation nor by the demands of his characters, but by Jeffers' inverted violences. The chaos is self-generated; the didacticism no less didactic for being nullifying and uncontrolled; the imagination is too often disturbed by intellectual hysteria.

Dear Judas (1929) is composed of two long and a few short poems, the two longer ones bearing a relation to each other in the contrasted aspects of love, the shorter ones condensing Jeffers' philosophy into some of his finest moments. Like his other work, *Dear Judas* exhibits Jeffers projecting blind and bewildering Nature, misconceiving man as a "spectral episode." Here again is energy threshing in meaninglessness; here is force in need of a faith.

Thurso's Landing (1932) consists of one long poem and several highly characteristic shorter ones. The title-poem must rank among Jeffers' most important creations—a poem in which sheer power and eloquence triumph above black and unrelieved melodrama. Here again the *dramatis personae* are nakedly symbols of tortured humanity, "all compelled, all unhappy, all helpless." The idea dominating the book is the *idée fixe* which runs through all of Jeffers' volumes: Life is horrible. Love, as we practice it, is inverted and incestuous; not one self-adoring man in a million expresses outward-going passion. Death is the beautiful capricious savior, "the gay child with the gypsy eyes." Civilization is a transient sickness. Were the world free of this botch of humanity, this walking disease of consciousness, it would be a cleaner place, one in which the noble, impersonal elements would be at home. In a few thousand years this may well happen, and life will no longer be a torture for the living. Meanwhile our nature, "ignoble in its quiet times, mean in its pleasures, slavish in the mass" can, in its stricken moments, occasionally "shine terribly against the dark magnificence of things." Meanwhile we can learn from hawks and headlands; we can learn to bear; we can endure. Sometimes the philosophy is implicit in the action of Jeffers' characters; sometimes it is explicit, and the poet steps out of the drama to say:

. . . No life
Ought to be thought important in the weave of the world, whatever it may show of
courage or endured pain.
It owns no other manner of shining but to bear pain; for pleasure is too little, our
inhuman God is too great, thought is too lost.

The shorter poems in *Give Your Heart to the Hawks* (1934) and *Solstice* (1935), like those in the preceding volumes, are Jeffers at his most characteristic; condensation forces his pessimism into a rhythm that is both long and compact, like a tightly coiled spring. Several of the finest appeared in the 1927 issue of *A Miscellany of American Poetry* and were added to the popular edition of *Roan Stallion, Tamar and Other Poems,* brought out by The Modern Library in 1935. This excellent reprint also contains an introduction by the author which is a valuable piece of self-appraisal, especially in its estimate of "originality." "It seemed to me," says Jeffers, "that Mallarmé and his followers, renouncing intelligibility in order to concentrate the music of poetry, had turned off the road into a narrowing lane. Their successors could only make further renunciations; ideas had gone, now meter had gone, imagery would have to go; then recognizable emotions would have to go; perhaps at last even words might have to go or give up their meaning and nothing be left but musical syllables. Every advance required the elimination of some aspect of reality, and what could it profit me to know the direction of modern poetry if I did not like the direction? It was too much like putting out your eyes to cultivate the sense of hearing, or cutting off the right hand to develop the left. These austerities were not for me; originality by amputation was too painful for me."

Three years after distressing himself about "originality" Jeffers began to write *Tamar,* the work which was one of the most original of his generation. Superficially, because of his loose musical line, Jeffers seems to resemble Whitman, but his spirit is the very opposite of that rude yea-sayer's. Where Whitman lifts himself in all-embracing affirmations, Jeffers loses himself in all-inclusive negations.

Such Counsels You Gave to Me and Other Poems (1937) repeats all the notes of Jeffers' previous work, but it contains a new attempt at clarification. Man is still "a spectral episode" and "humanity is needless"; but, even in an inhuman and valueless universe, man inconsistently, stupidly, seeks for values. *The Selected Poetry of Robinson Jeffers* (1938), a book of 620 pages, reveals this self-contradiction on a large scale; *Be Angry at the Sun* (1941) half conceals it in a fiercely restrained bitterness. There is, first of all, the glorification of tragedy, of the struggle toward self-realization and the "ennobling" power of pain. And there is the insistence that all struggle is useless, that all values are inconsequential in a universe which flees "the contagion of consciousness that infects this corner of space." Joy leads to destruction, and terror is the reward of truth.

The Double Axe and Other Poems (1948) is Jeffers' most vehemently self-defeating work. In a prose preface Jeffers insists that he does not hate mankind, that he presents a philosophic attitude "which might be called Inhumanist . . . the rejection of human solipsism and recognition of transhuman magnificence." But his poems—and in particular the 114-page title poem—reiterate that this planet is encumbered with a destructive creature who is not only irresponsible but irrelevant, a peeled ape teetering on his back legs, an absurd and temporary intrusion. "The human race is bound to defile," argues Jeffers. "Whatever is public—land, thoughts, or women—is dull, dirty and debauched." Yet, though mankind ought to be scrapped, "ground like fish-meal for soil-food," there still remains "the endless inhuman beauty of things—and endurance, endurance, death's nobler cousin."

The Double Axe caused an angry stir not so much because of the poems but because of Jeffers' prefatory statement that humanity would have been better off had the United States not "intervened" in the Second World War. *Hungerfield and Other Poems* (1954) is a continuation of his bitter misanthropy, a grim insistence that the world will be well only when our sick civilization dies and disappears.

One must, somehow, separate the idea and its expression, remembering that the poem transcends the experience and the personality that prompted it. Between Jeffers the philosopher and Jeffers the poet there is a significant dichotomy. The philosophy is negative, repetitious, dismal. The poetry, even when bitterest, is positive as any creative expression must be. It is varied in movement and color; it vibrates with a reckless fecundity; it is continually breaking through it own pattern to dangerous and unfathomed depths. This is not a work to be enjoyed without sacrificing that sense of ease dear to the casual reader; it is doubtful if, in the common sense, it can be "enjoyed" at all. But here is a full-throated poetry, remarkable in sheer drive and harrowing drama, a poetry we may never love but which we cannot forget.

COMPENSATION

Solitude that unmakes me one of men
In snow-white hands brings singular recompense,
Evening me with kindlier natures when
On the needled pinewood the cold dews condense

About the hour of Rigel fallen from heaven
In wintertime, or when the long night tides
Sigh blindly from the sand-dune backward driven,
Or when on stormwings of the northwind rides
The foamscud with the cormorants, or when passes
A horse or dog with brown affectionate eyes,
Or autumn frosts are pricked by earliest grasses,
Or whirring from her covert a quail flies.
Why, even in humanity, beauty and good
Show from the mountainside of solitude.

AGE IN PROSPECT

Praise youth's hot blood if you will, I think that happiness
Rather consists in having lived clear through
Youth and hot blood, on to the wintrier hemisphere
Where one has time to wait and to remember.

Youth and hot blood are beautiful, so is peacefulness.
Youth had some islands in it, but age is indeed
An island and a peak; age has infirmities,
Not few, but youth is all one fever.

To look around and to love in his appearances,
Though a little calmly, the universal God's
Beauty is better I think than to lip eagerly
The mother's breast or another woman's.

And there is no possession more sure than memory's;
But if I reach that gray island, that peak,
My hope is still to possess with eyes the homeliness
Of ancient loves, ocean and mountains,

And meditate the sea-mouth of mortality
And the fountain six feet down with a quieter thirst
Than now I feel for old age; a creature progressively
Thirsty for life will be for death too.

ANTE MORTEM

It is likely enough that lions and scorpions
Guard the end; life never was bonded to be endurable nor the act of dying
Unpainful; the brain burning too often
Earns, though it held itself detached from the object, often a burnt age.
No matter, I shall not shorten it by hand.
Incapable of body or unmoved of brain is no evil, one always went envying
The quietness of stones. But if the striped blossom
Insanity spread lewd splendors and lightning terrors at the end of the forest;
Or intolerable pain work its known miracle,
Exile the monarch soul, set a sick monkey in the office . . . remember me
Entire and balanced when I was younger,
And could lift stones, and comprehend in the praises the cruelties of life.

POST MORTEM

Happy people die whole, they are all dissolved in a moment, they have had what they wanted,
No hard gifts; the unhappy
Linger a space, but pain is a thing that is glad to be forgotten; but one who has given
His heart to a cause or a country,
His ghost may spaniel it a while, disconsolate to watch it. I was wondering how long the spirit
That sheds this verse will remain
When the nostrils are nipped, when the brain rots in its vault or bubbles in the violence of fire
To be ash in metal. I was thinking
Some stalks of the wood whose roots I married to the earth of this place will stand five centuries;
I held the roots in my hand,
The stems of the trees between two fingers; how many remote generations of women
Will drink joy from men's loins,
And dragged from between the thighs of what mothers will giggle at my ghost when it curses the axmen,
Gray impotent voice on the sea-wind,
When the last trunk falls? The women's abundance will have built roofs over all this foreland;
Will have buried the rock foundations
I laid here: the women's exuberance will canker and fail in its time and like clouds the houses
Unframe, the granite of the prime
Stand from the heaps: come storm and wash clean: the plaster is all run to the sea and the steel
All rusted; the foreland resumes
The form we loved when we saw it. Though one at the end of the age and far off from this place
Should meet my presence in a poem,
The ghost would not care but be here, long sunset shadow in the seams of the granite, and forgotten
The flesh, a spirit for the stone.

NOON

The pure air trembles, O pitiless God,
The air aches with flame on these gaunt rocks
Over the flat sea's face, the forest
Shakes in gales of piercing light.

But the altars are behind and higher
Where the great hills raise naked heads,
Pale antagonists in the reverberance
Of the pure air and the pitiless God.

On the domed skull of every hill
Who stand blazing with spread vans,
The arms uplifted, the eyes in ecstasy?

What wine has the God drunk, to sing
Violently in heaven, what wine his worshipers
Whose silence blazes? The light that is over
Light, the terror of noon, the eyes
That the eagles die at, have thrown down
Me and my pride, here I lie naked
In a hollow of the shadowless rocks,
Full of the God, having drunk fire.

CLOUDS OF EVENING

Enormous cloud-mountains that form over Point Lobos and into the sunset,
Figures of fire on the walls of tonight's storm,
Foam of gold in gorges of fire, and the great file of warrior angels:
Dreams gathering in the curdled brain of the earth—
The sky the brain-vault—on the threshold of sleep: poor earth, you, like your children
By inordinate desires tortured, make dreams?
Storms more enormous, wars nobler, more toppling mountains, more jeweled waters, more free
Fires on impossible headlands . . . as a poor girl
Wishing her lover taller and more desirous, and herself maned with gold,
Dreams the world right, in the cold bed, about dawn.
Dreams are beautiful; the slaves of form are beautiful also; I have grown to believe
A stone is a better pillow than many visions.

TO THE STONE-CUTTERS

Stone-cutters fighting time with marble, you foredefeated
Challengers of oblivion,
Eat cynical earnings, knowing rock splits, records fall down,
The square-limbed Roman letters
Scale in the thaws, wear in the rain. The poet as well
Builds his monument mockingly;
For man will be blotted out, the blithe earth die, the brave sun
Die blind, his heart blackening:
Yet stones have stood for a thousand years, and pained thoughts found
The honey of peace in old poems.

GALE IN APRIL

Intense and terrible beauty, how has our race with the frail naked nerves,
So little a craft swum down from its far launching?
Why now, only because the northwest blows and the headed grass billows,
Great seas jagging the west and on the granite

Blanching, the vessel is brimmed, this dancing play of the world is too much passion.
A gale in April so overfilling the spirit,
Though his ribs were thick as the earth's, arches of mountain, how shall one dare to live,
Though his blood were like the earth's rivers and his flesh iron,
How shall one dare to live? One is born strong, how do the weak endure it?
The strong lean upon death as on a rock,
After eighty years there is shelter and the naked nerves shall be covered with deep quietness.
O beauty of things, go on, go on, O torture
Of intense joy, I have lasted out my time, I have thanked God and finished,
Roots of millenial trees fold me in the darkness,
Northwest winds shake their tops, not to the root, not to the root, I have passed
From beauty to the other beauty, peace, the night splendor.

APOLOGY FOR BAD DREAMS

I

In the purple light, heavy with redwood, the slopes drop seaward,
Headlong convexities of forest, drawn in together to the steep ravine. Below, on the sea-cliff,
A lonely clearing; a little field of corn by the streamside; a roof under spared trees. Then the ocean
Like a great stone someone has cut to a sharp edge and polished to shining. Beyond it, the fountain
And furnace of incredible light flowing up from the sunk sun. In the little clearing a woman
Was punishing a horse; she had tied the halter to a sapling at the edge of the wood; but when the great whip
Clung to the flanks the creature kicked so hard she feared he would snap the halter! she called from the house
The young man her son; who fetched a chain tie-rope, they working together
Noosed the small rusty links round the horse's tongue
And tied him by the swollen tongue to the tree.
Seen from this height they are shrunk to insect size,
Out of all human relation. You cannot distinguish
The blood dripping from where the chain is fastened,
The beast shuddering; but the thrust neck and the legs
Far apart. You can see the whip fall on the flanks. . . .
The gesture of the arm. You cannot see the face of the woman.
The enormous light beats up out of the west across the cloud-bars of the trade-wind. The ocean
Darkens, the high clouds brighten, the hills darken together. Unbridled and unbelievable beauty
Covers the evening world . . . not covers, grows apparent out of it, as Venus down there grows out
From the lit sky. What said the prophet? "I create good: and I create evil: I am the Lord."

II

This coast crying out for tragedy like all beautiful places,
(The quiet ones ask for quieter suffering; but here the granite cliff the gaunt cypresses' crown
Demands what victim? The dykes of red lava and black what Titan? The hills like pointed flames
Beyond Soberanes, the terrible peaks of the bare hills under the sun, what immolation?)
This coast crying out for tragedy like all beautiful places: and like the passionate spirit of humanity
Pain for its bread: God's, many victims', the painful deaths, the horrible transfigurements: I said in my heart,
"Better invent than suffer: imagine victims
Lest your own flesh be chosen the agonist, or you
Martyr some creature to the beauty of the place." And I said,
"Burn sacrifices once a year to magic
Horror away from the house, this little house here
You have built over the ocean with your own hands
Beside the standing bowlders: for what are we,
The beast that walks upright, with speaking lips
And little hair, to think we should always be fed,
Sheltered, intact, and self-controlled? We sooner more liable
Than the other animals. Pain and terror, the insanities of desire; not accidents, but essential,
And crowd up from the core." I imagined victims for those wolves, I made the phantoms to follow.
They have hunted the phantoms and missed the house. It is not good to forget over what gulfs the spirit
Of the beauty of humanity, the petal of a lost flower blown seaward by the night-wind, floats to its quietness.

III

Bowlders blunted like an old bear's teeth break up from the headland; below them
All the soil is thick with shells, the tide-rock feasts of a dead people.
Here the granite flanks are scarred with ancient fire, the ghosts of the tribe
Crouch in the nights beside the ghost of a fire, they try to remember the sunlight,
Light has died out of their skies. These have paid something for the future
Luck of the country, while we living keep old griefs in memory: though God's
Envy is not a likely fountain of ruin, to forget evil calls down
Sudden reminders from the cloud: remembered deaths be our redeemers;
Imagined victims our salvation: white as the half moon at midnight
Someone flamelike passed me, saying, "I am Tamar Cauldwell, I have my desire,"
Then the voice of the sea returned, when she had gone by, the stars to their towers.
. . . Beautiful country, burn again, Point Pinos down to the Sur Rivers
Burn as before with bitter wonders, land and ocean and the Carmel water.

IV

He brays humanity in a mortar to bring the savor
From the bruised root: a man having bad dreams, who invents victims, is only the ape of that God.
He washes it out with tears and many waters, calcines it with fire in the red crucible,

Deforms it, makes it horrible to itself: the spirit flies out and stands naked, he sees the spirit.
He takes it in the naked ecstasy; it breaks in his hand, the atom is broken, the power that massed it
Cries to the power that moves the stars, "I have come home to myself, behold me.
I bruised myself in the flint mortar and burnt me
In the red shell, I tortured myself, I flew forth,
Stood naked of myself and broke me in fragments,
And here am I moving the stars that are me."
I have seen these ways of God: I know of no reason
For fire and change and torture and the old returnings.
He being sufficient might be still. I think they admit no reason; they are the ways of my love.
Unmeasured power, incredible passion, enormous craft: no thought apparent but burns darkly
Smothered with its own smoke in the human brain-vault: no thought outside: a certain measure in phenomena:
The fountains of the boiling stars, the flowers on the foreland, the ever-returning roses of dawn.

PROMISE OF PEACE

The heads of strong old age are beautiful
Beyond all grace of youth. They have strange quiet,
Integrity, health, soundness, to the full
They've dealt with life and been attempered by it.
A young man must not sleep; his years are war
Civil and foreign but the former's worse;
But the old can breathe in safety now that they are
Forgetting what youth meant, the being perverse,
Running the fool's gauntlet and being cut
By the whips of the five senses. As for me,
If I should wish to live long it were but
To trade those fevers for tranquillity,
Thinking though that's entire and sweet in the grave
How shall the dead taste the deep treasure they have?

BIRTH-DUES

Joy is a trick in the air; pleasure is merely contemptible, the dangled
Carrot the ass follows to market or precipice;
But limitary pain—the rock under the tower and the hewn coping
That takes thunder at the head of the turret—
Terrible and real. Therefore a mindless dervish carving himself
With knives will seem to have conquered the world.

The world's God is treacherous and full of unreason; a torturer, but also
The only foundation and the only fountain.
Who fights him eats his own flesh and perishes of hunger; who hides in the grave
To escape him is dead; who enters the Indian
Recession to escape him is dead; who falls in love with the God is washed clean
Of death desired and of death dreaded.

He has joy, but joy is a trick in the air; and pleasure, but pleasure is contemptible;
And peace; and is based on solider than pain.
He has broken boundaries a little and that will estrange him; he is monstrous, but not
To the measure of the God. . . . But I having told you—
However I suppose that few in the world have energy to hear effectively—
Have paid my birth-dues; am quits with the people.

SUMMER HOLIDAY

When the sun shouts and people abound
One thinks there were the ages of stone and the age of bronze
And the iron age; iron the unstable metal;
Steel made of iron, unstable as his mother; the towered-up cities
Will be stains of rust on mounds of plaster.
Roots will not pierce the heaps for a time, kind rains will cure them,
Then nothing will remain of the iron age
And all these people but a thigh-bone or so, a poem
Stuck in the world's thought, splinters of glass
In the rubbish dumps, a concrete dam far off in the mountain. . . .

CREDO

My friend from Asia has powers and magic, he plucks a blue leaf from the young blue-gum
And gazing upon it, gathering and quieting
The God in his mind, creates an ocean more real than the ocean, the salt, the actual
Appalling presence, the power of the waters.
He believes that nothing is real except as we make it.
I humbler have have found in my blood
Bred west of Caucasus a harder mysticism.
Multitude stands in my mind but I think that the ocean in the bone vault is only
The bone vault's ocean: out there is the ocean's;
The water is the water, the cliff is the rock, come shocks and flashes of reality. The mind
Passes, the eye closes, the spirit is a passage;
The beauty of things was born before eyes and sufficient to itself; the heart-breaking beauty
Will remain when there is no heart to break for it.

PELICANS

Four pelicans went over the house,
Sculled their worn oars over the courtyard: I saw that ungainliness
Magnifies the idea of strength.
A lifting gale of sea-gulls followed them; slim yachts of the element,
Natural growths of the sky, no wonder
Light wings to leave sea; but those grave weights toil, and are powerful,
And the wings torn with old storms remember
The cone that the oldest redwood dropped from, the tilting of continents,

The dinosaur's day, the lift of new sea-lines.
The omnisecular spirit keeps the old with the new also.
Nothing at all has suffered erasure.
There is life not of our time. He calls ungainly bodies
As beautiful as the grace of horses.
He is weary of nothing; he watches air-planes; he watches pelicans.

LOVE THE WILD SWAN

"I hate my verses, every line, every word,
Oh pale and brittle pencils ever to try
One grass-blade's curve, or the throat of one bird
That clings to twig, ruffled against white sky.
Oh cracked and twilight mirrors ever to catch
One color, one glinting flash, of the splendor of things.
Unlucky hunter, Oh bullets of wax,
The lion beauty, the wild-swan wings, the storm of the wings."
—This wild swan of a world is no hunter's game.
Better bullets than yours would miss the white breast,
Better mirrors than yours would crack in the flame.
Does it matter whether you hate your . . . self? At least
Love your eyes that can see, your mind that can
Hear the music, the thunder of the wings. Love the wild swan.

NIGHT

The ebb slips from the rock, the sunken
Tide-rocks lift streaming shoulders
Out of the slack, the slow west
Sombering its torch; a ship's light
Shows faintly, far out,
Over the weight of the prone ocean
On the low cloud.

Over the dark mountain, over the dark pinewood,
Down the long dark valley along the shrunken river,
Returns the splendor without rays, the shining shadow,
Peace-bringer, the matrix of all shining and quieter of shining.
Where the shore widens on the bay she opens dark wings
And the ocean accepts her glory. O soul worshipful of her
You, like the ocean, have grave depths where she dwells always,
And the film of waves above that takes the sun takes also
Her, with more love. The sun-lovers have a blond favorite,
A father of lights and noises, wars, weeping and laughter,
Hot labor, lust and delight and the other blemishes.
Quietness
Flows from her deeper fountain; and he will die; and she is immortal.

Far off from here the slender
Flocks of the mountain forest

Move among stems like towers
Of the old redwoods to the stream,
No twig crackling; dip shy
Wild muzzles into the mountain water
Among the dark ferns.

O passionately at peace you being secure will pardon
The blasphemies of glowworms, the lamp in my tower, the fretfulness
Of cities, the crescents of the planets, the pride of the stars.
This August night in a rift of cloud Antares reddens,
The great one, the ancient torch, a lord among lost children,
The earth's orbit doubled would not girdle his greatness, one fire
Globed, out of grasp of the mind enormous; but to you
O Night
What? Not a spark? What flicker of a spark in the faint far glimmer
Of a lost fire dying in the desert, dim coals of a sand-pit the Bedouins
Wandered from at dawn. . . . Ah singing prayer to what gulfs tempted
Suddenly are you more lost? To us the near-hand mountain
Be a measure of height, the tide-worn cliff at the sea-gate a measure of continuance.

The tide, moving the night's
Vastness with lonely voices,
Turns, the deep dark-shining
Pacific leans on the land,
Feeling his cold strength
To the outmost margins: you Night will resume
The stars in your time.

O passionately at peace when will that tide draw shoreward,
Truly the spouting fountains of light, Antares, Arcturus,
Tire of their flow, they sing one song but they think silence.
The striding winter-giant Orion shines, and dreams darkness.
And life, the flicker of men and moths and the wolf on the hill,
Though furious for continuance, passionately feeding, passionately
Remaking itself upon its mates, remembers deep inward
The calm mother, the quietness of the womb and the egg,
The primal and the latter silences: dear Night it is memory
Prophesies, prophecy that remembers, the charm of the dark.
And I and my people, we are willing to love the four-score years
Heartily; but as a sailor loves the sea, when the helm is for harbor.

Have men's minds changed,
Or the rock hidden in the deep of the waters of the soul
Broken the surface? A few centuries
Gone by, was none dared not to people
The darkness beyond the stars with harps and habitations.
But now, dear is the truth. Life is grown sweeter and lonelier,
And death is no evil.

SHINE, PERISHING REPUBLIC

While this America settles in the mold of its vulgarity, heavily thickening to empire,
And protest, only a bubble in the molten mass, pops and sighs out, and the mass
hardens,

I sadly smiling remember that the flower fades to make fruit, the fruit rots to make
earth.
Out of the mother; and through the spring exultances, ripeness and decadence; and
home to the mother.

You making haste, haste on decay: not blameworthy; life is good, be it stubbornly
long or suddenly
A mortal splendor: meteors are not needed less than mountains: shine, perishing
republic.

But for my children, I would have them keep their distance from the thickening
center; corruption
Never has been compulsory, when the cities lie at the monster's feet there are left
the mountains.

And boys, be in nothing so moderate as in love of man, a clever servant, insufferable
master.
There is the trap that catches noblest spirits, that caught—they say—God, when he
walked on earth.

DIVINELY SUPERFLUOUS BEAUTY

The storm-dances of gulls, the barking game of seals,
Over and under the ocean . . .
Divinely superfluous beauty
Rules the games, presides over destinies, makes trees grow
And hills tower, waves fall.
The incredible beauty of joy
Stars with fire the joining of lips, O let our loves too
Be joined, there is not a maiden
Burns and thirsts for love
More than my blood for you, by the shore of seals while the wings
Weave like a web in the air
Divinely superfluous beauty.

HURT HAWKS

The broken pillar of the wing jags from the clotted shoulder,
The wing trails like a banner in defeat,
No more to use the sky forever but live with famine
And pain in a few days: cat nor coyote
Will shorten the week of waiting for death, there is game without talons.

He stands under the oak-brush and waits
The lame feet of salvation: at night he remembers freedom

And flies in a dream, the dawns ruin it.
He is strong and pain is worse to the strong, incapacity is worse.
The curs of the day come and torment him
At distance, no one but death the redeemer will humble that head,
The intrepid readiness, the terrible eyes.
The wild God of the world is sometimes merciful to those
That ask mercy, not often to the arrogant.
You do not know him, you communal people, or you have forgotten him;
Intemperate and savage, the hawk remembers him;
Beautiful and wild, the hawks, and men that are dying remember him.

✣

I'd sooner, except the penalties, kill a man than a hawk; but the great redtail
Had nothing left but unable misery
From the bone too shattered for mending, the wing that trailed under his talons when he moved.
We had fed him six weeks, I gave him freedom,
He wandered over the foreland hill and returned in the evening, asking for death,
Not like a beggar, still eyed with the old
Implacable arrogance. I gave him the lead gift in the twilight.
What fell was relaxed,
Owl-downy, soft feminine feathers; but what
Soared: the fierce rush: the night-herons by the flooded river cried fear at its rising
Before it was quite unsheathed from reality.

PRESCRIPTION OF PAINFUL ENDS

Lucretius felt the change of the world in his time, the great republic coming to the height
Whence no way leads but downward, Plato in his time watched Athens
Dance the down path. The future is ever a misted landscape, no man foreknows it, but at cyclical turns
There is a change felt in the rhythm of events: as when an exhausted horse
Falters and recovers, then the rhythm of the running hoofbeats is altered, he will run miles yet,
But he must fall: we have felt it again in our own lifetime, slip, shift and speed-up
In the gallop of the world, and now suspect that, come peace or war, the progress of America and Europe
Becomes a long process of deterioration—starred with famous Byzantiums and Alexandrias,
Surely,—but downward. One desires at such times
To gather the insights of the age summit against future loss, against the narrowing minds and the tyrants,
The pedants, the mystagogues, the swarms of barbarians: time-conscious poems, poems for treasuries: Lucretius
Sings his great theory of natural origins and of wise conduct; Plato smiling carves dreams, bright cells
Of incorruptible wax to hive the Greek honey.

Our own time, much greater
and far less fortunate

Has acids for honey and for fine dreams
The immense vulgarities of misapplied science and decaying Christianity: therefore one christens each poem, in dutiful
Hope of burning off at least the top crust of the time's uncleanness, from the acid bottles.

MAY-JUNE, 1940

Foreseen for so many years: these evils, this monstrous violence, these massive agonies: no easier to bear.
We saw them with slow stone strides approach, everyone saw them; we closed our eyes against them, we looked
And they had come nearer. We ate and drank and slept, they came nearer. Sometimes we laughed, they were nearer. Now
They are here. And now a blind man foresees what follows them: degradation, famine, recovery and so forth, and the
Epidemic manias: but not enough death to serve us, not enough death. It would be better for men
To be few and live far apart, where none could infect another; then slowly the sanity of field and mountain
And the cold ocean and glittering stars might enter their minds.

Another
dream, another dream.
We shall have to accept certain limitations
In future, and abandon some humane dreams; only hard-minded, sleepless and realist, can ride this rock-slide
To new fields down the dark mountain; and we shall have to perceive that these insanities are normal;
We shall have to perceive that battle is a burning flower or like a huge music, and the dive-bomber's screaming orgasm
As beautiful as other passions; and that death and life are not serious alternatives. One has known all these things
For many years: there is greater and darker to know
In the next hundred.

And why do you cry, my dear, why do you cry?
It is all in the whirling circles of time.
If millions are born millions must die,
If England goes down and Germany up
The stronger dog will still be on top,
All in the turning of time.
If civilization goes down, that
Would be an event to contemplate.
It will not be in our time, alas, my dear,
It will not be in our time.

THE INQUISITORS

Coming around a corner of the dark trail . . . what was wrong with the valley?
Azevedo checked his horse and sat staring: it was all changed. It was occupied. There were three hills
Where none had been: and firelight flickered red on their knees between them: if they were hills:
They were more like Red Indians around a camp-fire grave and dark, mountain-high, hams on heels
Squating around a little fire of hundred-foot logs. Azevedo remembers he felt an ice-brook
Glide on his spine; he slipped down from the saddle and hid
In the brush by the trail, above the black redwood forest. There was the Little Sur South Fork,
Its forest valley; the man had come in at nightfall over Bowcher's Gap, and a high moon hunted
Through running clouds. He heard the rumble of a voice, heavy not loud, saying, "I gathered some,
You can inspect them." One of the hills moved a huge hand
And poured its contents on a table-topped rock that stood in the firelight; men and women fell out;
Some crawled and some lay quiet; the hills leaned to eye them. One said: "It seems hardly possible
Such fragile creatures could be so noxious." Another answered,
"True, but we've seen. But it is only recently they have the power." The third answered, "That bomb?"
"Oh," he said, "—and the rest." He reached across and picked up one of the mites from the rock, and held it
Close to his eyes, and very carefully with finger and thumbnail peeled it: by chance a young female
With long black hair: it was too helpless even to scream. He held it by one white leg and stared at it:
"I can see nothing strange: only so fragile." The third hill answered, "We suppose it is something
Inside the head." Then the other split the skull with his thumbnail, squinting his eyes and peering, and said,
"A drop of marrow. How could that spoil the earth?" "Nevertheless," he answered,
"They have that bomb. The blasts and the fires are nothing: freckles on the earth: the emanations
Might set the whole planet into a tricky fever
And destroy much." "Themselves," he answered. "Let them. Why not?" "No," he answered, "life."

Azevedo
Still watched in horror, and all three of the hills
Picked little animals from the rock, peeled them and cracked them, or toasted them
On the red coals, or split their bodies from the crotch upward
To stare inside. They said, "It remains a mystery. However," they said
"It is not likely they can destroy all life: the planet is capacious. Life would surely grow up again

From grubs in the soil, on the newt and toad level, and be beautiful again. And
again perhaps break its legs
On its own cleverness: who can forecast the future?" The speaker yawned, and
with his flat hand
Brushed the rock clean; the three slowly stood up,
Taller than Pico Blanco into the sky, their Indian-beaked heads in the moon-cloud,
And trampled their watchfire out and went away southward, stepping across the
Ventana mountains.

ORIGINAL SIN

The man-brained and man-handed ground-ape, physically
The most repulsive of all hot-blooded animals
Up to that time of the world: they had dug a pitfall
And caught a mammoth, but how could their sticks and stones
Reach the life in that hide? They danced around the pit, shrieking
With ape excitement, flinging sharp flints in vain, and the stench of their bodies
Stained the white air of dawn; but presently one of them
Remembered the yellow dancer, wood-eating fire
That guards the cave-mouth: he ran and fetched him, and others
Gathered sticks at the wood's edge; they made a blaze
And pushed it into the pit, and they fed it high, around the mired sides
Of their huge prey. They watched the long hairy trunk
Waver over the stifle-trumpeting pain,
And they were happy.
Meanwhile the intense color and nobility of sunrise,
Rose and gold and amber, flowed up the sky. Wet rocks were shining, a little wind
Stirred the leaves of the forest and the marsh flag-flowers; the soft valley between
the low hills
Became as beautiful as the sky; while in its midst, hour after hour, the happy
hunters
Roasted their living meat slowly to death.
These are the people.
This is the human dawn. As for me, I would rather
Be a worm in a wild apple than a son of man.
But we are what we are, and we might remember
Not to hate any person, for all are vicious;
And not to be astonished at any evil, all are deserved;
And not fear death; it is the only way to be cleansed.

T. S. Eliot

☙ Thomas Stearns Eliot was born in St. Louis, Missouri, September 26, 1888. He received his A.B. at Harvard, 1909, and his A.M., 1910. Subsequently, he studied at the Sorbonne and at Merton College, Oxford. In 1914 he settled in London where he became a teacher, lecturer, editor, and publisher. In 1927 he became a naturalized British subject and declared that he was "Anglo-Catholic in religion, royalist in politics, and classicist in literature."

Prufrock appeared in England in 1917. An American edition, including a number of other verses, was published under the title *Poems* in 1920. It was hailed, reviled, applauded, misunderstood, and imitated. There were indeed many imitators, particularly in England, where the younger men, rebounding from the affected simplicity of the Georgians, seized upon Eliot's disillusioned subtleties as a new gospel. Most of them patterned their lines upon the now famous "Sweeney" model, and by 1922 Eliot was one of the most discussed and disputed of living American poets. This early work reveals two sharply differentiated idioms. The more arresting inflection is in the impressionistic sets of quatrains that compose "Sweeney Among the Nightingales," "The Hippopotamus," "Burbank with a Baedeker." It is a witty if recondite inflection which is heard beneath the muffled allusions; the edged lines crackle with observations as shrewd as "the snarled and yelping seas," "this oval O cropped out with teeth," "laughter tinkling among the teacups," "the damp souls of housemaids." Occasionally Eliot's wit takes on a darker intensity; speaking of Donne's struggle to transcend the senses, he writes:

> He knew the anguish of the marrow,
> The ague of the skeleton;
> No contact possible of flesh
> Allayed the fever of the bone.

But there is another phase of Eliot, one that is disclosed in "The Love Song of J. Alfred Prufrock," the "Portrait of a Lady," and "La Figlia Che Piange," in which picture, philosophy, and music are surprisingly blended. "The Love Song of J. Alfred Prufrock," written while Eliot was still at Harvard, is a minor masterpiece; nothing in recent poetry (if we forget Laforgue and the other French poets to whom Eliot is manifestly indebted), nothing in English since the seventeenth century metaphysicals, has communicated so great a sense of ambiguous hurt and general frustration.

First and last Eliot represents a revolt from the "cheerfulness, optimism, and hopefulness" of the nineteenth century; his work is an implicit declaration that poetry must not only "be found *through* suffering, but can find its material only *in* suffering." Beauty itself is suspect in the modern world; Eliot insists that the poet should "be able to see beneath both beauty and ugliness; to see the boredom, and the horror, and the glory." In "The Love Song of J. Alfred Prufrock" Eliot shows the boredom and the horror, if not the glory, in contemporary society. The prematurely old Prufrock is a dilettante, culture-ridden and world-weary, aloof and disillusioned. He is inhibited by his own distorted memory and his confused desires; he recognizes passion, but he cannot rise to it. His isolation is emphasized by the strange opening simile ("when the evening is spread out against the sky like a patient etherized upon the table") with its mood of sick helplessness, and by the introductory lines from Dante's *Inferno:* "If I thought my answer were to one who ever could return to the world, this flame should shake no more; but since, if what I hear be true, none ever did return alive from this depth, without fear of infamy I answer thee." F. O. Matthiessen points out that the inscription from the *Inferno* underlines the closed circle of Prufrock's frightened loneliness. "Prufrock can give utterance in soliloquy to his debate with himself only because he knows no one will overhear him. The point of calling this poem a 'Love Song' lies in the irony that it will never be sung."

More important than Eliot's philosophy is his technique. It is a fascinating mixture of statement and suggestion, of passion and wit, of fact and symbol: the first extended use in English of the Symbolist method. The method, as Edmund Wilson showed in his valuable study *Axel's Castle,* is the result of an anti-scientific, romantic escapism; it consists chiefly in approximating the "indefiniteness of music," mingling "the grand and prosaic manners," and, generally, avoiding plain statements in favor of intimations. Instead of seeking the "jewel-like phrase" with its finality of definition, the Symbolists attempt to communicate "states of feeling." Eliot carries the method further by communicating—or at least registering—states of feeling that are complicated and highly personal. To achieve this he employs a complex verse, combining trivial and tawdry pictures with traditionally poetic subject-matter, linking the banalities of conversation to rich rhetoric, and interrupting the present with flash-backs of the past. This method, not unfamiliar to students of the films, makes for a nervous disintegration. The rapid and, seemingly, unrelated images, the discordant metaphors achieve an emotional response at the expense of a logical progression. But logic is not the objective. The reader is carried on by the rapidity of suggestions, by the swiftly accumulating ideas and echoes, chiefly by the play of cultural associations.

The contrast of the beautiful past with the repulsive present, the degradation of everything which enlarges the spirit, is given full scope in Eliot's *The Waste Land. The Waste Land* (1922) is Eliot's attempt to sound his recurring theme—the disillusion-frustration motif—on a major scale. The publication of this forty-page poem caused an outburst so violent and prolonged that the echoes of the controversy hung in the air for several years. On the one hand it was dismissed as "an impudent hoax," "filthy bedlam raving"; on the other it was exalted as "the greatest document of our day, showing the starvation of our entire civilization." *The Waste Land* is neither "erudite gibberish" nor is it "a great work, with one triumph after another." It is, in essence, a set of mangled, difficult, and (in spite of the arbitrary program of unification) separate failures and solitary successes. If its pages are splintered with broken phrases and distorted pictures, one must remember that Eliot is attempting to portray disintegration itself. Its dependence on associations in other literature makes it seem like an anthology of assimilations; its jumble of quotations (without inverted commas) from thirty-one sources gives the entire structure the look of a piece of literary carpentry; its allusiveness frantically attempts to connect the favorite myths of all time. It does, however, present a double picture: the cross-section of a tortured mind and the image of an arid world. Its sense of sterility, its refusal to face the growing complexity of the age was so significant—and so appealing to the escapists—that it became a term which characterized a period and added a new dimension to the language of poetry.

Eliot's influence was felt on both sides of the Atlantic. The younger poets repudiated his inverted romanticism masked as classicism, and his pessimism which scarcely troubled to conceal the death-wish, but they were fascinated by his technique. They scorned Eliot's withdrawal into Anglo-Catholicism, but they admired —and imitated—his power of suggestion. In England W. H. Auden, Stephen

Spender, and C. Day Lewis acknowledged his influence; in America his poetry affected the work of an entire generation. He lifted the prosaic tone to a pitch it had never attained.

In his turn, Eliot was strongly influenced by his "ancestors" in France. Reviewing Peter Quennell's *Baudelaire and the Symbolists* in 1930 he referred to Arthur Symons' *Symbolist Movement in Literature,* saying, "I myself owe Mr. Symons a great debt. But for having read his book I should not, in the year 1908, have heard of Laforgue and Rimbaud; I should probably not have begun to read Verlaine; and but for reading Verlaine, I should not have heard of Corbière. So the Symons book is one of those which have affected the course of my life." But, as Edmund Wilson points out, though Eliot's main theme (the inferiority of the present to the past) is found in Laforgue and the other Romantics, though the idea of juxtaposing many literatures and a medley of idioms was suggested by Ezra Pound, "yet Eliot manages to be more effective precisely where he might be expected to be least original—he succeeds in conveying his meanings, in communicating his emotions, in spite of all his learning or mysterious allusions, and whether we understand them or not. . . . He has been able to lend even to the rhythms, to the words themselves, of his great predecessors a new music and a new meaning." His borrowings are a proof of Eliot's retreat to the safety of literature; scholars have been surprised (and sometimes a little pained) to find many of Eliot's phrases not only in the minor Elizabethans, but (as Elizabeth Jackson discovered) in so curious a modern writer as Conan Doyle. The very "mottoes" or epigraphs are intended not only to comment upon the poems which they introduce, but to amplify their suggestiveness. "The Love Song of J. Alfred Prufrock" is prefaced by a quotation from Dante emphasizing the repressed Prufrock's ultra-fastidious and detached spirit; "Burbank with a Baedeker" is set off by the preceding jumble of phrases from Shakespeare, Browning, and Henry James referring to Venice; the quotation "Mistah Kurtz—he dead" from Conrad's *Heart of Darkness* intensifies the sense of loss and emptiness rising from the lines which follow—as F. O. Matthiessen remarks, it "epitomizes in a sentence the very tone of blasphemous hopelessness which issues from 'The Hollow Men.' "

In "The Hollow Men," which emphasizes the barrenness of *The Waste Land,* Eliot reached a dead end of doubt. "The Hollow Men" pictures a world exhausted —"shape without form, shade without color, paralyzed force, gesture without motion." Men gather on stony soil in a "valley of dying stars." They lean together, lacking initiative. They are without vision; they grope without thought. The confusion is intensified by the juxtaposition of a distorted nursery rhyme and a fragment from the Lord's Prayer. The finale completes the despair. Civilization, having lost its ideals and religion, has reached an impasse; man cannot even die heroically. The world ends not with a bang, but with a whimper.

After "The Hollow Men" Eliot, finding he could proceed no further with doubt, turned to faith. *Ash Wednesday* (1930), *The Rock: a Pageant Play* (1934), and *Murder in the Cathedral* (1935) express a hopefulness which Eliot's earlier poems repudiated. *The Family Reunion* (1939) is a drama in verse, the theme of which is the persistent sense of sin; the setting is contemporary, although the Eumenides appear in person. Eliot accepts the Christian religion and, beneath the austerity of the later work, sounds a compassion which is genuine and moving. Critics were particularly enthusiastic concerning *Ash Wednesday,* which begins in desperation, rises on hope, and rests in peaceful resignation. Here, said Edwin Muir, Eliot passes "from a historical conception of society to a religious one, or rather to that society within society in which he sees man's sole hope of salvation. A church is the only kind of institution in which the individual can hold communion not only with the living (the ideal of the Socialist and the Communist), but with the dead as well; and so membership of a church was perfectly consonant with Eliot's view of life and his development as a poet. *Ash Wednesday* is one of the most moving poems he has written, and perhaps the most perfect."

Murder in the Cathedral (1935), a dramatization of the murder of Thomas Becket in 1170, was written for production at the Canterbury Festival in 1935. The language is lucid, the action straightforward, and the poetry almost wholly free of the obliquity and harsh juxtaposition with which Eliot shocked an epoch out of its exhausted sentiments and offered new symbols for a new generation. Instead of a confusion of private references and literary allusions the verse has a simple unity, and the choruses are not only skillfully balanced but impassioned. The play was successfully produced in New York by the Federal Theater Project in 1938 and became a contemporary classic.

Collected Poems: 1907-1935 appeared in 1936. It comprehensively reveals Eliot struggling through his nightmares of vulgarity, crying aloud in an endless cactus land, and finally reaching his spiritual haven. Again the critics were divided. "Reading Eliot's new poems," wrote Malcolm Cowley, "was like excavating buried cities at the ends of the Syrian desert; they were full of imposing temples and perfectly proportioned statues of the gods; but there was nothing in the streets that breathed." Others suggested that Eliot, an American living in England, wrote like a man without a country and his poetry was a sublimation of the expatriate's sense of rootlessness. But most commentators accepted Eliot as a cultural phenomenon who was a constant challenge. His challenge, it was generally agreed, was to a civilization that had lost spiritual significance and had devoted itself to material standards and mechanical escapes. As he wrote in *The Rock:*

> And the wind shall say: "Here were decent godless people:
> Their only monument the asphalt road
> And a thousand lost golf balls."

"He despairs with humility and reverence," wrote Marjorie Brace. "He hopes without optimism; he seeks beyond hope and despair: a position alien to a time intricately dominated by the lure of power." After *Ash Wednesday* Eliot made the religious note the chief element of his poetry.

Eliot's later theme of pain and penitence, remorse and redemption, reaches its highest expression in *Four Quartets* (1943). The title prompted several reviewers to compare the work with Beethoven's later quartets in intention as well as execution. Beethoven fashioned a music to reach beyond music; Eliot planned a poetry to stretch the mind beyond the reasoning brain—"the hint half guessed, the gift half understood." In the third section ("The Dry Salvages") Eliot says explicitly:

> For most of us there is only the unattended
> Moment, the moment in and out of time,
> The distraction fit, lost in a shaft of sunlight.

. . . or music heard so deeply
That it is not heard at all, but you are the music
While the music lasts.

Each section of *Four Quartets* bears a title which is the name of a place associated with Eliot's experiences, and each stresses Eliot's main preoccupations: the sense of time and the sense of poetry. The style is both simpler and subtler than anything the author had previously written. The language ranges from conversational and flatly prosaic statements to rapt and mystical rhetoric. The allusions are remote, but not nearly as complex as those in *The Waste Land,* where, in the concluding eight lines, Eliot telescoped quotations from half a dozen languages, from sources as familiar as Mother Goose and as recondite as the Upanishad. Structurally *Four Quartets* is intricate with closely interwoven themes and variations. It unfolds design within design. Some of the patterns are fairly obvious: the manipulation of four-part harmonies; the mixed symbols of the four seasons and the four elements; the dexterous alternation of slow unrhymed monologues and rapidly rhymed lyrics. Seldom has a poet used repetition more skillfully. The refrain of time present and time past ("both perhaps present in time future"), the conflict between time and timelessness, is accompanied by a set of meditations on the difficulty of communication. Eliot complains of the twenty years between two wars largely wasted, "trying to learn to use words, and every attempt / Is a wholly new start, and a different kind of failure / Because one has only learnt to get the better of words / For the thing one no longer has to say." Therefore "the intolerable wrestle with words and meanings" is a struggle to recover "what has been lost and found and lost again"; each poem is a fresh uncertainty, "a raid on the inarticulate / With shabby equipment always deteriorating / In the general mess of imprecision of feeling."

Eliot's counterpoint of personal experience and private speculation is not easy to follow. Only the erudite reader will be able to thread his way through a montage of Milton, Dante, St. John of the Cross, the Bhagavad-Gita, and Eliot's own symbols. Nevertheless, the reader will find it hard to resist the emotional impact of *Four Quartets,* its burden of suffering and expiation, its grave beauty, and the music carrying the dominant idea of "dying into life."

In November, 1948, Eliot was awarded the Nobel Prize "for his work as a trail-blazing pioneer of modern poetry." He had already received the British Order of Merit. At sixty, Eliot was the most discussed of living poets. Ten full-length books were devoted to him; one of his commentators listed 263 critical studies, including theses, magazine articles, pamphlets, chapters, and volumes of appraisal—a number that was greatly increased after Eliot won the Nobel Prize.

In his sixties Eliot startled his critics and his admirers as a successful dramatist and, even more to their surprise, as a writer of comedies. *The Cocktail Party* (1950), *The Confidential Clerk* (1954), and *The Elder Statesman* (1958) are brilliant, ironic, and penetrating plays. In poetry smoothly flowing as good speech, Eliot combines smart repartee and somber philosophy, a criticism of contemporary society and an allegory of faith and salvation.

Of the many volumes devoted to Eliot, the best critical studies of the poet's work are *The Achievement of T. S. Eliot* (1947) by F. O. Matthiessen; *T. S. Eliot: A Study of His Writings by Several Hands* (1948) by B. Rajan; *T. S. Eliot: A*

Selected Critique (1948) by Leonard Unger; and *T. S. Eliot: The Design of His Poetry* (1949) by Elizabeth Drew.

Eliot's leadership in esthetic criticism has been debated, but he has established his place in several volumes, notably in *Selected Essays: 1917-1932. The Use of Poetry* (1933) was followed by *After Strange Gods: A Primer of Modern Heresy* (1934) and *Elizabethan Essays* (1934). Eliot abandoned the questioning attitude of his early work and assumed a position so conservative as to seem reactionary. Many of his admirers were alarmed by the lectures given at the University of Virginia and those collected in *The Idea of a Christian Society* (1940). Pointing out the destructive element in Eliot's Puritan conscience which, convinced of guilt, strives desperately toward Catholicism, Stephen Spender wrote, "It is in fact an Old Testament doctrine suited to intense nationalism and racial self-sufficiency." Horace Gregory, in a review written in 1936, anticipated Spender: "It is toward this danger that Eliot has been moving for the past five years, a danger which may at last obscure the values of his poetry and leave him, at the end of a career, an isolated symbol of post-war sensibility." Eliot was again attacked for *Notes Towards the Definition of Culture* (1949). It was charged that Eliot wrote in the roles of scientist and anthropologist without defining his terms. His philosophy was considered dogmatic and dubious; his conclusions were challenged; even his disciples questioned his pessimism: "Our own period is one of decline. The standards of culture are lower than they were fifty years ago. . . . I see no reason why the decay of culture should not proceed much further, and why we may not even anticipate a period, of some duration, of which it is possible to say that it will have *no* culture."

No one, however, questioned the poet's sensibility. Unlike Eliot's stiff and somewhat pontifical prose, the poetry is difficult but exciting. Eliot's theory, carried out in his practice, calls for unusual compression and ellipsis, a condensation so great that many moods and multiple allusions are expressed simultaneously. If the method demands intense concentration on the part of the reader, it rewards him with rich suggestiveness. The poet's progress from disgust through doubt to belief—from time to eternity, "at the still point of the turning world"—is registered in a poetry of the greatest seriousness and the highest integrity. If, like the prose, the poetry seems to be conditioned by a plethora of literary references and, because of its ambiguities, sometimes seems to lead the reader two ways at once, it stands not only as a significant document of its day but as a small body of troubled, often puzzling, but always poignant eloquence.

THE LOVE SONG OF J. ALFRED PRUFROCK

S'io credesse che mia risposta fosse
A persona che mai tornasse al mondo,
Questa fiamma staria senza piu scosse.
Ma perciocche giammai di questo fondo
Non torno vivo alcun, s'i'odo il vero,
Senza tema d'infamia ti rispondo.

Let us go then, you and I,
When the evening is spread out against the sky
Like a patient etherized upon a table;
Let us go, through certain half-deserted streets,

The muttering retreats
Of restless nights in one-night cheap hotels
And sawdust restaurants with oyster-shells:
Streets that follow like a tedious argument
Of insidious intent
To lead you to an overwhelming question. . . .
Oh, do not ask, "What is it?"
Let us go and make our visit.

In the room the women come and go
Talking of Michelangelo.

The yellow fog that rubs its back upon the window-panes,
The yellow smoke that rubs its muzzle on the window-panes,
Licked its tongue into the corners of the evening,
Lingered upon the pools that stand in drains,
Let fall upon its back the soot that falls from chimneys,
Slipped by the terrace, made a sudden leap,
And seeing that it was a soft October night,
Curled once about the house, and fell asleep.

And indeed there will be time
For the yellow smoke that slides along the street,
Rubbing its back upon the window-panes;
There will be time, there will be time
To prepare a face to meet the faces that you meet;
There will be time to murder and create,
And time for all the works and days of hands
That lift and drop a question on your plate;
Time for you and time for me,
And time yet for a hundred indecisions,
And for a hundred visions and revisions,
Before the taking of a toast and tea.

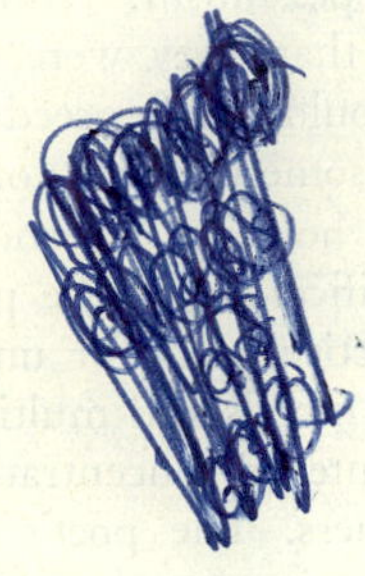

In the room the women come and go
Talking of Michelangelo.

And indeed there will be time
To wonder, "Do I dare?" and, "Do I dare?"
Time to turn back and descend the stair,
With a bald spot in the middle of my hair—
(They will say: "How his hair is growing thin!")
My morning coat, my collar mounting firmly to the chin,
My necktie rich and modest, but asserted by a simple pin—
(They will say: "But how his arms and legs are thin!")
Do I dare
Disturb the universe?
In a minute there is time
For decisions and revisions which a minute will reverse.

For I have known them all already, known them all:
Have known the evenings, mornings, afternoons,
I have measured out my life with coffee spoons;
I know the voices dying with a dying fall
Beneath the music from a farther room.
    So how should I presume?

And I have known the eyes already, known them all—
The eyes that fix you in a formulated phrase,
And when I am formulated, sprawling on a pin,
When I am pinned and wriggling on the wall,
Then how should I begin
To spit out all the butt-ends of my days and ways?
    And how should I presume?

And I have known the arms already, known them all—
Arms that are braceleted and white and bare
(But in the lamplight, downed with light brown hair!)
Is it perfume from a dress
That makes me so digress?
Arms that lie along a table, or wrap about a shawl,
    And should I then presume?
    And how should I begin?

✣

Shall I say, I have gone at dusk through narrow streets
And watched the smoke that rises from the pipes
Of lonely men in shirt-sleeves, leaning out of windows? . . .

I should have been a pair of ragged claws
Scuttling across the floors of silent seas.

✣

And the afternoon, the evening, sleeps so peacefully!
Smoothed by long fingers,
Asleep . . . tired . . . or it malingers,
Stretched on the floor, here beside you and me.
Should I, after tea and cakes and ices,
Have the strength to force the moment to its crisis?
But though I have wept and fasted, wept and prayed,
Though I have seen my head (grown slightly bald) brought in upon a platter,
I am no prophet—and here's no great matter;
I have seen the moment of my greatness flicker,
And I have seen the eternal Footman hold my coat, and snicker,
And in short, I was afraid.

And would it have been worth it, after all,
After the cups, the marmalade, the tea,
Among the porcelain, among some talk of you and me,

Would it have been worth while,
To have bitten off the matter with a smile,
To have squeezed the universe into a ball
To roll it toward some overwhelming question,
To say: "I am Lazarus, come from the dead,
Come back to tell you all, I shall tell you all"—
If one, settling a pillow by her head,
    Should say: "That is not what I meant at all;
    That is not it, at all."

And would it have been worth it, after all,
Would it have been worth while,
After the sunsets and the dooryards and the sprinkled streets,
After the novels, after the teacups, after the skirts that trail along the floor—
And this, and so much more?—
It is impossible to say just what I mean!
But as if a magic lantern threw the nerves in patterns on a screen:
Would it have been worth while
If one, settling a pillow or throwing off a shawl,
And turning toward the window, should say:
    "That is not it at all,
    That is not what I meant, at all."

✣

No! I am not Prince Hamlet, nor was meant to be;
Am an attendant lord, one that will do
To swell a progress, start a scene or two,
Advise the prince; no doubt, an easy tool,
Deferential, glad to be of use,
Politic, cautious, and meticulous;
Full of high sentence, but a bit obtuse;
At times, indeed, almost ridiculous—
Almost, at times, the Fool.

I grow old. . . . I grow old. . . .
I shall wear the bottoms of my trousers rolled.

Shall I part my hair behind? Do I dare to eat a peach?
I shall wear white flannel trousers, and walk upon the beach.
I have heard the mermaids singing, each to each.

I do not think that they will sing to me.

I have seen them riding seaward on the waves
Combing the white hair of the waves blown back
When the wind blows the water white and black.

We have lingered in the chambers of the sea
By sea-girls wreathed with seaweed red and brown
Till human voices wake us, and we drown.

THE WASTE LAND

"NAM Sibyllam quidem Cumis ego ipse oculis meis vidi in ampulla pendere, et cum illi pueri dicerent: Σίβυλλα τί θέλεις; *respondebat illa:* ἀποθανεῖν θέλω."

For Ezra Pound
il miglior fabbro

I. THE BURIAL OF THE DEAD

April is the cruellest month, breeding
Lilacs out of the dead land, mixing
Memory and desire, stirring
Dull roots with spring rain.
Winter kept us warm, covering
Earth in forgetful snow, feeding
A little life with dried tubers.
Summer surprised us, coming over the Starnbergersee
With a shower of rain; we stopped in the colonnade,
And went on in sunlight, into the Hofgarten, 10
And drank coffee, and talked for an hour.
Bin gar keine Russin, stamm' aus Litauen, echt deutsch.
And when we were children, staying at the archduke's,
My cousin's, he took me out on a sled,
And I was frightened. He said, Marie,
Marie, hold on tight. And down we went.
In the mountains, there you feel free.
I read, much of the night, and go south in the winter.

What are the roots that clutch, what branches grow
Out of this stony rubbish? Son of man, 20
You cannot say, or guess, for you know only
A heap of broken images, where the sun beats,
And the dead tree gives no shelter, the cricket no relief,
And the dry stone no sound of water. Only
There is shadow under this red rock,
(Come in under the shadow of this red rock),
And I will show you something different from either
Your shadow at morning striding behind you
Or your shadow at evening rising to meet you;
I will show you fear in a handful of dust. 30

Frisch weht der Wind
Der Heimat zu,
Mein Irisch Kind,
Wo weilest du?

"You gave me hyacinths first a year ago;
"They called me the hyacinth girl."
—Yet when we came back, late, from the Hyacinth garden,
Your arms full, and your hair wet, I could not
Speak, and my eyes failed, I was neither
Living nor dead, and I knew nothing, 40

Looking into the heart of light, the silence.
Od' und leer das Meer.

Madame Sosostris, famous clairvoyante,
Had a bad cold, nevertheless
Is known to be the wisest woman in Europe,
With a wicked pack of cards. Here, said she,
Is your card, the drowned Phoenician Sailor,
(Those are pearls that were his eyes. Look!)
Here is Belladonna, the Lady of the Rocks,
The lady of situations. 50
Here is the man with three staves, and here the Wheel,
And here is the one-eyed merchant, and this card,
Which is blank, is something he carries on his back,
Which I am forbidden to see. I do not find
The Hanged Man. Fear death by water.
I see crowds of people, walking round in a ring.
Thank you. If you see dear Mrs. Equitone,
Tell her I bring the horoscope myself:
One must be so careful these days.

Unreal City, 60
Under the brown fog of a winter dawn,
A crowd flowed over London Bridge, so many,
I had not thought death had undone so many.
Sighs, short and infrequent, were exhaled,
And each man fixed his eyes before his feet.
Flowed up the hill and down King William Street,
To where Saint Mary Woolnoth kept the hours
With a dead sound on the final stroke of nine.
There I saw one I knew, and stopped him, crying: "Stetson!
"You who were with me in the ships at Mylae! 70
"That corpse you planted last year in your garden,
"Has it begun to sprout? Will it bloom this year?
"Or has the sudden frost disturbed its bed?
"Oh keep the Dog far hence, that's friend to men,
"Or with his nails he'll dig it up again!
"You! hypocrite lecteur!—mon semblable,—mon frère!"

II. A GAME OF CHESS

The Chair she sat in, like a burnished throne,
Glowed on the marble, where the glass
Held up by standards wrought with fruited vines
From which a golden Cupidon peeped out 80
(Another hid his eyes behind his wing)
Doubled the flames of sevenbranched candelabra
Reflecting light upon the table as
The glitter of her jewels rose to meet it,
From satin cases poured in rich profusion;
In vials of ivory and coloured glass
Unstoppered, lurked her strange synthetic perfumes,

Unguent, powdered, or liquid—troubled, confused
And drowned the sense in odours; stirred by the air
That freshened from the window, these ascended   90
In fattening the prolonged candle-flames,
Flung their smoke into the laquearia,
Stirring the pattern on the coffered ceiling.
Huge sea-wood fed with copper
Burned green and orange, framed by the coloured stone,
In which sad light a carvèd dolphin swam.
Above the antique mantel was displayed
As though a window gave upon the sylvan scene
The change of Philomel, by the barbarous king
So rudely forced; yet there the nightingale   100
Filled all the desert with inviolable voice
And still she cried, and still the world pursues,
"Jug Jug" to dirty ears.
And other withered stumps of time
Were told upon the walls; staring forms
Leaned out, leaning, hushing the room enclosed.
Footsteps shuffled on the stair.
Under the firelight, under the brush, her hair
Spread out in fiery points
Glowed into words, then would be savagely still.   110

"My nerves are bad to-night. Yes, bad. Stay with me.
"Speak to me. Why do you never speak. Speak.
   "What are you thinking of? What thinking? What?
"I never know what you are thinking. Think."

I think we are in rats' alley
Where the dead men lost their bones.

"What is that noise?"
                    The wind under the door.
"What is that noise now? What is the wind doing?"
                    Nothing again nothing.   120
                                        "Do
"You know nothing? Do you see nothing? Do you remember
"Nothing?"
     I remember
Those are pearls that were his eyes.
"Are you alive, or not? Is there nothing in your head?"
                                                            But

O O O O that Shakespeherian Rag—
It's so elegant
So intelligent   130
"What shall I do now? What shall I do?"
"I shall rush out as I am, and walk the street
"With my hair down, so. What shall we do tomorrow?
"What shall we ever do?"

The hot water at ten.
And if it rains, a closed car at four.
And we shall play a game of chess,
Pressing lidless eyes and waiting for a knock upon the door.

When Lil's husband got demobbed, I said—
I didn't mince my words, I said to her myself, 140
HURRY UP PLEASE ITS TIME
Now Albert's coming back, make yourself a bit smart.
He'll want to know what you done with that money he gave you
To get yourself some teeth. He did, I was there.
You have them all out, Lil, and get a nice set,
He said, I swear, I can't bear to look at you.
And no more can't I, I said, and think of poor Albert,
He's been in the army four years, he wants a good time,
And if you don't give it him, there's others will, I said.
Oh is there, she said. Something o' that, I said. 150
Then I'll know who to thank, she said, and give me a straight look.
HURRY UP PLEASE ITS TIME
If you don't like it you can get on with it, I said,
Others can pick and choose if you can't.
But if Albert makes off, it won't be for lack of telling.
You ought to be ashamed, I said, to look so antique.
(And her only thirty-one.)
I can't help it, she said, pulling a long face,
It's them pills I took, to bring it off, she said.
(She's had five already, and nearly died of young George.) 160
The chemist said it would be all right, but I've never been the same.
You *are* a proper fool, I said.
Well, if Albert won't leave you alone, there it is, I said,
What you get married for if you don't want children?
HURRY UP PLEASE ITS TIME
Well, that Sunday Albert was home, they had a hot gammon,
And they asked me in to dinner, to get the beauty of it hot—
HURRY UP PLEASE ITS TIME
HURRY UP PLEASE ITS TIME
Goonight Bill. Goonight Lou. Goonight May. Goonight. 170
Ta ta. Goonight. Goonight.
Good night, ladies, good night, sweet ladies, good night, good night.

III. THE FIRE SERMON

The river's tent is broken: the last fingers of leaf
Clutch and sink into the wet bank. The wind
Crosses the brown land, unheard. The nymphs are departed.
Sweet Thames, run softly, till I end my song.
The river bears no empty bottles, sandwich papers,
Silk handkerchiefs, cardboard boxes, cigarette ends
Or other testimony of summer nights. The nymphs are departed.
And their friends, the loitering heirs of city directors; 180
Departed, have left no addresses.
By the waters of Leman I sat down and wept . . .

Sweet Thames, run softly till I end my song,
Sweet Thames, run softly, for I speak not loud or long.
But at my back in a cold blast I hear
The rattle of the bones, and chuckle spread from ear to ear.
A rat crept softly through the vegetation
Dragging its slimy belly on the bank
While I was fishing in the dull canal
On a winter evening round behind the gashouse 190
Musing upon the king my brother's wreck
And on the king my father's death before him.
White bodies naked on the low damp ground
And bones cast in a little low dry garret,
Rattled by the rat's foot only, year to year.
But at my back from time to time I hear
The sound of horns and motors, which shall bring
Sweeney to Mrs. Porter in the spring.
O the moon shone bright on Mrs. Porter
And on her daughter 200
They wash their feet in soda water
Et O ces voix d'enfants, chantant dans la coupole!

Twit twit twit
Jug jug jug jug jug jug
So rudely forc'd.
Tereu

Unreal City
Under the brown fog of a winter noon
Mr. Eugenides, the Smyrna merchant
Unshaven, with a pocket full of currants 210
C.i.f. London: documents at sight,
Asked me in demotic French
To luncheon at the Cannon Street Hotel
Followed by a weekend at the Metropole.

At the violet hour, when the eyes and back
Turn upward from the desk, when the human engine waits
Like a taxi throbbing waiting,
I Tiresias, though blind, throbbing between two lives,
Old man with wrinkled female breasts, can see
At the violet hour, the evening hour that strives 220
Homeward, and brings the sailor home from sea,
The typist home at teatime, clears her breakfast, lights
Her stove, and lays out food in tins.
Out of the window perilously spread
Her drying combinations touched by the sun's last rays,
On the divan are piled (at night her bed)
Stockings, slippers, camisoles, and stays.
I Tiresias, old man with wrinkled dugs
Perceived the scene, and foretold the rest—
I too awaited the expected guest. 230
He the young man carbuncular, arrives,

A small house agent's clerk, with one bold stare,
One of the low on whom assurance sits
As a silk hat on a Bradford millionaire.

The time is now propitious, as he guesses,
The meal is ended, she is bored and tired,
Endeavours to engage her in caresses
Which still are unreproved, if undesired.
Flushed and decided, he assaults at once;
Exploring hands encounter no defence; 240
His vanity requires no response,
And makes a welcome of indifference.
(And I Tiresias have foresuffered all
Enacted on this same divan or bed;
I who have sat by Thebes below the wall
And walked among the lowest of the dead.)
Bestows one final patronising kiss,
And gropes his way, finding the stairs unlit . . .

She turns and looks a moment in the glass,
Hardly aware of her departed lover; 250
Her brain allows one half-formed thought to pass:
"Well now that's done: and I'm glad it's over."
When lovely woman stoops to folly and
Paces about her room again, alone,
She smoothes her hair with automatic hand,
And puts a record on the gramophone.

"This music crept by me upon the waters"
And along the Strand, up Queen Victoria Street.
O City city, I can sometimes hear
Beside a public bar in Lower Thames Street, 260
The pleasant whining of a mandoline
And a clatter and a chatter from within
Where fishmen lounge at noon: where the walls
Of Magnus Martyr hold
Inexplicable splendour of Ionian white and gold.

The river sweats
Oil and tar
The barges drift
With the turning tide
Red sails 270
Wide
To leeward, swing on the heavy spar.
The barges wash
Drifting logs
Down Greenwich reach
Past the Isle of Dogs.
Weialala leia
Wallala leialala

Elizabeth and Leicester
Beating oars 280
The stern was formed
A gilded shell
Red and gold
The brisk swell
Rippled both shores
Southwest wind
Carried down stream
The peal of bells
White towers
Weialala leia 290
Wallala leialala

"Trams and dusty trees.
Highbury bore me. Richmond and Kew
Undid me. By Richmond I raised my knees
Supine on the floor of a narrow canoe."

"My feet are at Moorgate, and my heart
Under my feet. After the event
He wept. He promised 'a new start.'
I made no comment. What should I resent?"

"On Margate Sands. 300
I can connect
Nothing with nothing.
The broken fingernails of dirty hands.
My people humble people who expect
Nothing."
la la

To Carthage then I came

Burning burning burning burning
O Lord Thou pluckest me out
O Lord Thou pluckest 310

burning

IV. DEATH BY WATER

Phlebas the Phoenician, a fortnight dead,
Forgot the cry of gulls, and the deep sea swell
And the profit and loss.
A current under sea
Picked his bones in whispers. As he rose and fell
He passed the stages of his age and youth
Entering the whirlpool.
Gentile or Jew
O you who turn the wheel and look to windward, 320
Consider Phlebas, who was once handsome and tall as you.

V. WHAT THE THUNDER SAID

After the torchlight red on sweaty faces
After the frosty silence in the gardens
After the agony in stony places
The shouting and the crying
Prison and palace and reverberation
Of thunder of spring over distant mountains
He who was living is now dead
We who were living are now dying
With a little patience 330

Here is no water but only rock
Rock and no water and the sandy road
The road winding above among the mountains
Which are mountains of rock without water
If there were water we should stop and drink
Amongst the rock one cannot stop or think
Sweat is dry and feet are in the sand
If there were only water amongst the rock
Dead mountain mouth of carious teeth that cannot spit
Here one can neither stand nor lie nor sit 340
There is not even silence in the mountains
But dry sterile thunder without rain
There is not even solitude in the mountains
But red sullen faces sneer and snarl
From doors of mudcracked houses
If there were water
And no rock
If there were rock
And also water
And water 350
A spring
A pool among the rock
If there were the sound of water only
Not the cicada
And dry grass singing
But sound of water over a rock
Where the hermit-thrush sings in the pine trees
Drip drop drip drop drop drop drop
But there is no water

Who is the third who walks always beside you?
When I count, there are only you and I together 360
But when I look ahead up the white road
There is always another one walking beside you
Gliding wrapt in a brown mantle, hooded
I do not know whether a man or a woman
—But who is that on the other side of you?

What is that sound high in the air
Murmur of maternal lamentation

Who are those hooded hordes swarming
Over endless plains, stumbling in cracked earth
Ringed by the flat horizon only 370
What is the city over the mountains
Cracks and reforms and bursts in the violet air
Falling towers
Jerusalem Athens Alexandria
Vienna London
Unreal

A woman drew her long black hair out tight
And fiddled whisper music on those strings
And bats with baby faces in the violet light
Whistled, and beat their wings 380
And crawled head downward down a blackened wall
And upside down in air were towers
Tolling reminiscent bells, that kept the hours
And voices singing out of empty cisterns and exhausted wells.

In this decayed hole among the mountains
In the faint moonlight, the grass is singing
Over the tumbled graves, about the chapel
There is the empty chapel, only the wind's home.
It has no windows, and the door swings,
Dry bones can harm no one. 390
Only a cock stood on the rooftree
Co co rico co co rico
In a flash of lightning. Then a damp gust
Bringing rain

Ganga was sunken, and the limp leaves
Waited for rain, while the black clouds
Gathered far distant, over Himavant.
The jungle crouched, humped in silence.
Then spoke the thunder
DA 400
Datta: what have we given?
My friend, blood shaking my heart
The awful daring of a moment's surrender
Which an age of prudence can never retract
By this, and this only, we have existed
Which is not to be found in our obituaries
Or in memories draped by the beneficent spider
Or under seals broken by the lean solicitor
In our empty rooms
DA 410
Dayadhvam: I have heard the key
Turn in the door once and turn once only
We think of the key, each in his prison
Thinking of the key, each confirms a prison
Only at nightfall, aethereal rumours
Revive for a moment a broken Coriolanus

DA
Damyata: The boat responded
Gaily, to the hand expert with sail and oar
The sea was calm, your heart would have responded 420
Gaily, when invited, beating obedient
To controlling hands

I sat upon the shore
Fishing, with the arid plain behind me
Shall I at least set my lands in order?
London Bridge is falling down falling down falling down
Poi s' ascose nel foco che gli affina
Quando fiam uti chelidon—O swallow swallow
Le Prince d' Aquitaine à la tour abolie
These fragments I have shored against my ruins 430
Why then Ile fit you. Hieronymo's mad againe.
Datta. Dayadhvam. Damyata.
Shantih shantih shantih

NOTES BY T. S. ELIOT ON "THE WASTE LAND"

Not only the title, but the plan and a good deal of the incidental symbolism of the poem were suggested by Miss Jessie L. Weston's book on the Grail legend: *From Ritual to Romance* (Cambridge). Indeed, so deeply am I indebted, Miss Weston's book will elucidate the difficulties of the poem much better than my notes can do; and I recommend it (apart from the great interest of the book itself) to any who think such elucidation of the poem worth the trouble. To another work of anthropology I am indebted in general, one which has influenced our generation profoundly; I mean *The Golden Bough;* I have used especially the two volumes *Adonis, Attis, Osiris.* Anyone who is acquainted with these works will immediately recognise in the poem certain references to vegetation ceremonies.

I. THE BURIAL OF THE DEAD

Line 20. Cf. Ezekiel II, i.
23. Cf. Ecclesiastes XII, v.
31. V. Tristan und Isolde, I, verses 5-8.
42. Id. III, verse 24.
46. I am not familiar with the exact constitution of the Tarot pack of cards, from which I have obviously departed to suit my own convenience. The Hanged Man, a member of the traditional pack, fits my purpose in two ways: because he is associated in my mind with the Hanged God of Frazer, and because I associate him with the hooded figure in the passage of the disciples to Emmaus in Part V. The Phoenician Sailor and the Merchant appear later; also the "crowds of people," and Death by Water is executed in Part IV. The Man with Three Staves (an authentic member of the Tarot pack) I associate, quite arbitrarily, with the Fisher King himself.

60. Cf. Baudelaire:

"Fourmillante cité, cité pleine de rêves,
"Où le spectre en plein jour raccroche le passant."

63. Cf. Inferno III, 55-57:

"si lunga tratta
di gente, ch'io non avrei mai creduto
che morte tanta n'avesse disfatta."

64. Cf. Inferno IV, 25-27:

"Quivi, secondo che per ascoltare,
"non avea pianto, ma' che di sospiri,
"che l'aura eterna facevan tremare."

68. A phenomenon which I have often noticed.
74. Cf. the Dirge in Webster's *White Devil.*
76. V. Baudelaire, Preface to *Fleurs du Mal.*

II. A GAME OF CHESS

77. Cf. *Antony and Cleopatra,* II, ii, l. 190.
92. Laquearia. V. *Aeneid,* I, 726:
dependent lychni laquearibus aureis incensi, et noctem flammis funalia vincunt.
98. Sylvan scene. V. Milton, *Paradise Lost,* IV, 140.
99. V. Ovid, *Metamorphoses,* VI, Philomela.
100. Cf. Part III, l. 204.
115. Cf. Part III, l. 195.
118. Cf. Webster: "Is the wind in that door still?"
126. Cf. Part I, l. 37, 48.
138. Cf. the game of chess in Middleton's *Women beware Women.*

III. THE FIRE SERMON

176. V. Spenser, *Prothalamion.*
192. Cf. *The Tempest,* I, ii.
196. Cf. Marvell, *To His Coy Mistress.*
197. Cf. Day, *Parliament of Bees:*

"When of the sudden, listening, you shall hear,
"A noise of horns and hunting, which shall bring
"Actaeon to Diana in the spring,
"Where all shall see her naked skin . . ."

199. I do not know the origin of the ballad from which these lines are taken: it was reported to me from Sydney, Australia.

202. V. Verlaine, *Parsifal.*

210. The currants were quoted at a price "carriage and insurance free to London"; and the Bill of Lading etc. were to be handed to the buyer upon payment of the sight draft.

218. Tiresias, although a mere spectator and not indeed a "character," is yet the most important personage in the poem, uniting all the rest. Just as the one-eyed merchant, seller of currants, melts into the Phoenician Sailor, and the latter is not wholly distinct from Ferdinand Prince of Naples, so all the women are one woman, and the two sexes meet in Tiresias. What Tiresias *sees,* in fact, is the substance of the poem. The whole passage from Ovid is of great anthropological interest:

'. . . Cum Iunone iocos et maior vestra profecto est
Quam, quae contingit maribus,' dixisse, 'voluptas.'
Illa negat; placuit quae sit sententia docti
Quaerere Tiresiae: venus huic erat utraque nota.

Nam duo magnorum viridi coeuntia silva
Corpora serpentum baculi violaverat ictu
Deque viro factus, mirabile, femina septem
Egerat autumnos; octavo rursus eosdem
Videt et 'est vestrae si tanta potentia plagae,'
Dixit 'ut auctoris sortem in contraria mutet,
Nunc quoque vos feriam!' percussis anguibus isdem
Forma prior rediit genetivaque venit imago.
Arbiter hic igitur sumptus de lite iocosa
Dicta Iovis firmat; gravius Saturnia iusto
Nec pro materia fertur doluisse suique
Iudicis aeterna damnavit lumina nocte,
At pater omnipotens (neque enim licet inrita cuiquam
Facta dei fecisse deo) pro lumine adempto
Scire futura dedit poenamque levavit honore.

221. This may not appear as exact as Sappho's lines, but I had in mind the "longshore" or "dory" fisherman, who returns at nightfall.

253. V. Goldsmith, the song of *The Vicar of Wakefield.*

257. V. *The Tempest,* as above.

264. The interior of St. Magnus Martyr is to my mind one of the finest among Wren's interiors. See *The Proposed Demolition of Nineteen City Churches:* (P. S. King & Son, Ltd.).

266. The Song of the (three) Thames-daughters begins here. From line 292 to 306 inclusive they speak in turn. V. *Götterdämmerung* III, i: the Rhine-daughters.

279. V. Froude, *Elizabeth,* Vol. 1, ch. iv, letter of De Quadra to Philip of Spain: "In the afternoon we were in a barge, watching the games on the river. (The queen) was alone with Lord Robert and myself on the poop, when they began to talk nonsense, and went so far that Lord Robert at last said, as I was on the spot there was no reason why they should not be married if the queen pleased.

293. Cf. *Purgatorio,* V, 133:

"Ricorditi di me, che son la Pia;
"Siena mi fe', disfecemi Maremma."

307. V. St. Augustine's *Confessions:* "to Carthage then I came, where a cauldron of unholy loves sang all about mine ears."

308. The complete text of the Buddha's Fire Sermon (which corresponds in importance to the Sermon on the Mount) from which these words are taken, will be found translated in the late Henry Clarke Warren's *Buddhism in Translation* (Harvard Oriental Series). Mr. Warren was one of the great pioneers of Buddhist studies in the Occident.

309. From St. Augustine's *Confessions* again. The collocation of these two representatives of eastern and western asceticism, as the culmination of this part of the poem, is not an accident.

V. WHAT THE THUNDER SAID

In the first part of Part V three themes are employed: the journey to Emmaus, the approach to the Chapel Perilous (see Miss Weston's book) and the present decay of eastern Europe.

357. This is *Turdus aonalaschkae pallasii,* the hermit-thrush which I have heard in Quebec County. Chapman says (*Handbook of Birds of Eastern North America*) "it is most at home in secluded woodland and thickety retreats. . . . Its notes are

not remarkable for variety or volume, but in purity and sweetness of tone and exquisite modulation they are unequalled." Its "water-dripping song" is justly celebrated.

360. The following lines were stimulated by the account of one of the Antarctic expeditions (I forget which, but I think one of Shackleton's): it was related that the party of explorers, at the extremity of their strength, had the constant delusion that there was *one more member* than could actually be counted.

366-76. Cf. Hermann Hesse, *Blick ins Chaos:* "Schon ist halb Europa, schon ist zumindest der halbe Osten Europas auf dem Wege zum Chaos, fährt betrunken im heiligen Wahn am Abgrund entlang und singt dazu, singt betrunken und hymnisch wie Dmitri Karamasoff sang. Ueber diese Lieder lacht der Bürger beleidigt, der Heilige und Seher hört sie mit Tränen."

401. "Datta, dayadhvam, damyata" (Give, sympathize, control). The fable of the meaning of the Thunder is found in the *Brihadaranyaka—Upanishad,* 5, 1. A translation is found in Deussen's *Sechzig Upanishads des Veda,* p. 489.

407. Cf. Webster, *The White Devil,* V, vi:

> ". . . they'll remarry
> Ere the worm pierce your winding-sheet, ere the spider
> Make a thin curtain for your epitaphs."

411. Cf. *Inferno,* XXXIII, 46:

> "ed io sentii chiavar l'uscio di sotto
> all'orribile torre."

Also F. H. Bradley, *Appearance and Reality,* p. 346. "My external sensations are no less private to myself than are my thoughts or my feelings. In either case my experience falls within my own circle, a circle closed on the outside; and, with all its elements alike, every sphere is opaque to the others which surround it. . . . In brief, regarded as an existence which appears in a soul, the whole world for each is peculiar and private to that soul."

424. V. Weston: *From Ritual to Romance;* chapter on the Fisher King.

427. V. *Purgatorio,* XXVI, 148.

> " 'Ara vos prec per aquella valor
> 'que vos guida al som le l'escalina,
> 'sovegna vos a temps de ma dolor.'
> Poi s'ascose nel foco che gli affina."

428. V. *Pervigilium Veneris.* Cf. Philomela in Parts II and III.

429. V. Gerard de Nerval, Sonnet *El Desdichado.*

431. V. Kyd's *Spanish Tragedy.*

433. Shantih. Repeated as here, a formal ending to an Upanishad. "The Peace which passeth understanding" is our equivalent to this word.

THE HOLLOW MEN

Mistah Kurtz—he dead.
A penny for the Old Guy.

I

We are the hollow men
We are the stuffed men
Leaning together
Headpiece filled with straw. Alas!
Our dried voices, when
We whisper together
Are quiet and meaningless
As wind in dry grass
Or rats' feet over broken glass
In our dry cellar

Shape without form, shade without color,
Paralyzed force, gesture without motion;

Those who have crossed
With direct eyes, to death's other Kingdom
Remember us—if at all—not as lost
Violent souls, but only
As the hollow men
The stuffed men.

II

Eyes I dare not meet in dreams
In death's dream kingdom
These do not appear:
There, the eyes are
Sunlight on a broken column
There, is a tree swinging
And voices are
In the wind's singing
More distant and more solemn
Then a fading star.

Let me be no nearer
In death's dream kingdom
Let me also wear
Such deliberate disguises
Rat's coat, crowskin, crossed staves
In a field
Behaving as the wind behaves
No nearer—

Not that final meeting
In the twilight kingdom

III

This is the dead land
This is cactus land
Here the stone images
Are raised, here they receive
The supplication of a dead man's hand
Under the twinkle of a fading star.

Is it like this
In death's other kingdom
Waking alone
At the hour when we are
Trembling with tenderness
Lips that would kiss
Form prayers to broken stone.

IV

The eyes are not here
There are no eyes here
In this valley of dying stars
In this hollow valley
This broken jaw of our lost kingdoms

In this last of meeting places
We grope together
And avoid speech
Gathered on this beach of the tumid river

Sightless, unless
The eyes reappear
As the perpetual star
Multifoliate rose
Of death's twilight kingdom
The hope only
Of empty men.

V

Here we go round the prickly pear
Prickly pear prickly pear
Here we go round the prickly pear
At five o'clock in the morning.

Between the idea
And the reality
Between the motion
And the act
Falls the Shadow
For Thine is the Kingdom

Between the conception
And the creation
Between the emotion
And the response
Falls the Shadow
Life is very long

Between the desire
And the spasm
Between the potency
And the existence
Between the essence
And the descent
Falls the Shadow
For Thine is the Kingdom

For Thine is
Life is
For Thine is the

This is the way the world ends
This is the way the world ends
This is the way the world ends
Not with a bang but a whimper.

JOURNEY OF THE MAGI

"A cold coming we had of it,
Just the worst time of the year
For a journey, and such a long journey:
The ways deep and the weather sharp,
The very dead of winter."
And the camels galled, sore-footed, refractory,
Lying down in the melting snow.
There were times we regretted
The summer palaces on slopes, the terraces,
And the silken girls bringing sherbet.
Then the camel men cursing and grumbling
And running away, and wanting their liquor and women,
And the night-fires going out, and the lack of shelters,
And the cities hostile and the towns unfriendly
And the villages dirty and charging high prices:
A hard time we had of it.
At the end we preferred to travel all night,
Sleeping in snatches,
With the voices singing in our ears, saying
That this was all folly.

Then at dawn we came down to a temperate valley,
Wet, below the snow line, smelling of vegetation;
With a running stream and a water-mill beating the darkness,
And three trees on the low sky,
And an old white horse galloped away in the meadow.
Then we came to a tavern with vine-leaves over the lintel,
Six hands at an open door dicing for pieces of silver,
And feet kicking the empty wine-skins.
But there was no information, and so we continued
And arrived at evening, not a moment too soon
Finding the place; it was (you may say) satisfactory.

All this was a long time ago, I remember,
And I would do it again, but set down
This set down
This: were we led all that way for
Birth or Death? There was a Birth, certainly,
We had evidence and no doubt. I had seen birth and death,
But had thought they were different; this Birth was
Hard and bitter agony for us, like Death, our death.
We returned to our places, these Kingdoms,
But no longer at ease here, in the old dispensation,
With an alien people clutching their gods.
I should be glad of another death.

ASH-WEDNESDAY

I

Because I do not hope to turn again
Because I do not hope
Because I do not hope to turn
Desiring this man's gift and that man's scope
I no longer strive to strive towards such things
(Why should the aged eagle stretch its wings?)
Why should I mourn
The vanished power of the usual reign?

Because I do not hope to know again
The infirm glory of the positive hour
Because I do not think
Because I know I shall not know
The one veritable transitory power
Because I cannot drink
There, where trees flower, and springs flow, for there is nothing again

Because I know that time is always time
And place is always and only place
And what is actual is actual only for one time
And only for one place
I rejoice that things are as they are and
I renounce the blessèd face
And renounce the voice

Because I cannot hope to turn again
Consequently I rejoice, having to construct something
Upon which to rejoice

And pray to God to have mercy upon us
And I pray that I may forget
These matters that with myself I too much discuss
Too much explain
Because I do not hope to turn again
Let these words answer
For what is done, not to be done again,
May the judgment not be too heavy upon us

Because these wings are no longer wings to fly
But merely vans to beat the air
The air which is now thoroughly small and dry
Smaller and dryer than the will
Teach us to care and not to care
Teach us to sit still.

Pray for us sinners now and at the hour of our death
Pray for us now and at the hour of our death.

II

Lady, three white leopards sat under a juniper-tree
In the cool of the day, having fed to satiety
On my legs my heart my liver and that which had been contained
In the hollow round of my skull. And God said

Shall these bones live? shall these
Bones live? And that which had been contained
In the bones (which were already dry) said chirping:
Because of the goodness of this Lady
And because of her loveliness, and because
She honors the Virgin in meditation,
We shine with brightness. And I who am here dissembled
Proffer my deeds to oblivion, and my love
To the posterity of the desert and the fruit of the gourd.
It is this which recovers
My guts the strings of my eyes and the indigestible portions
Which the leopards reject. The Lady is withdrawn
In a white gown, to contemplation, in a white gown.
Let the whiteness of bones atone to forgetfulness.
There is no life in them. As I am forgotten
And would be forgotten, so I would forget
Thus devoted, concentrated in purpose. And God said
Prophesy to the wind, to the wind only, for only
The wind will listen. And the bones sang chirping
With the burden of the grasshopper, saying

Lady of silences
Calm and distressed
Torn and most whole
Rose of memory
Rose of forgetfulness
Exhausted and life-giving
Worried reposeful
The single Rose
Is now the Garden
Where all loves end
Terminate torment
Of love unsatisfied
The greater torment
Of love satisfied
End of the endless
Journey to no end
Conclusion of all that
Is inconclusible
Speech without word and
Word of no speech
Grace to the Mother
For the Garden
Where all love ends.

Under a juniper-tree the bones sang, scattered and shining
We are glad to be scattered, we did little good to each other,
Under a tree in the cool of the day, with the blessing of sand,
Forgetting themselves and each other, united
In the quiet of the desert. This is the land which ye
Shall divide by lot. And neither division nor unity
Matters. This is the land. We have our inheritance.

III

At the first turning of the second stair
I turned and saw below
The same shape twisted on the banister
Under the vapor in the fetid air
Struggling with the devil of the stairs who wears
The deceitful face of hope and of despair.

At the second turning of the second stair
I left them twisting, turning below;
There were no more faces and the stair was dark,
Damp, jaggèd, like an old man's mouth drivelling, beyond repair,
Or the toothed gullet of an agèd shark.

At the first turning of the third stair
Was a slotted window bellied like the fig's fruit
And beyond the hawthorn blossom and a pasture scene
The broadbacked figure drest in blue and green
Enchanted the maytime with an antique flute.
Blown hair is sweet, brown hair over the mouth blown,
Lilac and brown hair;
Distraction, music of the flute, stops and steps of the mind over the third stair,
Fading, fading; strength beyond hope and despair
Climbing the third stair.

Lord, I am not worthy
Lord, I am not worthy

but speak the word only.

IV

Who walked between the violet and the violet
Who walked between
The various ranks of varied green
Going in white and blue, in Mary's color,
Talking of trivial things
In ignorance and in knowledge of eternal dolour
Who moved among the others as they walked,
Who then made strong the fountains and made fresh the springs

Made cool the dry rock and made firm the sand
In blue of larkspur, blue of Mary's color,
Sovegna vos

Here are the years that walk between, bearing
Away the fiddles and the flutes, restoring
One who moves in the time between sleep and waking, wearing

White light folded, sheathed about her, folded.
The new years walk, restoring
Through a bright cloud of tears, the years, restoring
With a new verse the ancient rhyme. Redeem
The time. Redeem

The unread vision in the higher dream
While jewelled unicorns draw by the gilded hearse.

The silent sister veiled in white and blue
Between the yews, behind the garden god,
Whose flute is breathless, bent her head and sighed but spoke no word

But the fountain sprang up and the bird sang down
Redeem the time, redeem the dream
The token of the word unheard, unspoken

Till the wind shake a thousand whispers from the yew

And after this our exile

v

If the lost word is lost, if the spent word is spent
If the unheard, unspoken
Word is unspoken, unheard;
Still is the unspoken word, the Word unheard,
The Word without a word, the Word within
The world and for the world;
And the light shone in darkness and
Against the Word the unstilled world still whirled
About the center of the silent Word.

O my people, what have I done unto thee.

Where shall the word be found, where will the word
Resound? Not here, there is not enough silence,
Not on the sea or on the islands, not
On the mainland, in the desert or the rain land,
For those who walk in darkness
Both in the day time and in the night time
The right time and the right place are not here
No place of grace for those who avoid the face
No time to rejoice for those who walk among noise and deny the voice

Will the veiled sister pray for
Those who walk in darkness, who chose thee and oppose thee,
Those who are torn on the horn between season and season, time and time, between
Hour and hour, word and word, power and power, those who wait
In darkness? Will the veiled sister pray
For children at the gate
Who will not go away and cannot pray:
Pray for those who chose and oppose

O my people, what have I done unto thee.

Will the veiled sister between the slender
Yew trees pray for those who offend her
And are terrified and cannot surrender
And affirm before the world and deny between the rocks
In the last desert between the last blue rocks

The desert in the garden the garden in the desert
Of drouth, spitting from the mouth the withered apple-seed.

O my people.

VI

Although I do not hope to turn again
Although I do not hope
Although I do not hope to turn

Wavering between the profit and the loss
In this brief transit where the dreams cross
The dreamcrossed twilight between birth and dying
(Bless me father) though I do not wish to wish these things
From the wide window towards the granite shore
The white sails still fly seaward, seaward flying
Unbroken wings
And the lost heart stiffens and rejoices
In the lost lilac and the lost sea voices
And the weak spirit quickens to rebel
For the bent golden-rod and the lost sea smell
Quickens to recover
The cry of quail and the whirling plover
And the blind eye creates
The empty forms between the ivory gates
And smell renews the salt savor of the sandy earth

This is the time of tension between dying and birth
The place of solitude where three dreams cross
Between blue rocks
But when the voices shaken from the yew-tree drift away
Let the other yew be shaken and reply.

Blessed sister, holy mother, spirit of the fountain, spirit of the garden,
Suffer us not to mock ourselves with falsehood
Teach us to care and not to care
Teach us to sit still
Even among these rocks,
Our peace in His will
And even among these rocks
Sister, mother,
And spirit of the river, spirit of the sea,
Suffer me not to be separated

And let my cry come unto Thee.

BURNT NORTON

(*From "Four Quartets"*)

I

Time present and time past
Are both perhaps present in time future,
And time future contained in time past.

If all time is eternally present
All time is unredeemable.
What might have been is an abstraction
Remaining a perpetual possibility
Only in a world of speculation.
What might have been and what has been
Point to one end, which is always present.
Footfalls echo in the memory
Down the passage which we did not take
Towards the door we never opened
Into the rose-garden. My words echo
Thus, in your mind.
But to what purpose
Disturbing the dust on a bowl of rose-leaves
I do not know.
Other echoes
Inhabit the garden. Shall we follow?
Quick, said the bird, find them, find them,
Round the corner. Through the first gate,
Into our first world, shall we follow
The deception of the thrush? Into our first world.
There they were, dignified, invisible,
Moving without pressure, over the dead leaves,
In the autumn heat, through the vibrant air,
And the bird called, in response to
The unheard music hidden in the shrubbery,
And the unseen eyebeam crossed, for the roses
Had the look of flowers that are looked at.
There they were as our guests, accepted and accepting.
So we moved, and they, in a formal pattern,
Along the empty alley, into the box circle,
To look down into the drained pool.
Dry the pool, dry concrete, brown edged,
And the pool was filled with water out of sunlight,
And the lotos rose, quietly, quietly,
The surface glittered out of heart of light,
And they were behind us, reflected in the pool.
Then a cloud passed, and the pool was empty.
Go, said the bird, for the leaves were full of children,
Hidden excitedly, containing laughter.
Go, go, go, said the bird; human kind
Cannot bear very much reality.
Time past and time future
What might have been and what has been
Point to one end, which is always present.

II

Garlic and sapphires in the mud
Clot the bedded axle-tree.
The trilling wire in the blood
Sings below inveterate scars
And reconciles forgotten wars.

The dance along the artery
The circulation of the lymph
Are figured in the drift of stars
Ascend to summer in the tree
We move above the moving tree
In light upon the figured leaf
And hear upon the sodden floor
Below, the boarhound and the boar
Pursue their pattern as before
But reconciled among the stars.

At the still point of the turning world. Neither flesh nor fleshless;
Neither from nor towards; at the still point, there the dance is,
But neither arrest nor movement. And do not call it fixity,
Where past and future are gathered. Neither movement from nor towards,
Neither ascent nor decline. Except for the point, the still point,
There would be no dance, and there is only the dance.
I can only say, *there* we have been: but I cannot say where.
And I cannot say, how long, for that is to place it in time.

The inner freedom from the practical desire,
The release from action and suffering, release from the inner
And the outer compulsion, yet surrounded
By a grace of sense, a white light still and moving,
Erhebung without motion, concentration
Without elimination, both a new world
And the old made explicit, understood
In the completion of its partial ecstasy,
The resolution of its partial horror.
Yet the enchainment of past and future
Woven in the weakness of the changing body,
Protects mankind from heaven and damnation
Which flesh cannot endure.
Time past and time future
Allow but a little consciousness.
To be conscious is not to be in time
But only in time can the moment in the rose-garden,
The moment in the arbour where the rain beat,
The moment in the draughty church at smokefall
Be remembered; involved with past and future.
Only through time time is conquered.

III

Here is a place of disaffection
Time before and time after
In a dim light: neither daylight
Investing form with lucid stillness
Turning shadow into transient beauty
With slow rotation suggesting permanence
Nor darkness to purify the soul
Emptying the sensual with deprivation
Cleansing affection from the temporal.
Neither plenitude nor vacancy. Only a flicker

Over the strained time-ridden faces
Distracted from distraction by distraction
Filled with fancies and empty of meaning
Tumid apathy with no concentration
Men and bits of paper, whirled by the cold wind
That blows before and after time,
Wind in and out of unwholesome lungs
Time before and time after.
Eructation of unhealthy souls
Into the faded air, the torpid
Driven on the wind that sweeps the gloomy hills of London,
Hampstead and Clerkenwell, Campden and Putney,
Highgate, Primrose and Ludgate. Not here
Not here the darkness, in this twittering world.

Descend lower, descend only
Into the world of perpetual solitude,
World not world, but that which is not world,
Internal darkness, deprivation
And destitution of all property,
Desiccation of the world of sense,
Evacuation of the world of fancy,
Inoperancy of the world of spirit;
This is the one way, and the other
Is the same, not in movement
But abstention from movement; while the world moves
In appetency, on its metalled ways
Of time past and time future.

IV

Time and the bell have buried the day,
The black cloud carries the sun away.
Will the sunflower turn to us, will the clematis
Stray down, bend to us; tendril and spray
Clutch and cling?
Chill
Fingers of yew be curled
Down on us? After the kingfisher's wing
Has answered light to light, and is silent, the light is still
At the still point of the turning world.

V

Words move, music moves
Only in time; but that which is only living
Can only die. Words, after speech, reach
Into the silence. Only by the form, the pattern,
Can words or music reach
The stillness, as a Chinese jar still
Moves perpetually in its stillness.
Not the stillness of the violin, while the note lasts,
Not that only, but the co-existence,
Or say that the end precedes the beginning,
And the end and the beginning were always there

Before the beginning and after the end.
And all is always now. Words strain,
Crack and sometimes break, under the burden,
Under the tension, slip, slide, perish,
Decay with imprecision, will not stay in place,
Will not stay still. Shrieking voices
Scolding, mocking, or merely chattering,
Always assail them. The Word in the desert
Is most attacked by voices of temptation,
The crying shadow in the funeral dance,
The loud lament of the disconsolate chimera.

The detail of the pattern is movement,
As in the figure of the ten stairs.
Desire itself is movement
Not in itself desirable;
Love is itself unmoving,
Only the cause and end of movement,
Timeless, and undesiring
Except in the aspect of time
Caught in the form of limitation
Between un-being and being.
Sudden in a shaft of sunlight
Even while the dust moves
There rises the hidden laughter
Of children in the foliage
Quick now, here, now, always—
Ridiculous the waste sad time
Stretching before and after.

John Crowe Ransom

John Crowe Ransom was born in Pulaski, Tennessee, April 30, 1888, of Scotch-Irish descent. Pulaski, so Ransom states, is otherwise distinguished as being the County Seat of Giles County, the deathplace of Sam Davis, the Confederate martyr, and of the Ku Klux Klan. (Ransom's own great-uncle took part in the foundation of the latter.) Ransom, the son of a local minister, was educated in his own state and abroad: he received his B.A. at Vanderbilt University in 1909, his B.A. at Oxford in 1913. At the latter he was Rhodes Scholar from Tennessee, taking the "Greats" (classical) course. He taught at Vanderbilt from 1914 until 1937; he then transferred to Kenyon College, Ohio, where he founded *The Kenyon Review.* He was the chief instigator and one of the founders of *The Fugitive,* that experimental journal which did much to disprove Mencken's contention that the South was a vast "Sahara of the Beaux Arts." Although Ransom is realistically aware that the past is past, he cannot help yearning for a vanished richness, for an agrarianism that cannot be and a culture that never was.

Poems About God appeared in 1919, a raw first book with a tang of bitter humor. Here was no southern gentleman's proverbial courtliness, no unctuous and mincing gallantry; here was a bristling acerbity blurted in a strong if uncertain utterance. The lines range from the roughly powerful (reminding one of a coarser Robert Frost) to the surprisingly banal. During the five-year interval between *Poems About God* and his next volume, Ransom's poetry underwent an almost complete change. Little of the crudeness remains in *Chills and Fever,* by all odds the most distinguished volume of poetry published in 1924. Ransom, it was evident, reacted from the callow simplicities and the tradition of Wonder in words of one syllable; his verse is definitely for mature minds willing not only to allow a mature poet his mixed modes but willing to follow them. It is, at first glance, a curiously involved speech which Ransom uses to clothe his semi-whimsical, semi-ironic philosophy. But beneath his precise circumlocutions one is made aware of an extraordinarily sensitive lyricist. What adds zest to his verses is the mocking gravity of his speech—a gravity which is sometimes exaggerated to the verge of parody, if a philosopher can achieve that dubious art.

Ransom strikes his note with a sureness that is almost defiant. He is witty, but his wit is strengthened by passion; he turns from dialectical fencing to sudden emotion. Surprise is his forte; he can weave patterns that are, at one time, fanciful and learned. His account of a small boy's walk in deep woods ("First Travels of Max") is as fine a macabre piece as anything achieved by Amy Lowell. He can draw portraits of dream-lost mediocrities as sympathetically as Robinson, "Tom, Tom, the Piper's Son" being a second cousin to "Miniver Cheevy" and "Bewick Finzer." He can sound the mordant brasses in "Captain Carpenter," the muted violins in "Here Lies a Lady" and the prophetic trumpets in "Spiel of the Three Mountebanks" with equal precision. "Parting Without a Sequel" is memorable in its combination of emotion and mockery. "Piazza Piece" is, perhaps, the most characteristic of these poems; in a sonnet balanced as a lyric Ransom has revitalized—and localized—the old theme of Death and the Lady.

Such music, half soothing, half stinging, is new in our poetry; the modulations are strange, the cadences charming in their slight irregularities. Ransom knows how to employ the unresolved suspension; he delights in pairing such slant rhymes as "drunkard-conquered," "little-scuttle," "ready-study." But it is not merely the free use of dissonance and assonance which distinguishes his poems, it is what he does with these properties. "Antique Harvesters" breathes the very quixotic spirit of the old South and the Southron's devotion to that spirit; "Lady Lost" is a perfect harmonizing of teasing and tenderness; "Janet Waking" uncannily mingles sympathy and mock pathos.

Two Gentlemen in Bonds (1927) has the fresh combination of cavalier grace and surprising savagery uttered in a precise softness of speech. But the surprise is not only occasioned by his tempo which is both nervous and drawling. As Mark Van Doren wrote, "He has been at pains to salt his rhymes and pepper his diction with fresh, realistic words; he has wrenched his cadences to fit his wayward thought; he has written with an original and almost acid gayety."

Yet, for all of Ransom's variety, in spite of his ability to play equally well in the spangles of harlequin and the graver habit of *Kapellmeister,* this Southerner will never be a popular poet. His is too elegant a speech to meet with general favor; his vocabulary is meticulous to the point of being overelaborate, his utterance is often so finical as to seem pedantic. The fact that a great part of this particularity is not affectation, but a scholar's gentle mockery, will not save him from the disapproval or the neglect of the public which dreads polysyllabic poets. Nor can one blame the common reader. Several of Ransom's poems lose themselves in ellipses and remote allusions, a few are so rarefied as to be unintelligible without footnotes and a chart of cross references. His later work is both a growth and a departure. Such poems as "Prelude to an Evening," with its overtones of domestic worry, and "Painting: a Head" are a far cry from the philosophic-fanciful tone of "Here Lies a Lady." In this more difficult poetry Ransom seems to be hesitating between a veiled romanticism and an almost abstract intellectuality.

Nevertheless, even in a facile, overproductive age, there can be no doubt that these crisp narratives and teasing lyrics will find their niche. It will be neither a mean nor a long neglected one. Ransom has developed a new tone without straining for novelty; he has become an influence without becoming oracular. If the chief characteristic of Ransom's verse is irony, as Cleanth Brooks has pointed out, "it remains an instrument—it never becomes a mere attitude adopted by the poet for its own sake."

The combination of elegance and honesty which distinguishes Ransom's verse is even more striking in his prose. It characterizes *God without Thunder* (1930), which Ransom called an unorthodox defense of orthodoxy; his contribution to the agrarian symposium in *I'll Take My Stand* (1930); *The World's Body* (1938), a collection of animated literary studies; and *The New Criticism* (1941), an analytical examination of the critical theories of I. A. Richards, T. S. Eliot, Yvor Winters, and William Empson. *Selected Poems* (1945) contains forty of Ransom's best poems.

BELLS FOR JOHN WHITESIDE'S DAUGHTER

There was such speed in her little body,
And such lightness in her footfall,
It is no wonder that her brown study
Astonishes us all.

Her wars were bruited in our high window.
We looked among orchard trees and beyond,
Where she took arms against her shadow,
Or harried unto the pond

The lazy geese, like a snow cloud
Dripping their snow on the green grass,
Tricking and stopping, sleepy and proud,
Who cried in goose, Alas,

For the tireless heart within the little
Lady with rod that made them rise
From their noon apple-dreams, and scuttle
Goose-fashion under the skies!

But now go the bells, and we are ready;
In one house we are sternly stopped
To say we are vexed at her brown study,
Lying so primly propped.

LADY LOST

This morning, there flew up the lane
A timid lady-bird to our bird-bath
And eyed her image dolefully as death;
This afternoon, knocked on our windowpane
To be let in from the rain.

And when I caught her eye
She looked aside, but at the clapping thunder
And sight of the whole earth blazing up like tinder
Looked in on us again most miserably,
Indeed as if she would cry.

So I will go out into the park and say,
"Who has lost a delicate brown-eyed lady
In the West End Section? Or has anybody
Injured some fine woman in some dark way,
Last night or yesterday?

"Let the owner come and claim possession,
No questions will be asked. But stroke her gently
With loving words, and she will evidently
Resume her full soft-haired white-breasted fashion,
And her right home and her right passion."

BLUE GIRLS

Twirling your blue skirts, traveling the sward
Under the towers of your seminary,
Go listen to your teachers old and contrary
Without believing a word.

Tie the white fillets then about your lustrous hair
And think no more of what will come to pass
Than bluebirds that go walking on the grass
And chattering on the air.

Practice your beauty, blue girls, before it fail;
And I will cry with my loud lips and publish
Beauty which all our power shall never establish,
It is so frail.

For I could tell you a story which is true:
I know a lady with a terrible tongue,
Blear eyes fallen from blue,
All her perfections tarnished—and yet it is not long
Since she was lovelier than any of you.

HERE LIES A LADY

Here lies a lady of beauty and high degree.
Of chills and fever she died, of fever and chills,
The delight of her husband, her aunts, an infant of three,
And of medicos marveling sweetly on her ills.

For either she burned, and her confident eyes would blaze,
And her fingers fly in a manner to puzzle their heads—
What was she making? Why, nothing; she sat in a maze
Of old scraps of laces, snipped into curious shreds—

Or this would pass, and the light of her fire decline
Till she lay discouraged and cold as a thin stalk white and blown,
And would not open her eyes, to kisses, to wine.
The sixth of these states was her last; the cold settled down.

Sweet ladies, long may ye bloom, and toughly I hope ye may thole,
But was she not lucky? In flowers and lace and mourning,
In love and great honor we bade God rest her soul
After six little spaces of chill, and six of burning.

JANET WAKING

Beautifully Janet slept
Till it was deeply morning. She woke then
And thought about her dainty-feathered hen,
To see how it had kept.

One kiss she gave her mother,
Only a small one gave she to her daddy
Who would have kissed each curl of his shining baby;
No kiss at all for her brother.

"Old Chucky, Old Chucky!" she cried,
Running on little pink feet upon the grass
To Chucky's house, and listening. But alas,
Her Chucky had died.

It was a transmogrifying bee
Came droning down on Chucky's old bald head
And sat and put the poison. It scarcely bled,
But how exceedingly

And purply did the knot
Swell with the venom and communicate
Its rigor! Now the poor comb stood up straight
But Chucky did not.

So there was Janet
Kneeling on the wet grass, crying her brown hen

(Translated far beyond the daughters of men)
To rise and walk upon it.

And weeping fast as she had breath
Janet implored us, "Wake her from her sleep!"
And would not be instructed in how deep
Was the forgetful kingdom of death.

SPIEL OF THE THREE MOUNTEBANKS

THE SWARTHY ONE—
Villagers who gather round,
This is Fides, my lean hound.
Bring your bristled village curs
To try his fang and tooth, sweet sirs:
He will rend them, he is savage,
Thinking nothing but to ravage,
Nor with cudgel, fire, rope,
May ye control my misanthrope;
He would tear the moon in the sky
And fly at Heaven, could he fly.
And for his ravening without cease
I have had of him no peace.
Only once I bared the knife
To quit my devil of his life,
But listen, how I heard him say,
"Think you I shall die today?
Since your mother cursed and died,
I am keeping at your side,
We are firmly knit together,
Two ends tugging at one tether,
And you shall see when I shall die
That you are mortal even as I."
Bring your stoutest-hearted curs
If ye would risk him, gentle sirs.

THE THICK ONE—
Countrymen, here's a noble frame,
Humphrey is my elephant's name.
When my father's back was bent
Under steep impediment,
Humphrey came to my possession,
With patient strength for all his passion.
Have ye a mountain to remove?
It is Humphrey's dearest love.
Pile his burden to the skies,
Loose a pestilence of flies,
Foot him in the quick morass
Where no laden beast can pass:
He will staunch his weariless back
And march unswerving on the track.
Have ye seen a back so wide,
Such impenetrable hide?
Nor think ye by this Humphrey hill
Prince Hamlet bare his fardels ill?
Myself I like it not for us
To wear beneath an incubus;
I take offense, but in no rage
May I dispose my heritage;
Though in good time the vast and tough
Shall sink and totter soon enough.
So pile your population up:
They are a drop in Humphrey's cup;
Add all your curses to his pack
To make one straw for Humphrey's back.

THE PALE ONE—
If ye remark how poor I am,
Come, citizens, behold my lamb!
Have ye a lion, ounce, or scourge,
Or any beast of dainty gorge?
Agnus lays his tender youth
Between the very enemy's mouth,
And though he sniff his delicate meat,
He may not bruise that flesh nor eat,
He may not rend him limb from limb,
If Agnus do but bleat on him.
Fierce was my youth, but like a dream
I saw a temple, and a stream,
And where I knelt and washed my sore
This infant lamb stood on the shore,
He mounted with me from the river.
And still he cries, as brave as ever,
"Lay me down by the lion's side
To match my frailty with his pride;
Fain would I welter in my blood
To teach these lions true lionhood."
So daily Agnus would be slain
But daily is denied again,
And still the hungry lions range
While Agnus waits upon a change;

Only the coursing lions die
And in their deserts mortify.
So bring us lion, leopard, bear,
To try of Agnus without fear,
And ye less gentle than I am,
Come, be instructed of my Lamb.

FIRST TRAVELS OF MAX

As hath been, lo, these many generations,
The best of the Van Vroomans was the youngest;
And even he, in a chevroned sailor's blouse
And tawny curls far from subdued to the cap,
Had slapped old Katie and betaken himself
From games for children. That was because they told
Him never, never to set a wicked foot
Into Fool's Forest, where the devil dwelt.

"Become Saint Michael's sword!" said Max to the stick,
And to the stone, "Be a brand-new revolver!"
Then Max was glad that he had armed so wisely,
As darker grew the wood, and shrill with silence.
All good fairies were helpless here; at night
Whipped in an inch of their lives; weeping, forbidden
To play with strange scared truant little boys
Who didn't belong there. Snakes were allowed there
And lizards and adders—people of age and evil
That lay on their bellies and whispered—no bird nor rabbit.
There were more rotten trees than there were sound ones;
In that wood, timber was degenerate
And rotted almost faster than it grew.
There were no flowers nor apples; too much age.
The only innocent thing in there was Max,
And even he had cursed his little sisters.

The little black tarn rose up almost in his face—
It was as black and sudden as the pit
The Adversary digs in the bowels of earth;
Bubbles were on it, breath of the black beast
(Formed like a spider, white bag for entrails)
Who took that sort of blackness to inhabit
And dangle after bad men in Fool's Forest.
"Must they be bad?" said casuistical Max.
"Mightn't a good boy who stopped saying his prayers
Be allowed to slip into the spider's fingers?"
Max raised his sword—but what can swords do
Against the Prince of the Dark? Max sheathed his point
And crept around the pool.

In the middle of the wood was a Red Witch.
Max half expected her. He never expected
To find a witch's house so dirty and foolish,
A witch with a wide bosom yellow as butter,
Or a witch combing so many obscene things

From her black hair into her scarlet lap.
He never believed there would attempt to sing
The one that taught the rats to squeal and Bashan's
Bull to bellow.

"Littlest and last Van Vrooman, do you come too?"
She knew him, it appeared, would know him better,
The scarlet hulk of hell with a fat bosom,
Pirouetting at the bottom of the forest.
Certainly Max had come, but he was going,
Unequal contests never being commanded
On young knights only armed in innocency.
"When I am a grown man I will come here
And cut your head off!" That was very well;
Not a true heart beating in Christendom
Could have said more, but that for the present would do.
Max went straight home; and nothing chilled him more
Than the company kept him by the witch's laugh
And the witch's song, and the creeping of his flesh.

Max is more firmly domiciliated.
A great house is Van Vrooman, a green slope
South to the sun do the great ones inhabit
And a few children play on the lawn with the nurse.
Max has returned to his play, and you may find him,
His famous curls unsmoothed, if you will call
Where the Van Vroomans live, the tribe Van Vrooman
Live there, at least, when any are at home.

ANTIQUE HARVESTERS

(*Scene: Of the Mississippi the bank sinister, and of the Ohio the bank sinister*)

Tawny are the leaves turned, but they still hold.
It is the harvest; what shall this land produce?
A meager hill of kernels, a runnel of juice.
Declension looks from our land, it is old.
Therefore let us assemble, dry, gray, spare.
And mild as yellow air.

"I hear the creak of a raven's funeral wing."
The young men would be joying in the song
Of passionate birds; their memories are not long.
What is it thus rehearsed in sable? "Nothing."
Trust not but the old endure, and shall be older
Than the scornful beholder.

We pluck the spindling ears and gather the corn.
One spot has special yield? "On this spot stood
Heroes and drenched it with their only blood."
And talk meets talk, as echoes from the horn

Of the hunter—echoes are the old men's arts
Ample are the chambers of their hearts.

Here come the hunters, keepers of a rite.
The horn, the hounds, the lank mares coursing by
Under quaint archetypes of chivalry;
And the fox, lovely ritualist, in flight
Offering his unearthly ghost to quarry;
And the fields, themselves to harry.

Resume, harvesters. The treasure is full bronze
Which you will garner for the Lady, and the moon
Could tinge it no yellower than does this noon;
But the gray will quench it shortly—the fields, men, stones.
Pluck fast, dreamers; prove as you rumble slowly
Not less than men, not wholly.

Bare the arm too, dainty youths, bend the knees
Under bronze burdens. And by an autumn tone
As by a gray, as by a green, you will have known
Your famous Lady's image; for so have these.
And if one say that easily will your hands
More prosper in other lands,

Angry as wasp-music be your cry then:
"Forsake the Proud Lady, of the heart of fire,
The look of snow, to the praise of a dwindled choir,
Song of degenerate specters that were men?
The sons of the fathers shall keep her, worthy of
What these have done in love."

True, it is said of our Lady, she ageth.
But see, if you peep shrewdly, she hath not stooped;
Take no thought of her servitors that have drooped,
For we are nothing; and if one talk of death—
Why, the ribs of the earth subsist frail as a breath
If but God wearieth.

PIAZZA PIECE

—I am a gentleman in a dustcoat trying
To make you hear. Your ears are soft and small
And listen to an old man not at all;
They want the young men's whispering and sighing.
But see the roses on your trellis dying
And hear the spectral singing of the moon—
For I must have my lovely lady soon.
I am a gentleman in a dustcoat trying.

—I am a lady young in beauty waiting
Until my truelove comes, and then we kiss.
But what gray man among the vines is this

Whose words are dry and faint as in a dream?
Back from my trellis, sir, before I scream!
I am a lady young in beauty waiting.

CAPTAIN CARPENTER

Captain Carpenter rose up in his prime
Put on his pistols and went riding out
But had got wellnigh nowhere at that time
Till he fell in with ladies in a rout.

It was a pretty lady and all her train
That played with him so sweetly but before
An hour she'd taken a sword with all her main
And twined him of his nose for evermore.

Captain Carpenter mounted up one day
And rode straightway into a stranger rogue
That looked unchristian but be that as it may
The Captain did not wait upon prologue.

But drew upon him out of his great heart
The other swung against him with a club
And cracked his two legs at the shinny part
And let him roll and stick like any tub.

Captain Carpenter rode many a time
From male and female took he sundry harms
He met the wife of Satan crying "I'm
The she-wolf bids you shall bear no more arms."

Their strokes and counters whistled in the wind
I wish he had delivered half his blows
But where she should have made off like a hind
The bitch bit off his arms at the elbows.

And Captain Carpenter parted with his ears
To a black devil that used him in this wise
O jesus ere his threescore and ten years
Another had plucked out his sweet blue eyes.

Captain Carpenter got up on his roan
And sallied from the gate in hell's despite
I heard him asking in the grimmest tone
If any enemy yet there was to fight?

"To any adversary it is fame
If he risk to be wounded by my tongue
Or burnt in two beneath my red heart's flame
Such are the perils he is cast among.

"But if he can he has a pretty choice
From an anatomy with little to lose
Whether he cut my tongue and take my voice
Or whether it be my round red heart he choose."

It was the neatest knave that ever was seen
Stepping in perfume from his lady's bower
Who at this word put in his merry mien
And fell on Captain Carpenter like a tower.

I would not knock old fellows in the dust
But there lay Captain Carpenter on his back
His weapons were the old heart in his bust
And a blade shook between rotten teeth alack.

The rogue in scarlet and gray soon knew his mind
He wished to get his trophy and depart;
With gentle apology and touch refined
He pierced him and produced the Captain's heart.

God's mercy rest on Captain Carpenter now
I thought him Sirs an honest gentleman
Citizen husband soldier and scholar enow
Let jangling kites eat of him if they can.

But God's deep curses follow after those
That shore him of his goodly nose and ears
His legs and strong arms at the two elbows
And eyes that had not watered seventy years.

The curse of hell upon the sleek upstart
Who got the Captain finally on his back
And took the red red vitals of his heart
And made the kites to whet their beaks clack clack.

OLD MAN PONDERED

Three times he crossed our way where with me went
One who is fair and gentle, and it was strange,
But not once glancing did his vision range
Wayward on me, or my most innocent,
But strictly watched his own predicament.
How are old spirits so dead? His eye seemed true
As mine, he walked by it, it was as blue,
How came it monstered in its fixed intent?

But I will venture how. In his long years
Close-watched and dangerous, many a bright-barbed hate
Burning had smote against the optic gate
To enter and destroy. But the quick gears

Blinked shut the aperture. Else those grim leers
Had won to the inner chamber where sat Hope
To spin and pray, and made her misanthrope,
And bled her courage with a thousand spears.

Thus hate and scorn. And he must guard as well
Against alluring love, whose mild engine
Was perilous too for the lone sitter-in,
So hard consented to her little cell;
The tenderest looks vainly upon him fell,
Of dearest company, lest one light arrow
Be sharpened with a most immortal sorrow.
So had he kept his mansion shut of hell.

Firm and upright he walked for one so old,
Thrice-pondered; and I dare not prophesy
What age must bring me; for I look round bold
And seek my enemies out; and leave untold
The sideway watery dog's-glances I
Send fawning on you, thinking you will not scold.

PARTING, WITHOUT A SEQUEL

She has finished and sealed the letter
At last, which he so richly has deserved,
With characters venomous and hatefully curved,
And nothing could be better.

But even as she gave it,
Saying to the blue-capped functioner of doom,
"Into his hands," she hoped the leering groom
Might somewhere lose and leave it.

Then all the blood
Forsook the face. She was too pale for tears,
Observing the ruin of her younger years.
She went and stood

Under her father's vaunting oak
Who kept his peace in wind and sun, and glistened
Stoical in the rain; to whom she listened
If he spoke.

And now the agitation of the rain
Rasped his sere leaves, and he talked low and gentle,
Reproaching the wan daughter by the lintel;
Ceasing, and beginning again.

Away went the messenger's bicycle,
His serpent's track went up the hill forever.
And all the time she stood there hot as fever
And cold as any icicle.

PRELUDE TO AN EVENING

Do not enforce the tired wolf
Dragging his infected wound homeward
To sit tonight with the warm children
Naming the pretty kings of France.

The images of the invaded mind
Being as monsters in the dreams
Of your most brief enchanted headful,
Suppose a miracle of confusion:

That dreamed and undreamt become each other
And mix the night and day of your mind;
And it does not matter your twice crying
From mouth unbeautied against the pillow

To avert the gun of the same old soldier;
For cry, cock-crow, or the iron bell
Can crack the sleep-sense of outrage,
Annihilate phantoms who were nothing.

But now, by our perverse supposal,
There is a drift of fog on your mornings;
You in your peignoir, dainty at your orange cup,
Feel poising round the sunny room

Invisible evil, deprived and bold.
All day the clock will metronome
Your gallant fear; the needles clicking,
The heels detonating the stair's cavern.

Freshening the water in the blue bowls
For the buckberries, with not all your love,
You shall be listening for the low wind,
The warning sibilance of pines.

You like a waning moon, and I accusing
Our too banded Eumenides,
While you pronounce Noes wanderingly
And smooth the heads of the hungry children.

PAINTING: A HEAD

By dark severance the apparition head
Smiles from the air a capital on no
Column or a Platonic perhaps head
On a canvas sky depending from nothing;

Stirs up an old illusion of grandeur
By tickling the instinct of heads to be
Absolute and to try decapitation
And to play truant from the body bush;

But too happy and beautiful for those sorts
Of head (homekeeping heads are happiest)
Discovers maybe thirty unwidowed years
Of not dishonoring the faithful stem;

Is nameless and has authored for the evil
Historian headhunters neither book
Nor state and is therefore distinct from tart
Heads with crowns and guilty gallery heads;

So that the extravagant device of art
Unhousing by abstraction this once head
Was capital irony by a loving hand
That knew the no treason of a head like this;

Makes repentance in an unlovely head
For vinegar disparagement of flesh
Till, the hurt flesh recusing, the hard egg
Is shrunken to its own deathlike surface;

And an image thus: the body bears the head
(So hardly one they terribly are two)
Feeds and obeys and unto please what end?
Not to the glory of tyrant head but to

The increase of body. Beauty is of body.
The flesh contouring shallowly on a head
Is a rock-garden needing body's love
And best bodiness to colorify

The big blue birds sitting and sea-shell flats
And caves and on the iron acropolis
To spread the hyacinthine hair and rear
The olive garden for the nightingales.

Conrad Aiken

ঔ Conrad (Potter) Aiken was born at Savannah, Georgia, August 5, 1889. He attended Harvard, was chosen class poet during his senior year, received his A.B. in 1912, traveled extensively for three years, and since then devoted all his time to literature, living at South Yarmouth, Massachusetts, until 1921. In that year he moved his family to England; a few years later he bought a house on the Sussex coast at Rye. After a brief return to America in 1928 Aiken alternated between England and Massachusetts, finally settling in the latter.

The outstanding feature of Aiken's work is its rapid adaptability and its slow growth. His first volume, *Earth Triumphant and Other Tales in Verse* (1914), is the Keats tradition crossed, paraphrased, and vulgarized by Masefield. *Turns and Movies* (1916) is a complete change; Masefield is exchanged for Masters. But in the less conspicuous half of this book Aiken begins to speak with his true voice. Here he is the natural musician, playing with new rhythms, haunting cadences. *The Jig of Forslin* (1916) is an elaboration of his method. In this volume Aiken goes back to the narrative—or rather, to a series of loosely connected stories—and, reënforced by studies in analytical psychology, explores "the process of vicarious wish fulfillment by which civilized man enriches his circumscribed life."

Nocturne of Remembered Spring (1917), *The Charnel Rose* (1918) and *The House of Dust* (1920) are packed with a tired but often beautiful music. Even though it is enlivened by injections of T. S. Eliot's conversational idiom, the effect is frequently misty and monotonous. Rain seems to fall persistently through these volumes; dust blows down the street; the shadows blur; everything dissolves in a wash of boredom and forgetfulness. Even the poignance seems on the point of falling asleep, and the lyrics sound like echoes heard in a dream.

Often Aiken loses himself in this watery welter of language. In trying to create a closer *liaison* between poetry and music, he places so much importance on the rise and fall of syllables that his very excess of melody defeats his purpose. His verse, thus, gains greatly on the sensuous side, but loses, in its murmuring indefiniteness, that vitality of speech which is the very blood of poetry. It is a subaqueous music, strangely like the magic of Debussy.

This weakening overinsistence on sound does not prevent Aiken from attaining many exquisite effects. Primarily a lyric poet, he condenses an emotion in a few lines; some of his best moments are these "lapses" into tune. The music of the "Morning Song from 'Senlin'" (in *The Charnel Rose*) is rich with subtleties of rhythm. But it is much more than a lyrical movement. Beneath the flow and flexibility of these lines there is a summoning of the immensities that loom behind the casual moments of everyday.

Punch: The Immortal Liar (1921) is an almost complete *volte face.* After it seemed established that Aiken's gift was limited to the twitching of overrefined nerves, to a too ready response to gloomy subconsciousness, the poet strikes out toward a naked directness. Brilliant though the first half of this work is, it is the second part which burns steadily. Here Punch, stripped of his mask of braggadocio, is revealed as the solitary, frustrated dreamer; a pitiful puppet floundering in a net he cannot see; jerked and gesticulating without knowledge of the strings which direct him—a symbol, in short, of man as marionette. This second part of *Punch* contains not only Aiken's most delicate exposition of the inhibited soul, but some of the finest lyrics he has produced.

Priapus and the Pool (1922) is preponderantly lyrical, containing twenty-five songs, several of which are as skillful as those of any contemporary American singer. The succeeding volume, *The Pilgrimage of Festus* (1923), returns to the symphonic form; beneath its imaginative outlines it is an extended essay in epistemology. Festus is the lineal descendant of Aiken's own Senlin and a not distant relative of Ibsen's Peer Gynt. A revised and enlarged edition of *Priapus and the Pool* appeared in 1925.

Aiken, the keenest critic of his own poetry, has been quick to see its limitations as well as its potentialities. In a self-analysis in which he confessed that his verse has groped continually toward symphonic arrangement, Aiken wrote, "Here I give myself away as being in quest of a sort of absolute poetry, a poetry in which the intention is not so much to arouse an emotion, or to persuade of a reality, as to employ such emotion or sense of reality (tangentially struck) with the same cool detachment with which a composer employs notes or chords."

Here we are at the heart of the contradiction: the paradox that, though Aiken is undoubtedly one of the most musical of living poets, he is one of the least popular. An audience that prefers its emotion outright, that craves a palpable reality, resents (or, worse, ignores) the nuance "tangentially struck." The emphasis on overtone and implication creates, too often, an obscure pantomime; it is, as Aiken himself was quick to see, "a prestidigitation in which the juggler's bottles or balls are a little too apt, unfortunately, to be altogether invisible." What is even more obvious, an audience is quick to sense the performer's uncertainty. This—until the most recent work—has been Aiken's undoing. He has fancied himself as a symphonist when he was, preëminently, a lyricist, albeit a lyricist neither pure nor simple. More than any contemporary, except T. S. Eliot, who seems to have learned several tricks in dissonance from Aiken, he has evolved a subtly subjective poetry which flows as smoothly, as surprisingly, as the stream of the subconscious. He has given formlessness a form, has brought tortured self-analysis to a pitch of pure poetry, and (whether in the suspensions of the famous "Morning Song from 'Senlin'" or the more certain modulations of "Tetélestai") he has registered an immediacy of anguish. Aiken's growth in tonal surety must be evident to all but the tone-deaf. "The Road" is more than a compelling dream picture; in it Aiken contradicts his own credo and participates in the struggle of humanity. "At a Concert of Music" and "Annihilation" bring the earlier modulations to a perfect cadence.

Aiken's musical advance is cumulatively established by the *Selected Poems* (1929), which won the Pulitzer Prize for that year, *John Deth and Other Poems* (1930), and *Landscape West of Eden* (1933). All these deal with sets of symbols and dream pictures in a limbo of fantasy. *John Deth* is one of the most curious poems Aiken has written, and the lyrics which follow it ("Annihilation," "The Quarrel," "At a Concert of Music," with others) are among his completely successful pieces, something which cannot be said for *The Coming Forth by Day of Osiris Jones* (1931).

The music of such meditative lyrics is pitched lower in the somber "preludes" which began preoccupying Aiken before 1930 and of which he has written a hundred or more. Sixty-three of these were published in *Preludes for Memnon* (1931) and, though Memnon typified the sun, these poems seem chiefly addressed to darkness. The mood is disconsolate, the tone languorous to lugubrious. Most of the book suggests that abstract and "absolute" poetry to which Aiken has so often tuned his muted instruments, yet several of the individual poems ("This is not you?" "So, in the evening to the simple cloister," "But how it came from earth," "One star fell and another as we walked") are rich in movement and emotional intensity.

Time in the Rock (1936), which was sub-titled "Preludes to Definition," was received more cordially than *And in the Human Heart* (1940), a sequence of forty-three sonnets, which was faintly praised for its fluency and loudly damned for its shopworn rhetoric. Reviewing *And in the Human Heart* as a piece of outworn incantation, an attempt to trade "in rhetorical magic," Randall Jarrell wrote in *The New Republic,* "He is in love with a few dozen words, and their permutations and combinations have assumed for him a weight and urgency that would be quite incomprehensible to his readers, if it were not for the fact that most of these terms are the traditional magic-making words of English romantic poetry. . . . To him, now, the world exists as a thesaurus from which to derive the glittering and immaculate counters that arrange themselves, almost automatically, into a poem. Any similarity between the poems and reality is purely coincidental." But two weeks later Malcolm Cowley replied in the same journal, "Mr. Jarrell fails to discuss Mr. Aiken's real methods. He does not mention his subtly varied repetitions; and above all he does not say anything about the music of Mr. Aiken's verse." *Brownstone Eclogues* (1942) emphasizes and extends that music. *The Kid* (1947) is a set of rhymed metaphors on the American dream, a small-scale effort at large-scale myth-making.

Besides his poetry, Aiken has written some extraordinarily sensitive criticism. *Scepticisms* (1919) is a provocative and valuable set of studies. His anthologies—*Modern American Poets* (1922) and *American Poetry, 1671-1928*—suffer from Aiken's predilection for experimental and abstract verse, but are far superior to the ordinary compilation. He edited the first *Selected Poems of Emily Dickinson* which appeared in England in 1924. In that year his prose began to attract attention. *Bring! Bring!* (1925) and *Costumes by Eros* (1928) are collections of introspective short stories in a successful if not altogether new genre. *Blue Voyage* (1927) is less influenced, a novel closely woven and strangely unresolved. *Great Circle* (1933) is a tense study in psychopathological maladjustment, a theme which Aiken employs with skill and extraordinary effect. *King Coffin* (1935), a novel, is a brilliant study of a paranoiac and his "perfect" crime. *Collected Poems,* a book of almost nine hundred pages, appeared in 1953. *A Reviewer's ABC,* a collected critical volume, appeared in 1958.

BREAD AND MUSIC

Music I heard with you was more than music,
And bread I broke with you was more than bread;
Now that I am without you, all is desolate;
All that was once so beautiful is dead.

Your hands once touched this table and this silver,
And I have seen your fingers hold this glass.
These things do not remember you, belovèd,
And yet your touch upon them will not pass.

For it was in my heart you moved among them,
And blessed them with your hands and with your eyes;
And in my heart they will remember always,—
They knew you once, O beautiful and wise.

MIRACLES

Twilight is spacious, near things in it seem far,
And distant things seem near.
Now in the green west hangs a yellow star.
And now across old waters you may hear
The profound gloom of bells among still trees,
Like a rolling of huge bowlders beneath seas.

Silent as thought in evening contemplation
Weaves the bat under the gathering stars.
Silent as dew, we seek new incarnation,
Meditate new avatars.
In a clear dusk like this
Mary climbed up the hill to seek her son,
To lower him down from the cross, and kiss
The mauve wounds, every one.

Men with wings
In the dusk walked softly after her.
She did not see them, but may have felt
The winnowed air around her stir;
She did not see them, but may have known
Why her son's body was light as a little stone.
She may have guessed that other hands were there
Moving the watchful air.

Now, unless persuaded by searching music
Which suddenly opens the portals of the mind,
We guess no angels,
And are contented to be blind.
Let us blow silver horns in the twilight,
And lift our hearts to the yellow star in the green,
To find perhaps, if, while the dew is rising,
Clear things may not be seen.

MORNING SONG FROM "SENLIN"

It is morning, Senlin says, and in the morning
When the light drips through the shutters like the dew,

I arise, I face the sunrise,
And do the things my fathers learned to do.
Stars in the purple dusk above the rooftops
Pale in a saffron mist and seem to die,
And I myself on a swiftly tilting planet
Stand before a glass and tie my tie.

Vine-leaves tap my window,
Dew-drops sing to the garden stones,
The robin chirps in the chinaberry tree
Repeating three clear tones.

It is morning. I stand by the mirror
And tie my tie once more.
While waves far off in a pale rose twilight
Crash on a white sand shore.
I stand by a mirror and comb my hair:
How small and white my face!—
The green earth tilts through a sphere of air
And bathes in a flame of space.
There are houses hanging above the stars
And stars hung under a sea . . .
And a sun far off in a shell of silence
Dapples my walls for me. . . .

It is morning, Senlin says, and in the morning
Should I not pause in the light to remember God?
Upright and firm I stand on a star unstable,
He is immense and lonely as a cloud.
I will dedicate this moment before my mirror
To him alone, for him I will comb my hair.
Accept these humble offerings, clouds of silence!
I will think of you as I descend the stair.

Vine-leaves tap my window,
The snail-track shines on the stones;
Dew-drops flash from the chinaberry tree
Repeating two clear tones.

It is morning, I awake from a bed of silence,
Shining I rise from the starless waters of sleep.
The walls are about me still as in the evening,
I am the same, and the same name still I keep.
The earth revolves with me, yet makes no motion,
The stars pale silently in a coral sky.
In a whistling void I stand before my mirror,
Unconcerned, and tie my tie.

There are horses neighing on far-off hills
Tossing their long white manes,
And mountains flash in the rose-white dusk,
Their shoulders black with rains. . . .

It is morning, I stand by the mirror
And surprise my soul once more;
The blue air rushes above my ceiling,
There are suns beneath my floor. . . .

. . . It is morning, Senlin says, I ascend from darkness
And depart on the winds of space for I know not where;
My watch is wound, a key is in my pocket,
And the sky is darkened as I descend the stair.
There are shadows across the windows, clouds in heaven,
And a god among the stars; and I will go
Thinking of him as I might think of daybreak
And humming a tune I know. . . .

Vine-leaves tap at the window,
Dew-drops sing to the garden stones,
The robin chirps in the chinaberry tree
Repeating three clear tones.

THE ROOM

Through that window—all else being extinct
Except itself and me—I saw the struggle
Of darkness against darkness. Within the room
It turned and turned, dived downward. Then I saw
How order might—if chaos wished—become:
And saw the darkness crush upon itself,
Contracting powerfully; it was as if
It killed itself, slowly: and with much pain.
Pain. The scene was pain, and nothing but pain.
What else, when chaos draws all forces inward
To shape a single leaf? . . .
                                        For the leaf came
Alone and shining in the empty room;
After a while the twig shot downward from it;
And from the twig a bough; and then the trunk,
Massive and coarse; and last the one black root.
The black root cracked the walls. Boughs burst the window:
The great tree took possession.
                                        Tree of trees!
Remember (when time comes) how chaos died
To shape the shining leaf. Then turn, have courage,
Wrap arms and roots together, be convulsed
With grief, and bring back chaos out of shape.
I will be watching then as I watch now.
I will praise darkness now, but then the leaf.

THE PUPPET DREAMS

(*from "Punch: The Immortal Liar"*)

Sheba, now let down your hair,
And play upon it with your hands,
While girls from Tal and Mozambique
Parade before in sarabands,—

Play him songs inaudible
With white hands braceleted and slim,
Or shake your hair and let it fall
And softly darken him.

Cling to him, while cymbals far
Are sweetly smitten in the dusk,
And maenads, under a haughty star,
Break the white rose for its musk:

Cling to him, and with your lips
Feed his heart on crumbs of fire
That shall, perpetually, delight
But never slay desire!

✣

Open a window on the world
With all its sorrow, and then
When he has heard that sound a space,
Close it fast again. . . .

Sweet will it be, lapped round with ease
And music-troubled air,
To hear for a moment on the wind
A sound of far despair:

And then, to turn to lights again,
And fingers soft on strings,
While Sheba slips her bracelets off
And spreads her arms and sings. . . .

Sweet will it be, to hear far off
That gusty sound of pain,
And to remember, far away,
A world of death and rain:

And then, to close the window fast,
And laugh, and clap soft hands,
While girls from Tal and Mozambique
Parade in sarabands. . . .

Close now the window! Close it well!
That slow lament of pain
Was but the dissonance that makes
Dull music sweet again.

✣

There is a fountain in a wood
Where wavering lies a moon:
It plays to the slowly falling leaves
A sleepy tune.

. . . The peach-trees lean upon a wall
Of gold and ivory:
The peacock spreads his tail, the leaves
Fall silently. . . .

There, amid silken sounds and wine
And music idly broken,
The drowsy god observes his world
With no word spoken.

Arcturus, rise! Orion, fall! . . .
The white-winged stars obey. . . .
Or else he greets his Fellow-God;
And there, in the dusk, they play

A game of chess with stars for pawns
And a silver moon for queen:
Immeasurable as clouds, above
A chess-board world they lean

And thrust their hands amid their beards,
And utter words profound
That shake the star-swung firmament
With a fateful sound! . . .

. . . The peach-trees lean upon a wall
Of gold and ivory;
The peacock spreads his tail; the leaves
Fall silently. . . .

PORTRAIT OF A GIRL

This is the shape of the leaf, and this of the flower,
And this the pale bole of the tree
Which watches its bough in a pool of unwavering water
In a land we never shall see.

The thrush on the bough is silent, the dew falls softly,
In the evening is hardly a sound. . . .
And the three beautiful pilgrims who come here together
Touch lightly the dust of the ground.

Touch it with feet that trouble the dust but as wings do,
Come shyly together, are still,
Like dancers who wait in a pause of the music, for music
The exquisite silence to fill . . .

This is the thought of the first, and this of the second,
And this the grave thought of the third:
"Linger we thus for a moment, palely expectant,
And silence will end, and the bird

"Sing the pure phrase, sweet phrase, clear phrase in the twilight
To fill the blue bell of the world;
And we, who on music so leaflike have drifted together,
Leaflike apart shall be whirled

"Into what but the beauty of silence, silence forever? . . ."
. . . This is the shape of the tree,
And the flower and the leaf, and the three pale beautiful pilgrims:
This is what you are to me.

AND IN THE HANGING GARDENS—

And in the hanging gardens there is rain
From midnight until one, striking the leaves
And bells of flowers, and stroking boles of planes,
And drawing slow arpeggios over pools
And stretching strings of sound from eaves to ferns.
The princess reads. The gnave of diamonds sleeps.
The king is drunk, and flings a golden goblet
Down from the turret window (curtained with rain)
Into the lilacs.
And at one o'clock
The vulcan under the garden wakes and beats
The gong upon his anvil. Then the rain
Ceases, but gently ceases, dripping still,
And sound of falling water fills the dark
As leaves grow bold and upright, and as eaves
Part with water. The princess turns the page
Beside the candle, and between two braids
Of golden hair. And reads: "From there I went
Northward a journey of four days, and came
To a wild village in the hills, where none
Was living save the vulture and the rat
And one old man who laughed but could not speak.
The roofs were fallen in, the well grown over
With weed. And it was here my father died.

Then eight days further, bearing slightly west,
The cold wind blowing sand against our faces,
The food tasting of sand. And as we stood
By the dry rock that marks the highest point
My brother said: 'Not too late is it yet
To turn, remembering home.' And we were silent
Thinking of home." The princess shuts her eyes
And feels the tears forming beneath her eyelids
And opens them, and tears fall on the page.
The knave of diamonds in the darkened room
Throws off his covers, sleeps, and snores again.
The king goes slowly down the turret stairs
To find the goblet.

And at two o'clock
The vulcan in his smithy underground
Under the hanging gardens, where the drip
Of rain among the clematis and ivy
Still falls from sipping flower to purple flower
Smites twice his anvil, and the murmur comes
Among the roots and vines. The princess reads:
"As I am sick, and cannot write you more,
And have not long to live, I give this letter
To him, my brother, who will bear it south
And tell you how I died. Ask how it was,
There in the northern desert, where the grass
Was withered, and the horses, all but one,
Perished . . ." The princess drops her golden head
Upon the page between her two white arms
And golden braids. The knave of diamonds wakes
And at his window in the darkened room
Watches the lilacs tossing, where the king
Seeks for the goblet.

And at three o'clock
The moon inflames the lilac heads, and thrice
The vulcan, in his root-bound smithy, clangs
His anvil; and the sounds creep softly up
Among the vines and walls. The moon is round,
Round as a shield above the turret top.
The princess blows her candle out, and weeps
In the pale room, where scent of lilacs comes,
Weeping, with hands across her eyelids, thinking
Of withered grass, withered by sandy wind.
The knave of diamonds, in his darkened room,
Holds in his hands a key, and softly steps
Along the corridor, and slides the key
Into the door that guards her. Meanwhile, slowly,
The king, with raindrops on his beard and hands,
And dripping sleeves, climbs up the turret stairs,
Holding the goblet upright in one hand;
And pauses on the midmost step to taste
One drop of wine wherewith wild rain has mixed.

THE ROAD

Three then came forward out of darkness, one
An old man bearded, his old eyes red with weeping,
A peasant, with hard hands. "Come now," he said,
"And see the Road, for which our people die.
Twelve miles of road we've made, a little only,
Westward winding. Of human blood and stone
We build; and in a thousand years will come
Beyond the hills to sea."

I went with them,
Taking a lantern, which upon their faces
Showed years and grief; and in a time we came
To the wild road which wound among wild hills
Westward; and so along this road we stopped,
Silent, thinking of all the dead men there
Compounded with sad clay. Slowly we moved:
For they were old and weak, had given all
Their life to build this twelve poor miles of road,
Muddy, under the rain. And in my hand,
Turning the lantern here or there, I saw
Deep holes of water where the raindrop splashed,
And rainfilled footprints in the grass, and heaps
Of broken stone, and rusted spades and picks,
And helves of axes. And the old man spoke,
Holding my wrist: "Three hundred years it took
To build these miles of road: three hundred years;
And human lives unnumbered. But the day
Will come when it is done." Then spoke another,
One not so old, but old, whose face was wrinkled:
"And when it comes, our people will all sing
For joy, passing from east to west, or west
To east, returning, with the light behind them;
All meeting in the road and singing there."
And the third said: "The road will be their life;
A heritage of blood. Grief will be in it,
And beauty out of grief. And I can see
How all the women's faces will be bright.
In that time, laughing, they will remember us.
Blow out your lantern now, for day is coming."

My lantern blown out, in a little while
We climbed in long light up a hill, where climbed
The dwindling road, and ended in a field.
Peasants were working in the field, bowed down
With unrewarded work and grief and years
Of pain. And as we passed them, one man fell
Into a furrow that was bright with water
And gave a cry that was half cry, half song—
"The road . . . the road . . . the road . . ." And all then fell

Upon their knees and sang.
We four passed on
Over the hills, to westward. . . . Then I felt
How tears ran down my face, tears without end,
And knew that all my life henceforth was weeping,
Weeping, thinking of human grief, and human
Endeavor fruitless in a world of pain.
And when I held my hands up they were old;
I knew my face would not be young again.

ANNIHILATION

While the blue noon above us arches
And the poplar sheds disconsolate leaves,
Tell me again why love bewitches
And what love gives.

Is it the trembling finger that traces
The eyebrow's curve, the curve of the cheek?
The mouth that quivers, while the hand caresses,
But cannot speak?

No, not these, not in these is hidden
The secret, more than in other things:
Not only the touch of a hand can gladden
Till the blood sings.

It is the leaf that falls between us,
The bell that murmurs, the shadows that move
The autumnal sunlight that fades upon us,
These things are love.

It is the "No, let us sit here longer,"
The "Wait till tomorrow," the "Once I knew"—
These trifles, said as you touch my finger
And the clock strikes two.

The world is intricate, and we are nothing.
It is the complex world of grass,
The twig on the path, a look of loathing,
Feelings that pass—

These are the secret; and I could hate you
When, as I lean for another kiss,
I see in your eyes that I do not meet you,
And that love is this.

Rock meeting rock can know love better
Than eyes that stare or lips that touch.
All that we know in love is bitter,
And it is not much.

THE QUARREL

Suddenly, after the quarrel, while we waited,
Disheartened, silent, with downcast looks, nor stirred
Eyelid nor finger, hopeless both, yet hoping
Against all hope to unsay the sundering word:

While all the room's stillness deepened, deepened about us,
And each of us crept his thought's way to discover
How, with as little sound as the fall of a leaf,
The shadow had fallen, and lover quarreled with lover;

And while, in the quiet, I marveled—alas, alas—
At your deep beauty, your tragic beauty, torn
As the pale flower is torn by the wanton sparrow—
This beauty, pitied and loved, and now forsworn;

It was then, when the instant darkened to its darkest,—
When faith was lost with hope, and the rain conspired
To strike its gray arpeggios against our heartstrings,—
When love no longer dared, and scarcely desired:

It was then that suddenly, in the neighbor's room,
The music started: that brave quartette of strings
Breaking out of the stillness, as out of our stillness,
Like the indomitable heart of life that sings

When all is lost; and startled from our sorrow,
Tranced from our grief by that diviner grief,
We raised remembering eyes, each looked at other,
Blinded with tears of joy; and another leaf

Fell silently as that first; and in the instant
The shadow had gone, our quarrel became absurd;
And we rose, to the angelic voices of the music,
And I touched your hand, and we kissed, without a word.

AT A CONCERT OF MUSIC

Be still, while the music rises about us: the deep enchantment
  Towers, like a forest of singing leaves and birds,
Built for an instant by the heart's troubled beating,
  Beyond all power of words.

And while you are silent, listening, I escape you,
  And I run, by a secret path, through that bright wood
To another time, forgotten, and another woman,
  And another mood.
Then, too, the music's pure algebra of enchantment
  Wrought all about us a bird-voice-haunted grove.

Then, too, I escaped, as now, to an earlier moment
And a brighter love.

Alas! Can I never have peace in the shining instant?
The hard bright crystal of being, in time and space?
Must I always touch, in the moment, a remembered moment,
A remembered face?

Absolve me: I would adore you, had I the secret,
With all this music's power, for yourself alone:
I would try to answer, in the world's chaotic symphony,
Your one clear tone:

But alas, alas, being everything you are nothing;
The history of all my life is in your face;
And all I can grasp is an earlier, more haunted moment,
And a happier place.

TETÉLESTAI

I

How shall we praise the magnificence of the dead,
The great man humbled, the haughty brought to dust?
Is there a horn we should not blow as proudly
For the meanest of us all, who creeps his days,
Guarding his heart from blows, to die obscurely?
I am no king, have laid no kingdoms waste,
Taken no princes captive, led no triumphs
Of weeping women through long walls of trumpets;
Say rather, I am no one, or an atom;
Say rather, two great gods, in a vault of starlight,
Play ponderingly at chess, and at the game's end
One of the pieces, shaken, falls to the floor
And runs to the darkest corner; and that piece
Forgotten there, left motionless, is I. . . .
Say that I have no name, no gifts, no power,
Am only one of millions, mostly silent;
One who came with eyes and hands and a heart,
Looked on beauty, and loved it, and left it.
Say that the fates of time and space obscured me,
Led me a thousand ways to pain, bemused me,
Wrapped me in ugliness; and like great spiders
Dispatched me at their leisure. . . . Well, what then?
Should I not hear, as I lie down in dust,
The horns of glory blowing above my burial?

II

Morning and evening opened and closed above me:
Houses were built above me; trees let fall
Yellowing leaves upon me, hands of ghosts;
Rain has showered its arrows of silver upon me

Seeking my heart; winds have roared and tossed me;
Music in long blue waves of sound has borne me
A helpless weed to shores of unthought silence;
Time, above me, within me, crashed its gongs
Of terrible warning, sifting the dust of death;
And here I lie. Blow now your horns of glory
Harshly over my flesh, you trees, you waters!
You stars and suns, Canopus, Deneb, Rigel,
Let me, as I lie down, here in this dust,
Hear, far off, your whispered salutation!
Roar now above my decaying flesh, you winds,
Whirl out your earth-scents over this body, tell me
Of ferns and stagnant pools, wild roses, hillsides!
Anoint me, rain, let crash your silver arrows
On this hard flesh! I am the one who named you,
I lived in you, and now I die in you.
I your son, your daughter, treader of music,
Lie, broken, conquered. . . . Let me not fall in silence.

III

I, the restless one; the circler of circles;
Herdsman and roper of stars, who could not capture
The secret of self; I who was tyrant to weaklings,
Striker of children; destroyer of women; corrupter
Of innocent dreamers, and laugher at beauty; I,
Too easily brought to tears and weakness by music,
Baffled and broken by love, the helpless beholder
Of the war in my heart, of desire with desire, the struggle
Of hatred with love, terror with hunger; I
Who laughed without knowing the cause of my laughter, who grew
Without wishing to grow, a servant to my own body;
Loved without reason the laughter and flesh of a woman,
Enduring such torments to find her! I who at last
Grow weaker, struggle more feebly, relent in my purpose,
Choose for my triumph an easier end, look backward
At earlier conquests; or, caught in the web, cry out
In a sudden and empty despair, "Tetélestai!"
Pity me, now! I, who was arrogant, beg you!
Tell me, as I lie down, that I was courageous.
Blow horns of victory now, as I reel and am vanquished.
Shatter the sky with trumpets above my grave.

IV

. . . Look! this flesh how it crumbles to dust and is blown!
These bones, how they grind in the granite of frost and are nothing!
This skull, how it yawns for a flicker of time in the darkness,
Yet laughs not and sees not! It is crushed by a hammer of sunlight,
And the hands are destroyed. . . . Press down through the leaves of the jasmine,
Dig through the interlaced roots—nevermore will you find me;
I was no better than dust, yet you cannot replace me. . . .
Take the soft dust in your hand—does it stir: does it sing?

Has it lips and a heart? Does it open its eyes to the sun?
Does it run, does it dream, does it burn with a secret, or tremble
In terror of death? Or ache with tremendous decisions? . . .
Listen! . . . It says: "I lean by the river. The willows
Are yellowed with bud. White clouds roar up from the south
And darken the ripples; but they cannot darken my heart,
Nor the face like a star in my heart! . . . Rain falls on the water
And pelts it, and rings it with silver. The willow trees glisten,
The sparrow chirps under the eaves; but the face in my heart
Is a secret of music. . . . I wait in the rain and am silent."
Listen again! . . . It says: "I have worked, I am tired,
The pencil dulls in my hand; I see through the window
Walls upon walls of windows with faces behind them,
Smoke floating up to the sky, an ascension of sea-gulls.
I am tired. I have struggled in vain, my decision was fruitless,
Why then do I wait? with darkness, so easy, at hand! . . .
But tomorrow, perhaps. . . . I will wait and endure till tomorrow!" . . .
Or again: "It is dark. The decision is made. I am vanquished
By terror of life. The walls mount slowly about me
In coldness. I had not the courage. I was forsaken.
I cried out, was answered by silence . . . Tetélestai! . . ."

V

Hear how it babbles!—Blow the dust out of your hand,
With its voices and visions, tread on it, forget it, turn homeward
With dreams in your brain. . . . This, then, is the humble, the nameless,—
The lover, the husband and father, the struggler with shadows,
The one who went down under shoutings of chaos, the weakling
Who cried his "forsaken!" like Christ on the darkening hilltop! . . .
This, then, is the one who implores, as he dwindles to silence,
A fanfare of glory. . . . And which of us dares to deny him?

WHEN THE TREE BARES

When the tree bares, the music of it changes:
Hard and keen is the sound, long and mournful;
Pale are the poplar boughs in the evening light
Above my house, against a slate-cold cloud.
When the house ages and the tenants leave it,
Crickets sing in the tall grass by the threshold;
Spider, by the cold mantel, hangs his web.
Here, in a hundred years from that clear season
When first I came here, bearing lights and music,
To this old ghostly house my ghost will come,—
Pause in the half-light, turn by the poplar, glide
Above tall grasses through the broken door.
Who will say that he saw—or the dusk deceived him—
A mist with hands of mist blow down from the tree
And open the door and enter and close it after?
Who will say that he saw, as midnight struck
Its tremulous golden twelve, a light in the window,

And first heard music, as of an old piano,
Music remote, as if it came from the earth,
Far down; and then, in the quiet, eager voices?
". . . Houses grow old and die, houses have ghosts.
Once in a hundred years we return, old house,
And live once more." . . . And then the ancient answer,
In a voice not human, but more like the creak of boards
Or a rattle of panes in the wind—"Not as the owner,
But as a guest you come, to fires not lit
By hands of yours. . . . Through these long-silent chambers
Move slowly, turn, return, and bring once more
Your lights and music. It will be good to talk."

ONE STAR FELL AND ANOTHER

One star fell and another as we walked.
Lifting his hand toward the west, he said—
—How prodigal that sky is of its stars!
They fall and fall, and still the sky is sky.
Two more have gone, but heaven is heaven still.

Then let us not be precious of our thought,
Nor of our words, nor hoard them up as though
We thought our minds a heaven which might change
And lose its virtue, when the word had fallen.
Let us be prodigal, as heaven is;
Lose what we lose, and give what we may give,—
Ourselves are still the same. Lost you a planet—?
Is Saturn gone? Then let him take his rings
Into the Limbo of forgotten things.

O little foplings of the pride of mind,
Who wrap the phrase in lavender, and keep it
In order to display it: and you, who save our loves
As if we had not worlds of love enough—!

Let us be reckless of our words and worlds,
And spend them freely as the tree his leaves;
And give them where the giving is most blest.
What should we save them for,—a night of frost? . . .
All lost for nothing, and ourselves a ghost.

BUT HOW IT CAME FROM EARTH

But how it came from earth this little white
this waxen edge this that is sharp and white
this that is mortal and bright the petals bent
and all so curved as if for lovers meant
and why the earth unfolded in this shape
as coldly as words from the warm mouth escape

Or what it is that made the blood so speak
or what it was it wanted that made this
breath of curled air this hyacinth this word
this that is deeply seen profoundly heard
miracle of quick device
from fire and ice

Or why the snail puts out a horn to see
or the brave heart puts up a hand to take
or why the mind, as if to agonize,
will close, a century ahead, its eyes—
a hundred years put on the clock
its own mortality to mock—

Christ come, Confucius come, and tell us why
the mind delights before its death to die
embracing nothing as a lover might
in a terrific ecstasy of night—
and tell us why the hyacinth is sprung
from the world's dull tongue.

Did death so dream of life, is this its dream?
Does the rock think of flowers in its sleep?
Then words and flowers are only thoughts of stone
unconscious of the joy it thinks upon;
and we ourselves are only the rock's words
stammered in a dark dream of men and birds.

PRELUDE VI

This is not you? These phrases are not you?
That pomegranate of verses was not you?
The green bright leaf not you, nor the gold fruit
Burning amongst the leaves,—hot fruit of gold,—
Nor bird, nor bough, nor bole, nor heaven's blue? . . .
Alas, dear woman, I have sung in vain.

Let me dishevel then once more the leaves
Of Cupid's bright thesaurus, and there find
The word of words, the crimson seed of seeds,
The aureate sound of sounds; and out of this
Conceive once more your beauty, and in terms
Your feminine keen eye will not disdain.

For this is you: on April page it is,
Again on June, and once more on December;
On August page I find it twice; and March
Chronicles it in footnote; and July
Asserts it roundly. Thus, from page to page,
I find you many times in many terms.

It is a snowflake, which is like a star,
And melts upon the hand; it is a cobweb,
Shot with silver, that from the golden lip
Of April's dandelion hangs to the grass;
It is a raindrop,—of tremendous worth,—
Which slides the whole length of a lilac leaf. . . .

This is not you? These symbols are not you?
Not snowflake, cobweb, raindrop? . . . Woman, woman,
You are too literal, too strict with me.
What would you have? Some simple copper coin—
I love you, you are lovely, I adore you?
Or (better still) dumb silence, and a look?

No, no, this will not do; I am not one
For whom these silences are sovereign;
The pauses in the music are not music,
Although they make the music what it is.
Therefore I thumb once more the god's thesaurus,
For phrase and praise, and find it all for you.

It is a star which might be thought a snowflake,
Lost in a twinkling; it is a dandelion
Shrouded with silver brightness; it is a leaf
Which lets the raindrop go, but keeps its light. . . .
It is the purple veining in the white
That makes the pure throat of the iris pure. . . .

Yet you would have me say your hair is Helen's,—
Your gait angelic; while I turn from these
To the vast pages of that manuscript
On which the stars are stars, the world a world;
And there I find you written down, between
Arcturus and a primrose and the sea.

CLOISTER

So, in the evening, to the simple cloister:
This place of boughs, where sounds of water, softly,
Lap on the stones. And this is what you are:
Here, in this dusty room, to which you climb
By four steep flights of stairs. The door is closed:
The furies of the city howl behind you:
The last bell plunges rock-like to the sea:
The horns of taxis wail in vain. You come
Once more, at evening, to this simple cloister;
Hushed by the quiet walls, you stand at peace.

What ferns of thought are these, the cool and green,
Dripping with moisture, that festoon these walls?
What water-lights are these, whose pallid rings
Dance with the leaves, or speckle the pale stones?

What spring is this, that bubbles the cold sand,
Urging the sluggish grains of white and gold? . . .
Peace. The delicious silence throngs with ghosts
Of wingèd sound and shadow. These are you.

Now in the evening, in the simple cloister,
You stand and wait; you stand and listen, waiting
For wingèd sounds, and wingèd silences,
And long-remembered shadows. Here the rock
Lets down its vine of many-colored flowers:
Waiting for you, or waiting for the lizard
To move his lifted claw, or shift his eye
Quick as a jewel. Here the lizard waits
For the slow snake to slide among cold leaves.
And, on the bough that arches the deep pool,
Lapped in a sound of water, the brown thrush
Waits, too, and listens, till his silence makes
Silence as deep as song. And time becomes
A timeless crystal, an eternity,
In which the gone and coming are at peace.

What bird is this, whose silence fills the trees
With rich delight? What leaves and boughs are these,
What lizard, and what snake? . . . The bird is gone:
And while you wait, another comes and goes,—
Another and another; yet your eye,
Although it has not moved, can scarcely say
If birds have come and gone,—so quick, so brief,—
Or if the thrush who waits there is the same. . . .
The snake and lizard change, yet are the same:
The flowers, many-colored, on the vine,
Open and close their multitude of stars,—
Yet are the same. . . . And all these things are you.

Thus, in the evening, in the simple cloister,
Eternity adds ring to ring, the darker
Beyond the brighter; and your silence fills
With such a world of worlds,—so still, so deep,—
As never voice could speak, whether it were
The ocean's or the bird's. The night comes on:
You wait and listen, in the darkened room,
To all these ghosts of change. And they are you.

Edna St. Vincent Millay

☙ Edna St. Vincent Millay was born February 22, 1892, in Rockland, Maine. After a childhood spent in her native State, she attended Vassar College, from which she was graduated in 1917. Coming to New York, she supported herself by writing short stories under various pseudonyms (*Distressing Dialogues,* 1924, published under the name of "Nancy Boyd"), translating songs, acting with the Provincetown Players in the capacity of playwright and performer. After her marriage to Eugen Boissevain, she moved to a farm in the Berkshires, which she left only to travel and deliver occasional readings. She died there October 19, 1950.

Her first long poem, "Renascence," was the outstanding feature of *The Lyric Year* (1912), an anthology which revealed many new names. "Renascence" was written when Miss Millay was scarcely nineteen; it remains one of the most remarkable poems of this generation. Beginning like a casual rhyme, it proceeds to a set of climaxes. It is as if a child had, in the midst of ingenuousness, uttered some terrific truth.

Renascence, Miss Millay's first volume, was published in 1917. The small collection enlarges the tone of the title poem; here is a hunger for beauty so intense that no delight can appease it. Such poems as "God's World" and a few of the unnamed sonnets, capturing the breathless awe of "Renascence" in a smaller compass, vibrate with the emotion of romantic and rebellious youth.

A Few Figs from Thistles (originally published in 1920 and revised several times since then), although one of Miss Millay's most popular collections, is her least commendable. Here she presents herself as a flippant leader of Flaming Youth flaunting her right to be promiscuous, an emancipated woman who is also the naughty little girl determined to shock her elders.

Second April (1921) is a return to the triumph of her first book. In spite of certain lapses in which the poet seems to have adopted a fixed simper, *Second April* expresses that passion for identification with all of life which few poets in her generation have surpassed; she has made ecstasy articulate, and almost tangible. A new note, new at least for this singer, creeps into the lyrics, the note of gravity; here is dignity, almost an austerity, of emotion.

Three plays were published in 1921: *Two Slatterns and a King,* "a moral interlude" in adroit couplets, *The Lamp and the Bell,* a five-act drama which is a strange composite of native speech and Shakespearean echoes, and *Aria Da Capo,* a one-act play which, for all its brevity, is a profound satire on war and war-makers. A juvenile effort, *The Princess Marries the Page,* was exhumed from undergraduate days and published in 1932.

The Harp-Weaver and Other Poems (1924) wears its author's heart on its sleeve. But here Miss Millay begins to wear her heart with a difference. Rarely is she narcissistic or consciously arch; she speaks with a disillusion that contains more than a tinge of bitterness. Love, she announces, sometimes with a wry wistfulness, sometimes with a proud scorn, is not enough. If, she tells us, it is hard never to attain one's desires, it is even more painful to have them fulfilled. The title-poem, which was awarded the Pulitzer Prize for Poetry in 1922, barely saves itself from sentimentality. But the twenty-two sonnets which comprise Part Four of this book are not only representative of Miss Millay's best, but are among the finest modern examples of the form.

The Buck in the Snow and Other Poems (1928) is pitched in the key of loss. The heel-and-toe insouciance has disappeared; a new and more somber poet emerges from these pages. The happy vibrations of her early work have lengthened to a music that no longer celebrates eager dawn or headlong day but is tuned to the beginning of evening. Never has Miss Millay plucked so insistently on the autumnal string; never has she been so preoccupied with the water darkening, with the ceaseless "action of waves and the action of sorrow," with the lonely self, and the going down of "the sun that will not rise again." Her metaphysics of passion remain personal; she is still too much in love with lost love, with the shards of the broken pot, with the memory of a world forgotten, with the spirit of persecution, and the minutiae of unrelinquishing mortal mind. The mood is rarely anything but subjective and self-perturbed.

Exception, however, must be made in the case of a small part of the volume, especially the group which brings the book to its ascending close. The seven sonnets in *The Buck in the Snow* overcome the limitations of the poet as well as the limitations of the form. In "Sonnet to Gath" she has fashioned an irony far removed from impertinence; in "On Hearing a Symphony of Beethoven" she achieves the impossible, writing that rarest of things, a successful poem on a symphony, and holding, in fourteen lines, the music, the orchestra, the audience, and the triumphant catharsis which is Beethoven. Rising above its almost fatal first line, it turns inversions and generalities into a victory over rhetoric.

Fatal Interview (1931), a set of fifty-two love sonnets, was hailed with superlatives. Reviewers strained to outcry each other by comparing the sequence to Mrs. Browning's, Rosetti's, Sidney's, Petrarch's, Shakespeare's, mostly in Miss Millay's favor. Only a few voices registered a minority opinion. Theodore Morrison objected that "the sonnets give the air of being manufactured, of being wondrously clever, an extraordinary simulation rather than the true substance of poetry," and a reviewer in the *London Times* flatly asserted that "the sequence as a whole is rather verbally than truly impassioned. . . . We admire the rhetoric but find little real feeling to which to respond. It is always at the pitch of romantic extravagance."

Wine from These Grapes (1934) betrays, in spite of its author's craftsmanship, the same reliance on rhetoric which marred Fatal Interview. Here, too, the emotion is often inflated, the poem stretched beyond its capacity. There is, moreover, a certain magisterial utterance heard in the books published after 1924, which is suspiciously portentous. *Wine from These Grapes* is, technically, Miss Millay's most uncertain volume; philosophically, it is her most mature one. Here the poet turns from prettiness and the pangs of love, and concerns herself with the bewildered and self-torturing human spirit.

Conversation at Midnight (1937) is Miss Millay's outstanding failure. In the preceding work, the poet had usually spoken in character; she had alternately used the voice of the precocious, subtle child and the mind of the experienced, disillusioned woman. Now she determined to express herself like a man—like seven men. The result is a set of discussions prosy and pretentious. Miss Millay fails to make her men talk with conviction, for she creates neither real controversy nor actual character. She is not a thinker, though she tries hard to be one; she is intuitive, not intellectual. When she relies unhappily on intellect, she falls back upon clichés of thought as well as stereotypes of expression. The confusion is increased by the queer mixture of idioms; at one moment Miss Millay makes her dialecticians discourse in her favorite Elizabethan accent, the next moment she has them imitate Ogden Nash.

Huntsman, What Quarry? (1939) is an effort to return to the personal lyricism in which Miss Millay is most at home: the anatomy of love and defiance of age, a preoccupation which is candid if not self-critical. A few of the poems deal with subjects outside herself, but most of them dramatize a self which still hesitates to discard youth and accept maturity. Even her admirers were cautious in their praise; one of them, Gilbert Maxwell, wrote, "It seems regrettable that she has found in all these years no antidote for her animal fear of death and no substitute for that religious realization so perfectly projected in 'Renascence'." "What complicates its expression," wrote Louise Bogan, "is the influence of the hampering and sometimes destructive role of unofficial feminine laureate which Miss Millay has had to play for so long."

It was as laureate and political commentator, rather than as poet, that Miss Millay wrote *Make Bright the Arrows* (1940). The feeling which prompted the verse was intense, the outrage against the dictators and aggressors was deep and direct; but the reviewers could not help deprecating the facile couplets and journalistic carelessness. As Babette Deutsch wrote, "The subtitle of this thin collection ('1940 Notebook') might disarm the critic, but the fact that Miss Millay has permitted these verse commentaries on current history to appear between boards indicates that she believes in their permanent validity. This belief one must regretfully decline to share." *The Murder of Lidice* (1942) commemorates the Czechoslovak terror without invoking a corresponding emotion in the reader.

The legendary Miss Millay, the feminine Byron of the early 1920s, worshipped by her imitators, has not yet received final appraisal. One estimate rates her importance as high as her undoubted popularity; another deprecates her self-concern and concludes that she expresses "a twentieth century romantic temperament in a nineteenth century romantic vehicle." Critics of the future will be quick to discern the exaggeration, unevenness, and variety of Miss Millay's gifts; they will not fail to find, beyond the literary aptitude, the notes of authority.

RENASCENCE

All I could see from where I stood
Was three long mountains and a wood;
I turned and looked another way,
And saw three islands in a bay.
So with my eyes I traced the line
Of the horizon, thin and fine,
Straight around till I was come
Back to where I'd started from;
And all I saw from where I stood
Was three long mountains and a wood.
Over these things I could not see;
These were the things that bounded me;
And I could touch them with my hand,
Almost, I thought, from where I stand.
And all at once things seemed so small
My breath came short, and scarce at all.
But, sure, the sky is big, I said;
Miles and miles above my head;
So here upon my back I'll lie
And look my fill into the sky.
And so I looked, and, after all,
The sky was not so very tall.
The sky, I said, must somewhere stop,
And—sure enough!—I see the top!

The sky, I thought, is not so grand;
I 'most could touch it with my hand!
And, reaching up my hand to try,
I screamed to feel it touch the sky.

I screamed, and—lo!—Infinity
Came down and settled over me;
Forced back my scream into my chest,
Bent back my arm upon my breast,
And, pressing of the Undefined
The definition on my mind,
Held up before my eyes a glass
Through which my shrinking sight did pass
Until it seemed I must behold
Immensity made manifold;
Whispered to me a word whose sound
Deafened the air for worlds around,
And brought unmuffled to my ears
The gossiping of friendly spheres,
The creaking of the tented sky,
The ticking of Eternity.

I saw and heard, and knew at last
The How and Why of all things, past,
And present, and forevermore.
The universe, cleft to the core,
Lay open to my probing sense
That, sickening, I would fain pluck thence
But could not,—nay! But needs must suck
At the great wound, and could not pluck
My lips away till I had drawn
All venom out.—Ah, fearful pawn!
For my omniscience I paid toll
In infinite remorse of soul.
All sin was of my sinning, all
Atoning mine, and mine the gall
Of all regret. Mine was the weight
Of every brooded wrong, the hate
That stood behind each envious thrust,
Mine every greed, mine every lust.
And all the while for every grief,
Each suffering, I craved relief
With individual desire,—
Craved all in vain! And felt fierce fire
About a thousand people crawl;
Perished with each,—then mourned for all!
A man was starving in Capri;
He moved his eyes and looked at me;
I felt his gaze, I heard his moan,
And knew his hunger as my own.
I saw at sea a great fog-bank
Between two ships that struck and sank;
A thousand screams the heavens smote;
And every scream tore through my throat;
No hurt I did not feel, no death
That was not mine; mine each last breath
That, crying, met an answering cry
From the compassion that was I.
All suffering mine, and mine its rod;
Mine, pity like the pity of God.
Ah, awful weight! Infinity
Pressed down upon the finite me!
My anguished spirit, like a bird,
Beating against my lips I heard;
Yet lay the weight so close about
There was no room for it without.
And so beneath the weight lay I
And suffered death, but could not die.

Long had I lain thus, craving death,
When quietly the earth beneath
Gave way, and inch by inch, so great
At last had grown the crushing weight,
Into the earth I sank till I
Full six feet under ground did lie,
And sank no more,—there is no weight
Can follow here, however great.
From off my breast I felt it roll,
And as it went my tortured soul
Burst forth and fled in such a gust
That all about me swirled the dust.

Deep in the earth I rested now;
Cool is its hand upon the brow
And soft its breast beneath the head
Of one who is so gladly dead.
And all at once, and over all,
The pitying rain began to fall.
I lay and heard each pattering hoof
Upon my lowly, thatchèd roof.
And seemed to love the sound far more
Than ever I had done before.
For rain it hath a friendly sound
To one who's six feet underground;
And scarce the friendly voice or face:
A grave is such a quiet place.

The rain, I said, is kind to come
And speak to me in my new home.
I would I were alive again
To kiss the fingers of the rain,
To drink into my eyes the shine
Of every slanting silver line,
To catch the freshened, fragrant breeze

From drenched and dripping apple-trees.
For soon the shower will be done,
And then the broad face of the sun
Will laugh above the rain-soaked earth
Until the world with answering mirth
Shakes joyously, and each round drop
Rolls, twinkling, from its grass-blade top.
How can I bear it; buried here,
While overhead the sky grows clear
And blue again after the storm?
O, multi-colored, multiform,
Belovèd beauty over me,
That I shall never, never see
Again! Spring-silver, autumn-gold,
That I shall never more behold!
Sleeping your myriad magics through,
Close-sepulchered away from you!
O God, I cried, give me new birth,
And put me back upon the earth!
Upset each cloud's gigantic gourd
And let the heavy rain, down-poured
In one big torrent, set me free,
Washing my grave away from me!

I ceased; and, through the breathless hush
That answered me, the far-off rush
Of herald wings came whispering
Like music down the vibrant string
Of my ascending prayer, and—crash!
Before the wild wind's whistling lash
The startled storm-clouds reared on high
And plunged in terror down the sky,
And the big rain in one black wave
Fell from the sky and struck my grave.

I know not how such things can be,
I only know there came to me
A fragrance such as never clings
To aught save happy living things;
A sound as of some joyous elf
Singing sweet songs to please himself,
And, through and over everything,
A sense of glad awakening.
The grass, a tip-toe at my ear,
Whispering to me I could hear;
I felt the rain's cool finger-tips
Brushed tenderly across my lips,
Laid gently on my sealèd sight,
And all at once the heavy night
Fell from my eyes and I could see,—
A drenched and dripping apple-tree,
A last long line of silver rain,
A sky grown clear and blue again.
And as I looked a quickening gust
Of wind blew up to me and thrust
Into my face a miracle
Of orchard-breath, and with the smell,—
I know not how such things can be!—
I breathed my soul back into me.

Ah! Up then from the ground sprang I
And hailed the earth with such a cry
As is not heard save from a man
Who has been dead and lives again.
About the trees my arms I wound;
Like one gone mad I hugged the ground;
I raised my quivering arms on high;
I laughed and laughed into the sky,
Till at my throat a strangling sob
Caught fiercely, and a great heart-throb
Sent instant tears into my eyes;
O God, I cried, no dark disguise
Can e'er hereafter hide from me
Thy radiant identity!
Thou canst not move across the grass
But my quick eyes will see Thee pass,
Nor speak, however silently,
But my hushed voice will answer Thee.
I know the path that tells Thy way
Through the cool eve of every day;
God, I can push the grass apart
And lay my finger on Thy heart!

The world stands out on either side
No wider than the heart is wide;
Above the world is stretched the sky,—
No higher than the soul is high.
The heart can push the sea and land
Farther away on either hand;
The soul can split the sky in two,
And let the face of God shine through.
But East and West will pinch the heart
That cannot keep them pushed apart;
And he whose soul is flat—the sky
Will cave in on him by and by.

THE PEAR TREE

In this squalid, dirty dooryard,
  Where the chickens scratch and run,
White, incredible, the pear tree
  Stands apart and takes the sun,

Mindful of the eyes upon it,
  Vain of its new holiness,
Like the waste-man's little daughter
  In her first communion dress.

GOD'S WORLD

O world, I cannot hold thee close enough!
    Thy winds, thy wide gray skies!
    Thy mists that roll and rise!
Thy woods, this autumn day, that ache and sag
And all but cry with color! That gaunt crag
To crush! To lift the lean of that black bluff!
World, world, I cannot get thee close enough!

Long have I known a glory in it all,
    But never knew I this;
    Here such a passion is
As stretcheth me apart. Lord I do fear
Thou'st made the world too beautiful this year.
My soul is all but out of me,—let fall
No burning leaf; prithee, let no bird call.

WILD SWANS

I looked in my heart while the wild swans went over;—
  And what did I see I had not seen before?
  Only a question less or a question more;
Nothing to match the flight of wild birds flying.
Tiresome heart, forever living and dying!
  House without air! I leave you and lock your door!
Wild swans, come over the town, come over
The town again, trailing your legs and crying!

THE POET AND HIS BOOK

own, you mongrel, Death!
  Back into your kennel!
have stolen breath
  In a stalk of fennel!
ou shall scratch and you shall whine
  Many a night, and you shall worry
  Many a bone, before you bury
ne sweet bone of mine!

hen shall I be dead?
  When my flesh is withered,
nd above my head
  Yellow pollen gathered
ll the empty afternoon?
  When sweet lovers pause and wonder
  Who am I that lie thereunder,
idden from the moon?

his my personal death?—
  That my lungs be failing
To inhale the breath
  Others are exhaling?
This my subtle spirit's end?—
Ah, when the thawed winter splashes
Over these chance dust and ashes,
Weep not me, my friend!

Me, by no means dead
  In that hour, but surely
When this book, unread,
  Rots to earth obscurely,
And no more to any breast,
  Close against the clamorous swelling
  Of the thing there is no telling,
Are these pages pressed!

When this book is mold,
  And a book of many
Waiting to be sold
  For a casual penny,
In a little open case,
  In a street unclean and cluttered,

Where a heavy mud is spattered
From the passing drays,

Stranger, pause and look;
From the dust of ages
Lift this little book,
Turn the tattered pages,
Read me, do not let me die!
Search the fading letters, finding
Steadfast in the broken binding
All that once was I!

When these veins are weeds,
When these hollowed sockets
Watch the rooty seeds
Bursting down like rockets,
And surmise the spring again,
Or, remote in that black cupboard,
Watch the pink worms writhing upward
At the smell of rain,

Boys and girls that lie
Whispering in the hedges,
Do not let me die,
Mix me in your pledges;
Boys and girls that slowly walk
In the woods, and weep, and quarrel,
Staring past the pink wild laurel,
Mix me with your talk.

Do not let me die!
Farmers at your raking,
When the sun is high,
While the hay is making,
When, along the stubble strewn,
Withering on their stalks uneaten,
Strawberries turn dark and sweeten
In the lapse of noon;

Shepherds on the hills,
In the pastures, drowsing
To the tinkling bells
Of the brown sheep browsing;
Sailors crying through the storm;
Scholars at your study; hunters
Lost amid the whirling winter's
Whiteness uniform;

Men that long for sleep;
Men that wake and revel;—
If an old song leap
To your senses' level
At such moments, may it be
Sometimes, though a moment only,
Some forgotten, quaint and homely
Vehicle of me!

Women at your toil,
Women at your leisure
Till the kettle boil,
Snatch of me your pleasure,
Where the broom-straw marks the leaf;
Women quiet with your weeping
Lest you wake a workman sleeping,
Mix me with your grief!

Boys and girls that steal
From the shocking laughter
Of the old, to kneel
By a dripping rafter
Under the discolored eaves,
Out of trunks with hingeless covers
Lifting tales of saint and lovers,
Travelers, goblins, thieves,

Suns that shine by night,
Mountains made from valleys,—
Bear me to the light,
Flat upon your bellies
By the webby window lie,
Where the little flies are crawling,—
Read me, margin me with scrawling,
Do not let me die!

Sexton, ply your trade!
In a shower of gravel
Stamp upon your spade!
Many a rose shall ravel,
Many a metal wreath shall rust
In the rain, and I go singing
Through the lots where you are flinging
Yellow clay on dust!

SPRING

To what purpose, April, do you return again?
Beauty is not enough.
You can no longer quiet me with the redness
Of little leaves opening stickily.
I know what I know.
The sun is hot on my neck as I observe
The spikes of the crocus.
The smell of the earth is good.
It is apparent that there is no death.
But what does that signify?
Not only under ground are the brains of men
Eaten by maggots.

Life in itself
Is nothing,
An empty cup, a flight of uncarpeted stairs,
It is not enough that yearly, down this hill,
April
Comes like an idiot, babbling and strewing flowers.

PASSER MORTUUS EST

Death devours all lovely things;
Lesbia with her sparrow
Shares the darkness,—presently
Every bed is narrow.

Unremembered as old rain
Dries the sheer libation,
And the little petulant hand
Is an annotation.

After all, my erstwhile dear,
My no longer cherished,
Need we say it was not love,
Now that love has perished?

WHAT LIPS MY LIPS HAVE KISSED

What lips my lips have kissed, and where, and why,
I have forgotten, and what arms have lain
Under my head till morning; but the rain
Is full of ghosts tonight, that tap and sigh
Upon the glass and listen for reply;
And in my heart there stirs a quiet pain
For unremembered lads that not again
Will turn to me at midnight with a cry.

Thus in the winter stands the lonely tree,
Nor knows what birds have vanished one by one,
Yet knows its boughs more silent than before:
I cannot say what loves have come and gone;
I only know that summer sang in me
A little while, that in me sings no more.

PITY ME NOT

Pity me not because the light of day
At close of day no longer walks the sky;
Pity me not for beauties passed away
From field and thicket as the year goes by;
Pity me not the waning of the moon,
Nor that the ebbing tide goes out to sea,
Nor that a man's desire is hushed so soon,
And you no longer look with love on me.

This have I known always: love is no more
Than the wide blossom which the wind assails;
Than the great tide that treads the shifting shore,
Strewing fresh wreckage gathered in the gales.
Pity me that the heart is slow to learn
What the swift mind beholds at ever turn.

DEPARTURE

It's little I care what path I take,
And where it leads it's little I care;
But out of this house, lest my heart break,
I must go, and off somewhere.

It's little I know what's in my heart,
What's in my mind it's little I know,
But there's that in me must up and start,
And it's little I care where my feet go.

I wish I could walk for a day and a night,
And find me at dawn in a desolate place
With never the rut of a road in sight,
Nor the roof of a house, nor the eyes of a face.

I wish I could walk till my blood should spout,
And drop me, never to stir again,
On a shore that is wide, for the tide is out,
And the weedy rocks are bare to the rain.

But dump or dock, where the path I take
Brings up, it's little enough I care;
And it's little I'd mind the fuss they'll make,
Huddled dead in a ditch somewhere.

"Is something the matter, dear," she said,
"That you sit at your work so silently?"
"No, mother, no, 'twas a knot in my thread.
There goes the kettle, I'll make the tea."

I SHALL GO BACK

I shall go back again to the bleak shore
And build a little shanty on the sand
In such a way that the extremest band
Of brittle seaweed will escape my door
But by a yard or two, and nevermore
Shall I return to take you by the hand;
I shall be gone to what I understand
And happier than I ever was before.

The love that stood a moment in your eyes,
The words that lay a moment on your tongue,
Are one with all that in a moment dies,
A little under-said and over-sung;
But I shall find the sullen rocks and skies
Unchanged from what they were when I was young.

ELEGY

Let them bury your big eyes
In the secret earth securely,
Your thin fingers, and your fair,
Soft, indefinite-colored hair,—
All of these in some way, surely,
From the secret earth shall rise.
Not for these I sit and stare,
Broken and bereft completely;
Your young flesh that sat so neatly
On your little bones will sweetly
Blossom in the air.

But your voice,—never the rushing
Of a river underground,
Not the rising of the wind
In the trees before the rain,

Not the woodcock's watery call,
Not the note the white-throat utters,
Not the feet of children pushing
Yellow leaves along the gutters
In the blue and bitter fall,
Shall content my musing mind
For the beauty of that sound
That in no new way at all
Ever will be heard again.

Sweetly through the sappy stalk
Of the vigorous weed,
Holding all it held before,
Cherished by the faithful sun,
On and on eternally
Shall your altered fluid run,
Bud and bloom and go to seed;
But your singing days are done;
But the music of your talk
Never shall the chemistry
Of the secret earth restore.
All your lovely words are spoken.
Once the ivory box is broken,
Beats the golden bird no more.

JUSTICE DENIED IN MASSACHUSETTS[1]

Let us abandon then our gardens and go home
And sit in the sitting-room.
Shall the larkspur blossom or the corn grow under this cloud?
Sour to the fruitful seed
Is the cold earth under this cloud,
Fostering quack and weed, we have marched upon but cannot conquer;
We have bent the blades of our hoes against the stalks of them.

Let us go home, and sit in the sitting-room.
Not in our day
Shall the cloud go over and the sun rise as before,
Beneficent upon us
Out of the glittering bay,
And the warm winds be blown inward from the sea
Moving the blades of corn
With a peaceful sound.
Forlorn, forlorn,
Stands the blue hay-rack by the empty mow.
And the petals drop to the ground,
Leaving the tree unfruited.
The sun that warmed our stooping backs and withered the weed uprooted—
We shall not feel it again.
We shall die in darkness, and be buried in the rain.

What from the splendid dead
We have inherited—
Furrows sweet to the grain, and the weed subdued—
See now the slug and the mildew plunder.
Evil does overwhelm
The larkspur and the corn;
We have seen them go under.

Let us sit here, sit still,
Here in the sitting-room until we die;
At the step of Death on the walk, rise and go;

[1] Written after the final decision in the Sacco-Vanzetti case.

Leaving to our children's children this beautiful doorway,
And this elm,
And a blighted earth to till
With a broken hoe.

EUCLID ALONE HAS LOOKED ON BEAUTY BARE

Euclid alone has looked on Beauty bare.
Let all who prate of Beauty hold their peace,
And lay them prone upon the earth and cease
To ponder on themselves, the while they stare
At nothing, intricately drawn nowhere
In shapes of shifting lineage; let geese
Gabble and hiss, but heroes seek release
From dusty bondage into luminous air.

O blinding hour, O holy, terrible day,
When first the shaft into his vision shone
Of light anatomized! Euclid alone
Has looked on Beauty bare. Fortunate they
Who, though once only and then but far away,
Have heard her massive sandal set on stone.

ON HEARING A SYMPHONY OF BEETHOVEN

Sweet sounds, oh, beautiful music, do not cease!
Reject me not into the world again.
With you alone is excellence and peace,
Mankind made plausible, his purpose plain.
Enchanted in your air benign and shrewd,
With limbs a-sprawl and empty faces pale,
The spiteful and the stingy and the rude
Sleep like the scullions in the fairy-tale.
This moment is the best the world can give:
The tranquil blossom on the tortured stem.
Reject me not, sweet sounds! oh, let me live,
Till Doom espy my towers and scatter them,
A city spell-bound under the aging sun.
Music my rampart, and my only one.

SONNET TO GATH

Country of hunchbacks!—where the strong, straight spine
Jeered at by crooked children, makes his way
Through by-streets at the kindest hour of day,
Till he deplore his stature, and incline
To measure manhood with a gibbous line;
Till out of loneliness, being flawed with clay,
He stoop into his neighbor's house and say,
"Your roof is low for me—the fault is mine."

Dust in an urn long since, dispersed and dead
Is great Apollo; and the happier he;
Since who amongst you all would lift a head
At a god's radiance on the mean door-tree,
Saving to run and hide your dates and bread,
And cluck your children in about your knee?

THE CAMEO

Forever over now, forever, forever gone
That day. Clear and diminished like a scene
Carven in cameo, the lighthouse, and the cove between
The sandy cliffs, and the boat drawn up on the beach;
And the long skirt of a lady innocent and young,
Her hand resting on her bossom, her head hung;
And the figure of a man in earnest speech.

Clear and diminished like a scene cut in cameo
The lighthouse, and the boat on the beach, and the two shapes
Of the woman and the man; lost like the lost day
Are the words that passed, and the pain,—discarded, cut away
From the stone, as from the memory the heat of the tears escapes.

O troubled forms, O early love unfortunate and hard,
Time has estranged you into a jewel cold and pure;
From the action of the waves and from the action of sorrow forever secure,
White against a ruddy cliff you stand, chalcedony on sard.

OH, SLEEP FOREVER IN THE LATMIAN CAVE

O, sleep forever in the Latmian cave,
Mortal Endymion, darling of the Moon!
Her silver garments by the senseless wave
Shouldered and dropped and on the shingle strewn,
Her fluttering hand against her forehead pressed,
Her scattered looks that trouble all the sky,
Her rapid footsteps running down the west—
Of all her altered state, oblivious lie!
Whom earthen you, by deathless lips adored,
Wild-eyed and stammering to the grasses thrust,
And deep into her crystal body poured
The hot and sorrowful sweetness of the dust:
Whereof she wanders mad, being all unfit
For mortal love, that might not die of it.

SEE WHERE CAPELLA WITH HER GOLDEN KIDS

See where Capella with her golden kids
Grazes the slope between the east and north?
Thus when the builders of the pyramids
Flung down their tools at nightfall and poured forth

Homeward to supper and a poor man's bed,
Shortening the road with friendly jest and slur,
The risen She-Goat showing blue and red
Climbed the clear dusk, and three stars followed her.
Safe in their linen and their spices lie
The kings of Egypt; even as long ago
Under these constellations, with long eye
And scented limbs they slept, and feared no foe.
Their will was law; their will was not to die.
And so they had their way; or nearly so.

THE RETURN

Earth does not understand her child,
  Who from the loud gregarious town
Returns, depleted and defiled,
  To the still woods, to fling him down.

Earth cannot count the sons she bore:
  The wounded lynx, the wounded man
Come trailing blood unto her door;
  She shelters both as best she can.

But she is early up and out,
  To trim the year or strip its bones;
She has no time to stand about
  Talking of him in undertones

Who has no aim but to forget,
  Be left in peace, be lying thus
For days, for years, for centuries yet,
  Unshaven and anonymous;

Who, marked for failure, dulled by grief,
  Has traded in his wife and friend
For this warm ledge, this alder leaf:
  Comfort that does not comprehend.

Archibald MacLeish

Archibald MacLeish was born in Glencoe, northern Illinois, May 7, 1892. The son of a Scotch merchant and a Connecticut clergyman's daughter, he spent his boyhood on the lake shore, was educated in the public schools of his native town, a Connecticut preparatory school, Yale University, and Harvard Law School. He served in the Field Artillery in France during the War, became a lawyer in Boston and gave up the practice of law for literature, living in the Berkshires during the summer and in Paris during the winter. After his return to America, he spent most of the year in New York, where he became one of the editors of *Fortune*.

MacLeish's first volume, *Tower of Ivory* (1917), gave few hints of the original talent that was revealed in *The Happy Marriage* (1924), *The Pot of Earth* (1925) and the curious *Nobodaddy* (1925). There are influences apparent in all of these. *The Happy Marriage* owes not a little to Conrad Aiken and E. A. Robinson; *The Pot of Earth* relies on T. S. Eliot's structure as well as his free use of dissonance and peculiar juxtapositions. But MacLeish has something to say which is quite his own, something about man's uncertain place in the Unknown and, in these volumes, he is learning how to say it.

In *Streets in the Moon* (1926) the complete poet emerges. Here his subject-matter, conceived in amplitude, conveys an unusual "sense of infinity." But it is his idiom even more than his theme which makes MacLeish an important modern poet. He can, by the skillful use of repetition, achieve new effects in harmony, he can prompt a new beat in even so old a form as the sonnet, *vide* "The End of the World." "Ars Poetica" is more than an extension of poetic language; beneath its successful experiments in timing, interior rhyme and suspension, it says a number of pointed and profound things which have nothing to do with timeliness and changing tastes. The tone of these verses may be as new as this generation; the spirit which moves beneath them is as old as the sung phrase and the unspoken word.

The Hamlet of A. MacLeish (1928) is clearer in pattern and suppler in power than any of his other long poems. Its blemishes are those of confirmed modernity. Speaking of its author, Conrad Aiken says, "He is a kind of slave of tradition, with the difference that the traditions which enslave him are contemporary ones." MacLeish has not completely thrown off the influence of Eliot and various modern French poets, but his conceptions are so much his own that no one could mistake the originality of his design. In *The Hamlet of A. MacLeish,* the poet has plunged deeper into himself. The half-conscious breaks through; remote associations, shifting allusions, disordered griefs, phantasms, fag-ends of memories float up. By overtone and undercurrent, the reader is led to identify himself—as the author has done—with the eternal Hamlet, that conglomeration of lover, poet, procrastinator, ranter, doer, and doubter.

New Found Land (1930) contains only fourteen poems, yet some of MacLeish's richest verses are in this small book. The mood is elegaic, but the melancholy is provocative rather than lulling. The perceptions are unusually keen, the images highly charged, and the tone throughout is not only uplifted but noble. Some of MacLeish's critics made much of his nostalgia for the past, forgetting that no poet (no person, in fact) is free of it, and what distinguishes the poet is not his subject-matter but the way in which he employs his material. No one could question the distinction of "You, Andrew Marvell," that beautiful and uncanny exercise in suspension, one of the finest poems of the period, "Immortal Autumn," with its classical overtones, "Epistle to Be Left in the Earth," and others. In these poems—as in "Memorial Rain," which says more about War than any poetry since Owen's and Sassoon's—the style is elliptical but the figures are concrete; without strain or exaggeration MacLeish uses ordinary language to suggest extraordinary sensations and abstractions. Here, too, MacLeish is shown to be one of the most resourceful technicians of an experimental age; he employs all the approved forms and invents several of his own; extends the gamut of rhyme through dissonance and consonance to half-rhyme ("thin-continues," "sun-running," "dish-official," "star-harbor," etc.), rhyming consonants and unrhyming vowels ("lake-like," "vine-vane," "west-waste," etc.), and concealed internal rhyme.

Conquistador (1932) employs these effects on a wider scale for a larger purpose. Certain reviewers referred to the poem as being "loosely ductile" and "unrhymed." *Conquistador* happens to be highly formal, the form being nothing "looser" than terza rima. The rhyming trios, however, are unorthodox since MacLeish varies full rhyme with assonance ("market-carpenter-arsenal," "things-wind-insolent," etc.) and suspension. But it is not only in technique that *Conquistador* displays the poet's maturity; in accent and spirit it is a rich fulfillment of MacLeish's gifts. Richness of color, extension of musical devices, and a mastery of the long breath combine to produce the most accomplished saga-poem of the generation. Founded on Bernal Diaz's *True History of the Conquest of New Spain* and influenced by the accent of Pound's *Cantos,* especially Canto I, the narrative proceeds from one vivid detail to another. Sometimes the tale is disrupted as the aged narrator confuses time and events; yet even here the poem gains in movement, like the swift progression of a dream. Everything contributes to the vitality of this movement, most of all MacLeish's vocabulary. *Conquistador,* in spite of being cast in the key of reminiscence, is a record of life in action; and this parade of fighting and feasting, of blood, song, and quick surrenders is tuned to words that live and leap no less actively. No modern writer has used the device of Anglo-Saxon alliteration so well as MacLeish; we have to go back to *The Seafarer* to find narration so stripped in phrase, so speeded. The poem as a whole is a triumph in sonority and sustained power. It was awarded the Pulitzer Prize in 1933.

Poems 1924-1933 contains several new poems besides the best of those previously published, further experiments in stylistic subtlety. *Panic* (1935) is a play in flexible verse, which caused no little controversy when it was produced in New York. Neither the reactionaries nor the revolutionists where cheered by it, for MacLeish refused to join either camp, but none could dispute the eloquence of the mass choruses, the drive behind the dissolving scenes, and the universality of the passion which marked *Panic* as a significant revival of the poetic drama.

Public Speech (1936) includes twenty poems, about half of which are (as the title implies) tracts for the times. The poet has come a long way from the time when he announced that

> A poem should not mean
> But be.

Public Speech is definitely a poetry of meanings, even of convictions. No longer a modern Hamlet seeking to escape his situation, MacLeish participates in the problems of the present; he now declares that men are "brothers by life lived and are hurt for it." His style gathers strength. The delicacy is supported by dignity; the movement is vigorous without snapping its biceps. "Speech to a Crowd" and "The Reconciliation" are widely separated in subject matter but are united by a tone which is colloquial yet allusive.

Two verse plays for radio prove that MacLeish the poet is not only a wiser person than MacLeish the theorist, but a much more stimulating writer. *The Fall of the City* (1937) is a drama primarily for the ear rather than for the eye. The action takes place in the central plaza of a great city. Portents are in the air; a dead woman appears and prophesies. She tells them, not knowing what the words mean, that masterless men will take a master. The crowd is puzzled and fearful. A messenger appears warning the city that a ruthless conqueror is upon them. Orators, priests, and generals harangue the crowd, increasing uncertainty and inaction. Finally the conqueror appears; he comes out of the shadows and takes command. His visor opens, and the Announcer tells the listeners that there is no one in the armor; the metal is only a shell, absolutely empty; "the push of a stiff pole at the nipple would topple it." But the people lie on the ground. They do not or will not see. They shout as though they had won a victory; masterless men have found a master. The city falls.

The effectiveness of *The Fall of the City* is increased by the poet's recognition of the resources of radio and his employment of the Announcer as a combination of Greek Chorus and casual commentator. *Air Raid* (1938) is a worthy successor to the first poetry play written for the radio-spoken word. *The Fall of the City* is an allegory in terms of action; *Air Raid* is a prolonged action in terms of the morning headlines. MacLeish's favorite device, the employment of almost unbearable tension, is used here to remarkable effect.

In 1937 MacLeish collaborated with Ernest Hemingway, Lillian Hellman, and Joris Ivens on the film *The Spanish Earth*. During the year 1938 he was custodian of the Nieman Collection of Journalism at Harvard. In 1939 he was appointed Librarian of Congress. His work continued to increase in social consciousness. *Land of the Free* (1938) combines pictures and verse in a way that is experimental and dialectical: photographs of farmers, share-croppers, migrants, and other underprivileged Americans appear on the right-hand pages, while on the opposite pages MacLeish has furnished a text that is a cross between a running poem and a "sound track."

At fifty-seven MacLeish was appointed Boylston Professor of Rhetoric and Oratory at Harvard. By the time he had reached his sixties he had written twenty books of poetry, plays, essays, polemics, and political addresses. The Pulitzer Prize was awarded to him for the second time for *Collected Poems: 1917-1952,* a volume which also received the Bollingen Prize and the National Book Award. At sixty-six he became a popular as well as a successful playwright with *J.B.,* a modernization of the Book of Job, a theatricalized debate, which won the Pulitzer Prize for drama in 1959.

In spite of his achievements in technique, it is neither the novel form nor the phrase-making which distinguishes MacLeish. It is the discipline which he imposes on the flow of suggestions, on the very chaos of the unconscious, it is the rapid—and sometimes too immediate—employment of material almost too fluent to fix, which has made him one of the most debated poets of the period.

ARS POETICA

A poem should be palpable and mute
As a globed fruit

Dumb
As old medallions to the thumb

Silent as the sleeve-worn stone
Of casement ledges where the moss has grown—

A poem should be wordless
As the flight of birds

✣

A poem should be motionless in time
As the moon climbs

Leaving, as the moon releases
Twig by twig the night-entangled trees,

Leaving, as the moon behind the winter leaves,
Memory by memory the mind—

A poem should be motionless in time
As the moon climbs

✣

A poem should be equal to:
Not true

For all the history of grief
An empty doorway and a maple leaf

For love
The leaning grasses and two lights above the sea—

A poem should not mean
But be.

PROLOGUE

These alternate nights and days, these seasons
Somehow fail to convince me. It seems
I have the sense of infinity!

(In your dreams, O crew of Columbus,
O listeners over the sea
For that surf that breaks upon Nothing—)

Once I was waked by nightingales in the garden.
I thought, What time is it? I thought,
Time—Is it Time still?—Now is it Time?

(Tell me your dreams, O sailors:
Tell me, in sleep did you climb
The tall masts, and before you—)

At night the stillness of old trees
Is a leaning over, and the inertness
Of hills is a kind of waiting.

(In sleep, in a dream, did you see
The world's end? Did the water
Break—and no shore— Did you see?)

Strange faces come through the streets to me
Like messengers: and I have been warned
By the moving slowly of hands at a window.

O, I have the sense of infinity—
But the world, sailors, is round.
They say there is no end to it.

IN MY THIRTIETH YEAR

And I have come upon this place
By lost ways, by a nod, by words,
By faces, by the old man's face
At Morlaix lifted to the birds,

By hands upon the tablecloth
At Aldebori's, by the thin
Child's hands that opened to the moth
And let the flutter of the moonlight in,

By hands, by voices, by the voice
Of Mrs. Husman on the stair,
By Margaret's "If we had the choice
To choose or not—" through her thick hair,

By voices, by the creak and fall
Of footsteps on the upper floor,
By silence waiting in the hall
Between the door-bell and the door,

By words, by voices, a lost way—
And here above the chimney stack
The unknown constellations sway—
And by what way shall I go back?

MEMORIAL RAIN

Ambassador Puser the ambassador
Reminds himself in French, felicitous tongue,
What these (young men no longer) lie here for
In rows that once, and somewhere else, were young—

All night in Brussels the wind had tugged at my door:
I had heard the wind at my door and the trees strung
Taut, and to me who had never been before
In that country it was a strange wind blowing

Steadily, stiffening the walls, the floor,
The roof of my room. I had not slept for knowing
He too, dead, was a stranger in that land
And felt beneath the earth in the wind's flowing
A tightening of roots and would not understand,
Remembering lake winds in Illinois,
That strange wind. I had felt his bones in the sand
Listening.

—Reflects that these enjoy
Their country's gratitude, that deep repose,
That peace no pain can break, no hurt destroy,
That rest, that sleep—

At Ghent the wind rose.
There was a smell of rain and a heavy drag
Of wind in the hedges but not as the wind blows
Over fresh water when the waves lag
Foaming and the willows huddle and it will rain:
I felt him waiting.

—Indicates the flag
Which (may he say) enisles in Flanders' plain
This little field these happy, happy dead
Have made America—

In the ripe grain
The wind coiled glistening, darted, fled,
Dragging its heavy body: at Waereghem
The wind coiled in the grass above his head:
Waiting—listening—

—Dedicates to them
This earth their bones have hallowed, this last gift
A grateful country—

Under the dry grass stem
The words are blurred, are thickened, the words sift
Confused by the rasp of the wind, by the thin grating
Of ants under the grass, the minute shift
And tumble of dusty sand separating
From dusty sand. The roots of the grass strain,
Tighten, the earth is rigid, waits—he is waiting—

And suddenly, and all at once, the rain!
The people scatter, they run into houses, the wind
Is trampled under the rain, shakes free, is again
Trampled. The rain gathers, running in thinned
Spurts of water that ravel in the dry sand
Seeping into the sand under the grass roots, seeping
Between cracked boards to the bones of a clenched hand:
The earth relaxes, loosens; he is sleeping
He rests, he is quiet, he sleeps in a strange land.

WEATHER

The northeast wind was the wind off the lake
Blowing the oak leaves pale side out like
Aspen: blowing the sound of the surf far
Inland over the fences: blowing for
Miles over smell of earth the alien
Lake smell.
The southwest wind was thunder on
Afternoon: you saw the wind first in the vine
Over the side porch and the weather vane
Whirled on the barn and the doors slammed all together.
After the rain in the grass we used to gather
Wind-fallen cold white apples.
The west
Wind was the August wind, the wind over waste
Valleys over the waterless plains where still
Were skulls of buffalo, where in the sand stale
Dung lay of wild cattle. The west wind blew
Day after day as the winds on the plains blow
Burning the grass, turning the leaves brown, filling
Noon with the bronze of cicadas, far out falling
Dark on the colorless water, the lake where not
Waves were nor movement.
The north wind was at night
When no leaves and the husk on the oak stirs
Only nor birds then. The north wind was stars
Over the whole sky and snow in the ways
And snow on the sand where in summer the water was . . .
North here is the sea and westward the sea
And south the Tyrrhenian sea where the hills saw
Once the long oars and the helmsman. But here to me
The winds blow as always they blew in my
Country,
the winds blow out of Illinois,
Out of Missouri, out of Michigan. I know
The northeast wind: I know how the trees look—
The northeast wind is the wind over the lake
Blowing the oak leaves pale side out. . . .

IMMORTAL AUTUMN

I speak this poem now with grave and level voice
In praise of autumn of the far-horn-winding fall
I praise the flower-barren fields the clouds the tall
Unanswering branches where the wind makes sullen noise

I praise the fall it is the human season now
No more the foreign sun does meddle at our earth
Enforce the green and thaw the frozen soil to birth
Nor winter yet weigh all with silence the pine bough

But now in autumn with the black and outcast crows
Share we the spacious world the whispering year is gone
There is more room to live now the once secret dawn
Comes late by daylight and the dark unguarded goes

Between the mutinous brave burning of the leaves
And winter's covering of our hearts with his deep snow
We are alone there are no evening birds we know
The naked moon the tame stars circle at our eaves

It is the human season on this sterile air
Do words outcarry breath the sound goes on and on
I hear a dead man's cry from autumn long since gone

I cry to you beyond upon this bitter air.

YOU, ANDREW MARVELL

And here face down beneath the sun
And here upon earth's noonward height
To feel the always coming on
The always rising of the night

To feel creep up the curving east
The earthy chill of dusk and slow
Upon those under lands the vast
And ever-climbing shadow grow

And strange at Ecbatan the trees
Take leaf by leaf the evening strange
The flooding dark about their knees
The mountains over Persia change

And now at Kermanshah the gate
Dark empty and the withered grass
And through the twilight now the late
Few travelers in the westward pass

And Baghdad darken and the bridge
Across the silent river gone
And through Arabia the edge
Of evening widen and steal on

And deepen on Palmyra's street
The wheel rut in the ruined stone
And Lebanon fade out and Crete
High through the clouds and overblown

And over Sicily the air
Still flashing with the landward gulls
And loom and slowly disappear
The sails above the shadowy hulls

And Spain go under and the shore
Of Africa the gilded sand
And evening vanish and no more
The low pale light across that land

Nor now the long light on the sea—
And here face downward in the sun
To feel how swift how secretly
The shadow of the night comes on . . .

THE END OF THE WORLD

Quite unexpectedly as Vasserot
The armless ambidextrian was lighting
A match between his great and second toe
And Ralph the lion was engaged in biting
The neck of Madame Sossman while the drum
Pointed, and Teeny was about to cough
In waltz-time swinging Jocko by the thumb—
Quite unexpectedly the top blew off:

And there, there overhead, there, there, hung over
Those thousands of white faces, those dazed eyes,
There in the starless dark, the poise, the hover,
There with vast wings across the canceled skies,
There in the sudden blackness, the black pall
Of nothing, nothing, nothing—nothing at all.

THE TOO-LATE BORN

We too, we too, descending once again
The hills of our own land, we too have heard
Far off—Ah, que ce cor à longue haleine—
The horn of Roland in the passages of Spain,
The first, the second blast, the failing third,
And with the third turned back and climbed once more
The steep road southward, and heard faint the sound
Of swords, of horses, the disastrous war,
And crossed the dark defile at last, and found
At Roncevaux upon the darkening plain
The dead against the dead and on the silent ground
The silent slain—

EPISTLE TO BE LEFT IN THE EARTH

. . . It is colder now
there are many stars
we are drifting
North by the Great Bear
the leaves are falling
The water is stone in the scooped rocks
to southward
Red sun gray air
the crows are
Slow on their crooked wings
the jays have left us
Long since we passed the flares of Orion
Each man believes in his heart he will die
Many have written last thoughts and last letters
None know if our deaths are now or forever
None know if this wandering earth will be found

We lie down and the snow covers our garments
I pray you
you (if any open this writing)
Make in your mouths the words that were our names
I will tell you all we have learned
I will tell you everything
The earth is round
there are springs under the orchards
The loam cuts with a blunt knife
beware of

Elms in thunder
the lights in the sky are stars
We think they do not see
we think also
The trees do not know nor the leaves of the grasses
hear us
The birds too are ignorant
Do not listen
Do not stand at dark in the open windows
We before you have heard this
they are voices
They are not words at all but the wind rising
Also none among us has seen God
(. . . We have thought often
The flaws of sun in the late and driving weather
Pointed to one tree but it was not so)
As for the nights I warn you the nights are dangerous
The wind changes at night and the dreams come

It is very cold
there are strange stars near Arcturus

Voices are crying an unknown name in the sky

BURYING GROUND BY THE TIES

(*from "Frescoes for Mr. Rockefeller's City"*)

Ayee! Ai! This is heavy earth on our shoulders:
There were none of us born to be buried in this earth:
Niggers we were Portuguese Magyars Polacks:

We were born to another look of the sky certainly:
Now we lie here in the river pastures:
We lie in the mowings under the thick turf:

We hear the earth and the all-day rasp of the grasshoppers:
It was we laid the steel on this land from ocean to ocean:
It was we (if you know) put the U. P. through the passes

Bringing her down into Laramie full load
Eighteen mile on the granite anticlinal
Forty-three foot to the mile and the grade holding:

It was we did it: hunkies of our kind:
It was we dug the caved-in holes for the cold water:
It was we built the gully spurs and the freight sidings:

Who would do it but we and the Irishmen bossing us?
It was all foreign-born men there were in this country:
It was Scotsmen Englishmen Chinese Squareheads Austrians . . .

Ayee! but there's weight to the earth under it:
Not for this did we come out—to be lying here
Nameless under the ties in the clay cuts:

There's nothing good in the world but the rich will buy it:
Everything sticks to the grease of a gold note—
Even a continent—even a new sky!

Do not pity us much for the strange grass over us:
We laid the steel to the stone stock of these mountains:
The place of our graves is marked by the telegraph poles!

It was not to lie in the bottoms we came out
And the trains going over us here in the dry hollows . . .

PANIC

(from "Panic")

AN OLD MAN

Slowly the thing comes.
There are many signs: there are furnaces
Dead now that were burning
Thirty years in a town—
Never dark: there are foundries—
Fires drawn: trestles
Silent. The swifts nest in
Stacks that for generations
Flowed smoke. The patience of
Hawks is over the cities:
They circle in clean light where the
Smoke last year frightened them.

A WOMAN

The gears turn: twitter: are
Still now. The sound dies.
From the east with the sun's rising
Daily are fewer whistles:
Many mornings listening
One less or two.

A YOUNG MAN

The thing comes pursuing us
Creeping as death creeps in an
Old man: as sleep comes:
Leaving on one hill—
On the stand—the stalks silver—
Corn rotted in ear:
Leaving on land nearest us
Wagons abandoned: milk cows
Slaughtered for no sickness:
Rigs rusting at pit-heads:
Pumps frozen: switches
Green with the rain: the oil
Thickened: scale in boilers—
Good gear all of it:
Sound metal: faultless:
Idle now: never manned.

A GIRL

Men in the dusk—and they stand there
Letting the girls go by with the
Sweet scent: silent:
Leaning heavily: bent to the
Painted signs on the fences—
They that in other times
Calling after us climbed by the
Steep stair for the sight of a
Girl's knee delighting her.

A MAN

From what ill and what enemy
Armless shall we defend the
Evening—the night hours?

A MAN

No eyes of ours have
Ever knowing beheld it.
It comes not with the bells
Arousing towns: racing with
Smoke—with the wind's haste—
The tallest houses toppled.

A MAN

Comes not from the hospitals—
Odor of scattered lime—
Night burials climbing the
Empty streets by the markets.

A MAN

Not with the shot: with the barking of
Dogs before color of dawn—
The whistle over the lawn—the
Running footfalls stumbling.

A WOMAN

Nevertheless it comes.
Men die: houses
Fall among kitchen flowers.
Families scatter. Children
Wander the roads building of
Broken boxes shelter.
A land of great wealth and the
Old hungry: the young
Starving—but not with hunger.
None have beheld this enemy.
What arms can defend the
Evening—the night hours—
When fear: faceless: devours us?

A WOMAN

Blight—not on the grain!
Drought—not in the springs!
Rot—not from the rain!

A MAN

What shadow hidden or
Unseen hand in our midst
Ceaselessly touches our faces?

FINAL CHORUS

(*from "Panic"*)

AN OLD WOMAN (*exultantly*)

Bellies bitter with drinking the
Weak tears do you fear the
Fall of the walls and the sky
High over you shining there?

A MAN (*exultantly*)

Mouths bitter with hate and the
Aching of tears have you tasted the
New water that springs in the
Hollow of thirst in your fingers?

A MAN (*exultantly*)

Eyes blind with the sleet and the
Freezing of night have you seen how the
Wind's in the rising East and the
Mountains of morning increasing?

A WOMAN

The roof's fallen! The sun
Stands on the sky with his wonder.

A WOMAN

The wind—the wind's in the house!

A WOMAN

The walls open arousing us!

A MAN

Wildly as swollen river the
Dark will of the world
Flooded on rock rushes
Raving—bearing the brush down:
Breaking from ancient banks.
Cities are buried. The man
Drowns in his door who opposes it.

VOICES

Follow!

Give!

Go with the
Rushing of time in us!

Make of the
Silence of fate a trumpet!
Make of the time a drum!

March!

Shout!

A MAN

Run with the
Marching men: with the thunder of
Thousand heels on the earth—
Making of mortal burden a
Banner to shout and to break in the
Blazing of sunlight and shaken there!

VOICES

Take it!

Be taken!

The trumpet of
Time in our ears and the brazen and
Breaking shout of our days!

MANY VOICES

Man's fate is a drum!

THE RECONCILIATION

Time like the repetitions of a child's piano
Brings me the room again the shallow lamp the love
The night the silence the slow bell the echoed answer.

By no thing here or lacking can the eyes discover
The hundred winter evenings that have gone between
Nor know for sure the night is this and not that other.

The room is here the lamp is here: the mirror's leaning
Searches the same deep shadow where her knees were caught:
All these are here within the room as I have seen them.

Time has restored them all as in that rainy autumn:
Even the echoes of that night return to this—
All as they were when first the earthy evening brought them.

Between this night and that there is no human distance:
There is no space an arm could not out-reach by much—
And yet the stars most far apart are not more distant.

Between my hand that touched and her soft breast that touches
The irremediable past as deep as tone:
Wider than water: like all land and ocean stretches:

We touch and by that touching farness are alone.

SPEECH TO A CROWD

Tell me, my patient friends—awaiters of messages—
From what other shore: from what stranger:
Whence was the word to come? Who was to lesson you?

Listeners under a child's crib in a manger—
Listeners once by the oracles: now by the transoms—
Whom are you waiting for? Who do you think will explain?

Listeners thousands of years and still no answer—
Writers at night to Miss Lonely-Hearts: awkward spellers—
Open your eyes! There is only earth and the man!

There is only you: there is no one else on the telephone:
No one else is on the air to whisper:
No one else but you will push the bell.

No one knows if you don't: neither ships
Nor landing-fields decode the dark between:
You have your eyes and what your eyes see *is*.

The earth you see is really the earth you are seeing:
The sun is truly excellent: truly warm:
Women are beautiful as you have seen them—

Their breasts (believe it) like cooing of doves in a portico:
They bear at their breasts tenderness softly. Look at them!
Look at yourselves. You are strong. You are well formed.

Look at the world—the world you never took!
It is really true you may live in the world heedlessly:
Why do you wait to read it in a book then?

Write it yourselves! Write to yourselves if you need to!
Tell yourselves there is sun and the sun will rise:
Tell yourselves the earth has food to feed you:—

Let the dead men say that men must die!
Who better than you can know what death is?
How can a bone or a broken body surmise it?

Let the dead shriek with their whispering breath:
Laugh at them! Say the murdered gods may wake
But we who work have end of work together:

Tell yourselves the earth is yours to take!

Waiting for messages out of the dark you were poor.
The world was always yours: you will not take it.

Elizabeth J. Coatsworth

⥼§ Elizabeth J. Coatsworth was born in 1893 in Buffalo, New York. After extended travels she returned to America, where she divided her time between a cottage in Maine and an old house in Hingham, Massachusetts, where she lives with her husband, the author, Henry Beston.

Fox Footprints (1921) presents a group of Oriental images; *Atlas and Beyond* (1924) is more vivid and more original. A versatile mind fashioned *Compass Rose* (1929), *Country Poems* (1942), *The Creaking Stair* (1949), and *Night and the Cat* (1950), collections of poems which range from the homely to the heroic, from the mischievous to the macabre. The poet is particularly successful in evoking the varied feline moods which delight every ailurophile.

Besides writing novels and non-fiction, Miss Coatsworth is the author of twenty-seven juvenile books, one of which, *The Cat Who Went to Heaven,* won the Newbery Medal in 1930.

THE OLD MARE

Gray despair
Was on the old mare,
Grass turned bitter,
Sky a-glare,
And gnats like thoughts,
And thoughts like gnats,
Everywhere.

Her underlip
Hung pendulous wide,
Her ears twitched back,
Her dusty hide
Heaved with her heavy breathing
And her eyes rolled ominously
To one side.

The mule colt lay
In trampled grass,
Slick-tailed, long eared,
Bespeaking the ass
Carried so long in her body,
Born in travail and sweat—
Alien, alas.

But staggering
To unsteady feet
The mule colt fumbles
An unknown teat;
And the old mare relaxes and sighs,
Finding any motherhood
Most sweet.

DANIEL WEBSTER'S HORSES

If when the wind blows
Rattling the trees,
Clicking like skeletons'
Elbows and knees,

You hear along the road
Three horses pass—
Do not go near the dark
Cold window-glass.

If when the first snow lies
Whiter than bones
You see the mark of hoofs
Cut to the stones,

Hoofs of three horses
Going abreast—
Turn about, turn about,
A closed door is best!

Upright in the earth
Under the sod
They buried three horses
Bridled and shod,

Daniel Webster's horses—
He said as he grew old,
"Flesh, I love riding,
Shall I not love it, cold?

"Shall I not love to ride
Bone astride bone,
When the cold wind blows
And snow covers stone?

"Bury them on their feet
With bridle and bit.
They were fine horses—
See their shoes fit."

THE CIRCUS-POSTERED BARN

When Dobbin and Robin, unharnessed from the plow,
Stamp smoking to their stalls,
They pass beneath white horses with long manes
Shining upon the walls,
White horses airily leaping through great hoops
Along applauding tracks
Or carrying princesses in rosy tights
Upon their backs.

And Daisy, Madge and Buttercup
Raise their soft eyes,
Where through the darkness of the web-hung stable
Hippopotami arise,
Shaking the water from their enormous shoulders
Floundering in savage mud,
Showing those muzzles huge enough to ponder
An epic cud.

And Tom beside a rat-hole in the boarding
Meets the still stare
Of eyes fiercer than his eyes and a large lithe body
Above him there—
Despondent grow the inmates of the barnyard;
Not one achieves
The super-powers of those super-mammals
Beneath the eaves!

ON A NIGHT OF SNOW

Cat, if you go outdoors you must walk in the snow.
You will come back with little white shoes on your feet,
Little white slippers of snow that have heels of sleet.
Stay by the fire, my Cat. Lie still, do not go.
See how the flames are leaping and hissing low,
I will bring you a saucer of milk like a marguerite,
So white and so smooth, so spherical and so sweet—
Stay with me, Cat. Out-doors the wild winds blow.

Out-doors the wild winds blow. Mistress, and dark is the night.
Strange voices cry in the trees, intoning strange lore,
And more than cats move, lit by our eye's green light,
On silent feet where the meadow grasses hang hoar—
Mistress, there are portents abroad of magic and might,
And things that are yet to be done. Open the door!

A LADY COMES TO AN INN

Three strange men came to the inn,
One was a black man pocked and thin,
One was brown with a silver knife,
And one brought with him a beautiful wife.

That lovely woman had hair as pale
As French champagne or finest ale,
That lovely woman was long and slim
As a young white birch or a maple limb.

Her face was like cream, her mouth was a rose,
What language she spoke nobody knows,
But sometimes she'd scream like a cockatoo
And swear wonderful oaths that nobody knew.

Her great silk skirts like a silver bell
Down to her little bronze slippers fell,
And her low-cut gown showed a dove on its nest
In blue tattooing across her breast.

Nobody learned the lady's name
Nor the marvelous land from which they came,
But no one in all the countryside
Has forgotten those men and that beautiful bride.

Mark Van Doren

☙ Mark Van Doren was born at Hope, Illinois, June 13, 1894, and was educated at the University of Illinois and at Columbia. He taught English at Columbia, and became literary editor of *The Nation*. Since 1920 he has lived in New York except for the part of the year that he spends on his farm in Cornwall, Connecticut.

Besides his verses, he has published four volumes of criticism. *Henry David Thoreau, A Critical Study* (1916) and *The Poetry of John Dryden* (1920) are the best of his analytical appraisals. He took upon himself the huge labor of editing *An Anthology of World Poetry* (1928), which assembles the world's best poetry in the best English versions, and compiled *American Poets 1630-1930* (1932) and *The Oxford Book of American Prose* (1932). A novel called *The Transients* (1935) succeeded only in puzzling most of its readers.

Spring Thunder and Other Poems appeared in 1924. A glance through its pages reveals that Van Doren has been influenced by Robert Frost. He, too, writes of homely bucolic things: of water wheels which need mending, a mountain house in December, the coming of alfalfa, river snow, and dry meadows. His emotion, like Frost's, is restrained. But if neither his subjects nor his point of view is particularly individualized, his mellowness is his own, and the spirit which moves beneath the contours of his verse personifies even the simplest of his quatrains.

Now the Sky (1928) reveals Van Doren as a more metaphysical poet. He is still concerned with ferns, dark barns, deserted hollows, but he grows more and more preoccupied with "the crumbling away of former bright edges of courage and causeless decay." *Jonathan Gentry* (1933) is an impressive chronicle of five generations, interspersed with lyrics. It is a narrative poem which just misses being a great work, chiefly because of its author's unrestrained facility.

A Winter Diary (1935) is Van Doren's richest volume, even though the book represents an alternation of tradition and technical experiment. The title poem is a splendidly sustained narrative-soliloquy; it is almost twelve hundred lines long, yet there is not a forced or flat couplet. For sympathetic landscape and portrait painting there has been nothing like it in American poetry since Whittier's "Snow Bound."

The Last Look and Other Poems (1937), a scattering of sketches and fantasies undertaken lightly and sometimes superficially, was followed by *Collected Poems: 1922-1938,* which was awarded the Pulitzer Prize. *Shakespeare* (1939) combined a scholar's research and a poet's imagination in a persuasive study.

Nearing fifty, Van Doren became more prolific than ever. *The Mayfield Deer* (1941) attempts to create an American mythology, but fails to clarify, or even communicate, the confusing story of a backwoods tragedy. *The Seven Sleepers* (1944) is a volume of alternately tart, tender, and sententious lyrics. *The Careless Clock* (1947) consists of poems about children, poems which are perceptive and often complex and anything but conventional. *New Poems* (1948) are delicate and consciously restrained, a highly personal mixture of the metaphysical and the ironic. Van Doren's influences are dissimilar, his tone varies, but his manner is altogether his own. His later works include a play, *The Last Days of Lincoln* (1959) and a book of poems, *Morning Worship* (1960). *The Autobiography of Mark Van Doren* (1958) is the work of a modest, self-effacing and essentially noble being. Moreover, the work is that of a poet in that the phases of his life are illuminated by poetry alternating with prose.

FORMER BARN LOT

Once there was a fence here,
And the grass came and tried—
Leaning from the pasture—
To get inside.

But colt feet trampled it,
Turning it brown;
Until the farmer moved
And the fence fell down;

Then any bird saw,
Under the wire,
Grass nibbling inward
Like green fire.

IMMORTAL

The last thin acre of stalks that stood
Was never the end of the wheat.
Always something fled to the wood
As if the field had feet.

In front of the sickle something rose—
Mouse, or weasel, or hare;
We struck and struck, but our worst blows
Dangled in the air.

Nothing could touch the little soul
Of the grain. It ran to cover,
And nobody knew in what warm hole
It slept till the winter was over,

And early seeds lay cold in the ground.
Then—but nobody saw—
It burrowed back with never a sound,
And awoke the thaw.

THE PULSE

One thing is sure
When most are not:
That there is cold,
That there is hot,

That winter stars
Are swollen blue
And that bright summer
Bulges too—

Getting the same
Black sky with child;
And both are big,
And both are wild.

There is no error
In the frost;
With warmth away
No warmth is lost;

Waves are coming
Of a time
That has been written
In slow rhyme:

Hot and cold,
And cold and hot—
All things may fail,
But this one not.

Though hate and love
And mercy cease,
Under the rippling
Vapor-fleece

Of earth goes warmth
Pursuing cold
And neither is young
And neither is old.

THE DISTANT RUNNERS

Six great horses of Spain, set free after his death by De Soto's men, ran West and restored to America the wild race lost there some thousands of years ago.
—A legend.

Ferdinand De Soto lies
Soft again in river mud.
Birds again, as on the day
Of his descending, rise and go
Straightly West, and do not know
Of feet beneath that faintly thud.

If I were there in other time,
Between the proper sky and stream;
If I were there and saw the six
Abandoned manes, and ran along,
I could sing the fetlock song
That now is chilled within a dream.

Ferdinand De Soto, sleeping
In the river, never heard
Four-and-twenty Spanish hooves
Fling off their iron and cut the green,
Leaving circles new and clean
While overhead the wing-tips whirred.

Neither I nor any walker
By the Mississippi now
Can see the dozen nostrils open
Half in pain for death of men—
But half in gladness, neighing then
As loud as loping would allow.

On they rippled, tail and back,
A prairie day, and swallows knew
A dark, uneven current there.
But not a sound came up the wind,
And toward the night their shadow thinned
Before the black that flooded through.

If I were there to bend and look,
The sky would know them as they sped
And turn to see. But I am here,
And they are far, and time is old.
Within my dream the grass is cold;
The legs are locked; the sky is dead.

THE ESCAPE

Going from us at last,
He gave himself forever
Unto the mudded nest,
Unto the dog and the beaver.

Sick of the way we stood,
He pondered upon flying,
Or envied the triple thud
Of horses' hooves; whose neighing

Came to him sweeter than talk,
Whereof he too was tired.
No silences now he broke,
No emptiness explored.

Going from us, he never
Sent one syllable home.
We called him wild; but the plover
Watched him, and was tame.

THE WHISPERER

Be extra careful by this door,
No least, least sound, she said.
It is my brother Oliver's,
And he would strike you dead.

Come on. It is the top step now,
And carpet all the way.
But wide enough for only one,
Unless you carry me.

I love your face as hot as this.
Put me down, though, and creep.
My father! He would strangle you,
I think, like any sheep.

Now take me up again, again;
We're at the landing post.
You hear her saying Hush, and Hush?
It is my mother's ghost.

She would have loved you, loving me.
She had a voice as fine—
I love you more for such a kiss,
And here is mine, is mine.

And one for her—O, quick, the door!
I cannot bear it so.
The vestibule, and out—for now
Who passes that would know?

Here we could stand all night and let
Strange people smile and stare.
But you must go, and I must lie
Alone up there, up there.

Remember? But I understand.
More with a kiss is said.
And do not mind it if I cry,
Passing my mother's bed.

E. E. Cummings

⁂ E(dward) E(stlin) Cummings was born October 14, 1894, in Cambridge, Massachusetts. Son of Edward Cummings, who taught at Harvard and preached in Boston's South Congregational Church, Cummings attended Harvard, took his B.A. in 1915 and his M.A. in 1916. During World War I he served with the Ambulance Corps. Because of a censor's error, he was arrested and, because of the assertion of his own free will, he spent three months in a concentration camp. This experience formed the basis of his novel *The Enormous Room* (1922). After 1920 he lived in Paris where he secured recognition as painter and draftsman as well as a writer. Returning to America, he became a leader of the avantgarde; his versatility emphasized his eminence as irreconcilable experimenter.

From the beginning Cummings seemed to be preoccupied with typographical disarrangements. This is a pity, for much of his work suffers because of the distortions; that part of it which succeeds is often successful in spite of, and not because of, its form. Cummings is incapable of self-criticism; in middle age he resolutely continued the verve and brashness of adolescence.

His early books, *Tulips and Chimneys* (1923), *&* (1925), and *XLI Poems* (1925), are mixtures of extreme modernism, archaism, and stylistic affectations. Cummings' emotions, unlike the look of his eccentric pages, are not at all bizarre; often they are actually banal. A constant challenger, Cummings knows how to provoke the reader. Prompted by the French calligraphists, he arrests the attention by breaking up his sentences, even his words, with astonishing transpositions and elisions, with punctuation that interrupts and distorts the line, and a dozen other devices. Sometimes the disruptions are highly successful; sometimes they merely conceal an inflated sentimentality.

No Thanks (1935), privately printed, intensified Cummings' essential incongruities, his stretched irresponsibilities, and his paradox of traditional subject matter in ultra-modern treatment. The attention-getting devices were carried further than ever; stereotyped images were tricked out with parentheses, and interpolated commas wedged themselves irrelevantly into faintly protesting words. Allen Tate was one of those who insisted that Cummings had replaced "the old poetic conventions with equally limited conventions of his own."

But the critic must be wary in his eagerness to dispose of Cummings. Let the critic deride the poet as a sentimentalist, and he is faced by "Poem, or Beauty Hurts Mr. Vinal," one of the period's most savage thrusts against sentimental versifying. Let him dismiss Cummings as a cheapjack, and he is confronted with pieces as purely lyrical as "Somewhere I have never travelled," "Since feeling is first," "O sweet spontaneous earth."

Cummings' early work was reassembled in *Collected Poems* (1938). *Fifty Poems* (1941) was followed by *1 × 1* (1944). The work published in his fiftieth year shows no perceptible advance over the poems published in his early thirties. There is the same combination of persuasive phrases and precious rhetoric, of charm and wit. But the charm is marred by a determinedly scrambled syntax which, attempting to establish an individual idiom, only registers caprice, and the wit is not helped by the trickiness which, intended to arrest the eye, merely irritates it. Apart from typographical oddities, most of Cummings' poetry is devoted to the traditional subjects: spring, love, life, roses, etc.

In his sixties Cummings won several honors, including the National Book Award for his omnibus volume, *Poems: 1923-1954*. In 1953 he published *Six Nonlectures,* originally delivered at Harvard. *95 Poems* are those written in 1954-1958.

If Cummings is scarcely a revolutionary thinker, he is always a surprisingly creative craftsman. He is simultaneously the skillful draftsman, the leg-pulling clown, the sensitive commentator and the ornery boy. The nose-thumbing satirist is continually interrupted by the singer of brazenly tender lyrics. A modern of the moderns, he displays a seventeenth century obsession with desire and death; part Cavalier, part metaphysician, he is a shrewd manipulator of language, and his style —gracefully erotic or downright indecent—is strictly his own. It is a likely irony that Cummings will finally be appraised not as a typographical eccentric or as a startling exhibitionist, but as a thinly disguised and wholly unashamed romantic poet.

WHEN GOD LETS MY BODY BE

when god lets my body be

From each brave eye shall sprout a tree
fruit that dangles therefrom

the purpled world will dance upon
Between my lips which did sing

a rose shall beget the spring
that maidens whom passion wastes

will lay between their little breasts
My strong fingers beneath the snow

into strenuous birds shall go
my love walking in the grass

their wings will touch with her face
and all the while shall my heart be

With the bulge and nuzzle of the sea

SUNSET

stinging
gold swarms
upon the spires
silver
        chants the litanies the
great bells are ringing with rose
the lewd fat bells

                    and a tall

wind
is dragging
the
sea

with

dream

-S

IMPRESSION—IV

the hours rise up putting off stars and it is
dawn
into the street of the sky light walks scattering poems

on earth a candle is
extinguished   the city
wakes
with a song upon her
mouth having death in her eyes

and it is dawn
the world
goes forth to murder dreams. . . .

i see in the street where strong
men are digging bread
and i see the brutal faces of
people contented hideous hopeless cruel happy

and it is day,

in the mirror
i see a frail
man dreaming
dreams
dreams in the mirror

and it
is dusk   on earth

a candle is lighted
and it is dark.
the people are in their houses
the frail man is in his bed
the city

sleeps with death upon her mouth having a song in her eyes
the hours descend,
putting on stars. . . .
in the street of the sky night walks scattering poems

LA GUERRE

I

the bigness of cannon
is skillful,

but i have seen
death's clever enormous voice
which hides in a fragility
of poppies. . . .

i say that sometimes
on these long talkative animals
are laid fists of huger silence

I have seen all the silence
filled with vivid noiseless boys

at Roupy
i have seen
between barrages,

the night utter ripe unspeaking girls.

II

O sweet spontaneous
earth how often have
the
doting

fingers of
prurient philosophers pinched
and
poked
thee
, has the naughty thumb
of science prodded
thy
beauty , how
often have the religions taken
thee upon their scraggy knees
squeezing and

buffeting thee that thou mightest conceive
gods
(but
true
to the incomparable
couch of death thy
rhythmic
lover

thou answerest

them only with
spring)

CHANSON INNOCENT

in Just-
spring when the world is mud-
luscious the little
lame baloonman

whistles far and wee
and eddieandbill come
running from marbles and
piracies and it's
spring

when the world is puddle-wonderful

the queer
old baloonman whistles
far and wee

and bettyandisbel come dancing
from hop-scotch and jump-rope and

it's
spring
and
the
goat-footed

baloonman whistles
far
and
wee

ALWAYS BEFORE YOUR VOICE

Always before your voice my soul
half-beautiful and wholly droll
is as some smooth and awkward foal,
whereof young moons begin
the newness of his skin,

so of my stupid sincere youth
the exquisite failure uncouth
discovers a trembling and smooth
Unstrength, against the strong
silences of your song;

or as a single lamb whose sheen
of full unsheared fleece is mean
beside its lovelier friends, between
your thoughts more white than wool
My thought is sorrowful;

but my heart smote in trembling thirds
of anguish quivers to your words,
As to a flight of thirty birds
shakes with a thickening fright
the sudden fooled light.

it is the autumn of a year:
When the thin air is stooped with fear,
across the harvest whitely peer
empty of surprise
death's faultless eyes

(whose hand my folded soul shall know
while on faint hills do frailly go
The peaceful terrors of the snow,
and before your dead face
which sleeps, a dream shall pass)

and these my days their sounds and flowers
Fall in a pride of petaled hours,
like flowers at the feet of mowers
whose bodies strong with love
through meadows hugely move,

yet what am i that such and such
mysteries very simply touch
me, whose heart-wholeness overmuch
Expects of your hair pale,
a terror musical?

while in an earthless hour my fond
soul seriously yearns beyond
this fern of sunset frond on frond
opening in a rare
Slowness of gloried air. . . .

The flute of morning stilled in noon—
noon the implacable bassoon—
now Twilight seeks the thrill of moon,
washed with a wild and thin
despair of violin.

SONG

Thy fingers make early flowers of
all things.
thy hair mostly the hours love:
a smoothness which
sings, saying
(though love be a day)
do not fear, we will go amaying.

thy whitest feet crisply are straying.
Always
thy moist eyes are at kisses playing,
whose strangeness much
says; singing
(though love be a day)
for which girl art thou flowers bringing?

To be thy lips is a sweet thing
and small.
Death, thee i call rich beyond wishing
if this thou catch,
else missing.
(though love be a day
and life be nothing, it shall not stop kissing)

PORTRAIT VIII

Buffalo Bill's
defunct
who used to
ride a watersmooth-silver
stallion
and break onetwothreefourfive pigeonsjustlikethat
Jesus
he was a handsome man
and what i want to know is
how do you like your blueeyed boy
Mister Death

SONNET

a wind has blown the rain away and blown
the sky away and all the leaves away,
and the trees stand. I think i too have known
autumn too long

(and what have you to say,
wind wind wind—did you love somebody
and have you the petal of somewhere in your heart
pinched from dumb summer?
O crazy daddy
of death dance cruelly for us and start

the last leaf whirling in the final brain
of air!) Let us as we have seen see
doom's integration . . . a wind has blown the rain

away and the leaves and the sky and the
trees stand:
                    the trees stand. The trees,
suddenly wait against the moon's face.

THIS IS THE GARDEN

this is the garden: colors come and go,
frail azures fluttering from night's outer wing,
strong silent greens serenely lingering,
absolute lights like baths of golden snow.
This is the garden: pursèd lips do blow
upon cool flutes within wide glooms, and sing
(of harps celestial to the quivering string)
invisible faces hauntingly and slow.

This is the garden. Time shall surely reap,
and on Death's blade lie many a flower curled,
in other lands where other songs be sung;
yet stand They here enraptured, as among
the slow deep trees perpetual of sleep
some silver-fingered fountain steals the world.

POEM, OR BEAUTY HURTS MR. VINAL

take it from me kiddo
believe me
my country, 'tis of

you, land of the Cluett
Shirt Boston Garter and Spearmint
Girl With The Wrigley Eyes(of you
land of the Arrow Ide
and Earl &
Wilson
Collars)of you i
sing: land of Abraham Lincoln and Lydia E. Pinkham,
land above all of Just Add Hot Water And Serve—
from every B.V.D.

let freedom ring

amen. i do however protest, anent the un
-spontaneous and otherwise scented merde which
greets one(Everywhere Why)as divine poesy per
that and this radically defunct periodical. i would

suggest that certain ideas gestures
rhymes, like Gillette Razor Blades

having been used and reused
to the mystical moment of dullness, emphatically are
Not To Be Resharpened. (Case in point

if we are to believe these gently O sweetly
melancholy trillers amid the thrillers
these crepuscular violinsts among my and your
skyscrapers—Helen & Cleopatra were Just Too Lovely,
The Snail's On The Thorn enter Morn and God's
In His andsoforth

do you get me?)according
to such supposedly indigenous
throstles Art is O World O Life
a formula: example, Turn Your Shirttails Into
Drawers and If It Isn't An Eastman It Isn't A
Kodak therefore my friends let
us now sing each and all fortissimo A-
mer
i

ca, I
love,
You. And there're a
hun-dred-mil-lion-oth-ers, like
all of you successfully if
delicately gelded(or spaded)
gentlemen(and ladies)—pretty

littleliverpill-
hearted-Nujolneeding-There's-A-Reason
americans(who tensetendoned and with
upward vacant eyes, painfully
perpetually crouched, quivering, upon the
sternly allotted sandpile
—how silently
emit a tiny violetflavored nuisance: Odor?

ono.
comes out like a ribbon lies flat on the brush

ITEM

this man is o so
Waiter
this; woman is

please shut that
the pout And affectionate leer
interminable pyramidal, napkins
(this man is oh so tired of this
a door opens by itself

woman.) they so to speak were in

Love once?
now
her mouth opens too far
and: she attacks her Lobster without
feet mingle under the
mercy.
(exit the hors d'œuvres)

SINCE FEELING IS FIRST

since feeling is first
who pays any attention
to the syntax of things
will never wholly kiss you;

wholly to be a fool
while Spring is in the world

my blood approves,
and kisses are a better fate
than wisdom
lady i swear by all flowers. Don't cry
—the best gesture of my brain is less than
your eyelid's flutter which says

we are for each other: then
laugh, leaning back in my arms
for life's not a paragraph

And death i think is no parenthesis

SOMEWHERE I HAVE NEVER TRAVELLED

somewhere i have never travelled, gladly beyond
any experience, your eyes have their silence:
in your most frail gesture are things which enclose me,
or which i cannot touch because they are too near

your slightest look easily will unclose me
though i have closed myself as fingers,
you open always petal by petal myself as Spring opens
(touching skilfully, mysteriously) her first rose

or if your wish be to close me, i and
my life will shut very beautifully, suddenly,
as when the heart of this flower imagines
the snow carefully everywhere descending;
nothing which we are to perceive in this world equals
the power of your intense fragility: whose texture
compels me with the color of its countries,
rendering death and forever with each breathing

(i do not know what it is about you that closes
and opens; only something in me understands
the voice of your eyes is deeper than all roses)
nobody, not even the rain, has such small hands

IF THERE ARE ANY HEAVENS

if there are any heavens my mother will(all by herself)have
one. It will not be a pansy heaven nor
a fragile heaven of lilies-of-the-valley but
it will be a heaven of blackred roses

my father will be(deep like a rose
tall like a rose)

standing near my

(swaying over her
silent)
with eyes which are really petals and see

nothing with the face of a poet really which
is a flower and not a face with
hands
which whisper
This is my beloved my

(suddenly in sunlight
he will bow,

& the whole garden will bow)

ANYONE LIVED IN A PRETTY HOW TOWN

anyone lived in a pretty how town
(with up so floating many bells down)
spring summer autumn winter
he sang his didn't he danced his did.

Women and men(both little and small)
cared for anyone not at all
they sowed their isn't they reaped their same
sun moon stars rain

children guessed(but only a few
and down they forgot as up they grew
autumn winter spring summer)
that noone loved him more by more

when by now and tree by leaf
she laughed his joy she cried his grief
bird by snow and stir by still
anyone's any was all to her

someones married their everyones
laughed their cryings and did their dance
(sleep wake hope and then)they
said their nevers they slept their dream

stars rain sun moon
(and only the snow can begin to explain
how children are apt to forget to remember
with up so floating many bells down)

one day anyone died i guess
(and noone stooped to kiss his face)
busy folk buried them side by side
little by little and was by was

all by all and deep by deep
and more by more they dream their sleep
noone and anyone earth by april
wish by spirit and if by yes.

Women and men(both dong and ding)
summer autumn winter spring
reaped their sowing and went their came
sun moon stars rain

WHAT IF A MUCH OF A WHICH OF A WIND

what if a much of a which of a wind
gives the truth to summer's lie;
bloodies with dizzying leaves the sun
and yanks immortal stars awry?
Blow king to beggar and queen to seem
(blow friend to fiend:blow space to time)
—when skies are hanged and oceans drowned,
the single secret will still be man

what if a keen of a lean wind flays
screaming hills with sleet and snow:

strangles valleys by ropes of thing
and stifles forests in white ago?
Blow hope to terror;blow seeing to blind
(blow pity to envy and soul to mind)
—whose hearts are mountains,roots are trees,
it's they shall cry hello to the spring

what if a dawn of a doom of a dream
bites this universe in two,
peels forever out of his grave
and sprinkles nowhere with me and you?
Blow soon to never and never to twice
(blow life to isn't:blow death to was)
—all nothing's only our hugest home;
the most who die,the more we live

Genevieve Taggard

Genevieve Taggard was born November 28, 1894, in Waitsburg, Washington, attended the University of California, and taught at Bennington and Sarah Lawrence Colleges. She died in 1948.

For Eager Lovers (1922) triumphs over its banal title; the verse is unaffected, especially in such poems as "With Child" and "The Enamel Girl." Five other lyrical, highly personal volumes preceded her *Collected Poems: 1918-1938,* which was followed by two more collections. She was also the author of the searching if speculative biography, *The Life and Mind of Emily Dickinson* (1930).

WITH CHILD

Now I am slow and placid, fond of sun,
Like a sleek beast, or a worn one:
No slim and languid girl—not glad
With the windy trip I once had,
But velvet-footed, musing of my own,
Torpid, mellow, stupid as a stone.

You cleft me with your beauty's pulse, and now
Your pulse has taken body. Care not how
The old grace goes, how heavy I am grown,
Big with this loneliness, how you alone
Ponder our love. Touch my feet and feel
How earth tingles, teeming at my heel!
Earth's urge, not mine—my little death, not hers;
And the pure beauty yearns and stirs.

It does not heed our ecstasies, it turns
With secrets of its own, it own concerns,
Toward a windy world of its own, toward stark
And solitary places. In the dark,
Defiant even now, it tugs and moans
To be untangled from these mother's bones.

THE ENAMEL GIRL

Fearful of beauty, I always went
Timidly indifferent:

Dainty, hesitant, taking in
Just what was tiniest and thin;

Careful not to care
For burning beauty in blue air;

Wanting what my hand could touch—
That not too much;

Looking not to left or right
On a honey-silent night;

Fond of arts and trinkets, if
Imperishable and stiff.

They never played me false, nor fell
Into fine dust. They lasted well.

They lasted till you came, and then
When you went, sufficed again.

But for you, they had been quite
All I needed for my sight.

You faded. I never knew
How to unfold as flowers do,

Or how to nourish anything
To make it grow. I wound a wing

With one caress; with one kiss
Break most fragile ecstasies . . .

Now terror touches me when I
Dream I am touching a butterfly.

SOLAR MYTH

(Maui, the dutiful son and great hero, yields to his mother's entreaty and adjusts the center of the universe to her convenience. The days are too short for drying tapa. He is persuaded to slow down the speed of the spider-sun with a lasso of sisal rope.)

The golden spider of the sky
Leaped from the crater's rim;
And all the winds of morning rose
And spread, and followed him.

The circle of the day swept out,
His vast and splendid path;
The purple sea spumed in the west
His humid evening bath.

Thrice twenty mighty legs he had,
And over earth there passed
Shadows daily whipping by,
Faster, faster, fast . . .

For daily did he wax more swift,
And daily did he run
The span of heaven to the sea,
A lusty, rebel sun.

Then Maui's mother came to him
With weight of household woes:
"I cannot get my tapa dry
Before the daylight goes.

"Mornings I rise and spread with care
My tapa on the grass;
Evenings I gather it again
A damp and sodden mass."

Then Maui rose and climbed at night
The mountain. Dim and deep
Within the crater's bowl he saw
The sprawling sun asleep.

He looped his ropes, the mighty man,
He whirled his sisal cords;
They whistled like a hurricane
And cut the air like swords.

Up sprang the spider. Maui hurled
His lasso after him.
The spider fled. Great Maui stood
Firm on the mountain-rim.

The spider dipped and swerved and pulled
But struggle as he might,
Around one-half his whirl of legs
The sisal ropes cut tight.

He broke them off, the mighty man,
He dropped them in the sea,
Where there had once been sixty legs
There now were thirty-tree.

Maui counted them, and took
The pathway home; and came
Back to his mother, brooding,—strode
Like a lost man, and lame.

The tarnished spider of the sky
Limped slowly over heaven,
And with his going mourned and moaned
The missing twenty-seven.

On with a hollow voice he mourned,
Poured out his hollow woe;
Over each day the sound of him
Bellowing, went below.

Maui saw the gulls swarm up
And scream and settle on
The carcass of the limping thing
That once had been the sun.

But still he thought at length to have
His mother satisfied.
"Can't you put back his legs again
Now all my tapa's dried?"

"The days are long and dull," she said,
"I love to see them skim." . . .
Wearily the old sun shook
The black birds off of him.

DOOMSDAY MORNING

Deaf to God, who calls and walks
Until the earth aches with his tread
Summoning the sulky dead,
We'll wedge and stiffen under rocks
Or be mistaken for a stone,
And signal as children do, "Lie low,"
Wait and wait for God to go.

The risen will think we slumber on
Like slug-a-beds. When they have gone
Trouped up before the Judgment Throne
We in the vacant earth, alone,—
Abandoned by ambitious souls,
And deaf to God, who calls and walks
Like an engine overhead
Driving the disheveled dead,—
We will rise and crack the ground,
Tear the roots and heave the rocks,
And billow the surface where God walks,
And God will listen to the sound
And know that lovers are below
Working havoc, till they creep
Together, from their sundered sleep.

Then end, world! Let your final darkness fall!
And God may call . . . and call . . . and call.

TRY TROPIC

On the Properties of Nature for Healing an Illness

Try tropic for your balm,
Try storm,
And after storm, calm.
Try snow of heaven, heavy, soft, and slow,
Brilliant and warm.
Nothing will help, and nothing do much harm.

Drink iron from rare springs; follow the sun;
Go far
To get the beam of some medicinal star;
Or in your anguish run
The gauntlet of all zones to an ultimate one.
Fever and chill
Punish you still,
Earth has no zone to work against your ill.

Burn in the jeweled desert with the toad.
Catch lace
In evening mist across your haunted face;
Or walk in upper air the slanted road.
It will not lift that load;
Nor will large seas undo your subtle ill.

Nothing can cure and nothing kill
What ails your eyes, what cuts your pulse in two,
And not kill you.

DILEMMA OF THE ELM

In summer elms are made for me.
I walk ignoring them and they
Ignore my walking in a way
I like in any elegant tree.

Fountain of the elm is shape
For something I have felt and said. . . .
In winter to hear the lonely scrape
Of rooty branches overhead

Should make me only half believe
An elm had ever a frond of green—
Faced by the absence of a leaf
Forget the fair elms I have seen.

(A wiry fountain, black upon
The little landscape, pale-blue with snow—
Elm of my summer, obscurely gone
To leave me another elm to know.)

Instead, I paint it with my thought,
Not knowing, hardly, that I do;
The elm comes back I had forgot
I see it green, absurdly new,

Grotesquely growing in the snow.
In winter an elm's a double tree;
In winter all elms trouble me.

But in summer elms are made for me.
I can ignore the way they grow.

Robert Hillyer

☙ Robert (Silliman) Hillyer was born in East Orange, New Jersey, June 3, 1895. He attended Kent School and Harvard College. After graduating from the latter, he was an ambulance driver with the French army from 1917 to 1919 and was at Copenhagen as Fellow of the American-Scandinavian foundation in 1921. He was Assistant Professor of English at Trinity College, Boylston Professor of Rhetoric and Oratory at Harvard, and at his death in 1961, was Professor of English at the University of Delaware.

Hillyer's first book was as innocuous as its title, *Sonnets and Other Lyrics* (1917), following which came six volumes of varying merit. Hillyer's seventh, entitled with an appropriateness suspiciously like a pun *The Seventh Hill* (1928), is one of his best. *The Halt in the Garden* (1925) had a foreword by Arthur Machen and elicited high praise from Middleton Murry. Though the contours of this poetry are delicate to the point of elegance, the spirit upholding them has a sustaining strength. "Prothalamion," which is the peak of the volume, is typical. Upon a theme which has done duty since the beginning of art, in a form which is uncompromisingly classical, Hillyer constructed twenty-six stanzas, none of which fell below a high seriousness.

The Collected Verse of Robert Hillyer (1933) confirms the praise of those critics who found Hillyer's poetry conventional in form but "colored by something from within." It received the Pulitzer Prize in 1934, and the award drew attention to the longer poems as well as to the shorter lyrics.

A Letter to Robert Frost and Others (1937) contains the best writing and thinking Hillyer accomplished. His measures are disciplined, even "classical," the rhymes are precise, the couplets are as polished as Pope's. But the tone is the tone of the twentieth century with its abrupt address and its edged disposals of current shibboleths and frauds. *Pattern of a Day* (1940) is a further advance, a book of unpretentious but pointed connections. Hillyer's idiom is not startling, but it is worn with a difference. His poetry speaks in a deceptively quiet voice, beneath the suavity of which things are said that are quick and keen and far from soothing. Such a poem as "The Assassination" is skilfully modulated and dramatically surprising. The limitations of Hillyer's work remain implicit in his training, in his deliberate cultivation of tradition. *Poems for Music* (1947) contains the seventy best lyrics written by Hillyer during thirty years. A novel, *My Heart for Hostage,* was followed by *The Death of Captain Nemo,* a narrative in blank verse.

AS ONE WHO BEARS BENEATH HIS NEIGHBOR'S ROOF

As one who bears beneath his neighbor's roof
Some thrust that staggers his unready wit
And brooding through the night on such reproof
Too late conceives the apt reply to it,
So all our life is but an afterthought,
A puzzle solved long past the time of need,
And tardy wisdom that one failure bought
Finds no occasion to be used in deed.

Fate harries us; we answer not a word,
Or answering too late, we waste our breath;
Not even a belated quip is heard
From those who bore the final taunt of death;
And thus the Jester parries all retort:
His jest eternal, and our lives so short.

PASTORAL

So soft in the hemlock wood
The phoenix sang his lullaby,
Shepherds drowsed where they stood,
Slumber felled each passerby,
And lovers at their first caress
Slept in virgin loneliness.

Not for mortal eye to see
Naked life arise from embers;
Only the dark hemlock tree
Evergreen itself, remembers
How the Word came into being,
No man hearing, no man seeing.

From the taut bow of sleep
Shoots the phoenix toward the day,
Shepherds wake and call their sheep,
Wanderers go on their way.
Unaware how death went by,
Lovers under the hemlocks lie.

PROTHALAMION

(Second Section)

The hills turn hugely in their sleep
With sound of grinding rock and soil
While down their granite shoulders leap
The waterbrooks in white turmoil.
The vigil of Good Friday done,
Our second spring ascends the height;
The earth turns southward toward the sun,
And trees which guard the pascal door,
In leaf once more,
Once more are murmurous with strange de-
light.

For now is the world's Eastertide,
And born that they may die again
Arise from death the gods who died.
Osiris, slender as young grain,
Comes back to Isis; the shy lad
Adonis wakens by the stream;
And Jesus, innocently clad
In samite, walks beneath the trees,
Half ill-at-ease
That Judas and the Cross were but a dream.
And thou art she whom I have seen
Always, but never understood,
In broken shrines festooned with green,
In twilight chapels of the wood;
Or on the hills a shepherdess
Walked with the sun full on her face,
And though her body and her dress
Appareled her in meek disguise,
I dropped my eyes,
For still I knew the goddess by her pace.

I know thee now in morning light
Though thou art wrought of flesh and blood,
And though the mother of the night
Resumes at dawn her maidenhood;
And though love severed with his knife
The girdle of the million years
And yielded to importunate life
The toll she asks of those who still
Would journey, till
They pass her known and visible frontiers.

The children from beyond the sun
Come bounding down the hillside grass,
And in the joyous rout is one
Who smiles and will not let us pass.
He stands, the fairest of them all,
And in his loveliness I trace
Thy loveliness. His light footfall
Bends not the grass he treads upon;
But he is gone
Before my eyes have feasted on his face.

Let him go back beyond the air;
This spring is ours, it is not his;
Those eager lips would take their share
Of love's yet undiminished kiss.
Fairer than he, as young, as gay,
As much a child, forget all things,
All but this transitory day

Of love, all things but love, and give
Thy fugitive
Delights to me who fly but with thy wings.

In undulant desire we merge,
On tides of light we sport and rest;
We swerve up from the deeper surge
To hover on the trembling crest
Of joy, and when the wave has passed,
Then smooth is the wing to the abyss
Of quietness, where with a last
Eye-darkening smile, we say farewell
Until the spell
Shall be renewed. Forget all things but this.

No grass-blade bends, no shadow stirs;
Love mounted high, slumber is deep;
Deep is the spring beneath the firs,
A sweet and lonely place for sleep.
And waking, we shall cool our flesh
In depths so clear they seem as air;
Twofold in beauty, thou refresh
Thy body in that water, bright
With muted light,
And brighter still for thy reflection there.

While I along the bank shall find
The flowers that opened with the day
Still dew-drenched, and with these entwined
New fronds of fern or darker bay.
Or pausing in a shaft of sun
That strikes across the mottled glade
Watch thee too long, beloved one,
Watch thee with eyes grown big with tears
Because the years
Suddenly spoke and made my heart afraid.

Giver of immortality—
That was thy name within the shrine—
The Mighty Mother, Star of the Sea,
All syllables of love were thine
To wear as lesser women wear
The garlands of their fragile spring;
Why then within my heart this fear
Of time? why then amid the shout
Of life, this doubt
That clouds the new sun like an outspread wing?

We must not to a foe like time
Yield up our present. Take my hand
And up the morning we shall climb
Until the wooded valley land
Lies all beneath us in the drowse
Of love's meridial aftermath;
The trellis of entwining boughs
Trembles in the great joy of green,
But does not screen
The comfortable glimpse of homeward path.

We will not to our ancient foe
Yield all this happiness; it lies
Shielded from sickle and from snow
And all the menace of the skies.
At night I shall watch over thee,
The future safe beneath thy breast,
And after autumn there shall be
Dayspring, when for each other's sake
We shall awake
And follow Love beyond the unknown west.

THE ASSASSINATION

"Do you not find something very strange
About him?" asked the First Fate.
"Very strange indeed," answered the Second Fate,
"He is immune to change."
"Yes, he is always young," complained the First Fate.
"He never heeds us," said the Second,
"I, for example, have often called and beckoned."
"We must kill him while he sleeps."
"He does not sleep."
"Then we must make him weep."
"He does not weep."
"Or laugh?"
"Only at his own epitaph,—
Half tears and laughter half."

"Then how to death, that worst fate,
To doom him?" said the First Fate.
"Oh, he's a clever one, as we've long reckoned,"
Answered the Second.
"But we can cope
With such a fellow, can we not,
What?"
"Could we not, say with a falling girder,
Carelessly cause an unintended murder?"
"Why not?"
"He's dead. Who said we could not cope
With this young fool. What was his name?"
"His name?"
"Of course that's not within our scope,
But just the same . . ."
"Hope was his name."
"How funny, Hope."

A LETTER TO ROBERT FROST

Our friendship, Robert, firm through twenty years,
Dares not commend these couplets to your ears:
How celebrate a thing so rich and strange—
Two poets whose affection does not change;
Immune to all the perils Nature sends,
World war and revolution and kind friends.
Something there is that doesn't love a wall; [1]
Your apples and my pines knew none at all,
But grow together in that ghostly lot
Where your Vermont meets my Connecticut.
Ours is a startling friendship, because art,
Mother of quarrels who tears friends apart,
Has bound us ever closer, mind and heart.

Before the War, among those days that seem
Bathed in the slanting afterglow of dream,
Were happy autumn hours when you and I
Walked down that street still bright in memory.
I was a boy apprenticed to my rhymes,
Your fame already rose above our times,
Your shadow walking tall, my shorter gait,—
Both taller now, the difference as great.

Of wisdom I learned much, an artist's creed
Of work the flower, and worldly fame the weed;
I have forgotten phrases; it remains
As part of me, it courses in my veins.
From many conversations I remember
One on a windy day in late November.
The sly recluse of Amherst in those times
Moved me, in spite of questionable rhymes.

[1] See page 170.

We talked of women poets, nothing else,
From Sappho to our friend at Sevenels.[2]
"Miss Dickinson is best!" You shook your head.
"Perhaps a genius, but mad," you said.
Alas for Emily, alas for me,
That now I go much further than agree:
Once irresistible, now merely coy,
Her whims, her verbal airs and graces cloy.
Taste changes. Candid Louis Untermeyer
Consigns his past editions to the fire;
His new anthology, refined and thrifty,
Builds up some poets and dismisses fifty.
And every poet spared, as is but human,
Remarks upon his critical acumen.

Ah, could we know what vogue will be tomorrow,
What plumes of Paradise our pens could borrow!

Yet not alone among the modern names
Does Fashion choose; she rummages in Fame's.
One poet to be praised—and sometimes read—
She chooses, and the rest are safely dead.
One must be sacrificed if one is praised,
As Crashaw mounts, Shelley must be abased.
With what astonishment we witnessed Donne,
A poet we have always counted on,
Whisked from his niche among the second shelves
And placed with Chaucer, Shakespeare,—and ourselves!
While Blake departs, abandoned by the vogue,
To Beulah-land, where Reason is the rogue;
And Hopkins, fashion's choice to follow Donne,
Rattling his rusty iambs, climbs the sun.

Blest be thy name, O Vogue, that canst embalm
A minor poet with a potted palm;
Make me immortal in thy exegesis,—
Or failing that, at least a Doctor's thesis.

Yet, Robert, through the charlatans who swarm
Like blowing gnats before the social storm,
The stout immortals stand in this our time,
With manners, morals, metres,—even rhyme.
Not every age can triumph over death
In the bright train of Queen Elizabeth,
And our ingenious and cynic age
Has not quite lost the better heritage.
Take Robert Bridges, laureate forever,
Calm as the sea and flowing as a river,
Who knew his source and end, but also knew
The homely country he meandered through.
Who, when we thought his broadening current spent,

[2] "Sevenels," Brookline, Massachusetts: the home of Amy Lowell.

Flung high that sun-capped wave, his testament,
The Testament of Beauty. Of the few
Titles he gave his poems, all are true.
And Robinson, what other age but this
Has bred so classic an antithesis:
Mild in his manner, mocking in his eye,
Bold in appraisal, and in statement shy,
He knew all men,—the Man against the Sky.
And urbane Santayana, who alone
Among philosophers still seeks their Stone;
Whose irony, in golden prose alloyed
With doubt, yet yields not to the acid Freud;
Who after years of rightful fame defrauded,
Wrote one bad book at last,[3]—and all applauded.

If gold get rusty, what shall iron do?
If poets, prophets, critics, are untrue
Why blame the statesmen, who in turn reflect
On dusty mirrors the uncircumspect?
When poets laugh at metres, with applause,
Why punish citizens who laugh at laws?
All follies regimented are akin—
Free verse and Bolshevism and bad gin.
Surely a subtle spring, in flow or drought,
Waters one age or burns another out.
When worlds go mad, all things go mad together,
Nations, philosophers, the arts, the weather.

Beholding war, Nature, who brooks no rival
In blind destruction, threatens Man's survival.
While underground he plants his dynamite,
She answers with an earthquake overnight.
While from ingenious wings his bombs rain down,
She rips the clouds apart and cities drown.
Machine guns clatter, but her ticking worm
Of death bombards his armies with a germ.
Nor can the propaganda of slow doubt
That one by one puts all faith's candles out
Find Nature unprepared; her insect ranks
For Man's destructive unbelief give thanks.
The ant, the termite, and their brotherhood
Wait busily, as all good soviets should
To crack his concrete and to gnaw his wood,
And after war and storm have done their worst,
To view the last man, as they viewed the first.

From such dark thoughts only Dark Ages come;
I see not yet the end of Christendom;—
And if an end? In cloistered minds like yours
The classic wisdom of the past endures;
The ancient learning from the ancient guilt

[3] Santayana's *The Last Puritan.*

Survives, and from slim chances worlds are built.
Black-armored barons, after Rome declined,
Warred on each other and on soul and mind;
Yet while they slept, cell after lonely cell,
Nearsighted eyes bent to the pliant quill.
The barons' mail adorns Park Avenue,
Quite spurious;—the words remain as true
As when, frail thread amid a mad sword-dance,
They led men to the sunlit Renaissance.
The things that make outlive the things that mar,
Rome and Byzantium crashed,—but here we are;
And even the dark spectre of dark ages
Calls forth old warriors who shame our sages:
Which would you choose, to put it in a word,—
To die with Arthur? or to live with Ford?

Men are as cells within a mighty brain
Swept with one thought of happiness or pain;
Thus when the Thinker gazed beyond all time
Egypt and China blossomed at their prime,
Both worshipers of beauty and of peace.
That mood resolved. He meditated Greece,
Whose culture, wedded to the arts of war,
Brought beauty forth and slew the thing it bore.
Less fortunate we who brought forth the machine
And dare not slay it, lest the truth be seen
That we, now helplessly identified
With the machine, would perish if it died.
We watch each other, our fates intertwined:
It feeds us canned goods and we feed it mind;
It kills us and then calls us from the grave
With new machines, lest it should lack a slave.
In war, where no one wins but the machine,
I pondered as I brought the wounded in:
Of these three choices—death, deformity,
Or patched for war again, who would not die?
And now the final triumph: the star actor
In "Steel: a Tragedy," makes God a tractor.
Yet let us still believe, in thinking deeper,
These are but twitchings of a troubled Sleeper
In whom the nightmare rages, and who can
Tomorrow dream the incredible—a Man.

Why, Robert, look! it's after midnight. Always
At this hour I hear stirrings in the hallways.
You would not mind. If I recall aright
You and Miss Lowell would converse all night,
Seldom agreeing, always the best friends,
That poetry can shape to different ends;
Myself, too sleepy then as now, would run
To catch the last car back at half-past one.
Heigh-ho, I've seen worse things than morbid youth

Inscribes in his dark diary. The truth
Remains that my few perfect moments seem
Eternal, and the bad ones but a dream.
Like Johnson's friend, I woo philosophy,
But cheerfulness breaks in in spite of me.
So does the spirit sift a life away
Into its best, preparing for the day
When, from its golden nucleus, shall rise
That happy part attuned to happier skies.

But happier skies? That phrase is fustian stuff,—
This green Connecticut is good enough;
My shining acres and the house I built,
All mine, all earned, all mortgaged to the hilt.
If I may make some changes here and there
When halos play on my unhallowed hair,
New England winters well might be curtailed—
In May it snowed, and in July it hailed.
Rosebugs should all be banished, and with those
The people who see rosebugs on the rose.
And yet I shrink from this celestial boom,
Lest, with improvements, also I assume
Responsibility for things in bloom.
I might forget wax flowers of huckleberry,
I might leave out the fragrance of wild cherry;
In short, I am content to leave to God
The natural world. O that our statesmen would!

And so good night with lullaby, my friend,
Republics fall and even letters end,
And Horace at one elbow sings of home
Far more eternal than the hills of Rome;—
Caesar, in fact, must marvel, looking down,
To find an Ethiope in his Gallic crown.
And Gibbon, at my other elbow, gives
Wry testimony of what dies, what lives,—
A secret not to be imparted, but
Known to Vermont and to Connecticut:
New as tomorrow's dawn, old as the Nile,
In Nefertiti's tears and Shakespeare's smile,
And all so simple in an age of guile;
For Horace on his acres has no fears,
His empire grows through twenty hundred years.

Good night, I take unconscionable time
A-dying, but in rhymeless years a rhyme
Bids one converse beyond the crack of dawn,—
It now has cracked, and dew is on the lawn.
Since I write oftener than you, I vow
Another letter twenty years from now.

Louise Bogan

⇜ Louise Bogan was born in Livermore Falls, Maine, August 11, 1897, and was educated in country schools through New England and at the Girls' Latin School in Boston. Except for a year in Vienna and another in Santa Fé, she lived in New York and contributed critical articles to *The New Yorker.* She held the Chair of Poetry at the Library of Congress in 1945-46.

Body of This Death (1923) is one of the most brilliant first books of the period. The accent is not new; we have already heard it more crisply in Elinor Wylie's precise syllables. But if Miss Bogan lacks her forerunner's dazzling craftsmanship, she achieves effects not unworthy of her subtlety. There are less than thirty poems in her volume and only two of them cover more than a page. Yet every stanza gives evidence of a mind which is as sensitized as the eye is sharp, an intellect which, for all its burden of thought, expresses itself best in the lyric. The longer blank verse is only moderately interesting compared with such a vivid screen as "Decoration" or so cool and chiseled a piece as "Statue and Birds." Few of her contemporaries have surpassed the finesse of these—few indeed have equaled it—while the bright contempt of "Women" and the frozen imagery in "Medusa" seem destined for more than contemporary applause.

Dark Summer (1929) emphasizes the impression made by her first volume. The technique, no longer so scintillating, is simpler; the accents, deep, bell-like, vesperal, are more her own. The metaphysical note has strengthened, the beat of measured blood has become more pronounced. *The Sleeping Fury* (1937) is a still greater refinement of her gifts. Sometimes her spare definiteness reminds one of the later Yeats; sometimes the slow pace is too gravely retarded. But, with scarcely an exception, mood and measure are joined in strict accuracy.

Achievement in American Poetry (1951) was followed by *Collected Poems* (1954) which, with Léonie Adams' *Poems,* divided the Bollingen Prize. In 1959 she received a $5,000 award from the Academy of American Poets for distinguished accomplishment.

MEDUSA

I had come to the house, in a cave of trees,
Facing a sheer sky.
Everything moved,—a bell hung ready to strike,
Sun and reflection wheeled by.

When the bare eyes were before me
And the hissing hair,
Held up at a window, seen through a door.
The stiff bald eyes, the serpents on the forehead
Formed in the air.

This is a dead scene forever now.
Nothing will ever stir.
The end will never brighten it more than this,
Nor the rain blur.

The water will always fall, and will not fall,
And the tipped bell make no sound.
The grass will always be growing for hay
Deep on the ground.

And I shall stand here like a shadow
Under the great balanced day,
My eyes on the yellow dust that was lifting in the wind,
And does not drift away.

WOMEN

Women have no wilderness in them,
They are provident instead,
Content in the tight hot cell of their hearts
To eat dusty bread.

They do not see cattle cropping red winter grass,
They do not hear
Snow water going down under culverts
Shallow and clear.

They wait, when they should turn to journeys,
They stiffen, when they should bend.
They use against themselves that benevolence
To which no man is friend.

They cannot think of so many crops to a field
Or of clean wood cleft by an ax.
Their love is an eager meaninglessness
Too tense, or too lax.

They hear in every whisper that speaks to them
A shout and a cry.
As like as not, when they take life over their door-sills
They should let it go by.

DECORATION

A macaw preens upon a branch outspread
With jewelry of seed. He's deaf and mute.
The sky behind him splits like gorgeous fruit
And claw-like leaves clutch light till it has bled.
The raw diagonal bounty of his wings
Scrapes on the eye color too chafed. He beats
A flattered tail out against gauzy heats;
He has the frustrate look of cheated kings.
And all the simple evening passes by:
A gillyflower spans its little height
And lovers with their mouths press out their grief.
The bird fans wide his striped regality
Prismatic, while against a sky breath-white
A crystal tree lets fall a crystal leaf.

STATUE AND BIRDS

Here, in the withered arbor, like the arrested wind,
Straight sides, carven knees,
Stands the statue, with hands flung out in alarm
Or remonstrances.

Over the lintel sway the woven bracts of the vine
In a pattern of angles.
The quill of the fountain falters, woods rake on the sky
Their brusque tangles.

The birds walk by slowly, circling the marble girl,
The golden quails,
The pheasants closed up in their arrowy wings,
Dragging their sharp tails.

The inquietudes of the sap and of the blood are spent.
What is forsaken will rest.
But her heel is lifted,—she would flee,—the whistle of the birds
Fails on her breast.

THE ALCHEMIST

I burned my life that I might find
A passion wholly of the mind,
Thought divorced from eye and bone,
Ecstasy come to breath alone.
I broke my life to seek relief
From the flawed light of love and grief.

With mounting beat the utter fire
Charred existence and desire.
It died low, ceased its sudden thresh.
I had found unmysterious flesh—
Not the mind's avid substance—still
Passionate beyond the will.

SIMPLE AUTUMNAL

The measured blood beats out the year's delay.
The tearless eyes and heart forbidden grief,
Watch the burned, restless, but abiding leaf,
The brighter branches arming the bright day.

The cone, the curving fruit should fall away,
The vine-stem crumble, ripe grain know its sheaf.
Bonded to time, fires should have done, be brief,
But, serfs to sleep, they glitter and they stay.

Because not last nor first, grief in its prime
Wakes in the day, and knows of life's intent.
Anguish would break the seal set over time
And bring the baskets where the bough is bent.

Full seasons come, yet filled trees keep the sky,
And never scent the ground where they will lie.

CASSANDRA

To me, one silly task is like another.
I bare the shambling tricks of lust and pride.
This flesh will never give a child its mother,—
Song, like a wing, tears through my breast, my side,
And madness chooses out my voice again,
Again. I am chosen no hand saves:
The shrieking heaven lifted over men,
Not the dumb earth, wherein they set their graves.

COME, BREAK WITH TIME

Come, break with time,
You who were lorded
By a clock's chime
So ill afforded.
If time is allayed
Be not afraid.

I shall break, if I will.
Break, since you must.
Time has its fill,
Sated with dust.
Long the clock's hand
Burned like a brand.

Take the rocks' speed
And earth's heavy measure.
Let buried seed
Drain out time's pleasure,
Take time's decrees.
Come, cruel ease.

THE DREAM

O God, in the dream the terrible horse began
To paw at the air, and make for me with his blows.
Fear kept for thirty-five years poured through his mane,
And retribution equally old, or nearly, breathed through his nose.

Coward complete, I lay and wept on the ground
When some strong creature appeared, and leapt for the rein.
Another woman, as I lay half in a swound
Leapt in the air, and clutched at the leather and chain.

Give him, she said, something of yours as a charm.
Throw him, she said, some poor thing you alone claim.
No, no, I cried, he hates me; he's out for harm,
And whether I yield or not, it is all the same.

But, like a lion in a legend, when I flung the glove
Pulled from my sweating, my cold right hand,
The terrible beast, that no one may understand,
Came to my side, and put down his head in love.

David McCord

⇝§ David (Thompson Watson) McCord was born in New York City, November 15, 1897. His ancestry is Colonial, "brick end." He looks with some pride on his maternal forebears, particularly on Dr. John Morgan, First Surgeon-General, under Washington, of the Revolutionary Army, and discoverer of pus, though, as he says, "I don't see how anybody could have missed it." He has lived at both extremes of the continent; he went to private schools on Long Island and public schools in Oregon. He entered Harvard in 1917; went to Plattsburg, where he was Second Lieutenant in the Field Artillery; returned to college, where he specialized in physics and mathematics, planning to be an engineer, he graduated from Harvard in 1921, and became editor of the *Harvard Alumni Bulletin.*

After graduating he traveled extensively and worked at different occupations, the most important being his critical reviews, musical and dramatic, under H. T. Parker, for *The Boston Transcript.* This determined McCord's career as a writer. After his thirtieth year he alternated with ease and growing distinction between prose and poetry, between poetry and verse. *Oddly Enough* (1926) is a volume of characteristic essays. *Oxford Nearly Visited* (1929) and *Bay Window Ballads* (1935) are dexterous light verse which (especially in "Sonnets to Baedeker") attempt to graft American freedom on English form. *Floodgate* (1927) is composed of serious poetry, as is *The Crows* (1934), a far more important volume.

With *The Crows* a writer of delicate verse and distinguished prose emerges definitely as a poet. Perhaps McCord's outstanding "difference" is his blending of two tones: he not only combines but fuses light verse and pronounced poetry. Themes which another might develop into portentous effects are nimbly varied and played with a supple hand.

What Cheer (1945), an anthology of American and British light verse, was republished as *The Pocket Book of Humorous Verse. Odds Without Ends* appeared in 1954, *Selected Poems* in 1957.

THE CROWS

I

This morning, when I heard the crows
Blaming the rows
Of city houses, blaming the noise,
I knew no boys
Were chasing them from field to tree to field,
Or that the sentry, his sharp eye peeled
For danger from the farm,
Had spread wings and alarm,
And the whole flock, suddenly mutinous,
Gone flying over us.
There was no field nor acre
Which the proud city-maker
Had not dug to houses, set in stone,

Or scraped to the brown bone.
There was no traffic here
For crows this time of year
If not in summer when geranium pots
Flower the standard lots.
It must have been the spring that drew them by.
Lying in bed I didn't see them fly
In querulous talk
Above the sparrowed walk:
I only heard them cawing as you hear
Them in the longbow of the year,
When the dead chestnut breaks upon the hill,
And the dark woods come darker still
Because the light is younger where it shows
The clearest meadow and the blackest crows.

II

They were not come to stay.
Crows never caw that way,
Trailing the sound behind them as if scare
Pursued them down the altitudes of air,
Except to say once more:
March is outside the door
Flaming some old desire
As man turns uneasily from his fire.
March in the sky, least in the ground, that is:
The city is not his
Who looks for blades on brick
And the cold dead to quick.
On heavy wing
                    they cleared us
                                        in a file
Of wise old minsters who never smile.
Perhaps we seemed to them
Another theorem
Of parallels and planes
For corbel brains.
Perhaps they saw in smoke
The substituting oak,
And the last windward knoll
In calculus of coal.
We were the writhen horn
Above the wasting corn,
We were the western pass
To the deep eastern grass;
Perhaps they said:
                    the landfall of great seas,
Or to be feared, or to be tried as trees.
Lying in bed, I didn't hear it all:
They had to wake me through a city wall
With still the same cool critical catarrh
That I have heard afar

In greening wood or yellowing grain,
And knew that I should die just not to hear again.

III

Whatever it meant, they never came to rest.
Their going (as I guessed)
Had more the text of migratory souls
Than wings for other springs
and other goals.
We were too much a fact or too unreal
To break the steel,
The bullet-heart, that drove
Home to the meadow and the maple grove.
I might have tried to strip the cloudy dawn
From the right sky to see where they had gone,
As one will follow geese
Disturbing the mind's peace;
But I preferred the lack
Of their long day flown slowly into night
And the last crow blinding from my sight,
Black into black.
It was enough that I should hear by name
Mention of the spring before it came;
Rumor, which is all a city has
Of the seed's own grievance to be grass.
March, April, goes . . .
I heard the crows
Who less than man or bird
Beg the impending word.
I saw the raven head,
Questioning
(from my bed)
Searching horizons still
Over the dusty sill,
Leaving between two thoughts one consolate sign
Of what, too, once was mine.

Stephen Vincent Benét

Stephen Vincent Benét, the younger brother of William Rose Benét, was born at Bethlehem, Pennsylvania, in July, 1898. He was educated in various parts of the country, and graduated from Yale in 1919.

At seventeen he published a small book containing six dramatic portraits, *Five Men and Pompey* (1915), a remarkable set of monologues which, in spite of distinct traces of Browning and Kipling, was little short of astounding, coming from a schoolboy. In Benét's next volume, *Young Adventure* (1918), published before he was twenty, one hears something more than the speech of an infant prodigy; the precocious facility has developed into a keen and individual vigor. *Heavens and Earth* (1920) charts a greater imaginative sweep. Like his brother, the younger Benét is at his best in the decoratively grotesque; his fancy exults in running the scales between the whimsically bizarre and the lightly diabolic.

For a while Stephen Benét was too prolific to be self-critical. He published several novels (the best of which are *Jean Huguenot* and *Spanish Bayonet*), collaborated on two plays which flickered a few nights in New York, and, unconsciously perhaps, began imitating his contemporaries. *King David,* published in book form a few months after it won *The Nation's* poetry prize for 1923, is less Benét than usual; it seems unjust that at least half the prize for this poem was not awarded to Vachel Lindsay. *Tiger Joy* (1925) betrays haste; the poet allows his rhymes to dictate and often to blur the course of his imagery. But though *Tiger Joy* is padded out with negligible verse, it contains "The Golden Corpse," a splendid octave of sonnets, "The Mountain Whippoorwill" and "The Ballad of William Sycamore," two vigorous and thoroughly American ballads.

Stephen Benét's faculty for ballad-making stood him in good stead when he came to reconstruct the Civil War period in *John Brown's Body* (1928). With this work, the author, hitherto known only to a small circle, leaped into instant popularity. Within a few months, the book had reached more than one hundred thousand people, and Benét had proved that a long narrative poem if skillfully blended could hold attention as easily as a novel. It was awarded the Pulitzer Prize the year following its publication.

The weakness of *John Brown's Body* is in the treatment. Although his canvas is epical, the author sacrifices the unity of the epic by abruptly changing meters, by a cinematographic switching from one character to another, by interluding his narrative with lyrics, ballads, elegies, and even prose. Nor, in this intermingling, has he perfected a style of his own; the long cadences of Sandburg and the jingling beat of Lindsay occur throughout. It is, frankly, a work of assimilation rather than creation. Yet its virtues compensate for its defects. The historical events have been more powerfully projected by others, the battle-pictures are inferior to the fictional episodes—the forgotten George Parsons Lathrop has done better in "Keenan's Charge" —but the composite is so new, the issue so impartially treated, that the struggle takes on a vitality barely suggested by orthodox histories. Benét's achievement of showing the war through its impact on a large number of *dramatis personae*—of Jake Diefer, who sees the war in terms of his Pennsylvania farmland, of Spade, the runaway slave, of Breckenridge, the Tennessee mountaineer, of Connecticut-born Jack Ellyat—is no small triumph. If Benét sacrifices unity, he gains speed, sudden interest and the nervous contrasts which are continually stimulating. If no single passage contains that unanalyzable but unmistakable quality which permeates great poetry, the originality of the work, the vigor of its portraits, the interpolated lyrics, and the unflagging pace reveal an unusually rich talent.

Burning City (1936) is a strangely mixed collection; hortatory prophecies, nimble whimsicalities, and impassioned lyrics reveal a candor and conviction, but little sense of integration. The long "Litany for Dictatorships" is the most dramatic of the larger poems; it rises above the indebtedness to MacLeish and that poet's suspended conjunctions and characteristically dangling participles. The best of Benét's verse, however, is neither forensic nor inflated; it is nimbly lyrical and dexterously macabre. The nightmares of metropolitan life in the machine age are most effective; they combine whimsical mischief and genuine horror.

Thirteen O'Clock (1937) is an assembly of Benét's best short stories. Among other fantasies, it contains "The Devil and Daniel Webster," which has become a classic in its own time, and which has been made into a play, an opera (with music by Douglas Moore), and a moving picture, the last having been retitled *All That Money Can Buy*. The vein of tall tales and pseudo-folklore was continued in *Johnny Pye and the Fool-Killer* (1938).

Suffering from a heart ailment, Benét died March 13, 1943. Two volumes were published after his untimely death: *Western Star* (1943), part of an unfinished long narrative poem, which was awarded the Pulitzer Prize, and *The Last Circle* (1946), written during the last years of his life.

RAIN AFTER A VAUDEVILLE SHOW

The last pose flickered, failed. The screen's dead white
Glared in a sudden flooding of harsh light
Stabbing the eyes; and as I stumbled out
The curtains rose. A fat girl with a pout
And legs like hams, began to sing "His Mother."
Gusts of bad air rose in a choking smother;
Smoke, the wet steam of clothes, the stench of plush,
Powder, cheap perfume, mingled in a rush.
I stepped into the lobby—and stood still,
Struck dumb by sudden beauty, body and will.
Cleanness and rapture—excellence made plain—
The storming, thrashing arrows of the rain!
Pouring and dripping on the roofs and rods,
Smelling of woods and hills and fresh-turned sods,
Black on the sidewalks, gray in the far sky,
Crashing on thirsty panes, on gutters dry,
Hurrying the crowd to shelter, making fair
The streets, the houses, and the heat-soaked air,—
Merciful, holy, charging, sweeping, flashing,
It smote the soul with a most iron clashing!
Like dragons' eyes the street-lamps suddenly gleamed,
Yellow and round and dim-low globes of flame.
And, scarce-perceived, the clouds' tall banners streamed.
Out of the petty wars, the daily shame,
Beauty strove suddenly, and rose, and flowered. . . .
I gripped my coat and plunged where awnings lowered.
Made one with hissing blackness, caught, embraced,
By splendor and by striving and swift haste—
Spring coming in with thunderings and strife—
I stamped the ground in the strong joy of life!

WINGED MAN

The moon, a sweeping scimitar, dipped in the stormy straits,
The dawn, a crimson cataract, burst through the eastern gates,

The cliffs were robed in scarlet, the sands were cinnabar,
Where first two men spread wings for flight and dared the hawk afar.

There stands the cunning workman, the crafty, past all praise,
The man who chained the Minotaur, the man who built the Maze.
His young son is beside him and the boy's face is a light,
A light of dawn and wonder and of valor infinite.

Their great vans beat the cloven air, like eagles they mount up,
Motes in the wine of morning, specks in a crystal cup,
And lest his wings should melt apace old Daedalus flies low,
But Icarus beats up, beats up, he goes where lightnings go.

He cares no more for warnings, he rushes through the sky,
Braving the crags of ether, daring the gods on high,
Black 'gainst the crimson sunset, gold over cloudy snows,
With all Adventure in his heart the first winged man arose.

Dropping gold, dropping gold, where the mists of morning rolled,
On he kept his way undaunted, though his breaths were stabs of cold,
Through the mystery of dawning that no mortal may behold.

Now he shouts, now he sings in the rapture of his wings,
And his great heart burns intenser with the strength of his desire,
As he circles like a swallow, wheeling, flaming, gyre on gyre.

Gazing straight at the sun, half his pilgrimage is done,
And he staggers for a moment, hurries on, reels backward, swerves
In a rain of scattered feathers as he falls in broken curves.

Icarus, Icarus, though the end is piteous,
Yet forever, yea forever, we shall see thee rising thus,
See the first supernal glory, nor the ruin hideous.

You were Man, you who ran farther than our eyes can scan,
Man absurd, gigantic, eager for impossible Romance,
Overthrowing all Hell's legions with one warped and broken lance.

On the highest steeps of Space he will have his dwelling-place
In those far, terrific regions where the cold comes down like Death
Gleams the red glint of his pinions, smokes the vapor of his breath.

Floating downward, very clear, still the echoes reach the ear
Of a little tune he whistles and a little song he sings,
Mounting, mounting still, triumphant, on his torn and broken wings!

THE BALLAD OF WILLIAM SYCAMORE

(1790-1871)

My father, he was a mountaineer,
His fist was a knotty hammer;
He was quick on his feet as a running deer
And he spoke with a Yankee stammer.

My mother, she was merry and brave,
And so she came to her labor,
With a tall green fir for her doctor grave
And a stream for her comforting neighbor.

And some are wrapped in the linen fine,
And some like a godling's scion;
But I was cradled on twigs of pine
In the skin of a mountain lion.

And some remember a white, starched lap
And a ewer with silver handles;
But I remember a coonskin cap
And the smell of bayberry candles.

The cabin logs, with the bark still rough,
And my mother who laughed at trifles,
And the tall, lank visitors, brown as snuff,
With their long, straight squirrel-rifles.

I can hear them dance, like a foggy song,
Through the deepest one of my slumbers,
The fiddle squeaking the boots along
And my father calling the numbers.

The quick feet shaking the puncheon-floor,
The fiddle squeaking and squealing,
Till the dried herbs rattled above the door
And the dust went up to the ceiling.

There are children lucky from dawn till dusk,
But never a child so lucky!
For I cut my teeth on "Money Musk"
In the Bloody Ground of Kentucky!

When I grew tall as the Indian corn,
My father had little to lend me,
But he gave me his great, old powder-horn
And his woodsman's skill to befriend me.

With a leather shirt to cover my back,
And a redskin nose to unravel
Each forest sign, I carried my pack
As far as a scout could travel.

Till I lost my boyhood and found my wife,
A girl like a Salem clipper!
A woman straight as a hunting-knife
With eyes as bright as the Dipper!

We cleared our camp where the buffalo feed,
Unheard-of streams were our flagons;
And I sowed my sons like apple-seed
On the trail of the Western wagons.

They were right, tight boys, never sulky or
slow,
A fruitful, a goodly muster.
The eldest died at the Alamo.
The youngest fell with Custer.

The letter that told it burned my hand.
Yet we smiled and said, "So be it!"
But I could not live when they fenced the
land,
For it broke my heart to see it.

I saddled a red, unbroken colt
And rode him into the day there;
And he threw me down like a thunderbolt
And rolled on me as I lay there.

The hunter's whistle hummed in my ear
As the city-men tried to move me,
And I died in my boots like a pioneer
With the whole wide sky above me.

Now I lie in the heart of the fat, black soil,
Like the seed of a prairie-thistle;
It has washed my bones with honey and oil
And picked them clean as a whistle.

And my youth returns, like the rains of
Spring,
And my sons, like the wild-geese flying;
And I lie and hear the meadow-lark sing
And have much content in my dying.

Go play with the towns you have built of
blocks
The towns where you would have bound me!
I sleep in my earth like a tired fox,
And my buffalo have found me.

LOVE CAME BY FROM THE RIVERSMOKE

(*from "John Brown's Body"*)

Love came by from the riversmoke,
When the leaves were fresh on the tree,
But I cut my heart on the blackjack oak
Before they fell on me.

The leaves are green in the early spring,
They are brown as linsey now,
I did not ask for a wedding-ring
From the wind in the bending bough.

Fall lightly, lightly, leaves of the wild,
 Fall lightly on my care,
I am not the first to go with child
 Because of the blowing air.

I am not the first nor yet the last
 To watch a goosefeather sky,
And wonder what will come of the blast
 And the name to call it by.

Snow down, snow down, you whitefeather bird,
 Snow down, you winter storm,
Where the good girls sleep with a gospel word
 To keep their honor warm.

The good girls sleep in their modesty,
 The bad girls sleep in their shame
But I must sleep in a hollow tree
 Till my child can have a name.

I will not ask for the wheel and thread
 To spin the labor plain,
Or the scissors hidden under the bed
 To cut the bearing-pain.

I will not ask for the prayer in church
 Or the preacher saying the prayer,
But I will ask the shivering birch
 To hold its arms in the air.

Cold and cold and cold again,
 Cold in the blackjack limb,
The winds in the sky for his sponsor-men
 And a bird to christen him.

Now listen to me, you Tennessee corn,
 And listen to my word.
This is the first child ever born
 That was christened by a bird.

He's going to act like a hound let loose
 When he comes from the blackjack tree,
And he's going to walk in proud shoes
 All over Tennessee.

I'll feed him milk out of my own breast
 And call him Whistling Jack.
And his dad'll bring him a partridge nest,
 As soon as his dad comes back.

SONG OF THE RIDERS

(from "John Brown's Body")

The years ride out from the world like couriers gone to a throne
That is too far for treaty, or, as it may be, too proud;
The years marked with a star, the years that are skin and bone.
The years ride into the night like envoys sent to a cloud.

Perhaps they dismount at last, by some iron ring in the skies,
Dismount and tie their stallions and walk with an armored tread
Where an outlaw queen of the air receives strange embassies
Under a tree of wisdom between the quick and the dead.

Perhaps they are merely gone, as the white foam flies from the bit,
But the sparkling noise of their riding is ever in our ears.—
The men who came to the maze without foreknowledge of it,
The losers and the finders, under the riding years.

They pass, and the finders lose, the losers find for a space.
There are love and hate and delusion and all the tricks of the maze.
There are always losers and finders. There is no abiding place
And the years are unreturning. But, here and there, there were days.

Days when the sun so shone that the statue gave its cry
And a bird shook wings or a woman walked with a certain mirth,
When the staff struck out a spring from the leaves that had long been dry,
And the plow as before moved on from the hilltop, but its share had opened the
earth.

So the bird is caught for an instant, and so the bird escapes.
The years are not halted by it. The losers and finders wait.
The years move on toward the sunset, the tall far-trafficking shapes,
Each with a bag of news to lay at a ghostly gate.

Riders shaking the heart with the hoofs that will not cease,
Will you never lie stretched in marble, the hands crossed over the breast,
Some with hounds at your feet to show that you passed in peace,
And some with your feet on lions? It is time that you were at rest.

1935

All night they marched, the infantrymen under pack,
But the hands gripping the rifles were naked bone
And the hollow pits of the eyes stared, vacant and black,
When the moonlight shone.

The gas mask lay like a blot on the empty chest,
The slanting helmets were spattered with rust and mold,
But they burrowed the hill for the machine-gun nest
As they had of old.

And the guns rolled, and the tanks, but there was no sound,
Never the gasp or rustle of living men
Where the skeletons strung their wire on disputed ground. . . .
I knew them, then.

"It is seventeen years," I cried. "You must come no more.
We know your names. We know that you are the dead.
Must you march forever from France and the last, blind war?"
"Fool! From the next!" they said.

NIGHTMARE NUMBER THREE

We had expected everything but revolt
And I kind of wonder myself when they started thinking—
But there's no dice in that now.
I've heard fellows say
They must have planned it for years and maybe they did.
Looking back, you can find little incidents here and there,
Like the concrete-mixer in Jersey eating the wop
Or the roto press that printed "Fiddle-dee-dee!"

In a three-color process all over Senator Sloop,
Just as he was making a speech. The thing about that
Was, how could it walk upstairs? But it *was* upstairs,
Clicking and mumbling in the Senate Chamber.
They had to knock out the wall to take it way
And the wrecking-crew said it grinned.

It was only the best
Machines, of course, the superhuman machines,
The one's we'd built to be better than flesh and bone,
But the cars were in it, of course. . . .

and they hunted us
Like rabbits through the cramped streets on that Bloody Monday,
The Madison Avenue busses leading the charge.
The busses were pretty bad—but I'll not forget
The smash of glass when the Duesenberg left the show-room
And pinned three brokers to the Racquet Club steps,
Or the long howl of the horns when they saw the men run,
When they saw them looking for holes in the solid ground

I guess they were tired of being ridden in,
And stopped and started by pygmies for silly ends,
Of wrapping cheap cigarettes and bad chocolate bars,
Collecting nickels and waving platinum hair,
And letting six million people live in a town.
I guess it was that. I guess they got tired of us
And the whole smell of human hands.

But it was a shock
To climb sixteen flights of stairs to Art Zuckow's office
(Nobody took the elevators twice)
And find him strangled to death in a nest of telephones,
The octopus-tendrils waving over his head,
And a sort of quiet humming filling the air . . .
Do they eat? . . . There was red . . . But I did not stop to look.
And it's lonely, here on the roof.

For a while I thought
That window-cleaner would make it, and keep me company.
But they got him with his own hoist at the sixteenth floor
And dragged him in with a squeal.
You see, they cooperate. Well, we taught them that,
And it's fair enough, I suppose. You see, we built them.
We taught them to think for themselves.
It was bound to come. You can see it was bound to come.
And it won't be so bad, in the country. I hate to think
Of the reapers, running wild in the Kansas fields,
And the transport planes like hawks on a chickenyard,
But the horses might help. We might make a deal with the horses.
At least you've more chance, out there.

And they need us too.
They're bound to realize that when they once calm down.

They'll need oil and spare parts and adjustments and tuning up.
Slaves? Well, in a way, you know, we were slaves before.
There won't be so much real difference—honest there won't.
(I wish I hadn't looked into that beauty-parlor
And seen what was happening there.
But those are female machines and a bit high-strung.)
Oh, we'll settle down. We'll arrange it. We'll compromise.
It wouldn't make sense to wipe out the whole human race.
Why, I bet if I went to my old Plymouth now
(Of course, you'd have to do it the tactful way)
And said, "Look here! Who got you the swell French horn?"
He wouldn't turn me over to those police cars.
At least I don't *think* he would.
Oh, it's going to be jake.
There won't be so much real difference—honest, there won't—
And I'd go down in a minute and take my chance—
I'm a good American and I always liked them—
Except for one small detail that bothers me
And that's the food proposition. Because you see,
The concrete-mixer may have made a mistake,
And it looks like just high spirits.
But, if it's got so they like the flavor . . . well . . .

Horace Gregory

Horace Gregory was born April 10, 1898, in Milwaukee, Wisconsin, of English, Irish, and German descent. He attended the Milwaukee School of Fine Arts and, after a year of study under a tutor, went to the German English Academy, and then to the University of Wisconsin, from which he graduated in 1923. Then came six years of free lance writing, chiefly book-reviewing, in New York, where he married Marya Zaturenska, the poet. He was on the English faculty at Sarah Lawrence College from 1933 until 1961, when ill health forced him to resign.

Gregory at first was entirely under the spell of the classics; after reading Byron, he turned to Landor, Pope, and Dryden. At college his interests became completely Latinized, and, though he dropped his classicism after seeing the tenements and poverty-ridden alleys of the sodden Chelsea section of Whitman's "glorious Mannahatta," enough persisted so that he translated *The Poems of Catullus* (1931), rendering them, however, in the American idiom. There was a "first" book of traditional lyrics which Gregory destroyed upon his arrival in New York; a few years later he published *Chelsea Rooming House*.

Chelsea Rooming House (1930) is a half-detached, half-indignant work; a set of monologues dramatizing the lives of those crowded into the slums of New York's lower west side. Its observation is keen to the point of penetration; its sense of sympathy is surpassed only by the faintly restrained sense of outrage. There is no doubt about Gregory's social sentiments nor his political preferences, but he does not resort to polemics or propaganda. He persuades the reader by the integrity of his poetry. *No Retreat* (1933) is a more lyrical collection. "Poems for My Daughter" and "Good Friday" owe something to T. S. Eliot's juxtaposition of the classic-rhetorical and the sharply colloquial, but the basic tone is Gregory's, and "Valediction to My Contemporaries" is both biographically and esthetically authentic.

Chorus for Survival (1935) is the most frankly personal of Gregory's volumes. The intense self-participation is declared in the eloquent "Prologue," which is a sort of Prothalamion-1935 Model, with its nervous music. It lifts itself vividly in "Ask no return," nostalgically in the poems recalling the poet's youth by the Great Lakes, symbolically in the section in which Emerson points an American panorama, gravely in the concluding lines "For you, my son." Some may object to a certain obscurity of utterance, a confusion of image and effect. But such obscurity (where it exists) is not willful. Nor does it proceed from a desire to overcompensate for a paucity of the imagination. The figures follow so rapidly that the poet's mind leaps from one to the other, taking the ellipses in his stride, and the reader is sometimes unable to take the leap with him.

Poems: 1930-1940 (1941) is a selection from Gregory's other volumes with the addition of a new group of poems. The book is not a mere assembly of verses for various occasions, but a set of recurrent themes with clarifying key poems. Few of the poems can be read as straight narratives, for they indulge in a freedom of form and effect; they employ the montage of cinema, the interrupting voice of the radio, the summons of the quick-changing telephone dial. Like Eliot, Gregory is fond of the dissonant chord and the unresolved suspense; like Hart Crane, he crowds image upon image to increase sensation and suggest new perspectives. But he does not share Eliot's disillusions or Crane's disorganization. There is constant control as well as positive belief in Gregory's poetry; his faith is a social faith. Plain statement and elliptical suggestion are employed to create characters and dramas of quiet violence. The intensity disturbs continuity, but (the poet might well insist) so does modern life; the tone is appropriately tough and complex and strictly contemporary. Gregory's "M'Phail," like Eliot's "Prufrock" and Robinson's "Miniver Cheevy," is a symbol of the lost man, the failure who escapes from the actual world into a dream-world of feeble excitement and false grandeur. The later poems round out the earlier verse and give it a growing design; they reflect the forces of the past focussed upon the present.

Besides his poetry, Gregory has written *Pilgrim of the Apocalypse* (1933), a study of D. H. Lawrence, and, with his wife, *A History of American Poetry.*

THEY FOUND HIM SITTING IN A CHAIR

They found him sitting in a chair:
continual and rigid ease
poured downward through his lips and heart,
entered the lungs and spread until
paralysis possessed his knees.

The evanescent liquid still
bubbling overflows the glass
and no one heard the telephone

ringing while friends and strangers pass.
(Call taxis, wake the coroner,
police; the young ex-millionaire
is dead.) Examine unpaid bills,
insurance blanks and checks unfold
from refuse in a right-hand drawer
to read before the body's cold,

Lifelike, resembling what we were,
erect, alert the sun-tanned head:
polo or golf this afternoon?
And night, the country club or bar?

—drink down to end all poverty,
two millions gone,
and stir no more.

Because I know his kind too well,
his face is mine, and the release
of energy that spent his blood
is no certificate of peace,
but like a first shot heard in war.

And not for him, nor you, nor me
that safe oblivion, that cure
to make our lives intact: immure
old debts and keep old friends.

Even in death, my lips the same
whisper at midnight through the door
and through storm-breaking hemisphere,
rise at that hour and hear my name.

POEMS FOR MY DAUGHTER

Tell her I love
she will remember me
always, for she
is of my tissues made;
she will remember
these streets where the moon's shade
falls and my shadow mingles
with shadows sprung
from a midnight tree.
Tell her I love that I
am neither in earth nor sky,
stone nor cloud,
but only this
walled garden she knows well
and which her body is.

Her eyes alone shall make
me blossom for her sake;
contained within her, all
my days shall flower or die,
birthday or funeral
concealed where no man's eye
finds me unless she says:
He is my flesh and I
am what he was.

VALEDICTION TO MY CONTEMPORARIES

The return after ten years: New York, Chicago, Madison

Entrain airport New York Chicago west
piercing the sunset's terminal where day
breaks midnight into stars before the dawn
Superior Lake Erie Michigan:
seawind but no saltsea in this lake spray
clear eyes and nostrils: drink our health: the sand
our shores.

Stop signals home again!

Awake at morning, spring coiled in the body
and at the narrow window slit in stone,
skylight and sun.

Tilt the horizon down,
ride windward through Wisconsin miles of corn,
grazing the shallow valley and long plains.

O Alma Mater on the hill! What green hills, Cicero,
vanish, return. What stone embankments of hope, desire,
what little almost islands Sirmio
anchored within us rest, flower in sleep, Catullus,
welcomed home.

II

The University of Wisconsin: 1919

Here was the campus of our hearts, my friends,
Plato's green-treed republic of the air:
see what miraculous fruit its branches bear,
oceans of maple spray, green harbored, flowing
against the sky: and from these shores Greek towers . . .

See how the white dome trembles in the sun,
dissolves at noon three thousand years away
where the antique nightingale engraved in bronze
still sways unheard forever, now entwined
within the steel crescendos of the mind.

III

The indecisive peace after war which lasted until 1929

Those who return, return to empty halls,
the crystal image in the sky, pellucid
limbs that fade in shadows on these walls:

This peace was ours: the slow guns still resounding
peace: *drive homeward angels from Versailles*
in limousines sunk under no man's land.
Run the machine guns through the arras—dead?
Not dead but much alive.
How shall we find
the bodies of those unslain, exiled from war
but now returned, furloughs of exile signed
from all green ports on earth?
The birth certificate of love
declared obscene: Faith of no faith, Our Father,
do not destroy this faithlessness to friend
or enemy, lest we perish to no end.

IV

Alternate speeches: individual lovers walking in the shadow of Lucretius

Measure the atoms of our souls, O Roman
death's astronomer Lucretius.

Spires of light ascend
discarnate memories: the four years spanned
by the quick, sinewy shadow of his hand:
(And in this shadow where she stood,
flight in her hair!
the limbs reveal undress that virgins wear
to meet the bridegroom on the wedding stair,
do not unsay her testament, O love:

"Live for this hour and we who die today
kiss lips that bloom forever underground."
And did you call me by his name who died
naked, Parian attitudes of death
entwined your limbs and his: kiss and restore
his body's heat in mine, this earth his grave:
sleepless, his blood drives home
niagaras in our veins)

—O Mors Aeterna,
lean from the fiery ramparts of world's end,
time's end and love's last image scrolled
in quicksilver across the mind—descend
voice of a million tongues, your elegies
(some say that suicide usurped his blood)
resound no more. . . .

Mount stairways to the sun!
We have survived your heritage, these years
consuming time toward death too swift for tears.

V

The valediction

The course of empire westward to Cathay
rides in the east: the circle breaks in fire:
these charred remains of what we were expire,
(O incandescent speed!) the hands, lips, eyes
anonymous. Rise atque vale, rise:
another generation shall disown
these years in darkness each to four winds blown
(the deeds are obsolete as Helen's war) . . .

Good-by, Il Penseroso of our spring,
forgive our ashes and destroy the urn:
unwind the clock, empty the seasons down
rivers of memory—do not return!

ASK NO RETURN

Ask no return for love that's given
embracing mistress, wife or friend,
ask no return:
on this deep earth or in pale heaven,
awake and spend
hands, lips and eyes in love,
in darkness burn,
the limbs entwined until the soul ascend.

Ask no return of seasons gone:
the fire of autumn and the first hour of spring,
the short bough blossoming
through city windows when night's done,
when fears adjourn
backward in memory where all loves end
in self again, again the inward tree
growing against the heart
and no heart free.
From love that sleeps behind each eye
in double symmetry
ask no return,
even in enmity, look! I shall take your hand;
nor can our limbs disjoin in separate ways again,
walking, even at night on foreign land
through houses open to the wind, through cold and rain,
waking alive, meet, kiss and understand.

FOR YOU, MY SON

For you, my son,
I write of what we were:

Under cool skies, Wisconsin's April weather:
The lilac fragrance on our lips and hair,

Field and the lake where memories restore
Westward the wave to India, the passage
Chartered through night
                        and the returning dawn
Over the mast-head, spars:
                        New York,
Green Castle Gardens at thy side:
Brooklyn, the Battery, wide-breasted Whitman there,
Hand to the shoulder of the pioneer:
O many-footed echoing Manhattan,
Thy ships at harbor swaying with the tide.
Break here the lilac bough in April's weather,
Gather, foregather
                in the pale mist of Juneau's city,
And in the valley, dry Menomenee
(Where forests were, clay-banked the silver river:
The trail in memory across the plain)

Turn where the earth's plowed under,
There at the root, the lilac flowering
In tombs that open when remembered spring
Comes home again beneath the pine roof-tree.

And did you hear the voices
Out of sand beach, lake waves?
                        The sound of water
Leaping in the dark:
                remember shadowy limbs in darkness joined,
Pacing the forest to the inland sea.

Know what we were:
Our father's father
Ex-Dubliner, the tired eyes, bright laughter
Where the cold heart concealed disaster:

"How many times before we fall,
We fail:
I am a tall man, handsome for my years,

Erect three score, the six foot two and three hands taller
Mounting to steer the horses beggars ride.
And over Michigan the space too small
For any man my size:
Ex-patriarch, astronomer, engineer
From the black-green growing turf where I was born
The black-bird army wheeling close through cloud

(breaking the sky through sunlight, rain
until the violet, long archaic twilight
empties its shadows over hills again)

Building my bridges to oblivion,
Even here, across the lake, across the sea.
See the cold island where I was born,
Peace where there is no peace,
always the blind
Violent war behind each blinded eye,
And darling Emmett dead, the cause in blood
Against gray walls.
Priest over priest,
Walking in prayer to soothe the dead,
Over each friend betraying friend,
The dark stain spreading is a blood-clot in the mind.
Wherever I go now and even here
(Seeing sky break in spring new hemisphere)
There is no rest for me in the new land."

Know what we were: this is the hour
White-haired millionaire
Starts from the dream:
"The banks are broken, Gas has fallen;
Consolidated Ice and Frigidaire
Dropped down Chicago River;
River swimming with rats, the poor:
No virgin safe tonight, pack up your girls,
Call the militia, ride
Down blackened streets in hell
Machine-gun fire until the pickets fall.
Pity the poor, but not the undeserving poor,
The right arm raised in blood,
Whose hand is bleeding at my door,
The million strong
Army at my door and the lock sprung."

Turn here, my son
(No longer turn to what we were)
Build in the sunlight with strong men,
Beyond our barricade:
For even I remember the old war
And death in peace:
The neon sign 'Success' across our foreheads.

(Under the earth, shaken, as I am trembling now:
The small room where the body moves alone:
sleepless I saw the dream;
I saw my head upon the pillow
and the blood)

the naked bed, the folding chair
Voiceless we smile; we are not violent.

And this is fear, fear,
The empty heart and the closed lung.

The broken song:
My classmates a republic of old men,

Yet even here, my hand to you, my son.

We shall be envious: O bitter eyes
Inward to see the dead,
those dead, our dead,
The bitter dying where the old world is dead.

I tell you love returns
Changing the hour:
break here the lilac bough,
Scatter the ashes in the tomb before the slow
Wind gathers into storm.
Over the cities and the yellowing plain
In bitter drought:
wait for new rain, welcome the men
Who shall survive, outface despair,
Terror and hate
to build new fire
At an empty hearth,
Burn doubt and fear.

As the map changes, through the cold sky,
Lean from the cockpit, read
The flower of prairie grass in seed
(Though here is war
my hand points where the body
Leaps its dead, the million poor,
Steel-staved and broken
and no grave shall hold them
Either in stone or sea; nor urn nor sand,
Skyline of city walls, their monument,
And on this field, lockstep in millions joined,
New world in fire opens where they stand.)

Wake to the song,
Only the young
shall outlive this dark hour
And night down streets the body walks alone;
Then up the stair; your portrait is my mirror;
Your features mine, and yours the quick, bright hair,
Read here my testament
when I am done,
This book is yours, the page uncut
Farewell, my brother
Comrade, son.

THE POSTMAN'S BELL IS ANSWERED EVERYWHERE

God and the devil in these letters,
stored in tin trunks, tossed in wastebaskets,
or ticketed away in office files:
love, hate, and business, mimeograph sheets, circulars,
bills of lading, official communiqués,
accounts rendered. Even the anonymous letter says,
Do not forget.

And in that long list, Dean Swift to Stella,
Walpole to Hannah More, Carlyle to Jane—
and what were Caesar's "Gallic Wars" other than letters
of credit for future empire?
Do not forget me.
I shall wear laurels to face the world;
you shall remember the head in bronze,
profile on coin.

As the bell rings, here is the morning paper and more letters,
the post date 10 P.M. "It is an effort
for me to write; I have grown older.
I have two daughters and a son, and business prospers,
but my hair is white; why can't we meet for lunch?
It has been a long time since we met;
I doubt if you would know me if you glanced quickly
at my overcoat and hat, and saw them vanish
in a crowded street. . . ."

Do not forget. . . . "Oh, you must not forget
you held me in your arms while the small room
trembled in darkness; do you recall the slender, violet
light between the trees next morning through the park?
Since I'm a woman, how can I unlearn
the arts of love within a single hour,
how can I close my eyes before a mirror,
believe I am not wanted, that hands, lips, breast
are merely deeper shadows behind the door
where all is dark? . . ."

Or, "Forgive me if I intrude; the dream I had
last night was of your face; it was a child's face,
wreathed with the sun's hair, or pale in moonlight,
more of a child than woman; it followed me
wherever I looked, pierced everything I saw,
proved that you could not leave me, that I am always
at your side. . . ."

Or, "I alone am responsible for my own death." Or,
"I am White, Christian, Unmarried, 21." Or, "I am happy

to accept your invitation." Or, "Remember that evening at the Savoy-Plaza?" Or, "It was I who saw the fall of France."

As letters are put aside, another bell
rings in another day; it is, perhaps, not too late to remember
the words that leave us naked in their sight,
the warning,
"You have not forgotten me;
these lines were written by an unseen hand
twelve hours ago. Do not reply at this address; these are the last words I shall write."

THIS IS THE PLACE TO WAIT

(*from "The Passion of M'Phail"*)

When you are caught breathless in an empty station
and silence tells you that the train is gone,
as though it were something for which
you alone were not prepared
and yet was here and could not be denied;
when you whisper, Why was I late, what have I done?,
you know the waiting hour is at your side.

If the time becomes your own, you need not fear it;
if you can tell yourself the hour is not
the thing that takes you when you sit
staring through clinic waiting-room white walls
into the blank blue northern sky
frozen a quarter-mile above the street,
and you are held there by your veins and nerves
spreading and grasping as a grapevine curves
through the arms and back of
an enamelled iron riverside park seat,
you need not think, Why must I wait
until the doctors say:

"We have come to lock you up.
It's the psychology of things that has got you down;
if you complain, we shall take care of you
until you know at last you can't escape.
Is your dream
the dream of a child kept after school,
made to write a hundred times
what three times seven means,
while in your sleep, before you get the answer,
the blackness fills and swells with pictures
of Technicolor inkstain butterflies?
Is that ink blot a tiger
in a bonfire? Are these the spines
of ancient caterpillars?
Is this the shadow of a wildwood, leaping deer?

Is that what you see, or what you think you see?
Then we can tell you what you are,
what you can do, and what you ought to be,
as though your life were written down in court,
your name the last word on a questionnaire.
There is nothing private that we do not know;
you can't deny these figures on a chart
that follow you no matter where you go.
Each zero is an open, sleepless eye
piercing the hidden chambers of the heart,
and if you fail, or if you kill yourself,
we shall know why."

It is when the waiting forces you to stop
in stillness that you wish would not return
that you say, I am not the same as other men;
I must live to wake beyond the fears of hope
into an hour that does not quite arrive. . . .

And in that quiet, lost in space, almost remember
the difficult, newborn creature you once were,
in love with all the wonders of the world,
seeing a girl step, white and glittering as a fountain,
into cool evening air,
knowing you could not touch her,
or dare to still the floating, flawless motion
of that pale dress above its glancing knees,
brief as the sight of sun on Easter morning
dancing its joy of earth and spring and heaven
over the sleeping bodies of men in cities
and between the branches of the tallest trees.

It is then you tell yourself,
Everything I live for is not quite lost.
Even if you've waited someplace far too long,
if you can't call it peace, you call it rest;
if you can't call it luck, you call it fate;
you then know that when anything goes wrong,
perhaps it also happened in the past.

You light a cigarette, you carefully
blow out the match.

You know again you have to wait.

Hart Crane

Harold Hart Crane was born in Garrettsville, Ohio, July 21, 1899. From the beginning his life was unhappy. In youth his parents quarreled and separated; he sided with his mother, regarded his father as his enemy, and considered himself doomed by the "curse of sundered parentage." He never finished high school; he left home but was unable to find a place for himself. Sporadically he tried to earn a living. He was employed in a print shop; wrote copy in advertising offices; packed candy in his father's warehouse; worked briefly as a riveter in a Lake Erie ship-yard, a reporter on the *Cleveland Plain Dealer,* and manager of a tea-room. But it was impossible for him to stabilize himself. He began to live recklessly, love indiscriminately, and drink violently. He traveled to Europe and Mexico, hounding himself wherever he went with a sense of guilt and (as though in compensation) a mania of persecution. His genius did not go unrecognized, but he fought the very friends who appreciated him most. He had periods of great fecundity when his felicity with words was dazzling, but these times were followed by periods of agonizing sterility, neurotic behavior, and self-destructiveness. Emotional instability was increased by economic insecurity and sexual irregularity. He became a chronic alcoholic, purposely blunting his sensibilities, driving himself to disintegration. The death-wish was fulfilled in his thirty-third year. Having temporarily escaped his problem in Mexico, he could not face returning to an America which meant a return to responsibility. He jumped from a north-bound steamer in the Gulf of Mexico, April 28, 1932. The body was never recovered.

Crane's first poem was printed when he was seventeen; his first book, *White Buildings* (1926) appeared almost ten years later. Its verbal ingenuity was at once apparent; even those who found the book bizarre were forced to acknowledge its startling imagery and power of phrase. Much of it was roundly rhetorical, but it was rhetoric of a new order. It was influenced by Rimbaud, Poe, Eliot, and Wallace Stevens—experimenters in tonal allusiveness and the color value of words—but Crane often transcended his ingenuities. The very first lines of the book were illumining:

> As silent as a mirror is believed
> Realities plunge in silence by . . .

This, wrote Waldo Frank, was "a superb expression of chaos, and of the poet's need to integrate this chaos within the active mirror of self." The realities "plunge by" accompanied by such flashes of vision as "The seal's wide spindrift gaze toward Paradise," "where the cedar leaf divides the sky," "in sapphire arenas of the hills" and (writing of the sea) "this great wink of eternity." Alternating between delineation and complete departure from representation, the verse approximates and sometimes attains an "absolute" poetry, a poetry which lives on its own music, a music in which meaning is often incidental.

One of the sources of this verbal "absolutism" was not realized until some years after Crane's death. Recently, however, there was recovered the manuscript of an uneducated, poverty-stricken, and completely unknown poet, Samuel Greenberg. Greenberg had died in 1916, at the age of twenty-three, destitute and tubercular on Wards Island, New York. Through a friend, Crane saw Greenberg's notebooks; he was immediately excited by the elastic phraseology, the strange and often unintelligible eruption of words. He was enthralled by the uncontrolled rush of effects, particularly fascinated by the sea and flower images; he copied out many of the verses. Crane's preoccupation with sea and flowers may well date from that time; fragments of Greenberg's lines are paralleled and reconstructed in several of Crane's poems, notably in "Emblems of Conduct" and "Voyages II."

Although Crane did not object to being called an "absolutist," he was quick to defend himself from the charge of obscurity. The often-quoted letter to Harriet Monroe goes to considerable length to justify his odd syntax, his grammatical audacities, his complex and elliptical symbols. Admitting that he preferred suggestion to statement, he pushed suggestibility to the limit of communication. He believed that there was a "logic of metaphor" which antedated "our so-called pure logic, and which is the genetic basis of all speech." He cited a phrase from "Voyages II" as an example of his method, a composite of direct forcefulness and indirect allusion.

When I speak of "adagios of islands," the reference is to the motion of the boat through islands clustered thickly, the rhythm of the motion, etc. And it seems a much more direct and creative statement than any more "logical" employment of words such as "coasting slowly through the islands," besides ushering in a whole world of music.

In his mid-twenties Crane was groping toward a unifying theme, but it eluded him; more than most poets, he needed unity as well as economic security. In 1926 he found both: a centralizing idea and a philanthropist, the art patron Otto H. Kahn, who made it possible for him to create his largest work. *The Bridge* (1930) is a set of disparate poems united by national figures, legends, early history, modern inventions—all interwoven to express the "Myth of America." It was, in more ways than one, an answer to *The Waste Land;* for Crane, fascinated by Eliot's technique, fought Eliot's philosophy. "After this perfection of death," Crane wrote, "nothing is possible but a motion of some kind." It is significant that Crane turned to Eliot's opposites; the visions, the very mottoes, of *The Bridge* are those of Blake, The Book of Job, Emily Dickinson, and Walt Whitman. Strangeness of color and surprise of contrasts are still dominating principles, but a discipline which Crane never achieved in actual life controls singularity; a finer rhetoric, severe and mystical, plays about the central object.

The central theme, as Crane wrote in a letter to Otto Kahn, is an "organic panorama, showing the continuous and living evidence of the past in the inmost vital substance of the present." Although Crane was defeated by the problem of form, and his long poem lacks final integration, some of the individual sections are among the most eloquent poems of the period. Of "Van Winkle" Crane wrote:

The protagonist has left the room with its harbor sounds, and is walking to the subway. The rhythm is quickened; it is a transition between sleep and the imminent tasks of the day. Space is filled with the music of a hand organ and fresh sunlight, and one has the impression of the whole continent—from Atlantic to Pacific—freshly arisen and moving. The walk to the subway arouses reminiscences of childhood, also the "childhood" of the continental conquest, viz., the Conquistadores, Priscilla, Capt. John Smith, etc. These parallelisms unite in the figure of Rip Van Winkle (indigenous "Muse of Memory"), who finally becomes identified with the protagonist, and who boards the subway with the reader. He becomes the "guardian angel" of the journey into the past.

Concerning "The River," which, "past the din and slogans of the year," will take its place among the richest and most kaleidoscopic of contemporary poems, Crane declared:

The subway is simply a figurative, psychological "vehicle" for transporting the reader to the Middle West. He lands on the railroad tracks in the company of several tramps in the twilight. The extravagance of the first twenty-three lines of this section is an intentional burlesque on the cultural confusion of the present—a great conglomeration of noises analogous to the strident impression of a fast express rushing by. The rhythm is jazz. Thenceforward the rhythm settles down to a steady pedestrian gait, like that of wanderers plodding along. My tramps are psychological vehicles, also. Their wanderings, as you will notice, carry the reader into interior after interior, all of it funneled by the Mississippi. They are the left-overs of the pioneers in at least this respect—that abstractly their wanderings carry the reader through certain experiences roughly parallel to that of the traders, adventurers, Boone and others. I think I have caught some of the essential spirit of the Great Valley here, and in the process have approached the primal world of the Indian, which emerges with a full orchestra in the succeeding "Dance."

The river of steel, which begins in jagged syncopation and develops into gravely measured quatrains, turns into the "Father of Waters." It carries the poet to the primal American myth, with Pocahontas as the traditional nature-symbol representing the body of the continent. As Crane put it, describing the section called "The Dance":

Here one is on the pure mythical and smoky soil at last! Not only do I describe the conflict between the two races in this dance—I also become identified with the Indian and his world before it is over, which is the only method possible of ever really possessing the Indian and his world as a cultural factor. . . . Pocahontas (the continent) is the common basis of our meeting, she survives the extinction of the Indian, who finally, after being assumed into the elements of nature (as he understood them) persists only as a kind of "eye" in the sky, or as a star that hangs between day and night—"the twilight's dim perpetual throne."

"The Tunnel" and "Cape Hatteras" come close to realizing Crane's dream of accustoming poetry to images from contemporary life, of "acclimatizing" the machine with its "nasal whine of power." Crane spoke of "The Tunnel" as "the encroachment of machinery on humanity; a kind of purgatory in relation to the open sky"; "Cape Hatteras" was to be "a kind of ode to Whitman." In short Crane was attempting to write "an epic of the modern consciousness." In this attempt he failed; he packed every page with excesses of sound and sense, knowing no line could ever contain all he wanted to crowd into it.

But if *The Bridge* fails as a panoramic unit, it succeeds magnificently in many of its parts. Even its failures are failures of excess, of eagerness, sensationalism, and hysteria, but not impoverishment. Often it accomplishes the paradox of being both suggestive and factual; one moment it is flashy to the point of absurdity, the next moment it is brilliantly exact. *The Collected Poems of Hart Crane,* with an informative if somewhat rapt preface by Waldo Frank, was published posthumously in 1933. It includes a set of hitherto unpublished poems which are more representational than most of his other work. Crane was particularly fond of the Key West poems; he stressed their "happy impersonality."

Critics are still divided in their estimates of Crane. There are many who believe he hypnotized himself with drink and verbal intoxication. There are those who consider *The Bridge* his greatest accomplishment. And there are those who believe the early short poems, such as "Voyages" and "Praise for an Urn" his best. Speaking of the latter, Allen Tate wrote in his memoir, "Although his later development gave us a poetry that the period would be much the less rich for not having, he never again had such perfect mastery of his subject. And I think this was because he never afterwards knew precisely what his subject was. . . . Crane was the archetype of the modern American poet whose fundamental mistake lay in thinking that an irrational surrender of the intellect to the will would be the basis of a new mentality." Personal restlessness developed into tragic rootlessness.

Philip Horton's *Hart Crane: The Life of an American Poet* (1937) is devoted not only to the facts but to the critical and esthetic theories which compelled Crane. It shows that Crane sought desperately to record the kaleidoscopic play of the mind through a succession of pictures forming and dissolving in a continual flow of metaphors.

REPOSE OF RIVERS

The willows carried a slow sound,
A sarabande the wind mowed on the mead.
I could never remember
That seething, steady leveling of the marshes
Till age had brought me to the sea.

Flags, weeds. And remembrance of steep alcoves
Where cypresses shared the noon's
Tyranny; they drew me into hades almost.
And mammoth turtles climbing sulphur dreams
Yielded, while sun-silt rippled them
Asunder . . .

How much I would have bartered! the black gorge
And all the singular nestings in the hills
Where beavers learn stitch and tooth.
The pond I entered once and quickly fled—
I remember now its singing willow rim.

And finally, in that memory all things nurse;
After the city that I finally passed
With scalding unguents spread and smoking darts
The monsoon cut across the delta
At gulf gates . . . There, beyond the dykes

I heard wind flaking sapphire, like this summer,
And willows could not hold more steady sound.

TO BROOKLYN BRIDGE

(*Prelude to "The Bridge"*)

How many dawns, chill from his rippling rest
The seagull's wings shall dip and pivot him,
Shedding white rings of tumult, building high
Over the chained bay waters Liberty—

Then, with inviolate curve, forsake our eyes
As apparitional as sails that cross
Some page of figures to be filed away;
—Till elevators drop us from our day . . .

I think of cinemas, panoramic sleights
With multitudes bent toward some flashing scene
Never disclosed, but hastened to again,
Foretold to other eyes on the same screen;

And Thee, across the harbor, silver-paced
As though the sun took step of thee, yet left
Some motion ever unspent in thy stride,—
Implicitly thy freedom staying thee!

Out of some subway scuttle, cell or loft
A bedlamite speeds to thy parapets,
Tilting there momently, shrill shirt ballooning,
A jest falls from the speechless caravan.

Down Wall, from girder into street noon leaks,
A rip-tooth of the sky's acetylene;
All afternoon the cloud-flown derricks turn . . .
Thy cables breathe the North Atlantic still.

And obscure as that heaven of the Jews,
Thy guerdon . . . Accolade thou dost bestow
Of anonymity time cannot raise:
Vibrant reprieve and pardon thou dost show.

O harp and altar, of the fury fused,
(How could mere toil align thy choiring strings!)
Terrific threshold of the prophet's pledge,
Prayer of pariah, and the lover's cry,—

Again the traffic lights that skim thy swift
Unfractioned idiom, immaculate sigh of stars,
Beading thy path—condense eternity:
And we have seen night lifted in thine arms.

Under thy shadow by the piers I waited;
Only in darkness is thy shadow clear.
The City's fiery parcels all undone,
Already snow submerges an iron year . . .

O Sleepless as the river under thee,
Vaulting the sea, the prairies' dreaming sod,
Unto us lowliest sometime sweep, descend
And of the curveship lend a myth to God.

VOYAGES: II

—And yet this great wink of eternity,
Of rimless floods, unfettered leewardings,

Samite sheeted and processioned where
Her undinal vast belly moonward bends,
Laughing the wrapt inflections of our love;

Take this Sea, whose diapason knells
On scrolls of silver snowy sentences,
The sceptered terror of whose sessions rends
As her demeanors motion well or ill,
All but the pieties of lovers' hands.

And onward, as bells off San Salvador
Salute the crocus lusters of the stars,
In these poinsettia meadows of her tides,—
Adagios of islands, O my Prodigal,
Complete the dark confessions her veins spell.

Mark how her turning shoulders wind the hours,
And hasten while her penniless rich palms
Pass superscription of bent foam and wave,—
Hasten, while they are true,—sleep, death, desire,
Close round one instant in one floating flower.

Bind us in time, O seasons clear, and awe.
O minstrel galleons of Carib fire,
Bequeath us to no earthly shore until
Is answered in the vortex of our grave
The seal's wide spindrift gaze toward paradise.

VOYAGES : VI

Where icy and bright dungeons lift
Of swimmers their lost morning eyes,
And ocean rivers, churning, shift
Green borders under stranger skies,

Steadily as a shell secretes
Its beating leagues of monotone,
Or as many waters trough the sun's
Red kelson past the cape's wet stone;

O rivers mingling toward the sky
And harbor of the phoenix' breast—
My eyes pressed black against the prow,
—Thy derelict and blinded guest

Waiting, afire, what name, unspoke,
I cannot claim: let thy waves rear
More savage than the death of kings,
Some splintered garland for the seer.

Beyond siroccos harvesting
The solstice thunders, crept away,

Like a cliff swinging or a sail
Flung into April's inmost day—

Creation's blithe and petaled word
To the lounged goddess when she rose
Conceding dialogue with eyes
That smile unsearchable repose—

Still fervid covenant, Belle Isle,
—Unfolded floating dais before
Which rainbows twine continual hair—
Belle Isle, white echo of the oar!

The imaged word, it is, that holds
Hushed willows anchored in its glow.
It is the unbetrayable reply
Whose accent no farewell can know.

PRAISE FOR AN URN

It was a kind and northern face
That mingled in such exile guise
The everlasting eyes of Pierrot
And, of Gargantua, the laughter.

His thoughts, delivered to me
From the white coverlet and pillow,
I see now, were inheritances—
Delicate riders of the storm.

The slant moon on the slanting hill
Once moved us toward presentiments
Of what the dead keep, living still,
And such assessments of the soul

As, perched in the crematory lobby,
The insistent clock commented on,
Touching as well upon our praise
Of glories proper to the time.

Still, having in mind gold hair,
I cannot see that broken brow
And miss the dry sound of bees
Stretching across a lucid space.

Scatter these well-meant idioms
Into the smoky spring that fills
The suburbs, where they will be lost.
They are no trophies of the sun.

VAN WINKLE

(*from "The Bridge"*)

Macadam, gun-gray as the tunny's belt,
Leaps from Far Rockaway to Golden Gate:
Listen! the miles a hurdy-gurdy grinds—
Down gold arpeggios mile on mile unwinds.

Times earlier, when you hurried off to school,
—It is the same hour though a later day—
You walked with Pizarro in a copybook,
And Cortes rode up, reining tautly in—
Firmly as coffee grips the taste,—and away!

There was Priscilla's cheek close in the wind,
And Captain Smith, all beard and certainty,

And Rip Van Winkle, bowing by the way,—
"Is this Sleepy Hollow, friend—?" And he—

And Rip forgot the office hours,
and he forgot the pay;
Van Winkle sweeps a tenement
down town on Avenue A,—

The grind-organ says . . . Remember, remember
The cinder pile at the end of the backyard
Where we stoned the family of young
Garter snakes under . . . And the monoplanes
We launched—with paper wings and twisted
Rubber bands. . . . Recall—
the rapid tongues
That flittered from under the ash heap day
After day whenever your stick discovered
Some sunning inch of unsuspecting fiber—
It flashed back at your thrust, as clean as fire.

And Rip was slowly made aware
that he, Van Winkle, was not here
Nor there. He woke and swore he'd seen Broadway
a Catskill daisy chain in May—

So memory, that strikes a rhyme out of a box,
Or splits a random smell of flowers through glass—
Is it the whip stripped from the lilac tree
One day in spring my father took to me,
Or is it the Sabbatical, unconscious smile
My mother almost brought me once from church
And once only, as I recall—?

It flickered through the snow screen, blindly
It forsook her at the doorway; it was gone
Before I had left the window. It
Did not return with the kiss in the hall.

Macadam, gun-gray as the tunny's belt,
Leaps from Far Rockaway to Golden Gate . . .
Keep hold of that nickel for car-change, Rip,—
Have you got your paper—?
And hurry along, Van Winkle—it's getting late!

THE RIVER

(from "The Bridge")

Stick your patent name on a signboard
brother—all over—going west—young man
Tintex—Japalac—Certain-teed Overalls ads
and lands sakes! under the new playbill ripped
in the guaranteed corner—see Bert Williams what?

Minstrels when you steal a chicken just
save me the wing, for if it isn't
Erie it ain't for miles around a
Mazda—and the telegraphic night coming on Thomas

a Ediford—and whistling down the tracks
a headlight rushing with the sound—can you
imagine—while an EXPRESS makes time like
SCIENCE—COMMERCE and the HOLYGHOST
RADIO ROARS IN EVERY HOME WE HAVE THE NORTHPOLE
WALLSTREET AND VIRGINBIRTH WITHOUT STONES OR
WIRES OR EVEN RUNning brooks connecting ears
and no more sermons windows flashing roar
Breathtaking—as you like it . . . eh?

So the 20th Century—so
whizzed the Limited—roared by and left
three men, still hungry on the tracks, ploddingly
watching the tail lights wizen and converge, slip-
ping gimleted and neatly out of sight.
The last bear, shot drinking in the Dakotas,
Loped under wires that span the mountain stream.
Keen instruments, strung to a vast precision
Bind town to town and dream to ticking dream.
But some men take their liquor slow—and count
—Though they'll confess no rosary nor clue—
The river's minute by the far brook's year.
Under a world of whistles, wires and steam
Caboose-like they go ruminating through
Ohio, Indiana—blind baggage—
To Cheyenne tagging . . . Maybe Kalamazoo.

Time's renderings, time's blendings they construe
As final reckonings of fire and snow;
Strange bird-wit, like the elemental gist
Of unwalled winds they offer, singing low
My Old Kentucky Home and *Casey Jones,*
Some Sunny Day. I heard a road-gang chanting so.
And afterwards, who had a colt's eyes—one said,
"Jesus! Oh I remember watermelon days!" And sped
High in a cloud of merriment, recalled
"—And when my Aunt Sally Simpson smiled," he drawled—
"It was almost Louisiana, long ago."

"There's no place like Booneville though, Buddy,"
One said, excising a last burr from his vest,
"—For early trouting." Then peering in the can,
"—But I kept on the tracks." Possessed, resigned,
He trod the fire down pensively and grinned,
Spreading dry shingles of a beard. . . .

Behind
My father's cannery works I used to see

Rail-squatters ranged in nomad raillery,
The ancient men—wifeless or runaway
Hobo-trekkers that forever search
An empire wilderness of freight and rails.
Each seemed a child, like me, on a loose perch,
Holding to childhood like some termless play.
John, Jake, or Charley, hopping the slow freight
—Memphis to Tallahassee—riding the rods,
Blind fists of nothing, humpty-dumpty clods.

Yet they touch something like a key perhaps.
From pole to pole across the hills, the states
—They know a body under the wide rain;
Youngsters with eyes like fjords, old reprobates
With racetrack jargon,—dotting immensity
They lurk across her, knowing her yonder breast
Snow-silvered, sumac-stained or smoky blue,
Is past the valley-sleepers, south or west.
—As I have trod the rumorous midnights, too.

And past the circuit of the lamp's thin flame
(O Nights that brought me to her body bare!)
Have dreamed beyond the print that bound her name,
Trains sounding the long blizzards out—I heard
Wail into distances I knew were hers.
Papooses crying on the wind's long mane
Screamed redskin dynasties that fled the brain,
—Dead echoes! But I knew her body there,
Time like a serpent down her shoulder, dark,
And space, an eaglet's wing, laid on her hair.

Under the Ozarks, domed by Iron Mountain,
The old gods of the rain lie wrapped in pools
Where eyeless fish curvet a sunken fountain
And re-descend with corn from querulous crows.
Such pilferings make up their timeless eatage,
Propitiate them for their timber torn
By iron, iron—always the iron dealt cleavage!
They doze now, below axe and powder horn.

And Pullman breakfasters glide glistening steel
From tunnel into field—iron strides the dew—
Straddles the hill, a dance of wheel on wheel.
You have a half-hour's wait at Siskiyou,
Or stay the night and take the next train through.
Southward, near Cairo passing, you can see
The Ohio merging,—borne down Tennessee;
And if it's summer and the sun's in dusk
Maybe the breeze will lift the River's musk
—As though the waters breathed that you might know
Memphis Johnny, Steamboat Bill, Missouri Joe.
Oh, lean from the window, if the train slows down,

As though you touched hands with some ancient clown,
—A little while gaze absently below
And hum *Deep River* with them while they go.

Yes, turn again and sniff once more—look see,
O Sheriff, Brakeman and Authority—
Hitch up your pants and crunch another quid,
For you, too, feed the River timelessly.
And few evade full measure of their fate;
Always they smile out eerily what they seem.
I could believe he joked at heaven's gate—
Dan Midland—jolted from the cold brake-beam.

Down, down—born pioneers in time's despite,
Grimed tributaries to an ancient flow—
They win no frontier by their wayward plight,
But drift in stillness, as from Jordan's brow.

You will not hear it as the sea; even stone
Is not more hushed by gravity . . . But slow,
As loth to take more tribute—sliding prone
Like one whose eyes were buried long ago

The River, spreading, flows—and spends your dream.
What are you, lost within this tideless spell?
You are your father's father, and the stream—
A liquid theme that floating niggers swell.

Damp tonnage and alluvial march of days—
Nights turbid, vascular with silted shale
And roots surrendered down of moraine clays:
The Mississippi drinks the farthest dale.

O quarrying passion, undertowed sunlight!
The basalt surface drags a jungle grace
Ochreous and lynx-barred in lengthening might;
Patience! and you shall reach the biding place!

Over De Soto's bones the freighted floors
Throb past the City storied of three thrones.
Down two more turns the Mississippi pours
(Anon tall ironsides up from salt lagoons)

And flows within itself, heaps itself free.
All fades but one thin skyline 'round . . . Ahead
No embrace opens but the stinging sea;
The River lifts itself from its long bed,

Poised wholly on its dream, a mustard glow,
Tortured with history, its one will—flow!
—The Passion spreads in wide tongues, choked and slow,
Meeting the Gulf, hosannas silently below.

THE DANCE

(from "The Bridge")

The swift red flesh, a winter king—
Who squired the glacier woman down the sky?
She ran the neighing canyons all the spring;
She spouted arms; she rose with maize—to die.

And in the autumn drouth, whose burnished hands
With mineral wariness found out the stone
Where prayers, forgotten, streamed the mesa sands?
He holds the twilight's dim, perpetual throne.

Mythical brows we saw retiring—loth,
Disturbed and destined, into denser green.
Greeting they sped us, on the arrow's oath:
Now lie incorrigibly what years between. . . .

There was a bed of leaves, and broken play;
There was a veil upon you, Pocahontas, bride—
O Princess whose brown lap was virgin May;
And bridal flanks and eyes hid tawny pride.

I left the village for dogwood. By the canoe
Tugging below the mill-race, I could see
Your hair's keen crescent running, and the blue
First moth of evening take wing stealthily.

What laughing chains the water wove and threw!
I learned to catch the trout's moon whisper; I
Drifted how many hours I never knew,
But, watching, saw that fleet young crescent die,—

And one star, swinging, take its place, alone,
Cupped in the larches of the mountain pass—
Until, immortally, it bled into the dawn.
I left my sleek boat nibbling margin grass. . . .

I took the portage climb, then chose
A further valley-shed; I could not stop.
Feet nozzled watery webs of upper flows;
One white veil gusted from the very top.

O Appalachian Spring! I gained the ledge;
Steep, inaccessible smile that eastward bends
And northward reaches in that violet wedge
Of Adirondacks!—wisped of azure wands,

Over how many bluffs, tarns, streams I sped!
—And knew myself within some boding shade:

Grey tepees tufting the blue knolls ahead,
Smoke swirling through the yellow chestnut glade. . . .

A distant cloud, a thunder-bud—it grew,
That blanket of the skies: the padded foot
Within,—I hear it; 'til its rhythm drew,
—Siphoned the black pool from the heart's hot root!

A cyclone threshes in the turbine crest,
Swooping in eagle feathers down your back;
Know, Maquokeeta, greeting; know death's best;
—Fall, Sachem, strictly as the tamarack!

A birch kneels. All her whistling fingers fly.
The oak grove circles in a crash of leaves;
The long moan of a dance is in the sky.
Dance, Maquokeeta: Pocahontas grieves. . . .

And every tendon scurries toward the twangs
Of lightning deltaed down your saber hair.
Now snaps the flint in every tooth; red fangs
And splay tongues thinly busy the blue air. . . .

Dance, Maquokeeta! snake that lives before,
That casts his pelt, and lives beyond! Sprout, horn!
Spark, tooth! Medicine-man, relent, restore—
Lie to us—dance us back the tribal morn!

Spears and assemblies: black drums thrusting on—
O yelling battlements,—I, too, was liege
To rainbows currying each pulsant bone:
Surpassed the circumstance, danced out the siege!

And buzzard-circleted, screamed from the stake;
I could not pick the arrows from my side.
Wrapped in that fire, I saw more escorts wake—
Flickering, sprint up the hill, groins like a tide.

I heard the hush of lava wrestling your arms,
And stag teeth foam about the raven throat;
Flame cataracts of heaven in seething swarms
Fed down your anklets to the sunset's moat.

Oh, like the lizard in the furious noon,
That drops his legs and colors in the sun,
—And laughs, pure serpent, Time itself, and moon
Of his own fate, I saw thy change begun!

And saw thee dive to kiss that destiny
Like one white meteor, sacrosanct and blent

At last with all that's consummate and free
There, where the first and last gods keep thy tent.

* * *

Thewed of the levin, thunder-shod and lean,
Lo, through what infinite seasons dost thou gaze—
Across what bivouacs of thine angered slain,
And see'st thy bride immortal in the maize!

Totem and fire-gall, slumbering pyramid—
Though other calendars now stack the sky,
Thy freedom is her largesse, Prince, and hid
On paths thou knewest best to claim her by.

High unto Labrador the sun strikes free
Her speechless dream of snow, and stirred again,
She is the torrent and the singing tree;
And she is virgin to the last of men. . . .

West, west and south! winds over Cumberland
And winds across the llano grass resume
Her hair's warm sibilance. Her breasts are fanned—
O stream by slope and vineyard—into bloom!

And when the caribou slant down for salt
Do arrows thirst and leap? Do antlers shine
Alert, star-triggered in the listening vault
Of dusk?—And are her perfect brows to thine?

We danced, O Brave, we danced beyond their farms,
In cobalt desert closures made our vows . . .
Now is the strong prayer folded in thine arms,
The serpent with the eagle in the boughs.

POWER: CAPE HATTERAS

(*from "The Bridge"*)

The nasal whine of power whips a new universe . . .
Where spouting pillars spoor the evening sky,
Under the looming stacks of the gigantic power house
Stars prick the eyes with sharp ammoniac proverbs,
New verities, new inklings in the velvet hummed
Of dynamos where hearing's leash is strummed . . .
Power's script,—wound, bobbin-bound, refined—
Is stropped to the slap of belts on booming spools, spurred
Into the bulging bouillon, harnessed jelly of the stars.
Towards what? The forked crash of split thunder parts
Our hearing momentwise; but fast in whirling armatures,
As bright as frogs' eyes, giggling in the girth
Of steely gizzards—axle-bound, confined
In coiled precision, bunched in mutual glee
The bearings glint—O murmurless and shined
In oilrinsed circles of blind ecstasy!

Stars scribble on our eyes the frosty sagas,
The gleaming cantos of unvanquished space. . . .
O sinewy silver biplane, nudging the wind's withers!
There, from Kill Devils Hill at Kitty Hawk
Two brothers in their twinship left the dune;
Warping the gale, the Wright windwrestles veered
Capeward, then blading the wind's flank, banked and spun
What ciphers risen from prophetic script,
What marathons new-set between the stars!
The soul, by naphtha fledged into new reaches
Already knows the closer clasp of Mars,—
New latitudes, unknotting, soon give place
To what fierce schedules, rife of doom apace!

Behold the dragon's covey—amphibian, ubiquitous
To hedge the seaboard, wrap the headland, ride
The blue's unfeathered districts unto aether. . . .
While Iliads glimmer through eyes raised in pride
Hell's belt springs wider—into heaven's plumed side.
O bright circumferences, heights employed to fly
War's fiery kennel masked in downy offings,—
This tournament of space, the threshed and chiseled height,
Is baited by marauding circles, bludgeon flail
Of rancorous grenades whose screaming petals carve us
The wounds we wrap with theorems sharp as hail!

Wheeled swiftly, wings emerge from larval-silver hangars.
Taut motors surge, space-gnawing, into flight;
Through sparkling visibility, outspread, unsleeping
Wings clip the last peripheries of light. . . .
Tellurian wind-sleuths on dawn patrol,
Each plane a hurtling javelin of winged ordnance,
Bristle the heights above a screeching gale to hover;
Surely no eye that Sunward Escadrille can cover!
There, meaningful, fledged as the Pleiades
With razor sheen they zoom each rapid helix!
Up-chartered choristers of their own speeding
They, cavalcade on escapade, shear Cumulus—
Lay siege and hurdle Cirrus down the skies!
While Cetus-like, O thou Dirigibile, enormous Lounger
Of pendulous auroral beaches,—satellited wide
By convoy planes, moonferrets that rejoin thee
On fleeing balconies as thou dost glide,
—Hast splintered space!

THE TUNNEL

(from "The Bridge")

To find the Western path
Right thro' the Gates of Wrath
—BLAKE.

Performances, assortments, résumés—
Up Times Square to Columbus Circle lights

Channel the congresses, nightly sessions,
Refractions of the thousand theaters, faces—
Mysterious kitchens . . . You shall search them all.
Some day by heart you'll learn each famous sight
And watch the curtain lift in hell's despite;
You'll find the garden in the third act dead,
Finger your knees—and wish yourself in bed
With tabloid crime-sheets perched in easy sight.

Then let you reach your hat
and go.
As usual, let you—also
walking down—exclaim
to twelve upward leaving
a subscription praise
for what time slays . . .

Or can't you quite make up your mind to ride;
A walk is better underneath the L for a brisk
Ten blocks or so before? But you find yourself
Preparing penguin flexions of the arms—
As usual you will meet the scuttle yawn:
The subway yawns the quickest promise home.

Be minimum then, to swim the hiving swarms
Out of the Square, the Circle burning bright—
Avoid the glass doors gyring at your right,
Where boxed alone a second, eyes take fright
—Quite unprepared rush naked back to light:
And down beside the turnstile press the coin
Into the slot. The gongs already rattle.

And so
of cities you bespeak
subways, rivered under streets
and rivers . . . In the car
the overtone of motion
underground, the monotone
of motion is the sound
of other faces, also underground—

"Let's have a pencil Jimmy—living now
at Floral Park
Flatbush—on the fourth of July—
like a pigeon's muddy dream—potatoes
to dig in the field—travlin' the town too—
night after night—the Culver line—the
girls all shaping up—it used to be—"

Our tongues recant like beaten weather vanes.
This answer lives like verdigris, like hair

Beyond extinction, surcease of the bone;
And repetition freezes—"What
what do you want? getting weak on the links?
fandaddle daddy don't ask for change—IS THIS
FOURTEENTH? it's half-past six she said—if
you don't like my gate why did you
swing on it, why *didja*
swing on it
anyhow—"

And somehow anyhow swing—

The phonographs of hades in the brain
Are tunnels that re-wind themselves, and love
A burnt match skating in a urinal—
Somewhere above Fourteenth TAKE THE EXPRESS
To brush some new presentiment of pain—

"But I want service in this office SERVICE
I said—after
the show she cried a little afterwards but—"

Whose head is swinging from the swollen strap?
Whose body smokes along the bitten rails,
Bursts from a smoldering bundle far behind
In back forks of the chasms of the brain—
Puffs from a riven stump far out behind
In interborough fissures of the mind . . . ?

And why do I often meet your visage here,
Your eyes like agate lanterns—on and on
Below the toothpaste and the dandruff ads?
—And did their riding eyes right through your side,
And did their eyes like unwashed platters ride?
And Death, aloft—gigantically down
Probing through you toward me, O Evermore!
And when they dragged your retching flesh,
Your trembling hands that night through Baltimore—
That last night on the ballot rounds, did you,
Shaking—did you deny the ticket, Poe?

For Gravesend Manor change at Chambers Street.
The platform hurries along to a dead stop.
The intent escalator lifts a serenade
Stilly
Of shoes, umbrellas, each eye attending its shoe, then
Bolting outright somewhere above where streets
Burst suddenly in rain . . . The gongs recur:
Elbows and levers, guard and hissing door.
Thunder is galvothermic here below . . . The car

Wheels off. The train rounds, bending to a scream,
Taking the final level for the dive
Under the river—

And somewhat emptier than before,
Demented, for a hitching second, humps; then
Lets go . . . Towards corners of the floor
Newspapers wing, revolve and wing.
Blank windows gargle signals through the roar.

And does the Daemon take you home, also,
Wop washerwoman, with the bandaged hair?
After the corridors are swept, the cuspidors—
The gaunt sky-barracks cleanly now, and bare,
O Genoese, do you bring mother-eyes and hands
Back home to children and to golden hair?

Daemon, demurring and eventful yawn!
Whose hideous laughter is the bellows mirth
—Or the muffled slaughter of a day in birth—
O cruelly to inoculate the brinking dawn
With antennae toward worlds that spark and sink—
To spoon us out more liquid than the dim
Locution of the eldest star, and pack
The conscience naveled in the plunging wind,
Umbilical to call—and straightway die!
O caught like pennies beneath soot and steam,
Kiss of our agony thou gatherest;
Condensed, thou takest all—shrill ganglia
Impassioned with some song we fail to keep.

And yet, like Lazarus, to feel the slope,
The sod and billow breaking—lifting ground,
—A sound of waters bending astride the sky
Unceasing with some word that will not die!

✣

A tugboat, wheezing wreaths of steam,
Lunged past, with one galvanic blare stove up the river.
I counted the echoes assembling, one after one,
Searching, thumbing the midnight on the piers.
Lights, coasting left the oily tympanum of waters;
The blackness somewhere gouged glass on a sky.

And this thy harbor, O my City, I have driven under,
Tossed from the coil of ticking towers . . . Tomorrow,
And to be . . . Here by the River that is East—
Here at the waters' edge the hands drop memory;
Shadowless in that abyss they unaccounting lie.
How far away the star has pooled the sea—
Or shall the hands be drawn away, to die?

Kiss of our agony Thou gatherest,
O Hand of Fire
gatherest—

ROYAL PALM

Green rustlings, more-than-regal charities
Drift coolly from the tower of whispered light.
Amid the noontide's blazed asperities
I watched the sun's most gracious anchorite

Climb up as by communings, year on year
Uneaten of the earth or aught earth holds,
And the gray trunk, that's elephantine, rear
Its frondings sighing in aetherial folds.

Forever fruitless, and beyond that yield
Of sweat the jungle presses with hot love
And tendril till our deathward breath is sealed—
It grazes the horizons, launched above

Mortality—ascending emerald-bright,
A fountain at salute, a crown in view—
Unshackled, casual of its azured height,
As though it soared suchwise through heaven too.

THE AIR PLANT

(*Grand Cayman, W. I.*)

This tuft that thrives on saline nothingness,
Inverted octopus with heavenward arms
Thrust parching from a palm-bole hard by the cove—
A bird almost—of almost bird alarms,

Is pulmonary to the wind that jars
Its tentacles, horrific in their lurch.
The lizard's throat, held bloated for a fly,
Balloons but warily from this throbbing perch.

The needles and hacksaws of cactus bleed
A milk of earth when stricken off the stalk;
But this—defenseless, thornless, sheds no blood,
Scarce shadow even—but the air's thin talk.

Angelic Dynamo! Ventriloquist of the Blue!
While beachward creeps the shark-swept Spanish Main.
By what conjunctions do the winds appoint
Its apotheosis, at last—the hurricane!

THE HURRICANE

Lo, Lord, Thou ridest!
Lord, Lord, Thy swifting heart

Naught stayeth, naught now bideth
But's smithereened apart!

Ay! Scripture flee'th stone!
Milk-bright, Thy chisel wind

Rescindeth flesh from bone
To quivering whittlings thinned—

Swept—whistling straw! Battered,
Lord, e'en boulders now out-leap

Rock sockets, levin-lathered!
Nor, Lord, may worm out-deep

Thy drum's gambade, its plunge abscond!
Lord God, while summits crashing

Whip sea-kelp screaming on blond
Sky-seethe, high heaven dashing—

Thou ridest to the door, Lord!
Thou bidest wall nor floor, Lord!

AT MELVILLE'S TOMB

Often beneath the wave, wide from this ledge
The dice of drowned men's bones he saw bequeath
An embassy. Their numbers as he watched,
Beat on the dusty shore and were obscured.

And wrecks passed without sound of bells,
The calyx of death's bounty giving back
A scattered chapter, livid hieroglyph,
The portent wound in corridors of shells.

Then in the circuit calm of one vast coil,
Its lashings charmed and malice reconciled,
Frosted eyes there were that lifted altars;
And silent answers crept across the stars.

Compass, quadrant and sextant contrive
No farther tides . . . High in the azure steeps
Monody shall not wake the mariner.
This fabulous shadow only the sea keeps.

THE BROKEN TOWER

The bell-rope that gathers God at dawn
Dispatches me as though I dropped down the knell
Of a spent day—to wander the cathedral lawn
From pit to crucifix, feet chill on steps from hell.

Have you not heard, have you not seen that corps
Of shadows in the tower, whose shoulders sway
Antiphonal carillons launched before
The stars are caught and hived in the sun's ray?

The bells, I say, the bells break down their tower;
And swing I know not where. Their tongues engrave
Membrane through marrow, my long-scattered score
Of broken intervals. . . . And I, their sexton slave!

Oval encyclicals in canyons heaping
The impasse high with choir. Banked voices slain!
Pagodas, campaniles with reveilles outleaping—
O terraced echoes prostrate on the plain! . . .

And so it was I entered the broken world
To trace the visionary company of love, its voice
An instant in the wind (I know not whither hurled)
But not for long to hold each desperate choice.

My word I poured. But was it cognate, scored
Of that tribunal monarch of the air
Whose thigh embronzes earth, strikes crystal Word
In wounds pledged once to hope—cleft to despair?

The steep encroachments of my blood left me
No answer (could blood hold such a lofty tower
As flings the question true?)—or is it she
Whose sweet mortality stirs latent power?—

And through whose pulse I hear, counting the strokes
My veins recall and add, revived and sure
The angelus of wars my chest evokes:
What I hold healed, original now, and pure . . .

And builds, within, a tower that is not stone
(Not stone can jacket heaven)—but slip
Of pebbles—visible wings of silence sown
In azure circles, widening as they dip

The matrix of the heart, lift down the eye
That shrines the quiet lake and swells a tower . . .
The commodious, tall decorum of that sky
Unseals her earth, and lifts love in its shower.

Allen Tate

Allen Tate (whose full name, not often admitted, is John Orley Allen Tate) was born November 19, 1899, in Winchester, Clark County, Kentucky, and was educated at Vanderbilt University, where he was one of the founders of *The Fugitive* (1922-1925). Later he became editor of *The Sewanee Review,* a literary magazine that transcended its origins. An avowed believer in sectionalism, Tate's critical acumen ran parallel to his predilections in *Stonewall Jackson: The Good Soldier* (1928) and *Jefferson Davis: His Rise and Fall* (1929). Before he was sixty Tate was the author of sixteen volumes of poetry, criticism, biography, and fiction.

At the outset, with *Mr. Pope and Other Poems* (1928), Tate revealed a mind in which "a fierce latinity" mixed with a Gothic strength attains a strange efflorescence. Tate said that his method consists in playing the role of a hawk, "gradually circling around the subject, threatening it, filling it with suspense, and finally accomplishing its demise without ever quite using the ultimate violence upon it." Sometimes, however, in his circumlocutory or circumambient manner, the poet is likely to leave the climax unresolved, and the reader is uncertain whether, in spite of Tate's hawk-like swoop, the capture is always accomplished. Discarding the metaphor, the poem sometimes suffers from a critical introspection at war with the lyric impulse.

Tate's later work established him as one of the country's most distinguished poets and critics. *Reactionary Essays on Poetry and Ideas* (1936), *Reason in Madness* (1941), *On the Limits of Poetry* (1948) and particularly *The Forlorn Demon* (1953) are the work of a highly acute and probing sensibility. The particular estimates (as in the tribute to Hart Crane, the delicate analysis of Emily Dickinson, and the balanced appraisal of Ezra Pound) are generous as well as just.

Collected Essays (1959) and a selected *Poems* (1960) are cumulative proofs of Tate's power as creator and critic. Energetic in its technique as well as its teaching—much of Tate's life was spent as a teacher in various universities—the writing is both violent and disciplined, dramatic and moral, a belief "in the innate evil of human nature" (as he wrote in *The Fathers*) "and the need to face that evil." There is unquestionable authority in such single poems as "The Mediterranean," "Mother and Son," "The Cross," "The Swimmers," and "Ode to the Confederate Dead," one of the most remarkable poems of the period.

The Bollingen Prize for poetry was awarded to Tate in 1956.

ODE TO THE CONFEDERATE DEAD

Row after row with strict impunity
The headstones yield their names to the element,
The wind whirrs without recollection;
In the riven troughs the splayed leaves
Pile up, of nature the casual sacrament
To the seasonal eternity of death,
Then driven by the fierce scrutiny
Of heaven to their election in the vast breath,

They sough the rumor of mortality.
Autumn is desolation in the plot
Of a thousand acres, where these memories grow
From the inexhaustible bodies that are not
Dead, but feed the grass row after rich row.
Think of the autumns that have come and gone—
Ambitious November with the humors of the year,
With a particular zeal for every slab,
Staining the uncomfortable angels that rot
On the slabs, a wing chipped here, an arm there:
The brute curiosity of an angel's stare
Turns you like them to stone,
Transforms the heaving air,
Till plunged to a heavier world below
You shift your sea-space blindly,
Heaving, turning like the blind crab.

Dazed by the wind, only the wind
The leaves flying, plunge

You know who have waited by the wall
The twilight certainty of an animal;
Those midnight restitutions of the blood
You know—the immitigable pines, the smoky frieze
Of the sky, the sudden call; you know the rage—
The cold pool left by the mounting flood—
Of muted Zeno and Parmenides.
You who have waited for the angry resolution
Of those desires that should be yours tomorrow,
You know the unimportant shrift of death
And praise the vision
And praise the arrogant circumstance
Of those who fall
Rank upon rank, hurried beyond decision—
Here by the sagging gate, stopped by the wall.

Seeing, seeing only the leaves
Flying, plunge and expire

Turn your eyes to the immoderate past
Turn to the inscrutable infantry rising
Demons out of the earth—they will not last.
Stonewall, Stonewall—and the sunken fields of hemp,
Shiloh, Antietam, Malvern Hill, Bull Run.
Lost in that orient of the thick-and-fast
You will curse the setting sun.

Cursing only the leaves crying
Like an old man in a storm

You hear the shout—the crazy hemlocks point
With troubled fingers to the silence which
Smothers you, a mummy, in time. The hound bitch

Toothless and dying, in a musty cellar
Hears the wind only.
                                Now that the salt of their blood
Stiffens the saltier oblivion of the sea,
Seals the malignant purity of the flood,
What shall we, who count our days and bow
Our heads with a commemorial woe,
In the ribboned coats of grim felicity,
What shall we say of the bones, unclean,
Their verdurous anonymity will grow?
The ragged arms, the ragged heads and eyes
Lost in these acres of the insane green?
The gray lean spiders come; they come and go;
In a tangle of willows without light
The singular screech-owl's bright
Invisible lyric seeds the mind
With the furious murmur of their chivalry.

   We shall say only, the leaves
   Flying, plunge and expire

We shall say only, the leaves whispering
In the improbable mist of nightfall
That flies on multiple wing:
Night is the beginning and the end,
And in between the ends of distraction
Waits mute speculation, the patient curse
That stones the eyes, or like the jaguar leaps
For his own image in a jungle pool, his victim.

What shall we say who have knowledge
Carried to the heart? Shall we take the act
To the grave? Shall we, more hopeful, set up the grave
In the house? The ravenous grave?
                                                    Leave now
The turnstile and the decomposing wall:
The gentle serpent, green in the mulberry bush,
Riots with his tongue through the hush—
Sentinel of the grave who counts us all!

MOTHER AND SON

Now all day long the man who is not dead
Hastens the dark with inattentive eyes,
The lady of the white hand, of the erect head
Stares at the cover, leans for the son's replies
At last to her importunate womanhood—
That hand of death laid on the living bed;
Such is the fierce compositor of blood.

She waits; he lies upon the bed of sin
Where greed, avarice, anger writhed and slept
Till to their silence they were gathered in;

There, fallen with time, his tall and wicked kin
Once fired the passions that were never kept
In the permanent heart, and there his mother lay
To bear him on the impenetrable day.

Because of this she cannot will her hand
Up to the bed nor break the manacle
Her exile sets upon her harsh command
That he should say the time is beautiful,
Transfigured with her own devouring light:
The sick man craves the impalpable night.

Loosed betwixt eye and lid, the swimming beams
Of memory, that school of cuttlefish
Rise to the air, plunge to the cold streams,
Rising and plunging the half-forgotten wish
To tear his heart out in some slow disgrace
And freeze the hue of terror to her face.

Hate, misery and fear beat off his heart
To the dry fury of the woman's mind;
The son prone in his autumn, moves apart
A seed blown upon a returning wind:
O child, be vigilant till towards the South
On the flowered wall all the sweet afternoon
That reach of sun, swift as the cottonmouth
Strikes at the black crucifix on her breast
Where the cold dusk comes suddenly to rest—
Mortality will speak the victor soon!

The dreary flies lazy and casual
Stick to the ceiling, buzz along the wall—
O heart, the spider shuffles from the mold
Weaving between the pinks and grapes his pall.
The bright wallpaper imperishably old
Uncurls and flutters; it will never fall.

THE CROSS

There is a place that some men know,
I cannot see the whole of it,
Nor how men come there. Long ago
Flame burst out of a secret pit
Crushing the world with such a light
The day sky fell to moonless black,
The kingly sun to hateful night
For those, once seeing, turning back:
For love so hates mortality,
Which is the providence of life,
She will not let it blessèd be
But curses it with mortal strife.
Until beside the blinding rood
Within that world-destroying pit
—Like young wolves that have tasted blood
Of death, men taste no more of it:
So blind in so severe a place
(All life before in the black grave)
The last alternatives they face
Of life, without the life to save,
Being from all salvation weaned—
A stag charged both at heel and head:
Who would come back is turned a fiend
Instructed by the fiery dead.

THE MEDITERRANEAN

Quem das finem, rex magne, dolorum?

Where we went in the boat was a long bay
A sling-shot wide walled in by towering stone—
Peaked margin of antiquity's delay,
And we went there out of time's monotone:

Where we went in the black hull no light moved
But a gull white-winged along the feckless wave;
The breeze unseen but fierce as a body loved,
That boat drove onward like a willing slave.

Where we went in the small ship the seaweed
Parted and gave to us the murmuring shore
And we made feast and in our secret need
Devoured the very plates Aeneas bore:

Where derelict you see through the low twilight
The green coast that you thunder-tossed would win,
Drop sail, and hastening to drink all night
Eat dish and bowl—to take that sweet land in!

Where we feasted and caroused on the sandless
Pebbles, affecting our day of piracy,
What prophecy of eaten plates could landless
Wanderers fulfill by the ancient sea?

We for that time might taste the famous age
Eternal here yet hidden from our eyes
When lust of power undid its stuffless rage;
They, in a wineskin, bore earth's paradise.

—Let us lie down once more by the breathing side
Of ocean, where our live forefathers sleep
As if the Known Sea still were a month wide—
Atlantis howls but is no longer steep!

What country shall we conquer, what fair land
Unman our conquest and locate our blood?
We've cracked the hemispheres with careless hand!
Now, from the Gates of Hercules we flood

Westward, westward till the barbarous brine
Whelms us to the tired world where tasseling corn,
Fat beans, grapes sweeter than muscadine
Rot on the vine: in that land were we born.

THE SWIMMERS

SCENE: *Montgomery County,*
Kentucky, July 1911

Kentucky water, clear springs: a boy fleeing
To water under the dry Kentucky sun,
His four little friends in tandem with him, seeing

Long shadows of grapevine wriggle and run
Over the green swirl; mullein under the ear
Soft as Nausicaä's palm; sullen fun

Savage as childhood's thin harmonious tear:
O fountain, bosom source undying-dead
Replenish me the spring of love and fear

And give me back the eye that looked and fled
When a thrush idling in the tulip tree
Unwound the cold dream of the copperhead.

—Along the creek the road was winding; we
Felt the quicksilver sky. I see again
The shrill companions of that odyssey:

Bill Eaton, Charlie Watson, "Nigger" Layne
The doctor's son, Harry Duèsler who played
The flute; and Tate, with water on the brain.

Dog-days: the dusty leaves where rain delayed
Hung low on poison-oak and scuppernong,
And we were following the active shade

Of water, that bells and bickers all night long.
"No more'n a mile," Layne said. All five stood still.
Listening, I heard what seemed at first a song;

Peering, I heard the hooves come down the hill.
The posse passed, twelve horse; the leader's face
Was worn as limestone on an ancient sill.

Then, as sleepwalkers shift from a hard place
In bed, and rising to keep a formal pledge
Descend a ladder into empty space,

We scuttled down the bank below a ledge
And marched stiff-legged in our common fright
Along a hog-track by the riffle's edge:

Into a world where sound shaded the sight
Dropped the dull hooves again; the horsemen came
Again, all but the leader. It was night

Momently and I feared: eleven same
Jesus-Christers unmembered and unmade,
Whose Corpse had died again in dirty shame.

The bank then levelling in a speckled glade,
We stopped to breathe above the swimming-hole;
I gazed at its reticulated shade

Recoiling in blue fear, and felt it roll
Over my ears and eyes and lift my hair
Like seaweed tossing on a sunk atoll.

I rose again. Borne on the copper air
A distant voice green as a funeral wreath
Against a grave: "That dead nigger there."

The melancholy sheriff slouched beneath
A giant sycamore; shaking his head
He plucked a sassafras twig and picked his teeth:

"We come too late." He spoke to the tired dead
Whose ragged shirt soaked up the viscous flow
Of blood in which It lay discomfited.

A butting horse-fly gave one ear a blow
And glanced off, as the sheriff kicked the rope
Loose from the neck and hooked it with his toe

Away from the blood.—I looked back down the slope:
The friends were gone that I had hoped to greet.—
A single horseman came at a slow lope

And pulled up at the hanged man's horny feet;
The sheriff noosed the feet, the other end
The stranger tied to his pommel in a neat

Slip-knot. I saw the Negro's body bend
And straighten, as a fish-line cast transverse
Yields to the current that it must subtend.

The sheriff's Goddamn was a murmured curse
Not for the dead but for the blinding dust
That boxed the cortège in a cloudy hearse

And dragged it towards our town. I knew I must
Not stay till twilight in that silent road;
Sliding my bare feet into the warm crust,

I hopped the stonecrop like a panting toad
Mouth open, following the heaving cloud
That floated to the court-house square its load

Of limber corpse that took the sun for shroud.
There were three figures in the dying sun
Whose light were company where three was crowd.

My breath crackled the dead air like a shotgun
As, sheriff and the stranger disappearing,
The faceless head lay still. I could not run

Or walk, but stood. Alone in the public clearing
This private thing was owned by all the town,
Though never claimed by us within my hearing.

Léonie Adams

Léonie Adams was born in Brooklyn, New York, December 9, 1899, became a member of the class of 1922 at Barnard College, supported herself in New York, was awarded a "traveling fellowship" by the Guggenheim Foundation, and went abroad for two years in 1928. After her return she taught at various eastern universities. In 1948-49 she was Consultant in American Poetry at the Library of Congress; in 1954 she was, with Louise Bogan, co-winner of the

Bollingen Prize for her *Poems: A Selection;* in 1959 she received an award of $5,000 from the Academy of American Poets.

Many of the poems in her first volume, *Those Not Elect* (1925), were written while she was still an undergraduate. They are of two sorts: the simpler verses, direct and ecstatic, and the somewhat later, more metaphysical expressions of a rare and not lightly communicated wonder. Without imitating the Elizabethans, Miss Adams caught something of the quality of Webster and Vaughan. But whatever her style, whether she is direct as in "Home-Coming" or more difficult as in "The Horn," her sensitivity makes even the obscure passages a succession of inevitable images. Few poets have fixed the changing aspects of earth and sky, the fluid seasons, the constant variability of light with such certainty. Her most candid descriptions take on an unearthly and intensified air; even her statement of a landscape, or the performance of a tragedy, or "the pointed grass" drinking the light "till light brimmed even," or the old cheating of the sun is translated in lines both pure and suggestive.

Léonie Adams' second volume, *High Falcon* (1929) is abstract poetry in the purest sense; the word is more than a word; the letter is uplifted by pure spirit. The lyrical line, carried on wave after wave of music, transcends personality. The ecstasy, however, is no less ecstatic for being disembodied; every phrase carries its import of intensities, of vistas larger than the scene, of meaning beyond meaning. It is a rarefied atmosphere which Miss Adams breathes, and only a height-loving reader can venture with her into that fine air. "Twilit Revelation," "Bell Tower," "Sundown," "Country Summer" are a few of the poems in which the heart "extracts the spirit of the temporal." Neither sense nor the senses can wholly interpret this poetry, but every figure and accent compel us with authority. What, at first glance, seems obscurely metaphysical is resolved into a spiritual clarity that approaches clairvoyance.

"The Mount" synthesizes Miss Adams' qualities. One of her finest poems, it creates a new symbol of time; the sense of continuity is expressed through an image which is a little remote but quickly recognizable, holding a nice balance between the strange and the familiar.

Her utterance is unique, but it is no posture of "difference," no straining singularity. On the contrary, this is verse of the most reticent dignity, in which nothing, not even the mystical note, is overstressed. Herein lies Miss Adams' danger—or rather the danger to her imitators, for, since she is obviously "a poet's poet," she has been and will continue to be imitated. The surface pattern is easy enough to master: the withdrawn loveliness, the muted music, the faint Elizabethanism; but, lacking her rapt and actually reverent touch, the result would be only an echo of delicate diction. Miss Adams would undoubtedly gain a wider audience were she to mix a little more flesh with her spirit, but she would lose that virginal radiance which rises from springs more profound than those of the too nimbly gushing heart.

APRIL MORTALITY

Rebellion shook an ancient dust,
   And bones bleached dry of rottenness
Said: Heart, be bitter still, nor trust
   The earth, the sky, in their bright dress.

Heart, heart, dost thou not break to know
 This anguish thou wilt bear alone?
We sang of it an age ago,
 And traced it dimly upon stone.

With all the drifting race of men
 Thou also art begot to mourn
That she is crucified again,
 The lonely Beauty yet unborn.

And if thou dreamest to have won
 Some touch of her in permanence,
'Tis the old cheating of the sun,
 The intricate lovely play of sense.

Be bitter still, remember how
 Four petals, when a little breath
Of wind made stir the pear-tree bough,
 Blew delicately down to death.

HOME-COMING

When I stepped homeward to my hill
 Dusk went before with quiet tread;
The bare laced branches of the trees
 Were as a mist about its head.

Upon its leaf-brown breast, the rocks
 Like great gray sheep lay silent-wise;
Between the birch trees' gleaming arms
 The faint stars trembled in the skies.

The white brook met me half-way up
 And laughed as one that knew me well,
To whose more clear than crystal voice
 The frost had joined a crystal spell.

The skies lay like pale-watered deep.
 Dusk ran before me to its strand
And cloudily leaned forth to touch
 The moon's slow wonder with her hand.

THOUGHT'S END

I watched the hills drink the last color of light,
All shapes grow bright and wane on the pale air.
Till down the traitorous east there came the night,
And swept the circle of my seeing bare.
Its intimate beauty like a wanton's veil
Tore from the void as from an empty face.
I felt at being's rim all being fail,
And my one body pitted against space.

O heart more frightened than a wild bird's wings,
Beating at green, now is no fiery mark
Left on the quiet nothingness of things.
Be self no more against the flooding dark:
There thousandwise sown in that cloudy blot
Stars that are worlds look out and see you not.

DEATH AND THE LADY

Their bargain told again

Death to the Lady said
While she to dancing-measures still
Would move, while beauties on her lay,
Simply as dews the buds do fill,
Death said: "Stay!
Tell me, Lady,
If in your breast the lively breath
May flicker for a little space,
What ransom will you give to death,
Lady?" he said.
"O not one joy, O not one grace,
And what is your will to my will?
I can outwit parched fancies still."
To Death said the Lady.

Death to that Lady said,
When blood went numb and wearily,
"In innocency dear breath you drew,
And marrow and bloom you rendered me,"
She said: "True."
"How now, Lady?"
"My heart sucked up its sweet at will,
Whose scent when substance' sweet is past,
Is lovely still, is lovely still,
Death," she said.
"For bones' reprieve the dreams go last:
Soon, soon your flowery show did part,
But preciously I cull the heart,"
Death said to the Lady.

Death to that Lady said:
"Is then not all our bargain done?
Or why do you beckon me so fast
To chaffer for a skeleton
Flesh must cast,
Ghostly Lady?"
"For, Death, that I would have you drain
From my dead heart the blood that stands
So chilly in the withered vein.
And, Death," she said,

"Give me due bones into your hands."
"Beauties I claim at morning-prime,
But the lack-luster in good time,"
Death said to the Lady.

TWILIT REVELATION

This hour was set the time for heaven's descent
Come drooping toward us on the heavy air,
The sky, that's heaven's seat above us bent,
Blue faint as violet-ash, you near me there
In nether space so drenched in goblin blue,
I could touch Hesperus as soon as you.

Now I perceive you lapt in singling light,
Washed by that blue which sucks whole planets in,
And hung like those top jewels of the night,
A mournful gold too high for love to win.
And you, poor brief, poor melting star, you seem
Half sunk, and half to brighten in that stream.

And these rich-bodied hours of our delight
Show like a moth-wing's substance when the fall
Of confine-loosing, blue unending night
Extracts the spirit of this temporal.
So space can pierce the crevice wide between
Fast hearts, skies deep-descended intervene.

GHOSTLY TREE

O beech, unbind your yellow leaf, for deep
The honeyed time lies sleeping, and lead shade
Seals up the eyelids of its golden sleep.
Long are your flutes, chimes, little bells at rest,
And here is only the cold scream of the fox,
Only the hunter following on the hound,
And your quaint-plumagèd,
The bird that your green happy boughs lapped round,
Bends south its soft bright breast.

Before the winter and the terror break,
Scatter the leaf that broadened with the rose,
Not for a tempest, but a sigh to take.
Four nights to exorcise the thing that stood,
Bound by these frail which dangle at your branch,
They ran a frosty dagger to its heart,
And it, wan substance,
No more remembered it might cry, or start,
Or stain a point with blood.

THE HORN

In coming to the feast I found
A venerable silver-throated horn,
Which were I brave enough to sound,
Then all as from that moment born
Would breathe the honey of this clime,
And three times merry in their time,
Would praise the virtue of that horn.

The mist is risen like thin breath,
The young leaves of the ground smell chill,
So faintly as they strewn on death,
The road I came down a west hill.
But none can name as I can name
A little golden-bright thing flame,
Since bones have caught their marrow chill.

And in a thicket passed me by,
In the black brush a running hare,
Having a specter in his eye,
That sped in darkness to the snare;
And who but I can know in pride,
The heart set beating in the side
Has but the wisdom of a hare?

THE RIVER IN THE MEADOWS

Crystal parting the meads,
A boat drifted up it like a swan,
Tranquil, lovely, its bright front to the
  waters,
A slow swan is gone.

Full waters, O flowing silver,
Pure, level with the clover,
It will stain drowning a star,
With the moon it will brim over.

Running through lands dewy and shorn,
Cattle stoop at its brink,
And every fawny-colored throat
Will sway its bells and drink.

I saw a boat sailing the river
With a tranced gait; it seemed
Loosed by a spell from its moorings,
Or a thing the helmsman dreamed.

They said it would carry no traveler,
But the vessel would go down,
If a heart were heavy-winged,
Or the bosom it dwelt in, stone.

COUNTRY SUMMER

Now the rich cherry whose sleek wood
And top with silver petals traced,
Like a strict box its gems encased,
Has split from out that cunning lid,
All in an innocent green round,
Those melting rubies which it hid;
With moss ripe-strawberry-encrusted,
So birds get half, and minds lapse merry
To taste that deep-red lark's-bite berry,
And blackcap-bloom is yellow-dusted.

The wren that thieved it in the eaves
A trailer of the rose could catch
To her poor droopy sloven thatch,
And side by side with the wren's brood,—
O lovely time of beggars' luck—
Opens the quaint and hairy bud.
And full and golden is the yield
Of cows that never have to house.
But all night nibble under boughs,
Or cool their sides in the moist field.

Into the rooms flow meadow airs,
The warm farm-baking smell blows round
Inside and out and sky and ground
Are much the same; the wishing star,
Hesperus, kind and early-born,
Is risen only finger-far.
All stars stand close in summer air,
And tremble, and look mild as amber;
When wicks are lighted in the chamber
You might say stars were settling there.

Now straightening from the flowery hay,
Down the still light the mowers look;
Or turn, because their dreaming shook,
And they waked half to other days,
When left alone in yellow-stubble,
The rusty-coated mare would graze.
Yet thick the lazy dreams are born;
Another thought can come to mind,
But like the shivering of the wind,
Morning and evening in the corn.

THE MOUNT

"No, I have tempered haste,"
The joyous traveler said,
"The steed has passed me now
Whose hurrying hooves I fled.
My specter rides thereon,
I learned what mount he has,
Upon what summers fed;
And wept to know again,
Beneath the saddle swung,
Treasure for whose great theft
This breast was wrung.
His bridle bells sang out,
I could not tell their chime,
So brilliantly he rings,
But called his name as Time.
His bin was morning light,
Those straws which gild his bed
Are of the fallen West.
Although green lands consume
Beneath their burning tread,
In everlasting bright
His hooves have rest."

THIS MEASURE

This measure was a measure to my mind,
Still musical through the unlikely hush.
The cold goes wide as doors, and in will come
Those notes of May set ringing through the brush,
Where every voice by natural law is dumb.

How many seasons I have watched the boughs,
That first are happy-tongued and happy leaved,
Then bleed, as though an autumn were the last,
While that great life was with them undeceived,
Which all a wintering world seals home more fast.

Now visibly indeed I am assailed,
Yet I seem come clap on my very thing;
And now I learn I only asked as much:
It was in blooming weeks I lacked a spring
Rooted and blowing beyond sense or touch.

BELL TOWER

I have seen, O desolate one, the voice has its tower,
The voice also, builded at secret cost,
Its temple of precious tissue; not silent then,
Forever. Casting silence in your hour.
There marble boys are leant from the light throat,
Thick locks that hang with dew, and eyes dew-lashed,
Dazzled with morning,—angels of the wind,
With ear a-point for the enchanted note.

And these at length shall tip the hanging bell,
And first the sound must gather in deep bronze,
Till, rarer than ice, purer than a bubble of gold,
It fill the sky to beat on an airy shell.

KINGDOM OF HEAVEN

Bleak the February light
On the dark threshold spread,
The frost stood thick against the lock,
The clock for the great cold stopped dead,
When old wits idle with their luck
Lay singing in the bed,

That heard, while white frost span by night,
A pigeon happy with its bread.

And sang: I wakened to a sound
Which the streams make at thaw,
And pity on the shape I found
Inside a looking-glass with light.
For looking on my heart I saw,
A time before the break of day,
And looking won to second-sight,
And cast my character away.
The fields lie bound beneath the sky,
The hedge-top and the furrow freeze,
And still old plow-wheels sigh,
As sweet as bones which stretch from sleep,
And sooner than their sound is by,
Will come a noise of yellow bees
When the hay is nodding deep,
And some wise throat that laughs for ease.

Till there was a soft voice which spoke:
Hush, for every sound you tell
Is out of an old horn I blew.
I have come down to see who woke
On earth's cold brink when night was
through.
No wilder chance befell,
Then the starry breath I drew.
I am Gabriel.

SUNDOWN

This is the time lean woods shall spend
A steeped-up twilight, and the pale evening drink,
And the perilous roe, the leaper to the west brink,
Trembling and bright, to the caverned cloud descend.

Now shall you see pent oak gone gusty and frantic,
Stooped with dry weeping, ruinously unloosing
The sparse disheveled leaf, or reared and tossing
A dreary scarecrow bough in funeral antic.

Aye, tatter you and rend,
Oak heart, to your profession mourning, not obscure
The outcome, not crepuscular, on the deep floor,
Sable and gold match lusters and contend.

And rags of shrouding will not muffle the slain.
This is the immortal extinction, the priceless wound
Not to be staunched; the live gold leaks beyond,
And matter's sanctified, dipped in a gold stain.

NIGHT-PIECE

The moon above the milky field
Gleaning moves her one slant light,
The wind weeps from the cloud:
Then, weeping wind, unshroud
Pale Cassiopeia, blow
The true-swung pole-lamp bright.
To this room a midnight's come
Which speaks but with the beating clock,
While on glistening paws the mouse
Creeps night-master of the house.
Rust shall eat away the lock,
The door sag from the garner hoard,
And the sleeper lie unsphered.
Time's wheel frets on his finger still,
He bends no more his weight with time's.
He wept as long as wind,
And sleeps with an indifferent will.
Not airs, not climes unclose, behind
The lashes' scarcely faltering jet,
Which stars he sees since Hesper set.

LULLABY

Hush, lullay,
Your treasures all
Encrust with rust.

Your trinket pleasures
Fall
To dust.
Beneath the sapphire arch
Upon the grassy floor
Is nothing more
To hold,
And play is over old.
Your eyes
In sleepy fever gleam,
Your lids droop
To their dream.
You wander late alone,
The flesh frets on the bone,
Your love fails
In your breast.
Here is the pillow.
Rest.

Yvor Winters

Yvor Winters was born October 17, 1900, in Chicago. He attended the University of Chicago but, during his first year there, contracted tuberculosis and moved to the Southwest, where he taught in the grade schools and coal camps, receiving his B.A. and M.A. in Romance Languages from the University of Colorado. After teaching French and Spanish at the University of Idaho, he took his Ph.D. at Stanford University and taught there from 1928 on. He is married to Janet Lewis, the novelist.

His first two books, *The Immobile Wind* (1921) and *The Magpie's Shadow* (1922), show a poet unsure of his utterance, experimenting with the borrowed inflections of William Carlos Williams, Ezra Pound, and the Imagists. In *The Giant Weapon* (1943) and, most of all, in the revised *Collected Poems* (1960), the poet speaks in his own voice. It is a well-modulated voice, traditional, formal in the best sense, quiet but firm.

It was not Winters' poetry but his criticism which occasioned many attacks. As an essayist, he was nonchalantly controversial, stubbornly dogmatic, dispensing provocative obiter dicta, and challenging established reputations with dissenting opinions. "I laid," he said, "the foundation for more literary enmities . . . than I should judge have been enjoyed by any other writer of my generation." Nevertheless, *In Defense of Reason* (1947), a collection of three volumes of his criticism, overcomes opposition; an analysis of ideas governing styles, it is a cumulative and historical study. "To the extent that the evaluation of art has not become an extinct critical function in our time," wrote Stanley Edgar Hyman, one of Winters' most consistent critics, "credit must be largely due to the redoubtable labors of Yvor Winters." The six essays in *On Modern Poets,* reissued in 1959, are a set of drastic reappraisals by one who has been labeled "a maverick of literary criticism."

In 1961 the Bollingen Prize was awarded to Winters' *Collected Poems* as "the culmination of a poetic discipline."

JOHN SUTTER

was the patriarch of the shining land,
f the blond summer and metallic grain;
en vanished at the motion of my hand,
nd when I beckoned they would come again.

The earth grew dense with grain at my desire;
The shade was deepened at the springs and streams;
Moving in dust that clung like pillared fire,
The gathering herds grew heavy in my dreams.

Across the mountains, naked from the heights,
Down to the valley broken settlers came,
And in my houses feasted through the nights,
Rebuilt their sinews and assumed a name.

In my clear rivers my own men discerned
The motive for the ruin and the crime—
Gold heavier than earth, a wealth unearned,
Loot, for two decades, from the heart of Time.

Metal, intrinsic value, deep and dense,
Preanimate, inimitable, still,
Real, but an evil with no human sense,
Dispersed the mind to concentrate the will.

Grained by alchemic change, the human kind
Turned from themselves to rivers and to
rocks;
With dynamite broke metal unrefined;
Measured their moods by geologic shocks.

With knives they dug the metal out of stone;
Turned rivers back, for gold through ages
piled,
Drove knives to hearts, and faced the gold
alone;
Valley and river ruined and reviled;

Reviled and ruined me, my servant slew,
Strangled him from the figtree by my door.
When they had done what fury bade them do,
I was a cursing beggar, stripped and sore.

What end impersonal, what breathless age,
Incontinent of quiet and of years,
What calm catastrophe will yet assuage
This final drouth of penitential tears?

TIME AND THE GARDEN

The spring has darkened with activity.
The future gathers in vine, bush, and tree:
Persimmon, walnut, loquat, fig, and grape,
Degrees and kinds of color, taste, and shape.
These will advance in their due series, space
The season like a tranquil dwelling-place.
And yet excitement swells me, vein by vein:
I long to crowd the little garden, gain
Its sweetness in my hand and crush it small
And taste it in a moment, time and all!
These trees, whose slow growth measures off
my years,
I would expand to greatness. No one hears,
And I am still retarded in duress!
And this is like that other restlessness
To seize the greatness not yet fairly earned,
One which the tougher poets have discerned—
Gascoigne, Ben Jonson, Greville, Raleigh,
Donne,
Poets who wrote great poems, one by one,
And spaced by many years, each line an act
Through which few labor, which no men
retract.
This passion is the scholar's heritage,
The imposition of a busy age,
The passion to condense from book to book
Unbroken wisdom in a single look,
Though we know well that when this fix the
head,
The mind's immortal, but the man is dead.

TO A MILITARY RIFLE
1942

The times come round again;
The private life is small;
And individual men
Are counted not at all.
Now life is general,
And the bewildered Muse,
Thinking what she has done,
Confronts the daily news.

Blunt emblem, you have won:
With carven stock unbroke,
With core of steel, with crash
Of mass, and fading smoke;
Your fire leaves little ash;
Your balance on the arm
Points whither you intend;
Your bolt is smooth with charm.
When other concepts end,
This concept, hard and pure,
Shapes every mind therefor.
The time is yours, be sure,
Old Hammerheel of War.

I cannot write your praise
When young men go to die;
Nor yet regret the ways
That ended with this hour.
The hour has come. And I,
Who alter nothing, pray
That men, surviving you,
May learn to do and say
The difficult and true,
True shape of death and power.

TO THE HOLY SPIRIT

from a deserted graveyard
in the Salinas Valley

Immeasurable haze:
The desert valley spreads
Up golden river-beds
As if in other days.
Trees rise and thin away,
And past the trees, the hills,
Pure line and shade of dust,
Bear witness to our wills:
We see them, for we must;
Calm in deceit, they stay.

High noon returns the mind
Upon its local fact:
Dry grass and sand; we find
No vision to distract.
Low in the summer heat,
Naming old graves, are stones
Pushed here and there, the seat
Of nothing, and the bones
Beneath are similar:
Relics of lonely men,
Brutal and aimless, then,
As now, irregular.

These are thy fallen sons,
Thou whom I try to reach.
Thou whom the quick eye shuns,
Thou dost elude my speech.
Yet when I go from sense
And trace thee down in thought,
I meet thee, then, intense,
And know thee as I ought.
But thou art mind alone,
And I, alas, am bound
Pure mind to flesh and bone,
And flesh and bone to ground.

These had no thought: at most
Dark faith and blinding earth.
Where is the trammeled ghost?
Was there another birth?
Only one certainty
Beside thine unfleshed eye,
Beside the spectral tree,
Can I discern; these die.
All of this stir of age,
Though it elude my sense
Into what heritage
I know not, seems to fall,
Quiet beyond recall,
Into irrelevance.

Langston Hughes

☙ Langston Hughes was born February 1, 1902, in Joplin, Missouri. He was brought up in cities in the Middle West, graduated from Central High School in Cleveland, and at eighteen became a teacher of English in Mexico, where he lived for a year and a half. He spent a year at Columbia University and some time as a worker on the high seas. Hughes' next move was a foreign hegira to Paris in midwinter with seven dollars in his pocket. He stayed in France ten months, worked his way through Italy and Spain, and returned to New York with twenty-five cents. Working as a busboy in Washington, he was discovered by Vachel Lindsay, who read several of his poems to a fashionable audience in the very hotel in which Hughes carried trays of dishes.

The Weary Blues, Hughes' first volume, appeared in January, 1926. One of the poems had already won first prize in a contest conducted by *Opportunity,* a magazine which did great service in fostering creative work by Negroes. Hughes' poetry appearing at the same time as Countee Cullen's justified those who claimed we were witnessing a revival of Negro art. The Negroes themselves began to prove the quality of their inheritance. Johnson's *The Book of American Negro Poetry* appeared, three collections of American Negro spirituals disclosed the melodic fertility of the black singers, and various collections of "blues" revealed how greatly contemporary American composers were indebted to the complicated rhythms of the dark musicians. Hughes was the first to express the spirit of these blues in words. In his note to his second volume, *Fine Clothes to the Jew* (1927), he writes, "The *Blues,* unlike the *Spirituals,* have a strict poetic pattern: one long line repeated and a third line to rhyme with the first two. Sometimes the second line in repetition is slightly changed and sometimes, but very seldom, it is omitted. The mood of the *Blues* is almost always despondency, but when they are sung people laugh."

Although at least half of Hughes' work centers about the blues, much of his poetry is grim in an essentially urban manner. His portraits of Negro workmen (as evidenced in the remarkable "Brass Spittoons" with its similarity in symbols to Anna Hempstead Branch's "The Monk in the Kitchen") are more memorable than those produced by any of his compatriots. Hughes widened his appeal with the poetry of *Fields of Wonder* (1947) and *Montage of a Dream Deferred* (1951), short stories, *Simple Speaks His Mind* (1950) and *Laughing to Keep from Crying* (1952), *Ask Your Mama: 12 Moods for Jazz* (1961), and several compilations.

HOMESICK BLUES

De railroad bridge's
A sad song in de air.
De railroad bridge's
A sad song in de air.
Ever' time de trains pass
I wants to go somewhere.

I went down to de station;
Ma heart was in ma mouth.
Went down to de station;
Heart was in ma mouth;
Lookin' for a box car
To roll me to de South.

Homesick blues, Lawd,
'S a terrible thing to have.
Homesick blues is
A terrible thing to have.
To keep from cryin'
I opens ma mouth an' laughs.

BRASS SPITTOONS

Clean the spittoons, boy.
Detroit,
Chicago,
Atlantic City,
Palm Beach.
Clean the spittoons.
The steam in hotel kitchens,
And the smoke in hotel lobbies,
And the slime in hotel spittoons:
Part of my life.
Hey, boy!
A nickel,
A dime,
A dollar,
Two dollars a day.
Hey, boy!
A nickel,
A dime,
A dollar,
Two dollars
Buys shoes for the baby.
House rent to pay.
Church on Sunday.
My God!

Babies and church
and women and Sunday
all mixed up with dimes and
dollars and clean spittoons
and house rent to pay.
Hey, boy!

A bright bowl of brass is beautiful to the Lord.
Bright polished brass like the cymbals
Of King David's dancers,
Like the wine cups of Solomon.
Hey, boy!
A clean spittoon on the altar of the Lord.
A clean bright spittoon all newly polished,—
At least I can offer that.
Com'mere, boy!

SATURDAY NIGHT

Play it once.
O, play it some more.
Charlie is a gambler
An' Sadie is a whore
 A glass o' whiskey
 An' a glass o' gin:
 Strut, Mr. Charlie,
 Till de dawn comes in.
Pawn yo' gold watch
An' diamond ring.
Git a quart o' licker.
Let's shake dat thing!
 Skee-de-dad! De-dad!
 Doo-doo-doo!
 Won't be nothin' left
 When de worms git through.
 An' you's a long time
 Dead
 When you is
 Dead, too.
So beat dat drum, boy!
Shout dat song:
Shake 'em up an' shake 'em up
All night long.
 Hey! Hey!
 Ho . . . Hum!
 Do it, Mr. Charlie,
 Till de red dawn come.

JAZZ BAND IN A PARISIAN CABARET

Play that thing,
Jazz band!
Play it for the lords and ladies,
For the dukes and counts,
For the whores and gigolos,
For the American millionaires,
And the schoolteachers
Out for a spree.
Play it,
Jazz band!
You know that tune
That laughs and cries at the same time.
You know it.
 May I?
 Mais oui.
 Mein Gott!
 Parece una rumba.
Play it, jazz band!
You've got seven languages to speak in
And then some,
Even if you do come from Georgia.
 Can I go home wid yuh, sweetie?
 Sure.

DRUM

Bear in mind
That death is a drum
Beating for ever
Till the last worms come
To answer its call,
Till the last stars fall,
Until the last atom
Is no atom at all,
Until time is lost
And there is no air
And space itself
Is nothing nowhere.
Death is a drum,
A signal drum,
Calling all life
To Come! Come!
Come!

FLORIDA ROAD WORKERS

I'm makin' a road
For the cars
To fly by on.
Makin' a road
Through the palmetto thicket
For light and civilization
To travel on.

Makin' a road
For the rich old white men
To sweep over in their big cars
And leave me standin' here.

Sure,
A road helps all of us!
White folks ride—
And I get to see 'em ride.
I ain't never seen nobody
Ride so fine before.
Hey buddy!
Look at me.
I'm making a road!

Kenneth Fearing

⇝§ Kenneth Fearing was born in Chicago in 1902 and was graduated from the University of Wisconsin. After graduation, he worked in many capacities; he became a salesman, a millhand, a newspaper reporter, and a free-lance writer. In 1939 he taught poetry technique at the League of American Writers.

His first book of poems, *Angel Arms* (1929), flashes before the reader a set of close-ups of the contemporary scene in which "hatred and pity are exactly mixed." *Poems* (1935) and *Dead Reckoning* (1938) mark a further advance in swiftly paced and provocative verse. Fearing is not unaware of the provocation. In an introduction to his *Collected Poems* (1940) he says: "The idea underlying my poetry, as well as anything I write, is that it must be exciting." Fearing knows what he is about; if it does nothing else, his poetry excites. Its fault is a self-imposed restriction of tone; Fearing has purposely discarded "the entire bag of conventions and codes usually associated with poetry." While this is commendable (if possible), it forces upon the poet a limitation even more severe than the traditional demands. Worse, it makes for a prescribed attitude and a sense of final flatness. To save his work from monotony, Fearing ranges widely for his material; charwomen, gangsters, presidents of the Browning Writing League, Harry from the warehouse, Myrtle from the Five and Dime, checkers at the morgue, coupon-clippers, high-diving queens, fifth columnists, big business executives, and crystal-gazers are exposed against the modern setting. The idiom which Fearing uses is savagely appropriate: it is the glaring script of neon lights, the language of locked hotel rooms and casual death, the brusque statement of headlines, the jargon of advertising patter, the slang of the streets, chatter of pent-houses and hospitals, dialectics in the boiler-room, patois of mortgages and the movies. Fearing satirizes big business by his wry employment of metropolitan images and ironically twisted slogans. "Portrait" is a minor masterpiece of composite delineation; it is a bitter cartoon, but a broadly humorous and recognizable picture. "American Rhapsody (4)," far from comic, is as poignant as it is shrewd.

If this poetry does not achieve emphasis as poetry, it gains tension by its very pitch and tempo. Fearing is at his worst when he attempts the mystical-oracular; he loses himself and his reader in a blur of mumbled implications and vague, unfinished gestures. He is at his best in his characters and caricatures, in his ominous pictures of the depression, in the sense of spiritual estrangement, in the maladjusted terrors and the doomed suspense of a speeded-up civilization. The varied elements are brought to a climax in "Readings, Forecasts, Personal Guidance," a poem which combines vision and hard anguish.

Afternoon of a Pawnbroker (1944) and *Stranger at Coney Island* (1948) mix anger and irony. They pile up montages of casual horror, of a nightmare world populated by victims of incurable neuroses. The individual is helpless, lost in a chaos of the commonplace, but the poetry is continually exciting. The tension of Fearing's poetry is carried over into such novels of suspense as *"The Hospital, Dagger of the Mind,* and *The Big Clock.*

Fearing died of a chest tumor on June 26, 1961.

THE PEOPLE VS. THE PEOPLE

I have never seen him, this invisible member of the panel, this thirteenth juror, but
I have certain clues;
I know, after so many years of practice, though I cannot prove I know;
It is enough to say, I know that I know.

He is five feet nine or ten, with piercing, bright, triumphant eyes;
He needs glasses, which he will not wear, and he is almost certainly stone deaf.
(Cf. Blair vs. Gregg, which he utterly ruined.)
He is the juror forever looking out of the window, secretly smiling, when you
make your telling point.
The one who is wide awake when you think he is asleep. The man who naps with
his eyes wide open.
Those same triumphant eyes.
He is the man who knows. And knows that he knows.

His hair is meager and he wears wash ties, but these are not important points.
He likes the legal atmosphere, that is plain, because he is always there.
It is the decent, the orderly procedure that he likes.
He is the juror who arrived first, though you thought he was late; the one who
failed to return from lunch, though you had not noticed.
Let me put it like this: He is the cause of your vague uneasiness when you glance
about and see that the other twelve are all right.

I would know him if I were to see him, I could swear to his identity, if I actually
saw him once;
I nearly overheard him, when I was for the defense: "They never indict anyone
unless they are guilty";
And when I was the State: "A poor man (or a rich man) doesn't stand a chance."
Always, before the trial's end, he wants to know if the sergeant knew the moon
was full on that particular night.

And none of this matters, except I am convinced he is the unseen juror bribed,
bought, and planted by The People,
An enemy of reason and precedent, a friend of illogic,
Something, I now know, that I know that I really know—

And he or anyone else is welcome to my Blackstone, or my crowded shelves of
standard books,
In exchange for the monumental works I am convinced he has been writing
through the years:
"The Rules of Hearsay"; "The Laws of Rumor";
"An Omnibus Guide to Chance and Superstition," by One Who Knows.

PORTRAIT

The clear brown eyes, kindly and alert, with 12-20 vision, give confident regard
to the passing world through R. K. Lampert & Company lenses framed in gold;
His soul, however, is all his own;
Arndt Brothers necktie and hat (with feather) supply a touch of youth.

With his soul his own, he drives, drives, chats and drives,
The first and second bicuspids, lower right, replaced by bridge-work, while two
incisors have porcelain crowns;

(Render unto Federal, state and city Caesar, but not unto time;
Render nothing unto time until Amalgamated Death serves final notice, in proper
form;

The vault is ready;
The will has been drawn by Clagget, Clagget, Clagget & Brown;
The policies are adequate, Confidential's best, reimbursing for disability, partial or
complete, with double indemnity should the end be a pure and simple accident)

Nothing unto time,
Nothing unto change, nothing unto fate,
Nothing unto you, and nothing unto me, or to any other known or unknown party
or parties, living or deceased;

But Mercury shoes, with special arch supports, take much of the wear and tear;
On the course, a custombuilt driver corrects a tendency to slice;
Love's ravages have been repaired (it was a textbook case) by Drs. Schultz,
Lightner, Mannheim, and Goode,
While all of it is enclosed in excellent tweed, with Mr. Baumer's personal attention
to the shoulders and the waist;
And all of it now roving, chatting amiably through space in a Plymouth 6,
With his soul (his own) at peace, soothed by Walter Lippmann, and sustained by
Haig & Haig.

AMERICAN RHAPSODY (4)

First you bite your fingernails. And then you comb your hair again. And then you
wait. And wait.
(They say, you know, that first you lie. And then you steal, they say. And then,
they say, you kill.)

Then the doorbell rings. Then Peg drops in. And Bill. And Jane. And Doc.
And first you talk, and smoke, and hear the news and have a drink. Then you
walk down the stairs.
And you dine, then, and go to a show after that, perhaps, and after that a night
spot, and after that come home again, and climb the stairs again, and again go
to bed.

But first Peg argues, and Doc replies. First you dance the same dance and you
drink the same drink you always drank before.
And the piano builds a roof of notes above the world.

And the trumpet weaves a dome of music through space. And the drum makes a ceiling over space and time and night.
And then the table-wit. And then the check. Then home again to bed.
But first, the stairs.

And do you now, baby, as you climb the stairs, do you still feel as you felt back there?
Do you feel again as you felt this morning? And the night before? And then the night before that?

(They say, you know, that first you hear voices. And then you have visions, they say. Then, they say, you kick and scream and rave.)

Or do you feel: What is one more night in a lifetime of nights?
What is one more death, or friendship, or divorce out of two, or three? Or four? Or five?
One more face among so many, many faces, one more life among so many million lives?
But first, baby, as you climb and count the stairs (and they total the same) did you, sometime or somewhere, have a different idea?
Is this, baby, what you were born to feel, and do, and be?

READINGS, FORECASTS, PERSONAL GUIDANCE

It is not—I swear it by every fiery omen to be seen these nights in every quarter of the heavens, I affirm it by all the monstrous portents of the earth and of the sea—
It is not that my belief in the true and mystic science is shaken, nor that I have lost faith in the magic of the cards, or in the augury of dreams, or in the great and good divinity of the stars.
No, I know still whose science fits the promise to the inquirer's need, invariably, for a change: Mine. My science foretells the wished-for journey, the business adjustment, the handsome stranger. (Each of these is considered a decided change.)
And I know whose skill weighs matrimony, risks a flyer in steel or wheat against the vagaries of the moon.
(Planet of dreams, of mothers and of children, goddess of sailors and of all adventurers, forgive the liberty. But a man must eat.) My skill,
Mine, and the cunning and the patience. (Two dollars for the horoscope in brief and five for a twelve months' forecast in detail.)

No, it is this: The wonders that I have seen with my own eyes.

It is this: That still these people know, as I do not, that what has never been on earth before may still well come to pass,
That always, always there are new and brighter things beneath the sun,
That surely, in bargain basements or in walk-up flats, it must be so that still from time to time they hear wild angel voices speak.
It is this: That I have known them for what they are,
Seen thievery written plainly in their planets, found greed and murder and worse in their birth dates and their numbers, guilt etched in every line of every palm;

But still a light burns through the eyes they turn to me, a need more moving than the damned and dirty dollars (which I must take) that form the pattern of their larger hopes and deeper fears.

And it comes to this: That always I feel another hand, not mine, has drawn and turned the card to find some incredible ace,
Always another word I did not write appears in the spirit parchment prepared by me,
Always another face I do not know shows in the dream, the crystal globe, or the flame.

And finally, this: Corrupt, in a world bankrupt and corrupt, what have I got to do with these miracles?
If they want miracles, let them consult someone else.
Would they, in extremity, ask them of a physician? Or expect them, in desperation, of an attorney? Or of a priest? Or of a poet?

Nevertheless, a man must eat.
Mrs. Raeburn is expected at five. She will communicate with a number of friends and relatives long deceased.

Marya Zaturenska

Marya Zaturenska was born in September, 1902, in Kiev, Russia. Her father came here after the Russo-Japanese War but had difficulty bringing over his wife and two children. The child Marya was eight years old when she came to the United States, and conditions were such that at thirteen she had to leave school and find work. Since she had no training of any kind, she had to accept all sorts of odd jobs in factories and department stores. Starting to write poetry in her early teens, she attended night high school, secured several scholarships, attended the University of Wisconsin, and qualified as a librarian. In 1925 she married the poet Horace Gregory.

Marya Zaturenska's earliest verse was readily accepted by the magazines, but the poet's critical instinct prevented exploitation as an infant prodigy. Her insights, fresh and vivid, are apparent in *Threshold and Hearth* (1934). Fluid though this writing is, it is never facile; it moves with a power which is highly imaginative but always restrained. The restraint is so characteristic that it misled the critics. Even when *Cold Morning Sky* (1937) won the Pulitzer Prize for poetry the reviewers spoke of her precisions as "detached," "abstract," and "removed from the immediate world." In spite of its distinction, her work was so little known that her name was not even listed in the 1940 edition of Millett's comprehensive *Contemporary American Authors.*

The Listening Landscape (1941) is the very best of her verse, richest in feeling, ripest in expression. In common with the preceding volumes it is deceptive in its smoothness; beneath the calm exterior there is a prevailing and penetrative glow. Here the quick communication and sure craft go hand in hand. "Interview in

Midsummer" is an uncanny trance-like monolog, but what is unsaid is envisioned in any woman's universe; "The White Dress" is an extraordinary evocation, the growth of a symbol from haunting beauty to horrible possession; "The Lovers" is, in skillful repetitions and contrapuntal images, one of the most musical love-poems of our time. Even the "classical" poems, such as the "Head of Medusa," bring full life to mythological figures, not only reanimating a legend but creating a new and complex character.

There is in this poetry a combination which no contemporary has quite achieved: a fusion of definite picture and indefinite symbolism, of word-music and parable. Experience is transmuted, resolved, and transcended; "The Daisy" is only one example of subtlety resolved into simplicity. The lyrical impulse is extended in individualized images and personal landscapes; it searches but it never forgets to sing. If the tone is sometimes faraway, it is because this poet is occupied with a sense of timelessness.

Hers is an art of vivid condensation, of wide allusions in compact phrases: "the swan-feathered snow," "the heart's best weather," "the grass blade's thin precision," "the lip-red poppy scenting earth with sleep," "the intricate unholiness of pain." Superficially these lyrics may seem to be pastoral-historical—the tradition of Marvell, Waller, and Clare—but the synthesis is as remarkable as it is new: a combination of shining observation and shadowed allegory. In spirit as well as substance this verse has a form of its own, a shape delicate and pure. The best of *The Golden Mirror* (1944) was reprinted in *Selected Poems* (1954), which was followed by the lucid *Terraces of Light* (1960).

THE DAISY

Having so rich a treasury, so fine a hoard
Of beauty water-bright before my eyes,
I plucked the daisy only, simple and white
In its fringed frock and brooch of innocent gold.

So is all equilibrium restored:
I leave the noontide wealth of richer bloom
To the destroyer, the impatient ravisher,
The intemperate bee, the immoderate bird.

Of all this beauty felt and seen and heard
I can be frugal and devout and plain,
Deprived so long of light and air and grass,
The shyest flower is sweetest to uncover.

How poor I was: and yet no richer lover
Discovered joy so deep in earth and water;
And in the air that fades from blue to pearl,
And in a flower white-frocked like my small daughter.

THE LOVERS

My glittering sky, high, clear, profound,
Be thou my Alps. I'll be thy summer.

I'll be thy summer and the ground
Where all thy garlands, all thy honors found
In the sky's mirror, fire and dew contend,
Which shall excel, which shall transcend.

Be thou my mountain heights, I'll be the plain,
Warm, simple, sweet, complaisant to the rain,
Complaisant to the rain and wind, the common day.
I'll be the daisy field where happy children play,
Where happy children play, where the world's voice is heard
In a tree, in the grass, in the storm, in a bird.

Be thou the diamond water-crisp, and I the fire
Rosy and quick within the ruby's flame,
Within the ruby's flame inscribe my name
Sensitive on the spirit's delicate wire,
Send occult messages no human tongue can say.
Be thou the night, I'll be the day.

I'll be the day, so fresh, so morning bright,
And thy youth's dawning and the fields of light,
The fields of light that change dark to bright.
Thou my tranquillity, I thy delight,
Thou the thin light of opals on my wrist
And I the evening tinted heaven brooding amethyst.

Be thou the waterbrook and I the hart
Drinking in coolness from rain moistened heat,
Drinking in coolness where the willows part,
And where the willows part, two diverse shadows meet.
Be thou the sheltered pool, and I the busy street
And we the shades that one another greet.

Change then forever, be forever the same,
Who have one road, one destiny, one name,
One destiny, one name, jewel, dew, fire (never the same),
The mountain and the river, city and plain.
Separate, distinct, divided, parted, meeting ever
What the eye loses, let the heart recover.

THE WHITE DRESS

Imperceptively the world became haunted by her white dress.
Walking in forest or garden, he would start to see,
Her flying form; sudden, swift, brief as a caress
The flash of her white dress against a darkening tree.

And with forced unconcern, withheld desire, and pain
He beheld her at night; and when sleepless in his bed,
Her light footfalls seemed loud as cymbals; deep as his disdain,
Her whiteness entered his heart, flowed through from feet to head.

Or it was her face at a window, her swift knock at the door,
Then she appeared in her white dress, her face as white as her gown;
Like snow in midsummer she came and left the rich day poor;
And the sun chilled and grew higher, remote, and the moon slipped down.

So the years passed; more fierce in pursuit her image grew;
She became the dream abjured, the ill uncured, the deed undone,
The life one never lived, the answer one never knew,
Till the white shadow swayed the moon, stayed the expiring sun,

Until at his life's end, the shadow of the white face, the white dress
Became his inmost thought, his private wound, the word unspoken,
All that he cherished in failure, all that had failed his success;
She became the crystal orb, half-seen, untouched, unbroken.

There on his death bed, kneeling at the bed's foot, he trembling saw,
The image of the Mother-Goddess, enormous, archaic, cruel,
Overpowering the universe, creating her own inexorable law,
Molded of stone, but her fire and ice flooded the room like a pool.

And she was the shadow in the white dress, no longer slight and flying,
But solid as death. Her cold, firm, downward look,
Brought close to the dissolving mind the marvellous act of dying,
And on her lap, the clasped, closed, iron book.

HEAD OF MEDUSA

How long she waited for her executioner!
She who froze life to stone, whose hissing hair
Once grew as waved and flowing as the sea,
Ash-damp and dreadful now. The fabulous mystery, the shame,
Forever in that cave where man nor beast came

Came and returned to life; so great the curse
Of the invulnerable enemy whose eyes immerse
Medusa's soul in this foul universe,
Turns her warm body passionate, fleshed with fire,
Into this loathsome thing no men desire.

Cast in the final loneliness she must lie
Knowing that all who look on her will die
(The savage sorrow frozen in her sigh)
Even as she meets the look of fear and hate.
Their blood dries and their flesh must expiate.

But now her Perseus comes, foe or deliverer?
Bringing the welcome end. For whom her serpents stir,
Brute force and animal terror, the soul's tormentor
Subside; low-water calm, slow, unperceptively
Comes he who sets her free.

And now the end nears. Through steelpoint warm blood
Shall flow in purification. Her world made clean and good,
Through pain the Immortal's hatred is withstood.
Even now in the gold shield
One faces her, his life-blood uncongealed.

Prepares for the quick stroke that sets her free
From the cold terror in all eyes that see.
Even now the slayer's hand displays the mystery
That once vainglorious and guilty head,
Emptied of all its sorrow and its dread!

WOMAN AT THE PIANO

Rippling in the ocean of that darkening room,
The music poured from the thin hands, widening, gathering
The floods of descending night; flying from the keys
The sound of memory, then the woman singing
Vibrant and full, the resonant echoes scattered
Into a stranger's language, into a foreign country.

The rococo clock on the mantel strikes out its chimes
The night wind sighing through the open windows,
Sends in its signals, wishes, memories.
The withdrawn room grows immense with hallucination
Clear woman's voice, long fingers whitely straying
Over the speaking keys do you hear the answer?
Will the male voice answer? see stirring through the walls
Behind the rustling curtains in the declining light
How another voice still silent seems to tremble.

Patience is all. Unloved, unlovable, lonely,
It sits on the neglected sofa, watches the fingers
Draw out the significant music, hears the finale
Shatter the torpor of the dying room.
Now the trees through open windows aspire and flame
Now there are footsteps, echoes, reveries
Now two voices sound in the room where only one
Wove intricate sweetness from the simple keys.
Two voices ring in the dawn, the morning enters.

THE TEMPEST

As in a Watteau fete of rose and silver blue,
The intense colors lift the dreamy world
Into a sharper vision than it knew,
The graceful figures vast in miniature.

And deepens overhead the dainty, sweeping azure.

So in the cold and limpid morning air,
When but a hint of sun was felt, we breathed the storm

Companioned by June light. It tinged the warm,
Half-sleeping flowers. Unseen, but everywhere
We felt the tempest's uncreated form,

Gathering its might, its bright and nervous flare.

See how its silver hand disturbs the clouds
And the soul's solitude in anger wakes
The waving revery of grass, and whispering shakes
The airy heavens into the drifting lakes,

While rain falls gently from the savage eyes.

And silken-sharp the dazzling thunder falls
Upon the startled land. The rising, falling dart
Sudden and piercing on the summer's heart;
And while from tree to tree the voice of fire calls

The unleashed tempest shakes the garden walls.

Ogden Nash

Ogden Nash was born August 19, 1902, in Rye, New York, of a distinguished and seemingly ubiquitous family. He claims to have had ten thousand cousins in North Carolina; his great-great-grandfather was Revolutionary Governor of the state, and the latter's brother, General Francis Nash, gave his name to Nashville, Tennessee. Ogden Nash spent a year at St. George's School in Rhode Island, where, he says, he lost his entire nervous system carving lamb for a table of fourteen-year-olds. He entered Harvard in the class of 1924, but left after one year.

To continue his biography in his own words: "Came to New York to make my fortune as a bond salesman; in two years I sold one bond—to my godmother. However, I saw a lot of good movies. Next went to work writing car cards. After two years of that I landed in the advertising department of Doubleday. That was 1925, and I doubledayed until 1931." After 1931, Nash engaged in a succession of varied activities: he was on the staff of *The New Yorker;* became associated with two publishing firms; married and lived in Baltimore; had two daughters and moved to Hollywood, where he wrote—or rewrote—scenarios.

Nash's liveliest effects are in *Free Wheeling* (1931), *The Bad Parent's Garden of Verse* (1936), and *I'm a Stranger Here Myself* (1938), but all his volumes are characterized by rollicking spirits, easy satire, and a slightly insane manner. The style is bantering, deceptively haphazard, but the end is often a kind of social criticism. For most readers, however, Nash's charm lies in his irresponsible absurdities, in the impudent rhymes which do not quite rhyme, in his way of giving a new twist to an old subject. He can be surprisingly shrewd and nonsensical at the same time; his technique is unique, a completely new form of verse.

The Face Is Familiar (1940) contains two hundred eighty poems selected from

Nash's preceding volumes. The half-irresponsible, half-ironic manner is continued in *Good Intentions* (1942), *Many Long Years Ago* (1945), *Parents Keep Out* (1951), and *Private Dining Room* (1953). With S. J. Perelman Nash wrote a musical comedy, *One Touch of Venus.*

THE RHINOCEROS

The rhino is a homely beast,
For human eyes he's not a feast,
But you and I will never know
Why nature chose to make him so.
Farewell, farewell, to you old rhinoceros,
I'll stare at something less prepoceros!

ADVENTURES OF ISABEL

Isabel met an enormous bear;
Isabel, Isabel, didn't care.
The bear was hungry, the bear was ravenous,
The bear's big mouth was cruel and cavernous.
The bear said, Isabel, glad to meet you,
How do, Isabel, now I'll eat you!
Isabel, Isabel, didn't worry;
Isabel didn't scream or scurry.
She washed her hands and she straightened her hair up,
Then Isabel quietly ate the bear up.

Once on a night as black as pitch
Isabel met a wicked old witch.
The witch's face was cross and wrinkled,
The witch's gums with teeth were sprinkled.
Ho, ho, Isabel! the old witch crowed,
I'll turn you into an ugly toad!
Isabel, Isabel, didn't worry;
Isabel didn't scream or scurry.
She showed no rage and she showed no rancor,
But she turned the witch into milk and drank her.

Isabel met a hideous giant,
Isabel continued self-reliant.
The giant was hairy, the giant was horrid,
He had one eye in the middle of his forehead.
Good morning, Isabel, the giant said,
I'll grind your bones to make my bread.
Isabel, Isabel, didn't worry;
Isabel didn't scream or scurry.
She nibbled the zwieback that she always fed off,
And when it was gone, she cut the giant's head off.

Isabel met a troublesome doctor,
He punched and poked till he really shocked her.

The doctor's talk was of coughs and chills,
And the doctor's satchel bulged with pills.
The doctor said unto Isabel,
Swallow this, it will make you well.
Isabel, Isabel, didn't worry;
Isabel didn't scream or scurry.
She took those pills from the pill-concoctor,
And Isabel calmly cured the doctor.

GOLLY, HOW TRUTH WILL OUT!

How does a person get to be a capable liar?
That is something that I respectfully inquiar,
Because I don't believe a person will ever set the world on fire
Unless they are a capable lire.
Some wise man said that words were given to us to conceal our thoughts,
But if a person has nothing but truthful words why their thoughts haven't even the protection of a pair of panties or shoughts,
And a naked thought is ineffectual as well as improper,
And hasn't a chance in the presence of a glib chinchilla-clad whopper.
One of the greatest abilities a person can have, I guess,
Is the ability to say Yes when they mean No and No when they mean Yes.
Oh to be Machiavellian, oh to be unscrupulous, oh, to be glib!
Oh to be ever prepared with a plausible fib!
Because then a dinner engagement or a contract or a treaty is no longer a fetter,
Because liars can just logically lie their way out of it if they don't like it or if one comes along that they like better;
And do you think their conscience prickles?
No, it tickles.
And please believe that I mean every one of these lines as I am writing them
Because once there was a small boy who was sent to the drugstore to buy some bitter stuff to put on his nails to keep him from biting them,
And in his humiliation he tried to lie to the clerk
And it didn't work,
Because he said My mother sent me to buy some bitter stuff for a friend of mine's nails that bites them, and the clerk smiled wisely and said I wonder who that friend could be,
And the small boy broke down and said Me,
And it was me, or at least I was him,
And all my subsequent attempts at subterfuge have been equally grim,
And that is why I admire a suave prevarication because I prevaricate so awkwardly and gauchely,
And that is why I can never amount to anything politically or socially.

SONG TO BE SUNG BY THE FATHER OF INFANT FEMALE CHILDREN

My heart leaps up when I behold
A rainbow in the sky;
Contrariwise, my blood runs cold
When little boys go by.

For little boys as little boys,
No special hate I carry,
But now and then they grow to men,
And when they do, they marry.
No matter how they tarry,
Eventually they marry.
And, swine among the pearls,
They marry little girls.

Oh, somewhere, somewhere, an infant plays,
With parents who feed and clothe him.
Their lips are sticky with pride and praise,
But I have begun to loathe him.
Yes, I loathe with a loathing shameless
This child who to me is nameless.
This bachelor child in his carriage
Gives never a thought to marriage,
But a person can hardly say knife
Before he will hunt him a wife.

I never see an infant (male),
A-sleeping in the sun,
Without I turn a trifle pale
And think, is he the one?
Oh, first he'll want to crop his curls,
And then he'll want a pony,
And then he'll think of pretty girls
And holy matrimony.
He'll put away his pony,
And sigh for matrimony.
A cat without a mouse
Is he without a spouse.

Oh, somewhere he bubbles, bubbles of milk,
And quietly sucks his thumbs;
His cheeks are roses painted on silk,
And his teeth are tucked in his gums.
But alas, the teeth will begin to grow,
And the bubbles will cease to bubble;
Given a score of years or so,
The roses will turn to stubble.
He'll sell a bond, or he'll write a book,
And his eyes will get that acquisitive look,
And raging and ravenous for the kill,
He'll boldly ask for the hand of Jill.
This infant whose middle
Is diapered still
Will want to marry
My daughter Jill.

Oh sweet be his slumber and moist his middle!
My dreams, I fear, are infanticiddle.
A fig for embryo Lohengrins!

I'll open all of his safety pins,
I'll pepper his powder and salt his bottle,
And give him readings from Aristotle,
Sand for his spinach I'll gladly bring,
And tabasco sauce for his teething ring,
And an elegant, elegant alligator
To play with in his perambulator.
Then perhaps he'll struggle through fire and water
To marry somebody *else's* daughter!

THE EVENING OUT

You have your hat and coat on and she says she will be right down,
And you hope so because it is getting late and you are dining on the other side of town,
And you are pretty sure she can't take long,
Because when you left her she already looked as neat and snappy as a Cole Porter song,
So you stand around thinking of various things and wondering why good rye costs more than Scotch.
And after a while you begin to look at your watch,
And so goes ten minutes, and then fifteen minutes, and then half an hour,
And you listen for the sound of water running because you suspect she may have gone back for a bath or a shower,
Or maybe she is taking a nap,
Or possibly getting up a subscription for the benefit of the children of the mouse that she said mean things about last night but she is now sorry got caught in a trap,
Or maybe she decided her hair was a mess and is now shampooing it,
But whatever she is up to, she is a long time doing it,
And finally she comes down and says she is sorry she couldn't find the right lipstick, that's why she was so slow,
And you look at her and she looks marvelous but not a bit more marvelous than she did when you left her forty-five minutes ago,
And you tell her she looks ravishing and she says No, she is a sight,
And you reflect that you are now an hour late, but at any rate she is now groomed for the rest of the night,
So you get to your destination and there's the ladies dressing room and before you know it she's in it,
But she says she'll be back in a minute,
And so she is, but not to tarry,
No, only to ask you for her bag, which she has forgotten she had asked you to carry,
So you linger in the lobby
And wish you had a nice portable hobby,
And you try to pass the time seeing how much you can remember of the poetry you learned in school, both good verse and bad verse,
And eventually she re-aapears just about as you have decided she was in the middle of *Anthony Adverse,*

And she doesn't apologize, but glances at you as if you were Bluebeard or Scrooge,
And says why didn't you tell her she had on too much rouge?
And you look to see what new tint she has acquired,
And she looks just the same as she did before she retired,
So you dine, and reach the theater in time for the third act, and then go somewhere to dance and sup,
And she says she looks like a scarecrow, she has to go straighten up,
So then you don't see her for quite a long time,
But at last you see her for a moment when she comes out to ask if you will lend her a dime,
The moral of all which is that you will have just as much of her company and still save considerable on cover charges and beverages and grub
If instead of taking her out on the town, you settle her in a nice comfortable dressing room and then go off and spend the evening at the Club.

THE SEVEN SPIRITUAL AGES OF MRS. MARMADUKE MOORE

Mrs. Marmaduke Moore, at the age of ten
(Her name was Jemima Jevons then),
Was the quaintest of little country maids.
Her pigtails slapped on her shoulderblades;
She fed the chickens, and told the truth
And could spit like a boy through a broken tooth.
She could climb a tree to the topmost perch,
And she used to pray in the Methodist church.

At the age of twenty her heart was pure,
And she caught the fancy of Mr. Moore.
He broke his troth (to a girl named Alice),
And carried her off to his city palace,
Where she soon forgot her childhood piety
And joined in the orgies of high society.
Her voice grew English, or, say, Australian,
And she studied to be an Episcopalian.

At thirty our lives are still before us,
But Mr. Moore had a friend in the chorus.
Connubial bliss was overthrown
And Mrs. Moore now slumbered alone.
Hers was a nature that craved affection;
She gave herself up to introspection;
Then, finding theosophy rather dry,
Found peace in the sweet Bahai and Bahai.

Forty! and still an abandoned wife.
She felt old urges stirring to life.
She dipped her locks in a bowl of henna
And booked a passage through to Vienna.

She paid a professor a huge emolument
To demonstrate what his ponderous volume meant.
Returning, she preached to the unemployed
The gospel according to St. Freud.

Fifty! she haunted museums and galleries,
And pleased young men by augmenting their salaries.
Oh, it shouldn't occur, but it does occur,
That poets are made by fools like her.
Her salon was full of frangipani,
Roumanian, Russian and Hindustani,
And she conquered par as well as bogey
By reading a book and going Yogi.

Sixty! and time was on her hands—
Maybe remorse and maybe glands.
She felt a need for a free confession
To publish each youthful indiscretion,
And before she was gathered to her mothers,
To compare her sinlets with those of others,
Mrs. Moore gave a joyous whoop,
And immersed herself in the Oxford group.

That is the story of Mrs. Moore,
As far as it goes. But of this I'm sure—
When seventy stares her in the face
She'll have found some other state of grace.
Mohammed may be her Lord and master,
Or Zeus, or Mithros, or Zoroaster.
For when a lady is badly sexed
God knows what God is coming next.

THE PURIST

I give you now Professor Twist,
A conscientious scientist.
Trustees exclaimed, "He never bungles!"
And sent him off to distant jungles.
Camped on a tropic riverside,
One day he missed his loving bride.
She had, the guide informed him later,
Been eaten by an alligator.
Professor Twist could not but smile.
"You mean," he said, "a crocodile."

Countee Cullen

◆§ Countee Cullen was born in New York City, May 30, 1903. He was educated in the New York schools and at New York University, and was graduated with the class of 1925. A year later he received his M.A. at Harvard.

Color (1925) and *Copper Sun* (1927) suffer not only from the poet's influences but from his own juvenilia. There is, however, no gainsaying his gift of epigram and the neatness of his execution. Lacking the deep racial quality of Langston Hughes, Cullen's is a more literary accomplishment. If his verse is not as black as it might be painted, it is bold in concept and metaphor. "Heritage," which, in spite of reminiscences of Ralph Hodgson and Edna Millay, marks the peak of his first volume, still stands as one of the finest poems produced by an American Negro; it ranks with the best by James Weldon Johnson and Langston Hughes.

The Ballad of the Brown Girl (1927) appeared in the same year as his comprehensive anthology of Negro verse, *Caroling Dusk*, in which Cullen showed unexpected editorial acumen. *The Black Christ* (1930) suffers from the double handicap of formula in style and formula in feeling. Its program is ambitious and promises force; but here is no fire, only fluency. The poet seems to be victimized by his own epithets, and these lack surprise or conviction.

The Medea and Other Poems (1935) puts the Euripidean tragedy into powerful prose although the choruses were in verse. It was set to music by Virgil Thompson. *My Lives and How I Lost Them* (1942) is a whimsical fantasy in which the author "collaborates" with a cat. Cullen's most representative work dealt with pain and oppression, with defeat and desperate courage. He selected the best of his poems, *On These I Stand* (1947), shortly before his death, January 8, 1946.

SIMON THE CYRENIAN SPEAKS

He never spoke a word to me,
And yet He called my name.
He never gave a sign to see,
And yet I knew and came.

At first I said, "I will not bear
His cross upon my back—
He only seeks to place it there
Because my skin is black."

But He was dying for a dream,
And He was very meek;
And in His eyes there shone a gleam
Men journey far to seek.

It was Himself my pity bought;
I did for Christ alone
What all of Rome could not have wrought
With bruise of lash or stone.

THREE EPITAPHS

For My Grandmother

This lovely flower fell to seed.
Work gently, sun and rain—
She held it as her dying creed
That she would grow again.

For a Virgin Lady

For forty years I shunned the lust
Inherent in my clay:
Death only was so amorous
I let him have his way.

A Lady I Know

She thinks that even up in heaven
Her class lies late and snores,
While poor black cherubs rise at seven
To do celestial chores.

HERITAGE

What is Africa to me:
Copper sun or scarlet sea,
Jungle star or jungle track,
Strong bronzed men, or regal black
Women from whose loins I sprang
When the birds of Eden sang?
One three centuries removed
From the scenes his fathers loved,
Spicy grove, cinnamon tree,
What is Africa to me?

So I lie, who all day long
Want no sound except the song
Sung by wild barbaric birds
Goading massive jungle herds,
Juggernauts of flesh that pass
Trampling tall defiant grass
Where young forest lovers lie,
Plighting troth beneath the sky.
So I lie, who always hear,
Though I cram against my ear
Both my thumbs and keep them there,
Great drums throbbing through the air.
So I lie, whose fount of pride,
Dear distress, and joy allied,
Is my somber flesh and skin,
With the dark blood dammed within
Like great pulsing tides of wine
That, I fear, must burst the fine
Channels of the chafing net
Where they surge and foam and fret.

Africa? A book one thumbs
Listlessly, till slumber comes.
Unremembered are her bats
Circling through the night, her cats
Crouching in the river reeds,
Stalking gentle flesh that feeds
By the river brink; no more
Does the bugle-throated roar
Cry that monarch claws have leapt
From the scabbards where they slept.
Silver snakes that once a year
Doff the lovely coats you wear,
Seek no covert in your fear
Lest a mortal eye should see;
What's your nakedness to me?
Here no leprous flowers rear
Fierce corollas in the air;
Here no bodies sleek and wet,
Dripping mingled rain and sweat,
Tread the savage measures of
Jungle boys and girls in love.

What is last year's snow to me,
Last year's anything? The tree
Budding yearly must forget
How its past arose or set—
Bough and blossom, flower, fruit,
Even what shy bird with mute
Wonder at her travail there,
Meekly labored in its hair.
One three centuries removed
From the scenes his fathers loved,
Spicy grove, cinnamon tree,
What is Africa to me?

So I lie, who find no peace
Night or day, no slight release
From the unremittent beat
Made by cruel padded feet
Walking through my body's street.
Up and down they go, and back,
Treading out a jungle track.
So I lie, who never quite
Safely sleep from rain at night—
I can never rest at all
When the rain begins to fall;
Like a soul gone mad with pain
I must match its weird refrain;

Ever must I twist and squirm,
Writhing like a baited worm,
While its primal measures drip
Through my body, crying, "Strip!
Doff this new exuberance.
Come and dance the Lover's Dance!"
In an old remembered way
Rain works on me night and day.

Quaint, outlandish heathen gods
Black men fashion out of rods,
Clay and brittle bits of stone,
In a likeness of their own,
My conversion came high-priced;
I belong to Jesus Christ,
Preacher of humility;
Heathen gods are naught to me.
Father, Son and Holy Ghost,
So I make an idle boast;
Jesus of the twice-turned cheek,
Lamb of God, although I speak
With my mouth thus, in my heart
Do I play a double part.
Even at Thy glowing altar
Must my heart grow sick and falter
Wishing He I served were black,
Thinking then it would not lack
Precedent of pain to guide it,
Let who would or might deride it;
Surely then this flesh would know
Yours had borne a kindred woe.
Lord, I fashion dark gods, too,
Daring even to give You
Dark despairing features where,
Crowned with dark rebellious hair,
Patience wavers just so much as
Mortal grief compels, while touches
Quick and hot, of anger, rise
To smitten cheek and weary eyes.
Lord, forgive me if my need
Sometimes shapes a human creed.

All day long and all night through,
One thing only must I do:
Quench my pride and cool my blood,
Lest I perish in the flood.
Lest a hidden ember set
Timber that I thought was wet
Burning like the dryest flax,
Melting like the merest wax,
Lest the grave restore its dead.
Not yet has my heart or head
In the least way realized
They and I are civilized.

Merrill Moore

Merrill Moore was born in Columbia, Tennessee, September 11, 1903. Although he served an interneship in Boston and practiced there, his backgrounds are entirely Southern: his father, John Trotwood Moore, the historian, was from Alabama; his mother from Missouri. He was educated in Nashville, received his B.A. at Vanderbilt University in 1924, his M.D. in 1928, and was one of the group that founded *The Fugitive*. He died of cancer September 20, 1957.

His work is vividly modern and its seems, at first glance, a paradox that this experimental poet has chosen the most classic form as his medium. Typography and tradition notwithstanding, *The Noise That Time Makes* (1929) is composed entirely of sonnets—and it is an open secret that Merrill Moore at the age of twenty-five had composed no less than nine thousand such sonnets. Nor is it a fiction that Moore learned shorthand in order to get more of his fourteen-liners done between classroom and laboratory. It should be said that neither Wyatt nor Philip Sidney would have sponsored had they even recognized Moore's employment of the key with which Shakespeare is supposed to have unlocked his heart. *The Noise That Time Makes* bears the first fruits of what might be considered a new hybrid: the American sonnet.

The characterization is not far-fetched, for Moore's cis-Atlantic accent, the native syncopated speed—so different from English and Italian tempi—the abrupt approach and swift abandonment are not only occasioned by local backgrounds but are the very essence of these poems. As a sonneteer in the strict sense, Moore commits every known heresy and invents several new ones. His rhyme-schemes seem as haphazard as they are numerous—the rhymes themselves are suspiciously unorthodox. His lines, instead of conforming to a precise meter, stretch themselves flexibly as their author throws in four or five extra syllables with prodigal nonchalance. His stanzas, instead of splitting neatly into customary octave and sestet, divide themselves anywhere with what seems sheer perversity. But there is nothing arbitrary about these "American sonnets." The innovations are essentially reasonable, and the reasons for them are quite simple. Merrill Moore's sonnets are, in some ways, the most spontaneous ever written in America, and their "naturalness" is reflected in their structure. The rhythms are based on the rise and fall of the breath rather than on the beat of the metronome. It is not scansion but stress which determines the line-length.

The charm of such poetry is the continual freshness which gives it the quality of improvisation. This is, likewise, a danger; for when Moore, seated before his instrument, lets his fingers wander as they list, his spontaneous playing extends itself into a fluency which is neither a virtue nor virtuosity. But the best of his lines reveal the serious eye and sensitive touch. "What if small birds are peppering the sky," "allowing fish-like thoughts to escape in thin streams trickling through the mind," "birds' indeclinable twitter"—the sonnets are full of such swift exactitudes. Suiting their pace to subjects limited only by a seemingly unlimited imagination, scarcely two of these poems are alike in shape or theme. "Shot Who? Jim Lane!" is as realistic as it is sectional; "Warning to One" is a tribute etched with acid; "How She Resolved to Act" is intuitive as it is whimsical; "The Book of How" quietly mingles the casual and the colossal.

Six Sides to a Man (1935), like its predecessor, presents no sequence but, with kaleidoscopic changes, a set of unrelated patterns. It is as if a flood of quickly igniting thoughts were impelled by recollections, sights, sounds, smells, the look and feel of words, with all their complex associations. These associations, intuitions, and memories both help and hinder each other, and in the clash the poem appears. This paradox of creation and conflict, this order out of chaos, is common to every poet; in Moore's case the process is somewhat more self-revealing. The factor that frequently deranges his aim is probably that his intuitions and unconscious associations are not in league with and often even opposed to his conscious intention.

M (1938), as the title indicates, actually includes one thousand poems, one thousand autobiographical sonnets. Using the sonnet as a foscusing lens, the greatest mass production poet of his age directs the camera-eye, and presents a multitude of allusions, fantasies, case histories, brilliant pictures, and psychological shadows.

This, obviously, is not a poetry of perfection but of casual disassociation. It attains diverse and sometimes dazzling effects rather than integrated finish. It pushes its way through experience and dreams; it cannot stop to correct errors in taste and proportion. But Moore's mind is expansive, almost explosive—at thirty-seven he had published only a small part of the 50,000 sonnets he had written.

Clinical Sonnets (1949), *Case Record from a Sonnetorium* (1951), *The Hill of Venus* (1957), were followed by the posthumous *Poems of American Life* (1958).

OLD MEN AND OLD WOMEN GOING HOME ON THE STREET CAR

Carrying their packages of groceries in particular
With books under their arms that maybe they will read
And possibly understand, old women lead
Their weaker selves up to the front of the car.

And old men who for thirty years have sat at desks
Survey them harmlessly.
They regard each other
As forgotten sister looks at forgotten brother
On their way between two easily remembered tasks
And that is positively all there is to it.

But it was not that way thirty years ago!
Before desks and counters had tired their backs and feet,

When life for them was a bowl of odorous fruit
That they might take their pick of, then turn and go,
Saying, "This tastes so good!" or, "This smells so sweet!"

IT IS WINTER, I KNOW

What if small birds are peppering the sky,
Scudding south with the clouds to an ultimate tip on lands
Where they may peck worms and slugs from moist sands
Rather muddily mixed with salt?
Or if wind dashes by
Insufferably filled with birds' indeclinable twitter
Not deigning to toy with the oak-twigs that it passes
And treading but lightly on all the delicate grasses
Under trees where crickets are silent, where mad leaves flutter?

It is winter, I know, there are too many Nays now confronting
The obdurate soul that would trick itself into believing
That buds are still ripe, that cells are all ready for cleaving;
It can only be winter, winter alone, when blunting
Winds rush over the ice, scattering leaves from their weeds
To rattle the sycamore tree's dry-shriveled seeds.

SHOT WHO? JIM LANE!

When he was shot he toppled to the ground
As if the toughened posts that were his thighs
Had felt that all that held them up were lies,
Weak lies, that suddenly someone had found

Out all that was true about them.
It did not seem
Like the crashing of a stalwart forest oak
But like a frail staff that a sharp wind broke
Or something insubstantial in a dream.

I never thought Jim Lane would fall like that.

He'd sworn that bullets must be gold to find him;
That when they came toward him he made them mind him
By means he knew,
just as a barn-yard cat
Can keep a pack of leaping dogs at bay
By concentrating and looking a certain way.

WARNING TO ONE

Death is the strongest of all living things
And when it happens do not look in the eyes
For a dead fire or a lack-luster there,
But listen for the words that fall from lips
Or do not fall. Silence is not death;
It merely means that the one who is conserving breath
Is not concerned with tattle and small quips.

Watch the quick fingers and the way they move
During unguarded moments—words of love
And love's caresses may be cold as ice
And cold the glitter of engagement rings;
Death is the sword that hangs on a single hair,
And that thin tenuous hair is no more than love
And yours is the silly head it hangs above.

HOW SHE RESOLVED TO ACT

"I shall be careful to say nothing at all
About myself or what I know of him
Or the vaguest thought I have—no matter how dim,
Tonight if it so happen that he call."

And not ten minutes later the door-bell rang
And into the hall he stepped as he always did
With a face and a bearing that quite poorly hid
His brain that burned and his heart that fairly sang
And his tongue that wanted to be rid of the truth.

As well as she could, for she was very loath
To signify how she felt, she kept very still,
But soon her heart cracked loud as a coffee mill
And her brain swung like a comet in the dark
And her tongue raced like a squirrel in the park.

PANDORA AND THE MOON

Minds awake in bodies that were asleep
Caused the winged troubles to be born
That made Pandora one time feel forlorn,
Because, in spite of the box, she could not keep
Her troubles there, the worrisome animalcules
Fluttered out never to be regained,
For every method of evil especially trained
And subject neither to God's nor the devil's rules.

What shall she do? Nothing; sit and ponder;
Watch the dying leaves drop from the tree
Until they all are gone and she may see
The same moon then that used to make her wonder
At the unbelievable stories she sits and reads.
And if she succeeds in that then she succeeds.

VILLAGE NOON: MID-DAY BELLS

When both hands of the town clock stood at twelve
Eve ceased spinning, Adam ceased to delve.
A lusty cockerel crowed that noon had come,
The shadows stood beneath the trees and some
Were motionless a moment—then the people
Busied themselves for food, and in the steeple
Ubiquitous pigeons roucoulayed and slept
Above the watch the dogs below them kept
For nothing—or a dust cloud down the road
That might mean feet or might mean wheels or not.

Then as the noon sun with its ardor glowed
On man and beast and field and dwelling place
The hands moved past noon to another spot
And Time moved on a little way in Space.

UNKNOWN MAN IN THE MORGUE

Tortured body, lie at rest alone
Finally on the long and merciless
Slab of now cool lava-molten stone,
And wait our mutual and final guess
At your identity, nameless, homeless one.

No suburb avenue, no numbered house
We know for you; no date of birth nor death
Are yours, though somewhere visitors may carouse
In a forgotten room where once you lived,
Fathered, soned and brothered, lovered, wived.
But here you come unfollowed to this place,
With an anonymous grimace on your face
In death, whose last name and whose last address
Will now be yours in your last loneliness.

THE BOOK OF HOW

After the stars were all hung separately out
For mortal eyes to see that care to look
The one who did it sat down and wrote a book
On how he did it. It took him about
As long to write the book as to do the deed
But he said, "It's things like this we mostly need."
And the angels approved but the devils screamed with laughter,
For they knew exactly what would follow after.

For somehow he managed entirely to omit
The most important facts in accomplishing it,
Where he got the ladder to reach the stars
And how he lighted them, especially Mars,
And what he hung them on when he got them there
Eternally distant and luminous in the air.

AND TO THE YOUNG MEN

And to the young men awaiting their sacrifice
You brought water in an invisible pail
And promised them the plans would surely fail
That were written against them, recorded in the stars.
And you brought straw and padded the cold bars
Of the prison beds whereon the young men lay,
And sung to some at night and fanned by day
Those who were fevering into paradise.

But even then you did not do enough.
For you remember a boy, the silent one?
With a silent eye, who scarcely loved the sun,
And felt too keenly the winter wind's dry sough?
Well, you should have brought him cresses from a far stream
Over which nymphs and under which naiads dream.

THE NOISE THAT TIME MAKES

The noise that Time makes in passing by
Is very slight but sometimes you can hear it,
Having not necessarily to be near it,
Needing only the slightest effort to try.
Hold the receiver of a telephone
To your ear when no one is talking on the line
And what at first may sound to you like a whine
Of wind over distant wires is Time's own
Garments brushing against a windy cloud.
That same noise again though not so well
May be heard by taking a small cockle-shell
From the sand and holding it against your head.
Then you can hear Time's footsteps as they pass
Over the earth brushing the eternal grass.

Richard Eberhart

◆§ Richard (Ghormley) Eberhart was born April 5, 1904, in Austin, Minnesota. He received his B.A. from Dartmouth College, his M.A. from St. John's College (University of Cambridge), and studied at the Harvard Graduate School. At twenty-six he tutored the son of the King of Siam when the ruler came to America for an eye operation. He later taught English at St. Mark's School in Southborough, Massachusetts, for nine years. During World War II he served in the Navy as aerial gunnery instructor and, after his discharge, managed to combine the functions of poet, teacher, and lecturer as well as manager of his wife's family business, which manufactured floor polishes. Between poems he wrote *Helpful Hints to Homemakers,* a pamphlet in praise of Butcher's Wax.

Eberhart's first volume, *A Bravery of Earth* (1930), appeared in his twenty-sixth year. Since that time he has published nine books of poetry and has been the recipient of many prizes, including the Shelley Memorial Award and the Harriet Monroe Award. He taught at various universities and was Consultant in Poetry at the Library of Congress in 1959-1961.

Eberhart's poetry is marked by a loose and frequently awkward manipulation of romantic concepts which sometimes slip into specious moralizing. "I tend to philosophize about everything," he wrote, "to conclude nothing, to sit on the fence, to espouse seer-states if I can, or whirlpools of violent contemplation, the fiery centers of creative consciousness." The idiom is paradoxical: plain, often prosaic, but working its way into a rhetoric of its own, a rhetoric that attains moments of rhapsody. Eberhart seems unaware of the distance or even the difference between his high and his low passages. When he succeeds he is almost clairvoyant, direct and disturbing; when he fails he flounders in a morass of flat but entangling prose. "Eberhart lacks the power to control his material," wrote Geoffrey Moore in a review of *Collected Poems: 1930–1960.* "With the key to his success, which is his brilliant verbal gift and with which he unlocks the reader's imagination, he also locks the door in their faces."

If one cannot accept Eberhart's worst, his descents into philosophic commonplaces and bathos, one must welcome his best, which is both brilliant and Blakean. What Robert Lowell calls his "stately, jagged innocence" distinguishes such poems as "The Groundhog," "The Horse Chestnut Tree," "Seals, Terns, Time," "Rainscapes, Hydrangeas, Roses, and Singing Birds," and illuminates such opening lines as "If I could only live at the pitch that is near madness," "Now is the air made of chiming balls," "I walked out to the graveyard to see the dead," "My golden and my fierce assays," "Where are those high and haunting skies?" "The grave's seed will get some monstrous bloom," "In prison of established craze," and "My bones flew apart. They flew to the sky." Eberhart's is a spontaneous poetry which, searching for a "moral answer," elicits a series of affirmative replies.

THE HORSE CHESTNUT TREE

Boys in sporadic but tenacious droves
Come with sticks, as certainly as Autumn,
To assault the great horse chestnut tree.

There is a law governs their lawlessness.
Desire is in them for a shining amulet
And the best are those that are highest up.

They will not pick them easily from the ground.
With shrill arms they fling to the higher branches,
To hurry the work of nature for their pleasure.

I have seen them trooping down the street
Their pockets stuffed with chestnuts shucked, unshucked.
It is only evening keeps them from their wish.

Sometimes I run out in a kind of rage
To chase the boys away: I catch an arm,
Maybe, and laugh to think of being the lawgiver.

I was once such a young sprout myself
And fingered in my pocket the prize and trophy.
But still I moralize upon the day

And see that we, outlaws on God's property,
Fling out imagination beyond the skies,
Wishing a tangible good from the unknown.

And likewise death will drive us from the scene
With the great flowering world unbroken yet,
Which we held in idea, a little handful.

THE GROUNDHOG

n June, amid the golden fields,
saw a groundhog lying dead.
ead lay he; my senses shook,
nd mind outshot our naked frailty.
There lowly in the vigorous summer
is form began its senseless change,
nd made my senses waver dim
eeing nature ferocious in him.
nspecting close his maggots' might
nd seething cauldron of his being,
alf with loathing, half with a strange love,
poked him with an angry stick.
he fever rose, became a flame
nd Vigour circumscribed the skies,
mmense energy in the sun,
nd through my frame a sunless trembling.
y stick had done nor good nor harm.
hen stood I silent in the day
atching the object, as before;
nd kept my reverence for knowledge
rying for control, to be still,
To quell the passion of the blood;
Until I had bent down on my knees
Praying for joy in the sight of decay.
And so I left; and I returned
In Autumn strict of eye, to see
The sap gone out of the groundhog,
But the bony sodden hulk remained.
But the year had lost its meaning,
And in intellectual chains
I lost both love and loathing,
Mured up in the wall of wisdom.
Another summer took the fields again
Massive and burning, full of life,
But when I chanced upon the spot
There was only a little hair left,
And bones bleaching in the sunlight
Beautiful as architecture;
I watched them like a geometer,
And cut a walking stick from a birch.
It has been three years, now.
There is no sign of the groundhog.
I stood there in the whirling summer,
My hand capped a withered heart,

And thought of China and of Greece,
Of Alexander in his tent;
Of Montaigne in his tower,
Of Saint Theresa in her wild lament.

SEALS, TERNS, TIME

The seals at play off Western Isle
In the loose flowing of the summer tide
And burden of our strange estate—

Resting on the oar and lolling on the sea,
I saw their curious images,
Hypnotic, sympathetic eyes

As the deep elapses of the soul.
O ancient blood, O blurred kind forms
That rise and peer from elemental water:

I loll upon the oar, I think upon the day,
Drawn by strong, by the animal soft bonds
Back to a dim pre-history;

While off the point of Jagged Light
In hundreds, gracefully, the fork-tailed terns
Draw swift esprits across the sky.

Their aspirations dip in mine,
The quick order of their changing spirit,
More freedom than the eye can see.

Resting lightly on the oarlocks,
Pondering, and balanced on the sea,
A gauze and spindrift of the world,

I am in compulsion hid and thwarted,
Pulled back in the mammal water,
Enticed to the release of the sky.

A NEW ENGLAND BACHELOR

My death was arranged by special plans in Heaven
And only occasioned comment by ten persons in Adams, Mass.
The best thing ever said about me
Was that I was deft at specifying trump.
I was killed by my father
And married to my mother
But born too early to know what happened to me,
And as I was an only child
I erected selfishness into a personal religion,
Sat thinking forty years saying nothing.
I observed all. I loved to drink gin,
Would not have thought to go farther
Into arcane episodes of the heavier drugs,
And, being New England, always remained sober.
However, I confess now, I was
Always afraid of women,
I don't know why, it was just the way it was,
I could never get very close to any woman.
Knowledge and intelligence allowed me
The grand rationalization of this; also, I respected
Delicacy, but would not go too far in any direction.
I thought I was a good man. I was.
I did not obstruct the state, nor religion,
But I saw through both and maintained my independence.
I kept my counsels among the learned.
My learning was more private and precious than worldly.
The world had no sense of the devious,
So my private vicissitudes were mine alone.

I say all this with a special sort of grace
For I avoided many of the pitfalls of fallen man

And while I did not have heroic size, the
Creative grandeur, nor mastership of the mind
I earned my bread by cynicism alone,
And blow you all a kiss from the tomb.

RAINSCAPES, HYDRANGEAS, ROSES, AND SINGING BIRDS

Rain thunderstorms over the Potomac, in Georgetown,
Descend blistering June to the coolest aftermath
Of birds clamant, wet roses burgeoning to open
And airplanes hungering for the skies again.

I could not call it landscape. It is too intimate.
Here the lush nature of the summer world
Reads a strength of vines into any doubt,
States nature is hale despite the canting absolute.

Call to the caterpillar in furry brevity,
To the heavy bee dramatic over the tigerlily,
To the cardinal stripped of every perfidy,
To the cocktail party glancing from the glasses

And say that rainscapes, hydrangeas, roses and
Singing birds parade a splendour of late afternoon
In June in fleshtime in the saunter of early summer.
Children propel their skyey laughter to the future.

I am the proliferation of nature,
Non-political, affirmative, tumultuous,
I am the rainscape, hydrangeas, the rose and
The singing bird and bard, triumphing tumescent

In this hour of the earthly Paradise.
Opulence is as indifferent as death itself.
I would rather be and sing this positive hour
Than groan in nightscape nightmare makeshift errors. Now

The storm is lifting and the pale, late, subservient sun
Salutes the skies with a rosy, infallible glow
Of delicate and parson-haunted ineffable benediction
As I think of my days in the earth, memory long aglow.

Robert Penn Warren

Robert Penn Warren was born April 24, 1905, in Guthrie, Todd County, Kentucky, the background of his novel, *Night Rider,* and of much of his poetry. His education was widely scattered. He received his B.A. from Vanderbilt University, where he was the youngest member of *The Fugitive* group, and his M.A. from the University of California; he held a fellowship at Yale, where he did graduate work, went to Oxford as a Rhodes Scholar, received a B. Litt. degree at twenty-five, and returned to the United States to teach at

Louisiana State University, the University of Minnesota, and the Yale Drama School. He was Poetry Consultant at the Library of Congress in 1944-45.

Although Warren is a notable novelist—*All the King's Men* (1946), a fictionalized study of the mind and times of an American demagogue, which won the Pulitzer Prize for fiction; *World Enough and Time* (1950); *Band of Angels* (1955); *The Cave* (1959)—and a provocative critic—*Coleridge's Rime of The Ancient Mariner* (1946) and, with Cleanth Brooks, *Understanding Poetry* (1938)—he is preeminently a poet.

In Warren's poetry the critical and creative impulses are fused; *Twenty-Six Poems* (1935) and *Eleven Poems on the Same Theme* (1942) are charged with intensity, a sense of terror bred by the corruption of the modern world and a sharing of its guilt. *Brother to Dragons* (1953) is a horror story in verse, centering about a brutal murder, a psychological study of evil, in which Thomas Jefferson is one of the chief speakers. *Promises* (1957), which won the Pulitzer Prize for poetry as well as the National Book award, and *You, Emperors and Others* (1960) are rich proofs of an unusual ability to join the narrative and the lyric.

A poet who makes his stories sing, Warren is at his best in a kind of rough balladry. Macabre legends, half-mad evocations, and lurid folk tales mingle with boyhood recollections, wisps and strays of memory. The manner fluctuates between tart and tender; it is by turns casually ironic and painfully violent, grim and, in the poems to his daughter, unashamedly affecting. In spite of Warren's productivity, his is not a facile poetry. On the contrary, it is complex and intricately coordinated, the reflection of experiences intensified and analyzed through the medium of a keen and disturbing sensibility.

PONDY WOODS

The buzzards over Pondy Woods
Achieve the blue tense altitudes,
Black figments that the woods release,
Obscenity in form and grace,
Drifting high through the pure sunshine
Till the sun in gold decline.

Big Jim Todd was a slick blackbuck
Laying low in the mud and muck
Of Pondy Woods when the sun went down
In gold, and the buzzards tilted down
A windless vortex to the black-gum trees
To sit along the quiet boughs,
Devout and swollen, at their ease.

By the buzzard roost Big Jim Todd
Listened for hoofs on the corduroy road
Or for the foul and sucking sound
A man's foot makes on the marshy ground.
Past midnight, when the moccasin
Slipped from the log and, trailing in
Its obscured waters, broke
The dark algae, one lean bird spoke.

"Nigger, you went this afternoon
For your Saturday spree at the Blue Goose saloon,
So you've got on your Sunday clothes,
On your big splay feet got patent-leather shoes.
But a buzzard can smell the thing you've done;
The posse will get you—run, nigger, run—
There's a fellow behind you with a big shot-gun.

Nigger, nigger, you'll sweat cold sweat
In your patent-leather shoes and Sunday clothes
When down your track the steeljacket goes
Mean and whimpering over the wheat.

"Nigger, your breed ain't metaphysical."
The buzzard coughed. His words fell
In the darkness, mystic and ambrosial.
"But we maintain our ancient rite,
Eat gods by day and prophesy by night.
We swing against the sky and wait;
You seize the hour, more passionate
Than strong, and strive with time to die—
With Time, the beaked tribe's astute ally.

"The Jew-boy died. The Syrian vulture swung
Remotely above the cross whereon he hung
From dinner-time to supper-time, and all
The people gathered there watched him until
The lean brown chest no longer stirred,
Then idly watched the slow majestic bird
That in the last sun above the twilit hill
Gleamed for a moment at the height and slid
Down the hot wind and in the darkness hid:
Nigger, regard the circumstance of breath:
'Non omnis moriar,' the poet saith."

Pedantic, the bird clacked its gray beak,
With a Tennessee accent to the classic phrase;
Jim understood, and was about to speak,
But the buzzard drooped one wing and filmed the eyes.

At dawn unto the Sabbath wheat he came,
That gave to the dew its faithless yellow flame
From kindly loam in recollection of
The fires that in the brutal rock once strove.
To the ripe wheat fields he came at dawn.
Northward the printed smoke stood quiet above
The distant cabins of Squiggtown.
A train's far whistle blew and drifted away
Coldly; lucid and thin the morning lay
Along the farms, and here no sound
Touched the sweet earth miraculously stilled.
Then down the damp and sudden wood there belled
The musical white-throated hound.

In Pondy Woods in the August drouth
Lurks fever and the cottonmouth.
And buzzards over Pondy Woods
Achieve the blue tense altitudes,

Drifting high in the pure sunshine
Till the sun in gold decline;
Then golden and hieratic through
The night their eyes burn two by two.

PRO SUA VITA

Nine months I waited in the dark beneath
Her tried heart for this precious breath,

And month by month since I left her breast
Her breath and blood I have given in waste,

Till now at length some peace she has got
That her breath and blood in me have not.

In the strictured nights of glimmering snow
The blood drives quick though breath is slow,

And through the August afternoon
Flees the breath faintly but too soon.

So blood is lost to the brutal gardens
Where the iron petal of dark frost hardens,

And breath, when the storm-black trees bowed under,
Waited the fanged astounding thunder.

Shall I say to my father then
Among the belted best of men:

"Fellow, you tupped her years ago
That tonight my boots might crunch the snow.

"And, woman, you show your son to wait
Till the breath and distraught blood abate;

"As my father began the tale of waste
When the sullen head slept on your breast,

"So the rigid hills had been forgot
In darkness, if God had wasted not."

LETTER OF A MOTHER

Under the green lamp-light her letter there
Lies among cluttered papers, rusted pens,
Books and handkerchiefs, tobacco tins.
Shuffle of feet ascends the darkened stair.

The son, defined upon the superscription,
Inherits now his cubicled domain,
And reads. Indeed, should he possess again
The loneliness of time's slow mitigation?

Or spell the name, which is himself, and say:
"By now this woman's milk is out of me.
I have a debt of flesh, assuredly,
Which score the mintage of the breath might pay. . . .

"A certain weight of cunning flesh devised
So hunger is bred in the bitter bone
To cleave about his precious skeleton
Held mortmain of her womb and merchandised

"Unto the dark: a subtile engine, propped
In the sutured head beneath the coronal seam,
Whose illegal prodigality of dream
In shaking the escheat heart is quick estopped.

"Such is the substance of this legacy:
A fragile vision fed of acrid blood,
Whose sweet process may bloom in gratitude
For the worthier gift of her mortality."

But still the flesh cries out unto the black
Void, across the plains insistently
Where rivers wash their wastage to the sea. . . .
The mother flesh that cannot summon back

The tired child it would again possess
As shall a womb more tender than her own
That builds not tissue or the little bone,
But dissolves them to itself in weariness.

HISTORY AMONG THE ROCKS

(*from "Kentucky Mountain Farm"*)

There are many ways to die
Here among the rocks in any weather:
Wind, down the eastern gap, will lie
Level along the snow, beating the cedar,
And lull the drowsy head that it blows over
To startle a crystalline, cold dream forever.

The hound's black paw will print the grass in May,
And sycamores rise down a dark ravine,
Where a creek in flood, sucking the rock and clay,
Will tumble the sycamore, the laurel, away.
Think how a body, naked and lean

And white as the splintered sycamore, would go
Tumbling and turning, hushed in the end,
With hair afloat in waters that gently bend
To ocean where the blind tides flow.

Under the shadow of ripe wheat,
By flat limestone, will coil the copperhead,
Fanged as the sunlight, hearing the reaper's feet.
But there are other ways, the lean men said:
In these autumn orchards once young men lay dead—
Gray coats, blue coats. Young men on the mountainside
Clambered, fought. Heels muddied the rocky spring.
Their reason is hard to guess, remembering
Blood on their black mustaches in moonlight,
Cold musket-barrels glittering with frost.
Their reason is hard to guess and a long time past;
The apple falls, falling in the quiet night.

LETTER FROM A COWARD TO A HERO

What did the day bring?
The sharp fragment,
The shard,
The promise half-meant,
The impaired thing,
At dusk the hard word,
Good action by good will marred . . .
All
In the trampled stall:

I think you deserved better;
Therefore I am writing you this letter.

The scenes of childhood were splendid,
And the light that there attended,
But is rescinded:
The cedar,
The lichened rocks,
The thicket where I saw the fox,
And where I swam, the river.
These things are hard
To reconstruct:
The word
Is memory's gelded usufruct.
But piety is simple,
And should be ample.

Though late at night we have talked,
I cannot see what ways your feet in childhood walked.
In what purlieus was courage early caulked?

Guns blaze in autumn and
The quail falls and

Empires collide with a bang
That shakes the pictures where they hang
And democracy shows signs of dry rot
And Dives has and Lazarus not
And the time is out of joint:
But a good pointer holds the point
And is not gun-shy;
But I
Am gun-shy.

Though young, I do not like loud noise:
The sudden backfire,
The catcall of boys,
Drums beating for
The big war,
Or clocks that tick at night, and will not stop.
If you ever lose your compass and map
Or a mouse gets in the wall,
For sleep try love or veronal,
Though some prefer, I know, philology.
Does the airman scream in the flaming trajectory?

You have been strong in love and hate.
Disaster owns less speed than you have got,
But he will cut across the back lot
To lurk and lie in wait.
Admired of children, gathered for their games,
Disaster, like the dandelion, blooms,
And the delicate film is fanned
To seed the shaven lawn.
Rarely, you've been unmanned;
I have not seen your courage put to pawn.

At the blind hour of unaided grief,
Of addition and subtraction,
Of compromise,
Of the smoky lecher, the thief,
Of regretted action,
At the hour to close the eyes,
At the hour when lights go out in the houses . . .
Then wind rouses
The kildees from their sodden ground:
Their commentary is part of the wind's sound.
What is that other sound,
Surf or distant cannonade?
You are what you are without our aid.
No doubt, when corridors are dumb
And the bed is made,
It is your custom to recline,
Clutching between the forefinger and thumb
Honor, for death shy valentine.

THE OWL

Here was the sound of water falling only,
Which is not sound but silence musical
Tumbling forever down the gorge's wall.
Like late milkweed that blooms beside the lonely
And sunlit stone, peace bloomed all afternoon.
Where time is not is peace; and here the shadow,
That crept to him across the Western meadow
And climbed the hill to mark the dropping sun,
Seemed held a space, washed downward by the water
Whose music flowed against the flow of time.
It could not be. Dark fell along the stream,
And like a child grown suddenly afraid,
With shaking knees, hands bloody on the stone,
Toward the upland gleaming fields he fled.
Light burned against their rim, was quickly gone.

Later he would remember this, and start.
And once or twice again his tough old heart
Knew sickness that the rabbit's heart must know,
When star by star the great wings float,
And down the moonlit track below
Their mortal silken shadow sweeps the snow.
O scaled bent claw, infatuate deep throat!

LETTER TO A FRIEND

Our eyes have viewed the burnished vineyards where
No leaf falls, and the grape, unripening, ripes.
It was a dream without fruition as
Without our terror. We have seen it;

And seen the ever-rounding vaulty-structured
Ocean moveless, and the mortised keel
Unmoving o'er the sunlit lichened wave.
That voyage, then each to each we said, had rendered

Courage superfluous, hope a burden.
But living still, we live by them, and only
Thus, or thus, stuttering, eke them out,
Our huddled alms to crammed Necessity.

Fears rise, old wranglers out of sleep, and go:
The caterpillar knows its leaf, the mole
Its hummock, who has known his heart, or knows
The trigger of this action, set and sprung?

In this, the time of toads' engendering,
I write to you, to you unfrighted yet
Before the blunt experiment of Time.
Your triumph is not commensurate with stone.

AUBADE FOR HOPE

Dawn: and foot on the cold stair treading or
Thump of wood on the unswept hearth-stone is
Comment on the margin of consciousness,
A dirty thumb-smear by the printed page.

Thumb-smear: nay other, for the blessed light
Acclaimèd thus, as a ducal progress by
The scared cur, wakes them who wallowed in
The unaimed faceless appetite of dream.

All night the ice sought out the rotten bough:
In sleep they heard. And now they stir, as east
Beyond the formal gleam of landscape sun
Has struck the senatorial hooded hill.

Light; the groaning stair; the match aflame;
The negro woman's hand, horned gray with cold,
That lit the wood; a child's eyes sullen
In the August street . . . I name some things that shall,

As voices speaking from a farther room,
Muffled, bespeak us yet for time and hope:
For Hope that like a blockhead grandam ever
Above the ash and spittle croaks and leans.

BEARDED OAKS

The oaks, how subtle and marine,
Bearded, and all the layered light
Above them swims; and thus the scene,
Recessed, awaits the positive night.

So, waiting, we in the grass now lie
Beneath the languorous tread of light:
The grasses, kelp-like, satisfy
The nameless motions of the air.

Upon the floor of light, and time,
Unmurmuring, of polyp made,
We rest; we are, as light withdraws,
Twin atolls on a shelf of shade.

Ages to our construction went,
Dim architecture, hour by hour:
And violence, forgot now, lent
The present stillness all its power.

The storm of noon above us rolled,
Of light the fury, furious gold,
The long drag troubling us, the depth:
Dark is unrocking, unrippling, still.

Passion and slaughter, ruth, decay
Descend, minutely whispering down,
Silted through swaying streams, to lay
Foundation for our voicelessness.

All our debate is voiceless here,
As all our rage, the rage of stone;
If hope is hopeless, then fearless fear,
And history is thus undone.

Our feet once wrought the hollow street
With echo when the lamps were dead
At windows; once our headlight glare
Disturbed the doe that, leaping, fled.

I do not love you less that now
The caged heart makes iron stroke,
Or less that all that light once gave
The graduate dark should now revoke.

We live in time so little time
And we learn all so painfully,
That we may spare this hour's term
To practice for eternity.

PURSUIT

The hunckback on the corner, with gum and shoelaces,
Has his own wisdom and pleasures, and may not be lured
To divulge them to you, for he has merely endured
Your appeal for his sympathy and your kind purchases;
And wears infirmity but as the general who turns
Apart, in his famous old greatcoat there on the hill
At dusk when the rapture and cannonade are still,
To muse withdrawn from the dead, from his gorgeous subalterns;
Or stares from the thicket of his familiar pain, like a fawn
That meets you a moment, wheels, in imperious innocence is gone.

Go to the clinic. Wait in the outer room
Where like an old possum the snag-nailed hand will hump
On its knee in murderous patience, and the pomp
Of pain swells like the Indies, or a plum.
And there you will stand, as on the Roman hill,
Stunned by each withdrawn gaze and severe shape,
The first barbarian victor stood to gape
At the sacrificial fathers, white-robed, still;
And even the feverish old Jew stares stern with authority
Till you feel like one who has come too late, or improperly clothed, to a party.

The doctor will take you now. He is burly and clean;
Listening, like lover or worshiper, bends at your heart;
But cannot make out just what it tries to impart;
So smiles; says you simply need a change of scene.
Of scene, of solace: therefore Florida,
Where Ponce de Leon clanked among the lilies,
Where white sails skit on blue and cavort like fillies,
And the shoulder gleams in the moonlit corridor.
A change of love: if love is a groping Godward, though blind,
No matter what crevice, cranny, chink, bright in dark, the pale tentacle find.

In Florida consider the flamingo,
Its color passion but its neck a question;
Consider even that girl the other guests shun
On beach, at bar, in bed, for she may know
The secret you are seeking, after all;
Or the child you humbly sit by, excited and curly,
That screams on the shore at the sea's sunlit hurlyburly,
Till the mother calls its name, toward nightfall.
Till you sit alone: in the dire meridians, off Ireland, in fury
Of spume-tooth and dawnless sea-heave, salt rimes the lookout's devout eye.

Till you sit alone—which is the beginning of error—
Behind you the music and the lights of the great hotel:
Solution, perhaps, is public, despair personal,
But history held to your breath clouds like a mirror.
There are many states, and towns in them, and faces,

But meanwhile, the little old lady in black, by the wall,
Who admires all the dancers, and tells you how just last fall
Her husband died in Ohio, and damp mists her glasses;
She blinks and croaks, like a toad or a Norn, in the horrible light,
And rattles her crutch, which may put forth a small bloom, perhaps white.

WHEN THE CENTURY DRAGGED

When the century dragged, like a great wheel stuck at dead center;
When the wind that had hurled us our half-century sagged now,
And only velleity of air somewhat snidely nagged now,
With no certain commitment to compass, or quarter: you chose to enter.

You enter an age when the neurotic clock-tick
Of midnight competes with the heart's pulsed assurance of power.
You have entered our world at scarcely its finest hour,
And smile now life's gold Apollonian smile at a sick dialectic.

You enter at the hour when the dog returns to his vomit,
And fear's moonflower spreads, white as girl-thigh, in dusk of compromise;
When posing for pictures, arms linked, the same smile in their eyes,
Good and Evil, to iron out all differences, stage their meeting at summit.

You come in the year when promises are broken,
And petal fears the late, as fruit the early frost-fall;
When the young expect little, and old endure total recall,
But discover no logic to justify what they had taken, or forsaken.

But to take and forsake now you're here, and the heart will compress
Like stone when we see that rosy heel learn,
With its first step, the apocalyptic power to spurn
Us, and our works and days, and onward, prevailing, pass

To pause, in high pride of undisillusioned manhood,
At the gap that gives on the new century, and land,
And with calm heart and level eye command
That dawning perspective and possibility of human good.

Stanley Kunitz

⁂ Stanley (Jasspon) Kunitz was born July 29, 1905, in Worcester, Massachusetts. Because of a partner's misappropriation of funds, his father had committed suicide before his son was born, and his mother opened a dry-goods store to repay the family debts. Educated in the Worcester High School, where he edited the school magazine, he was graduated *summa cum laude* from Harvard University, where he had been awarded the Garrison Medal for Poetry.

In his mid-twenties he was co-editor with Howard Haycraft of a series of biographical books beginning with *British Authors Before 1800* and *American Au-*

thors: 1600-1900. His career as editor was interrupted by World War II when he entered the Army as a private and was discharged as a staff sergeant in 1945. At forty he became a teacher; he taught at Bennington College, conducted summer seminars, and organized literary workshops at various centers in New York.

A poet of singular reticence, Kunitz is so modest that he does not make any reference to himself in *Twentieth Century Authors,* which he edited and which includes scores of writers far less noteworthy than he. Although his fellow-poets unreservedly praised his *Intellectual Things* (1930) and *Passport to the War* (1944), he remained not only neglected but rejected. Five publishers declined to publish his *Selected Poems: 1928-1958,* which won the Pulitzer Prize in 1959. In the same year Kunitz was widely acclaimed. Besides the Pulitzer Prize, the poet who had been passed by also received a grant from the National Institute of Arts and Letters and a two-year grant from the Ford Foundation.

At first glance Kunitz's poetry seems formal, scholastic, and almost too carefully polished. "At times," wrote John Ciardi, "one must labor to follow the subtleties of his perception. The point is that the labor will not be in vain." For the most part, however, little labor is required to appreciate the skill and suggestiveness of his achievement. "The Thief" is as straightforward in telling as a documentary which is both graphic and wry; "End of Summer" and "When the Light Falls" are simple, sensuous lyrics; it needs only a little imagination to sound the metaphysical depths of "The Science of the Night." This is a poetry which is both dramatic and meditative, classical and, at the same time, experimental.

THE SCIENCE OF THE NIGHT

I touch you in the night, whose gift was you,
My careless sprawler,
And I touch you cold, unstirring, star-bemused,
That are become the land of your self-strangeness.
What long seduction of the bone has led you
Down the imploring roads I cannot take
Into the arms of ghosts I never knew,
Leaving my manhood on a rumpled field
To guard you where you lie so deep
In absent-mindedness,
Caught in the calcium snows of sleep?

And even should I track you to your birth
Through all the cities of your mortal trial,
As in my jealous thought I try to do,
You would escape me—from the brink of earth
Take off to where the lawless auroras run,
You with your wild and metaphysic heart.
My touch is on you, who are light-years gone.

We are not souls but systems, and we mov
In clouds of our unknowing
like great nebulae
Our very motives swirl and have their star
With father lion and with mother crab.

Dreamer, my own lost rib,
Whose planetary dust is blowing
Past archipelagoes of myth and light,
What far Magellans are you mistress of
To whom you speed the pleasure of you art?
As through a glass that magnifies my loss
I see the lines of your spectrum shifting rec
The universe expanding, thinning out,
Our worlds flying, oh flying, fast apart.

From hooded powers and from abstrac flight
I summon you, your person and your prid
Fall to me now from outer space,
Still fastened desperately to my side;
Through gulfs of streaming air
Bring me the mornings of the milky ways
Down to my threshold in your drowsy eye
And by virtue of your honeyed word

Restore the liquid language of the moon,
That in gold mines of secrecy you delve.
Awake!
My whirling hands stay at the noon,
Each cell within my body holds a heart
And all my hearts in unison strike twelve.

WHEN THE LIGHT FALLS

When the light falls, it falls on her
In whose rose-gilded chamber
A music strained through mind
Turns everything to measure.

The light that seeks her out
Finds answering light within,
And the two join hands and dance
On either side of her skin.

The lily and the swan
Attend her whiter pride,
While the courtly laurel kneels
To kiss his mantling bride.

Under each cherry-bough
She spreads her silken cloths
At the rumor of a wind,
To gather up her deaths,

For the petals of her heart
Are shaken in a night,
Whose ceremonial art
Is dying into light.

END OF SUMMER

An agitation of the air,
A perturbation of the light
Admonished me the unloved year
Would turn on its hinge that night.

I stood in the disenchanted field
Amid the stubble and the stones,
Amazed, while a small worm lisped to me
The song of my marrow-bones.

Blue poured into summer blue,
A hawk broke from his cloudless tower,
The roof of the silo blazed, and I knew
That part of my life was over.

Already the iron door of the north
Clangs open: birds, leaves, snows
Order their populations forth,
And a cruel wind blows.

THE THIEF

In a Roman tram, where the famous Roman mob,
Wrung from the bowels of the hippodrome,
Mauled into shape its many-elbowed god
To fight for exit through its civil wars,
Somebody Roman picked my pocket clean.
A pagan and a Christian curse on him!
Somebody Roman, may he find tonight
In the street of the serpents or the lion's mouth,
Strewn on a wine-soaked board,
More than he reached for, more than cash,
Green trumpeters, for whom the legions march
Through solid stone. (Meanwhile the Carthaginians
Play redskins in the ambush of the sea
To whom must be meted out the standard destruction:
It is a heavy responsibility.)
Let the *ladrone* sneer
As the leathered fold yields him my haunt of years,
The papers of a life I wanted lost,
Memos, addresses, the snapshot of a child,
To plague him through his alley nights until
He begs for mercy for the thing well-robbed.
Worlds in my pocket older than his own,
May they erupt on him like hissing gold,
Tooth of the pythoness, chimaera's scales,
Stones of the temple and Isaiah's beard—
Toss him, sweet furies, from Tarpeia's Rock!

More even than my purse,
And that's no laughing matter, it is my pride
That has been hurt: a fine Italian hand,
With its mimosa touch, has made me feel
Blind-skinned, indelicate, a fool Americano
Touring a culture like a grand museum,
People and statues interchangeable shows,
Perception blunted as one's syntax fails.

Why am I here? Some thirty years ago
A set of lantern slides I saw at school
Of these antiquities gave me an image
Of the rare serene that brimmed my eyes,
For nothing pleased me then in my legacy;
But the past that tempted me, the frozen pure,
Was a pedagogic lie. All's motion here,
And motion like emotion is impure,
A flower flawed by mutability,
Religion by its ruins, and yet thereby
More lovely and more graced, perhaps
More true. Still, still, the chariot wheels
Turn, the assassin motorcyclists charge,
Wolves prowl in the streets under arcades of bells,
Tiberius grovels through his dungeon halls
Dreaming of boy-sized fishes in his bath;
Behind the balcony of the Cardinal's palace,
Smelling the laureled Mamertine blood,
A baldpate awaits his rhetorical cue,
And the clouds drift
Through a triumph of broken columns.

Pick-pocket, pick-thank music plucks the strings
For the rag-madonna with perdurable babe
Most dolorously hallowing the square
Where Caesar walks three steps to meet Bernini,
Whose sumptuous art runs wild
From gate to gate, pausing in tiptoe-joy
Only to light a torch of fountains, to set
His tritons dancing, or at a blest façade
To cast up from his wrist a flight of angels,
Volute on volute, wing on climbing wing.
In the middle of my life I heard the waters playing.

Mater Cloaca, feast thee well, I pray,
On what has been subtracted from my fate—
Ten days of lectures, thirty days abroad:
In this excess that's Rome I'll not mope long,
Wearing my heart less Roman than baroque,
Though damn it all! I wish I'd lived in style,
Jogged in *carrozze* round and round the town,
Guzzled Spumante by the bucketful,
Bought wagons of daffodils to please my dear.
Now that I face the moment and the loss,
Driven to language on the Ides of March
Here in my blistered room
Where the wind flaps my ceiling like a sail
(A miracle, no doubt, to be left at that!)
I recognize the gods' capricious hand
And write this poem for money, rage, and love.

Phyllis McGinley

⤙§ Phyllis McGinley was born March 21, 1905, in Ontario, Oregon. "The nearest town, about six miles away," she recalls, "looked like a scene from a TV western—muddy Main Street, hitching posts, false-fronted stores. My brother and I rode ponies to school about three miles from home." Her father died when she was twelve, and her mother took the family to her native Ogden, Utah, where her daughter attended the Convent of the Sacred Heart and the University of Utah. While still in college, Phyllis McGinley began selling poetry to national publications and, after teaching for a year, came to New York in 1928. She supported herself teaching high school English in New Rochelle, working for an advertising agency, and writing at night. When *The New Yorker* began publishing her poems she moved to Manhattan, married, and wrote regularly, painstakingly, and profitably.

By 1960 she was the author of twenty volumes of prose and verse, including several juveniles, and the recipient of various awards and trophies. *Times Three*

(1960), her verse selected from three decades, carried an appreciative foreword by W. H. Auden, who, like Miss McGinley, had helped break down the once rigid line between light verse and serious poetry. It received the Pulitzer Prize in 1961 and was an unusually popular award.

Miss McGinley's subject matter, like her style, is larger than is apparent at first glance; it is compact with ironic sidelights and sharp appraisals. Her attitude is that of amused resignation, a tolerance of man's foibles and a prodigal interest in the fluctuations of emotional fashions. She breaks through the ambiguous barrier between playful verse and pure poetry with such penetrations as the mock-serious address to a dentist in "Intimations of Mortality," the satirical comments on pulpit publicity in "The Day After Sunday," the summoning of a period of depression and the picture of a threadbare time in "Trinity Place," and the grim jocularity of "The Theology of Jonathan Edwards," with its appropriately punning finale.

In an age preoccupied with the debased and distorted, Phyllis McGinley concerns herself with the shapes of what is everyone's occupational commonplace. A feminine wit—she has been characterized as both kitten and tiger—she is almost abnormally normal. In contrast to those who are at ease only with the bizarre, she is at home with what others have rejected as too familiar and too unimportant for poetry.

THE DAY AFTER SUNDAY

Always on Monday, God's in the morning papers,
    His Name is a headline, His Works are rumored abroad.
Having been praised by men who are movers and shapers,
    From prominent Sunday pulpits, newsworthy is God.

On page 27, just opposite Fashion Trends,
    One reads at a glance how He scolded the Baptist a little,
Was firm with the Catholics, practical with the Friends,
    To Unitarians pleasantly noncommittal.

In print are His numerous aspects, too: God smiling,
    God vexed, God thunderous, God whose mansions are pearl,
Political God, God frugal, God reconciling
    Himself with science, God guiding the Camp Fire Girl.

Always on Monday morning the press reports
    God as revealed to His vicars in various guises—
Benevolent, stormy, patient, or out of sorts.
    God knows which God is the God God recognizes.

INTIMATIONS OF MORTALITY

On being told by the dentist that "this will be over soon"

Indeed, it will soon be over, I shall be done
    With the querulous drill, the forceps, the clove-smelling cotton.
I can go forth into fresher air, into sun,
    This narrow anguish forgotten.

In twenty minutes or forty or half an hour,
  I shall be easy, and proud of my hard-got gold.
But your apple of comfort is eaten by worms, and sour.
  Your consolation is cold.

This will not last, and the day will be pleasant after.
  I'll dine tonight with a witty and favorite friend.
No doubt tomorrow I shall rinse my mouth with laughter.
  And also that will end.

The handful of time that I am charily granted
  Will likewise pass, to oblivion duly apprenticed.
Summer will blossom and autumn be faintly enchanted.
  Then time for the grave, or the dentist.

Because you are shrewd, my man, and your hand is clever,
  You must not believe your words have a charm to spell me.
There was never a half of an hour that lasted forever.
  Be quiet. You need not tell me.

THE THEOLOGY OF JONATHAN EDWARDS

Whenever Mr. Edwards spake
  In church about Damnation,
The very benches used to quake
  For awful agitation.

Good men would pale and roll their eyes
  While sinners rent their garments
To hear him so anatomize
  Hell's orgiastic torments,

The blood, the flames, the agonies
  In store for frail or flighty
New Englanders who did not please
  A whimsical Almighty.

Times were considered out of tune
  When half a dozen nervous
Female parishioners did not swoon
  At every Sunday service;

And, if they had been taught aright,
  Small children, carried bedwards,
Would shudder lest they meet that night
  The God of Mr. Edwards.

Abraham's God, the Wrathful One,
  Intolerant of error—
Not God the Father or the Son
  But God the Holy Terror.

TRINITY PLACE

The pigeons that peck at the grass in Trinity Churchyard
  Are pompous as bankers. They walk with an air, they preen
Their prosperous feathers. They smugly regard their beauty.
  They are plump, they are sleek. It is only the men who are lean.

The pigeons scan with disfavor the men who sit there,
  Listless in sun or shade. The pigeons sidle
Between the gravestones with shrewd, industrious motions.
  The pigeons are busy. It is only the men who are idle.

The pigeons sharpen their beaks on the stones, and they waddle
  In dignified search of their proper, their daily bread.
Their eyes are small with contempt for the men on the benches.
  It is only the men who are hungry. The pigeons are fed.

Theodore Roethke

Theodore Roethke was born May 25, 1908, in Saginaw, Michigan. He was educated at the University of Michigan and Harvard University and taught at Lafayette College, Pennsylvania State University—he was also varsity tennis coach at both institutions—Bennington College, and the University of Washington. Since his first book, *Open House* (1941), he has been the recipient of almost all the honors a poet can hope to win, including two Guggenheim Fellowships, an award by the American Academy of Arts and Letters, and the Pulitzer prize for *The Waking* (1953). In 1959 his collected verse, *Words for the Wind* brought him three more rewards: The Edna St. Vincent Millay Award, the Bollingen Prize, and the National Book Award.

Roethke's range is astonishing. He summons childhood with rhymes as lightly capering as Lear's and metaphors as wildly fanciful and curiously dissolving as the Surrealists'; he can write with equal persuasion as a man discovering the innocence and majesty of love and as a meditative old woman watching the wind ruffle the backs of small birds. His first indebtednesses (Eliot, Pound, and a touch of Thomas) are not only apparent but casually acknowledged: "I take this cadence from a man called Yeats." Nevertheless, Roethke, having absorbed and transmuted his influences, is completely himself in a variety of packed lyrics, long soliloquies, and nonsense verses. His inventiveness allows him to handle horror as easily as humor. "The ferocity of Roethke's imagination," wrote Stanley Kunitz, "makes most contemporary poetry seem pale and tepid by contrast." "Many people," concluded W. H. Auden, "have the experience of feeling physically soiled and humiliated by life; some quickly put it out of their minds, others gloat narcistically on its unimportant details; but both to remember and to transform its humiliation into something beautiful, as Mr. Roethke does, is rare."

Roethke's acts of transformation are as remarkable in his few failures as his simple successes. Particularly brilliant are the later poems, such as "Meditation at Oyster River," where, in rolling Whitmanic rhythms, he has tried to catch the convoluted movement of the mind itself. Whether Roethke expresses himself in a searching soliloquy, a symbolic song, a solemn villanelle, or a sudden abstraction, he achieves a speaking music that, in its very originality, is as suggestive as it is provocative.

I KNEW A WOMAN

I knew a woman, lovely in her bones,
When small birds sighed, she would sigh back at them;
Ah, when she moved, she moved more ways than one:
The shapes a bright container can contain!
Of her choice virtues only gods should speak,
Or English poets who grew up on Greek
(I'd have them sing in chorus, cheek to cheek).

How well her wishes went! She stroked my chin,
She taught me Turn, and Counter-turn, and Stand;

She taught me Touch, that undulant white skin;
I nibbled meekly from her proffered hand;
She was the sickle; I, poor I, the rake,
Coming behind her for her pretty sake
(But what prodigious mowing we did make).

Love likes a gander, and adores a goose:
Her full lips pursed, the errant note to seize;
She played it quick, she played it light and loose;
My eyes, they dazzled at her flowing knees;
Her several parts could keep a pure repose,
Or one hip quiver with a mobile nose
(She moved in circles, and those circles moved).

Let seed be grass, and grass turn into hay:
I'm martyr to a motion not my own;
What's freedom for? To know eternity.
I swear she cast a shadow white as stone.
But who would count eternity in days?
These old bones live to learn her wanton ways:
(I measure time by how a body sways).

ELEGY FOR JANE

(*My student, thrown by a horse*)

I remember the neckcurls, limp and damp as tendrils,
And her quick look, a sidelong pickerel smile;
And how, once startled into talk, the light syllables leaped
  for her,
And she balanced in the delight of her thought,
A wren, happy, tail in the wind,
Her song trembling the twigs and small branches,
The shade sang with her;
The leaves, their whispers turned to kissing;
And the mould sang in the bleached valleys under the rose.

Oh, when she was sad, she cast herself down into such a pure
  depth,
Even a father could not find her:
Scraping her cheek against straw;
Stirring the clearest water.

My sparrow, you are not here,
Waiting like a fern, making a spiney shadow.
The sides of wet stones cannot console me,
Nor the moss, wound with the last light.

If only I could nudge you from this sleep,
My maimed darling, my skittery pigeon.
Over this damp grave I speak the words of my love:
I, with no rights in this matter,
Neither father nor lover.

THE WAKING

I wake to sleep, and take my waking slow.
I feel my fate in what I cannot fear.
I learn by going where I have to go.

We think by feeling. What is there to know?
I hear my being dance from ear to ear.
I wake to sleep, and take my waking slow.

Of those so close beside me, which are you?
God bless the Ground! I shall walk softly there,
And learn by going where I have to go.

Light takes the Tree; but who can tell us how?
The lowly worm climbs up a winding stair;
I wake to sleep, and take my waking slow.

Great Nature has another thing to do
To you and me; so take the lively air,
And, lovely, learn by going where to go.

This shaking keeps me steady. I should know.
What falls away is always. And is near.
I wake to sleep, and take my waking slow.
I learn by going where I have to go.

FOUR FOR SIR JOHN DAVIES

1 *The Dance*

Is that dance slowing in the mind of man
That made him think the universe could hum?
The great wheel turns its axle when it can;
need a place to sing, and dancing-room,
And I have made a promise to my ears
'll sing and whistle romping with the bears.

For they are all my friends: I saw one slide
Down a steep hillside on a cake of ice,—
Or was that in a book? I think with pride:
A caged bear rarely does the same thing twice
In the same way: O watch his body sway!—
This animal remembering to be gay.

tried to fling my shadow at the moon,
The while my blood leaped with a wordless song.
Though dancing needs a master, I had none
To teach my toes to listen to my tongue.
But what I learned there, dancing all alone,
Was not the joyless motion of a stone.

I take this cadence from a man named Yeats;
I take it, and I give it back again:
For other tunes and other wanton beats
Have tossed my heart and fiddled through my brain.
Yes, I was dancing-mad, and how
That came to be the bears and Yeats would know.

2 *The Partner*

Between such animal and human heat
I find myself perplexed. What is desire?—
The impulse to make someone else complete?
That woman would set sodden straw on fire.
Was I the servant of a sovereign wish,
Or ladle rattling in an empty dish?

We played a measure with commingled feet:
The lively dead had taught us to be fond.
Who can embrace the body of his fate?
Light altered light along the living ground.
She kissed me close, and then did something else.
My marrow beat as wildly as my pulse.

I'd say it to my horse: we live beyond
Our outer skin. Who's whistling up my sleeve?
I see a heron prancing in his pond;
I know a dance the elephants believe.
The living all assemble! What's the cue?—
Do what the clumsy partner wants to do!

Things loll and loiter. Who condones the lost?
This joy outleaps the dog. Who cares? Who cares?
I gave her kisses back, and woke a ghost.
O what lewd music crept into our ears!
The body and the soul know how to play
In that dark world where gods have lost their way.

3 *The Wraith*

Incomprehensible gaiety and dread
Attended what we did. Behind, before,
Lay all the lonely pastures of the dead;

The spirit and the flesh cried out for more.
We two, together, on a darkening day
Took arms against our own obscurity.

Did each become the other in that play?
She laughed me out, and then she laughed
me in;
In the deep middle of ourselves we lay;
When glory failed, we danced upon a pin.
The valley rocked beneath the granite hill;
Our souls looked forth, and the great day
stood still.

There was a body, and it cast a spell,—
God pity those but wanton to the knees,—
The flesh can make the spirit visible;
We woke to find the moonlight on our toes.
In the rich weather of a dappled wood
We played with dark and light as children
should.

What shape leaped forward at the sensual
cry?—
Sea-beast or bird flung toward the ravaged
shore?
Did space shake off an angel with a sigh?
We rose to meet the moon, and saw no more.
It was and was not she, a shape alone,
Impaled on light, and whirling slowly down.

4 *The Vigil*

Dante attained the purgatorial hill,
Trembled at hidden virtue without flaw,
Shook with a mighty power beyond his will,—
Did Beatrice deny what Dante saw?
All lovers live by longing, and endure:
Summon a vision and declare it pure.

Though everything's astonishment at last,
Who leaps to heaven at a single bound?
The links were soft between us; still, we
kissed;
We undid chaos to a curious sound:
The waves broke easy, cried to me in white;
Her look was morning in the dying light.

The visible obscures. But who knows when?
Things have their thought: they are the
shards of me;
I thought that once, and thought comes
round again;
Rapt, we leaned forth with what we could
not see.
We danced to shining; mocked before the
black
And shapeless night that made no answer
back.

The world is for the living. Who are they?
We dared the dark to reach the white and
warm.
She was the wind when wind was in my way;
Alive at noon, I perished in her form.
Who rise from flesh to spirit know the fall:
The word outleaps the world, and light is all.

IN A DARK TIME

I

In a dark time, the eye begins to see:
I meet my shadow in the deepening shade;
I hear my echo in the echoing wood,
A lord of nature weeping to a tree.
I live between the heron and the wren,
Beasts of the hill and serpents of the den.

II

What's madness but nobility of soul
At odds with circumstance? The day's on
fire!
I know the purity of pure despair,
My shadow pinned against a sweating wall.
That place among the rocks—is it a cave
Or winding path? The edge is what I have.

III

A steady storm of correspondences!—
A night flowing with birds, a ragged moon
And in broad day the midnight come again
A man goes far to find out what he is—
Death of the self in a long tearless night,
All natural shapes blazing unnatural light.

IV

Dark, dark my light, and darker my desire
My soul, like some heat-maddened summer
fly,
Keeps buzzing at the sill. Which I is *I*?
A fallen man, I climb out of my fear.
The mind enters itself, and God the mind,
And one is One, free in the tearing wind.

LIGHT LISTENED

O what could be more nice
Than her ways with a man?
She kissed me more than twice
Once we were left alone.
Who'd look when he could feel?
She'd more sides than a seal.

The close air faintly stirred.
Light deepened to a bell,
The love-beat of a bird.
She kept her body still
And watched the weather flow.
We live by what we do.

All's known, all, all around:
The shape of things to be;
A green thing loves the green
And loves the living ground.
The deep shade gathers night;
She changed with changing light.

We met to leave again
The time we broke from time;
A cold air brought its rain,
The singing of a stem.
She sang a final song;
Light listened when she sang.

MEDITATION AT OYSTER RIVER

I

Over the low, barnacled, elephant-colored rocks
Come the first tide ripples, moving, almost without sound, toward me,
Running along the narrow furrows of the shore, the rows of dead clamshells;
Then a runnel behind me, creeping closer,
Alive with tiny striped fish, and young crabs climbing in and out of the water.

No sound from the bay. No violence.
Even the gulls quiet on the far rocks,
Silent, in the deepening light,
Their cat-mewing over,
Their child-whimpering.

At last one long undulant ripple,
Blue black from where I am sitting,
Makes almost a wave over a barrier of small stones,
Slapping lightly against a sunken log.
I dabble my toes in the brackish foam sliding forward,
Then retire to a rock higher up on the cliffside.

The wind slackens, light as a moth fanning a stone—
A twilight wind, light as a child's breath,
Turning not a leaf, not a ripple.

The dew revives on the beach grass;
The salt-soaked wood of a fire crackles;
A fish raven turns on its perch (a dead tree in the river mouth),
Its wings catching a last glint of the reflected sunlight.

II

The self persists like a dying star,
In sleep, afraid. Death's face rises afresh,
Among the shy beasts—the deer at the salt lick,

The doe, with its sloped shoulders, loping across the highway,
The young snake, poised in green leaves, waiting for its fly,
The hummingbird, whirring from quince blossom to morning-glory—
With these I would be.

And with water: the waves coming forward without cessation,
The waves, altered by sandbars, beds of kelp, miscellaneous driftwood,
Topped by cross-winds, tugged at by sinuous undercurrents,
The tide rustling in, sliding between the ridges of stone,
The tongues of water creeping in quietly.

III

In this hour,
In this first heaven of knowing,
The flesh takes on the pure poise of the spirit,
Acquires, for a time, the sandpiper's insouciance,
The hummingbird's surety, the kingfisher's cunning.

I shift on my rock, and I think:
Of the first trembling of a Michigan brook in April,
Over a lip of stone, the tiny rivulet;
And that wrist-thick cascade tumbling from a cleft rock,
Its spray holding a double rainbow in early morning,
Small enough to be taken in, embraced, by two arms;
Or the Tittabawasee, in the time between winter and spring,
When the ice melts along the edges in early afternoon
And the mid-channel begins cracking and heaving from the pressure beneath,
The ice piling high against the ironbound spiles,
Gleaming, freezing hard again, creaking at midnight,
And I long for the blast of dynamite,
The sudden sucking roar as the culvert loosens its debris of branches and sticks—
Welter of tin cans, pails, old bird's nests, a child's shoe riding a log—
As the piled ice breaks away from the battered spiles
And the whole river begins to move forward, its bridges shaking.

IV

Now, in this waning of light,
I rock with the motion of morning;
In the cradle of all that is,
I'm lulled into half sleep
By the lapping of waves,
The cries of the sandpiper.

Water's my will and my way,
And the spirit runs, intermittently,
In and out of the small waves,
Runs with the intrepid shore birds—
How graceful the small before danger!

In the first of the moon,
All's a scattering,
A shining.

James Agee

☙ James Agee was born in Knoxville, Tennessee, November 27, 1909. Although his early schooling was in Franklin County, Tennessee, the center of "The Fugitives," Agee did not enter Vanderbilt and never came under the influence of the Nashville group. Instead he came north, attended Exeter for three years and spent four years at Harvard. Subsequently he came to New York, where he worked on *Fortune,* where his chief "namable" interests were "music, words, the present, the future, and 'documentary' movies," and contributed to *The Nation.*

His first book, *Permit Me Voyage* (1934), with a foreword by Archibald MacLeish, was published in Agee's twenty-fifth year. It is an unusual book, remarkable in its vigor and its unevenness, but the directness shines through the derivations. The title poem, the opening group of lyrics, and the twenty-five sonnets are the book's real reason for being. All of them are interesting and many are admirable; they show a dexterous balance of passion and restraint, of novelty and authority.

Agee had spent some of his school vacations working in the wheat fields of Kansas and Nebraska; he was well equipped for a journalistic assignment to discover and disclose the daily lives of Southern sharecroppers. The result was the tremendously moving documentary, *Let Us Now Praise Famous Men,* which, written in 1940 with devastating photographs by Walker Evans, was reissued twenty years later as a resuscitated classic, "a poetic tract for its times."

In his late thirties Agee left journalism for Hollywood. He had been motion picture reviewer for *Time* and *The Nation,* and he had planned experimental scripts. He made successful and highly popular adaptations of C. S. Forester's *The African Queen,* Stephen Crane's *The Bride Comes to Yellow Sky,* and *The Night of the Hunter.* He was making voluminous notes for a novel when he died of a heart attack in his forty-sixth year in New York on May 16, 1955.

Two years after his death, Agee's most important work, *A Death in the Family,* was issued. It is an unfinished masterpiece—one part, published as *The Morning Watch,* an impressionistic portrait of a sensitive small town boy, had appeared in 1951—and Agee's friends had put the volume together from a mass of uncoordinated manuscripts. The book is both dramatic and meditative, an alternation of tragic event and idyllic monologue, a poignant narrative and a prose poem. It was awarded the Pulitzer Prize for the most distinguished work of fiction published in 1957.

The recognition accorded *A Death in the Family*—a greater acclaim than Agee had received during his life—prompted the publication of another posthumous volume: *Agee on Film* (1958), a collection of pieces written for *Time* and *The Nation,* and including "Comedy's Greatest Era," which had evoked a nationwide nostalgic response when it first appeared in *Life.*

LYRICS

No doubt left. Enough deceiving.
Now I know you do not love.
Now you know I do not love.

Now we know we do not love.
No more doubt. No more deceiving.

Yet there is pity in us for each other
And better times are almost fresh as true.
The dog returns. And the man to his mother.
And tides. And you to me. And I to you.
And we are cowardly kind the cruelest way,
Feeling the cliff unmorsel from our heels
And knowing balance gone, we smile, and stay
A little, whirling our arms like desperate wheels.

✣

Not met and marred with the year's whole turn of grief,
But easily on the mercy of the morning
Fell this still folded leaf:
Small that never Summer spread
Demented on the dusty heat;
And sweet that never Fall
Wrung sere and tarnished red;
Safe now that never knew
Stunning Winter's bitter blue
It fell fair in the fair season:

Therefore with reason
Dress all in cheer and lightly put away
  With music and glad will
This little child that cheated the long day
  Of the long day's ill:
Who knows this breathing joy, heavy on us all,
  Never, never, never.

✣

I loitered weeping with my bride for gladness
Her walking side against and both embracing
Through the brash brightening rain that now the season changes
White on the fallen air that now my fallen
the fallen girl her grave effaces.

SONNETS

I

So it begins. Adam is in his earth
Tempted, and fallen, and his doom made sure,
O, in the very instant of his birth:
Whose deathly nature must all things endure.
The hungers of his flesh, and mind, and heart,
That governed him when he was in the womb,
These ravenings multiply in every part:
And shall release him only to the tomb.
Meantime he works the earth, and builds up nations,
And trades, and wars, and learns, and worships chance,

And looks to God, and weaves the generations
Which shall his many hungerings advance
When he is sunken dead among his sins.
Adam is in this earth. So it begins.

II

Our doom is in our being. We began
In hunger eager more than ache of hell:
And in that hunger became each a man
Ravened with hunger death alone may spell:
And in that hunger live, as lived the dead,
Who sought, as now we seek, in the same ways,
Nobly, and hatefully, what angel's-bread
Might ever stand us out these short few days.
So is this race in this wild hour confounded:
And though you rectify the big distress,
And kill all outward wrong where wrong abounded,
Your hunger cannot make this hunger less
Which breeds all wrath and right, and shall not die
In earth, and finds some hope upon the sky.

XIX

Those former loves wherein our lives have run
Seeing them shining, following them far,
Were but a hot deflection of the sun,
The operation of a migrant star.
In that wrong time when still a shape of earth
Severed us far and stood our sight between,
Those loves were effigies of love whose worth
Was all our wandering nothing to have seen:
So toward those steep projections on our sky
We toiled though partners to their falsity
Who faintly in that falseness could descry
What now stands forth too marvelous to see:
Who one time loved in them the truth concealed:
And now must leave them in the truth revealed.

XX

Now stands our love on that still verge of day
Where darkness loiters leaf to leaf releasing
Lone tree to silvering tree: then slopes away
Before the morning's deep-drawn strength increasing
Till the sweet land lies burnished in the dawn:
But sleeping still: nor stirs a thread of grass:
Large on the low hill and the spangled lawn
The pureleaved air dwells passionless as glass:
So stands our love new found and unaroused,
Appareled in all peace and innocence,
In all lost shadows of love past still drowsed
Against foreknowledge of such immanence
As now, with earth outshone and earth's wide air,
Shows each to other as this morning fair.

PERMIT ME VOYAGE

Take these who will as may be: I
Am careless now of what they fail:
My heart and mind discharted lie
And surely as the nervèd nail

Appoints all quarters on the north
So now it designates him forth
My sovereign God my princely soul
Whereon my flesh is priestly stole:

Whenceforth shall my heart and mind
To God through soul entirely bow,
Therein such strong increase to find
In truth as is my fate to know:

Small though that be great God I know
I know in this gigantic day
What God is ruined and I know
How labors with Godhead this day:

How from the porches of our sky
The crested glory is declined:
And hear with that translated cry
The stridden soul is overshined:

And how this world of wildness through
True poets shall walk who herald you:
Of whom God grant me of your grace
To be, that shall preserve this race.

Permit me voyage, Love, into your hands.

SONG WITH WORDS

When Eve first saw the glistering day
  Watch by the wan world side
She learned her worst and down she lay
  In the streaming land and cried.

When Adam saw the mastering night
  First board the wan world's lifted breast
He climbed his bride with all his might
  And sank to tenderest rest.

And night took both and day brought high
The children that must likewise die:
And all our grief and every joy
To time's deep end shall time destroy:

And weave us one and wave us under
Where is neither faith nor wonder.

TWO SONGS ON THE ECONOMY OF ABUNDANCE

Temperance Note: and Weather Prophecy

  Watch well The Poor in this late hour
  Before the wretched wonder stop:
  Who march among a thundershower
  And never touch a drop.

Red Sea

  How long this way: that everywhere
  We make our march the water stands
  Apart and all our wine is air
  And all our ease the emptied sands?

IN HEAVY MIND

In heavy mind I strayed the field
The chilly damp and devious air
The restiveness the rags of snow
The mulled and matted blackness where

The summer overthroned with leaves
Had shown its cloudy loveliest
And I had lain along the shade
In tears that fully undistressed

Me among men upon the earth
In flowering sky of every doubt
But only so much natural joy
Might flare the flesh, thaw the wick out:

But now was logy with the weight of brain
Flat in the eyes and of my love most low,
Hate toward, and clambering thought, and
  failure sure,
And life a lean long while, the starving slow

When, not to see, some previous bird
Made whistling from a bramble tree:
And all my will was not enough
To hold the heavens out of me.

RAPID TRANSIT

Squealing under city stone
  The millions on the millions run,
Every one a life alone,
  Every one a soul undone:

There all the poisons of the heart
  Branch and abound like whirling brooks,
And there through every useless art
  Like spoiled meats on a butcher's hooks

Pour forth upon their frightful kind
  The faces of each ruined child:
The wrecked demeanors of the mind
  That now is tamed, and once was wild.

Kenneth Patchen

Kenneth Patchen was born December 3, 1911, in Niles, Ohio. When he was four his parents (Scotch-French-English) moved to near-by Warren, where he was raised and attended high school. At seventeen Patchen went to work with his father's crew in the steel-mills; most of his relatives worked either in the mills of the Mahoning Valley or in the coal mines of Pennsylvania and West Virginia. Out of work and briefly "schooled" at Alexander Meiklejohn's Experimental College, University of Wisconsin, Patchen spent several years drifting from one end of the country to the other, working at anything that came to hand. He was awarded a Guggenheim Fellowship in 1936.

His first volume, *Before the Brave* (1936), was crammed with revolutionary fervor and technical experiment. Unfortunately its ardor was overinsistently strained and too often its oratory was a crescendo of screams. It was succeeded by a richer and far more genuinely startling volume, *First Will & Testament* (1939), which included about one hundred poems, three surrealistic dramas, and the beginning of a projected epic planned to fill several volumes. *First Will & Testament* is sensational in its tempo, amazing in its gusto, and unique in its uncanny combination of delicacy and disorganization. The tone is savage disillusionment, but not apathy; it is rebellious and ribald, indignant and desperate, but clean-cut even in its fury.

Much of Patchen's work is conceived in the limbo of nightmare, in a world where the humor is worse than the horror. Frenzy rules here; phantasmagoria triumphs in slapstick satire, casual killings, and sinister obscenity. But there is more to Patchen than his power to evoke ugliness, violence, and nonchalant treachery. Only a poet of unusual sensibility could have fashioned the nuances of "In Memory of Kathleen," "Do the Dead Know What Time It Is?", "The Deer and the Snake," and the cold terror of "Street Corner College."

Before he was fifty, Patchen, in spite of continued ill health, was the author of some twenty-five volumes of prose, verse, and combinations of the two. *Memoirs of a*

Shy Pornographer (1945) and *Sleepers Awake* (1946) are many-voiced novels, diaries, and "amusements" in a technique comparable to the polyphony of James Joyce. Paul Rosenfeld praised Patchen's "exploitation of the vernacular"; Henry Miller hailed Patchen as an unmistakable genius; Robert Penn Warren declared that *The Dark Kingdom* (1942) proved he was not only a poet but a seer. Other volumes were similarly arresting, especially *Cloth of the Tempest* (1943), *To Say If You Love Someone* (1948), and *Because It Is* (1960).

IN MEMORY OF KATHLEEN

How pitiful is her sleep.
Now her clear breath is still.
There is nothing falling tonight,
Bird or man,
As dear as she;
Nowhere that she should go
Without me. None but my calling.
Nothing but the cold cry of the snow.

How lonely does she seem.
I, who have no heaven,
Defenseless, without lands,
Must try a dream
Of the seven
Lost stars and how they put their hands
Upon her eyes that she might ever know
Nothing worse than the cold cry of snow.

DO THE DEAD KNOW WHAT TIME IT IS?

The old guy put down his beer.
Son, he said,
  (and a girl came over to the table where we were:
  asked us by Jack Christ to buy her a drink.)
Son, I am going to tell you something
The like of which nobody ever was told.
  (and the girl said, I've got nothing on tonight;
  how about you and me going to your place?)
I am going to tell you the story of my mother's
Meeting with God.
  (and I whispered to the girl: I don't have a room,
  but maybe . . .)
She walked up to where the top of the world is
And He came right up to her and said
So at last you've come home.
  (but maybe what?
  I thought I'd like to stay here and talk to you.)
My mother started to cry and God
Put His arms around her.
  (about what?

Oh, just talk . . . we'll find something.)
She said it was like a fog coming over her face
And light was everywhere and a soft voice saying
You can stop crying now.
(what can we talk about that will take all night?
and I said that I didn't know.)
You can stop crying now.

THE DEER AND THE SNAKE

The deer is humble, lovely as God made her
I watch her eyes and think of wonder owned

These strange priests enter the cathedral of woods
And seven Marys clean their hands to woo her

Foot lifted, dagger-sharp—her ears
Poised to their points like a leaf's head.

But the snake strikes, in a velvet arc
Of murderous speed—assassin beautiful

As mountain water at which a fawn drank.
Stand there, forever, while the poison works

While I stand counting the arms of your Cross
Thinking that many Christs could hang there, crying.

STREET CORNER COLLEGE

Next year the grave grass will cover us.
We stand now, and laugh;
Watching the girls go by;
Betting on slow horses; drinking cheap gin.
We have nothing to do; nowhere to go; nobody.

Last year was a year ago; nothing more.
We weren't younger then; nor older now.

We manage to have the look that young men have;
We feel nothing behind our faces, one way or other.

We shall probably not be quite dead when we die.
We were never anything all the way; not even soldiers.

We are the insulted, brother, the desolate boys.
Sleepwalkers in a dark and terrible land,
Where solitude is a dirty knife at our throats.
Cold stars watch us, chum,
Cold stars and the whores.

LIKE A MOURNINGLESS CHILD

The rescuing gate is wide
On villages that drift through the sun.
I do not listen to sleep anymore.
Cows pasture on stalks of green hours
And a haze of joyous deer drinks eternity.
Bells make blue robes for the wind to wear.
Summer whistles for his dogs of tree and flower.
The old faith plays jacks with idiots on church lawns
I am so close to good. I have no need to see God.

WE GO OUT TOGETHER

We go out together into the staring town
And buy cheese and bread and little jugs with flowered labels.

Everywhere is a tent where we put on our whirling show.

A great deal has been said of the handless serpents
Which war has set loose in the gay milk of our heads

But because you braid your hair and taste like honey of heaven
We go together into town and buy wine and yellow candles.

FROM MY HIGH LOVE

From my high love I look at that poor world there;
I know that murder is the first prince in that tribe.

The towering sucking terror . . .
Schoolboys over whom the retching crows sing.
There is no lack of hell in that mad nest.
Gray horns hoot dismally in skeleton paws . . .

There is a little inn in the valley.
I wet my finger and put it to the wind;
Death whistles at his pitiless fun.

On the inn wall I tack our two hearts;
Let not the bullet go through one before the other.

Elizabeth Bishop

☙ Elizabeth Bishop was born February 8, 1911, in Worcester, Massachusetts. Brought up in New England and Nova Scotia, she was graduated from Vassar College and has traveled widely. For some time she spent part of each year in Key West, which may account for the peculiar quality of her images which combine New England severity with tropical floridity. In 1946 she received the Houghton Mifflin Literary Fellowship for a book of poems, *North & South,* although most of the poems were written before 1942.

At first glance Miss Bishop appears to be a painter, an impressionist who, with a line here, a stroke there, evokes a continual play of substance and shadow. But the visual effects are largely intellectual, and Miss Bishop is seen to be both a colorist and a wit whose adroitness recalls the subtlety of Marianne Moore. Irony lurks behind many of the images, but they do not depend on technique and intellect only. Even the most abstract figures are alive with emotion. "The Imaginary Iceberg," "The Man-Moth," "The Fish," a miniature Moby Dick, and others are half-satirical, half-sympathetic disposals which combine unusually careful observation and a vividly alert imagination. Miss Bishop's work scintillates with such lines as "The palm trees clatter in the stiff breeze like the bills of the pelicans" and "the storm roaming the sky uneasily like a dog looking for a place to sleep in." *Poems,* a small but brilliant collection including her first volume, received the Pulitzer Prize in 1956.

THE FISH

I caught a tremendous fish
and held him beside the boat
half out of water, with my hook
fast in a corner of his mouth.
He didn't fight.
He hadn't fought at all.
He hung a grunting weight,
battered and venerable
and homely. Here and there
his brown skin hung in strips
like ancient wall-paper,
and its pattern of darker brown
was like wall-paper:
shapes like full-blown roses
stained and lost through age.
He was speckled with barnacles,
fine rosettes of lime,
and infested
with tiny white sea-lice,
and underneath two or three
rags of green weed hung down.
While his gills were breathing in
the terrible oxygen
—the frightening gills
fresh and crisp with blood,
that can cut so badly—
I thought of the coarse white flesh
packed in like feathers,
the big bones and the little bones,
the dramatic reds and blacks
of his shiny entrails,
and the pink swim-bladder
like a big peony.
I looked into his eyes
which were far larger than mine
but shallower, and yellowed,
the irises backed and packed
with tarnished tinfoil
seen through the lenses
of old scratched isinglass.
They shifted a little, but not
to return my stare.
—It was more like the tipping
of an object toward the light.
I admired his sullen face,
the mechanism of his jaw,
and then I saw
that from his lower lip
—if you could call it a lip—
grim, wet, and weapon-like,
hung five old pieces of fish-line,
or four and a wire leader
with the swivel still attached,
with all their five big hooks
grown firmly in his mouth.
A green line, frayed at the end
where he broke it, two heavier lines,
and a fine black thread
still crimped from the strain and snap
when it broke and he got away.
Like medals with their ribbons
frayed and wavering,
a five-haired beard of wisdom
trailing from his aching jaw.
I stared and stared
and victory filled up

the little rented boat,
from the pool of bilge
where oil had spread a rainbow
around the rusted engine
to the bailer rusted orange,
the sun-cracked thwarts,
the oarlocks on their strings,
the gunnels—until everything
was rainbow, rainbow, rainbow!
And I let the fish go.

THE IMAGINARY ICEBERG

We'd rather have the iceberg than the ship,
Although it meant the end of travel.
Although it stood stock still like cloudy rock
And all the sea were moving marble.
We'd rather have the iceberg than the ship;
We'd rather own this breathing plain of snow
Though the ship's sails were laid upon the sea
As the snow lies undissolved upon the water.
O solemn, floating field,
Are you aware an iceberg takes repose
With you, and when it wakes may pasture on your snows?

This is a scene a sailor'd give his eyes for.
The ship's ignored. The iceberg rises
And sinks again; its glassy pinnacles
Correct elliptics in the sky.
This is a scene where he who treads the boards
Is artlessly rhetorical. The curtain
Is light enough to rise on finest ropes
That airy twists of snow provide.
The wits of these white peaks
Spar with the sun. Its weight the iceberg dares
Upon a shifting stage and stands and stares.

This iceberg cuts its facets from within.
Like jewelry from a grave
It saves itself perpetually and adorns
Only itself, perhaps the snows
Which so surprise us lying on the sea.
Goodbye, we say, goodbye, the ship steers off
Where waves give in to one another's waves
And clouds run in a warmer sky.
Icebergs behoove the soul
(Both being self-made from elements least visible)
To see them so: fleshed, fair, erected indivisible.

THE MAN-MOTH[1]

Here, above,
cracks in the buildings are filled with battered moonlight.
The whole shadow of Man is only as big as his hat.
It lies at his feet like a circle for a doll to stand on,

[1] Newspaper misprint for "mammoth."

and he makes an inverted pin, the point magnetized to the moon.
He does not see the moon; he observes only her vast properties,
feeling the queer light on his hands, neither warm nor cold,
of a temperature impossible to record in thermometers.

But when the Man-Moth
pays his rare, although occasional, visit to the surface,
the moon looks rather different to him. He emerges
from an opening under the edge of one of the sidewalks
and nervously begins to scale the faces of buildings.
He thinks the moon is a small hole at the top of the sky,
proving the sky quite useless for protection.
He trembles, but must investigate as high as he can climb.

Up the façades,
his shadow dragging like a photographer's cloth behind him,
he climbs fearfully, thinking that this time he will manage
to push his small head through that round clean opening
and be forced through, as from a tube, in black scrolls on the light.
(Man, standing below him, has no such illusions.)
But what the Man-Moth fears most he must do, although
he fails, of course, and falls back scared but unhurt.

Then he returns
to the pale subways of cement he calls his home. He flits,
he flutters, and cannot get aboard the silent trains
fast enough to suit him. The doors close swiftly.
The Man-Moth always seats himself facing the wrong way
and the train starts at once at its full, terrible speed,
without a shift in gears or a gradation of any sort.
He cannot tell the rate at which he travels backwards.

Each night he must
be carried through artificial tunnels and dream recurrent dreams.
Just as the ties recur beneath his train, these underlie
his rushing brain. He does not dare look out the window,
for the third rail, the unbroken draught of poison,
runs there beside him. He regards it as disease
he has inherited susceptibility to. He has to keep
his hands in pockets, as others must wear mufflers.

If you catch him,
hold up a flashlight to his eye. It's all dark pupil,
an entire night itself, whose haired horizon tightens
as he stares back, and closes up the eye. Then from the lids
one tear, his only possession, like the bee's sting, slips.
Slyly he palms it, and if you're not paying attention
he'll swallow it. However, if you watch, he'll hand it over,
cool as from underground springs and pure enough to drink.

LITTLE EXERCISE

Think of the storm roaming the sky uneasily
like a dog looking for a place to sleep in,
listen to it growling.

Think how they must look now, the mangrove keys
lying out there unresponsive to the lightning
in dark, coarse-fibred families,

where occasionally a heron may undo his head,
shake up his feathers, make an uncertain comment
when the surrounding water shines.

Think of the boulevard and the little palm trees
all stuck in rows, suddenly revealed
as fistfuls of limp fish-skeletons.

It is raining there. The boulevard
and its broken sidewalks with weeds in every crack,
are relieved to be wet, the sea to be freshened.

Now the storm goes away again in a series
of small, badly lit battle-scenes,
each in "Another part of the field."

Think of someone sleeping in the bottom of a row-boat
tied to a mangrove root or the pile of a bridge;
think of him as uninjured, barely disturbed.

J. V. Cunningham

☙ J(ames) V(incent) Cunningham was born August 23, 1911, in Cumberland, Maryland, but grew up in Montana, where he spent his winters in town and his summers on a dry-land ranch. "I find," he says, "that the imagery of my poems is often derived from the wheatfields and rattlesnakes of those years." After graduating in Classics from Stanford University, he taught at various universities as far apart as the University of Virginia and the University of Hawaii, taught mathematics to the Air Force for a year during World War II, and became chairman of the department of English at Brandeis University.

His three volumes of poems (*The Helmsman, The Judge Is Fury,* and *Dr. Drink*) were republished in *The Exclusions of a Rhyme* (1960), a collection that is scholarly but not pedantic, witty, at times bawdy, and always precise in its felicities. None of his contemporaries excels Cunningham in his handling of the epigram.

Besides his poetry Cunningham is the author of *The Quest of the Opal* (1950) and *Woe or Wonder: The Emotional Effect of Shakespearian Tragedy* (1951).

MONTANA PASTORAL

I am no shepherd of a child's surmises.
I have seen fear where the coiled serpent rises,

Thirst where the grasses burn in early May
And thistle, mustard, and the wild oat stay.

There is dust in this air. I saw in the heat
Grasshoppers busy in the threshing wheat.

So to this hour. Through the warm dusk I drove
To blizzards sifting on the hissing stove,

And found no images of pastoral will,
But fear, thirst, hunger, and this huddled chill.

COFFEE

When I awoke with cold
And looked for you, my dear,
And the dusk inward rolled,
Not light or dark, but drear,

Unabsolute, unshaped,
That no glass can oppose,
I fled not to escape
Myself, but to transpose.

I have so often fled
Wherever I could drink
Dark coffee and there read
More than a man would think

That I say I waste time
For contemplation's sake:
In an uncumbered clime
Minute inductions wake,

Insight flows in my pen.
I know nor fear nor haste.
Time is my own again.
I waste it for the waste.

THREE EPIGRAMS

I married in my youth a wife.
She was my own, my very first,
She gave the best years of her life.
I hope nobody gets the worst.

*

Here lies New Critic who would fox us
With his poetic paradoxes.
Though he lies here rigid and quiet,
If he could speak he would deny it.

*

I had gone broke, and got set to come back,
And lost, on a hot day and a fast track,
On a long shot at long odds, a black mare
By Hatred out of Envy by Despair.

Delmore Schwartz

☙ Delmore Schwartz was born December 8, 1913, in Brooklyn, New York. Most of his education was spent in studying philosophy at the University of Wisconsin, New York University, and Harvard; he became a teacher and began his pedagogical career as Instructor in English Composition at Harvard University. He was awarded a Guggenheim Fellowship in his twenty-sixth year.

Schwartz had already published in the more advanced monthlies and the critical quarterlies, but his first volume came as something of a sensation. *In Dreams*

Begin Responsibilities (1938) combined a versatility and technical surety which occasioned a spontaneous salvo of enthusiasm from critics not usually given to superlatives. Allen Tate wrote that Schwartz's poetic style was "the only genuine innovation since Pound and Eliot came upon the scene twenty-five years ago." F. O. Matthiessen spoke of his "fertility of invention, his energy and ambitious resourcefulness."

In Dreams Begin Responsibilities is made up of a short story, a long philosophical poem ("Coriolanus and his Mother: The Dream of One Performance"), a play in prose and verse, and two groups which the author modestly called "Poems of Experiment and Imitation." The long poem is an eloquent and searching effort; the lyrics are almost continuously successful. Here Schwartz moves among the complexities of his material with extraordinary ease. In verse that is both intellectual and musical he presents a rounded portrait of a young man shaken by the war between brute fact and bewildering fantasy, between intellect and emotion. No young poet, perhaps no poet of the period, has so skilfully registered the threat of change and the cruelty of time. Schwartz's poems are variations on the leading theme:

> Time is the school in which we learn,
> Time is the fire in which we burn.

And again:

> We cannot stand still: Time is dying;
> We are dying: Time is farewell!

The original idiom, the personal gesture which is unmistakable, commands with increased certainty *Shenandoah* (1941), a play in which the speaker-chorus addresses the audience in verse while the characters in the drama discuss the action in prose. *Shenandoah* is a fusion of allegory, philosophy, and autobiographical overtones, although the action is almost entirely fictive. Once more the central motif is the conflict between time and the individual; the lines beginning "Let us consider where the great men are" present a condensed cultural background of the period. They are, moreover, an impressionistic statement of a poet growing up in the 1930s, studying modern literature, and emerging from his influences. Here again is natural eloquence without the support of induced rhetoric.

Genesis (1943) is the genesis of a human being, a work in which Schwartz's desperate concern with time is crossed by the ego's struggle to maintain its unique selfhood. This motif was already sounded in "Coriolanus and his Mother"; in *Genesis* the poet tries to track down the multiple and remote causes which determine any event in a life. The way in which the story unfolds is novel. The narrative is in prose, but the commentary (a chorus which "explains" the things remembered) is in verse. Thus, when the boy reads *Tarzan of the Apes,* Darwin and Huxley are summoned as two of the cultural "divinities" which have caused such a book as *Tarzan* to be written. Thus theology and the mythology of our times are curiously but logically interwoven.

The Imitation of Life (1943), a volume of critical essays, was followed by another book of prose, *The World Is a Wedding* (1948), a collection of witty, sometimes angry, and always sensitive short stories. *Summer Knowledge* (1959), a collection of new and selected poems, was awarded the Bollingen Prize in 1960, Schwartz being the youngest winner since the prize was established in 1948.

FOR RHODA

Calmly we walk through this April's day,
Metropolitan poetry here and there,
In the park sit pauper and *rentier,*
The screaming children, the motor car
Fugitive about us, running away,
Between the worker and the millionaire.
Number provides all distances,
It is Nineteen Thirty-Seven now,
Many great dears are taken away,
What will become of you and me
(This is the school in which we learn . . .)
Besides the photo and the memory?
(. . . that time is the fire in which we burn.)

(This is the school in which we learn . . .)
What is the self amid this blaze?
What am I now that I was then
Which I shall suffer and act again,
The theodicy I wrote in my high school days
Restored all life from infancy,
The children shouting are bright as they run
(This is the school in which they learn . . .)
Ravished entirely in their passing play!
(. . . that time is the fire in which they burn.)

Avid its rush, that reeling blaze!
Where is my father and Eleanor?
Not where are they now, dead seven years,
But what they were then?
No more? No more?
From Nineteen-Fourteen to the present day,
Bert Spira and Rhoda consume, consume
Not where they are now (where are they now?)
But what they were then, both beautiful;
Each minute bursts in the burning room,
The great globe reels in the solar fire,
Spinning the trivial and unique away.
(How all things flash! How all things flare!)
What am I now that I was then?
May memory restore again and again
The smallest color of the smallest day:
Time is the school in which we learn,
Time is the fire in which we burn.

TIRED AND UNHAPPY, YOU THINK OF HOUSES

Tired and unhappy, you think of houses
Soft-carpeted and warm in the December evening,
While snow's white pieces fall past the window,
And the orange firelight leaps.

A young girl sings
That song of Gluck where Orpheus pleads with Death;
Her elders watch, nodding their happiness
To see time fresh again in her self-conscious eyes:
The servants bring the coffee, the children retire,
Elder and younger yawn and go to bed,
The coals fade and glow, rose and ashen,
It is time to shake yourself! and break this
Banal dream, and turn your head
Where the underground is charged, where the weight
Of the lean buildings is seen,
Where close in the subway rush, anonymous
In the audience, well-dressed or mean,
So many surround you, ringing your fate,
Caught in an anger exact as a machine!

FOR THE ONE WHO WOULD TAKE MAN'S LIFE IN HIS HANDS

Tiger Christ unsheathed his sword,
Threw it down, became a lamb.
Swift spat upon the species, but
Took two women to his heart.
Samson who was strong as death
Paid his strength to kiss a slut.
Othello that stiff warrior
Was broken by a woman's heart.
Troy burned for a sea-tax, also for
Possession of a charming whore.
What do all examples show?
What must the finished murderer know?

You cannot sit on bayonets,
Nor can you eat among the dead.
When all are killed, you are alone,
A vacuum comes where hate has fed.
Murder's fruit is silent stone,
The gun increases poverty.
With what do these examples shine?
The soldier turned to girls and wine.
Love is the tact of every good,
The only warmth, the only peace.

"What have I said?" asked Socrates,
"Affirmed extremes, cried yes and no,
Taken all parts, denied myself,
Praised the caress, extolled the blow,
Soldier and lover quite deranged
Until their motions are exchanged.
—What do all examples show?
What can any actor know?
The contradiction in every act,
The infinite task of the human heart."

IN THE NAKED BED, IN PLATO'S CAVE

In the naked bed, in Plato's cave,
Reflected headlights slowly slid the wall,
Carpenters hammered under the shaded window,
Wind troubled the window curtains all night long,
A fleet of trucks strained uphill, grinding,
Their freights covered, as usual.
The ceiling lightened again, the slanting diagram
Slid slowly forth.
                                        Hearing the milkman's chop,
His striving up the stair, the bottle's chink,
I rose from bed, lit a cigarette,
And walked to the window. The stony street
Displayed the stillness in which buildings stand,
The street-lamp's vigil and the horse's patience.
The winter sky's pure capital
Turned me back to bed with exhausted eyes.

Strangeness grew in the motionless air. The loose
Film grayed. Shaking wagons, hooves' waterfalls,
Sounded far off, increasing, louder and nearer.
A car coughed, starting. Morning, softly
Melting the air, lifted the half-covered chair
From underseas, kindled the looking-glass,
Distinguished the dresser and the white wall.
The bird called tentatively, whistled, called,
Bubbled and whistled, so! Perplexed, still wet
With sleep, affectionate, hungry and cold. So, so,
O son of man, the ignorant night, the travail
Of early morning, the mystery of beginning
Again and again,
                                        While Time is unforgiven.

LET US CONSIDER WHERE THE GREAT MEN ARE

(*from "Shenandoah"*)

Let us consider where the great men are
Who will obsess the child when he can read:
Joyce teaches in Trieste in a Berlitz school,
Learns to pronounce the puns in *Finnegan's Wake*—
Eliot works in a bank, and there he learns
The profit and the loss,
                                        the death of cities—
Pound howls at him, finds what expatriates
Can find,
                        culture in chaos all through time,
Like a Picasso show.
                                        Rilke endures
Of silence and of solitude the unheard music
In empty castles which great knights have left

(Like Beethoven, hewing in memory
The ineffable forests of the last quartets)—
Trotzky in exile, too, in London walks
With Lenin, hears him speak exile's half-truth:
"Look: that's *their* Westminster there," as if
The father's features were the son's whole soul—
Yeats too, like Rilke, on old lords' estates,
Seeks for the permanent amid the loss,
Daily and desperate, of love, of friends,
Of every thought with which his age began—
Kafka in Prague works in an office, learns
How bureaucratic Life,
how far off God,
A white-collar class theology—
Perse is in Asia as a diplomat,
Finding the violent energy with which
Civilization creates itself and moves—
Yet with these images he cannot see
The moral apathy after the Munich Pact,
The unnatural silence on the Maginot Line,
Yet he cannot foresee the Fall of France—
Mann too, in Davos-Platz, finds in the sick
The triumph of the artist and the intellect—
All over Europe these exiles find in art
What exile is: art becomes exile too,
A secret and a code studied in secret,
Declaring the agony of modern life:
This child will learn of life from these great men,
He will participate in their solitude,
And maybe in the end, on such a night
As this, return to the starting-point, his name,
Showing himself as such, among his friends.

Muriel Rukeyser

Muriel Rukeyser was born in New York City, December 15, 1913. She began her education in Ethical Culture and Fieldston School, entered Vassar with the class of 1934, left college after two years, and attended summer sessions at Columbia for two years more. In 1932 she became literary editor of *The Student Review* and a member of committees investigating Negro and labor problems; she was arrested during the second Scottsboro trial in Alabama. She worked her way through the ground-course at Roosevelt Aviation School, but was not allowed to pilot a plane as her parents refused to sign a contract permitting a minor to fly. It was at this time that she wrote her first important long poem, "Theory of Flight," which became the title-poem of her first volume. Work in statistics took her in 1936 to England, from where a London magazine sent her to report the People's Olympics in Barcelona, which were to open on the day the Spanish Civil War began. In 1941 she joined the staff of the monthly *Decision.*

Theory of Flight (1935) is startling without being theatrical, intense yet governed, alternating between autobiography and impersonality. This poet not only uses the material of modern life, but uses it without self-consciousness. For her the trucks rumbling along the city streets are a more native, a more natural prelude to day than the lark at heaven's gate; the airplane is a more legitimate if more ominous symbol of man's longing for freedom than fluttering Psyches, butterflies, and picturesquely released doves. Her images, dramatic and often militant, are appropriate to one born in a period of national struggle and economic warfare. The very poignance of her dialogues—"Effort at Speech Between Two People" was written when she was a sophomore—reveals the tension and terror of the contemporary world.

U. S. I (1938) is an assimilation of influence and an effort at difficult integration. Echoes can be recognized—chiefly reminders of Hart Crane and W. H. Auden—but the poet's own voice comes through with conviction if not always with clarity. Intentness and originality progress further in *A Turning Wind* (1939); written between her twenty-third and twenty-fifth years, the book indicates continuing growth and complexity. The power of the communication is perceived even before it is understood; the meaning, sometimes muffled by the very rush of words, declares itself in the shifting tempi, the abrupt change of mood and action, the hurtling emotion in runaway fever.

Continuing the series of "Lives" sketched in the preceding volume, Miss Rukeyser turned to John Brown as a symbol of the American past and a manifesto for her generation. The motto of *The Soul and Body of John Brown* (1940) is from Joel: "Multitudes, multitudes in the valley of decision." It is a quotation which has a terrible choice of meanings, for the chapter from which it is taken is a prologue to the Day of Judgment—and it is our day which will be judged, judged by our own multitudes "in the valley of decision." The symbolism is emphasized with the entry of another Hebrew prophet, Ezekiel; for Ezekiel, thundering about the doom of nations, foretold the end of slavery and foreshadowed a spiritual resurrection. Joel . . . Ezekiel . . . John Brown . . . Miss Rukeyser synthesizes their apocalyptic visions, repudiates the self-willed doom of the appeasers and defeatists, and, feeling the line of the past, urges more freedom. She calls valiantly for reawakened life. The cry is to the spirit of Joel-John Brown-Ezekiel: "Threaten us alive!" Imposing 1940 upon 1859, the poem becomes a chorale in contrasts. The prophetic voices, echoed in the buzz of guitar (a truer symbol of American song than the traditional lute or classic lyre) call for more life: "in all the harm, calling . . . challenging this hatred—

a wish to be again
threatened alive, in agonies of decision,
part of our nation, of a fanatic sun.

Beast in View (1944) and *The Green Wave* (1948) display Miss Rukeyser's fertility and fluency. In these books, as in her *Selected Poems* (1951) and *Body of Waking* (1958), meaning and music are expressed in swift intensities which are also capable of sounding peaceful philosophic depths.

The poet's vigorous mind is further revealed in a prose biography of the scientist *Willard Gibbs* (1942), a poetic interpretation of Wendell Willkie's career, *One Life* (1954), and *Come Back, Paul* (1955), a juvenile, which she illustrated.

CEILING UNLIMITED

The cattle-trains edge along the river, bringing morning on a white vibration
breaking the darkness split with beast-cries: a milk-wagon proceeds
down the street leaving the cold bottles: the Mack truck pushes
around the corner, tires hissing on the washed asphalt. A clear sky
growing candid and later bright.
Ceiling unlimited. Visibility unlimited.

They stir on the pillows, her leg moving, her face swung windowward
vacant with sleep still, modeled with light's coming; his dark head
among the softness of her arm and breast, nuzzled in dreams,
mumbling the old words, hardly roused. They return to silence.
At the airport, the floodlights are snapped off.

Turning, he says, "Tell me how's the sky this morning?" "Fair," she answers,
"no clouds from where I lie; bluer and bluer." "And later and later—
god, for some sleep into some noon, instead of all these mornings
with my mouth going stiff behind the cowling and wind brushing
away from me and my teeth freezing against the wind."
Light gales from the northwest: tomorrow, rain.

The street is long, with a sprinkling of ashcans; panhandlers
begin to forage among banana-peels and cardboard boxes.
She moves to the window, tall and dark before a brightening sky,
full with her six months' pregnancy molded in ripeness.
Stands, watching the sky's blankness.

Very soon: "How I love to see you when I wake," he says.
"How the child's meaning in you is my life's growing."
She faces him, hands brought to her belly's level, offering,
wordless, looking upon him. She carries his desire well.
Sun rises: 6:38 A.M. Sun sets. . . .

"Flying is what makes you strange to me, dark as Asia,
almost removed from my world even in your closenesses:
that you should be familiar with those intricacies
and a hero in mysteries which all the world has wanted."
Wind velocity changing from 19 to 30.

"No, that's wrong," and he laughs, "no personal hero's left
to make a legend. Those centuries have gone. If I fly,
why, I know that countries are not map-colored, that seas
belong to no one, that war's a pock-marking on Europe:"
The Weather Bureau's forecast, effective until noon.

"Your friends sleep with strange women desperately,
drink liquor and sleep heavily to forget those skies.
You fly all day and come home truly returning
to me who know only land. And we will have this child."
New York to Boston: Scattered to broken clouds.

"The child will have a hard time to be an American,"
he says slowly, "fathered by a man whose country is air,
who believes there are no heroes to withstand
wind, or a loose bolt, or a tank empty of gas."
To Washington: Broken clouds becoming overcast.

"It will be a brave child," she answers, smiling.
"We will show planes to it, and the bums in the street.
You will teach it to fly, and I will love it.
very much." He thinks of his job, dressing.
Strong west northwest winds above 1000 feet.

He thinks how many men have wanted flight.
He ties his tie, looking into his face.
Finishes breakfast, hurrying to be gone,
crossing the river to the airport and his place.
To Cleveland: Broken clouds to overcast.

She does not imagine how the propeller turns
in a blinding speed, swinging the plane through space;
she never sees the cowling rattle and slip
forward and forward against the grim blades' grinding.
Cruising speed 1700 R.P.M.

Slipping, a failing desire; slipping like death
insidious against the propeller, until the blades shake,
bitten by steel, jagged against steel, broken,
and his face angry and raked by death, staring.
Strong west northwest or west winds above 2000 feet.

She watches the clock as his return time hurries,
the schedule ticking off, eating the short minutes.
She watches evening advance; she knows the child's stirring.
She knows night. She knows he will not come.
Ceiling unlimited. Visibility unlimited.

EFFORT AT SPEECH BETWEEN TWO PEOPLE

Speak to me. Take my hand. What are you now?
I will tell you all. I will conceal nothing.
When I was three, a little child read a story about a rabbit
who died, in the story, and I crawled under a chair:
a pink rabbit: it was my birthday, and a candle
burnt a sore spot on my finger, and I was told to be happy.

Oh, grow to know me. I am not happy. I will be open:
Now I am thinking of white sails against a sky like music,
like glad horns blowing, and birds tilting, and an arm about me.
There was one I loved, who wanted to live, sailing.

Speak to me. Take my hand. What are you now?
When I was nine, I was fruitily sentimental,
fluid: and my widowed aunt played Chopin,

and I bent my head on the painted woodwork, and wept.
I want now to be close to you.   I would
link the minutes of my days close, somehow, to your days.

I am not happy.   I will be open.
I have liked lamps in evening corners, and quiet poems.
There has been fear in my life.   Sometimes I speculate
On what a tragedy his life was, really.

Take my hand.   Fist my mind in your hand.   What are you now?
When I was fourteen, I had dreams of suicide,
and I stood at a steep window, at sunset, hoping toward death:
if the light had not melted clouds and plains to beauty,
if light had not transformed that day, I would have leapt,
I am unhappy.   I am lonely.   Speak to me.

I will be open.   I think he never loved me:
he loved the bright beaches, the little lips of foam
that ride small waves, he loved the veer of gulls:
he said with a gay mouth: I love you.   Grow to know me.

What are you now?   If we could touch one another,
if these our separate entities could come to grips,
clenched like a Chinese puzzle . . . yesterday
I stood in a crowded street that was live with people,
and no one spoke a word, and the morning shone.
Everyone silent, moving. . . . Take my hand.   Speak to me.

THE SOUL AND BODY OF JOHN BROWN

Multitudes, multitudes in the valley of decision!
—JOEL, IV, 14

His life is in the body of the living.
When they hanged him the first time, his image leaped
into the blackened air. His grave was the floating faces
of the crowd, and he refused them in release,
rose open-eyed to autumn, a fanatic
beacon of fierceness leaping to meet them there,
match the white prophets of the storm,
the streaming meteors of the war.

Dreaming Ezekiel, threaten me alive!

Voices: Why don't you rip up that guitar?
Or must we listen to those blistering strings?

The trial of heroes follows their execution. The striding
wind of western nations carried new rain, new lightning,
destroyed in magnificence with noon shining straight down,
Swaying the fiery pines.—He wanted freedom. Could not himself be free
until more grace reached a corroded world. Our guilt his own.
Under the cloak of the century drops the trap—
There in October's fruition-fire, three
tall images of himself: one as he stood on the ground,

one as he stood on sudden air, and one
standing to our fatal topmost hills
faded through dying altitudes, and low
through faces living under the dregs of the air,
deprived childhood and thwarted youth and change:
fantastic sweetness gone to rags
and incorruptible anger blurred by age.

Compel the steps of lovers, watch them lie silvery
attractive in naked embrace over the brilliant gorge,
and open them to love: enlarge their welcome
to sharp-faced countrysides, vicious familiar windows
where lopped-off worlds say *I am promise,* holding
the stopgap slogans of a thin season offering only
the false initials, blind address, dummy name—
enemies who reply in smiles, mild slavers, moderate whores
—There is a gorge to remember, where the soldiers came
in a terrible answer of lechery after death.
—He said at last, with a living perfect look,
"I designed to have done the same thing again
on a larger scale." Sleepless, he sees his tree
grow in the land, a wish to leap these mountains.
They are not mountains, but men and women sleeping.

O my scene! my mother!
America who offers many births.

Over the tiers of barriers, compel the steps of armies
who will arrive with horizon sharpness rising
in quick embrace toward the people who greet them, love
faltering in our hills among the symptoms of ice,
small lights of the shifting winter, the rapid snow-blue stars.
—This must be done by armies. Nothing is free.—He knows
direct attacks, refuses to speak again,
"If I tell them the truth,
they will say I speak in symbols."

White landscapes emphasize his nakedness
reflected in countries of naked who shiver and stare at fires,
their backs to the face that unrolls new worlds around them.
—They go down the valleys. They shamble in the streets.
Blind to the sun-storming image echoed in their eyes.
—They dread the surface of their victim life,
lying helpless and savage in shade parks,
asking the towers only what beggars dare:
food, fire, water, and air.

Spring: the great hieroglyph: the mighty, whose first hour
collects the winter invalids, whose cloudless
pastures train swarms of mutable apple-trees
to blond delusions of light, the touch of whiter
more memorable breasts each evening, the resistant

male shoulders riding under sold terrible eyes.
The soldier-face persists, the victorious head
kissing those breasts asks for more miracles—
Untarnished hair! Set them free! "Without the snap of a gun—"
More failures—but the season is a garden after sickness;
Then the song begins,
"The clearing of the sky
brings fulness to heroes—
Call Death out of the city
and ring the summer in."

Whether they sleep alone. Whether they understand darkness
of mine or tunnel or store. Whether they lay branches
with Western skill to entice their visions out of fire.
Whether she lie awake, whether he walk in guilt
down silenced corridors, leaving no fingerprints.
Whether he weaken searching for power in pamphlets,
or shut out every fantasy but the fragile eyelid to
commemorate delight . . .
They believe in their dreams.

They more and more, secretly, tell their dreams.
They listen oftener for certain words, look deeper
in faces for features of one remembered image.
They almost forget the face. They cannot miss the look.
It waits until faces have gathered darkness,
and country guitars a wide and subtle music.
It rouses love. It has mastered its origin:
Death was its method. It will surpass its
furious birth when it is known again.

Dreaming Ezekiel, threaten me alive!

Greengrown with the sun on it. All the living summer.
They tell their dreams on the cool hill reclining,
after a twilight daytime painting machines on the sky,
the spite of tractors and the toothless cannon.
—The cities of horror are down. These are called born,
and Hungry Hill's to them a plain again.
—They stand in the factory, deal out identical
gestures of reaching—cathedral-color-rose
resumes the bricks as the walls go leaning—bend
away from the windows, blank in bellwavering air,
reach out, mechanical cat's-claw reaping sky.

I know your face, deepdrowned
prophet, and seablown eyes.

Darkflowing peoples. A tall tree, prophet, fallen,
your arms in their flesh laid on the mountains, all
your branches in the scattered valleys down.
Your boughs lie broken in channels of the land,

dim anniversaries written on many clouds.
—There is no partial help. Lost in the face of a child,
lost in the factory repetitions, lost
on the steel plateaus, in a ghost distorted.
—Calling More Life. In all the harm calling.
Pointing disaster of death and lifting up the bone,
heroic drug and the intoxication gone.

I see your mouth calling
before the words arrive.

The strings repeat it, buzz of guitars, a streamy
summernoon song, the whitelight of the meaning
filling American valleys. More life, saying: this rich,
this hatred, this Hallelloo—risk it upon yourselves.
—Free all the dangers of promise, clear the image
of freedom for the body of the world.—
After the tree is fallen and has become the land,
when the hand in the earth declined rises and touches air,
after the walls go down and all the faces turn,
the diamond shoals of eyes demanding life
deep in the prophet eyes, a wish to be again
threatened alive, in agonies of decision
part of our nation of our fanatic sun.

A LEG IN A PLASTER CAST

When at last he was well enough to take the sun
he leaned on the nearest railing and summed up his sins,
criminal weaknesses, deeds done and undone.
He knew he was healing. He guessed he was sane.

The convalescent gleam upon his skin,
with his supported leg and an unknown
recovery approaching let him block out pain.
The world promised recovery from his veins.

People said, "Sin"; in the park everyone
mentioned one miracle. "We must all be reborn."
Across an accidental past the horns
blasted through stone and barriers of sense

and the sound of a plaster cast knocking on stone.
He recognized the sound of fearful airmen
returning, forerunners, and he could not run.
He knew they were not flying home alone.

He stood in a down-torn town of men and women
whose wasted days poured on their heads as rain,
as sin, as fire—too lame, too late to turn,
for there, the air, everywhere full of planes.

THE MEETING

One o'clock in the letter-box
very black and I will go home early.
Now I have put off my dancing-dress
and over a sheet of distance write my love.
I walk in the city with my pride of theme
while the lean girls at their betrayal smiling
dance, do their sea-green dance, and laugh in dancing.
And all the stars fade out of my sky.

Early in the morning on a windy ocean.
My sleep opens upon your face to kiss and find
and take diversion of the meeting waters,
the flameless sky of peace, blue-sided white air.
I leave you as the trivial birds careen
in separation, a dream of easy parting.
I see you through a door. The door sails away,
and all the ships move into the real sea.

Let that far day arrive, that evening stain!
Down the alleys of the night I trail a cloak;
field-dusk and mountain-dusk and final darkness—
each absence brings me nearer to that night
when I stone-still in desire standing
shall see the masked body of love enter the garden
to reach the night-burning, the perpetual fountain.
And all the birds fly out of my scene.

MADBOY'S SONG

Fly down, Death : Call me :
I have become a lost name.

One I loved, she put me away,
        Fly down, Death;
Myself renounced myself that day,
        Fly down, Death.

My eyes in whom she looked so deep
        Long ago flowed away,
My hands which slept on her asleep
        Withered away,
My living voice I meant to keep,
        Faded and gray.

Fly down, Death : Call me :
I have become a lost name.

Evening closes in whispers,
    Dark words buried in flame.
My love, my mother, my sister,
    I know there is no blame;

But you have your living voice,
  Speak my forgotten name.

Fly down, Death : Call me :
I have become a lost name.

Don't come for me in a car
To drive me through the town;
Don't rise up out of the water,
Once is enough to drown;
Only drop out of the sky,
For I am fallen down.

Fly down, Death.

HOLY FAMILY

A long road and a village.
A bloody road and a village.
A road away from war.
Born, born, we know how it goes.

A man and woman riding.
Riding, the new-born child.
White sky, clever and wild.
Born, born, we know how it goes.

A child rides into the forest
on its mother's arms.
The air screams the alarms.
Born, born, we know how it goes.

The wheel goes back.
How is it with the child?
How is it with the world?
Born, born, we know how it goes.

Never look at the child.
Give it to bloody ground.
By this dream we are bound.
Born, born, we know how it goes.

Riding between these hills,
woman and man alone
enter the battle-line.
Born, born, we know how it goes.

They childless disappear
among the fighting men.
Two thousand years until they come again.
Born, born, we know how it goes.

AJANTA

(The title refers to the caves of that name in India, on whose walls appear the great frescoes, with their religious analogy between space and the space of the body, and their acceptance of reality which may be filled with creation.)

Came in my full youth to the midnight cave
nerves ringing; and this thing I did alone.
Wanting my fulness and not a field of war,
for the world considered annihilation, a star
called Wormwood rose and flickered, shattering
bent light over the dead boiling up in the ground,
the biting yellow their corrupted lives
streaming to war, denying all our words.
Nothing was left among the tainted weather
but world-walking and the shadowless Ajanta.
Hallucination and the metal laugh
in clouds, and the mountain-spectre riding storm.
Nothing was certain but a moment of peace,
a hollow behind the unbreakable waterfall.
All the way to the cave, the teeming forms of death,
and death, the price of the body, cheap as air.
I blessed my heart on the expiation journey
for it had never been unable to suffer:
when I met the man whose face looked like the future,
when I met the whore with the dying red hair,
the child myself who is my murderer.
So came I between heaven and my grave
past the serene smile of the *voyeur,* to
this cave where the myth enters the heart again.

II. THE CAVE

Space to the mind, the painted cave of dream.
This is not a womb, nothing but good emerges:
this is a stage, neither unreal nor real
where the walls are the world, the rocks and palaces
stand on a borderland of blossoming ground.
If you stretch your hand, you touch the slope of the world
reaching in interlaced gods, animals, and men.
There is no background. The figures hold their peace
in a web of movement. There is no frustration,
every gesture is taken, everything yields connections.
The heavy sensual shoulders, the thighs, the blood-born flesh
and earth turning into color, rocks into their crystals,
water to sound, fire to form; life flickers
uncounted into the supple arms of love.
The space of these walls is the body's living space;
tear open your ribs and breathe the color of time
where nothing leads away, the world comes forward
in flaming sequences. Pillars and prisms. Riders
and horses and the figures of consciousness,
red cow grows long, goes running through the world.

Flung into movement in carnal purity,
these bodies are sealed—warm lip and crystal hand
in a jungle of light. Color-sheeted, seductive
foreboding eyelid lowered on the long eye,
fluid and vulnerable. The spaces of the body
are suddenly limitless, and riding flesh
shapes constellations over the golden breast,
confusion of scents and illuminated touch—
monster touch, the throat printed with brightness,
wide outlined gesture where the bodies ride.
Bells, and the spirit flashing. The religious bells,
bronze under the sunlight like beasts ringing,
bronze in the closed air, the memory of walls,
great sensual shoulders in the web of time.

III. LES TENDRESSES BESTIALES

A procession of caresses alters the ancient sky
until new constellations are the body shining:
There's the Hand to steer by, there the horizon Breast,
and the Great Stars kindling the fluid hill.
All the rooms open into magical boxes,
nothing is tilted, everything flickers
sexual and exquisite.
The panther with its throat along my arm
turns black and flows away.
Deep in all streets passes a faceless whore
and the checkered men are whispering one word.
The face I know becomes the night-black rose.
The sharp face is now an electric fan
and says one word to me.
The dice and the alcohol and the destruction
have drunk themselves and cast.
Broken bottle of loss, and the glass
turned bloody into the face.
Now the scene comes forward, very clear.
Dream-singing, airborne, surrenders the recalled,
the gesture arrives riding over the breast,
singing, singing, tender atrocity,
the silver derelict wearing fur and claws.
Oh love, I stood under the apple branch,
I saw the whipped bay and the small dark islands,
and night sailing the river and the foghorn's word.
My life said to you: I want to love you well.
The wheel goes back and I shall live again,
but the wave turns, my birth arrives and spills
over my breast the world bearing my grave,
and your eyes open in earth. You touched my life.
My life reaches the skin, moves under your smile,
and your shoulders and your throat and your face and your thighs
flash.

I am haunted by interrupted acts,
introspective as a leper, enchanted

by a repulsive clew,
a gross and fugitive movement of the limbs.
Is this the love that shook the lights to flame?
Sheeted avenues thrash in the wind,
torn streets, the savage parks.
I am plunged deep. Must find the midnight cave.

IV. BLACK BLOOD

A habit leading to murder, smoky laughter
hated at first, but necessary later.
Alteration of motives. To stamp in terror
around the deserted harbor, down the hill
until the woman laced into a harp
screams and screams and the great clock strikes,
swinging its giant figures past the face.
The Floating Man rides on the ragged sunset
asking and asking. Do not say, Which loved?
Which was beloved? Only, Who most enjoyed?
Armored ghost of rage, screaming and powerless.
Only find me and touch my blood again.
Find me. A girl runs down the street
singing Take me, yelling Take me Take
Hang me from the clapper of a bell
and you as hangman ring it sweet tonight,
for nothing clean in me is more than cloud
unless you call it.—As I ran I heard
a black voice beating among all that blood:
"Try to live as if there were a God."

V. THE BROKEN WORLD

Came to Ajanta cave, the painted space of the breast,
the real world where everything is complete,
there are no shadows, the forms of incompleteness.
The great cloak blows in the light, rider and horse arrive,
the shoulders turn and every gift is made.
No shadows fall. There is no source of distortion.
In our world, a tree casts the shadow of a woman,
a man the shadow of a phallus, a hand raised
the shadow of the whip.
Here everything is itself,
here all may stand on summer earth.
Brightness has overtaken every light,
and every myth netted itself in flesh.
New origins, and peace given entire
and the spirit alive.
In the shadowless cave
the naked arm is raised.
Animals arrive,
interlaced, and gods
interlaced, and men
flame-woven.
I stand and am complete.

Crawls from the door,
black at my two feet
the shadow of the world.
World, not yet one,
enters the heart again.
The naked world, and the old noise of tears,
the fear, the expiation and the love,
a world of the shadowed and alone.
The journey, and the struggles of the moon.

Karl Shapiro

☙ Karl (Jay) Shapiro was born November 10, 1913, in Baltimore, Maryland. He attended the University of Virginia and Johns Hopkins University. In March, 1941, he was inducted into the Army and, during the Second World War, served as a sergeant overseas. From 1942 until 1945, he was stationed in the South Pacific; his first two books were put together while he was there and published without the author's assistance.

Person, Place and Thing (1942) was hailed as one of the most startling first books of the period. Shapiro's brusque and sometimes tortured irony was matched by a sensitivity which, though understanding, was never sentimental. Mark Van Doren praised his "acute sense of form and a wit that never fails"; Selden Rodman acclaimed him as "a true spokesman of our generation." Such poems as "The Dome of Sunday," "Travelogue for Exiles," and "The Twins," are the work of a man deeply concerned with the dilemmas of his day but who writes about them neither as a sociologist nor an evangelist. His hatred of injustice and resentment against the traditional "romantic" attitude matured into *V-Letter and Other Poems* (1944), which was awarded the Pulitzer Prize. It was evident that Shapiro had not wholly outgrown his influences, chiefly Eliot and Auden—there is even an echo of Swinburne in the rhythm and excessive alliteration of the following lines from "The Gun":

We have wounded the wind with a wire and stung in the sky
A white hole that is small and unseen as the bite of the asp.

But "The Leg," "The Puritan," "Elegy for a Dead Soldier," and other poems of the war marked Shapiro's progress and established his own sharp idiom. Writing continually in conflict, he avoided the temptation of becoming a "war poet." In his introduction to *V-Letter,* he wrote that "the most resounding slogans ring dead after a few years. We learn that war is an affection of the human spirit. . . . In the totality of striving and suffering we come to see the great configuration abstractly, with oneself at the center reduced in size but not in meaning, like a V-letter. . . . I tried to write freely, one day as a Christian, the next as a Jew, the next as a soldier who sees the gigantic slapstick of modern war. Certainly our contemporary man should feel divested of the stark attitudes of the last generation, the stance of the political intellectual, the proletarian, the expert, the salesman, the world-traveler, the pundit-poet."

Essay on Rime (1945) is a blank verse examination of the confusion in modern poetry: the confusion in prosody, the confusion in language, and the confusion in belief. The unknowing reader might think this work of more than two thousand decasyllabic lines to be the labor of a dusty academician amassing data for his Ph.D.; actually it was written by a soldier thousands of miles away from any library. Possibly because of that isolation, it is a more living commentary than any carefully footnoted appraisal. "This book," wrote F. O. Matthiessen, "may well be the most remarkable contribution to American art yet to have come out of the war. . . . What makes the result such exciting reading is that here we have no formal estimate; we have rather the direct statement of what a poet really knows and believes." A genuinely critical work, it is also a sketchy one; it is not without its own confusions, personal prejudices, and occasional didacticisms. But it is spontaneous, full of debatable ideas and contradictions, a provocative *tour de force*.

Shapiro's preoccupation with the poet's function and his fondness for the didactic note led to dubious results in the title poem of *Trial of a Poet and Other Poems* (1947). His attacks on the schools of modernism which Shapiro found deleterious and his condemnation of most of the intellectuals were extended in *Beyond Criticism* (1953) and in his lectures at various universities. A selected *Poems: 1940-1953*, displaying his use of mythic symbolism as well as the more effective urban realism, was followed by *Poems of a Jew* (1958).

THE LEG

Among the iodoform, in twilight-sleep,
What have I lost? he first inquires,
Peers in the middle distance where a pain,
Ghost of a nurse, hastily moves, and day,
Her blinding presence pressing in his eyes
And now his ears. They are handling him
With rubber hands. He wants to get up.

One day beside some flowers near his nose
He will be thinking, *When will I look at it?*
And pain, still in the middle distance, will reply
At what? and he will know it's gone,
O where! and begin to tremble and cry.
He will begin to cry as a child cries
Whose puppy is mangled under a screaming wheel.

Later, as if deliberately, his fingers
Begin to explore the stump. He learns a shape
That is comfortable and tucked in like a sock.
This has a sense of humor, this can despise
The finest surgical limb, the dignity of limping,
The nonsense of wheel-chairs. Now he smiles to the wall:
The amputation becomes an acquisition.

For the leg is wondering where he is (all is not lost)
And surely he has a duty to the leg;

He is its injury, the leg is his orphan,
He must cultivate the mind of the leg,
Pray for the part that is missing, pray for peace
In the image of man, pray, pray for its safety,
And after a little it will die quietly.

The body, what is it, Father, but a sign
To love the force that grows us, to give back
What in Thy palm is senselessness and mud?
Knead, knead the substance of our understanding
Which must be beautiful in flesh to walk,
That if Thou take me angrily in hand
And hurl me to the shark, I shall not die!

THE PURITAN

In tender May when the sweet laugh of Christ
Sounds in the fields, and bitter sorrows die,
Death wanes and lovers kiss and everything
Made perfect dances in the earth and sky,
Then near the Maypole where the children sing
A shadow falls, the hand and the hoarse cry
Of one whom winter more than well sufficed.

He is the Puritan under whose tall hat
Evil is nested like an ugly toad,
And in his eye he holds the basilisk,
And in his weathered hand the knotted goad;
Brimstone is on his tongue, for he will risk
Hellfire to pleasure; sin is his abode,
A barn and Bible his best habitat.

He dwells in evil; beauty of the day,
Or drifting snows of spring or flowers wet
Or touch of woman's hand are not for him;
The flesh of pleasure which he must forget
Walks in his sleep, awakens him more grim;
Deeper he falls into the Devil's debt,
And harder must he rant and harder pray.

Till every stone that manifests a pose
Beckons him lewdly, binds him to the stake
Where the cold fires of suspicion burn,
And he would gladly die for his name's sake
And call it righteous; tortures he would learn
To teach that flesh must sting and bones must ache
And hell claim all that happiness bestows.

His is the heresy of gloom, to all
That's grace a sin, to God a stumbling-block,
And to himself damnation. Year by year
He sees the hypocrisy of nature mock

His steadfastness, and in old age his fear
Of beauty strikes him dead, becomes a rock
Fixed like a gargoyle on a cathedral wall.

TRAVELOGUE FOR EXILES

Look and remember. Look upon this sky;
Look deep and deep into the sea-clean air,
The unconfined, the terminus of prayer.
Speak now and speak into the hallowed dome.
What do you hear? What does the sky reply?
The heavens are taken: this is not your home.

Look and remember. Look upon this sea;
Look down and down into the tireless tide.
What of a life below, a life inside,
A tomb, a cradle in the curly foam?
The waves arise; sea-wind and sea agree
The waters are taken: this is not your home.

Look and remember. Look upon this land,
Far, far across the factories and the grass.
Surely, there, surely, they will let you pass.
Speak then and ask the forest and the loam.
What do you hear? What does the land command?
The earth is taken: this is not your home.

THE TWINS

Likeness has made them animal and shy.
See how they turn their full gaze left and right,
Seeking the other, yet not moving close;
Nothing in their relationship is gross,
But soft, conspicuous, like giraffes. And why
Do they not speak except by sudden sight?

Sisters kiss freely and unsubtle friends
Wrestle like lovers; brothers loudly laugh:
These in a dreamier bondage dare not touch.
Each is the other's soul and hears too much
The heartbeat of the other; each apprehends
The sad duality and the imperfect half.

The one lay sick, the other wandered free,
But like a child to a small plot confined
Walked a short way and dumbly reappeared.
Is it not all-in-all of what they feared,
The single death, the obvious destiny
That maims the miracle their will designed?

For they go emptily from face to face,
Keeping the instinctive partnership of birth

A ponderous marriage and a sacred name;
Theirs is the pride of shouldering each the same
The old indignity of Esau's race
And Dromio's denouement of tragic mirth.

THE DOME OF SUNDAY

With focus sharp as Flemish-painted face
In film of varnish brightly fixed
And through a polished hand-lens deeply seen,
Sunday at noon through hyaline thin air
Sees down the street,
And in the camera of my eye depicts
Row-houses and row-lives:
Glass after glass, door after door the same,
Face after face the same, the same,
The brutal visibility the same;

As if one life emerging from one house
Would pause, a single image caught between
Two facing mirrors where vision multiplies
Beyond perspective,
A silent clatter in the high-speed eye
Spinning out photo-circulars of sight.

I see slip to the curb the long machines
Out of whose warm and windowed rooms pirouette
Shellacked with silk and light
The hard legs of our women.
Our women are one woman, dressed in black.
The carmine printed mouth
And cheeks as soft as muslin-glass belong
Outright to one dark dressy man
Merely a swagger at her curvy side.

This is their visit to themselves:
All day from porch to porch they weave
A nonsense pattern through the even glare,
Stealing in surfaces
Cold vulgar glances at themselves.

And high up in the heated room all day
I wait behind the plate glass pane for one,
Hot as a voyeur for a glimpse of one,
The vision to blot out this woman's sheen;
All day my sight records expensively
Row-houses and row-lives.

But nothing happens; no diagonal
With melting shadow falls across the curb:
Neither the blinded negress lurching through fatigue,
Nor exiles bleeding from their pores,
Nor that bright bomb slipped lightly from its rack
To splinter every silvered glass and crystal prism,
Witch-bowl and perfume bottle
And billion candle-power dressing-bulb,
No direct hit to smash the shatter-proof
And lodge at last the quivering needle
Clean in the eye of one who stands transfixed
In fascination of her brightness.

OCTOBER I

That season when the leaf deserts the bole
And half-dead see-saws through the October air
Falling face-downward on the walks to print
The decalcomania of its little soul—
Hardly has the milkman's sleepy horse
On wooden shoes echoed across the blocks,
When with its back jaws open like a dredge
The van comes lumbering up the curb to someone's door and knocks.

And four black genii muscular and shy
Holding their shy caps enter the first room

Where someone hurriedly surrenders up
The thickset chair, the mirror half awry,
Then to their burdens stoop without a sound.
One with his bare hands rends apart the bed,
One stuffs the china-barrel with stale print,
To bear the sofa toward the door with dark funereal tread.

The corner lamp, the safety eye of night,
Enveloped in the sun blinks and goes blind
And soon the early risers pick their way
Through kitchenware and pillows bolt upright.
The bureau on the sidewalk with bare back
And wrinkling veneer is most disgraced,
The sketch of Paris suffers in the wind,
Only the bike, its nose against the wall, does not show haste.

Two hours—the movers mop their neck and look
Filing through dust and echoes back and forth.
The halls are hollow and all the floors are cleared
Bare to the last board, to the most secret nook;
But on the street a small chaos survives
That slowly now the leviathan ingests,
And schoolboys and stenographers stare at
The truck, the house, the husband in his hat who stands and rests.

He turns with miserable expectant face
And for the last time enters. On the wall
A picture-stain spreads from the nail-hole down.
Each object live and dead has left its trace.
He leaves his key; but as he quickly goes
This question comes behind: Did someone die?
Is someone rich or poor, better or worse?
What shall uproot a house and bring this care into his eye?

POET

Il arrive que l'esprit demande la poésie

Left leg flung out, head cocked to the right,
Tweed coat or army uniform, with book,
Beautiful eyes, who is this walking down?
Who, glancing at the pane of glass looks sharp
And thinks it is not he—as when a poet
Comes swiftly on some half-forgotten poem
And loosely holds the page, steady of mind,
Thinking it is not his?

And when will *you* exist?—Oh, it is I,
Incredibly skinny, stooped, and neat as pie,
Ignorant as dirt, erotic as an ape,
Dreamy as puberty—with dirty hair!

Into the room like kangaroo he bounds,
Ears flopping like the most expensive hound's;
His chin received all questions as he bows
Mouthing a green bon-bon.

Has no more memory than rubber. Stands
Waist-deep in heavy mud of thought and broods
At his own wetness. When he would get out,
To his surprise he lifts in air a phrase
As whole and clean and silvery as a fish.
Which jumps and dangles on his damned hooked grin,
But like a name-card on a man's lapel
Calls him a conscious fool.

And childlike he remembers all his life
And cannily constructs it, fact by fact,
As boys paste postage stamps in careful books,
Denoting pence and legends and profiles,
Nothing more valuable.—And like a thief,
His eyes glassed over and concealed with guilt,
Fondles his secrets like a case of tools,
And waits in empty doors.

By men despised for knowing what he is,
And by himself. But he exists for women.
As dolls to girls, as perfect wives to men,
So he to women. And to himself a thing,
All ages, epicene, without a trade.
To girls and wives always alive and fated;
To men and scholars always dead like Greek
And always mistranslated.

Towards exile and towards shame he lures himself,
Tongue winding on his arm, and thinks like Eve
By biting apple will become most wise.
Sentio ergo sum: he feels his way
And words themselves stand up for him like Braille
And punch and perforate his parchment ear.
All language falls like Chinese on his soul,
Image of song unsounded.

This is the coward's coward that in his dreams
Sees shapes of pain grow tall. Awake at night
He peers at sounds and stumbles at a breeze.
And none holds life less dear. For as a youth
Who by some accident observes his love
Naked and in some natural ugly act,
He turns with loathing and with flaming hands,
Seared and betrayed by sight.

He is the business man, on beauty trades,
Dealer in arts and thoughts who, like the Jew,

Shall rise from slums and hated dialects
A tower of bitterness. Shall be always strange,
Hunted and then sought after. Shall be sat
Like an ambassador from another race
At tables rich with music. He shall eat flowers,
Chew honey and spit out gall. They shall all smile
 And love and pity him.

His death shall be by drowning. In that hour
When the last bubble of pure heaven's air
Hovers within his throat, safe on his bed,
A small eternal figurehead in terror,
He shall cry out and clutch his days of straw
Before the blackest wave. Lastly, his tomb
Shall list and founder in the troughs of grass.
 And none shall speak his name.

John Berryman

John Berryman was born October 25, 1914, in McAlester, Oklahoma, although his family was not southwestern, but northern and southern. He was educated in various states, chiefly in Connecticut and New York, as well as at Clare College, Cambridge. He taught at Harvard and Princeton.

His first important publication, "Twenty Poems," was in the first series of *Five Young American Poets* (1940), which was followed by a pamphlet, *Poems* (1942). His work was labeled (or libeled) "cerebral," and, although he employed rhyme easily, the rhythms were jagged and often broken. *The Dispossessed* (1948), a full-length volume, reveals a larger and more matured poet. The pitch is low, restrained and even resigned, somber and speculative. But Berryman's brooding is deep and his sensibility is rare. "Winter Landscape" is a perfect transcript of the mood as well as the quality of a Brueghel painting. "Parting as Descent" is a brief but brilliant record of an anguished moment; the joy of "Canto Amor" reproves the critics who implied that Berryman was preoccupied with pain. "The Statue" and "The Ball Poem" move characteristically on several levels. A semi-epical, book-length poem, *Homage to Mistress Bradstreet* (1956) puzzled many readers but was acknowledged as an intricate and outstanding accomplishment.

Besides his poetry, Berryman has published much criticism, has edited a *Selected Poems of Ezra Pound,* and has written a biography of Stephen Crane (1950), which is both comprehensive and critical.

WINTER LANDSCAPE

The three men coming down the winter hill
In brown, with tall poles and a pack of hounds
At heel, through the arrangement of the trees,

Past the five figures at the burning straw,
Returning cold and silent to their town,

Returning to the drifted snow, the rink
Lively with children, to the older men,
The long companions they can never reach,
The blue light, men with ladders, by the church
The sledge and shadow in the twilit street,

Are not aware that in the sandy time
To come, the evil waste of history
Outstretched, they will be seen upon the brow
Of that same hill: when all their company
Will have been irrecoverably lost,

These men, this particular three in brown
Witnessed by birds will keep the scene and say
By their configuration with the trees,
The small bridge, the red houses and the fire,
What place, what time, what morning occasion

Sent them into the wood, a pack of hounds
At heel and the tall poles upon their shoulders,
Thence to return as now we see them and
Ankle-deep in snow down the winter hill
Descend, while three birds watch and the fourth flies.

PARTING AS DESCENT

The sun rushed up the sky; the taxi flew;
There was a kind of fever on the clock
That morning. We arrived at Waterloo
With time to spare and couldn't find my track.

The bitter coffee in a small café
Gave us our conversation. When the train
Began to move, I saw you turn away
And vanish, and the vessels in my brain

Burst, the train roared, the other travellers
In flames leapt, burning on the tilted air
Che si cruccia, I heard the devils curse
And shriek with joy in that place beyond prayer.

THE BALL POEM

What is the boy now, who has lost his ball,
What what is he to do? I saw it go
Merrily bouncing, down the street, and then
Merrily over—there it is in the water!
No use to say "O there are other balls":

An ultimate shaking grief fixes the boy
As he stands rigid, trembling, staring down
All his young days into the harbour where
His ball went. I would not intrude on him,
A dime, another ball, is worthless. Now
He senses first his responsibility
In a world of possessions. People will take balls,
Balls will be lost always, little boy,
And no one buys a ball back. Money is external.
He is learning, far behind his desperate eyes,
The epistemology of loss, how to stand up.
Knowing what every man must one day know
And most know many days, how to stand up.
And gradually light returns to the street,
A whistle blows, the ball is out of sight,
Soon part of me will explore the deep and dark
Floor of the harbour. I am everywhere,
I suffer and move, my mind and my heart move
With all that move me, under the water
Or whistling, I am not a little boy.

CANTO AMOR

Dream in a dream the heavy soul somewhere
struck suddenly & dark down to its knees.
A griffin sighs off in the orphic air.

If (Unknown Majesty) I not confess
praise for the rack the rock the live sailor
under the blue sea,—yet I may You bless

always for hér, in fear & joy for hér
whose gesture summons ever when I grieve
me back and is my mage and minister.

—Muses, whose worship I may never leave
but for this pensive woman, now I dare,
teach me her praise! with her my praise re-
ceive.—

Three years already of the round world's war
had rolled by stoned & disappointed eyes
when she and I came where we were made
for.

Pale as a star lost in returning skies,
more beautiful than midnight stars more frail
she moved towards me like chords, a sacri-
fice;

entombed in body trembling through the veil
arm upon arm, learning our ancient wound,
we see our one soul heal, recovering pale.

Then priestly sanction, then the drop of
sound.
Quickly part to the cavern ever warm
deep from the march, body to body bound,

descend (my soul) out of dismantling storr
into the darkness where the world is made
Come back to the bright air. Love is multi
form.

Heartmating hesitating unafraid
although incredulous, she seemed to fill
the lilac shadow with light wherein sh
played,

whom sorry childhood had made sit qui
still,
an orphan silence, unregarded sheen,
listening for any small soft note, not hopefu

caricature: as once a maiden Queen,
flowering power comeliness kindness grac
shattered her mirror, wept, would not
seen.

These pities moved. Also above her face
serious or flushed, swayed her fire-gold
not earthly hair, now moonless to unlace,

resistless flame, now in a sun more cold
great shells to whorl about each secret ear,
mysterious histories, strange shores, unfol

New musics! One the music that we hear
this is the music which the masters make
out of their minds, profound solemn & clear.

And then the other music, in whose sake
all men perceive a gladness but we are drawn
less for that joy than utterly to take

our trial, naked in the music's vision,
the flowing ceremony of trouble and light,
all Loves becoming, none to rest upon.

Such Mozart made,—an ear so delicate
he fainted at a trumpet-call, a child
so delicate. So merciful that sight,

so stern, we follow rapt who ran awild.

Marriage is the second music, and thereof
we hear what we can bear, faithful & mild.

Therefore the streaming torches in the grove
through dark or bright, swiftly & now more
 near
cherish a festival of anxious love.

Dance for this music, Mistress to music dear,
more, that full storm through the disordered
 wood
ravens at midnight of my thirtieth year

and only the trial of our music should
still this irresolute air, only your voice
spelling the tempest may compel our good:

Sing then beyond my song: whirl & rejoice!

Randall Jarrell

⁂ Randall Jarrell was born May 6, 1914, in Nashville, Tennessee, spent his childhood in California, and, after that, lived in Arizona, Texas, and Tennessee. Educated at Vanderbilt University, he made his living by teaching English at Kenyon College, the University of Texas, Sarah Lawrence, and the Woman's College of the University of North Carolina. He also taught at the Salzburg Seminar in American Civilization, and for one year was literary editor of *The Nation,* in which his lively if astringent reviews appeared. In 1942 he enlisted in the Air Force, flew for a while, was "washed out" and spent most of the war as CNT (Celestial Navigation Trainer) operator at a field in Arizona, where he trained B-29 crews.

Blood for a Stranger (1942) is a first book in which the acerb critic is controlled by the sensitive poet. Jarrell alternates suave measures with brusque rhythms and achieves a wry music, a checked melodiousness, without straining for effect. This unforced intensity grows steadily in *Little Friend, Little Friend* (1945) and *Losses* (1948). The poems vibrate with an emotion which is tender and tragic, full of unsentimental pity which can smoulder with bitter outrage. An unusual intelligence is always in command, lucid, swift, witty, energetic, and vividly suggestive.

Whatever Jarrell touches is given a precise impact. John Crowe Ransom wrote that Jarrell had "an angel's velocity and range with language"; the late Theodore Spencer said that his "energy, satiric bitterness, and weight prove him to be one of the most interesting poets of his generation." Such tributes were justified by the increasing substance and subtlety of the poems in *The Seven-League Crutches* (1951), *Selected Poems* (1955), and *The Woman at the Washington Zoo* (1960), which won the National Book Award in 1961.

Jarrell, who was Consultant in Poetry for two years at the Library of Congress, is also the author of *Pictures from an Institution* (1954), a satirical and coruscating novel, and *Poetry and the Age* (1953), a collection of alertly critical studies.

A CAMP IN THE PRUSSIAN FOREST

I walk beside the prisoners to the road.
Load on puffed load,
Their corpses, stacked like sodden wood,
Lie barred or galled with blood

By the charred warehouse. No one comes today
In the old way
To knock the fillings from their teeth;
The dark, coned, common wreath

Is plaited for their grave—a kind of grief.
The living leaf
Clings to the planted profitable
Pine if it is able;

The boughs sigh, mile on green, calm, breathing mile,
From this dead file
The planners ruled for them . . . One year
They sent a million here:

Here men were drunk like water, burnt like wood.
The fat of good
And evil, the breast's star of hope
Were rendered into soap.

I paint the star I sawed from yellow pine—
And plant the sign
In soil that does not yet refuse
Its usual Jews

Their first asylum. But the white, dwarfed star—
This dead white star—
Hides nothing, pays for nothing; smoke
Fouls it, a yellow joke,

The needles of the wreath are chalked with ash,
A filmy trash
Litters the black woods with the death
Of men; and one last breath

Curls from the monstrous chimney . . . I laugh aloud
Again and again;
The star laughs from its rotting shroud
Of flesh. O star of men!

PILOTS, MAN YOUR PLANES

(*A Jill is a Japanese torpedo-plane.*)

Dawn; and the jew's-harp's sawing seesaw song
Plucks at the starlight where the planes are folded
At the lee of their blank, wind-whipped, hunting road—
A road in air, the road to nowhere
Turreted and bucketed with guns, long undermined
With the thousand necessary deaths that breathe
Like fire beside a thousand men, who sleep
Hunched in the punk of Death: slow, dreaming sparks
That burrow through the block-long, light-split gloom
Of their great hangar underground and oversea
Into the great tanks, dark forever; past the steam
Of turbines, laundries—under rockets,
Bakeries, war-heads, the steel watch-like fish,
To the hull's last plates and atmosphere:
The sea sways with the dazed, blind, groping sway
Of the raw soul drugged with sleep, the chancy life
Troubling with dreams its wars, its own earned sea
That stretches year on year, death after death,
And hemisphere on blind black hemisphere
Into the stubborn corners of its earth.

Here in the poor, bleak, guessing haze of dawn
The giant's jew's-harp screeches its two notes
Over and over, over and over; from the roar
Of the fighters waved into the blazing clouds
The lookout lifts his scrubbed tetanic stare
Into the East of light, the empty day.
But on the tubes the raiders oscillate
A mile in every nine or thirteen seconds
To the target's first premonitory bursts;
To the boy with a ball of coffee in his stomach,
Snapping the great light buckles on his groin,
Shifting his raft's hot-water-bottle weight
As he breasts the currents of the bellowing deck
And, locked at last into the bubble, Hope,
Is borne along the foaming windy road
To the air where he alone is still
Above the world's cold, absent, searching roll.

The carrier meshed in its white whirling wake,
The gray ship sparkling from the blue-black sea,
The little carrier—erupts in flak,
One hammering, hysterical, tremendous fire.
Flickering through flashes, the stained rolling clouds,
The air jarred like water tilted in a bowl,
The red wriggling tracers—colonies
Whose instant life annexes the whole sky—

Hunt out the one end they have being for,
Are metamorphosed into one pure smear
Of flame, and die
In the maniacal convulsive spin
Of the raider with a wing snapped off, the plane
Trailing its flaming kite's-tail to the wave.
A miss's near, near bloom, a hill of foam,
Is bulged skyward, crashes back; crest after crest
Patterns the ships' cat's-craddle wakes, the racing
Swells that hiss outward from a plane's quenched flame:
There is traced in the thousand meetings of the grave
Of matter and of matter, man and man,
The print of the running feet upon the waves . . .
The Jill threads her long, blind, unbearable
Way into fire (the waves lick past her, her whole sky
Is tracer and the dirt of flak, the fire
Flung from the muzzles riddling sea and sky),
Comes on, comes on, comes on; and the fighter flames to her
Through his own flak, the hammering guns
Stitch one long line along his wing, his gear
Falls, his dive staggers as his tracer strikes,
And he breaks off and somersaults into the sea.
Under the canopy's dark strangling green,
The darkening canopy, he struggles free
To float into the choking white, to breathe—
His huge leg floating and immovable,
His goggles blackened with his own bright blood—
On the yellow raft, to see his carrier
Still firing, but itself a fire, its planes
Flung up like matches from the stern's white burst.
Now rockets arch above the deck's great blaze,
Shells break from it, trail after trail; its steel
Melts in steam into the sea, its tanks explode
In one last overwhelming sound; and silently
The ship, a flame, sinks home into the sea.
The pilot holds his striped head patiently
Up out of the dancing smother of the sea
And weeps with hatred, longing, agony—
The sea rises and settles; and the ship is gone.

The planes fly off looking for a carrier,
Destroyers curve in their long hunting arcs
Through the dead of the carrier: the dazed, vomiting,
Oil-blackened and fire-blistered, saved or dying men
Cling with cramped shaking fingers to the lines
Lowered from their old life: the pilot,
Drugged in a blanket, straining up to gulp
From the mug that scrapes like chalk against his mouth,
Knows, knows at last; he yawns the chattering yawn
Of effort and anguish, of hurt hating helplessness—
Yawns sobbingly, his head falls back, he sleeps.

THE DEATH OF THE BALL TURRET GUNNER

From my mother's sleep I fell into the State,
And I hunched in its belly till my wet fur froze.
Six miles from earth, loosed from its dream of life,
I woke to black flak and the nightmare fighters.
When I died they washed me out of the turret with a hose.

BURNING THE LETTERS

(*The wife of a pilot killed in the Pacific is speaking several years after his death. She was once a Christian, a Protestant.*)

Here in my head, the home that is left for you,
You have not changed; the flames rise from the sea
And the sea changes: the carrier, torn in two,
Sinks to its planes—the corpses of the carrier
Are strewn like ashes on the star-reflecting sea;
Are gathered, sewn with weights, are sunk.
The gatherers disperse.
Here to my hands
From the sea's dark, incalculable calm,
The unchanging circle of the universe,
The letters float: the set yellowing face
Looks home to me, a child's at last,
From the cut-out paper; and the licked
Lips part in their last questioning smile.
The poor labored answers, still unanswering;
The faded questions—questioning so much,
I thought then—questioning so little;
Grew younger, younger, as my eyes grew old,
As that dreamed-out and wept-for wife,
Your last unchanging country, changed
Out of your own rejecting life—a part
Of accusation and of loss, a child's eternally—
Into my troubled separate being.

A child has her own faith, a child's.
In its savage figures—worn down, now, to death—
Men's one life issues, neither out of earth
Nor from the sea, the last dissolving sea,
But out of death: by man came death
And his Life wells from death, the death of Man.
The hunting flesh, the broken blood
Glimmer within the tombs of earth, the food
Of the lives that burrow under the hunting wings
Of the light, of the darkness: dancing, dancing,
The flames grasp flesh with their last searching grace—
Grasp as the lives have grasped: the hunted
Pull down the hunter for his unused life
Parted into the blood, the dark, veined bread

Later than all law. The child shudders, aging:
The peering savior, stooping to her clutch,
His talons cramped with his own bartered flesh,
Pales, flickers, and flares out. In the darkness—darker
With the haunting after-images of light—
The dying God, the eaten Life
Are the nightmare I awaken from to night.

(The flames dance over life. The mourning slaves
In their dark secrecy, come burying
The slave bound in another's flesh, the slave
Freed once, forever, by another's flesh:
The Light flames, flushing the passive face
With its eternal life.)

The lives are fed
Into the darkness of their victory;
The ships sink, forgotten; and the sea
Blazes to darkness: the unsearchable
Death of the lives lies dark upon the life
That, bought by death, the loved and tortured lives,
Stares westward, passive, to the blackening sea.
In the tables of the dead, in the unopened almanac,
The head, charred, featureless—the unknown mean—
Is thrust from the waters like a flame, is torn
From its last being with the bestial cry
Of its pure agony. O death of all my life,
Because of you, because of you, I have not died,
By your death I have lived.

The sea is empty.
As I am empty, stirring the charred and answered
Questions about your home, your wife, your cat
That stayed at home with me—that died at home
Gray with the years that gleam above you there
In the great green grave where you are young
And unaccepting still. Bound in your death,
I choose between myself and you, between your life
And my own life: it is finished.

Here in my head
There is room for your black body in its shroud,
The dog-tags welded to your breastbone, and the flame
That winds above your death and my own life
And the world of my life. The letters and the face
That stir still, sometimes, with your fiery breath—
Take them, O grave! Great grave of all my years,
The unliving universe in which all life is lost,
Make yours the memory of that accepting
And accepted life whose fragments I cast here.

JEWS AT HAIFA

The freighter, gay with rust,
Coasts to a bare wharf of the harbor.
From the funnel's shade (the arbor
Of gourds from which the prophet, without trust,
Watched his old enemies,
The beings of this earth) I scrutinize

The hundreds at the rail
Lapped in the blue blaze of this sea
Who stare till their looks fail
At the earth that they are promised; silently
See the sand-bagged machine-guns,
The red-kneed soldiers blinking in the sun.

A machine-gun away
Are men with our faces: we are torn
With the live blaze of day—
Till we feel shifting, wrenched apart, the worn
Named stones of our last knowledge:
That all men wish our death. Here on the edge

Of the graves of Europe
We believe: truly, we are not dead;
It seems to us that hope
Is possible—that even mercy is permitted
To men on this earth,
To Jews on this earth. . . . But at Cyprus, the red earth,

The huts, the trembling wire
That wreathes us, are to us familiar
As death. All night, the fires
Float their sparks up to the yellow stars;
From the steel, stilted tower
The light sweeps over us. We whisper: "Ours."

Ours; and the stones slide home.
There is no hope; "in all this world
There is no other wisdom
Than ours: we have understood the world,"
We think; but hope, in dread
Search for one doubt, and whisper: "Truly, we are not dead."

A COUNTRY LIFE

A bird that I don't know,
Hunched on this light-pole like a scarecrow,
Looks sideways out into the wheat
The wind waves under the waves of heat.

The field is yellow as egg-bread dough
Except where (just as though they'd let
It live for looks) a locust billows
In leaf-green and shade-violet,
A standing mercy.
The bird calls twice, "*Red* clay, *red* clay";
Or else he's saying, "Directly, directly."
If someone came by I could ask,
Around here all of them must know—
And why they live so and die so—
Or why, for once, the lagging heron
Flaps from the little creek's parched cresses
Across the harsh-grassed, gullied meadow
To the black, rowed evergreens below.

They know and they don't know.
To ask, a man must be a stranger—
And asking, much more answering, is dangerous;
Asked about it, who would not repent
Of all he ever did and never meant,
And think a life and its distresses,
Its random, clutched-for, homefelt blisses,
The circumstances of an accident?
The farthest farmer in a field,
A gaunt plant grown, for seed, by farmers,
Has felt a longing, lorn urbanity
Jailed in his breast; and, just as I,
Has grunted, in his old perplexity,
A standing plea.

From the tar of the blazing square
The eyes shift, in their taciturn
And unavowing, unavailing sorrow.
Yet the intonation of a name confesses
Some secrets that they never meant
To let out to a soul; and what words would not dim
The bowed and weathered heads above the denim
Or the once-too-often-washed wash dresses?

They are subdued to their own element.
One day
The red, clay face
Is lowered to the naked clay;
After some words, the body is forsaken. . . .
The shadows lengthen, and a dreaming hope
Breathes, from the vague mound, *Life;*
From the grove under the spire
Stars shine, and a wandering light
Is kindled for the mourner, man.
The angel kneeling with the wreath
Sees, in the moonlight, graves.

HOPE

The spirit killeth, but the
letter giveth life.

The week is dealt out like a hand
That children pick up card by card.
One keeps getting the same hand.
One keeps getting the same card.

But twice a day—except on Saturday—
But every day—except on Sunday—
The wheel stops, there is a catch in Time:
With a hiss of soles, a rattle of tin,
My own gray Daemon pauses on the stair,
My own bald Fortune lifts me by the hair.

Woe's me! Woe's me! In Folly's mailbox
Still laughs the postcard, Hope:
Your uncle in Australia
Has died and you are Pope.
For many a soul has entertained
A Mailman unawares—
And as you cry, "Impossible,"
A step is on the stairs.

One keeps getting the same dream
Delayed, marked Postage Due,
The bill that one has paid
Delayed, marked Payment Due,

Twice a day, in a rotting mailbox,
The white grubs are new:
And Faith once more is mine
Faithfully, but Charity
Writes hopefully about a new
Asylum—but Hope is as good as new.

Woe's me! Woe's me! In Folly's mailbox
Still laughs the postcard, Hope:
Your uncle in Australia
Has died and you are Pope.
For many a soul has entertained
A Mailman unawares—
And as you cry, "Impossible,"
A step is on the stairs.

THE REFUGEES

In the shabby train no seat is vacant.
The child in the ripped mask
Sits undisturbed in the waste
Of the smashed compartment. But how shall I escape?

These had lives like mine. What was it they possessed
That they were willing to trade for this?

There is blood, dried now, along the mask
Of the child who yesterday possessed
A country welcomer than this.
Did he? All night into the waste
The train moves silently, the vacant
Breath rises, vanishes—Escape, escape!

One pays, for this freedom, all that one possessed;
Here all the purses are vacant.
Sleep; and the emptying hearts escape
Even their own wish—turn back to this
Nothing that hides, with its calm cancelling mask,
The days and the faces: the world they waste.

What else are the lives but a journey to the vacant
Satisfaction of death? And the mask
They wear tonight through their waste
Is death's rehearsal. *For I too shall escape,*
We read in the faces; and what is there we possessed
That we were unwilling to trade for this?

Barbara Howes

Barbara Howes was born in Boston, Massachusetts, in 1914. Graduating from Bennington College, she went to New York, where she edited the quarterly, *Chimera.* After spending some time abroad, she married the poet, William Jay Smith, and, with their two young sons, took up residence in North Pownal, Vermont.

Recipient of several awards, including a Guggenheim Fellowship, Barbara Howes showed her distinctive quality in her first two volumes, *The Undersea Farmer* (1948) and *In the Cold Country* (1954). Her third volume, *Light and Dark* (1959), strengthens the impression made by their predecessors, the impact of a seventeenth century poet with a twentieth century turn of mind. Her images are always original, deceptively smooth and quiet, but edged with sharp expressiveness; her lines are graceful but firm. The poet employs some of the most rigid classical forms to frame her modern material. "Death of a Vermont Farm Woman" is a rondeau; "The Triumph of Death" is a villanelle; "Early Supper" consists of three triolets. In the less rigid forms, as in "Portrait of the Artist," "On a Bougainvillæa Vine at the Summer Palace," and "On Galveston Beach," she is equally adept at fusing outer form and inner substance with perception and imagination.

In addition to prizes awarded by *Poetry: A Magazine of Verse,* she was presented with the Poetry Grant by Brandeis University in 1958.

PORTRAIT OF THE BOY AS ARTIST

Were he composer, he would surely write
A quartet for three orchestras, one train:
After the penny-whistle's turn, he might—
With ten bull-fiddles purring the refrain—
Dub in a lion to outroar the night.

Were he a painter, he would loose such bolts
Of color as would scare the sun, abash
Rainbows: a palomino-coated colt
Gallops on every speckled plain: a gashed
Knee bleeds rubies: frogs are emerald.

Were he a poet with the gift of tongues,
He'd scale the Andes in a metaphor,
Race Theseus in the labyrinth, among
Larks and angels act as troubadour,
For Daniel Boone shout at the top of his lungs.

Clear-eyed he sallies forth upon the field,
Holding close to his ear the shell of the world.

DEATH OF A VERMONT FARM WOMAN

Is it time now to go away?
July is nearly over; hay
Fattens the barn, the herds are strong,
Our old fields prosper; these long
Green evenings will keep death at bay.

Last winter lingered; it was May
Before a flowering lilac spray
Barred cold for ever. I was wrong.
Is it time now?

Six decades vanished in a day!
I bore four sons: one lives; they
Were all good men; three dying young
Was hard on us. I have looked long
For these hills to show me where peace lay.
Is it time now?

THE TRIUMPH OF DEATH

Illusion forms before us like a grove
Of aspen hazing all the summer air
As we approach a new plateau of love.

With discs of light and shade, vibration of
Leaf-candelabra, dim, all-tremulous there,
Illusion forms before us like a grove

And bends in welcome: with each step we move
Nearer, quick with desire, quick to dare.
As we approach a new plateau of love,

New passion, new adventure wait above
And call to our drumming blood; all unaware
Illusion forms before us like a grove

In a mirage, we reach out to take Love
In our arms, compelled by one another's stare.
As we approach a new plateau of love

The aspen sigh in mockery: then have
We come this way before? Staining the air,
Illusion forms before us like a grove
As we approach a new plateau of love.

ON A BOUGAINVILLÆA VINE AT THE SUMMER PALACE

Under the sovereign crests of dead volcanoes,
See how the lizards move in courtly play;
How when the regnant male
Fills the loose bagpipe of his throat with air,
His mate will scale
Some vine portcullis, quiver, halt, then peer—
Eyes sharp as pins—
At that grandee posed stiff with self-esteem,
His twiglike tail acurve.

What palaces lie hid in vines! She sees
Chameleon greenrooms opening on such
Elite boudoirs,
Flowers as bright as massacres; should she
Not try their spiring tendrils
That like string
Hammocks are slung upon the open air?
Tensing his tiny jaw, he seems to smile;
And while all nature sways,
Lightly rides his delicate trapeze.

A virid arrow parts
The leaves—she's at
His side. Then darts away; he following,
They lose themselves within the redolent shade. . . .
Quiet the palace lies
Under the sun's green thumb,
As if marauding winter would never come.

ON GALVESTON BEACH

The sky was battened down
Low all around us. We stood up
Into a sea of air,
First-comers to this Sicilian element,
Prospectors motionless in a bowl of blue.

Down-at-mouth at the rim,
The barely-breathing sea
Neighbored flat sand; it waited
As a pier does for some sightseer
Of horizons to wander out.

If the sky is indeed a bowl
Pressed over us by a huge hand,
We have fellow-creatures everywhere. The
Sand in its patient minuteness,
That lean duck, his neck a hook, bobbing for fish,
Or those great mushrooms of the Gulf,
Jetsam jellyfish, in whose gills
Lie strands of aquamarine;
Their lives, so humpbacked and so white,
Resemble death. We stand awhile and watch
Waves worry them toward shore,
Before striking out in their sea.

Ruth Stone

⁂ Ruth Stone was born June 8, 1915, in Roanoke, Virginia, grew up in Indianapolis, Indiana, attended the University of Illinois, and was, for a while, assistant to the literary and dramatic editor of the *Indianapolis Star*. Her marriage to the writer, Walter Stone, brought her to Cambridge, Massachusetts and, when her husband taught at Vassar College, to Poughkeepsie, New York. After his death in 1959, she divided her time between Middletown, Connecticut, where she became an editor of the Wesleyan University Press and, with her three daughters, a home in Vermont.

Mrs. Stone won the Kenyon Review Fellowship in Poetry in 1955; her first volume, *In an Iridescent Time* (1959) was published four years later and displayed a style that is both bold and delicate. The title poem (originally called "Laundry" when it appeared in *The New Yorker*), "Orchard," and "Vernal Equinox" communicate a special touch, a reminiscence of childhood in a tone that is tender without being mawkish, while "The Magnet" is a brisk and lightly ribald ballad. Mrs. Stone's technique is tight; her lines are direct and the implications never waver. The firmness, however, is not the result of rigidity but is the diction of a discriminating mind and a disciplined heart.

IN AN IRIDESCENT TIME

My mother, when young, scrubbed laundry in a tub,
She and her sisters on an old brick walk
Under the apple trees, sweet rub-a-dub.
The bees came round their heads, the wrens made talk.
Four young ladies each with a rainbow board
Honed their knuckles, wrung their wrists to red,
Tossed back their braids and wiped their aprons wet.
The Jersey calf beyond the back fence roared;
And all the soft days, swarms about their pet
Buzzed at his big brown eyes and bullish head.
Four times they rinsed, they said. Some things they starched,
Then shook them from the baskets two by two,
And pinned the fluttering intimacies of life
Between the lilac bushes and the yew:
Brown gingham, pink, and skirts of Alice blue.

THE MAGNET

I loved my lord, my black-haired lord, my young love
Thin faced, pointed like a fox,
And he, singing and sighing, with the bawdy went crying
Up the hounds, through thicket he leaped, through bramble,
And crossed the river on rocks.
And there alongside the sheep and among the ewes and lambs,
With terrible sleep he cunningly laid his hoax.

Ah fey, and ill-gotten, and wicked his tender heart,
Even as they with their bahs and their niggles, rumped up the thistle and bit
With their delicate teeth the flowers and the seeds and the leaf,
He leaped with a cry as coarse as the herders, "Come I will start,
Come now my pretties, and dance, to the hunting horn and the slit
Of your throbbing throats, and make me a coat out of grief."
And they danced, he was fey, and they danced, and the coat they made
Turned all of an innocent mind, and a single love, into beasts afraid.

Was it is I called him back? was it hunger? was it the world?
Not my tears, not those cries of the murdered, but 'twas the fox
Hid in the woods who called, and the smell of the fox, burned in his mind,
The fox in his den, smiling, around his red body his fine plume curled,
Out of the valley and across the river, leaving his sheep's hair, he left the maligned flocks,
I heard him coming through brambles, through narrow forests, I bid my nights unwind,
I bid my days turn back, I broke my windows, I unsealed my locks.

VERNAL EQUINOX

Daughters, in the wind's boisterous roughing,
Pray the tickle's equal to the coat tearing,

And the wearing equal to the puffing,
As you match breath and tugging after the winter
In the thaw and the first heat of the sun's splinter.

In your first ramble, daughters, with your laughing
Loosed from the freeze when the grass is seeping,
Save your dimpled knees in the headstrong leaping.

And under his cloak, if you run with the north wind
When there is the smell of hibernation in him
And the black half-frozen waters of a dam,
Watch for his cruelty, he traps the lamb.

Daughters under the birches in the green weeping,
In the rain and lightning of the west wind's keeping,
Daughters, does, with tawny flanks shy stamping,
Nibble his water-quick land with your hoofs tamping,
And dance, do not rest, or he'll have you sleeping.

And daughters whose hearts are going
Higher, higher with your wild hair blowing
Into his high-riding giant's bellows,
Observe the tremble of the weeping willows.

Peter Viereck

Peter Viereck was born August 5, 1916, in New York City. He attended Horace Mann School and, at twenty-one, was graduated *summa cum laude* from Harvard, where he was Phi Beta Kappa, and won prizes for his prose and verse. During 1937-38 he was a Fellow at Christ Church, Oxford, and, a few years later, was awarded the M.A. and Ph.D. in history from Harvard. During the Second World War he served overseas in the African and Italian campaigns and, later, taught at the "G. I. University" at Florence. After receiving his honorable discharge in 1945, he returned to Harvard, where he was Instructor in Literature and German. He became Assistant Professor at Smith and Associate Professor at Mount Holyoke.

Viereck's first book was not a book of poems but a book of political essays: *Metapolitics: From the Romantics to Hitler* (1941). Written at twenty-five, this brilliant analysis of the cultural backgrounds of fascism was translated into several languages. Viereck's range was enlarged in *Terror and Decorum* (1948), a book of energetic and, at times, exuberant poems. Viereck writes about the Dawn Horse and the function of the poet with an equal mixture of gravity and mockery. He puts the scrawled phrase "Kilroy was here" into rhyme with adventurous daring and epic spirit. He is amusing and arousing in the same breath. He is an experimenter who rarely yields to the speciously spectacular, a writer who respects tradition without being submerged by it, a wit who is, at the same time, a serious and, sometimes, too self-conscious poet.

Terror and Decorum, which won the Pulitzer Prize in 1949, was followed by four other volumes of poetry: *Strike Through the Mask* (1950), *The First Morning* (1952), *The Persimmon Tree* (1956), chiefly lyrics and pastorals, and *The Tree Witch* (1961), a fantasy which is part drama and part social satire.

A commentator and critic, Viereck is also the author of *Conservatism Revisited* (1949), a study of present-day politics, *Shame and Glory of the Intellectuals* (1952), an appraisal of American culture, *Dream and Responsibility* (1953), and other prose.

KILROY

[Editor's note: An example of an unfaked epic spirit emerging from the war was the expression "Kilroy was here," scribbled everywhere by American soldiers and implying that nothing was too adventurous or remote.]

Also Ulysses once—that other war.
(Is it because we find his scrawl
Today on every privy door
That we forget his ancient role?)
Also was there—he did it for the wages—
When a Cathay-drunk Genoese set sail.
Whenever "longen folk to goon on pilgrimages,"
Kilroy is there;
he tells The Miller's Tale.

At times he seems a paranoic king
Who stamps his crest on walls and says "My Own!"
But in the end he fades like a lost tune,
Tossed here and there, whom all the breezes sing.
"Kilroy was here"; these words sound wanly gay,
Haughty yet tired with long marching.
He is Orestes—guilty of what crime?—
For whom the Furies still are searching;
When they arrive, they find their prey
(Leaving his name to mock them) went away.
Sometimes he does not flee from them in time:
"Kilroy was—"
with his blood a dying man
Wrote half the phrase out in Bataan.

Kilroy, beware. "HOME" is the final trap
That lurks for you in many a wily shape:
In pipe-and-slippers plus a Loyal Hound
Or fooling around, just fooling around.
Kind to the old (their warm Penelope)
But fierce to boys,
thus "home" becomes that sea,

Horribly disguised, where you were always drowned—
(How could suburban Crete condone
The yarns you would have V-mailed from the sun?)—
And folksy fishes sip Icarian tea.

One stab of hopeless wings imprinted your
Exultant Kilroy-signature
Upon sheer sky for all the world to stare:
"I was there! I was there! I was there!"

God is like Kilroy. He, too, sees it all;
That's how He knows of every sparrow's fall;
That's why we prayed each time the tightropes cracked
On which our loveliest clowns contrived their act.
The G. I. Faustus who was

everywhere
Strolled home again. "What was it like outside?"
Asked Can't, with his good neighbors Ought and But
And pale Perhaps and grave-eyed Better Not;
For "Kilroy" means: the world is very wide.
He was there, he was there, he was there!

And in the suburbs Can't sat down and cried.

VALE FROM CARTHAGE

(*Spring, 1944*)

I, now at Carthage. He, shot dead at Rome.
Shipmates last May. "And what if one of us,"
I asked last May, in fun, in gentleness,
"Wears doom, like dungarees, and doesn't know?"
He laughed, "Not see Times Square again?" The foam,
Feathering across that deck a year ago,
Swept those five words—like seeds—beyond the seas
Into his future. There they grew like trees;
And as he passed them there next spring, they laid
Upon his road of fire their sudden shade.
Though he had always scraped his mess-kit pure
And scrubbed redeemingly his barracks floor,
Though all his buttons glowed their ritual-hymn
Like cloudless moons to intercede for him,
No furlough fluttered from the sky. He will
Not see Times Square—he will not see—he will
Not see Times

change; at Carthage (while my friend,
Living those words at Rome, screamed in the end)
I saw an ancient Roman's tomb and read
"*Vale*" in stone. Here two wars mix their dead:
Roman, my shipmate's dream walks hand in hand
With yours tonight ("New York again" and "Rome"),

Like widowed sisters bearing water home
On tired heads through hot Tunisian sand
In good cool urns, and says, "I understand."
Roman, you'll see your Forum Square no more;
What's left but this to say of any war?

LOVE SONG TO EOHIPPUS

(Dictionary definition: "EOHIPPUS, Greek for dawn-horse, small graceful prehistoric ancestor of modern equine family; size of rabbit; had four toes, no hoofs.")

Dance, dance in this museum case,
Ballet-star of our mammal race,
Attar and avatar of grace.

Sweet Eohippus, "dawn horse" in
That golden Attic tongue which now
Like you and Helen is extinct,
Like Cheshire cat of fading grin,
Like Carthage and like Villon's snow,
With death and beauty gently linked.

Yet all are deathless in their fashion:
You live in science, they in song,
You in museums, she in Homer.
She cannot help but live while passion
Still lives; your dancing lives as long
As grace; "extinct" is a misnomer.

Because sly Darwin liked the Fit
And Mendel, good gray monk, sowed peas,
Dame Evolution said benignly,
"My child, get bigger," and you did;
"Look here, those silly toes must cease!",
And you grew hoofs and frisked equinely.

When you were dodging dinosaurs
So recklessley, they were gigantic;
But look how Nature turns the tables:
Now they, who scared you with their roars,
Have changed to lizards, wee and frantic,
And you're immense and live in stables.

Ballet-star of our mammal race,
Last lingering of earth's first grace,
Dance on in this museum case.

BLINDMAN'S BUFF

Night-watchmen think of dawn and things auroral.
Clerks wistful for Bermudas think of coral.
The poet in New York still thinks of laurel.

(But lovers think of death and touch each other
As if to prove that love is still alive.)

The Martian space-crew, in an Earthward dive,
Think of their sweet unearthly earth Up There,
Where darling monsters romp in airless air.
(Two lovers think of death and touch each other,
Fearing that day when only one's alive.)

We think of cash, but cash does not arrive.
We think of fun, but fate will not connive.
We never mention death. Do we survive?
(The lovers think of death and touch each other
To live their love while love is yet alive.)

Prize-winners are so avid when they strive;
They race so far; they pile their toys so high.
Only a cad would trip them. Yet they die.
(The lovers think of death and touch each other;
Of all who live, these are the most alive.)

When all the lemming-realists contrive
To swim—where to?—in life's enticing tide,
Only a fool would stop and wait outside.
(The lovers stop and wait and touch each other.
Who twinly think of death are twice alive.)

Plump creatures smack their lips and think they thrive;
The hibernating bear, but half alive,
Dreams of free honey in a stingless hive.
He thinks of life at every lifeless breath.
(The lovers think of death.)

POET

"Toute forme crée, même par l'homme, est immortelle. Car la forme est indépendante de la matière, et ce ne sont pas les molécules qui constituent la forme."

(*Baudelaire: Mon Cœur Mis à Nu*)

The night he died, earth's images all came
To gloat in liberation round his tomb.
Now vengeful colors, stones, and faces dare
        To argue with his metaphor;
And stars his fancy painted on the skies
Drop down like swords
                                        to pierce his too wide eyes.

Words that begged favor at his court in vain—
Lush adverbs, senile rhymes in tattered gowns—
        Send notes to certain exiled nouns
And mutter openly against his reign.
While rouged clichés hang out red lights again.

Hoarse refugees report from far-flung towns
That exclamation-marks are running wild
And prowling half-truths carried off a child.

But he lives on in Form, and Form shall shatter
 This tuneless mutiny of Matter.
His bones are dead; his voice is horribly strong
Those famed vibrations of life's dancing dust,
Whose thrice-named pangs are "birth" and "death" and "lust,"
Are but the split iambics of his song.
Scansion of flesh in endless ebb and flow,
Mere grace-notes of that living thousand-year
Tyrannic metronome whose every gear
Is some shy craftsman buried long ago.
What terror crowns the sweetness of all song?

What hardness leaps at us from each soft tune
And hammers us to shapes we never planned?
This was a different dying from our own.
 Call every wizard in the land—
Bell, book, and test tube; let the dark be rife
With every exorcism we command.
In vain. This death is stronger than our life.

In vain we drive stakes through such a haunter
Or woo with spiced applaudings such a heart.
His news of April do but mock our Winter
Like maps of heaven breathed on window-frost
By cruel clowns in codes whose key is lost.
Yet some sereneness in our rage has guessed
That we are being blessed and blessed and blessed
When least we know it and when coldest art
 Seems hostile,
 useless,
 or apart.

 Not worms, not worms in such a skull
But rhythms, rhythms writhe and sting and crawl.
He sings the seasons round, from bud to snow.
And all things are because he willed them so.

Robert Lowell

Robert (Traill Spence) Lowell was born March 1, 1917 in Boston, Massachusetts. He attended St. Mark's School, Harvard, and Kenyon, where he taught briefly, and Louisiana State University. In 1943 he twice attempted to enlist but he was rejected. When he was drafted he refused to serve on the grounds that the country was out of danger and that the indiscriminate bombing of civilians was unprincipled and unbridled murder. As a conscientious objector, he served five months in a federal prison.

Like James Russell Lowell, his great-grandfather's brother, and Amy Lowell, a distant cousin, Robert Lowell was a consistent nonconformer. His first slender book, *Land of Unlikeness* (1944), showed a Puritan Lowell in revolt. Many of Lowell's poems were not only exciting but exasperated—angry love letters to New England. *Lord Weary's Castle* (1946), which contained some pages from the earlier volume, was awarded the Pulitzer Prize. In 1947, before Lowell was thirty, the poet won two other signal honors: he was given a Guggenheim Fellowship and a grant of $1000 by the National Institute of Arts and Letters.

It is immediately apparent that Robert Lowell's poetry does not make for easy reading; the images are so congested, the allusions so complex that the uninitiated reader is likely to be confused. But it is also apparent that this is a poetry of deep passion and fierce tension; the impact is violent, the intensity of a traditional Protestant turned Catholic. Beneath the surface formalism of the verse, there is a deep protest against what New England has become, against the commercialism of the age and degeneration of the community.

The poets were especially loud in praise of Lowell's vibrancy and inventiveness. John Berryman wrote: "Robert Lowell seems to me the most powerful poet who has appeared in England or America for some years, master of a freedom in the Catholic subject without peer since Hopkins." Peter Viereck added: "He may become the great American poet of the 1950's, for he seems the best qualified to restore to our literature its sense of the tragic and the lofty."

Lowell's fellow-craftsmen were not less enthusiastic after the publication of *The Mills of the Kavanaghs* (1951), which included a dramatic narrative of some six hundred lines, and *Life Studies,* which contained a thirty-five-page prose autobiography and won the National Book Award in 1960. "Whenever I read a book by Robert Lowell," wrote Elizabeth Bishop, "I have a chilling sensation of here-and-now, of exact contemporaneity. . . . If more people read poetry, if it were more exportable and translatable, surely his poems would go far towards changing, or at least unsettling, minds made up against us. Somehow or other, in the midst of our worst century so far, we have produced a magnificent poet."

It was generally granted that Lowell's method was elliptical, but there was no escaping the moral purpose of his work. His is a tortured outcry against the corruption of the times; a grim need to find a faith in a world torn between frivolity and failure. If there is uncertainty in the writing there is no softness or insincerity. Technically Lowell is remarkably resourceful; he combines classic form and daring experiment. Obeying a logic of its own, Lowell's verse is unpredictable; the quickly accumulating images, the sudden transitions, the fierce rhetoric recall Hart Crane as well as the baroque metaphysicians of the seventeenth century. ("Falling Asleep Over the Aeneid" is prefaced by Lowell's note: "An old man in Concord forgets to go to morning service. He falls asleep while reading Vergil, and dreams that he is Aeneas at the funeral of Pallas, an Italian prince.") But Lowell's poetry could have been written nowhere but in New England, and at no other time than now.

THE HOLY INNOCENTS

Listen, the hay-bells tinkle as the cart
Wavers on rubber tires along the tar
And cindered ice below the burlap mill
And ale-wife run. The oxen drool and start
In wonder at the fenders of a car
And blunder hugely up St. Peter's hill.
These are the undefiled by woman—their
Sorrow is not the sorrow of this world:
King Herod shrieking vengeance at the curled
Up knees of Jesus choking in the air,

A king of speechless clods and infants. Still
The world out-Herods Herod; and the year,
The nineteen-hundred forty-fifth of grace,
Lumbers with losses up the clinkered hill
Of our purgation; and the oxen near
The worn foundations of their resting place,
The holy manger where their bed is corn
And holly torn for Christmas. If they die,
As Jesus, in the harness, who will mourn?
Lamb of the shepherds, Child, how still you lie.

COLLOQUY IN BLACK ROCK

Here the jack-hammer jabs into the ocean;
My heart, you race and stagger and demand
More blood-gangs for your nigger-brass percussions,
Till I, the stunned machine of your devotion,
Clanging upon this cymbal of a hand,
Am rattled screw and footloose. All discussions

End in the mud-flat detritus of death.
My heart, beat faster, faster. In Black Mud
Hungarian workmen give their blood
For the martyre Stephen, who was stoned to death.

Black Mud, a name to conjure with: O mud
For watermelons gutted to the crust,
Mud for the mole-tide harbor, mud for mouse,
Mud for the armored Diesel fishing tubs that thud
A year and a day to wind and tide; the dust
Is on this skipping heart that shakes my house,

House of our Saviour who was hanged till death.
My heart, beat faster, faster. In Black Mud
Stephen the martyre was broken down to blood:
Our ransom is the rubble of his death.

Christ walks on the black water. In Black Mud
Darts the kingfisher. On Corpus Christi, heart,
Over the drum-beat of St. Stephen's choir

I hear him, *Stupor Mundi,* and the mud
Flies from his hunching wings and beak—my heart,
The blue kingfisher dives on you in fire.

AS A PLANE TREE BY THE WATER

Darkness has called to darkness, and disgrace
Elbows about our windows in this planned
Babel of Boston where our money talks
And multiplies the darkness of a land
Of preparation where the Virgin walks
And roses spiral her enamelled face
Or fall to splinters on unwatered streets.
Our Lady of Babylon, go by, go by,
I was once the apple of your eye;
Flies, flies are on the plane tree, on the streets.

The flies, the flies, the flies of Babylon
Buzz in my ear-drums while the devil's long
Dirge of the people detonates the hour
For floating cities where his golden tongue
Enchants the masons of the Bable Tower
To raise tomorrow's city to the sun
That never sets upon these hell-fire streets
Of Boston, where the sunlight is a sword
Striking at the withholder of the Lord:
Flies, flies are on the plane tree, on the streets.

Flies strike the miraculous waters of the iced
Atlantic and the eyes of Bernadette
Who saw Our Lady standing in the cave
At Massabielle, saw her so squarely that
Her vision put out reason's eyes. The grave
Is open-mouthed and swallowed up in Christ.
O walls of Jericho! And all the streets
To our Atlantic wall are singing: "Sing,
Sing for the resurrection of the King."
Flies, flies are on the plane tree, on the streets.

THE DEATH OF THE SHERIFF

"forsitan et Priami fuerint quae fata, requiras?"

Noli Me Tangere

We park and stare. A full sky of the stars
Wheels from the pumpkin setting of the moon
And sparks the windows of the yellow farm
Where the red-flannelled madmen look through bars
At windmills thrashing snowflakes by an arm
Of that Atlantic. Soon
The undertaker who collects antiques
Will let his motor idle at the door

And set his pine-box on the parlor floor.
Our homicidal sheriff howled for weeks;
We kiss. The State had reasons: on the whole,
It acted out of kindness when it locked
Its servant in this place and had him watched
Until an ordered darkness left his soul
A *tabula rasa;* when the Angel knocked
The sheriff laid his notched
Revolver on the table for the guest.
Night draws us closer in its bearskin wrap
And our loved sightless smother feels the tap
Of the blind stars descending to the west

To lay the Devil in the pit our hands
Are draining like a windmill. Who'll atone
For the unsearchable quicksilver heart
Where spiders stare their eyes out at their own
Spitting and knotted likeness? We must start:
Our aunt, his mother, stands
Singing *O Rock of Ages,* as the light
Wanderers show a man with a white cane
Who comes to take the coffin in his wain,
The thirsty Dipper on the arc of night.

WHERE THE RAINBOW ENDS

I saw the sky descending, black and white,
Not blue, on Boston where the winters wore
The skulls to jack-o'-lanterns on the slates,
And Hunger's skin-and-bone retrievers tore
The chickadee and shrike. The thorn tree waits
Its victim and tonight
The worms will eat the deadwood to the foot
Of Ararat: the scythers, Time and Death,
Helmed locusts, move upon the tree of breath;
The wild ingrafted olive and the root

Are withered, and a winter drifts to where
The Pepperpot, ironic rainbow, spans
Charles River and its scales of scorched-earth miles
I saw my city in the Scales, the pans
Of judgment rising and descending. Piles
Of dead leaves char the air—
And I am a red arrow on this graph
Of Revelations. Every dove is sold.
The Chapel's sharp-shinned eagle shifts its hold
On serpent-Time, the rainbow's epitaph.

In Boston serpents whistle at the cold.
The victim climbs the altar steps and sings:
"Hosannah to the lion, lamb, and beast
Who fans the furnace-face of IS with wings:

I breathe the ether of my marriage feast."
At the high altar, gold
And a fair cloth. I kneel and the wings beat
My cheek. What can the dove of Jesus give
You now but wisdom, exile? Stand and live,
The dove has brought an olive branch to eat.

FALLING ASLEEP OVER THE AENEID

The sun is blue and scarlet on my page,
And *yuck-a, yuck-a, yuck-a, yuck-a,* rage
The yellowhammers mating. Yellow fire
Blankets the captives dancing on their pyre,
And the scorched lictor screams and drops his rod.
Trojans are singing to their drunken God,
Ares. Their helmets catch on fire. Their files
Clank by the body of my comrade—miles
Of filings! Now the scythe-wheeled chariot rolls
Before their lances long as vaulting poles,
And I stand up and heil the thousand men,
Who carry Pallas to the bird-priest. Then
The bird-priest groans, and as his birds foretold,
I greet the body, lip to lip. I hold
The sword that Dido used. It tries to speak,
A bird with Dido's sworded breast. Its beak
Clangs and ejaculates the Punic word
I hear the bird-priest chirping like a bird.
I groan a little. "Who am I, and why?"
It asks, a boy's face, though its arrow-eye
Is working from its socket. "Brother, try,
O Child of Aphrodite, try to die:
To die is life." His harlots hang his bed
With feathers of his long-tailed birds. His head
Is yawning like a person. The plumes blow;
The beard and eyebrows ruffle. Face of snow,
You are the flower that country girls have caught,
A wild bee-pillaged honey-suckle brought
To the returning bridegroom—the design
Has not yet left it, and the petals shine;
The earth, its mother, has, at last, no help:
It is itself. The broken-winded yelp
Of my Phoenician hounds, that fills the brush
With snapping twigs and flying, cannot flush
The ghost of Pallas. But I take his pall,
Stiff with its gold and purple, and recall
How Dido hugged it to her, while she toiled,
Laughing—her golden threads, a serpent coiled
In cypress. Now I lay it like a sheet;
It clinks and settles down upon his feet,
The careless yellow hair that seemed to burn
Beforehand. Left foot, right foot—as they turn,

More pyres are rising: armored horses, bronze,
And gagged Italians, who must file by ones
Across the bitter river, when my thumb
Tightens into their wind-pipes. The beaks drum;
Their headman's cow-horned death's-head bites its tongue,
And stiffens, as it eyes the hero slung
Inside his feathered hammock on the crossed
Staves of the eagles that we winged. Our cost
Is nothing to the lovers, whoring Mars
And Venus, father's lover. Now his car's
Plumage is ready, and my marshals fetch
His squire, Acoetes, white with age, to hitch
Aethon, the hero's charger, and its ears
Prick, and it steps and steps, and stately tears
Lather its teeth; and then the harlots bring
The hero's charms and baton—but the King,
Vain-glorious Turnus, carried off the rest.
"I was myself, but Ares thought it best
The way it happened." At the end of time,
He sets his spear, as my descendants climb
The knees of Father Time, his beard of scalps,
His scythe, the arc of steel that crowns the Alps.
The elephants of Carthage hold those snows,
Turms of Numidian horse unsling their bows,
The flaming turkey-feathered arrows swarm
Beyond the Alps. "Pallas," I raise my arm
And shout, "Brother, eternal health. Farewell
Forever." Church is over, and its bell
Frightens the yellowhammers, as I wake
And watch the whitecaps wrinkle up the lake.
Mother's great-aunt, who died when I was eight,
Stands by our parlor sabre. "Boy, it's late.
Vergil must keep the Sabbath." Eighty years!
It all comes back. My Uncle Charles appears.
Blue-capped and bird-like. Phillips Brooks and Grant
Are frowning at his coffin, and my aunt,
Hearing his colored volunteers parade
Through Concord, laughs, and tells her English maid
To clip his yellow nostril hairs, and fold
His colors on him. . . . It is I, I hold
His sword to keep from falling, for the dust
On the stuffed birds is breathless, for the bust
Of young Augustus weighs on Vergil's shelf:
It scowls into my glasses at itself.

WAKING IN THE BLUE

The night attendant, a B. U. sophomore,
rouses from the mare's-nest of his drowsy head
propped on *The Meaning of Meaning*.
He catwalks down our corridor.

Azure day
makes my agonized blue window bleaker.
Crows maunder on the petrified fairway.
Absence! My heart grows tense
as though a harpoon were sparring for the kill.
(This is the house for the "mentally ill.")

What use is my sense of humor?
I grin at Stanley, now sunk in his sixties,
once a Harvard all-American fullback,
(if such were possible!)
still hoarding the build of a boy in his twenties,
as he soaks, a ramrod
with the muscle of a seal
in his long tub,
vaguely urinous from the Victorian plumbing.
A kingly granite profile in a crimson golf-cap,
worn all day, all night,
he thinks only of his figure,
of slimming on sherbet and ginger ale—
more cut off from words than a seal.

This is the way day breaks in Bowditch Hall at McLean's;
the hooded night lights bring out "Bobbie,"
Porcellian '29,
a replica of Louis XVI
without the wig—
redolent and roly-poly as a sperm whale,
as he swashbuckles about in his birthday suit
and horses at chairs.

These victorious figures of bravado ossified young.

In between the limits of day,
hours and hours go by under the crew haircuts
and slightly too little nonsensical bachelor twinkle
of the Roman Catholic attendants.
(There are no Mayflower
screwballs in the Catholic Church.)

After a hearty New England breakfast,
I weigh two hundred pounds
this morning. Cock of the walk,
I strut in my turtle-neck French sailor's jersey
before the metal shaving mirrors,
and see the shaky future grow familiar
in the pinched, indigenous faces
of these thoroughbred mental cases,
twice my age and half my weight.
We are all old-timers,
each of us holds a locked razor.

SKUNK HOUR

(For Elizabeth Bishop)

Nautilus Island's hermit
heiress still lives through winter in her Spartan cottage;
her sheep still graze above the sea.
Her son's a bishop. Her farmer
is first selectman in our village;
she's in her dotage.

Thirsting for
the hierarchic privacy
of Queen Victoria's century,
she buys up all
the eyesores facing her shore,
and lets them fall.

The season's ill—
we've lost our summer millionaire,
who seemed to leap from an L. L. Bean
catalogue. His nine-knot yawl
was auctioned off to lobstermen.
A red fox stain covers Blue Hill.

And now our fairy
decorator brightens his shop for fall;
his fishnet's filled with orange cork,
orange, his cobbler's bench and awl;
there is no money in his work,
he'd rather marry.

One dark night,
my Tudor Ford climbed the hill's skull;
I watched for love-cars. Lights turned down,
they lay together, hull to hull,
where the graveyard shelves on the town. . . .
My mind's not right.

A car radio bleats,
"Love, O careless love. . . ." I hear
my ill-spirit sob in each blood cell,
as if my hand were at its throat. . . .
I myself am hell;
nobody's here—

only skunks, that search
in the moonlight for a bite to eat.
They march on their soles up Main Street:
white stripes, moonstruck eyes' red fire
under the chalk-dry and spar spire
of the Trinitarian Church.

I stand on top
of our back steps and breathe the rich air—
a mother skunk with her column of kittens swills the garbage pail.
She jabs her wedge-head in a cup
of sour cream, drops her ostrich tail,
and will not scare.

William Jay Smith

⁂ William Jay Smith was born April 22, 1918, in Winnfield, Louisiana, which his father's family had helped to found; on his mother's side he is (he says precisely) one-sixteenth Cherokee. Brought up in Army posts as the son of an enlisted man, he attended Washington University in St. Louis, served in World War II as Navy personnel and liaison officer, and continued his studies at Columbia University and (as a Rhodes Scholar) Oxford, as well as in France and Italy. Married to the poet Barbara Howes, he taught at Washington University, Columbia University, and Williams College. In 1960 he was elected a Democratic member of the Vermont House of Representatives.

The best of *Poems* (1947) and *Celebration at Dark* (1950) were combined with uncollected work in *Poems: 1947-1957* and disclosed an unusually versatile mind and manner. Smith is, by turns, macabre and metaphysical; he is equally at home in serious commentary on the state of the world and in nimble nonsense about anything. The whimsical delicacy of "A Pavane for the Nursery" is as native to Smith as the contrasting flat declarations of "Plain Talk" and "American Primitive." Léonie Adams characterized his touch when she said that he possessed "an airy lyricism of a sort rare now."

Smith is also the translator of Valéry Larbaud's *Poems of a Multimillionaire* (1955) and *Selected Writings of Jules Laforgue* (1956), the author of a literary curiosity, *The Spectra Hoax* (1961), several books for children, notably *Laughing Time* (1955), and various typographical amusements.

AMERICAN PRIMITIVE

Look at him there in his stovepipe hat,
His high-top shoes, and his handsome collar;
Only my Daddy could look like that,
And I love my Daddy like he loves his Dollar.

The screen door bangs, and it sounds so funny—
There he is in a shower of gold;
His pockets are stuffed with folding money,
His lips are blue, and his hands feel cold.

He hangs in the hall by his black cravat,

The ladies faint, and the children holler:
Only my Daddy could look like that,
And I love my Daddy like he loves his Dollar.

A PAVANE FOR THE NURSERY

Now touch the air softly,
Step gently. One, two . . .
I'll love you till roses
Are robin's-egg blue;
I'll love you till gravel
Is eaten for bread,
And lemons are orange,
And lavender's red.

Now touch the air softly,
Swing gently the broom.
I'll love you till windows
Are all of a room;
And the table is laid,
And the table is bare,
And the ceiling reposes
On bottomless air.

I'll love you till Heaven
Rips the stars from his coat,
And the Moon rows away in
A glass-bottomed boat;
And Orion steps down
Like a diver below,
And Earth is ablaze,
And Ocean aglow.

So touch the air softly,
And swing the broom high.
We will dust the gray mountains,
And sweep the blue sky;
And I'll love you as long
As the furrow the plow,
As However is Ever,
And Ever is Now.

PLAIN TALK

"There are people so dumb," my father said,
"That they don't know beans from an old bedstead.
They can't tell one thing from another,
Ella Cinders from Whistler's Mother,
A porcupine quill from a peacock feather,
A buffalo-flop from Florentine leather.
Meatless shanks boiled bare and blue,
They bob up and down like bones in a stew;
Don't know their arse from a sassafras root,
And couldn't pour piss from a cowhide boot
With complete directions on the heel."

That's how *he* felt. That's how *I* feel.

THE LOVERS

Above, through lunar woods a goddess flees
Between the curving trunks of slender trees;
Bare Mazda bulbs outline the bone-white rooms

Where, on one elbow, rousing by degrees,
They stare, a sheet loose-folded round their knees,
Off into space, as from Etruscan tombs.

THE TEMPEST

Let England knowe our willingnesse, for that our worke is goode,
We hope to plant a Nation, where none before hath stood.
—R. Rich in *Newes from Virginia*

Imagine that July morning: Cape Henry and Virginia
There but one week off; black winds having gathered
All the night before,
The gray clouds thickened, and the storm,
From out the wild Northeast, bore
Down upon them, beating light from heaven.
The cries of all on board were drowned in wind,
And wind in thunder drowned;
With useless sails upwound,
The Sea Adventure rode upon rivers of rain
To no known destination.
Bison-black, white-tongued, the waves
Swept round;
Green-meadow beautiful, the sea below swung up
To meet them, hollow filling hollow,
Till sound absorbed all sound;
Lashed about gnatlike in the dark,
The men with candle flame
Sought out the leaks along the hull.

While oakum spewed, one leak they found
Within the gunnery room, and this they stopped
With slabs of beef;
Their food they fed that leak, that wound,
But it continued still to bleed, and bled
Until its blood was everywhere,
And they could see their own blood
Rush to join it,
And the decks were wet and red;
And greater leaks sprang open in the hold.

Ripped silk—sound magnified ten million times—
The winds were shreds,
Each shred a bleeding tongue
Torn from a howling mouth.
By great waves borne
West, East, North, South,
They sought deliverance:
God-fearing, God-bereft,
They bore His rage.
And yet the water spoke—roar answered roar—
A bleat, a surge, a mounting groan;
Gut-green, hyena-toothed, the waves lashed ever higher—
Stone grinding buckling stone
Up from the heaving ocean floor.

Each moment seemed the last:
The ship, but faintly stirring,
Tumbled in its net,
While caged the compass whirled
And whipstaff flew.
Four nights, three days,
With neither rest nor food,
Stripped galley slaves, they worked the pumps full force
To hurl the water back upon itself;
And steered a trackless course,
St. Elmo's fire round-streaming through the haze,
Shooting from shroud to shroud,
Brushing with hairy jets of flame the yardarm
As it might green blades of prairie grass
Or the tips of bisons' horns.

Then, on the fourth day, having given up
All but themselves the ship contained—
Trunks, chests, food, firearms, beer and wine—
When they prepared to hack
The mainmast, to batten down all hatches
And commit the vessel to the sea,
They saw far off—sweet introduction of good hope—
A wavering light-green, brooding calm,
Trees moving with the waves—and it was land.
And so the ship rode on, rode out the gale,
And brought them, wrecked but living, to the island there,
Where safely, under more compliant skies,
They might chart out that voyage to a shore
On which with confidence a nation would arise.

Richard Wilbur

☙ Richard Wilbur was born March 1, 1921, in New York City. His parents moved to part of a country estate in New Jersey while he was still a child and there he and his brother grew up, he says, "among woods, orchards, corn-fields, horses, hogs, cows, and haywagons. A friend recently remarked that my poems are unfashionably favorable toward nature, and I must blame this warp on a rural, pleasant, and somewhat solitary boyhood." A born poet, he was stimulated by his father, an artist, and his mother, whose father and grandfather were editors and publishers. It was only natural that, when Wilbur attended Amherst, he should become editor of the college newspaper.

After marrying and serving on various fronts during World War II, he attended Harvard's graduate school, received his M.A. in 1942, taught at Harvard, and lived in nearby Lincoln with his wife and children, until he moved to Middletown, Connecticut, where he taught at Wesleyan and served as one of the mentors of the university's new publishing program.

Before he had reached his mid-thirties, Wilbur had won the Prix de Rome Fellowship as well as other prizes and had published three volumes of poetry, *The Beautiful Changes* (1947), *Ceremony and Other Poems* (1950), *Things of This World* (1956), which was awarded the Pulitzer Prize in 1957, and a spirited translation of Molière's *The Misanthrope* (1955). *Advice to a Prophet and Other Poems* appeared in 1961.

Sometimes characterized as one of the "New Formalists," Wilbur is unusually fastidious—"elegant" is the adjective most often applied to his poetry—but there is firmness behind the finesse. Wilbur is a virtuoso performer; a reviewer in the London *Times Literary Supplement* wrote that his poems "have produced an impression of rather finicky cleverness" but that they were full of felicities, that he combined a seventeenth century ingenuity with a peculiarly modern manner, and that his best work achieved "an effect through some form of contrast between actuality and the metaphysical conception of his imagination."

It is a half-wondering, half-whimsical imagination with which Wilbur perceives what Whitman called "the glory of the commonplace"—a washline, a morning newspaper, a park statue, a child digging, a railroad station. His is an instant response to the small aspects of the "things of this world"; his visual and imaginative powers unite in a sensibility that sparkles and shimmers with alert play. Apart from its own virtues, Wilbur's poetry serves as a bridge between the traditionalists of an earlier generation and the experimentalists of his own.

"A WORLD WITHOUT OBJECTS IS A SENSIBLE EMPTINESS"

The tall camels of the spirit
Steer for their deserts, passing the last groves loud
With the sawmill shrill of the locust, to the whole honey of the arid
Sun. They are slow, proud,

And move with a stilted stride
To the land of sheer horizon, hunting Traherne's
Sensible emptiness, there where the brain's lantern-slide
Revels in vast returns.

O connoisseurs of thirst,
Beasts of my soul who long to learn to drink
Of pure mirage, those prosperous islands are accurst
That shimmer on the brink

Of absence; auras, lustres,
And all shinings need to be shaped and borne.
Think of those painted saints, capped by the early masters
With bright, jauntily-worn

Aureate plates, or even
Merry-go-round rings. Turn, O turn
From the fine sleights of the sand, from the long empty oven
Where flames in flamings burn

Back to the trees arrayed
In bursts of glare, to the halo-dialing run
Of the country creeks, and the hills' bracken tiaras made
Gold in the sunken sun,

Wisely watch for the sight
Of the supernova burgeoning over the barn,
Lampshine blurred in the steam of beasts, the spirit's right
Oasis, light incarnate.

BELL SPEECH

The selfsame toothless voice for death or bridal:
It has been long since men would give the time
To tell each someone's-change with a special chime,
And a toll for every year the dead walked through.
And mostly now, above this urgent idle
Town, the bells mark time, as they can do.

This bavardage of early and of late
Is what is wanted, and yet the bells beseech
By some excess that's in their stricken speech
Less meanly to be heard. Were this not so,
Why should Great Paul shake every window plate
To warn me that my pocket watch is slow?

Whether or not attended, bells will chant
With a clear dumb sound, and wide of any word
Expound our hours, clear as the waves are heard
Crashing at Mount Desert, from far at sea,
And dumbly joining, as the night's descent
Makes deltas into dark of every tree.

Great Paul, great pail of sound, still dip and draw
Dark speech from the deep and quiet steeple well,
Bring dark for doctrine, do but dim and quell
All voice in yours, while earth will give you breath.
Still gather to a language without flaw
Our loves, and all the hours of our death.

LOVE CALLS US TO THE THINGS OF THIS WORLD

The eyes open to a cry of pulleys,
And spirited from sleep, the astounded soul
Hangs for a moment bodiless and simple
As false dawn.
Outside the open window
The morning air is all awash with angels.

Some are in bed-sheets, some are in blouses,
Some are in smocks: but truly there they are.

Now they are rising together in calm swells
Of halcyon feeling, filling whatever they wear
With the deep joy of their impersonal breathing;

Now they are flying in place, conveying
The terrible speed of their omnipresence, moving
And staying like white water, and now of a sudden
They swoon down into so rapt a quiet
That nobody seems to be there.
The soul shrinks

From all that it is about to remember,
From the punctual rape of every blessèd day,
And cries,
"Oh, let there be nothing on earth but laundry,
Nothing but rosy hands in the rising steam
And clear dances done in the sight of heaven."

Yet, as the sun acknowledges
With a warm look the world's hunks and colors,
The soul descends once more in bitter love
To accept the waking body, saying now
In a changed voice as the man yawns and rises,
"Bring them down from their ruddy gallows;
Let there be clean linen for the backs of thieves;
Let lovers go fresh and sweet to be undone,
And the heaviest nuns walk in a pure floating
Of dark habits,
keeping their difficult balance."

AFTER THE LAST BULLETINS

After the last bulletins the windows darken
And the whole city founders readily and deep,
Sliding on all its pillows
To the thronged Atlantis of personal sleep,

And the wind rises. The wind rises and bowls
The day's litter of news in the alleys. Trash
Tears itself on the railings,
Soars and falls with a soft crash,

Tumbles and soars again. Unruly flights
Scamper the park, and taking a statue for dead
Strike at the positive eyes,
Batter and flap the stolid head

And scratch the noble name. In empty lots
Our journals spiral in a fierce noyade
Of all we thought to think,
Or caught in corners cramp and wad

And twist our words. And some from gutters flail
Their tatters at the tired patrolman's feet,
Like all that fisted snow
That cried beside his long retreat

Damn you! damn you! to the emperor's horse's heels.
Oh none too soon through the air white and dry
Will the clear announcer's voice
Beat like a dove, and you and I

From the heart's anarch and responsible town
Return by subway-mouth to life again,
Bearing the morning papers,
And cross the park where saintlike men,

White and absorbed, with stick and bag remove
The litter of the night, and footsteps rouse
With confident morning sound
The songbirds in the public boughs.

IN THE SMOKING-CAR

The eyelids meet. He'll catch a little nap.
The grizzled crew-cut head drops to his chest.
It shakes above the briefcase on his lap.
Close voices breathe, "Poor sweet, he did his best."

"Poor sweet, poor sweet," the bird-hushed glades repeat,
Through which in quiet pomp his litter goes,
Carried by native girls with naked feet.
A sighing stream concurs in his repose.

Could he but think, he might recall to mind
The righteous mutiny or sudden gale
That beached him here; the dear ones left behind . . .
So near the ending, he forgets the tale.

Were he to lift his eyelids now, he might
Behold his maiden porters, brown and bare.
But even here he has no appetite.
It is enough to know that they are there.

Enough that now a honeyed music swells,
The gentle, mossed declivities begin,
And the whole air is full of flower-smells.
Failure, the longed-for valley, takes him in.

ADVICE TO A PROPHET

When you come, as you soon must, to the streets of our city,
Mad-eyed from stating the obvious,
Not proclaiming our fall but begging us
In God's name to have self-pity,

Spare us all word of the weapons, their force and range,
The long numbers that rocket the mind;
Our slow, unreckoning hearts will be left behind,
Unable to fear what is too strange.

Nor shall you scare us with talk of the death of the race.
How should we dream of this place without us?—
The sun mere fire, the leaves untroubled about us,
A stone look on the stone's face?

Speak of the world's own change. Though we cannot conceive
Of an undreamt thing, we know to our cost
How the dreamt cloud crumbles, the vines are blackened by frost,
How the view alters. We could believe,

If you told us so, that the white-tailed deer will slip
Into perfect shade, grown perfectly shy,
The lark avoid the reaches of our eye,
The jack-pine lose its knuckled grip

On the cold ledge, and every torrent burn
As Xanthus once, its gliding trout
Stunned in a twinkling. What should we be without
The dolphin's arc, the dove's return,

These things in which we have seen ourselves and spoken?
Ask us, prophet, how we shall call
Our natures forth when that live tongue is all
Dispelled, that glass obscured or broken,

In which we have said the rose of our love and the clean
Horse of our courage, in which beheld
The singing locust of the soul unshelled,
And all we mean or wish to mean.

Ask us, ask us whether with the worldless rose
Our hearts shall fail us; come demanding
Whether there shall be lofty or long standing
When the bronze annals of the oak-tree close.

Vassar Miller

Vassar Miller was born July 19, 1924, in Houston, Texas, where she obtained all her schooling. From the University of Houston she received her B.S. degree in 1947 and her M.A. degree three years later.

Handicapped from birth by cerebral palsy, Miss Miller triumphed over pain and cruel difficulties by dedicating herself to the strictest discipline of poetry. At a time when so much writing seemed a plunge into the welter of the inchoate, she devoted herself to the most delicately balanced concepts and the most orthodox rhymes. The forms she chose to embody her most intricate statements in *Adam's Footprint* (1956) and *Wage War on Silence* (1960) are equally orthodox; they conform to a spirit that is both self-searching and secure. Her religious lyrics have been compared to those of Herbert and Hopkins; her sonnets, adhering to the formal tradition, strain at their bounds to express the inexpressible.

Critics have attempted to describe the convincing and even compulsive quality of her thought. Speaking impersonally, Miss Miller ventured to say that "poetry, like all art, has a trinitarian function: creative, redemptive, and sanctifying. It is creative because it takes the raw materials of fact and feeling and makes them into that which is neither fact nor feeling. It is redemptive because it can transform the pain and ugliness of life into joy and beauty. It is sanctifying because it thus gives the transitory at least a relative form and meaning. Hence poetry, whether avowedly so or not, is always religious; it is akin to prayer, an act of love."

WITHOUT CEREMONY

Except ourselves, we have no other prayer;
Our needs are sores upon our nakedness.
We do not have to name them; we are here.
And You who can make eyes can see no less.
We fall, not on our knees, but on our hearts,
A posture humbler far and more downcast;
While Father Pain instructs us in the arts
Of praying, hunger is the worthiest fast.
We find ourselves where tongues cannot wage war
On silence (farther, mystics never flew)
But on the common wings of what we are,
Borne on the wings of what we bear, toward You,
Oh Word, in whom our wordiness dissolves,
When we have not a prayer except ourselves.

CHRISTMAS MOURNING

On Christmas Day I weep
Good Friday to rejoice.
I watch the Child asleep.
Does He half dream the choice
The Man must make and keep?

At Christmastime I sigh
For my Good Friday hope.
Outflung the Child's arms lie
To span in their brief scope
The death the Man must die.

Come Christmastide I groan
To hear Good Friday's pealing.
The Man, racked to the bone,
Has made His hurt my healing,
Has made my ache His own.

Slay me, pierced to the core
With Christmas penitence
So I who, new-born, soar
To that Child's innocence,
May wound the Man no more.

BOUT WITH BURNING

I have tossed hours upon the tides of fever,
Upon the billows of my blood have ridden,
Where fish of fancy teem as neither river
Nor ocean spawns from India to Sweden.
Here while my boat of body burnt has drifted
Along her sides crawled tentacles of crabs
Sliming her timbers; on the waves upwafted
Crept water rats to gnaw her ropes and ribs.
Crashing, she has dived, her portholes choking
With weed and ooze, the swirls of black and green
Gulping her inch by inch, the seagulls' shrieking
Sieved depth through depth to silence. Till blast-blown,
I in my wreck beyond storm's charge and churning
Have waked marooned upon the coasts of morning.

JUDAS

Always I lay upon the brink of love,
Impotent, waiting till the waters stirred,
And no one healed my weakness with a word;
For no one healed me who lacked words to prove
My heart, which, when the kiss of Mary wove
His shroud, my tongueless anguish spurred
To cool dissent, and which, each time I heard
John whisper to Him, moaned, but could not move.

While Peter deeply drowsed within love's deep
I cramped upon its margin, glad to share
The sop Christ gave me, yet its bitter bite
Dried up my ducts. Praise Peter, who could weep
His sin away, but never see me where
I hang, huge teardrop on the cheek of night.

DEFENSE RESTS

I want
a love to hold
in my hand because love
is too much for the heart to bear
alone.

Then stop
mouthing to me
"Faith and Sacraments" when
the Host feather-heavy weighs down
my soul.

So I
blaspheme! My Lord,
John's head on your breast or
Mary's lips on your feet, would you
agree?

If this
is not enough—
upon Your sweat, Your thirst,
Your nails, and nakedness I rest
my case.

W. D. Snodgrass

W(illiam) D(ewitt) Snodgrass was born January 5, 1926, in Wilkinsburg, Pennsylvania. The family soon moved to Beaver Falls, where William acted in high school dramas, played on the tennis team, and performed on the orchestra's drums. He attended Geneva College for a year, after which he joined the Navy. Receiving his discharge with the rank of Yeoman Third Class, he attended Iowa State College, where he concentrated on Renaissance literature and flowered, wrote Robert Lowell, "in the most sterile of sterile places, a post-war, cold-war, mid-western university's poetry workshop for graduate student poets." Upon attaining his master's degree he taught at Cornell University, the University of Rochester and, in 1959, at Wayne State University in Detroit.

The title of Snodgrass's volume, *Heart's Needle,* is taken from an Irish phrase: "An only daughter is the needle of the heart." The contents consist of only 60 pages. Most of the poems are autobiographical—recollections of his service in the Navy, sessions with his psychiatrist, his adjustments and maladjustments in the academic arena, repercussions of an unsuccessful first marriage, and the delicate relationship with his young daughter. It was his first book, and it received the Pulitzer Prize in 1960. Snodgrass also received several other rewards including a grant from the National Institute of Arts and Letters.

Snodgrass uses the traditional form in an untraditional way. His sense of individual and moral responsibility is accentuated by the discipline of his images. His idiom is sharp, usually colloquial, but poetically precise. He has, wrote Stanley Kunitz, "the gift of transforming ordinary experience, including the domestic, into a decisive act of the imagination, remarkable for its pace and controlled emotion."

TEN DAYS LEAVE

He steps down from the dark train, blinking; stares
At trees like miracles. He will play games
With boys or sit up all night touching chairs.
Talking with friends, he can recall their names.

Noon burns against his eyelids, but he lies
Hunched in his blankets; he is half awake
But still lacks nerve to open up his eyes;
Supposing it were just his old mistake?

But no; it seems just like it seemed. His folks
Pursue their lives like toy trains on a track.
He can foresee each of his father's jokes
Like words in some old movie that's come back.

He is like days when you've gone some place new
To deal with certain strangers, though you never
Escape the sense in everything you do,
"We've done this all once. Have I been here, ever?"

But no; he thinks it must recall some old film, lit
By lives you want to touch; as if he'd slept
And must have dreamed this setting, peopled it,
And wakened out of it. But someone's kept

His dream asleep here like a small homestead
Preserved long past its time in memory
Of some great man who lived here and is dead.
They have restored his landscape faithfully:

The hills, the little houses, the costumes:
How real it seems! But he comes, wide awake,
A tourist whispering through the priceless rooms
Who must not touch things or his hand might break

Their sleep and black them out. He wonders when
He'll grow into his sleep so sound again.

SONG

Sweet beast, I have gone prowling,
   a proud rejected man
who lived along the edges
   catch as catch can;
in darkness and in hedges
   I sang my sour tone
and all my love was howling
   conspicuously alone.

I curled and slept all day
   or nursed my bloodless wounds
until the squares were silent
   where I could make my tunes
singular and violent.
   Then, sure as hearers came
I crept and flinched away.
   And, girl, you've done the same.

A stray from my own type,
   led along by blindness,
my love was near to spoiled
   and curdled all my kindness.
I find no kin, no child;
   only the weasel's ilk.
Sweet beast, cat of my own stripe,
   come and take my milk.

FROM "HEART'S NEEDLE"

Child of My Winter

Child of my winter, born
When the new fallen soldiers froze
In Asia's steep ravines and fouled the snows,
When I was torn

By love I could not still,
By fear that silenced my cramped mind
To that cold war where, lost, I could not find
My peace in my will,

All those days we could keep
Your mind a landscape of new snow
Where the chilled tenant-farmer finds, below,
His fields asleep

In their smooth covering, white
As quilts to warm the resting bed
Of birth or pain, spotless as paper spread
For me to write,

And thinks: Here lies my land
Unmarked by agony, the lean foot
Of the weasel tracking, the thick trapper's boot;
And I have planned

My chances to restrain
The torments of demented summer or
Increase the deepening harvest here before
It snows again.

THE MEN'S ROOM IN THE COLLEGE CHAPEL

Here, in the most Unchristian basement
of this "fortress for the Christian mind,"
they close these four gray walls, shut out shame,
and scribble of sex and excrement,
draw bestial pictures and sign their names—
the old, lewd defiance of mankind.

The subversive human in his cell—
burn his vile books, stamp out his credo,
lock him away where no light falls,
and no live word can go back to tell
where he's entombed like Monte Cristo—
yet, he'll carve his platform in the walls.

In need, men have painted the deep caves
to summon their animal, dark gods:
even the reviled, early Christians
prayed in catacombs to outlawed Good,
laid their honored dead and carved out graves
with pious mottos of resistance.

This is the last cave, where the soul
turns in its corner like a beast
nursing its wounds, where it contemplates
vengeance, how it shall gather to full
strength, what lost cause shall it vindicate,
returning, masterless and twisted.

MEMENTOS

Sorting out letters and piles of my old
Cancelled checks, old clippings, and yellow note cards
That meant something once, I happened to find
Your picture. *That* picture. I stopped there cold,
Like a man raking piles of dead leaves in his yard
Who has turned up a severed hand.

Yet, that first second, I was glad: you stand
Just as you stood—shy, delicate, slender,
In the long gown of green lace netting and daisies
That you wore to our first dance. The sight of you stunned
Us all. Our needs seemed simpler, then;
And our ideals came easy.

Then through the war and those two long years
Overseas, the Japanese dead in their shacks
Among dishes, dolls, and lost shoes—I carried
This glimpse of you, there, to choke down my fear,
Prove it had been, that it might come back.
That was before we got married.

—Before we drained out one another's force
With lies, self-denial, unspoken regret
And the sick eyes that blame; before the divorce
And the treachery. Say it: before we met.
Still, I put back your picture. Someday, in due course,
I will find that it's still there.

LYING AWAKE

This moth caught in the room tonight
Squirmed up, sniper-style, between
The rusty edges of the screen;
Then, long as the room stayed light,

Lay here, content, in some cornerhole.
Now that we've settled into bed
Though, he can't sleep. Overhead,
He throws himself at the blank wall.

Each night hordes of these flutterers haunt
And climb my study windowpane;
Fired by reflection, their insane
Eyes gleam; they know what they want.

How do the petulant things survive?
Out in the fields they have a place

And proper work, furthering the race;
Why this blind fanatical drive

Indoors? Why rush at every spark,
Cigar, headlamp, or railway warning
To break off your wings and starve by morning?
And what could a moth fear in the dark

Compared with what you meet inside?
Still, he rams the fluorescent face
Of the clock, thinks that's another place
Of light and families, where he'll hide.

We ought to trap him in a jar,
Or come, like the white-coats, with a net
And turn him out toward living. Yet
We don't; we take things as they are.

Anne Sexton

Anne Sexton was born in 1928 in Newton, Massachusetts, attended public and private schools, including Garland Junior College, and eloped at the age of nineteen. For a short while she lived on a farm in upper New York while her husband went to college, then in Boston and San Francisco while her husband was in the Navy. In her early twenties she worked as a librarian and fashion model.

Although she started to write poems in high school, she soon stopped and did not attempt poetry again until 1957, when she was twenty-eight. She then studied with Robert Lowell at Boston University and was awarded the Robert Frost Fellowship at the Bread Loaf Writers' Conference in 1959.

Her first volume, *To Bedlam and Part Way Back* (1960), is provocative in every sense. Her subject matter—guilt, loss, mental distress—will trouble the reader, yet, in its calm clarity, it delights even while it disturbs. This poetry is poignant and sometimes painful, the impact of a spirit so agitated that it has been pushed across the borders of sanity. This is made plain not only by the forthright title but also by several poems of almost heartbreaking intensity. "You, Doctor Martin" is merely one of the poems which prove that, said Robert Lowell, "she is a realist who describes her very personal experiences with an almost Russian abundance and accuracy." The touch is seldom heavy, the tone is never lugubrious.

"Funnel" is a charming retrospective portrait of her New England ancestry—"back from that great-grandfather I have come"—while "Some Foreign Letters" is another family reminiscence which is as intimate as it is immediate. Such poems as "In the Deep Museum" and "The Truth the Dead Know," written subsequent to her first volume, show an increase in power, the translation of bitter endurances—a stay in an asylum, a separation of mother and child, the death of parents—into a poetic catharsis. They turn, as Geoffrey Hartman said in *The Kenyon Review,* "wounds into words."

YOU, DOCTOR MARTIN

You, Doctor Martin, walk
from breakfast to madness. Late August,
I speed through the antiseptic tunnel
where the moving dead still talk
of pushing their bones against the thrust
of cure. And I am queen of this summer hotel
or the laughing bee on a stalk

of death. We stand in broken
lines and wait while they unlock
the door and count us at the frozen gates
of dinner. The shibboleth is spoken
and we move to gravy in our smock
of smiles. We chew in rows, our plates
scratch and whine like chalk

in school. There are no knives
for cutting your throat. I make
moccasins all morning. At first my hands
kept empty, unraveled for the lives
they used to work. Now I learn to take
them back, each angry finger that demands
I mend what another will break

tomorrow. Of course, I love you;
you lean above the plastic sky,
god of our block, prince of all the foxes.
The breaking crowns are new
that Jack wore. Your third eye
moves among us and lights the separate boxes
where we sleep or cry.

What large children we are
here. All over I grow most tall
in the best ward. Your business is people,
you call at the madhouse, an oracular
eye in our nest. Out in the hall
the intercom pages you. You twist in the pull
of the foxy children who fall

like floods of life in frost.
And we are magic talking to itself,
noisy and alone. I am queen of all my sins
forgotten. Am I still lost?
Once I was beautiful. Now I am myself,
counting this row and that row of moccasins
waiting on the silent shelf.

SOME FOREIGN LETTERS

I knew you forever and you were always old,
soft white lady of my heart. Surely you would scold
me for sitting up late, reading your letters,
as if these foreign postmarks were meant for me.
You posted them first in London, wearing furs
and a new dress in the winter of eighteen-ninety.
I read how London is dull on Lord Mayor's Day,
where you guided past groups of robbers, the sad holes
of Whitechapel, clutching your pocketbook, on the way
to Jack the Ripper dissecting his famous bones.
This Wednesday in Berlin, you say, you will
go to a bazaar at Bismarck's house. And I
see you as a young girl in a good world still,
writing three generations before mine. I try
to reach into your page and breathe it back . . .
but life is a trick, life is a kitten in a sack.

This is the sack of time your death vacates.
How distant you are on your nickel-plated skates
in the skating park in Berlin, gliding past
me with your Count, while a military band
plays a Strauss waltz. I loved you last,
a pleated old lady with a crooked hand.
Once you read *Lohengrin* and every goose
hung high while you practiced castle life
in Hanover. Tonight your letters reduce
history to a guess. The Count had a wife.
You were the old maid aunt who lived with us.
Tonight I read how the winter howled around
the towers of Schloss Schwöbber, how the tedious
language grew in your jaw, how you loved the sound
of the music of the rats tapping on the stone
floors. When you were mine you wore an earphone.

This is Wednesday, May 9th, near Lucerne,
Switzerland, sixty-nine years ago. I learn
your first climb up Mount San Salvatore;
this is the rocky path, the hole in your shoes,
the yankee girl, the iron interior
of her sweet body. You let the Count choose
your next climb. You went together, armed
with alpine stocks, with ham sandwiches
and seltzer wasser. You were not alarmed
by the thick woods of briars and bushes,
nor the rugged cliff, nor the first vertigo
up over Lake Lucerne. The Count sweated
with his coat off as you waded through top snow.
He held your hand and kissed you. You rattled
down on the train to catch a steamboat for home;
or other postmarks: Paris, Verona, Rome.

This is Italy. You learn its mother tongue.
I read how you walked on the Palatine among
the ruins of the palaces of the Caesars;
alone in the Roman autumn, alone since July.
When you were mine they wrapped you out of here
with your best hat over your face. I cried
because I was seventeen. I am older now.
I read how your student ticket admitted you
into the private chapel of the Vatican and how
you cheered with the others, as we used to do
on the Fourth of July. One Wednesday in November
you watched a balloon, painted like a silver ball,
float up over the Forum, up over the lost emperors,
to shiver its little modern cage in an occasional
breeze. You worked your New England conscience out
beside artisans, chestnut vendors and the devout.

Tonight I will learn to love you twice;
learn your first days, your mid-Victorian face.
Tonight I will speak up and interrupt
your letters, warning you that wars are coming,
that the Count will die, that you will accept
your America back to live like a prim thing
on the farm in Maine. I tell you, you will come
here, to the suburbs of Boston, to see the blue-nose
world go drunk each night, to see the handsome
children jitterbug, to feel your left ear close
one Friday at Symphony. And I tell you,
you will tip your boot feet out of that hall,
rocking from its sour sound, out onto
the crowded street, letting your spectacles fall
and your hair net tangle as you stop passers-by
to mumble your guilty love while your ears die.

FUNNEL

The family story tells, and it was told true,
of my great-grandfather who begat eight
genius children and bought twelve almost new
grand pianos. He left a considerable estate
when he died. The children honored their
separate arts, two became moderately famous,
three married and fattened their delicate share
of wealth and brilliance. The sixth one was
a concert pianist. She had a notable career
and wore cropped hair and walked like a man,
or so I heard when prying a childhood ear
into the hushed talk of the straight Maine clan.
One died a pinafore child, she stays her five
years forever. And here is one that wrote—

I sort his odd books and wonder his once alive
words and scratch out my short marginal notes
and finger my accounts.

Back from that great-grandfather I have come
to tidy a country graveyard for his sake,
to chat with the custodian under a yearly sun
and touch a ghost sound where it lies awake.

I like best to think of that Bunyan man
slapping his thighs and trading the yankee sale
for one dozen grand pianos. It fit his plan
of culture to do it big. On this same scale
he built seven arking houses and they still stand.
One, five stories up, straight up like a square
box, still dominates its costal edge of land.
It is rented cheap in the summer musted air
to sneaker-footed families who pad through
its rooms and sometimes finger the yellow keys
of an old piano that wheezes bells of mildew.
Like a shoe factory amid the spruce trees
it squats; flat roof and rows of windows spying
through the mist. Where those eight children danced
their starfished summers, the thirty-six pines sighing,
that bearded man walked giant steps and chanced
his gifts in numbers.

Back from that great-grandfather I have come
to puzzle a bending gravestone for his sake,
to question this diminishing and feed a minimum
of children their careful slice of suburban cake.

THE TRUTH THE DEAD KNOW

for my mother, born March 1902, died March 1959
and my father, born February 1900, died June 1959

Gone, I say, and walk from church,
refusing the stiff procession to the grave,
letting the dead ride alone in the hearse.
It is June. I am tired of being brave.

We drive to The Cape. I cultivate
myself where the sun gutters from the sky,
where the sea swings in like an iron gate
and we touch. In another country people die.

My darling, the wind falls in like stones
from the whitehearted water and when we touch
we enter touch entirely. No one's alone.
Men kill for this, or for as much.

And what of the dead? They lie without shoes
in their stone boats. They are more like stone
than the sea would be if it stopped. They refuse
to be blessed, throat, eye and knucklebone.

IN THE DEEP MUSEUM

My God, my God, what queer corner am I in?
Didn't I die, blood running down the post,
lungs gagging for air, die there for the sin
of anyone, my sour mouth giving up the ghost?
Surely my body is done? Surely I died?
And yet, I know, I'm here. What place is this?
Cold and queer, I sting with life. I lied.
Yes, I lied. Or else in some damned cowardice
my body would not give me up. I touch
fine cloth with my hands and my cheeks are cold.
If this is hell, then hell could not be much,
neither as special or as ugly as I was told.

What's that I hear, snuffling and pawing its way
toward me? Its tongue knocks a pebble out of place
as it slides in, a sovereign. How can I pray?
It is panting: it is an odor with a face
like the skin of a donkey. It laps my sores.
It is hurt, I think, as I touch its little head.
It bleeds. I have forgiven murderers and whores
and now I must wait like old Jonah, not dead
nor alive, stroking a clumsy animal. A rat.
His teeth test me; he waits like a good cook,
knowing his own ground. I forgive him that,
as I forgave my Judas the money he took.

Now I hold his soft red sore to my lips
as his brothers crowd in, hairy angels who take
my gift. My ankles are a flute. I lose hips
and wrists. For three days, for love's sake,
I bless this other death. Oh, not in air—
in dirt. Under the rotting veins of its roots,
under the markets, under the sheep bed where
the hill is food, under the slippery fruits
of the vineyard, I go. Unto the bellies and jaws
of rats I commit my prophecy and fear.
Far below The Cross, I correct its flaws.
We have kept the miracle. I will not be here.

Index of Authors and Titles

The names of authors and the page references to the sections devoted to their work are shown in italics. Titles of poems are shown in roman.

MODERN BRITISH POETRY

New and Enlarged Edition

NEW AND ENLARGED EDITION

Modern British Poetry

EDITED BY *Louis Untermeyer*

HARCOURT, BRACE & WORLD, INC.
NEW YORK • BURLINGAME

Printed in the United States of America

Library of Congress Catalog Card Number: 62-12184

LIST OF COPYRIGHTS

Four Seas Company for the selections from *War and Love* by Richard Aldington and *The Mountainy Singer* by Seasamh MacCathmhaoil (Joseph Campbell).

Laurence J. Gomme for the selections from *Verses*, copyright, 1916, by Hilaire Belloc.

Grove Press, Inc. for "In Love for Long," "The Animals," "The Good Man in Hell," "The Labyrinth," "The Combat," and "The Horses" from *Collected Poems of Edwin Muir*, published by Grove Press, Inc., copyright © 1957 by Edwin Muir.

Harcourt, Brace & World, Inc. for the selections from *Secrets*, copyright 1924, and *Selected Poems* by W. H. Davies; *The Contemplative Quarry*, copyright 1921, by Anna Wickham; *The Unknown Goddess*, copyright 1925, by Humbert Wolfe; and *Awake! And Other Wartime Poems*, copyright 1942, by W. R. Rodgers; "Missing Dates," "This Last Pain," "Rolling the Lawn," "Just a Smack at Auden," and "Homage to the British Museum" from *Collected Poems*, copyright, 1935, 1940, 1949, by William Empson; "Naming of Parts," "Chard Whitlow," and "Sailor's Harbor" from *A Map of Verona and Other Poems*, copyright, 1947 by Henry Reed. All these poems reprinted by permission of Harcourt, Brace & World, Inc.

Harper & Brothers for the selections from *Hawthorn and Lavender* by W. E. Henley.

Harper's Magazine for "Under Which Lyre" by W. H. Auden.

William Heinemann for the selections from *Poems* by Isaac Rosenberg.

The Hogarth Press for the selections from *New Signatures* by W. H. Auden, and *A Time to Dance* by C. Day Lewis.

Henry Holt and Company for the selections from *Wild Earth*, copyright 1916, by Padraic Colum; *Peacock Pie*, copyright 1914, *The Listeners*, copyright 1916, *The Veil*, copyright 1922 and *Collected Poems*, copyright 1941, by Walter De la Mare; *A Shropshire Lad* and *Last Poems* by A. E. Housman; and *Poems*, copyright 1917, by Edward Thomas. Reprinted by permission of Henry Holt and Company.

Alfred A. Knopf, Inc. for the selections from *The Collected Poems of William H. Davies*, copyright 1916; *Cautionary Tales for Children* by Hilaire Belloc, *The Bad Child's Book of Beasts* by Hilaire Belloc; *The Waggoner* by Edmund Blunden; *Fairies and Fusiliers* by Robert Graves; *Argonaut and Juggernaut* by Osbert Sitwell; *Rustic Elegies* by Edith Sitwell, and *The Sleeping Beauty* by Edith Sitwell.

The Liveright Company for the selections from *Dublin Days*, copyright 1923, by L. A. G. Strong.

Longmans, Green & Co., Ltd. for "Canal Bank Walk," "The Self-Slaved," "The One," "Question to Life," and "Intimate Parnassus" from *Come Dance With Kitty Stobling and Other Poems*, copyright © 1960 by Patrick Kavanagh. Reprinted by permission of Patrick Kavanagh and the publishers.

The Macmillan Company for the selections from *Selected Poems* by "Æ" (George W. Russell), copyright 1935; *Creatures* by Padraic Colum, copyright 1927; *Fires* by Wilfrid Wilson Gibson, copyright 1912, and *Borderlands and Thoroughfares*, copyright 1915, by Wilfrid Wilson Gibson; *Collected Poems* by Thomas Hardy; *Poems* by Ralph Hodgson; *Good Friday and Other Poems*, copyright 1916, and *Salt-Water Ballads* by John Masefield; the passage (in this volume entitled "Rounding the Horn") from "Dauber" and two poems from *The Story of a Round-House* copyright 1913; and *Collected Poems*, copyright 1918, 1925, by John Masefield; *Saturday Market* by Charlotte Mew; *A Trophy of Arms*, copyright 1936, by Ruth Pitter, *A Mad Lady's Garland*, copyright 1935, by Ruth Pitter, *The Spirit Watches*, copyright 1940, by Ruth Pitter; *Collected Poems* by James Stephens, copyright 1926; *Poems* by William Butler Yeats, *Later Poems*, copyright 1924, by William Butler Yeats, *The Tower*, copyright 1928, by William Butler Yeats, and *Collected Poems*, copyright 1932, by William Butler Yeats. "The Second Coming" from *The Collected Poems of W. B. Yeats: Definitive Edition*, copyright 1924 by The Macmillan Company, renewed 1952 by Bertha Georgie Yeats. "Byzantium" and "A Dialogue of Self and Soul" from *The Collected Poems of W. B. Yeats: Definitive Edition*, copyright 1933 by The Macmillan Company and used with their permission. All these poems reprinted by permission of the publishers, The Macmillan Company.

Macmillan and Co., Ltd. (London) for the selections from *Collected Poems* by Thomas Hardy and *Late Lyrics and Earlier* by Thomas Hardy.

The Marvell Press for "Coming," "Next Please," "No Road," "Spring," "Arrivals," "Departures," and "Church Going" from *The Less Deceived* by Philip Larkin, copyright 1955, 1958 by The Marvell Press and reprinted by permission of The Marvell Press, Hessle, Yorkshire, England.

Elkin Matthews for the poem from *Chambers of Imagery* by Gordon Bottomley.

John Murray for "Inevitable," "Slough," "Arrest of Oscar Wilde," "Remorse," and "The Cottage Hospital" from *John Betjeman's Collected Poems*, copyright © John Betjeman 1958, published in the United States by Houghton Mifflin Company. Reprinted by permission of John Murray. For the selections from *Poetical Works* by Robert Bridges.

New Directions for the selections from *The World I Breathe*, copyright 1939, by Dylan Thomas, and *New Poems*, copyright 1943, by Dylan Thomas; *New Directions in Prose and Poetry: 1940; The New British Poets*, edited by Kenneth Rexroth; and *Sacred and Secular Elegies*, copyright 1943, by George Barker; for the selections from *Poems* by Wilfred Owen. "Do Not Go Gentle Into That Good Night" and "A Refusal to Mourn the Death by Fire of a Child in London" from *Collected Poems of Dylan Thomas*. Copyright 1939, 1942, 1946 by New Directions. Copyright 1952, 1953 by Dylan Thomas, © 1957 by New Directions. Reprinted by permission of New Directions.

Ivan Obolensky, Inc. for "The Crane," "The Jam Trap," and "In Defense of Metaphysics" from *Seeing Is Believing* by Charles Tomlinson, © 1958 by Charles Tomlinson. Reprinted by permission of the author and the publisher.

Oxford University Press for the selections from *The Poems of Gerard Manley Hopkins,* copyright 1918, 1930. Reprinted by permission of the Oxford University Press and the poet's family. Also for the selections from *Short Is the Time,* copyright 1940, 1943, by C. Day Lewis.

James B. Pinker for the selections from *Whipperginny* and for other poems by Robert Graves.

The Poetry Bookshop (London) for the selections from *Spring Morning* and *Autumn Midnight* by Frances Cornford; *The Farmer's Bride* and *The Rambling Sailor* by Charlotte Mew; *Strange Meetings, Children of Love,* and *Real Property* by Harold Monro. Also for the poems reprinted, with the authors' permissions, from the volumes of *Georgian Poetry.*

Random House, Inc. for the selections from *Poems,* copyright 1934, by W. H. Auden, *On This Island,* copyright 1937, by W. H. Auden, *Another Time,* copyright 1940, by W. H. Auden, *For the Time Being,* copyright 1944, by W. H. Auden, *The Collected Poetry of W. H. Auden,* copyright 1945; *Collected Poems,* copyright 1935, by C. Day Lewis; *Poems: 1925-1940,* copyright 1937, 1940, by Louis MacNeice, *Springboard,* copyright 1945, by Louis MacNeice; *Poems,* copyright 1934, by Stephen Spender; *The Still Centre,* copyright 1939, by Stephen Spender; *Ruins and Visions,* copyright 1942, by Stephen Spender; *Poems of Dedication,* copyright 1947, by Stephen Spender; *The Edge of Being,* copyright 1949, by Stephen Spender; and *The Complete Works of J. M. Synge.* Reprinted by permission of, and by special arrangement with, Random House, Inc.

Henry Reed for "The Auction Sale" from *Encounter.*

Grant Richards for the selections from *The Hundred and One Harlequins* by Sacheverell Sitwell.

Routledge & Kegan Paul Ltd. for "Greenwich Observatory," "William Yeats in Limbo," "Early Spring," "Neutrality," and "The Gardener" from *The Collected Poems of Sydney Keyes.* Copyright 1945, 1951. Reprinted by permission of the publisher.

Siegfried Sassoon for the selections from his *Selected Poems, Recreations,* and *Vigils.*

Charles Scribner's Sons for the selections from the *Collected Poems of Alice Meynell, Poems* by William Ernest Henley, and the works of Robert Louis Stevenson.

Martin Secker for the selections from *Collected Poems* by James Elroy Flecker.

Sidgwick and Jackson, Ltd. for the selections from *The Waggoner,* copyright 1920, by Edmund Blunden, and *The Dark Fire,* copyright 1918, by W. J. Turner.

Frederick A. Stokes Company for the selections from *Collected Poems by Alfred Noyes,* copyright 1906 by Alfred Noyes, copyright 1913, by Frederick A. Stokes Company.

The Vanguard Press for the selections from *The Song of the Cold,* copyright 1948, by Edith Sitwell.

The Viking Press, Inc. for the selections from *The Song of Lazarus* by Alex Comfort, copyright 1945 by Alex Comfort; *Chamber Music* by James Joyce, copyright 1918 by B. W. Huebsch, 1946 by Nora Joyce; *Amores* by D. H. Lawrence, copyright 1916 by David Herbert Lawrence, 1944 by Frieda Lawrence; *New Poems* by D. H. Lawrence, copyright 1920 by B. W. Huebsch, Inc., 1948 by Frieda Lawrence; *Look! We Have Come Through!* by D. H. Lawrence; *Collected Poems* by Siegfried Sassoon; *The Espalier* by Sylvia Townsend Warner, and *Time Importuned* by Sylvia Townsend Warner. "The Ship of Death" from *Last Poems* by D. H. Lawrence. Copyright 1933 by Frieda Lawrence. Reprinted by permission of The Viking Press, Inc.

Ann Watkins, Inc. for "Still Falls the Rain" from *Street Song,* copyright 1942, by Edith Sitwell, "Dirge for the New Sunrise" and "Song: Now That Fate Is Dead and Gone" from *The Song of the Cold,* copyright 1948 by Edith Sitwell.

A. P. Watt & Son for "To Bring the Dead to Life," "The White Goddess," "Cry Faugh!" and "To Juan at the Winter Solstice" from *Collected Poems 1955* by Robert Graves. © 1955 Roturman S. A. and published by Doubleday & Co., Inc.

Three of the posthumous poems of Thomas Hardy are reprinted by permission of Mrs. Hardy and Mr. Sidney Cockerell, his executors. The poems of James Elroy Flecker are reprinted by permission of his executors. The poems of Alice Meynell are reprinted with the consent of her husband, Wilfred Meynell. The poems of Harold Monro are reprinted with his consent and that of his widow, Alida Klemantaski, Mrs. Harold Monro. The poems of Charlotte Mew are reprinted with her consent and her executors'.

Foreword
to the New and Enlarged Edition

⥈ Since the first edition of this anthology was printed more than forty years ago, two world wars have shattered the security of mankind. The final results are still unpredictable. Instead of establishing peace, they created new battlefronts, quickened "cold" as well as fierce colonial wars, and intensified the spreading conflict of opposed ideologies throughout the world.

It is against this background that the new edition of *Modern British Poetry* has been prepared. As before, the editor aims to show the range of English poetry over a century which includes highly experimental as well as accomplished traditional writing. The emphasis is on reappraisal, so that the work is not only inclusive but critical. To accomplish this, it has been necessary to omit several interesting poets. The editor regrets the omissions, but comforts himself with the thought that even a work of encyclopedic dimensions would not be inclusive enough to satisfy every reader. Researchers and students of the period may find the omitted poets in earlier editions of this collection.

This edition has been revised still further. The biographical and bibliographical notes have been brought sharply up-to-date. The preface has been amplified. Recent innovations which attempt to extend the domain of poetry have been recorded. More than ever, the volume hopes to reflect the variety of experience and vision, the sense of discovery which is the essential power of poetry.

Although the editor believes he has favored no group, movement, or tendency at the expense of any other, he admits that he is less impressed by the repetition of accepted subjects and generally approved poetic formulas, however skillful, than by a distinctive inflection, even though it may lead to oddity, as in the case of Hopkins. This personal idiom, this "difference," may be difficult to define but it is impossible to mistake.

The choice of poems may seem willful to some, but the selection has not been arbitrary. The editor cannot pretend that he has infallibly chosen only the best, but he maintains that he has included nothing that does not represent some phase of the period and does not reveal some aspect of the poet. To achieve this he has mingled the well-known with the unfamiliar. A good poem remains a good poem no matter how often it has been reprinted, but its presence in anthologies is not necessarily a proof of its goodness. New blood is needed not only to quicken the life stream of culture but to keep it fresh and powerful.

It must be repeated that this collection is anything but a complete summary. Since the end of the Victorian era the work of the poets of England and Ireland has been so voluminous, the departures in form and subject matter have been so varied, that no editor would dare claim finality for his labors. Perhaps it is just as well; it might be asserted that finality, even if attainable, is undesirable. The duty of the anthologist, as one anthologist sees it, is to stimulate, not to satisfy, to whet the reader's appetite, not to surfeit it.

Such a collection as this, if its purpose is achieved, should excite the reader's curiosity and rouse him to a closer reading of the poet's own volumes. The following pages are, as already implied, little more than a guide, a critical introduction, to characteristic figures and leading poetic tendencies.

This anthology begins with Thomas Hardy, born in 1840; and the editor acknowledges a special indebtedness to that great figure not only for his general austere example, but for personal advice in the preparation of the early editions of this volume. Thanks must also be given to most of the living poets, too many to list, who have furnished invaluable data, helped in the final choice of selections, and in several instances have supplied new poems in manuscript.

Contents

W. J. TURNER *(1889-1946)*, 344

ISAAC ROSENBERG *(1890-1918)*, 349

RICHARD ALDINGTON *(1892-1962)*, 353

OSBERT SITWELL *(1892-)*, 355

HUGH MAC DIARMID *(1892-)*, 359

WILFRED OWEN *(1893-1918)*, 361

SYLVIA TOWNSEND WARNER *(1893-)*, 369

MODERN BRITISH POETRY

New and Enlarged Edition

Preface

☙ To say this is a collection of modern poetry calls at once for a definition of the term, and it is doubtful whether there is a less exact and more abused adjective in the language than "modern." In the case of this compilation the limits of the term are determined if not defined by the dates 1840-1960, or from the advent of Thomas Hardy in the midst of Victorianism to the emergence of the "post-war" poets who reflect the impasse and precarious balance of the world today.

One line of the arbitrary boundary—a deadline by which any poet born before 1840 is excluded—has been chosen for three reasons. First, it permits the other end to round out something more than a full century of poetic accomplishment, so that the book acts as a comparison as well as a companion to *Modern American Poetry*. Second, it begins with Thomas Hardy, a pioneer in candor, one of the first to express the scientific thought of the times in a poetry at once vigorous, uncompromising, and austere—a poetry which anticipated the direct speech of the contemporary generation. Third, the division brings us close to the end of four-square, Victorian conservatism and the beginning of the energetic experimentalism which still engages us.

Most of the great Victorian figures are thus eliminated; reaction takes the place of reflection. Nothing, it has been said, is more permanent than the spirit of change, and we have come a long way since the time when a poet was seriously praised (in 1870) because he held "the proud honor of never uttering one single line which an English mother once would wish unwritten or an English girl would wish unread." The poet was Tennyson who (in *Idylls of the King*) reduced Malory's Round Table to the board of a royal family in the best suburban manner, proving that no laureate could have been more appropriate to the era. But if Tennyson, as G. K. Chesterton dryly remarked, "did hold a great many of the same views as Queen Victoria, though he was gifted with a more fortunate literary style," it was his style even more than his views from which his successors revolted. He presented a conventionalized tightness of sentiment; Swinburne offered an equally conventionalized looseness of rhetoric. Taste tired of both. They suggested the extremes which Yeats defined in another connection, "Sentimentality is deceiving one's self; rhetoric is deceiving other people." Artificial emotions were waning. The inversions, the elaborate diction, the strained affections were doomed by the demand for truth.

This was not achieved overnight. Within the larger curve traced in this volume, there are the records of conflicting tendencies. In general—if I may be permitted an arbitrary grouping—these smaller movements may be classified as (1) The end of Victorianism and the growth of a purely decorative art, (2) The Pre-Raphaelites and Swinburne, (3) The rise and decline of the esthetic philosophy, (4) The muscular influence of Henley, (5) William Butler Yeats and the Celtic revival in Ireland, (6) Rudyard Kipling and the ascendancy of mechanism in art, (7) John Masefield and the return of the rhymed narrative, (8) The war and its effects upon the Georgians, (9) The aftermath and the new bucolic poetry, (10) The "literature of nerves," and (11) The "post-war" group. It may be interesting to follow these developments in somewhat closer detail.

THE END OF VICTORIANISM

The age commonly called Victorian came to an end in England about 1880. It was an age distinguished by many true idealists and many false ideals. It was, in spite of its notable artists, on an entirely different level from the epoch preceding. Its poetry was, in the main, not universal but parochial; its romanticism was gilt and tinsel; its realism was kin to its showy glass pendants, red plush, parlor chromos and antimacassars. The period was full of a pessimistic resignation (the note popularized by Fitzgerald's Omar Khayyám) and a kind of negation which, refusing to see any glamor in the present world, turned to the Middle Ages, to King Arthur, to the legend of Troy—to the suave surroundings of a dream-world instead of the hard contours of actual experience.

At its worst, it was a period of smugness, of placid and pious sentimentality, epitomized by the rhymed sermons of Martin Farquhar Tupper, whose *Proverbial Philosophy* was devoured, with all its cloying and indigestible sweetmeats, by tens of thousands. The same tendency is apparent, though a little less objectionably, in the moralizing lays of Lord Thomas Macaulay, in the theatrically emotionalized verses of Robert Buchanan, Edwin Arnold and Sir Lewis Morris, even in the lesser work of Alfred Lord Tennyson.

The poets of a generation before this time were fired with such ideas as freedom, an adoration of nature, an insatiable hunger for truth in all its forms and manifestations. The characteristic poets of the Victorian Era, says Max Plowman, "wrote under the dominance of churchliness, of 'sweetness and light,' and a thousand lesser theories that have not truth but comfort for their end."

The revolt against the tawdriness of the period had already begun; the best of Victorianism can be found not in men who were typically Victorian, but in pioneers like Browning and insurrectionary spirits like Swinburne, Rossetti, William Morris, who were completely out of sympathy with their time.

THE PRE-RAPHAELITES AND SWINBURNE

That band of painters and poets who called themselves quaintly The Pre-Raphaelite Brotherhood hurried the demise of Victorianism. Their work was a continual denial of its forms; their poems aspired to be paintings, their paintings poems. Under the leadership of William Morris The Pre-Raphaelites enlisted the coöperation of Burne-Jones, the Rossettis, and the insecure loyalty of Swinburne. Morris, the most practical member of the group, sought to make over an entire culture; he designed everything from chintzes to stained-glass windows, created furniture, wrought iron, printed books, manufactured glass, needlework, tapestries, tools—all as a protest against the rapid commercialism of a period whose prosperity was essentially shoddy. Morris was a consistent protestant in his poetry and his politics. In the rôle of poet he rebuked the smallness of his times with epics like *The Earthly Paradise;* in the rôle of propagandist he answered narrow individualism with *News from Nowhere,* picturing an ideal England in which the principles of communism had triumphed. Here Morris, dreaming of a medieval Utopia, confused the future with the past. With a simplicity surpassed only by his energy, he turned back to passion in suits of antique armor and to gallants whose heroism was suspiciously like heroics.

Morris failed, partly because the trend toward standardized production was too sweeping to take account of his theories, partly because he himself was not so much concerned with humanity as with things. He advocated a knightly Socialism not because it would make a more beautiful race but more decorative objects. His sagas show that his preoccupation was with literature instead of life; and, by an ungrateful paradox, a literature that is preferred to life has a swift mortality.

Swinburne suffered from a similar defect. Flying from the prim domesticity sanctified by Tennyson, Swinburne rushed to the unholy (and purely literary) arms of Dolores, Faustine, Félise, Fragoletta, to the neo-paganism of *Atalanta in Calydon,* to the lush intransigence of *Songs Before Sunrise,* to Gautier and Hugo and Baudelaire, to a quick succession of enthusiasms and influences. But it was neither Swinburne's political convictions nor his vaguely revolutionary tendencies which made the young men of his day go about "chanting to one another these new, astonishing melodies." It was his mastery of the lightning phrase, cutting through murky philosophizing and wave-like rhythms arising and crashing on startled shores; it was his headlong fervor coming immediately after a decade of cautious hesitancy. Most of all, from a literary-historical point of view, it was his technique which affected the entire conception of English metrics. English poetry had been slavishly devoted to its norm, the *iamb;* Swinburne, by a lavish use of the dactyl, the choriambus and the anapest, gave poetry a new motion, a polyphonic freedom, an orchestral sweep and sonority. He enlarged the potentialities of English prosody. "Nor," writes Edmund Gosse, "was his singular vogue due only to this extraordinary metrical ingenuity; the effect of his artistic personality was itself intoxicating, even delirious. He was the poet of youth insurgent against all the restraints of conventionality and custom."

The "purest" poet of the group was one only loosely affiliated with it, the quiet sister of Dante Gabriel, Christina Rossetti. Her delicate reticences have been often portrayed, but it remained for Frances Winwar, in *Poor Splendid Wings: The Rossettis and Their Circle,* to depict the outer softness and the inner sharpness, "protecting, like a coat of armor, something she held above the treasures of the world." Struggling between the desires of her womanhood and a congenital refusal to face life, her philosophy grew more and more ascetic. Denial and loss became her favorite themes, she grew increasingly preoccupied with the thought of death as the undemanding lover, the final appeasement. But the thought of sundering to which she always returned, the tremulous abnegation, stirred the depths of her music and inspired her most memorable poetry.

RISE AND DECLINE OF THE ESTHETIC PHILOSOPHY

A somewhat more fashionable revolt ensued. Oscar Wilde, dilettante *de luxe,* attempted to make the 'Nineties draw up an esthetic declaration of independence; the beauty thus championed, taking a leaf from the French symbolists, was to be "its own excuse for being." Wilde's was, in the most outspoken manner, the first use of estheticism as a slogan; the battle-cry of the group was actually the now outworn but then revolutionary "Art for Art's sake"! And, so sick were people of the pinchbeck ornaments of the immediate past, that the slogan won. At least, temporarily.

The Yellow Book, the organ of the révoltés, appeared (1894-1897), representing a reasoned if limited reaction. The Rhymers' Club was the nucleus, and its members—among them Ernest Dowson, Lionel Johnson, Victor Plarr, John Davidson, Arthur Symons, William Butler Yeats—met at the Cheshire Cheese where, over their cakes and ale, they fondly hoped to restore the spirit of the Elizabethan age. Unfortunately they lacked both the gusto and the initiative of their Mermaid Tavern models. Where the Elizabethans were all for size, the sad young men were all for subtlety; instead of being large and careless, they were cramped and self-conscious, writing with one eye on the British public which they hoped to startle, and the other on the French poets whom they hoped to impress. But, underneath the desire to shock the middle-classes their standards were as prescribed as those they derided. To be mildly heretical was their unwritten orthodoxy; instead of being sentimental about virgins they were sentimental about street-walkers. Prostitutes were "soiled doves" and the street-lamps under which they plied their trade were "the iron lilies of the Strand."

Until its collapse after the trial of Wilde, the Esthetic Movement gathered a show of strength which was, however, weakened by its central fallacy. It tried to drag life down to literature instead of bringing literature up to life. The young men's prophet was Walter Pater; their stronghold the ivory tower; their program a mixture of Anglican intellectuality and Parnassian impressionism. "But," as C. E. Andrews and M. O. Percival point out in *Poetry of the Nineties,* "they left behind the intellectual side of Pater, and the 'gem-like flame' was fed purely by emotions. The esthetes' search for beauty became a search for sensations. They did not face the whole of life . . . but they selected from life its strange colors and its strange experiences. They loved to see in the real world glimpses that *seemed* exotic and remote."

Almost the first act of the "new" men was to rouse and outrage their immediate predecessors. This end-of-the-century desire to shock, which was so strong and natural an impulse, still has a place of its own as an antidote. Mid-Victorian propriety and self-satisfaction crumbled under the swift audacities of rebellious spirits. The old walls fell; the public, once so apathetic to *belles-lettres,* was more than attentive to every phase of literary experimentation. The last decade of the nineteenth century was so tolerant of novelty in art and ideas, that it would seem, says Holbrook Jackson in his penetrative summary, *The Eighteen-Nineties,* "as though the declining century wished to make amends for several decades of artistic monotony. It may indeed be something more than a coincidence that placed this decade at the close of a century, and *fin de siècle* may have been at once a swan song and a death-bed repentance."

Thereafter, the movement (if such it may be called) surfeited with its own excesses fell into the mere poses of revolt; it degenerated into a half-hearted defense of artificialities.

It scarcely needed W. S. Gilbert (in *Patience*) or Robert Hichens (in *The Green Carnation*) to satirize its distorted attitudinizing. It strained itself to death; it became its own burlesque of the bizarre, an extravaganza of extravagance. "The period" (I am again quoting Holbrook Jackson) "was as certainly a period of decadence as it was a period of renaissance. The decadence was to be seen in a perverse and finicking glorification of the fine arts and mere artistic virtuosity on the one hand, and a militant commercial movement on the other. . . . The eroticism which became so prevalent in the verse of many of the younger poets was minor because it was little more than a pose—not because it was erotic. . . . It was a passing mood which gave the poetry of the hour a hothouse fragrance; a perfume faint, yet unmistakable and strange."

But most of the elegant and disillusioned young men overshot their mark. Vulgar health reasserted itself; an inherent though long-repressed vitality sought new channels. Arthur Symons deserted his hectic Muse, Richard Le Gallienne abandoned his preciosity, and the group began to disintegrate. The esthetic philosophy was wearing thin; it had already begun to fray and reveal its essential shabbiness. Wilde, himself, possessed the three things which he said the English would never forgive—youth, power, and enthusiasm. But in trying to make an exclusive cult of beauty, Wilde had also tried to make it evade actuality; he urged that art should not, in any sense, be a part of life but an escape from it. "The proper school to learn art in is not Life—but Art." And in the same essay ("The Decay of Lying") he wrote, "All bad Art comes from returning to Life and Nature, and elevating them into ideals." Elsewhere he declared his motto: "The first duty in life is to be as artificial as possible. What the second duty is no one has discovered."

Such a cynical and, in essence, silly philosophy could not go unchallenged. Its snobbish fastidiousness, its very pretense, was bound to arouse the blood of common reality. This negative attitude received its answer in the work of that determined yea-sayer, W. E. Henley.

WILLIAM ERNEST HENLEY

Henley repudiated languid estheticism; he scorned a mincing art which was out of touch with the world. His was a large and sweeping affirmation. He felt that mere existence was glorious: life was coarse, difficult, often dangerous and dirty, but splendid at the heart. Art, he knew, could not be separated from the dreams and hungers of man; it could not flourish only on its own essences or technical accomplishments. To live, poetry would have to share the fears, angers, hopes and struggles of the prosaic world. So Henley came like a salt breeze blowing through a perfumed, heavily screened studio. He sang loudly (often, indeed, too loudly) of the joy of living and the courage of the "unconquerable soul." He was a powerful influence not only as a poet but as a critic and editor. In the latter capacity he gathered about him such men as Robert Louis Stevenson, Rudyard Kipling, Thomas Hardy, H. G. Wells, William Butler Yeats, T. E. Brown, J. M. Barrie. None of these men were his disciples, some were much older, but none came into contact with him without being influenced in some way by his sharp and positive personality. A pioneer and something of a prophet, he was one of the first to champion the paintings of Whistler and to proclaim the genius of Rodin.

Historically considered, Henley represents another transition; his is the bridge between the loose optimism of Browning and the applied imperialism of Kipling. Both extremes find a voice—and a prolonged one—in his work. "Life! More life!" he shouted with the over-eagerness of one afflicted by physical infirmities. "More life!"—particularly English life which, with the authority of sword and gospel, must be broadcast over both hemispheres—but life, no matter how undisciplined, at any cost. And the more boisterous the better.

Life—give me life until the end,
That at the very top of being,
The battle-spirit shouting in my blood,
Out of the reddest hell of the fight
I may be snatched and flung
Into the everlasting lull,
The immortal, incommunicable dream.

But Henley's verse was not always shrill. When he forgot to be muscular, he fashioned ballades and rondeaus with a dexterity scarcely surpassed by Swinburne, lyrics of surprisingly delicate texture, free verse that anticipated a movement two generations later, and "voluntaries" of the city on the Thames with Whistlerian glamor. Further than that, Henley's noisy periods are redeemed by his passionate enthusiasm for nobility in whatever cause it was joined. He loved the world in all its moods. Bus-drivers, hospital interiors, scrubwomen, a panting train, the mystery and squalor of London's alleys, all found a voice in his lines; his later work contains more than a hint of the delight in science and machinery which was later to be sounded more fully in the work of Rudyard Kipling.

THE CELTIC REVIVAL AND J. M. SYNGE

In 1889, William Butler Yeats published his *Wanderings of Oisin;* in the same year Douglas Hyde, scholar and folk-lorist, brought out his *Book of Gaelic Stories.*

The revival of Gaelic and the renascence of Irish literature may be said to date from the publication of those two books. The fundamental idea of both men and their followers was the same. It was to create a literature which would express the national consciousness of Ireland through a purely national art. They began to reflect the strange background of dreams, politics, hopelessness, and heroism which is proverbially Irish. This community of fellowship and aims is to be found in the varied but allied work of William Butler Yeats,

"Æ" (George W. Russell), Moira O'Neill, Lionel Johnson, Katharine Tynan, Padraic Colum, and others. The first fervor gone, a period of dullness set in. After reanimating the old myths, surcharging the legendary heroes with a new significance, it seemed that the movement was losing itself in a literary mysticism. But there followed an increasing concern with the peasant, the migratory laborer, the tramp; an interest that was a reaction against the influence of Yeats and his then arbitrary, over-symbolized otherworldliness. In 1904, the Celtic Revival reached its height with John Millington Synge, who was not only the greatest dramatist of the Irish Theater, but (to quote such contrary critics as George Moore and Harold Williams) "one of the greatest dramatists who has written in English." Synge's poetry, brusque and all too small in quantity, was a minor occupation with him, yet the quality and power of it is unmistakable. Its content was not great, but the raw vigor in it served as a bold banner—a sort of a brilliant Jolly Roger—for the younger men of a subsequent period.

In the introduction to *The Playboy of the Western World,* Synge declared, "When I was writing *The Shadow of the Glen* some years ago, I got more aid than any learning could have given me from a chink in the floor of the old Wicklow house where I was staying that let me hear what was being said by the servant girls in the kitchen. This matter is, I think, of some importance; for in countries where the imagination of the people and the language they use, is rich and living, it is possible for a writer to be rich and copious in his words —and at the same time to give the reality which is at the root of all poetry, in a natural and comprehensive form." This not only explains Synge's impulse but his idiom, possibly the raciest in modern literature.

Synge's poetic power is unquestionably greatest in his plays. In *The Well of the Saints, The Playboy of the Western World,* and *Riders to the Sea* there is more beauty of form, more richness of language than in any piece of dramatic writing since the Elizabethans. Yeats, when he first heard Synge's early one-act play, *The Shadow of the Glen,* is said to have exclaimed "Euripides." A half year later when Synge read him *Riders to the Sea,* Yeats again confined his enthusiasm to a single word:—"Aeschylus!" Time has shown that Yeats's exaggeration was not wholly a compatriot's *beau geste.*

Although Synge's poetry was not his major concern, numbering only twenty-four original pieces and eighteen translations, it had a surprising effect. It marked a point of departure, a reaction against the too-polished verse of his immediate predecessors as well as the dehumanized mysticism of many of his associates. In that memorable preface to his *Poems* he wrote what was a manifesto and at the same time a classic *credo* for all that called itself the "new" poetry. "I have often thought," it begins, "that at the side of poetic diction, which everyone condemns, modern verse contains a great deal of poetic material, using 'poetic' in the same special sense. The poetry of exaltation will be always the highest, but when men lose their poetic feeling for ordinary life and cannot write poetry of ordinary things, their exalted poetry is likely to lose its strength of exaltation in the way that men cease to build beautiful churches when they have lost happiness in building shops. . . . Even if we grant that exalted poetry can be kept successfully by itself, the strong things of life are needed in poetry also, to show that what is exalted or tender is not made by feeble blood."

WILLIAM BUTLER YEATS

William Butler Yeats began by being part of the Celtic movement; before he was sixty he had inspired a movement of his own. With the publication of his *Collected Poems* in 1933 he was acclaimed Ireland's uncrowned laureate and was considered by many the finest poet of his day. Yeats's early poetry was in the style popularized by the Celtic twilight with all its musing and mistiness. Such volumes as *Crossways* (1889), *The Rose* (1893), *The Wind Among the Reeds* (1899), illustrate his gift for pure song. With *The Green Helmet* (1910) a more colloquial tone entered his verse and in *Responsibilities* (1914) a new articulation manifested itself. Yeats had met Ezra Pound and was greatly impressed with the young American's idiom. His later work grew firmer in thought, more complex in harmony. Common speech mingled wit and wisdom in a way scarcely suggested by his early poetry.

The publication of *Collected Poems,* when Yeats was in his sixty-eighth year, was the signal for an international salute; poets of every school and tendency united to acclaim Yeats's increased power. Charles Powell wrote in the *Manchester Guardian,* "In Mr. Yeats there is, perhaps, the clearest link between the modern and the more traditional. There is no poet writing today, old or new, who gets so surely through to reality or who has so vitally the contemporary consciousness. . . . Now that he has established something like an equipoise between the intellect and the imagination, his poetry has the energy of life that is at once passionate and serene."

Even before Yeats's death in 1939 it was evident that he had helped to make and destroy a movement. He had begun by believing that a new culture would grow with the common man, but he confessed his disillusion. "I could not foresee that a new class would change the nature of the Irish movement. . . . Power passed to small shopkeepers, to men who had risen above the traditions of the countryman without learning those of cultivated life and who, because of their poverty, ignorance, and superstitious piety, are much subject to all kinds of fear. Immediate victory, immediate utility, became everything, and we artists, who are the servants not of any cause but of mere naked life . . . became, as elsewhere in Europe, protesting individual voices."

Yeats had hoped to speak to and for the average man, but he had in mind "the divine average." Events destroyed his hopes. He wrote Lady Gregory that "we must accept the baptism of the gutter," yet he defended aristocracy in art as in life. He had championed the ordinary individual, but he revolted from the commercial middle classes who "fumble in the greasy till/ And add the halfpence to the pence." Reluctantly he gave up his early dream of awaking Ireland, and concluded:

Romantic Ireland's dead and gone,
It's with O'Leary in the grave.

Faced with the physical terror of revolt he declared scornfully:

> Hurrah for revolution! Let the cannon shoot!
> The beggar upon horseback lashes the beggar upon foot.

Although Yeats never quite repudiated his "aristocratic" affiliations, he delighted to employ the "vulgar" tone; he discarded the early elaborateness for a final sharpness. He turned away from the poetry of incantation for a plain-speaking verse, from the mystic rose and wild swans to a more personal symbolism, to swords and towers and winding stairs. He borrowed from his juniors, even from those he disliked (Pound and Auden, for example), and he never disdained to learn from them. He did more; he used his experience, his changing taste, and his poetic instinct to surpass them all.

HARDY, HOUSMAN, AND HOPKINS

The nineteenth century ended on a dwindling note, a thin echo of the confident imperialism with which it began. The revolt against Victorianism was anticipated by the skepticism of Darwin and the agnosticism of John Stuart Mill; the end of the century was marked by a resistance to everything which Victoria had established, symbolized, and sanctified. One of the most undaunted questioners of the conventions was Thomas Hardy, a Victorian in everything but spirit. Hardy acknowledged the shifting backgrounds, the increased tempo, and the dictates of modern science, but he accepted them without joy and with little hope. His predecessors and most of his contemporaries regarded Nature not only as the friend of man but as the Great Mother, the Divine Healer. Hardy had no such illusions; he agreed with Matthew Arnold who had written:

> Man must begin, know this, where Nature ends;
> Nature and man can never be fast friends.

Although Hardy did not believe in the lovingkindness of Nature, he did not conclude, as some of his critics have maintained, that it was evil. Nature was not malevolent, but indifferent. God was equally unconcerned, Hardy added grimly, with man's personal life, even with humanity's "destiny." If He should stop to observe the antics of man, one of his minor creations, He would smile ironically at the distorted human standards presumed to be reflections of eternal "values." Man may "explain" God's labors, but God himself, "sense-sealed," wrought His work without logic, even without suspicion that He had evolved a creature with sufficient consciousness "to ask for reasons why."

This is a far cry from the unflinching certainties and devout standards of the Victorians. Hardy offered little comfort to the smug church-goers who believed themselves "in tune with the Infinite" and the complacent citizens who prided themselves upon living in "the best of all possible worlds." Not that Hardy was hopeless about humanity. On the contrary, he admired its accomplishments in the face of adversity; mankind, he implied, was all the greater when it struggled against overwhelming odds. In its very failures, more than in its occasional triumphs, humanity's stature increased; it became tragic and, hence, noble.

A similar note of stubborn heroism was sounded in the poetry of A. E. Housman. Like Hardy, Housman was a quiet but forceful pessimist. A cloistered Latin scholar and teacher, Housman wrote with detachment about individual betrayal and cosmic grief. Evil is a constant, says Housman—"the troubles of our proud and angry dust are from eternity and shall not fail"—but evil must be borne. Cruelty is natural in this our world, but it can, somehow, be endured.

> Therefore, since the world has still
> Much good, but much less good than ill,
> And while the sun and moon endure
> Luck's a chance, but trouble's sure,
> I'd face it as a wise man would,
> And train for ill and not for good.

This was a startling note, a new expression of the old stoic bitterness. In laconic lines Housman affirmed Hardy's contention that the sense of suffering makes for strength, an immunity against too much pain. His incongruously blithe verse assured the reader that, though man is "a stranger and afraid in the world he never made," there are compensations. For example, there is always enough love, laughter, and liquor to go round—and the latter

> . . . does more than Milton can
> To justify God's ways to man.

An attitude completely opposed to that of Hardy and Housman was taken by Gerard Manley Hopkins. God's ways to man were justified by His sense of love and, even more generously, by His gift of Beauty—by a world where thrush's eggs look like "little low heavens," where a common horse-shoe becomes a "bright and battering sandal," where the stars are "fire-folk sitting in the air," a world "barbarous in beauty," prodigal in energy "charged with the grandeur of God."

Hopkins, a devout but highly imaginative Jesuit, embodied a religious confidence at a time when skepticism was in favor. In brilliantly original verse he brought a new manner to the old tradition. Almost unknown in his day, neglected by practically all his contemporaries, Hopkins influenced another generation by the richness of his style, the splendor of his vocabulary, and his way of packing every phrase with far-reaching allusions.

RUDYARD KIPLING

New tendencies are contagious. But they also disclose themselves simultaneously in places and people where there has been no point of contact. Even before Synge proclaimed the wild beauty in rude life, Kipling was illuminating the wealth of poetic material in things hitherto regarded as too commonplace for poetry. Before literary England had quite recovered from a surfeit of Victorian priggishness and Pre-Raphaelite preciosity, the young Kipling came out of India with high spirits and a great tide of life, sweeping all before him. An obscure Anglo-Indian journalist, the publication of his *Barrack-room Ballads* in 1892 brought him sudden notice. By 1895, he was internationally famous. Plunging through the past as through a withered underbrush, he sprang into the open field of the present. Its mechanical obstacles did not deter him. Kipling gloried in the material world; he did more—he glorified it. He pierced the tough exteriors of seemingly prosaic things—things like machinery, bridge-building, cockney soldiers, slang, steam, the dirty by-products of science (witness "M'Andrews Hymn" and "The Bell Buoy")—and uncovered their hidden glamor. "Romance is gone," sighed most of his contemporaries, whereupon Kipling countered:

> . . . and all unseen
> Romance brought up the nine-fifteen.

Reality is Kipling's romanticism; he rolls drums and sounds clarions for another "crowded hour of glorious life." He composes marches for soldiers, explorers, mechanics, foot-sloggers—for life in action. Motion itself is apostrophized in his verse. Where the world is going is of no particular concern to Kipling; that it moves as a beneficent Britannia directs is gratifying, but that it moves is sufficient to rouse Kipling's enthusiasm.

Kipling, with his perception of ordinary people in terms of ordinary life, is one of the strongest links between the Wordsworth-Browning era and the apostles of vigor, beginning with Masefield. There are serious defects in Kipling's work, particularly in his more facile poetry. He falls into a journalistic ease with a tendency to jingle; he is fond of a militaristic drum-banging as blatant as the insularity he condemns. His best work vibrates with an intensity that transforms the tawdry, that lifts the vulgar and incidental to the universal—the universal, that is, in terms of the British Empire.

JOHN MASEFIELD

All art is a twofold reviving—a reappraisal of subject and a reanimating of form. Poetry becomes perennially "new" by returning to the old with a different consciousness, a greater awareness. In 1911, when art was again searching for novelty, John Masefield created something startling and new by going back to 1385 and *The Canterbury Tales.* Employing both the Chaucerian model and a form similar to the practically forgotten Byronic stanza, Masefield wrote in rapid succession, *The Everlasting Mercy* (1911), *The Widow in the Bye Street* (1912), *Dauber* (1912), *The Daffodil Fields* (1913)—four long rhymed narratives. Expressive of every rugged phase of life, these poems responded to Synge's proclamation that "the strong things of life are needed in poetry also . . . and it may almost be said that before verse can be human again it must be brutal."

Masefield brought back to poetry a mixture of beauty and brutality which is its most human and enduring quality. He brought back that rich and vulgar vividness which is the life-blood of Chaucer, of Shakespeare, of Burns, of Villon, of Heine. As a purely descriptive poet, he won a place with the masters of seascape and landscape. As an imaginative realist, he showed those who were stumbling from one wild eccentricity to another that humanity itself was wilder, stranger, far more thrilling than anything in the world—or out of it. Few things in contemporary poetry are as powerful as the regeneration of Saul Kane (in *The Everlasting Mercy*) or the story of *Dauber,* the tale of a tragic sea-voyage and a dreamer who wanted to be a painter. The vigorous description of rounding Cape Horn in the latter poem is a masterpiece in itself.

THE WAR AND THE GEORGIANS

In 1914, the line of demarcation between Masefield and the younger men was not sharp. Realism was again in the ascendancy. So definite a style as Masefield's was bound to be imitated. It even attracted W. W. Gibson, who deserted bowery arcades to follow the rude trail Masefield had blazed. Gibson reënforced the interest in actuality by turning from a preoccupation with shining knights, faultless queens, ladies in distress, and all the paraphernalia of hackneyed medieval romances, to write about ferrymen, berry-pickers, stone-cutters, farmers, printers, circus-men, carpenters—dramatizing (and often theatricalizing) the primitive emotions of ordinary people in *Livelihood, Daily Bread,* and *Fires.* Candor had been asking new questions. It found unexpected answers in the war; repressed emotionalism discovered a new and terrible outlet.

The first volume of the biennial *Georgian Poetry* had just appeared when the war caught up the youth of England in a gust of national fervor. Not only the young men but their seniors joined what seemed then to be "the Great Adventure," only to find that it was, as one of them has since called it, "the Late Great Nightmare." After the early flush of romanticism had passed, the voices of bitter disillusion were heard. Not at first, for censorship was omnipresent. But Siegfried Sassoon's fierce satires and burning denunciations could not be stilled; the mocking lines of Robert Graves began to be quoted; Wilfred Owen's posthumous poems painted a picture the very opposite of the journalistic jingo verses which attempted to paint civilization's greatest horror in bright and cheerful colors.

Rupert Brooke, the most popular of his group, remains, in most minds, as the type of romantic warrior, a symbolic figure not uncommon at the beginning of the first World War. But his poetry, as well as his correspondence, contains evidence that, had he survived the first few years of warfare, his verse —had he written at all—would have been akin to the unromanticized passion of those who, like Sassoon and Rosenberg and Owen, saw the horror at close range and at length. Even his comrade, Charles Hamilton Sorley, that marvelous boy killed at twenty, hearing the news of Brooke's enlistment, wrote: "Rupert Brooke is far too obsessed with his own sacrifice, regarding the going to war of himself (and others) as a highly intense, remarkable and sacrificial exploit, whereas it is merely the conduct demanded of him (and others) by the turn of circumstances, where non-compliance with this demand would have made life intolerable. He has clothed his attitude in fine words: but his is, nevertheless, the sentimental attitude."

EFFECTS OF THE WAR

Meanwhile the Georgians had rediscovered the direct speech of Wordsworth; but they relied uncritically upon the spirit of his pastoral lyrics. They echoed his assurances of natural beauty, and extended his confidence in the benign power of the country scene. They avoided the uglier implications of rural life, the losing struggles with the soil, poverty and hunger, the spiritual barrenness, and the economic failures. Theirs was a poetry of happy dawns, song-filled dusks, peace-breathing nights.

The more original poets outgrew the group. The fierce and self-flagellating D. H. Lawrence had little enough in common with his fellows at the beginning; at the end he spoke in a language which most of them preferred not to comprehend. Walter De la Mare, a neo-Gothic romancer lost in the actual present, created a fabulous world of ghosts, of unfulfilled longings and unhappy memories, in which the very landscape was haunted. Ralph Hodgson masked a far-reaching imagination in deceptive simplicities. Charlotte Mew and Anna Wickham, two women never admitted into the Georgian anthologies, combined a searching gravity with fretted energy. James Stephens and Humbert Wolfe mingled whimsical fantasy and impudent versatility.

The effect of the first World War on the established poets was definite and disastrous. The Georgian group issued two more volumes (there were five in all, the last being *Georgian Poetry 1920-1922*), but the spirit had gone out of it. Rupert Brooke and Edward Thomas had been silenced by death. The work of Walter De la Mare grew increasingly somber; John Masefield no longer contributed; D. H. Lawrence—never a Georgian at heart and admitted to the volumes with a few circumspect poems—turned to prose and bitter *pensées;* Lascelles Abercrombie wrote little after 1919; Ralph Hodgson ceased to write at all. Only W. H. Davies, living in a world which, seemingly common-pastoral, was really a world of his own, continued to warble his delighted, thought-free bird-notes. The loss to the group of these men—or the loss of their power—was not compensated by the addition of Martin Armstrong, William Kerr, J. D. C. Pellow, Edward Shanks, Thomas Moult, and other fashioners of what Sassoon called "crocus-crowded lyrics."

AFTERMATH

Peace brought back but few of the younger poets. The most brilliant of them, Charles Hamilton Sorley, was killed on the threshold of an indubitably great future. The career of Isaac Rosenberg, author of an amazing poetic drama, was ended almost before it had begun. Rupert Brooke died in the midst of his singing; so did Edward Thomas, Francis Ledwidge, Cameron Wilson. Wilfred Owen was struck down just as he had found his own full-throated utterance. It is impossible to calculate how much was lost to English poetry by the death of these singers.

One after-effect was particularly noticeable. English literature suffered not only from individual losses but from general shock. This shock affected the writers of every school and diverted where it did not arrest the current of contemporary verse. It threw Masefield back to pontifical sonnets and the classic drama of half a century ago; it silenced such of its War-poets as refused to continue to write about "the collective madness" and yet could think of little else. It created the sharp division between the new group of English pastoral poets and the still younger intellectuals. The reactions of the two contradictory movements are easy to understand. Wishing to escape the mechanistic urban civilization which had scarred Europe with ruins, many of the poets turned hopefully to the traditional curlew-calling, plover-haunted English countryside. The machine is a dead thing spreading death, they cried; only the soil brings forth. "We have had enough of destructive ingenuities; let us go back to creative simplicities." Following, more or less consciously, the example of the naïf poet, W. H. Davies, a small cohort of writers began to sing exclusively about the charms of childhood, sunsets, and rural delights. But where Davies' innocence was natural, the simplicity of most of the Georgians was predetermined. Much of the resulting poetry was inspired by the wish to avoid past memories rather than by a spontaneous affection for the present scene; much of it was a sort of protracted convalescence.

The Georgian group developed a vocabulary built on the colloquial, but it failed to emphasize any conviction behind it. Although it was devoted to real objects, it favored a gentlemanly realism. It was, as L. A. G. Strong has written, "soothing, reassuring. Its outbursts of indignation were directed against precisely the right objects, and were timed for precisely the right moment." The technique was always enviably neat—a finical contrast to the vivid bucolic records of Edward Thomas—and the conceits were properly restrained. Sometimes they reached extremes of insipidity; one of the collections enshrines this *reductio ad absurdum,* in which a literary shepherd composes such unintentionally comic strophes as:

I lingered at a gate and talked
A little with a lonely lamb.
He told me of the great still night,
Of calm starlight,
And of the lady moon, who'd stoop
For a kiss sometimes. . . .
Of how, when sheep grew old,
As their faith told
They went without a pang
To far green fields, where fall
Perpetual streams that call
To deathless nightingales.

THE "LITERATURE OF NERVES"

Opposed to the rustic tendency, a group emerged headed by the three Sitwells, Edith, Osbert, and Sacheverell. Revolting from the false naïveté of the Georgians—particularly that part of it dominated by J. C. Squire of *The London Mercury* and derisively nicknamed the Squirearchy—the expression at first took the form of satire. Sometimes the burlesque was broad, sometimes the allusions were so erudite and private that only the initiate found them intelligible. The Sitwells advertised themselves liberally, even caricatured their offerings as the "queer" products of a disordered age, bellowed their verses through megaphones, and capitalized their well-organized unpopularity. Their poetry was not always compounded of wildness prepense; it was mad only north-north-west, and soon it became evident that what they had to say was of some significance to their times. Their artificial figures began to breathe; their pastiche was humanized. Nostalgia welled up beneath the elegances, reminiscent of the 'Nineties, and (again reminding us of the *fin de siècle* esthetes) this yearning for a happier world clothed itself in foreign symbolism. Differing from the Parnassian poets, they did not depict their objects—or objectives—by direct statement. Like the Symbolists, they relied on the power of elision and suggestion; they compelled readers to participate in the process of creation and made them fill the gaps between thought and figure, between meaning and mystery.

The movement was primarily intellectual and inflexible. It attempted to develop through the senses, but it distrusted the emotions and was bound to a manner. It was conceived in the latest fashion—the fashion of rebellion without responsibility, cynicism without satire—and fashion changes with unfortunate rapidity.

For several years the "anti-Georgians" sent up rockets of esoteric brilliance. Nor did all of these explosions end in a shower of burnt sticks. Whatever their defects, they were faults of excess; their idiom (particularly Edith Sitwell's and Peter Quennell's) was like no other's. Much of it, high-pitched and exacerbated, belongs to the literature of nerves. But it was provocative and never dull.

THE POST-WAR POETS

A more serious group of poets arose in the early nineteen thirties. These youths had seen space shrink with the airplane while radio annihilated all borders. They had watched governments turn more nationalistic and men grow more unneighborly. Part of a world-wide depression, they entered a decade so financially bankrupt and morally insolvent that it was sometimes known as the Threadbare 'Thirties.

The men of the nineteen thirties were not optimistic, but they had hopes; they dreamed of a new society risen from the ashes of the old. As writers they had more than youth and poetry in common; they shared the fear that they were born in one war and doomed to die in another. Their vocabulary, their taste, their technique, most of all their social and political convictions, offered the greatest possible contrasts to those of the Georgians and the Sitwellians. They owed much to two experimental predecessors: Gerard Manley Hopkins, that richly associative and daring poet, and the American T. S. Eliot, who so strongly influenced English poetry at the beginning of the twentieth century. Eliot prepared the way, celebrating and satirizing the end of a cycle, the cultural decay of a period and a system. But Eliot retreated into Anglo-Catholicism and increasingly obscure allegories. Here the younger Englishmen broke with him; they refused to follow his desperate evasions and defeatism. They borowed from Eliot's style but repudiated his thought.

The most important members of the post-war group were W. H. Auden, Stephen Spender, Cecil Day Lewis, and Louis MacNeice. Their volumes appeared almost simultaneously in the early thirties; they shared the same point of view toward art and nature, politics and poetry. Considering their contribution, Alastair Miller in *The Saturday Review of Literature* wrote: "Nature is no longer considered anthropomorphically, nor love religiously. The poet no longer looks out of his windw in the country and, blinding himself to the railway track, sees a beneficent Providence creating the pleasures and necessities of men: he sees electric pylons conveying imprisoned power, telegraph wires defying distance, motor ploughs forcing fertility into the soil. There is no disrespect, as is sometimes maintained, for primroses and budding trees; but they are not accepted as a solution of, or consolation for, human misery." Stephen Spender makes this particularly explicit in his "Landscape near an Aerodrome" which begins:

> More beautiful and soft than any moth
> With burring furred antennae feeling its huge path
> Through dusk, the air-liner with shut-off engines
> Glides over suburbs and the sleeves set trailing tall
> To point the wind.

In "The Express" Spender pictures "the first powerful plain manifesto, the black statement of pistons," and at the end of one of his sonnets he emphasizes the post-war poet's attitude:

> Real were iron lines, and, smashing the grass
> The cars in which we ride, and real our compelled time:
> Painted on enamel beneath moving glass
> Unreal were cows, the wave-winged storks, the line:
> These burned in a clear world from which we pass
> Like *rose* and *love* in a forgotten rhyme.

C. Day Lewis, in his revealing essay, "A Hope for Poetry," makes plain the salient characteristic of post-war verse technique. "The deliberate insertion into a lyrical context of pieces of slang and 'prosaic' words; the juxtaposition of highly charged 'poetical' images and dull, commonplace images; the use of bathos—all these have been taken over from the Symbolists, largely through the instrumentality of Eliot; and the verse that results offers an uneven, conversational surface shot through with gleams of lyricism, rather thaan a uniformly lyrical texture. . . . The desire for intensity and for freshness of language which leads these poets to syntactical ellipses, produces also that preoccupation with internal rhyme and assonance which may succeed in reestablishing poetry as a delight to the ear."

As Lewis concludes, no amount of technical experiment can of itself produce poetry, but the experimentation was conducted with an energy and optimism that was startling. The poetic art in England received a sudden increase in vitality. It was quickened so exuberantly that those who challenged its philosophy could not dispute its stimulative effect. Quoting some lines of

W. H. Auden, Hugh Walpole wrote, "The Waste Land is, at last, to be cultivated. . . . The real importance comes from the undoubted fact that these poets accept life rather than curse or despise it." Auden, the most forceful if also the least simple, not only inspired Day Lewis and Spender, but seems to have engendered a poetry revival by himself.

THE STREAM OF CONSCIOUSNESS AND SURREALISM

The younger poets were accused of irreverence, lack of standards, and obscurity of aim. They were not without defenders. Writing in *Recent Poetry: 1923-1933,* Alida Monro agreed that the poet who is the product of the twentieth century may not be understood by persons born during the 'Sixties, 'Seventies, and 'Eighties of the last century, but she added: "At no time in the history of man has there been so sudden and violent a change in his environment and circumstances as has taken place in the past twenty-five years. It is far easier, in some ways, to understand the past, even the past of two hundred years ago, than it is to understand our own time, or to try to imagine what life may be like twenty years hence. It is, then, not remarkable that, oppressed by every fresh scientific discovery, with the Great War behind, with the Greater and more horrible War before him, the poet today should be preoccupied with subjects and forms that do not seem to fit into the preconceived notions of what constitutes poetry according to the canons of an age in literature that is now as dead as is the Augustan age."

Caught in a world that was growing increasingly terrifying, a few poets sought to escape reality by avoiding a program of ideas. Life and art had become too demanding for them; they hoped to liberate themselves from everything, even from logic, by letting themselves drift on the erratic stream of consciousness. They substituted intuition for thinking, tension for fluency, and improvisation for form. Much of the poetry produced was so allusive as to seem to move in all directions at once. The first few lines of a cryptogrammatic poem by W. H. Empson illustrate the method:

> The god arkitect whose coping with the Flood
> Groyned the white stallion arches of the main
>   (And miner deeps that in the dome of the brain
>   Take Iris' arches' pupillage and Word)
> Walked on the bucking water like a bird
> And, guard, went round its ramparts and its ball
>   (Columbus' egg sat on earth's garden wall
>   And held the equitation of his bar;
>   Waves beat his bounds until he foamed a star
>   And mapped with fire the skyline that he ploughed),
> Trod and divined the inwheeling serene cloud—
>   (And who knows if Narcissus dumb and bent—)
> Shed and fermented to a firmament. . . .

Surrealism was the result, an extreme manifestation of the tendency to discard logic and coherence, to pass literally "beyond realism." Henry Miller, one of the most experimental of American writers, declared that surrealism was a self-defeating movement, "a confession of intellectual and spiritual bankruptcy, a reflection of the death process, a quickening of the foredoomed end of civilization." The beginning of a poem by Dylan Thomas, using the surrealist method at its best, is revealing in its daring technique and verbal ambiguity:

> Into her lying down head
> His enemies entered bed,
> Under the encumbered eyelid,
> Through the rippled drum of the hair-buried ear;
> And Noah's rekindled now unkind dove
> Flew man-bearing there.
> Last night in a raping wave
> Whales quaked loose from the green grave
> In fountains of origin gave up their love,
> Along her innocence glided
> Juan aflame and savagely young King Lear,
> Queen Catherine howling bare
> And Samson drowned in his hair—
> The colossal intimacies of silent
> Once seen strangers or shades on a stair. . . .

One senses the feeling and direction of the images in these lines; the emotion is apparent, although the phrases present a gathering confusion. Perhaps confusion is the purpose, for the intention itself is left vague, ambiguous instead of exact. The surrealists contended that ambiguity was not only more provocative than precision, but a more honest reflection of the times and therefore more rewarding to the reader. But the attempt to picture a chaotic inner world was doomed; it was dwarfed by the greater chaos of the second World War.

"THE AGE OF ANXIETY"

The stream of consciousness never developed into a main current; it wandered haphazardly and finally went underground. Surrealism became a passing curiosity. Extreme stylistic subtlety was followed by a return to simplicity. After attempting to speak publicly in what seemed a private code, the poets clarified their utterance and their intentions. They proclaimed a fresh affirmation; they announced a renewed interest in, and a desire to reach, the common man. Spender, as spokesman, declared that nothing could withstand "the palpable and obvious love of man." Auden echoed: "We must love one another or die." They praised candor instead of complexity, and celebrated those who were visionaries, pioneers, leaders in nobility. Auden, hoping for salvation from within rather than violent upheaval from without, paid tribute to Freud, who attempted to unite "the unequal moieties fractured by our own well-meaning sense of justice," and William Butler Yeats: "In the deserts of the heart/ Let the healing fountain start,/ In the prison of his days/ Teach the free man how to praise." Spender in "I think continually of those who were truly great" exalted those who "left the vivid air signed with their honor."

By the end of the nineteen thirties, the hopes and affirmations were challenged by a universal denial. The total war which began in September, 1939, unleashed unprecedented horrors and threatened contemporary culture. Dictatorships upset the balance of power; the military state—a state of mind as well as a form of misgovernment—violated nations and betrayed humanity.

The feeling of tension increased as the war grew in length and intensity. The arts seemed haunted by ghosts of undefined but devastating guilt. Poetry echoed the mind's despair aand the heart's desolation. A sense of universal shame became an expression of personal apprehension. W. H. Auden characterized his time in a bitter book-length poem entitled *The Age of Anxiety*.

During the 1930s poetry had become confused with politics. Auden and Spender had been prime movers among those who, revolted by the spread of Fascism and the threat of totalitarian victories, looked hopefully toward the promise of Communism and a new social order. Their attacks on the old order were bitter and often persuasive, but their enthusiasm for the new dispensation waned. After the debacle in Spain and the violent extremes in Russian policy, they were forced back upon personal rather than political problems: the difficulties of the disillusioned individual in a disordered world. The spirit, however, remained indomitable and their writing, amplified in scope as well as depth, proved once more that creation, not chaos, was a constant.

THE NEW CRITICISM AND THE NEW POETS

Concomitant with a new note in poetry there arose an antiseptic tone and technique in criticism. It owed much to the taste and practice of Ezra Pound and T. S. Eliot in both their poetry and criticism. I. A. Richards, followed by William Empson and perhaps paralleled in zigzag by F. R. Leavis—and later abetted by the Americans R. P. Blackmur, Cleanth Brooks, Yvor Winters and others to whom John Crowe Ransom devoted a work entitled *The New Criticism*—were largely responsible for the notion that poetry was written not so much for delight as for the covert expression of multiple meanings. Being such, poetry obviously required dissection and thus this school became so busy searching for devious meanings, remote associations, and levels of irony and ambiguity that, in a zeal for *explication de texte,* it took the life out of narratives, dismembered sonnets, and twisted twelve-line lyrics through twenty paragraphs of tortured prose. Its methods are catalogued in a formidable American handbook of the late forties—Rene Wellek and Austin Warren's *Theory of Literature.*

Beginning in the late 1930s a new group of poet-critics supplemented and supplanted the "new criticism." *Auden and After* (1942) announced the change and carried the challenging subtitle, "The Liberation of Poetry"; *The New British Poetry* (1949) disclosed some seventy poets, most of whom were little known; the new edition of *The Chatto Book of Modern Poetry* (1959) presented still more recent names. Among the poets who aroused readers with fresh creative energy were George Barker, Patrick Kavanagh, W. R. Rodgers, Henry Reed, Alex Comfort, Norman Nicholson, Sidney Keyes, Kathleen Raine, and Philip Larkin. The explosive exuberance of Dylan Thomas was overwhelming and overcame even those who could not understand him, while such older poets as Edwin Muir and Robert Graves were rediscovered and acclaimed by a new audience.

The flight from reality had ended; the battle for freedom of expression had been won. New ideas framed in new images gave metaphors a power beyond logic and a speed they had never attained. Intuition strengthened by experience produced a poetry which was dynamic, immediate, and intensified. Once again the poet fulfilled his function. He sharpened the reader's perception, increased his appreciation, and heightened his awareness not only of life's accepted simplicities but also its endless complexities.

Thomas Hardy

☙ Thomas Hardy was born at Upper Bockhampton, near Dorchester, June 2, 1840, of parents in humble circumstances, his father being a stone-mason. His schooling was fitful. When sixteen, he was apprenticed to an ecclesiastical architect. Later, he left his native village and worked in London, where he won the prize offered by the Royal Institute of British Architects. This was in 1863. A few years after, he abandoned architecture and, in 1871, his first novel, *Desperate Remedies,* was published anonymously. It was a failure, little attention being paid to the author until the publication of *Under the Greenwood Tree.* From that time on his success as a writer was assured.

It was not until he was almost sixty—in 1898, to be precise—that Hardy abandoned prose and challenged attention as a poet, verse having been the form of expression with which he began and, as many (including the editor and Hardy himself) believe, the form by which he will be remembered longest. Technically considered, the rhythms of his verse are, at first reading, irritatingly rude; his syntax is often clumsy; his language involved. But, beneath the surface crudities—and many of them are efforts to achieve particular effects—Hardy's poetry is as disciplined as it is original. If its idiom is sometimes overweighted, it corresponds to the large design and complexities of his thought. "It has," says Dorothy Martin, in an essay on Hardy's lyrics, "an elemental power which, in its wide range of emotion, its sense of inner conflict between mind and heart, affords something like a counterpart in poetry to the art of Rodin in sculpture. To the horror of the orthodox, it has outwardly the same challenging roughnesses and acerbities; it has also the same profundity and stimulating power for those who, refusing to be put off by a difficult exterior, push on to the inner spirit of which this exterior is the vigorous, provocative but fitting expression."

As has been said, by Hardy himself, he "was *compelled* to give up verse for prose," but at no time did he prefer the many works of fiction which won him an international reputation. On the contrary, he was bitter that necessity had forced him to discontinue the creation of poetry for the writing of novels, and in private life would refer to the latter as "pot-boilers" and "wretched stuff." Nevertheless, between the ages of thirty-four and fifty-seven, Hardy published eleven novels and three collections of stories, of which *The Return of the Native* and *The Mayor of Casterbridge* are the sharpest in characterization although *Tess of the D'Urbervilles* (1891) and *Jude the Obscure* (1896) caused more comment. The former started a controversy which grew into an attack, chiefly because of the social criticism which had been implicit in his previous work but which was now openly expressed. With greater violence, almost with vituperation, Hardy was called to account for *Jude the Obscure.* This further example of critical stupidity hurt Hardy so deeply that he said it "cured him of all interest in novel-writing."

Two years later he turned definitely and exclusively to poetry, publishing *Wessex Poems* (1898) with his own drawings, and *Poems of the Past and Present* (1902). Both volumes were respectfully but unenthusiastically received. Then, when Hardy was sixty-four years old and critics had decided that his power had waned, he published the first part of *The Dynasts* (1904), that epic which was to spread itself on the largest canvas of his time. By 1908 the work was complete, a huge drama of the Napoleonic Wars in three books, nineteen acts, and one hundred and thirty scenes. This triumph is the apotheosis of the poet. Of it, the *London Times* wrote: "A work which combines as only a work of genius could combine, a poetic philosophy with minute historical knowledge and a shrewd eye for the tragical and comical ways of men and women." Lascelles Abercrombie, a most conservative appraiser, unhesitatingly called it "the biggest and most consistent exhibition of fatalism in literature." Hardy himself liked, so he informed the editor, two or three of the lyrics in *The Dynasts* (particularly "Trafalgár") as well as anything in his *Collected Poems*.

As Hardy grew older, his poems increased, and his powers with them. Explaining the large number of verses written after his sixtieth year, he said that he would merely "go to a drawer and take something out." But, although it is true that he resuscitated and refurbished many lyrics of an earlier period, Hardy continued to create new ones no less knotted, no less characteristically acrid, delicately nostalgic, pungently bitter-sweet, until he was almost ninety. When he was seventy-nine his *Collected Poems* (1919) displayed the range and fecundity but not the end of his gifts. As an octogenarian, he published *Late Lyrics and Earlier* (1922), *Human Shows: Far Phantasies, Songs and Trifles* (1925), and *Winter Words in Various Moods and Metres,* which, though appearing posthumously, had been arranged and selected by Hardy before his death.

Hardy's death in his eighty-eighth year on January 11, 1928, deprived contemporary England of its most honored author. Although his ashes were placed in Westminster Abbey, his heart (as requested in his Will) was buried in the churchyard of his own village, in the soil he loved so faithfully.

His work resists a pat synthesis. Hardy wrote in almost every manner, good and bad, in every meter, old and new, mixing novelty and banality, dropping heavy cacophonies into the lightest melodies, balancing the profound with the trivial, the cosmic with the comic. Most readers prefer him in that curiously lyric-narrative style which he perfected, but his intensities escape category. Each of his collections runs the gamut of life and its reflection in literature, and his style follows the scale. Modern and ancient, his technique is as advanced as the youngest contemporary's, as formal as a poetic ballet-master's. "In the Servants' Quarters" is a splendid instance of Hardy's talk-flavored verse, which ascends from casual speech on a *crescendo* of dramatic effect, to a half-expected yet startling climax. In quite another manner, his *Satires of Circumstance* (reminding an American reader of Masters' *Spoon River Anthology,* which it anticipated by a generation) are epigrammatic vignettes in which he condensed whole domestic dramas. "The Dark-Eyed Gentleman," on the other hand, is as simple-spontaneous as a folk-tune and quite unlike Hardy's other verse.

Hardy's resources are seemingly endless. At one moment he plays the pathetic fanciful as in "The Tree and the Lady," the next moment he strikes the ironically bizarre in "Ah, Are You Digging on My Grave?" "In Time of 'The Breaking of Nations'" packs an epic into twelve quiet-colored lines; "Snow in the Suburbs" is a purely objective delineation in black and white; "When I Set Out for Lyonnesse" (one of Hardy's favorites among his own poems) is pure song; "The Oxen" turns a superstition to tender humor. And, though each of these is a lyric and all are straightforward in rhythm, each has its own dexterous difference in meter. It has passed unnoted, but Hardy even ventured into the French forms for occasional effects; "The Roman Road" is as neat a rondeau as Austin Dobson ever fashioned; "Winter in Durnover Field" and "Birds at Winter Nightfall" are thoroughly Hardyesque and yet precise if unusual triolets.

Hardy's questioning the beneficence of Nature led to accusations of pessimism, a charge that he continually but ineffectually denied. Actually the poet was an unorthodox moralist whose heart went out to the things, people, and elements he loved. These elements—as he says ironically in "New Year's Eve," affirmatively in "The Subalterns"—are not actuated either by blind hate or blinder chance, but are subject to laws beyond the rules of logic. Hardy denied no God, but sensed design in chaos. Even when he could not rationalize a universe struggling to establish order in imperfection, he praised it, "hoping it might be so."

In the brief note preceding Hardy's contribution in *Great Names* (1926) Siegfried Sassoon wrote, "Without laboring the analogy between poetry and religion, it may be said that sham poetry is as pernicious as sham religion; and that for poets a merely poetical state of mind is as dangerous as a religious belief based on superficial religious emotion. That is why Hardy's poetry of experience is so significant. He records with microscopic exactitude, preserving a flawless artistic integrity. In his short poems he fuses all that he has learned from the past and endured in the present, in a supreme imaginative vision with masterly and original craft in words and subtle ironic sense. He realizes that the true satisfaction of life lies in imaginative conflict. Whatever their ultimate purpose, men are alive only while they struggle. When they grow aware of the futility of their effort, and yet strive to fashion something from it, they become noble and tragic. Such is Hardy; but his despair is mitigated by tenderness and pity for his fellows. . . . With a wistful understanding he surveys the human scene."

No consideration of Hardy could end on a finer coda. Throughout Hardy's work there shines a greater triumph than the technician's: a triumphant personality.

Three excellent studies of Hardy, presenting the novelist and poet from three distinctly different points of view, are those by Lionel Johnson (1894), Lascelles Abercrombie (1912), and Ernest Brennecke (1925).

IN TIME OF "THE BREAKING OF NATIONS"

Only a man harrowing clods
  In a slow silent walk,
With an old horse that stumbles and nods
  Half asleep as they stalk.

Only thin smoke without flame
  From the heaps of couch grass:
Yet this will go onward the same
  Though Dynasties pass.

Yonder a maid and her wight
  Come whispering by;
War's annals will fade into night
  Ere their story die.

THE DARKLING THRUSH

I leaned upon a coppice gate
  When Frost was specter-gray,
And Winter's dregs made desolate
  The weakening eye of day.

The tangled bine-stems scored the sky
  Like strings from broken lyres,
And all mankind that haunted nigh
  Had sought their household fires.

The land's sharp features seemed to be
  The Century's corpse outleant;
His crypt the cloudy canopy,
  The wind his death-lament.
The ancient pulse of germ and birth
  Was shrunken hard and dry,
And every spirit upon earth
  Seemed fervorless as I.

At once a voice burst forth among
  The bleak twigs overhead
In a full-hearted evensong
  Of joy illimited;
An aged thrush, frail, gaunt and small,
  In blast-beruffled plume,
Had chosen thus to fling his soul
  Upon the growing gloom.

So little cause for carolings
  Of such ecstatic sound
Was written on terrestrial things
  Afar or nigh around,
That I could think there trembled through
  His happy good-night air
Some blessed hope, whereof he knew
  And I was unaware.

THE MAN HE KILLED

"Had he and I but met
  By some old ancient inn,
We should have sat us down to wet
  Right many a nipperkin!

"But ranged as infantry,
  And staring face to face,
I shot at him as he at me,
  And killed him in his place.

"I shot him dead because—
  Because he was my foe,
Just so: my foe of course he was;
  That's clear enough; although

"He thought he'd 'list, perhaps,
  Off-hand-like—just as I—
Was out of work—had sold his traps—
  No other reason why.

"Yes; quaint and curious war is!
  You shoot a fellow down
You'd treat, if met where any bar is,
  Or help to half-a-crown."

IN THE SERVANTS' QUARTERS

"Man, you too, aren't you, one of these rough followers of the criminal?
All hanging hereabout to gather how he's going to bear
Examination in the hall." She flung disdainful glances on
The shabby figure standing at the fire with others there,
    Who warmed them by its flare.

"No, indeed, my skipping maiden: I know nothing of the trial here,
Or criminal, if so he be.—I chanced to come this way,
And the fire shone out into the dawn, and morning airs are cold now;
I, too, was drawn in part by charms I see before me play,
    That I see not every day."

"Ha, ha!" then laughed the constables who also stood to warm themselves,
The while another maiden scrutinized his features hard,
As the blaze threw into contrast every knot and line that wrinkled them,
Exclaiming, "Why, last night when he was brought in by the guard,
    You were with him in the yard!"

"Nay, nay, you teasing wench, I say! You know you speak mistakenly.
Cannot a tired pedestrian who has legged it long and far
Here on his way from northern parts, engrossed in humble marketings,
Come in and rest awhile, although judicial doings are
Afoot by morning star?"

"'O come, come!" laughed the constables. "Why, man, you speak the dialect
He uses in his answers; you can hear him up the stairs.
So own it. We sha'n't hurt ye. There, he's speaking now! His syllables
Are those you sound yourself when you are talking unawares,
As this pretty girl declares."

"And you shudder when his chain clinks!" she rejoined. "O yes, I noticed it.
And you winced, too, when those cuffs they gave him echoed to us here.
They'll soon be coming down, and you may then have to defend yourself
Unless you hold your tongue, or go away and keep you clear
When he's led to judgment near!"

"No! I'll be damned in hell if I know anything about the man!
No single thing about him more than everybody knows!
Must not I even warm my hands but I am charged with blasphemies?" . . .
—His face convulses as the morning cock that moment crows,
And he droops, and turns, and goes.

NEUTRAL TONES

We stood by a pond that winter day,
And the sun was white, as though chidden of God,
And a few leaves lay on the starving sod;
They had fallen from an ash, and were gray.

Your eyes on me were as eyes that rove
Over tedious riddles solved years ago;
And some words played between us to and fro
On which lost the more by our love.

The smile on your mouth was the deadest thing
Alive enough to have strength to die;
And a grin of bitterness swept thereby
Like an ominous bird a-wing. . . .

Since then, keen lessons that love deceives,
And wrings with wrong, have shaped to me
Your face, and the God-curst sun, and a tree,
And a pond edged with grayish leaves.

NEW YEAR'S EVE

"I have finished another year," said God,
"In gray, green, white and brown;
I have strewn the leaf upon the sod,
Sealed up the worm within the clod,
And let the last sun down."

"And what's the good of it?" I said,
"What reasons made you call
From formless void this earth we tread,
When nine-and-ninety can be read
Why nought should be at all?

"Yea, Sire; why shaped you us, 'who in
This tabernacle groan'—
If ever a joy be found herein,
Such joy no man had wished to win
If he had never known!"

Then he: "My labors—logicless—
You may explain; not I:
Sense-sealed I have wrought, without a guess
That I evolved a Consciousness
To ask for reasons why.

"Strange that ephemeral creatures who
  By my own ordering are,
Should see the shortness of my view,
Use ethic tests I never knew,
  Or made provision for!"

He sank to raptness as of yore,
  And opening New Year's Day
Wove it by rote as theretofore,
And went on working evermore
  In his unweeting way.

THE NIGHT OF TRAFALGÁR

(from "The Dynasts")

In the wild October night-time, when the wind raved round the land,
And the Back-sea met the Front-sea, and our doors were blocked with sand,
And we heard the drub of Dead-man's Bay, where bones of thousands are,
We knew not what the day had done for us at Trafalgár.
Had done,
Had done,
For us at Trafalgár!

"Pull hard, and make the Nothe, or down we go!" one says, says he.
We pulled; and bedtime brought the storm; but snug at home slept we.
Yet all the while our gallants after fighting through the day,
Were beating up and down the dark, sou'-west of Cadiz Bay.
The dark,
The dark,
Sou'-west of Cadiz Bay!

The victors and the vanquished then the storm it tossed and tore,
As hard they strove, those worn-out men, upon that surly shore;
Dead Nelson and his half-dead crew, his foes from near and far,
Were rolled together on the deep that night at Trafalgár!
The deep,
The deep,
That night at Trafalgár!

WEATHERS

This is the weather the cuckoo likes,
    And so do I;
When showers betumble the chestnut spikes,
    And nestlings fly;
And the little brown nightingale bills his best,
And they sit outside the "Traveler's Rest,"
And maids come forth sprig-muslin drest,
And citizens dream of the South and West,
    And so do I.

This is the weather the shepherd shuns,
    And so do I;
When beeches drip in browns and duns,
    And thresh, and ply;
And hill-hid tides throb, throe on throe,
And meadow rivulets overflow,
And drops on gate-bars hang in a row,
And rooks in families homeward go,
    And so do I.

"AH, ARE YOU DIGGING ON MY GRAVE?"

"Ah, are you digging on my grave
  My beloved one?—planting rue?"
—"No: yesterday he went to wed
One of the brightest wealth has bred,
'It cannot hurt her now,' he said,
  'That I should not be true.'"

"Then who is digging on my grave?
  My nearest, dearest kin?"
—"Ah, no: they sit and think, 'What use!
What good will planting flowers produce?
No tendance of her mound can loose
  Her spirit from Death's gin.' "

"But someone digs upon my grave?
  My enemy?—prodding sly?"
—"Nay: when she heard you had passed the
    Gate
That shuts on all flesh soon or late,
She thought you no more worth her hate,
  And cares not where you lie."

"Then, who is digging on my grave?
  Say—since I have not guessed!"
—"O it is I, my mistress dear,
Your little dog, who still lives near,
And much I hope my movements here
  Have not disturbed your rest?"

"Ah, yes! *You* dig upon my grave. . . .
  Why flashed it not on me
That one true heart was left behind!
What feeling do we ever find
To equal among human kind
  A dog's fidelity!"

"Mistress, I dug upon your grave
  To bury a bone, in case
I should be hungry near this spot
When passing on my daily trot.
I am sorry, but I quite forgot
  It was your resting-place."

FIVE "SATIRES OF CIRCUMSTANCE"

In Church

"And now to God the Father," he ends,
And his voice thrills up to the topmost tiles:
Each listener chokes as he bows and bends,
And emotion pervades the crowded aisles.
Then the preacher glides to the vestry-door,
And shuts it, and thinks he is seen no more.

The door swings softly ajar meanwhile,
And a pupil of his in the Bible class,
Who adores him as one without gloss or guile,
Sees her idol stand with a satisfied smile
And reënact at the vestry-glass
Each pulpit gesture in deft dumb-show
That had moved the congregation so.

By Her Aunt's Grave

"Sixpence a week," says the girl to her lover,
"Aunt used to bring me, for she could confide
In me alone, she vowed. It was to cover
The cost of her headstone when she died.
And that was a year ago last June;
I've not yet fixed it. But I must soon."

"And where is the money now, my dear?"
"O, snug in my purse. . . . Aunt was *so* slow
In saving it—eighty weeks, or near.". . .
"Let's spend it," he hints. "For she won't know.
Theres a dance tonight at the *Load of Hay*."
She passively nods. And they go that way.

At the Altar-Rail

"My bride is not coming, alas!" says the groom,
And the telegram shakes in his hand. "I own
It was hurried! We met at a dancing-room
When I went to the Cattle-Show alone,
And then, next night, where the Fountain leaps,
And the Street of the Quarter-Circle sweeps.

"Aye, she won me to ask her to be my wife—
'Twas foolish perhaps!—to forsake the ways
Of the flaring town for a farmer's life.
She agreed. And we fixed it. Now she says:
'It's sweet of you, dear, to prepare me a nest,
But a swift, short, gay life suits me best.
What I really am you have never gleaned;
I had eaten the apple ere you were weaned.' "

In the Restaurant

"But hear. If you stay, and the child be born,
It will pass as your husband's with the rest,
While, if we fly, the teeth of scorn
Will be gleaming at us from east to west;
And the child will come as a life despised.
I feel an elopement is ill-advised!"

"O you realize not what it is, my dear,
To a woman! Daily and hourly alarms
Lest the truth should out. How can I stay here
And nightly take him into my arms!
Come to the child no name or fame,
Let us go, and face it, and bear the shame."

At the Draper's

"I stood at the back of the shop, my dear,
  But you did not perceive me.
Well, when they deliver what you were shown
  I shall know nothing of it, believe me!"

And he coughed and coughed as she paled and said,
  "O, I didn't see you come in there—
Why couldn't you speak?"—"Well, I didn't. I left
  That you should not notice I'd been there.

"You were viewing some lovely things. *'Soon required*
  For a widow, of latest fashion';
And I knew 'twould upset you to meet the man
  Who had to be cold and ashen

"And screwed in a box before they could dress you
  'In the last new note in mourning,'
As they defined it. So, not to distress you,
  I left you to your adorning."

AFTERWARDS

When the Present has latched its postern behind my tremulous stay,
  And the May month flaps its glad green leaves like wings,
Delicate-filmed as new-spun silk, will the neighbors say,
  "He was a man who used to notice such things"?

If it be in the dusk when, like an eyelid's soundless blink,
  The dewfall-hawk comes crossing the shades to alight
Upon the wind-warped upland thorn, a gazer may think,
  "To him this must have been a familiar sight."

If I pass during some nocturnal blackness, mothy and warm,
  When the hedgehog travels furtively over the lawn,
One may say, "He strove that such innocent creatures should come to no harm,
  But he could do little for them; and now he is gone."

If, when hearing that I have been stilled at last, they stand at the door,
  Watching the full-starred heavens that winter sees,
Will this thought rise on those who will meet my face no more,
  "He was one who had an eye for such mysteries"?

And will any say when my bell of quittance is heard in the gloom,
  And a crossing breeze cuts a pause in its outrollings,
Till they rise again, as they were a new bell's boom,
  "He hears it not now, but used to notice such things"?

BIRDS AT WINTER NIGHTFALL

Around the house the flakes fly faster,
And all the berries now are gone
From holly and cotoneaster
Around the house. The flakes fly!—faster
Shutting indoors that crumb-outcaster
We used to see upon the lawn
Around the house. The flakes fly faster,
And all the berries now are gone!

WINTER IN DURNOVER FIELD

SCENE.—*A wide stretch of fallow ground recently sown with wheat, and frozen to iron hardness. Three large birds walking about thereon, and wistfully eyeing the surface. Wind keen from north-east: sky a dull gray.*

Rook: Throughout the field I find no grain;
  The cruel frost encrusts the cornland!
Starling: Aye: patient pecking now is vain
  Throughout the field, I find . . .
Rook: No grain!
Pigeon: Nor will be, comrade, till it rain,
  Or genial thawings loose the lorn land
  Throughout the field.
Rook: I find no grain:
  The cruel frost encrusts the cornland!

THE ROMAN ROAD

The Roman Road runs straight and bare
As the pale parting-line in hair
Across the heath. And thoughtful men
Contrast its days of Now and Then,
And delve, and measure, and compare;

Visioning on the vacant air
Helmed legionnaires, who proudly rear
The Eagle, as they pace again
The Roman Road.

But no tall brass-helmed legionnaire
Haunts it for me. Uprises there
A mother's form upon my ken,
Guiding my infant steps, as when
We walked that ancient thoroughfare,
The Roman Road.

MY SPIRIT WILL NOT HAUNT THE MOUND

My spirit will not haunt the mound
Above my breast,
But travel, memory-possessed,
To where my tremulous being found
Life largest, best.

My phantom-footed shape will go
When nightfall grays
Hither and thither along the ways
I and another used to know
In backward days.

And there you'll find me, if a jot
You still should care
For me, and for my curious air;
If otherwise, then I shall not,
For you, be there.

WHEN I SET OUT FOR LYONNESSE

When I set out for Lyonnesse,
A hundred miles away,
The rime was on the spray,
And starlight lit my lonesomeness
When I set out for Lyonnesse
A hundred miles away.

What could bechance at Lyonnesse
While I should sojourn there
No prophet durst declare,
Nor did the wisest wizard guess
What would bechance at Lyonnesse
While I should sojourn there.

When I came back from Lyonnesse
With magic in my eyes,
All marked with mute surmise
My radiance rare and fathomless,
When I came back from Lyonnesse
With magic in my eyes.

THE DARK-EYED GENTLEMAN

I pitched my day's leazings[1] in Crimmercrock Lane,
To tie up my garter and jog on again,
When a dear dark-eyed gentleman passed there and said,
In a way that made all o' me color rose-red,
"What do I see—
O pretty knee!"
And he came and he tied up my garter for me.

'Twixt sunset and moonrise it was, I can mind:
Ah, 'tis easy to lose what we nevermore find!—
Of the dear stranger's home, of his name, I knew nought,
But I soon knew his nature and all that it brought.
Then bitterly
Sobbed I that he
Should ever have tied up my garter for me!

[1] "Leazings"; bundles of gleaned corn.

Yet now I've beside me a fine lissom lad,
And my slip's nigh forgot, and my days are not sad;
My own dearest joy is he, comrade, and friend,
He it is who safe-guards me, on him I depend;
No sorrow brings he,
And thankful I be
That his daddy once tied up my garter for me!

THE SUBALTERNS

"Poor wanderer," said the leaden sky,
"I fain would lighten thee,
But there be laws in force on high
Which say it must not be."

"I would not freeze thee, shorn one," cried
The North, "knew I but how
To warm my breath, to slack my stride;
But I am ruled as thou."

"Tomorrow I attack thee, wight,"
Said Sickness. "Yet I swear
I bear thy little ark no spite,
But am bid enter there."

"Come hither, Son," I heard Death say;
"I did not will a grave
Should end thy pilgrimage today,
But I, too, am a slave!"

We smiled upon each other then,
And life to me wore less
Of that fell guise it wore ere when
They owned their passiveness.

THE OXEN

Christmas Eve, and twelve of the clock,
"Now they are all on their knees,"
An elder said as we sat in a flock
By the embers in hearthside ease.

We pictured the meek mild creatures where
They dwelt in their strawy pen,
Nor did it occur to one of us there
To doubt they were kneeling then.

So fair a fancy few would weave
In these years! Yet, I feel,
If someone said on Christmas Eve,
"Come; see the oxen kneel

"In the lonely barton[1] by yonder coomb[2]
Our childhood used to know,"
I should go with him in the gloom,
Hoping it might be so.

THE TREE AND THE LADY

I have done all I could
For that lady I knew! Through the heats I have shaded her,
Drawn to her songsters when summer has jaded her,
Home from the heath or the wood.

At the mirth-time of May,
When my shadow first lured her, I'd donned my new bravery
Of greenth: 'twas my all. Now I shiver in slavery,
Icicles grieving me gray.

Plumed to every twigs end
I could tempt her chair under me. Much did I treasure her
During those days she had nothing to pleasure her;
Mutely she used me as friend.

[1] Barton: farmyard.
[2] Coomb: valley, hollow.

I'm a skeleton now,
And she's gone, craving warmth. The rime sticks like skin to me;
Through me Arcturus peers; Nor'lights shoot into me;
Gone is she, scorning my bough!

SNOW IN THE SUBURBS

Every branch big with it,
Bent every twig with it;
Every fork like a white web-foot;
Every street and pavement mute:
Some flakes have lost their way, and grope back upward, when
Meeting those meandering down they turn and descend again.
The palings are glued together like a wall,
And there is no waft of wind with the fleecy fall.

A sparrow enters the tree
Whereon immediately
A snow-lump thrice his own slight size
Descends on him and showers his head and eyes.
And overturns him,
And near inurns him,
And lights on a nether twig, when its brush
Starts off a volley of other lodging lumps with a rush.

The steps are a blanched slope,
Up which, with feeble hope,
A black cat comes, wide-eyed and thin;
And we take him in.

THE SELF-UNSEEING

Here is the ancient floor,
Footworn and hollowed and thin,
Here was the former door
Where the dead feet walked in.

She sat here in her chair,
Smiling into the fire;
He who played stood there,
Bowing it higher and higher.

Childlike, I danced in a dream;
Blessings emblazoned that day;
Everything glowed with a gleam,
Yet we were looking away!

A PLACID MAN'S EPITAPH

As for my life, I've led it
With fair content and credit:

It said: "Take this." I took it:
Said: "Leave." And I forsook it.
If I had done without it
None would have cared about it,
Or said: "One has refused it
Who might have meetly used it."

WAITING BOTH

A star looks down at me,
And says: "Here I and you
Stand, each in our degree:
What do you mean to do—
    Mean to do?"

I say: "For all I know,
Wait, and let Time go by,
Till my change come."—"Just so,"
The star says: "So mean I—
    So mean I."

HAP

If but some vengeful god would call to me
From up the sky, and laugh: "Thou suffering thing,
Know that thy sorrow is my ecstasy,
That thy love's loss is my hate's profiting!"

Then would I bear it, clench myself, and die,
Steeled by the sense of ire unmerited;
Half-eased in that a Powerfuller than I
Had willed and meted me the tears I shed.

But not so. How arrives it joy lies slain,
And why unblooms the best hope ever sown?
—Crass Casualty obstructs the sun and rain,
And dicing Time for gladness casts a moan. . . .
These purblind Doomsters had as readily strown
Blisses about my pilgrimage as pain.

THE CONVERGENCE OF THE TWAIN

(*Lines on the loss of the "Titanic"*)

I

In a solitude of the sea
Deep from human vanity,
And the Pride of Life that planned her, stilly couches she.

II

Steel chambers, late the pyres
Of her salamandrine fires,
Cold currents thrid, and turn to rhythmic tidal lyres.

III

Over the mirrors meant
To glass the opulent
The sea-worm crawls—grotesque, slimed, dumb, indifferent.

IV

Jewels in joy designed
To ravish the sensuous mind
Lie lightless, all their sparkles bleared and black and blind.

V

Dim moon-eyed fishes near
Gaze at the gilded gear
And query: "What does this vaingloriousness down here?"

VI

Well: while was fashioning
This creature of cleaving wing,
The Immanent Will that stirs and urges everything

VII

Prepared a sinister mate
For her—so gaily great
A Shape of Ice, for the time far and dissociate.

VIII

And as the smart ship grew
In stature, grace, and hue,
In shadowy silent distance grew the Iceberg too.

IX

Alien they seemed to be;
No mortal eye could see
The intimate welding of their later history,

X

Or sign that they were bent
By paths coincident
On being anon twin halves of one august event,

XI

Till the Spinner of the Years
Said "Now!" And each one hears,
And consummation comes, and jars two hemispheres

Gerard Manley Hopkins

⋞§ Gerard Manley Hopkins was born in Essex, July, 28, 1844, became a Jesuit, and taught Greek and Greek meters at University College in Dublin. He was, in addition, a painter and a musician of no little ability, and his various gifts equipped him to be an innovator in poetic structure. Although he wrote much during an intensely spiritual life, none of his poetry appeared during his lifetime, and it was not until thirty years after his death that his extraordinary verse was collected. Hopkins died in 1889 and the world was not given the *Poems of Gerard Hopkins, Now First Published, with Notes by Robert Bridges* until 1918. Many of the verses in this posthumous volume were deciphered from manuscript by the Poet-Laureate and it is to him that one must be grateful for rescuing the work of a most original mind from oblivion.

A casual reader of Hopkins should expect obstacles; he must be prepared for difficulties that, at first, seem insuperable. He must be willing to accept a series of musical dissonances, compared to which the most cacophonous passages in Browning are limpid and bird-like. He must penetrate obscurities which are cloudy to the point of confusion. But he will be rewarded. Behind the tortured constructions and heaped-up epithets there is magnificence. In spite of the verbal excesses and idiomatic oddities there is an originality of vision which is nothing less than startling. In its intimate fancifulness, the imagery sometimes reminds one of the more controlled extravagances of Emily Dickinson. Like the New England poetess, Hopkins' poetry is sometimes eccentric, but it is always logical, never arbitrary or perverse, and sometimes breathless with ecstasy.

Hopkins himself worked out a curious scheme of prosody (he even invented a system of signs to make plain the effects he wished to achieve) and his lines (as his own preface tells us) are "written in Running Rhythm, the common rhythm in English use, some in Sprung Rhythm (a free beat strongly suggestive of later *vers libre*) and some in a mixture of both." The peculiar beauty in his poems makes it lamentable that Hopkins (to quote his editor) "died when, to judge by his latest work, he was beginning to concentrate the force of all his luxuriant experiments in rhythm and diction, and castigate his art into a more reserved style." Even in the cloudiest of his effects there is a splendor, a rush of rhyme, a cataract of color, attained by scarcely any of his plainer-speaking contemporaries.

The most outspoken admirer of this highly imaginative and highly elliptical poetry must admit its structural awkwardness. Hopkins himself wrote, "No doubt my poetry errs on the side of oddness. I hope in time to have a more balanced and Miltonic style. But as air, melody, is what strikes me most of all in music, and design in painting, so design, pattern, or what I am in the habit of calling *inscape* is what above all I aim at in poetry. Now it is the virtue of design, pattern, or 'inscape' to be distinctive, and it is the vice of distinctiveness to become queer. This vice I cannot have escaped." Yet Dr. Robert Bridges has made too much of Hopkins' mannerisms. If these poems, Bridges comments, "were to be arraigned for errors of what might be called taste, they might be convicted of occasional affectation in metaphor, as where the hills are 'as a stallion stalwart, very-violet-sweet' " . . .

As Robert Graves and Laura Riding inquire in *A Survey of Modernist Poetry,* "Why cannot what Dr. Bridges calls a fault of taste, an affectation, in the description of hills as 'a stallion stalwart, very-violet-sweet' be, with the proper sympathy for Hopkins' enthusiasm, appreciated as a phrase reconciling the two seemingly opposed qualities of mountains, their male, animal-like roughness and strength and, at the same time, their ethereal quality under soft light for which the violet in the gentle eye of the horse makes exactly the proper association?" That Bridges never understood Hopkins is proved by Bridges' other comments in the introduction, and emphasized by Hopkins' letters—Bridges having (significantly, it seems) destroyed his side of the correspondence.

Continually daring, Hopkins' work has never the note of ostentatious bravado. His boldness is instinctive; even such extraordinary departures as "Hurrahing in Harvest" and "Felix Randal" are extensions of the sonnet form but not violations of its spirit.

One of the more enthusiastic disciples (C. Day Lewis) has compared Hopkins to Shakespeare, not only because of Hopkins' continual "re-creation of word and image," but because of the exuberant quality of his images.

> I caught this morning morning's minion, king-
> dom of daylight's Dauphin, dapple-dawn-drawn Falcon, in his riding
> Of the rolling level underneath him steady air.

In such lines Hopkins explores the limbo which divides the ridiculous from the sublime. Here is a riotous alliteration which even the prodigal Swinburne might have hesitated to use, and yet Hopkins lifts the device into grandeur. Here, and almost everywhere in his poetry, is the concealed music, the subtle modulation, which breaks down the current poetic speech and forms it into a new language. "The poetic language of an age," Hopkins wrote, improving on Wordsworth, "should be the current language heightened, to any degree heightened and unlike itself, but not an obsolete one." Such heightening sometimes causes the reader to confess his inability to follow the poet's vision, but, as Day Lewis remarked in *A Hope for Poetry,* "what obscurity we may find is due, not to a clouded imagination or an unsettled intellect, but to his lightning dashes from image to image, so quick that we are unable at first to perceive the points of contact."

Hopkins' epithets may seem erratic but they are actually if oddly precise. As with his punctuation, he could give a rule for everything, even for the frequent and deliberate omission of the relative pronoun which he dropped not only "to crowd out every merely grammatical or toneless element" but to stress the heavy accents of his verse. "The Habit of Perfection," "The Starlight Night," "The Golden Echo," its companion piece, "The Leaden Echo," and "God's Grandeur" will not be shaken out of the mind. If "emphasis seems to oust euphony" in a struggle of intense contractions, his style, pushed by the extremities of his theories, is a triumph of elisions. Far from being a "fascinating failure" (T. Earle Welby's summary), his poetry lifts exact if unfamiliar verity of phrase to a burning beauty.

Hopkins having found an audience thirty-five years after his death, his least fragments were collated and an enlarged edition of his *Poems* was issued in 1930. A year later there appeared *The Letters of Gerard Manley Hopkins to Robert Bridges* (1935) and *The Correspondence of Gerard Manley Hopkins and Richard Watson Dixon* (1935), two volumes rich in delicate humor, insight, and discrimination, possibly the finest criticism written in English. Memorable are his disposals of Dickens, Wordsworth, Tennyson—he called the Idylls "Charades of the Middle Ages"—and Swinburne of the "delirium-tremendous imagination." And who, after once reading his estimate of Browning, can forget that Browning has "a way of talking and making his people talk with the air and spirit of a man bouncing up from table with his mouth full of bread and cheese and saying that he meant to stand no blasted nonsense." A third augmented edition of *Poems* appeared in 1948.

Gerard Manley Hopkins: A Biography (1930) by G. F. Lahey, and *Three Friends,* by Robert Bridges, memoirs of Digby Mackworth Dolben, Richard Watson Dixon and Henry Bradley, shed further light on this rich personality.

One of the most erudite critics and certainly the most inventive poet of his day—such was the man who refused to fight for fame because, as a Jesuit, he had vowed to serve God. Like the things he loved most, he, too, was "counter, original, spare, strange," possibly the most original genius of his generation. Everywhere in his work there is a new extravagance of metaphor. The opulence is not carefully built up; it is reckless, almost agonized, as though the poet could not lay his hands on figures rich and rapid enough to express the speed of his intuitions. To Hopkins everything was happy and magnificent. The world was not merely colorful but prodigal, "barbarous in beauty." Nature was a divine turmoil, and God was an eternal exuberance.

THOU ART INDEED JUST, LORD

Thou art indeed just, Lord, if I contend
With thee; but, sir, so what I plead is just.
Why do sinners' ways prosper? and why must
Disappointment all I endeavour end?
Wert thou my enemy, O thou my friend,
How wouldst thou worse, I wonder, than thou dost
Defeat, thwart me? Oh, the sots and thralls of lust
Do in spare hours more thrive than I that spend,
Sir, life upon thy cause. See, banks and brakes
Now, leavèd how thick! lacèd they are again
With fretty chervil, look, and fresh wind shakes
Them; birds build—but not I build; no, but strain,
Time's eunuch, and not breed one work that wakes.
Mine, O thou lord of life, send my roots rain.

PIED BEAUTY

Glory be to God for dappled things—
  For skies of couple-color as a brinded cow;
    For rose-moles all in stipple upon trout that swim;
Fresh-firecoal chestnut-falls; finches' wings;
  Landscapes plotted and pieced—fold, fallow, and plow;
    And all trades, their gear and tackle and trim.
All things counter, original, spare, strange;
  Whatever is fickle, freckled (who knows how?)
    With swift, slow; sweet, sour; adazzle, dim;
He fathers-forth whose beauty is past change:
      Praise Him.

THE HABIT OF PERFECTION

Elected Silence, sing to me
And beat upon my whorlèd ear,
Pipe me to pastures still, and be
The music that I care to hear.

Shape nothing, lips; be lovely-dumb;
It is the shut, the curfew sent
From there where all surrenders come
Which only makes you eloquent.

Be shellèd, eyes, with double dark
And find the uncreated light:
This ruck and reel which you remark
Coils, keeps, and teases simple sight.

Palate, the hutch of tasty lust,
Desire not to be rinsed with wine:
The can must be so sweet, the crust
So fresh that come in fasts divine!

Nostrils, your careless breath that spend
Upon the stir and keep of pride,
What relish shall the censers send
Along the sanctuary side!

O feel-of-primrose hands, O feet
That want the yield of plushy sward,
But you shall walk the golden street
And you unhouse and house the Lord.

And, Poverty, be thou the bride
And now the marriage feast begun,
And lily-colored clothes provide
Your spouse, not labored-at nor spun.

THE LEADEN ECHO

How to keep—is there any, any, is there none such, nowhere known, some bow or
 brooch or braid or brace, lace, latch or catch or key to keep
Back beauty, keep it, beauty, beauty, beauty, . . . from vanishing away?
Oh, is there no frowning of these wrinkles, ranked wrinkles deep,
Down? no waving-off of these most mournful messengers, still messengers, sad and
 stealing messengers of gray?
No, there's none, there's none—oh, no, there's none!
Nor can you long be, what you now are, called fair—
Do what you may do, do what you may,
And wisdom is early to despair:

Be beginning; since, no, nothing can be done
To keep at bay
Age and age's evils—hoar hair,
Ruck and wrinkle, drooping, dying, death's worst, winding sheets, tombs and worms, and tumbling to decay;
So be beginning, be beginning to despair.
Oh, there's none—no, no, no, there's none:
Be beginning to despair, to despair,
Despair, despair, despair, despair.

THE GOLDEN ECHO

Spare!
There is one, yes, I have one (Hush there!);
Only not within seeing of the sun,
Not within the singeing of the strong sun,
Tall sun's tingeing, or treacherous the tainting of the earth's air,
Somewhere elsewhere there is ah, well, where! one,
One. Yes, I can tell such a key, I do know such a place,
Where whatever's prized and passed of us, everything that's fresh and fast-flying of us, seems to us sweet of us and swiftly away with, done away with, undone,
Undone, done with, soon done with, and yet dearly and dangerously sweet
Of us, the wimpled-water-dimpled, not-by-morning-matchèd face,
The flower of beauty, fleece of beauty, too too apt to, ah! to fleet,
Never fleets more, fastened with the tenderest truth
To its own best being and its loveliness of youth: it is an everlastingness of, O it is an all youth!
Come then, your ways and airs and looks, locks, maiden gear, gallantry and gayety and grace,
Winning ways, airs innocent, maiden manners, sweet looks, loose locks, long locks, lovelocks, gaygear, going gallant, girlgrace—
Resign them, sign them, seal them, send them, motion them with breath,
And with sighs soaring, soaring sighs deliver
Them; beauty-in-the-ghost, deliver it, early now, long before death
Give beauty back, beauty, beauty, beauty, back to God, beauty's self and beauty's giver.
See; not a hair is, not an eyelash, not the least lash lost; every hair
Is, hair of the head, numbered.
Nay, what we had lighthanded left in surely the mere mold
Will have waked and have waxed and have walked with the wind whatwhile we slept,
This side, that side hurling a heavyheaded hundredfold
What while we, while we slumbered.
O then, weary then why should we tread? O why are we so haggard at the heart, so care-coiled, care-killed, so fagged, so fashed, so cogged, so cumbered,
When the thing we freely forfeit is kept with fonder a care,
Fonder a care kept than we could have kept it, kept
Far with fonder a care (and we, we should have lost it) finer, fonder
A care kept.—Where kept? Do but tell us where kept, where.—
Yonder.—What high as that! We follow, now we follow.—Yonder, yes, yonder, yonder,
Yonder.

GOD'S GRANDEUR

The world is charged with the grandeur of God.
  It will flame out, like shining from shook foil;
  It gathers to a greatness, like the ooze of oil
Crushed. Why do men then now not reck his rod?
Generations have trod, have trod, have trod;
  And all is seared with trade; bleared, smeared with toil;
  And wears man's smudge and shares man's smell: the soil
Is bare now, nor can foot feel, being shod.

And for all this, nature is never spent;
  There lives the dearest freshness deep down things;
And though the last lights off the black West went
  Oh, morning, at the brown brink eastward, springs—
Because the Holy Ghost over the bent
  World broods with warm breast and with ah! bright wings.

THE STARLIGHT NIGHT

Look at the stars! look, look up at the skies!
  O look at all the fire-folk sitting in the air!
  The bright boroughs, the circle-citadels there!
Down in dim woods the diamond delves! the elves'-eyes!
The gray lawns cold where gold, where quickgold lies!
  Wind-beat whitebeam! airy abeles set on a flare!
  Flake-doves sent floating forth at a farmyard scare!
Ah, well! it is all a purchase, all is a prize.
Buy then! bid then!—What?—Prayer, patience, alms, vows.
Look, look: a May-mess, like on orchard boughs!
  Look! March-bloom, like on mealed-with-yellow sallows!
These are indeed the barn; withindoors house
The shocks. This piece-bright paling shuts the spouse
  Christ home, Christ and his mother and all his hallows.

SPRING

Nothing is so beautiful as spring—
  When weeds, in wheels, shoot long and lovely and lush;
  Thrush's eggs look little low heavens, and thrush
Through the echoing timber does so rinse and wring
The ear, it strikes like lightning to hear him sing;
  The glassy peartree leaves and blooms, they brush
  The descending blue; that blue is all in a rush
With richness; the racing lambs too have fair their fling.

What is all this juice and all this joy?
  A strain of the earth's sweet being in the beginning
In Eden garden.—Have, get, before it cloy,
  Before it cloud, Christ, lord, and sour with sinning,
Innocent mind and Mayday in girl and boy,
  Most, O maid's child, thy choice and worthy the winning.

HURRAHING IN HARVEST

Summer ends now; now, barbarous in beauty, the stooks arise
  Around; up above, what wind-walks! what lovely behavior
  Of silk-sack clouds! has wilder, willful-wavier
Meal-drift molded ever and melted across skies?

I walk, I lift up, I lift up heart, eyes,
  Down all that glory in the heavens to glean our Saviour;
  And, eyes, heart, what looks, what lips yet gave you a
Rapturous love's greeting of realer, of rounder replies?

And the azurous hung hills are his world-wielding shoulder
  Majestic—as a stallion stalwart, very-violet-sweet!—
These things, these things were here and but the beholder
  Wanting; which two when they once meet,
The heart rears wings bold and bolder
  And hurls for him, O half hurls earth for him off under his feet.

THE CAGED SKYLARK

As a dare-gale skylark scanted in a dull cage
  Man's mounting spirit in his bone-house, mean house, dwells—
  That bird beyond the remembering his free fells;
This in drudgery, day-laboring-out life's age.

Though aloft on turf or perch or poor low stage,
  Both sing sometimes the sweetest, sweetest spells,
  Yet both droop deadly sometimes in their cells
Or wring their barriers in bursts of fear or rage.

Not that the sweet-fowl, song-fowl, needs no rest—
Why, hear him, hear him babble and drop down to his nest,
  But his own nest, wild nest, no prison.

Man's spirit will be flesh-bound when found at best,
But uncumbered: meadow-down is not distressed
  For a rainbow footing it nor he for his bones risen.

MOONRISE

I awoke in the Midsummer not to call night, in the white and the walk of the
    morning:
The moon, dwindled and thinned to the fringe of a finger-nail held to the candle,
Or paring of paradisaïcal fruit, lovely in waning but lusterless,
Stepped from the stool, drew back from the barrow, of dark Maenefa the mountain;
A cusp still clasped him, a fluke yet fanged him, entangled him, not quit utterly.
This was the prized, the desirable sight, unsought, presented so easily,
Parted me leaf and leaf, divided me, eyelid and eyelid of slumber.

FELIX RANDAL

Felix Randal the farrier, O he is dead then? my duty all ended,
Who have watched his mold of man, big-boned and hardy-handsome
Pining, pining, till time when reason rambled in it and some
Fatal four disorders, fleshed there, all contended?

Sickness broke him. Impatient he cursed at first, but mended
Being anointed and all; though a heavenlier heart began some
Months earlier, since I had our sweet reprieve and ransom
Tendered to him. Ah, well, God rest him all road ever he offended!

This seeing the sick endears them to us, us too it endears.
My tongue had taught the comfort, touch had quenched thy tears,
Thy tears that touched my heart, child, Felix, poor Felix Randal;

How far from then forethought of, all thy more boisterous years,
When thou at the random grim forge, powerful amidst peers,
Didst fettle for the great gray drayhorse his bright and battering sandal!

TO HIS WATCH

(unfinished)

Mortal my mate, bearing my rock-a-heart
Warm beat with cold beat company, shall I
Earlier or you fail at our force, and lie
The ruins of, rifled, once a world of art?
The telling time our task is; time's some part,
Not all, but we were framed to fail and die—
One spell and well that one. There, ah, thereby
Is comfort's carol of all or woe's worst smart.

Field-flown the departed day no morning brings
Saying "This was yours" with her, but new one, worse,
And then that last and shortest . . .

THE CUCKOO

Repeat that, repeat,
Cuckoo, bird, and open ear wells, heart-springs, delightfully sweet,
With a ballad, with a ballad, a rebound
Off trundled timber and scoops of the hillside ground, hollow hollow hollow ground:
The whole landscape flushes on a sudden at a sound.

HEAVEN-HAVEN

A Nun Takes the Veil

I have desired to go
Where springs not fail,
To fields where flies no sharp and sided hail,
And a few lilies blow.

And I have asked to be
Where no storms come,
Where the green swell is in the havens dum
And out of the swing of the sea.

THE WINDHOVER

To Christ Our Lord

I caught this morning morning's minion, king-
  dom of daylight's dauphin, dapple-dawn-drawn Falcon, in his riding
  Of the rolling level underneath him steady air, and striding
High there, how he rung upon the rein of a wimpling wing
In his ecstasy! then off, off forth on swing,
  As a skate's heel sweeps smooth on a bow-bend: the hurl and gliding
  Rebuffed the big wind. My heart in hiding
Stirred for a bird,—the achieve of, the mastery of the thing!

Brute beauty and valor and act, oh, air, pride, plume, here
  Buckle! AND the fire that breaks from thee then, a billion
Times told lovelier, more dangerous, O my chevalier!

  No wonder of it: sheer plod makes plough down sillion
Shine, and blue-bleak embers, ah my dear,
  Fall, gall themselves, and gash gold-vermillion.

INVERSNAID

This darksome burn, horseback brown,
His rollrock highroad roaring down,
In coop and in comb the fleece of his foam
Flutes and low to the lake falls home.

A windpuff-bonnet of fawn-froth
Turns and twindles over the broth
Of a pool so pitchblack, fell-frowning,
It rounds and rounds Despair to drowning.

Degged with dew, dappled with dew
Are the groins of the braes that the brook treads through,
Wiry heathpacks, flitches of fern,
And the beadbonny ash that sits over the burn.

What would the world be, once bereft
Of wet and of wildness? Let them be left,
O let them be left, wildness and wet;
Long live the weeds and the wilderness yet.

WHAT I DO IS ME

As kingfishers catch fire, dragonflies draw flame;
As tumbled over rim in roundy wells
Stones ring; like each tucked string tells, each hung bell's
Bow swung finds tongue to fling out broad its name;
Each mortal thing does one thing and the same:
Deals out that being indoors each one dwells;

Selves—goes itself; *myself* it speaks and spells,
Crying *What I do is me: for that I came.*

I say more: the just man justices;
Keeps grace: that keeps all his goings graces;
Acts in God's eye what in God's eye he is—
Christ—for Christ plays in ten thousand places,
Lovely in limbs, and lovely in eyes not his
To the Father through the features of men's faces.

NO WORST, THERE IS NONE

No worst, there is none. Pitched past pitch of grief,
More pangs will, schooled at forepangs, wilder wring.
Comforter, where, where is your comforting?
Mary, mother of us, where is your relief?
My cries heave, herds-long; huddle in a main, a chief
Woe, world-sorrow; on an age-old anvil wince and sing—
Then lull, then leave off. Fury had shrieked "No ling-
ering! Let me be fell: force I must be brief."

O the mind, mind has mountains; cliffs of fall
Frightful, sheer, no-man-fathomed. Hold them cheap
May who ne'er hung there. Nor does long our small
Durance deal with that steep or deep. Here! creep,
Wretch, under a comfort serves in a whirlwind: all
Life death does end and each day dies with sleep.

MY OWN HEART

My own heart let me more have pity on; let
Me live to my sad self hereafter kind,
Charitable; not live this tormented mind
With this tormented mind tormenting yet.
I cast for comfort I can no more get
By groping round my comfortless, than blind
Eyes in their dark can day or thirst can find
Thirst's all-in-all in all a world of wet.

Soul, self; come, poor Jackself, I do advise
You, jaded, let be; call off thoughts awhile
Elsewhere; leave comfort root-room; let joy size
At God knows when to God knows what; whose smile
's not wrung, see you; unforseen times rather—as skies
Betweenpie mountains—lights a lovely mile.

Robert Bridges

⁂ Robert (Seymour) Bridges was born October 23, 1844. He was educated at Eton and Corpus Christi, Oxford, and, after having traveled, studied medicine, taking the post of Casualty Surgeon at St. Bartholomew's Hospital, London. He retired from the medical profession in 1882 to devote himself entirely to literature. Although many more prominent poets were suggested for the office, the classic restraint of his verse won him the highest official honor: he became Poet Laureate in 1913. So often has the Laureateship been nothing more than a political prize that is gratifying to observe that the award went to one distinguished for nothing more zealous than his art. As essayist, he wrote considerably for the Society of Pure English which, largely through his efforts, was founded in 1913. His interests were unusually varied and included cricket, hymnology (he collaborated in the editing of a hymnal), spoken English, reformed spelling, the encouragement of fellow poets (Hopkins, for example), and music, especially music for the harpsichord. He died, after a short illness, in his eighty-sixth year, on April 21, 1930.

The subjects of his many volumes are indicative of his expression; a few of the titles are: *Prometheus the Firegiver; Eros and Psyche; Achilles in Scyros; The Feast of Bacchus. Poems* appeared as early as 1873. The distinguishing features of his *Shorter Poems* (1894) are a subtlety of rhythm, a precise command of metrical delicacies. It is, in fact, as a metrician that his work is most interesting; even his most academic lines bear a beauty of pattern. Apart from the skill of versification, there are many delights for the most casual reader in his collected *Poetical Works* (excluding the dramas) which appeared in 1913.

Robert Hillyer, the American poet and teacher, has made a study of Bridges' poems and a particularly delicate analysis of his major work. "Until the publication of *The Testament of Beauty* (1929)," writes Mr. Hillyer, "the genius of Robert Bridges was known to comparatively few. In spite of the prolonged neglect of his earlier works on the part of the large public, most of the poets of England and a few in America recognized him as a master. The *Shorter Poems* were accounted the height of lyric artistry. Some of these, such as 'A Passer-by,' 'London Snow,' and 'Awake, My Heart, to Be Loved,' found a more general audience; but, for the most part, Bridges remained a poet's poet until the publication of *The Testament of Beauty.*

"Both those who admire and those who dislike the poetry of Bridges agree on one point: that technically he was one of the masters of English verse. His experiments within the tradition are bolder and more informed than most of those outside it. His skill has often been cited against him by the school of modern critics who prefer verse to be slip-shod or, as they would express it, 'unacademic.' Starting early with Gerard Manley Hopkins and other friends a systematic study of what could be done in English meters without breaking down the instrument, he explored possibilities which, though not so obviously startling as Hopkins' 'sprung rhythm,' were subtly quite as adventurous. His main impulse came from classical prosody, and his early adaptations of quantity to English metrics have never been equaled. In his later work, notably in the 'loose Alexandrines' of *The Testament of Beauty,* he combined with this strong quantitative influence an element wholly derived from our own ancient verse; that is, great liberty in the number of syllables within the single line.

"Space forbids any detailed analysis of this great work. It has been compared to Wordsworth's *Prelude* and to Lucretius's *De Rerum Natura.* The main theme, based on Christian teleology, is the evolution of the human soul toward perfection, the reunion of all things in God through the growth of spiritual love. The poet shows how in Man the blind instincts of Nature become transformed, through influences such as that of beauty, into spiritual forces. Thus, the indiscriminate mating of lower forms of life rises to love inspired by the beauty of the beloved, and in higher natures becomes completely transmuted, as in Dante's love for Beatrice. The theme is developed by the high logic of poetry, which combines with the philosopher's learning and reasoning, the persuasion of beauty itself."

A PASSER-BY

Whither, O splendid ship, thy white sails crowding,
  Leaning across the bosom of the urgent West,
That fearest nor sea rising nor sky clouding,
  Whither away, fair rover, and what thy quest?
  Ah! soon, when Winter has all our vales opprest,
When skies are cold and misty, and hail is hurling,
  Wilt thou glide on the blue Pacific, or rest
In a summer haven asleep, thy white sails furling.

I there before thee, in the country that well thou knowest,
  Already arrived am inhaling the odorous air:
I watch thee enter unerringly where thou goest,
  And anchor queen of the strange shipping there,
  Thy sails for awnings spread, thy masts bare;
Nor is aught from the foaming reef to the snow-capp'd, grandest
  Peak, that is over the feathery palms, more fair
Than thou, so upright, so stately, and still thou standest.

And yet, O splendid ship, unhail'd and nameless,
  I know not if, aiming a fancy, I rightly divine
That thou hast a purpose joyful, a courage blameless,
  Thy port assured in a happier land than mine.
  But for all I have given thee, beauty enough is thine,
As thou, aslant with trim tackle and shrouding,
  From the proud nostril curve of a prow's line
In the offing scatterest foam, thy white sails crowding.

AWAKE, MY HEART, TO BE LOVED

Awake, my heart, to be loved, awake, awake!
The darkness silvers away, the morn doth break,
It leaps in the sky: unrisen lusters slake
The o'ertaken moon. Awake, O heart, awake!

She too that loveth awaketh and hopes for thee;
Her eyes already have sped the shades that flee,
Already they watch the path thy feet shall take:
Awake, O heart, to be loved, awake, awake!

And if thou tarry from her,—if this could be,—
She cometh herself, O heart, to be loved, to thee;
For thee would unashamèd herself forsake:
Awake to be loved, my heart, awake, awake!

Awake! the land is scattered with light, and see,
Uncanopied sleep is flying from field and tree:
And blossoming boughs of April in laughter shake;
Awake, O heart, to be loved, awake, awake!

Lo all things wake and tarry and look for thee:
She looketh and saith, "O sun, now bring him to me.
Come more adored, O adored, for his coming's sake,
And awake, my heart, to be loved: awake, awake!"

O WEARY PILGRIMS

(from "The Growth of Love")

O weary pilgrims, chanting of your woe,
That turn your eyes to all the peaks that shine,
Hailing in each the citadel divine
The which ye thought to have entered long ago;
Until at length your feeble steps and slow
Falter upon the threshold of the shrine,
And your hearts overburdened doubt in fine
Whether it be Jerusalem or no:
Disheartened pilgrims, I am one of you;
For, having worshiped many a barren face,
I scarce now greet the goal I journeyed to:
I stand a pagan in the holy place;
Beneath the lamp of truth I am found untrue,
And question with the God that I embrace.

THOU DIDST DELIGHT MY EYES

Thou didst delight my eyes:
Yet who am I? nor first
Nor last nor best, that durst
Once dream of thee for prize;
Nor this the only time
Thou shalt set love to rhyme.

Thou didst delight my ear:
Ah! little praise; thy voice
Makes other hearts rejoice,
Makes all ears glad that hear;
And short my joy: but yet,
O song, do not forget.

For what wert thou to me?
How shall I say? The moon,
That poured her midnight noon
Upon his wrecking sea;—
A sail, that for a day
Has cheered the castaway.

WINTER NIGHTFALL

The day begins to droop,—
  Its course is done:
But nothing tells the place
  Of the setting sun.

The hazy darkness deepens,
  And up the lane
You may hear, but cannot see,
  The homing wain.

An engine pants and hums
  In the farm hard by:
Its lowering smoke is lost
  In the lowering sky.

The soaking branches drip,
  And all night through
The drooping will not cease
  In the avenue.

A tall man there in the house
  Must keep his chair:
He knows he will never again
  Breathe the spring air:

His heart is worn with work;
  He is giddy and sick
If he rise to go as far
  As the nearest rick:

He thinks of his morn of life,
  His hale, strong years;
And braves as he may the night
  Of darkness and tears.

LONDON SNOW

When men were all asleep the snow came flying,
In large white flakes falling on the city brown,
Stealthily and perpetually settling and loosely lying,
  Hushing the latest traffic of the drowsy town;
Deadening, muffling, stifling its murmurs failing;
Lazily and incessantly floating down and down;
  Silently sifting and veiling road, roof and railing;
Hiding difference, making unevenness even,
Into angles and crevices softly drifting and sailing.
  All night it fell, and when full inches seven
It lay in the depth of its uncompacted lightness,
The clouds blew off from a high and frosty heaven;
  And all woke earlier for the unaccustomed brightness
Of the winter dawning, the strange unheavenly glare:
The eye marveled—marveled at the dazzling whiteness;
  The ear harkened to the stillness of the solemn air;
No sound of wheel rumbling nor of foot falling,
And the busy morning cries came thin and spare.
  Then boys I heard, as they went to school, calling;
They gathered up the crystal manna to freeze
Their tongues with tasting, their hands with snow-balling;
  Or rioted in a drift, plunging up to the knees;
Or peering up from under the white-mossed wonder,
"O look at the trees!" they cried. "O look at the trees!"
  With lessened load, a few carts creak and blunder,
Following along the white deserted way,
A country company long dispersed asunder:
  When now already the sun, in pale display
Standing by Paul's high dome, spread forth below

His sparkling beams, and awoke the stir of the day.
  For now doors open, and war is waged with the snow;
And trains of somber men, past tale of number,
Tread down brown paths, as toward their toil they go:
  But even for them awhile no cares encumber
Their minds diverted; the daily word is unspoken,
The daily thoughts of labor and sorrow slumber
At the sight of the beauty that greets them, for the charm they
    have broken.

NIGHTINGALES

Beautiful must be the mountains whence ye come,
And bright in the fruitful valleys the streams wherefrom
      Ye learn your song:
Where are those starry woods? O might I wander there,
  Among the flowers, which in that heavenly air
      Bloom the year long!

Nay, barren are those mountains and spent the streams:
Our song is the voice of desire, that haunts our dreams,
      A throe of the heart,
Whose pining visions dim, forbidden hopes profound,
  No dying cadence nor long sigh can sound,
      For all our art.

Alone, aloud in the raptured ear of men
We pour our dark nocturnal secret; and then,
      As night is withdrawn
From these sweet-springing meads and bursting boughs of May,
  Dream, while the innumerable choir of day
      Welcome the dawn.

I HAVE LOVED FLOWERS

I have loved flowers that fade,
Within whose magic tents
Rich hues have marriage made
With sweet unmemoried scents:
A honeymoon delight,—
A joy of love at sight,
That ages in an hour:—
My song be like a flower!

I have loved airs that die
Before their charm is writ
Along a liquid sky
Trembling to welcome it.
Notes that with pulse of fire
Proclaim the spirit's desire,
Then die, and are nowhere:—
My song be like an air!

Die, song, die like a breath,
And wither as a bloom:
Fear not a flowery death,
Dread not an airy tomb!
Fly with delight, fly hence!
'Twas thine love's tender sense
To feast; now on thy bier
Beauty shall shed a tear.

NIMIUM FORTUNATUS

I have lain in the sun,
I have toil'd as I might,
I have thought as I would,
And now it is night.

My bed full of sleep,
My heart of content
For friends that I met
The way that I went.

I welcome fatigue
While frenzy and care
Like thin summer clouds
Go melting in air.

To dream as I may
And awake when I will
With the song of the birds
And the sun on the hill.

Or death—were it death—
To what should I wake
Who loved in my home
All life for its sake?

What good have I wrought?
I laugh to have learned
That joy cannot come
Unless it be earned;

For a happier lot
Than God giveth me
It never hath been
Nor ever shall be.

William Ernest Henley

William Ernest Henley was born August 23, 1849, at Gloucester, and was educated at the Grammar School of Gloucester. From childhood he was afflicted wtih a tuberculous disease which finally necessitated the amputation of a foot. His *Hospital Sketches,* those vivid precursors of free verse, were a record of the time when he was at the infirmary at Edinburgh; they are sharp with the sights, sensations, even the smells, of the sick-room. In spite (or, more probably, because) of his continued poor health, Henley never ceased to worship strength and energy; courage and a triumphant belief shine out of the athletic *London Voluntaries* (1892) and the light lyrics in *Hawthorn and Lavender* (1901).

The buoyancy, rousing at first, becomes wearing; it is too insistent, a little shrill. When Henley ceased to overrate animal energy he was no less himself, and a better poet. When not banging drums and flashing swords, he could distill the essence of a lyric, turn a triolet or ballade with the most expert practitioner of the French forms, paint impressionistic side-lights of intimate London, and, in such pieces as "Madame Life," combine grimness and gay *bizarrerie.*

The mixture of lightness and lustiness dates from his early youth. An infectious idiom, it flowered under his first influence, which was that of his schoolmaster, T. E. Brown, and remained to the end.

The bulk of Henley's poetry is not great in volume. He has himself explained the small quantity of his work in a Preface to his *Poems,* first published in 1888. "A principal reason," he says, "is that, after spending the better part of my life in the pursuit of poetry, I found myself (about 1877) so utterly unmarketable that I had to own myself beaten in art, and to indict myself to journalism for the next ten years." Later on, he began to write again—"old dusty sheaves were dragged to light; the work of selection and correction was begun; I burned much; I found that, after all, the lyrical instinct had slept—not died."

As editor he was fearless, prejudiced, violent in preferences and antipathies, and always sincere. His unflinching candor won over even those who completely disagreed with him. His friendships were many; one of the closest was with Robert Louis Stevenson, with whom he wrote three plays published in 1892. (Henley is only slightly disguised as the characteristic "Burly" in Stevenson's essay, "Talk and Talkers.") He compiled a book of poems for boys, *Lyra Heroica* (1891), and collaborated on a dictionary of English slang. Though continually in conflict, he remained belligerent until 1894; in that year the death of his six-year-old daughter broke the heart of one whose head had been "bloody but unbowed."

In 1901 he published *Hawthorn and Lavender,* releasing a far finer though smaller music than he had ever uttered. His unrhythmed rhythms, reminiscent of Heine's *North Sea* cycles, anticipated in color and accent the subsequent vogue of *vers libre.* Although he was not one of the great poets of his period, his period, as well as ours, would be incomplete without him. After a brilliant and varied career devoted mostly to journalism, Henley died in 1903.

INVICTUS

Out of the night that covers me,
  Black as the Pit from pole to pole,
I thank whatever gods may be
  For my unconquerable soul.

In the fell clutch of circumstance
  I have not winced nor cried aloud.
Under the bludgeonings of chance
  My head is bloody, but unbowed.

Beyond this place of wrath and tears
  Looms but the horror of the shade,
And yet the menace of the years
  Finds, and shall find me, unafraid.

It matters not how strait the gate,
  How charged with punishments the scroll,
I am the master of my fate:
  I am the captain of my soul.

THE BLACKBIRD

The nightingale has a lyre of gold,
  The lark's is a clarion call,
And the blackbird plays but a boxwood flute,
  But I love him best of all.

For his song is all of the joy of life,
  And we in the mad, spring weather,
We two have listened till he sang
  Our hearts and lips together.

A BOWL OF ROSES

It was a bowl of roses:
  There in the light they lay,
Languishing, glorying, glowing
  Their life away.

And the soul of them rose like a presence,
  Into me crept and grew,
And filled me with something—someone—
  O, was it you?

BEFORE

Behold me waiting—waiting for the knife.
A little while, and at a leap I storm
The thick sweet mystery of chloroform,
The drunken dark, the little death-in-life.
The gods are good to me: I have no wife,
No innocent child, to think of as I near
The fateful minute; nothing all-too dear
Unmans me for my bout of passive strife.
Yet I am tremulous and a trifle sick,
And, face to face with chance, I shrink a little:
My hopes are strong, my will is something weak.
Here comes the basket? Thank you. I am ready.
But, gentlemen my porters, life is brittle:
You carry Caesar and his fortunes—Steady!

BALLADE

Made in the Hot Weather

Fountains that frisk and sprinkle
The moss they overspill;
Pools that the breezes crinkle;
The wheel beside the mill,
With its wet, weedy frill;
Wind-shadows in the wheat;
A water-cart in the street;
The fringe of foam that girds
An islet's ferneries;
A green sky's minor thirds—
To live, I think of these!

Of ice and glass the tinkle,
Pellucid, silver-shrill;
Peaches without a wrinkle;
Cherries and snow at will,
From china bowls that fill
The senses with a sweet
Incuriousness of heat;
A melon's dripping sherds;
Cream-clotted strawberries;
Dusk dairies set with curds—
To live, I think of these!

Vale-lily and periwinkle;
Wet stone-crop on the sill;
The look of leaves a-twinkle
With windlets clear and still;
The feel of a forest rill
That wimples fresh and fleet
About one's naked feet;
The muzzles of drinking herds;
Lush flags and bulrushes;
The chirp of rain-bound birds—
To live, I think of these!

Envoy

Dark aisles, new packs of cards,
Mermaidens' tails, cool swards,
Dawn dews and starlit seas,
White marbles, whiter words—
To live, I think of these!

WE'LL GO NO MORE A-ROVING

We'll go no more a-roving by the light of the moon.
November glooms are barren beside the dusk of June.
The summer flowers are faded, the summer thoughts are sere.
We'll go no more a-roving, lest worse befall, my dear.

We'll go no more a-roving by the light of the moon.
The song we sang rings hollow, and heavy runs the tune.
Glad ways and words remembered would shame the wretched year.
We'll go no more a-roving, nor dream we did, my dear.

We'll go no more a-roving by the light of the moon.
If yet we walk together, we need not shun the noon.
No sweet thing left to savor, no sad thing left to fear,
We'll go no more a-roving, but weep at home, my dear

MADAM LIFE

Madam Life's a piece in bloom
Death goes dogging everywhere:
She's the tenant of the room,
He's the ruffian on the stair.

You shall see her as a friend,
You shall bilk him once and twice;
But he'll trap you in the end,
And he'll stick you for her price.

With his kneebones at your chest,
And his knuckles in your throat,
You would reason—plead—protest!
Clutching at her petticoat;

But she's heard it all before,
Well she knows you've had your fun,
Gingerly she gains the door,
And your little job is done.

OUT OF TUNE

The spring, my dear,
Is no longer spring.
Does the blackbird sing
What he sang last year?
Are the skies the old
Immemorial blue?
Or am I, or are you,
Grown cold?

Though life be change,
It is hard to bear
When the old sweet air
Sounds forced and strange,
To be out of tune,
Plain You and I . . .
It were better to die,
And soon!

FALMOUTH[1]

O, Falmouth is a fine town with ships in the bay,
And I wish from my heart it's there I was today;
I wish from my heart I was far away from here,
Sitting in my parlor and talking to my dear.
For it's home, dearie, home—it's home I want to be.
Our topsails are hoisted, and we'll away to sea.
O, the oak and the ash and the bonnie birken tree
They're all growing green in the old countrie.

In Baltimore a-walking a lady I did meet
With her babe on her arm, as she came down the street;
And I thought how I sailed, and the cradle standing ready
For the pretty little babe that has never seen its daddie.
And it's home, dearie, home . . .

O, if it be a lass, she shall wear a golden ring;
And if it be a lad, he shall fight for his king:
With his dirk and his hat and his little jacket blue
He shall walk the quarter-deck as his daddie used to do.
And it's home, dearie, home . . .

[1] The burden and the third stanza are adapted from an old song.

O, there's a wind a-blowing, a-blowing from the west,
And that of all the winds is the one I like the best,
For it blows at our backs, and it shakes our pennon free,
And it soon will blow us home to the old countrie.
For it's home, dearie, home—it's home I want to be.
Our topsails are hoisted, and we'll away to sea.
O, the oak and the ash and the bonnie birken tree
They're all growing green in the old countrie.

ENGLAND, MY ENGLAND

What have I done for you,
England, my England?
What is there that I would not do,
England, my own?
With your glorious eyes austere,
As the Lord were walking near,
Whispering terrible things and dear
As the Song on your bugles blown,
England—
Round the world on your bugles blown!

Where shall the watchful Sun,
England, my England,
Match the master-work you've done,
England, my own?
When shall he rejoice again
Such a breed of mighty men
As come forward, one to ten,
To the Song on your bugles blown,
England—
Down the years on your bugles blown?

Ever the faith endures,
England, my England:—
"Take and break us: we are yours,
"England, my own!
"Life is good, and joy runs high
"Between English earth and sky:
"Death is death; but we shall die
"To the Song on your bugles blown,
"England—
"To the stars on your bugles blown!"

They call you proud and hard,
England, my England:
You with worlds to watch and ward,
England, my own!
You whose mailed hand keeps the keys
Of such teeming destinies
You could know nor dread nor ease
Were the Song on your bugles blown,
England,
Round the Pit on your bugles blown!

Mother of Ships whose might,
England, my England,
Is the fierce old Sea's delight,
England, my own,
Chosen daughter of the Lord,
Spouse-in-Chief of the ancient sword,
There's the menace of the Word
In the Song on your bugles blown,
England—
Out of heaven on your bugles blown!

O GATHER ME THE ROSE

O gather me the rose, the rose,
While yet in flower we find it,
For summer smiles, but summer goes,
And winter waits behind it.

For with the dream foregone, foregone,
The deed forborne for ever,
The worm Regret will canker on,
And time will turn him never.

So were it well to love, my love,
And cheat of any laughter
The fate beneath us and above,
The dark before and after.

The myrtle and the rose, the rose,
The sunshine and the swallow,
The dream that comes, the wish that goes
The memories that follow!

TO ROBERT LOUIS STEVENSON

A child,
Curious and innocent,
Slips from his Nurse, and rejoicing
Loses himself in the Fair.

Thro' the jostle and din
Wandering, he revels,
Dreaming, desiring, possessing;
Till, of a sudden
Tired and afraid, he beholds
The sordid assemblage
Just as it is; and he runs
With a sob to his Nurse
(Lighting at last on him),
And in her motherly bosom
Cries him to sleep.

Thus thro' the World,
Seeing and feeling and knowing,
Goes Man: till at last,
Tired of experience, he turns
To the friendly and comforting breast
Of the old nurse, Death.

MARGARITAE SORORI

A late lark twitters from the quiet skies;
And from the west,
Where the sun, his day's work ended,
Lingers as in content,
There falls on the old, gray city
An influence luminous and serene,
A shining peace.

The smoke ascends
In a rosy-and-golden haze. The spires
Shine, and are changed. In the valley
Shadows rise. The lark sings on. The sun,
Closing his benediction,
Sinks, and the darkening air
Thrills with a sense of the triumphing
night—
Night with her train of stars
And her great gift of sleep.

So be my passing!
My task accomplished and the long day done,
My wages taken, and in my heart
Some late lark singing,
Let me be gathered to the quiet west,
The sundown splendid and serene,
Death.

Robert Louis Stevenson

⁂ Robert Louis Stevenson was born at Edinburgh in 1850 and attended the university there. From infancy he was afflicted with illness, nearly dying of gastric fever at the age of eight, a sickness which left him constitutionally weak. The rest of his life was a struggle between his work and a search for health in Switzerland, America, and the South Seas. He was at first trained to be a lighthouse engineer, following the profession of his family. However, he studied law instead, was admitted to the bar in 1875, and abandoned law for literature a few years later. After wandering several years about Europe, he recorded his peregrinations in *An Inland Voyage* (1878) and *Travels with a Donkey* (1879). Although he had written much before his thirtieth year, it was not until the publication of *Treasure Island* (1883) that he became popular. In 1885 he published, with misgivings, *A Child's Garden of Verses;* and again won public favor a year later with that *tour de force, The Strange Case of Dr. Jekyll and Mr. Hyde.*

In 1887, after a prolonged breakdown, he left England never to return. In rapid succession he tried the Adirondacks, New Jersey, California, and, in 1888 sailed, as Sidney Colvin said, "on what was only intended to be an excursion, but turned into a voluntary exile, prolonged until the hour of his death." He lived in Honolulu, Australia, and finally Samoa, where, after a long fight, he succumbed to tuberculosis in 1894.

Though primarily a novelist, Stevenson has left one book which is equally at home in the nursery and the library: *A Child's Garden of Verses* is second only to Mother Goose's own collection in simplicity and universal appeal. With the exception of these favorite verses and a posthumous *New Poems* (1918), *Underwoods* (1887) and *Ballads* (1890) comprise his entire poetic output. As a genial essayist, he is usually ranked with Charles Lamb. As a romancer, his fame rests on *Kidnapped,* the unfinished masterpiece, *Weir of Hermiston,* and that classic of youth, *Treasure Island.*

Stevenson's writing is inseparable from his charm and the personal appeal of his life-story. He is persuasive, not profound, too concerned with his craft, but never dull, and finally winning.

SUMMER SUN

Great is the sun, and wide he goes
Through empty heaven without repose;
And in the blue and glowing days
More thick than rain he showers his rays.

Though closer still the blinds we pull
To keep the shady parlor cool,
Yet he will find a chink or two
To slip his golden fingers through.

The dusty attic, spider-clad,
He, through the keyhole, maketh glad;
And through the broken edge of tiles
Into the laddered hay-loft smiles.

Meantime his golden face around
He bares to all the garden ground,
And sheds a warm and glittering look
Among the ivy's inmost nook.

Above the hills, along the blue,
Round the bright air with footing true,
To please the child, to paint the rose,
The gardener of the World, he goes.

WINTER TIME

Late lies the wintry sun a-bed,
A frosty, fiery sleepy-head;
Blinks but an hour or two; and then,
A blood-red orange, sets again.

Before the stars have left the skies
At morning in the dark I rise;
And, shivering in my nakedness,
By the cold candle, bathe and dress.

Close by the jolly fire I sit
To warm my frozen bones a bit;
Or, with a reindeer-sled, explore
The colder countries round the door.

When to go out, my nurse doth wrap
Me in my comforter and cap;
The cold wind burns my face, and blows
Its frosty pepper up my nose.

Black are my steps on silver sod;
Thick blows my frosty breath abroad;
And tree and house, and hill and lake,
Are frosted like a wedding-cake.

THE CELESTIAL SURGEON

If I have faltered more or less
In my great task of happiness;
If I have moved among my race
And shown no glorious morning face;
If beams from happy human eyes
Have moved me not; if morning skies,
Books, and my food, and summer rain
Knocked on my sullen heart in vain:—
Lord, thy most pointed pleasure take
And stab my spirit broad awake;
Or, Lord, if still too obdurate I,
Choose thou, before that spirit die,
A piercing pain, a killing sin,
And to my dead heart run them in!

ROMANCE

I will make you brooches and toys for your delight
Of bird-song at morning and star-shine at night.
I will make a palace fit for you and me,
Of green days in forests and blue days at sea.

I will make my kitchen, and you shall keep your room,
Where white flows the river and bright blows the broom
And you shall wash your linen and keep your body white
In rainfall at morning and dewfall at night.

And this shall be for music when no one else is near,
The fine song for singing, the rare song to hear!
That only I remember, that only you admire,
Of the broad road that stretches and the roadside fire.

REQUIEM

Under the wide and starry sky
Dig the grave and let me lie:
Glad did I live and gladly die,
And I laid me down with a will.

This be the verse you 'grave for me:
Here he lies where he long'd to be;
Home is the sailor, home from sea,
And the hunter home from the hill.

GO, LITTLE BOOK

Go, little book, and wish to all
Flowers in the garden, meat in the hall,
A bin of wine, a spice of wit,
A house with lawns enclosing it,
A living river by the door,
A nightingale in the sycamore.

Alice Meynell

☙ Alice (Christiana Thompson) Meynell was born in 1850, educated at home and spent a great part of her early life in Italy. Later, she married Wilfred Meynell, friend, editor, and literary executor of Francis Thompson. For eighteen years she contributed to the *Weekly Register* of which her husband was editor; for twelve years was co-editor with him on *Merrie England;* wrote countless essays, columns for other periodicals, issued several volumes of poetry, took on responsibilities not the least of which was the sponsorship of Francis Thompson which saved him from ruin—all with a huge family growing up about her. There were seven Meynell children, among them being Francis, who became a typographer and poet, Viola, the novelist and essayist, Monica, the critical, and Everard, author of *The Life of Francis Thompson.* As described in the authorized Memoir *Alice Meynell* (1929) by her daughter, Viola, the children, aping their elders, conceived editing as a species of indoor sport and made up papers of their own. In one of these, the youngsters, attempting to answer Mrs. Meynell's critics, unconsciously appraised her:

"Her thought is a thought which very few writers got. It is mystical but excucite. She is a little obscure to readers who are not up in literature sufficiently to understand mystical touches. . . . Hers is a very docile temperament and thoroughly sympathetic. When she is singing a sympathetic song you can tell that she must have some excellent powers in her head."

The child Monica, touched with the family passion for salvation and trying to save her mother from literature, put the case against "ecstasy" in these delightful sentences:

"Dear Mother,—I hope you will in time give up your absurd thoughts about literature. It makes my mind quite feverish when I think of the exhaltation your undergoing. I'm getting quite frightened about calling you 'dear Mother' because you will begin to take it quite seriously. Just because Mr. Henley and those sort of unsencere men say you write well simply because they know if they don't flatter you they'll never get anything for their paper. Now mother take my advise and don't be quite so estatic, you'll get on just as well in the world and much better because you'll be respected. Now just see. MONNIE."

Whatever form Alice Meynell chose, her work was always a reflection of her spirit. She scorned sentimentality, "the facile literary opportunity," despised slovenliness, "the fashion of an animated strut of style," and kept herself aloof from them. Her later years were spent collecting her poems, revising her early prose and publishing the best of it in *Essays.* She died in 1923.

Preludes was published in 1876. Since then, various collections of her poems and essays have appeared at irregular intervals, and, in 1923, Charles Scribner's Sons published *The Poems of Alice Meynell.* From the earliest restrained verses to the later more ornate conceits, one strain is dominant: the music of religious emotion. It is, obviously, emotion controlled, almost intellectualized. Yet the poetry is never dull. The reader is always aware of a nature disciplined, but which, for all its self-imposed strictures, is rich in feeling, exquisite in communication.

Selected Poems of Alice Meynell (1931), with a valuable introductory note by Wilfred Meynell, is a careful winnowing of her best, although one of her finest short lyrics ("Chimes") is omitted. The book begins appropriately with the quietly original and wholly beautiful "A Letter from a Girl to Her Own Old Age" and ends with tributes from Ruskin, Meredith, Coventry Patmore, Chesterton and others.

Dante Gabriel Rossetti considered her "Renouncement" one of the three finest sonnets ever written by women. "Christ in the Universe," "To a Daisy," and "A Thrush Before Dawn," show a literary as well as spiritual kinship with Francis

Thompson; but where Thompson is lavish to the point of gaudiness, Mrs. Meynell's fastidiousness dictates a fine economy.

TO A DAISY

Slight as thou art, thou art enough to hide,
  Like all created things, secrets from me,
  And stand a barrier to eternity.
And I, how can I praise thee well and wide
From where I dwell—upon the hither side?
  Thou little veil for so great mystery,
  When shall I penetrate all things and thee,
And then look back? For this I must abide,
Till thou shalt grow and fold and be unfurled
Literally between me and the world.
  Then I shall drink from in beneath a spring,
And from a poet's side shall read his book.
O daisy mine, what will it be to look
  From God's side even on such a simple thing?

THE SHEPHERDESS

She walks—the lady of my delight—
  A shepherdess of sheep.
Her flocks are thoughts. She keeps them white;
  She guards them from the steep;
She feeds them on the fragrant height,
  And folds them in for sleep.

She roams maternal hills and bright
  Dark valleys safe and deep.
Into that tender breast at night,
  The chastest stars may peep.
She walks—the lady of my delight—
  A shepherdess of sheep.

She holds her little thoughts in sight,
  Though gay they run and leap.
She is so circumspect and right;
  She has her soul to keep.
She walks—the lady of my delight—
  A shepherdess of sheep.

THE WIND IS BLIND

"Eyeless, in Gaza, at the mill, with slaves."
—MILTON'S SAMSON.

    The wind is blind.
The earth sees sun and moon; the height
Is watch-tower to the dawn; the plain

Shines to the summer; visible light
Is scattered in the drops of rain.

The wind is blind.
The flashing billows are aware;
With open eyes the cities see;
Light leaves the ether, everywhere
Known to the homing bird and bee.

The wind is blind,
Is blind alone. How has he hurled
His ignorant lash, his sinless dart,
His eyeless rush upon the world,
Unseeing, to break his unknown heart!

The wind is blind.
And the sail traps him, and the mill
Captures him; and he cannot save
His swiftness and his desperate will
From those blind uses of the slave.

NOVEMBER BLUE

The golden tint of the electric lights seems to give a complementary color to the air in the early evening. —ESSAY ON LONDON.

O heavenly color, London town
Has blurred it from her skies;
And, hooded in an earthly brown,
Unheaven'd the city lies.
No longer, standard-like, this hue
Above the broad road flies;
Nor does the narrow street the blue
Wear, slender pennon-wise.

But when the gold and silver lamps
Color the London dew,
And, misted by the winter damps,
The shops shine bright, anew—
Blue comes to earth, it walks the street,
It dyes the wide air through;
A mimic sky about their feet
The throng go crowned with blue.

CHIMES

Brief, on a flying night
From the shaken tower,
A flock of bells take flight,
And go with the hour.

Like birds from the cote to the gales,
  Abrupt—O hark!
A fleet of bells set sails,
  And go to the dark.

Sudden the cold airs swing,
  Alone, aloud,
A verse of bells takes wing
  And flies with the cloud.

A LETTER FROM A GIRL TO HER OWN OLD AGE

Listen, and when thy hand this paper presses,
O time-worn woman, think of her who blesses
What thy thin fingers touch, with her caresses.

O mother, for the weight of years that break thee!
O daughter, for slow time must yet awake thee,
And from the changes of my heart must make thee!

O fainting traveler, morn is gray in heaven.
Dost thou remember how the clouds were driven?
And are they calm about the fall of even?

Pause near the ending of thy long migration;
For this one sudden hour of desolation
Appeals to one hour of thy meditation.

Suffer, O silent one, that I remind thee
Of the great hills that stormed the sky behind thee,
Of the wild winds of power that have resigned thee.

Know that the mournful plain where thou must wander
Is but a gray and silent world; but ponder
The misty mountains of the morning yonder.

Listen:—the mountain winds with rain were fretting,
And sudden gleams the mountain-tops besetting.
I cannot let thee fade to death, forgetting.

What part of this wild heart of mine I know not
Will follow with thee where the great winds blow not,
And where the young flowers of the mountain grow not.

Yet let my letter with thy lost thoughts in it
Tell what the way was when thou didst begin it,
And win with thee the goal when thou shalt win it.

I have not writ this letter of divining
To make a glory of thy silent pining,
A triumph of thy mute and strange declining.

Only one youth, and the bright life was shrouded;
Only one morning, and the day was clouded;
And one old age with all regrets is crowded.

O hush, O hush! Thy tears my words are steeping.
O hush, hush, hush! So full, the fount of weeping?
Poor eyes, so quickly moved, so near to sleeping?

Pardon the girl; such strange desires beset her.
Poor woman, lay aside the mournful letter
That breaks thy heart; the one who wrote, forget her:

The one who now thy faded features guesses,
With filial fingers thy gray hair caresses,
With morning tears thy mournful twilight blesses.

THE OCTOBER REDBREAST

Autumn is weary, halt, and old;
Ah, but she owns the song of joy!
Her colors fade, her woods are cold.
Her singing-bird's a boy, a boy.

In lovely Spring the birds were bent
On nests, on use, on love, forsooth!
Grown-up were they. This boy's content,
For his is liberty, his is youth.

The musical stripling sings for play
Taking no thought, and virgin-glad.
For duty sang those mates in May.
This singing-bird's a lad, a lad.

A THRUSH BEFORE DAWN

A voice peals in this end of night
A phrase of notes resembling stars,
Single and spiritual notes of light.
What call they at my window-bars?
The South, the past, the day to be,
An ancient infelicity.

Darkling, deliberate, what sings
This wonderful one, alone, at peace?
What wilder things than song, what things
Sweeter than youth, clearer than Greece,
Dearer than Italy, untold
Delight, and freshness centuries old?

And first first-loves, a multitude,
The exaltation of their pain;
Ancestral childhood long renewed;
And midnights of invisible rain;
And gardens, gardens, night and day,
Gardens and childhood all the way.

What Middle Ages passionate,
O passionless voice! What distant bells
Lodged in the hills, what palace state
Illyrian! For it speaks, it tells,
Without desire, without dismay
Some morrow and some yesterday.

All-natural things! But more—Whence came
This yet remoter mystery?
How do these starry notes proclaim
A graver still divinity?
This hope, this sanctity of fear?
O innocent throat! O human ear!

RENOUNCEMENT

I must not think of thee; and, tired yet strong,
  I shun the thought that lurks in all delight—
  The thought of thee—and in the blue Heaven's height,
And in the sweetest passage of a song.

O just beyond the fairest thoughts that throng
  This breast, the thought of thee waits hidden yet bright;
  But it must never, never come in sight;
I must stop short of thee the whole day long.

But when sleep comes to close each difficult day,
  When night gives pause to the long watch I keep,
    And all my bonds I needs must loose apart,

Must doff my will as raiment laid away,
  With the first dream that comes with the first sleep
    I run, I run, I am gathered to thy heart.

CHRIST IN THE UNIVERSE

  With this ambiguous earth
His dealings have been told us. These abide:
The signal to a maid, the human birth,
The lesson, and the young Man crucified.

  But not a star of all
The innumerable hosts of stars has heard
How He administered this terrestrial ball.
Our race have kept their Lord's entrusted Word.

  Of His earth-visiting feet
None knows the secret, cherished, perilous,
The terrible, shamefast, frightened, whispered, sweet,
Heart-shattering secret of His way with us.

  No planet knows of this.
Our wayside planet, carrying land and wave,
Love and life multiplied, and pain and bliss,
Bears, as chief treasure, one forsaken grave.

  Nor, in our little day,
May His devices with the heavens be guessed;
His pilgrimage to thread the Milky Way,
Or His bestowals there, be manifest.

  But, in the eternities,
Doubtless we shall compare together, hear
A million alien Gospels, in what guise
He trod the Pleiades, the Lyre, the Bear.

O be prepared, my soul!
To read the inconceivable, to scan
The million forms of God those stars unroll
When, in our turn, we show to them a Man.

Oscar Wilde

⁂ Oscar (Fingall O'Flahertie) Wilde was born at Dublin, Ireland, October 16, 1856, and even as an undergraduate at Oxford was marked for a brilliant career. When he was scarcely twenty-one years of age, he won the Newdigate Prize with his poem "Ravenna." Devoting himself almost entirely to prose, he speedily became known as a writer of brilliant epigrammatic essays and even more brilliant paradoxical plays, such as *An Ideal Husband* and *The Importance of Being Earnest.* Wilde's aphorisms and flippancies were quoted everywhere; his fame as a wit was only surpassed by his notoriety as an esthete, the scandal of his trial, and the final prison sentence.

Most of his poems in prose (such as "The Happy Prince," "The Birthday of the Infanta," and "The Fisherman and His Soul") are more imaginative and richly colored than his rococo verse which suffers from deliberate decadence. But in one long poem, "The Ballad of Reading Gaol" (1898), he sounded his simplest and most enduring note. Prison was, in some ways, a regeneration for Wilde. It not only produced "The Ballad of Reading Gaol," but made possible his finest piece of writing, "De Profundis," only a small part of which has been published. "Salomé," which has made the author's name a household word, was originally written in French in 1892 and later translated into English by Lord Alfred Douglas, accompanied by the famous illustrations by Aubrey Beardsley. More recently, this heated drama, based on the story of Herod and Herodias, was made into an opera by Richard Strauss and performed in a dozen countries and several languages.

Wilde's society plays, flashing and cynical, were the forerunners of Bernard Shaw's audacious and far more searching ironies. One sees the origin of a whole school of drama in such epigrams as "The history of woman is the history of the worst form of tyranny the world has ever known: the tyranny of the weak over the strong. It is the only tyranny that lasts." Or "There is only one thing in the world worse than being talked about, that is not being talked about."

Wilde's flair for publicity, avowed in the last quotation, was gratified to the full. No man of his time was more talked about. The end of the Esthetic Movement came coincidentally—and ironically—with the trial of Oscar Wilde and his indictment for a social crime. His predilection for extremes caused his artistic ruin: in youth he was ultra-Keatsian; in early manhood, ultra-Rossettian; in maturity, ultra-Wilde—and he pushed preciosity to the limits of the absurd. He believed in nothing, not even himself, except for the passing effect; he was essentially the "Pierrot of the minute"—a Pierrot whose shifting passions and impertinences convinced no one. Even his Pierroticism was a pose.

"Impression du Matin" and "Symphony in Yellow" are among the poems which suggest a verbal Whistler, with whom Wilde waged many an epigrammatic battle, and "Hélas" is an unusually honest fragment of self-analysis.

Wilde borrowed from Swinburne no little of his spirit and as much of his technique as he could master. But Swinburne's rebelliousness, though vague and general, was sincere; Wilde, the antithesis of a rebel by instinct, was a social snob who clung to his insurgence for the entrée it won him in properly breathless gatherings. His success was without dignity, his failure without pathos.

Wilde died at Paris, November 30, 1900, his body being buried in the Cemetery of Bagneux. On July 20, 1909, it was transferred to the great Cemetery of Père Lachaise, where later a striking monument by Epstein was erected to his memory.

REQUIESCAT

Tread lightly, she is near
  Under the snow,
Speak gently, she can hear
  The daisies grow.

All her bright golden hair
  Tarnished with rust,
She that was young and fair
  Fallen to dust.

Lily-like, white as snow,
  She hardly knew
She was a woman, so
  Sweetly she grew.

Coffin-board, heavy stone,
  Lie on her breast;
I vex my heart alone,
  She is at rest.

Peace, peace; she cannot hear
  Lyre or sonnet;
All my life's buried here.
  Heap earth upon it.

IMPRESSION DU MATIN

The Thames nocturne of blue and gold
  Changed to a harmony in gray;
  A barge with ocher-colored hay
Dropt from the wharf: and chill and cold

The yellow fog came creeping down
  The bridges, till the houses' walls
  Seemed changed to shadows, and St. Paul's
Loomed like a bubble o'er the town.

Then suddenly arose the clang
  Of waking life; the streets were stirred
  With country wagons; and a bird
Flew to the glistening roofs and sang.

But one pale woman all alone,
  The daylight kissing her wan hair,
  Loitered beneath the gas lamps' flare,
With lips of flame and heart of stone.

HÉLAS

To drift with every passion till my soul
Is a stringed lute on which all winds can play,
Is it for this that I have given away
Mine ancient wisdom, and austere control?
Methinks my life is a twice-written scroll
Scrawled over on some boyish holiday
With idle songs for pipe and virelay,
Which do but mar the secret of the whole.
Surely there was a time I might have trod
The sunlit heights, and from life's dissonance
Struck one clear chord to reach the ears of
  God:
Is that time dead? lo! with a little rod
I did but touch the honey of romance—
And must I lose a soul's inheritance?

MAGDALEN WALKS

The little white clouds are racing over the sky,
  And the fields are strewn with the gold of the flower of March,
  The daffodil breaks under foot, and the tasseled larch
Sways and swings as the thrush goes hurrying by.

A delicate odor is borne on the wings of the morning breeze,
  The odor of deep wet grass, and of brown new-furrowed earth,
  The birds are singing for joy of the Spring's glad birth,
Hopping from branch to branch on the rocking trees.

And all the woods are alive with the murmur and sound of Spring,
  And the rose-bud breaks into pink on the climbing briar,
  And the crocus-bed is a quivering moon of fire
Girdled round with the belt of an amethyst ring.

And the plane of the pine-tree is whispering some tale of love
  Till it rustles with laughter and tosses its mantle of green,
  And the gloom of the wych-elm's hollow is lit with the iris sheen
Of the burnished rainbow throat and the silver breast of a dove.

See! the lark starts up from his bed in the meadow there,
  Breaking the gossamer threads and the nets of dew,
  And flashing adown the river, a flame of blue!
The kingfisher flies like an arrow, and wounds the air.

And the sense of my life is sweet! though I know that the end is nigh:
  For the ruin and rain of winter will shortly come,
  The lily will lose its gold, and the chestnut-bloom
In billows of red and white on the grass will lie.

And even the light of the sun will fade at the last,
  And the leaves will fall, and the birds will hasten away,
  And I will be left in the snow of a flowerless day
To think on the glories of Spring, and the joys of a youth long past.

Yet be silent, my heart! do not count it a profitless thing
  To have seen the splendor of the sun, and of grass, and of flower!
  To have lived and loved! for I hold that to love for an hour
Is better for man and woman than cycles of blossoming Spring.

E TENEBRIS

Come down, O Christ, and help me! reach thy hand,
  For I am drowning in a stormier sea
  Than Simon on thy lake of Galilee:
The wine of life is spilt upon the sand,
My heart is as some famine-murdered land
  Whence all good things have perished utterly,
  And well I know my soul in Hell must lie
If I this night before God's throne should stand.
"He sleeps perchance, or rideth to the chase,
  Like Baal, when his prophets howled that name
  From morn to noon on Carmel's smitten height."
Nay, peace, I shall behold, before the night,
  The feet of brass, the robe more white than flame,
The wounded hands, the weary human face.

SYMPHONY IN YELLOW

An omnibus across the bridge
  Crawls like a yellow butterfly,
  And, here and there, a passer-by
Shows like a little restless midge.

Big barges full of yellow hay
  Are moved against the shadowy wharf,
  And, like a yellow silken scarf,
The thick fog hangs along the quay.

The yellow leaves begin to fade
  And flutter from the Temple elms,
  And at my feet the pale green Thames
Lies like a rod of rippled jade.

THE HARLOT'S HOUSE

We caught the tread of dancing feet,
We loitered down the moonlit street,
And stopped beneath the harlot's house.

Inside, above the din and fray,
We heard the loud musicians play
The "Treues Liebes Herz" of Strauss.

Like strange mechanical grotesques,
Making fantastic arabesques,
The shadows raced across the blind.

We watched the ghostly dancers spin
To sound of horn and violin,
Like black leaves wheeling in the wind.

Like wire-pulled automatons,
Slim silhouetted skeletons
Went sidling through the slow quadrille.

They took each other by the hand,
And danced a stately saraband;
Their laughter echoed thin and shrill.

Sometimes a clockwork puppet pressed
A phantom lover to her breast,
Sometimes they seemed to try to sing.

Sometimes a horrible marionette
Came out, and smoked its cigarette
Upon the steps like a live thing.

Then, turning to my love, I said,
"The dead are dancing with the dead,
The dust is whirling with the dust."

But she—she heard the violin,
And left my side and entered in:
Love passed into the house of lust.

Then suddenly the tune went false,
The dancers wearied of the waltz,
The shadows ceased to wheel and whirl.

And down the long and silent street,
The dawn, with silver-sandaled feet,
Crept like a frightened girl.

FROM "THE SPHINX"

How subtle-secret is your smile! Did you love none then? Nay, I know
Great Ammon was your bedfellow! He lay with you beside the Nile!

The river-horses in the slime trumpeted when they saw him come
Odorous with Syrian galbanum and smeared with spikenard and with thyme.

He came along the river bank like some tall galley argent-sailed,
He strode across the waters, mailed in beauty, and the waters sank.

He strode across the desert sand: he reached the valley where you lay:
He waited till the dawn of day: then touched your black breasts with his hand.

You kissed his mouth with mouth of flame: you made the hornèd god your own:
You stood behind him on his throne: you called him by his secret name.

You wihspered monstrous oracles into the caverns of his ears:
With blood of goats and blood of steers you taught him monstrous miracles.

White Ammon was your bedfellow! Your chamber was the steaming Nile!
And with your curved archaic smile you watched his passion come and go.

FROM "THE BALLAD OF READING GAOL"

He did not wear his scarlet coat,
For blood and wine are red,
And blood and wine were on his hands
When they found him with the dead,
The poor dead woman whom he loved,
And murdered in her bed.

He walked amongst the Trial Men
In a suit of shabby gray;
A cricket cap was on his head,
And his step seemed light and gay;
But I never saw a man who looked
So wistfully at the day.

I never saw a man who looked
With such a wistful eye
Upon that little tent of blue
Which prisoners call the sky,
And at every drifting cloud that went
With sails of silver by.

I walked, with other souls in pain,
Within another ring,
And was wondering if the man had done
A great or little thing,
When a voice behind me whispered low,
"That fellow's got to swing."

Dear Christ! the very prison walls
Suddenly seemed to reel,
And the sky above my head became
Like a casque of scorching steel;
And, though I was a soul in pain,
My pain I could not feel.

I only knew what hunted thought
Quickened his step, and why
He looked upon the garish day
With such a wistful eye:
The man had killed the thing he loved,
And so he had to die.

*

Yet each man kills the thing he loves,
By each let this be heard,
Some do it with a bitter look,
Some with a flattering word,
The coward does it with a kiss,
The brave man with a sword!

Some kill their love when they are young,
And some when they are old;
Some strangle with the hands of Lust,
Some with the hands of Gold:
The kindest use a knife, because
The dead so soon grow cold.

Some love too little, some too long,
Some sell, and others buy;
Some do the deed with many tears,
And some without a sigh:
For each man kills the thing he loves,
Yet each man does not die.

He does not die a death of shame
On a day of dark disgrace,
Nor have a noose about his neck,
Nor a cloth upon his face,
Nor drop feet foremost through the floor
Into an empty space.

He did not wring his hands nor weep,
Nor did he peak or pine,
But he drank the air as though it held
Some healthful anodyne;
With open mouth he drank the sun
As though it had been wine!

And I and all the souls in pain,
Who tramped the other ring,
Forgot if we ourselves had done
A great or little thing,
And watched with gaze of dull amaze
The man who had to swing.

And strange it was to see him pass
With a step so light and gay,

And strange it was to see him look
  So wistfully at the day,
And strange it was to think that he
  Had such a debt to pay.

*

For oak and elm have pleasant leaves
  That in the spring-time shoot:
But grim to see is the gallows-tree
  With its adder-bitten root,
And, green or dry, a man must die
  Before it bears its fruit!

The loftiest place is that seat of grace
  For which all worldlings try:
But who would stand in hempen band
  Upon a scaffold high,
And through a murderer's collar take
  His last look at the sky?

It is sweet to dance to violins
  When Love and Life are fair:
To dance to flutes, to dance to lutes
  Is delicate and rare:
But it is not sweet with nimble feet
  To dance upon the air!

So with curious eyes and sick surmise
  We watched him day by day,
And wondered if each one of us
  Would end the self-same way,
For none can tell to what red Hell
  His sightless soul may stray.

At last the dead man walked no more
  Amongst the Trial Men,
And I knew that he was standing up
  In the black dock's dreadful pen,
And that never would I see his face
  In God's sweet world again.

Like two doomed ships that pass in storm
  We had crossed each other's way:
But we made no sign, we said no word,
  We had no word to say;
For we did not meet in the holy night,
  But in the shameful day.

A prison wall was round us both,
  Two outcast men we were:
The world had thrust us from its heart,
  And God from out His care:
And the iron gin that waits for Sin
  Had caught us in its snare.

John Davidson

John Davidson was born at Barrhead, Renfrewshire, in 1857. His *Ballads and Songs* (1895) and *New Ballads* (1897) attained a sudden but too short-lived popularity; his great promise was quenched by an apathetic public and by his own growing disillusion and despair. Neither the later *Holiday and Other Poems* (1906) nor the ambitious trilogy, *God and Mammon* (the first volume of which appeared in 1907) received anything more than frozen respect. His somber poetry never tired of repeating his favorite theme: "Man is but the Universe grown conscious." Author of some four "testaments," six plays, three novels, and various collections of poems and essays, Davidson died by his own hand at Penzance in 1909.

The theme of "A Ballad of a Nun" is one which has attracted many writers since the Middle Ages, but Davidson has given it a turn which makes the tale sound far fresher than Vollmoeller's employment of it in *The Miracle.* "A Ballad of Hell," Davidson's only "popular" poem, is wholly his own material.

Davidson's work may be divided into three stages. His first phase, announced in *The North Wall* (1885), was conscious cleverness. In the second stage he tried to reach sophisticated audiences, attempting the metropolitan note with sketches, plays, and novels in the manner of the febrile Nineties. It was not until *Ballads and Songs* and *The Last Ballad* (1899) that he struck what for him and his readers was the true note. "A Ballad of Hell" and "A Ballad of a Nun," among others, are infused with the old ballad spirit; they have the traditional reach and vigor, modernized without becoming topical, pointed but not over-personalized.

After 1900 Davidson's work suffered. As his biographer R. M. Wenley puts it, "cosmogonic passion overwhelming him, the artist pales before the prophet in travail." Somberness developed into pessimism, pessimism into self-persecution. He identified himself with the unhappy James Thomson, another maladjusted soul; he became paranoiac, losing himself in "strange passions, outlandish affaires, overstrung rhetoric." Over-emphasizing extremes, his later work was not only neurotic but melodramatic. Hysteria tainted a half-Nietzschean, half-Calvinistic philosophy; his twisted apprehension of the "hero" concept of history (in which he seemed to himself one of the defeated martyrs) was, as Wenley remarks, "like other Neo-Romantics'—from Nietzsche *in excelsis* to D'Annunzio *in inferis*."

But it is only in his last phase that Davidson turned from singing to shrieking. His huge and misshapen trilogies are forgotten; his exaggerated colors have faded; the ballads and a few of the lyrics remain. They have persistent if not permanent stuff.

A BALLAD OF HELL

"A letter from my love today!
  Oh, unexpected, dear appeal!"
She struck a happy tear away,
  And broke the crimson seal.

"My love, there is no help on earth,
  No help in heaven; the dead-man's bell
Must toll our wedding; our first hearth
  Must be the well-paved floor of hell."

The color died from out her face,
  Her eyes like ghostly candles shone;
She cast dread looks about the place,
  Then clenched her teeth and read right on.

"I may not pass the prison door;
  Here must I rot from day to day,
Unless I wed whom I abhor,
  My cousin, Blanche of Valencay.

"At midnight with my dagger keen,
  I'll take my life; it must be so.
Meet me in hell tonight, my queen,
  For weal and woe."

She laughed, although her face was wan,
  She girded on her golden belt,
She took her jeweled ivory fan,
  And at her glowing missal knelt.

Then rose, "And am I mad?" she said:
  She broke her fan, her belt untied;
With leather girt herself instead,
  And stuck a dagger at her side.

She waited, shuddering in her room,
  Till sleep had fallen on all the house.
She never flinched; she faced her doom:
  They two must sin to keep their vows.

Then out into the night she went,
  And, stooping, crept by hedge and tree;
Her rose-bush flung a snare of scent,
  And caught a happy memory.

She fell, and lay a minute's space;
  She tore the sward in her distress;
The dewy grass refreshed her face;
  She rose and ran with lifted dress.

She started like a morn-caught ghost
  Once when the moon came out and stood
To watch; the naked road she crossed,
  And dived into the murmuring wood.

The branches snatched her streaming cloak;
  A live thing shrieked; she made no stay!
She hurried to the trysting-oak—
  Right well she knew the way.

Without a pause she bared her breast,
And drove her dagger home and fell,
And lay like one that takes her rest,
And died and wakened up in hell.

She bathed her spirit in the flame,
And near the center took her post;
From all sides to her ears there came
The dreary anguish of the lost.

The devil started at her side,
Comely, and tall, and black as jet.
"I am young Malespina's bride;
Has he come hither yet?"

"My poppet, welcome to your bed."
"Is Malespina here?"
"Not he! Tomorrow he must wed
His cousin Blanche, my dear!"

"You lie, he died with me tonight."
"Not he! it was a plot" . . . "You lie."
"My dear, I never lie outright."
"We died at midnight, he and I."

The devil went. Without a groan
She, gathered up in one fierce prayer,
Took root in hell's midst all alone,
And waited for him there.

She dared to make herself at home
Amidst the wail, the uneasy stir.
The blood-stained flame that filled the dome,
Scentless and silent, shrouded her.

How long she stayed I cannot tell;
But when she felt his perfidy,
She marched across the floor of hell;
And all the damned stood up to see.

The devil stopped her at the brink:
She shook him off; she cried, "Away!"
"My dear, you have gone mad, I think."
"I was betrayed: I will not stay."

Across the weltering deep she ran;
A stranger thing was never seen:
The damned stood silent to a man;
They saw the great gulf set between.

To her it seemed a meadow fair;
And flowers sprang up about her feet.
She entered heaven; she climbed the stair
And knelt down at the mercy-seat.

Seraphs and saints with one great voice
Welcomed that soul that knew not fear.
Amazed to find it could rejoice,
Hell raised a hoarse, half-human cheer.

IMAGINATION

(*from "New Year's Eve"*)

There is a dish to hold the sea,
A brazier to contain the sun,
A compass for the galaxy,
A voice to wake the dead and done!

That minister of ministers,
Imagination, gathers up
The undiscovered Universe,
Like jewels in a jasper cup.

Its flame can mingle north and south;
Its accent with the thunder strive;
The ruddy sentence of its mouth
Can make the ancient dead alive.

The mart of power, the fount of will,
The form and mold of every star,
The source and bound of good and ill,
The key of all the things that are,

Imagination, new and strange
In every age, can turn the year;
Can shift the poles and lightly change
The mood of men, the world's career.

THE UNKNOWN

(*Villanelle*)

To brave and to know the unknown
Is the high world's motive and mark,
Though the way with snares be strewn.

The earth itself alone
Wheels through the light and the dark
Onward to meet the unknown.

Each soul, upright or prone,
While the owl sings or the lark,
Must pass where the bones are strewn.

Power on the loftiest throne
  Can fashion no certain ark
That shall stem and outride the unknown.

Beauty must doff her zone,
  Strength trudge unarmed and stark
Though the way with eyes be strewn.

This only can atone,
  The high world's motive and mark,
To brave and to know the unknown
Though the way with fire be strewn.

A BALLAD OF A NUN

From Eastertide to Eastertide
  For ten long years her patient knees
Engraved the stones—the fittest bride
  Of Christ in all the diocese.

She conquered every earthly lust;
  The abbess loved her more and more;
And, as a mark of perfect trust,
  Made her the keeper of the door.

High on a hill the convent hung,
  Across a duchy looking down,
Where everlasting mountains flung
  Their shadows over tower and town.

The jewels of their lofty snows
  In constellations flashed at night;
Above their crests the moon arose;
  The deep earth shuddered with delight.

Long ere she left her cloudy bed,
  Still dreaming in the orient land,
On many a mountain's happy head
  Dawn lightly laid her rosy hand.

The adventurous sun took heaven by storm;
  Clouds scattered largesses of rain;
The sounding cities, rich and warm,
  Smoldered and glittered in the plain.

Sometimes it was a wandering wind,
  Sometimes the fragrance of the pine,
Sometimes the thought how others sinned,
  That turned her sweet blood into wine.

Sometimes she heard a serenade
  Complaining sweetly far away:
She said, "A young man woos a maid";
  And dreamt of love till break of day.

Then she would ply her knotted scourge
  Until she swooned; but evermore
She had the same red sin to purge,
  Poor, passionate keeper of the door!

For still night's starry scroll unfurled,
  And still the day came like a flood:
It was the greatness of the world
  That made her long to use her blood.

In winter-time when Lent drew nigh,
  And hill and plain were wrapped in snow
She watched beneath the frosty sky
  The nearest city nightly glow.

Like peals of airy bells outworn
  Faint laughter died above her head
In gusts of broken music borne:
  "They keep the Carnival," she said.

Her hungry heart devoured the town:
  "Heaven save me by a miracle!
Unless God sends an angel down,
  Thither I go though it were Hell."

Fillet and veil in strips she tore;
  Her golden tresses floated wide;
The ring and bracelet that she wore
  As Christ's betrothed, she cast aside.

"Life's dearest meaning I shall probe;
  Lo! I shall taste of love at last!
Away!" She doffed her outer robe,
  And sent it sailing down the blast.

Her body seemed to warm the wind;
  With bleeding feet o'er ice she ran:
"I leave the righteous God behind;
  I go to worship sinful man."

She reached the sounding city's gate;
  No question did the warder ask:
He passed her in: "Welcome, wild mate!"
  He thought her some fantastic mask.

Half-naked through the town she went;
  Each footstep left a bloody mark;
Crowds followed her with looks intent;
  Her bright eyes made the torches dark.

Alone and watching in the street
  There stood a grave youth nobly dressed;
To him she knelt and kissed his feet;
  Her face her great desire confessed.

Straight to his house the nun he led:
  "Strange lady, what would you with me?"
"Your love, your love, sweet lord," she said;
  "I bring you my virginity."

He healed her bosom with a kiss;
  She gave him all her passion's hoard;
And sobbed and murmured ever, "This
  Is life's great meaning, dear, my lord.

"I care not for my broken vows;
  Though God should come in thunder soon,
I am sister to the mountains now,
  And sister to the sun and moon."

Through all the towns of Belmarie
  She made a progress like a queen.
'She is," they said, "whate'er she be,
  The strangest woman ever seen.

"From fairyland she must have come,
  Or else she is a mermaiden."
Some said she was a ghoul, and some
  A heathen goddess born again.

But soon her fire to ashes burned;
  Her beauty changed to haggardness;
Her golden hair to silver turned;
  The hour came of her last caress.

At midnight from her lonely bed
  She rose, and said, "I have had my will."
The old ragged robe she donned, and fled
  Back to the convent on the hill.

Half-naked as she went before,
  She hurried to the city wall,
Unnoticed in the rush and roar
  And splendor of the Carnival.

She ran across the icy plain;
  Her worn blood curdled in the blast;
Each footstep left a crimson stain;
  The white-faced moon looked on aghast.

She said between her chattering jaws,
  "Deep peace is mine, I cease to strive;
Oh, comfortable convent laws,
  That bury foolish nuns alive!

"A trowel for my passing-bell,
  A little bed within the wall,
A coverlet of stones; how well
  I there shall keep the Carnival!"

Like tired bells chiming in their sleep,
  The wind faint peals of laughter bore;
She stopped her ears and climbed the steep
  And thundered at the convent door.

It opened straight: she entered in,
  And at the wardress' feet fell prone:
"I come to purge away my sin;
  Bury me, close me up in stone."

The wardress raised her tenderly;
  She touched her wet and fast-shut eyes:
"Look, sister; sister, look at me;
  Look; can you see through my disguise?"

She looked and saw her own sad face,
  And trembled, wondering, "Who art
    thou?"
"God sent me down to fill your place:
  I am the Virgin Mary now."

And with the word, God's mother shone:
  The wanderer whispered, "Mary, hail!"
The vision helped her to put on
  Bracelet and fillet, ring and veil.

"You are sister to the mountains now,
  And sister to the day and night;
Sister to God." And on the brow
  She kissed her thrice, and left her sight,

While dreaming in her cloudy bed,
  Far in the crimson orient land,
On many a mountain's happy head
  Dawn lightly laid her rosy hand.

Francis Thompson

⁂ Francis Thompson was born in Ashton in Lancashire in 1859. The son of a doctor, he was intended for the profession and took the medical course at Owens College, Manchester. He had, however, no interest in medicine, but from youth evinced a passion for religion, particularly for the ritual of Catholicism.

His attempts to earn a living were a succession of failures. He was employed as a book-agent, and sold no books; he was apprenticed to the boot trade, and spent many hours of his apprenticeship in public libraries; he enlisted as a soldier, and was discharged as incompetent. He went to London, as Francis Meynell says, "not so much to seek his fortune as to escape his bad fortune. He lost in the gamble, but literature gained. He lived for four years as errand man, seller of matches, holder of horses' heads. Soon he became too shabby to gain admittance into the public libraries, so that when one says that desire of reading was with him a passion, one restores to its literal meaning that abused word. He slept on the Embankment, and 'saw the traffic of Jacob's ladder Pitched betwixt Heaven and Charing Cross.' A woman of the streets took pity on him and kept him alive by her charity—the spirit and the deed. He began to write—now for the first time. His poem, 'Dream Tryst,' written on blue sugar wrapping, found after many months an editorial welcome. Thereafter he was persuaded, though with difficulty, to come off the streets; and even to give up for many years the laudanum he had been taking. For the remaining nineteen years of his life he had an existence at any rate three-quarters protected from the physical tragedies of his starved and homeless young manhood."

Francis Meynell does not name the persons who gave Thompson "an editorial welcome" and who provided him with the shelter which made it possible for him to continue writing and, for that matter, living. These persons were Wilfred Meynell (later to become Thompson's editor and executor) and the poet Alice Meynell (see page 59), who named their son Francis after the genius who became his godfather.

Thompson's first volume, *Poems,* appeared in 1893, disclosing beneath a surface of wild metaphors and violent neologisms an affinity with the august. This volume was followed by *Sister Songs* (1895) and *New Poems* (1897). In these, as well as in the essays on De Quincey and Shelley, there was tropical strangeness. Plenitude is here not only in the large concept but in the small detail. Here are metaphors as bold as

> . . . laden with its lampèd clusters bright
> The fiery-fruited vineyard of this night.

and

> I broke through the doors of sunset,
> Ran before the hooves of sunrise.

The "Anthem of Earth," from which the last quotation is taken, is second only to Thompson's highest achievement. "The Hound of Heaven," which Coventry Patmore declared "one of the very few 'great' odes the language can boast," has captured more readers than any religious poem of this century. In a mystic circle, in which the God-pursuing is the God-pursued, the poem moves with the unhurried majesty of a Bach Chorale, building verse upon fugual verse into an unterrestrial architecture. Recognition of a divine order is celebrated with an almost divine excess. Everything, like Thompson's bright laburnum, spills its "honey of wild flame."

Thompson's poetry was embedded in his philosophy to an unusual degree; he saw all things related and linked by immortal power. It was a super-Berkeley who wrote:

> . . . thou canst not stir a flower
> Without troubling of a star.

Thompson's philosophy, however, exalted though it was, could not maintain him on the heights. Rapture and despair fought within him. "Down the arcane where Night would perish in night," he wandered, lost in "incredible excess"; the heart's cry in "The Dread of Height" sounds the ecstatic reaches and profound depths which his spirit touched. His suspensions were unresolved. But if neither man nor nature granted him final solution, the Church offered him serenity, and no singer has ever put the Catholic creed to more inspired measures.

Influenced at first by the dazzling Crashaw and the conceits of the seventeenth century metaphysicians, Thompson allowed himself the fullest play of purple-pompous tropes. He was as prodigal with strange colors and curious words as a child; the words he applied to characterize Shelley might be used with even greater justice to describe Thompson himself: "To the last, in a degree uncommon even among poets, he retained the idiosyncrasy of childhood, expanded and matured without differentiation. To the last, he was the enchanted child."

Riotous images and extravagant archaisms were Thompson's delight and his defect; he toyed with a style that loved to toss the stars and swing constellations by the hair. His was, not infrequently, a baroque magnificence. He often confused glitter with gold, painting the sublime in terms of the theatrical, falling from the grand manner into the grand-opera manner. At worst, Thompson overdressed his lines with a showy vocabulary; at his best, he attained sublimity. Such poems as "A Fallen Yew," "Ode to the Setting Sun," "Any Saint," "In No Strange Land," and, first and last, "The Hound of Heaven," provide a noble shrine for a noble vision. Here he captured, if only for glowing moments, a glory of which most of his contemporaries were not even aware.

Thompson died, after a fragile and spasmodic life, in St. John's Wood, London, in November, 1907. Since that time, several *Selected Poems* have revealed Thompson's pomp and prodigality to a new generation; an inexpensive *Complete Poetical Works* may be found in The Modern Library.

DAISY

Vhere the thistle lifts a purple crown
  Six foot out of the turf,
.nd the harebell shakes on the windy hill—
  O breath of the distant surf!—

'he hills look over on the South,
  And southward dreams the sea;
And with the sea-breeze hand in hand
  Came innocence and she.

Where'mid the gorse the raspberry
  Red for the gatherer springs;
Two children did we stray and talk
  Wise, idle, childish things.

She listened with big-lipped surprise,
  Breast-deep 'mid flower and spine:

Her skin was like a grape whose veins
  Run snow instead of wine.

She knew not those sweet words she spake,
  Nor knew her own sweet way;
But there's never a bird, so sweet a song
  Thronged in whose throat all day.

Oh, there were flowers in Storrington
  On the turf and on the spray;
But the sweetest flower on Sussex hills
  Was the Daisy-flower that day!

Her beauty smoothed earth's furrowed face.
  She gave me tokens three:—
A look, a word of her winsome mouth,
  And a wild raspberry.

A berry red, a guileless look,
  A still word,—strings of sand!
And yet they made my wild, wild heart
  Fly down to her little hand.

For standing artless as the air
  And candid as the skies,
She took the berries with her hand
  And the love with her sweet eyes.

The fairest things have fleetest end,
  Their scent survives their close:
But the rose's scent is bitterness
  To him that loved the rose.

She looked a little wistfully,
  Then went her sunshine way:—
The sea's eye had a mist on it,
  And the leaves fell from the day.

She went her unremembering way,
  She went and left in me
The pang of all the partings gone,
  And partings yet to be.

She left me marveling why my soul
  Was sad that she was glad;
At all the sadness in the sweet,
  The sweetness in the sad.

Still, still I seemed to see her, still
  Look up with soft replies,
And take the berries with her hand,
  And the love with her lovely eyes.

Nothing begins, and nothing ends,
  That is not paid with moan,
For we are born in other's pain,
  And perish in our own.

TO A SNOWFLAKE

What heart could have thought you?—
Past our devisal
(O filigree petal!)
Fashioned so purely,
Fragilely, surely,
From what Paradisal
Imagineless metal,
Too costly for cost?
Who hammered you, wrought you,
From argentine vapor?—

"God was my shaper.
Passing surmisal,
He hammered, He wrought me,
From curled silver vapor,
To lust of his mind:—
Thou couldst not have thought me!
So purely, so palely,
Tinily, surely,
Mightily, frailly,
Insculped and embossed,
With His hammer of wind,
And His graver of frost."

AN ARAB LOVE-SONG

The hunchèd camels of the night[1]
Trouble the bright
And silver waters of the moon.
The Maiden of the Morn will soon
Through Heaven stray and sing,
Star gathering.

[1] Cloud-shapes observed by travelers in the East.

Now while the dark about our loves is strewn,
Light of my dark, blood of my heart, O come!
And night will catch her breath up, and be dumb.

Leave thy father, leave thy mother
And thy brother;
Leave the black tents of thy tribe apart!
Am I not thy father and thy brother,
And thy mother?
And thou—what needest with thy tribe's black tents
Who hast the red pavilion of my heart?

ALL'S VAST

O nothing, in this corporal earth of man,
That to the imminent heaven of his high soul
Responds with color and with shadow, can
Lack correlated greatness. If the scroll
Where thoughts lie fast in spell of hieroglyph
Be mighty through its mighty inhabitants;
If God be in His Name; grave potence if
The sounds unbind of hieratic chants;
All's vast that vastness means. Nay, I affirm
Nature is whole in her least things exprest,
Nor know we with what scope God builds the worm.
Our towns are copied fragments from our breast;
And all man's Babylons strive but to impart
The grandeurs of his Babylonian heart.

EPILOGUE

(from "A Judgment in Heaven")

Heaven, which man's generations draws,
Nor deviates into replicas,
Must of as deep diversity
In judgment as creation be.
There is no expeditious road
To pack and label men for God,
And save them by the barrel-load.
Some may perchance, with strange surprise,
Have blundered into Paradise.
In vasty dusk of life abroad,
They fondly thought to err from God,
Nor knew the circle that they trod;
And, wandering all the night about,
Found them at morn where they set out.
Death dawned; Heaven lay in prospect wide:—
Lo! they were standing by His side!

THE POPPY

(To Monica)

Summer set lip to earth's bosom bare,
And left the flushed print in a poppy there:
Like a yawn of fire from the grass it came,
And the fanning wind puffed it to flapping flame.

With burnt mouth, red like a lion's, it drank
The blood of the sun as he slaughtered sank,
And dipped its cup in the purpurate shine
When the Eastern conduits ran with wine.

Till it grew lethargied with fierce bliss,
And hot as a swinked gypsy is,
And drowsed in sleepy savageries,
With mouth wide a-pout for a sultry kiss.

A child and man paced side by side,
Treading the skirts of eventide;
But between the clasp of his hand and hers
Lay, felt not, twenty withered years.

She turned, with the rout of her dusk South hair,
And saw the sleeping gypsy there:
And snatched and snapped it in swift child's whim,
With—"Keep it, long as you live!"—to him.

And his smile, as nymphs from their laving meres,
Trembled up from a bath of tears;
And joy, like a mew sea-rocked apart,
Tossed on the waves of his troubled heart.

For *he* saw what she did not see,
That—as kindled by its own fervency—
The verge shriveled inward smolderingly:
And suddenly 'twixt his hand and hers
He knew the twenty withered years—
No flower, but twenty shriveled years.

"Was never such thing until this hour,"
Low to his heart he said; "the flower
Of sleep brings wakening to me,
And of oblivion, memory.

"Was never this thing to me," he said,
"Though with bruisèd poppies my feet are red!"
And again to his own heart very low:
"O child! I love, for I love and know;

"But you, who love nor know at all
The diverse chambers in Love's guest-hall,
Where some rise early, few sit long:
In how differing accents hear the throng
His great Pentecostal tongue;

"Who know not love from amity,
Nor my reported self from me;
A fair fit gift is this, meseems,
You give—this withering flower of dreams.

"O frankly fickle, and fickly true,
Do you know what the days will do to you?
To your love and you what the days will do,
O frankly fickle, and fickly true?

"You have loved me, Fair, three lives—or days:
'Twill pass with the passing of my face.
But where *I* go, your face goes too,
To watch lest I play false to you.

"I am but, my sweet, your foster-lover,
Knowing well when certain years are over
You vanish from me to another;
Yet I know, and love, like the foster-mother.

"So frankly fickle, and fickly true!
For my brief life-while I take from you
This token, fair and fit, meseems,
For me—this withering flower of dreams."

The sleep-flower sways in the wheat its head,
Heavy with dreams, as that with bread:
The goodly grain and the sun-flushed sleeper
The reaper reaps, and Time the reaper.

I hang 'mid men my needless head,
And my fruit is dreams, as theirs is bread:
The goodly men and the sun-hazed sleeper
Time shall reap, but after the reaper
The world shall glean of me, me the sleeper.

Love, love! your flower of withered dream
In leavèd rhyme lies safe, I deem,
Sheltered and shut in a nook of rhyme,
From the reaper man, and his reaper Time.

Love! *I* fall into the claws of Time:
But last within a leavèd rhyme
All that the world of me esteems—
My withered dreams, my withered dreams.

THE SUN

(from "Ode to the Setting Sun")

Who lit the furnace of the mammoth's heart?
Who shagged him like Pilatus' ribbèd flanks?
Who raised the columned ranks
Of that old pre-diluvian forestry,
Which like a continent torn oppressed the sea,
When the ancient heavens did in rains depart,
While the high-dancèd whirls
Of the tossed scud made hiss thy drenchèd curls?
Thou rear'dst the enormous brood;
Who hast with life imbued
The lion maned in tawny majesty,
The tiger velvet-barred,
The stealthy-stepping pard,
And the lithe panther's flexous symmetry?

How came the entombèd tree a light-bearer,
Though sunk in lightless lair?
Friend of the forgers of earth,
Mate of the earthquake and thunders volcanic,
Clasped in the arms of the forces Titanic
Which rock like a cradle the girth
Of the ether-hung world;
Swart son of the swarthy mine,
When flame on the breath of his nostrils feeds
How is his countenance half-divine,
Like thee in thy sanguine weeds?
Thou gavest him his light,
Though sepultured in night
Beneath the dead bones of a perished world;
Over his prostrate form
Though cold, and heat, and storm,
The mountainous wrack of a creation hurled.

Who made the splendid rose
Saturate with purple glows;
Cupped to the marge with beauty; a perfume-press
Whence the wind vintages
Gushes of warmèd fragrance richer far
Than all the flavorous ooze of Cyprus' vats?
Lo, in yon gale which waves her green cymar,
With dusky cheeks burnt red
She sways her heavy head,
Drunk with the must of her own odorousness;
While in a moted trouble the vexed gnats
Maze, and vibrate, and tease the noontide hush.
Who girt dissolvèd lightnings in the grape?
Summered the opal with an Irised flush?
Is it not thou that dost the tulip drape,

And huest the daffodilly,
Yet who hast snowed the lily,
And her frail sister, whom the waters name,
Dost vestal-vesture 'mid the blaze of June,
Cold as the new-sprung girlhood of the moon
Ere Autumn's kiss sultry her cheek with flame?
Thou sway'st thy sceptered beam
O'er all delight and dream,
Beauty is beautiful but in thy glance:
And like a jocund maid
In garland-flowers arrayed,
Before thy ark Earth keeps her sacred dance.

A FALLEN YEW

It seemed corrival of the world's great prime,
Made to un-edge the scythe of Time,
And last with stateliest rhyme.

No tender Dryad ever did indue
That rigid chiton of rough yew,
To fret her white flesh through:

But some god like to those grim Asgard lords,
Who walk the fables of the hordes
From Scandinavian fjords,

Upheaved its stubborn girth, and raised unriven,
Against the whirl-blast and the levin,
Defiant arms to Heaven.

When doom puffed out the stars, we might have said,
It would decline its heavy head,
And see the world to bed.

For this firm yew did from the vassal leas,
And rain and air, its tributaries,
Its revenues increase,

And levy impost on the golden sun,
Take the blind years as they might run,
And no fate seek or shun.

But now our yew is strook, is fallen—yea,
Hacked like dull wood of every day
To this and that, men say.

Never!—To Hades' shadowy shipyards gone,
Dim barge of Dis, down Acheron
It drops, or Lethe wan.

Stirred by its fall—poor destined bark of Dis!—
Along my soul a bruit there is
Of echoing images,

Reverberations of mortality:
  Spelt backward from its death, to me
    Its life reads saddenedly.

Its breast was hollowed as the tooth of eld;
  And boys, there creeping unbeheld,
    A laughing moment dwelled.

Yet they, within its very heart so crept,
  Reached not the heart that courage kept
    With winds and years beswept.

And in its boughs did close and kindly nest
  The birds, as they within its breast,
    By all its leaves caressed.

But bird nor child might touch by any art
  Each other's or the tree's hid heart,
    A whole God's breadth apart;

The breadth of God, the breadth of death and life!
  Even so, even so, in undreamed strife
    With pulseless Law, the wife,—

The sweetest wife on sweetest marriage-day,—
  Their souls at grapple in mid-way,
    Sweet to her sweet may say:

"I take you to my inmost heart, my true!"
  Ah, fool! but there is one heart you
    Shall never take him to!

The hold that falls not when the town is got,
  The heart's heart, whose immurèd plot
    Hath keys yourself keep not!

Its ports you cannot burst—you are withstood—
  For him that to your listening blood
    Sends precepts as he would.

Its gates are deaf to Love, high summoner;
  Yea, love's great warrant runs not there:
    You are your prisoner.

Yourself are with yourself the sole consortress
  In that unleaguerable fortress;
    It knows you not for portress.

Its keys are at the cincture hung of God;
  Its gates are trepidant to His nod;
    By Him its floors are trod.

And if His feet shall rock those floors in wrath,
  Or blest aspersion sleek His path,
    Is only choice it hath.

Yea, in that ultimate heart's occult abode
To lie as in an oubliette of God,
Or in a bower untrod,

Built by a secret Lover for His Spouse;—
Sole choice is this your life allows,
Sad tree, whose perishing boughs
So few birds house!

A COUNSEL OF MODERATION

On him the unpetitioned heavens descend,
Who heaven on earth proposes not for end;
The perilous and celestial excess
Taking with peace, lacking with thankfulness.
Bliss in extreme befits thee not until
Thou'rt not extreme in bliss; be equal still:
Sweets to be granted think thyself unmeet
Till thou have learned to hold sweet not too sweet.

This thing not far is he from wise in art
Who teacheth; nor who doth, from wise in heart.

ANY SAINT

(*Condensed*)

His shoulder did I hold
Too high that I, o'erbold
Weak one,
Should lean thereon.

But He a little hath
Declined His stately path
And my
Feet set more high;

That the slack arm may reach
His shoulder, and faint speech
Stir
His unwithering hair.

And bolder now and bolder
I lean upon that shoulder,
So dear
He is and near:

And with His aureole
The tresses of my soul
Are blent
In wished content.

Yea, this too gentle Lover
Hath flattering words to move her
To pride
By his sweet side.

Ah, Love! somewhat let be—
Lest my humility
Grow weak
When Thou dost speak.

Rebate Thy tender suit,
Lest to herself impute
Some worth
Thy bride of earth!

A maid too easily
Conceits herself to be
Those things
Her lover sings;

And being straitly wooed,
Believes herself the Good
And Fair
He seeks in her.

Turn something of Thy look,
And fear me with rebuke,
That I
May timorously

Take tremors in Thy arms,
And with contrivèd charms
Allure
A love unsure.

Not to me, not to me,
Builded so flawfully,
O God,
Thy humbling laud!

Not to this man, but Man,—
Universe in a span;
Point
Of the spheres conjoint;

In whom eternally
Thou, Light, dost focus Thee!—
Didst pave
The way o' the wave.

*

Thou meaning, couldst thou see,
Of all which dafteth thee;
So plain,
It mocks thy pain.

Stone of the Law indeed,
Thine own self couldst thou read;
Thy bliss
Within thee is.

Compost of Heaven and mire,
Slow foot and swift desire!
Lo,
To have Yes, choose No;

*

To feel thyself and be
His dear nonentity—
Caught
Beyond human thought

In the thunder-spout of Him,
Until thy being dim,
And be
Dead deathlessly.

Stoop, stoop; for thou dost fear
The nettle's wrathful spear,
So slight
Art thou of might!

Rise; for Heaven hath no frown
When thou to thee pluck'st down,
Strong clod!
The neck of God.

THE HOUND OF HEAVEN

I fled Him, down the nights and down the days;
I fled Him, down the arches of the years;
I fled Him, down the labyrinthine ways
Of my own mind; and in the mist of tears
I hid from Him, and under running laughter.
Up vistaed hopes I sped;
And shot, precipitated,
Adown Titanic glooms of chasmèd fears,
From those strong Feet that followed, followed after.
But with unhurrying chase,
And unperturbèd pace,
Deliberate speed, majestic instancy,
They beat—and a Voice beat
More instant than the Feet—
"All things betray thee, who betrayest Me."

I pleaded, outlaw-wise,
By many a hearted casement, curtained red,
Trellised with intertwining charities
(For, though I knew His love Who followèd,

Yet was I sore adread
Lest, having Him, I must have naught beside);
But, if one little casement parted wide,
The gust of His approach would clash it to:
Fear wist not to evade, as Love wist to pursue.
Across the margent of the world I fled,
And troubled the gold gateways of the stars,
Smiting for shelter on their clangèd bars;
Fretted to dulcet jars
And silvern chatter the pale ports o' the moon.
I said to Dawn: Be sudden—to Eve: Be soon;
With thy young skiey blossoms heap me over
From this tremendous Lover—
Float thy vague veil about me, lest He see!
I tempted all His servitors, but to find
My own betrayal in their constancy,
In faith to Him their fickleness to me,
Their traitorous trueness, and their loyal deceit.
To all swift things for swiftness did I sue;
Clung to the whistling mane of every wind.
But whether they swept, smoothly fleet,
The long savannahs of the blue;
Or whether, Thunder-driven,
They clanged his chariot 'thwart a heaven,
Plashy with flying lightnings round the spurn o' their feet:—
Fear wist not to evade as Love wist to pursue.
Still with unhurrying chase,
And unperturbèd pace,
Deliberate speed, majestic instancy,
Came on the following Feet,
And a Voice above their beat—
"Naught shelters thee, who wilt not shelter Me."

I sought no more that after which I strayed
In face of man or maid;
But still within the little children's eyes
Seems something, something that replies,
They at least are for me, surely for me!
I turned me to them very wistfully;
But just as their young eyes grew sudden fair
With dawning answers there,
Their angel plucked them from me by the hair.
"Come then, ye other children, Nature's—share
With me" (said I) "your delicate fellowship;
Let me greet you lip to lip,
Let me twine with you caresses,
Wantoning
With our Lady-Mother's vagrant tresses,
Banqueting

With her in her wind-walled palace,
Underneath her azured daïs,
Quaffing, as your taintless way is,
From a chalice
Lucent-weeping out of the dayspring."
So it was done:
I in their delicate fellowship was one—
Drew the bolt of Nature's secrecies.
I knew all the swift importings
On the willful face of skies;
I knew how the clouds arise
Spumèd of the wild sea-snortings;
All that's born or dies
Rose and drooped with; made them shapers
Of mine own moods, or wailful or divine;
With them joyed and was bereaven.
I was heavy with the even,
When she lit her glimmering tapers
Round the day's dead sanctities.
I laughed in the morning's eyes.
I triumphed and I saddened with all weather,
Heaven and I wept together,
And its sweet tears were salt with mortal mine;

Against the red throb of its sunset-heart
I laid my own to beat,
And share commingling heat;
But not by that, by that, was eased my human smart.
In vain my tears were wet on Heaven's gray cheek.
For ah! we know not what each other says,
These things and I; in sound *I* speak—
Their sound is but their stir, they speak by silences.
Nature, poor stepdame, cannot slake my drouth;
Let her, if she would owe me,
Drop yon blue bosom-veil of sky, and show me
The breasts o' her tenderness:
Never did any milk of hers once bless
My thirsting mouth.
Nigh and nigh draws the chase,
With unperturbèd pace,
Deliberate speed, majestic instancy;
And past those noisèd Feet
A Voice comes yet more fleet—
"Lo! naught contents thee, who content'st not Me."

'Naked I wait Thy love's uplifted stroke!
My harness piece by piece Thou hast hewn from me,
And smitten me to my knee;
I am defenseless utterly.
I slept, methinks, and woke,

And, slowly gazing, find me stripped in sleep.
In the rash lustihead of my young powers,
    I shook the pillaring hours
And pulled my life upon me; grimed with smears,
I stand amid the dust o' the mounded years—
My mangled youth lies dead beneath the heap.
My days have crackled and gone up in smoke,
Have puffed and burst as sun-starts on a stream.
    Yea, faileth now even dream
The dreamer, and the lute the lutanist;
Even the linked fantasies, in whose blossomy twist
I swung the earth a trinket at my wrist,
Are yielding; cords of all too weak account
For earth with heavy griefs so overplused.
    Ah! is Thy love indeed
A weed, albeit an amaranthine weed,
Suffering no flowers except its own to mount?
    Ah! must—
    Designer infinite!—
Ah! must Thou char the wood ere Thou canst limn with it?
My freshness spent its wavering shower i' the dust;
And now my heart is as a broken fount,
Wherein tear-drippings stagnate, spilt down ever
    From the dank thoughts that shiver
Upon the sighful branches of my mind.
    Such is; what is to be?
The pulp so bitter, how shall taste the rind?
I dimly guess what Time in mists confounds;
Yet ever and anon a trumpet sounds
From the hid battlements of Eternity;
Those shaken mists a space unsettle, then
Round the half-glimpsèd turrets slowly wash again.
    But not ere him who summoneth
    I first have seen, enwound
With glooming robes purpureal, cypress-crowned;
His name I know, and what his trumpet saith.
Whether man's heart or life it be which yields
    Thee harvest, must Thy harvest-fields
    Be dunged with rotten death?

      Now of that long pursuit
      Comes on at hand the bruit;
    That Voice is round me like a bursting sea:
      "And is thy earth so marred,
      Shattered in shard on shard?
    Lo, all things fly thee, for thou fliest Me!
    Strange, piteous, futile thing!
Wherefore should any set thee love apart?
Seeing none but I makes much of naught" (He said),
"And human love needs human meriting:
    How hast thou merited—

Of all man's clotted clay the dingiest clot?
Alack, thou knowest not
How little worthy of any love thou art!
Whom wilt thou find to love ignoble thee
Save Me, save only Me?
All which I took from thee I did but take,
Not for thy harms,
But just that thou might'st seek it in My arms.
All which thy child's mistake
Fancies as lost, I have stored for thee at home:
Rise, clasp My hand, and come!"

Halts by me that footfall:
Is my gloom, after all,
Shade of His hand, outstretched caressingly?
"Ah, fondest, blindest, weakest,
I am He Whom thou seekest!
Thou dravest love from thee, who dravest Me."

FROM "GRACE OF THE WAY"

Now of that vision I, bereaven,
This knowledge keep, that may not dim:
Short arm needs man to reach to Heaven,
So ready is Heaven to stoop to him.

TO OLIVIA

I fear to love thee, Sweet, because
Love's the ambassador of loss;
White flake of childhood, clinging so
To my soiled raiment, thy shy snow
At tenderest touch will shrink and go.
Love me not, delightful child.
My heart, by many snares beguiled,
Has grown timorous and wild.
It would fear thee not at all,
Wert thou not so harmless-small.
Because thy arrows, not yet dire,
Are still unbarbed with destined fire,
I fear thee more than hadst thou stood
Full-panoplied in womanhood.

"IN NO STRANGE LAND"[1]

O world invisible, we view thee,
O world intangible, we touch thee,
O world unknowable, we know thee,
Inapprehensible, we clutch thee!

Does the fish soar to find the ocean,
The eagle plunge to find the air—
That we ask of the stars in motion
If they have rumor of thee there?

Not where the wheeling systems darken,
And our benumbed conceiving soars!—
The drift of pinions, would we hearken,
Beats at our own clay-shuttered doors.

The angels keep their ancient places;
Turn but a stone, and start a wing!
'Tis ye, 'tis your estrangèd faces,
That miss the many-splendored thing.

But, when so sad thou canst not sadder,
Cry;—and upon thy so sore loss
Shall shine the traffic of Jacob's ladder
Pitched betwixt Heaven and Charing Cross.

Yea, in the night, my Soul, my daughter,
Cry,—clinging Heaven by the hems;
And lo, Christ walking on the water
Not of Gennesareth, but Thames!

[1] These verses, unpublished during his lifetime, were found among Francis Thompson's papers after his death.

ENVOY

Go, songs, for ended is our brief, sweet play;
  Go, children of swift joy and tardy sorrow:
And some are sung, and that was yesterday,
  And some unsung, and that may be tomorrow.

Go forth; and if it be o'er stony way,
  Old joy can lend what newer grief must borrow:
And it was sweet, and that was yesterday,
  And sweet is sweet, though purchasèd with sorrow.

Go, songs, and come not back from your far way:
  And if men ask you why ye smile and sorrow,
Tell them ye grieve, for your hearts know Today,
  Tell them ye smile, for your eyes know Tomorrow.

A. E. Housman

A(lfred) E(dward) Housman was born March 26, 1859, and educated at Oxford where he received his M.A. He was a Higher Division Clerk in the British Patent Office for ten years (1882-1892), leaving the office to become a teacher. Professor of Latin at University College, London, from 1892 to 1911, at Cambridge after 1911, one of the great classical scholars of his day, he died April 30, 1936.

In 1895 Housman offered for publication a manuscript entitled *Poems by Terence Hearsay*—a title which accounts for the personal reference in the "Epilogue" on page 100. The poems were rejected. Housman changed the title, and another publisher brought the book out as *A Shropshire Lad*. Only five hundred copies were printed; the publisher refused to print a second edition except at the poet's expense. The critical reception was fair, but sales were sluggish. It was not until 1914, during the war, that their militant masculine spirit made the poems immensely popular.

The extraordinary success of *A Shropshire Lad* is comparable to that of Fitzgerald's *Rubáiyát of Omar Khayyám*. Both works reveal a mood of pessimism and defeat. The philosophy would ordinarily have found little favor, but it was expressed in quotable phrases and captivating music. Fitzgerald and Housman wrote with such skill that they charmed readers who might otherwise have been repelled by the intellectual content of the poetry. The spell was woven less by the meaning than by the sheer charm of the brisk and brilliant measures.

A Shropshire Lad is limited in range and idea. Nature is not kind; lovers are untrue; men cheat and girls betray; lads, though lightfoot, drink and die; an occasional drum calls to a conflict without reason, a struggle without hope. Nevertheless, courage is dominant, declared over and over in such poems as "Réveillé," "When Smoke Stood Up from Ludlow," "The Chestnut Casts His Flambeaux," and Housman's bitter but fearless philosophy reaches the heights in his "Epilogue."

Purely as writing, however, *A Shropshire Lad* is incomparable. Owing nothing to any poet of his own generation and showing few influences other than Heine's, Housman's verse is condensed to the uttermost, stripped of every superfluous ornament, pared and precise. Not the least of his triumph is the mingling of pungent humor and poignance. Possibly the outstanding virtue is the seemingly artless but extraordinarily skillful simplicity of tone. This is song sharpened, acid-flavored, yet always song.

A Shropshire Lad was first published in 1896 when Housman was thirty-seven, although several of the lyrics were written when the poet was younger. After a silence of twenty-six years, there appeared his *Last Poems* (1922). The title is significant, Housman saying, "I publish these poems, few though they are, because it is not likely that I shall ever be impelled to write much more. I can no longer expect to be revisited by the continuous excitement under which in the early months of 1895 I wrote the greater part of my other book, nor indeed could I well sustain it if it came." Most of the second volume belongs to an earlier period, to the years between 1895 and 1910. Here in *Last Poems* the Shropshire lad lives again to pipe his mournful-merry tunes; here again the rose-lipt maiden kisses carelessly as ever, and the heart out of the bosom is given in vain. Here Wenlock Edge is still in trouble, young men shoulder the sky and face the hills whose comfort cannot delay "the beautiful and deathstruck year." The pessimism assumes a half-careless, half-heroic note.

A Shropshire Lad sounded the note of a wry surrender:

Be still, be still, my soul; it is but for a season:
  Let us endure an hour and see injustice done.

Aye, look, high heaven and earth ail from the prime foundation;
  All thoughts to rive the heart are here, and all in vain:
Horror and scorn and hate and fear and indignation—
  Oh, why did I awake? When shall I sleep again?

And in *Last Poems* the no less disillusioned spirit cries:

We of a certainty are not the first
  Have sat in taverns while the tempest hurled
Their hopeful plans to emptiness, and cursed
  Whatever brute or blackguard made the world.

The rhythms of *Last Poems* are a trifle slower, the cadences somewhat more acrid, but Housman's command of his instrument is still unfaltering. Some critics have pointed out Housman's "echoes" and John Sparrow, in *The Nineteenth Century,* has traced certain general resemblances and a few specific phrases to earlier writers, especially Shakespeare, Heine, and the Greek lyrists. But Housman's touch is so definitely his own, his accent so individualized that the occasional (and usually intentional) allusions are absorbed in the English poet's idiom. Who else could modernize the story of Jesus as concisely as Housman has done in "The Carpenter's Son"; who but he could have turned such simple material as "Loveliest of Trees" to the words and music of possibly the finest lyric in the English language? Each reader will have his favorites, and those admirers who know the two volumes almost by heart will even resent learning that Thomas Hardy considered "Is My Team Ploughing" one of the most dramatic short poems in the language.

A posthumous *More Poems* (1936) was edited by Housman's brother Laurence; this and the preceding volumes were assembled, together with some hitherto unpublished verse, in a comprehensive *Collected Poems* (1940). The introductions to his editions of Manilius, Juvenal, and Lucan reveal Housman's passion for chiseled form and his contempt for careless work. His scholarly papers are edged with sarcasm and bristle with cold contempt; he wrote of a certain teacher, "When X has acquired a scrap of misinformation he cannot rest till he has imparted it." A similar tone, trenchant and controversial, is heard in *The Name and Nature of Poetry* (1933), a lecture which conceals as much about the process of creation as it reveals. For example, when asked to define poetry Housman replied, "I could no more define poetry than a terrier can define a rat, but I thought we both recognized the object by the symptoms which it provokes in us. . . . Experience has taught me, when I am shaving, to keep watch over my thoughts, because if a line of poetry strays into my memory, my skin bristles so that the razor ceases to act." But it is as a poet that Housman will live, and his verse already seems marked for permanence. A dozen or more of his poems have the authority that comes only with age and tradition. They are fastidious; they are small; they are limited in range, restricted in outlook, and sometimes inflexible because of their overdisciplined line. But they haunt the mind, and many of them are as nearly perfect as lyrics can hope to be.

The most informative as well as the most informal account of Housman's life was written by Laurence Housman and entitled *My Brother, A. E. Housman.*

RÉVEILLÉ

Wake: the silver dusk returning
   Up the beach of darkness brims,
And the ship of sunrise burning
   Strands upon the eastern rims.

Wake: the vaulted shadow shatters,
   Trampled to the floor it spanned,
And the tent of night in tatters
   Straws the sky-pavilioned land.

Up, lad, up, 'tis late for lying:
   Hear the drums of morning play;
Hark, the empty highways crying
   "Who'll beyond the hills away?"

Towns and countries woo together,
   Forelands beacon, belfries call;
Never lad that trod on leather
   Lived to feast his heart with all.

Up, lad: thews that lie and cumber
   Sunlit pallets never thrive;
Morns abed and daylight slumber
   Were not meant for man alive.

Clay lies still, but blood's a rover;
  Breath's a ware that will not keep.
Up, lad: when the journey's over
  There'll be time enough to sleep.

WITH RUE MY HEART IS LADEN

With rue my heart is laden
  For golden friends I had,
For many a rose-lipt maiden
  And many a lightfoot lad.

By brooks too broad for leaping
  The lightfoot boys are laid;
The rose-lipt girls are sleeping
  In fields where roses fade.

INTO MY HEART

Into my heart an air that kills
  From yon far country blows:
What are those blue remembered hills,
  What spires, what farms are those?

That is the land of lost content,
  I see it shining plain:
The happy highways where I went
  And cannot come again.

WHEN I WAS ONE-AND-TWENTY

When I was one-and-twenty
  I heard a wise man say,
"Give crowns and pounds and guineas
  But not your heart away;
Give pearls away and rubies
  But keep your fancy free."
But I was one-and-twenty,
  No use to talk to me.

When I was one-and-twenty
  I heard him say again,
"The heart out of the bosom
  Was never given in vain;
'Tis paid with sighs a-plenty
  And sold for endless rue."
And I am two-and-twenty,
  And oh, 'tis true, 'tis true.

TO AN ATHLETE DYING YOUNG

The time you won your town the race
We chaired you through the market-place;
Man and boy stood cheering by,
And home we brought you shoulder-high.

Today, the road all runners come,
Shoulder-high we bring you home,
And set you at your threshold down,
Townsman of a stiller town.

Smart lad, to slip betimes away
From fields where glory does not stay,
And early though the laurel grows
It withers quicker than the rose.

Eyes the shady night has shut
Cannot see the record cut,
And silence sounds no worse than cheers
After earth has stopped the ears:

Now you will not swell the rout
Of lads that wore their honors out,
Runners whom renown outran
And the name died before the man.

So set, before its echoes fade,
The fleet foot on the sill of shade,
And hold to the low lintel up
The still-defended challenge-cup.

And round that early-laureled head
Will flock to gaze the strengthless dead,
And find unwithered on its curls
The garland briefer than a girl's.

LOVELIEST OF TREES

Loveliest of trees, the cherry now
Is hung with bloom along the bough,
And stands about the woodland ride
Wearing white for Eastertide.

Now, of my threescore years and ten,
Twenty will not come again,
And take from seventy springs a score,
It only leaves me fifty more.

And since to look at things in bloom
Fifty springs are little room,
About the woodlands I will go
To see the cherry hung with snow.

IS MY TEAM PLOUGHING

"Is my team ploughing,
  That I used to drive
And hear the harness jingle
  When I was man alive?"

Aye, the horses trample,
  The harness jingles now;
No change though you lie under
  The land you used to plough.

"Is football playing
  Along the river shore,
With lads to chase the leather,
  Now I stand up no more?"

Aye, the ball is flying,
  The lads play heart and soul;
The goal stands up, the keeper
  Stands up to keep the goal.

"Is my girl happy,
  That I thought hard to leave,
And has she tired of weeping
  As she lies down at eve?"

Aye, she lies down lightly,
  She lies not down to weep:
Your girl is well contented.
  Be still, my lad, and sleep.

"Is my friend hearty,
  Now I am thin and pine;
And has he found to sleep in
  A better bed than mine?"

Aye, lad, I lie easy,
  I lie as lads would choose;
I cheer a dead man's sweetheart.
  Never ask me whose.

WHEN SMOKE STOOD UP FROM LUDLOW

When smoke stood up from Ludlow,
  And mist blew off from Teme,
And blithe afield to ploughing
  Against the morning beam
  I strode beside my team,

The blackbird in the coppice
  Looked out to see me stride,
And hearkened as I whistled
  The trampling team beside,
  And fluted and replied:

"Lie down, lie down, young yeoman;
  What use to rise and rise?
Rise man a thousand mornings
  Yet down at last he lies,
  And then the man is wise."

I heard the tune he sang me,
  And spied his yellow bill;

I picked a stone and aimed it
And threw it with a will:
And then the bird was still.

Then my soul within me
Took up the blackbird's strain,
And still beside the horses
Along the dewy lane
It sang the song again:

"Lie down, lie down, young yeoman;
The sun moves always west;
The road one treads to labor
Will lead one home to rest,
And that will be the best."

WHEN I WATCH THE LIVING MEET

When I watch the living meet,
And the moving pageant file
Warm and breathing through the street
Where I lodge a little while,

If the heats of hate and lust
In the house of flesh are strong,
Let me mind the house of dust
Where my sojourn shall be long.

In the nation that is not
Nothing stands that stood before;
There revenges are forgot,
And the hater hates no more;

Lovers lying two and two
Ask not whom they sleep beside,
And the bridegroom all night through
Never turns him to the bride.

OH, SEE HOW THICK THE GOLDCUP FLOWERS

Oh, see how thick the goldcup flowers
Are lying in field and lane,
With dandelions to tell the hours
That never are told again,
Oh, may I squire you round the meads
And pick you posies gay?
—'Twill do no harm to take my arm.
"You may, young man, you may."

Ah, spring was sent for lass and lad,
'Tis now the blood runs gold,
And man and maid had best be glad
Before the world is old.
What flowers today may flower tomorrow,
But never as good as new.
—Suppose I wound my arm right round.
" 'Tis true, young man, 'tis true."

Some lads there are, 'tis shame to say,
That only court to thieve,
And once they bear the bloom away
'Tis little enough they leave.
Then keep your heart for men like me
And safe from trustless chaps.
My love is true and all for you.
"Perhaps, young man, perhaps."

Oh, look in my eyes then, can you doubt?
—Why, 'tis a mile from town.
How green the grass is all about!
We might as well sit down.
—Ah, life, what is it but a flower?
Why must true lovers sigh?
Be kind, have pity, my own, my pretty,—
"Good-by, young man, good-by."

THE LADS IN THEIR HUNDREDS

The lads in their hundreds to Ludlow come in for the fair,
There's men from the barn and the forge and the mill and the fold,
The lads for the girls and the lads for the liquor are there,
And there with the rest are the lads that will never be old.

There's chaps from the town and the field and the till and the cart,
And many to count are the stalwart, and many the brave,
And many the handsome of face and the handsome of heart,
And few that will carry their looks or their truth to the grave.

I wish one could know them, I wish there were tokens to tell
  The fortunate fellows that now you can never discern;
And then one could talk with them friendly and wish them farewell
  And watch them depart on the way that they will not return.

But now you may stare as you like and there's nothing to scan;
  And brushing your elbow unguessed-at and not to be told
They carry back bright to the coiner the mintage of man,
  The lads that will die in their glory and never be old.

WHEN THE LAD FOR LONGING SIGHS

When the lad for longing sighs,
  Mute and dull of cheer and pale,
If at death's own door he lies,
  Maiden, you can heal his ail.

Lovers' ills are all to buy:
  The wan look, the hollow tone,
The hung head, the sunken eye,
  You can have them for your own.

Buy them, buy them: eve and morn
  Lovers' ills are all to sell.
Then you can lie down forlorn;
  But the lover will be well.

THE IMMORTAL PART

Vhen I meet the morning beam,
)r lay me down at night to dream,
hear my bones within me say,
Another night, another day.

When shall this slough of sense be cast,
his dust of thoughts be laid at last,
he man of flesh and soul be slain
nd the man of bone remain?

This tongue that talks, these lungs that shout,
hese thews that hustle us about,
his brain that fills the skull with schemes,
nd its humming hive of dreams,—

These today are proud in power
nd lord it in their little hour:
ıe immortal bones obey control
dying flesh and dying soul.

" 'Tis long till eve and morn are gone:
Slow the endless night comes on,
And late to fullness grows the birth
That shall last as long as earth.

"Wanderers eastward, wanderers west,
Know you why you cannot rest?
'Tis that every mother's son
Travails with a skeleton.

"Lie down in the bed of dust;
Bear the fruit that bear you must;
Bring the eternal seed to light,
And morn is all the same as night.

"Rest you so from trouble sore,
Fear the heat o' the sun no more,
Nor the snowing winter wild,
Now you labor not with child.

"Empty vessel, garment cast,
We that wore you long shall last.
—Another night, another day."
  So my bones within me say.

Therefore they shall do my will
Today while I am master still,
And flesh and soul, now both are strong,
Shall hale the sullen slaves along,

Before this fire of sense decay,
This smoke of thought blow clean away,
And leave with ancient night alone
The steadfast and enduring bone.

ON WENLOCK EDGE

On Wenlock Edge the wood's in trouble;
His forest fleece the Wrekin heaves;
The gale, it plies the saplings double,
And thick on Severn snow the leaves.

'Twould blow like this through holt and hangar
When Uricon the city stood:
'Tis the old wind in the old anger,
But then it threshed another wood.

Then, 'twas before my time, the Roman
At yonder heaving hill would stare:
The blood that warms an English yeoman,
The thoughts that hurt him, they were there.

There, like the wind through woods in riot,
Through him the gale of life blew high;
The tree of man was never quiet:
Then 'twas the Roman, now 'tis I.

The gale, it plies the saplings double,
It blows so hard, 'twill soon be gone:
Today the Roman and his trouble
Are ashes under Uricon.

OH, WHEN I WAS IN LOVE WITH YOU

Oh, when I was in love with you,
Then I was clean and brave,
And miles around the wonder grew
How well did I behave.

And now the fancy passes by,
And nothing will remain,
And miles around they'll say that I
Am quite myself again.

ALONG THE FIELD AS WE CAME BY

Along the field as we came by
A year ago, my love and I,
The aspen over stile and stone
Was talking to itself alone.
"Oh, who are these that kiss and pass?
A country lover and his lass;
Two lovers looking to be wed;
And time shall put them both to bed,
But she shall lie with earth above,
And he beside another love."

And sure enough beneath the tree
There walks another love with me,
And overhead the aspen heaves
Its rainy-sounding silver leaves;
And I spell nothing in their stir,
But now perhaps they speak to her,
And plain for her to understand
They talk about a time at hand
When I shall sleep with clover clad,
And she beside another lad.

ON THE IDLE HILL OF SUMMER

On the idle hill of summer,
Sleepy with the flow of streams,
Far I hear the steady drummer
Drumming like a noise in dreams.

Far and near and low and louder
On the roads of earth go by,
Dear to friends and food for powder,
Soldiers marching, all to die.

East and west on fields forgotten
Bleach the bones of comrades slain,
Lovely lads and dead and rotten;
None that go return again.

Far the calling bugles hollo,
High the screaming fife replies,
Gay the files of scarlet follow:
Woman bore me, I will rise.

BREDON HILL

In summertime on Bredon
The bells they sound so clear;
Round both the shires they ring them
In steeples far and near,
A happy noise to hear.

Here of a Sunday morning
My love and I would lie,
And see the colored counties,
And hear the larks so high
About us in the sky.

The bells would ring to call her
In valleys miles away:
"Come all to church, good people;
Good people, come and pray."
But here my love would stay.

And I would turn and answer
Among the springing thyme,
"Oh, peal upon our wedding,

And we will hear the chime,
  And come to church in time."

But when the snows at Christmas
  On Bredon top were strown,
My love rose up so early
  And stole out unbeknown
  And went to church alone.

They tolled the one bell only,
  Groom there was none to see,
The mourners followed after,
  And so to church went she,
  And would not wait for me.

The bells they sound on Bredon,
  And still the steeples hum.
"Come all to church, good people,—"
  Oh, noisy bells, be dumb;
  I hear you, I will come.

LANCER

I 'listed at home for a lancer,
  Oh who would not sleep with the brave?
I 'listed at home for a lancer
  To ride on a horse to my grave.

And over the seas we were bidden
  A country to take and to keep;
And far with the brave I have ridden,
  And now with the brave I shall sleep.

For round me the men will be lying
  That learned me the way to behave,
And showed me my business of dying:
  Oh who would not sleep with the brave?

They ask and there is not an answer;
Says I, I will 'list for a lancer,
  Oh who would not sleep with the brave?

And I with the brave shall be sleeping
  At ease on my mattress of loam,
When back from their taking and keeping
  The squadron is riding at home.

The wind with the plumes will be playing,
  The girls will stand watching them wave,
And eyeing my comrades and saying
  Oh who would not sleep with the brave?

They ask and there is not an answer;
Says you, I will 'list for a lancer,
  O who would not sleep with the brave?

THE CHESTNUT CASTS HIS FLAMBEAUX, AND THE FLOWERS

The chestnut casts his flambeaux, and the flowers
  Stream from the hawthorn on the wind away,
The doors clap to, the pane is blind with showers.
  Pass me the can lad; there's an end of May.

There's one spoilt spring to scant our mortal lot,
  One season ruined of our little store.
May will be fine next year as like as not:
  Oh, aye, but then we shall be twenty-four.

We for a certainty are not the first
  Have sat in taverns while the tempest hurled
Their hopeful plans to emptiness, and cursed
  Whatever brute and blackguard made the world.

It is in truth iniquity on high
  To cheat our sentenced souls of aught they crave,
And mar the merriment as you and I
  Fare on our long fool's errand to the grave.

Iniquity it is; but pass the can.
  My lad, no pair of kings our mothers bore;
Our only portion is the estate of man:
  We want the moon, but we shall get no more.

If here today the cloud of thunder lours
Tomorrow it will hie on far behests;
The flesh will grieve on other bones than ours
Soon, and the soul will mourn in other breasts.

The troubles of our proud and angry dust
Are from eternity, and shall not fail.
Bear them we can, and if we can we must.
Shoulder the sky, my lad, and drink your ale.

EIGHT O'CLOCK

He stood, and heard the steeple
Sprinkle the quarters on the morning town.
One, two, three, four, to market-place and people
It tossed them down.

Strapped, noosed, nighing his hour,
He stood and counted them and cursed his luck;
And then the clock collected in the tower
Its strength, and struck.

EPILOGUE

"Terence, this is stupid stuff;
You eat your victuals fast enough;
There can't be much amiss, 'tis clear,
To see the rate you drink your beer.
But oh, good Lord, the verse you make,
It gives a chap the belly-ache.
The cow, the old cow, she is dead;
It sleeps well, the horned head:
We poor lads, 'tis our turn now
To hear such tunes as killed the cow.
Pretty friendship 'tis to rhyme
Your friends to death before their time
Moping melancholy mad:
Come, pipe a tune to dance to, lad."

Why, if 'tis dancing you would be,
There's brisker pipes than poetry.
Say, for what were hop-yards meant,
Or why was Burton built on Trent?
Oh, many a peer of England brews
Livelier liquor than the Muse,
And malt does more than Milton can
To justify God's ways to man.
Ale, man, ale's the stuff to drink
For fellows whom it hurts to think:
Look into the pewter pot
To see the world as the world's not.
And faith, 'tis pleasant till 'tis past:
The mischief is that 'twill not last.
Oh, I have been to Ludlow fair
And left my necktie God knows where.
And carried half way home, or near,
Pints and quarts of Ludlow beer:
Then the world seemed none so bad,
And I myself a sterling lad;
And down in lovely muck I've lain,
Happy till I woke again.
Then I saw the morning sky:
Heigho, the tale was all a lie;
The world, it was the old world yet,
I was I, my things were wet,
And nothing now remained to do
But begin the game anew.

Therefore, since the world has still
Much good, but much less good than ill,
And while the sun and moon endure
Luck's a chance, but trouble's sure,
I'd face it as a wise man would,
And train for ill and not for good.
'Tis true, the stuff I bring for sale
Is not so brisk a brew as ale:
Out of a stem that scored the hand
I wrung it in a weary land.
But take it: if the smack is sour,
The better for the embittered hour;

It should do good to heart and head
When your soul is in my soul's stead;
And I will friend you, if I may,
In the dark and cloudy day.

There was a king reigned in the East:
There, when kings will sit to feast,
They get their fill before they think
With poisoned meat and poisoned drink.
He gathered all that springs to birth
From the many-venomed earth;
First a little, thence to more,
He sampled all her killing store;
And easy, smiling, seasoned sound,
Sate the king when healths went round.
They put arsenic in his meat
And stared aghast to watch him eat;
They poured strychnine in his cup
And shook to see him drink it up:
They shook, they stared as white's their
  shirt:
Them it was their poison hurt.
I tell the tale that I heard told.
Mithridates, he died old.

OTHERS, I AM NOT THE FIRST

Others, I am not the first,
Have willed more mischief than they durst:
If in the breathless night I too
Shiver now, 'tis nothing new.

More than I, if truth were told,
Have stood and sweated hot and cold,
And through their reins in ice and fire
Fear contended with desire.

Agued once like me were they,
But I like them shall win my way
Lastly to the bed of mould
Where there's neither heat nor cold.

But from my grave across my brow
Plays no wind of healing now,
And fire and ice within me fight
Beneath the suffocating night.

THE CARPENTER'S SON

Here the hangman stops his cart:
Now the best of friends must part
Fare you well, for ill fare I:
Live, lads, and I will die.

"Oh, at home had I but stayed
'Prenticed to my father's trade,
Had I stuck to plane and adze,
I had not been lost, my lads.

"Then I might have built perhaps
Gallows-trees for other chaps,
Never dangled on my own,
Had I but left ill alone.

"Now, you see, they hang me high,
And the people passing by
Stop to shake their fists and curse;
So 'tis come from ill to worse.

"Here hang I, and right and left
Two poor fellows hang for theft:
All the same's the luck we prove,
Though the midmost hangs for love.

"Comrades, all, that stand and gaze,
Walk henceforth in other ways;
See my neck and save your own:
Comrades all, leave ill alone.

"Make some day a decent end,
Shrewder fellows than your friend.
Fare you well, for ill fare I:
Live, lads, and I will die."

BE STILL, MY SOUL, BE STILL

Be still, my soul, be still; the arms you bear are brittle,
  Earth and high heaven are fixt of old and founded strong.
Think rather,—call to thought, if now you grieve a little,
  The days when we had rest, O soul, for they were long.

Men loved unkindness then, but lightless in the quarry
  I slept and saw not; tears fell down, I did not mourn;
Sweat ran and blood sprang out and I was never sorry:
  Then it was well with me, in days ere I was born.

Now, and I muse for why and never find the reason,
I pace the earth, and drink the air, and feel the sun.
Be still, be still, my soul; it is but for a season:
Let us endure an hour and see injustice done.

Ay, look: high heaven and earth ail from the prime foundation;
All thoughts to rive the heart are here, and all are vain:
Horror and scorn and hate and fear and indignation—
Oh, why did I awake? When shall I sleep again?

FROM FAR, FROM EVE

From far, from eve and morning
And yon twelve-winded sky,
The stuff of life to knit me
Blew hither: here am I.

Now—for a breath I tarry
Nor yet disperse apart—
Take my hand quick and tell me,
What have you in your heart.

Speak now, and I will answer;
How shall I help you, say;
Ere to the wind's twelve quarters
I take my endless way.

I HOED AND TRENCHED

I hoed and trenched and weeded,
And took the flowers to fair:
I brought them home unheeded;
The hue was not the wear.

So up and down I sow them
For lads like me to find,
When I shall lie below them,
A dead man out of mind.

Some seeds the birds devour,
And some the season mars,
But here and there will flower
The solitary stars,

And fields will yearly bear them
As light-leaved spring comes on,
And luckless lads will wear them
When I am dead and gone.

THE ISLE OF PORTLAND

The star-filled stars are smooth tonight
From France to England strown;
Black towers above the Portland light
The felon-quarried stone.

On yonder island, not to rise,
Never to stir forth free,
Far from his folk a dead lad lies
That once was friends with me.

Lie you easy, dream you light,
And sleep you fast for aye;
And luckier may you find the night
Than ever you found the day.

THE LAWS OF GOD, THE LAWS OF MAN

The laws of God, the laws of man,
He may keep that will and can;
Not I: let God and man decree
Laws for themselves and not for me;
And if my ways are not as theirs
Let them mind their own affairs.
Their deed I judge and much condemn,
Yet when did I make laws for them?
Please yourselves, say I, and they
Need only look the other way.
But no, they will not; they must still
Wrest their neighbour to their will,
And make me dance as they desire
With jail and gallows and hell-fire.
And how am I to face the odds
Of man's bedevilment and God's?
I, a stranger and afraid
In a world I never made.
They will be master, right or wrong;
Though both are foolish, both are strong
And since, my soul, we cannot fly
To Saturn nor to Mercury,
Keep we must, if keep we can,
These foreign laws of God and man.

THE NEW MISTRESS

"Oh, sick I am to see you, will you never let me be?
You may be good for something, but you are not good for me.
Oh, go where you are wanted, for you are not wanted here."
And that was all the farewell when I parted from my dear.

I will go where I am wanted, to a lady born and bred
Who will dress me free for nothing in a uniform of red;
She will not be sick to see me if I only keep it clean:
I will go where I am wanted for a soldier of the Queen.

I will go where I am wanted, for the sergeant does not mind;
He may be sick to see me but he treats me very kind:
He gives me beer and breakfast and a ribbon for my cap,
And I never knew a sweetheart spend her money on a chap.

I will go where I am wanted, where there's room for one or two,
And the men are none too many for the work there is to do;
Where the standing line wears thinner and the dropping dead lie thick;
And the enemies of England, they shall see me and be sick.

FAREWELL

"Farewell to barn and stack and tree,
  Farewell to Severn shore.
Terence, look your last at me,
  For I come home no more.

"The sun burns on the half-mown hill,
  By now the blood is dried;
And Maurice among the hay lies still
  And my knife is in his side.

"My mother thinks us long away;
  'Tis time the field were mown.
She had two sons at rising day,
  To-night she'll be alone.

"And here's a bloody hand to shake,
  And oh, man, here's good-bye;
We'll sweat no more on scythe and rake,
  My bloody hands and I.

"I wish you strength to bring you pride,
  And love to keep you clean,
And I wish you luck, come Lammastide,
  At racing on the green.

"Long for me the rick will wait,
  And long will wait the fold,
And long will stand the empty plate,
  And dinner will be cold."

William Butler Yeats

⸎ William Butler Yeats, son of John B. Yeats, the Irish artist, was born at Sandymount, Ireland, June 13, 1865. He studied art for a short time at the Royal Dublin Society, but his childhood was spent in the wild district of Sligo. He was educated at Godolphin School, Hammersmith, and Erasmus Smith School, Dublin. In 1888 he came to London where he lived many years. Later in life he spent much time abroad, in Paris, on the Italian Riviera, always returning to his Ireland as the source of his inspiration. He died, after a brief illness, at Roquebrune, near Nice, January 28, 1939; his body was taken to his native Ireland.

It is not easy to summarize Yeats' contribution, for his activities have been so varied and his work does not divide in fixed periods nor fit into convenient categories. He was folk-lorist, playwright, pamphleteer, editor, experimenter in Spiritualism—and above these rôles, prompting them all, he was a poet.

In the capacity of folk-lorist he prepared the collections of old wives' tales and mythical legends: *Fairy and Folk Tales* (1888) and *Representative Irish Tales* (1891). As essayist he wrote *The Celtic Twilight* (1893); as editor he collaborated with Edwin T. Ellis on an invaluable edition of *The Works of William Blake* (1893); as playwright, he helped organize a native theater and impel the movement known as the Celtic revival.

It was through the "Young Ireland" society that Yeats became identified with an Irish literary theater. He dreamed of a national poetry which would be traditional yet dramatic, written in simple English but spiritually Irish. He founded and edited a paper, the first number appearing in May, 1899, to expound his views. He collaborated with George Moore, with whom he had become associated, wrote his first original play in prose, *Katheleen ni Houlihan* (1902), and became one of the leaders of the movement, his chief associates being J. M. Synge, Douglas Hyde, Moore, and Lady Gregory. He worked incessantly for the cause both as propagandist and playwright; his *Plays for an Irish Theatre* (1913) containing *Where There Is Nothing, The Hour-Glass, Kathleen ni Houlihan, The Pot of Broth, The King's Threshold,* and *On Baile's Strand.*

Others who followed Yeats intensified the Irish drama; they established a closer contact between the peasant and poet. No one, however, had so great a part as Yeats in the actual shaping of modern drama in Ireland. His *Deirdre* (1907), a beautiful retelling of the great Gaelic legend, is far more dramatic than the earlier plays; it is particularly interesting to read as a complement to Synge's more idiomatic play on the same theme, *Deirdre of the Sorrows.*

The poet was already at work—*Mosada: A Poem* was published in 1886, in Yeats' twenty-first year—but he was not yet ready to declare himself definitely. Before his verse marked the rise of a new Irish school he was one of the group contributing to the *fin de siècle* publication *The Yellow Book;* he became the friend of Lionel Johnson and Oscar Wilde, and with them founded the Rhymer's Club; he was represented in both its anthologies. But, as he has told in his autobiographical volumes, *Reveries over Childhood and Youth* (1915) and *The Trembling of the*

Veil (1922), he was forced to walk about London because he could not afford the bus fare, and tea with hospitable friends was not only a social function but a meal that kept him from days of hunger. Accepting his enforced asceticism he turned it into a discipline, and those critics who consider his mysticism a later affectation might well study this period of Yeats' life and trace its essential reality.

It was in London, at the age of twenty-four, that he decided to devote himself to poetry, and it was there that his first representative volume was published in 1889, *The Wanderings of Oisin.* There appeared in rapid succession *The Countess Kathleen and Various Lyrics* (1892), a drama with appended verses; *A Book of Irish Verse* (1895); *The Wind Among the Reeds* (1899), which contains some of Yeats' finest early lyrics; and *The Shadowy Waters* (1900), another poetic play.

By this time Yeats had established himself as a poet of delicate effects and inconclusive loveliness. His was both a vague and personal music—the translation of faery charms and elfin songs into traditionally romantic yet highly individualized lyrics. The very music of the early lyrics—favored by those who prefer sensuousness to depth of feeling—is a limitation. They are almost too musical; they sacrifice strength of thought and utterance to limpidity. In this period Yeats presumably depended on a small set of colorful symbols, symbols which were both arbitrary and facile. It seemed that Yeats had found his métier and that he would continue to sound the charming if restricted gamut of fancy. But the poet revolted against fancifulness; he turned away from the comfort of sheer sentiment and the reliance on rhetoric. "Sentimentality," he said, "is deceiving one's self; rhetoric is deceiving other people."

With *Responsibilities* (1914) and *The Wild Swans at Coole* (1919) a change in tone is immediately apparent. The idiom is sharper, the imagery sparser. The language, no longer richly colored, is almost bare of ornament, the tone pitched on a conversational plane. This contrast to the earlier poetry was emphasized in *Later Poems* (1922), *Michael Robartes and the Dancer* (1923), *The Tower* (1928), and *The Winding Stair* (1932). One likes to believe that it was the later work which won Yeats the Nobel Prize for literature in 1924. In the comprehensive *Collected Poems* of 1933 the complete change is fully revealed not only in the quality of the later work but in the alterations Yeats had made in the earlier poems, often substituting the exact and sometimes harsh word for the smooth and dreamlike one.

In changing the wavering outlines of his poetry to a more rigorous line Yeats did not sacrifice music. On the contrary, the revisions disclose a music which is, at the same time, subtler and more precise. The poet has freed himself from his preoccupations with shadowy waters, Gaelic gods, and the mystic Rose's multiple meanings; he has emerged from his "labyrinth of images." Not that he has discarded symbolism, but his symbols now have a greater value; they are intellectually finer and firmer. Originally influenced by Blake and the French Symbolists, he finally accomplished a "more subtle rhythm, a more organic form."

I made my song a coat
Covered with embroideries
Out of old mythologies
From heel to throat;
But the fools caught it,

Wore it in the world's eyes
As though they'd wrought it.
Song, let them take it,
For there's more enterprise
In walking naked.

Here Yeats says explicitly what so many of the later poems imply. He repudiates his imitators and mocks his own early mythological manner. Instead of the purple patches and the multicolored "cloths of Heaven" Yeats seems less interested in talking to poets and more concerned with the simple people he used to live among. Desire for direct communication must have prompted such a poem as the one which begins

Although I see him still
The freckled man who goes
To a gray place on the hill

and ends

I shall have written him one
Poem maybe as cold
And passionate as the dawn.

"Leda" (a modern poem in spite of its classical subject), "The Wild Swans at Coole," some of the political poems, "Among School Children," and "Sailing to Byzantium" are among the many verses illustrating the deeper contemplative manner with which "the last of the romantics," as Yeats called himself, rose from remote fantasies into immediate experience. More intensely self-searching the poet turns, regretfully but resolutely, to a new set of symbols expressing his adjustment with the actual world. "Sailing to Byzantium" shows the conflict and its solution with particular clarity. Cleanth Brooks, in "A Note on Symbol and Conceit" (in *The American Review* for May, 1934), summarizes it thus: "The poet's own country is a land of natural beauty, beauty of the body. But his own body is old. The soul must, therefore, sing the louder to compensate for the old and dying flesh.

An aged man is but a paltry thing,
A tattered coat upon a stick, unless
Soul clap its hands and sing, and louder sing
For every tatter in its mortal dress.

But there is no singing school for the soul except in studying the works of the soul. 'And therefore' he has sailed to Byzantium, for the artists of Byzantium do not follow the forms of nature but intellectual forms, ideal patterns. He appears to them to

Consume my heart away; sick with desire
And fastened to a dying animal

and by severing him from the dying world of the body, to gather him into what is at least 'the artifice of eternity.'

"A comparison of this clumsy paraphrase with the poem in its entirety illustrates better than anything else why the poet must write as he does—how much we lose by substituting concepts for his richer 'symbols.' Byzantium is, for instance, a very rich symbol. It may be thought a very indefinite one. But richness and complexity are not vagueness, and it will be easy to show that the symbol has its precision. It means many things, but if one misses the connection with intellectual art, one has missed the poem. The whole poem demands, as do the poems of Donne and Marvell, mental agility on the part of the reader."

As Yeats grew old his intellectual power increased. "I am content to follow to its source every event in action or in thought," Yeats wrote in "A Dialogue of Self and Soul," and he concluded the poem with Blake-like divination:

> When such as I cast out remorse
> So great a sweetness flows into the breast
> We must laugh and we must sing,
> We are blest by everything,
> Everything we look upon is blest.

The Winding Stair (1932), *The King of the Great Clock Tower* (1935), published in Yeats's seventieth year, and the posthumous *Last Poems and Plays* (1940), contain the utterances of a man not afraid to taste unpalatable truths and even less afraid to say that they are bitter. The later poems are weighted with a sense of isolation, with the disillusionments of the age—and of old age—with defeated dreams, with the decay of beauty, with the death of friends, and the degeneration of the contemporary world. Yet, though Yeats voiced his horror and even his disgust in the later work, he did not despair. The ladder of happy fantasy was gone, but, even at the end, he was willing to begin the long ascent again.

> "I must lie down where all the ladders start,
> In the foul rag-and-bone shop of the heart."

Letters on Poetry from W. B. Yeats to Dorothy Wellesley (1940) posthumously reveal the poet's limitations, prejudices, and persuasions. But the ordinary reader will be fascinated by the mingled wit and profundity. The letters are studded with such epigrams as: "People much occupied with morality always lose heroic ecstasy." "The correction of prose, because it has no fixed laws, is endless; a poem comes right with a click like a closing box." Yeats distrusted change, yet he shifted his point of view as radically as he changed his idiom. He learned to suspect national panaceas and millennial dreams; in "The Second Coming" he wrote:

> Mere anarchy is loosed upon the world,
> The blood-dimmed tide is loosed, and everywhere
> The ceremony of innocence is drowned;
> The best lack all conviction, while the worst
> Are full of passionate intensity.

Failing to find any certainty in politics, he sought for solutions in occult lore, in spiritualism, even in crystal-gazing. To the last he held that "nature, races, and individual men are unified by an image," and insisted that when men desert one myth they will substitute another. This is proved by his verse. If his symbolism is complicated and questionable, the directness of his best poetry is undeniable.

Yeats's own memories and meditations are in his *Autobiographies* (1926). Joseph Hone wrote the poet's official biography, but the best analyses of his work are in Edmund Wilson's *Axel's Castle* (1931), Stephen Spender's *The Destructive Element* (1935), David Daiches's *Poetry and the Modern World* (1940), and Richard Ellmann's scholarly and intensive study, *Yeats: The Man and the Masks* (1948).

THE LAKE ISLE OF INNISFREE

I will arise and go now, and go to Innisfree,
And a small cabin build there, of clay and wattles made;
Nine bean rows will I have there, a hive for the honey bee,
And live alone in the bee-loud glade.

And I shall have some peace there, for peace comes dropping slow,
Dropping from the veils of the morning to where the cricket sings;
There midnight's all a glimmer, and noon a purple glow,
And evening full of the linnet's wings.

I will arise and go now, for always night and day
I hear lake water lapping with low sounds by the shore;
While I stand on the roadway, or on the pavements gray,
I hear it in the deep heart's core.

AEDH WISHES FOR THE CLOTHS OF HEAVEN

Had I the heavens' embroidered cloths,
Enwrought with golden and silver light,
The blue and the dim and the dark cloths
Of night and light and the half-light,
I would spread the cloths under your feet:
But I, being poor, have only my dreams;
I have spread my dreams under your feet;
Tread softly because you tread on my dreams.

THE SONG OF WANDERING AENGUS

I went out to the hazel wood,
Because a fire was in my head,
And cut and peeled a hazel wand,
And hooked a berry to a thread,
And when white moths were on the wing,
And moth-like stars were flickering out,
I dropped the berry in a stream
And caught a little silver trout.

When I had laid it on the floor
I went to blow the fire a-flame,
But something rustled on the floor,
And someone called me by my name:
It had become a glimmering girl
With apple blossoms in her hair
Who called me by my name and ran
And faded through the brightening air.

Though I am old with wandering
Through hollow lands and hilly lands,

I will find out where she has gone,
And kiss her lips and take her hands;
And walk among long dappled grass,
And pluck till time and times are done,
The silver apples of the moon,
The golden apples of the sun.

AEDH TELLS OF THE ROSE IN HIS HEART

All things uncomely and broken, all things worn out and old,
The cry of a child by the roadway, the creak of a lumbering cart,
The heavy steps of the plowman, splashing the wintry mold,
Are wronging your image that blossoms a rose in the deeps of my heart.

The wrong of unshapely things is a wrong too great to be told;
I hunger to build them anew and sit on a green knoll apart,
With the earth and the sky and the water, remade, like a casket of gold
For my dreams of your image that blossoms a rose in the deeps of my heart.

FAIRY SONG

(*from "The Land of Heart's Desire"*)

The wind blows out of the gates of the day,
The wind blows over the lonely of heart,
And the lonely of heart is withered away,
While the faëries dance in a place apart,
Shaking their milk-white feet in a ring,
Tossing their milk-white arms in the air:
For they hear the wind laugh, and murmur and sing
Of a land where even the old are fair,
And even the wise are merry of tongue;
But I heard a reed of Coolaney say,
"When the wind has laughed and murmured and sung,
The lonely of heart is withered away!"

WHEN YOU ARE OLD

When you are old and gray and full of sleep,
And nodding by the fire, take down this book,
And slowly read, and dream of the soft look
Your eyes had once, and of their shadows deep;

How many loved your moments of glad grace,
And loved your beauty with love false or true;
But one man loved the pilgrim soul in you,
And loved the sorrows of your changing face.

And bending down beside the glowing bars
Murmur, a little sadly, how love fled
And paced upon the mountains overhead
And hid his face amid a crowd of stars.

THE CAP AND BELLS

A Queen was beloved by a jester,
  And once when the owls grew still
He made his soul go upward
  And stand on her window sill.

In a long and straight blue garment,
  It talked before morn was white,
And it had grown wise by thinking
  Of a footfall hushed and light.

But the young queen would not listen;
  She rose in her pale nightgown,
She drew in the brightening casement
  And pushed the brass bolt down.

He bade his heart go to her,
  When the bats cried out no more,
In a red and quivering garment
  It sang to her through the door.

The tongue of it sweet with dreaming
  Of a flutter of flower-like hair,
But she took up her fan from the table
  And waved it off on the air.

"I've cap and bells," he pondered,
  "I will send them to her and die."
And as soon as the morn had whitened
  He left them where she went by.

She laid them upon her bosom,
  Under a cloud of her hair,
And her red lips sang them a love song.
  The stars grew out of the air.

She opened her door and her window,
  And the heart and the soul came through,
To her right hand came the red one,
  To her left hand came the blue.

They set up a noise like crickets,
  A chattering wise and sweet,
And her hair was a folded flower,
  And the quiet of love her feet.

THE INDIAN UPON GOD

I passed along the water's edge below the humid trees,
My spirit rocked in evening light, the rushes round my knees,
My spirit rocked in sleep and sighs; and saw the moorfowl pace
All dripping on a grassy slope, and saw them cease to chase
Each other round in circles, and heard the eldest speak:
Who holds the world between His bill and made us strong or weak
Is an undying moorfowl, and He lives beyond the sky.
The rains are from His dripping wing, the moonbeams from His eye.
I passed a little further on and heard a lotus talk:
Who made the world and ruleth it, He hangeth on a stalk,
For I am in His image made, and all this tinkling tide
Is but a sliding drop of rain between His petals wide.
A little way within the gloom a roebuck raised his eyes
Brimful of starlight, and he said: *The Stamper of the Skies,*
He is a gentle roebuck; for how else, I pray, could He
Conceive a thing so sad and soft, a gentle thing like me?
I passed a little further on and heard a peacock say:
Who made the grass and made the worms and made my feathers gay,
He is a monstrous peacock, and He waveth all the night
His languid tail above us, lit with myriad spots of light.

AN OLD SONG RESUNG[1]

Down by the salley gardens my love and I did meet;
She passed the salley gardens with little snow-white feet.
She bid me take love easy, as the leaves grow on the tree;
But I, being young and foolish, with her would not agree.

In a field by the river my love and I did stand,
And on my leaning shoulder she laid her snow-white hand.
She bid me take life easy, as the grass grows on the weirs;
But I was young and foolish, and now am full of tears.

THE ROSE OF THE WORLD

Who dreamed that beauty passes like a dream?
  For these red lips, with all their mournful pride,
  Mournful that no new wonder may betide,
Troy passed away in one high funeral gleam,
  And Usna's children died.

We and the laboring world are passing by:
  Amid men's souls, that waver and give place,
  Like the pale waters in their wintry race,
Under the passing stars, frame of the sky,
  Lives on this lonely face.

Bow down, archangels, in your dim abode:
Before you were, or any hearts to beat,
  Weary and kind, one lingered by His seat;
He made the world to be a grassy road
  Before her wandering feet.

THE SORROW OF LOVE

The quarrel of the sparrows in the eaves,
The full round moon and the star-laden sky,
And the loud song of the ever-singing leaves,
Has hid away earth's old and weary cry.

And then you came with those red mournful lips,
And with you came the whole of the world's tears,
And all the trouble of her laboring ships,
And all the trouble of her myriad years.

And now the sparrows warring in the eaves,
The curd-pale moon, the white stars in the sky,
And the loud chaunting of the unquiet leaves,
Are shaken with earth's old and weary cry.

[1] "This," Yeats wrote in a footnote in one of the early editions, "is an extension of three lines sung to me by an old woman of Ballisodare."

THE SONG OF THE OLD MOTHER

I rise in the dawn, and I kneel and blow
Till the seed of the fire flicker and glow.
And then I must scrub, and bake, and sweep,
Till stars are beginning to blink and peep;
But the young lie long and dream in their bed
Of the matching of ribbons, the blue and the red,
And their day goes over in idleness,
And they sigh if the wind but lift up a tress.
While I must work, because I am old
And the seed of the fire gets feeble and cold.

THE BALLAD OF FATHER GILLIGAN

The old priest Peter Gilligan
Was weary night and day;
For half his flock were in their beds,
Or under green sods lay.

Once, while he nodded on a chair,
At the moth-hour of eve,
Another poor man sent for him,
And he began to grieve.

"I have no rest, nor joy, nor peace,
"For people die and die";
And after cried he, "God forgive!
"My body spake, not I."

He knelt, and leaning on the chair
He prayed and fell asleep;
And the moth-hour went from the fields,
And stars began to peep.

They slowly into millions grew,
And leaves shook in the wind;
And God covered the world with shade,
And whispered to mankind.

Upon the time of sparrow chirp
When the moths came once more,
The old priest Peter Gilligan
Stood upright on the floor.

"Mavrone, mavrone! the man has died,
"While I slept on the chair";
He roused his horse out of its sleep
And rode with little care.

He rode now as he never rode,
By rocky lane and fen;
The sick man's wife opened the door;
"Father! You come again!"

"And is the poor man dead?" he cried.
"He died an hour ago."
The old priest Peter Gilligan
In grief swayed to and fro.

"When you were gone, he turned and died
"As merry as a bird."
The old priest Peter Gilligan
He knelt him at that word.

"He who hath made the night of stars
"For souls, who tire and bleed,
"Sent one of His great angels down
"To help me in my need.

"He who is wrapped in purple robes,
"With planets in His care,
"Had pity on the least of things
"Asleep upon a chair."

THE WILD SWANS AT COOLE

The trees are in their autumn beauty,
The woodland paths are dry,
Under the October twilight the water
Mirrors a still sky;

Upon the brimming water among the stones
Are nine and fifty swans.

The nineteenth Autumn has come upon me
Since I first made my count;
I saw, before I had well finished,
All suddenly mount
And scatter, wheeling, in great broken rings
Upon their clamorous wings.

I have looked upon those brilliant creatures,
And now my heart is sore.
All's changed since I, hearing at twilight,
The first time on this shore,
The bell-beat of their wings above my head,
Trod with a lighter tread.

Unwearied still, lover by lover,
They paddle in the cold,
Companionable streams or climb the air;
Their hearts have not grown old;
Passion or conquest, wander where they will,
Attend upon them still.

But now they drift on the still water
Mysterious, beautiful;
Among what rushes will they build,
By what lake's edge or pool
Delight men's eyes, when I awake some day
To find they have flown away?

LEDA AND THE SWAN

A sudden blow: the great wings beating still
Above the staggering girl, her thighs caressed
By the dark webs, her nape caught in his bill,
He holds her helpless breast upon his breast.

How can those terrified vague fingers push
The feathered glory from her loosening thighs?
And how can body, laid in that white rush,
But feel the strange heart beating where it lies?

A shudder in the loins engenders there
The broken wall, the burning roof and tower
And Agamemnon dead.

Being so caught up,
So mastered by the brute blood of the air,
Did she put on his knowledge with his power
Before the indifferent beak could let her drop?

SAILING TO BYZANTIUM

I

That is no country for old men. The young
In one another's arms, birds in the trees,
—Those dying generations—at their song,
The salmon-falls, the mackerel-crowded seas,
Fish, flesh, or fowl, commend all summer long
Whatever is begotten, born, and dies.
Caught in that sensual music all neglect
Monuments of unaging intellect.

II

An aged man is but a paltry thing,
A tattered coat upon a stick, unless
Soul clap its hands and sing, and louder sing
For every tatter in its mortal dress,
Nor is there singing school but studying
Monuments of its own magnificence;
And therefore I have sailed the seas and come
To the holy city of Byzantium.

III

O sages standing in God's holy fire
As in the gold mosaic of a wall,
Come from the holy fire, perne [1] in a gyre,
And be the singing-masters of my soul.
Consume my heart away; sick with desire
And fastened to a dying animal
It knows not what it is; and gather me
Into the artifice of eternity.

IV

Once out of nature I shall never take
My bodily form from any natural thing,
But such a form as Grecian goldsmiths make
Of hammered gold and gold enameling
To keep a drowsy Emperor awake;
Or set upon a golden bough to sing
To lords and ladies of Byzantium
Of what is past, or passing, or to come.

AMONG SCHOOL CHILDREN

I

I walk through the long schoolroom questioning;
A kind old nun in a white hood replies;
The children learn to cipher and to sing,
To study reading-books and history,

[1] Perne: Change attitude.

To cut and sew, be neat in everything
In the best modern way—the children's eyes
In momentary wonder stare upon
A sixty-year-old smiling public man.

II

I dream of a Ledaean body, bent
Above a sinking fire, a tale that she
Told of a harsh reproof, or trivial event
That changed some childish day to tragedy—
Told, and it seemed that our two natures blent
Into a sphere from youthful sympathy,
Or else, to alter Plato's parable,
Into the yolk and white of the one shell.

III

And thinking of that fit of grief or rage
I look upon one child or t'other there
And wonder if she stood so at that age—
For even daughters of the swan can share
Something of every paddler's heritage—
And had that color upon cheek or hair,
And thereupon my heart is driven wild:
She stands before me as a living child.

IV

Her present image floats into the mind—
Did Quattrocento finger fashion it
Hollow of a cheek as though it drank the wind
And took a mess of shadows for its meat?
And I though never of Ledaean kind
Had pretty plumage once—enough of that,
Better to smile on all that smile, and show
There is a comfortable kind of scarecrow.

V

What youthful mother, a shape upon her lap
Honey of generation had betrayed,
And that must sleep, shriek, struggle to escape
As recollection or the drug decide,
Would think her son, did she but see that shape
With sixty or more winters on its head,
A compensation for the pang of his birth,
Or the uncertainty of his setting forth?

VI

Plato thought nature but a spume that plays
Upon a ghostly paradigm of things;
Soldier Aristotle played the taws
Upon the bottom of a king of kings;

World-famous golden-thighed Pythagoras
Fingered upon a fiddle-stick or strings
What a star sang and careless Muses heard:
Old clothes upon old sticks to scare a bird.

VII

Both nuns and mothers worship images,
But those the candles light are not as those
That animate a mother's reveries,
But keep a marble or a bronze repose.
And yet they too break hearts—O Presences
That passion, piety or affection knows,
And that all heavenly glory symbolize—
O self-born mockers of man's enterprise;

VIII

Labor is blossoming or dancing where
The body is not bruised to pleasure soul,
Nor beauty born out of its own despair,
Nor blear-eyed wisdom out of midnight oil
O Chestnut tree, great rooted blossomer,
Are you the leaf, the blossom or the bole?
O body swayed to music, O brightening glance,
How can we know the dancer from the dance?

THE LEADERS OF THE CROWD

They must to keep their certainty accuse
All that are different of a base intent;
Pull down established honor; hawk for news
Whatever their loose phantasy invent
And murmur it with bated breath, as though
The abounding gutter had been Helicon
Or calumny a song. How can they know
Truth flourishes where the student's lamp has shone,
And there alone, that have no solitude?
So the crowd come they care not what may come.
They have loud music, hope every day renewed
And heartier loves; that lamp is from the tomb.

AN IRISH AIRMAN FORESEES HIS DEATH

I know that I shall meet my fate
Somewhere among the clouds above;
Those that I fight I do not hate,
Those that I guard I do not love;
My country is Kiltartan Cross,
My countrymen Kiltartan's poor,
No likely end could bring them loss
Or leave them happier than before.
Nor law, nor duty bade me fight,
Nor public men, nor cheering crowds,
A lonely impulse of delight
Drove to this tumult in the clouds;
I balanced all, brought all to mind,
The years to come seemed waste of breath,
A waste of breath the years behind
In balance with this life, this death.

TO A FRIEND WHOSE WORK HAS COME TO NOTHING

Now all the truth is out,
Be secret and take defeat
From any brazen throat,
For how can you compete,
Being honor bred, with one
Who, were it proved he lies,
Were neither shamed in his own
Nor in his neighbors' eyes?
Bred to a harder thing
Than Triumph, turn away
And like a laughing string
Whereon mad fingers play
Amid a place of stone,
Be secret and exult,
Because of all things known
That is most difficult.

THE SECOND COMING

Turning and turning in the widening gyre
The falcon cannot hear the falconer;
Things fall apart; the centre cannot hold;
Mere anarchy is loosed upon the world,
The blood-dimmed tide is loosed, and everywhere
The ceremony of innocence is drowned;
The best lack all conviction, while the worst
Are full of passionate intensity.

Surely some revelation is at hand;
Surely the Second Coming is at hand.
The Second Coming! Hardly are those words out
When a vast image out of *Spiritus Mundi*
Troubles my sight: somewhere in sands of the desert
A shape with lion body and the head of a man,
A gaze blank and pitiless as the sun,
Is moving its slow thighs, while all about it
Reel shadows of the indignant desert birds.
The darkness drops again; but now I know
That twenty centuries of stony sleep
Were vexed to nightmare by a rocking cradle,
And what rough beast, its hour come round at last,
Slouches towards Bethlehem to be born?

BYZANTIUM

The unpurged images of day recede;
The Emperor's drunken soldiery are abed;
Night resonance recedes, night-walkers' song
After great cathedral gong;
A starlit or a moonlit dome disdains
All that man is,
All mere complexities,
The fury and the mire of human veins.

Before me floats an image, man or shade,
Shade more than man, more image than a shade;
For Hades' bobbin bound in mummy-cloth
May unwind the winding path;
A mouth that has no moisture and no breath
Breathless mouths may summon;
I hail the superhuman;
I call it death-in-life and life-in-death.

Miracle, bird or golden handiwork,
More miracle than bird or handiwork,
Planted on the star-lit golden bough,
Can like the cocks of Hades crow,
Or, by the moon embittered, scorn aloud
In glory of changeless metal

Common bird or petal
And all complexities of mire or blood.

At midnight on the Emperor's pavement flit
Flames that no faggot feeds, nor steel has lit,
Nor storm disturbs, flames begotten of flame,
Where blood-begotten spirits come
And all complexities of fury leave,
Dying into a dance,
An agony of trance,
An agony of flame that cannot singe a sleeve.

Astraddle on the dolphin's mire and blood,
Spirit after spirit! The smithies break the flood,
The golden smithies of the Emperor!
Marbles of the dancing floor
Break bitter furies of complexity,
Those images that yet
Fresh images beget,
That dolphin-torn, that gong-tormented sea.

A DIALOGUE OF SELF AND SOUL

I

My Soul. I summon to the winding ancient stair;
Set all your mind upon the steep ascent,
Upon the broken, crumbling battlement,
Upon the breathless starlit air,
Upon the star that marks the hidden pole;
Fix every wandering thought upon
That quarter where all thought is done:
Who can distinguish darkness from the soul?

My Self. The consecrated blade upon my knees
Is Sato's ancient blade, still as it was,
Still razor-keen, still like a looking-glass
Unspotted by the centuries;
That flowering, silken, old embroidery, torn
From some court-lady's dress and round
The wooden scabbard bound and wound,
Can, tattered, still protect, faded adorn.

My Soul. Why should the imagination of a man
Long past his prime remember things that are
Emblematical of love and war?
Think of ancestral night that can,
If but imagination scorn the earth
And intellect its wandering
To this and that and t'other thing,
Deliver from the crime of death and birth.

My Self. Montashigi, third of his family, fashioned it
Five hundred years ago, about it lie

Flowers from I know not what embroidery—
Heart's purple—and all these I set
For emblems of the day against the tower
Emblematical of the night,
And claim as by a soldier's right
A charter to commit the crime once more.

My Soul. Such fullness in that quarter overflows
And falls into the basin of the mind
That man is stricken deaf and dumb and blind,
For intellect no longer knows
Is from the *Ought,* or *Knower* from the *Known*—
That is to say, ascends to Heaven;
Only the dead can be forgiven;
But when I think of that my tongue's a stone.

II

My Self. A living man is blind and drinks his drop.
What matter if the ditches are impure?
What matter if I live it all once more?
Endure that toil of growing up;
The ignominy of boyhood; the distress
Of boyhood changing into man;
The unfinished man and his pain
Brought face to face with his own clumsiness;
The finished man among his enemies?—
How in the name of Heaven can he escape
That defiling and disfigured shape
The mirror of malicious eyes
Casts upon his eyes until at last
He thinks that shape must be his shape?
And what's the good of an escape
If honour find him in the wintry blast?

I am content to live it all again
And yet again, if it be life to pitch
Into the frog-spawn of a blind man's ditch,
A blind man battering blind men;
Or into that most fecund ditch of all,
The folly that man does
Or must suffer, if he woos
A proud woman not kindred of his soul.

I am content to follow to its source,
Every event in action or in thought;
Measure the lot; forgive myself the lot!
When such as I cast out remorse
So great a sweetness flows into the breast
We must laugh and we must sing,
We are blest by everything,
Everything we look upon is blest.

Rudyard Kipling

⚜ (Joseph) Rudyard Kipling was born at Bombay, India, December 30, 1865. Both his parents were English; his father, John Lockwood Kipling, was curator of the Lahore Museum and an illustrator of some note. At six young Kipling was taken to Westward Ho, in North Devon, and his experiences at the English school furnished the basis for the grimly amusing *Stalky and Co.* (1899). Returning to India, he engaged in journalism; at seventeen he became sub-editor of the *Lahore Civil and Military Gazette.* At twenty-one Kipling published his first volume, *Departmental Ditties* (1886), a book of light verse. A year later he challenged attention as a story-teller with *Plain Tales from the Hills* (1887). Before he was twenty-four he had brought out six small collections of stories which showed his mastery in the form. They were astonishing in their vigor, accurate observation, and swift inventiveness. A new province was added to fiction: a realistic *Arabian Nights* transplanted to India and cultivated by an Englishman.

With maturity, Kipling's gift grew in power and range. His soldier stories embodied characters which rank with those of Dickens. His stories for children—*The Jungle Books* (1894-95), *Captains Courageous* (1897) and *Just So Stories* (1902)—became contemporary classics. He appealed equally to youth and age with *Kim* (1901), *Puck of Pook's Hill* (1906), *Rewards and Fairies* (1910).

Between his twenty-third and twenty-sixth year Kipling traveled to China, Japan, India, and America. In England he found himself famous at twenty-seven. On a return visit to the United States in 1892 Kipling married an American, Caroline Starr Balestier, sister of Wolcott Balestier, with whom he wrote *The Naulahka,* 1891, and lived for a few years in Brattleboro, Vermont. Here he wrote several of his most popular works, and it seems likely that he would have remained in America if a quarrel with another brother-in-law, Beatty Balestier, and threats of legal action, had not driven him back to England. Sensitive to criticism and increasingly wary of social contacts, Kipling buried himself in a little Sussex village. He had lost a daughter; the death of a son during the World War embittered and almost silenced him. Although he had received the Nobel Prize for literature in 1907, changes in taste caused a reaction against Kipling's militant "imperialism," which had once influenced British sentiment and, to some extent, its policies. Nevertheless, Kipling's work continued to grow in subtlety, if not in quantity, and he was at work on a collection of autobiographical notes when he died a few weeks after his seventieth birthday, January 17, 1936.

Considered solely as a poet, Kipling is one of the most vigorous figures of his time. He shared the experiences of all classes of people, and his verse spoke for civilians as well as soldiers, office-holders and vagabond adventurers. His brisk lines communicate a common joy in the snapping of a banner, the tingle of salt spray, the lurch and rumble of the sea; his poetry is woven of the stuff of myths, but it never loses its hold on actualities. Kipling himself in his poem "The Benefactors" (from *The Years Between* [1919]) writes:

Ah! What avails the classic bent
And what the cultured word,
Against the undoctored incident
That actually occurred?

What attracted the average reader to Kipling was this attitude to the world's work. Where others sang of lilies and leisure, Kipling celebrated difficulties, duty, hard labor; where others evoked Greek nymphs, he hailed bridge-builders, engineers, sweating stokers—all those who exulted in the job. If he sometimes lost his head in a general hurrahing, his high spirits carried off specious prophesying and brought sing-song meters to a pitch of excitement. Life was all gusto. *A Choice of Kipling's Verse* (1941) was compiled, surprisingly enough, by T. S. Eliot.

If Kipling's energy is boisterous it is irresistible. His varied poems, ranging from the lustry *Barrack-Room Ballads* to the quieter verse in *The Five Nations, The Seven Seas* and the later work, were collected in a remarkable one-volume *Inclusive Edition* (1885-1918), an indispensable part of any student's library. Subsequent to this collection, a new volume, *The Years Between,* was published in 1919.

The best and worst of Kipling are obvious to the least critical reader. His worst is inherent in a heartiness which is too loud and too prolonged, a vehemence which changes robustiousness into rowdiness. Max Beerbohm excoriated this Kipling in the cartoon showing an irate little man, helmeted and spectacled, blowing a tin trumpet, waving a Union Jack, and dancing himself into a paroxysm of patriotic fury. This Kipling, overcome by the conquering chauvinism of the Colonist, loses his sense of values, belittling the weak to the tune of British imperialism. The tune, one must admit, is an attractive one, and even those who object to its burden of bombast have learned to whistle it by heart. The rhythms are often the beat of journalistic verse, but they communicate to the "average man" something he seeks and which he would not recognize in finer measures. It is indisputable that Kipling too often tries to force beauty in a rape of violence. But there are also those poems in which, as T. Earle Welby says in *A Popular History of English Poetry,* "he has been humbler and more passive, and in which beauty is a voluntary captive. One emotion has never failed to inspire him, the inverted nostalgia of the man returned home and yearning for far and once familiar scenes of exile. It arouses all the poet in him, puts wistfulness into his generally brazen music, clears his style of semi-Biblical claptrap, and sets his extraordinary descriptive talent to work more legitimately than usual." Such a descriptive talent is illustrated by "Mandalay," "Fuzzy Wuzzy," "Chant-Pagan," "The Return," even by such a stanza as:

Rivers at night that cluck an' jeer,
Plains which the moonshine turns to sea,
Mountains which never let you near,
An' stars to all eternity;
An' the quick-breathin' dark that fills
The 'ollows of the wilderness,
When the wind worries through the 'ills—
These may 'ave taught me more or less.

Such work shows that Kipling, though a poet, is something besides a poet. He is not so much a writer for those who enjoy writing—although his craftsmanship will repay study—as he is the singer of those who have never risen to an understanding of song. After World War I it became the fashion to disparage Kipling's work as well as his philosophy. When his name was mentioned it was accompanied by a deprecatory shrung or a remark about the decline of his fame; in 1935 a New York newspaper referred to him as "the forgotten man of English letters."

Reaction follows reaction, and if Kipling is underpraised today for the very qualities which were overpraised thirty years ago his hour will strike again. Few poems have revealed a richer and more resigned understanding of the soil and those whose live close to it than "The Land"; the wanderlust has never been so poignantly expressed as in "For to Admire." His ballads have not only the swing but the vitality of the ancient Border Ballads, and it is altogether possible that he will outlast most of his contemporaries, and go down to posterity as a people's poet, a balladist whose songs were the popular tunes of one age and the folk-classics of another.

GUNGA DIN

You may talk o' gin an' beer
When you're quartered safe out 'ere,
An' you're sent to penny-fights an' Aldershot it;
But when it comes to slaughter
You will do your work on water,
An' you'll lick the bloomin' boots of 'em that's got it.
Now in Injia's sunny clime,
Where I used to spend my time
A-servin' of 'Er Majesty the Queen,
Of all them black-faced crew
The finest man I knew
Was our regimental *bhisti,*[1] Gunga Din.

It was "Din! Din! Din!
You limping lump o' brick-dust, Gunga Din!
Hi! *slippy hitherao!*
Water, get it! *Panee lao*[2]
You squidgy-nosed old idol, Gunga Din!"

The uniform 'e wore
Was nothin' much before,
An' rather less than 'arf o' that be'ind,
For a twisty piece o' rag
An' a goatskin water-bag
Was all the field-equipment 'e could find.
When the sweatin' troop-train lay
In a sidin' through the day,
Where the 'eat would make your bloomin' eyebrows crawl,
We shouted *"Harry By!"*[3]

[1] The *bhisti,* or water-carrier, attached to regiments in India, is often one of the most devoted of the Queen's servants. He is also appreciated by the men.

[2] Bring water swiftly.

[3] Tommy Atkins' equivalent for "O Brother!"

Till our throats were bricky-dry,
Then we wopped 'im 'cause 'e couldn't serve us all.

> It was "Din! Din! Din!
> You 'eathen, where the mischief 'ave you been?
> You put some *juldee*[1] in it,
> Or I'll *marrow*[2] you this minute,
> If you don't fill up my helmet, Gunda Din!"

'E would dot an' carry one
Till the longest day was done,
An' 'e didn't seem to know the use o' fear.
If we charged or broke or cut,
You could bet your bloomin' nut,
'E'd be waitin' fifty paces right flank rear.
With 'is *mussick*[3] on is back,
'E would skip with our attack,
An' watch us till the bugles made "Retire."
An' for all 'is dirty 'ide,
'E was white, clear white, inside
When 'e went to tend the wounded under fire!

> It was "Din! Din! Din!"
> With the bullets kickin' dust-spots on the green.
> When the cartridges ran out,
> You could 'ear the front-files shout:
> "Hi! ammunition-mules an' Gunga Din!"

I sha'n't forgit the night
When I dropped be'ind the fight
With a bullet where my belt-plate should 'a' been.
I was chokin' mad with thirst,
An' the man that spied me first
Was our good old grinnin', gruntin' Gunga Din.
'E lifted up my 'ead,
An' 'e plugged me where I bled,
An' 'e guv me 'arf-a-pint o' water—green;
It was crawlin' an' it stunk,
But of all the drinks I've drunk,
I'm gratefulest to one from Gunga Din.

> It was "Din! Din! Din!
> 'Ere's a beggar with a bullet through 'is spleen;
> 'E's chawin' up the ground an' 'e's kickin' all around:
> For Gawd's sake, git the water, Gunga Din!"

'E carried me away
To where a *dooli* lay,
An' a bullet come an' drilled the beggar clean.
'E put me safe inside,
An' just before 'e died:
"I 'ope you liked your drink," sez Gunga Din.

[1] Speed. [2] Hit you. [3] Water-skin.

So I'll meet 'im later on
In the place where 'e is gone—
Where it's always double drill and no canteen;
'E'll be squattin' on the coals
Givin' drink to pore damned souls,
An' I'll get a swig in Hell from Gunga Din!

Din! Din! Din!
You Lazarushian-leather Gunga Din!
Tho' I've belted you an' flayed you,
By the livin' Gawd that made you,
You're a better man than I am, Gunga Din!

32

DANNY DEEVER

"What are the bugles blowin' for?" said Files-on-Parade.
"To turn you out, to turn you out," the Color-Sergeant said.
"What makes you look so white, so white?" said Files-on-Parade.
"I'm dreadin' what I've got to watch," the Color-Sergeant said.
For they're hangin' Danny Deever, you can 'ear the Dead March play,
The regiment's in 'ollow square—they're hangin' him today;
They've taken of his buttons off an' cut his stripes away,
An' they're hangin' Danny Deever in the mornin'.

"What makes the rear-rank breathe so 'ard?" said Files-on-Parade.
"It's bitter cold, it's bitter cold," the Color-Sergeant said.
"What makes that front-rank man fall down?" says Files-on-Parade.
"A touch of sun, a touch of sun," the Color-Sergeant said.
They are hangin' Danny Deever, they are marchin' of 'im round.
They 'ave 'alted Danny Deever by 'is coffin on the ground:
An 'e'll swing in 'arf a minute for a sneakin' shootin' hound—
O they're hangin' Danny Deever in the mornin'!

" 'Is cot was right-'and cot to mine," said Files-on-Parade.
" 'E's sleepin' out an' far tonight," the Color-Sergeant said.
"I've drunk 'is beer a score o' times," said Files-on-Parade.
" 'E's drinkin' bitter beer alone," the Color-Sergeant said.
They are hangin' Danny Deever, you must mark 'im to 'is place,
For 'e shot a comrade sleepin'—you must look 'im in the face;
Nine 'undred of 'is county an' the regiment's disgrace,
While they're hangin' Danny Deever in the mornin.'

"What's that so black agin the sun?" said Files-on-Parade.
"It's Danny fightin' 'ard for life," the Color-Sergeant said.
"What's that that whimpers over'ead?" said Files-on-Parade.
"It's Danny's soul that's passin' now," the Color-Sergeant said.
For they're done with Danny Deever, you can 'ear the quickstep play,
The regiment's in column, an' they're marchin' us away;
Ho! the young recruits are shakin', an' they'll want their beer today,
After hangin' Danny Deever in the mornin'.

MANDALAY

By the old Moulmein Pagoda, lookin' eastward to the sea,
There's a Burma girl a-settin', an' I know she thinks o' me;
For the wind is in the palm-trees, an' the temple-bells they say:
"Come you back, you British soldier; come you back to Mandalay!"
    Come you back to Mandalay,
    Where the old Flotilla lay:
    Can't you 'ear their paddles chunkin' from Rangoon to Mandalay?
    On the road to Mandalay,
    Where the flyin'-fishes play,
    An' the dawn comes up like thunder outer China 'crost the Bay!

'Er petticut was yaller an' 'er little cap was green,
An' 'er name was Supi-yaw-let—jes' the same as Theebaw's Queen,
An' I seed her fust a-smokin' of a whackin' white cheroot,
An' a-wastin' Christian kisses on an 'eathen idol's foot:
    Bloomin' idol made o' mud—
    What they called the Great Gawd Budd—
    Plucky lot she cared for idols when I kissed 'er where she stud!
    On the road to Mandalay—

When the mist was on the rice-fields an' the sun was droppin' slow,
She'd git 'er little banjo an' she'd sing *"Kulla-lo-lo!"*
With 'er arm upon my shoulder an' her cheek agin my cheek
We useter watch the steamers an' the *hathis* pilin' teak.
    Elephints a-pilin' teak
    In the sludgy, squdgy creek,
    Where the silence 'ung that 'eavy you was 'arf afraid to speak!
    On the road to Mandalay—

But that's all shove be'ind me—long ago an' fur away,
An' there ain't no 'busses runnin' from the Bank to Mandalay;
An' I'm learnin' 'ere in London what the ten-year sodger tells:
"If you've 'eard the East a-callin', why, you won't 'eed nothin' else."
    No! you wont 'eed nothin' else
    But them spicy garlic smells
    An' the sunshine an' the palm-trees an' the tinkly temple bells!
    On the road to Mandalay—

I am sick o' wastin' leather on these gritty pavin'-stones,
An' the blasted Henglish drizzle wakes the fever in my bones;
Tho' I walks with fifty 'ousemaids outer Chelsea to the Strand,
An' they talks a lot o' lovin', but wot do they understand?
    Beefy face an' grubby 'and—
    Law! wot *do* they understand?
    I've a neater, sweeter maiden in a cleaner, greener land!
    On the road to Mandalay—

Ship me somewheres east of Suez where the best is like the worst,
Where there aren't no Ten Commandments, an' a man can raise a thirst;

For the temple-bells are callin', an' it's there that I would be—
By the old Moulmein Pagoda, lookin' lazy at the sea—
    On the road to Mandalay,
    Where the old Flotilla lay,
    With our sick beneath the awnings when we went to Mandalay!
    Oh, the road to Mandalay,
    Where the flyin'-fishes play,
    An' the dawn comes up like thunder outer China 'crost the Bay!

"FUZZY-WUZZY"

(Soudan Expeditionary Force)

We've fought with many men acrost the seas,
  An' some of 'em was brave an' some was not:
The Paythan an' the Zulu an' Burmese;
  But the Fuzzy was the finest o' the lot.
We never got a ha'porth's change of 'im:
  'E squatted in the scrub an' 'ocked our 'orses,
'E cut our sentries up at Sua*k*im,
  An' 'e played the cat an' banjo with our forces.
    So 'ere's *to* you, Fuzzy-Wuzzy, at your 'ome in the Sowdan;
    You're a pore benighted 'eathen but a first-class fightin' man;
    We gives you your certifikit, an' if you want it signed
    We'll come an' 'ave a romp with you whenever you're inclined.

We took our chanst among the Kyber 'ills,
  The Boers knocked us silly at a mile,
The Burman guv us Irriwaddy chills,
  An' a Zulu *impi* dished us up in style:
But all we ever got from such as they
  Was pop to what the Fuzzy made us swaller;
We 'eld our bloomin' own, the papers say,
  But man for man the Fuzzy knocked us 'oller.
    Then 'ere's *to* you, Fuzzy-Wuzzy, an' the missis and the kid;
    Our orders was to break you, an' of course we went an' did.
    We sloshed you with Martinis, an' it wasn't 'ardly fair;
    But for all the odds agin you, Fuzzy-Wuz, you bruk the square.

'E 'asn't got no papers of 'is own,
  'E 'asn't got no medals nor rewards,
So we must certify the skill 'e's shown
  In usin of 'is long two-'anded swords;
When 'e's 'oppin' in an' out among the bush
  With 'is coffin-'eaded shield an' shovel-spear,
A 'appy day with Fuzzy on the rush
  Will last a 'ealthy Tommy for a year.
    So 'ere's *to* you, Fuzzy-Wuzzy, an' your friends which is no more,
    If we 'adn't lost some messmates we would 'elp you to deplore;
    But give an' take's the gospel, an' we'll call the bargain fair,
    For if you 'ave lost more than us, you crumpled up the square!

'E rushes at the smoke when we let drive,
An', before we know, 'e's 'ackin' at our 'ead;
'E's all 'ot sand an' ginger when alive,
An' 'e's generally shammin' when 'e's dead.
'E's a daisy, 'e's a ducky, 'e's a lamb!
'E's a injia-rubber idiot on the spree,
'E's the on'y thing that doesn't care a damn
For the Regiment o' British Infantree.
So 'ere's *to* you, Fuzzy-Wuzzy, at your 'ome in the Sowdan;
You're a pore benighted 'eathen but a first-class fightin' man;
An 'ere's *to* you, Fuzzy-Wuzzy, with your 'ayrick 'ead of 'air—
You big black boundin' beggar—for you bruk a British square.

TOMMY

I went into a public-'ouse to get a pint o' beer,
The publican 'e up an' sez, "We serve no red-coats here."
The girls be'ind the bar they laughed an' giggled fit to die,
I outs into the street again, an' to myself sez I:
O it's Tommy this, an' Tommy that, an' "Tommy go away";
But it's "Thank you, Mister Atkins," when the band begins to play,
The band begins to play, my boys, the band begins to play,
O it's "Thank you, Mister Atkins," when the band begins to play.

I went into a theater as sober as could be,
They give a drunk civilian room, but 'adn't none for me;
They sent me to the gallery or round the music-'alls,
But when it comes to fightin', Lord! they'll shove me in the stalls.
For it's Tommy this, an' Tommy that, an' "Tommy wait outside";
But it's "Special train for Atkins," when the trooper's on the tide,
The troopship's on the tide, my boys, etc.

O makin' mock o' uniforms that guard you while you sleep
Is cheaper than them uniforms, an' they're starvation cheap;
An' hustlin' drunken sodgers when they're goin' large a bit
Is five times better business than paradin' in full kit.
Then it's Tommy this, an' Tommy that, an' "Tommy 'ow's yer soul?"
But it's "Thin red line of 'eroes" when the drums begin to roll,
The drums begin to roll, my boys, etc.

We aren't no thin red 'eroes, nor we aren't no blackguards too,
But single men in barricks, most remarkable like you;
An' if sometimes our conduck isn't all your fancy paints,
Why, single men in barricks don't grow into plaster saints.
While it's Tommy this, an' Tommy that, an' "Tommy fall be'ind";
But it's "Please to walk in front, sir," when there's trouble in the wind,
There's trouble in the wind, my boys, etc.

You talk o' better food for us an' schools, an' fires, an' all:
We'll wait for extry rations if you treat us rational.
Don't mess about the cook-room slops, but prove it to our face
The Widow's uniform is not the soldier-man's disgrace.

But it's Tommy this, an' Tommy that, an' "Chuck him out, the brute!"
But it's "Savior of 'is country" when the guns begin to shoot;
An' it's Tommy this, an' Tommy that, an' anything you please;
An' Tommy ain't a bloomin' fool—you bet that Tommy sees!

THE LADIES

I've taken my fun where I've found it;
  I've rogued an' I've ranged in my time;
I've 'ad my pickin' o' sweet'earts,
  An' four o' the lot was prime.
One was an 'arf-caste widow,
  One was a woman at Prome,
One was the wife of a *jemadar-sais,*
  An' one is a girl at 'ome.

Now I aren't no 'and with the ladies,
  For, takin' 'em all along,
You never can say till you've tried 'em,
  An' then you are like to be wrong.
There's times when you'll think that you mightn't,
  There's times when you'll know that you might;
But the things you will learn from the Yellow an' Brown,
  They'll 'elp you a lot with the White!

I was a young un at 'Oogli,
  Shy as a girl to begin;
Aggie de Castrer she made me,
  An' Aggie was clever as sin;
Older than me, but my first un—
  More like a mother she were—
Showed me the way to promotion an' pay,
  An' I learned about women from 'er!

Then I was ordered to Burma,
  Actin' in charge o' Bazar,
An' I got me a tiddy live 'eathen
  Through buyin' supplies off 'er pa.
Funny an' yellow an' faithful—
  Doll in a teacup she were,
But we lived on the square, like a true-married pair,
  An' I learned about women from 'er!

Then we was shifted to Neemuch
  (Or I might ha' been keepin' 'er now),
An' I took with a shiny she-devil,
  The wife of a nigger at Mhow;
Taught me the gypsy-folks' *bolee;*
  Kind o' volcano she were,
For she knifed me one night 'cause I wished she was white,
  An' I learned about women from 'er!

Then I come 'ome in the trooper,
'Long of a kid o' sixteen—
Girl from a convent at Meerut,
The straightest I ever 'ave seen.
Love at first sight was 'er trouble,
She didn't know what it were;
An' I wouldn't do such, 'cause I liked 'er too much,
But—I learned about women from 'er!

I've taken my fun where I've found it,
An' now I must pay for my fun,
For the more you 'ave known o' the others
The less you will settle to one;
An' the end of it's sittin' and thinkin',
An' dreamin' Hell-fires to see;
So be warned by my lot (which I know you will not),
An' learn about women from me!

What did the Colonel's Lady think?
Nobody never knew.
Somebody asked the Sergeant's wife,
An' she told 'em true!
When you get to a man in the case,
They're like as a row of pins—
For the Colonel's Lady an' Judy O'Grady
Are sisters under their skins!

BOOTS

(*Infantry Columns of the Earlier War*)

We're foot—slog—slog—slog—sloggin' over Africa!
Foot—foot—foot—foot—sloggin' over Africa—
(Boots—boots—boots—boots, movin' up an' down again!)
There's no discharge in the war!

Seven—six—eleven—five—nine-an'-twenty mile today—
Four—eleven—seventeen—thirty-two the day before—
(Boots—boots—boots—boots, movin' up an' down again!)
There's no discharge in the war!

Don't—don't—don't—don't—look at what's in front of you
(Boots—boots—boots—boots, movin' up an' down again);
Men—men—men—men—men go mad with watchin' 'em,
An' there's no discharge in the war!

Try—try—try—try—to think o' something different—
Oh—my—God—keep—me from goin' lunatic!
(Boots—boots—boots—boots, movin' up an' down again!)
There's no discharge in the war!

Count—count—count—count—the bullets in the bandoliers;
If—your—eyes—drop—they will get atop o' you
(Boots—boots—boots—boots, movin' up an' down again)—
There's no discharge in the war!

We—can—stick—out—'unger, thirst, an' weariness,
But—not—not—not—not the chronic sight of 'em—
Boots—boots—boots—boots, movin' up an' down again,
An' there's no discharge in the war!

'Tain't—so—bad—by—day because o' company,
But night—brings—long—strings o' forty thousand million
Boots—boots—boots—boots, movin' up an' down again.
There's no discharge in the war!

I—'ave—marched—six—weeks in 'Ell an' certify
It—is—not—fire—devils, dark or anything
But boots—boots—boots, movin' up an' down again,
An' there's no discharge in the war!

THE RETURN

Peace is declared, and I return
To 'Ackneystadt, but not the same;
Things 'ave transpired which made me learn
The size and meanin' of the game.
I did no more than others did,
I don't know where the change began;
I started as a average kid,
I finished as a thinkin' man.

If England was what England seems
An' not the England of our dreams,
But only putty, brass, an' paint,
'Ow quick we'd drop 'er! But she ain't!

Before my gappin' mouth could speak
I 'eard it in my comrade's tone;
I saw it on my neighbor's cheek
Before I felt it flush my own.
An' last it come to me—not pride,
Nor yet conceit, but on the 'ole
(If such a term may be applied)
The makin's of a bloomin' soul.

Rivers at night that cluck an' jeer,
Plains which the moonshine turns to sea,
Mountains that never let you near,
An' stars to all eternity;

An' the quick-breathin' dark that fills
  The 'ollows of the wilderness,
When the wind worries through the 'ills—
  These may 'ave taught me more or less.

Towns without people, ten times took,
  An' ten times left an' burned at last;
An' starvin' dogs that come to look
  For owners when a column passed;
An' quiet, 'omesick talks between
  Men, met by night, you never knew
Until—'is face—by shellfire seen—
  Once—an' struck off. They taught me, too.

The day's lay-out—the mornin' sun
  Beneath your 'at-brim as you sight;
The dinner-'ush from noon till one,
  An' the full roar that lasts till night;
An' the pore dead that look so old
  An' was so young an hour ago,
An' legs tied down before they're cold—
  These are the things which make you know.

Also Time runnin' into years—
  A thousand Places left be'ind—
An' Men from both two 'emispheres
  Discussin' things of every kind;
So much more near than I 'ad known,
  So much more great than I 'ad guessed—
An' me, like all the rest, alone—
  But reachin' out to all the rest!

So 'ath it come to me—not pride,
  Nor yet conceit, but on the 'ole
(If such a term may be applied)
  The makin's of a bloomin' soul.
But now, discharged, I fall away
  To do with little things again. . . .
Gawd, 'oo knows all I cannot say,
  Look after me in Thamesfontein!

If England was what England seems
  An' not the England of our dreams,
But only putty, brass, an' paint,
  'Ow quick we'd chuck 'er! But she ain't!

THE CONUNDRUM OF THE WORKSHOPS

When the flush of a newborn sun fell first on Eden's green and gold,
Our father Adam sat under the Tree and scratched with a stick in the mold;
And the first rude sketch that the world had seen was joy to his mighty heart,
Till the Devil whispered behind the leaves: "It's pretty, but is it Art?"

Wherefore he called to his wife and fled to fashion his work anew—
The first of his race who cared a fig for the first, most dread review;
And he left his lore to the use of his sons—and that was a glorious gain
When the Devil chuckled: "Is it Art?" in the ear of the branded Cain.

They builded a tower to shiver the sky and wrench the stars apart,
Till the Devil grunted behind the bricks: "It's striking, but is it Art?"
The stone was dropped by the quarry-side, and the idle derrick swung,
While each man talked of the aims of art, and each in an alien tongue.

They fought and they talked in the north and the south, they talked and they fought in the west,
Till the waters rose on the jabbering land, and the poor Red Clay had rest—
Had rest till the dank blank-canvas dawn when the dove was preened to start,
And the Devil bubbled below the keel: "It's human, but is it Art?"

The tale is old as the Eden Tree—as new as the new-cut tooth—
For each man knows ere his lip-thatch grows he is master of Art and Truth;
And each man hears as the twilight nears, to the beat of his dying heart,
The Devil drum on the darkened pane: "You did it, but was it Art?"

We have learned to whittle the Eden Tree to the shape of a surplice-peg,
We have learned to bottle our parents twain in the yolk of an addled egg,
We know that the tail must wag the dog, as the horse is drawn by the cart;
But the Devil whoops, as he whooped of old: "It's clever, but is it Art?"

When the flicker of London's sun falls faint on the club-room's green and gold,
The sons of Adam sit them down and scratch with their pens in the mold—
They scratch with their pens in the mold of their graves, and the ink and the anguish start
When the Devil mutters behind the leaves: "It's pretty, but is it Art?"

Now, if we could win to the Eden Tree where the four great rivers flow,
And the wreath of Eve is red on the turf as she left it long ago,
And if we could come when the sentry slept, and softly scurry through,
By the favor of God we might know as much—as our father Adam knew.

EVARRA AND HIS GODS

Read here,
This is the story of Evarra—man—
Maker of Gods in lands beyond the sea.
Because the city gave him of her gold,
Because the caravans brought turquoises,
Because his life was sheltered by the King,
So that no man should maim him, none should steal,
Or break his rest with babble in the streets
When he was weary after toil, he made
An image of his God in gold and pearl,
With turquoise diadem and human eyes,
A wonder in the sunshine, known afar
And worshiped by the King; but drunk with pride,

Because the city bowed to him for God,
He wrote above the shrine: *"Thus Gods are made,*
And whoso makes them otherwise shall die."
And all the city praised him. . . . Then he died.

Read here the story of Evarra—man—
Maker of Gods in lands beyond the sea.
Because his city had no wealth to give,
Because the caravans were spoiled afar,
Because his life was threatened by the King,
So that all men despised him in the streets,
He hacked the living rock, with sweat and tears,
And reared a God against the morning-gold,
A terror in the sunshine, seen afar,
And worshiped by the King; but, drunk with pride,
Because the city fawned to bring him back,
He carved upon the plinth: *"Thus Gods are made,*
And whoso makes them otherwise shall die."
And all the people praised him. . . . Then he died.

Read here the story of Evarra—man—
Maker of Gods in lands beyond the sea.
Because he lived among the simple folk,
Because his village was between the hills,
Because he smeared his cheeks with blood of ewes,
He cut an idol from a fallen pine,
Smeared blood upon its cheeks, and wedged a shell
Above its brow for eye, and gave it hair
Of trailing moss, and plaited straw for crown.
And all the village praised him for his craft,
And brought him butter, honey, milk, and curds.
Wherefore, because the shoutings drove him mad,
He scratched upon that log: *"Thus Gods are made,*
And whoso makes them otherwise shall die."
And all the people praised him. . . . Then he died.

Read here the story of Evarra—man—
Maker of Gods in lands beyond the sea.
Because his God decreed one clot of blood
Should swerve a hair's-breadth from the pulse's path,
And chafe his brain, Evarra mowed alone,
Rag-wrapped, among the cattle in the fields,
Counting his fingers, jesting with the trees,
And mocking at the mist, until his God
Drove him to labor. Out of dung and horns
Dropped in the mire he made a monstrous God,
Abhorrent, shapeless, crowned with plantain tufts.
And when the cattle lowed at twilight-time,
He dreamed it was the clamor of lost crowds,
And howled among the beasts: *"Thus Gods are made,*
And whoso makes them otherwise shall die."
Thereat the cattle bellowed. . . . . Then he died.

Yet at the last he came to Paradise,
And found his own four Gods, and that he wrote;
And marveled, being very near to God,
What oaf on earth had made his toil God's law,
Till God said, mocking: "Mock not. These be thine."
Then cried Evarra: "I have sinned!"—"Not so.
If thou hadst written otherwise, thy Gods
Had rested in the mountain and the mine,
And I were poorer by four wondrous Gods,
And thy more wondrous law, Evarra. Thine,
Servant of shouting crowds and lowing kine."
Thereat with laughing mouth, but tear-wet eyes,
Evarra cast his Gods from Paradise.

This is the story of Evarra—man—
Maker of Gods in lands beyond the sea.

LA NUIT BLANCHE

A Much-Discerning Public hold
The Singer generally sings
Of personal and private things,
And prints and sells his past for gold.

Whatever I may here disclaim,
The very clever folk I sing to
Will most indubitably cling to
Their pet delusion, just the same.

I had seen, as dawn was breaking
And I staggered to my rest,
Tari Devi softly shaking
From the Cart Road to the crest.
I had seen the spurs of Jakko
Heave and quiver, swell and sink.
Was it Earthquake or tobacco,
Day of Doom or Night of Drink?

In the full, fresh, fragrant morning
I observed a camel crawl,
Laws of gravitation scorning,
On the ceiling and the wall;
Then I watched a fender walking,
And I heard gray leeches sing,
And a red-hot monkey talking
Did not seem the proper thing.

Half the night I watch the Heavens
Fizz like '81 champagne—
Fly to sixes and to sevens,
Wheel and thunder back again;
And when all was peace and order
Save one planet nailed askew,
Much I wept because my warder
Would not let me set it true.

After frenzied hours of waiting,
When the Earth and Skies were dumb,
Pealed an awful voice dictating
An interminable sum,
Changing to a tangled story—
"What she said you said I said—"
Till the Moon arose in glory,
And I found her . . . in my head;

Then a Face came, blind and weeping,
And It couldn't wipe Its eyes,
And It muttered I was keeping
Back the moonlight from the skies;
So I patted it for pity,
But it whistled shrill with wrath,
And a huge black Devil City
Poured its peoples on my path.

So I fled with steps uncertain
On a thousand-year long race,
But the bellying of the curtain
Kept me always in one place;
While the tumult rose and maddened
To the roar of Earth on fire,
Ere it ebbed and sank and saddened
To a whisper tense as wire.

In intolerable stillness
Rose one little, little star,
And it chuckled at my illness,
And it mocked me from afar;
And its brethren came and eyed me,
Called the Universe to aid,
Till I lay, with naught to hide me,
'Neath the Scorn of All Things Made.

Dun and saffron, robed and splendid,
  Broke the solemn, pitying Day,
And I knew my pains were ended,
  And I turned and tried to pray;
But my speech was shattered wholly,
  And I wept as children weep,
Till the dawn-wind, softly, slowly,
  Brought to burning eyelids sleep.

AN ASTROLOGER'S SONG

To the Heavens above us
  Oh, look and behold
The Planets that love us
  All harnessed in gold!
What chariots, what horses
  Against us shall bide
While the Stars in their courses
  Do fight on our side?

All thought, all desires,
  That are under the sun,
Are one with their fires,
  As we also are one:
All matter, all spirit,
  All fashion, all frame,
Receive and inherit
  Their strength from the same.

(Oh, man that deniest
  All power save thine own,
Their power in the highest
  Is mightily shown.
Not less in the lowest
  That power is made clear.
Oh, man, if thou knowest,
  What treasure is here!)

Earth quakes in her throes
  And we wonder for why!
But the blind planet knows
  When her ruler is nigh;
And, attuned since Creation
  To perfect accord,
She thrills in her station
  And yearns to her Lord.

The waters have risen,
  The springs are unbound—
The floods break their prison,
  And ravin around.
No rampart withstands 'em,
  Their fury will last,
Till the Sign that commands 'em
  Sinks low or swings past.

Through abysses unproven
  And gulfs beyond thought,
Our portion is woven,
  Our burden is brought.
Yet They that prepare it,
  Whose Nature we share,
Make us who must bear it
  Well able to bear.

Though terrors o'ertake us
  We'll not be afraid.
No power can unmake us
  Save that which has made.
Nor yet beyond reason
  Or hope shall we fall—
All things have their season,
  And Mercy crowns all!

Then doubt not, ye fearful—
  The Eternal is King—
Up, heart, and be cheerful,
  And lustily sing:—
What chariots, what horses
  Against us shall bide
While the Stars in their courses
  Do fight on our side?

RECESSIONAL

God of our fathers, known of old,
  Lord of our far-flung battle-line,
Beneath whose awful hand we hold
  Dominion over palm and pine—
Lord God of Hosts, be with us yet,
Lest we forget—lest we forget!

The tumult and the shouting dies;
  The captains and the kings depart:
Still stands Thine ancient sacrifice,
  An humble and a contrite heart.
Lord God of Hosts, be with us yet,
Lest we forget—lest we forget!

Far-called, our navies melt away;
  On dune and headland sinks the fire:

Lo, all our pomp of yesterday
  Is one with Nineveh and Tyre!
Judge of the Nations, spare us yet,
Lest we forget—lest we forget!

If, drunk with sight of power, we loose
  Wild tongues that have not Thee in awe,
Such boastings as the Gentiles use,
  Or lesser breeds without the Law—
Lord God of Hosts, be with us yet,
Lest we forget—lest we forget!

For heathen heart that puts her trust
  In reeking tube and iron shard,
All valiant dust that builds on dust,
  And, guarding, calls not Thee to guard,
For frantic boast and foolish word—
Thy Mercy on Thy People, Lord!

THE LAST CHANTEY

"And there was no more sea"

Thus said the Lord in the Vault above the Cherubim,
  Calling to the Angels and the Souls in their degree:
    "Lo! Earth has passed away
    On the smoke of Judgment Day.
  That Our word may be established shall We gather up the sea?"

Loud sang the souls of the jolly, jolly mariners:
  "Plague upon the hurricane that made us furl and flee!
    But the war is done between us,
    In the deep the Lord hath seen us—
  Our bones we'll leave the barracout', and God may sink the sea!"

Then said the soul of Judas that betrayed Him:
  "Lord, hast Thou forgotten Thy covenant with me?
    How once a year I go
    To cool me on the floe?
  And Ye take my day of mercy if Ye take away the sea."

Then said the soul of the Angel of the Off-shore Wind:
  (He that bits the thunder when the bull-mouthed breakers flee):
    "I have watch and ward to keep
    O'er Thy wonders on the deep,
  And Ye take mine honor from me if Ye take away the sea!"

Loud sang the souls of the jolly, jolly mariners:
  "Nay, but we were angry, and a hasty folk are we.
    If we worked the ship together
    Till she foundered in foul weather,
  Are we babes that we should clamor for a vengeance on the sea?"

Then said the souls of the slaves that men threw overboard:
  "Kenneled in the picaroon a weary band were we;
    But Thy arm was strong to save,
    And it touched us on the wave,
  And we drowsed the long tides idle till Thy Trumpets tore the sea."

Then cried the soul of the stout Apostle Paul to God:
  "Once we frapped a ship, and she labored woundily.

There were fourteen score of these,
And they blessed Thee on their knees,
When they learned Thy Grace and Glory under Malta by the sea!"

Loud sang the souls of the jolly, jolly mariners,
Plucking at their harps, and they plucked unhandily:
"Our thumbs are rough and tarred,
And the tune is something hard—
May we lift a Deepsea Chantey such as seamen use at sea?"

Then said the souls of the gentlemen-adventurers—
Fettered wrist to bar all for red iniquity:
"Ho, we revel in our chains
O'er the sorrow that was Spain's;
Heave or sink it, leave or drink it, we were masters of the sea!"

Up spake the soul of a gray Gothavn 'speckshioner—
(He that led the flenching in the fleets of fair Fundee):
"Oh, the ice-blink white and near,
And the bowhead breaching clear!
Will Ye whelm them all for wantonness that wallow in the sea?"

Loud sang the souls of the jolly, jolly mariners,
Crying: "Under Heaven, here is neither lead nor lea!
Must we sing for evermore
On the windless, glassy floor?
Take back your golden fiddles and we'll beat to open sea!"

Then stooped the Lord, and He called the good sea up to Him,
And 'stablished its borders unto all eternity,
That such as have no pleasure
For to praise the Lord by measure,
They may enter into galleons and serve Him on the sea.

Sun, Wind, and Cloud shall fail not from the face of it,
Stinging, ringing spindrift, nor the fulmar flying free;
And the ships shall go abroad
To the Glory of the Lord
Who heard the silly sailor-folk and gave them back their sea!

SESTINA OF THE TRAMP-ROYAL

Speakin' in general, I 'ave tried 'em all—
The 'appy roads that take you o'er the world.
Speakin' in general, I 'ave found them good
For such as cannot use one bed too long,
But must get 'ence, the same as I 'ave done,
An' go observin' matters till they die.

What do it matter where or 'ow we die,
So long as we've our 'ealth to watch it all—
The different ways that different things are done,

An' men an' women lovin' in this world;
Takin' our chances as they come along,
An' when they ain't, pretendin' they are good?

In cash or credit—no, it aren't no good;
You 'ave to 'ave the 'abit or you'd die,
Unless you lived your life but one day long,
Nor didn't prophesy nor fret at all,
But drew your tucker some'ow from the world,
An' never bothered what you might ha' done.

But, Gawd, what things are they I 'aven't done!
I've turned my 'and to most, an' turned it good,
In various situations round the world—
For 'im that doth not work must surely die;
But that's no reason man should labor all
'Is life on one same shift—life's none so long.

Therefore, from job to job I've moved along.
Pay couldn't 'old me when my time was done,
For something in my 'ead upset it all,
Till I 'ad dropped whatever 't was for good,
An' out at sea, be'eld the dock-lights die,
An' met my mate—the wind that tramps the world!

It's like a book, I think, this bloomin' world,
Which you can read and care for just so long,
But presently you feel that you will die
Unless you get the page you're readin' done,
An' turn another—likely not so good;
But what you're after is to turn 'em all.

Gawd bless this world! Whatever she 'ath done—
Excep' when awful long—I've found it good.
So write, before I die, " 'E liked it all!"

THE LAND

When Julius Fabricius, Sub-Prefect of the Weald,
In the days of Diocletian owned our Lower River-field,
He called to him Hobdenius—a Briton of the Clay,
Saying, "What about that River-piece for layin' in to hay?"

And the aged Hobden answered: "I remember as a lad
My father told your father that she wanted dreenin' bad.
An' the more that you neeglect her the less you'll get her clean.
Have it jest *as* you've a mind to, but, if I was you, I'd dreen."

So they drained it long and crossways in the lavish Roman style.
Still we find among the river-drift their flakes of ancient tile,
And in drouthy middle August, when the bones of meadows show,
We can trace the lines they followed sixteen hundred years ago.

Then Julius Fabricius died as even Prefects do,
And after certain centuries, Imperial Rome died too.
Then did robbers enter Britain from across the Northern main
And our Lower River-field was won by Ogier the Dane.

Well could Ogier work his war-boat—well could Ogier wield his brand—
Much he knew of foaming waters—not so much of farming land.
So he called to him a Hobden of the old unaltered blood,
Saying: "What about that River-bit, she doesn't look so good."

And that aged Hobden answered: " 'Tain't for *me* to interfere,
But I've known that bit o' meadow now for five and fifty year.
Have it *jest* as you've a mind to, but I've proved it time on time,
If you want to change her nature you have *got* to give her lime!"

Ogier sent his wains to Lewes, twenty hours' solemn walk,
And drew back great abundance of the cool, gray, healing chalk.
And old Hobden spread it broadcast, never heeding what was in't;
Which is why in cleaning ditches, now and then we find a flint.

Ogier died. His sons grew English. Anglo-Saxon was their name,
Till out of blossomed Normandy another pirate came;
For Duke William conquered England and divided with his men,
And our Lower River-field he gave to William of Warenne.

But the Brook (you know her habit) rose one rainy Autumn night
And tore down sodden flitches of the bank to left and right.
So, said William to his Bailiff as they rode their dripping rounds:
"Hob, what about that River-bit—the Brook's got up no bounds?"

And that aged Hobden answered: "Tain't my business to advise,
But ye might ha' known 'twould happen from the way the valley lies.
When ye can't hold back the water you must try and save the sile.
Hev it jest as you've a *mind* to, but if I was you I'd spile."

They spiled along the water-course with trunks of willow-trees
And planks of elms behind 'em and immortal oaken knees.
And when the spates of Autumn whirl the gravel-beds away
You can see their faithful fragments iron-hard in iron clay.

Georgii Quinti, Anno Sexto, I, who own the River-field,
Am fortified with title-deeds, attested, signed and sealed,
Guaranteeing me, my assigns, my executors and heirs
All sorts of powers and profits which—are neither mine nor theirs.

I have rights of chase and warren, as my dignity requires.
I can fish—but Hobden tickles. I can shoot—but Hobden wires.
I repair, but he reopens, certain gaps which, men allege,
Have been used by every Hobden since a Hobden swapped a hedge.

Shall I dog his morning progress o'er the track-betraying dew?
Demand his dinner-basket into which my pheasant flew?
Confiscate his evening faggot into which the conies ran,
And summons him to judgment? I would sooner summons Pan.

His dead are in the churchyard—thirty generations laid.
Their names went down in Domesday Book when Domesday Book was made.
And the passion and the piety and prowess of his line
Have seeded, rooted, fruited in some land the Law calls mine.

Not for any beast that burrows, nor for any bird that flies,
Would I lose his large sound council, miss his keen amending eyes.
He is bailiff, woodman, wheelwright, field-surveyor, engineer,
And if flagrantly a poacher—'tain't for me to interfere.

"Hob, what about that River-bit?" I turn to him again
With Fabricius and Ogier and William of Warenne.
"Hev it jest as you've a mind to, *but*"—and so he takes command.
For whoever pays the taxes, old Mus' Hobden owns the land.

FOR TO ADMIRE

The Injian Ocean sets an' smiles
So sof', so bright, so bloomin' blue;
There aren't a wave for miles an' miles
Excep' the jiggle from the screw.
The ship is swep', the day is done,
The bugle's gone for smoke and play;
An' black agin' the settin' sun
The Lascar sings, *"Hum deckty hai!"*[1]

For to admire an' for to see,
For to be'old this world so wide—
It never done no good to me,
But I can't drop it if I tried!

I see the sergeants pitchin' quoits,
I 'ear the women laugh an' talk,
I spy upon the quarter-deck
The orficers an' lydies walk.
I thinks about the things that was,
An' leans an' looks acrost the sea,
Till spite of all the crowded ship
There's no one lef' alive but me.

The things that was which I 'ave seen,
In barrick, camp, an' action too,
I tells them over by myself,
An' sometimes wonders if they're true;
For they was odd—most awful odd—
But all the same now they are o'er,
There must be 'eaps o' plenty such,
An' if I wait I'll see some more.

[1] "I'm looking out."

Oh, I 'ave come upon the books,
An' frequent broke a barrick rule,
An' stood beside an' watched myself
Be'avin like a bloomin' fool.
I paid my price for findin' out,
Nor never grutched the price I paid,
But sat in Clink without my boots,
Admirin' 'ow the world was made.

Be'old a crowd upon the beam,
An' 'umped above the sea appears
Old Aden, like a barrick-stove
That no one's lit for years an' years!
I passed by that when I began,
An' I go 'ome the road I came,
A time-expired soldier-man
With six years' service to 'is name.

My girl she said, "Oh, stay with me!"
My mother 'eld me to 'er breast.
They've never written none, an' so
They must 'ave gone with all the rest—
With all the rest which I 'ave seen
An' found an' known an' met along.
I cannot say the things I feel,
And so I sing my evenin' song:

For to admire an' for to see,
For to be'old this world so wide—
It never done no good to me,
But I can't drop it if I tried!

L'ENVOI

What is the moral? Who rides may read.
When the night is thick and the tracks are
 blind
A friend at a pinch is a friend indeed,
But a fool to wait for the laggard behind.
Down to Gehenna or up to the Throne,
He travels the fastest who travels alone.

White hands cling to the tightened rein,
Slipping the spur from the booted heel,
Tenderest voices cry "Turn again!"
Red lips tarnish the scabbarded steel.
High hopes faint on a warm hearth stone—
He travels the fastest who travels alone.

One may fall but he falls by himself—
Falls by himself with himself to blame.
One may attain and to him is pelf—
Loot of the city in Gold or Fame.
Plunder of earth shall be all his own
Who travels the fastest and travels alone.

Wherefore the more ye be holpen and stayed,
Stayed by a friend in the hour of toil,
Sing the heretical song I have made—
His be the labour and yours be the spoil.
Win by his aid and the aid disown—
He travels the fastest who travels alone!

"Æ"

George William Russell was born April 10, 1867, in the small town of Lurgan, County Armagh, Ireland. At sixteen he studied painting in the School of Art in Dublin, and became the close friend of W. B. Yeats and, later, James Stephens. While working as an accountant in a draper's establishment, he read much in Oriental mystical literature, becoming the leader of a small theosophical group. At that time he wrote an aricle for *The Irish Theosophist* under the pseudonym "Æon" but the compositor omitted the two last letters and the piece appeared under the diphthong "Æ," a pen-name which Russell adopted.

In 1897 he became active in Irish politics. For several years he devoted himself to establishing coöperative societies, aiding rural communities, editing (in 1904) *The Irish Homestead* and (in 1923) *The Irish Statesman.* There were two distinct, almost opposed, sides to Russell. There was the political and practical side which took him all over Ireland, founding poultry and creamery coöperatives, and made him goad his countrymen out of their ruinously antiquated methods of farming. There was the mystical side which prompted him to join the Theosophists, to see the inanimate earth as a powerfully living organism, and "to run in and out of a house of dream." Russell always maintained he had a double identity, and he kept his two selves clearly separated.

Besides being a public speaker, propagandist, and sociologist, Russell was a painter; his landscapes have the misty-mystical color of his verse, serene and appropriately vague in their otherworldliness. He was the author of several volumes of prose ranging from *Coöperatives and Nationality* (1912) to *The Avatars* (1933). *Song and Its Fountains* (1932) voices his poetic credo.

It was as poet that Russell established himself beyond national borders. The best of his early poetry is in *Homeward: Songs by the Way* (1894) and *The Earth Breath* (1897). Thirteen subsequent volumes revealed, as Yeats wrote, "a kind of scented flame consuming them from within." The choicest of these were collected in *Selected Poems* (1935). The poetry is a curious contradiction of the things for which Russell fought. Completely unconcerned with agrarian issues or, for that matter, any other problems, his poetry maintains that the world is an unreal world, an insubstantial shadow, in which dreams and visions are the only true guides. It is the poetry of one who is drunk with abstract Beauty, devoted to "the Heavenly Brooding" and a sense of the Everlasting.

In spite of a struggle with disease—he was afflicted with cancer—Russell continued working until the end. He died after an operation at Bournemouth, England, July 17, 1935.

SELF-DISCIPLINE

When the soul sought refuge in the place of rest,
Overborne by strife and pain beyond control,
From some secret hollow, whisper soft-confessed,
Came the legend of the soul.

Some bright one of old time laid his sceptre down,
So his heart might learn of sweet and bitter truth;
Going forth bereft of beauty, throne, and crown,
And the sweetness of his youth.

So the old appeal and fierce revolt we make
Through the world's hour dies within our primal will;
And we justify the pain and hearts that break,
And our lofty doom fulfil.

PAIN

Men have made them gods of love,
Sun-gods, givers of the rain,
Deities of hill and grove:
I have made a god of Pain.

Of my god I know this much,
And in singing I repeat,
Though there's anguish in his touch,
Yet his soul within is sweet.

TRUTH

The hero first thought it;
To him 'twas a deed:
To those who retaught it,
A chain on their speed.

The fire that we kindled,
A beacon by night,
When darkness has dwindled
Grows pale in the light.

For life has no glory
Stays long in one dwelling,
And time has no story
That's true twice in telling.

And only the teaching
That never was spoken
Is worthy thy reaching,
The fountain unbroken.

TRAGEDY

A man went forth one day at eve;
The long day's toil for him was done;
The eye that scanned the page could leave
Its task until tomorrow's sun.

Upon the threshold as he stood
Flared on his tired eyes the sight,
Where host on host the multitude
Burned fiercely in the dusky height.

The starry lights at play—at play—
The giant children of the blue
Heaped scorn upon his trembling clay,
And with their laughter pierced him through.

They seemed to say in scorn of him:
"The power we have was once in thee.
King, is thy spirit grown so dim,
That thou art slave and we are free?"

As out of him the power—the power—
The free, the fearless, whirled in play,
He knew himself that bitter hour
The close of all his royal day.

And from the stars' exultant dance
Within the fiery furnace glow,
Exile of all the vast expanse,
He turned him homeward sick and slow.

THE GREAT BREATH

Its edges foamed with amethyst and rose,
Withers once more the old blue flower of day:
There where the ether like a diamond glows,
Its petals fade away.

A shadowy tumult stirs the dusky air;
Sparkle the delicate dews, the distant snows;
The great deep thrills—for through it everywhere
The breath of Beauty blows.

I saw how all the trembling ages past,
Molded to her by deep and deeper breath,
Near'd to the hour when Beauty breathes her last
And knows herself in death.

FROLIC

The children were shouting together
And racing along the sands,
A glimmer of dancing shadows,
A dovelike flutter of hands.

The stars were shouting in heaven,
The sun was chasing the moon:
The game was the same as the children's,
They danced to the self-same tune.

The whole of the world was merry,
One joy from the vale to the height,
Where the blue woods of twilight encircled
The love-lawns of the light.

THE SECRET

One thing in all things have I seen:
One thought has haunted earth and air:
Clangor and silence both have been
Its palace chambers. Everywhere

I saw the mystic vision flow
And live in men and woods and streams,
Until I could no longer know
The dream of life from my own dreams.

Sometimes it rose like fire in me
Within the depths of my own mind,
And spreading to infinity,
It took the voices of the wind:

It scrawled the human mystery—
Dim heraldry—on light and air;
Wavering along the starry sea
I saw the flying vision there.

Each fire that in God's temple lit
Burns fierce before the inner shrine,
Dimmed as my fire grew near to it
And darkened at the light of mine.

At last, at last, the meaning caught—
The Spirit wears its diadem;
It shakes its wondrous plumes of thought
And trails the stars along with them.

THE UNKNOWN GOD

Far up the dim twilight fluttered
  Moth-wings of vapor and flame:
The lights danced over the mountains,
  Star after star they came.

The lights grew thicker unheeded,
  For silent and still were we;
Our hearts were drunk with a beauty
  Our eyes could never see.

CONTINUITY

No sign is made while empires pass,
The flowers and stars are still His care,
The constellations hid in grass,
The golden miracles in air.

Life in an instant will be rent,
Where death is glittering blind and wild—
The Heavenly Brooding is intent
To that last instant on Its child.

It breathes the glow in brain and heart,
Life is made magical. Until
Body and spirit are apart,
The Everlasting works Its will.

In that wild orchid that your feet
In their next falling shall destroy,
Minute and passionate and sweet
The Mighty Master holds His joy.

Though the crushed jewels droop and fade,
The Artist's labors will not cease,
And of the ruins shall be made
Some yet more lovely masterpiece.

EPILOGUE

Well, when all is said and done
Best within my narrow way,
May some angel of the sun
Muse memorial o'er my clay:

"Here was Beauty all betrayed
From the freedom of her state;
From her human uses stayed
On an idle rhyme to wait.

"Ah, what deep despair might move
If the beauty lit a smile,
Or the heart was warm with love
That was pondering the while.

"He has built his monument
With the winds of time at strife,
Who could have, before he went,
Written in the Book of Life.

"To the stars from which he came
Empty-handed he goes home;
He who might have wrought in flame
Only traced upon the foam."

EXILES

The gods have taken alien shapes upon them,
Wild peasants driving swine
In a strange country. Through the swarthy faces
The starry faces shine.

Under grey tattered skies they strain and reel there:
Yet cannot all disguise
The majesty of fallen gods, the beauty,
The fire beneath their eyes.

They huddle at night within low, clay-built cabins;
And, to themselves unknown,
They carry with them diadem and sceptre
And move from throne to throne.

GERMINAL

Call not thy wanderer home as yet
  Though it be late.
Now is his first assailing of
  The invisible gate.
Be still through that light knocking. The hour
  Is thronged with fate.

To that first tapping at the invisible door
  Fate answereth.
What shining image or voice, what sigh
  Or honied breath,
Comes forth, shall be the master of life
  Even to death.

Satyrs may follow after. Seraphs
  On crystal wing
May blaze. But the delicate first comer
  It shall be King.
They shall obey, even the mightiest,
  That gentle thing.

All the strong powers of Dante were bowed
  To a child's mild eyes,
That wrought within him travail
  From depths up to skies,
Inferno, Purgatorio,
  And Paradise.

Amid the soul's grave councillors
  A petulant boy
Laughs under the laurels and purples, the elf
  Who snatched at his joy,
Ordering Caesar's legions to bring him
  The world for his toy.

In ancient shadows and twilights
  Where childhood had strayed,
The world's great sorrows were born
  And its heroes were made.
In the lost boyhood of Judas
  Christ was betrayed.

Let thy young wanderer dream on:
  Call him not home.
A door opens, a breath, a voice
  From the ancient room,
Speaks to him now. Be it dark or bright
  He is knit with his doom.

Ernest Dowson

⁂ Ernest Dowson was born at Belmont Hill in Kent, August 2, 1867. His great-uncle was Alfred Domett (Browning's "Waring"), one time Prime Minister of New Zealand. Dowson, practically an invalid all his life, lived intermittently in London, Paris, Normandy, and on the Riviera. He was reckless with himself and, as disease weakened him more and more, hid in miserable surroundings; for almost two years he lived in sordid supper-houses known as "cabmen's shelters."

He formed only one passion but that one was final and devastating. He fell in love with a restaurant-keeper's daughter, paid court to her with the most delicate reserve, and she—impatient alike of his words and his reticences—married a waiter. The shock to Dowson was profound. He grew more and more withdrawn, even his contacts with fellow-members of the Rhymers' Club became slighter. He sank into despondency and dissipation; he literally drank himself to death.

Dowson's delicate and fantastic poetry was an attempt to escape from a reality too brutal for him. It is not only typically *fin de siécle;* it is, as any psychoanalytical critic will recognize, curiously autobiographical. He, himself, was his own pitiful "Pierrot of the Minute," throwing "roses, riotously with the throng"—even though the throng was ignorant of him. His passionate lyric, "I have been faithful to thee, Cynara! in my fashion," a triumph of despair and disillusion, is an outburst in which Dowson epitomized himself. "One of the greatest lyrical poems of our time," writes Arthur Symons; "in it he has for once said everything, and he has said it to an intoxicating and perhaps immortal music."

Yet, in spite of the fact that this familiar poem has been quoted in almost every contemporary collection, several of Dowson's less well-known poems strike a higher and far more resonant note. Among such poems are "Extreme Unction," possibly the finest expression of his Catholicism, and "A Last Word," which expresses his revulsion from the "perverse and aimless band."

Dowson's poems of decadence are no less typical than his religious poems; both, unlike the product of much of his period, are sincere. His mysticism, no less than his idealization of preciosity, is an esthetic one. Unable to find fulfillment in either, he wavered, as C. E. Andrews and M. O. Percival say in *Poetry of the Nineties,* "between heaping garlands upon the altars of Aphrodite and lighting candles to the Blessed Virgin."

Dowson died obscure in 1900, one of the least effectual but one of the most gifted of modern minor poets. His life was a tragedy of a weak nature buffeted by a strong and merciless environment. His poetry, highly special but never specious, survives.

A LAST WORD

Let us go hence: the night is now at hand;
  The day is overworn, the birds all flown;
  And we have reaped the crops the gods have sown;
Despair and death; deep darkness o'er the land,

Broods like an owl; we cannot understand
  Laughter or tears, for we have only known
  Surpassing vanity: vain things alone
Have driven our perverse and aimless band.

Let us go hence, somewhither strange and cold,
  To Hollow Lands where just men and unjust
  Find end of labor, where's rest for the old,
Freedom to all from love and fear and lust.
Twine our torn hands! O pray the earth enfold
Our life-sick hearts and turn them into dust.

NON SUM QUALIS ERAM BONAE SUB REGNO CYNARAE

Last night, ah, yesternight, betwixt her lips and mine
There fell thy shadow, Cynara! thy breath was shed
Upon my soul between the kisses and the wine;
And I was desolate and sick of an old passion,
  Yea, I was desolate and bowed my head:
I have been faithful to thee, Cynara! in my fashion.

All night upon mine heart I felt her warm heart beat,
Night-long within mine arms in love and sleep she lay;
Surely the kisses of her bought red mouth were sweet;
But I was desolate and sick of an old passion,
  When I awoke and found the dawn was gray;
I have been faithful to thee, Cynara! in my fashion.

I have forgot much, Cynara! gone with the wind,
Flung roses, roses riotously with the throng,
Dancing, to put thy pale, lost lilies out of mind;
But I was desolate and sick of an old passion,
  Yea, all the time, because the dance was long:
I have been faithful to thee, Cynara! in my fashion.

I cried for madder music and for stronger wine,
But when the feast is finished and the lamps expire,
Then falls thy shadow, Cynara! the night is thine;
And I am desolate and sick of an old passion,
  Yea, hungry for the lips of my desire:
I have been faithful to thee, Cynara! in my fashion.

SPLEEN

I was not sorrowful, I could not weep,
And all my memories were put to sleep.

I watched the river grow more white and strange,
All day till evening I watched it change.

All day till evening I watched the rain
Beat wearily upon the window-pane.

I was not sorrowful, but only tired
Of everything that ever I desired.

Her lips, her eyes, all day became to me
The shadow of a shadow utterly.
All day mine hunger for her heart became
Oblivion, until the evening came.

And left me sorrowful, inclined to weep,
With all my memories that could not sleep.

TO ONE IN BEDLAM

With delicate, mad hands, behind his sordid bars,
Surely he hath his posies, which they tear and twine;
Those scentless wisps of straw that, miserable, line
His strait, caged universe, whereat the dull world stares,

Pedant and pitiful. O, how his rapt gaze wars
With their stupidity! Know they what dreams divine
Lift his long, laughing reveries like enchanted wine,
And make his melancholy germane to the stars?

O lamentable brother! if those pity thee,
Am I not fain of all thy lone eyes promise me;
Half a fool's kingdom, far from men who sow and reap,
All their days, vanity? Better than mortal flowers,
Thy moon-kissed roses seem: better than love or sleep,
The star-crowned solitude of thine oblivious hours!

EXTREME UNCTION

pon the eyes, the lips, the feet,
On all the passages of sense,
he atoning oil is spread with sweet
Renewal of lost innocence.

he feet, that lately ran so fast
To meet desire, are soothly sealed;
he eyes that were so often cast
On vanity, are touched and healed.

rom troublous sights and sounds set free;
In such a twilight hour of breath
Shall one retrace his life, or see
Through shadows the true face of death?

Vials of mercy! Sacring oils!
I know not where nor when I come,
Nor through what wanderings and toils,
To crave of you Viaticum.

Yet, when the walls of flesh grow weak,
In such an hour, it well may be,
Through mist and darkness, light will break,
And each anointed sense will see!

YOU WOULD HAVE UNDERSTOOD ME

You would have understood me had you waited;
I could have loved you, dear! as well as he:
Had we not been impatient, dear! and fated
Always to disagree.

What is the use of Speech? Silence were fitter:
Lest we should still be wishing things unsaid.
Though all the words we ever spake were bitter,
Shall I reproach you, dead?

Nay, let this earth, your portion, likewise cover
All the old anger, setting us apart:
Always, in all, in truth was I your lover;
Always, I held your heart.

I have met other women who were tender,
As you were cold, dear! with a grace as rare.
Think you, I turned to them, or made surrender,
I who had found you fair?

Had we been patient, dear! ah, had you waited,
I had fought death for you, better than he:
But from the very first, dear! we were fated
Always to disagree.

Late, late, I come to you, now death discloses
Love that in life was not to be our part:
On your low lying mound between the roses,
Sadly I cast my heart.

I would not waken you: nay! this is fitter;
Death and the darkness give you unto me;
Here we who loved so, were so cold and bitter,
Hardly can disagree.

VILLANELLE OF MARGUERITES

"A little, passionately, not at all?"
She casts the snowy petals on the air;
And what care we how many petals fall?

Nay, wherefore seek the seasons to forestall?
It is but playing, and she will not care,
A little, passionately, not at all!

She would not answer us if we should call
Across the years; her visions are too fair;
And what care we how many petals fall!

She knows us not, nor recks if she enthrall
With voice and eyes and fashion of her hair,
A little, passionately, not at all!

Knee-deep she goes in meadow-grasses tall,
Kissed by the daisies that her fingers tear;
And what care we how many petals fall!

We pass and go; but she shall not recall
What men we were, nor all she made us bear;
"A little, passionately, not at all!"
And what care we how many petals fall!

ENVOY

(Vitae summa brevis spem nos vetat incohare longam)

They are not long, the weeping and the laughter,
Love and desire and hate;
I think they have no portion in us after
We pass the gate.

They are not long, the days of wine and roses:
Out of a misty dream
Our path emerges for a while, then closes
Within a dream.

Lionel Johnson

Born in 1867, at Broadstairs in Kent, Lionel (Pigot) Johnson received a classical education at Oxford; his poetry is a reflection of his studies in Greek and Latin literatures. Though he allied himself with the modern Irish poets, his Celtic origin is a literary myth; Johnson, having been converted to Catholicism in 1891, became imbued with Catholic and Irish traditions. Yeats, who became his intimate friend, says it was Johnson's habit to sleep all day and read and write all night, the ordinary world about him having no significance to the recluse. "In my library," Johnson said, "I have all the knowledge I need of the world."

Before any of his poetry was collected in a volume, he published a book on *The Art of Thomas Hardy* (1894) which, though planned before the appearance of *Jude the Obscure* or *The Dynasts*, remains one of the most sensitive studies of Hardy yet written. His verse, published originally among the bizarre novelties of *The Yellow Book*, was curiously cool and removed; he seemed, as one of his associates had said, a young monk surrounded by dancing pagans. "Divine austerity" is the goal to which his verse aspires. While sometimes over-decorated, it is chastely designed, and, like that of the Cavalier poets of the seventeenth century, fiercely devotional. Today, with such poems as "Mystic and Cavalier," "The Precept of Silence," and "The Dark Angel," he seems the most important of his group; his voice has found echoes in recent poetry, particularly in the poems of Yeats.

Johnson was one of the many poets to whom conversion to the Church supplied not only a new color but a new impetus. It is a subject rich in speculation why this period should have yielded so many artists who turned to the Catholic Church for inspiration in their life and work; among the most eminent converts, besides Johnson, were Alice Meynell, Ernest Dowson, Oscar Wilde, and Aubrey Beardsley.

Poems (1895) and *Ireland* (1897) were published during his lifetime; a posthumous collection of essays, *Post Liminium,* appeared in 1911. A collected edition of his poems was brought out in 1915. Johnson died tragically in 1902.

MYSTIC AND CAVALIER

Go from me: I am one of those who fall.
What! hath no cold wind swept your heart at all,
In my sad company? Before the end,
Go from me, dear my friend!

Yours are the victories of light: your feet
Rest from good toil, where rest is brave and sweet:
But after warfare in a mourning gloom,
I rest in clouds of doom.

Have you not read so, looking in these eyes?
Is it the common light of the pure skies
Lights up their shadowy depths? The end is set:
Though the end be not yet.

When gracious music stirs, and all is bright,
And beauty triumphs through a courtly night;
When I too joy, a man like other men:
Yet, am I like them, then?

And in the battle, when the horsemen sweep
Against a thousand deaths, and fall on sleep:
Who ever sought that sudden calm, if I
Sought not? yet could not die!

Seek with thine eyes to pierce this crystal sphere:
Canst read a fate there, prosperous and clear?
Only the mists, only the weeping clouds,
Dimness and airy shrouds.

Beneath, what angels are at work? What powers
Prepare the secret of the fatal hours?
See! the mists tremble, and the clouds are stirred:
When comes the calling word?

The clouds are breaking from the crystal ball,
Breaking and clearing: and I look to fall.
When the cold winds and airs of portent sweep,
My spirit may have sleep.

O rich and sounding voices of the air!
Interpreters and prophets of despair:
Priests of a fearful sacrament! I come
To make with you mine home.

TO MORFYDD

A voice on the winds,
A voice by the waters,
Wanders and cries:
Oh! what are the winds?
And what are the waters?
Mine are your eyes!

Western the winds are,
And western the waters,
Where the light lies:
Oh! what are the winds?
And what are the waters?
Mine are your eyes!

Cold, cold grow the winds,
And wild grow the waters,
Where the sun dies:
Oh! what are the winds?
And what are the waters?
Mine are your eyes!

And down the night winds,
And down the night waters,
The music flies:
Oh! what are the winds?
And what are the waters?
Cold be the winds,
And wild be the waters,
So mine be your eyes!

BY THE STATUE OF KING CHARLES AT CHARING CROSS

Somber and rich, the skies,
Great glooms, and starry plains;
Gently the night wind sighs;
Else a vast silence reigns.

The splendid silence clings
Around me: and around
The saddest of all Kings,
Crown'd, and again discrown'd.

Comely and calm, he rides
Hard by his own Whitehall.
Only the night wind glides:
No crowds, no rebels, brawl.

Gone, too, his Court: and yet,
The stars his courtiers are:
Stars in their stations set;
And every wandering star.

Alone he rides, alone,
The fair and fatal King:
Dark night is all his own,
That strange and solemn thing.

Which are more full of fate:
The stars, or those sad eyes?
Which are more still and great:
Those brows, or the dark skies?

Although his whole heart yearn
In passionate tragedy,
Never was face so stern,
With sweet austerity.

Vanquish'd in life, his death
By beauty made amends:
The passing of his breath
Won his defeated ends.

Brief life and hapless? Nay:
Through death, life grew sublime,
Speak after sentence? Yea:
And to the end of time.

Armor'd he rides, his head
Bare to the stars of doom;
He triumphs now, the dead,
Beholding London's gloom.

Our wearier spirit faints,
Vex'd in the world's employ:
His soul was of the saints;
And art to him was joy.

King, tried in fires of woe!
Men hunger for thy grace:
And through the night I go,
Loving thy mournful face.

Yet, when the city sleeps,
When all the cries are still,
The stars and heavenly deeps
Work out a perfect will.

TO A TRAVELER

The mountains, and the lonely death at last
Upon the lonely mountains: O strong friend!
The wandering over, and the labor passed,
    Thou art indeed at rest:
    Earth gave thee of her best,
    That labor and this end.

Earth was thy mother, and her true son thou:
Earth called thee to a knowledge of her ways,
Upon the great hills, up the great streams: now:
    Upon earth's kindly breast
    Thou art indeed at rest:
    Thou, and thine arduous days.

Fare thee well, O strong heart! The tranquil night
Looks calmly on thee: and the sun pours down
His glory over thee, O heart of might!
    Earth gives thee perfect rest:
    Earth, whom thy swift feet pressed:
    Earth, whom the vast stars crown.

THE DARK ANGEL

Dark Angel, with thine aching lust
To rid the world of penitence:
Malicious Angel, who still dost
My soul such subtile violence!

Because of thee, no thought, no thing,
Abides for me undesecrate:
Dark Angel, ever on the wing,
Who never reachest me too late!

When music sounds, then changest thou
Its silvery to a sultry fire:
Nor will thine envious heart allow
Delight untortured by desire.

Through thee, the gracious Muses turn
To Furies, O mine Enemy!
And all the things of beauty burn
With flames of evil ecstasy.

Because of thee, the land of dreams
Becomes a gathering place of fears.
Until tormented slumber seems
One vehemence of useless tears.

When sunlight glows upon the flowers,
Or ripples down the dancing sea:
Thou, with thy troop of passionate powers,
Beleaguerest, bewilderest, me.

Within the breath of autumn woods,
Within the winter silences:
Thy venomous spirit stirs and broods,
O Master of impieties!

The ardor of red flames is thine,
And thine the steely soul of ice:
Thou poisonest the fair design
Of nature, with unfair device.

Apples of ashes, golden bright;
Waters of bitterness, how sweet!
O banquet of a foul delight,
Prepared by thee, dark Paraclete!

Thou art the whisper in the gloom,
The hinting tone, the haunting laugh:
Thou art the adorner of my tomb,
The minstrel of mine epitaph.

I fight thee, in the Holy Name!
Yet, what thou dost is what God saith:
Tempter! should I escape thy flame,
Thou wilt have helped my soul from Death:

The second Death, that never dies,
That cannot die, when time is dead:
Live Death, wherein the lost soul cries,
Eternally uncomforted.

Dark Angel, with thine aching lust!
Of two defeats, of two despairs;
Less dread, a change to drifting dust,
Than thine eternity of cares.

Do what thou wilt, thou shalt not so,
Dark Angel! triumph over me:
Lonely, unto the Lone I go;
Divine, to the Divinity.

THE PRECEPT OF SILENCE

I know you: solitary griefs,
Desolate passions, aching hours!
I know you: tremulous beliefs,
Agonized hopes, and ashen flowers!

The winds are sometimes sad to me;
The starry spaces, full of fear:
Mine is the sorrow on the sea,
And mine the sigh of places drear.

Some players upon plaintive strings
Publish their wistfulness abroad:
I have not spoken of these things,
Save to one man, and unto God.

Laurence Binyon

(Robert) Laurence Binyon was born at Lancaster, August 10, 1869, son of a clergyman, and a cousin of the poet and playwright, Stephen Phillips. Educated at Trinity College, Oxford, Binyon won the Newdigate Prize in his twenty-first year with the long poem *Persephone.* The publication of this poem was followed by *Primavera* (1890), a collaboration with his cousin and two friends; a tragedy in four acts entitled *Attila;* studies of Dutch etchers of the seventeenth century; and *The Popularization of Art* (1896).

Although Binyon's energy and versatility was apparent, his early poetry showed little distinction until he published *London Visions,* which, in an enlarged edition in 1908, revealed a gift of characterization and a turn of speech in surprising contrast to his previous academic *Lyrical Poems* (1894). His *Odes* (1901) contains his ripest work; two poems in particular, "The Threshold" and "The Bacchanal of Alexander," are glowing and unusually spontaneous.

Binyon's talent continued to grow; age gave his verse a new sharpness. Sixty poems were published in *The Secret* (1920), most of which reflect the poet's dignity with a definiteness which he never before attained. *Selected Poems* (1924) is an excellently arranged sequence which includes Binyon's finest work, with the exception of *The Sirens* (1927), a long, elaborate ode in which the slow-paced rhythms have wide scope.

Binyon's *Collected Poems* (1931), in two volumes, reveal his progress from purely scholarly patterns to flexibility. The later verses are deepened with an unusual power of thought and with a restrained music.

For fifty years—from 1893 until his death in 1943—Binyon was head of the Department of Printed Books in the British Museum. One volume of his critical studies—*English Poetry in its Relation to Painting and the Other Arts* (1919)—is especially rewarding to those interested in the kinship of the arts.

THE LITTLE DANCERS

Lonely, save for a few faint stars, the sky
Dreams; and lonely, below, the little street
Into its gloom retires, secluded and shy.
Scarcely the dumb roar enters this soft retreat;
And all is dark, save where come flooding rays
From a tavern window; there, to the brisk measure
Of an organ that down in an alley merrily plays,
Two children, all alone and no one by,
Holding their tattered frocks, thro' an airy maze
Of motion lightly threaded with nimble feet
Dance sedately; face to face they gaze,
Their eyes shining, grave with a perfect pleasure.

O WORLD, BE NOBLER

O world, be nobler, for her sake!
  If she but knew thee what thou art,
What wrongs are borne, what deeds are done
In thee, beneath thy daily sun,
  Know'st thou not that her tender heart
For pain and very shame would break?
  O World, be nobler, for her sake!

NOTHING IS ENOUGH

Nothing is enough!
No, though our all be spent—

Heart's extremest love,
Spirit's whole intent,
All that nerve can feel,
All that brain invent,—
Still beyond appeal
Will Divine Desire
Yet more excellent
Precious cost require
Of this mortal stuff,—
Never be content
Till ourselves be fire.
Nothing is enough!

BEAUTY

I think of a flower that no eye has ever seen,
That springs in a solitary air.
Is it no one's joy? It is beautiful as a queen
Without a kingdom's care.

We have built houses for Beauty, and costly shrines,
And a throne in all men's view:
But she was far on a hill where the morning shines
And her steps were lost in the dew.

A SONG

For Mercy, Courage, Kindness, Mirth,
There is no measure upon earth.
Nay, they wither, root and stem,
If an end be set to them.

Overbrim and overflow,
If your own heart you would know;
For the spirit born to bless
Lives but in its own excess.

THE HOUSE THAT WAS

Of the old house, only a few crumbled
Courses of brick, smothered in nettle and dock,
Or a squared stone, lying mossy where it tumbled.
Sprawling bramble and saucy thistle mock
What once was firelit floor and private charm
Whence, seen in a windowed picture, were hills fading
At dusk, and all was memory-colored and warm,
And voices talked, secure from the wind's invading.

Of the old garden, only a stray shining
Of daffodil flames amid April's cuckoo-flowers,

Or a cluster of aconite mixt with weeds entwining!
  But, dark and lofty, a royal cedar towers
By homely thorns; and whether the white rain drifts
  Or sun scorches, he holds the downs in ken,
The western vales; his branchy tiers he lifts,
  Older than many a generation of men.

Charlotte Mew

⟡ Charlotte (Mary) Mew was born November 15, 1869, the daughter of an architect of distinction, who died when she was an infant. Little is generally known of her life except that it was a long struggle not only with poverty but with adversity and private sorrows that finally overcame her. In her late fifties, through the joint efforts of Hardy, De la Mare, and Masefield, she was granted a Civil List pension. Though she loved the country, she was forced to live almost continually in London, in the very heart of Bloomsbury, becoming more and more of a recluse. One of her few excursions was a week-end at Max Gate, where she was the guest of Thomas Hardy, who considered her the best woman poet of her day. The death of her mother was a blow from which she never recovered; the death of her sister hastened her end. As Sidney C. Cockerell wrote, "Charlotte and Anne Mew had more than a little in them of what made another Charlotte and Anne, and their sister Emily, what they were. They were indeed like two Brontë sisters reincarnate."

Charlotte Mew died by her own hand in a nursing home March 24, 1928.

In the obituary note which Sidney Cockerell wrote for the *London Times* few new facts came to light. It was learned that Charlotte Mew wrote much more than was suspected, but "how much she destroyed at house-movings and during periods of overwhelming depression, we shall never know. There can be no doubt that her fastidious self-criticism proved fatal to much work that was really good, and that the printed poems are far less than a tithe of what she composed. These first appeared in various periodicals. In 1916, seventeen of them were collected into a thin volume which was issued by the Poetry Book Shop for a shilling. In 1921 this volume, named *The Farmer's Bride,* after the opening poem, was re-issued with the addition of 11 new poems, 28 in all. Perhaps not more than another 20 have seen the light. But, although the visible output was so small, the quality was in each case poignant and arresting. These poems are written as though with the life-blood of a noble and passionate heart."

One of Charlotte Mew's first discoverers was Alida Klemantaski (later Mrs. Harold Monro), who was not only responsible for the publication of *The Farmer's Bride,* but for the printing of the posthumous *The Rambling Sailor* (1929) to which she furnished a Memoir. The first book was brought out in America under the title of *Saturday Market* in 1921. Had Miss Mew printed nothing but the original booklet, it would have been sufficient to rank her among the most distinctive and intense of living poets. Hers is the distillation, the essence of emotion, rather than the stirring up of passion. Her most remarkable work is in dramatic projections and monologues (unfortunately too long to quote) like "The Changeling," with its fantastic pathos, and that powerful meditation, "Madeleine in Church." But lyrics as swift as "Sea Love," or as ageless as "Song," with its simple finality, or as hymn-like as "I Have Been Through the Gates" are equally sure of their place in English literature. They are, in common with all of Charlotte Mew's work, disturbing in their direct beauty; full of a speech that is noble and profound without ever becoming pompous. Apart from her other qualities (not the least of which is her control of an unusually long and extraordinarily flexible line) Miss Mew's work is a series of triumphs in condensation.

"To a Child in Death," a strangely premonitory poem, "In the Fields," and "Old Shepherd's Prayer" are among those given in manuscript by Charlotte Mew to the editor shortly before her death. These, with thirty other posthumous poems, appeared in a definitive *Collected Poems* (1954).

IN THE FIELDS

Lord, when I look at lovely things which pass,
Under old trees the shadow of young leaves
Dancing to please the wind along the grass,
Or the gold stillness of the August sun on the August sheaves;
Can I believe there is a heavenlier world than this?
And if there is
Will the strange heart of any everlasting thing
Bring me these dreams that take my breath away?
They come at evening with the home-flying rooks and the scent of hay,
Over the fields. They come in Spring.

SEA LOVE

Tide be runnin' the great world over:
'Twas only last June month I mind that we
Was thinkin' the toss and the call in the breast of the lover
So everlastin' as the sea.

Here's the same little fishes that sputter and swim,
Wi' the moon's old glim on the gray, wet sand;
An' him no more to me nor me to him
Than the wind goin' over my hand.

I HAVE BEEN THROUGH THE GATES

His heart, to me, was a place of palaces and pinnacles and shining towers;
I saw it then as we see things in dreams,—I do not remember how long I slept;
I remember the trees, and the high, white walls, and how the sun was always on the towers;
The walls are standing today, and the gates: I have been through the gates, I have groped, I have crept
Back, back. There is dust in the streets, and blood; they are empty; darkness is over them;

His heart is a place with the lights gone out, forsaken by great winds and the
heavenly rain, unclean and unswept,
Like the heart of the holy city, old, blind, beautiful Jerusalem,
Over which Christ wept.

TO A CHILD IN DEATH

You would have scoffed if we had told you yesterday
Love made us feel—or so it was with me—like some great bird
Trying to hold and shelter you in its strong wing;—
A gay little shadowy smile would have tossed us back such a solemn word,
And it was not for that you were listening
When so quietly you slipped away
With half the music of the world unheard.
What shall we do with this strange Summer, meant for you,—
Dear, if we see the Winter through
What shall be done with Spring—?
This, this is the victory of the grave; here is death's sting.
That it is not strong enough, our strongest wing.

But what of His who like a Father pitieth—?
His Son was also, once, a little thing,
The wistfulest child that ever drew breath,
Chased by a sword from Bethlehem and in the busy house at Nazareth
Playing with little rows of nails, watching the carpenter's hammer swing,
Long years before His hands and feet were tied
And by a hammer and the three great nails He died,
Of youth, of Spring,
Of sorrow, of loneliness, of victory the king,
Under the shadow of that wing.

SONG

Love, Love today, my dear,
Love is not always here;
Wise maids know how soon grows sere
The greenest leaf of Spring;
But no man knoweth
Whither it goeth
When the wind bloweth
So frail a thing.

Love, Love, my dear, today,
If the ship's in the bay,
If the bird has come your way
That sings on summer trees;
When his song faileth
And the ship saileth
No voice availeth
To call back these.

THE FARMER'S BRIDE

Three summers since I chose a maid,
Too young maybe—but more's to do
At harvest-time than bide and woo.
  When us was wed she turned afraid
Of love and me and all things human;
Like the shut of a winter's day.
Her smile went out, and 'twasn't a woman—
  More like a little frightened fay.
    One night, in the Fall, she runned away.

"Out 'mong the sheep, her be," they said,
"Should properly have been abed;
But sure enough she wasn't there
Lying awake with her wide brown stare.
So over seven-acre field and up-along across the down
We chased her, flying like a hare
Before our lanterns. To Church-Town
  All in a shiver and a scare
We caught her, fetched her home at last
  And turned the key upon her, fast.

She does the work about the house
As well as most, but like a mouse:
  Happy enough to chat and play
  With birds and rabbits and such as they,
  So long as men-folk keep away.
"Not near, not near!" her eyes beseech
When one of us comes within reach.
  The women say that beasts in stall
  Look round like children at her call.
  I've hardly heard her speak at all.

Shy as a leveret, swift as he,
Straight and slight as a young larch tree,
Sweet as the first wild violets, she
To her wild self. But what to me?

The short days shorten and the oaks are brown,
  The blue smoke rises to the low gray sky,
One leaf in the still air falls slowly down,
  A magpie's spotted feathers lie
On the black earth spread white with rime,
The berries redden up to Christmas-time.
  What's Christmas-time without there be
  Some other in the house than we!

  She sleeps up in the attic there
  Alone, poor maid. 'Tis but a stair
Betwixt us. Oh! my God! the down,
The soft young down of her, the brown,
The brown of her—her eyes, her hair, her hair . . .

BESIDE THE BED

Someone has shut the shining eyes, straightened and folded
  The wandering hands quietly covering the unquiet breast:
So, smoothed and silenced you lie, like a child, not again to be questioned or scolded:
  But, for you, not one of us believes that this is rest.

Not so to close the windows down can cloud and deaden
  The blue beyond: or to screen the wavering flame subdue its breath:
Why, if I lay my cheek to your cheek, your gray lips, like dawn, would quiver and redden,
  Breaking into the old, odd smile at this fraud of death.

Because all night you have not turned to us or spoken
  It is time for you to wake; your dreams were never very deep:
I, for one, have seen the thin bright, twisted threads of them dimmed suddenly and broken.
  This is only a most piteous pretense of sleep!

FROM "MADELEINE IN CHURCH"

How old was Mary out of whom you cast
  So many devils? Was she young or perhaps for years
She had sat staring, with dry eyes, at this and that man going past
  Till suddenly she saw You on the steps of Simon's house
    And stood and looked at You through tears.
      I think she must have known by those
    The thing, for what it was that had come to her.
    For some of us there is a passion, I suppose,
    So far from earthly cares and earthly fears
    That in its stillness you can hardly stir
      Or in its nearness lift your hand,
    So great that you have simply got to stand
    Looking at it through tears, through tears.
    Then straight from these there broke the kiss.
      I think You must have known by this
    The thing, for what it was that had come to You:
      She did not love You like the rest,
    It was in her own way, but at the worst, the best,
      She gave you something altogether new.
     And through it all, from her, no word,
      She scarcely saw You, scarcely heard:
    Surely You knew when she so touched You with her hair,
      Or by the wet cheek lying there,
And while her perfume clung to You from head to feet all through the day
    That You can change the things for which we care,
    But even You, unless You kill us, not the way.

    This then was peace for her, but passion too.
    I wonder was it like a kiss that once I knew,

The only one that I would care to take
Into the grave with me, to which if there were afterwards, to wake
Almost as happy as the carven dead
In some dim chancel lying head to head
We slept with it, but face to face, the whole night through—
One breath, one throbbing quietness, as if the thing behind our lips was endless life,
Lost, as I woke, to hear in the strange earthly dawn, his "Are you there?"
And lie still, listening to the wind outside, among the firs.

So Mary chose the dream of Him for what was left to her of night and day.
It is the only truth: it is the dream in us that neither life nor death nor any other thing can take away:
But if she had not touched Him in the doorway of the dream could she have cared so much?
She was a sinner, we are what we are: the spirit afterwards, but first, the touch.

And He has never shared with me my haunted house beneath the trees
Of Eden and Calvary, with its ghosts that have not any eyes for tears,
And the happier guests, who would not see, or if they did, remember these,
Though they lived here a thousand years.
Outside, too gravely looking at me, He seems to stand,
And looking at Him if my forgotten spirit came
Unwillingly back, what could it claim
Of those calm eyes, that quiet speech,
Breaking like a slow tide upon the beach,
The scarred, not quite human hand?—
Unwillingly back to the burden of old imaginings
When it has learned so long not to think, not to be,
Again, again it would speak as it has spoken to me of things
That I shall not see!

AGAIN

One day, not here, you will find a hand
Stretched out to you as you walk down some heavenly street;
You will see a stranger scarred from head to feet;
But when he speaks to you you will not understand,
Nor yet who wounded him nor why his wounds are sweet.
And saying nothing, letting go his hand,
You will leave him in the heavenly street—
So we shall meet!

OLD SHEPHERD'S PRAYER

Up to bed by the window, where I be lyin',
Comes bells and bleats of the flock wi' they two children's clack.
Over, from under the eaves there's the starlings flyin',
And down in yard, fit to burst his chain, yapping out at Sue I do hear young Mac.

Turning around like a falled-over sack
I can see team plowin' in Whithy-bush field and meal carts startin' up road to
Church-Town;
Saturday arternoon then men goin' back
And the women from market, trapin' home over the down.

Heavenly Master, I wud like to wake to they same green places
Where I'd be know'd for breakin' dogs and follerin' sheep.
And if I may not walk in th' old ways and look on th' old faces
I wud sooner sleep.

THE TREES ARE DOWN

—and he cried with a loud voice:
Hurt not the earth, neither the sea, nor the trees—
(Revelation.)

They are coming down the great plane-trees at the end of the gardens.
For days there has been the grate of the saw, the swish of the branches as they fall,
The crash of trunks, the rustle of trodden leaves,
With the "Whoops" and the "Whoas," the loud common talk, the loud common
laughs of the men, above it all.

I remember one evening of a long past Spring
Turning in at a gate, getting out of a cart, and finding a large dead rat in the
mud of the drive.
I remember thinking: alive or dead, a rat was a god-forsaken thing,
But at least, in May, that even a rat should be alive.

The week's work here is as good as done. There is just one bough
On the roped bole, in the fine gray rain,
Green and high
And lonely against the sky.
(Down now!—)
And but for that,
If an old dead rat
Did once, for a moment, unmake the Spring, I might never have thought of him
again.

It is not for a moment the Spring is unmade today;
These were great trees, it was in them from root to stem:
When the men with the "Whoops" and the "Whoas" have carted the whole of the
whispering loveliness away
Half the Spring, for me, will have gone with them.

It is going now, and my heart has been struck with the hearts of the planes;
Half my life it has beat with these, in the sun, in the rains,
In the March wind, the May breeze,
In the great gales that came over to them across the roofs from the great seas.
There was only a quiet rain when they were dying;
They must have heard the sparrows flying,
And the small creeping creatures in the earth where they were lying—
But I, all day, I heard an angel crying:
"Hurt not the trees."

HERE LIES A PRISONER

Leave him: he's quiet enough: and what matter
Out of his body or in, you can scatter
The frozen breath of his silenced soul, of his outraged soul to the winds that rave:
Quieter now than he used to be, but listening still to the magpie chatter
Over his grave.

NOT FOR THAT CITY

Not for that city of the level sun,
Its golden streets and glittering gates ablaze—
The shadeless, sleepless city of white days,
White nights, or nights and days that are as one—
We weary, when all is said, all thought, all done.
We strain our eyes beyond this dusk to see
What, from the threshold of eternity,
We shall step into. No, I think we shun
The splendor of that everlasting glare,
The clamor of that never-ending song.
And if for anything we greatly long,
It is for some remote and quiet stair
Which winds to silence and a space of sleep
Too sound for waking and for dreams too deep.

ABSENCE

Sometimes I know the way
You walk, up over the bay;
It is a wind from that far sea
That blows the fragrance of your hair to me.

Or in this garden when the breeze
Touches my trees
To stir their dreaming shadows on the grass
I see you pass.

In sheltered beds, the heart of every rose
Serenely sleeps tonight. As shut as those
Your guarded heart; as safe as they from the beat, beat
Of hooves that tread dropped roses in the street.

Turn never again
On these eyes blind with a wild rain
Your eyes; they were stars to me.
There are things stars may not see.

But call, call, and though Christ stands
Still with scarred hands
Over my mouth, I must answer. So,
I will come—He shall let me go!

ON THE ASYLUM ROAD

Theirs is the house whose windows—every pane—
  Are made of darkly stained or clouded glass:
Sometimes you come upon them in the lane,
  The saddest crowd that you will ever pass.

But still we merry town or village folk
  Throw to their scattered stare a kindly grin,
And think no shame to stop and crack a joke
  With the incarnate wages of man's sin.

None but ourselves in our long gallery we meet,
  The moor-hen stepping from her reeds with dainty feet,
    The hare-bell bowing on his stem,
Dance not with us; their pulses beat
  To fainter music; nor do we to them
    Make their life sweet.

The gayest crowd that they will ever pass
  Are we to brother-shadows in the lane:
Our windows, too, are clouded glass
  To them, yes, every pane!

Hilaire Belloc

⁂ (Joseph) Hilaire (Pierre) Belloc, who has been described as "a Frenchman, an Englishman, an Oxford man, a country gentleman, a soldier, a satirist, a democrat, a novelist, and a practical journalist," was born near Paris, July 27, 1870. Four of his great-uncles were generals under Napoleon; his father was an eminent French lawyer; his mother, an Englishwoman, was a leader in the feminist movement which finally secured votes for women. After leaving school Belloc served as a driver in the 8th Regiment of French Artillery at Toul. Later he became a naturalized British subject, finished his education at Balliol College, Oxford, and in 1906 entered the House of Commons as Liberal Member for South Salford. He was a member of Parliament from 1906 to 1910.

Besides his other multifarious activities, he was the author (by 1940) of about one hundred volumes. These books range the gamut of literature: from travel-sketches to essays significantly entitled *On Nothing and Kindred Subjects* (1908), *On Everything* (1909), *On Anything* (1910), and simply *On* (1923); from *A Book of Beasts* (1896) to a *History of England,* three volumes of which were published by 1927. He wrote several books of satirical fiction, one of which, *Mr. Clutterbuck's Election* (1908), exposed British underground politics, and which bristled with affable Bellocosity.

Belloc's *Path to Rome* (1902) is a high-spirited travel book; his historical studies and biographies of *Robespierre* and *Marie Antoinette* (1909) are classics of their kind. His nonsense-rhymes (*Cautionary Tales, The Bad Child's Book of Beasts,* and *More Beasts for Worse Children*) are comparable to Edward Lear's. As a serious poet, Belloc is engaging but somewhat less original. Although his humorous and burlesque stanzas are refreshing, Belloc is most himself when he writes of malt liquor and his beloved Sussex. "The South County" and the "Lines to a Don" in defense of his friend Chesterton are the most persuasive of his earnest poems. "Tarantella," with its internal rhymes and shifting rhythms, is a skilful approximation of the dance which gives the poem its name. His poetic as well as spiritual kinship with that other protagonist of a burly Catholicism, G. K. Chesterton, is obvious. He died of severe burns in his Sussex home, July 16, 1953.

Like Chesterton, Belloc is equally at home in a highly personal prose and in brightly ringing rhyme. He likes to grumble, but he does not groan. He is crotchety, often quarrelsome—in company with Chesterton he violently resents progress—but he is fiercely loyal to his loves in art, religion, and history. His faith is evident in the tributes and epigrams in *Collected Poems* (1923) as well as in the varied papers in *The Silence of the Sea and Other Essays* (1940).

WEST SUSSEX DRINKING SONG

They sell good Beer at Haslemere
  And under Guildford Hill.
At Little Cowfold as I've been told
  A beggar may drink his fill:
There is a good brew in Amberley too,
  And by the bridge also;
But the swipes they take in at Washington Inn
  Is the very best Beer I know.

Chorus:

With my here it goes, there it goes,
  All the fun's before us:
The Tipple's Aboard and the night is young,
The door's ajar and the Barrel is sprung,
I am singing the best song ever was sung,
  And it has a rousing chorus.

If I were what I never can be,
  The master or the squire:
If you give me the hundred from here to the sea,
  Which is more than I desire:
Then all my crops should be barley and hops,
  And did my harvest fail
I'd sell every rood of mine acres, I would,
  For a bellyful of good Ale.

[*Chorus*]

TARANTELLA

Do you remember an Inn,
Miranda?
Do you remember an Inn?

And the tedding and the spreading
Of the straw for a bedding,
And the fleas that tease in the High Pyrenees,
And the wine that tasted of the tar?
And the cheers and the jeers of the young muleteers
(Under the vine of the dark verandah)?
Do you remember an Inn, Miranda,
Do you remember an Inn?
And the cheers and the jeers of the young muleteers
Who hadn't got a penny,
And who weren't paying any,
And the hammer at the doors and the din?
And the *hip! hop! hap!*
Of the clap
Of the hands to the twirl and the swirl
Of the girl gone chancing,
Glancing,
Dancing,
Backing and advancing,
Snapping of the clapper to the spin
Out and in—
And the *ting, tong, tang* of the guitar!
Do you remember an Inn,
Miranda?
Do you remember an Inn?

Never more;
Miranda,
Never more.
Only the high peaks hoar:
And Aragon a torrent at the door.
No sound
In the walls of the halls where falls
The tread
Of the feet of the dead to the ground,
No sound:
But the boom
Of the far waterfall like doom.

THE SOUTH COUNTRY

When I am living in the Midlands
That are sodden and unkind,
I light my lamp in the evening:
My work is left behind;
And the great hills of the South Country
Come back into my mind.

The great hills of the South Country
They stand along the sea;

And it's there walking in the high woods
  That I could wish to be,
And the men that were boys when I was a boy
  Walking along with me.

The men that live in North England
  I saw them for a day:
Their hearts are set upon the waste fells,
  Their skies are fast and gray;
From their castle-walls a man may see
  The mountains far away.

The men that live in West England
  They see the Severn strong,
A-rolling on rough water brown
  Light aspen leaves along.
They have the secret of the rocks,
  And the oldest kind of song.

But the men that live in the South Country
  Are the kindest and most wise,
They get their laughter from the loud surf,
  And the faith in their happy eyes
Comes surely from our Sister the Spring
  When over the sea she flies;
The violets suddenly bloom at her feet,
  She blesses us with surprise.

I never get between the pines
  But I smell the Sussex air;
Nor I never come on a belt of sand
  But my home is there.
And along the sky the line of the Downs
  So noble and so bare.

A lost thing could I never find,
  Nor a broken thing mend:
And I fear I shall be all alone
  When I get towards the end.
Who will there be to comfort me
  Or who will be my friend?

I will gather and carefully make my friends
  Of the men of the Sussex Weald;
They watch the stars from silent folds,
  They stiffly plow the field.
By them and the God of the South Country
  My poor soul shall be healed.

If I ever become a rich man,
  Or if ever I grow to be old,
I will build a house with deep thatch
  To shelter me from the cold,

And there shall the Sussex songs be sung
And the story of Sussex told.

I will hold my house in the high wood
Within a walk of the sea,
And the men that were boys when I was a boy
Shall sit and drink with me.

HA'NACKER MILL

Sally is gone that was so kindly,
Sally is gone from Ha'nacker Hill.
And the Briar grows ever since then so blindly
And ever since then the clapper is still,
And the sweeps have fallen from Ha'nacker Mill.

Ha'nacker Hill is in Desolation:
Ruin a-top and a field unplowed,
And Spirits that call on a fallen nation,
Spirits that loved her calling aloud:
Spirits abroad in a windy cloud.

Spirits that call and no one answers;
Ha'nacker's down and England's done.
Wind and Thistle for pipe and dancers
And never a plowman under the Sun.
Never a plowman. Never a one.

FOUR BEASTS

The Big Baboon

The Big Baboon is found upon
The plains of Cariboo;
He goes about with nothing on
(A shocking thing to do.)
But if he dressed respectably
And let his whiskers grow
How like this Big Baboon would be
To Mister So-and-So!

The Yak

As a friend to the children commend me the Yak;
You will find it exactly the thing:
It will carry and fetch, you can ride on its back,
Or lead it about with a string.

The Tartar who dwells on the plains of Thibet
(A desolate region of snow)
Has for centuries made it a nursery pet,
And surely the Tartar should know!

Then tell your papa where the Yak can be got,
And if he is awfully rich
He will buy you the creature—or else he will not.
(I cannot be positive which.)

The Lion

The Lion, the Lion, he dwells in the waste,
He has a big head and a very small waist;
But his shoulders are stark, and his jaws they are grim,
And a good little child will not play with him.

The Tiger

The Tiger, on the other hand, is kittenish and mild,
He makes a pretty playfellow for any little child;
And mothers of large families (who claim to common sense)
Will find a Tiger well repays the trouble and expense.

LINES TO A DON

emote and ineffectual Don
'hat dared attack my Chesterton,
Vith that poor weapon, half-impelled,
'nlearnt, unsteady, hardly held,
'nworthy for a tilt with men—
our quavering and corroded pen;
on poor at Bed and worse at Table,
on pinched, Don starved, Don miserable;
on stuttering, Don with roving eyes,
on nervous, Don of crudities;
on clerical, Don ordinary,
on self-absorbed and solitary;
on here-and-there, Don epileptic;
on puffed and empty, Don dyspeptic;
on middle-class, Don sycophantic,
on dull, Don brutish, Don pedantic;
on hypocritical, Don bad,
on furtive, Don three-quarters mad;
on (since a man must make an end),
on that shall never be my friend.

*

on different from those regal Dons!
ith hearts of gold and lungs of bronze,
ho shout and bang and roar and bawl
e Absolute across the hall,
sail in amply bellowing gown
ormous through the Sacred Town,
aring from College to their homes
ep cargoes of gigantic tomes;
Dons admirable! Dons of Might!
Uprising on my inward sight
Compact of ancient tales, and port
And sleep—and learning of a sort.
Dons English, worthy of the land;
Dons rooted; Dons that understand.
Good Dons perpetual that remain
A landmark, walling in the plain—
The horizon of my memories—
Like large and comfortable trees.

Don very much apart from these,
Thou scapegoat Don, thou Don devoted,
Don to thine own damnation quoted,
Perplexed to find thy trivial name
Reared in my verse to lasting shame.
Don dreadful, rasping Don and wearing
Repulsive Don—Don past all bearing,
Don of the cold and doubtful breath,
Don despicable, Don of death;
Don nasty, skimpy, silent, level;
Don evil; Don that serves the devil.
Don ugly—that makes fifty lines.
There is a Canon which confines
A Rhymed Octosyllabic Curse
If written in Iambic Verse
To fifty lines. I never cut;
I far prefer to end it—but
Believe me I shall soon return.
My fires are banked, but still they burn
To write some more about the Don
That dared attack my Chesterton.

SONNET

We will not whisper, we have found the place
Of silence and the endless halls of sleep.
Of that which breathes alone throughout the deep
The end and the beginning; and the face
Between the level brows of whose blind eyes
Lie plenary contentment, full surcease
Of violence, and the passionless long peace
Wherein we lose our human lullabies.

Look up and tell the immeasurable height
Betwen the vault of the world and your dear head;
That's death, my little sister, and the night
Which was our Mother beckons us to bed,
  Where large oblivion in her house is laid
  For us tired children, now our games are played.

SIX EPIGRAMS

On Lady Poltagrue, a Public Peril

The Devil, having nothing else to do,
Went off to tempt My Lady Poltagrue.
My Lady, tempted by a private whim,
To his extreme annoyance, tempted him.

On a Dead Hostess

Of this bad world the loveliest and the best
Has smiled and said "Good Night," and gone to rest.

On Hygiene

Of old when folk lay sick and sorely tried,
The doctors gave them physic, and they died.
But here's a happier age: for now we know
Both how to make men sick and keep them so.

On His Books

When I am dead, I hope it may be said:
"His sins were scarlet, but his books were read."

Epitaph on the Politician

Here, richly, with ridiculous display,
The Politician's corpse was laid away.
While all of his acquaintance sneered and slanged,
I wept: for I had longed to see him hanged.

For False Heart

I said to Heart, "How goes it?" Heart replied:
"Right as a Ribstone Pippin!" But it lied.

W. H. Davies

◆§ According to his own biography, W(illiam) H(enry) Davies was born in a public-house called Church House at Newport, in the County of Monmouthshire, April 20, 1870, of Welsh parents. He was, until Bernard Shaw "discovered" him, a cattleman, a berry-picker, a panhandler—in short, a vagabond. In a preface to Davies' *The Autobiography of a Super-Tramp* (1906), Shaw describes how the manuscript came into his hands:

"In the year 1905 I received by post a volume of poems by one William H. Davies, whose address was The Farm House, Kennington, S.E. I was surprised to learn that there was still a farmhouse left in Kennington; for I did not then suspect that The Farm House, like the Shepherdess Walks and Nightingale Lane and Whetstone Parks of Bethnal Green and Holborn, is so called nowadays in irony, and is, in fact, a doss-house, or hostelry, where single men can have a night's lodging, for, at most, sixpence. . . . The author, as far as I could guess, had walked into a printer's or stationer's shop; handed in his manuscript; and ordered his book as he might have ordered a pair of boots. It was marked 'price, half a crown.' An accompanying letter asked me very civilly if I required a half-crown book of verses; and if so, would I please send the author the half-crown: if not, would I return the book. This was attractively simple and sensible. I opened the book, and was more puzzled than ever; for before I had read three lines I perceived that the author was a real poet. His work was not in the least strenuous or modern; there was indeed no sign of his ever having read anything otherwise than as a child reads. . . . Here, I saw, was a genuine innocent, writing odds and ends of verse about odds and ends of things; living quite out of the world in which such things are usually done, and knowing no better (or rather no worse) than to get his book made by the appropriate craftsman and hawk it round like any other ware."

It is more than likely that Davies' first notoriety as a tramp-poet who had ridden the rails in the United States and had had his right foot cut off by a train in Canada, obscured his merit as a singer. Even his early *The Soul's Destroyer* (1907) revealed that simplicity which is as *naïf* as it is unexpected.

Between 1906, when Davies published his first book, and 1935, the poet issued twenty-two volumes, five of autobiography, seventeen of verse. Besides these, there were four different *Collected Poems,* appearing in 1916, 1923, 1929, and 1935. The difficulty of strictly evaluating this verse is the greater since the Welsh-English poet depended on repetitions of a few ideas, and rarely trusted his imagination with any but the most tested themes. *Love Poems* (1935) is a typical mixture of Davies' plain-song sagacities and painful banalities. It needs all one's faith in a poet to forgive him such a stanza as:

The sun has his spots, the moon has her shadows,
  The sea has his wrinkles, the land has her warts;
Sweet faith has her doubts and lovers their quarrels,
  And nothing is perfect in all its parts.

But Davies merits our faith, for his best, like the best of the Caroline poets, moves us not only because of the innocence of vision but because of the adequacy of communicating it. If, in his later work, his thought is confused and tempts Davies out of his depth, his ear remains quick and sensitive as the thrush he celebrates:

> That speckled thrush, that stands so still,
> Is listening for the worms to stir;
> He hears a worm—what marvelous ears
> That he can live by ear alone,
> And save his eyes to guard his fears!

Collected Poems (1935) contains some five hundred poems in which good, indifferent, and bad mingle so inextricably that the reader must accept Davies *en masse* or reject him *in toto*. One can no more imagine Davies self-critical than one can imagine him in the labor of creation, his "labor" being about as arduous as a bird's and his song being no less recreational. The figure is not far-fetched, for no poetry has ever been more obviously bird-like. But, it may be asked with a proper regard for ornithology, what bird? Not the lark, for Davies is no Shelley hurling himself and his cry far above the comfortable altitudes of man. Not the nightingale, for his is not Keats' clear passion nor Swinburne's operatic coloratura. It is the English robin that Davies most resembles or the American goldfinch, whose song, limited in range, is cleanly, sharply pitched. Without the variability of greater singers, his notes are only three or four, but the tones are so cool, the delivery so fresh that we would not exchange the crisp spontaneity even for the versatile brilliance of the hermit-thrush. No less than thirty-three poems begin: "When I in praise of babies speak," "When on a summer morn I wake," "When I came forth this morn I saw," "When I am old," "When I complained," "When . . ."

It is easy enough to deride such naïveté, easy enough to confuse Davies with his compatriots who pipe their placid week-end pastorals. But, although a Georgian in point of time, Davies shakes himself free of "Georgianism," that false simplicity sicklied o'er with the pale cast of thoughtlessness. He does not study his subjects from the outside; it is doubtful if he studies them at all; he is always within his bucolics. Thus his sympathies are as genuine as they are ingenuous. His sense of wonder is as direct, as unmistakable as an untutored child's. He looks at clouds, cowslips, lovely ladies, glow-worms, sheep, dogs, dolls, and daisies, as though they had never existed prior to his observation; and he puts them to rhyme as unselfconsciously as though never before had they been employed in verse. Davies rediscovers the common objects which everyone takes for granted; he regards them with an air of surprise and what is more, communicates his astonished wonder.

Observe the poem entitled "A Great Time" and note what details prompt his adjective. Beauty to Davies is not in the elaboration but in the mere being; greatness is, therefore, implicit in the coming together of a rainbow and a cuckoo. These are his auguries of innocence; for him, also, "a dog starv'd at his master's gate Predicts the ruin of the State." His rapport with lamb and bat and game-cock may lead us to imply a kinship with Blake, but he is, at the best, a Blake in words of one syllable. Where Blake projects apocalypses and flaming images, Davies offers a panorama of quiet pictures; we drop from passionate vision into pleasant reverie.

Davies was planning another volume of homely and spontaneous verse when he died at his home in Gloucestershire, September 26, 1940.

THE HOUR OF MAGIC

This is the hour of magic, when the Moon
With her bright wand has charmed the tallest tree
To stand stone-still with all his million leaves!
I feel around me things I cannot see;
I hold my breath, as Nature holds her own.
And do the mice and birds, the horse and cow,
Sleepless in this deep silence, so intense,
Believe a miracle has happened now,
And wait to hear a sound they'll recognize,
To prove they still have life with earthly ties?

A GREETING

Good morning, Life—and all
Things glad and beautiful.
My pockets nothing hold,
But he that owns the gold,
The Sun, is my great friend—
His spending has no end.

Hail to the morning sky,
Which bright clouds measure high;
Hail to you birds whose throats
Would number leaves by notes;
Hail to you shady bowers,
And you green fields of flowers.

Hail to you women fair,
That make a show so rare
In cloth as white as milk—
Be't calico or silk:
Good morning, Life—and all
Things glad and beautiful.

DAYS TOO SHORT

'hen primroses are out in Spring,
And small, blue violets come between;
When merry birds sing on boughs green,
nd rills, as soon as born, must sing;

When butterflies will make side-leaps,
As though escaped from Nature's hand
Ere perfect quite; and bees will stand
pon their heads in fragrant deeps;

When small clouds are so silvery white
Each seems a broken rimmèd moon—
When such things are, this world too soon,
For me, doth wear the veil of Night.

THE MOON

Thy beauty haunts me heart and soul,
O thou fair Moon, so close and bright;
Thy beauty makes me like the child
That cries aloud to own thy light:
The little child that lifts each arm
To press thee to her bosom warm.

Though there are birds that sing this night
With thy white beams across their throats,
Let my deep silence speak for me
More than for them their sweetest notes:
Who worships thee till music fails
Is greater than thy nightingales.

THE VILLAIN

While joy gave clouds the light of stars,
That beamed where'er they looked;
And calves and lambs had tottering knees,
Excited, while they sucked;
While every bird enjoyed his song,
Without one thought of harm or wrong—
I turned my head and saw the wind,
Not far from where I stood,
Dragging the corn by her golden hair,
Into a dark and lonely wood.

THE EXAMPLE

Here's an example from
A Butterfly;
That on a rough, hard rock
Happy can lie;
Friendless and all alone
On this unsweetened stone.

Now let my bed be hard,
No care take I;
I'll make my joy like this
Small Butterfly,
Whose happy heart has power
To make a stone a flower.

THE TWO STARS

Day has her star, as well as Night,
One star is black, the other white.
I saw a white star burn and pant
And swirl with such a wildness, once—
That I stood still, and almost stared
Myself into a trance!

The star of Day, both seen and heard,
Is but a little, English bird:
The Lark, whose wings beat time to his
Wild rapture, sings, high overhead;
When silence comes, we almost fear
That Earth receives its dead.

THE DOG

The dog was there, outside her door,
She gave it food and drink,
She gave it shelter from the cold:
It was the night young Molly robbed
An old fool of his gold.

"Molly," I said, "you'll go to hell—"
And yet I half believed
That ugly, famished, tottering cur
Would bark outside the gates of Heaven,
To open them for Her!

JENNY WREN

Her sight is short, she comes quite near;
A foot to me's a mile to her;
And she is known as Jenny Wren,
The smallest bird in England. When
I heard that litle bird at first,
Methought her frame would surely burst
With earnest song. Oft had I seen
Her running under leaves so green,
Or in the grass when fresh and wet,
As though her wings she would forget.
And, seeing this, I said to her—
"My pretty runner, you prefer
To be a thing to run unheard
Through leaves and grass, and not a bird!"
'Twas then she burst, to prove me wrong,
Into a sudden storm of song;
So very loud and earnest, I
Feared she would break her heart and die,
"Nay, nay," I laughed, "be you no thing
To run unheard, sweet scold, but sing!
O I could hear your voice near me,
Above the din in that oak tree,
When almost all the twigs on top
Had starlings chattering without stop."

AMBITION

I had Ambition, by which sin
The angels fell;
I climbed and, step by step, O Lord,
Ascended into Hell.

Returning now to peace and quiet,
And made more wise,
Let my descent and fall, O Lord,
Be into Paradise.

THE HERMIT

What moves that lonely man is not the boom
Of waves that break against the cliff so strong;
Nor roar of thunder, when that traveling voice
Is caught by rocks that carry far along.

'Tis not the groan of oak tree in its prime,
When lightning strikes its solid heart to dust.
Nor frozen pond when, melted by the sun,
It suddenly doth break its sparkling crust.

What moves that man is when the blind bat taps
His window where he sits alone at night;
Or when the small bird sounds like some great beast
Among the dead, dry leaves so frail and light;

Or when the moths on his night-pillow beat
Such heavy blows he fears they'll break his bones;
Or when a mouse inside the papered walls,
Comes like a tiger crunching through the stones.

WHEN YON FULL MOON

When yon full moon's with her white fleet of stars,
And but one bird makes music in the grove;
When you and I are breathing side by side,
Where our two bodies make one shadow, love;

Not for her beauty will I praise the moon,
But that she lights thy purer face and throat;
The only praise I'll give the nightingale
Is that she draws from thee a richer note.

For, blinded with thy beauty, I am filled,
Like Saul of Tarsus, with a greater light;
When he had heard that warning voice in Heaven,
And lost his eyes to find a deeper sight.

Come, let us sit in that deep silence then,
Launched on love's rapids, with our passions proud,
That makes all music hollow—though the lark
Raves in his windy heights above a cloud.

SHEEP

When I was once in Baltimore,
A man came up to me and cried,
"Come, I have eighteen hundred sheep,
And we will sail on Tuesday's tide.

"If you will sail with me, young man,
"I'll pay you fifty shillings down;
These eighteen hundred sheep I take
From Baltimore to Glasgow town."

He paid me fifty shillings down,
I sailed with eighteen hundred sheep;
We soon had cleared the harbor's mouth,
We soon were in the salt sea deep.

The first night we were out at sea
Those sheep were quiet in their mind;
The second night they cried with fear—
They smelt no pastures in the wind.

They sniffed, poor things, for their green fields,
They cried so loud I could not sleep;
For fifty thousand shillings down
I would not sail again with sheep.

THE MIND'S LIBERTY

The mind, with its own eyes and ears,
May for these others have no care;
No matter where this body is,
The mind is free to go elsewhere.
My mind can be a sailor, when
This body's still confined to land;
And turn these mortals into trees,
That walk in Fleet Street or the Strand.

So, when I'm passing Charing Cross,
Where porters work both night and day,
I ofttimes hear sweet Malpas Brook,
That flows thrice fifty miles away.
And when I'm passing near St. Paul's,
I see, beyond the dome and crowd,
Twm Barlum, that green pap in Gwent,
With its dark nipple in a cloud.

A GREAT TIME

Sweet Chance, that led my steps abroad,
Beyond the town, where wild flowers grow—
A rainbow and a cuckoo, Lord!
How rich and great the times are now!
Know, all ye sheep
And cows that keep
On staring that I stand so long
In grass that's wet from heavy rain—
A rainbow and a cuckoo's song
May never come together again;
May never come
This side the tomb.

THE ELEMENTS

No house of stone
Was built for me;
When the Sun shines—
I am a bee.

No sooner comes
The Rain so warm,
I come to light—
I am a worm.

When the Winds blow,
I do not strip,
But set my sails—
I am a ship.

When Lightning comes,
It plays with me
And I with it—
I am a tree.

When drowned men rise
At Thunder's word,
Sings Nightingale—
I am a bird.

LEAVES

Peace to these little broken leaves,
That strew our common ground;
That chase their tails, like silly dogs,
As they go round and round.

For though in winter boughs are bare,
Let us not once forget
Their summer glory, when these leaves
Caught the great Sun in their strong net;
And made him, in the lower air,
Tremble—no bigger than a star!

SONGS OF JOY

Sing out, my Soul, thy songs of joy;
Such as a happy bird will sing
Beneath a Rainbow's lovely arch
In early spring.

Think not of Death in thy young days;
Why shouldst thou that grim tyrant fear,
And fear him not when thou art old,
And he is near.

Strive not for gold, for greedy fools
Measure themselves by poor men never;
Their standards still being richer men,
Makes them poor ever.

Train up thy mind to feel content,
What matters then how low thy store!
What we enjoy, and not possess,
Makes rich or poor.

Filled with sweet thought, then happy I
Take not my state from others' eyes;
What's in my mind—not on my flesh
Or theirs—I prize.

Sing, happy Soul, thy songs of joy;
Such as a Brook sings in the wood,
That all night had been strengthened by
Heaven's purer flood.

TO A LADY FRIEND

Since you have turned unkind,
Then let the truth be known:
We poets give our praise
To any weed or stone,
Or sulking bird that in
The cold, sharp wind is dumb;
To this, or that, or you—
Whatever's first to come.

You came my way the first,
When the life-force in my blood—
Coming from none knows where—
Had reached its highest flood;
A time when anything,
No matter old or new,
Could bring my song to birth—
Sticks, bones, or rags, or you!

LEISURE

What is this life if, full of care,
We have no time to stand and stare.

No time to stand beneath the boughs
And stare as long as sheep or cows.

No time to see, when woods we pass,
Where squirrels hide their nuts in grass.

No time to see, in broad daylight,
Streams full of stars, like skies at night.

No time to turn at Beauty's glance,
And watch her feet, how they can dance.

No time to wait till her mouth can
Enrich that smile her eyes began.

A poor life this if, full of care,
We have no time to stand and stare.

J. M. Synge

☙ John M. Synge, the most brilliant star of the Celtic revival, was born at Rathfarnham, near Dublin, in 1871, his maternal grandfather, Robert Traill, being famous for a splendid translation of Josephus. As a child in Wicklow, Synge was already fascinated by the strange idioms and rhythmic speech he heard there, a native utterance which was his delight and which was rare material for his greatest work. He did not use this folk-language merely as he heard it; he was an artist first, and, as an artist, he bent and shaped the rough matter, selecting with fastidiousness, so that in his plays every speech is, as he himself declared all good speech should be, "as fully flavored as a nut or apple." Even in *The Tinker's Wedding* (1907), the least important of his plays, Synge's peculiarly inflected sentences vivify every scene; one is arrested by snatches of illuminated prose like:

"That's a sweet tongue you have, Sarah Casey; but if sleep's a grand thing, it's a grand thing to be waking up a day the like of this, when there's a warm sun in it, and a kind of air, and you'll hear the cuckoos singing and crying out on the top of the hill."

For some time, Synge's career was uncertain. He went to Germany half intending to become a professional musician. There he studied the theory of music, perfecting himself meanwhile in Gaelic and Hebrew, winning prizes in both of these languages. He took up Heine with great interest, familiarized himself with the peasant-dramas of Anzengruber, and was planning to translate the ballads of the old German minnesingers into Anglo-Irish dialect. Then he went to Paris.

Yeats found him in France in 1898 and advised him to go to the Aran Islands, to live there as if he were one of the people. "Express a life," said Yeats, "that has never found expression." Synge went. He became part of the life of Aran, living upon salt fish and eggs, talking Irish for the most part, but listening also to that beautiful English which, to quote Yeats again, "has grown up in Irish-speaking districts and takes its vocabulary from the time of Malory and of the translators of the Bible, but its idiom and vivid metaphor from Irish." The result of this close contact can be seen in five dramas which are like nothing produced in Synge's own time; in them the imagination of the artist is linked with the imaginings of the people.

In *Riders to the Sea* (1903), *The Well of the Saints* (1905), and *The Playboy of the Western World* (1907), there is a richness of imagery, a new language startling in its vigor; a wildness and passion that contrast strangely with the suave mysticism and delicate spirituality of the playwright's associates in the Irish Theatre.

Synge's *Poems and Translations* (1910), a volume which was not issued until after his death, contains not only his few hard and earthy verses, but also the famous preface embodying his theory of poetry. The translations, which have been rendered in a highly intensified prose, are as racy as anything in his plays; his versions of Villon and Petrarch are remarkable for their adherence to the original though they radiate the adapter's own personality.

Synge died of an old illness, just as his reputation had broken down borders, at a private hospital in Dublin, March 24, 1909.

PRELUDE

Still south I went and west and south again,
Through Wicklow from the morning till the night,
And, far from cities and the sights of men,
Lived with the sunshine and the moon's delight.

I knew the stars, the flowers, and the birds,
The gray and wintry sides of many glens,
And did but half remember human words,
In converse with the mountains, moors and fens.

BEG-INNISH

Bring Kateen-beug and Maurya Jude
To dance in Beg-Innish,[1]
And when the lads (they're in Dunquin)
Have sold their crabs and fish,
Wave fawny shawls and call them in,
And call the little girls who spin,
And seven weavers from Dunquin,
To dance in Beg-Innish.

[1] The accent is on the last syllable.

I'll play you jigs, and Maurice Kean,
Where nets are laid to dry,
I've silken strings would draw a dance
From girls are lame or shy;
Four strings I've brought from Spain and France
To make your long men skip and prance,
Till stars look out to see the dance
Where nets are laid to dry.

We'll have no priest or peeler in
To dance in Beg-Innish;
But we'll have drink from M'riarty Jim
Rowed round while gannets fish,
A keg with porter to the brim,
That every lad may have his whim,
Till we up sails with M'riarty Jim
And sail from Beg-Innish.

IN KERRY

We heard the thrushes by the shore and sea,
And saw the golden stars' nativity,
Then round we went the lane by Thomas Flynn,
Across the church where bones lie out and in;
And there I asked beneath a lonely cloud
Of strange delight, with one bird singing loud,
What change you'd wrought in graveyard, rock and sea,
To wake this new wild paradise for me....
Yet knew no more than knew those merry sins
Had built this stack of thigh-bones, jaws and shins.

A QUESTION

I asked if I got sick and died, would you
With my black funeral go walking too,
If you'd stand close to hear them talk or pray
While I'm let down in that steep bank of clay.

And, No, you said, for if you saw a crew
Of living idiots pressing round that new
Oak coffin—they alive, I dead beneath
That board—you'd rave and rend them with your teeth.

ON AN ISLAND

You've plucked a curlew, drawn a hen,
Washed the shirts of seven men,
You've stuffed my pillow, stretched the sheet,
And filled the pan to wash your feet,

You've cooped the pullets, wound the clock,
And rinsed the young men's drinking crock;
And now we'll dance to jigs and reels,
Nailed boots chasing girls' naked heels,
Until your father'll start to snore,
And Jude, now you're married, will stretch on the floor.

DREAD

Beside a chapel I'd a room looked down,
Where all the women from the farms and town
On Holy-days and Sundays used to pass
To marriages, and christenings, and to Mass.

Then I sat lonely watching score and score,
Till I turned jealous of the Lord next door....
Now by this window, where there's none can see,
The Lord God's jealous of yourself and me.

IN MAY

In a nook
That opened south,
You and I
Lay mouth to mouth.

A snowy gull
And sooty daw
Came and looked
With many a caw;

"Such," I said,
"Are I and you,
When you've kissed me
Black and blue!"

A TRANSLATION FROM PETRARCH

(*He is Jealous of the Heavens and the Earth*)

What a grudge I am bearing the earth that has its arms about her, and is holding that face away from me, where I was finding peace from great sadness.

What a grudge I am bearing the Heavens that are after taking her, and shutting her in with greediness, the Heavens that do push their bolt against so many.

What a grudge I am bearing the blessed saints that have got her sweet company, that I am always seeking; and what a grudge I am bearing against Death, that is standing in her two eyes, and will not call me with a word.

A TRANSLATION FROM WALTER VON DER VOGELWEIDE

I never set my two eyes on a head was so fine as your head, but I'd no way to be looking down into your heart.

It's for that I was tricked out and out—that was the thanks I got for being so steady in my love.

I tell you, if I could have laid my hands on the whole set of the stars, the moon and the sun along with it, by Christ I'd have given the lot to her. No place have I set eyes on the like of her; she's bad to her friends, and gay and playful with those she'd have a right to hate. I ask you can that behaviour have a good end come to it?

TWO TRANSLATIONS FROM VILLON

1

(*Prayer of the Old Woman, Villon's Mother*)

Mother of God that's Lady of the Heavens, take myself, the poor sinner, the way I'll be along with them that's chosen.

Let you say to your own Son that He'd have a right to forgive my share of sins, when it's the like He's done, many's the day, with big and famous sinners. I'm a poor aged woman, was never at school, and is no scholar with letters, but I've seen pictures in the chapel with Paradise on one side, and harps and pipes in it, and the place on the other side, where sinners do be boiled in torment; the one gave me great joy, the other a great fright and scaring; let me have the good place, Mother of God, and it's in your faith I'll live always.

It's yourself that bore Jesus, that has no end or death, and He the Lord Almighty, that took our weakness and gave Himself to sorrows, a young and gentle man. It's Himself is our Lord surely, and it's in that faith I'll live always.

2

(*An Old Woman's Lamentations*)

The man I had a love for—a great rascal would kick me in the gutter—is dead thirty years and over it, and it is I am left behind, grey and aged. When I do be minding the good days I had, minding what I was one time, and what it is I'm come to, and when I do look on my own self, poor and dry, and pinched together, it wouldn't be much would set me raging in the streets.

Where is the round forehead I had, and the fine hair, and the two eyebrows, and the eyes with a big gay look out of them would bring folly from a great scholar? Where is my straight, shapely nose, and two ears, and my chin with a valley in it, and my lips were red and open?

Where are the pointed shoulders were on me, and the long arms and nice hands to them? Where is my bosom was as white as any, or my straight rounded sides?

It's the way I am this day—my forehead is gone away into furrows, the hair of my head is grey and whitish, my eyebrows are tumbled from me, and my two eyes have died out within my head—those eyes that would be laughing to the men—my nose has a hook on it, my ears are hanging down, and my lips are sharp and skinny.

That's what's left over from the beauty of a right woman—a bag of bones, and legs the like of two shrivelled sausages going beneath it.

It's of the like of that we old hags do be thinking, of the good times are gone away from us, and we crouching on our hunkers by a little fire of twigs, soon kindled and soon spent, we that were the pick of many.

QUEENS

Seven dog-days we let pass
Naming Queens in Glenmacnass,
All the rare and royal names
Wormy sheepskin yet retains:
Etain, Helen, Maeve, and Fand,
Golden Deirdre's tender hand;
Bert, the big-foot, sung by Villon,
Cassandra, Ronsard found in Lyon.
Queens of Sheba, Meath, and Connaught,
Coifed with crown, or gaudy bonnet;
Queens whose finger once did stir men,
Queens were eaten of fleas and vermin,
Queens men drew like Mona Lisa,
Or slew with drugs in Rome and Pisa.
We named Lucrezia Crivelli,
And Titian's lady with amber belly,
Queens acquainted in learned sin,
Jane of Jewry's slender shin:
Queens who cut the bogs of Glanna,
Judith of Scripture, and Gloriana,
Queens who wasted the East by proxy,
Or drove the ass-cart, a tinker's doxy.
Yet these are rotten—I ask their pardon—
And we've the sun on rock and garden;
These are rotten, so you're the Queen
Of all are living, or have been.

TO THE OAKS OF GLENCREE

My arms are round you, and I lean
Against you, while the lark
Sings over us, and golden lights and green
Shadows are on your bark.

There'll come a season when you'll stretch
Black boards to cover me;
Then in Mount Jerome I will lie, poor wretch,
With worms eternally.

Ralph Hodgson

Ralph Hodgson was born in Yorkshire in 1871. Though he has been most reticent regarding the facts of his life, separating the poet from the casual man by the intimation that "the poet should live in his poetry," this much has been gathered: He lived for a while in America; he worked as a pressman in Fleet Street; he was a professional draughtsman, employed on the pictorial staff of an evening paper; he edited *Fry's Magazine;* he has bred bull terriers and, as a leading authority, has judged them; pugilism is one of his private enthusiasms. In 1924, Hodgson accepted an invitation to visit Japan as lecturer in English literature at Sendai University, about two hundred miles from Tokyo. In 1928 the invitation was renewed and again accepted. In 1940 Hodgson came to America and bought a farm near Canton, Ohio.

Although Hodgson has earned a livelihood in many capacities, he kept his writing severely apart; he refused to stain his pen with hack-work of any sort. He has given only his highest moments to his art, believing with Housman that lyric poetry—and Hodgson is one of the purest lyric poets of his age—is not a casual recreation. Writing little and publishing less, Hodgson was unknown until he was thirty-six; his first book, *The Last Blackbird and Other Lines,* appeared in 1907. In 1913, he went into partnership with Lovat Fraser and Holbrook Jackson to publish broadsides and chapbooks; many of his most famous poems appeared in the exquisite booklets issued by their press and illustrated by Fraser, "The Sign of Flying Fame." *Eve, The Bull, The Song of Honor, The Mystery and Other Poems* (1913-1914) found a wide circle of delighted readers in this format. A collected edition (entitled simply *Poems*) was published in 1917 and reissued in America some months later.

Hodgson's verses, full of the love of all natural things, a love that goes out to

"an idle rainbow
No less than laboring-seas,"

establish, like Davies' and De la Mare's, the wonder of essentially simple objects, or they (as in "Time, You Old Gypsy Man") personify abstractions.

One of the most graceful of word-magicians, Ralph Hodgson will retain his freshness as long as there are lovers of fresh and timeless songs. It is difficult to think of any showing of contemporary English poetry that could omit "Eve," "The Bull," "The Song of Honor," and that memorable snatch of music, "Time, You Old Gypsy Man." One succumbs to the charm of "Eve" at the first reading; here is the oldest of all legends told with a surprising simplicity and still more surprising difference. This Eve is neither the conscious sinner nor the symbolic Mother of men; she is, in Hodgson's candid lines, any young English country girl filling her basket, regarding the world and the serpent itself with a frank and childlike wonder.

Outstanding in Hodgson's work is his sympathy with animal life. This wide humanitarianism is implicit in poems like "The Bull," but it is explicit in his outrage against the slaughter of birds for fine feathers ("Stupidity Street") and the irony of "The Bells of Heaven."

Influences are far to seek in this work, although one scents rather than sees a trace of Christina Rossetti's "Goblin Market" in "Eve" and Christopher Smart's "Song to David" in "The Song of Honor."

At eighty-three Hodgson received the Queen's Gold Medal for Poetry, and at eighty-seven published another slim volume, *The Skylark and Other Poems* (1958).

REASON

Reason has moons, but moons not hers
Lie mirrored on her sea,
Confusing her astronomers,
But O! delighting me.

EVE

Eve, with her basket, was
Deep in the bells and grass,
Wading in bells and grass
Up to her knees.
Picking a dish of sweet
Berries and plums to eat,
Down in the bells and grass
Under the trees.

Mute as a mouse in a
Corner the cobra lay,
Curled round a bough of the
Cinnamon tall....
Now to get even and
Humble proud heaven and
Now was the moment or
Never at all.

"Eva!" Each syllable
Light as a flower fell,
"Eva!" he whispered the
Wondering maid,
Soft as a bubble sung
Out of a linnet's lung,
Soft and most silverly
"Eva!" he said.

Picture that orchard sprite;
Eve, with her body white,
Supple and smooth to her
Slim finger tips;
Wondering, listening,
Listening, wondering,
Eve with a berry
Half-way to her lips.

Oh, had our simple Eve
Seen through the make-believe!
Had she but known the
Pretender he was!

Out of the boughs he came,
Whispering still her name,
Tumbling in twenty rings
Into the grass.

Here was the strangest pair
In the world anyhere,
Eve in the bells and grass
Kneeling, and he
Telling his story low....
Singing birds saw them go
Down the dark path to
The Blasphemous Tree.

Oh, what a clatter when
Titmouse and Jenny Wren
Saw him successful and
Taking his leave!
How the birds rated him,
How they all hated him!
How they all pitied
Poor motherless Eve!

Picture her crying
Outside in the lane,
Eve, with no dish of sweet
Berries and plums to eat,
Haunting the gate of the
Orchard in vain....
Picture the lewd delight
Under the hill tonight—
"Eva!" the toast goes round,
"Eva!" again.

TIME, YOU OLD GYPSY MAN

Time, you old gypsy man,
Will you not stay,
Put up your caravan
Just for one day?

All things I'll give you
Will you be my guest,
Bells for your jennet
Of silver the best,
Goldsmiths shall beat you
A great golden ring,
Peacocks shall bow to you,
Little boys sing,
Oh, and sweet girls will
Festoon you with may.
Time, you old gypsy,
Why hasten away?

Last week in Babylon,
Last night in Rome,
Morning, and in the crush
Under Paul's dome;
Under Paul's dial
You tighten your rein—
Only a moment,
And off once again;

Off to some city
Now blind in the womb,
Off to another
Ere that's in the tomb.

Time, you old gypsy man,
  Will you not stay,
Put up your caravan
  Just for one day?

THE BIRDCATCHER

When flighting time is on, I go
With clap-net and decoy,
A-fowling after goldfinches
And other birds of joy;

I lurk among the thickets of
The Heart where they are bred,
And catch the twittering beauties as
They fly into my Head.

THE MOOR

The world's gone forward to its latest fair
And dropt an old man done with by the way,
To sit alone among the bats and stare
At miles and miles and miles of moorland bare
Lit only with last shreds of dying day.

Not all the world, not all the world's gone by:
Old man, you're like to meet one traveler still,
A journeyman well kenned for courtesy
To all that walk at odds with life and limb;
If this be he now riding up the hill
Maybe he'll stop and take you up with him. . . .

"But thou art Death?" "Of Heavenly Seraphim
None else to seek thee out and bid thee come."
"I only care that thou are come from Him,
Unbody me—I'm tired—and get me home."

AFTER

"How fared you when you mortal were?
  "What did you see on my peopled star?"
"Oh well enough," I answered her,
  "It went for me where mortals are!

"I saw blue flowers and the merlin's flight
  "And the rime on the wintry tree,
"Blue doves I saw and summer light
  "On the wings of the cinnamon bee."

THE SONG OF HONOR

I climbed the hill as light fell short,
And rooks came home in scramble sort,
And filled the trees and flapped and fought
And sang themselves to sleep;
An owl from nowhere with no sound
Swung by and soon was nowhere found,
I heard him calling half-way round,
Holloing loud and deep;
A pair of stars, faint pins of light,
Then many a star, sailed into sight,
And all the stars, the flower of night,
Were round me at a leap;
To tell how still the valleys lay
I heard the watchdog miles away
And bells of distant sheep.
I heard no more of bird or bell,
The mastiff in a slumber fell,
I stared into the sky,
As wondering men have always done
Since beauty and the stars were one,
Though none so hard as I.

It seemed, so still the valleys were,
As if the whole world knelt at prayer,
Save me and me alone;
So pure and wide that silence was
I feared to bend a blade of grass,
And there I stood like stone.

There, sharp and sudden, there I heard—
Ah! some wild lovesick singing bird
Woke singing in the trees?
The nightingale and babble-wren
Were in the English greenwood then,
And you heard one of these?
The babble-wren and nightingale
Sang in the Abyssinian vale
That season of the year!
Yet, true enough, I heard them plain,
I heard them both again, again,
As sharp and sweet and clear
As if the Abyssinian tree
Had thrust a bough across the sea,
Had thrust a bough across to me
With music for my ear!

I heard them both, and, oh! I heard
The song of every singing bird
That sings beneath the sky,
And with the song of lark and wren
The song of mountains, moths and men
And seas and rainbows vie!

I heard the universal choir,
The Sons of Light exalt their Sire
With universal song,
Earth's lowliest and loudest notes,
Her million times ten million throats
Exalt Him loud and long,
And lips and lungs and tongues of Grace
From every part and every place
Within the shining of His face,
The Universal throng.

I heard the hymn of being sound
From every well of honor found
In human sense and soul:
The song of poets when they write
The testament of Beautysprite
Upon a flying scroll,
The song of painters when they take
A burning brush for Beauty's sake
And limn her features whole—

The song of men divinely wise
Who look and see in starry skies
Not stars so much as robins' eyes,
And when these pale away
Hear flocks of shiny pleiades
Among the plums and apple trees
Sing in the summer day—

The song of all both high and low
To some blest vision true,
The song of beggars when they throw
The crust of pity all men owe
To hungry sparrows in the snow,
Old beggars hungry too—
The song of kings of kingdoms when
They rise above their fortune men,
And crown themselves anew—

The song of courage, heart and will
And gladness in a fight,
Of men who face a hopeless hill
With sparkling and delight,
The bells and bells of song that ring
Round banners of a cause or king
From armies bleeding white—

The song of sailors every one
When monstrous tide and tempest run
At ships like bulls at red,
When stately ships are twirled and spun
Like whipping tops and help there's none
And mighty ships ten thousand ton
Go down like lumps of lead—

And song of fighters stern as they
At odds with fortune night and day,
Crammed up in cities grim and gray
As thick as bees in hives,
Hosannas of a lowly throng
Who sing unconscious of their song,
Whose lips are in their lives—

And song of some at holy war
With spells and ghouls more dread by far
Than deadly seas and cities are,
Or hordes of quarreling kings—
The song of fighters great and small
The song of petty fighters all
And high heroic things—

The song of lovers—who knows how
Twitched up from place and time
Upon a sigh, a blush, a vow,
A curve or hue of cheek or brow,
Borne up and off from here and now
Into the void sublime!

And crying loves and passions still
In every key from soft to shrill
And numbers never done,
Dog-loyalties to faith and friend,
And loves like Ruth's of old no end,
And intermissions none—

And burst on burst for beauty and
For numbers not behind,
From men whose love of motherland
Is like a dog's for one dear hand,
Sole, selfless, boundless, blind—
And song of some with hearts beside
For men and sorrows far and wide,
Who watch the world with pity and pride
And warm to all minkind—

And endless joyous music rise
From children at their play,
And endless soaring lullabies
From happy, happy mothers' eyes,
And answering crows and baby cries,
How many who shall say!
And many a song as wondrous well
With pangs and sweets intolerable
From lonely hearths too gray to tell,
God knows how utter gray!
And song from many a house of care
When pain has forced a footing there
And there's a Darkness on the stair
Will not be turned away—

And song—that song whose singers come
With old kind tales of pity from
The Great Compassion's lips,
That make the bells of Heaven to peal
Round pillows frosty with the feel
Of Death's cold finger tips—

The song of men all sorts and kinds,
As many tempers, moods and minds
As leaves are on a tree,
As many faiths and castes and creeds,
As many human bloods and breeds
As in the world may be;

The song of each and all who gaze
On Beauty in her naked blaze,
Or see her dimly in a haze,
Or get her light in fitful rays
And tiniest needles even,
The song of all not wholly dark,
Not wholly sunk in stupor stark
Too deep for groping Heaven—

And alleluias sweet and clear
And wild with beauty men mishear,
From choirs of song as near and dear
To Paradise as they,
The everlasting pipe and flute
Of wind and sea and bird and brute,
And lips deaf men imagine mute
In wood and stone and clay,
The music of a lion strong
That shakes a hill a whole night long,
A hill as loud as he,
The twitter of a mouse among
Melodious greenery,
The ruby and the night-owl's song,
The nightingale's—all three,

The song of life that wells and flows
From every leopard, lark and rose
And everything that gleams or goes
Lack-luster in the sea.

I heard it all, each, every note
Of every lung and tongue and throat,
Aye, every rhythm and rhyme
Of everything that lives and loves
And upward ever upward moves
From lowly to sublime!
Earth's multitudinous Sons of Light,
I heard them lift their lyric might
With each and every chanting sprite
That lit the sky that wondrous night
As far as eye could climb!

I heard it all, I heard the whole
Harmonious hymn of being roll
Up through the chapel of my soul
And at the altar die,
And in the awful quiet then
Myself I heard, Amen, Amen,
Amen I heard me cry!
I heard it all and then although
I caught my flying senses, oh,
A dizzy man was I!
I stood and stared; the sky was lit,
The sky was stars all over it,
I stood, I knew not why,
Without a wish, without a will,
I stood upon that silent hill
And stared into the sky until
My eyes were blind with stars and still
I stared into the sky.

THE LATE, LAST ROOK

The old gilt vane and spire receive
The last beam eastward striking;
The first shy bat to peep at eve
Has found her to his liking.
The western heaven is dull and gray,
The last red glow has followed day.

The late, last rook is housed and will
With cronies lie till morrow;
If there's a rook loquacious still
In dream he hunts a furrow,
And flaps behind a specter team,
Or ghostly scarecrows walk his dream.

THE BULL

See an old unhappy bull,
Sick in soul and body both,
Slouching in the undergrowth
Of the forest beautiful,
Banished from the herd he led,
Bulls and cows a thousand head.

Cranes and gaudy parrots go
Up and down the burning sky;
Tree-top cats purr drowsily
In the dim-day green below;
And troops of monkeys, nutting some,
All disputing, go and come;
And things abominable sit
Picking offal buck or swine,
On the mess and over it
Burnished flies and beetles shine,
And spiders big as bladders lie
Under hemlocks ten foot high;

And a dotted serpent curled
Round and round and round a tree,
Yellowing its greenery,
Keeps a watch on all the world,
All the world and this old bull
In the forest beautiful.

Bravely by his fall he came:
One he led, a bull of blood
Newly come to lustihood,
Fought and put his prince to shame,
Snuffed and pawed the prostrate head
Tameless even while it bled.

There they left him, every one,
Left him there without a lick,
Left him for the birds to pick,
Left him for the carrion,
Vilely from their bosom cast
Wisdom, worth and love at last.
When the lion left his lair
And roared his beauty through the hills,
And the vultures pecked their quills
And flew into the middle air,
Then this prince no more to reign
Came to life and lived again.
He snuffed the herd in far retreat,
He saw the blood upon the ground,
And snuffed the burning airs around

Still with beevish odors sweet,
While the blood ran down his head
And his mouth ran slaver red.
Pity him, this fallen chief,
All his splendor, all his strength
All his beauty's breadth and length
Dwindled down with shame and grief,
Half the bull he was before,
Bones and leather, nothing more.

See him standing dewlap-deep
In the rushes at the lake,
Surly, stupid, half asleep,
Waiting for his heart to break
And the birds to join the flies
Feasting at his bloodshot eyes,—
Standing with his head hung down
In a stupor, dreaming things:
Green savannas, jungles brown,
Battlefields and bellowings,
Bulls undone and lions dead
And vultures flapping overhead.
Dreaming things: of days he spent
With his mother gaunt and lean
In the valley warm and green,
Full of baby wonderment,
Blinking out of silly eyes
At a hundred mysteries;
Dreaming over once again
How he wandered with a throng
Of bulls and cows a thousand strong,
Wandered on from plain to plain,
Up the hill and down the dale,
Always at his mother's tail;
How he lagged behind the herd,
Lagged and tottered, weak of limb,
And she turned and ran to him
Blaring at the loathly bird
Stationed always in the skies,
Waiting for the flesh that dies.

Dreaming maybe of a day,
When her drained and drying paps
Turned him to the sweets and saps,
Richer fountains by the way,
And she left the bull she bore
And he looked to her no more;
And his little frame grew stout,
And his little legs grew strong,
And the way was not so long;
And his little horns came out,
And he played at butting trees
And bowlder-stones and tortoises,
Joined a game of knobby skulls
With the youngsters of his year,
All the other little bulls,
Learning both to bruise and bear,
Learning how to stand a shock
Like a little bull of rock.

Dreaming of a day less dim,
Dreaming of a time less far,
When the faint but certain star
Of destiny burned clear for him,
And a fierce and wild unrest
Broke the quiet of his breast,
And the gristles of his youth
Hardened in his comely pow,
And he came to fighting growth,
Beat his bull and won his cow,
And flew his tail and trampled off
Past the tallest, vain enough.
And curved about in splendor full
And curved again and snuffed the airs
As who should say, Come out who dares!
And all beheld a bull, a Bull,
And knew that here was surely one
That backed for no bull, fearing none.
And the leader of the herd
Looked and saw, and beat the ground,
And shook the forest with his sound,
Bellowed at the loathly bird
Stationed always in the skies,
Waiting for the flesh that dies.

Dreaming, this old bull forlorn,
Surely dreaming of the hour
When he came to sultan power,
And they owned him master-horn,
Chiefest bull of all among
Bulls and cows a thousand strong,
And in all the trampling herd
Not a bull that barred his way,
Not a cow that said him nay,
Not a bull or cow that erred
In the furnace of his look
Dared a second, worse rebuke;
Not in all the forest wide,
Jungle, thicket, pasture, fen,
Not another dared him then,
Dared him and again defied;

Not a sovereign buck or boar
Came a second time for more.
Not a serpent that survived
Once the terrors of his hoof,
Risked a second time reproof,
Came a second time and lived,
Not a serpent in its skin
Came again for discipline;

Not a leopard bright as flame,
Flashing fingerhooks of steel,
That a wooden tree might feel,
Met his fury once and came
For a second reprimand,
Not a leopard in the land,
Not a lion of them all,
Not a lion of the hills,
Hero of a thousand kills,
Dared a second fight and fall,
Dared that ram terrific twice,
Paid a second time the price. . . .

Pity him, this dupe of dream,
Leader of the herd again
Only in his daft old brain,
Once again the bull supreme
And bull enough to bear the part
Only in his tameless heart.

Pity him that he must wake.
Even now the swarm of flies
Blackening his bloodshot eyes
Bursts and blusters round the lake,
Scattered from the feast half-fed,
By great shadows overhead,
And the dreamer turns away
From his visionary herds
And his splendid yesterday,
Turns to meet the loathly birds
Flocking round him from the skies,
Waiting for the flesh that dies.

THE BELLS OF HEAVEN

'Twould ring the bells of Heaven
The wildest peal for years,
If Parson lost his senses
And people came to theirs,
And he and they together
Knelt down with angry prayers
For tamed and shabby tigers
And dancing dogs and bears,
And wretched, blind pit ponies,
And little hunted hares.

THE HAMMERS

Noise of hammers once I heard
Many hammers, busy hammers,
Beating, shaping night and day,
Shaping, beating dust and clay
To a palace; saw it reared;
Saw the hammers laid away.

And I listened, and I heard
Hammers beating, night and day,
In the palace newly reared,
Beating it to dust and clay:
Other hammers, muffled hammers,
Silent hammers of decay.

STUPIDITY STREET

I saw with open eyes
Singing birds sweet
Sold in the shops
For the people to eat,
Sold in the shops of
Stupidity Street.

I saw in a vision
The worm in the wheat,
And in the shops nothing
For people to eat:
Nothing for sale in
Stupidity Street.

THE MYSTERY

He came and took me by the hand
Up to a red rose tree,
He kept His meaning to Himself
But gave a rose to me.

I did not pray Him to lay bare
The mystery to me,
Enough the rose was Heaven to smell,
And His own face to see.

THE GIPSY GIRL

"Come, try your skill, kind gentlemen,
A penny for three tries!"
Some threw and lost, some threw and won
A ten-a-penny prize.

She was a tawny gipsy girl,
A girl of twenty years,
I liked her for the lumps of gold
That jingled from her ears;

I liked the flaring yellow scarf
Bound loose about her throat,
I liked her showy purple gown
And flashy velvet coat.

A man came up, too loose of tongue,
And said no good to her;
She did not blush as Saxons do,
Or turn upon the cur;

She fawned and whined, "Sweet gentleman
A penny for three tries!"
—But, oh, the den of wild things in
The darkness of her eyes!

GHOUL CARE

Sour fiend, go home and tell the Pit
For once you met your master,—
A man who carried in his soul
Three charms against disaster,
The Devil and disaster.

Away, away, and tell the tale
And start your whelps a-whining,
Say "In the greenwood of his soul
A lizard's eye was shining,
A little eye kept shining."

Away, away, and salve your sores,
And set your hags a-groaning,
Say "In the greenwood of his soul
A drowsy bee was droning,
A dreamy bee was droning."

Prodigious Bat! Go start the walls
Of Hell with horror ringing,
Say "In the greenwood of his soul
There was a goldfinch singing,
A pretty goldfinch singing."

And then come back, come, if you please,
A fiercer ghoul and ghaster,
With all the glooms and smuts of Hell
Behind you, I'm your master!
You know I'm still your master.

Walter De la Mare

Walter (John) De la Mare was born at Charlton, in Kent, in 1873. He was educated at St. Paul's school in London and was employed for eighteen years in the English branch of The Standard Oil Company of America. Later he retired to the village of Taplow near London. He died in Twickenham on June 22, 1956.

His first volume, *Songs of Childhood* (1902), was published under the pseudonym of "Walter Ramal," an anagram of part of his name. The first volume published under his own name was the novel *Henry Brocken* (1904), a form to which he returned with phenomenal success in *Memoirs of a Midget* (1921), a permanent addition to the world's small stock of philosophic fiction.

By 1929 De la Mare was the author of some twenty-three volumes which seem to fall into four categories: (1) The poetry of metaphysical phantasy. (2) The poems to and of children. (3) The mixture of prose and verse achieved in *Ding Dong Bell* (1924). (4) The introspective prose.

Although not the most important, his most popular verse is that which is centered in the child's sphere. As Harold Williams has written, "De la Mare is the singer of a young and romantic world, understanding and perceiving as a child." This poet paints simple scenes of miniature loveliness; he uses fragments of fairy-like delicacy and, with the least consequential matter, achieves a grace remarkable in its appeal. "In a few words, seemingly artless and unsought" (to quote Williams again) "he can express a pathos or a hope as wide as man's life."

De la Mare is an astonishing joiner of words; in *Peacock Pie* (1913) and *Down-a-Down Derry* (1922) he surprises us again and again by transforming what began as a child's nonsense-rhyme into a thrilling snatch of music. A score of times he takes events as casual as the feeding of chickens, or the swallowing of physic, berry-picking, eating, hair-cutting—and turns them into magic. These poems read like lyrics of William Shakespeare rendered by Mother Goose. The trick of revealing the ordinary in whimsical colors, of catching the commonplace off its guard, as in "Martha" and "The Sleeper," is the first of De la Mare's two chief gifts.

This poet's second gift is his sense of the supernatural, of the fantastic otherworld that lies on the edges of our consciousness. Sometimes, as in "At the Keyhole" and "The Mocking Fairy," the sinister turns into the lightly *macabre;* often the unbelievable, as in "Sam" and "Berries," is more homely-natural than the real. *The Listeners* (1912) is a book that, like all the best of De la Mare, is full of half-heard whispers. Moonlight and mystery seem soaked in the lines, and a cool wind from Nowhere blows over them. That most suggestive of modern verses, "The Listeners," and the brief music of "An Epitaph" are two examples among many. In the first of these poems there is an uncanny splendor. What we have here is the effect, the thrill, the overtones, of a ghost story rather than the narrative itself—the less than half-told adventure of some new Childe Roland heroically challenging a heedless universe. Never have silence and black night been reproduced more creepily, nor has the symbolism of man's courage facing the cryptic riddle of life been more memorably expressed.

De la Mare's chief distinction, however, lies not so much in what he says as in how he says it; he can take outworn words like "thridding," "athwart," "amaranthine" and make them live again in a poetry that is of no time and of all time. He writes, it has been said, as much for antiquity as for posterity; he is a poet who is distinctively in the world and yet not wholly of it.

Motley and Other Poems (1918) was followed by *Collected Poems, 1901-1918,* published in 1920, and *The Veil and Other Poems* (1921). *Come Hither* (1923), a collection apparently designed for children, is actually for mature minds. In all of these—even in the anthology—De la Mare betrays a speculation which is kin to a preoccupation: the paradox of mortality and immortality. Henry Newbolt, in *New Paths on Helicon,* recognizes this pervading quality, but perfers to call it "an inveterate habit of questioning. . . . Even the descriptions in which he excels are of the nature of a search: he attempts, like the Pre-Raphaelite painters, to pierce by intensity of vision through to the reality behind the visible word."

The Fleeting and Other Poems (1934) displays less of De la Mare's technical virtuosity than its forerunners; the awareness of the dream world, so characteristic of De la Mare, is a little strained and the spirit seems tired. But the vocabulary is still supple, the harmonies delicate and often exquisite. *Collected Poems* (1941) displays, more effectively than any of De la Mare's separate volumes, the poet's creation of his own limbo, a fitful region between the natural and the supernatural order of things. *Love* (1946) is a nostalgic garland of prose and verse.

It is a curiously remembering quality which characterizes De la Mare. He is spellbound by the magic of dreams—his *Behold, This Dreamer* (1939) is the largest anthology ever published about dreams "so various in their shocking disregard of our tastes and ideals"—fascinated by the borderland between hallucination and true vision, by the conflict between the outer event and the inner eye, by mystery *as* mystery. It is as if De la Mare, unable to remain a child, so feared adult reality that his whole work becomes a defense against it, a retreat into bitter-sweet remembrances of things past, into a domain (half faery fantasy, half nightmare reality) where everything is veiled in an unearthly loveliness and the impossible is more likely to happen than not.

It is in this hushed and recessive mood that De la Mare triumphs. Whether he is examining the extra-rational, or harking back to irresponsible childhood and irresistible romance, or exploring territories of spectral solitude, his poetry is soaked in a pervasive and musical melancholy. *The Burning Glass* (1945), full of ghostly, wistful romanticism, contains some of his saddest and some of his most serene poems. His "motto" may be found in a verse from the ancient "Tom o' Bedlam":

With a host of furious fancies
Whereof I am commander;
With a burning spear,
And a horse of air,
To the wilderness I wander.

It is as a determined "knight of ghosts" that De la Mare journeys into the terra incognita of time and spaciousness. He is one of the poets who have ventured "ten leagues beyond the wide world's end" and have returned to tell us something incredible yet, somehow, believable about that uncharted and illimitable universe.

THE SONG OF FINIS

At the edge of All the Ages
  A Knight sate on his steed,
His armor red and thin with rust,
  His soul from sorrow freed;
And he lifted up his visor
  From a face of skin and bone,
And his horse turned head and whinnied
  As the twain stood there alone.

No bird above that steep of time
  Sang of a livelong quest;
No wind breathed,
    Rest:
"Lone for an end!" cried Knight to steed,
  Loosed an eager rein—
Charged with his challenge into Space:
  And quiet did quiet remain.

THE LISTENERS

"Is there anybody there?" said the Traveler,
  Knocking on the moonlit door;
And his horse in the silence champed the grasses
  Of the forest's ferny floor.
And a bird flew up out of the turret,
  Above the Traveler's head:
And he smote upon the door again a second time;
  "Is there anybody there?" he said.
But no one descended to the Traveler;
  No head from the leaf-fringed sill
Leaned over and looked into his gray eyes,
  Where he stood perplexed and still.
But only a host of phantom listeners
  That dwelt in the lone house then
Stood listening in the quiet of the moonlight
  To that voice from the world of men:
Stood thronging the faint moonbeams on the dark stair
  That goes down to the empty hall,
Hearkening in an air stirred and shaken
  By the lonely Traveler's call.
And he felt in his heart their strangeness,
  Their stillness answering his cry,

While his horse moved, cropping the dark turf,
'Neath the starred and leafy sky;
For he suddenly smote on the door, even
Louder, and lifted his head:—
"Tell them I came, and no one answered,
That I kept my word," he said.
Never the least stir made the listeners,
Though every word he spake
Fell echoing through the shadowiness of the still house
From the one man left awake:
Aye, they heard his foot upon the stirrup,
And the sound of iron on stone,
And how the silence surged softly backward,
When the plunging hoofs were gone.

AN EPITAPH

Here lies a most beautiful lady,
Light of step and heart was she;
I think she was the most beautiful lady
That ever was in the West Country.

But beauty vanishes; beauty passes;
However rare—rare it be;
And when I crumble, who will remember
This lady of the West Country?

THE TRUANTS

Ere my heart beats too coldly and faintly
To remember sad things, yet be gay,
I would sing a brief song of the world's little children
Magic hath stolen away.

The primroses scattered by April,
The stars of the wide Milky Way,
Cannot outnumber the hosts of the children
Magic hath stolen away.

The buttercup green of the meadows,
The snow of the blossoming may,
Lovelier are not than the legions of children
Magic hath stolen away.

The waves tossing surf in the moonbeam,
The albatross lone on the spray,
Alone knew the tears wept in vain for the children
Magic hath stolen away.

In vain: for at hush of the evening,
When the stars twinkle into the gray,
Seems to echo the far-away calling of children
Magic hath stolen away.

OLD SUSAN

When Susan's work was done, she'd sit
With one fat guttering candle lit,
And window opened wide to win
The sweet night air to enter in;
There, with a thumb to keep her place
She'd read, with stern and wrinkled face.
Her mild eyes gliding very slow
Across the letters to and fro,
While wagged the guttering candle flame
In the wind that through the window came.
And sometimes in the silence she
Would mumble a sentence audibly,
Or shake her head as if to say,
"You silly souls, to act this way!"
And never a sound from night I'd hear,
Unless some far-off cock crowed clear;
Or her old shuffling thumb should turn
Another page; and rapt and stern,
Through her great glasses bent on me,
She'd glance into reality;
And shake her round old silvery head,
With—"You!—I thought you was in bed!"—
Only to tilt her book again,
And rooted in Romance remain.

MARTHA

"Once . . . once upon a time . . ."
  Over and over again,
Martha would tell us her stories,
  In the hazel glen.

Hers were those clear gray eyes
  You watch, and the story seems
Told by their beautifulness
  Tranquil as dreams.

She'd sit with her two slim hands
  Clasped round her bended knees;
While we on our elbows lolled,
  And stared at ease.

Her voice and her narrow chin,
  Her grave small lovely head,
Seemed half the meaning
  Of the words she said.

"Once . . . once upon a time . . ."
  Like a dream you dream in the night,
Fairies and gnomes stole out
  In the leaf-green light.

And her beauty far away
  Would fade, as her voice ran on,
Till hazel and summer sun
  And all were gone:—

All fordone and forgot;
  And like clouds in the height of the sky,
Our hearts stood still in the hush
  Of an age gone by.

SOMEONE

Someone came knocking
  At my wee, small door;
Someone came knocking,
  I'm sure—sure—sure;
I listened, I opened,
  I looked to left and right,
But nought there was a-stirring
  In the still dark night;
Only the busy beetle
  Tap-tapping in the wall,
Only from the forest
  The screech-owl's call,
Only the cricket whistling
  While the dewdrops fall,
So I know not who came knocking,
  At all, at all, at all.

THE SLEEPER

As Ann came in one summer's day,
  She felt that she must creep,
So silent was the clear cool house,
  It seemed a house of sleep.
And sure, when she pushed open the door,
  Rapt in the stillness there,
Her mother sat with stooping head,
  Asleep upon a chair;
Fast—fast asleep; her two hands laid
  Loose-folded on her knee,
So that her small unconscious face
  Looked half unreal to be:
So calmly lit with sleep's pale light
  Each feature was; so fair
Her forehead—every trouble was
  Smooth'd out beneath her hair.

But though her mind in dream now moved,
  Still seemed her gaze to rest
From out beneath her fast-sealed lids,
  Above her moving breast,
On Ann, as quite, quite still she stood;
  Yet slumber lay so deep
Even her hands upon her lap
  Seemed saturate with sleep.
And as Ann peeped, a cloudlike dread
  Stole over her, and then,
On stealthy, mouselike feet she trod,
  And tiptoed out again.

THE OLD MEN

Old and alone sit we,
Caged, riddle-rid men;
Lost to earth's "Listen!" and "See!"
Thought's "Wherefore?" and "When?"
Only far memories stray
Of a past once lovely, but now
Wasted and faded away,
Like green leaves from the bough.
Vast broods the silence of night;
And the ruinous moon
Lifts on our faces her light,
Whence all dreaming is gone.
We speak not; trembles each head;
In their sockets our eyes are still;
Desire as cold as the dead,
Without wonder or will.
And one, with a lanthorn, draws near,
At clash with the moon in our eyes:
"Where art thou?" he asks: "I am here!"
One by one we arise.
And none lifts a hand to withhold
A friend from the touch of that foe:
Heart cries unto heart, "Thou art old!"
Yet reluctant we go.

AT THE KEYHOLE

"Grill me some bones," said the Cobbler,
  "Some bones, my pretty Sue;
I'm tired of my lonesome with heels and
    soles,
Springsides and uppers too;
A mouse in the wainscot is nibbling;
A wind in the keyhole drones;
And a sheet webbed over my candle,
    Susie,
  Grill me some bones!"

"Grill me some bones," said the Cobbler,
  "I sat at my tic-tac-to;
And a footstep came to my door and stopped
And a hand groped to and fro;
And I peered up over my boot and last;
And my feet went cold as stones:—
I saw an eye at the keyhole, Susie!—
  Grill me some bones!"

THE MOCKING FAIRY

"Won't you look out of your window, Mrs. Gill?"
  Quoth the Fairy, nidding, nodding in the garden;
"Can't you look out of your window, Mrs. Gill?"
  Quoth the Fairy, laughing softly in the garden;
But the air was still, the cherry boughs were still,
And the ivy-tod[1] 'neath the empty sill,
And never from her window looked out Mrs. Gill
  On the Fairy shrilly mocking in the garden.

"What have they done with you, your poor Mrs. Gill?"
  Quoth the Fairy brightly glancing in the garden;
"Where have they hidden you, you poor old Mrs. Gill?"
  Quoth the Fairy dancing lightly in the garden;
But night's faint veil now wrapped the hill,
Stark 'neath the stars stood the dead-still Mill,
And out of her cold cottage never answered Mrs. Gill
  The Fairy mimbling mambling in the garden.

[1] Tod = dense foliage.

SAM

When Sam goes back in memory,
It is to where the sea
Breaks on the shingle, emerald-green,
In white foam, endlessly;
He says—with small brown eye on mine—
"I used to keep awake,
And lean from my window in the moon,
Watching those billows break.
And half a million tiny hands,
And eyes, like sparks of frost,
Would dance and come tumbling into the moon,
On every breaker tossed.
And all across from star to star,
I've seen the watery sea,
With not a single ship in sight,
Just ocean there, and me;
And heard my father snore. And once,
As sure as I'm alive,
Out of those wallowing, moon-flecked waves
I saw a mermaid dive;
Head and shoulders above the wave,
Plain as I now see you,
Combing her hair, now back, now front,
Her two eyes peeping through;
Calling me, 'Sam!'—quietlike—'Sam!' . . .
But me . . . I never went,
Making believe I kind of thought
'Twas someone else she meant . . .
Wonderful lovely there she sat,
Singing the night away,
All in the solitudinous sea
Of that there lonely bay.
P'raps," and he'd smooth his hairless mouth,
"P'raps, if 'twere now, my son,
P'raps, if I heard a voice say, 'Sam!'
Morning would find me gone."

BERRIES

There was an old woman
Went blackberry picking
Along the hedges
From Weep to Wicking.
Half a pottle—
No more she had got,
When out steps a Fairy
From her green grot;
And says, "Well, Jill,
Would 'ee pick 'ee mo?"
And Jill, she curtseys,
And looks just so.
"Be off," says the Fairy,
"As quick as you can,
Over the meadows
To the little green lane,
That dips to the hayfields
Of Farmer Grimes:
I've berried those hedges
A score of times;
Bushel on bushel
I'll promise 'ee, Jill,

This side of supper
  If 'ee pick with a will."
She glints very bright,
  And speaks her fair;
Then lo, and behold!
  She had faded in air.

Be sure Old Goodie
  She trots betimes
Over the meadows
  To Farmer Grimes.
And never was queen
  With jewelry rich
As those same hedges
  From twig to ditch;
Like Dutchmen's coffers,
  Fruit, thorn, and flower—
They shone like William
  And Mary's Bower.
And be sure Old Goodie
  Went back to Weep,
So tired with her basket
  She scarce could creep.

When she comes in the dusk
  To her cottage door,
There's Towser wagging
  As never before,
To see his Missus
  So glad to be
Come from her fruit-picking
  Back to he.
As soon as next morning
  Dawn was gray,
The pot on the hob
  Was simmering away;
And all in a stew
  And a hugger-mugger
Towser and Jill
  A-boiling of sugar,
And the dark clear fruit
  That from Faërie came
For syrup and jelly
  And blackberry jam.

Twelve jolly gallipots
  Jill put by;
And one little teeny one,
  One inch high;
And that she's hidden
  A good thumb deep,
Half way over
  From Wicking to Weep.

ALL BUT BLIND

All but blind
  In his chambered hole
Gropes for worms
  The four-clawed Mole.

All but blind
  In the evening sky,
The hooded Bat
  Twirls softly by.

All but blind
  In the burning day
The Barn-Owl blunders
  On her way.

And blind as are
  These three to me,
So, blind to Someone
  I must be.

SUMMER EVENING

The sandy cat by the Farmer's chair
Mews at his knee for dainty fare;
Old Rover in his moss-greened house
Mumbles a bone, and barks at a mouse.
In the dewy fields the cattle lie
Chewing the cud 'neath a fading sky.
Dobbin at manger pulls his hay:
Gone is another summer's day.

THERE BLOOMS NO BUD IN MAY

There blooms no bud in May
Can for its white compare
With snow at break of day,
On fields forlorn and bare.

For shadow it hath rose,
Azure, and amethyst;
And every air that blows
Dies out in beauteous mist.

It hangs the frozen bough
With flowers on which the night
Wheeling her darkness through
Scatters a starry light.

Fearful of its pale glare
In flocks the starlings rise;
Slide through the frosty air,
And perch with plaintive cries.

Only the inky rook,
Hunched cold in ruffled wings,
Its snowy nest forsook,
Caws of unnumbered Springs.

THE SCARECROW

All winter through I bow my head
  Beneath the driving rain;
The North wind powders me with snow
  And blows me black again;
At midnight 'neath a maze of stars
  I flame with glittering rime,
And stand, above the stubble, stiff
  As mail at morning-prime.
But when that child, called Spring, and all
  His host of children, come,
Scattering their buds and dew upon
  These acres of my home,
Some rapture in my rags awakes;
  I lift void eyes and scan
The skies for crows, those ravening foes
  Of my strange master, Man.
I watch him striding lank behind
  His clashing team, and know
Soon will the wheat swish body high
  Where once lay sterile snow;
Soon shall I gaze across a sea
  Of sun-begotten grain,
Which my unflinching watch hath sealed
  For harvest once again.

THE GHOST

"Who knocks?" "I, who was beautiful,
Beyond all dreams to restore,
I, from the roots of the dark thorn am hither,
And knock on the door."

"Who speaks?" "I—once was my speech
Sweet as the bird's on the air.
When echo lurks by the waters to heed;
'Tis I speak thee fair."

"Dark is the hour!" "Aye, and cold."
"Lone is my house." "Ah, but mine?"
"Sight, touch, lips, eyes yearned in vain."
"Long dead these to thine. . . ."

Silence. Still faint on the porch
Brake the flames of the stars.
In gloom groped a hope-wearied hand
Over keys, bolts, and bars.

A face peered. All the grey night
In chaos of vacancy shone;
Nought but vast sorrow was there—
The sweet cheat gone.

SILVER

Slowly, silently, now the moon
Walks the night in her silver shoon;
This way, and that, she peers, and sees
Silver fruit upon silver trees;
One by one the casements catch
Her beams beneath the silvery thatch;
Couched in his kennel, like a log,
With paws of silver sleeps the dog;
From their shadowy cote the white breasts
  peep
Of doves in a silver-feathered sleep;
A harvest mouse goes scampering by,
With silver claws and a silver eye;
And moveless fish in the water gleam,
By silver reeds in a silver stream.

THE SONG OF SHADOWS

Sweep thy faint strings, Musician,
  With thy long lean hand;
Downward the starry tapers burn,
  Sinks soft the waning sand;
The old hound whimpers couched in sleep,
  The embers smolder low;
Across the walls the shadows
  Come, and go.

Sweep softly thy strings, Musician,
  The minutes mount to hours;
Frost on the windless casement weaves
  A labyrinth of flowers;

Ghosts linger in the darkening air,
  Hearken at the open door;
Music hath called them, dreaming,
  Home once more.

NOD

Softly along the road of evening,
  In a twilight dim with rose,
Wrinkled with age, and drenched with dew
  Old Nod, the shepherd, goes.

His drowsy flock streams on before him,
  Their fleeces charged with gold,
To where the sun's last beam leans low
  On Nod the shepherd's fold.

The hedge is quick and green with briar,
  From their sand the conies creep;
And all the birds that fly in heaven
  Flock singing home to sleep.

His lambs outnumber a noon's roses,
  Yet, when night's shadows fall,
His blind old sheep-dog, Slumber-soon,
  Misses not one of all.

His are the quiet steeps of dreamland,
  The waters of no-more-pain;
His ram's bell rings 'neath an arch of stars,
  "Rest, rest, and rest again."

THE LAST CHAPTER

I am living more alone now than I did;
This life tends inward, as the body ages;
And what is left of its strange book to read
Quickens in interest with the last few pages.

Problems abound. Its authorship? A sequel?
Its hero-villain, whose ways so little mend?
The plot? still dark. The style? a shade unequal.
And what of the denouement? And the end?

No, no, have done! Lay the thumbed thing aside;
Forget its horrors, folly, incitement, lies;
In silence and in solitude abide,
And con what yet may bless your inward eyes.

Pace, still, for pace with you, companion goes,
Though now, through dulled and inattentive ear,
No more—as when a child's—your sick heart knows
His infinite energy and beauty near.

His, too, a World, though viewless save in glimpse;
He, too, a book of imagery bears;
And as your halting foot beside him limps,
Mark you whose badge and livery he wears.

PEACE

Night arches England, and the winds are still;
Jasmine and honeysuckle steep the air;
Softly the stars that are all Europe's fill
Her heaven-wide dark with radiancy fair;
That shadowed moon now waxing in the west,
Stirs not a rumor in her tranquil seas;

Mysterious sleep has lulled her heart to rest,
Deep even as theirs beneath her churchyard trees.

Secure, serene; dumb now the nighthawk's threat;
The gun's low thunder drumming o'er the tide;
The anguish pulsing in her stricken side . . .
All is at peace. Ah, never, heart, forget
For this her youngest, best, and bravest died,
These bright dews once were mixed with blood and sweat.

G. K. Chesterton

⊰ That brilliant journalist, novelist, essayist, publicist and lyricist, Gilbert Keith Chesterton, was born at Campden Hill, Kensington, May 29, 1874, and began his literary life by reviewing books on art for various magazines. He is best known as a writer of paradoxical essays on anything and everything, such as *Tremendous Trifles* (1909), *Varied Types* (1905), and *All Things Considered* (1910). But he was also a stimulating critic; a keen appraiser, as shown in his volume *Heretics* (1905) and his analytical studies of Robert Browning, Charles Dickens, and George Bernard Shaw; a writer of strange and grotesque romances like *The Napoleon of Notting Hill* (1906), *The Man Who Was Thursday* (1908), which Chesterton himself has sub-titled "A Nightmare," and that mad extravaganza with songs for a sublimated comic-opera, *The Flying Inn* (1914). This being insufficient to exhaust his creative energy, he was also the author of several books of fantastic short stories, ranging from the whimsical narratives in *The Club of Queer Trades* (1905) to that amazing sequence begun with *The Innocence of Father Brown* (1911), which is a series of religious detective stories.

Besides being the creator of all these, Chesterton found time to be a prolific if sometimes too acrobatic newspaperman, a lay preacher in disguise (witness *Orthodoxy* [1908], *What's Wrong with the World* [1910], *The Ball and the Cross* [1909]) and a pamphleteer. He was also—his admirers say, primarily—a poet. His first volume of verse, *The Wild Knight and Other Poems* (1900), a collection of quaintly flavored affirmative verses, was followed by *The Ballad of the White Horse* (1911), one long poem which, in spite of Chesterton's ever-present sermonizing, is possibly the most stirring creation he ever achieved.

Scarcely less notable is the ringing "Lapanto" from his later, more epigrammatic *Poems* (1915) which, anticipating the clanging verses of Vachel Lindsay's "The Congo," is one of the finest of modern chants. The syllables beat, as though on brass; the armies sing; the feet tramp; the drums snarl; the tides of marching crusaders surge through such lines as

Strong gongs groaning as the guns boom far,
Don John of Austria is going to the war;
Stiff flags straining in the night-blasts cold
In the gloom black-purple, in the glint old-gold;
Torchlight crimson on the copper kettle-drums,
Then the tuckets, then the trumpets, then the cannon, and he comes. . . .

Subsequent volumes established the poet's rollicking reactions. Aware that something was wrong with the economic system, he revolted against both capitalism and socialism, and proclaimed a new order which was curiously like an old disorder: a confused and romanticized medievalism. Here Chesterton revealed his irrational rationalism. He wrote like an adult who lived in a world of childish fantasy, a serious thinker who thought only in terms of paradox, a philosopher who defended the obvious with the zeal of a fanatic crucified for heresy. When Chesterton died on June 14, 1936, he was the author of more than one hundred volumes of fiction, poetry, plays, biographies, criticisms, essays, and studies.

A clue to Chesterton's tricky humor is contained in some of his later titles: *The Unthinkable Theory of Professor Green* (1925), *The Moderate Murderer* (1929), *The Poet and the Lunatics* (1929), *A Defence of Nonsense* (1911), and *The Scandal of Father Brown* (1935). His charm is the charm of gusto, a zest which does not stop to appraise its defects. His criticism of Mrs. Browning's style might well be applied to Chesterton himself: "Whenever her verse is bad, it is bad from some violence of comparison, some kind of debauch of cleverness. Her nonsense never arises from weakness, but from a confusion of powers. . . . She cannot leave anything alone, she cannot write a line, without a conceit. She gives the reader the impression that she never declined a fancy."

ECCLESIASTES

There is one sin: to call a green leaf gray,
  Whereat the sun in heaven shuddereth.
There is one blasphemy: for death to pray,
  For God alone knoweth the praise of death.

There is one creed: 'neath no world-terror's wing
  Apples forget to grow on apple-trees.
There is one thing is needful—everything—
  The rest is vanity of vanities.

LEPANTO

White founts falling in the Courts of the sun,
And the Soldan of Byzantium is smiling as they run;
There is laughter like the fountains in that face of all men feared,
It stirs the forest darkness, the darkness of his beard;
It curls the blood-red crescent, the crescent of his lips;
For the inmost sea of all the earth is shaken with his ships.
They have dared the white republics up the capes of Italy,
They have dashed the Adriatic round the Lion of the Sea,
And the Pope has cast his arms abroad for agony and loss,
And called the kings of Christendom for swords about the Cross.
The cold queen of England is looking in the glass;
The shadow of the Valois is yawning at the Mass;
From evening isles fantastical rings faint the Spanish gun,
And the Lord upon the Golden Horn is laughing in the sun.

Dim drums throbbing, in the hills half heard,
Where only on a nameless throne a crownless prince has stirred,

Where, risen from a doubtful seat and half-attainted stall,
The last knight of Europe takes weapons from the wall,
The last and lingering troubadour to whom the bird has sung,
That once went singing southward when all the world was young.
In that enormous silence, tiny and unafraid,
Comes up along a winding road the noise of the Crusade.
Strong gongs groaning as the guns boom far,
Don John of Austria is going to the war;
Stiff flags straining in the night-blasts cold
In the gloom black-purple, in the glint old-gold,
Torchlight crimson on the copper kettle-drums,
Then the tuckets, then the trumpets, then the cannon, and he comes.
Don John laughing in the brave beard curled,
Spurning of his stirrups like the thrones of all the world,
Holding his head up for a flag of all the free.
Love-light of Spain—hurrah!
Death-light of Africa!
Don John of Austria
Is riding to the sea.

Mahound is in his paradise above the evening star,
(Don John of Austria is going to the war.)
He moves a mighty turban on the timeless houri's knees,
His turban that is woven of the sunsets and the seas.
He shakes the peacock gardens as he rises from his ease,
And he strides among the tree-tops and is taller than the trees;
And his voice through all the garden is a thunder sent to bring
Black Azrael and Ariel and Ammon on the wing.
Giants and the Genii,
Multiplex of wing and eye,
Whose strong obedience broke the sky
When Solomon was king.

They rush in red and purple from the red clouds of the morn,
From the temples where the yellow gods shut up their eyes in scorn;
They rise in green robes roaring from the green hells of the sea
Where fallen skies and evil hues and eyeless creatures be,
On them the sea-valves cluster and the gray sea-forests curl,
Splashed with a splendid sickness, the sickness of the pearl;
They swell in sapphire smoke out of the blue cracks of the ground,—
They gather and they wonder and give worship to Mahound.
And he saith, "Break up the mountains where the hermit-folk can hide,
And sift the red and silver sands lest bone of saint abide,
And chase the Giaours flying night and day, not giving rest,
For that which was our trouble comes again out of the west.
We have set the seal of Solomon on all things under sun,
Of knowledge and of sorrow and endurance of things done.
But a noise is in the mountains, in the mountains; and I know
The voice that shook our palaces—four hundred years ago:
It is he that saith not 'Kismet'; it is he that knows not Fate;
It is Richard, it is Raymond, it is Godfrey at the gate!

It is he whose loss is laughter when he counts the wager worth,
Put down your feet upon him, that our peace be on the earth."
For he heard drums groaning and he heard guns jar,
(*Don John of Austria is going to the war.*)
Sudden and still—hurrah!
Bolt from Iberia!
Don John of Austria
Is gone by Alcalar.

St. Michael's on his Mountain in the sea-roads of the north
(*Don John of Austria is girt and going forth.*)
Where the gray seas glitter and the sharp tides shift
And the sea-folk labor and the red sails lift.
He shakes his lance of iron and he claps his wings of stone;
The noise is gone through Normandy; the noise is gone alone;
The North is full of tangled things and texts and aching eyes,
And dead is all the innocence of anger and surprise,
And Christian killeth Christian in a narrow dusty room,
And Christian dreadeth Christ that hath a newer face of doom,
And Christian hateth Mary that God kissed in Galilee,—
But Don John of Austria is riding to the sea.
Don John calling through the blast and the eclipse,
Crying with the trumpet, with the trumpet to his lips,
Trumpet that sayeth *ha!*
Domino Gloria!
Don John of Austria
Is shouting to the ships.

King Philip's in his closet with the Fleece about his neck
(*Don John of Austria is armed upon the deck.*)
The walls are hung with velvet that is black and soft as sin,
And little dwarfs creep out of it and little dwarfs creep in.
He holds a crystal phial that has colors like the moon,
He touches, and it tingles, and he trembles very soon,
And his face is as a fungus of a leprous white and gray
Like plants in the high houses that are shuttered from the day,
And death is in the phial and the end of noble work,
But Don John of Austria has fired upon the Turk.
Don John's hunting, and his hounds have bayed—
Booms away past Italy the rumor of his raid.
Gun upon gun, ha! ha!
Gun upon gun, hurrah!
Don John of Austria
Has loosed the cannonade.

The Pope was in his chapel before day or battle broke,
(*Don John of Austria is hidden in the smoke.*)
The hidden room in man's house where God sits all the year,
The secret window whence the world looks small and very dear.
He sees as in a mirror on the monstrous twilight sea
The crescent of his cruel ships whose name is mystery;

They fling great shadows foe-wards, making Cross and Castle dark,
They veil the plumèd lions on the galleys of St. Mark;
And above the ships are palaces of brown, black-bearded chiefs,
And below the ships are prisons, where with multitudinous griefs,
Christian captives, sick and sunless, all a laboring race repines
Like a race in sunken cities, like a nation in the mines.
They are lost like slaves that swat, and in the skies of morning hung
The stair-ways of the tallest gods when tyranny was young.
They are countless, voiceless, hopeless as those fallen or fleeing on
Before the high Kings' horses in the granite of Babylon.
And many a one grows witless in his quiet room in hell
Where a yellow face looks inward through the lattice of his cell,
And he finds his God forgotten, and he seeks no more a sign—
(*But Don John of Austria has burst the battle-line!*)
Don John pounding from the slaughter-painted poop,
Purpling all the ocean like a bloody pirate's sloop,
Scarlet running over on the silvers and the golds,
Breaking of the hatches up and bursting of the holds,
Thronging of the thousands up that labor under sea
White for bliss and blind for sun and stunned for liberty.
Vivat Hispania!
Domino Gloria!
Don John of Austria
Has set his people free!

Cervantes on his galley sets the sword back in the sheath
(*Don John of Austria rides homeward with a wreath.*)
And he sees across a weary land a straggling road in Spain,
Up which a lean and foolish knight for ever rides in vain,
And he smiles, but not as Sultans smile, and settles back the blade . . .
(*But Don John of Austria rides home from the Crusade.*)

A PRAYER IN DARKNESS

This much, O heaven—if I should brood or rave,
  Pity me not; but let the world be fed,
  Yea, in my madness if I strike me dead,
Heed you the grass that grows upon my grave.

If I dare snarl between this sun and sod,
  Whimper and clamor, give me grace to own,
  In sun and rain and fruit in season shown,
The shining silence of the scorn of God.

Thank God the stars are set beyond my power,
  If I must travail in a night of wrath;
  Thank God my tears will never vex a moth,
Nor any curse of mine cut down a flower.

Men say the sun was darkened: yet I had
  Thought it beat brightly, even on—Calvary:
  And He that hung upon the Torturing Tree
Heard all the crickets singing, and was glad.

ELEGY IN A COUNTRY CHURCHYARD

The men that worked for England
They have their graves at home;
And bees and birds of England
About the cross can roam.

But they that fought for England,
Following a falling star,
Alas, alas, for England
They have their graves afar.

And they that rule in England
In stately conclave met,
Alas, alas, for England
They have no graves as yet.

THE DONKEY

When fishes flew and forests walked
  And figs grew upon thorn,
Some moment when the moon was blood,
  Then surely I was born;

With monstrous head and sickening cry
  And ears like errant wings,
The devil's walking parody
  On all four-footed things.

The tattered outlaw of the earth,
  Of ancient crooked will;
Starve, scourge, deride me: I am dumb,
  I keep my secret still.

Fools! For I also had my hour;
  One far fierce hour and sweet:
There was a shout about my ears,
  And palms before my feet!

THE PRAISE OF DUST

"What of vile dust?" the preacher said.
  Methought the whole world woke,
The dead stone lived beneath my foot,
  And my whole body spoke.

"You, that play tyrant to the dust,
  And stamp its wrinkled face,
This patient star that flings you not
  Far into homeless space,

"Come down out of your dusty shrine
  The living dust to see,
The flowers that at your sermon's end
  Stand blazing silently.

"Rich white and blood-red blossom; stones,
  Lichens like fire encrust;
A gleam of blue, a glare of gold,
  The vision of the dust.

"Pass them all by: till, as you come
  Where, at a city's edge,
Under a tree—I know it well—
  Under a lattice ledge,

"The sunshine falls on one brown head.
  You, too, O cold of clay,
Eater of stones, may haply hear
  The trumpets of that day.

"When God to all his paladins
  By his own splendor swore
To make a fairer face than heaven,
  Of dust and nothing more."

WINE AND WATER

Old Noah he had an ostrich farm and fowls on the largest scale,
He ate his egg with a ladle in an egg-cup big as a pail,
And the soup he took was Elephant Soup, and the fish he took was Whale,
But they all were small to the cellar he took when he set out to sail,
And Noah he often said to his wife when he sat down to dine,
"I don't care where the water goes if it doesn't get into the wine."

The cataract of the cliff of heaven fell blinding off the brink
As if it would wash the stars away as suds go down a sink,
The seven heavens came roaring down for the throats of hell to drink,
And Noah he cocked his eye and said, "It looks like rain, I think,

The water has drowned the Matterhorn as deep as a Mendip mine,
But I don't care where the water goes if it doesn't get into the wine."

But Noah he sinned, and we have sinned; on tipsy feet we trod,
Till a great big, black teetotaler was sent to us for a rod,
And you can't get wine at a P. S. A., or chapel, or Eisteddfod.
For the Curse of Water has come again because of the wrath of God,
And water is on the Bishop's board and the Higher Thinker's shrine,
But I don't care where the water goes if it doesn't get into the wine.

THE SWORD OF SURPRISE

Sunder me from my bones, O sword of God,
Till they stand stark and strange as do the trees;
That I whose heart goes up with the soaring woods
May marvel as much at these.

Sunder me from my blood that in the dark
I hear that red ancestral river run,
Like branching buried floods that find the sea
But never find the sun.

Give me miraculous eyes to see my eyes,
Those rolling mirrors made alive in me,
Terrible crystal more incredible
Than all the things they see.

Sunder me from my soul, that I may see
The sins like streaming wounds, the life's brave beat
Till I shall save myself, as I would save
A stranger in the street.

THE HOUSE OF CHRISTMAS

There fared a mother driven forth
  Out of an inn to roam;
In the place where she was homeless
  All men are at home.
The crazy stable close at hand,
With shaking timber and shifting sand,
Grew a stronger thing to abide and stand
  Than the square stones of Rome.

For men are homesick in their homes,
  And strangers under the sun,
And they lay their heads in a foreign land
  Whenever the day is done.
Here we have battle and blazing eyes,
And chance and honor and high surprise;
But our homes are under miraculous skies
  Where the yule tale was begun.

A child in a foul stable,
  Where the beasts feed and foam;
Only where He was homeless
  Are you and I at home;
We have hands that fashion and heads that know,
But our hearts we lost—how long ago!
In a place no chart nor ship can show
  Under the sky's dome.

This world is wild as an old wives' tale,
  And strange the plain things are,
The earth is enough and the air is enough
  For our wonder and our war;
But our rest is as far as the fire-drake swings,
And our peace is put in impossible things
Where clashed and thundered unthinkable wings
  Round an incredible star.

To an open house in the evening
  Home shall men come,
To an older place than Eden
  And a taller town than Rome;
To the end of the way of the wandering star,
To the things that cannot be and that are,
To the place where God was homeless
  And all men are at home.

Gordon Bottomley

Gordon Bottomley was born at Keighley in 1874 and educated at the Grammar School. He is best known as a dramatist, his volumes —and there are ten of them dating from 1904—having elicited high praise upon publication. When the dramas were collected in two volumes, *King Lear's Wife and Other Plays* (1920) and *Gruach and Britain's Daughter* (1921), the tributes were still more enthusiastic. Referring to *Gruach,* which is a portrait of the Lady Macbeth at the time of her first meeting with the Thane, Lascelles Abercrombie wrote, "It was remarkable enough that Mr. Bottomley should have proved himself capable of worthily inventing a prelude to 'Lear'; it is astonishing that the success should be repeated in a prelude to 'Macbeth.' But it has become clear now that at no time in the history of English poetry since the seventeenth century has the requisite combination of dramatic and poetic talents existed until now in the person of Mr. Bottomley."

His poetry, collected in *Chambers of Imagery, First Series* (1907), *Second Series* (1912), displays the same command of vivid characterization and imaginative vigor one finds in his poetic dramas. What lends technical, if contemporary, interest to both volumes is that they anticipated the effects of the Imagists long before the group created a movement. A comprehensive collection, *Poems of Thirty Years*

(1925), synthesizes the combination of force and delicacy which is Bottomley's own. "The End of the World" (which should be read in connection with Abercrombie's play of the same title) is typical, simple in language, dramatic in effect, and extraordinarily supple in rhythm. Here, as in his dramas, the fine intricacies of phrase are paralleled by a knit power of thought. Bottomley died in 1948.

THE END OF THE WORLD

The snow had fallen many nights and days;
The sky was come upon the earth at last,
Sifting thinly down as endlessly
As though within the system of blind planets
Something had been forgot or overdriven.
The dawn now seemed neglected in the gray,
Where mountains were unbuilt and shadowless trees
Rootlessly paused or hung upon the air.
There was no wind, but now and then a sigh
Crossed that dry falling dust and rifted it
Through crevices of slate and door and casement.
Perhaps the new moon's time was even past.
Outside, the first white twilights were too void
Until a sheep called once, as to a lamb,
And tenderness crept everywhere from it;
But now the flock must have strayed far away.
The lights across the valley must be veiled,
The smoke lost in the grayness or the dusk.
For more than three days now the snow had thatched
That cow-house roof where it had ever melted
With yellow stains from the beasts' breath inside;
But yet a dog howled there, though not quite lately.
Someone passed down the valley swift and singing,
Yes, with locks spreaded like a son of morning;
But if he seemed too tall to be a man
It was that men had been so long unseen,
Or shapes loom larger through a moving snow.
And he was gone and food had not been given him.
When snow slid from an overweighted leaf
Shaking the tree, it might have been a bird
Slipping in sleep or shelter, whirring wings;
Yet never bird fell out, save once a dead one—
And in two days the snow had covered it.
The dog had howled again—or thus it seemed
Until a lean fox passed and cried no more.
All was so safe indoors where life went on
Glad of the close enfolding snow—O glad
To be so safe and secret at its heart,
Watching the strangeness of familiar things.
They knew not what dim hours went on, went by,
For while they slept the clock stopt newly wound
As the cold hardened. Once they watched the road,
Thinking to be remembered. Once they doubted

If they had kept the sequence of the days,
Because they heard not any sound of bells.
A butterfly, that hid until the Spring
Under a ceiling's shadow, dropt, was dead.
The coldness seemed more nigh, the coldness deepened
As a sound deepens into silences;
It was of earth and came not by the air;
The earth was cooling and drew down the sky.
The air was crumbling. There was no more sky.
Rails of a broken bed charred in the grate,
And when he touched the bars he thought the sting
Came from their heat—he could not feel such cold . . .
She said, "O do not sleep,
Heart, heart of mine, keep near me. No, no; sleep.
I will not lift his fallen, quiet eyelids,
Although I know he would awaken then—
He closed them thus but not of his own will.
He can stay with me while I do not lift them."

DAWN

A thrush is tapping a stone
With a snail-shell in its beak;
A small bird hangs from a cherry
Until the stem shall break.
No waking song has begun,
And yet birds chatter and hurry
And throng in the elm's gloom
Because an owl goes home.

EAGER SPRING

Whirl, snow, on the blackbird's chatter;
You will not hinder his song to come.
East wind, sleepless, you cannot scatter
Quince-bud, almond-bud,
Little grape-hyacinth's
Clustering brood.
Nor unfurl the tips of the plum.
No half-born stalk of a lily stops;
There is sap in the storm-torn bush;
And, ruffled by gusts in a snow-blurred copse,
"Pity to wait" sings a thrush.

Love, there are few Springs left for us;
They go, and the count of them as they go
Makes surer the count that is left for us.
More than the East wind, more than the snow,
I would put back these hours that bring
Buds and bees and are lost;
I would hold the night and the frost,
To save for us one more Spring.

EAGLE SONG

(from "Suilven and the Eagle")

O deep, creating Light,
My energy, my desire,
Receive me into you in the height
And force me to aspire.

Alone I am made for you;
I alone rise and gaze
With lidless eyes, alone pursue
Like spiring flame your ways.

I am that part of life
Which will not live but to dare:
When I must rest from joyful strife
I climb the lonely air,

And climbing strive again.
On fellow life I prey,
Know that immaterial pain
Passes and things remain

In me or outside me,
Which deepen in that fierce way
Life, and by wisdom and cruelty
Continue it for a day.

Out of the fathomless height,
Come, show to me here
This thing I have held in my breast all night,
Desired, devoted, dear.
On strange, small limb and brow
Come, Light, now.

Edward Thomas

☙ Philip Edward Thomas was born in 1878 and educated at Lincoln College, Oxford. Before he turned to verse, Thomas had a large following as author of travel books, biographies, and pot-boilers. Hating his hack-work, yet unable to free himself of it, he had so repressed his creative ability that he had grown doubtful concerning his power. It needed something foreign to animate and release what was native in him. When Robert Frost, the New England poet, went abroad in 1912 for two years and became an intimate of Thomas's, the English critic began to write poetry.

Thomas's verse was first published under the pseudonym "Edward Eastaway." It immediately attracted the attention of a small circle, but (as with his American preceptor) editors were slow to recognize the distinction of the poet's rusticities. Loving, like Frost, the *minutiae* of existence, the quaint and casual turns of ordinary life, Thomas caught the magic of the English countryside in its unpoeticized quietude. Many of his poems are full of a slow, sad contemplation of life and a reflection of its brave futility. It is not exactly disillusion; it is rather an absence of illusion. *Poems* (1917), dedicated to Robert Frost, is full of Thomas's fidelity to little things, things as unglorified as the unfreezing of the "rock-like mud," a child's path, a list of quaint-sounding villages, birds' nests uncovered by the autumn wind, dusty nettles. Thomas somehow manages to combine close observation of the familiar with a sense of strangeness.

Thomas was killed at Arras at an observatory outpost on Easter Monday, 1917. *Last Poems,* published posthumously in 1919, has less of Frost's idiom (apparent in such poems as "Fifty Faggots," "Tall Nettles," "Haymaking") and more of Thomas's darkening concern. Faithful to a beauty unseen or scorned by others, his heart "floats through the window to a tree down in the misting, quiet vale":

> Not like a peewit that returns to wail
> For something it has lost, but like a dove
> That slants unswerving to its home and love.
> There I find my rest, and through the dark air
> Flies what yet lives in me. Beauty is there.

This poetry is a constant search for neglected loveliness: the vortex in an eddy of dead leaves, the dying sun in a fading sunflower, the sedgewarbler's pipe, a music of songlessness. Aldous Huxley characterized it as "a nameless emotion of quiet happiness shot through with melancholy."

Collected Poems, a richly inclusive volume with an introduction by Walter De la Mare, was published in 1922. Thomas must be reckoned among the most natural—and most English—of nature poets. As De la Mare wrote, "When Edward Thomas was killed in Flanders, a mirror of England was shattered of so pure a crystal that a clearer and tenderer reflection can be found no otherwhere than in these poems." Behind the accuracy of observation there is an emotional tensity, a vision of things seen "not with but through the eye."

Thomas's biography has been twice told by his wife, Helen Thomas, in *World Without End* and *As It Was.* The best essay, laudatory but analytical, is to be found in Aldous Huxley's *On the Margin* (1923).

THE NEW HOUSE

Now first, as I shut the door,
I was alone
In the new house; and the wind
Began to moan.

Old at once was the house,
And I was old;
My ears were teased with the dread
Of what was foretold,

Nights of storm, days of mist, without end;
Sad days when the sun
Shone in vain: old griefs and griefs
Not yet begun.

All was foretold me; naught
Could I foresee;
But I learned how the wind would sound
After these things should be.

TALL NETTLES

Tall nettles cover up, as they have done
These many springs, the rusty harrow, the plow
Long worn out, and the roller made of stone:
Only the elm butt tops the nettles now.

This corner of the farmyard I like most:
As well as any bloom upon a flower
I like the dust on the nettles, never lost
Except to prove the sweetness of a shower.

IF I SHOULD EVER BY CHANCE

If I should ever by chance grow rich
I'll buy Codham, Cockridden, and Childerditch,
Roses, Pyrgo, and Lapwater,
And let them all to my elder daughter.
The rent I shall ask of her will be only
Each year's first violets, white and lonely,
The first primroses and orchises—
She must find them before I do, that is.
But if she finds a blossom on furze
Without rent they shall all for ever be hers,
Codham, Cockridden, and Childerditch,
Roses, Pyrgo, and Lapwater,—
I shall give them all to my elder daughter.

COCK-CROW

Out of the wood of thoughts that grows by night
To be cut down by the sharp ax of light,—
Out of the night, two cocks together crow,
Cleaving the darkness with a silver blow:

And bright before my eyes twin trumpeters stand,
Heralds of splendor, one at either hand,
Each facing each as in a coat of arms:—
The milkers lace their boots up at the farms.

THE PENNY WHISTLE

The new moon hangs like an ivory bugle
In the naked frosty blue;
And the ghylls of the forest, already blackened
By Winter, are blackened anew.

The brooks that cut up and increase the forest,
As if they had never known
The sun, are roaring with black hollow voices
Betwixt rage and a moan.

But still the caravan-hut by the hollies
Like a kingfisher gleams between;
Round the mossed old hearths of the charcoal-burners,
First primroses ask to be seen.

The charcoal-burners are black, but their linen
Blows white on the line;
And white the letter the girl is reading
Under that crescent fine:

And her brother who hides apart in a thicket,
Slowly and surely playing
On a whistle an olden nursery melody,
Says far more than I am saying.

THE TRUMPET

Rise up, rise up,
And, as the trumpet blowing
Chases the dreams of men,
As the dawn glowing
The stars that left unlit
The land and water,
Rise up and scatter
The dew that covers
The print of last night's lovers—
Scatter it, scatter it!

While you are listening
To the clear horn,
Forget, men, everything
On this earth newborn,
Except that it is lovelier
Than any mysteries.
Open your eyes to the air
That has washed the eyes of stars
Through all the dewy night:
Up with the light,
To the old wars;
Arise, arise!

DIGGING

Today I think
Only with scents,—scents dead leaves yield
And bracken and wild carrot's seed,
And the square mustard field;

Odors that rise
When the spade wounds the root of a tree
Rose, currant, raspberry, or goutweed,
Rhubarb or celery;

The smoke's smell, too,
Flowing from where a bonfire burns
The dead, the waste, the dangerous,
And all to sweetness turns.

It is enough
To smell, to crumble the dark earth,
While the robin sings over again
Sad songs of Autumn mirth.

THAW

Over the land freckled with snow half-thawed
The speculating rooks at their nests cawed,
And saw from elm-tops, delicate as flower of grass,
What we below could not see, Winter pass.

GALLOWS

There was a weasel lived in the sun
With all his family,
Till a keeper shot him with his gun
And hung him up on a tree,
Where he swings in the wind and the rain,
In the sun and in the snow,
Without pleasure, without pain
On the dead oak tree bough.

There was a crow who was no sleeper,
But a thief and a murderer
Till a very late hour; and this keeper
Made him one of the things that were,
To hang and flap in the rain and wind,
In the sun and in the snow.
There are no more sins to be sinned
On the dead oak tree bough.

There was a magpie, too,
Had a long tongue and a long tail;
He could both talk and do—
But what did that avail?
He, too, flaps in the wind and rain
Alongside weasel and crow.
Without pleasure, without pain,
On the dead oak tree bough.

And many other beasts
And birds, skin, bone and feather,
Have been taken from their feasts
And hung up there together,
To swing and have endless leisure
In the sun and in the snow,
Without pain, without pleasure,
On the dead oak tree bough.

FIFTY FAGGOTS

There they stand, on their ends, the fifty faggots
That once were underwood of hazel and ash
In Jenny Pink's copse. Now, by the hedge
Close packed they make a thicket fancy alone
Can creep through with the mouse and wren. Next Spring
A blackbird or a robin will nest there,
Accustomed to them, thinking they will remain
Whatever is forever to a bird:
This Spring it is too late; the swift has come.
'Twas a hot day for carrying them up:
Better they will never warm me, though they must
Light several Winters' fires. Before they are done
The war will have ended, many other things
Have ended, maybe, that I can no more
Foresee or more control than robin and wren.

HAYMAKING

After night's thunder far away had rolled,
The fiery day had a sweet kernel of cold,
And in the perfect blue the clouds uncurled,
Like the first gods before they made the world
And misery, swimming the stormless sea
In beauty and in divine gayety.
The smooth white empty road was lightly strewn
With leaves—the holly's Autumn falls in June—
And fir cones standing stiff up in the heat.
The mill-foot water tumbled white and lit
With tossing crystals, happier than any crowd
Of children pouring out of school aloud.
And in the little thickets where a sleeper
For ever might lie lost, the nettle-creeper
And garden warbler sang unceasingly;
While over them shrill shrieked in his fierce glee
The swift with wings and tail as sharp and narrow
As if the bow had flown off with the arrow.
Only the scent of woodbine and hay new-mown
Traveled the road. In the field sloping down,
Park-like to where its willows showed the brook,
Haymakers rested. The tosser lay forsook
Out in the sun; and the long wagon stood
Without its team, it seemed it never would
Move from the shadow of that single yew.
The team, as still, until their task was due,
Beside the laborers enjoyed the shade
That three squat oaks mid-field together made
Upon a circle of grass and weed uncut,
And on the hollow, once a chalk-pit, but
Now brimmed with nut and elder-flower so clean.
The men leaned on their rakes, about to begin,
But still. And all were silent. All was old,
This morning time, with a great age untold,
Older than Clare and Cobbett, Morland and Crome
Than, at the field's far edge, the farmer's home,
A white house crouched at the foot of a great tree.
Under the heavens that know not what years be
The men, the beasts, the trees, the implements
Uttered even what they will in times far hence—
All of us gone out of the reach of change—
Immortal in a picture of an old grange.

OUT IN THE DARK

Out in the dark over the snow
The fallow fawns invisible go
With the fallow doe;

And the winds blow
Fast as the stars are slow.

Stealthily the dark haunts round
And, when a lamp goes, without sound
At a swifter bound
Than the swiftest hound,
Arrives, and all else is drowned;

And I and star and wind and deer,
Are in the dark together,—near,
Yet far,—and fear
Drums on my ear
In that sage company drear.

How weak and little is the light,
All the universe of sight,
Love and delight,
Before the might,
If you love it not, of night.

John Masefield

⁂ John Masefield was born June 1, 1878, in Ledbury, Herefordshire. His father, a lawyer, died while Masefield was still a child; at fourteen the boy was indentured to a merchant ship and became a wanderer for several years. At one time (in 1895, to be exact) he worked for a few months as a sort of third assistant barkeeper in Luke O'Connor's saloon, the Columbia Hotel, on the corner of Sixth and Greenwich Avenues, New York City. Later he worked in a carpet factory in Yonkers, and earned his living at various odd jobs. In 1897, he returned to England where he made friends with Synge in London, living, for a time, in Bloomsbury. Reading Chaucer's *The Parlement of Foules* in 1896 Masefield determined to be a poet. After the death of Robert Bridges in 1930 he was appointed Poet Laureate.

The results of his wanderings showed in his early works, *Salt-Water Ballads* (1902), *Ballads* (1903), frank, often crude, but rightly measured poems of sailors written in their own speech, and *A Mainsail Haul* (1905), a collection of short nautical stories. In these books Masefield occasionally overemphasized passion and brutality, yet, underneath the violence, he captured a highly colored realism.

It was not until he published *The Everlasting Mercy* (1911) that Masefield became famous. Followed quickly by long narrative poems, *The Widow in the Bye Street* (1912), *Dauber* (1912), and *The Daffodil Fields* (1913), these works vibrate with a blend of physical exulting and spiritual exaltation. It is typical of Masefield that the very rudeness is lifted to a plane of religious intensity. The religious undercurrent did not save the volumes from causing a scandal. The combination of profanity and ecstasy, sordid melodrama and spiritual elevation created a sensation;

they overwhelmed the critics as well as ordinary readers. Masefield's sympathy with workers and "common characters" often brought him to the verge of sentimentality —his dramatis personae usually "got religion" and reformed—but Masefield was one of the first to make the Georgian movement seem a movement of innovation, even of protest. Moreover he succeeded (if only temporarily) in bringing narrative verse back to favor. The popularity of his rude and sometimes shocking story-poems was appreciated because of their gusto; they achieved a blend of personal strength and irresponsible vigor. But the World War, which outdid Masefield in intensity, did not stimulate a literature of violence. On the contrary, force lost its power and gave way to a literature of exhaustion.

The exhaustion is apparent in the work which Masefield wrote after the first World War, in which he served with the Red Cross in France and on the Gallipoli Peninsula. After the Armistice, most of the Georgian poets turned from bugle calls to pastorals and exchanged the field of battle for fields of buttercups and daisies. Masefield joined the movement of escape. Logically enough, he wrote classical sonnets, religious verse, and new versions of old myths such as *King Cole* (1921) and *A Tale of Troy* (1932). But in sacrificing the early vigor of epithet and plot he also sacrificed individuality. Critical opinion changed. It began to be suspected that the rebellious Georgian was little more than a roughened Victorian.

Masefield attempted to recapture his high spirits in *Reynard the Fox* (1919) and *Right Royal* (1920). The vigor is there, but a sense of strain pervades the too packed, too rapidly propelled stanzas; influenced by Chaucer, they are marred by excess. "There is," says Middleton Murry, speaking of *Reynard the Fox,* "in Chaucer, a naturalness, a lack of emphasis, a confidence that the object will not fail to make its own impression, beside which Mr. Masefield's demonstration and underlining seem almost *malsain* . . . tainted by the desperate *bergerie* of the Georgian era. Chaucer is at home with his speech and at home with his world; by his side Mr. Masefield seems nervous and uncertain about both." But though the Chaucerian influence is obvious, it is not wholly a handicap to Masefield; it stimulates him to overcome a nostalgia, roused (if overanimated) by the English countryside. It is said that *Reynard the Fox* did more than any other single poem to earn him the Laureateship.

After 1930 Masefield grew less and less self-critical, and his work suffered from prolixity. *Midsummer Night* (1928) still has the narrative sweep of the earlier poems, but *Minnie Maylow's Story and Other Tales and Scenes* (1931) is a sort of British Night's Entertainment neither interesting in idea nor technique. The thirteen "tales and scenes" ranging from the Chaucerian "Adamas and Eva" to the outworn theme of "Tristan and Isolt," will not bear close scrutiny. *A Tale of Troy* (1932) shows Masefield, for no discernible reason, retelling the drama of the Trojan War. *End and Beginning* (1933) is a poem-drama of the last days and execution of Mary, Queen of Scots, the title being from her prophetic remark when notified of her death sentence, "In the end is my beginning." A generous *Collected Poems* was issued in 1923 and enlarged in 1935. The former is the more commendable since it contains the best of his poetry from youth to maturity and does not include the later tedious work. Besides his poetry, Masefield wrote more than a dozen plays (including translations from Racine); a standard work on *Shakespeare* (1911); about twelve volumes of essays and studies, which range from *Sea Life in*

Nelson's Time (1905) through *The Battle of the Somme* (1919) to *Chaucer* (1931); several books for boys, and "adventure" novels which capture the early robustiousness.

In his early sixties Masefield turned to reminiscences and retelling of old tales; an account of his working days in America was entitled *In the Mill* (1941). A later and more comprehensive autobiography, *So Long to Learn* (1952), tries, said Masefield, "to set down what matters have been helpful to me in the finding, framing, and telling of stories in prose and verse, according to the tale and power within me."

A CONSECRATION

Not of the princes and prelates with periwigged charioteers
Riding triumphantly laureled to lap the fat of the years,—
Rather the scorned—the rejected—the men hemmed in with the spears;

The men of the tattered battalion which fights till it dies,
Dazed with the dust of the battle, the din and the cries.
The men with the broken heads and the blood running into their eyes.

Not the be-medaled Commander, beloved of the throne,
Riding cock-horse to parade when the bugles are blown,
But the lads who carried the koppie and cannot be known.

Not the ruler for me, but the ranker, the tramp of the road,
The slave with the sack on his shoulders pricked on with the goad,
The man with too weighty a burden, too weary a load.

The sailor, the stoker of steamers, the man with the clout,
The chantyman bent at the halliards putting a tune to the shout,
The drowsy man at the wheel and the tired look-out.

Others may sing of the wine and the wealth and the mirth,
The portly presence of potentates goodly in girth;—
Mine be the dirt and the dross, the dust and scum of the earth!

Theirs be the music, the color, the glory, the gold;
Mine be a handful of ashes, a mouthful of mold.
Of the maimed, of the halt and the blind in the rain and the cold—
Of these shall my songs be fashioned, my tales be told.

AMEN.

SEA-FEVER

I must down to the seas again, to the lonely sea and the sky,
And all I ask is a tall ship and a star to steer her by,
And the wheel's kick and the wind's song and the white sail's shaking
And a gray mist on the sea's face and a gray dawn breaking.

I must down to the seas again, for the call of the running tide
Is a wild call and a clear call that may not be denied;
And all I ask is a windy day with the white clouds flying,
And the flung spray and the blown spume, and the sea-gulls crying.

I must down to the seas again to the vagrant gypsy life.
To the gull's way and the whale's way where the wind's like a whetted knife;
And all I ask is a merry yarn from a laughing fellow-rover,
And quiet sleep and a sweet dream when the long trick's over.

A WANDERER'S SONG

A wind's in the heart of me, a fire's in my heels,
I am tired of brick and stone and rumbling wagon-wheels;
I hunger for the sea's edge, the limits of the land,
Where the wild old Atlantic is shouting on the sand.

Oh I'll be going, leaving the noises of the street,
To where a lifting foresail-foot is yanking at the sheet;
To a windy, tossing anchorage where yawls and ketches ride,
Oh I'll be going, going, until I meet the tide.

And first I'll hear the sea-wind, the mewing of the gulls,
The clucking, sucking of the sea about the rusty hulls,
The songs at the capstan in the hooker warping out,
And then the heart of me'll know I'm there or thereabout.

Oh I am sick of brick and stone, the heart of me is sick,
For windy green, unquiet sea, the realm of Moby Dick;
And I'll be going, going, from the roaring of the wheels,
For a wind's in the heart of me, a fire's in my heels.

SORROW OF MYDATH

Weary the cry of the wind is, weary the sea,
Weary the heart and the mind and the body of me.
Would I were out of it, done with it, would I could be
    A white gull crying along the desolate sands!

Outcast, derelict soul in a body accurst,
Standing drenched with the spindrift, standing athirst,
For the cool green waves of death to arise and burst
    In a tide of quiet for me on the desolate sands!

Would that the waves and the long white hair of the spray
Would gather in splendid terror and blot me away
To the sunless place of the wrecks where the waters sway
    Gently, dreamily, quietly over desolate sands!

TOMORROW

Oh yesterday the cutting edge drank thirstily and deep,
The upland outlaws ringed us in and herded us as sheep,
They drove us from the stricken field and bayed us into keep;
        But tomorrow,
    By the living God, we'll try the game again!

Oh yesterday our little troop was ridden through and through,
Our swaying, tattered pennons fled, a broken, beaten few,
And all a summer afternoon they hunted us and slew;
But tomorrow,
By the living God, we'll try the game again!

And here upon the turret-top the bale-fire glowers red,
The wake-lights burn and drip about our hacked, disfigured dead,
And many a broken heart is here and many a broken head;
But tomorrow,
By the living God, we'll try the game again!

THE WEST WIND

It's a warm wind, the west wind, full of birds' cries;
I never hear the west wind but tears are in my eyes.
For it comes from the west lands, the old brown hills,
And April's in the west wind, and daffodils.

It's a fine land, the west land, for hearts as tired as mine,
Apple orchards blossom there, and the air's like wine.
There is cool green grass there, where men may lie at rest,
And the thrushes are in song there, fluting from the nest.

"Will ye not come home, brother? ye have been long away,
It's April, and blossom time, and white is the may;
And bright is the sun, brother, and warm is the rain,—
Will ye not come home, brother, home to us again?

"The young corn is green, brother, where the rabbits run,
It's blue sky, and white clouds, and warm rain and sun.
It's song to a man's soul, brother, fire to a man's brain,
To hear the wild bees and see the merry spring again.

"Larks are singing in the west, brother, above the green wheat,
So will ye not come home, brother, and rest your tired feet?
I've a balm for bruised hearts, brother, sleep for aching eyes,"
Says the warm wind, the west wind, full of birds' cries.

It's the white road westwards is the road I must tread
To the green grass, the cool grass, and rest for heart and head,
To the violets and the warm hearts and the thrushes' song,
In the fine land, the west land, the land where I belong.

ROUNDING THE HORN

(*from "Dauber"*)

Then came the cry of "Call all hands on deck!"
The Dauber knew its meaning; it was come:
Cape Horn, that tramples beauty into wreck,
And crumples steel and smites the strong man dumb.

Down clattered flying kites and staysails; some
Sang out in quick, high calls: the fair-leads skirled,
And from the south-west came the end of the world . . .

"Lay out!" the Bosun yelled. The Dauber laid
Out on the yard, gripping the yard, and feeling
Sick at the mighty space of air displayed
Below his feet, where mewing birds were wheeling.
A giddy fear was on him; he was reeling.
He bit his lip half through, clutching the jack.
A cold sweat glued the shirt upon his back.

The yard was shaking, for a brace was loose.
He felt that he would fall; he clutched, he bent,
Clammy with natural terror to the shoes
While idiotic promptings came and went.
Snow fluttered on a wind-flaw and was spent;
He saw the water darken. Someone yelled,
"Frap it; don't stay to furl! Hold on!" He held.

Darkness came down—half darkness—in a whirl;
The sky went out, the waters disappeared.
He felt a shocking pressure of blowing hurl
The ship upon her side. The darkness speared
At her with wind; she staggered, she careered;
Then down she lay. The Dauber felt her go,
He saw her yard tilt downwards. Then the snow

Whirled all about—dense, multitudinous, cold—
Mixed with the wind's one devilish thrust and shriek,
Which whiffled out men's tears, defeated, took hold,
Flattening the flying drift against the cheek.
The yards buckled and bent, man could not speak.
The ship lay on her broadside; the wind's sound
Had devilish malice at having got her downed.

How long the gale had blown he could not tell,
Only the world had changed, his life had died.
A moment now was everlasting hell.
Nature an onslaught from the weather side,
A withering rush of death, a frost that cried,
Shrieked, till he withered at the heart; a hail
Plastered his oilskins with an icy mail. . . .

"Up!" yelled the Bosun; "up and clear the wreck!"
The Dauber followed where he led; below
He caught one giddy glimpsing of the deck
Filled with white water, as though heaped with snow.
He saw the streamers of the rigging blow
Straight out like pennons from the splintered mast,
Then, all sense dimmed, all was an icy blast.

Roaring from nether hell and filled with ice,
Roaring and crashing on the jerking stage,
An utter bridle given to utter vice,
Limitless power mad with endless rage
Withering the soul; a minute seemed an age.
He clutched and hacked at ropes, at rags of sail,
Thinking that comfort was a fairy tale,

Told long ago—long, long ago—long since
Heard of in other lives—imagined, dreamed—
There where the basest beggar was a prince.
To him in torment where the tempest screamed,
Comfort and warmth and ease no longer seemed
Things that a man could know; soul, body, brain,
Knew nothing but the wind, the cold, the pain.

C. L. M.

n the dark womb where I began
Iy mother's life made me a man.
Through all the months of human birth
Ier beauty fed my common earth.
cannot see, nor breathe, nor stir,
ut through the death of some of her.

)own in the darkness of the grave
he cannot see the life she gave.
'or all her love, she cannot tell
Vhether I use it ill or well,
Ior knock at dusty doors to find
Ier beauty dusty in the mind.

f the grave's gates could be undone,
he would not know her little son,
am so grown. If we should meet,
he would pass by me in the street,
Unless my soul's face let her see
My sense of what she did for me.

What have I done to keep in mind
My debt to her and womankind?
What woman's happier life repays
Her for those months of wretched days?
For all my mouthless body leech'd
Ere Birth's releasing hell was reach'd?

What have I done, or tried, or said
In thanks to that dear woman dead?
Men triumph over women still,
Men trample women's rights at will,
And man's lust roves the world untamed.

O grave, keep shut lest I be shamed.

CARGOES

Quinquireme of Nineveh from distant Ophir
Rowing home to haven in sunny Palestine,
With a cargo of ivory,
And apes and peacocks,
Sandalwood, cedarwood, and sweet white wine.

Stately Spanish galleon coming from the Isthmus,
Dipping through the Tropics by the palm-green shores,
With a cargo of diamonds,
Emeralds, amethysts,
Topazes, and cinnamon, and gold moidores.

Dirty British coaster with a salt-caked smoke-stack
Butting through the Channel in the mad March days,
With a cargo of Tyne coal,
Road-rail, pig-lead,
Firewood, iron-ware, and cheap tin trays.

CAPTAIN STRATTON'S FANCY

Oh some are fond of red wine, and some are fond of white,
And some are all for dancing in the pale moonlight;
But rum alone's the tipple and the heart's delight
Of the old bold mate of Henry Morgan.

Oh some are fond of Spanish wine, and some are fond of French,
And some'll swallow tay and stuff fit only for a wench;
But I'm for right Jamaica till I roll beneath the bench,
Says the old bold mate of Henry Morgan.

Oh some are for the lily, and some are for the rose,
But I am for the sugar-cane that in Jamaica grows;
For it's that makes the bonny drink to warm my copper nose,
Says the old bold mate of Henry Morgan.

Oh some are fond of fiddles and a song well sung,
And some are all for music for to lilt upon the tongue;
But mouths were made for tankards, and for sucking at the bung,
Says the old bold mate of Henry Morgan.

And some are fond of dancing, and some are fond of dice,
And some are all for red lips and pretty lasses' eyes;
But a right Jamaica puncheon is a finer prize
To the old bold mate of Henry Morgan.

Oh some that's good and godly ones they hold that it's a sin
To troll the jolly bowl around and let the dollars spin;
But I'm for toleration and for drinking at an inn,
Says the old bold mate of Henry Morgan.

Oh some are sad and wretched folk that go in silken suits,
And there's a mort of wicked rogues that live in good reputes;
So I'm for drinking honestly, and dying in my boots,
Like an old bold mate of Henry Morgan.

NIGHT ON THE DOWNLAND

Night is on the downland, on the lonely moorland,
On the hills where the wind goes over sheep-bitten turf,
Where the bent grass beats upon the unplowed poorland
And the pine-woods roar like the surf.

Here the Roman lived on the wind-barren lonely,
Dark now and haunted by the moorland fowl;
None comes here now but the peewit only,
And moth-like death in the owl.

Beauty was here on this beetle-droning downland;
The thought of a Caesar in the purple came
From the palace by the Tiber in the Roman townland
To this wind-swept hill with no name.

Lonely Beauty came here and was here in sadness,
Brave as a thought on the frontier of the mind,
In the camp of the wild upon the march of madness,
The bright-eyed Queen of the Blind.

Now where Beauty was are the wind-withered gorses,
Moaning like old men in the hill-wind's blast;
The flying sky is dark with running horses,
And the night is full of the past.

ON GROWING OLD

Be with me, Beauty, for the fire is dying;
My dog and I are old, too old for roving.
Man, whose young passion sets the spindrift flying,
Is soon too lame to march, too cold for loving.
I take the book and gather to the fire,
Turning old yellow leaves; minute by minute
The clock ticks to my heart. A withered wire,
Moves a thin ghost of music in the spinet.
I cannot sail your seas, I cannot wander
Your cornland, nor your hill-land, nor your valleys
Ever again, nor share the battle yonder
Where the young knight the broken squadron rallies.
Only stay quiet while my mind remembers
The beauty of fire from the beauty of embers.

Beauty, have pity! for the strong have power,
The rich their wealth, the beautiful their grace,
Summer of man its sunlight and its flower.
Spring-time of man all April in a face.
Only, as in the jostling in the Strand,
Where the mob thrusts or loiters or is loud,
The beggar with the saucer in his hand
Asks only a penny from the passing crowd,
So, from this glittering world with all its fashion,
Its fire, and play of men, its stir, its march,
Let me have wisdom, Beauty, wisdom and passion,
Bread to the soul, rain when the summers parch.
Give me but these, and though the darkness close
Even the night will blossom as the rose.

SONNET

Flesh, I have knocked at many a dusty door,
Gone down full many a windy midnight lane,
Probed in old walls and felt along the floor,
Pressed in blind hope the lighted window-pane,
But useless all, though sometimes when the moon
Was full in heaven and the sea was full,
Along my body's alleys came a tune
Played in the tavern by the Beautiful.
Then for an instant I have felt at point
To find and seize her, whosoe'er she be,
Whether some saint whose glory doth anoint
Those whom she loves, or but a part of me,
Or something that the things not understood
Make for their uses out of flesh and blood.

SONNET

Is there a great green commonwealth of Thought
Which ranks the yearly pageant, and decides
How Summer's royal progress shall be wrought,
By secret stir which in each plant abides?
Does rocking daffodil consent that she,
The snowdrop of wet winters, shall be first?
Does spotted cowslip with the grass agree
To hold her pride before the rattle burst?
And in the hedge what quick agreement goes,
When hawthorn blossoms redden to decay,
That Summer's pride shall come, the Summer's rose,
Before the flower be on the bramble spray?
Or is it, as with us, unresting strife,
And each consent a lucky gasp for life?

LAUGH AND BE MERRY

Laugh and be merry, remember, better the world with a song,
Better the world with a blow in the teeth of a wrong.
Laugh, for the time is brief, a thread the length of a span.
Laugh, and be proud to belong to the old proud pageant of man.

Laugh and be merry: remember, in olden time,
God made Heaven and Earth for joy He took in a rhyme,
Made them, and filled them full with the strong red wine of His mirth,
The splendid joy of the stars: the joy of the earth.

So we must laugh and drink from the deep blue cup of the sky,
Join the jubilant song of the great stars sweeping by,
Laugh, and battle, and work, and drink of the wine outpoured
In the dear green earth, the sign of the joy of the Lord.

Laugh and be merry together, like brothers akin,
Guesting awhile in the rooms of a beautiful inn,
Glad till the dancing stops, and the lilt of the music ends.
Laugh till the game is played; and be you merry, my friends.

THE CHOICE

The Kings go by with jeweled crowns;
Their horses gleam, their banners shake, their spears are many.
The sack of many-peopled towns
Is all their dream:
The way they take
Leaves but a ruin in the brake,
And, in the furrow that the plowmen make,
A stampless penny; a tale, a dream.

The Merchants reckon up their gold,
Their letters come, their ships arrive, their freights are glories;
The profits of their treasures sold
They tell and sum;
Their foremen drive
Their servants, starved to half-alive,
Whose labors do but make the earth a hive
Of stinking stories; a tale, a dream.

The Priests are singing in their stalls,
Their singing lifts, their incense burns, their praying clamors;
Yet God is as the sparrow falls,
The ivy drifts;
The votive urns
Are all left void when Fortune turns,
The god is but a marble for the kerns
To break with hammers; a tale, a dream.

O Beauty, let me know again
The green earth cold, the April rain, the quiet waters figuring sky,
The one star risen.
So shall I pass into the feast
Not touched by King, Merchant, or Priest;
Know the red spirit of the beast,
Be the green grain;
Escape from prison.

THE PASSING STRANGE

t of the earth to rest or range
petual in perpetual change,
e unknown passing through the strange.

ter and saltness held together
tread the dust and stand the weather,
d plow the field and stretch the tether,

To pass the wine-cup and be witty,
Water the sands and build the city,
Slaughter like devils and have pity,

Be red with rage and pale with lust,
Make beauty come, make peace, make
trust,
Water and saltness mixed with dust;

Drive over earth, swim under sea,
Fly in the eagle's secrecy,
Guess where the hidden comets be;

Know all the deathy seeds that still
Queen Helen's beauty, Caesar's will,
And slay them even as they kill;

Fashion an altar for a rood,
Defile a continent with blood,
And watch a brother starve for food:

Love like a madman, shaking, blind,
Till self is burnt into a kind
Possession of another mind;

Brood upon beauty, till the grace
Of beauty with the holy face
Brings peace into the bitter place;

Probe in the lifeless granites, scan
The stars for hope, for guide, for plan;
Live as a woman or a man;

Fasten to lover or to friend,
Until the heart break at the end
The break of death that cannot mend:

Then to lie useless, helpless, still,
Down in the earth, in dark, to fill
The roots of grass or daffodil.

Down in the earth, in dark, alone,
A mockery of the ghost in bone,
The strangeness, passing the unknown.

Time will go by, that outlasts clocks,
Dawn in the thorps will rouse the cocks,
Sunset be glory on the rocks:

But it, the thing, will never heed
Even the rootling from the seed
Thrusting to suck it for its need.

*

Since moons decay and suns decline,
How else should end this life of mine?
Water and saltness are not wine.

But in the darkest hour of night,
When even the foxes peer for sight,
The byre-cock crows; he feels the light.

So, in this water mixed with dust,
The byre-cock spirit crows from trust
That death will change because it must.

For all things change: the darkness chang
The wandering spirits change their ranges,
The corn is gathered to the granges.

The corn is sown again, it grows;
The stars burn out, the darkness goes;
The rhythms change, they do not close.

They change, and we, who pass like foam,
Like dust blown through the streets of Ro
Change ever, too; we have no home,

Only a beauty, only a power,
Sad in the fruit, bright in the flower,
Endlessly erring for its hour,

But gathering as we stray, a sense
Of Life, so lovely and intense,
It lingers when we wander hence,

That those who follow feel behind
Their backs, when all before is blind,
Our joy, a rampart to the mind.

Harold Monro

☙ Harold Monro was born in Brussels in 1879 and educated at Caius College, Cambridge. He described himself as "author, publisher, editor and book-seller." Monro founded The Poetry Bookshop in London in 1912, a unique establishment having as its object a practical relation between poetry and the public: it kept in stock nothing but poetry, the drama, and books connected with the subjects. His quarterly, *Poetry and Drama* (discontinued during the war and revived in 1919 as *The Chapbook*), was in a sense the organ of the younger men; and his shop, in which he lived for the last twenty years of his life except while he was in the army, became a literary center. In spite of changing fashions Monro remained an influence, the "rare Ben Jonson" of a modern Mermaid Tavern, until his death in 1932.

Monro's poetry depicts the play between the world of reality and the limbo of fantasy. *Before Dawn* (1911) has little of his peculiar mysticism, but *Children of Love* (1914), *Trees* (1915) and *Strange Meetings* (1917) present, with indubitable originality, the relation of man, not only to the earth he rose from, but to the inanimate things among which he moves. Even the most whimsical poems disclose an emotional intensity beneath the skillful rhythms. Monro's kettles are as animated as his cats; his machines, domestic furniture, ordinary interiors are both surprising and natural—surprising in the revelation of what might well be their "inner selves," natural in the way their speech is communicated.

Monro has been criticized as being a poet by intention but not a singer by intuition. Defending certain of the more determined "modernist" poets—and, by implication, himself—Monro has written, "It will be no use to say that their poetry 'does not sing.' It is not meant to. The word *Song* has been abandoned and swept out, with *Ode, Sonnet, Quatrain*, and other similar verbal lumber. The test of intellect is more important to them than tests of prosody, or tradition. The passing event and its effect on the mind is everything to them. . . . Thus they think in terms of the whole poem rather than of the single line, and thus they are often unquotable except in *extenso*." While this is interesting (and only partially true) Monro's own poetry is at its best when intellect is subservient to imagination and music.

Real Property (1922) represents a further advance. Although Monro has not lost his whimsical appraisal of "still life," the note is graver, the implications larger. Some of the poems, as Monro states in a prefatory note, are "tainted with slight Georgian affectations." But such verses as the metaphysical "Earthliness" (too long for quotation) and the simpler poems of Part Two, four of which are reprinted in the group below, mark this poet as one of the most original though, undeservedly, one of the least popular creators of the period.

The Earth for Sale (1928) is a continuation and extension of the more somber speculations. Besides his poetry, Monro is the author of *Some Contemporary Poets* (1920), a set of sharply critical estimates.

EVERY THING

Since man has been articulate,
Mechanical, improvidently wise
(Servant of Fate),
He has not understood the little cries
And foreign conversations of the small
Delightful creatures that have followed him
Not far behind;
Has failed to hear the sympathetic call
Of Crockery and Cutlery, those kind
Reposeful Teraphim
Of his domestic happiness; the Stool
He sat on, or the Door he entered through:
He has not thanked them, overbearing fool!
What is he coming to?

But you should listen to the talk of these.
Honest they are, and patient they have kept;
Served him without his Thank you or his Please . . .
I often heard
The gentle Bed, a sigh between each word,
Murmuring, before I slept.
The Candle, as I blew it, cried aloud,
Then bowed,
And in a smoky argument
Into the darkness went.
The Kettle puffed a tentacle of breath:—
"Pooh! I have boiled his water, I don't know
Why; and he always says I boil too slow.
He never calls me 'Sukie, dear,' and oh,
I wonder why I squander my desire
Sitting submissive on his kitchen fire."

Now the old Copper Basin suddenly
Rattled and tumbled from the shelf,
Bumping and crying: "I can fall by myself;
Without a woman's hand
To patronize and coax and flatter me,
I understand
The lean and poise of gravitable land."
It gave a raucous and tumultuous shout,
Twisted itself convulsively about,
Rested upon the floor, and, while I stare,
It stares and grins at me.

The old impetuous Gas above my head
Begins irascibly to flare and fret,
Wheezing into its epileptic jet,
Reminding me I ought to go to bed.

The rafters creak; an Empty-Cupboard door
Swings open; now a wild Plank of the floor

Breaks from its joist, and leaps behind my foot.
Down from the chimney, half a pound of Soot
Tumbles and lies, and shakes itself again.
The Putty cracks against the window-pane.
A piece of Paper in the basket shoves
Another piece, and toward the bottom moves.
My independent Pencil, while I write,
Breaks at the point: the ruminating Clock
Stirs all its body and begins to rock,
Warning the waiting presence of the Night,
Strikes the dead hour, and tumbles to the plain
Ticking of ordinary work again.

You do well to remind me, and I praise
Your strangely individual foreign ways.
You call me from myself to recognize
Companionship in your unselfish eyes.
I want your dear acquaintances, although
I pass you arrogantly over, throw
Your lovely sounds, and squander them along
My busy days. I'll do you no more wrong.

Purr for me, Sukie, like a faithful cat.
You, my well-trampled Boots, and you, my Hat,
Remain my friends: I feel, though I don't speak,
Your touch grow kindlier from week to week.
It well becomes our mutual happiness
To go toward the same end more or less.
There is not much dissimilarity,
Not much to choose, I know it well, in fine,
Between the purposes of you and me,
And your eventual Rubbish Heap, and mine.

FROM "WEEK-END"

I

The train! The twelve o'clock for paradise.
  Hurry, or it will try to creep away.
Out in the country everyone is wise:
  We can be wise only on Saturday.
There you are waiting, little friendly house:
  Those are your chimney-stacks with you between,
Surrounded by old trees and strolling cows,
  Staring through all your windows at the green.
Your homely floor is creaking for our tread;
  The smiling tea-pot with contented spout
Thinks of the boiling water, and the bread
  Longs for the butter. All their hands are out

To greet us, and the gentle blankets seem
Purring and crooning: "Lie in us, and dream."

II

The key will stammer, and the door reply,
  The hall wake, yawn, and smile; the torpid stair
Will grumble at our feet, the table cry:
  "Fetch my belongings for me; I am bare."
A clatter! Something in the attic falls.
  A ghost has lifted up his robes and fled.
The loitering shadows move along the walls;
  Then silence very slowly lifts his head.
The starling with impatient screech has flown
  The chimney, and is watching from the tree.
They thought us gone for ever: mouse alone
  Stops in the middle of the floor to see.
Now all you idle things, resume your toil.
Hearth, put your flames on. Sulky kettle, boil.

THE BIRD AT DAWN

What I saw was just one eye
In the dawn as I was going:
A bird can carry all the sky
In that little button glowing.

Never in my life I went
So deep into the firmament.

He was standing on a tree,
All in blossom overflowing;
And he purposely looked hard at me,
At first, as if to question merrily:
"Where are you going?"
But next some far more serious thing to say:
I could not answer, could not look away.

Oh, that hard, round, and so distracting eye:
Little mirror of all sky!—
And then the after-song another tree
Held, and sent radiating back on me.

If no man had invented human word,
And a bird-song had been
The only way to utter what we mean,
What would we men have heard,
What understood, what seen,
Between the trills and pauses, in between
The singing and the silence of a bird?

CHILDREN OF LOVE

The holy boy
Went from his mother out in the cool of day
Over the sun-parched fields
And in among the olives shining green and shining gray.

There was no sound,
No smallest voice of any shivering stream.
Poor sinless little boy,
He desired to play, and to sing; he could only sigh and dream.

Suddenly came
Running along to him naked, with curly hair,
That rogue of the lovely world,
That other beautiful child whom the virgin Venus bare.

The holy boy
Gazed with those sad blue eyes that all men know.
Impudent Cupid stood
Panting, holding an arrow and pointing his bow.

("Will you not play?
Jesus, run to him, run to him, swift for our joy.
Is he not holy, like you?
Are you afraid of his arrows, O beautiful dreaming boy?")

And now they stand
Watching one another with timid gaze;
Youth has met youth in the wood,
But holiness will not change its melancholy ways.

Cupid at last
Draws his bow and softly lets fly a dart.
Smile for a moment, sad world!—
It has grazed the white skin and drawn blood from the sorrowful heart.

Now for delight,
Cupid tosses his locks and goes wantonly near;
But the child that was born to the cross
Has let fall on his cheek, for the sadness of life a compassionate tear.

Marvelous dream!
Cupid has offered his arrows for Jesus to try;
He has offered his bow for the game,
But Jesus went weeping away, and left him there wondering why.

STRANGE MEETINGS

If Suddenly a Clod of Earth

If suddenly a clod of earth should rise,
And walk about, and breathe, and speak, and love,
How one would tremble, and in what surprise
Gasp: "Can *you* move"?

I see men walking and I always feel:
"Earth! How have you done this? What can you be?"
I can't learn how to know men, or conceal
How strange they are to me.

A Flower Is Looking

A flower is looking through the ground,
Blinking at the April weather;
Now a child has seen the flower:
Now they go and play together.

Now it seems the flower will speak,
And will call the child its brother—
But, oh strange forgetfulness!—
They don't recognize each other.

SOLITUDE

When you have tidied all things for the night,
And while your thoughts are fading to their sleep,
You'll pause a moment in the late firelight,
Too sorrowful to weep.

The large and gentle furniture has stood
In sympathetic silence all the day
With that old kindness of domestic wood;
Nevertheless the haunted room will say:
"Someone must be away."

The little dog rolls over half awake,
Stretches his paws, yawns, looking up at you,
Wags his tail very slightly for your sake,
That you may feel he is unhappy too.

A distant engine whistles, or the floor
Creaks, or the wandering night-wind bangs a door

Silence is scattered like a broken glass.
The minutes prick their ears and run about,
Then one by one subside again and pass
Sedately in, monotonously out.

You bend your head and wipe away a tear.
Solitude walks one heavy step more near.

MILK FOR THE CAT

When the tea is brought at five o'clock,
And all the neat curtains are drawn with care,
The little black cat with bright green eyes
Is suddenly purring there.

At first she pretends, having nothing to do,
She has come in merely to blink by the grate,
But, though tea may be late or the milk may be sour,
She is never late.

And presently her agate eyes
Take a soft large milky haze,
And her independent casual glance
Becomes a stiff hard gaze.

Then she stamps her claws or lifts her ears
Or twists her tail and begins to stir,
Till suddenly all her little body becomes
One breathing trembling purr.

The children eat and wriggle and laugh;
The two old ladies stroke their silk:
But the cat is grown small and thin with desire,
Transformed to a creeping lust for milk.

The white saucer like some full moon descends
At last from the clouds of the table above;
She sighs and dreams and thrills and glows,
Transfigured with love.

She nestles over the shining rim,
Buries her chin in the creamy sea;
Her tail hangs loose; each drowsy paw
Is doubled under each bending knee.

A long dim ecstasy holds her life;
Her world is an infinite shapeless white,
Till her tongue has curled the last holy drop,
Then she sinks back into the night,

Draws and dips her body to heap
Her sleepy nerves in the great arm-chair,
Lies defeated and buried deep
Three or four hours unconscious there.

DOG

O little friend, your nose is ready; you sniff,
Asking for that expected walk,
(Your nostrils full of the happy rabbit-whiff)
And almost talk.

And so the moment becomes a moving force;
Coats glide down from their pegs in the humble dark;
You scamper the stairs,
Your body informed with the scent and the track and the mark
Of stoats and weasels, moles and badgers and hares.

We are going *Out.* You know the pitch of the word,
Probing the tone of thought as it comes through fog
And reaches by devious means (half-smelt, half-heard)
The four-legged brain of a walk-ecstatic dog.

Out through the garden your head is already low.
You are going your walk, you know,
And your limbs will draw
Joy from the earth through the touch of your padded paw.

Now, sending a look to us behind,
Who follow slowly the track of your lovely play,
You fetch our bodies forward away from mind
Into the light and fun of your useless day.

Thus, for your walk, we took ourselves, and went
Out by the hedge, and tree, to the open ground.
You ran, in delightful strata of wafted scent,
Over the hill without seeing the view;
Beauty is hinted through primitive smells to you:
And that ultimate Beauty you track is but rarely found.

*

Home . . . and further joy will be waiting there:
Supper full of the lovely taste of bone,
You lift up your nose again, and sniff, and stare
For the rapture known
Of the quick wild gorge of food, then the still lie-down;
While your people will talk above you in the light
Of candles, and your dreams will merge and drown
Into the bed-delicious hours of night.

MAN CARRYING BALE

The tough hand closes gently on the load;
  Out of the mind a voice
Calls "Lift!" and the arms, remembering well their work,
  Lengthen and pause for help.
Then a slow ripple flows along the body,
While all the muscles call to one another:
  "Lift!" and the bulging bale
  Floats like a butterfly in June.

So moved the earliest carrier of bales,
  And the same watchful sun
Glowed through his body feeding it with light.
  So will the last one move,
And halt, and dip his head, and lay his load
Down, and the muscles will relax and tremble . . .
  Earth, you designed your man
Beautiful both in labor and repose.

THE NIGHTINGALE NEAR THE HOUSE

Here is the soundless cypress on the lawn:
It listens, listens. Taller trees beyond
Listen. The moon at the unruffled pond
  Stares. And you sing, you sing.

That star-enchanted song falls through the air
From lawn to lawn down terraces of sound,
Darts in white arrows on the shadowed ground;
  And all the night you sing.

My dreams are flowers to which you are a bee
As all night long I listen, and my brain
Receives your song; then loses it again
  In moonlight on the lawn.

Now is your voice a marble high and white,
Then like a mist on fields of paradise,
Now is a raging fire, then is like ice,
  Then breaks, and it is dawn.

CITY-STORM

The heavy sounds are over-sweet
That droop above the hooded street,
At any moment ripe to fall and lie,
And when the Wind will swagger up the town
They'll bend a moment, then will fly
All clattering down.

Troupes come and go of urchin breeze:
They flick your face or smack the trees,
Then round the corner spin and leap
With whistling cries,
Rake their rubbish in a heap
And throw it in your eyes.

(Much preparation of the earth and air
Is needed everywhere
Before that first large drop of rain can fall.)

Smells of the Sea, or inland Grass,
Come staring through the town and pass.
Brilliant old Memories drive in state
Along the way, but cannot wait;
And many a large unusual bird
Hovers across the sky, half-heard.

But listen. It is He;
At last he comes:
Gigantic tyrant panting through the street,
Slamming the windows of our little homes,

Banging the doors, knocking the chimneys
down.
Oh, his loud tramp: how scornfully he can
meet
Great citizens, and lash them with his sleet!
Everything will be altered in our town.
He'll wipe the film of habit clean away,
While he remains,
His cloak is over everything we do,
And the whole town complains:—

A somber scroll;
An inner room.
A crystal bowl:
Waters of gloom.
Oh, the darkened house—
Into silence creep!
The world is cold.
All people weep.

THE HURRIER

O furrowed plaintive face,
No time for peace?
Your grim appointment will not wait?
No, our great earthly clock
Ticks through your spine, and locomotion
wags
An angry tail.
Quick, do not miss the toiling trailing tram.
Hurry, or you are lost, for anywhere
Hunger may lurk and leer.
You may have been elected, mid so many,
To be his prey,
Even today.
On horned imagination drive your limbs.
It will need your whole life to be at peace:
Then all appointments cease.
But now you neither have the time for death,
Nor time conveniently to draw your breath.

W. W. Gibson

W(ilfrid) W(ilson) Gibson was born in 1880 at Hexham, Northumberland, and, by his fiftieth year, was the author of some twenty-two books of poems and five volumes of poetic plays and dialogues. The first five or six of these were pseudo-Tennysonian, imitative in manner and sentimental in tone. Their titles give the key: *Urlyn the Harper* (1902), *The Queen's Vigil* (1902), *The Golden Helm* (1903), *The Nets of Love* (1905).

With *Daily Bread* (1910), *Fires* (1912), and *Borderlands* (1914) Gibson executed a complete right-about-face and, with dramatic brevity, wrote a series of poems mirroring the dreams, pursuits, and fears of common humanity. *Thoroughfares* (1914) marks an advance in technique and power. In *Livelihood* (1917) Gibson seems to be theatricalizing and merely exploiting his working-people, yet several of his later lyrics recapture the quality of such poems as "The Old Man," "The Stone" and "The Machine." *Hill-Tracks* (1918) attempts to hold (as Edward Thomas actually did hold) the beauty of village-names through the glamor of the English countryside. *Neighbors* (1920) again takes up the strain of a somewhat too conscious poeticizing of the casual. *Islands* (1932) and *Fuel* (1934) prolong the attempt.

Gibson's later work suffers from his facility; a thinning out of power, even of feeling, is evident in *Krindlesyke* (1922), *Kestrel Edge* (1924) and *I Heard a Sailor* (1925). The best of Gibson is in the first *Collected Poems* (1923), which was followed by other collections, including a volume of plays, *Within Four Walls* (1950).

PRELUDE

As one, at midnight, wakened by the call
Of golden-plovers in their seaward flight,
Who lies and listens, as the clear notes fall
Through tingling silence of the frosty night—
Who lies and listens, till the last note fails,
And then, in fancy, faring with the flock
Far over slumbering hills and dreaming dales,
Soon hears the surges break on reef and rock;
And, hearkening, till all sense of self is drowned
Within the mightier music of the deep,
No more remembers the sweet piping sound
That startled him from dull, undreaming sleep;
So I, first waking from oblivion, heard,
With heart that kindled to the call of song,
The voice of young life, fluting like a bird,
And echoed that light lilting; till, ere long,
Lured onward by that happy, singing-flight,
I caught the stormy summons of the sea,
And dared the restless deeps that, day and night,
Surge with the life-song of humanity.

THE STONE

And will you cut a stone for him,
o set above his head?
nd will you cut a stone for him—
stone for him?" she said.

hree days before, a splintered rock
lad struck her lover dead—
lad struck him in the quarry dead,
Vhere, careless of the warning call,
le loitered, while the shot was fired—
lively stripling, brave and tall,
nd sure of all his heart desired . . .
flash, a shock,
rumbling fall . . .
nd, broken 'neath the broken rock,
lifeless heap, with face of clay;
nd still as any stone he lay,
/ith eyes that saw the end of all.

went to break the news to her;
nd I could hear my own heart beat
'ith dread of what my lips might say
ut, some poor fool had sped before;
nd flinging wide her father's door,
ad blurted out the news to her,
ad struck her lover dead for her,
Had struck the girl's heart dead in her,
Had struck life lifeless, at a word,
And dropped it at her feet:
Then hurried on his witless way,
Scarce knowing she had heard.

And when I came, she stood alone,
A woman turned to stone:
And, though no word at all she said,
I knew that all was known.
Because her heart was dead,
She did not sigh nor moan,
His mother wept:
She could not weep,
Her lover slept:
She could not weep.
Three days, three nights,
She did not stir:
Three days, three nights,
Were one to her,
Who never closed her eyes
From sunset to sunrise,
From dawn to evenfall:
Her tearless, staring eyes,
That seeing naught, saw all.

The fourth night when I came from work,
I found her at my door.

"And will you cut a stone for him?"
She said: and spoke no more:
But followed me, as I went in,
And sank upon a chair;
And fixed her gray eyes on my face,
With still, unseeing stare.
And, as she waited patiently,
I could not bear to feel
Those still, gray eyes that followed me,
Those eyes that plucked the heart from me,
Those eyes that sucked the breath from me
And curdled the warm blood in me,
Those eyes that cut me to the bone,
And pierced my marrow like cold steel.

And so I rose, and sought a stone;
And cut it, smooth and square:
And, as I worked, she sat and watched,
Beside me, in her chair.
Night after night, by candlelight,
I cut her lover's name:
Night after night, so still and white,
And like a ghost she came;
And sat beside me in her chair;
And watched with eyes aflame.

She eyed each stroke;
And hardly stirred:
She never spoke
A single word:
And not a sound or murmur broke
The quiet, save the mallet-stroke.

With still eyes ever on my hands,
With eyes that seemed to burn my hands,
My wincing, overwearied hands,
She watched, with bloodless lips apart,
And silent, indrawn breath:
And every stroke my chisel cut,
Death cut still deeper in her heart:
The two of us were chiseling,
Together, I and death.

And when at length the job was done,
And I had laid the mallet by,
As if, at last, her peace were won,
She breathed his name; and, with a sigh,
Passed slowly through the open door:
And never crossed my threshold more.

Next night I labored late, alone,
To cut her name upon the stone.

SIGHT

By the lamplit stall I loitered, feasting my eyes
On colors ripe and rich for the heart's desire—
Tomatoes, redder than Krakatoa's fire,
Oranges like old sunsets over Tyre,
And apples golden-green as the glades of Paradise.

And as I lingered, lost in divine delight,
My heart thanked God for the goodly gift of sight
And all youth's lively senses keen and quick . . .
When suddenly, behind me in the night,
I heard the tapping of a blind man's stick.

THE WHITE DUST

I felt no tremor and I caught no sounds;
But a fresh crack scored my ceiling: white dust dropped,
Sprinkling my polished table . . .
Underground,
Fathoms beneath my comfortable room,
In the pit's dripping gloom,
A new drift's rock-roof, insecurely propped,
Had settled; and, in settling, crushed just then

The life out of six men:
Six hearts had stopped . . .

But I, unguessing, looked up fretfully
At the fresh crack, and rose impatiently
To wipe the dust from my mahogany.

Alfred Noyes

◆§ Alfred Noyes was born at Staffordshire, September 16, 1880, one of the few contemporary poets who have been fortunate enough to write a kind of poetry that is not only readable but extraordinarily saleable.

His first book, *The Loom of Years* (1902), was published when he was only 22 years old, and *Poems* (1904) emphasized the promise of this first publication. Swinburne, grown old and living in retirement, was so struck with Noyes's talent that he had the young poet out to read to him. Unfortunately, Noyes never developed his gifts as deeply as his admirers expected. His poetry, extremely straightforward and rhythmical, degenerated too often into sentimentalities and cheap tirades; the later work attempted to express programs and profundities far beyond Noyes's limited power.

What is most appealing about his best verse is its ease and heartiness; this singer's gift lies in the almost personal bond established between the poet and his public. It may be said that many people have such a good time reading his vivacious lines because Noyes had such a good time writing them. Rhyme in a thumping rhythm seems to be not merely his trade but his morning exercise. Noyes's own relish quickens the glees and catches like *Forty Singing Seamen* (1907), the lusty choruses in *Tales of the Mermaid Tavern* (1913), the seemingly inspired nonsense of the earlier *Forest of Wild Thyme* (1905).

The least popular work of Noyes is, as a unified product, his most remarkable performance. It is an epic in twelve books of blank verse, *Drake* (1908), a pageant of the sea and England's drama upon it. It is a spirited echo of the maritime Elizabethans, a vivid orchestral work interspersed with lyric passages and brisk songs. The companion volume, an attempted reconstruction of the literary phase of the same period, is less successful; but these *Tales of the Mermaid Tavern* (which introduce Shakespeare, Marlowe, Drayton, Raleigh, Ben Jonson, and other immortals) are colorful, if somewhat too insistently rollicking and smoothly lilting.

Noyes's eight volumes were assembled in 1913 and published in two books of *Collected Poems*. The third volume of his rapidly accumulating *Collected Poems* appeared in 1920, the fourth in 1927. In 1922 Noyes began *The Torch-Bearers,* "An Epic Trilogy," a sort of outline of man's accomplishment rendered in verse.

In his early sixties Noyes visited America on a transcontinental tour and remained in California until he was seventy, when he returned to England. Besides his poetry he had written several prose works, including *Aspects of Poetry* and an autobiography, *Two Worlds for Memory* (1953). He died June 28, 1958.

Although most of his smooth-running rhymes seemed doomed to rush to an early death—are, in fact, already extinct—Noyes will remain a poet pleasant to read because of his "Sherwood," the lilt of "The Barrel-Organ," the galloping "The Highwayman" and a handful of other ballads.

SHERWOOD

Sherwood in the twilight, is Robin Hood awake?
Gray and ghostly shadows are gliding through the brake;
Shadows of the dappled deer, dreaming of the morn,
Dreaming of a shadowy man that winds a shadowy horn.

Robin Hood is here again: all his merry thieves
Hear a ghostly bugle-note shivering through the leaves,
Calling as he used to call, faint and far away,
In Sherwood, in Sherwood, about the break of day.

Merry, merry England has kissed the lips of June;
All the wings of fairyland were here beneath the moon;
Like a flight of rose-leaves fluttering in a mist
Of opal and ruby and pearl and amethyst.

Merry, merry England is waking as of old,
With eyes of blither hazel and hair of brighter gold:
For Robin Hood is here again beneath the bursting spray
In Sherwood, in Sherwood, about the break of day.

Love is in the greenwood building him a house
Of wild rose and hawthorn and honeysuckle boughs;
Love is in the greenwood: dawn is in the skies;
And Marian is waiting with a glory in her eyes.

Hark! The dazzled laverock climbs the golden steep:
Marian is waiting: is Robin Hood asleep?
Round the fairy grass-rings frolic elf and fay,
In Sherwood, in Sherwood, about the break of day.

Oberon, Oberon, rake away the gold,
Rake away the red leaves, roll away the mold,
Rake away the gold leaves, roll away the red,
And wake Will Scarlet from his leafy forest bed.

Friar Tuck and Little John are riding down together
With quarter-staff and drinking-can and gray goose-feather;
The dead are coming back again; the years are rolled away
In Sherwood, in Sherwood, about the break of day.

Softly over Sherwood the south wind blows;
All the heart of England hid in every rose
Hears across the greenwood the sunny whisper leap,
Sherwood in the red dawn, is Robin Hood asleep?

Hark, the voice of England wakes him as of old
And, shattering the silence with a cry of brighter gold,
Bugles in the greenwood echo from the steep,
Sherwood in the red dawn, is Robin Hood asleep?

Where the deer are gliding down the shadowy glen
All across the glades of fern he calls his merry men;
Doublets of the Lincoln green glancing through the May,
In Sherwood, in Sherwood, about the break of day;

Calls them and they answer: from aisles of oak and ash
Rings the *Follow! Follow!* and the boughs begin to crash;
The ferns begin to flutter and the flowers begin to fly;
And through the crimson dawning the robber band goes by.

Robin! Robin! Robin! All his merry thieves
Answer as the bugle-note shivers through the leaves:
Calling as he used to call, faint and far away,
In Sherwood, in Sherwood, about the break of day.

THE BARREL-ORGAN

There's a barrel-organ caroling across a golden street
  In the City as the sun sinks low;
And the music's not immortal; but the world has made it sweet
  And fulfilled it with the sunset glow;
And it pulses through the pleasures of the City and the pain
  That surround the singing organ like a large eternal light;
And they've given it a glory and a part to play again
  In the Symphony that rules the day and night.
And now it's marching onward through the realms of old romance,
  And trolling out a fond familiar tune,
And now it's roaring cannon down to fight the King of France,
  And now it's prattling softly to the moon.
And all around the organ there's a sea without a shore
  Of human joys and wonders and regrets;
To remember and to recompense the music evermore
  For what the cold machiney forgets . . .

Yes; as the music changes,
  Like a prismatic glass,
It takes the light and ranges
  Through all the moods that pass:
Dissects the common carnival
  Of passions and regrets,
And gives the world a glimpse of all
  The colors it forgets.

And there *La Traviata* sighs
  Another sadder song;
And there *Il Trovatore* cries
  A tale of deeper wrong;

And bolder knights to battle go
  With sword and shield and lance,
Than ever here on earth below
  Have whirled into—a dance!—

Go down to Kew in lilac-time, in lilac-time, in lilac-time;
  Go down to Kew in lilac-time (it isn't far from London!)
And you shall wander hand in hand with Love in summer's wonderland;
  Go down to Kew in lilac-time (it isn't far from London!)

The cherry-trees are seas of bloom and soft perfume and sweet perfume,
  The cherry-trees are seas of bloom (and oh, so near to London!)
And there they say, when dawn is high and all the world's a blaze of sky
  The cuckoo, though he's very shy, will sing a song for London.

The nightingale is rather rare and yet they say you'll hear him there
  At Kew, at Kew in lilac-time (and oh, so near to London!)
The linnet and the throstle, too, and after dark the long halloo
  And golden-eyed *tu-whit, tu-whoo* of owls that ogle London.

For Noah hardly knew a bird of any kind that isn't heard
  At Kew, at Kew in lilac-time (and oh, so near to London!)
And when the rose begins to pout and all the chestnut spires are out
  You'll hear the rest without a doubt, all chorusing for London:—

Come down to Kew in lilac-time, in lilac-time, in lilac-time;
  Come down to Kew in lilac-time (it isn't far from London!)
And you shall wander hand in hand with Love in summer's wonderland;
  Come down to Kew in lilac-time (it isn't far from London!)

And then the troubadour begins to thrill the golden street,
  In the City as the sun sinks low;
And in all the gaudy busses there are scores of weary feet
Marking time, sweet time, with a dull mechanic beat,
And a thousand hearts are plunging to a love they'll never meet,
Through the meadows of the sunset, through the poppies and the wheat,
  In the land where the dead dreams go.

Verdi, Verdi, when you wrote *Il Trovatore* did you dream
  Of the City when the sun sinks low,
Of the organ and the monkey and the many-colored stream
On the Picadilly pavement, of the myriad eyes that seem
To be litten for a moment with a wild Italian gleam
As *A che la morte* parodies the world's eternal theme
  And pulses with the sunset-glow?

There's a thief, perhaps, that listens with a face of frozen stone
  In the City as the sun sinks low;
There's a portly man of business with a balance of his own,
There's a clerk and there's a butcher of a soft reposeful tone,
And they're all of them returning to the heavens they have known:
They are crammed and jammed in busses and—they're each of them alone
  In the land where the dead dreams go.

There's a laborer that listens to the voices of the dead
   In the City as the sun sinks low;
And his hand begins to tremble and his face is rather red
As he sees a loafer watching him and—there he turns his head
And stares into the sunset where his April love is fled,
For he hears her softly singing and his lonely soul is led
   Through the land where the dead dreams go . . .

There's a barrel-organ caroling across a golden street
   In the City as the sun sinks low;
Though the music's only Verdi there's a world to make it sweet
Just as yonder yellow sunset where the earth and heaven meet
Mellows all the sooty City! Hark, a hundred thousand feet
Are marching on to glory through the poppies and the wheat
   In the land where the dead dreams go.

So it's Jeremiah, Jeremiah,
   What have you to say
When you meet the garland girls
   Tripping on their way?

All around my gala hat
   I wear a wreath of roses
(A long and lonely year it is
   I've waited for the May!)
If anyone should ask you,
   The reason why I wear it is—
My own love, my true love, is coming home today.

And it's buy a bunch of violets for the lady
   (*It's lilac-time in London; it's lilac-time in London!*)
Buy a bunch of violets for the lady;
   While the sky burns blue above:

On the other side the street you'll find it shady
   (*It's lilac time in London; it's lilac-time in London!*)
But buy a bunch of violets for the lady,
   And tell her she's your own true love.

There's a barrel-organ caroling across a golden street
   In the City as the sun sinks glittering and slow;
And the music's not immortal; but the world has made it sweet
And enriched it with the harmonies that make a song complete
In the deeper heavens of music where the night and morning meet,
   As it dies into the sunset glow;
And it pulses through the pleasures of the City and the pain
   That surround the singing organ like a large eternal light,
And they've given it a glory and a part to play again
   In the Symphony that rules the day and night.

And there, as the music changes,
The song runs round again;
Once more it turns and ranges
Through all its joy and pain:
Dissects the common carnival
Of passions and regrets;
And the wheeling world remembers all
The wheeling song forgets.

Once more *La Traviata* sighs
Another sadder song:
Once more *Il Trovatore* cries
A tale of deeper wrong;
Once more the knights to battle go
With sword and shield and lance
Till once, once more, the shattered foe
Has whirled into—a dance!

Come down to Kew in lilac-time, in lilac-time, in lilac-time;
Come down to Kew in lilac-time (it isn't far from London!)
And you shall wander hand in hand with Love in summer's wonderland,
Come down to Kew in lilac-time (it isn't far from London!)

EPILOGUE

(from "The Flower of Old Japan")

Carol, every violet has
Heaven for a looking-glass!

Every little valley lies
Under many-clouded skies;
Every little cottage stands
Girt about with boundless lands.
Every little glimmering pond
Claims the mighty shores beyond—
Shores no seaman ever hailed,
Seas no ship has ever sailed.

All the shores when day is done
Fade into the setting sun,
So the story tries to teach
More than can be told in speech.

Beauty is a fading flower,
Truth is but a wizard's tower,
Where a solemn death-bell tolls,
And a forest round it rolls.
We have come by curious ways
To the light that holds the days;
We have sought in haunts of fear
For that all-enfolding sphere:
And lo! it was not far, but near.
We have found, O foolish-fond,
The shore that has no shore beyond.
Deep in every heart it lies
With its untranscended skies;
For what heaven should bend above
Hearts that own the heaven of love?

Carol, Carol, we have come
Back to heaven, back to home.

Padraic Colum

⤙ Padraic Columm was born at Longford, Ireland (in the same county as Oliver Goldsmith), December 8, 1881, and was educated at the local schools. At twenty he was a member of the group that created the Irish National Theatre.

Colum began as a dramatist with *Broken Soil* (1904), *The Land* (1905), *Thomas Muskerry* (1910), and this early dramatic influence has colored much of his work; in fact, his best poetry is in the form of dramatic lyrics. *Wild Earth,* his most quoted collection of verse, first appeared in 1909, and an amplified edition of it was published in America in 1916. Colum himself had come to America (where he has lived ever since) shortly before that date; his *Dramatic Poems* appeared in 1922. *Creatures* (1927), utterly different in theme from its predecessors, is held together by the same gift of condensation. Though Colum's animals are less obviously divine than his gods, his treatment of them is no less devotional. He combines an innocence of vision with wisdom of experience. *Old Pastures* (1930) and *Flower Pieces* (1939) are sensitive and ingratiating.

As a recorder, Colum has been equally successful as an autobiographer, a folklorist, and a popular adapter of myths and legends for young people. In 1953 he was awarded the Gregory Medal by the Irish Academy of Letters.

THE PLOWER

Sunset and silence! A man: around him earth savage, earth broken;
Beside him two horses—a plow!

Earth savage, earth broken, the brutes, the dawn man there in the sunset,
And the Plow that is twin to the Sword, that is founder of cities!

"Brute-tamer, plow-maker, earth-breaker! Can'st hear?
  "There are age between us.
"Is it praying you are as you stand there alone in the sunset?

"Surely our sky-born gods can be naught to you, earth-child and earth-master?
"Surely your thoughts are of Pan, or of Wotan, or Dana?

"Yet, why give thought to the gods? Has Pan led your brutes where they stumble?
"Has Dana numbed pain of the child-bed, or Wotan put hands to your plow?

"What matter your foolish reply! O man, standing lone and bowed earthward,
"Your task is a day near its close. Give thanks to the night-giving God."

*

Slowly the darkness falls, the broken lands blend with the savage;
The brute-tamer stands by the brutes, a head's breadth only above them.

A head's breadth? Aye, but therein is hell's depth, and the height up to heaven,
And the thrones of the gods and their halls, their chariots, purples, and splendors.

AN OLD WOMAN OF THE ROADS

O, to have a little house!
To own the hearth and stool and all!
The heaped-up sods upon the fire,
The pile of turf against the wall!

To have a clock with weights and chains
And pendulum swinging up and down!
A dresser filled with shining delph,
Speckled and white and blue and brown!

I could be busy all the day
Clearing and sweeping hearth and floor,
And fixing on their shelf again
My white and blue and speckled store!

I could be quiet there at night
Beside the fire and by myself,
Sure of a bed and loth to leave
The ticking clock and the shining delph!

Och! but I'm weary of mist and dark,
And roads where there's never a house nor bush,
And tired I am of bog and road,
And the crying wind and the lonesome hush!

And I am praying to God on high,
And I am praying Him night and day,
For a little house—a house of my own—
Out of the wind's and the rain's way.

INTERIOR

The little moths are creeping
Across the cottage pane;
On the floor the chickens gather,
And they make talk and complain.

And she sits by the fire
Who has reared so many men;
Her voice is low like the chickens'
With the things she says again.

"The sons that come back do be restless,
They search for the thing to say;
Then they take thought like the swallows,
And the morrow brings them away.

"In the old, old days, upon Innish,
The fields were lucky and bright,
And if you lay down you'd be covered
By the grass of one soft night."

She speaks and the chickens gather,
And they make talk and complain,
While the little moths are creeping
Across the cotttage pane.

A DROVER

To Meath of the pastures,
From wet hills by the sea,
Through Leitrim and Longford,
Go my cattle and me.

I hear in the darkness
Their slipping and breathing—
I name them the by-ways
They're to pass without heeding;

Then the wet, winding roads,
Brown bogs with black water;
And my thoughts on white ships
And the King o' Spain's daughter.

Oh! farmer, strong farmer!
You can spend at the fair;
But your face you must turn
To your crops and your care.

And soldiers, red soldiers!
You've seen many lands;
But you walk two by two,
And by captain's commands.

Oh! the smell of the beasts,
The wet wind in the morn;
And the proud and hard earth
Never broken for corn;

And the crowds at the fair,
The herds loosened and blind,
Loud words and dark faces
And the wild blood behind.

(Oh! strong men, with your best
I would strive breast to breast,
I could quiet your herds
With my words, with my words.)

I will bring you my kine,
Where there's grass to the knee;
But you'll think of scant croppings
Harsh with salt of the sea.

WILD ASS

The wild ass lounges, legs struck out
In vagrom unconcern:
The tombs of Achaemenian kings
Are for those hooves to spurn.

And all of rugged Tartary
Lies with him on the ground.
The Tartary that knows no awe
That has nor ban nor bound.

The wild horse from the herd is plucked
To bear a saddle's weight;
The boar is one keeps covert, and
The wolf runs with a mate.

But he's the solitary of space,
Curbless and unbeguiled;
The only being that bears a heart
Not recreant to the wild.

Joseph Campbell

(SEOSAMH MacCATHMHAOIL)

Joseph Campbell was born in Belfast in 1881, and was not only a poet but an artist; he made all the illustrations for *The Rushlight* (1906), a volume of his own poems. Writing under the Gaelic form of his name, he published half a dozen books of verse, the most striking of which is *The Mountainy Singer* (1909).

He went to America, where, for a time, he was instructor at Fordham University, and died July 13, 1944.

I AM THE MOUNTAINY SINGER

I am the mountainy singer—
The voice of the peasant's dream,
The cry of the wind on the wooded hill,
The leap of the fish in the stream.

Quiet and love I sing—
The cairn on the mountain crest,
The *cailin* in her lover's arms,
The child at its mother's breast.

Beauty and peace I sing—
The fire on the open hearth,
The *cailleach* spinning at her wheel,
The plow in the broken earth.

Travail and pain I sing—
The bride on the childing bed,
The dark man laboring at his rhymes,
The ewe in the lambing shed.

Sorrow and death I sing—
The canker come on the corn,
The fisher lost in the mountain loch,
The cry at the mouth of morn.

No other life I sing,
For I am sprung of the stock
That broke the hilly land for bread,
And built the nest in the rock!

THE OLD WOMAN

As a white candle
In a holy place,
So is the beauty
Of an aged face.

As the spent radiance
Of the winter sun,
So is a woman
With her travail done,

Her brood gone from her,
And her thoughts as still
As the waters
Under a ruined mill.

Lascelles Abercrombie

Lascelles Abercrombie was born in 1881, at Ashton-upon-Mersey, near Manchester. He was educated at Malcolm College and Manchester University. After that, he engaged in a variety of professions; he taught literature at the University in Liverpool and in London. He succumbed to a long illness in 1938.

Like Masefield, Abercrombie gained his reputation rapidly. Unknown until 1909, upon the publication of *Interludes and Poems,* he was recognized as one of the true metaphysical poets of his period. *Emblems of Love* (1912), the ripest collection of his dialogues, justified the enthusiasm of his admirers.

Many of Abercrombie's poems, the best of which are too long to quote, are founded on scriptural themes, but his blank verse is biblical neither in mood nor in manner. It is the undercurrent rather than the surface of his verse which moves with a strong religious conviction. Abercrombie's images are daring and brilliant; his lines, sometimes too closely packed, glow with an intensity that is spiritual and yet recognizably human.

As a dramatist, Abercrombie had achieved a series of literary but scarcely popular successes with *Deborah* (1914), *Four Short Plays* (1921), and *Phoenix* (1923), brilliantly written though not eminently actable pieces. His knotted, almost tortured, style presents many difficulties to the performers as well as to audiences; but, once the speech is mastered, a swift intellectuality and a dramatic sense are disclosed beneath the obvious eloquence.

It is only the superficially dense style which keeps Abercrombie an unpopular, almost an unread, poet. Actually his diction, though thickened, is extraordinarily flexible; his characters, if overburdened with analysis, are vividly imagined; and, as Edward Thomas wrote, "the march or leap or stagger or hesitation of the syllables correspond to varying emotions with thrilling delicacy."

It seems a pity that the poet who conceived the ecstatic action of *The Sale of St. Thomas* (1911), the racing vigor of "Witchcraft: New Style," and the brilliant couplets of "Epilogue," should interest so few readers. Lacking a responsive following, Abercrombie turned almost entirely to prose. During his illness he wrote no less than six volumes about prosody and the technique of verse; *The Theory of Poetry* (1924) is one of the most illuminating books on the subject.

SONG

(from "Judith")

Balkis was in her marble town,
And shadow over the world came down.
Whiteness of walls, towers and piers,
That all day dazzled eyes to tears,
Turned from being white-golden flame,
And like the deep-sea blue became.
Balkis into her garden went;
Her spirit was in discontent
Like a torch in restless air.
Joylessly she wandered there,
And saw her city's azure white
Lying under the great night,
Beautiful as the memory
Of a worshiping world would be
In the mind of a god, in the hour
When he must kill his outward power;
And, coming to a pool where trees
Grew in double greeneries,
Saw herself, as she went by
The water, walking beautifully,
And saw the stars shine in the glance
Of her eyes, and her own fair countenance
Passing, pale and wonderful,
Across the night that filled the pool.
And cruel was the grief that played
With the queen's spirit; and she said:
"What do I here, reigning alone?
For to be unloved is to be alone.
There is no man in all my land
Dare my longing understand;
The whole folk like a peasant bows
Lest its look should meet my brows
And be harmed by this beauty of mine.
I burn their brains as I were sign
Of God's beautiful anger sent
To master them with punishment
Of beauty that must pour distress
On hearts grown dark with ugliness.
But it is I am the punisht one.
Is there no man, is there none,
In whom my beauty will but move
The lust of a delighted love;
In whom some spirit of God so thrives
That we may wed our lonely lives?
Is there no man, is there none?"—
She said, "I will go to Solomon."

EPILOGUE

What shall we do for Love these days?
How shall we make an altar-blaze
To smite the horny eyes of men
With the renown of our Heaven,
And to the unbelievers prove
Our service to our dear god, Love?
What torches shall we lift above
The crowd that pushes through the mire,
To amaze the dark heads with strange fire?
I should think I were much to blame,
If never I held some fragrant flame
Above the noises of the world,
And openly 'mid men's hurrying stares,
Worshipt before the sacred fears
That are like flashing curtains furl'd
Across the presence of our lord Love.
Nay, would that I could fill the gaze
Of the whole earth with some great praise
Made in a marvel for men's eyes,
Some tower of glittering masonries,
Therein such a spirit flourishing
Men should see what my heart can sing:
All that Love hath done to me
Built into stone, a visible glee;
Marble carried to gleaming height
As moved aloft by inward delight;
Not as with toil of chisels hewn,
But seeming poised in a mighty tune.

For of all those who have been known
To lodge with our kind host, the sun,
I envy one for just one thing:
In Cordova of the Moors
There dwelt a passion-minded King,
Who set great bands of marble-hewers
To fashion his heart's thanksgiving
In a tall palace, shapen so
All the wondering world might know
The joy he had of his Moorish lass.
His love, that brighter and larger was
Than the starry places, into firm stone
He sent, as if the stone were glass
Fired and into beauty blown.
    Solemn and invented gravely
In its bulk the fabric stood,
Even as Love, that trusteth bravely
In its own exceeding good
To be better than the waste
Of time's devices; grandly spaced,
Seriously the fabric stood.
But over it all a pleasure went
Of carven delicate ornament,
Wreathing up like ravishment,
Mentioning in sculptures twined
The blitheness Love hath in his mind;
And like delighted senses were
The windows, and the columns there
Made the following sight to ache
As the heart that did them make.
Well I can see that shining song
Flowering there, the upward throng
Of porches, pillars and windowed walls,
Spires like piercing panpipe calls,
Up to the roof's snow-cloudy flight;
All glancing in the Spanish light
White as water of arctic tides,
Save an amber dazzle on sunny sides.
You had said, the radiant sheen
Of that palace might have been
A young god's fantasy, ere he came
His serious worlds and suns to frame;
Such an immortal passion
Quiver'd among the slim hewn stone.
And in the nights it seemed a jar
Cut in the substance of a star,
Wherein a wine, that will be poured
Some time for feasting Heaven, was stored.
    But within this fretted shell,
The wonder of Love made visible,
The King a private gentle mood
There placed, of pleasant quietude.
For right amidst there was a court,
Where always muskèd silences
Listened to water and to trees;
And herbage of all fragrant sort,—
Lavender, lad's love, rosemary,
Basil, tansy, centaury,—
Was the grass of that orchard, hid
Love's amazements all amid.
Jarring the air with rumor cool,
Small fountains played into a pool
With sound as soft as the barley's hiss
When its beard just sprouting is;
Whence a young stream, that trod on moss,
Prettily rippled the court across.
And in the pool's clear idleness,
Moving like dreams through happiness,
Shoals of small bright fishes were;
In and out weed-thickets bent
Perch and carp, and sauntering went

With mounching jaws and eyes a-stare;
Or on a lotus leaf would crawl,
A brinded loach to bask and sprawl,
Tasting the warm sun ere it dipt
Into the water; but quick as fear
Back his shining brown head slipt
To crouch on the gravel of his lair,
Where the cooled sunbeams broke in wrack,
Spilt shatter'd gold about his back.
So within that green-veiled air,
Within that white-walled quiet, where
Innocent water thought aloud,—
Childish prattle that must make
The wise sunlight with laughter shake
On the leafage overbowed,—
Often the King and his love-lass
Let the delicious hours pass.
All the outer world could see
Graved and sawn amazingly
Their love's delighted riotise,
Fixt in marble for all men's eyes;
But only these twain could abide
In the cool peace that withinside
Thrilling desire and passion dwelt;
They only knew the still meaning spelt
By Love's flaming script, which is
God's word written in ecstasies.
And where is now that palace gone,
All the magical skill'd stone,
All the dreaming towers wrought
By Love as if no more than thought
The unresisting marble was?
How could such a wonder pass?
Ah, it was but built in vain
Against the stupid horns of Rome,
That pusht down into the common loam
The loveliness that shone in Spain.
But we have raised it up again!
A loftier palace, fairer far,
Is ours, and one that fears no war.
Safe in marvelous walls we are;
Wondering sense like builded fires,
High amazement of desires,
Delight and certainty of love,
Closing around, roofing above
Our unapproacht and perfect hour
Within the splendors of love's power.

WOMAN'S BEAUTY

(from "Vashti")

What thing shall be held up to woman's beauty?
Where are the bounds of it? Yea, what is all
The world, but an awning scaffolded amid
The waste perilous Eternity, to lodge
This Heaven-wander'd princess, woman's beauty?
The East and West kneel down to thee, the North
And South; and all for thee their shoulders bear
The load of fourfold space. As yellow morn
Runs on the slippery waves of the spread sea,
Thy feet are on the griefs and joys of men
That shine to be thy causey. Out of tears
Indeed, and blitheness, murder and lust and love,
Whatever has been passionate in clay,
Thy flesh was tempered. Behold in thy body
The yearnings of all men measured and told,
Insatiate endless agonies of desire
Given thy flesh, the meaning of thy shape!
What beauty is there, but thou makest it?
How is earth good to look on, woods and fields,
The season's garden, and the courageous hills,
All this green raft of earth moored in the seas?
The manner of the sun to ride the air,

The stars God has imagined for the night?
What's this behind them that we cannot near,
Secret still on the point of being blabbed,
The ghost in the world that flies from being named
Where do they get their beauty from, all these?
They do but glaze a lantern lit for man,
And woman's beauty is the flame therein.

WITCHCRAFT: NEW STYLE

The sun drew off at last his piercing fires.
Over the stale warm air, dull as a pond
And moveless in the gray quieted street,
Blue magic of a summer evening glowed.
The sky, that had been dazzling stone all day,
Hollowed in smooth hard brightness, now dissolved
To infinite soft depth, and smoldered down
Low as the roofs, dark burning blue, and soared
Clear to that winking drop of liquid silver,
The first exquisite star. Now the half-light
Tidied away the dusty litter parching
Among the cobbles, veiled in the color of distance
Shabby slates and brickwork moldering, turned
The hunchback houses into patient things
Resting; and golden windows now began.

A little brisk gray slattern of a woman,
Pattering along in her loose-heeled clogs,
Pusht the brass-barred door of a public-house;
The spring went hard against her; hand and knee
Shoved their weak best. As the door poised ajar,
Hullabaloo of talking men burst out,
A pouring babble of inflamed palaver,
And overriding it and shouted down
High words, jeering or downright, broken like
Crests that leap and stumble in rushing water.
Just as the door went wide and she stept in,
"She cannot do it!" one was bawling out:
A glaring hulk of flesh with a bull's voice.
He fingered with his neckerchief, and stretcht
His throat to ease the anger of dispute,
Then spat to put a full stop to the matter.
The little woman waited, with one hand
Propping the door, and smiled at the loud man.
They saw her then; and the sight was enough
To gag the speech of every drinker there:
The din fell down like something chopt off short.
Blank they all wheeled towards her, with their mouths
Still gaping as though full of voiceless words.
She let the door slam to; and all at ease,

Amused, her smile wrinkling about her eyes,
Went forward; they made room for her quick enough.
Her chin just topt the counter; she gave in
Her bottle to the potboy, tuckt it back,
Full of bright tawny ale, under her arm,
Rapt down the coppers on the planisht zinc,
And turned: and no word spoken all the while.
The first voice, in that silent crowd, was hers,
Her light snickering laugh, as she stood there
Pausing, scanning the sawdust at her feet.
Then she switcht round and faced the positive man
Whose strong "She cannot do it!" all still felt
Huskily shouting in their guilty ears.
"She can't, eh? She can't do it?"—Then she'd heard!
The man, inside his ruddy insolent flesh,
Had hoped she did not hear. His barrel chest
Gave a slight cringe, as though the glint of her eyes
Prickt him. But he stood up to her awkwardly bold,
One elbow on the counter, gripping his mug
Like a man holding on to a post for safety.

The Man You can't do what's not nature: nobody can.
The Woman And louts like you have nature in your pocket?
The Man I don't say that —
The Woman If you kept saying naught,
No one would guess the fool you are.
Second Man Almost
My very words!
The Woman O you're the knowing man!
The spark among the cinders!
First Man You can't fetch
A free man back, unless he wants to come.
The Woman Nay, I'll be bound he doesn't want to come!
Third Man And he won't come: he told me flat he wouldn't.
The Woman Are you there too?
Third Man And if he does come back
It will be devilry brought him.
The Woman I shall bring him;—
Tonight.
First Man How will he come?
The Woman Running: unless
He's broke his leg, and then he'll have to come
Crawling. But he will come.
First Man How do you know
What he may choose to do, three countries off?
The Woman He choose?
Third Man You haven't got him on a lead.
The Woman Haven't I though!
Second Man That's right: it's what I said.
The Woman Aye, there are brains in your family.

First Man You have
Some sort of pull on him, to draw him home?
The Woman You may say that: I have hold of his mind.
And I can slack it off or fetch it taut,
And make him dance a score of miles away
An answer to the least twangling thrum
I play on it. He thought he lurkt at last
Safely; and all the while, what has he been?
An eel on the end of a night-line; and it's time
I hauled him in. You'll see, tonight I'll land him.
Third Man Bragging's a light job.
The Woman You daren't let me take
Your eyes in mine!—Haul, did I say? no need:
I give his mind a twitch, and up he comes
Tumbling home to me. Whatever work he's at,
He drops the thing he holds like redhot iron
And runs—runs till he falls down like a beast
Pole-axt, and grunts for breath; then up and on,
No matter does he know the road or not:
The strain I put on his mind will keep him going
Right as a homing-pigeon.
First Man Devilry
I call it.
The Woman And you're welcome.
Second Man But the law
Should have a say here.
The Woman What, isn't he mine,
My own? There's naught but what I please about it.
Third Man Why did you let him go?
The Woman To fetch him back!
For I enjoy this, mind. There's many a one
Would think to see me, There goes misery!
There's a queer starveling for you!—and I do
A thing that makes me like a saint in glory,
The life of me the sound of a great tune
Your flesh could never hear: I can send power
Delighting out of me! O, the mere thought
Has made my blood go smarting in my veins,
Such a flame glowing along it!—And all the same
I'll pay him out for sidling off from me.
But I'll have supper first.

When she was gone,
Their talk could scarcely raise itself again
Above a grumble. But at last a cry
Sharp-pitcht came startling in from the street: at once
Their moody talk exploded into flare
Of swearing hubbub, like gunpowder dropt
On embers; mugs were clapt down, out they bolted
Rowdily jostling, eager for the event.
All down the street the folk thronged out of doors,

But left a narrow track clear in the middle;
And there a man came running, a tall man
Running desperately and slowly, pounding
Like a machine, so evenly, so blindly;
And regularly his trotting body wagged.
Only one foot clattered upon the stones;
The other padded in his dogged stride:
The boot was gone, the sock hung frayed in shreds
About his ankle, the foot was blood and earth;
And never a limp, not the least flinch, to tell
The wounded pulp hit stone at every step.
His clothes were tattered and his rent skin showed,
Harrowed with thorns. His face was pale as putty,
Thrown far back; clots of drooping spittle foamed
On his mustache, and his hair hung in tails,
Mired with sweat; and sightless in their sockets
His eyeballs turned up white, as dull as pebbles.
Evenly and doggedly he trotted,
And as he went he moaned. Then out of sight
Round a corner he swerved, and out of hearing.
—"The law should have a say to that, by God!"

EPITAPH

Sir, you should notice me: I am the Man;
I am Good Fortune: I am satisfied.
All I desired, more than I could desire,
I have: everything has gone right with me.
Life was a hiding-place that played me false;
I croucht ashamed, and still was seen and scorned:
But now I am not seen. I was a fool,
And now I know what wisdom dare not know:
For I know Nothing. I was a slave, and now
I have ungoverned freedom and the wealth
That cannot be conceived: for I have Nothing.
I lookt for beauty and I longed for rest,
And now I have perfection: nay, I am
Perfection: I am Nothing, I am dead.

James Stephens

James Stephens was born in Dublin in February, 1882. His youth was difficult, his livelihood precarious. Stephens was "discovered" in an office and saved from clerical slavery by George Russell ("Æ"). Always a poet, many of Stephen's most poetic moments are in his highly colored prose. Yet, although the finest of his novels, *The Crock of Gold* (1912), contains more wild fantasy and quaint imagery than his verse, his *Insurrections* (1909) and *The Hill of Vision* (1912) reveal a rebellious spirit that is at once hotly ironic and coolly whimsical. *Green Branches* (1916) and *Reincarnations* (1918)—the latter being free adaptations from the Gaelic—are further persuasive volumes of his verse.

Collected Poems (1926) discloses two strongly differentiated personalities. There is the familiar and well-beloved Irish gamin, intimate with goats and gods, the playboy of the roads, deferential to rabbits and lesser folk, impudent to the universe. There is, also, the less popular but more sizeable poet, the thoughtful author of "The Crest Jewel," "In Waste Places," "The Main-Deep" with its surging rhythm held in a few syllables, and "A Prelude and a Song" which moves with the gentle solemnity of a river. Traces of Blake are in the later Stephens; the poet, discarding his light grotesquerie, becomes the seer. A less amusing singer is the result, but a more impassioned one. In youth Stephens delighted in gay mischiefs, pranking with unnatural phenomena; in maturity he is concerned with nothing less than elemental truths.

Both personalities combine in the prose fiction for which Stephens is famous. *Deirdre* (1923) and *In the Land of Youth* (1924) continue the re-creations from the Irish folk- and fairy-tales. *Hunger* (1918), originally published under the pseudonym "James Esse," was incorporated in the somber collection of short stories *Etched in Moonlight* (1928) which, curiously enough, was poorly received in England but an enormous success in America. An edition of his *Irish Fairy Tales* was arranged for children.

Strict Joy (1931) is a small book containing a dozen new poems, yet its very range is characteristic. Stephens lightly runs the scale from badinage to mysticism and seldom strikes an uncertain note, never a false one.

Kings and the Moon (1938) is another deceptive little volume. It is so simply written as to seem banal, so unaffected in thought as to appear sentimental. But the simplicity is attained by severe restraint, by clear perception instead of poetic diction, by the refusal to inflate an emotion or pad a line.

Stephens's final characteristic is his delightful blend of incongruities—he successfully mingles the bizarre and the charming, the buoyant and the profound. It is sometimes difficult to separate the elfin from the human in Stephens—Fred B. Millett has characterized Stephens' spirit as "that of a sensitive and uncannily observant gnome"—but Stephens charms by the very uncertainty, by the tricks of his imagination and the sudden warmth of his sympathy. Stephens died December 26, 1950.

EVENING

The drowsy sun went slowly to his rest
Gathering all his dusty gold again
Into one place:
He did not leave a trace
Upon the sky except one distant stain,
Scarce to be seen, upon the quiet west:
So evening came, and darkness, and the sound
Of moving feet upon the whispering ground.

Like timid girls the shades went pacing down
The spreading slopes apparelled soberly
In vestments grey;
And far away
The last red color faded to a brown,
So faint, so far, the eye could scarcely see:
And then the skirts of evening swung upon
That distant little light, and it was gone.

The bee sped home, the beetle's wing of horn
Went booming by, the darkness every side
Gathered around
On sky and air and ground;
And all the pliant trees sang far and wide
In cadenced lift of leaves a song of morn:
And then the moon's white circle, faint and thin,
Looked steady on the earth—*there is no sin.*

THE LAKE

He could see the little lake
Cuddled on a mountain's arm,
And the rushes were a-shake,
On the margin of the lake.

And the gloom of evening threw
On the surface of the lake,
Just a shadow on the blue
Where the night came creeping through.

There was silence all around,
Not a whisper stirred the lake,
And the trees made not a sound
Standing silent in the ground.

Then a moon of beauty swept
One slim finger on the lake,
And the glory of it crept
Past the lilies where they slept,

And just where a lily flung
Its broad flag upon the lake
Was a dead face pale and young
And the wet hair spread and swung;

And the moon beamed mild and dim
On that dead face in the lake,
Then it grew fierce, wide and grim,
And a mad moon glared at Him.

THE SHELL

And then I pressed the shell
Close to my ear
And listened well,
And straightway like a bell
Came low and clear
The slow, sad murmur of the distant seas,
Whipped by an icy breeze
Upon a shore
Wind-swept and desolate.
It was a sunless strand that never bore
The footprint of a man,
Nor felt the weight
Since time began
Of any human quality or stir
Save what the dreary winds and waves incur.
And in the hush of waters was the sound
Of pebbles rolling round,
For ever rolling with a hollow sound.
And bubbling sea-weeds as the waters go
Swish to and fro
Their long, cold tentacles of slimy gray.
There was no day,
Nor felt the weight
Setting the stars alight
To wonder at the moon:
Was twilight only and the frightened croon,
Smitten to whimpers, of the dreary wind
And waves that journeyed blind—
And then I loosed my ear . . . O, it was sweet
To hear a cart go jolting down the street.

WHAT THOMAS AN BUILE SAID IN A PUB

I saw God. Do you doubt it?
  Do you dare to doubt it?
I saw the Almighty Man. His hand
Was resting on a mountain, and
He looked upon the World and all about it:
I saw Him plainer than you see me now,
  You mustn't doubt it.

He was not satisfied;
  His look was all dissatisfied.
His beard swung on a wind far out of sight
Behind the world's curve, and there was light
Most fearful from His forehead, and He sighed,
"That star went always wrong, and from the start
  I was dissatisfied."

He lifted up His hand—
  I say He heaved a dreadful hand
Over the spinning Earth. Then I said, "Stay,
You must not strike it, God; I'm in the way;
And I will never move from where I stand."
He said, "Dear child, I feared that you were dead,"
  And stayed His hand.

TO THE FOUR COURTS, PLEASE

The driver rubbed at his nettly chin
With a huge, loose forefinger, crooked and black,
And his wobbly, violet lips sucked in,
And puffed out again and hung down slack:
One fang shone through his lop-sided smile,
In his little pouched eye flickered years of guile.

And the horse, poor beast, it was ribbed and forked,
And its ears hung down, and its eyes were old,
And its knees were knuckly, and as we talked
It swung the stiff neck that could scarcely hold
Its big, skinny head up—then I stepped in,
And the driver climbed to his seat with a grin.

God help the horse and the driver too,
And the people and beasts who have never a friend,
For the driver easily might have been you,
And the horse be me by a different end.
And nobody knows how their days will cease,
And the poor, when they're old, have little of peace.

LITTLE THINGS

Little things that run and quail
And die in silence and despair;

Little things that fight and fail
And fall on earth and sea and air;

All trapped and frightened little things
The mouse, the coney, hear our prayer.

As we forgive those done to us,
The lamb, the linnet, and the hare,

Forgive us all our trespasses,
Little creatures everywhere.

THE RED-HAIRED MAN'S WIFE

I have taken that vow—
  And you were my friend
But yesterday—now
  All that's at an end,
And you are my husband, and claim me, and I must depend.

Yesterday I was free,
  Now you, as I stand
Walk over to me
  And take hold of my hand.
You look at my lips, your eyes are too bold, your smile is too bland.

My old name is lost,
  My distinction of race:
Now the line has been crossed,
  Must I step to your pace?
Must I walk as you list, and obey and smile up in your face?

All the white and the red
  Of my cheeks you have won;
All the hair of my head,
  And my feet, tho' they run,
Are yours, and you own me and end me just as I begun.

Must I bow when you speak,
  Be silent and hear,
Inclining my cheek
  And incredulous ear
To your voice, and command, and behest, hold your lightest wish dear?

I am woman, but still
  Am alive, and can feel
Every intimate thrill
  That is woe or is weal.
I, aloof, and divided, apart, standing far, can I kneel?

If not, I shall know,
  I shall surely find out,
And your world will throw
  In disaster and rout;
I am woman and glory and beauty, I mystery, terror, and doubt.

I am separate still,
  I am I and not you:
And my mind and my will,
  As in secret they grew,
Still are secret, unreached and untouched and not subject to you.

HATE

ly enemy came nigh,
nd I
tared fiercely in his face.
ly lips went writhing back in a grimace,
nd stern I watched him with a narrow eye.
hen, as I turned away, my enemy,
hat bitter heart and savage, said to me:
Some day, when this is past,
Vhen all the arrows that we have are cast,
Ve may ask one another why we hate,
nd fail to find a story to relate.
may seem to us then a mystery
hat we could hate each other."
Thus said he,
nd did not turn away,
Vaiting to hear what I might have to say.
ut I fled quickly, fearing if I stayed
might have kissed him as I would a maid.

THE WATCHER

A rose for a young head,
A ring for a bride,
Joy for the homestead
Clean and wide—
Who's that waiting
In the rain outside?

A heart for an old friend,
A hand for the new:
Love can to earth lend
Heaven's hue—
Who's that standing
In the silver dew?

A smile for the parting,
A tear as they go,
God's sweethearting
Ends just so—
Who's that watching
Where the black winds blow?

He who is waiting
In the rain outside,
He who is standing
Where the dew drops wide,
He who is watching
In the wind must ride
(Tho' the pale hands cling)
With the rose
And the ring
And the bride,
Must ride
With the red of the rose,
And the gold of the ring,
And the lips and the hair of the bride.

RIGHTEOUS ANGER

The lanky hank of a she in the inn over there
Nearly killed me for asking the loan of a glass of beer:
May the devil grip the whey-faced slut by the hair,
And beat bad manners out of her skin for a year.

That parboiled imp, with the hardest jaw you will see
On virtue's path, and a voice that would rasp the dead,
Came roaring and raging the minute she looked at me,
And threw me out of the house on the back of my head!

If I asked her master he'd give me a cask a day;
But she with the beer at hand, not a gill would arrange!
May she marry a ghost and bear him a kitten and may
The High King of Glory permit her to get the mange.

ODELL

My mind is sad and weary thinking how
The griffins of the Gael went over the sea

From noble Eiré, and are fighting now
In France and Flanders and in Germany.

If they, 'mid whom I sported without dread,
Were home I would not mind what foe might do,
Or fear tax-man Odell would seize my bed
To pay the hearth-rate that is overdue.

I pray to Him who, in the haughty hour
Of Babel, threw confusion on each tongue,
That I may see our princes back in power,
And see Odell, the tax-collector, hung.

BLUE BLOOD

(*After O'Bruaidar*)

We thought at first, this man is a king for sure,
Or the branch of a mighty and ancient and famous lineage—
That silly, sulky, illiterate, black-avised boor
Who was hatched by foreign vulgarity under a hedge.

The good men of Clare were drinking his health in a flood,
And gazing with me in awe of the princely lad,
And asking each other from what bluest blueness of blood
His daddy was squeezed, and the pa of the da of his dad?

We waited there, gaping and wondering, anxiously,
Until he'd stop eating and let the glad tidings out,
And the slack-jawed booby proved to the hilt that he
Was lout, son of lout, by old lout, and was da to a lout!

THE MAIN-DEEP

The long rólling,
Steady-póuring,
Deep-trenchéd
Green billow:

The wide-topped,
Unbróken,
Green-glacid,
Slow-sliding.

Cold-flushing,
On—on—on—
Chill-rushing,
Hush-hushing,

Hush—hushing. . . .

IN WASTE PLACES

As a naked man I go
Through the desert, sore afraid;
Holding high my head, although
I'm as frightened as a maid.

The lion crouches there! I saw
In barren rocks his amber eye!
He parts the cactus with his paw!
He stares at me as I go by!

He would pad upon my trace
If he thought I was afraid!
If he knew my hardy face
Veils the terrors of a maid.

He rises in the night-time, and
He stretches forth! He snuffs the air!

He roars! He leaps along the sand!
He creeps! He watches everywhere!

His burning eyes, his eyes of bale
Through the darkness I can see!
He lashes fiercely with his tail!
He makes again to spring at me!

I am the lion, and his lair!
I am the fear that frightens me!
I am the desert of despair!
And the night of agony!

Night or day, whate'er befall,
I must walk that desert land,
Until I dare my fear and call
The lion out to lick my hand.

GOOD AND BAD

Good and bad and right and wrong,
Wave the silly words away:
This is wisdom to be strong,
This is virtue to be gay:
Let us sing and dance until
We shall know the final art,
How to banish good and ill
With the laughter of the heart.

THE OUTCAST

Shy and timid, Gloom to me
Said, I am lost! How shall I go?
There is no place for Misery,
Welcome for Woe!

And to him,
Desolate and fey,
My stricken heart
Found nought to say.

But soon: Be thou my Joy, I said:
Give me your hand, rest here your head:
Come to my home, and eat my bread,
And rest thee from annoy.

For I shall give thee all of mine,
Until my all be sealéd thine,
And thou shalt be, in little time,
A Child of Joy.

Now, on my heart, as on a throne,
Gloom, as heavy as a stone,
Sits, and I go dark till he
Is Joy, and gives Joy back to me.

THE CREST JEWEL

I

The leaf will wrinkle to decay
And crumble into dust away!

The rose, the lily, grow to eld,
And are, and are no more, beheld!

Nothing will stay! For, as the eye
Rests upon an object nigh,

It is not there to look upon!
It is mysteriously gone!

And, in its place, another thing
Apes its shape and fashioning!

II

All that the sun will breathe today
The moon will lip and wear away

Tonight. And all will re-begin
Tomorrow as the dawn comes in.

Is no beginning, middle-trend
Or argument to that or end.

No cause and no effect, and no
Reason why it should be so.

Or why it might be otherwise
To other minds or other eyes.

III

The soul can dream itself to be
Adrift upon an endless sea

Of day and night. The soul can seem
To be all things that it can dream!

Yet needs but look within to find
That which is steady in the wind,

That which the fire does not appal,
Which good and ill mourn not at all

Which does not seek, or lack, or try.
And was not born, and cannot die!

IV

It has been writ in wisdom old—
This is the last word to be told:

—There is no dissolution! No
Creation! There are none in woe!

There is no teacher, teaching, taught!
Are none who long for, lack for aught!

Are none who pine for freedom! None
Are liberated under sun!

—And this is absolutely true
In Him who dreams in me and you.

James Joyce

☙ James Augustine Aloysius Joyce was born February 2, 1882, in Dublin. Educated for the priesthood, he attended Jesuit schools in Ireland for thirteen years. At twenty he revolted, wrote a blasphemous broadside, left his country and repudiated his countrymen, "the most belated race in Europe."

From that time Joyce's life (according to Herbert Gorman, Joyce's official biographer) became "a constant struggle against terrific odds, prejudices, mob smugness, poverty, and physical disability." His work was censored, officially banned, and even burned; his books, forbidden by several governments, were illicitly published all over the world, and Joyce received no royalties from the pirated publications. He studied medicine in Paris; almost became a professional singer; taught languages in Trieste and Switzerland; wandered about the Continent until he finally settled in Paris. Illness and overwork necessitated ten eye operations in twenty years; before he was forty Joyce was practically blind. Writing was a painful effort for him; a few lines at a time scrawled on a large sheet of paper was all he could manage.

Joyce's literary début was quiet and undistinguished: *Chamber Music* (1907), a small volume of pseudo-Elizabethan verse in the traditional lyric manner. His next book, *Dubliners* (1914), marked the beginning of the artist's twofold struggle for recognition and for the right to pursue his own methods—methods which, depending upon the point of view, were lauded as pioneering or attacked as mere arrogance.

In his early thirties Joyce definitely broke with tradition in *A Portrait of the Artist as a Young Man* (1916), a welter of characters and theories, a kaleidoscope of the weird and the commonplace. Its central character became a chief figure in Joyce's *Ulysses* (1922), banned for many years from the United States. *Ulysses,* an autobiographical extension of reality, is one of the strangest novels ever written and one of the most extraordinary works of the age. It became a storm-center. It was reviled as the work of an obscene madman and praised as the utterance of an unqualifiedly great genius. With all its complexities, *Ulysses* is crystal-clear compared to *Finnegan's Wake* (1939). *Finnegan's Wake* seems to be a collision between the language of speech and the language of literature, a colossal series of telescopic phrases, vast figures which dissolve into allusions, and a constant elaboration of half-intelligible puns.

The enormous labor demanded by his cryptic work was too much for Joyce. He succumbed in a losing fight against blindness, illness, and poverty; he died in Zurich, Switzerland, January 13, 1941, a few weeks before his fifty-ninth birthday. Richard Ellmann's *James Joyce* (1959) is the most penetrating biography.

Pomes Penyeach (1927) is delicate and genuinely lyrical, strangely reminiscent of the seventeenth century singers. Like the early *Chamber Music,* the verse is conventional in theme, orthodox in treatment, harmonically simple, and the very antithesis of everything for which Joyce is celebrated.

STRINGS IN THE EARTH

Strings in the earth and air
 Make music sweet;
Strings by the river where
 The willows meet.

There's music along the river
 For Love wanders there,
Pale flowers on his mantle,
 Dark leaves on his hair.

All softly playing,
 With head to the music bent,
And fingers straying
 Upon an instrument.

I HEAR AN ARMY

I hear an army charging upon the land,
 And the thunder of horses plunging, foam about their knees:
Arrogant, in black armor, behind them stand,
 Disdaining the reins, with fluttering whips, the charioteers.

They cry unto the night their battle-name:
 I moan in sleep when I hear afar their whirling laughter.
They cleave the gloom of dreams, a blinding flame,
 Clanging, clanging upon the heart as upon an anvil.

They come shaking in triumph their long, green hair:
 They come out of the sea and run shouting by the shore.
My heart, have you no wisdom thus to despair?
 My love, my love, my love, why have you left me alone?

O SWEETHEART, HEAR YOU

O sweetheart, hear you
  Your lover's tale;
A man shall have sorrow
  When friends him fail.

For he shall know then
  Friends be untrue
And a little ashes
  Their words come to.

But one unto him
  Will softly move
And softly woo him
  In ways of love.

His hand is under
  Her smooth round breast;
So he who has sorrow
  Shall have rest.

ALL DAY I HEAR

All day I hear the noise of waters
  Making moan,
Sad as the sea-bird is when, going
  Forth alone,
He hears the winds cry to the waters'
  Monotone.

The gray winds, the cold winds are blowing
  Where I go.
I hear the noise of many waters
  Far below.
All day, all night, I hear them flowing
  To and fro.

SONG

O, it was out by Donnycarney,
  When the bat flew from tree to tree,
My love and I did walk together,
  And sweet were the words she said to me.

Along with us the summer wind
  Went murmuring—O, happily!—
But softer than the breath of summer
  Was the kiss she gave to me.

ON THE BEACH AT FONTANA

Wind whines and whines the shingle,
The crazy pierstakes groan;
A senile sea numbers each single
Slimesilvered stone.

From whining wind and colder
Gray sea I wrap him warm
And touch his trembling fineboned shoulder
And boyish arm.

Around us fear, descending
Darkness of fear above
And in my heart how deep unending
Ache of love!

FLOOD

Goldbrown upon the sated flood
The rockvine clusters lift and sway,
Vast wings above the lambent waters brood
Of sullen day.

A waste of waters ruthlessly
Sways and uplifts its weedy mane
Where brooding day stares down upon the sea
In dull disdain.

Uplift and sway, O golden vine,
Your clustered fruits to love's full flood,
Lambent and vast and ruthless as in thine
Incertitude!

James Elroy Flecker

Another remarkable poet whose early death was a blow to English literature was James Elroy Flecker. Born in London, November 5, 1884, he studied at Trinity College, Oxford, specialized in Oriental languages at Cambridge, and went to Constantinople in the Consular Service in 1910. The fact that the remainder of his life was spent in the East has a direct bearing on Flecker's work: his play *Hassan,* one of the most powerful and brilliantly colored modern dramas, is the definite reflection of his adopted Orientalism.

Possibly due to low vitality, Flecker found little to interest him but a reaction against realism in verse, a delight in verbal craftsmanship, and a passion for technical perfection—especially the deliberate technique of the French Parnassians, whom he worshiped. Flecker was opposed to any art that was emotional or that "taught" anything. "The poet's business," he declared, "is not to save the soul of man, but to make it worth saving." Flecker's desire to be objective rather than passionate was scarcely consistent with his actual creation, even though he maintained that "the Parnassians raised the technique of their art to a height which enabled them to express the subtlest ideas in powerful and simple verse." Technique and manner were his abstract gods.

The advent of the war began to make Flecker's verse more personal and romantic. The tuberculosis that finally killed him at Davos Platz, Switzerland, January 3, 1915, forced him from an Olympian disinterest to a deep concern with life and death. He passionately denied that he was weary of living "as the pallid poets are," and he was attempting higher flights of song when his singing ceased altogether.

Flecker's two notable volumes are *The Golden Journey to Samarkand* (1913) and *The Old Ships* (1915). *Collected Poems,* with an autobiographical introduction and notes by J. C. Squire, was published in 1917 and drew fresh attention to Flecker's half-classical, half-romantic, and always vivid style.

THE OLD SHIPS

I have seen old ships sail like swans asleep
Beyond the village which men still call Tyre,
With leaden age o'ercargoed, dipping deep
For Famagusta and the hidden sun
That rings black Cyprus with a lake of fire;
And all those ships were certainly so old—
Who knows how oft with squat and noisy gun,
Questing brown slaves or Syrian oranges,
The pirate Genoese
Hell-raked them till they rolled
Blood, water, fruit and corpses up the hold.
But now through friendly seas they softly run,
Painted the mid-sea blue or shore-sea green,
Still patterned with the vine and grapes in gold.

But I have seen,
Pointing her shapely shadows from the dawn
An image tumbled on a rose-swept bay,
A drowsy ship of some yet older day;
And, wonder's breath indrawn,
Thought I—who knows—who knows—but in that same
(Fished up beyond Aeaea, patched up new
—Stern painted brighter blue—)
That talkative, bald-headed seaman came
(Twelve patient comrades sweating at the oar)
From Troy's doom-crimson shore,
And with great lies about his wooden horse
Set the crew laughing, and forgot his course.

It was so old a ship—who knows, who knows?
—And yet so beautiful, I watched in vain
To see the mast burst open with a rose,
And the whole deck put on its leaves again.

STILLNESS

When the words rustle no more,
And the last work's done,
When the bolt lies deep in the door,

And Fire, our Sun,
Falls on the dark-laned meadows of the floor;

When from the clock's last chime to the next chime
Silence beats his drum,
And Space with gaunt gray eyes and her brother Time
Wheeling and whispering come,
She with the mold of form and he with the loom of rhyme:

Then twittering out in the night my thought-birds flee,
I am emptied of all my dreams:
I only hear Earth turning, only see
Ether's long bankless streams,
And only know I should drown if you
Laid not your hand on me.

THE WAR SONG OF THE SARACENS

We are they who come faster than fate: we are they who ride early or late:
We storm at your ivory gate: Pale Kings of the Sunset, beware!
Not on silk nor in samet we lie, not in curtained solemnity die
Among women who chatter and cry, and children who mumble a prayer.
But we sleep by the ropes of the camp, and we rise with a shout, and we tramp
With the sun or the moon for a lamp, and the spray of the wind in our hair.

From the lands, where the elephants are, to the forts of Merou and Balghar,
Our steel we have brought and our star to shine on the ruins of Ruhm.
We have marched from the Indus to Spain, and, by God, we will go there again;
We have stood on the shore of the plain where the Waters of Destiny boom.
A mart of destruction we made at Jalúla where men were afraid,
For death was a difficult trade, and the sword was a broker of doom;

And the Spear was a Desert Physician who cured not a few of ambition.
And drave not a few to perdition with medicine bitter and strong;
And the shield was a grief to the fool and as bright as a desolate pool,
And as straight as the rock of Stamboul when their cavalry thundered along:
For the coward was drowned with the brave when our battle sheered up like a wave,
And the dead to the desert we gave, and the glory to God in our song.

TENEBRIS INTERLUCENTEM

A linnet who had lost her way
Sang on a blackened bough in Hell,
Till all the ghosts remembered well
The trees, the wind, the golden day.

At last they knew that they had died
When they heard music in that land,
And someone there stole forth a hand
To draw a brother to his side.

TO A POET A THOUSAND YEARS HENCE

I who am dead a thousand years,
And wrote this sweet archaic song,
Send you my words for messengers
The way I shall not pass along.

I care not if you bridge the seas,
Or ride secure the cruel sky,
Or build consummate palaces
Of metal or of masonry.

But have you wine and music still,
And statues and a bright-eyed love,
And foolish thoughts of good and ill,
And prayers to them who sit above?

How shall we conquer? Like a wind
That falls at eve our fancies blow,
And old Maeonides the blind
Said it three thousand years ago.

O friend unseen, unborn, unknown,
Student of our sweet English tongue,
Read out my words at night, alone:
I was a poet, I was young.

Since I can never see your face,
And never shake you by the hand,
I send my soul through time and space
To greet you. You will understand.

THE TOWN WITHOUT A MARKET

There lies afar behind a western hill
The Town without a Market, white and still;
For six feet long and not a third as high
Are those small habitations. There stood I,
Waiting to hear the citizens beneath
Murmur and sigh and speak through tongueless teeth.
When all the world lay burning in the sun
I heard their voices speak to me. Said one:
"Bright lights I loved and colors, I who find
That death is darkness, and has struck me blind."
Another cried: "I used to sing and play,
But here the world is silent, day by day."
And one: "On earth I could not see or hear,
But with my fingers touched what I was near,
And knew things round and soft, and brass from gold,
And dipped my hand in water, to feel cold,
And thought the grave would cure me, and was glad

When the time came to lose what joy I had."
Soon all the voices of a hundred dead
Shouted in wrath together. Someone said,
"I care not, but the girl was sweet to kiss
At evening in the meadows." "Hard it is,"
Another cried, "to hear no hunting horn.
Ah me! the horse, the hounds, and the great gray morn
When I rode out a-hunting." And one sighed,
"I did not see my son before I died."
A boy said, "I was strong and swift to run:
Now they have tied my feet; what have I done?"
A man, "But it was good to arm and fight
And storm their cities in the dead of night."
An old man said, "I read my books all day,
But death has taken all my books away."
And one, "The popes and prophets did not well
To cheat poor dead men with false hopes of hell.
Better the whips of fire that hiss and rend
Than painless void proceeding to no end."
I smiled to hear them restless, I who sought
Peace. For I had not loved, I had not fought,
And books are vanities, and manly strength
A gathered flower. God grants us peace at length!
I heard no more, and turned to leave their town
Before the chill came, and the sun went down.
Then rose a whisper, and I seemed to know
A timorous man, buried long years ago.
"On Earth I used to shape the Thing that seems.
Master of all men, give me back my dreams.
Give me the world that never failed me then,
The hills I made and peopled with tall men,
The palace that I built and called my home,
My cities which could break the pride of Rome,
The three queens hidden in the sacred tree,
And those white cloudy folk who sang to me,
O death, why hast thou covered me so deep?
I was thy sister's child, the friend of Sleep."

Then said my heart, Death takes and cannot give.
Dark with no dream is hateful: let me live!

THE BALLAD OF HAMPSTEAD HEATH

om Heaven's Gate to Hampstead Heath
Young Bacchus and his crew
me tumbling down, and o'er the town
Their bursting trumpets blew.

e silver night was wildly bright,
And madly shone the moon
hear a song so clear and strong,
With such a lovely tune.

From London's houses, huts and flats,
Came busmen, snobs, and Earls,
And ugly men in bowler hats
With charming little girls.

Sir Moses came with eyes of flame,
Judd, who is like a bloater,
The brave Lord Mayor in coach and pair,
King Edward, in his motor.

Far in a rosy mist withdrawn
  The God and all his crew,
Silenus pulled by nymphs, a faun,
  A satyr drenched in dew,

Smiled as they wept those shining tears
  Only Immortals know,
Whose feet are set among the stars,
  Above the shifting snow.

And one spake out into the night,
  Before they left for ever,
"Rejoice, rejoice!" and his great voice
  Rolled like a splendid river.

He spake in Greek, which Britons speak
  Seldom, and circumspectly;
But Mr. Judd, that man of mud,
  Translated it correctly.

And when they heard that happy word,
  Policemen leapt and ambled:
The busmen pranced, the maidens danced,
  The men in bowlers gambolled.

A wistful Echo stayed behind
  To join the mortal dances,
But Mr. Judd, with words unkind,
  Rejected her advances,

And passing down through London Tow
  She stopped, for all was lonely,
Attracted by a big brass plate
  Inscribed: FOR MEMBERS ONLY.

And so she went to Parliament,
  But those ungainly men
Woke up from sleep, and turned about,
  And fell asleep again.

Anna Wickham

Anna Wickham was born in Wimbledon, Surrey, in 1884. She went to Australia at six, returned when she was twenty-one, studied for Opera in Paris with De Reszke and suddenly, after a few years of marriage, became a poet. In a burst of creative energy she wrote nine hundred poems in four years.

Her first two books (*The Contemplative Quarry,* 1915, and *The Man with a Hammer,* 1916) were republished in America in one volume, *The Contemplative Quarry* (1921). This was followed by *The Little Old House* (1922). Another volume, *The Noiseless Propeller,* was prepared, but its publication was postponed. The most casual reading of Anna Wickham's work reveals the strength of her candor. The poems could scarcely be put in the category of "charming" verse; they are astringent and sometimes harsh, gnarled frequently by their own violences of mood. But there is no disputing their incisiveness and integrity. Mrs. Wickham's lines present the picture of woman struggling between dreams and domesticity; they are acutely sensitive, restless, analytical. The very tone of her poetry reflects the disturbed music and the nervous protests of her age.

Sometimes her verse tends toward introverted self-questioning, but usually it is as just in phrase as it is fearless in thought. Much of her poetry is a poetry of the senses, and in this she seems kin to D. H. Lawrence. But where Lawrence, lost and suffering in the "mazes of the female mystery," is sexually tormented, Anna Wickham, unhampered in her sensuality, delights even in her torments. She turns upon men for maintaining a traditional attitude, not to the real women of today, but to creatures half-historical, half-illusory; she berates women for fostering this tendency, thus weakening men and enchaining themselves.

We, vital women, are no more content
Bound, first to passion, then to sentiment.
Of you, the masters, slaves in our poor eyes
Who most are moved by women's tricks and lies,
We ask our freedom. In good sooth,
We only ask to know and speak the truth!

Yet Mrs. Wickham does more than "only ask to know and speak the truth." Her angers and revulsions cannot choke the lyric impulse. Time and again she makes songs that are sweet without being sentimental, almost perfect in their simple cadences, shrewd yet lightly persuasive.

For the most part she is torn between being the instrument of love and love itself; making, with a wry determination, an unhappy compromise between the conflicting claims of modernity and maternity. She is rarely objective; even such dramatic projections as "Meditation at Kew" and the acrid humor of "Nervous Prostration" are too bitter to be impersonal. Out of all her poems, the plangent as well as the powerful, rises this cry which is also an apologia:

Let it be something for my song,
If it is sometimes swift and strong.

"Self-Analysis," "Divorce," and "The Affinity" are this remarkable and unappreciated poet *in petto*. Divided between her desire for mastery and being mastered, for perfection and her distrust of it, she typifies the woman who has repudiated order but is frustrated in lawlessness; even her domesticity, which she celebrates, is, if not self-condemning, self-contradicting.

Although Mrs. Wickham has written longer poems, her terse, pungently flavored lyrics are most characteristic of her. She is a psychologist by intention, but a psychologist who has not forgotten how to sing. At her worst she offers an interesting exhibit of the age; at her best she displays a genius for the firm epithet and quick-thrusting phrase—and an unforgettable power of emotion.

CREATRIX

Let us thank Almighty God
For the woman with the rod.
Who was ever and is now
Strong, essential as the plow.
She shall goad and she shall drive,
So to keep man's soul alive.
Amoris with her scented dress
Beckons, in pretty wantonness;
But the wife drives, nor can man tell
What hands so urge, what powers compel.

SONG

I was so chill, and overworn, and sad,
To be a lady was the only joy I had.
I walked the street as silent as a mouse,
Buying fine clothes, and fittings for the house.

But since I saw my love
I wear a simple dress,
And happily I move
Forgetting weariness.

SELF-ANALYSIS

The tumult of my fretted mind
Gives me expression of a kind;

But it is faulty, harsh, not plain—
My work has the incompetence of pain.

I am consumed with a slow fire,
For righteousness is my desire;
Towards that good goal I cannot whip my will,
I am a tired horse that jibs upon a hill.

I desire Virtue, though I love her not—
I have no faith in her when she is got:
I fear that she will bind and make me slave
And send me songless to the sullen grave.

I am like a man who fears to take a wife,
And frets his soul with wantons all his life.
With rich, unholy foods I stuff my maw;
When I am sick, then I believe in law.

I fear the whiteness of straight ways—
I think there is no color in unsullied days.
My silly sins I take for my heart's ease,
And know my beauty in the end disease.

Of old there were great heroes, strong in fight,
Who, tense and sinless, kept a fire alight:
God of our hope, in their great name,
Give me the straight and ordered flame!

SEHNSUCHT

Because of body's hunger are we born,
And by contriving hunger are we fed;
Because of hunger is our work well done,
As so are songs well sung, and things well said.
Desire and longing are the whips of God—
God save us all from death when we are fed.

WEAPONS

Up the crag
In the screaming wind,
Naked and bleeding
I fought blind.

Then at dawn
On the snowy height
I seized a spear
By the eastern light.

On I trudged
In the eye of the sun,
Past the cromlech
I found a gun.

Then I strayed
In the cities of men,
In the house of my Love
I found a pen!

THE LAST ROUND

Clasp you the God within yourself
And hold it fast;
After all combats shall ye come
To this good fight at last.

God is a mighty wrestler
He battles in the night;
Not till the end shall it be known
What foe you fight.

When God in you is overthrown
He'll show a light
And claim the victor for his own
And crown the fight.

TO A CRUCIFIX

O courteous Christ—Kind guest, most gracious host,
Which of these ugly things had pained you most
That silly priests repeat your words for gain
Or in your house hang symbols of your pain?

How had you withered at the servile breath
Spent in the praises of your common death,
Scorning these claims to honor and to pride
For such a death as multitudes have died.

Not in the cross was such indignity
As these acclaiming Christian ages see,
When you who lived for cure and for relief
Are most remembered for your wounds and grief.

FRIEND CATO

When the master sits at ease
He joys in generalities;
In aphorisms concerning all things human,
But most of all concerning woman.
Saying, "Women are this or that.
Woman is round, or high, or square, or flat."

Sir, a shepherd knows his sheep apart,
And mothers know young babes by heart.
To taste no little shade of difference
Is sign of undiscerning sense.
Cato, in pity, hear our just demur,
Man to be critic, must be connoisseur.

THE SONG-MAKER

I would live for a day and a night,
In the rigorous land where everything's right.
Then I would sit and make a song,
In the leisurely land where everything's wrong.

DEDICATION OF THE COOK

If any ask why there's no great She-Poet,
Let him come live with me, and he will know it:
If I'd indite an ode or mend a sonnet,
I must go choose a dish or tie a bonnet;

For she who serves in forced virginity
Since I am wedded will not have me free;
And those new flowers my garden is so rich in
Must die for clammy odors of my kitchen.

Yet had I chosen Dian's barrenness
I'm not full woman, and I can't be less,
So could I state no certain truth for life,
Can I survive and be my good man's wife?

Yes! I will make the servant's cause my own
That she in pity leave me hours alone
So I will tend her mind and feed her wit
That she in time have her own joy of it;
And count it pride that not a sonnet's spoiled
Lacking her choice betwixt the baked and boiled.
So those young flowers my garden is so rich in
Will blossom from the ashes of my kitchen!

MEDITATION AT KEW

Alas! for all the pretty women who marry dull men,
Go into the suburbs and never come out again,
Who lose their pretty faces, and dim their pretty eyes,
Because no one has skill or courage to organize.

What do these pretty women suffer when they marry?
They bear a boy who is like Uncle Harry,
A girl, who is like Aunt Eliza, and not new,
These old, dull races must breed true.

I would enclose a common in the sun,
And let the young wives out to laugh and run;
I would steal their dull clothes and go away,
And leave the pretty naked things to play.

Then I would make a contract with hard Fate
That they see all the men in the world and choose a mate,
And I would summon all the pipers in the town
That they dance with Love at a feast, and dance him down.

From the gay unions of choice
We'd have a race of splendid beauty, and of thrilling voice.
The World whips frank, gay love with rods,
But frankly, gayly shall we get the gods.

THE TIRED WOMAN

O my Lover, blind me,
Take your cords and bind me,
Then drive me through a silent land
With the compelling of your open hand!

There is too much of sound, too much for sight,
In thundrous lightnings of this night,
There is too much of freedom for my feet,
Bruised by the stones of this disordered street.

I know that there is sweetest rest for me,
In silent fields, and in captivity.
O Lover! drive me through a stilly land
With the compelling of your open hand.

DIVORCE

A voice from the dark is calling me.
In the close house I nurse a fire.
Out in the dark, cold winds rush free,
To the rock heights of my desire.
I smother in the house in the valley below,
Let me out to the night, let me go, let me go!

Spirits that ride the sweeping blast,
Frozen in rigid tenderness,
Wait! For I leave the fire at last,
My little-love's warm loneliness.
I smother in the house in the valley below,
Let me out in the night, let me go, let me go!

High on the hills are beating drums,
Clear from a line of marching men
To the rock's edge the hero comes.
He calls me, and he calls again.
On the hill there is fighting, victory, or quick death,
In the house is the fire, which I fan with sick breath
I smother in the house in the valley below,
Let me out in the dark, let me go, let me go!

AFTER ANNUNCIATION

Rest, little Guest,
Beneath my breast.
Feed, sweet Seed,
At your need.

I took Love for my lord
And this is my reward,
My body is good earth,
That you, dear Plant, have birth.

THE CHERRY-BLOSSOM WAND

I will pluck from my tree a cherry-blosom wand,
And carry it in my merciless hand,

So I will drive you, so bewitch your eyes,
With a beautiful thing that can never grow wise.

Light are the petals that fall from the bough,
And lighter the love that I offer you now;
In a spring day shall the tale be told
Of the beautiful things that will never grow old.

The blossoms shall fall in the night wind,
And I will leave you so, to be kind:
Eternal in beauty are short-lived flowers,
Eternal in beauty, these exquisite hours.

I will pluck from my tree a cherry-blossom wand,
And carry it in my merciless hand,
So I will drive you, so bewitch your eyes,
With a beautiful thing that shall never grow wise.

SOUL'S LIBERTY

He who has lost soul's liberty
Concerns himself for ever with his property,
As, when the folk have lost both dance and song,
Women clean useless pots the whole day long.

Thank God for war and fire
To burn the silly objects of desire,
That from the ruin of a church thrown down
We see God clear and high above the town.

TO MEN

(*Variation on Ella Wheeler Wilcox, after a poem of the same name*)

Sirs—though we fail you—let us live;
Be just, have pity, and forgive.
Think how poor Mother Eve was brought
To being as God's afterthought.

God had a vast expanse of clay
To fashion Adam's primal day;
Yet was the craftsman's limit shown
His image could not live alone.

Yet God supports eternal life
Without the comfort of a wife;
So it was proved e'er we began
God had miscalculated man.

And of his fault, he took a part
Formed woman's brain and woman's heart
Of Imperfection—vainly planned—
To love, to serve, to understand.

How can you wonder, if we stray
Through coward night and sloven day
When power in us can but reflect
God's wifelessness and man's defect.

Had lonely God when earth was new
Some blest remembrances of two,
He had not made one half of life
A shambles and a hell-stung strife.

*

Do you remember, O my Dear,
The seventh night of our first year,
The night, when my first son was give[n]
With ecstasy to tutor Heaven—

Had God loved thus, all Hell were blin[d]
And famine, lust and murder kind.
Come, my co-adjutor, beloved smith,
Raise thou thy hammer—break the myth

There is no marvel of creation
Exists beyond our full relation—
Yet God shall strengthen from his sins
To breed us new and breed us twins.

Thou bungling artificer, yet
Thou shalt be artist and beget
And on the form of Chaos lie
To wash the earth and raise the sky.

Not equal I, but counterpart
And in relation is my heart
Perfect with man's—as with his mind—
Mine is all strong to loose and bind.

Come then, my husband, here and rest
On my so well-remolded breast.
At morning we'll go out and see
How well God works for you and me.

THE SINGER

If I had peace to sit and sing,
Then I could make a lovely thing;
But I am stung with goads and whips,
So I build songs like iron ships.

Let it be something for my song,
If it is sometimes swift and strong.

ENVOI

God, thou great symmetry,
Who put a biting lust in me
From whence my sorrows spring,
For all the frittered days
That I have spent in shapeless ways,
Give me one perfect thing.

D. H. Lawrence

D(avid) H(erbert) Lawrence was born September 17, 1885, in the colliery town of Eastwood, a drab hamlet on the border between Derbyshire and Nottinghamshire. The son of workers, his novels return again and again to the rural and industrial backgrounds of his boyhood. Lawrence obtained a scholarship at the Nottingham High School and at sixteen became a pupil-teacher. After a short appointment in a London school, he abandoned teaching for literature. He traveled considerably in search of health and, during his last fifteen years, lived in Italy, New Mexico, and Southern France.

Even in his mid-twenties—in *The White Peacock* (1909), *Love Poems and Others* (1913) and, first of all, in *Sons and Lovers* (1913)—Lawrence pronounced the strain with which he was to be so closely identified. The two volumes of *Collected Poems* (1929) are autobiographically candid, completely characterizing. No one in his generation pursued the cry of sex so passionately, so painfully as D. H. Lawrence; and no one was more confused by it. A magnificently equipped craftsman, a writer *pur sang,* his gamut never extended. His novels, with two unimportant exceptions and, more explicitly, his poems are concerned with little else than the dark fire, the broken body, the struggle, death and resurrection of crucified flesh, the recurring cycle of fulfillment and frustration. This is Lawrence's theme, a theme which he varied with great skill, but one which he could neither leave nor fully control. It is not merely his passion, it is his obsession.

This is as far as Lawrence goes. And he could go no farther except in that limbo where sex and love are desperately confused. He could not separate his spirit from his loins; he was, at the same time, mentally detached and emotionally victimized.

His agony grew sharper, his solution vaguer. This, it seems, was the core of Lawrence's *malaise.* There is something about his excitation which is uncomfortably flagellant; his sudden heats and swift revulsions are too neurotic to evoke more than pity; hysteria, in many of the poems, is subdued but not silenced.

But there is something here beyond the sex-fearful, sex-fascinated being; something beyond the self-worshiping, self-deluded artist, and that is Lawrence's intensity. Whatever its faults, the pitch and register of his work is poetry. Impotence itself has power in his propulsive verse. A poet of sensibilities which are refined to the point of being always wounded, a recorder of kaleidoscopic images and sensory nuances, Lawrence at forty-four had made a permanent if painful contribution to literature. There are passages in his novels—especially in *The Rainbow* (1915) and *Women in Love* (1921)—that have the accent and the sweep of poetry; these are poems that fasten on the mind and will not be shaken off. It is rather a curious commentary that his objective or "fictional" poems are among his best. Nothing that he has written, none of his verse is more surely projected than the dramatic lyrics in dialect: "A Youth Mowing," "Violets," "Whether or Not," that remarkable sequence which a ruder Browning might have fathered and which is a completely rounded tale, a poignantly condensed novel.

Lawrence is more the enmeshed self, less the detached poet in "A Young Wife," "Love on the Farm," "Wedding Morn," and the irritated fragments in *Pansies* (1929). Here speaks "the hot blood's blindfold art," chaotically, characteristically, but always eloquently.

After a struggle of many years, Lawrence succumbed to tuberculosis. His wish that he be taken to New Mexico, either to die or to recuperate, could not be granted and he died March 2, 1930, at Vence, France. Immediately thereafter reappraisals set in: Lawrence was subjected to new examinations as poet, prophet, and pamphleteer. No less than four "intimate" biographers, including his wife, attempted the almost impossible task of presenting Lawrence as he seemed to the world and himself—and succeeded only in presenting him as he appeared to Mabel Dodge Luhan, Middleton Murry, Catherine Carswell, and Freda Lawrence. Horace Gregory was more critical in his study of Lawrence's symbols, estimating the man in relation to his work in *Pilgrim of the Apocalypse.* Lawrence's early stories were collected with a Memoir by David Garnett; posthumous and partly finished stories were issued for several years after his death. *Last Poems,* a volume of some three hundred pages with an introduction by Richard Aldington, appeared in 1933. The book consists of the greater part of two large manuscripts found among Lawrence's papers. It ranges from the sharp, snarling, and often trivial pensées, which Lawrence liked to call "Pansies," to long premonitory poems on death, poems which voice a new dignity.

Few writers had roused more violent and controversial issues; four of his books had been suppressed, a show of his paintings (an art to which Lawrence turned in his forties) was raided. Though he was unusually fecund, opposition kindled a bitter flame in him and his creative passion turned to propaganda. *Fantasia of the Unconscious* is a fantastic variation on Jung; *Studies in Classic American Literature* is a queerly proportioned but provocative plea for the recognition of a native spirit; *Pornography and Obscenity* (1929) is a tract, an argument for the appreciation of the realities as against the hypocrisies of sexual morality.

But his polemical writing is, after all, the least of his work. In the best of his novels and poems he achieved a style that was dynamic, inflamed, savagely honest. A conscientious barbarian, he was, as Stuart Sherman wrote, "a revolutionist in favor of an individualistic, aristocratic barbarianism." He seldom wrote badly. True, his preoccupation was sex (he was described as "the novelist of the over- and the under-sexed"); he dealt almost entirely with the intensification or the perversion of the sexual instinct. But his deeper obsession, the "inner theme," was the possession and maintenance of masculine power and the understanding of men's and women's basic relations with each other. He clarified, though he did not altogether resolve, the complexities in two essays published in *We Need One Another* (1933). Here Lawrence pleaded for a relinquishing of the over-inflated ego and a realization of the sexes' spiritual dependence—"the great flow of the relationship goes on, undying, and this is the flow of living sex, the relation that lasts a lifetime, and of which sex-desire is only one vivid, most vivid, manifestation."

This conviction was fully expressed only toward the end of Lawrence's life; most of his writing lacks such clarity. One homily was apparent in all his works: The world has gone stale, feebly promiscuous, prettily fetid. Small spurts of lust instead of a long passion; talk instead of acts. The world has ceased to be masculine. Its discontent, like its nervous art, its soft-rotten culture, its middle-class *malaise,* is all the outcome of womanishness. Women, pretending to need us, have used us up; women have destroyed us with merciless softness. All we cherish has become effeminized, vitiated with the white poison of their approval and the black venom of their jealousy. Suffering from a "mind-perverted, will-perverted, ego-perverted love," the world will be happy only when man—overcivilized man—regains the free power and security which are the well-spring of emotional vitality. The defect in thinking is obvious. It is not "maleness" which troubles the artist but his consciousness of it. It is this lack of peace which Lawrence instinctively resented and which kept him enslaved to his narrow freedom. Coming up from that lower English world "where the good form and restraint of the public school tradition was a gag to be spat out once the speaker gained the strength of self-confidence," Lawrence, rising by self-improvement, could never resist improving others. In this he was, beneath his libertarian manner, the Puritan. "He came up," said Henry S. Canby, "when the bourgeois Victorian morality was losing its vigor, and he preached his new gospel of virility just as the Methodists preached revivalism to the Angelicans." His methods were extravagant, often exacerbated, but they were vitally his own. He had, above all, the faculty of making the reader revalue his own standards. Whatever status as an artist the future may assign him, there can be no question that he was a force.

A YOUTH MOWING

There are four men mowing down by the Isar;
I can hear the swish of the scythe-strokes, four
Sharp breaths taken; yea, and I
Am sorry for what's in store.

The first man out of the four that's mowing
Is mine, I claim him once and for all;
Though it's sorry I am, on his young feet, knowing
None of the trouble he's led to stall.

As he sees me bring the dinner, he lifts
His head as proud as a deer that looks
Shoulder-deep out of the corn; and wipes
His scythe-blade bright, unhooks

The scythe-stone and over the stubble to me.
Lad, thou hast gotten a child in me,
Laddie, a man thou'lt ha'e to be,
Yea, though I'm sorry for thee.

LIGHTNING

I felt the lurch and halt of her heart
  Next my breast, where my own heart was beating;
And I laughed to feel it plunge and bound,
And strange in my blood-swept ears was the sound
  Of the words I kept repeating,
Repeating with tightened arms, and the hot blood's blind-fold art.

Her breath flew warm against my neck,
  Warm as a flame in the close night air;
And the sense of her clinging flesh was sweet
Where her arms and my neck's blood-surge could meet.
  Holding her thus, did I care
That the black night hid her from me, blotted out every speck?

I leaned me forward to find her lips,
  And claim her utterly in a kiss,
When the lightning flew across her face,
And I saw her for the flaring space
  Of a second, afraid of the clips
Of my arms, inert with dread, wilted in fear of my kiss.

A moment, like a wavering spark,
  Her face lay there before my breast,
Pale love lost in a snow of fear,
And guarded by a glittering tear,
  And lips apart with dumb cries;
A moment, and she was taken again in the merciful dark.

I heard the thunder, and felt the rain,
  And my arms fell loose, and I was dumb.
Almost I hated her, she was so good,
Hated myself, and the place, and my blood,
  Which burned with rage, as I bade her come
Home, away home, ere the lightning floated forth again.

SUSPENSE

The wind comes from the north
Blowing little flocks of birds
Like spray across the town,
And a train roaring forth
Rushes stampeding down
South, with flying curds
Of steam, from the darkening north.

Whither I turn and set
Like a needle steadfastly,
Waiting ever to get
The news that she is free;
But ever fixed, as yet,
To the lode of her agony.

A YOUNG WIFE

The pain of loving you
Is almost more than I can bear.

I walk in fear of you.
The darkness starts up where
You stand, and the night comes through
Your eyes when you look at me.

Ah, never before did I see
The shadows that live in the sun!

Now every tall glad tree
Turns round its back to the sun
And looks down on the ground, to see
The shadow it used to shun.

At the foot of each glowing thing
A night lies looking up.

Oh, and I want to sing
And dance, but I can't lift up
My eyes from the shadows: dark
They lie spilt round the cup.

What is it?—Hark
The faint fine seethe in the air!

Like the seething sound in a shell!
It is death still seething where
The wild-flower shakes its bell
And the skylark twinkles blue—

The pain of loving you
Is almost more than I can bear.

CHERRY ROBBERS

Under the long dark boughs, like jewels red
  In the hair of an Eastern girl
Hangs strings of crimson cherries, as if had bled
  Blood-drops beneath each curl.

Under the glistening cherries, with folded wings
  Three dead birds lie:
Pale-breasted throstles and a blackbird, robberlings
  Stained with red dye.

Against the haystack a girl stands laughing at me,
  Cherries hung round her ears.
Offers me her scarlet fruit: I will see
  If she has any tears.

A WINTER'S TALE

Yesterday the fields were only gray with scattered snow,
And now the longest grass leaves hardly emerge;
Yet her deep footsteps mark the snow, and go
On toward the pines at the hill's white verge.

I cannot see her, since the mist's pale scarf
Obscures the dark wood and the dull orange sky;
But she's waiting, I know, impatient and cold, half
Sobs struggling into her frosty sigh.

Why does she come so promptly, when she must know
She's only the nearer to the inevitable farewell?
The hill is steep, on the snow my steps are slow—
Why does she come, when she knows what I have to tell?

LOVE ON THE FARM

What large, dark hands are those at the window
Grasping in the golden light
Which weaves its way through the evening wind
  At my heart's delight?

Ah, only the leaves! But in the west
I see a redness suddenly come
Into the evening's anxious breast—
  'Tis the wound of love goes home!

The woodbine creeps abroad
Calling low to her lover:
  The sun-lit flirt who all the day
  Has poised above her lips in play
  And stolen kisses, shallow and gay
  Of pollen, now has gone away—
    She wooes the moth with her sweet, low word;
And when above her his moth-wings hover
Then her bright breast she will uncover
And yield her honey-drop to her lover.

Into the yellow, evening glow
Saunters a man from the farm below;
Leans, and looks in at the low-built shed
Where the swallow has hung her marriage bed.
  The bird lies warm against the wall.
  She glances quick her startled eyes
  Towards him, then she turns away
  Her small head, making warm display
  Of red upon the throat. Her terrors sway
  Her out of the nest's warm, busy ball,
  Whose plaintive cry is heard as she flies
  In one blue stoop from out the sties
  Into the twilight's empty hall.

Oh, water-hen, beside the rushes,
Hide your quaintly scarlet blushes,
Still your quick tail, lie still as dead,
Till the distance folds over his ominous tread!

The rabbit presses back her ears,
Turns back her liquid, anguished eyes
And crouches low; then with wild spring
Spurts from the terror of his oncoming;
To be choked back, the wire ring
Her frantic effort throttling:
  Piteous brown ball of quivering fears!
Ah, soon in his large, hard hands she dies,
And swings all loose from the swing of his walk!
Yet calm and kindly are his eyes
And ready to open in brown surprise
Should I not answer to his talk
Or should he my tears surmise.

I hear his hand on the latch, and rise from my chair
Watching the door open; he flashes bare
His strong teeth in a smile, and flashes his eyes
In a smile like triumph upon me; then careless-wise
He flings the rabbit soft on the table board
And comes toward me: he! the uplifted sword
Of his hand against my bosom! and oh, the broad
Blade of his glance that asks me to applaud
His coming! With his hand he turns my face to him
And caresses me with his fingers that still smell grim
Of rabbit's fur! God, I am caught in a snare!
I know not what fine wire is round my throat;
I only know I let him finger there
My pulse of life, and let him nose like a stoat
Who sniffs with joy before he drinks the blood.

And down his mouth comes to my mouth! and down
His bright dark eyes come over me, like a hood
Upon my mind! his lips meet mine, and a flood
Of sweet fire sweeps across me, so I drown
Against him, die, and find death good.

PIANO

Softly, in the dusk, a woman is singing to me;
Taking me back down the vista of years, till I see
A child sitting under the piano, in the boom of the tingling strings
And pressing the small, poised feet of a mother who smiles as she sings.

In spite of myself, the insidious mastery of song
Betrays me back, till the heart of me weeps to belong
To the old Sunday evenings at home, with winter outside
And hymns in the cozy parlor, the tinkling piano our guide.

So now it is vain for the singer to burst into clamor
With the great black piano appassionato. The glamour
Of childish days is upon me, my manhood is cast
Down in the flood of remembrance, I weep like a child for the past.

GREEN

The dawn was apple-green,
  The sky was green wine held up in the sun,
The moon was a golden petal between.

She opened her eyes, and green
They shone, clear like flowers undone
For the first time, now for the first time seen.

A WHITE BLOSSOM

A tiny moon as small and white as a single jasmine flower
Leans all alone above my window, on night's wintry bower,
Liquid as lime-tree blossom, soft as brilliant water or rain
She shines, the first white love of my youth, passionless and in vain.

WEDDING MORN

The morning breaks like a pomegranate
  In a shining crack of red;
Ah, when tomorrow the dawn comes late
  Whitening across the bed
It will find me at the marriage gate
  And waiting while light is shed
On him who is sleeping satiate
  With a sunk, unconscious head.

And when the dawn comes creeping in,
  Cautiously I shall raise
Myself to watch the daylight win
  On my first of days,
As it shows him sleeping a sleep he got
  With me, as under my gaze
He grows distinct, and I see his hot
  Face freed of the wavering blaze.

Then I shall know which image of God
  My man is made toward;
And I shall see my sleeping rod
  Or my life's reward;
And I shall count the stamp and worth
  Of the man I've accepted as mine,
Shall see an image of heaven or of earth
  On his minted metal shine.

Oh, and I long to see him sleep
  In my power utterly;
So I shall know what I have to keep. . . .
  I long to see
My love, that spinning coin, laid still
  And plain at the side of me
For me to reckon—for surely he will
  Be wealth of life to me.

And then he will be mine, he will lie
  Revealed to me;
Patent and open beneath my eye
  He will sleep of me;
He will lie negligent, resign
  His truth to me, and I
Shall watch the dawn light up for me
  This fate of mine.

And as I watch the wan light shine
  On his sleep that is filled of me,
On his brow where the curved wisps clot and
    twine
  Carelessly,
On his lips where the light breaths come
    and go
  Unconsciously,
On his limbs in sleep at last laid low
  Helplessly,
I shall weep, oh, I shall weep, I know
  For joy or for misery.

WHETHER OR NOT

I

Dunna thee tell me it's his'n, mother,
  Dunna thee, dunna thee!
—Oh, ay, he'll come an' tell thee his-sèn,
  Wench, wunna he?

Tha doesna mean ter say ter me, mother,
  He's gone wi' that—
—My gel, owt'll do for a man i' th' dark;
  Tha's got it flat!

But 'er's old, mother, 'er's twenty year
  Older nor him—
—Ay, an' yaller as a crowflower; an' yet i' th' dark
  Er'd do for Tim.

Tha niver believes it, does ter, mother?
  It's somebody's lies.
—Ax 'im thy-sèn, wench; a widder's lodger!
  It's no surprise.

II

A widow o' forty-five
Wi' a bitter, dirty skin,
To ha' 'ticed a lad o' twenty-five,
An' 'im to 'ave been took in!

A widow o' forty-five
As 'as sludged like a horse all 'er life
Till 'er's tough as whit-leather, to slive[1]
Atween a lad an' 'is wife!

A widow o' forty-five!
A glum old otchel, wi' long
Witch teeth, an' 'er hawk-eyes, as I've
Mistrusted all along!

An' me as 'as kept my-sèn
Shut like a daisy bud,
Clean an' new an' nice, so's when
He wed he'd ha'e summat good!

An' 'im as nice an' fresh
As any man i' th' force,
To ha' gone an' given his clean young flesh
To a woman that coarse!

III

You're stout to brave this snow, Miss Stainwright,
  Are you makin' Brinsley way?
—I'm off up th' line to Underwood
  Wi' a dress as is wanted today.

[1] To slive = to slip, to interfere.

Oh, are you goin' to Underwood?
  'Appen then you've 'eered!
—What's that as 'appen I've 'eered on, Missis?
  Speak up, you nedn't be feared.

Why, your young man an' Widow Naylor,
  'Er as 'e lodges wi'!
They say he's got 'er wi' childt; but there—
  It's nothing to do wi' me!

Though if it's true, they'll turn 'im out
  O' th' p'lice force, without fail;
An' if it's *not* true, you may back your life
  They'll listen to *her* tale.

—Well, I'm believin' no tale, Missis,
  I'm seein' for my-sèn.
An' when I know for sure, Missis,
  I'll talk *then*.

IV

Nay, robin red-breast, tha needna
  Sit noddin' thy head at me!
My breast's as red as thine, I reckon,
  Flayed red, if tha could but see.

Nay, yo' blessed pee-whips,
  Yo' needna scraight[1] at me!
I'm scraightin' my-sèn but arena goin'
  Ter let iv'rybody see.

Tha *art* smock-raveled, bunny,
  Larropin' neck an' crop
I' th' snow! but I's warrant thee
  I'm further ower th' top.

V

Now sithee theer at th' reelroad crossin'
Warmin' 'is-sèn at the stool o' fire
Under the tank as fills th' ingines,
If there isn't my dearly-beloved liar!

My constable, wi' 'is buttoned breast
As stout as the truth, my Sirs! an' 'is face
As bold as a robin! It's much he cares
For this nice old shame an' disgrace.

Oh, but 'e drops 'is flag when 'e sees me!
Yi, an' 'is face goes white! Oh, yes,
Tha can stare at me wi' thy fierce blue eyes;
Tha won't stare me out, I guess.

[1] Scraight = cry.

VI

Whativer brings thee out so far
  In a' this depth o' snow?
—I'm takin' 'ome a weddin'-dress,
  If yer mun know.

Why, is there a weddin' at Underwood
  As tha ne'd trudge up 'ere?
—It's Wider Naylor's weddin'-dress,
  'Er'll be wantin' it, I 'ear.

'Er doesna want no weddin'-dress—
  —Why—? but what dost mean?
—Doesn't ter know what I mean, Timmy?
  Yi, tha must ha' bin 'ard ter wean!

Tha'rt a good-un at suckin'-in yet, Timmy!
  But tell me, isn't it true
As 'er'll be wantin' my weddin'-dress
  In a wik or two?

—Tha's no 'casions ter ha'e me on,
  Lizzie; what's done is done.
—*Done,* I should think so! An' might I ask
  When tha begun?

It's thee as 'as done it, as much as me,
  So there, an' I tell thee flat.
—Me gotten a childt ter thy landlady?
  —Tha's gotten thy answer pat.

As tha allus 'ast; but let me tell thee
  Hasna ter sent me whoam, when I
Was a'most burstin' mad o' my-sèn,
  An' walkin' in agony?

After I'd kissed thee at night, Lizzie,
  An' tha's laid against me, an' melted
Into me, melted right into me, Lizzie,
  Till I was verily swelted.

An' if my landlady seed me like it,
  An' if 'er clawkin' eyes
Went through me as the light went out,
  Is it any cause for surprise?

—No cause for surprise at all, my lad;
  After kissin' an cuddlin' wi' me, tha could
Turn thy mouth on a woman like that!
  I hope it did thee good.

—Ay, it did; but afterwards
  I could ha' killed 'er.
—Afterwards! how many times afterwards
  Could ter ha' killed 'er?

Say no more, Liz, dunna thee;
  'Er's as good as thee.
—Then I'll say good-by to thee, Timothy;
  Take 'er i'stead o' me.

I'll ta'e thy word good-by, Liz,
  Though I shonna marry 'er.
Nor 'er nor nub'dy.—It is
  Very brave of you, Sir!

—T' childt maun ta'e its luck, it mun,
  An' 'er maun ta'e *'er* luck.
F'r I tell yer I h'arena marryin' none
  On yer; yo'n got what yer took!

—That's spoken like a man, Timmy,
  That's spoken like a man!
" 'E up an' fired 'is pistol,
  An' then away 'e ran!"

I damn well shanna marry 'er,
  Nor yo', so chew it no more!
I'll chuck the flamin' lot o' you—
  —Yer nedn't 'ave swore!

VII

There's 'is collar round th' candlestick,
An' there's the dark-blue tie I bought 'im!
An' these is the woman's kids 'es's so fond on,
An' 'ere comes the cat as caught 'im!

I dunno wheer 'is eyes was—a gret
Round-shouldered hag! My Sirs, to think
Of 'im stoopin' to 'er! You'd wonder 'e could
Throw 'imself down *that* sink!

I expect yer know who I am, Mrs. Naylor?
  Who y'are? yis, you're Lizzie Stainwright.
An' 'appen you'd guess then what I've come for?
  —'Appen I mightn't, 'appen I might.

Yer knowed as I was courtin' Tim Merfin?
  —Yis, I knowed 'e wor courtin' thee.
An' yet yer've bin carryin' on wi' 'im!
  —Ay, an' 'im wi' me.

Well, now yer've got ter pay for it.
  —If I han, what's that ter thee?
'E isn't goin' ter marry yer.
  —Tha wants 'im thy-sèn, I see.

It 'asn't nothin' to do with me.
  —Then what art colleyfoglin' for?
I'm not 'avin' your orts an' slarts.
  Which on us said you wor?

But I want you to know 'e's not *marryin'* you.
  —Tha wants 'im thy-sèn too bad.
Though I'll see as 'e pays you, an' does what's right.
  —Tha'rt for doin' a lot wi' t' lad!

VIII

To think I should 'ave ter 'affle an' caffle
  Wi' a woman, an' name 'er a price
For lettin' me marry the lad as I thought
  Ter marry wi' cabs an' rice!

But we'll go unbeknown ter th' registrar,
  An' give *'er* the money there is;
For I won't be beholden to such as 'er,
  I won't, or my name's not Liz.

IX

Ta'e off thy duty stripes, Tim,
  An' come in 'ere wi' me;
Ta'e off thy p'liceman's helmet
  An' look at me.

I wish tha hadna done it, Tim,
  I do, an' that I do!
For whenever I look thee i' th' face, I s'll see
  Her face too.

I wish I could wesh 'er off'n thee;
  'Appen I can, if I try.
But tha'll ha'e ter promise ter be true ter me
  Till I die. . . .

X

Twenty pounds o' thy own tha hast, an' fifty pound ha'e I;
Thine shall go ter pay the woman, an' wi' my bit we'll buy
All as we s'll want for furniture when tha leaves this place;
An' we'll be married at th' registrar—now lift thy face.

Lift thy face an' look at me, man! canna ter look at me?
Sorry I am for this business, an' sorry if ever I've driven thee
To do such a thing; though it's a poor tale, it is, that I'm bound to say,
Afore I can ta'e thee I've got a widder o' forty-five ter pay!

Dunna thee think but what I've loved thee; I've loved thee too well.
An' 'deed an' I wish as this tale o' thine wor niver my tale to tell!
Deed an' I wish I c'd 'a' stood at th' altar wi' thee an' bin proud o' thee!
That I could 'a' bin first woman ter thee, as th'art first man ter me!

But we maun ma'e the best on't. So now rouse up an' look at me.
Look up an' say tha'rt sorry tha did it; say tha'rt sorry for me.
They'll turn thee out o' th' force, I doubt me; if they do, we can see
If my father can get thee a job on t'bank. Say tha'rt sorry, Timmy!

XI

Ay, I'm sorry, I'm sorry,
  But what o' that!
Ay, I'm sorry! Tha needa worry
  Nor fret thy fat.

I'm sorry for thee, I'm sorry f'r 'er,
  I'm sorry f'r us a'.
But what then? Tha wants me, does ter
  After a'?

Ah'n put my-sèn i' th' wrong, Liz,
  An' 'er as well.
An' tha'rt that right, tha knows; 'tis
  Other folks in hell.

Tha *art* so sure tha'rt right, Liz!
  That damned sure!
But 'ark thee 'ere, that widder woman
  's less graspin', if 'er's poor.

What 'er gen, 'er gen me
  Beout a thought.
'Er gen me summat; I shanna
  Say it wor nought.

I'm sorry for th' trouble, ay
  As comes on us a'.
But sorry for what I had? why
  I'm not, that's a'.

As for marryin', I shanna marry
  Neither on yer.
Ah've 'ad a' as I can carry
  From you an' from 'er.

So I s'll go an' leave yer,
  Both on yer,
I don't like yer, Liz, I want ter
  Get away from yer.

An' I don't really like 'er neither,
  Even though I've 'ad
More from 'er than from you; but either
  Of yer's too much for this lad.

Let me go! what's good o' talkin'?
  Let's a' ha' done.
Talk about love o' women!
  Ter me it's no fun.

I s'll say good-by, Liz, to yer,
  Yer too much i' th' right for me.
An wi' 'er somehow it isn't right.
  So good-by, an' let's let be!

AWARE

Slowly the moon is rising out of the ruddy haze,
Divesting herself of her golden shift, and so
Emerging white and exquisite; and I in amaze
See in the sky before me, a woman I did not know
I loved, but there she goes, and her beauty hurts my heart;
I follow her down the night, begging her not to depart.

KISSES IN THE TRAIN

I saw the midlands
  Revolve through her hair;
The fields of autumn
  Stretching bare,
And sheep on the pasture
  Tossed back in a scare.

And still as ever
  The world went round,
My mouth on her pulsing
  Neck was found,
And my breast to her beating
  Breast was bound.

But my heart at the center
  Of all, in a swound
Was still as a pivot,
  As all the ground
On its prowling orbit
  Shifted round.

And still in my nostrils
  The scent of her flesh,
And still my wet mouth
  Sought her afresh;
And still one pulse
  Through the world did thresh.

And the world all whirling
  Around in joy
Like the dance of a dervish
  Did destroy
My sense—and my reason
  Spun like a toy.

But firm at the center
  My heart was found;
Her own to my perfect
  Heart-beat bound,
Like a magnet's keeper
  Closing the round.

SPRING MORNING

Ah, through the open door
Is there an almond tree
Aflame with blossom!
    —Let us fight no more.

Among the pink and blue
Of the sky and the almond flowers
A sparrow flutters.
—We have come through.

It is really spring!—See
When he thinks himself alone
How he bullies the flowers.
—You and me

How happy we'll be!—See him,
He clouts the tufts of flowers
In his impudence.
—But, did you dream

It would be so bitter? Never mind
It is finished, the spring is here.
And we're going to be summer-happy
And summer-kind.

We have died, we have slain and been slain
We are not our old selves any more.
I feel new and eager
To start again.

It is gorgeous to live and forget.
And to feel quite new.
See the bird in the flowers?—he's making
A rare to-do!

He thinks the whole blue sky
Is much less than the bit of blue egg
He's got in his nest—we'll be happy
You and I, I and you.

With nothing to fight any more—
In each other, at least.
See, how gorgeous the world is
Outside the door!

TREES IN THE GARDEN

Ah in the thunder air
how still the trees are!

And the lime-tree, lovely and tall, every leaf silent
hardly looses even a last breath of perfume.

And the ghostly, creamy colored little tree of leaves
white, ivory white among the rambling greens,
how evanescent, variegated elder, she hesitates on the green grass
as if, in another moment, she would disappear
with all her grace of foam!

And the larch that is only a column, it goes up too tall to see:
and the balsam-pines that are blue with the gray-blue blueness of things from the sea,
and the young copper beech, its leaves red-rosy at the ends
how still they are together, they stand so still
in the thunder air, all strangers to one another
as the green grass glows upwards, strangers in the garden.

MORNING WORK

A gang of labourers on the piled wet timber
That shines blood-red beside the railway siding
Seem to be making out of the blue of the morning
Something faery and fine, the shuttles sliding,
The red-gold spools of their hands and faces shuttling
Hither and thither across the morn's crystalline frame
Of blue: trolls at the cave of ringing cerulean mining,
And laughing with work, living their work like a game.

SHIP OF DEATH

I sing of autumn and the falling fruit
and the long journey towards oblivion.

The apples falling like great drops of dew
to bruise themselves an exit from themselves.

Have you built your ship of death, oh, have you?
Build then your ship of death, for you will need it!

Can man his own quietus make
with a bare bodkin?

With daggers, bodkins, bullets, man can make
a bruise or break of exit for his life
but is that a quietus, oh tell me, is it quietus?

Quietus is the goal of the long journey
the longest journey towards oblivion.

Slips out the soul, invisible one, wrapped still
in the white shirt of the mind's experiences
and folded in the dark-red, unseen
mantle of the body's still mortal memories.

Frightened and alone, the soul slips out of the house
or is pushed out
to find himself on the crowded, arid margins of existence.

Oh, it is not so easy, I tell you it is not so easy
to set softly forth on the longest journey, the longest journey.

It is easy to be pushed out of the silvery city of the body
through any breach in the wall,
thrust out onto the grey grey beaches of shadow
the long marginal stretches of existence, crowded with lost souls
that intervene between our tower and the shaking sea of the beyond.

Oh build your ship of death, oh build it in time
and build it lovingly, and put it between the hands of your soul.

Once outside the gate of the walled silvery life of days
once outside, upon the grey marsh beaches, where lost souls moan
in millions, unable to depart
having no boat to launch upon the shaken, soundless
deepest and longest of seas,
once outside the gate
what will you do, if you have no ship of the soul?

Oh pity the dead that are dead, but cannot take
the journey, still they moan and beat
against the silvery adamant walls of this our exclusive existence.

They moan and beat, they gnash, they rage
they fall upon the new outcoming souls with rage
and they send arrows of anger, bullets and bombs of frustration
over the adamant walls of this, our by-no-means impregnable existence.

Pity, oh pity the poor dead that are only ousted from life
and crowd there on the grey mud beaches of the margins
gaunt and horrible
waiting, waiting till at last the ancient boatman with the common barge
shall take them abroad, towards the great goal of oblivion.

Pity the poor gaunt dead that cannot die
into the distance with receding oars
but must roam like outcast dogs on the margins of life,
and think of them, and with the soul's deep sigh
waft nearer to them the bark of delivery.

But for myself, but for my soul, dear soul
let me build a little ship with oars and food
and little dishes, and all accoutrements
dainty and ready for the departing soul.

And put it between the hands of the trembling soul.
So that when the hour comes, and the last door closes behind him
he shall slip down the shores invisible
between the half-visible hordes
to where the furthest and the longest sea
touches the margins of our life's existence
with wincing unwilling waves.

And launching there his little ship,
wrapped in the dark-red mantle of the body's memories
the little, slender soul sits swiftly down, and takes the oars
and draws away, away, away, towards the dark depths
fathomless deep ahead, far, far from the grey shores
that fringe with shadow all this world's existence.

Over the sea, over the farthest sea
on the longest journey
past the jutting rocks of shadow
past the lurking, octopus arms of agonised memory
past the strange whirlpools of remembered greed
through the dead weed of a life-time's falsity,
slow, slow my soul, in his little ship
on the most soundless of all seas
taking the longest journey.

Pulling the long oars of a life-time's courage,
drinking the confident water from the little jug
and eating the brave bread of a wholesome knowledge
row, little soul, row on
on the longest journey, towards the greatest goal

Neither straight nor crooked, neither here nor there
but shadows folded on deeper shadows
and deeper, to a core of sheer oblivion
like the convolutions of shadow-shell
or deeper, like the foldings and involvings of a womb.

Drift on, drift on, my soul, towards the most pure
most dark oblivion.
And at the penultimate porches, the dark-red mantle
of the body's memories slips and is absorbed
into the shell-like, womb-like convoluted shadow.

And round the great final bend of unbroken dark
the skirt of the spirit's experience has melted away
the oars have gone from the boat, and the little dishes
gone, gone, and the boat dissolves like pearl
as the soul at last slips perfect into the goal, the core
of sheer oblivion and of utter peace,
the womb of silence in the living night.

Ah peace, ah lovely peace, most lovely lapsing
of this my soul into the plasm of peace.

Oh lovely last, last lapse of death, into pure oblivion
at the end of the longest journey
peace, complete peace!
But can it be that also it is procreation?

Oh build your ship of death
oh, build it!
Oh, nothing matters but the longest journey.

Humbert Wolfe

☙§ Humbert Wolfe was born at Milan in Italy, January 5, 1885. As he himself declared, he "lost no time in crossing to Bradford in the West Riding of Yorkshire, which town he reached during the same year and remained there till he left it for Oxford some 18 years later. Wrote sporadic and increasingly unsatisfactory verse from the age of 16 till his appointment to the British Civil Service in 1909."

Before he was fifty Wolfe had published a score of books, all, with two exceptions, in verse. Their chief quality is neither the satire which Wolfe used so incisively nor the grace of which he was somewhat too fond, but a confusion of the two. The surface characteristics are modern, but modern only in certain tricks of typography and employment of "suspended" rhymes. There is, above all, a fancy that delights to improvise on major themes which somehow slide into minor cadences. It is this contradiction which marks even the most definite of his volumes, an indetermination from which Wolfe was unable to escape. It is as if the "pale musicianer" of whom he speaks had composed a robust theme—and arranged it as a pretty duet for dulcimer and *viola d'amore.*

Wolfe's two best volumes are the early *Kensington Gardens* (1924) and the larger *Requiem* (1927). In the first, the fantasies enchant with their delicacy. The squirrel "like a small gray coffee-pot," the half-metal tulip "clean as a lady, cool as glass," the city financier with his "table-land of shiny hat," the "flushed example" of the rose with her "dazzling inch of scent"—all these are seen and communicated in such a way that the reader enjoys the mingling of recognition and surprise. *Requiem* is the most reflective of all Wolfe's work and the nearest to a synthesis. This symphonic and almost fugual creation retains Wolfe's exactitude of epithet embodied in a graver music than he usually employed.

Homage to Meleager (1930) and *Others Abide* (1927) display Wolfe as the translator of many epigrams from the Greek, a task for which he was eminently capable. *X at Oberammergau* (1935) again attempts to construct a major poem upon minor effects. The theme is timely: the conflict between personal good and universal evil. The design is large: the Gospel narrative and a Passion Play translated to the present scene. Unfortunately Wolfe's treatment fails to meet the demands of his subject.

It was evident that Wolfe was overworked. He had been one of the most responsible and hard-pressed Civil Servants. He was made a Commander of the Order of the British Empire in 1918 and a Companion of the Bath in 1925. The Second World War added more burdens than he could bear. He died of a heart attack on his fifty-fifth birthday, January 5, 1940.

In his lifetime Wolfe was underpraised for the tart dissonances and light fancies which were natural to him, overpraised for the symphonic elaborations which were scarcely his forte. He made the mistake of going in for fragility on a large scale; he tried to build cosmic allegories on every whimsicality. He will, however, outlive many louder poets by virtue of his frail-spun, faintly acid lyrics.

THE GRAY SQUIRREL

Like a small gray
coffee-pot,
sits the squirrel.
He is not

all he should be,
kills by dozens
trees, and eats
his red-brown cousins.

The keeper, on the
other hand
, who shot him, is
a Christian, and

loves his enemies,
which shows
the squirrel was not
one of those.

GREEN CANDLES

"There's someone at the door," said gold candlestick:
"Let her in quick, let her in quick!"
"There is a small hand groping at the handle.
Why don't you turn it?" asked green candle.

"Don't go, don't go," said the Heppelwhite chair,
Lest you find a strange lady there."
Yes, stay where you are," whispered the white wall:
There is nobody there at all."

I know her little foot," gray carpet said:
Who but I should know her light tread?"
She shall come in," answered the open door,
And not," said the room, "go out any more."

TULIP

Clean as a lady,
cool as glass,
fresh without fragrance
the tulip was.

The craftsman, who carved her
of metal, prayed:
"Live, oh thou lovely!"
Half metal she stayed.

LOVE IS A KEEPER OF SWANS

Love is a keeper of swans!
Helen! amid what dark wherries
are you steering the silver boat,
that for all the love of Paris,
and his lips against your throat,
passed out of Troy with windless vans?

And, fairest of Italians,
where do you glimmer, Beatrice?
What light of heaven stains your wings
with gold that were all fleur de lys?
And do you hear when Dante sings?
"Love is a keeper of swans."

Love is a keeper of swans.
Have you left the barren plain,
and stormed a gold-eagle's eyrie?
Queen-swan of the eagle strain,
what mountain has you, Mary?
And is its name, as ever, still romance?

And you, bright cynet of immortal Hans,
you need not join your sisters yet.
You have all time. Why should you hasten?
What though the lake with reeds be set,
one reed is murmuring, oh, listen!
"Love is a keeper of swans."

MAN

The feathers in a fan
are not so frail as man;
the green embossèd leaf
than man is no more brief.
His life is not so loud
as the passing of a cloud;
his death is quieter
than harebells when they stir.
The years that have no form
and substance are as warm,
and space has hardly less
supreme an emptiness.
And yet man being frail
does on himself prevail,

and with a single thought
can bring the world to naught,
as being brief he still
bends to his fleeting will
all time and makes of it
the shadow of his wit.
Soundles in life and death
although he vanisheth,
the echo of a song
makes all the stars a gong.
Cold, void, and yet the grim
darkness is hot with him,
and space is but the span
of the long love of man.

THE WATERS OF LIFE

When, hardly moving, you decorate night's hush
with the slim pencil of your grace, retrieving
the clean flat stroke of some old Grecian brush
that painted dancers fair beyond believing;

when, leaning back the harvest of your hair
under the moon with beauty as still as hers,
your body's wonder writes upon the air
the perfect cadence of consummate verse,

I think, if this upon the air be shaken,
brief as a falling blossom, it can but be
that Time records, by beauty overtaken,
in one gold instant, immortality,

and that the patterns you weave upon the night
have such swift passion, such essential heat,
that all the painter sees, the poet can write,
are but pale shadows of your dancing feet.

THIS IS NOT DEATH

Lay aside phrases; speak as in the night
a child in terror might.
Confess that you are lonely, that you heard
some foot or hand that stirred,
that, holding your own breath, you almost hear
the midnight breath of Fear,
that tearless, soundless in your heart you pray:
"God! give me back the day!"
Yes! God can give it back, but not the one
that you have dreamed upon.
The black will turn to gray, the gray to blue
distance, but not for you,
and not for you the cheerful voice of men
will warm the heart again.
Nor will your friends or enemies intrude
upon that solitude
where only shadows drift and cross and pass,
seen sideways in your glass.

Make not complaint. For neither prayer nor tear
has its old power here.
This is not silence rounded by the deep
deliverance of sleep,
but by the empty spaces where the will
to wake again is still.
You chose, and you abide the choice, apart,
saying to your own heart:
"Beat if you must, though softly," to the brain:
"Must you imagine pain?"
And last of all say to the sobbing breath:
"No, fool, this is not death."

ILIAD

False dreams, all false,
mad heart, were yours.
The word, and nought else,
in time endures.
Not you long after,
perished and mute,
will last, but the defter
viol and lute.
Sweetly they'll trouble
the listeners
with the cold dropped pebble
of painless verse.
Not you will be offered,
but the poet's false pain.
You have loved and suffered,
mad heart, in vain.
What love doth Helen
or Paris have
where they lie still in
a nameless grave?
Her beauty's a wraith,
and the boy Paris
muffles in death
his mouth's cold cherries.
Yes! these are less,
that were love's summer,
than one gold phrase
of old blind Homer.
Not Helen's wonder
nor Paris stirs,
but the bright, untender
hexameters.
And thus, all passion
is nothing made,
but a star to flash in
an Iliad.
Mad heart, you were wrong!
No love of yours,
but only what's sung,
when love's over, endures.

Frances Cornford

⇜§ Frances (Darwin) Cornford, daughter of Sir Francis Darwin, the third son of Charles Darwin, was born in 1886 at Cambridge. She married Francis Macdonald Cornford, Fellow and Lecturer of Trinty College, Cambridge, in 1909.

Her first volume, *Poems* (1910), though unaffected, showed little trace of individuality. With *Spring Morning* (1915) a much more distinct personality expressed itself. Hers is a firmly realized, clean-edged verse, with a clarity of utterance which is also found in the more suggestive *Autumn Midnight* (1923). Her later verse in *Different Days* (1928) is no less spontaneous than the simple "A Wasted Day," the acute and onomatopoetic "The Watch," and the delightfully teasing triolet "To a Fat Lady Seen from the Train." It is, however, more measured; gravity has been added without the loss of charm. Whether grave or mocking Mrs. Cornford's tone maintains a quiet distinction.

In *Mountains and Molehills* (1935), with distinctive woodcuts by Gwen Raverat, Mrs. Cornford continues to write of the English countryside with a quaint difference, of thoughts in a night nursery, of a back view particular yet universal, of Cambridge autumns, of madmen and fairies—a seemingly heterogeneous set of variations on traditional themes. A modest but distinctive *Collected Poems* was published in 1954.

THE COUNTRY BEDROOM

My room's a square and candle-lighted boat,
In the surrounding depths of night afloat.
My windows are the portholes, and the seas
The sound of rain on the dark apple-trees.

Sea-monster-like beneath, an old horse blows
A snort of darkness from his sleeping nose,
Below, among drowned daisies. Far off, hark!
Far off, one owl amidst the waves of dark.

TO A FAT LADY SEEN FROM THE TRAIN

O why do you walk through the fields in gloves,
  Missing so much and so much?
O fat white woman whom nobody loves,
Why do you walk through the fields in gloves,
When the grass is soft as the breast of doves
  And shivering sweet to the touch?
O why do you walk through the fields in gloves,
  Missing so much and so much?

THE WATCH

I wakened on my hot, hard bed;
Upon the pillow lay my head;
Beneath the pillow I could hear
My little watch was ticking clear.
I thought the throbbing of it went
Like my continual discontent;
I thought it said in every tick:
I am so sick, so sick, so sick:
O death, come quick, come quick, come quick,
Come quick, come quick, come quick, come quick. . . .

A WASTED DAY

I spoiled the day;
  Hotly, in haste

All the calm hours
  I gashed and defaced.

Let me forget,
  Let me embark
—Sleep for my boat—
  And sail through the dark.

Till a new day
  Heaven shall send,
Whole as an apple,
  Kind as a friend.

AT NIGHT

My brain is like the ravaged shores—the sand
Torn cruelly by footsteps from the land.
O hushing waves; O profound sea of sleep,
Send your curved ripples surely-lapping. Creep,
Pour on the scarrèd surface of my brain;
With your vast pity, wash it smooth again.

THE UNBESEECHABLE

(*To be set to music*)

"Time stands still
  With gazing on her face,"
Sang Dowland to his lute,
  Full of courtly grace.

Now that his musician's face
  And her face are dust,
Still I cry, Stand still:
  Still cry I must.

Stand still, Time,
  Hold, hold your pace;
Stiller stand than the smile
  On Pharaoh's face.

Stiller than December's frost
  That takes the heart with wonder,
Or the pause that comes between
  Lightning and thunder.

Time, stand still,
  Hush now your tread,
Stiller, stiller than a room
  Where lies the sheeted dead.

Where, though it's busy noon,
  Naught comes or goes;
Where the tree of endless peace
  To the ceiling grows.

O Time, Time—
  Stark and full of pain
Why drag me into space,
  A dog upon a chain?

I who would float with you,
  A ship sailing white,
Who cannot tell which power is hers
  And which the wind's delight.

So my refreshèd soul
  Time would adore,
If for one moment's breath
  Time were no more.

But, with Dowland's broken lute
  And his forgotten rhyme,
Still I cry, Stand still,
  Stand still, Time.

THE HILLS

Out of the complicated house, come I
To walk beneath the sky.
Here mud and stones and turf, here everything
Is mutely comforting.
Now hung upon the twigs and thorns appear
A host of lovely rain-drops cold and clear.
And on the bank
Or deep in brambly hedges dank
The small birds nip about, and say:
"Brothers, the Spring is not so far away!"
The hills like mother-giantesses old
Lie in the cold,
And with a complete patience, let
The cows come cropping on their bosoms wet,
And even tolerate that such as I
Should wander by
With paltry leathern heel which cannot harm
Their bodies' calm;
And, with a heart they cannot know, to bless
The enormous power of their peacefulness.

Siegfried Sassoon

Siegfried (Loraine) Sassoon was born September 8, 1886. He was educated at Marlborough and Clare College, Cambridge, and, during the War, was a captain in the Royal Welsh Fusiliers. He fought in France and Palestine; he won the Military Cross for bringing in wounded on the battlefield.

Sassoon's literary development seems as contradictory as it is curious. Descended from Persian Jews on his father's side, from a traditional English country family on his mother's, Sassoon's boyhood was spent alternating between fox and rhyme hunting. He was divided between a love of rugged activity and a fondness for pale, Dowsonesque lyrics. Several volumes ranging from parody to the verge of preciosity were issued anonymously and privately printed. The earliest book, *Poems* (1906), was published in Sassoon's twentieth year and is, according to its author, "mostly weak imitations of Tennyson, Swinburne, and Rossetti." A sense of their unreality drove him to larger work, *The Daffodil Murderer* (1913), a poem which, beginning as a burlesque of Masefield, ended in serious self-expression.

By this time the poet had chaffed himself out of his juvenile admirations for Stephen Phillips and the Pre-Raphaelites, and strong feeling demanded a powerful expression. The war compelled it. With *The Old Huntsman* (1917) Sassoon came into his own idiom, taking his place immediately as "one of England's most brilliant rising stars." The first poem, a pseudo-Masefieldian monologue, was followed by a series of war poems, undisguised in their reality and bitterness. Every line of these quivering stanzas bore the mark of a sensitive and outraged nature; there was scarcely a phrase that did not protest against the "glorification" and false glamor of war.

Counter-Attack appeared in 1918. In this volume, Sassoon turned from ordered loveliness to the gigantic brutality of war. At heart a lyric idealist, the bloody years intensified and twisted his tenderness till what was subborn and satiric in him forced its way to the top. In *Counter-Attack* Sassoon found his angry outlet. Most of these poems are choked with passion; many of them are torn out, roots and all, from the very core of an intense conviction. They rush on, not so much because of the poet's art but almost in spite of it. A suave utterance, a neatly-joined structure would be out of place and even inexcusable in such verses as the title-poem, "The Rear-Guard," "Base Details," "Does It Matter?"—verses that are composed of love and indignation. "Let no one ever," Robert Nichols in his preface quotes Sassoon as saying, "from henceforth say one word in any way countenancing war. It is dangerous even to speak of how here and there the individual may gain some hardship of soul by it. For war is hell, and those who institute it are criminals. Were there even anything to say for it, it should not be said; for its spiritual disasters far outweigh any of its advantages. . . ." Nichols adds his approval to these sentences, saying, "For myself, this is the truth. War does not ennoble, it degrades."

Early in 1920, Sassoon visited America. At the same time, he brought out his *Picture Show* (1920), a vigorous answer to those who feared that Sassoon had "written himself out" or had begun to burn away in his own fire. Had Rupert

Brooke lived, he might have written many of these lacerated but somehow exalted lines. "The Dug-Out" and "Everyone Sang" are splendid examples of how much poignance and (in the latter) winged joy can be held in less than a dozen lines. Sassoon's three volumes are the most vital and unsparing records of the war we have had. They synthesize in poetry what Barbusse's *Under Fire* and Remarque's *All Quiet on the Western Front* spread out in panoramic prose or Sheriff's *Journey's End* compacted in his stripped tragedy.

Recreations, a privately distributed volume, printed at Christmas, 1923, for his friends, shows Sassoon in a more playfully intellectual vein. Another, even more strictly limited publication, *Lingual Exercises for Advanced Vocabularians,* was issued in 1925. Most of the contents of the two volumes appeared in *Satirical Poems* (1926). Less direct than his deeper notes, these poems display another interesting though not so compelling aspect of Sassoon's genius. *Poems of Pinchbeck Lyre* (1931), issued anonymously, is a revival of Sassoon's talent for parody; this small but bitter collection is a set of diabolical burlesques of Humbert Wolfe.

The Heart's Journey (1928) and *Vigils* (1935) represent a further maturing. They seem the work of another poet, but it is the essential Sassoon. Here is the distillation of the post-war years, of silence and sorrow, of long conflict and final unity. Here are the visionary ideals of youth sharpened and purified through pain; here is bitter knowledge saved from bitterness by the spirit of faith; here, in short, Sassoon's Songs of Innocence are mingled with his Songs of Experience. This spiritual autobiography reveals the old fire, but a fire subdued. It has dignity, a gentle ecstasy which places it in the line of great religious poetry. With almost monosyllabic simplicity of word and music, Sassoon shares the power of the mystic; he achieves a sense of identification with all things—be they inanimate objects like a lamp or a book, intangible concepts like music, or his fellowmen, living or dead—fusing every element in a rapt and universal love.

Memoirs of a Fox-Hunting Man (1928), first published anonymously, was awarded the two most coveted literary prizes in England: the Hawthornden Prize and the James Tait Black Memorial Prize in 1929. *Memoirs of an Infantry Officer,* its sequel, appeared in 1930.

Sherston's Progress (1936) and *The Old Century and Seven More Years* (1938) are further explorations in autobiography. *Rhymed Ruminations* (1941) was followed by a comprehensive *Collected Poems* (1949). *The Path to Peace* (1961) marks Sassoon's conversion to the Roman Catholic Church in his seventy-first year.

DREAMERS

Soldiers are citizens of death's gray land,
  Drawing no dividend from time's tomorrows.
In the great hour of destiny they stand,
  Each with his feuds, and jealousies, and sorrows.
Soldiers are sworn to action; they must win
  Some flaming, fatal climax with their lives.
Soldiers are dreamers; when the guns begin
  They think of firelit homes, clean beds, and wives.

I see them in foul dug-outs, gnawed by rats,
  And in the ruined trenches, lashed with rain,

Dreaming of things they did with balls and bats,
  And mocked by hopeless longing to regain
Bank-holidays, and picture shows, and spats,
  And going to the office in the train.

THE REAR-GUARD

Groping along the tunnel, step by step,
He winked his prying torch with patching glare
From side to side, and sniffed the unwholesome air.

Tins, boxes, bottles, shapes too vague to know,
A mirror smashed, the mattress from a bed;
And he, exploring fifty feet below
The rosy gloom of battle overhead.
Tripping, he grabbed the wall; saw someone lie
Humped at his feet, half-hidden by a rug,
And stooped to give the sleeper's arm a tug.
"I'm looking for headquarters." No reply.
"God blast your neck!" (For days he'd had no sleep.)
"Get up and guide me through this stinking place."
Savage, he kicked a soft, unanswering heap,
And flashed his beam across the livid face
Terribly glaring up, whose eyes yet wore
Agony dying hard ten days before;
And fists of fingers clutched a blackening wound.
Alone he staggered on until he found
Dawn's ghost that filtered down a shafted stair
To the dazed, muttering creatures underground
Who hear the boom of shells in muffled sound.
At last, with sweat of horror in his hair,
He climbed through darkness to the twilight air,
Unloading hell behind him step by step.

BASE DETAILS

If I were fierce and bald and short of breath,
  I'd live with scarlet Majors at the Base,
And speed glum heroes up the line to death.
  You'd see me with my puffy petulant face,
Guzzling and gulping in the best hotel,
  Reading the Roll of Honor. "Poor young chap,"
I'd say—"I used to know his father well.
  Yes, we've lost heavily in this last scrap."
And when the war is done and youth stone dead,
I'd toddle safely home and die—in bed.

ATTACK

At dawn the ridge emerges massed and dun
In the wild purple of the glowering sun

Smoldering through spouts of drifting smoke that shroud
The menacing scarred slope; and, one by one,
Tanks creep and topple forward to the wire.
The barrage roars and lifts. Then, clumsily bowed
With bombs and guns and shovels and battle-gear,
Men jostle and climb to meet the bristling fire.
Lines of gray, muttering faces, masked with fear,
They leave their trenches, going over the top,
While time ticks blank and busy on their wrists,
And hope, with furtive eyes and grappling fists,
Flounders in mud. O Jesu, make it stop!

COUNTER-ATTACK

We'd gained our first objective hours before
While dawn broke like a face with blinking eyes,
Pallid, unshaved and thirsty, blind with smoke.
Things seemed all right at first. We held their line,
With bombers posted, Lewis guns well placed,
And clink of shovels deepening the shallow trench.
The place was rotten with dead; green clumsy legs
High-booted, sprawled and groveled along the saps;
And trunks, face downward in the sucking mud,
Wallowed like trodden sand-bags, loosely filled;
And naked, sodden buttocks, mats of hair,
Bulged, clotted heads, slept in the plastering slime.
And then the rain began—the jolly old rain!

A yawning soldier knelt against the bank,
Staring across the morning blear with fog;
He wondered when the Allemands would get busy;
And then, of course, they started with five-nines
Traversing, sure as fate, and never a dud.
Mute in the clamor of shells he watched them burst
Spouting dark earth and wire with gusts from hell,
While posturing giants dissolved in drifts of smoke.
He crouched and flinched, dizzy with galloping fear,
Sick for escape,—loathing the strangled horror
And butchered, frantic gestures of the dead.

An officer came blundering down the trench:
"Stand-to and man the fire-step!" On he went. . . .
Gasping and bawling, "Fire-step . . . counter-attack!"
Then the haze lifted. Bombing on the right
Down the old sap: machine guns on the left;
And stumbling figures looming out in front.
"O Christ, they're coming at us!" Bullets spat,
And he remembered his rifle . . . rapid fire . . .
And started blazing wildly . . . then a bang
Crumpled and spun him sideways, knocked him out
To grunt and wriggle: none heeded him: he choked

And fought the flapping veils of smothering gloom,
Lost in a blurred confusion of yells and groans . . .
Down, and down, and down, he sank and drowned,
Bleeding to death. The counter-attack had failed.

DOES IT MATTER?

Does it matter?—losing your legs? . . .
For people will always be kind,
And you need not show that you mind
When the others come in after hunting
To gobble their muffins and eggs.

Does it matter?—losing your sight? . . .
There's such splendid work for the blind;
And people will always be kind,
As you sit on the terrace remembering
And turning your face to the light.

Do they matter?—those dreams from the pit? . . .
You can drink and forget and be glad,
And people won't say that you're mad;
For they'll know that you've fought for your country,
And no one will worry a bit.

THE DUG-OUT

Why do you lie with your legs ungainly huddled,
And one arm bent across your sullen, cold,
Exhausted face? It hurts my heart to watch you,
Deep-shadowed from the candle's guttering gold;
And you wonder why I shake you by the shoulder;
Drowsy, you mumble and sigh and turn your head. . . .
You are too young to fall asleep for ever;
And when you sleep you remind me of the dead.

INVOCATION

Come down from heaven to meet me when my breath
Chokes, and through drumming shafts of stifling death
I stumble toward escape, to find the door
Opening on morn where I may breathe once more
Clear cock-crow airs across some valley dim
With whispering trees. While dawn along the rim
Of night's horizon flows in lakes of fire,
Come down from heaven's bright hill, my song's desire.

Belov'd and faithful, teach my soul to wake
In glades deep-ranked with flowers that gleam and shake

And flock your paths with wonder. In your gaze
Show me the vanquished vigil of my days.
Mute in that golden silence hung with green,
Come down from heaven and bring me in your eyes
Remembrance of all beauty that has been,
And stillness from the pools of Paradise.

AFTERMATH

Have you forgotten yet? . . .
For the world's events have rumbled on since those gagged days,
Like traffic checked a while at the crossing of city ways:
And the haunted gap in your mind has filled with thoughts that flow
Like clouds in the lit heavens of life; and you're a man reprieved to go,
Taking your peaceful share of Time, with joy to spare.
But the past is just the same,—and War's a bloody game. . . .
Have you forgotten yet? . . .
Look down, and swear by the slain of the War that you'll never forget.

Do you remember the dark months you held the sector at Mametz,—
The nights you watched and wired and dug and piled sand-bags on parapets?
Do you remember the rats; and the stench
Of corpses rotting in front of the front-line trench,—
And dawn coming, dirty-white, and chill with a hopeless rain?
Do you ever stop and ask, "Is it all going to happen again?"

Do you remember that hour of din before the attack,—
And the anger, the blind compassion that seized and shook you then
As you peered at the doomed and haggard faces of your men?
Do you remember the stretcher-cases lurching back
With dying eyes and lolling heads, those ashen-gray
Masks of the lads who once were keen and kind and gay?

Have you forgotten yet? . . .
Look up, and swear by the slain of the War that you'll never forget!

EVERYONE SANG

Everyone suddenly burst out singing;
And I was filled with such delight
As prisoned birds must find in freedom
Winging wildly across the white
Orchards and dark green fields; on; on;
  and out of sight.

Everyone's voice was suddenly lifted,
And beauty came like the setting sun.
My heart was shaken with tears, and horror
Drifted away. . . . O, but everyone

Was a bird; and the song was wordless; the
singing will never be done.

FALLING ASLEEP

Voices moving about in the quiet house:
Thud of feet and a muffled shutting of doors:
Everyone yawning. Only the clocks are alert.

Out in the night there's autumn-smelling gloom
Crowded with whispering trees; across the park
A hollow cry of hounds like lonely bells:
And I know that the clouds are moving across the moon;
The low, red, rising moon. Now herons call
And wrangle by their pool; and hooting owls
Sail from the wood above pale stooks of oats.

Waiting for sleep, I drift from thoughts like these;
And where today was dream-like, build my dreams.
Music . . . there was a bright white room below,
And someone singing a song about a soldier,
One hour, two hours ago: and soon the song
Will be *"last night":* but now the beauty swings
Across my brain, ghost of remembered chords
Which still can make such radiance in my dream
That I can watch the marching of my soldiers,
And count their faces; faces; sunlit faces.

Falling asleep . . . the herons, and the hounds. . . .
September in the darkness; and the world
I've known; all fading past me into peace.

THE WISDOM OF THE WORLD

The wisdom of the world is this; to say, *"There is
No other wisdom but to gulp what time can give"* . . .
To guard no inward vision winged with mysteries;
To hear no voices haunt the hurrying hours we live;
To keep no faith with ghostly friends; never to know
Vigils of sorrow crowned when loveless passions fade . . .
From wisdom such as this to find my gloom I go,
Companioned by those powers who keep me unafraid.

EVERYMAN

The weariness of life that has no will
To climb the steepening hill:
The sickness of the soul for sleep, and to be still.

And then once more the impassioned pygmy fist
Clenched cloudward and defiant;

The pride that would prevail, the doomed protagonist,
Grappling the ghostly giant.

Victim and venturer, turn by turn; and then
Set free to be again
Companion in repose with those who once were men.

CONCLUSION

An image dance of change
Throngs my dim-sighted flesh,
To music's air-built mesh
Move thoughts forever strange.
I am so woven of sense
And subtlety uncharted
That I must vanish hence
Blind-souled and twilight-hearted.

Soon death the hooded lover
Shall touch my house of clay,
And life-lit eyes discover
That in the warbling gray
I have been early waking,
And while the dawn was breaking
Have stolen afield to find
That secrecy which quivers
Beyond the skies and rivers
And cities of the mind.

Till then my thought shall strive
That living I may not lose
The wonder of being alive,
Nor Time's least gift refuse.
For, though the end be night,
This wonder and this white
Astonishment of sight
Make hours of magic shine;
And heaven's a blaze and bloom
Of transience and divine
Inheritance of doom.

PREHISTORIC BURIALS

These barrows of the century-darkened dead,—
Memorials of oblivion, these turfed tombs
Of muttering ancestries whose fires, once red,
Now burn for me beyond mysterious glooms,
I pass them, day by day, while daylight fills
My sense of sight on these time-haunted hills.

Could I but see those burials that began
Whole History,—flint and bronze and iron beginnings,—
When under the wide Wiltshire sky, crude man
Warred with his world and augured our world-winnings!
Could I but enter that unholpen brain,
Cabined and comfortless and insecure,
Ruling some settlement on Salisbury Plain
And offering blood to blind primeval powers,—
Dim Caliban whose doom was to endure
Earth's ignorant nullity made strange with flowers.

LIMITATIONS

If you could crowd them into forty lines!
Yes; you can do it once you get a start:
All that you want is waiting in your head,
For long ago you've learnt it off by heart.

Begin: your mind's the room where you have slept,
(Don't pause for rhymes), till twilight woke you early.
The window stands wide-open, as it stood
When tree-tops loomed enchanted for a child
Hearing the dawn's first thrushes through the wood
Warbling (you know the words) serene and wild.

You've said it all before: you dreamed of Death,
A dim Apollo in the bird-voiced breeze
That drifts across the morning veiled with showers,
While golden weather shines among dark trees.

You've got your limitations; let them sing,
And all your life will waken with a cry:
Why should you halt when rapture's on the wing
And you've no limit but the cloud-flocked sky? . . .

But some chap shouts, "Here, stop it; that's been done!"
As God might holloa to the rising sun,
And then relent, because the glorying rays
Remind Him of green-glinting Eden days,
And Adam's trustful eyes as he looks up
From carving eagles on his beechwood cup.

Young Adam knew his job; he could condense
Life to an eagle from the unknown immense. . . .
Go on, whoever you are, your lines can be
A whisper in the music from the weirs
Of song that plunge and tumble toward the sea
That is the uncharted mercy of our tears.

*

I told you it was easy! . . . Words are fools
Who follow blindly, once they get a lead.
But thoughts are kingfishers that haunt the pools
Of quiet; seldom-seen: and all you need
Is just that flash of joy above your dream.
So, when those forty platitudes are done,
You'll hear a bird-note calling from the stream
That wandered through your childhood; and the sun
Will strike old flaming wonder from the waters. . . .
And there'll be forty lines not yet begun.

GRANDEUR OF GHOSTS

When I have heard small talk about great men
I climb to bed; light my two candles; then
Consider what was said; and put aside
What Such-a-one remarked and Someone-else replied.

They have spoken lightly of my deathless friends,
(Lamps for my gloom, hands guiding where I stumble,)
Quoting, for shallow conversational ends,
What Shelley shrilled, what Blake once wildly muttered. . . .

How can they use such names and not be humble?
I have sat silent; angry at what they uttered.
The dead bequeathed them life; the dead have said
What these can only memorize and mumble.

ALONE

"*When I'm alone*"—the words tripped off his tongue
As though to be alone were nothing strange.
"*When I was young,*" he said; "*when I was young. . . .*"

I thought of age, and loneliness, and change.
I thought how strange we grow when we're alone,
And how unlike the selves that meet and talk,
And blow the candles out, and say good night.
Alone. . . . The word is life endured and known.
It is the stillness where our spirits walk
And all but inmost faith is overthrown.

PRESENCES PERFECTED

I looked on that prophetic land
Where, manifested by their powers,
Presences perfected stand
Whom night and day no more command
With shine and shadow of earthly hours.

I saw them. Numberless they stood
Half-way toward heaven, that men might mark
The grandeur of their ghostlihood
Burning divinely on the dark.

Names had they none. Through spirit alone
They triumphed, the makers of mankind,
Whose robes like flames were round them blown
By winds which raved from the unknown
Erebus of earth's ancestral mind.

ELECTED SILENCE

Where voices vanish into dream,
I have discovered, from the pride
Of temporal trophydoms, this theme,
That silence is the ultimate guide.

Allow me now much musing-space
  To shape my secrecies alone:
Allow me life apart, whose heart
  Translates instinctive tragi-tone.

How solitude can hear! O see
  How stillness unreluctant stands
Enharmonized with cloud and tree . . .
  O earth and heaven not made with hands!

Rupert Brooke

Possibly the most famous of the younger Georgians, Rupert Brooke was born at Rugby, August 3, 1887, where his father was assistant master at the school. As a youth, Brooke was fastidious, finicky in dress, but keenly interested in athletics; he played cricket, football, and tennis, and swam as well as most professionals. He was six feet tall, his finely molded head topped with a crown of loose hair of lively brown: "a golden young Apollo," said Edward Thomas. Another friend wrote, "To look at, he was part of the youth of the world." His beauty encouraged a naturally romantic disposition; his poems are a blend of delight in the splendor of actuality and disillusion in a loveliness that dies. The shadow of John Donne lies over many of his early and more than a few of his later pages, while the accent of Housman (*vide* "The Chilterns") prompts the conversational tone which Brooke adopted, extended, and popularized.

At first Brooke affected a tired sophistication not uncommon to the young poet of the times. However, the bored cynicisms, the fashionable ennuis were purged, when after several years of travel (he had been to Germany, Italy and Honolulu) the War came, turning Brooke away from

"A world grown old and cold and weary . . .
And half men, and their dirty songs and dreary,
And all the little emptiness of love."

Brooke enlisted with a relief that was like a rebirth; he sought new energy in the struggle "where the worst friend and enemy is but Death." After seeing service in Belgium, 1914, he spent the following winter in a training-camp in Dorsetshire and sailed with the British Mediterranean Expeditionary Force in February, 1915, to take part in the unfortunate Dardanelles Campaign.

Brooke never reached his destination. He died of blood-poison at Skyros in the Aegean, April 23, 1915. His early death was one of England's great literary losses; Lascelles Abercrombie, W. W. Gibson (with both of whom he had been associated on the quarterly, *New Numbers*), Walter De la Mare, Winston Spencer Churchill, and a host of others united to pay tribute to the most brilliant and passionate of the younger poets.

Brooke's sonnet-sequence, *1914* (from which "The Soldier" is taken), appeared with prophetic irony, a few weeks before his death. It contains the accents of immortality. "The Old Vicarage, Grantchester," "Heaven" and "Fish" are characteristic of the lighter and more playful side of Brooke's temperament. The metaphysician, not yet free of Donne, speaks in the mingled fancy and philosophy of "Dining-Room Tea," in several of the sonnets, and "Second Best." Both phases are combined in "The Great Lover," of which Abercrombie has written, "It is life he loves, and not in any abstract sense, but all the infinite little familiar details of life, remembered and catalogued with delightful zest."

Brooke published only two volumes during his lifetime. After his death, both volumes, with several posthumous poems, were issued as *Collected Poems of Rupert Brooke,* with a Memoir, in 1915. With a few exceptions, when Brooke yielded to the merely clever, his poetry is alert with the sparkle of his personality. It is the self-aware, self-examining mind that rules his emotions; his verse is a triumph of the intellectual imagination. "The theme of his poetry," says Walter De la Mare, "is the life of the mind, the senses, the feelings—life here and now. . . . His world stands out sharp and distinct, like the towers and pinnacles of a city under the light of a sunny sky." Brooke's delight was not in the shadows of revery and meditation, but in the swift play of ideas, in energetic action and reaction.

Thus Brooke was as thorough in his inconsistencies as in his sincerities. Impulse was his god—and his goad. He worshipped glamor and turned from it in revulsion, in a kind of sea- and beauty-sickness; he celebrated (in "Dust") the immortality of love and (in "Kindliness" and the sonnet already quoted) ridiculed its empty impermanence; turned from the intellect to sheer imagination—and abandoned fantasy for an ordered philosophy. His later work indicates that Brooke had tired of shifting extremes. It is impossible to predict what integration might have come with maturity. He was dead at twenty-seven.

THE GREAT LOVER

I have been so great a lover: filled my days
So proudly with the splendor of Love's praise,
The pain, the calm, and the astonishment,
Desire illimitable, and still content,
And all dear names men use, to cheat despair,
For the perplexed and viewless streams that bear
Our hearts at random down the dark of life.
Now, ere the unthinking silence on that strife
Steals down, I would cheat drowsy Death so far,
My night shall be remembered for a star
That outshone all the suns of all men's days.
Shall I not crown them with immortal praise
Whom I have loved, who have given me, dared with me
High secrets, and in darkness knelt to see
The inenarrable godhead of delight?
Love is a flame:—we have beaconed the world's night.
A city:—and we have built it, these and I.
An emperor:—we have taught the world to die.
So, for their sakes I loved, ere I go hence,
And the high cause of Love's magnificence,

And to keep loyalties young, I'll write those names
Golden for ever, eagles, crying flames,
And set them as a banner, that men may know,
To dare the generations, burn, and blow
Out on the wind of Time, shining and streaming. . . .

These I have loved:
White plates and cups, clean-gleaming,
Ringed with blue lines; and feathery, faëry dust;
Wet roofs, beneath the lamp-light; the strong crust
Of friendly bread; and many-tasting food;
Rainbows; and the blue bitter smoke of wood;
And radiant raindrops couching in cool flowers;
And flowers themselves, that sway through sunny hours;
Dreaming of moths that drink them under the moon;
Then, the cool kindliness of sheets, that soon
Smooth away trouble; and the rough male kiss
Of blankets; grainy wood; live hair that is
Shining and free; blue-massing clouds; the keen
Unpassioned beauty of a great machine;
The benison of hot water; furs to touch;
The good smell of old clothes; and other such—
The comfortable smell of friendly fingers,
Hair's fragrance, and the musty reek that lingers
About dead leaves and last year's ferns. . . .
Dear names,
And thousand others throng to me! Royal flames;
Sweet water's dimpling laugh from tap or spring;
Holes in the ground; and voices that do sing:
Voices in laughter, too; and body's pain,
Soon turned to peace; and the deep-panting train;
Firm sands; the little dulling edge of foam
That browns and dwindles as the wave goes home;
And washen stones, gay for an hour; the cold
Graveness of iron; moist black earthen mold;
Sleep; and high places; footprints in the dew;
And oaks; and brown horse-chestnuts, glossy-new;
And new-peeled sticks; and shining pools on grass;—
All these have been my loves. And these shall pass,
Whatever passes not, in the great hour,
Nor all my passion, all my prayers, have power
To hold them with me through the gate of Death.
They'll play deserter, turn with the traitor breath,
Break the high bond we made, and sell Love's trust
And sacramental covenant to the dust.
—Oh, never a doubt but, somewhere, I shall wake,
And give what's left of love again, and make
New friends now strangers. . . .
But the best I've known
Stays here, and changes, breaks, grows old, is blown

About the winds of the world, and fades from brains
Of living men, and dies.
Nothing remains.
O dear my loves, O faithless, once again
This one last gift I give: that after men
Shall know, and later lovers, far-removed
Praise you, "All these were lovely"; say, "He loved."

THE CHILTERNS

Your hands, my dear, adorable,
Your lips of tenderness
—Oh, I've loved you faithfully and well,
Three years, or a bit less.
It wasn't a success.

Thank God, that's done! and I'll take the road,
Quit of my youth and you,
The Roman road to Wendover
By Tring and Lilley Hoo,
As a free man may do.

For youth goes over, the joys that fly,
The tears that follow fast;
And the dirtiest things we do must lie
Forgotten at the last;
Even love goes past.

What's left behind I shall not find,
The splendor and the pain;
The splash of sun, the shouting wind,
And the brave sting of rain,
I may not meet again.

But the years, that take the best away,
Give something in the end;
And a better friend than love have they,
For none to mar or mend,
That have themselves to friend.

I shall desire and I shall find
The best of my desires;
The autumn road, the mellow wind
That soothes the darkening shires.
And laughter, and inn-fires.

White mist about the black hedgerows,
The slumbering Midland plain,
The silence where the clover grows,
And the dead leaves in the lane,
Certainly, these remain.

And I shall find some girl perhaps,
And a better one than you,
With eyes as wise, but kindlier,
And lips as soft, but true.
And I daresay she will do.

THE HILL

Breathless, we flung us on the windy hill,
Laughed in the sun, and kissed the lovely grass.
You said, "Through glory and ecstasy we pass;
Wind, sun, and earth remain, the birds sing still,
When we are old, are old. . . ." And when we die
All's over that is ours; and life burns on
Through other lovers, other lips," said I,
"Heart of my heart, our heaven is now, is won!"
"We are Earth's best, that learnt her lesson here.
Life is our cry. We have kept the faith!" we said;
"We shall go down with unreluctant tread
Rose-crowned into the darkness! . . ." Proud we were,
And laughed, that had such brave true things to say.
And then you suddenly cried, and turned away.

DUST

Vhen the white flame in us is gone,
And we that lost the world's delight
Stiffen in darkness, left alone
To crumble in our separate night;

Vhen your swift hair is quiet in death,
And through the lips corruption thrust
Ias stilled the labor of my breath—
When we are dust, when we are dust!—

Not dead, not undesirous yet,
Still sentient, still unsatisfied,
Ve'll ride the air, and shine and flit,
Around the places where we died,

nd dance as dust before the sun,
And light of foot, and unconfined,
Iurry from road to road, and run
About the errands of the wind.

nd every mote, on earth or air,
Will speed and gleam down later days,
nd like a secret pilgrim fare
By eager and invisible ways,

or ever rest, nor ever lie,
Till, beyond thinking, out of view,
One mote of all the dust that's I
Shall meet one atom that was you.

Then in some garden hushed from wind,
Warm in a sunset's afterglow,
The lovers in the flowers will find
A sweet and strange unquiet grow

Upon the peace; and, past desiring,
So high a beauty in the air,
And such a light, and such a quiring,
And such a radiant ecstasy there,

They'll know not if it's fire, or dew,
Or out of earth, or in the height,
Singing, or flame, or scent, or hue,
Or two that pass, in light, to light,

Out of the garden higher, higher . . .
But in the instant they shall learn
The shattering fury of our fire,
And the weak passionless hearts will burn

And faint in that amazing glow,
Until the darkness close above;
And they will know—poor fools, they'll know!—
One moment, what it is to love.

SONNET

Oh! Death will find me, long before I tire
Of watching you; and swing me suddenly
Into the shade and loneliness and mire
Of the last land! There, waiting patiently,

One day, I think, I'll feel a cool wind blowing,
See a slow light across the Stygian tide,
And hear the Dead about me stir, unknowing,
And tremble. And I shall know that you have died,

And watch you, a broad-browed and smiling dream,
Pass, light as ever, through the lightless host,
Quietly ponder, start, and sway, and gleam—
Most individual and bewildering ghost!—

And turn, and toss your brown delightful head
Amusedly, among the ancient Dead.

THE SOLDIER

If I should die, think only this of me;
That there's some corner of a foreign field
That is for ever England. There shall be
In that rich earth a richer dust concealed;
A dust whom England bore, shaped, made aware,
Gave, once, her flowers to love, her ways to roam,
A body of England's breathing English air,
Washed by the rivers, blest by suns of home.

And think, this heart, all evil shed away,
A pulse in the eternal mind, no less
Gives somewhere back the thoughts by England given;
Her sights and sounds; dreams happy as her day;
And laughter, learnt of friends; and gentleness,
In hearts at peace, under an English heaven.

HEAVEN

Fish (fly-replete, in depth of June
Dawdling away their wat'ry noon)
Ponder deep wisdom, dark or clear,
Each secret fishy hope or fear.
Fish say, they have their Stream and Pond;
But is there anything Beyond?
This life cannot be All, they swear,
For how unpleasant, if it were!
One may not doubt that, somehow, good
Shall come of Water and of Mud;
And, sure, the reverent eye must see
A Purpose in Liquidity.
We darkly know, by Faith we cry,
The future is not Wholly Dry.
Mud unto Mud!—Death eddies near—
Not here the appointed End, not here!
But somewhere, beyond Space and Time,
Is wetter water, slimier slime!
And there (they trust) there swimmeth One
Who swam ere rivers were begun,
Immense, of fishy form and mind,
Squamous, omnipotent and kind;
And under that Almighty Fin
The littlest fish may enter in.
Oh! never fly conceals a hook,
Fish say, in the Eternal Brook,
But more than mundane weeds are there,
And mud, celestially fair;
Fat caterpillars drift around,
And Paradisal grubs are found;
Unfading moths, immortal flies,
And the worm that never dies.
And in that Heaven of all their wish,
There shall be no more land, say fish.

SECOND BEST

Here in the dark, O heart;
Alone with the enduring Earth, and Night,
And Silence, and the warm strange smell of clovers;
Clear-visioned, though it break you; far apart
From the dead best, the dear and old delight;
Throw down your dreams of immortality,
O faithful, O foolish lover!
Here's peace for you, and surety; here the one
Wisdom—the truth!—"All day the good glad sun
Showers love and labor on you, wine and song;
The greenwood laughs, the wind blows, all day long

Till night." And night ends all things.
Then shall be
No lamp relumed in heaven, no voices crying,
Or changing lights, or dreams and forms that hover!
(And, heart, for all your sighing,
That gladness and those tears, are over, over. . . .)

And has the truth brought no new hope at all,
Heart, that you're weeping yet for Paradise?
Do they still whisper, the old weary cries?
" 'Mid youth and song, feasting and carnival,
Through laughter, through the roses, as of old
Comes Death, on shadowy and relentless feet,
Death, unappeasable by prayer or gold;
Death is the end, the end!"
Proud, then, clear-eyed and laughing, go to greet
Death as a friend!

Exile of immortality, strongly wise,
Strain through the dark with undesirous eyes
To what may lie beyond it. Sets your star,
O heart, for ever! Yet, behind the night,
Waits for the great unborn, somewhere afar,
Some white tremendous daybreak. And the light,
Returning, shall give back the golden hours,
Ocean a windless level, Earth a lawn
Spacious and full of sunlit dancing-places,
And laughter, and music, and among the flowers,
The gay child-hearts of men, and the child-faces,
O heart, in the great dawn!

THE BUSY HEART

Now that we've done our best and worst, and parted,
I would fill my mind with thoughts that will not rend.
(O heart, I do not dare go empty-hearted)
I'll think of Love in books, Love without end;
Women with child, content; and old men sleeping;
And wet strong plowlands, scarred for certain grain;
And babes that weep, and so forget their weeping;
And the young heavens, forgetful after rain;
And evening hush, broken by homing wings;
And Song's nobility, and Wisdom holy,
That live, we dead. I would think of a thousand things,
Lovely and durable, and taste them slowly,
One after one, like tasting a sweet food.
I have need to busy my heart with quietude.

DINING-ROOM TEA

When you were there, and you, and you,
Happiness crowned the night; I too,
Laughing and looking, one of all,
I watched the quivering lamplight fall
On plate and flowers and pouring tea
And cup and cloth; and they and we
Flung all the dancing moments by
With jest and glitter. Lip and eye
Flashed on the glory, shone and cried,
Improvident, unmemoried;
And fitfully, and like a flame
The light of laughter went and came.
Proud in their careless transcience moved
The changing faces that I loved.

Till suddenly, and otherwhence,
I looked upon your innocence.
For lifted clear and still and strange
From the dark woven flow of change
Under a vast and starless sky
I saw the immortal moment lie.
One instant I, an instant, knew
As God knows all. And it and you,
I, above Time, oh, blind! could see
In witless immortality.

I saw the marble cup; the tea,
Hung on the air, an amber stream;
I saw the fire's unglittering gleam,
The painted flame, the frozen smoke.
No more the flooding lamplight broke
On flying eyes and lips and hair;
But lay, but slept unbroken there,
On stiller flesh, and body breathless,
And lips and laughter stayed and deathless,
And words on which no silence grew.
Light was more alive than you.

For suddenly, and otherwhence,
I looked on your magnificence.
I saw the stillness and the light,
And you, august, immortal, white,
Holy and strange; and every glint
Posture and jest and thought and tint
Freed from the mask of transiency,
Triumphant in eternity,
Immote, immortal.
Dazed at length
Human eyes grew, mortal strength
Wearied; and Time began to creep.
Change closed about me like a sleep.
Light glinted on the eyes I loved.
The cup was filled. The bodies moved.
The drifting petal came to ground.
The laughter chimed its perfect round,
The broken syllable was ended.
And I, so certain and so friended,
How could I cloud, or how distress,
The heaven of your unconsciousness?
Or shake at Time's sufficient spell,
Stammering of lights unutterable?
The eternal holiness of you,
The timeless end, you never knew,
The peace that lay, the light that shone.
You never knew that I had gone
A million miles away, and stayed
A million years. The laughter played
Unbroken round me; and the jest
Flashed on. And we that knew the best
Down wonderful hours grew happier yet.
I sang at heart, and talked, and ate,
And lived from laugh to laugh, I too,
When you were there, and you, and you.

THE OLD VICARAGE, GRANTCHESTER

(Café des Westens, Berlin. May, 1912)

Just now the lilac is in bloom,
All before my little room;
And in my flower-beds, I think,
Smile the carnation and the pink;
And down the borders, well I know,
The poppy and the pansy blow . . .
Oh! there the chestnuts, summer through,
Beside the river make for you
A tunnel of green gloom, and sleep
Deeply above; and green and deep
The stream mysterious glides beneath,
Green as a dream and deep as death.
—Oh, damn! I know it! and I know
How the May fields all golden show,
And when the day is young and sweet,
Glide gloriously the bare feet
That run to bathe . . .
Du lieber Gott!
Here am I, sweating, sick, and hot,

nd there the shadowed waters fresh
eap up to embrace the naked flesh.
emperamentvoll German Jews
rink beer around;—and *there* the dews
re soft beneath a morn of gold.
ere tulips bloom as they are told;
nkempt about those hedges blows
n English unofficial rose;
nd there the unregulated sun
opes down to rest when day is done,
nd wakes a vague unpunctual star,
slippered Hesper; and there are
eads towards Haslingfield and Coton
here *das Betreten's* not *verboten.*

θε γενοίμην . . . would I were
Grantchester, in Grantchester!—
me, it may be, can get in touch
ith Nature there, or Earth, or such.
nd clever modern men have seen
Faun a-peeping through the green,
nd felt the Classics were not dead,
o glimpse a Naiad's reedy head,
r hear the Goat-foot piping low; . . .
ut these are things I do not know.
only know that you may lie
ay long and watch the Cambridge sky,
nd, flower-lulled in sleepy grass,
ear the cool lapse of hours pass,
ntil the centuries blend and blur
Grantchester, in Grantchester. . . .
ill in the dawnlit waters cool
is ghostly Lordship swims his pool,
nd tries the strokes, essays the tricks,
ong learnt on Hellespont, or Styx.
an Chaucer hears his river still
hatter beneath a phantom mill.
ennyson notes, with studious eye,
ow Cambridge waters hurry by . . .
nd in that garden, black and white,
reep whispers through the grass all night;
nd spectral dance, before the dawn,
hundred vicars down the lawn;
urates, long dust, will come and go
n lissom, clerical, printless toe;
nd oft between the boughs is seen
he sly shade of a Rural Dean . . .
ill, at a shiver in the skies,
anishing with Satanic cries,
he prim ecclesiastical rout
eaves but a startled sleeper-out,
Gray heavens, the first bird's drowsy calls,
The falling house that never falls.

God! I will pack, and take a train,
And get me to England once again!
For England's the one land, I know,
Where men with Splendid Hearts may go;
And Cambridgeshire, of all England,
The shire for Men who Understand;
And of *that* district I prefer
The lovely hamlet Grantchester.
For Cambridge people rarely smile,
Being urban, squat, and packed with guile;
And Royston men in the far South
Are black and fierce and strange of mouth;
At Over they fling oaths at one,
And worse than oaths at Trumpington,
And Ditton girls are mean and dirty,
And there's none in Harston under thirty,
And folks in Shelford and those parts
Have twisted lips and twisted hearts,
And Barton men make Cockney rhymes,
And Coton's full of nameless crimes,
And things are done you'd not believe
At Madingley on Christmas Eve.
Strong men have run for miles and miles,
When one from Cherry Hinton smiles,
Strong men have blanched, and shot their
wives,
Rather than send them to St. Ives;
Strong men have cried like babes, bydam,
To hear what happened in Babraham.
But Grantchester! ah, Grantchester!
There's peace and holy quiet there,
Great clouds along pacific skies,
And men and women with straight eyes,
Lithe children lovelier than a dream,
A bosky wood, a slumb'rous stream,
And little kindly winds that creep
Round twilight corners, half asleep.
In Grantchester their skins are white;
They bathe by day, they bathe by night;
The women there do all they ought;
The men observe the Rules of Thought;
They love the Good; they worship Truth;
They laugh uproariously in youth;
(And when they get to feeling old,
They up and shoot themselves, I'm told) . . .

Ah God! to see the branches stir
Across the moon at Grantchester!

To smell the thrilling-sweet and rotten
Unforgettable, unforgotten
River-smell, and hear the breeze
Sobbing in the little trees.
Say, do the elm-clumps greatly stand
Still guardians of that holy land?
The chestnuts shade, in reverend dream,
The yet unacademic stream?
Is dawn a secret shy and cold
Anadyomene, silver-gold?
And sunset still a golden sea
From Haslingfield to Madingley?
And after, ere the night is born,
Do hares come out about the corn?
Oh, is the water sweet and cool,
Gentle and brown, above the pool?
And laughs the immortal river still
Under the mill, under the mill?
Say, is there Beauty yet to find?
And Certainty? And Quiet kind?
Deep meadows yet, for to forget
The lies, and truths, and pain? . . . oh! yet
Stands the Church clock at ten to three?
And is there honey still for tea?

Edith Sitwell

Edith Sitwell, daughter of Sir George and Lady Ida Sitwell, granddaughter of the Earl of Landesborough, was born at Scarborough, Yorkshire, in 1887. She was educated, as she puts it, "in secrecy" and in 1914 came to London, where she has lived ever since. A portrait of her, painted by Alvaro Guevara, hangs in the Tate Gallery. In her forties she occupied herself with prose, with a life of Pope, a history of Bath, and a critical anthology.

In 1916, she began the editing of *Wheels,* a determinedly modern anthology which outraged most of the conservative critics. Her own poems provided an even greater series of shocks. After a mild and undistinguished début—*The Mother and Other Poems* (1915)—Miss Sitwell published, in a succession so speedy as to seem little less than rapid-fire, *Clown's Houses* (1918), *The Wooden Pegasus* (1920), *Façade* (1922), *Bucolic Comedies* (1923).

In these volumes—particularly in the last two—Miss Sitwell limits her gamut; but, within her range, there is no poet quite like her. Her favorite instrument seems to be the xylophone, and it is amazing what effects she produces from its restricted timbre. Miss Sitwell is a virtuoso in the communication of a half-wooden, half-glassy tone which is seldom without brilliance. It has been objected that Miss Sitwell's poetry is artificial, and this may be true. But the criticism is not as devastating as it seems, for hers is obviously, and purposefully, an artificial world. It is a curious, semi-mechanical heaven and earth over which her keen eye ranges, a landscape in which Miss Sitwell sees, as none before her has seen, skies of paper, seas of wool, the "reynard-colored sun," the world "like a bare egg laid by the feathered air," the "coltish wind nuzzling the hand," trees "hissing like green geese," "barley-sugar children,"—she even hears Silence "like a slow-leaking tap." If Miss Sitwell's is nothing but a clock-work, conjuring-trick sort of poetry—and it is often more than that—there has rarely been so brilliant an exhibition of verbal legerdemain.

But, it must be reiterated, Miss Sitwell is more than an adroit juggler of startling phrases. Purely as a craftsman in nonsense, she has written some of the most delectable nonsense verses of the age; her grotesque nursery rhymes are, in their own genre, as memorable as De la Mare's. The secret of her serious poetry is scarcely more difficult to capture. After an initial bewilderment (due chiefly to the galloping pace) the wit of her comments, her strange associations, and the romanticism of an essentially feminine mind disclose themselves beneath the glitter.

Beginning with *The Sleeping Beauty* (1924) Miss Sitwell began to alter her bright idiom. Here, as in the succeeding *Troy Park* (1925) and *Rustic Elegies* (1927), she achieves an intensity which her other work, for all its felicities, never expressed. She delights to juxtapose actualities and impossibilities, shifting suddenly from patent absurdity to piercing sympathy. She is Donne one moment, Lewis Carroll the next. To apply the term "mystic" to her will surprise only those who have never cared to see through the glassy surface of her verse. To such readers, Miss Sitwell will remain the artificer of a *papier-mâché* universe, where grass is shrill, fire furry, where the creaking air, combed seas, and spangled emotions are equally automatic and heartless.

In the later volumes her occupation with the human drama is more apparent. Man's hunger for beauty is no longer a pitiful joke in a vegetable existence, but an insatiate passion. The pictures become autobiographical; "Colonel Fantock" reveals the poet in her simplest mood, and those who know her brothers Osbert and Sacheverell will have no difficulty identifying "Dagobert" and "Peregrine."

Gold Coast Customs and Other Poems (1930) repeats the pattern which Miss Sitwell's work has formed: a combination of contempt and nostalgia. The Swiftian scorn is for a fatuous world she refuses to join, and the nostalgia is for the quiet, aristocratic world left in childhood. *Collected Poems* (1930), more clearly than any single volume, emphasizes Miss Sitwell's alternation of wayward metaphysics and methodical madness. The poet reveals herself as a grown-up child, absurd, wise and determinedly innocent, who insists on translation of all objects in terms of her characters. Thus, in "Aubade," Miss Sitwell pictures the world as seen through the mind of a half-dreaming, half-doltish kitchen maid. Jane's sad bucolic stupidity colors the country morning. Coming down with her "cockscomb ragged hair" to light the fire, she feels each drop of rain hardening into a "dull blunt wooden stalactite"; she faces weeding in "eternities" of kitchen-garden where the flowers "cluck" (since most of them are cockscombs) and mock at her; even the flames remind her of the carrots and turnips which she is continually cleaning and cooking, and her own spirits hang limp as the "milk's weak mind."

Street Song (1942) and *The Song of the Cold* (1948) present a further departure. Were it not for the incorporation of some of the early verses in the latter volume, the reader would find it hard to believe that the new and old poems were composed by the same author. The poems written during and after the war discard the marionettes and macabre jingles for disturbing symbols and deeply human values. In "Still Falls the Rain" Miss Sitwell, writing from bombed London, uses two lines from the end of Marlowe's *Doctor Faustus* to dramatize the conflict between the world of legend and the world of nightmare reality. In "Dirge for the New Sunrise" and other later poems she exchanges the stylized opulence and kaleidoscopic images of her surrealist nursery tunes for an utterance which is solemn, incantatory, and sometimes too determinedly oracular.

Gardeners and Astronomers: New Poems (1953) was followed by an enlarged *Collected Poems* (1957), which appeared in the same year that she was named Dame of the Grand Cross of the Order of the British Empire by Queen Elizabeth II.

Besides her poetry, Miss Sitwell has written criticism, fiction, history—as depicted in the nostalgic *Bath* (1932)—and several volumes of biography, the most characteristic of which are *Alexander Pope* (1930) and *The English Eccentrics* (1933).

INTERLUDE

Amid this hot green glowing gloom
A word falls with a raindrop's boom.

Like baskets of ripe fruit in air
The bird-songs seem, suspended where

Those goldfinches—the ripe warm lights
Peck slyly at them—take quick flights.

My feet are feathered like a bird
Among the shadows scarcely heard;

I bring you branches green with dew
And fruits that you may crown anew

Your whirring waspish-gilded hair
Amid this cornucopia—

Until your warm lips bear the stains
And bird-blood leap within your veins.

AUBADE

Jane, Jane,
Tall as a crane,
The morning light creaks down again.

Comb your cockscomb-ragged hair;
Jane, Jane, come down the stair.

Each dull blunt wooden stalactite
Of rain creaks, hardened by the light,

Sounding like an overtone
From some lonely world unknown.

But the creaking empty light
Will never harden into sight,

Will never penetrate your brain
With overtones like the blunt rain.

The light would show (if it could harden)
Eternities of kitchen-garden,

Cockscomb flowers that none will pluck,
And wooden flowers that 'gin to cluck.

In the kitchen you must light
Flames as staring, red and white

As carrots or as turnips, shining
Where the cold dawn light lies whining.

Cockscomb hair on the cold wind
Hangs limp, turns the milk's weak mind....

Jane, Jane,
Tall as a crane,
The morning light creaks down again!

SIR BEELZEBUB

WHEN
Sir
Beelzebub called for his syllabub in the hotel in Hell
Where Proserpine first fell,
Blue as the gendarmerie were the waves of the sea,

(Rocking and shocking the bar-maid).

Nobody comes to give him his rum but the
Rim of the sky hippopotamus-glum
Enhances the chances to bless with a benison
Alfred Lord Tennyson crossing the bar laid
With cold vegetation from pale deputations
Of temperance workers (all signed in Memoriam)
Hoping with glory to trip up the Laureate's feet,

(Moving in classical meters)....

Like Balaclava, the lava came down from the
Roof, and the sea's blue wooden gendarmerie
Took them in charge while Beelzebub roared for his rum.

... None of them come!

THE KING OF CHINA'S DAUGHTER

The King of China's daughter,
She never would love me
Though I hung my cap and bells upon
Her nutmeg tree.
For oranges and lemons,
The stars in bright blue air,
(I stole them long ago, my dear)
Were dangling there.
The Moon did give me silver pence,
The Sun did give me gold,

And both together softly blew
And made my porridge cold;
But the King of China's daughter
Pretended not to see,
When I hung my cap and bells upon
Her nutmeg tree.

SOLO FOR EAR-TRUMPET

The carriage brushes through the bright
Leaves (violent jets from life to light).
Strong polished speed is plunging, heaves
Between the showers of bright hot leaves.
The window-glasses glaze our faces
And jar them to the very basis,—
But they could never put a polish
Upon my manners, or abolish
My most distinct disinclination
For calling on a rich relation!
In her house,—bulwark built between
The life man lives and visions seen,—
The sunlight hiccups white as chalk,
Grown drunk with emptiness of talk,
And silence hisses like a snake,
Invertebrate and rattling ache. . . .

Till suddenly, Eternity
Drowns all the houses like a sea,
And down the street the Trump of Doom
Blares,—barely shakes this drawing-room
Where raw-edged shadows sting forlorn
As dank dark nettles. Down the horn
Of her ear-trumpet I convey
The news that: "It is Judgment Day!"
"Speaker louder; I don't catch, my dear."
I roared: *"It is the Trump we hear!"*
"The *What?*"—"The TRUMP!" . . .
"I shall complain—
Those boy-scouts practicing again!"

GARDENER JANUS CATCHES A NAIAD

Baskets of ripe fruit in air
The bird-songs seem suspended where

Between the hairy leaves trills dew
All tasting of fresh green anew.

Ma'am, I've heard your laughter flare
Through your waspish-gilded hair:

Feathered masks,
Pots of peas,—
Janus asks
Nought of these,
Creaking water
Brightly stripèd
Now I've caught her—
Shrieking biped.
Flute sounds jump
And turn together,
Changing clumps
Of glassy feather.
In among the
Pots of peas
Naiad changes—
Quick as these.

SPINNING SONG

The miller's daughter
Combs her hair,
Like flocks of dove
As soft as vair. . . .

Oh, how those soft flocks flutter down
Over the empty grassy town.

Like a queen in a crown
Of gold light, she
Sits 'neath the shadows'
Flickering tree—

Till the old dame went the way she came,
Playing bobcherry with a candle-flame.

Now Min the cat
With her white velvet gloves
Watches where sat
The mouse with her loves—

(Old and malicious Mrs. Grundy
Whose washing day is from Monday to Monday.)

"Not a crum," said Min,
"To a mouse I'll be giving.
For a mouse must spin
To earn her living."

So poor Mrs. Mouse and her three cross Aunts
Nibble snow that rustles like gold wheat plants.

And the miller's daughter
Combs her locks,
Like running water
Those dove-soft flocks;

And her mouth is sweet as a honey flower cold
But her heart is heavy as bags of gold.

The shadow-mice said
We will line with down
From those doves, our bed
And our slippers and gown,

For everything comes to the shadows at last
If the spinning-wheel Time move slow or fast."

PANOPE

How lovely are the tombs of the dead nymphs
On the heroic shore—the glittering plinths
Of jacynth . . . hyacinthine waves profound
Sigh of the beauty out of sight and sound

And many a golden foot that pressed the sand—
Panope walking like the pomp of waves
With plumaged helmet near the fountain caves
The panoply of suns on distant strand—

Is only now an arena for the worm,
Her golden flesh lies in the dust's frail storm

And beauty water-bright for long is laid
Deep in the empire of eternal shade—

Only the sighing waves know now the plinth
Of those deep tombs that were of hyacinth.

But still the echoes of that helmeted bright hair
Are like the pomp of tropic suns, the blare
That from the inaccessible horizon runs—
The eternal music of heroic suns
When their strong youth comes freshened from deep seas—
And the first music heard among the trees.

COLONEL FANTOCK

Thus spoke the lady underneath the tree:
I was a member of a family
Whose legend was of hunting—(all the rare
And unattainable brightness of the air)—
A race whose fabled skill in falconry
Was used on the small song-birds and a winged
And blinded Destiny. . . . I think that only
Winged ones know the highest eyrie is so lonely.

There in a land austere and elegant
The castle seemed an arabesque in music;
We moved in an hallucination born
Of silence, which like music gave us lotus
To ear, perfuming lips and our long eyelids
As we trailed over the sad summer grass
Or sat beneath a smooth and mournful tree.

And Time passed, suavely, imperceptibly.

But Dagobert and Peregrine and I
Were children then; we walked like shy gazelles
Among the music of thin flower-bells.
And life still held some promise,—never ask
Of what,—but life seemed less a stranger then
Than ever after in this cold existence.
I always was a little outside life,—
And so the things we touch could comfort me,
I loved the shy dreams we could hear and see—
For I was like one dead, like a small ghost,
A little cold air wandering and lost.

All day within the straw-roofed arabesque
Of the towered castle and the sleepy gardens wandered
We; those delicate paladins, the waves
Told us fantastic legends that we pondered.
And the soft leaves were breasted like a dove,
Crooning old mournful tales of untrue love.

When night came sounding like the growth of trees,
My great-grandmother bent to say good night,
And the enchanted moonlight seemed transformed
Into the silvery tinkling of an old

And gentle music-box that played a tune
Of Circean enchantments and far seas.
Her voice was lulling like the splash of these
When she had given me her good night kiss
There, in her lengthened shadow, I saw this
Old military ghost with mayfly whiskers,—
Poor harmless creature, blown by the cold wind,
Boasting of unseen, unreal victories
To a harsh unbelieving world unkind,—
For all the battles that this warrior fought
Were with cold poverty and helpless age—
His spoils were shelters from the winter's rage.
And so forever through his braggart voice,
Through all that martial trumpet's sound, his soul
Wept a little sound, so pitiful,
Knowing that he is outside life for ever
With no one that will warm or comfort him. . . .
He is not even dead, but Death's buffoon
On a bare stage, a shrunken pantaloon.—
His military banner never fell,
Nor his account of victories, the stories
Of old apocryphal misfortunes, glories
Which comforted his heart in later life
When he was the Napoleon of the schoolroom
And all the victories he gained were over
Little boys who would not learn to spell.

All day within the sweet and ancient gardens
He had my childish self for audience—
Whose body flat and strange, whose pale straight hair
Made me appear as though I had been drowned—
(We all have the remote air of a legend)—
And Dagobert my brother whose large strength,
Great body and grave beauty still reflect
The Angevin dead kings from whom we spring;
And sweet as the young tender winds that stir
In thickets where the earliest flower-bells sing
Upon the boughs, was his just character;
And Peregrine the youngest with a naïve
Shy grace like a faun's, whose slant eyes seemed
The warm green light beneath eternal boughs.
His hair was like the fronds of feathers, life
In him was changing ever, springing fresh
As the dark songs of birds . . . the furry warmth
And purring sound of fires was in his voice
Which never failed to warm and comfort me.

And there were haunted summers in Troy Park
When all the stillness budded into leaves;
We listened like Ophelia drowned in blond
And fluid hair, beneath stag-antlered trees;

Then in the ancient park the country-pleasant
Shadows fell as brown as any pheasant,
And Colonel Fantock seemed like one of these.
Sometimes for comfort in the castle kitchen
He drowsed, where with a sweet and velvet lip
The snapdragons within the fire
Of their red summer never tire.
And Colonel Fantock liked our company.
For us he wandered over each old lie,
Changing the flowering hawthorn full of bees
Into the silver helm of Hercules,
For us defended Troy from the top stair
Outside the nursery, when the calm full moon
Was like the sound within the growth of trees.
But then came one cruel day in deepest June
When pink flowers seemed a sweet Mozartian tune,
And Colonel Fantock pondered o'er a book.
A gay voice like a honeysuckle nook,—
So sweet,—said, "It is Colonel Fantock's age
Which makes him babble." . . . Blown by winter's rage
The poor old man then knew his creeping fate,
The darkening shadow that would take his sight
And hearing; and he thought of his saved pence
Which scarce would rent a grave . . . that youthful voice
Was a dark bell which ever clanged "Too late"—
A creeping shadow that would steal from him
Even the little boys who would not spell—
His only prisoners. . . . On that June day
Cold Death had taken his first citadel.

STILL FALLS THE RAIN

The Raids, 1940. Night and Dawn

Still falls the Rain—
Dark as the world of man, black as our loss—
Blind as the nineteen hundred and forty nails
Upon the cross.

Still falls the Rain
With a sound like the pulse of the heart that is changed to the hammer-beat
In the Potter's Field, and the sound of the impious feet

On the Tomb:
                    Still falls the Rain
In the Field of Blood where the small hopes breed and the human brain
Nurtures its greed, that worm with the brow of Cain.

Still falls the Rain
At the feet of the Starved Man hung upon the Cross.

Christ that each day, each night, nails there, have mercy on us—
On Dives and on Lazarus:
Under the rain the sore and the gold are as one.

Still falls the Rain—
Still falls the blood from the Starved Man's wounded Side:
He bears in His Heart all wounds,—those of the light that died,
The last faint spark
In the self-murdered heart, the wounds of the sad uncomprehending dark,

The wounds of the baited bear,—
The blind and weeping bear whom the keepers beat
On his helpless flesh . . . the tears of the hunted hare.

Still falls the Rain—
Then—O Ile leape up to my God: who pulles me doune—
See, see where Christ's blood streames in the firmament:
It flows from the Brow we nailed upon the tree
Deep to the dying, to the thirsting heart
That holds the fires of the world,—dark-smirched with pain
As Caesar's laurel crown.

Then sounds the voice of One who like the heart of man
Was once a child who among beasts has lain—
"Still do I love, still shed my innocent light, my Blood, for thee."

SONG

Now that Fate is dead and gone
And that Madness reigns alone,
Still the Furies shake the fires
Of their torches in the street
Of my blood. . . . And still they stand
In the city's street that tires
Of the tread of Man.

Three old rag-pickers are they—
Clothed with grandeur by the light
As a queen, but blind as Doom
Fumbling for the rag of Man
In an empty room.

Now they take the place of Fate
In whom the flames of Madness ran
Since her lidless eyes were cursed
With the world-expunging sight
Of the heart of Man.

How simple was the time of Cain
Before the latter Man-made Rain
Washed away all loss and gain
And the talk of right and wrong—
Murdered now and gone!

And the Ghost of Man is red
From the sweep of the world's blood . . .
In this late equality
Would you know the Ghost of Man
From the Ghost of the Flea?

But still the fires of the great Spring
In the desolate fields proclaim
Eternity . . . those wild fires shout
Of Christ the New Song.

Run those fires from field to field;
I walk alone and ghostly
Burning with Eternity's
Fires, and quench the Furies' song
In flame that never tires.

DIRGE FOR THE NEW SUNRISE

(Fifteen minutes past eight o'clock, on the morning of Monday, the 6th of August, 1945.)

Bound to my heart as Ixion to the wheel,
Nailed to my heart as the thief upon the cross,
I hang between our Christ and the gap where the world was lost

And watch the phantom Sun in Famine Street—
The ghost of the heart of Man . . . red Cain,
And the more murderous brain
Of Man, still redder Nero that conceived the death
Of his mother Earth, and tore
Her womb, to know the place where he was conceived.

But no eyes grieved—
For none were left for tears:
They were blinded as the years
Since Christ was born. Mother or Murderer, you have given or taken life—
Now all is one!

There was a morning when the holy Light
Was young. . . . The beautiful First Creature came
To our water-springs, and thought us without blame.

Our hearts seemed safe in our breasts and sang to the Light—
The marrow in the bone
We dreamed was safe . . . the blood in the veins, the sap in the tree
Were springs of Deity.

But I saw the little Ant-men as they ran
Carrying the world's weight of the world's filth
And the filth in the heart of Man—
Compressed till those lusts and greeds had a greater heat than that of the Sun.

And the ray from the heat came soundless, shook the sky
As if in search for food, and squeezed the stems
Of all that grows on the earth till they were dry.
—And drank the marrow of the bone:
The eyes that saw, the lips that kissed, are gone,
Or black as thunder lie and grin at the murdered Sun.

The living blind and seeing dead together lie
As if in love . . . There was no more hating them—
And no more love: Gone is the heart of Man.

Edwin Muir

☙ Edwin Muir was born May 15, 1887, in Deerness on the mainland of Orkney. His father was a farmer who could not fit into the industrial pattern, and Edwin, youngest of a family of six, entered a law office when he was fourteen. He clerked in various positions until he was thirty-one, at which time he became an assistant editor on the *New Age* and married Willa Anderson, with whom he collaborated on translations of modern German authors.

Muir spent much time abroad. He wandered through Italy, Austria, and Czechoslovakia, was director of the British Institute in Prague and in Rome, lectured at Harvard, became Warden of Newbattle Abbey College, and lived the last thirty years of his life in Scotland. He died at seventy-one, January 4, 1959.

Writing in the traditional manner, Muir originated no new techniques, yet his extremely varied writings—novels, biographies, essays, travel books, and a rich autobiography, *The Story and the Fable* (1940)—disclose a mind which is original without straining for originality, a mind engaged on a quest for "the drowned original of the soul." In *World Within World,* Stephen Spender, recounting meetings with Muir, remarks, "On each occasion I was struck by the integrity of purpose in his life and work . . . a purpose which converted a life of shifting jobs into a spiritual pilgrimage."

It is this sense of "a spiritual pilgrimage" which makes Muir's *Collected Poems* (1960) so dreamlike and, at the same time, so vividly graphic. "The Labyrinth" is both a retelling of a favorite myth and a powerful evocation of the winding course of Muir's own life; "In Love for Long," "The Good Man in Hell," "The Combat" and "The Animals" are not only deep and sometimes enigmatical explorations, but also extraordinary contrasts in moods and symbols. "The Horses" is a poem which must excite the most casual reader with its prophetic terror and beauty.

This is a poetry which combines grace and wisdom with the greatest naturalness. Never having been fashionable, it cannot go out of fashion and, in its quiet authority, seems certain to survive.

THE GOOD MAN IN HELL

If a good man were ever housed in Hell
   By needful error of the qualities,
Perhaps to prove the rule or shame the devil,
   Or speak the truth only a stranger sees,

Would he, surrendering quick to obvious hate,
   Fill half eternity with cries and tears,
Or watch beside Hell's little wicket gate
   In patience for the first ten thousand years,

Feeling the curse climb slowly to his throat
   That, uttered, dooms him to rescindless ill,

Forcing his praying tongue to run by rote,
Eternity entire before him still?

Would he at last, grown faithful in his station,
Kindle a little hope in hopeless Hell,
And sow among the damned doubts of damnation,
Since here someone could live and could live well?

One doubt of evil would bring down such a grace,
Open such a gate, all Eden could enter in,
Hell be a place like any other place,
And love and hate and life and death begin.

IN LOVE FOR LONG

I've been in love for long
With what I cannot tell
And will contrive a song
For the intangible
That has no mould or shape,
From which there's no escape.

It is not even a name,
Yet it is all constancy;
Tried or untried, the same,
It cannot part from me;
A breath, yet as still
As the established hill.

It is not any thing,
And yet all being is;
Being, being, being,
Its burden and its bliss.
How can I ever prove
What it is I love?

This happy happy love
Is sieged with crying sorrows,
Crushed beneath and above
Between to-days and morrows;
A little paradise
Held in the world's vice.

And there it is content
And careless as a child,
And in imprisonment
Flourishes sweet and wild;
In wrong, beyond wrong,
All the world's day long.

This love a moment known
For what I do not know
And in a moment gone
Is like the happy doe
That keeps its perfect laws
Between the tiger's paws
And vindicates its cause.

THE LABYRINTH

Since I emerged that day from the labyrinth,
Dazed with the tall and echoing passages,
The swift recoils, so many I almost feared
I'd meet myself returning at some smooth corner,
Myself or my ghost, for all there was unreal
After the straw ceased rustling and the bull
Lay dead upon the straw and I remained,
Blood-splashed, if dead or alive I could not tell
In the twilight nothingness (I might have been
A spirit seeking his body through the roads
Of intricate Hades)—ever since I came out
To the world, the still fields swift with flowers, the trees

All bright with blossom, the little green hills, the sea,
The sky and all in movement under it,
Shepherds and flocks and birds and the young and old,
(I stared in wonder at the young and the old,
For in the maze time had not been with me;
I had strayed, it seemed, past sun and season and change,
Past rest and motion, for I could not tell
At last if I moved or stayed; the maze itself
Revolved around me on its hidden axis
And swept me smoothly to its enemy,
The lovely world)—since I came out that day,
There have been times when I have heard my footsteps
Still echoing in the maze, and all the roads
That run through the noisy world, deceiving streets
That meet and part and meet, and rooms that open
Into each other—and never a final room—
Stairways and corridors and antechambers
That vacantly wait for some great audience,
The smooth sea-tracks that open and close again,
Tracks undiscoverable, indecipherable,
Paths on the earth and tunnels underground,
And bird-tracks in the air—all seemed a part
Of the great labyrinth. And then I'd stumble
In sudden blindness, hasten, almost run,
As if the maze itself were after me
And soon must catch me up. But taking thought,
I'd tell myself, 'You need not hurry. This
Is the firm good earth. All roads lie free before you.'
But my bad spirit would sneer, 'No, do not hurry.
No need to hurry. Haste and delay are equal
In this one world, for there's no exit, none,
No place to come to, and you'll end where you are,
Deep in the centre of the endless maze.'

I could not live if this were not illusion.
It is a world, perhaps; but there's another.
For once in a dream or trance I saw the gods
Each sitting on the top of his mountain-isle,
While down below the little ships sailed by,
Toy multitudes swarmed in the harbours, shepherds drove
Their tiny flocks to the pastures, marriage feasts
Went on below, small birthdays and holidays,
Ploughing and harvesting and life and death,
And all permissible, all acceptable,
Clear and secure as in a limpid dream.
But they, the gods, as large and bright as clouds,
Conversed across the sounds in tranquil voices
High in the sky above the untroubled sea;
And their eternal dialogue was peace
Where all these things were woven; and this our life
Was as a chord deep in that dialogue,

As easy utterance of harmonious words,
Spontaneous syllables bodying forth a world.

That was the real world; I have touched it once,
And now shall know it always. But the lie,
The maze, the wild-wood waste of falsehood, roads
That run and run and never reach an end,
Embowered in error—I'd be prisoned there
But that my soul has birdwings to fly free.

Oh these deceits are strong almost as life.
Last night I dreamt I was in the labyrinth,
And woke far on. I did not know the place.

THE COMBAT

It was not meant for human eyes,
That combat on the shabby patch
Of clods and trampled turf that lies
Somewhere beneath the sodden skies
For eye of toad or adder to catch.

And having seen it I accuse
The crested animal in his pride,
Arrayed in all the royal hues
Which hide the claws he well can use
To tear the heart out of the side.

Body of leopard, eagle's head
And whetted beak, and lion's mane,
And frost-grey hedge of feathers spread
Behind—he seemed of all things bred.
I shall not see his like again.

As for his enemy, there came in
A soft round beast as brown as clay;
All rent and patched his wretched skin;
A battered bag he might have been,
Some old used thing to throw away.

Yet he awaited face to face
The furious beast and the swift attack.
Soon over and done. That was no place
Or time for chivalry or for grace.
The fury had him on his back.

And two small paws like hands flew out
To right and left as the trees stood by.
One would have said beyond a doubt
This was the very end of the bout,
But that the creature would not die.

For ere the death-stroke he was gone,
Writhed, whirled, huddled into his den,
Safe somehow there. The fight was done,
And he had lost who had all but won.
But oh his deadly fury then.

A while the place lay blank, forlorn,
Drowsing as in relief from pain.
The cricket chirped, the grating thorn
Stirred, and a little sound was born.
The champions took their posts again.

And all began. The stealthy paw
Slashed out and in. Could nothing save
These rags and tatters from the claw?
Nothing. And yet I never saw
A beast so helpless and so brave.

And now, while the trees stand watching, still
The unequal battle rages there.
The killing beast that cannot kill
Swells and swells in his fury till
You'd almost think it was despair.

THE ANIMALS

They do not live in the world,
Are not in time and space.
From birth to death hurled
No word do they have, not one
To plant a foot upon,
Were never in any place.

For with names the world was called
Out of the empty air,
With names was built and walled,
Line and circle and square,
Dust and emerald;

Snatched from deceiving death
By the articulate breath.

But these have never trod
Twice the familiar track,
Never never turned back
Into the memoried day.

All is new and near
In the unchanging Here
Of the fifth great day of God,
That shall remain the same,
Never shall pass away.

On the sixth day we came.

THE HORSES

Barely a twelvemonth after
The seven days war that put the world to sleep,
Late in the evening the strange horses came.
By then we had made our covenant with silence,
But in the first few days it was so still
We listened to our breathing and were afraid.
On the second day
The radios failed; we turned the knobs; no answer.
On the third day a warship passed us, heading north,
Dead bodies piled on the deck. On the sixth day
A plane plunged over us into the sea. Thereafter
Nothing. The radios dumb;
And still they stand in corners of our kitchens,
And stand, perhaps, turned on, in a million rooms
All over the world. But now if they should speak,
If on a sudden they should speak again,
If on the stroke of noon a voice should speak,
We would not listen, we would not let it bring
That old bad world that swallowed its children quick
At one great gulp. We would not have it again.
Sometimes we think of the nations lying asleep,
Curled blindly in impenetrable sorrow,
And then the thought confounds us with its strangeness.
The tractors lie about our fields; at evening
They look like dank sea-monsters couched and waiting.
We leave them where they are and let them rust:
'They'll moulder away and be like other loam'.
We make our oxen drag our rusty ploughs,
Long laid aside. We have gone back
Far past our fathers' land.

And then, that evening
Late in the summer the strange horses came.
We heard a distant tapping on the road,
A deepening drumming; it stopped, went on again
And at the corner changed to hollow thunder.
We saw the heads
Like a wild wave charging and were afraid.
We had sold our horses in our fathers' time
To buy new tractors. Now they were strange to us
As fabulous steeds set on an ancient shield
Or illustrations in a book of knights.
We did not dare go near them. Yet they waited,

Stubborn and shy, as if they had been sent
By an old command to find our whereabouts
And that long-lost archaic companionship.
In the first moment we had never a thought
That they were creatures to be owned and used.
Among them were some half-a-dozen colts
Dropped in some wilderness of the broken world,
Yet new as if they had come from their own Eden.
Since then they have pulled our ploughs and borne our loads,
But that free servitude still can pierce our hearts.
Our life is changed; their coming our beginning.

W. J. Turner

Walter James (Redfern) Turner was born in Melbourne, Australia, in 1889. He was educated at Scotch College, Melbourne, and, at seventeen, made the long journey to Europe. He studied in Germany and, shortly afterward, came to England, where, except for intervals of travel, he lived until his death in 1946.

His activities have been numerous. He was literary editor of *The Daily Herald,* dramatic critic of *The London Mercury,* and musical critic for three English weeklies. In the last rôle, his essays have been collected in three volumes, the first being *Music and Life* (1921). Later Turner made a reputation as an incisive dramatist with the imaginative *The Man Who Ate the Popomack* (1922) and the satiric *Smaragda's Lover* (1924).

But it is as a poet that Turner first attracted and still challenges attention. *The Hunter and other Poems* (1916) contains other matter besides the whimsical "Romance," which has been much quoted. *The Dark Fire* (1918) suggests if it does not sound depths; repressed passion adds a somber note to the fancies. Turner's subsequent volumes, *Paris and Helen* (1921), *In Time Like Glass* (1921) and *Landscape of Cytherea* (1923), suffer from an overproductive and uncritical ease, but many of the individual poems are on a level with the author's successful work. A dramatic poem, *The Seven Days of the Sun* (1925), was followed by the simpler, more persuasive *New Poems* (1928). A critical study of Beethoven was published in 1927.

Pursuit of Psyche (1931) and *Jack and Jill* (1934) came as a surprise to all except Turner's insistent admirers. *Jack and Jill* has a freshness of idea and a technical proficiency which command instant attention. *Pursuit of Psyche,* Turner's most ambitious project, concerns (as the title suggests) the search for the spirit through the varying forms of human desire. The ten cantos suffer from the lack of a fiery imagination which should unify the whole—the poem has organization without integration—but its parts are admirable. There are reminders of Abercrombie's *Emblems of Love* not only in the philosophy but in the phrasing. Beauty fills

This common function of all living things
With a pure value, vivid as the pact
The rosebush makes with summer, or the wings
The dove makes with the wind, or water when ice is still.

But Turner is, at the same time, more abstract and more lyrical than Abercrombie. The shorter poems are particularly convincing, and such pieces as "Talking with Soldiers," "The Music of a Tree," and "The Lion" pronounce an imagination altogether his own, an imagination which has not been sufficiently praised.

Blow for Balloons (1935), Turner's first novel, is a mixture of naïve egotism, penetration, poetry, and general literary sans-culottisme—a headlong fantasy, the best part of which is the author's account of his boyhood in Australia. Turner's music criticism, acute and authoritative, is at its best in *Berlioz* (1934) and *Mozart* (1938).

ROMANCE

When I was but thirteen or so
  I went into a golden land,
Chimborazo, Cotopaxi
  Took me by the hand.

My father died, my brother too,
  They passed like fleeting dreams,
I stood where Popocatapetl
  In the sunlight gleams.

I dimly heard the master's voice
  And boys far-off at play,—
Chimborazo, Cotopaxi
  Had stolen me away.

I walked in a great golden dream
  To and fro from school—
Shining Popocatapetl
  The dusty streets did rule.

I walked home with a gold dark boy
  And never a word I'd say,
Chimborazo, Cotopaxi
  Had taken my speech away.

I gazed entranced upon his face
  Fairer than any flower—
O shining Popocatapetl,
  It was thy magic hour:

The houses, people, traffic seemed
  Thin fading dreams by day;
Chimborazo, Cotopaxi
  They had stolen my soul away!

SONG

Lovely hill-torrents are
  At cold winterfall;
Among the earth's silence, they
  Stonily call.

Gone Autumn's pageantry;
  Through woods all bare
With strange, locked voices
  Shining they stare!

THE ROBBER

The Trees were taller than the night,
  And through my window square,
Earth-stupefied, great oranges
  Drowsed in the leaf-carved air.

Into that tree-top crowded dream
  A white arm stretched, and soon
Those green-gold oranges were plucked,
  Were sucked pale by the Moon.

And white and still that robber lay
  On the frail boughs asleep,
Eating the solid substance through
  In silence clear and deep.

Suddenly he went, and then
  The wood was dark as death:
Come back, O robber; robber, come;
  These gray trees are but breath:

These gray trees are but breath, the Night
  Is a wind-walled, dream-filled Hall!
But on the mirror of the air
  The wood wreathed dark and tall.

No movement and no sound there was
  Within that silent House.
Behind a cloud, the Robber laughed
  In a mad white carouse.

TALKING WITH SOLDIERS

The mind of the people is like mud,
From which arise strange and beautiful things,
But mud is none the less mud,
Though it bear orchids and prophesying Kings,
Dreams, trees, and water's bright babblings.

It has found form and color and light,
The cold glimmer of the ice-wrapped Poles:
It has called a far-off glow: Arcturus,
And some pale weeds: lilies of the valley.

It has imagined Virgil, Helen and Cassandra,
The sack of Troy, and the weeping for Hector—
Rearing stark up 'mid all this beauty
In the thick, dull neck of Ajax.

There is a dark Pine in Lapland,
And the great, figured Horn of the Reindeer
Moving soundlessly across the snow,
Is its twin brother, double-dreamed,
In the mind of a far-off people.

It is strange that a little mud
Should echo with sounds, syllables, and letters,
Should rise up and call a mountain Popocatapetl,
And a green-leafed wood Oleander.

These are the ghosts of invisible things;
There is no Lapland, no Helen and no Hector,
And the Reindeer is a darkening of the brain,
And Oleander is but oleander.

Mary Magdalena and the vine Lachryma Christi
Were like ghosts up the ghost of Vesuvius,
As I sat and drank wine with the soldiers,
As I sat in the Inn on the mountain,
Watching the shadows in my mind.

The mind of the people is like mud:
Where are the imperishable things,
The ghosts that flicker in the brain—
Silent women, orchids, and prophesying Kings,
Dreams, trees, and water's bright babblings!

THE LION

Strange spirit with inky hair,
  Tail tufted stiff in rage,
I saw with sudden stare
  Leap on the printed page.

The stillness of its roar
  From midnight deserts torn
Clove silence to the core
  Like the blare of a great horn.

I saw the sudden sky;
  Cities in crumbling sand;
The stars fall wheeling by;
  The lion roaring stand:

The stars fall wheeling by,
  Their silent, silver stain
Cold on his glittering eye,
  Cold on his carven mane.

The full-orbed Moon shone down,
  The silence was so loud,
From jaws wide-open thrown
  His voice hung like a cloud.

Earth shrank to blackest air;
  That spirit stiff in rage
Into some midnight lair
  Leapt from the printed page.

THE MUSIC OF A TREE

Once, walking home, I passed beneath a Tree,
It filled the dark like stone statuary,
  It was so quiet and still,
  Its thick green leaves a hill
Of strange and faint earth-branching melody:

Over a wall it hung its leaf-starred wood,
And as I lonely there beneath it stood,
  In that sky-hollow street
  Where rang no human feet,
Sweet music flowed and filled me with its flood;

And all my weariness then fell away,
The houses were more lovely than by day;
  The Moon and that old Tree
  Sang there, and secretly,
With throbbing heart, tip-toe I stole away.

IN TIME LIKE GLASS

In Time like glass the stars are set,
And seeming-fluttering butterflies
Are fixed fast in Time's glass net
With mountains and with maids' bright eyes.

Above the cold Cordilleras hung
The winged eagle and the Moon:
The gold, snow-throated orchid sprung
From gloom where peers the dark baboon:

The Himalayas' white, rapt brows;
The jewel-eyed bear that threads their caves;
The lush plains' lowing herds of cows;
That Shadow entering human graves:

All these like stars in Time are set,
They vanish but can never pass;
The Sun that with them fades is yet
Fast-fixed as they in Time like glass.

INDIA

They hunt, the velvet tigers in the jungle,
The spotted jungle full of shapeless patches—
Sometimes they're leaves, sometimes they're hanging flowers,
Sometimes they're hot gold patches of the sun:
They hunt, the velvet tigers in the jungle!

What do they hunt by glimmering pools of water,
By the round silver Moon, the Pool of Heaven?—
In the striped grass, amid the barkless trees—
The stars scattered like eyes of beasts above them!

What do they hunt, their hot breath scorching insects?
Insects that blunder blindly in the way,
Vividly fluttering—they also are hunting,
Are glittering with a tiny ecstasy!

The grass is flaming and the trees are growing,
The very mud is gurgling in the pools,
Green toads are watching, crimson parrots flying,
Two pairs of eyes meet one another glowing—
They hunt, the velvet tigers in the jungle.

SILENCE

It was a bright day and all the trees were still
In the deep valley, and the dim Sun glowed;
The clay in hard-baked fire along the hill
Leapt through dark trunks to apples green and gold,
Smooth, hard and cold, they shone like lamps of stone.

They were bright bubbles bursting from the trees,
Swollen and still among the dark green boughs;
On their bright skins the shadows of the leaves
Seemed the faint ghosts of summers long since gone,
Faint ghosts of ghosts, the dreams of ghostly eyes.

There was no sound between those breathless hills.
Only the dim Sun hung there, nothing moved;
The thronged, massed, crowded multitude of leaves
Hung like dumb tongues that loll and gasp for air:
The grass was thick and still between the trees.

There were big apples lying on the ground,
Shining, quite still, as though they had been stunned
By some great violent spirit stalking through,
Leaving a deep and supernatural calm
Round a dead beetle upturned in a furrow.

A valley filled with dark, quiet, leaf-thick trees,
Loaded with green, cold, faintly shining suns;
And in the sky a great dim burning disc!—
Madness it is to watch these twisted trunks
And to see nothing move and hear no sound.

Let's make a noise, Hey! . . . Hey! . . . Hullo!
  Hullo!

THE SUN

The sun has come, I know,
  For yesterday I stood
  Beside it in the wood—
But O how pale, how softly did it glow.
I stooped to warm my hands
  Before its rain-washed gold;
  But it was pebble-cold,
Startled to find itself in these dark lands.

Isaac Rosenberg

Isaac Rosenberg was born at Bristol on November 25, 1890. At the age of seven his parents brought him to London; at fourteen he was compelled to leave school and work for his living. Later some friends interested themselves in the boy who had begun to show great talent as a writer and draftsman, and made it possible for the young Jew from the East End to attend the Slade School. After three years of art schooling, during which Rosenberg won prizes, ill health forced him to leave England. In 1914, he went to South Africa, to a married sister in Capetown. It was there that he definitely decided to become a poet. He attempted to support himself by writing and lecturing, but his efforts were without success and, in less than a year, he was back in London. War had broken out. Sick and unhappy, Rosenberg enlisted in 1915. Early in 1916, he was sent to France, totally unfitted for military life. Nevertheless, his endurance was amazing; he hated war with all the force of his keen mind and disabled body, but he never whined. He was killed in action on April 1, 1918.

As a poet, Rosenberg is greater in promise than achievement. Most of the privately printed *Night and Day* (1912), although published at the age of twenty-two, was written in his 'teens. Even the succeeding *Youth* (1915) suffers from verbal awkwardness; a fear of falling into weak writing led him to complicate his images until they are, for the most part, turgid and overburdened. But in *Moses* (1916), and in the posthumous war-poems, the passionate young poet speaks in his own half-savage voice. Here and there a passage suggests Abercrombie, who Rosenberg admired greatly; but the images are so fiercely fresh, the accent so personal, that there is no mistaking the strength and originality of Rosenberg's gift.

Rosenberg's three small books, as well as a quantity of uncollected verse including an unfinished play, were published in one volume, *Poems,* in 1922, edited by Gordon Bottomley and introduced by Lawrence Binyon. An enlarged *Collected Works of Issac Rosenberg* (1937) includes his prose, letters, some drawings, and many poems never before published. In the foreword Siegfried Sassoon recognized in Rosenberg a fusion of English and Hebrew culture. "Behind all his poetry there is a racial quality—biblical and prophetic. His experiments were a strenuous effort for impassioned expression; his imagination had a sinewy and muscular aliveness. Often he saw things in terms of sculpture, but he did not carve or chisel; he *modelled* words with fierce energy and aspiration, finding ecstasy in form, dreaming in grandeurs of superb light and deep shadow. . . . Watching him working with words, I find him a poet of movement. Words which express movement are often used by him and are essential to his natural utterance."

EXPRESSION

Call—call—and bruise the air:
Shatter dumb space!
Yea! We will fling this passion
    everywhere;
Leaving no place

For the superb and grave
Magnificent throng,
The pregnant queens of quietness
    that brave
And edge our song

Of wonder at the light
(Our life-leased home),
Of greeting to our housemates.
    And in might
Our song shall roam

Life's heart, a blossoming fire
Blown bright by thought,
While gleams and fades the infinite
    desire,
Phantasmed naught.

Can this be caught and caged?
Wings can be clipt
Of eagles, the sun's gaudy measure
    gauged,
But no sense dipt

In the mystery of sense.
The troubled throng
Of words break out like smothered
    fire through dense
And smouldering wrong.

CHAGRIN

Caught still as Absalom,
Surely the air hangs
From the swayless cloud-boughs,
Like hair of Absalom
Caught and hanging still.

From the imagined weight
Of spaces in a sky
Of mute chagrin, my thoughts
Hang like branch-clung hair

To trunks of silence swung,
With the choked soul weighing down
Into thick emptiness.
Christ! end this hanging death,
For endlessness hangs therefrom.

Invisibly—branches break
From invisible trees—
The cloud-woods where we rush,
Our eyes holding so much,
Which we must ride dim ages round
Ere the hands (we dream) can touch,
We ride, we ride, before the morning
The secret roots of the sun to tread,
And suddenly
We are lifted of all we know
And hang from implacable boughs.

BREAK OF DAY IN THE TRENCHES

The darkness crumbles away—
It is the same old druid Time as ever.
Only a live thing leaps my hand—
A queer sardonic rat—
As I pull the parapet's poppy
To stick behind my ear.
Droll rat, they would shoot you if they knew
Your cosmopolitan sympathies.
Now you have touched this English hand
You will do the same to a German—
Soon, no doubt, if it be your pleasure
To cross the sleeping green between.
It seems you inwardly grin as you pass
Strong eyes, fine limbs, haughty athletes
Less chanced than you for life,
Bonds to the whims of murder,
Sprawled in the bowels of the earth,
The torn fields of France.
What do you see in our eyes
At the shrieking iron and flame
Hurled through still heavens?
What quaver—what heart aghast?
Poppies whose roots are in man's veins
Drop, and are ever dropping;
But mine in my ear is safe,
Just a little white with the dust.

ON RECEIVING NEWS OF THE WAR

Snow is a strange white word.
No ice or frost
Has asked of bud or bird
For Winter's cost.

Yet ice and frost and snow
From earth to sky
This Summer land doth know.
No man knows why.

In all men's hearts it is.
Some spirit old
Hath turned with malign kiss
Our lives to mould.

Red fangs have torn His face.
God's blood is shed.

He mourns from His lone place
His children dead.

O! ancient crimson curse!
Corrode, consume.
Give back this universe
Its pristine bloom.

I AM THE BLOOD

I am the blood
Streaming the veins of sweet-
ness; sharp and sweet,
Beauty has pricked the live
veins of my soul
And sucked all being in.

I am the air
Prowling the room of beauty,
climbing her soft
Walls of surmise, her ceilings
that close in.
She breathes me as her breath.

I am the death
Whose monument is beauty,
and forever,
Although I lie unshrouded
in life's tomb,
She is my cenotaph.

THE ONE LOST

I mingle with your bones;
You steal in subtle noose
This lighted dust Jehovah loans
And now I lose.

What will the Lender say
When I shall not be found,
Safe-sheltered at the Judgment Day,
Being in you bound?

He'll hunt through wards of Heaven,
Call to uncoffined earth,
"Where is this soul, unjudged, not given
Dole for good's dearth?"

And I, lying so safe
Within you, hearing all,
To have cheated God shall laugh,
Freed by your thrall.

THE JEW

Moses, from whose loins I sprung,
Lit by a lamp in his blood
Ten immutable rules, a moon
For mutable lampless men.

The blond, the bronze, the ruddy,
With the same heaving blood,
Keep tide to the moon of Moses.
Then why do they sneer at me?

THE DEAD HEROES

Flame out, you glorious skies,
Welcome our brave;
Kiss their exultant eyes;
Give what they gave.

Flash, mailèd seraphim,
Your burning spears;
New days to outflame their dim
Heroic years.

Thrills their baptismal tread
The bright proud air;
The embattled plumes outpread
Burn upwards there.

Flame out, flame out, O Song!
Star, ring to star!
Strong as our hurt is strong,
Our children are.

Their blood is England's heart;
By their dead hands,
It is their noble part
That England stands.

England—Time gave them thee;
They gave back this
To win Eternity
And claim God's kiss.

Richard Aldington

Richard Aldington was born in England in 1892, and educated at Dover College and London University. His first poems were published in England in 1909; *Images Old and New* appeared in 1915. Aldington and "H. D." (the chief American Imagist) were conceded to be two of the foremost Imagist poets; their sensitive and clean-cut lines put to shame their scores of imitators. Both appeared, with four others, under Amy Lowell's ægis in the three issues of *Some Imagist Poets,* published from 1915 to 1917.

Aldington's *War and Love* (1918) is somewhere more regular in pattern; the poems in this latter volume are less consciously programmatic but more searching. Recently, Aldington, in common with most of the *vers libristes,* has been writing in regular rhythms and fixed forms. *Images of Desire* (1919) was followed by *Exile and Other Poems* (1923) which contains whole sections of surprisingly archaic, pseudo-Elizabethan songs. *A Fool i' the Forest* (1925) is a return to Aldington's earlier manner with the addition of foreign dissonances. Though the influence of Eliot is obvious, this phantasmagoria is in many ways Aldington's most important work. Juxtaposing classic calm with the incongruities of a mechanical civilization, Aldington projects an agony unrelated to either ancient or modern backgrounds. This agony was amplified in Aldington's first novel, *Death of a Hero* (1929), a novel dealing with three generations, beginning in the snug little England of the Victorian Nineties; a work kaleidoscopic in effect and, as might be imagined, rich in musical variety. *Roads to Glory* (1931), *All Men Are Enemies* (1933), and *Women Must Work* (1934) are his decreasingly important books of prose. His *Collected Poems* was published in 1928. He died in France, July 28, 1962.

Critics differ concerning Aldington's position as a poet; none disputes his eminence as a translator. Among his many translations (of which more than twenty were published prior to 1929) are *The Poems of Anyte of Tegea, The Poems of Meleager,* Cyrano de Bergerac's *Voyages to the Moon and the Sun.* His autobiography, *Life for Life's Sake* (1941) is a lively record of the literary movements and influences from 1912 to 1940. His *Collected Poems* appeared in 1949; his biography of Wellington (1946) was awarded the Tait Black Memorial Prize.

IMAGES

I

ke a gondola of green scented fruits
rifting along the dank canals of Venice,
ou, O exquisite one,
ave entered into my desolate city.

II

he blue smoke leaps
ke swirling clouds of birds vanishing.
So my love leaps forth toward you,
Vanishes and is renewed.

III

A rose-yellow moon in a pale sky
When the sunset is faint vermilion
In the mist among the tree-boughs
Art thou to me, my beloved.

IV

A young beech tree on the edge of the forest
Stands still in the evening,

Yet shudders through all its leaves in the light air
And seems to fear the stars—
So are you still and so tremble.

V

The red deer are high on the mountain,
They are beyond the last pine trees.
And my desires have run with them.

VI

The flower which the wind has shaken
Is soon filled again with rain;
So does my heart fill slowly with tears,
O Foam-Driver, Wind-of-the-Vineyards,
Until you return.

THE FAUN SEES SNOW FOR THE FIRST TIME

Zeus,
Brazen-thunder-hurler,
Cloud-whirler, son-of-Kronos,
Send vengeance on these Oreads
Who strew
White frozen flecks of mist and cloud

Over the brown trees and the tufted grass
Of the meadows, where the stream
Runs black through shining banks
Of bluish white.

Zeus,
Are the halls of heaven broken up
That you flake down upon me
Feather-strips of marble?

Dis and Styx!
When I stamp my hoof
The frozen-cloud specks jam into the cleft
So that I reel upon two slippery points. . . .

Fool, to stand here cursing
When I might be running!

AT THE BRITISH MUSEUM

I turn the page and read:
"I dream of silent verses where the rhyme
Glides noiseless as an oar."

The heavy musty air, the black desks,
The bent heads and rustling noises
In the great dome
Vanish . . .
And
The sun hangs in the cobalt-blue sky,
The boat drifts over the lake shallows,
The fishes skim like umber shadows
through undulating weeds,
The oleanders drop their rosy
petals on the lawns,
And the swallows dive and swirl and whistle
About the cleft battlements of Can Grande's
castle. . . .

EVENING

The chimneys, rank on rank,
Cut the clear sky;
The moon,
With a rag of gauze about her loins,
Poses among them, an awkward Venus—

And here am I looking wantonly at her
Over the kitchen sink.

VICARIOUS ATONEMENT

This is an old and very cruel god. . . .

We will endure;
We will try not to wince
When he crushes and rends us.

If indeed it is for your sakes,
If we perish or moan in torture,
Or stagger under sordid burdens
That you may live—
Then we can endure.

If our wasted blood
Makes bright the page
Of poets yet to be;
If this our tortured life
Save from destruction's nails
Gold words of a Greek long dead;
Then we can endure,
Then hope,
Then watch the sun rise
Without utter bitterness.

But, O thou old and very cruel god,
Take if thou canst this bitter cup from

POSSESSION

I must possess you utterly
And utterly must you possess me;
So even if that dreamer's tale
Of heaven and hell be true
There shall be two spirits rived together
Either in whatever peace be heaven
Or in the icy whirlwind that is hell
For those who loved each other more than God—
So that the other spirits shall cry out:
"Ah! Look how the ancient love yet holds to them
That these two ghosts are never driven apart
But kiss with shadowy kisses and still take
Joy from the mingling of their misty limbs!"

AFTER TWO YEARS

She is all so slight
And tender and white
  As a May morning.
She walks without hood
At dusk. It is good
  To hear her sing.

It is God's will
That I shall love her still
  As he loves Mary,
And night and day
I will go forth to pray
  That she love me.

She is as gold
Lovely, and far more cold.
  Do thou pray with me,
For if I win grace
To kiss twice her face
  God has done well to me.

Osbert Sitwell

Osbert Sitwell (brother of Sacheverell and Edith Sitwell) was born in London, December 6, 1892, was educated at Eton, and became an officer in the Grenadier Guards, with whom he served in France for various periods from 1914 to 1917. After contesting the 1918 election at Scarborough in the Liberal interests, he devoted himself to literature.

His first contributions appeared in *Wheels* (an annual anthology of a few of the younger radical writers, edited by his sister) and disclosed an ironic touch. That impression was strengthened by *Argonaut and Juggernaut* (1920), where Sitwell's cleverness and satire are intensified if not fused. *Out of the Flame* (1923) reenforces this judgment. It is in two parts; a contrast, not a combination. There is the world of ideal beauty which the poet loves and the world of idle luxury which rouses his critical spleen and satirical hate.

After 1923 this author distinguished himself in prose, registering a deep impression with the short stories in *Triple Fugue* (1924) and the novel *Before the Bombardment* (1926). Sharing the nostalgia of his sister, Edith, he also returns to his childhood for much of the material in *England Reclaimed: A Book of Eclogues* (1927). Satire is still here, but it is satire softened with sympathy. If he laughs at such rustic figures as Mr. Goodbeare and Moping Fred, he smiles with Mr. and Mrs. Nutch, the gamekeepers, gardeners and the homely gentles of the countryside. The author aims at "recording a broad panorama, essentially English, but which seems now, by force of circumstance, to be slipping away into the past." *The Collected Poems and Satires of Osbert Sitwell* (1931) contrasts stylized witticsms with ingratiating period pieces.

Penny Foolish (1935) assembles Sitwell's enthusiasms and irritations—English public school, games, and war being among the latter, and the telephone among the former. His reminiscences ran to four autobiographical volumes—*Laughter in the Next Room; Great Morning; The Scarlet Tree; Left Hand, Right Hand!*—and were followed by the family memoirs of *Noble Essences* (1950).

FOUNTAINS

Proud fountains, wave your plumes,
Spread out your phoenix-wing,
Let the tired trees rejoice
Beneath your blossoming
(Tired trees, you whisper low).

High up, high up, above
These green and drooping sails,
A fluttering young wind
Hovers and dives, but fails
To steal a foaming feather.

Sail, like a crystal ship,
Above your sea of glass;
Then, with your quickening touch,
Transmute the things that pass
(Come down, cool wind, come down).

All humble things proclaim,
Within your magic net,
Their kinship to the Gods.
More strange and lovely yet
All lovely things become.

Dead, sculptured stone assumes
The life, from which it came;
The kingfisher is now
A moving tongue of flame,
A blue, live tongue of flame—

While birds, less proud of wing,
Crouch, in wind-ruffled shade,
Hide shyly, then pour out
Their jealous serenade;
. . . Close now your golden wings!

ELEGY FOR MR. GOODBEARE

Do you remember Mr. Goodbeare, the carpenter,
Godfearing and bearded Mr. Goodbeare,
Who worked all day
At his carpenter's tray,
Do you remember Mr. Goodbeare?
Mr. Goodbeare, that Golconda of gleaming fable,
Lived, thin-ground between orchard and stable,
Pressed thus close against Alfred, his rival—
Mr. Goodbeare, who had never been away.

Do you remember Mr. Goodbeare,
Mr. Goodbeare, who never touched a cup?
Do you remember Mr. Goodbeare,
Who remembered a lot?
  Mr. Goodbeare could remember
    When things were properly kept up:
  Mr. Goodbeare could remember
    The christening and the coming-of-age:
  Mr. Goodbeare could remember
    The entire and roasted ox:
  Mr. Goodbeare could remember
    When the horses filled the stable,
  And the port-wine-colored gentry rode after the tawny fox:
  Mr. Goodbeare could remember
    The old lady in her eagle rage,
      Which knew no bounds:
  Mr. Goodbeare could remember
    When the escaped and hungering tiger
  Flickered lithe and fierce through Foxton Wood,
  When old Sir Nigel took his red-tongued, clamoring hounds,
  And hunted it then and there,
    As a Gentleman Should.

Do you remember Mr. Goodbeare,
Mr. Goodbeare who never forgot?
Do you remember Mr. Goodbeare,
That wrinkled and golden apricot,

Dear, bearded, godfearing Mr. Goodbeare
Who remembered remembering such a lot?

Oh, do you remember, do you remember,
As I remember and deplore,
That day in drear and far-away December
When dear, godfearing, bearded Mr. Goodbeare
Could remember
No more?

ON THE COAST OF COROMANDEL

On the coast of Coromandel
Dance they to the tunes of Handel;
Chorally, that coral coast
Correlates the bone to ghost,
Till word and limb and note seem one,
Blending, binding act to tone.

All day long they point the sandal
On the coast of Coromandel.
Lemon-yellow legs all bare
Pirouette to peruqued air
From the first green shoots of morn,
Cool as northern hunting-horn,
Till the nightly tropic wind
With its rough-tongued, grating rind
Shatters the frail spires of spice.
Imaged in the lawns of rice
(Mirror-flat and mirror green
Is that lovely water's sheen)
Saraband and rigadoon
Dance they through the purring noon,
While the lacquered waves expand
Golden dragons on the sand—
Dragons that must, steaming, die
From the hot sun's agony—
When elephants, of royal blood,
Plod to bed through lilied mud,
Then evening, sweet as any mango,
Bids them do a gay fandango,
Minuet, jig or gavotte.
How they hate the turkey-trot,
The nautch-dance and the highland fling,
Just as they will never sing
Any music save by Handel
On the coast of Coromandel!

Hugh MacDiarmid

☙ Hugh MacDiarmid (whose real name is Christopher Murray Grieve) was born in Scotland in 1892. From the beginning it was evident that he was a radical in politics and an experimenter in poetry. His volumes, from *Penny Wheep* to *Stony Limits and Other Poems* (1934) are as uneven as they are Communistic. Much of these are written in MacDiarmid's own particular Scots, but even his straight English is a confusion of satire and sentimentality, rough humor and metaphysical refinements, rugged strength and lyric clarity.

A selection of MacDiarmid's poetry was published in the United States in 1946. Entitled *Speaking for Scotland,* it proved that MacDiarmid was Scotland's most considerable modern poet. "He has effected, almost single-handed, a literary revolution," wrote David Daiches; "he has destroyed one Scottish tradition and founded another." In 1941 he edited a *Golden Treasury of Scottish Poetry;* two years later hc published his autobiography, *Lucky Poet.*

WITH A LIFTING OF THE HEAD

Scotland, when it is given to me
As it will be
To sing the immortal song
The crown of all my long
Travail with thee,
I know in that high hour
I'll have, and use, the power
Sublime contempt to blend
With its ecstatic end—
As who, in love's embrace,
Forgetfully may frame
Above the poor slut's face
Another woman's name.

PARLEY OF BEASTS

Auld Noah was at hame wi' them a',
The lion and the lamb,
Pair by pair they entered the Ark,
And he took them as they cam'.

If twa a' ilka beist there is
Into this room s'ud come,
Wad I could welcome them like him,
And no' stand gowpin' dumb!

Be chief wi' them and they wi' me
And a' wi' ane anither,

As Noah and his couples were
There in the Ark thegither.

It's fain I'd mell wi' tiger and tit,
Wi' elephant and eel,
But noo-a'days e'en wi' ain's sel
At hame it's hard to feel.

CATTLE SHOW

I shall go among red faces and virile voices,
See stylish sheep, with fine heads and well-wooled,
And great bulls mellow to the touch,
Brood mares of marvellous approach, and geldings
With sharp and flinty bones and silken hair.

And through th' enclosure draped in red and gold
I shall pass on to spheres more vivid yet
Where countesses' coque feathers gleam and glow
And, swathed in silks, the painted ladies are
Whose laughter plays like summer lightning there.

TO A SEA EAGLE

I used to walk on solid gr'und
Till it fell awa' frae my feet
And, left in the void, I'd instantly
To get accustomed wi't.

Watchin' your prood flight noo I feel
As a man may dae wi' a bairn,
For withoot ony show at a'
In deeper abysses I'm farin'.

Aye, withoot ony show at a',
Save whiles a song I may sing
Gets in resonance wi' the sun
And ootshines't like a turnin' wing.

ON THE OXFORD BOOK OF VICTORIAN VERSE

Most poets to a muse that is stone-deaf cry.
This English poetry that they vaunt so high,
What is it except for two or three men
Whose best work is beyond all but a few men's ken?

Stupidity will not accept the fact, and so
Cheek by jowl with Shakespeare and Milton must go
Even in famous anthologies the incredibly small,
A Domett, Toke Lynch, and Wathen Mark Call.

A horde no man is the better for reading,
A horde no man is the worse for not heeding,
Create with these the notion that poetry's less rare
Than it is; that there's something for most men there.

Something—but what? Poetry's not written for men
And lies always beyond all but all men's ken
—Only fools—countless fools—are deceived by the claims
Of a Menella Bute Smedley and most other names.

So when this book is revised for reissue
Let us have you included lest somebody should miss you.
Here with your peers—Spoof, Dubb, and Blong,
Smiffkins, Pimple, and Jingle. *Oh Lord! how long?*

THE SKELETON OF THE FUTURE

(At Lenin's Tomb)

Red granite and black diorite, with the blue
Of the labradorite crystals gleaming like precious stones
In the light reflected from the snow; and behind them
The eternal lightning of Lenin's bones.

Wilfred Owen

Wilfred Owen's biography is pitifully brief. He was born at Oswestry on the 18th of March, 1893, was educated at the Birkenhead Institute, matriculated at London University in 1910, obtained a private tutorship in 1913 near Bordeaux and remained there for two years. In 1915, in spite of delicate health, he joined the Artist's Rifles, served in France from 1916 to June, 1917, when he was invalided home. Fourteen months later, he returned to the Western Front, was awarded the Military Cross for gallantry in October, and was killed while trying to get his men across the Sambre Canal—with tragic irony—a week before the armistice, on November 4, 1918.

Owen's name was unknown to the world until his friend Siegfried Sassoon unearthed the contents of his posthumous volume, *Poems* (1920). It was evident at once that here was one of the most important contributions to the literature of the War, expressed by a poet whose courage was surpassed only by his integrity of mind and nobility of soul. The restrained passion as well as the pitiful outcries in Owen's poetry have a spiritual kinship with Sassoon's stark verses. They reflect that second stage of the War, when the glib patter wears thin and the easy patriotics have a sardonic sound in the dug-outs and trenches. "He never," writes Sassoon, "wrote his poems (as so many war poets did) to make the effect of a personal gesture. He pitied others; he did not pity himself."

In a scrap which serves as an unfinished preface, Owen wrote, "This book is not about heroes. English poetry is not yet fit to speak of them. Nor is it about deeds or lands, nor anything about glory, honor or dominion. . . .

except War.
Above all, this book is not concerned with Poetry,
The subject of it is War, and the pity of War.
The Poetry is in the pity."

"Strange Meeting," "Miners," and the poignant "Futility" illustrate, beneath their emotional content, Owen's great fondness for assonance. He was continually experimenting with devices to enrich or take the place of rhyme, testing alliterative consonants as substitutes for the prepared and often monotonous matching of vowels. Almost half of his volume is a record of such unique and surprisingly successful experiments. But it is the nobility, the profound sympathy, compassionate without ever becoming maudlin, that gives Owen's verse a place among the authentic poetry of his day. "Dulce et Decorum Est" is obviously a reaction against the "glory" of war; but it is bigger than its subject, something far beyond a protest, surpassing its program.

It is difficult to choose among Owen's few but compelling poems. "Apologia pro Poemate Meo," "Greater Love," "Anthem for Doomed Youth" and the rhymed suspensions already mentioned will live beyond the tragic events during which they were created. They influenced the post-war poets (*vide* C. Day Lewis' *A Hope for Poetry*) in theme as well as technique; time has already found a place for them.

A new and enlarged edition entitled *The Poems of Wilfred Owen* was published in 1931 with an introduction by Edmund Blunden. This complete collection included many poems hitherto unprinted, notably "The Unreturning," "Arms and the Boy"—both full of Owen's peculiar broken music—and "From My Diary," in which Owen added initial consonantal dissonances (Blunden calls them "pararhymes") to the usual end-rhymes. They emphasize that Owen's death at twenty-five was one of modern poetry's greatest losses.

FUTILITY

Move him into the sun—
Gently its touch awoke him once,
At home, whispering of fields unsown.
Always it woke him, even in France.
Until this morning and this snow.
If anything might rouse him now
The kind old sun will know.

Think how it wakes the seeds—
Woke, once, the clay of a cold star.
Are limbs so dear-achieved, are sides
Full-nerved,—still warm,—too hard to stir?
Was it for this the clay grew tall?
—Oh, what made fatuous sunbeams toil
To break earth's sleep at all?

APOLOGIA PRO POEMATE MEO

I, too, saw God through mud—
The mud that cracked on cheeks when wretches smiled.
War brought more glory to their eyes than blood,
And gave their laughs more glee than shakes a child.

Merry it was to laugh there—
Where death becomes absurd and life absurder.
For power was on us as we slashed bones bare
Not to feel sickness or remorse of murder.

I, too, have dropped off fear—
Behind the barrage, dead as my platoon,
And sailed my spirit surging, light and clear,
Past the entanglement where hopes lay strewn;

And witnessed exultation—
Faces that used to curse me, scowl for scowl,
Shine and lift up with passion of oblation,
Seraphic for an hour, though they were foul.

I have made fellowships—
Untold of happy lovers in old song.
For love is not the binding of fair lips
With the soft silk of eyes that look and long,

By joy, whose ribbon slips,—
But wound with war's hard wire whose stakes are strong;
Bound with the bandage of the arm that drips;
Knit in the welding of the rifle-thong.

I have perceived much beauty
In the hoarse oaths that kept our courage straight;
Heard music in the silentness of duty;
Found peace where shell-storms spouted reddest spate

Nevertheless, except you share
With them in hell the sorrowful dark of hell,
Whose world is but the trembling of a flare,
And heaven but as the highway for a shell,

You shall not hear their mirth:
You shall not come to think them well content
By any jest of mine. These men are worth
Your tears: You are not worth their merriment.

ANTHEM FOR DOOMED YOUTH

What passing-bells for these who die as cattle?
Only the monstrous anger of the guns.
Only the stuttering rifles' rapid rattle

Can patter out their hasty orisons.
No mockeries for them; no prayers nor bells,
Nor any voice of mourning save the choirs,—
The shrill, demented choirs of wailing shells;
And bugles calling for them from sad shires.

What candles may be held to speed them all?
Not in the hands of boys, but in their eyes
Shall shine the holy glimmers of good-bys.
The pallor of girls' brows shall be their pall;
Their flowers the tenderness of patient minds,
And each slow dusk a drawing-down of blinds.

DULCE ET DECORUM EST

Bent double, like old beggars under sacks,
Knock-kneed, coughing like hags, we cursed through sludge,
Till on the haunting flares we turned our backs,
And towards our distant rest began to trudge.
Men marched asleep. Many had lost their boots,
But limped on, blood-shod. All went lame, all blind;
Drunk with fatigue; deaf even to the hoots
Of gas-shells dropping softly behind.

Gas! Gas! Quick, boys!—An ecstasy of fumbling,
Fitting the clumsy helmets just in time,
But someone still was yelling out and stumbling
And flound'ring like a man in fire or lime.
Dim through the misty panes and thick green light,
As under a green sea, I saw him drowning.

In all my dreams before my helpless sight
He plunges at me, guttering, choking, drowning.

If in some smothering dreams, you too could pace
Behind the wagon that we flung him in,
And watch the white eyes wilting in his face,
His hanging face, like a devil's sick of sin,
If you could hear, at every jolt, the blood
Come gargling from the froth-corrupted lungs
Bitten as the cud
Of vile, incurable sores on innocent tongues,—
My friend, you would not tell with such high zest
To children ardent for some desperate glory,
The old lie: *Dulce et decorum est*
Pro patria mori.[1]

FROM MY DIARY, JULY 1914

Leaves
    Murmuring by myriads in the shimmering trees.

[1] "It is sweet and dignified to die for one's country."

Lives
  Wakening with wonder in the Pyrenees.
Birds
  Cheerily chirping in the early day.
Bards
  Singing of summer scything thro' the hay.
Bees
  Shaking the heavy dews from bloom and frond.
Boys
  Bursting the surface of the ebony pond.
Flashes
  Of swimmers carving thro' the sparkling cold.
Fleshes
  Gleaming with wetness to the morning gold.
A mead
  Bordered about with warbling water brooks.
A maid
  Laughing the love-laugh with me; proud of looks.
The heat
  Throbbing between the upland and the peak.
Her heart
  Quivering with passion to my pressed cheek.
Braiding
  Of floating flames across the mountain brow.
Brooding
  Of stillness; and a sighing of the bough.
Stirs
  Of leaflets in the gloom; soft petal-showers;
Stars
  Expanding with the starr'd nocturnal flowers.

THE UNRETURNING

Suddenly night crushed out the day and hurled
Her remnants over cloud-peaks, thunder-walled.
Then fell a stillness such as harks appalled
When far-gone dead return upon the world.

There watched I for the Dead; but no ghost woke.
Each one whom Life exiled I named and called.
But they were all too far, or dumbed, or thralled;
And never one fared back to me or spoke.

Then peered the indefinite unshapen dawn
With vacant gloaming, sad as half-lit minds,
The weak-limned hour when sick men's sighs are drained.
And while I wondered on their being withdrawn,
Gagged by the smothering wing which none unbinds,
I dreaded even a heaven with doors so chained.

GREATER LOVE

Red lips are not so red
    As the stained stones kissed by the English dead.
Kindness of wooed and wooer
Seems shame to their love pure.
O Love, your eyes lose lure
    When I behold eyes blinded in my stead!

Your slender attitude
    Trembles not exquisite like limbs knife-skewed,
Rolling and rolling there
Where God seems not to care;
Till the fierce love they bear
    Cramps them in death's extreme decrepitude.

Your voice sings not so soft,—
    Though even as wind murmuring through raftered loft,—
Your dear voice is not clear,
Gentle, and evening clear,
As theirs whom none now hear
    Now earth has stopped their piteous mouths that coughed.

Heart, you were never hot,
    Nor large, nor full like hearts made great with shot;
And though your hand be pale,
Paler are all which trail
Your cross through flame and hail:
    Weep, you may weep, for you may touch them not.

MINERS

There was a whispering in my hearth,
  A sigh of the coal,
Grown wistful of a former earth
  It might recall.

I listened for a tale of leaves
  And smothered ferns,
Proud forests, and the low sly lives
  Before the fawns.

My fire might show steam-phantoms simmer
  From Time's old caldron,
Before the birds made nests in summer,
  Or men had children.

But the coals were murmuring of their mine.
  And moans down there,
Of boys that slept wry sleep, and men
  Writhing for air.

I saw white bones in the cinder-shard,
  Bones without number.
For many hearts with coal are charred,
  And few remember.

I thought of all that worked dark pits
  Of war, and died
Digging the rock where Death reputes
  Peace lies indeed:

Comforted years will sit soft-chaired,
  In rooms of amber,
The years will stretch their hands, well
    cheered
  By our life's ember;

The centuries will burn rich loads
  With which we groaned,
Whose warmth shall lull their dreamy lic
  While songs are crooned;
But they will not dream of us poor lads
  Lost in the ground.

ARMS AND THE BOY

Let the boy try along this bayonet-blade
How cold steel is, and keen with hunger of blood;
Blue with all malice, like a madman's flash;
And thinly drawn with famishing for flesh.

Lend him to stroke these blind, blunt bullet-heads
Which long to nuzzle in the heart of lads,
Or give him cartridges of fine zinc teeth,
Sharp with the sharpness of grief and death.

For his teeth seem for laughing round an apple.
There lurk no claws behind his fingers supple;
And god will grow no talons at his heels,
Nor antlers through the thickness of his curls.

STRANGE MEETING

It seemed that out of the battle I escaped
Down some profound dull tunnel, long since scooped
Through granites which Titanic wars had groined.
Yet also there encumbered sleepers groaned,
Too fast in thought or death to be bestirred.
Then, as I probed them, one sprang up, and stared
With piteous recognition in fixed eyes,
Lifting distressful hands as if to bless.
And by his smile, I knew that sullen hall;
By his dead smile I knew I stood in Hell.
With a thousand fears that vision's face was grained;
Yet no blood reached there from the upper ground,
And no guns thumped, or down the flues made moan.
"Strange, friend," I said, "here is no cause to mourn."
"None," said the other, "save the undone years,
The hopelessness. Whatever hope is yours,
Was my life also; I went hunting wild
After the wildest beauty in the world,
Which lies not calm in eyes, or braided hair,
But mocks the steady running of the hour,
And if it grieves, grieves richlier than here.
For by my glee might many men have laughed,
And of my weeping something has been left,
Which must die now. I mean the truth untold,
The pity of war, the pity war distilled.
Now men will go content with what we spoiled,
Or, discontent, boil bloody, and be spilled.
They will be swift with swiftness of the tigress,
None will break ranks, though nations trek from progress.
Courage was mine, and I had mystery,
Wisdom was mine, and I had mastery;
To miss the march of this retreating world

Into vain citadels that are not walled.
Then when much blood had clogged their chariot-wheels
I would go up and wash them from sweet wells,
Even with truths that lie too deep for taint.
I would have poured my spirit without stint
But not through wounds; not on the cess of war.
Foreheads of men have bled where no wounds were.
I am the enemy you killed, my friend.
I knew you in this death; for so you frowned
Yesterday through me as you jabbed and killed.
I parried; but my hands were loath and cold.
Let us sleep now. . . ."

THE SEND-OFF

Down the close, darkening lanes they sang their way
To the siding-shed,
And lined the train with faces grimly gay.
Their breasts were stuck all white with wreath and spray
As men's are, dead.

Dull porters watched them, and a casual tramp
Stood staring hard,
Sorry to miss them from the upland camp.
Then, unmoved, signals nodded, and a lamp
Winked to the guard.

So secretly, like wrongs hushed-up, they went.
They were not ours:
We never heard to which front these were sent.
Nor there if they yet mock what women meant
Who gave them flowers.

Shall they return to beatings of great bells
In wild trainloads?
A few, a few, too few for drums and yells,
May creep back, silent, to still village wells
Up half-known roads.

THE SHOW

My soul looked down from a vague height with Death,
As unremembering how I rose or why,
And saw a sad land, weak with sweats of dearth,
Gray, cratered like the moon with hollow woe,
And fitted with great pocks and scabs of plagues.

Across its beard, that horror of harsh wire,
There moved thin caterpillars, slowly uncoiled.
It seemed they pushed themselves to be as plugs
Of ditches, where they writhed and shrivelled, killed.

By them had slimy paths been trailed and scraped
Round myriad warts that might be little hills.
From gloom's last dregs these long-strung creatures crept,
And vanished out of dawn down hidden holes.

(And smell came up from those foul openings
As out of mouths, or deep wounds deepening.)

On dithering feet upgathered, more and more,
Brown strings towards strings of gray, with bristling spines,
All migrants from green fields, intent on mire.
Those that were gray, of more abundant spawns,
Ramped on the rest and ate them and were eaten.
I saw their bitten backs curve, loop, and straighten,
I watched those agonies curl, lift, and flatten.

Whereat, in terror what that sight might mean,
I reeled and shivered earthward like a feather.
And Death fell with me, like a deepening moan.
And He, picking a manner of worm, which half had hid
Its bruises in the earth, but crawled no further,
Showed me its feet, the feet of many men,
And the fresh-severed head of it, my head.

Sylvia Townsend Warner

⁂ Sylvia Townsend Warner was born December 1893 at Harrow on the Hill, Middlesex, where her father was a schoolmaster. From 1916 to 1926 she worked on the preparation of the critical edition of *Tudor Church Music,* a vast and learned compilation in ten volumes, of which she was one of four editors. Research work in the music of the fifteenth and sixteenth centuries was not only her occupation but her preoccupation, and it was not until 1922 that she started writing as a by-product.

Although she first attracted wide attention with the fanciful *Lolly Willowes: or The Loving Huntsman,* which was the first "book-of-the-month" in America in 1926, her literary début was made with a volume of verse, *The Espalier* (1925). There followed two more books of prose, quaintly misnamed novels by the publishers: *Mr. Fortune's Maggot* (1927) and *The True Heart* (1929). Three years after her first volume, her second book of poems appeared, *Time Importuned* (1928).

Although her work seems to fall into two categories, it actually forms a unified expression. The poems, objective, sharply characterized, compact with drama, are condensed stories; the novels are poetry from beginning to end. *Lolly Willowes* is a fantasy which alternates between the unshamedly tender and the lightly terrible. *Mr. Fortune's Maggot* adds compassionate understanding to extravaganza; fantasy turns here to philosophy whose motto implies surrender instead of possession in love. The title-story of *The Salutation* (1932) is a sequel to *Mr. Fortune's Maggot,* exquisite in style, tragic in effect. *The True Heart* is the simplest and the deepest of her larger works. Seemingly an idyll of Victorian England, it is really one of the oldest love stories, the classic tale of Psyche and Eros retold. Although no critic seems to have noted the fact, Miss Warner has supplied sufficient hints; "Sukey" is obviously an Anglicized Psyche; the mad Love, Eros, is the witless "Eric"; Venus is less than half-disguised as "Mrs. Seaborn."

Thus all of Miss Warner's work is a paradoxical union of subtlety and simplicity, with no sense of strain between these opposites. Each quality is equally characteristic of this author; if the mode tends toward increasing simplicity, it is as though the subtle brain were being counseled if not always controlled by the simple —and the true—heart.

The element which holds these contraries in so nice a balance is the rightness, the so-to-speak connoisseurship of Miss Warner's taste. She can be utterly exquisite when elegance dictates the mood; her coarseness is no less in place when theme and measure demand rudeness. Thus *Time Importuned* has the same sparse imagery and no little of the earth smell of which *The Espalier* is redolent, but the rustic note is not so broad; the rough country humor which underlines her bucolic comedies turns to rustic elegies without effort or affectation. "Nelly Trim," a poem which touches the ballad with nothing short of magnificence, finds its complement in "The Rival"; the neat incisiveness of "The Alarum" is matched by the bittersweetness of "Song."

Craftsmen will be quick to detect Miss Warner's innovations. She is particularly resourceful in her use of the unrhymed line; she is as adroit in her mingling of assonantal and dissonantal rhyme as Wilfred Owen and Humbert Wolfe. But it is unwise to place too much emphasis on technique. Each reader will discover a different quality on which to lay stress: the poet's marked accent; or her half-modern, half-archaic blend of naïvete and erudition; or the low-pitched but tart tone of voice, like a feminine Thomas Hardy.

Opus 7 (1931) is, in spite of its unimaginative title, a highly imaginative tale in precise couplets of one Rebecca Random who, with her "green thumb," has a way with flowers, but who has no love for them except as a means of supplying herself with gin. It is both a delicate and a diabolic long poem, realistic and revenant, musing and epigrammatic. It is as though the ghost of Pope had seized Miss Warner's pen and, allowing her to control her own fancy, had added a series of commentaries to prove that the proper student of mankind was woman. *Whether a Dove or Seagull* (1933) contains more than a hundred poems, half of which are by Miss Warner and half by her friend Valentine Ackland. The authors believed that by issuing their separate work under one cover the element of contrast would add to the pleasure of the reader; by withholding their signatures from the poems they attained the freshness as well as the provocation of anonymity. The book contains some of Miss Warner's finest poems.

In her forties Miss Warner grew more prolific without losing her discriminating touch. *More Joy in Heaven* (1935) and *A Garland of Straw* (1943) are collections of short stories; *The Cat's Cradle Book* (1940) contains subtle and mischievous fables; *Summer Will Show* (1936), *The Corner That Held Them* (1948) and *The Flint Anchor* (1954) are highly imaginative novels.

Greatly gifted, Miss Warner just misses greatness. Ironic, critical, compassionate, her mind rules her heart a fraction too well. But, although she rarely gives herself to a self-forgetting, world-forsaking ecstasy, Miss Warner is one who combines raillery and tragedy, light airs and grave implications.

FOUR EPITAPHS

ohn Bird, a laborer, lies here,
Vho served the earth for sixty year
Vith spade and mattock, drill and plow;
ut never found it kind till now.

*

an unwedded wandering dame,
or quiet into the country came:
ere, hailed it; but did not foretell
d stay so long and rest so well.

*

Richard Kent, beneath these stones,
eltered my old and trembling bones;
ut my best manhood, quick and brave,
ies buried in another grave.

*

er grieving parents cradled here
nn Monk, a gracious child and dear.
ord, let this epitaph suffice:
arly to Bed and Early to Rise.

COUNTRY THOUGHT

Idbury bells are ringing
And Westcote has just begun,
And down in the valley
Ring the bells of Bledington.

To hear all the church-bells
Ring-ringing together,
Chiming so pleasantly
As if nothing were the matter.

The notion might come
To some religious thinker,
That The Lord God Almighty
Is a traveling tinker,

Who travels through England
From north to south,
And sits him at the roadside
With a pipe in his mouth,

A-tinkling and a-tinkering
To mend up the souls
That week-day wickedness
Has worn into holes.

And yet there is not
One tinker, but Three—
One at Westcote, One at Bledington
And One at Idbury.

NELLY TRIM

"Like men riding,
The mist from the sea
Drives down the valley
And baffles me."
"Enter, traveler,
Whoever you be."

By lamplight confronted
He staggered and peered;
Like a wet bramble
Was his beard.
"Sit down, stranger,
You look a-feared."

Shudders rent him
To the bone,
The wet ran off him
And speckled the stone.
"Dost bide here alone, maid?"
"Yes, alone."

As he sat down
In the chimney-nook
Over his shoulder
He cast a look,
As if the night
Were pursuing; she took

A handful of brash
To mend the fire,
He eyed her close
As the flame shot higher;
He spoke—and the cattle
Moved in the byre.

"Though you should heap
Your fire with wood,
'Twouldn't warm me
Nor do no good,
Unless you first warm me
As a maiden should."

With looks unwavering,
With breath unstirred,
She took off her clothes
Without a word,
And stood up naked
And white as a curd.

He breathed her to him
With famished sighs,
Against her bosom
He sheltered his eyes,
And warmed his hands
Between her thighs.

Strangely assembled
In the quiet room,
Alone alight
Amidst leagues of gloom,
So brave a bride,
So sad a groom;

And strange love-traffic
Between these two;
Nor mean, nor shamefaced—
As though they'd do
Something more solemn
Than they knew:

As though by this greeting
Which chance had willed
'Twixt him so silent
And her so stilled,
Some pledge or compact
Were fulfilled,

Made for all time
In times unknown,
'Twixt man and woman
Standing alone
In mirk night
By a tall stone.

His wayfaring terrors
All cast aside,
Brave now the bridegroom
Quitted the bride;
As he came, departing—
Undenied.

But once from darkness
Turned back his sight
To where in the doorway
She held a light:
"Good-by to you, maiden."
"Stranger, good night."

Long time has this woman
Been bedded alone.
The house where she slept
Lies stone on stone:
She'd not know her ash-tree,
So warped has it grown.

But yet this story
Is told of her
As a memorial;
And some aver
She'd comfort thus any
Poor traveler.

A wanton, you say—
Yet where's the spouse,
However true
To her marriage-vows,
To whom the lot
Of the earth-born allows

More than this?—
To comfort the care
Of a stranger, bound
She knows not where,
And afraid of the dark,
As his fathers were.

THE ALARUM

With its rat's tooth the clock
Gnaws away delight.
Piece by piece, piece by piece
It will gnaw away tonight,

Till the coiled spring released
Rouses me with a hiss
To a day, to another night
Less happy than this.

And yet my own hands wound it
To keep watch while I slept;
For though they be with sorrow
Appointments must be kept.

AFTER HE HAD GONE

After he had gone the wind rose,
Buffeting the house and rumbling in the chimney,
And I thought: It will roar against him like a lion
As onward he goes.

Seven miles before him, all told—
Chilled will be the lips I kissed so warm at parting,
Kissed in vain; for he's forth into the wind, and kisses
Won't keep out the cold.

Closer should I have kissed, fondlier prayed:
Pleasant is the room in the wakeful firelight,
And within is the bed, arrayed with peace and safety.
Would he had stayed!

ELIZABETH

"Elizabeth the Beloved"—
So much says the stone
That is all with weather defaced,
With moss overgrown.

But if to husband or child,
Brother or sire, most dear
Is past deciphering;
This only is clear:

That once she was beloved,
Was Elizabeth,
And is now beloved no longer,
If it be not of Death.

TRIUMPH OF SENSIBILITY

Tiger, strolling at my side,
hy have you unbound the zone
f your individual pride?
hy so meek did you come sneaking
fter me as I walked alone?

ince the goat and since the deer
ait the shattering death you wield
a constancy of fear,
By your stripes, my strange disciple,
Am I also to be healed?"

"Woman, it was your tender heart
Did my bloody heart compel.
Master-mistress of my art,
Past my wit of wrath your pity,
Ruthless and inexorable.

"I hunt flesh by fallible sense;
You a more exquisite prey pursue
With a finer prescience,
And lap up another's unhappiness:
Woman, let me learn of you."

SAD GREEN

The glass falls lower,
And lowers the wet sky,
And by a fire sit I
Hearing the lawn-mower

Nearing and waning—
Howbeit out of tune
The essential voice of June,
Patient and uncomplaining;

For though by frost and thunder
Summer be overthrown,
The grass plat must be mown
And the daisies kept under.

SONG

She has left me, my pretty,
Like a fleeting of apple-blows
She has left her loving husband.
And who she has gone to
The Lord only knows.

She has left me, my pretty,
A needle in a shirt,
Her pink flannelette bedgown,
And a pair of pattens
Caked over with dirt.

I care not for the pattens,
Let 'em lie in the mold;
But the pretty pink bedgown
Will comfort my lumbago
When midnights are cold;

And the shirt I will wear it,
And the needle may bide.
Let it prick, let it rankle,
Let my flesh remember
How she lay against my side!

SONG FROM THE BRIDE OF SMITHFIELD

A thousand guileless sheep have bled,
A thousand bullocks knelt in fear,
To daub my Henry's cheek with red
And round the curl above his ear.

And wounded calves hung up to drip
Have in slow sweats distilled for him
To dew that polishes his lip,
The inward balm that oils each limb.

In vain I spread my maiden arts,
In vain for Henry's love I pine.
He is too skilled in bleeding hearts
To turn this way and pity mine.

THE RIVAL

The farmer's wife looked out of the dairy:
She saw her husband in the yard;
She said: "A woman's life is hard,
The chimney smokes, the churn's contrary
She said:
"I of all women am the most ill-starred.

"Five sons I've borne and seven daughters,
And the last of them is on my knee.
Finer children you could not see.
Twelve times I've put my neck in the halte
You'd think
So much might knit my husband's love to m

"But no! Though I should serve him doub
He keeps another love outdoors,
Who thieves his strength, who drains h
stores,
Who haunts his mind with fret and troubl
I pray
God's curse may light on such expensi
whores.

"I am grown old before my season,
Weather and care have worn me down;
Each year delves deeper in my frown,
I've lost my shape and for good reaso
But she
Yearly puts on young looks like an East
gown.

"And year by year she has betrayed him
With blight and mildew, rain and drough
Smut, scab, and murrain, all the rout;
But he forgets the tricks she's played him
When first
The fields give a good smell and the leav
put out.

"Aye, come the Spring, and the gulls keenin
Over her strumpet lap he'll ride,
Watching those wasteful fields and wide,
Where the darkened tilth will soon be gree
ing,
With looks
Fond and severe, as looks the groom
bride."

KILLING NO MURDER

You, master of delays,
Need no artillery but days
One after one
Loosed off in blank against hope's garrison;
No art,
Save doing nothing, to undo a heart.

MODO AND ALCIPHRON

n the Lybian desert I
aw a hermit's carcass lie,
nd a melancholy fiend
ver the battered bosom leaned.

lack as a widow dead for love,
Motionless he drooped above;
nly his tail from side to side
witched the sand with narrow stride.

Grievest thou, imp, to see thy spoil
ie thus quenched on burning soil?
insed the brain, and the loin's lust
afely reconciled with dust?

Or perchance thy mournful hide
reads how well the lash will chide
Vhen Pope Satan makes thee skip
or a negligent stewardship?"

Vith a sullen silence he
aised his head, and looked at me,
ooked me through, and looked away,
ot for all that I could say

ooked again. Quoth I, I've matched
atience with yours; and so I watched
he slow, sun-swollen daytime through
o mark what this strange fiend would do

ramped and cold I woke from sleep
o hear the fiend begin to weep.
winkling in starlight the tears ran
long his beard, and he began:

Dead is the holy Alciphron!
Modo's occupation's gone.
ll my pretty joys are sped,
entle Alciphron is dead!

"Never was there saint so mild
And so easily beguiled;
'Twas pure pleasure to torment
Anything so innocent.

"Danced I, gleaming in a dress
Of nimble maiden nakedness,
His prompt heart with hastening beat
Drummed the measure for my feet,

"And his glances whipped me round,
Till toppling in a dizzy swound
With long recovery I would twine
About him like the conjugal vine,

"While my forked and flickering tongue,
Constant as summer lightning, hung
On the scant flesh that wrapped his bones,
Till sighs long-husbanded, chuckling groans,

"Vouched for the pleasures he endured;
By thorns such pleasures must be cured,
And when most thick the thin blood fell
I knew that I had pleased him well.

"Then at other times I'd sit
Praising his spiritual wit,
Assuring him how deftly he
Could comprehend the Trinity,

"Flesh Christ, with never a trespassing glide
To error on this or t'other side,
Show how original sin doth breed
Inherent in the genital seed,

"And every tinkling sophist quell,
Who questions that the troops of hell
Pester the saint upon his knees,
Actual and numerous as his fleas.

"But most of all 'twas my delight
To cajole him from the elected night
Wherewith the christian cowls his sense
From the allurement and offense

"Of a lost planet. I would be
Damnation singing from a tree
With voice more wildly ravishing
For being damned, or in a spring

"With chill adulteries surprise
Him parched; often I thieved his eyes
To love me in lizard, or in braid
Of sun begetting from a shade

"A spawn of dancing babies—all
Accursed as their original.
In many a salad I laid a snare
Of joy that he on such poor fare

"Fared well, or else on wafts of thyme
Into the warded brain would climb
Unchallenged, or tweaked him by the nose
With the remembrance of a rose.

"Thus did we wrestle, and never chaste
Turtles did rarer dalliance taste,
Thus mixed our opposites, as true
As plighted dock and nettle do,

'Thus to all time example gave
Of the mutual comfort saint should have
With devil, devil with saint, and thus
I clean forgot how envious

"In his unmated splendor sits
He, the Tyrant—"
As oak splits
Before the ax, and falls with loud
Indignant groan, so groaned, so bowed,

The fiend, and lay in silence long;
But once or twice against the throng
Of stars raised up a blackening fist;
Then mourned, as mourning from a mist:

"Alas, how faithless man can be
To a friend's eternity!
Into untiring malice doomed,
Virtue as long-breathed I presumed;

"With never a care save which art next
To ply I looked on time unvexed,
Nor, in this plenty of sand, did doubt
The tale of his was running out.

"So Alciphron grew old, though I
Knew it not. This gew-gawed sky
Its virgin hood of gray had on,
And light was scarce, when Alciphron

"Awoke, and laid his hand on me,
And stared east. *Haec dies,* said he,
Quam fecit Dominus. I too
Looked east, and saw a path run throug

"The kindling cloud. It bruised my gaze
To meet the intolerable blaze,
The ostentatious Rose, the blare
And uproar of light which threatened ther

"But Alciphron beheld and smiled,
Crowing for pleasure like a child
Who views its promised sugarplum:
Then, with a crash which has left dumb

"All thunder since, about us came
A simpering angel in a flame,
Who seized upon redemption's prey,
And bore him, like a child, away.

"Thus, O woe, I'm left alone
With this unanswering flesh and bone.
All my pretty joys are sped,
Gentle Alciphron is dead!

"Nothing is left me of my joy
But this contemptuous broken toy.
Modo's occupation's gone,
Dead is the holy Alciphron!"

THE ABSENCE

How happy I can be with my love awa
No care comes all day;
Like a dapple of clouds the hours pass by,
Time stares from the sky
But does not see me where I lie in the hay,
So still do I lie.

Like points of dew the stars well in the ski
Taller the trees rise.
Dis-shadowed, unselved, I wander slow,
My thoughts flow and flow,
But whither tending I know not, nor ne
surmise,
So softly I go,

Till to my quiet bed I must undress—
Then I say, Alas!
That he whom, too anxious or too gay,
I torment all day
Can never know me in my harmlessness
While he is away.

BUILDING IN STONE

God is still glorified—
To him the wakeful arch holds up in prayer,
Nightly dumb glass keeps vigil to declare
His East, and Eastertide;

The constant pavement lays
Its flatness for his feet, each pier acquaints
Neighbor, him housed; time-thumbed, forgotten saints
Do not forget to praise;

All parcels of the whole,
Each hidden, each revealed, each thrust and stress,
Antiphonally interlocked, confess
Him, stay, and him, control.

Whether upon the fens
Anchored, with all her canvas and all her shrouds,
Ely signal him to willows and clouds
And cattle, or whether Wren's

Unperturbed dome, above
The city roaring with mechanic throat
And climbing in layer on layer of Babel, float
Like an escaping dove,

Or whether in countryside
Stationed all humble and holy churches keep
Faith with the faith of those who lie asleep,
God is still glorified;

Since by the steadfastness
Of his most mute creation man conjures
—Man, so soon hushed—the silence which endures
To bear in mind, and bless.

THE GREEN VALLEY

Here in the green scooped valley I walk to and fro
In all my journeyings I have not seen
A place so tranquil, so green;
And yet I think I have seen it long ago,
The grassy slopes, and the cart-track winding, so.

O now I remember it well, now all is plain,
Why twitched my memory like a dowser's rod
At waters hidden under sod.
When I was a child they told me of Charlemagne,
Of Gan the traitor, and Roland outmatched and slain.

Weeping for Roland then, I scooped in my spirit

A scant green Roncesvalles, a holy ground,
Which here in Dorset I've found:
But finding, I knew it not. The years disinherit
Their children. The horn is blown, but I do not hear it.

Charles Hamilton Sorley

Charles Hamilton Sorley, who promised great things, was born at Old Aberdeen in May, 1895. Son of Professor Sorley of Cambridge, he studied at Marlborough College and University College, Oxford. He was finishing his studies abroad and was on a walking-tour along the banks of the Moselle when war came. Sorley returned home to receive an immediate commission in the 7th Battalion of the Suffolk Regiment. In August, 1915, at the age of twenty, he was made a captain. On October 13, 1915, he was killed in action near Hulluch.

Jingoism, violent propaganda, falsely patriotic slogans could not obscure his piercing vision. "There is no such thing as a just war," he wrote. "What we are doing is casting out Satan by Satan." At nineteen, while he was training at Shorncliffe, he dared to write, "England—I am sick of the sound of the word. In training to fight for England, I am training to fight for that deliberate hypocrisy, that terrible middle-class sloth of outlook and appalling 'imaginative indolence' that has marked us out from generation to generation. . . . Indeed I think that after the War all brave men will renounce their country and confess that they are strangers and pilgrims on the earth." Such electrifying sentences, as well as his independent appreciations of Masefield, Richard Jefferies, and Thomas Hardy, are to be found in the posthumous *Letters of Charles Sorley* (1919). These letters perform the same service to Sorley the poet as the letters of Keats perform in rounding out that greater poet who also died at the beginning of manhood.

Sorley left but one book, *Marlborough and Other Poems,* a posthumous collection, edited by his father, published in 1916. The verse contained in it is sometimes rough but never rude. Although he admired Masefield, loveliness rather than liveliness was his aim. Restraint, tolerance, and a dignity unusual for a boy of twenty distinguish his verse. There is scarcely a line in Sorley's work which does not breathe the spirit of compelling exaltation.

Whether it blows with breezy youth in "The Song of the Ungirt Runners" or burns with steady ardor in the sonnets, his poetry is, in the fullest sense, radiant. What Sorley might have accomplished is apparent though indefinable. He died before he was twenty-one.

TWO SONNETS

I

Saints have adored the lofty soul of you.
Poets have whitened at your high renown.
We stand among the many millions who
Do hourly wait to pass your pathway down.

You, so familiar, once were strange: we tried
To live as of your presence unaware.
But now in every road on every side
We see your straight and steadfast signpost there.

I think it like that signpost in my land
Hoary and tall, which pointed me to go
Upward, into the hills, on the right hand,
Where the mists swim and the winds shriek and blow,
A homeless land and friendless, but a land
I did not know and that I wished to know.

II

Such, such is Death: no triumph: no defeat:
Only an empty pail, a slate rubbed clean,
A merciful putting away of what has been.

And this we know: Death is not Life effete,
Life crushed, the broken pail. We who have seen
So marvelous things know well the end not yet.
Victor and vanquished are a-one in death:
Coward and brave: friend, foe. Ghosts do not say,
"Come, what was your record when you drew breath?"
But a big blot has hid each yesterday
So poor, so manifestly incomplete.
And your bright Promise, withered long and sped,
Is touched; stirs, rises, opens and grows sweet
And blossoms and is you, when you are dead.

THE SONG OF THE UNGIRT RUNNERS

We swing ungirded hips,
And lightened are our eyes,
The rain is on our lips,
We do not run for prize.
We know not whom we trust
Nor whitherward we fare,
But we run because we must
Through the great wide air.

The waters of the seas
Are troubled as by storm.
The tempest strips the trees
And does not leave them warm.
Does the tearing tempest pause?
Do the tree tops ask it why?
So we run without a cause
'Neath the big bare sky.

The rain is on our lips,
We do not run for prize.

But the storm the water whips
And the wave howls to the skies.
The winds arise and strike it
And scatter it like sand,
And we run because we like it
  Through the broad bright land.

TO GERMANY

You are blind like us. Your hurt no man designed,
And no man claimed the conquest of your land.
But gropers both, through fields of thought confined,
We stumble and we do not understand.
You only saw your future bigly planned,
And we the tapering paths of our own mind,
And in each other's dearest ways we stand,
And hiss and hate. And the blind fight the blind.

When it is peace, then we may view again
With new-won eyes each other's truer form
And wonder. Grown more loving-kind and warm
We'll grasp firm hands and laugh at the old pain,
When it is peace. But until peace, the storm,
The darkness and the thunder and the rain.

ROOKS

There where the rusty iron lies,
  The rooks are cawing all the day.
Perhaps no man, until he dies,
  Will understand them, what they say.

The evening makes the sky like clay.
  The slow wind waits for night to rise.
The world is half content. But they

Still trouble all the trees with cries,
  That know, and cannot put away,
The yearning to the soul that flies
  From day to night, from night to day.

ALL THE HILLS AND VALES

All the hills and vales along
Earth is bursting into song,
And the singers are the chaps
Who are going to die perhaps.
    O sing, marching men,
    Till the valleys ring again.

Give your gladness to earth's keeping,
So be glad, when you are sleeping.

Cast away regret and rue,
Think what you are marching to.
Little live, great pass.
Jesus Christ and Barabbas
Were found the same day.
This died, that went his way.
So sing with joyful breath.
For why, you are going to death.
Teeming earth will surely store
All the gladness that you pour.

Earth that never doubts nor fears,
Earth that knows of death, not tears,
Earth that bore with joyful ease
Hemlock for Socrates,
Earth that blossomed and was glad
'Neath the cross that Christ had,
Shall rejoice and blossom too
When the bullet reaches you.
Wherefore, men marching
On the road to death, sing!
Pour your gladness on earth's head,
So be merry, so be dead.

From the hills and valleys earth
Shouts back the sound of mirth,
Tramp of feet and lilt of song
Ringing all the road along.
Ringing, swinging, glad song-throwing,
Earth will echo still when foot
Lies numb and voice mute.
On, marching men, on
To the gates of death with song.
Sow your gladness for earth's reaping,
So you may be glad, though sleeping.
Strew your gladness on earth's bed,
So be merry, so be dead.

Robert Graves

☙ Robert (Ranke) Graves, son of the Irish poet and song-writer Alfred Percival Graves, was born July 26, 1895. He was educated at Charterhouse and Oxford, after which he joined the British Expeditionary Force and served three times in France, in the same regiment as Siegfried Sassoon. His activities were as numerous as incongruous. He won a prize at the Olympic games, lost his capital as an unsuccessful shopkeeper, was the biographer of Colonel T. E. Lawrence, and taught literature in Cairo.

Graves was one of the writers who, roused by the War and giving himself to his country, refused to glorify warfare or chant new hymns of hate. Like Sassoon, Graves reacted against the storm of fury and blood-lust, but, fortified by a lighter and more whimsical spirit, where Sassoon is violent, Graves is volatile; where Sassoon grew bitter, Graves was almost blithe in his irony.

An easy gaiety rises from *Fairies and Fusiliers* (1917), a surprising and healing humor that is warmly individual. In *Country Sentiment* (1919) Graves turns to a more rustic simplicity. But a buoyant fancy ripples beneath the most archaic of his ballads and a quaintly original turn of mind saves them from their own echoes.

With *Country Sentiment,* Graves, so one was ready to believe, had established his characteristics. His gift was charming rather than startling, playful and lightly *macabre* rather than profound; qualities, which, while not those of a great poet, were distinctly those of an enjoyable one. The young poet seemed happy in his combinations (and mutations) of two traditionally English forms: the ballad and the Mother Goose rhyme. "A Frosty Night," "Star-Talk," "True Johnny," "It's a Queer Time," "Neglectful Edward," "I Wonder What It Feels Like to Be Drowned?" are some of the measures written out of a surplus and careless fertility, with little effort, scarcely with thought, and with one eye winking at the Nursery.

In his thirties, temporarily putting aside the direct lyric impulse, Graves threw himself into controversies. He issued broadsides from his home in Majorca. He began to probe and analyze the ways, means, and results of the creative process—his own as well as others'. No less than seven volumes were devoted to interpretation and technique; *On English Poetry* (1922), *The Meaning of Dreams* (1924), *Poetic Unreason* (1925), *Contemporary Techniques of Poetry* (1925), *Another Future of Poetry* (1926), *A Survey of Modernist Poetry,* the last in collaboration with Laura Riding (1928). His volumes of verse during this period reflect changing preoccupations. *The Pier Glass* (1921), *Whipperginny* (1923), *Mock Beggar Hall* (1924), *Welchman's Hose* (1925), *The Marmosite's Miscellany,* issued by "John Doyle" (1925), turn from fancy to philosophy, from Skelton to Freud.

Much of this intellectual turmoil is reflected in *Good-Bye to All That* (1929) and *But It Still Goes On* (1930), two autobiographies which poignantly, ironically, and not always successfully wave farewell to Graves' youth. Without bravado and with surprisingly little bitterness the poet describes the sordid side of war, the drudgery of trench life and the abuses of officialdom, but his pages are intensified with a hatred of injustice in all its forms.

After forty, Graves gave himself energetically to reappraisals of history, legend, and myth. *I, Claudius* (1934) and *Claudius the God* (1935) were followed by the searching prose of *Wife to Mr. Milton* (1943), *Hercules, My Shipmate* (1945), the controversial *King Jesus* (1946), the erudite *The White Goddess* (1948) which T. S. Eliot hailed as "a prodigious, monstrous, stupefying, indescribable book," and *Watch the Northwind Rise* (1949), a witty fantasy of a future utopia run by witchcraft. The poet was always apparent in all these books as well as in *Poems: 1938-1945* and *Collected Poems: 1914-1947*—volumes which increased his stature.

At sixty-five Graves was the prolific author of some twenty-five books of poems, a dozen novels, and more than two dozen miscellaneous volumes: biographies, essays, short stories, adaptations, interpretations, criticisms, causeries and mischievous retellings of *The Greek Myths* (1955). Upon the publication of a new *Collected Poems; 1959* his place was assured. It was an isolated place. "Not only has he never been a member of a school or followed any prevailing fashion," wrote J. M. Cohen in his book-length study, *Robert Graves* (1960), "but even in his generation he stands alone, too young to have experienced the impact of Continental symbolism and not young enough to have been affected by the social stress which determined the initial poetic course of Auden and his group." "Having written poetry for forty-five years and been for the greater part of that time not exactly neglected but often regarded as peripheral," reported Walter Allen in a *London Letter,* "he is suddenly recognized by the younger poets as *the* living English poet."

Although Graves truculently derided the obscurantists (see *The Crowning Privilege,* delivered as lectures during his tenure at Oxford), his own poetry is not always easy to comprehend. For example "To Juan at the Winter Solstice" is one of his more magical poems; but in order to appreciate its cryptic lines the reader must have an acquaintance with mythology, the many-titled queen-goddesses, the kings who must die and be reborn at the winter solstice, the basic legends which have a central meaning—"there is one story and one story only"—and an understanding of *The White Goddess* which maintains that the leading theme of poetry is the relations, often tragic, of men and women.

The belated salvos were unaccompanied by the usual murmurs of dissent. It was generally agreed that Graves had an obstinate integrity and an innate ability to capture and communicate the essence of poetry. "He is helplessly original," declared Richard Wilbur when introducing Graves at the American Academy of Arts and Letters. "His poems issue directly from a self-trusting and inimitable sensibility . . . They are 'occasional'—that is, however handsomely made, they have the air of being spontaneous answers to actual experience."

NEGLECTFUL EDWARD

Nancy

Edward, back from the Indian Sea,
"What have you brought for Nancy?"

Edward

"A rope of pearls and a gold earring,
And a bird of the East that will not sing.
A carven tooth, a box with a key—"

Nancy

"God be praised you are back," says she,
"Have you nothing more for your Nancy?"

Edward

"Long as I sailed the Indian Sea
I gathered all for your fancy:
Toys and silk and jewels I bring,

And a bird of the East that will not sing:
What more can you want, dear girl, from me?"

Nancy

"God be praised you are back," said she,
"Have you nothing better for Nancy?"

Edward

"Safe and home from the Indian Sea,
And nothing to take your fancy?"

Nancy

"You can keep your pearls and your gold earring,
And your bird of the East that will not sing,
But, Ned, have you nothing more for me
Than heathenish gew-gaw toys?" says she,
"Have you nothing better for Nancy?"

IT'S A QUEER TIME

It's hard to know if you're alive or dead
When steel and fire go roaring through your head.
One moment you'll be crouching at your gun
Traversing, mowing heaps down half in fun:
The next, you choke and clutch at your right breast—
No time to think—leave all—and off you go . . .
To Treasure Island where the Spice winds blow,
To lovely groves of mango, quince and lime—
Breathe no good-by, but ho, for the Red West!
It's a queer time.

You're charging madly at them yelling "Fag!"
When somehow something gives and your feet drag.
You fall and strike your head; yet feel no pain
And find . . . you're digging tunnels through the hay
In the Big Barn, 'cause it's a rainy day.
Oh, springy hay, and lovely beams to climb!
You're back in the old sailor suit again.
It's a queer time.

Or you'll be dozing safe in your dug-out—
A great roar—the trench shakes and falls about—
You're struggling, gasping, struggling, then . . . *hullo!*
Elsie comes tripping gayly down the trench,
Hanky to nose—that lyddite makes a stench—
Getting her pinafore all over grime.
Funny! because she died ten years ago!
It's a queer time.

The trouble is, things happen much too quick;
Up jump the Boches, rifles thump and click,

You stagger, and the whole scene fades away:
Even good Christians don't like passing straight
From Tipperary or their Hymn of Hate
To Alleluiah-chanting, and the chime
Of golden harps . . . and . . . I'm not well today . . .
It's a queer time.

A PINCH OF SALT

When a dream is born in you
With a sudden clamorous pain,
When you know the dream is true
And lovely, with no flaw nor stain,
O then, be careful, or with sudden clutch
You'll hurt the delicate thing you prize so much.

Dreams are like a bird that mocks,
Flirting the feathers of his tail.
When you seize at the salt box,
Over the hedge you'll see him sail.
Old birds are neither caught with salt nor chaff:
They watch you from the apple bough and laugh.

Poet, never chase the dream.
Laugh yourself, and turn away.
Mask your hunger; let it seem
Small matter if he come or stay;
But when he nestles in your hand at last,
Close up your fingers tight and hold him fast.

STAR-TALK

"Are you awake, Gemelli,
This frosty night?"
"We'll be awake till réveillé,
Which is Sunrise," say the Gemelli,
"It's no good trying to go to sleep:
If there's wine to be got we'll drink it deep,
But sleep is gone tonight,
But sleep is gone tonight."

"Are you cold too, poor Pleiads,
This frosty night?"
"Yes, and so are the Hyads:
See us cuddle and hug," say the Pleiads,
"All six in a ring: it keeps us warm:
We huddle together like birds in a storm:
It's bitter weather tonight,
It's bitter weather tonight."

"What do you hunt, Orion,
 This starry night?"
"The Ram, the Bull and the Lion,
And the Great Bear," says Orion,
"With my starry quiver and beautiful belt
I am trying to find a good thick pelt
 To warm my shoulders tonight,
 To warm my shoulders tonight."

"Did you hear that, Great She-bear,
 This frosty night?"
"Yes, he's talking of stripping *me* bare
Of my own big fur," says the She-bear,
"I'm afraid of the man and his terrible arrow:
The thought of it chills my bones to the marrow,
 And the frost so cruel tonight!
 And the frost so cruel tonight!"

"How is your trade, Aquarius,
 This frosty night?"
"Complaints is many and various
And my feet are cold," says Aquarius,
"There's Venus objects to Dolphin-scales,
And Mars to Crab-spawn found in my pails,
 And the pump has frozen tonight,
 And the pump has frozen tonight."

I WONDER WHAT IT FEELS LIKE TO BE DROWNED?

Look at my knees,
That island rising from the steamy seas!
The candle's a tall lightship; my two hands
Are boats and barges anchored to the sands,
With mighty cliffs all round;
They're full of wine and riches from far lands. . . .
I wonder what it feels like to be drowned?

I can make caves,
By lifting up the island and huge waves
And storms, and then with head and ears well under
Blow bubbles with a monstrous roar like thunder,
A bull-of-Bashan sound.
The seas run high and the boats split asunder . . .
I wonder what it feels like to be drowned?

The thin soap slips
And slithers like a shark under the ships.
My toes are on the soap-dish—that's the effect
Of my huge storms; an iron steamer's wrecked.

The soap slides round and round;
He's biting the old sailors, I expect. . . .
I wonder what it feels like to be drowned?

ESCAPE

(*August 6, 1916. Officer Previously Reported Died of Wounds, Now Reported Wounded: Graves, Capt. R., Royal Welch Fusiliers*)

. . . But I *was* dead, an hour or more:
I woke when I'd already passed the door
That Cerberus guards and half-way down the road
To Lethe, as an old Greek sign-post showed.
Above me, on my stretcher swinging by,
I saw new stars in the sub-terrene sky,
A Cross, a Rose in Bloom, a Cage with Bars,
And a barbed Arrow feathered with fine stars.
I felt the vapors of forgetfulness
Float in my nostrils: Oh, may Heaven bless
Dear Lady Proserpine, who saw me wake
And, stooping over me, for Henna's sake
Cleared my poor buzzing head and sent me back
Breathless, with leaping heart along the track.
After me roared and clattered angry hosts
Of demons, heroes, and policemen-ghosts.
"Life, life! I can't be dead, I won't be dead:
Damned if I'll die for anyone," I said . . .
Cerberus stands and grins above me now,
Wearing three heads, lion and lynx and sow.
"Quick, a revolver! but my Webley's gone,
Stolen . . . no bombs . . . no knife . . . (the crowd swarms on,
Bellows, hurls stones) . . . not even a honeyed sop . . .
Nothing . . . Good Cerberus . . . Good dog . . . But stop!
Stay! . . . A great luminous thought . . . I do believe
There's still some morphia that I bought on leave."
Then swiftly Cerberus' wide mouths I cram
With Army biscuit smeared with Tickler's jam;
And Sleep lurks in the luscious plum and apple.
He crunches, swallows, stiffens, seems to grapple
With the all-powerful poppy . . . then a snore,
A crash; the beast blocks up the corridor
With monstrous hairy carcase, red and dun—
Too late: for I've sped through.
O Life! O Sun!

THE TRAVELER'S CURSE AFTER MISDIRECTION

(*from the Welsh*)

May they wander stage by stage
Of the same vain pilgrimage,
Stumbling on, age after age,
Night and day, mile after mile,
At each and every step, a stile;
At each and every stile, withal,
May they catch their feet and fall;
At each and every fall they take,

May a bone within them break;
And may the bones that break within
Not be, for variation's sake,
Now rib, now thigh, now arm, now shin,
But always, without fail, THE NECK.

SONG: ONE HARD LOOK

Small gnats that fly
In hot July
And lodge in sleeping ears,
Can rouse therein
A trumpet's din
With Day of Judgment fears.

Small mice at night
Can wake more fright
Than lions at midday.
A straw will crack
The camel's back;
There is no easier way.

One smile relieves
A heart that grieves
Though deadly sad it be,
And one hard look
Can close the book
That lovers love to see.

A FROSTY NIGHT

Mother

Alice, dear, what ails you,
  Dazed and white and shaken?
Has the chill night numbed you?
  Is it fright you have taken?

Alice

Mother, I am very well,
  I felt never better,
Mother, do not hold me so,
  Let me write my letter.

Mother

Sweet, my dear, what ails you?

Alice

  No, but I am well;
The night was cold and frosty,
  There's no more to tell.

Mother

Aye, the night was frosty,
  Coldly gaped the moon,
Yet the birds seemed twittering
  Through green boughs of June.

Soft and thick the snow lay,
  Stars danced in the sky.
Not all the lambs of May-day
  Skip so bold and high.

Your feet were dancing, Alice,
  Seemed to dance on air,
You looked a ghost or angel
  In the starlight there.

Your eyes were frosted starlight,
  Your heart fire and snow.
Who was it said, "I love you"?

Alice

  Mother, let me go!

IN THE WILDERNESS

Christ of His gentleness
Thirsting and hungering,
Walked in the wilderness;
Soft words of grace He spoke
Unto lost desert-folk
That listened wondering.
He heard the bitterns call
From ruined palace-wall,
Answered them brotherly.
He held communion
With the she-pelican
Of lonely piety.
Basilisk, cockatrice,
Flocked to his homilies,
With mail of dread device,
With monstrous barbèd slings,
With eager dragon-eyes;
Great bats on leathern wings
And poor blind broken things,
Foul in their miseries.
And ever with Him went,
Of all His wanderings
Comrade, with ragged coat,
Gaunt ribs—poor innocent—

Bleeding foot, burning throat,
The guileless old scapegoat;
For forty nights and days
Followed in Jesus' ways,
Sure guard behind Him kept,
Tears like a lover wept.

A FORCED MUSIC

Of Love he sang, full hearted one,
But when the song was done,
The King demanded more,
Aye, and commanded more.
The boy found nothing for encore,
Words, melodies—none,
Ashamed the song's glad rise and plaintive fall
Had so charmed King and Queen and all.

He sang the same verse once again
But urging less Love's pain.
With altered time and key
He showed variety,
Seemed to refresh the harmony
Of his only strain,
So still the glad rise and the plaintive fall
Could charm the King, the Queen and all.

He of his song then wearying ceased,
But was not yet released:
The Queen's request was "More,"
And her behest was "More."
He played of random notes some score,
Then suddenly let his twangling harp down fall
And fled in tears from King and Queen and all.

LOST LOVE

His eyes are quickened so with grief,
He can watch a grass or leaf
Every instant grow; he can
Clearly through a flint wall see,
Or watch the startled spirit flee
From the throat of a dead man:
Across two counties he can hear,
And catch your words before you speak;
The woodlouse or the maggot's weak
Clamor rings in his sad ear;
And noise so slight it would surpass
Credence:—drinking sound of grass,
Worm-talk, clashing jaws of moth
Chumbling tiny holes in cloth:
The groan of ants who undertake
Gigantic loads for honor's sake,
Their sinews creak, their breath comes thin:
Whir of spiders when they spin,

And minute, whispering, mumbling sighs
Of idle grubs and flies.
This man is quickened so with grief,
He wanders god-like or like thief
Inside and out, below, above,
Without relief seeking lost love.

TO BRING THE DEAD TO LIFE

To bring the dead to life
Is no great magic.
Few are wholly dead:
Blow on a dead man's embers
And a live flame will start.

Let his forgotten griefs be now,
And now his withered hopes;
Subdue your pen to his handwriting
Until it proves as natural
To sign his name as yours.

Limp as he limped,
Swear by the oaths he swore;
If he wore black, affect the same;
If he had gouty fingers,
Be yours gouty too.

Assemble tokens intimate of him—
A seal, a cloak, a pen:
Around these elements then build
A home familiar to
The greedy revenant.

So grant him life, but reckon
That the grave which housed him
May not be empty now:
You in his spotted garments
Shall yourself lie wrapped.

TO JUAN AT THE WINTER SOLSTICE

There is one story and one story only
That will prove worth your telling,
Whether as learned bard or gifted child;
To it all lines or lesser gauds belong
That startle with their shining
Such common stories as they stray into.

Is it of trees you tell, their months and virtues,
Or strange beasts that beset you,
Of birds that croak at you the Triple will?

Or of the Zodiac and how slow it turns
Below the Boreal Crown,
Prison of all true kings that ever reigned?

Water to water, ark again to ark,
From woman back to woman:
So each new victim treads unfalteringly
The never altered circuit of his fate,
Bringing twelve peers as witness
Both to his starry rise and starry fall.

Or is it of the Virgin's silver beauty,
All fish below the thighs?
She in her left hand bears a leafy quince;
When with her right she crooks a finger, smiling,
How may the King hold back?
Royally then he barters life for love.

Or of the undying snake from chaos hatched,
Whose coils contain the ocean,
Into whose chops with naked sword he springs,
Then in black water, tangled by the reeds,
Battles three days and nights,
To be spewed up beside her scalloped shore?

Much snow is falling, winds roar hollowly,
The owl hoots from the elder,
Fear in your heart cries to the loving-cup:
Sorrow to sorrow as the sparks fly upward.
The log groans and confesses:
There is one story and one story only.

Dwell on her graciousness, dwell on her smilling,
Do not forget what flowers
The great boar trampled down in ivy time.
Her brow was creamy as the crested wave,
Her sea-blue eyes were wild
But nothing promised that is not performed.

THE WHITE GODDESS

All saints revile her, and all sober men
Ruled by the God Apollo's golden mean—
In scorn of which we sailed to find her
In distant regions likeliest to hold her
Whom we desired above all things to know,
Sister of the mirage and echo.

It was a virtue not to stay,
To go our headstrong and heroic way
Seeking her out at the volcano's head,

Among pack ice, or where the track had faded
Beyond the cavern of the seven sleepers:
Whose broad high brow was white as any leper's,
Whose eyes were blue, with rowan-berry lips,
With hair curled honey-coloured to white hips.

Green sap of Spring in the young wood a-stir
Will celebrate the Mountain Mother,
And every song-bird shout awhile for her;
But we are gifted, even in November
Rawest of seasons, with so huge a sense
Of her nakedly worn magnificence
We forget cruelty and past betrayal,
Heedless of where the next bright bolt may fall.

CRY FAUGH!

Caria and Philistia considered
Only pre-marital adventures wise;
The bourgeois French argue contrariwise.

Socrates and Plato burked the issue
(Namely, how man-and-woman love should be)
With homosexual ideology.

Apocalyptic Israelites, foretelling
The Imminent End, called only for a chaste
Sodality: all dead below the waist.

Curious, various, amoral, moral—
Confess, what elegant square or lumpish hamlet
Lives free from nymphological disquiet?

'Yet males and females of the lower species
Contrive to eliminate the sexual problem,'
Scientists ponder: 'Why not learn from them?'

Cry faugh! on science, ethics, metaphysics,
On antonyms of sacred and profane—
Come walk with me, love, in a golden rain

Past toppling colonnades of glory,
The moon alive on each uptilted face:
Proud remnants of a visionary race.

L. A. G. Strong

Leonard Alfred George Strong was born on March 8, 1896, in the parish of Plympton, in Devon. "One of his parents," Strong informed the editor some years ago, "is Irish, the other is half English and half Irish, so that he is fairly entitled to describe himself as a mongrel. He spent his childhood partly on Southern Dartmoor and partly on the borders between Dublin and Wicklow. From a preparatory school at Plymouth, he went with a scholarship to Brighton College, and thence, five years later, won an open Classical Scholarship at Wadham College, Oxford. Illness interrupting his career, he finally graduated in 1920 and taught at Summer Fields, a famous preparatory school near Oxford. Delicate health has confined him to a spectator's part in his favorite sports. Swimming is the only form of violent exercise he has been able to keep up—perhaps because, as legend has it, one of his ancestors, Teig Riarch O'Dowda, King of Connaught, captured and married a mermaid, thereby endowing his descendants with a taste for the sea!"

In 1930 Strong left Oxford and full-time teaching and came down to London and set up shop as a writer. He had behind him the considerable English success of his novel *Dewer Rides* (1929). A complete literary man, Strong's first American reputation came through his poetry. *Dublin Days* (1921), *Selected Poems* (1931), and *Call to the Swans* (1936) were all well received. A prolific novelist and short story writer, Strong worked more surely in the short story. *Travellers* (1945), a short story collection, received the James Tait Black Memorial Prize. Two works of nonfiction are especially noteworthy: *The Sacred River* (1949), one of the sounder books on James Joyce, and *The Writer's Trade* (1953), a professional's account of a beguiling and problematic profession. Strong, who died in 1958, had a virtuosity which would seem peculiar to the English literary life. There was little to which he could not turn his hand. Not only was he poet, novelist, and critic, a writer of detective stories, a BBC radio and television script writer as well as a broadcaster, a teacher of "verse-speaking" in a London drama school, but also he was a director of the distinguished London publishing firm of Metheun.

OLD DAN'L

Out of his cottage to the sun
Bent double comes old Dan'l,
His chest all over cotton wool,
His back all over flannel.

"Winter will finish him," they've said
Each winter now for ten:
But come the first warm day of Spring
Old Dan'l's out again.

ZEKE

Gnarly and bent and deaf's a pos',
Pore old Ezekiel Purvis
Goeth crippin' slowly up the 'ill
To the Commoonion Survis.

And tappy, tappy up the haisle
Goeth stick and brassy ferule:
And Passen[1] 'ath to stoopy down
An' 'oller in ees yerole.

AN OLD WOMAN, OUTSIDE THE ABBEY THEATER

In this Theayter they has plays
On us, and high-up people comes
And pays to see things playin' here
They'd run like hell from in the slums.

[1] Parson.

RUFUS PRAYS

In the darkening church
  Where but a few had stayed
At the Litany Desk
  The idiot knelt and prayed.

Rufus, stunted, uncouth,
  The one son of his mother.
"Eh, I'd sooner 'ave Rufie,"
  She said, "than many another:

" 'E's useful about the 'ouse,
  And so gentle as 'e can be.
An' 'e gets up early o' mornin's
  And makes me a cup o' tea."

The formal evensong
  Had passed over his head:
He sucked his thumb, and squinted,
  And dreamed, instead.

Now while the organ boomed
  To the few who still were there,
At the Litany Desk
  The idiot made his prayer:

"Gawd bless Mother,
  'N make Rufie a good lad:
Take Rufie to Heaven
  'N forgive him when 'e's bad.

" 'N early mornin's in Heaven
  'E'll make mother's tea,
'N a cup for the Lord Jesus
  'N a cup for Thee."

THE MAD WOMAN OF PUNNET'S TOWN

A-swell within her billowed skirts
  Like a great ship with sails unfurled,
The mad woman goes gallantly
  Upon the ridges of her world.

With eagle nose and wisps of gray
  She strides upon the westward hills,
Swings her umbrella joyously
  And waves it to the waving mills.

Talking and chuckling as she goes
  Indifferent both to sun and rain,
With all that merry company:
  The singing children of her brain.

LOWERY COT

This is the house where Jesse White
Run staring in one misty night,
And said he seed the Holy Ghost
Out to Lowery finger-post.

Said It rised up like a cloud
Muttering to Itself out loud,
And stood tremendous on the hill
While all the breathing world was still.

They put en shivering to bed,
And in three days the man was dead.
Gert solemn visions such as they
Be overstrong for mortal clay.

THE DOOR

One in the boat cried out
Pointing to land,
For the sun leaped clear of the mist
And a rainbow spanned
With one vast arch the mountain, the tre
  and the sand.

The mountain stood like a huge
Ghost in a cloud;
The startled trees were caught
In a wavering crowd;
And the four in their glittering oilskins cri
  aloud

As that pure and soaring arch
More marvelous grew,
And the sandhills stared beneath it
Wild and new,
And down the unearthly beaches lamenti
  flew

Gull upon gull distraught
Blown through that Door,
Handful on handful flung
High over the shore.
Such desperate beauty they never had se
  before.

MARCH EVENING

This pool, the quiet sky,
Is rippled with a chime.
Night gathers, and the cry

Of lambs in the far fold
Comes to us as we climb:
The moorland air is cold.

Ghost-pale the grass, and bare
The bowlder-scattered crest.
A frightened rabbit starts—
With quickening eyes and hearts
We turn about, and stare
Into the open west.

The Cornish hills lie small,
So huge the sky has grown.
We can look down on all
Western and southern ground,
And see the Eddystone,
Pricking the seaward pall,
Wink over Plymouth Sound.

Below us, dim and deep,
Mist-hidden, murmuring,
The valley winds away:
Beneath its shadow Spring
Lies light asleep
In dreams of coming day,
With cuckoos on the wing
And steep banks blossoming.

Again the quiet sky
Is troubled with a chime
That spreads in rings of sound.
We sigh, and think, What rhyme
That man has ever bound
Can hold a sigh?

Edmund Blunden

Edmund (C.) Blunden was born in 1896, and educated at Queen's College, Oxford. During the War he served as lieutenant in the Royal Sussex Regiment. His bucolic poems were a direct revulsion from his experiences as a soldier. In 1916 he published three small volumes of pastorals which appeared as one book, *The Wagoner and other Poems*, in 1920. In the same year, he edited, with Alan Porter, *The Poems of John Clare,* most of the verses being deciphered from a mass of old manuscript. Two years later, he published *The Shepherd* (1922), which was awarded the Hawthornden Prize for that year. He was Professor of English Literature at Tokyo University from 1924 to 1927.

The most casual glance at his volumes discloses that Blunden's use of the pastoral note is not, as it is with some of his contemporaries, a mere literary device. Here, the verse is gnarled and twisted as the bent trees of which he loves to write; there is rude country air in his lines and even the words have the smell of apple orchards. It has been objected that Blunden depends too often on unusual and obsolescent terms, but—as Robert Bridges wrote in a pamphlet on *The Dialectical Words in Blunden's Poems* (1921)—"his poetry cannot be imagined without them, and the strength and beauty of the effects must be estimated in his successes and not in his failures."

Blunden's subsequent poetry is milder; a softness but not a flabbiness of texture clothes *To Nature* (1923), *Masks of Time* (1925) and *Retreat* (1928). These verses, lacking the earthy flavor of the early poems, lose the spiciness that dialect confers, but they retain the contemplative quality of Blunden's mind and a dignity which inheres both in the tradition and in the man. *Near and Far* (1929), on the other hand, is composed of pretty trifles which did Blunden's reputation no good. The contents, betraying a monotonous solemnity, are, as Peter Quennell remarked, "a drowsy methodical grinding out of familiar tunes."

In spite of his attainments, Blunden remained known to only a small circle until 1929. In that year he published his large prose work, *Undertones of War,* which was received with instant enthusiasm in Europe and America and took its place among such vivid anti-militaristic documents as Remarque's *All Quiet on the Western Front,* Zweig's *The Case of Sergeant Grischa,* Hemingway's *A Farewell to Arms,* and E. E. Cummings' *The Enormous Room.*

The Poems of Edmund Blunden (1932) collects all the poetry written by Blunden between 1914 and 1930. Nature and war are the chief themes and, though one sometimes wishes for more abandon, no reader can be deaf to the admirable diction and the grave music. *Poems: 1930-1940* and *Shells by a Stream* (1945) reflect the author's gentle clarity but suffer from an obsession with vanished innocence. Blunden is also the author of books on Hardy and Shelley.

(The definitions appended to the poems are by Robert Bridges.)

THE POOR MAN'S PIG

Already fallen plum-bloom stars the green
And apple-boughs as knarred[1] as old toads' backs
Wear their small roses ere a rose is seen;
The building-thrush watches old Job who stacks

The bright-peeled osiers on the sunny fence,
The pent sow grunts to hear him stumping by,
And tries to push the bolt and scamper thence,
But her ringed snout still keeps her to the sty.

Then out he lets her run; away she snorts
In bundling gallop for the cottage door,
With hungry hubbub begging crusts and orts.[2]
Then like a whirlwind bumping round once more;
Nuzzling the dog, making the pullets run,
And sulky as a child when her play's done.

A COUNTRY GOD

When groping farms are lanterned up
And stolchy[3] plowlands hid in grief,
And glimmering byroads catch the drop
That weeps from sprawling twig and leaf,
And heavy-hearted spins the wind
Among the tattered flags of Mirth,—
Then who but I flit to and fro,
With shuddering speech, with mope and mow,
And glass the eyes of earth?

[1] *Knarred,* a word meaning "wrinkled," is a country-cousin to our "gnarled."
[2] *Orts* are fragments or scraps of refuse.
[3] *Stolchy* is such an excellent onomatopoetic word that it scarcely needs explanation. But there is an old English verb *stolch:* "to tread down in wet land or mud."

Then haunt I by some moaning brook
  Where lank and snaky brambles swim,
Or where the hill pines swartly look
  I whirry[1] through the dark and hymn
A dull-voiced dirge and threnody,
  An echo of the sad world's drone
That now appals the friendly stars—
O wail for blind brave youth, whose wars
  Turn happiness to stone.

How rang the cavern-shades of old
  To my melodious pipes, and then
My bright-haired bergomask patrolled
  Each lawn and plot for laughter's din:
Never a sower flung broadcast,
  No hedger brished[2] nor scythesman swung,
Nor maiden trod the purpling press,
But I was by to guard and bless
  And for their solace sung.

But now the sower's hand is writhed
  In livid death, the bright rhythm stolen,
The gold grain flatted and unscythed,
  The boards in the vineyard, gnarled and sullen,
Havocking the grapes; and the pouncing wind
  Spins the spattered leaves of the glen
In a mockery dance, death's hue-and-cry;
With all my murmurous pipes flung by
  And summer not to come again.

THE BARN

in-sunken roof, grown green and thin
r sparrows' nests and starlings' nests;
isheveled eaves; unwieldy doors,
racked rusty pump, and oaken floors,
nd idly-penciled names and jests
Upon the posts within.

e light pales at the spider's lust,
e wind tangs[3] through the shattered pane:
empty hop-poke spreads across
e gaping frame to mend the loss
d keeps out sun as well as rain,
Mildewed with clammy dust.

e smell of apples stored in hay
d homely cattle-cake is there.
Use and disuse have come to terms,
The walls are hollowed out by worms,
But men's feet keep the mid-floor bare
  And free from worse decay.

All merry noise of hens astir
Or sparrows squabbling on the roof
Comes to the barn's broad open door;
You hear upon the stable floor
Old hungry Dapple strike his hoof,
  And the blue fan-tail's whir.

The barn is old, and very old,
But not a place of spectral fear.
Cobwebs and dust and speckling sun
Come to old buildings every one.
Long since they made their dwelling here,
  And here you may behold

[1] *Whirry* is another sound-word, not to be confused with "worry." It means "to fly rapidly with noise"—a combination of "whir" and "hurry."

[2] *Brished* is country dialect for "brush"—principally used in connection with trimming trees and hedges.

[3] *Tangs*—an old term (differing from our word meaning "taste") denoting a barb or a sting. Blunden uses it here as a verb.

Nothing but simple wane and change;
Your tread will wake no ghost, your voice
Will fall on silence undeterred.
No phantom wailing will be heard,
Only the farm's blithe cheerful noise;
The barn is old, not strange.

EASTERN TEMPEST

This flying angel's torrent cry
Will hurl the mountains through the sky!
A wind like fifty winds at once
Through the bedragoned kingdom runs,
And hissing rain slants icy stings
At many a wretch afield who clings
His cloak of straw, with glistening spines
Like a prodigious porcupine's.
The reptile grasses by his path
Wind sleek as unction from that Wrath
Which with its glassy claw uproots
The broad-leaved *kiri,* flays and loots
Torn and sprung sinews, leaves for dead
The young crops with the shining head,
While blotched blunt melons darkly dot
The slaughtered swathes like cannon-shot.
The lotus in the pond upheaves
Its sacred, slow, appealing leaves,
And many a bush with wrestling jerk
Defies the demon's murderous work—
Yet nature stares white-lipped, to read
In Chance's eye what desperate deed?
A kinder god discerns, replies,
And stills the land's storm-shouts to sighs;
The clouds in massy folds apart
Disclose the day's bright bleeding heart,
Huge plumes and scarves black-tossing wide
As if a Kubla Khan had died!
From flame to flame the vision glows,
Till all the pools of heaven unclose
The lotus-light, the hue, the balm
Of wisdom infinitely calm.

THE MIDNIGHT SKATERS

The hop-poles stand in cones,
The icy pond lurks under,
The pole-tops touch the star-gods' thrones
And sound the gulfs of wonder,
But not the tallest there, 'tis said,
Could fathom to this pond's black bed.

Then is not Death at watch
Within those secret waters?
What wants he but to catch
Earth's heedless sons and daughters?
With but a crystal parapet
Between, he has his engines set.

Then on, blood shouts, on, on,
Twirl, wheel and whip above him,
Dance on this ball-floor thin and wan,
Use him as though you love him;
Court him, elude him, reel and pass,
And let him hate you through the glass.

THE RECOVERY

From the dark mood's control
I free this man; there's light still in th
West.
The most virtuous, chaste, melodious soul
Never was better blest.

Here medicine for the mind
Lies in a gilded shade; this feather stirs
And my faith lives; the touch of this tree
Rind,—
And temperate sense recurs.

No longer the loud pursuit
Of self-made clamors dulls the ear; here
dwell
Twilight societies, twig, fungus, root,
Soundless, and speaking well.

Beneath the accustomed dome
Of this chance-planted, many-centuried tr
The snake-marked earthy multitudes a
come
To breathe their hour like me.

The leaf comes curling down,
Another and another, gleam on gleam;
Above, celestial leafage glistens on,
Borne by time's blue stream.

The meadow- stream will serve
For my refreshment; that high glory yiel
Imaginings that slay; the safe paths curve
Through unexalted fields

Like these, where now no more
My early angels walk and call and fly,
But the mouse stays his nibbling, to explo
My eye with his bright eye.

Sacheverell Sitwell

⁂ Sacheverell Sitwell, brother of Edith and Osbert Sitwell, was born in 1897 at Scarborough and educated at Eton. As soon as he was of military age, he joined the Grenadier Guards as second lieutenant. After the War he attended Balliol College, Oxford, for a short time, but came to London before completing his courses, confining his activities to literature.

From the first, his poetry was experimental, but even the early *The People's Palace* contained his gesture. *The Hundred and One Harlequins* (1922) and *The Thirteenth Caesar* (1924) are less dependent on influences, although the accents of such dissimilar poets as Vachel Lindsay and T. S. Eliot arise from his pages. Here the youngest of the Sitwells displays a lively imagination, a delight in toying with the subject as well as distorting it, a glittering, if sometimes too self-conscious, cleverness.

His more recent work shows him milder in manner and idiom. Less distinctive than his strepitant sister and brother, he seems to be developing a more traditional vein. His larger efforts would seem to dispute this; "Canons of Giant Art" and "Doctor Donne and Gargantua" are exercises in the approved modern manner. But they are not the poet. Try as he will with all the resources of the brain, his art is not in them. His art (and for that manner his heart) finds its response in unaffected song, a group of twenty-five lyrics being the core of *The Cyder Feast* (1927). Apart from a dissonance or two, an inverted image, a strained or dislocated adjective, these horticultural verses might have been written in the eighteenth century.

It is curious to note how the more modern "modernists" turn their eyes not to formless futurism, but to a precise past. Thus we find T. S. Eliot rediscovering Dryden and Lancelot Andrewes, Humbert Wolfe looting the Greek Anthology, Edith Sitwell turning from Gertrude Stein and Dr. Steiner to pen an introduction to the didactic rhymes of Jane Taylor. And here, in *The Cyder Feast,* in the midst of the "alchemy of dank leaves," one finds the youngest Sitwell writing "Four Variations upon William Browne of Tavistock," "Variations on a Theme by Robert Herrick," "Variation upon a Couplet of Alexander Pope," "An Adaption from John Milton." Moreover most of the poems not adapted or "varied" betray accents of a period that is scarcely Sitwellian. "Tulip Tree" and "Kingcups" are two examples among many. *Canons of Giant Art* (1933) continues the classical "heroic" strain.

The eruption of a kind of architectural fancy is natural in one who has established himself as an authority on the genesis of the rococo, notably in *Southern Baroque Art* (1924), *German Baroque Art* (1927), and *The Gothick North* (1929). *Selected Poems* (1948) was introduced with a proud preface by Osbert Sitwell.

FOUNTAINS

This night is pure and clear as thrice refinèd silver.
Silence, the cape of Death, lies heavy
Round the bare shoulders of the hills.
Faint throbs and murmurs

At moments growing to a mutter, then subsiding,
Fill the night with mystery and panic.
The honey-tongued arguings of fountains
Stir the air with flutes and gentle voices.

The graven fountain-masks suffer and weep—
Curved with a smile, the poor mouths
Clutch at a half-remembered song
Striving to forget the agony of ever laughing,—
Laughing while they hear the secrets
Echoed from the depths of Earth beneath them.

This half-remembered song—
This flow of sad-restrainèd laughter
Jars with the jets of youthful water
Springing from the twisted masks,
For this is but the birth of water;
And singing joyfully
It springs upon the world
And wanders ceaselessly
Along its jeweled valleys to the sea,
Rattling like rolls of drums
The shells and pebbles down its bed.

The endless argument of water ceases,
A few drops fall heavily, splashing on the marble:
A Sultan with his treasures
Seeking to gain the goodwill of his love,
Pouring before her chains of crackling pearls
And weeping heavy jealous tears
Because she will not heed him.

THE RED-GOLD RAIN

(*Orange Tree by Day*)

Sun and rain at work together
Ripened this for summer weather;
Sun gave it color tawny red
And rain its life as though it bled;
In the long days full of fire
Its fruit will cool us when we tire.
Against the house-wall does it grow
With smooth stem like a fountain's flow,
Dark are its leaves, a colder shade
Than ever rock or mountain made;
When the wind plays soft they sing,
For here the birds' songs never ring,
Quite still the fruit that in a golden shower
Will fall one day to flood this tower.

"PSITTACHUS EOIS IMITATRIX ALES AB INDIS"—*Ovid*

The parrot's voice snaps out—
No good to contradict—
What he says he'll say again:
Dry facts, like biscuits,—

His voice and vivid colors
Of his breast and wings
Are immemorably old;
Old dowagers dressed in crimpèd satin
Boxed in their rooms
Like specimens beneath a glass
Inviolate—and never changing,
Their memory of emotions dead:
The ardor of their summers

Sprayed like camphor
On their silken parasols
Intissued in a cupboard.

Reflective, but with never a new thought
The parrot sways upon his ivory perch—
Then gravely turns a somersault
Through rings nailed in the roof—
Much as the sun performs his antics
As he climbs the aerial bridge
We only see
Through crystal prisms in a falling rain.

TULIP TREE

Whose candles light the tulip tree?
What is this subtle alchemy,
That builds an altar in one night
And touches the green boughs with light?
Look at the shaped leaves below
And see the scissor-marks they show,
As if a tailor had cut fine
The marking of their every line!

These are no leaves of prudery
Hiding what all eyes should see;
No Adam and no Eve lie hid
Below this leafy coverlid:
The long limbs of that flower-hid girl
Would need no leaves to twist and curl,
The markings of that leaf-hid boy
Want no flowers to mar and cloy.

And so these cut leaves and their lights
Live only for the tulip-rites
At this altar of bright fires
Sweet-scented lest their ardor tires;
Leaf, and flower, and scent are all
Alive for this lit interval:
Between two winters are they born
To make great summer seem forlorn.

KINGCUPS

When poetry walked the live, spring wood,
Hid, ghostlike, in the leaves' green hood
She came to a slant fence of sun,
Whose golden timbers, one by one,
Trod into a marsh's toils
And here she stayed her flowery spoils;
But pitying the marshes' plight
She shook her lap and wide and bright
Great kingcups to that waste she threw
Where nothing lived and nothing grew;
Now, where poetry passed, there stays
The light of suns, the fire of days,
And these cups for kings to hold
Make summer with their wide-eyed gold.

THE RIVER GOD

Leap out, chill water, over reeds and brakes,
Flash bright your sword
Out of my hand that never shakes,
Your voice rings louder than my whispered word,
For my song is but a murmur down the wind and water
No louder than the leaves that make my chequered shade,
Cooling the bank on which I'm laid.
My urn I move not, lest the blade may break,
Its round lip no more dropping water,
When this, my river, at its source will die
And sinking through the sand will bare each daughter,
Born of this glassy world, though now they lie
On the green bank high above that falling flood,
And wait like snow for sun or rain to move them.
I could not help them, were my stream to stop,
Until it springs again from out my urn,
But now it floods the pool and wells up high,
Sparkling like the sun's gold eye,

While from this plenitude it flows away
And hides those nymphs again below its glass.
Heaped on the hills, till with the sun they flow,
Safe runs the river now made sure with snow,
Snow, as those nymphs cool, as white my locks,
Which, while they also fall, tell time like clocks.

FROM "AGAMEMNON'S TOMB"

One by one, as harvesters, all heavy laden,
The bees sought their corridor into the dome
With honey of the asphodel, the flower of death,
Or thyme, rain-sodden, and more sweet for that;
Here was their honeycomb, high in the roof,
I heard sweet summer from their drumming wings,
Though it wept and rained and was the time of tears;
They made low music, they murmured in the tomb,
As droning nuns through all a shuttered noon,
Who prayed in this place of death, and knew it not.

How sweet such death, with honey from the flowers,
A little air, a little light, and drone of wings,
To long monotony, to prison of the tomb!
But he did not know it. His bones, picked clean,
Were any other bones. The trick is in our mind:
They love not a bed, nor raiment for their bones,
They are happy on cold stone or in the aching water,
And neither care, nor care not, they are only dead.
It once was Agamemnon, and we think him happy:
O false, false hope! How empty his happiness,
All for a fine cavern and the hum of bees.

Ruth Pitter

Ruth Pitter was born in Ilford, a village in the Essex forest, November 7, 1897. Daughter of a schoolteacher, she was educated at Coborn School, Bow, London. There (to continue her informal autobiographical note) she learned to cook "and got a certain amount of natural science, and a faint but indelible smear of Latin. Matriculated, and as war came when I was nearly through my Intermediate Arts year, and I had no predilections as regards a career, I went to the War Office and worked for nearly two years at 25 shillings a week." The first World War over, Miss Pitter learned woodwork and painting, went into business, and made a specialty of hand-painted trays. The second World War bombed her shop out of existence.

Ruth Pitter wrote verse at the age of five and published her first book in her twenty-third year. She never had a large popular success, although she was continually acclaimed by her fellow poets. *A Trophy of Arms* (1936) was prefaced by

James Stephens; *A Mad Lady's Garland* (1935) carried two introductions, one by Hilaire Belloc and the other by the poet laureate John Masefield. Beset by increasing difficulties and an ungenial mental climate, Miss Pitter steadfastly refused to dramatize her conflicts. Calm, even dream-like, the surface of her poetry is deceptive. The texture is smooth and graceful; the idiom is quietly conventional; the statements are seemingly casual. But the craftsmanship is unusually disciplined, and the tone is unmistakably the tone of a high order of poetry.

The Spirit Watches (1940) indicates a firm control of fluid material as well as constant growth. The fanciful soliloquies have changed to intense meditations, the mocking parodies have turned into earnest wit. Miss Pitter is that rare thing: a mystic with a sense of humor, an initiate whose revelations are immediate, eager, and seldom arcane. *The Ermine* (1953) received the Heinemann Foundation Award, and in 1955 Miss Pitter was awarded the Queen's Gold Medal for Poetry.

THE TASK

everse the flight of Lucifer,
lurl back to heaven the fallen star;
ecall Eve's fate, establish her
gain where the first glories are:
gain where Eden's rivers are.

hrust back contention, merge in one
/arring dualities, make free
'ight of the moon, day of the sun;
nd the old war of land and sea,
ying, There shall be no more sea.

With love of love now make an end;
Let male and female strive no more;
Let good and bad their quarrel mend
And with an equal voice adore;
The lion with the lamb adore.

Bow softly saint, rise humble sin,
Fall from your throne, creep from your den:
The king, the kingdom is within,
That is for evermore, amen:
Was dead and is alive. Amen.

THE COFFIN-WORM

The Worm unto his love: lo, here's fresh store;
Want irks us less as men are pinched the more.
Why dost thou lag? thou pitiest the man?
Fall to, the while I teach thee what I can.
Men in their lives full solitary be:
We are their last and kindest company.
Lo, where care's claws have been! those marks are grim;
Go, gentle Love, erase the scar from him.
Hapless perchance in love (most men are so),
Our quaint felicity he could not know:
We and our generation shall sow love
Throughout that frame he was not master of;
Flatter his wishful beauties; in his ear
Whisper he is at last beloved here;
Sing him (and in no false and siren strain)
We will not leave him while a shred remain
On his sweet bones. Then shall our labor cease,
And the imperishable part find peace,
Even from love. Meanwhile how blest he lies,
Love in his heart, his empty hands, his eyes.

THE UNICORN

Hate me or love, I care not, as I pass
To those hid citadels
Where in the depth of my enchanted glass
The changeless image dwells;
To where for ever blooms the nameless tree;
For ever, alone and fair,
The lovely Unicorn beside the sea
Is laid, and slumbers there.

Give or withhold, all's nothing, as I go
On to those glimmering grounds
Where falling secretly and quiet as snow
The silent music sounds;
Where earth is withered away before the
eyes,
And heaven hangs in the air,
For in the oak the bird of paradise
Alights, and triumphs there.

Slay me or spare, it matters now: I fly
Ever, for ever rest
Alone and with a host: in the void sky
There do I build my nest:
I lay my beams from star to star, and make
My house where all is bare;
Hate, slay, withhold, I rear it for thy sake
And thou art with me there.

THE ETERNAL IMAGE

Her angel looked upon God's face
As eagles gaze upon the sun,
Fair in the everlasting place.

And saw that everything is one
And moveless, in the eternal light:
Never completed, not begun.

She on the earth, with steadfast sight,
Stood like an image of the Muse
Amid the falling veils of night:

Her feet were silvered in the dews,
Dew fell upon her darkling tree,
And washed the plain with whitish hues.

Standing so still, what does she see?
She sees the changeless creature shine
Apparelled in eternity:

She knows the constancy divine;
The whole of life sees harvested,
And frozen into crystalline

And final form, the quick, the dead,
All that has ever seemed to change,
Possess at once the pale and red:

All that from birth to death may range
Newborn and dead she sees, nor says
The vision to be sad or strange.

How may this serve her mortal ways?
Truly it cannot buy her bread
Nor ease the labor of her days:

But calm her waking, quiet her bed.
For she has seen the perfect round
That binds the infant to the dead,

And one by one draws underground
All men; and still, and one by one,
Into the air the living bound,

Never completed, not begun.
With burning hair, with moveless grace,
As eagles gaze against the sun

Her angel looks upon God's face.

TIME'S FOOL

Time's fool, but not heaven's: yet hope not for any return.
The rabbit-eaten dry branch and the halfpenny candle
Are lost with the other treasure: the sooty kettle
Thrown away, become redbreast's home in the hedge, where the nettle
Shoots up, and bad bindweed wreathes rust-fretted handle.
Under that broken thing no more shall the dry branch burn.

Poor comfort all comfort: once what the mouse had spared
Was enough, was delight, there where the heart was at home;
The hard cankered apple holed by the wasp and the bird,
The damp bed, with the beetle's tap in the headboard heard,
The dim bit of mirror, three inches of comb:
Dear enough, when with youth and with fancy shared.

I knew that the roots were creeping under the floor,
That the toad was safe in his hole, the poor cat by the fire,
The starling snug in the roof, each slept in his place:
The lily in splendor, the vine in her grace,
The fox in the forest, all had their desire,
As then I had mine, in the place that was happy and poor.

THE SWAN BATHING

Now to be clean he must abandon himself
To that fair yielding element whose lord he is.
There where she is strongest, in mid-current,
Facing the stream, he half sinks, who knows how?
His armed head, his prow wave-worthy, he dips under:
The meeting streams glide rearward, fill the hollow
Of the proud wings; then as if fainting he falls sidelong,
Prone, without shame, reveals the shiplike belly,
Tumbling reversed, with limp black paddles waving,
And down, gliding abandoned, helplessly wallows,
The head and neck, wrecked mast and pennon, trailing.

It is enough: satisfied he rears himself,
Sorts with swift movement his disordered tackle,
Rises, again the master: and so seated
Riding, he spreads his wings and flogs the water
Lest she should triumph; in a storm of weeping
And a great halo of her tears transfigured,
With spreading circles of his force he smites her,
Till remote tremblings heave her rushy verges
And all her lesser lives are rocked with rumour.

Now they are reconciled; with half-raised pinion
And backward-leaning head pensively sailing,

With silver furrow the reflected evening
Parting, he softly goes; and one cold feather
Drifts, and is taken gently by the rushes:
By him forgotten, and by her remembered.

Richard Hughes

☙ Richard Hughes was born in 1900 of a Welsh family settled in England. Educated at Charterhouse School and Oriel College, Oxford, his first play, *The Sisters' Tragedy,* was produced in London in 1922 while Hughes was still an undergraduate. In the same year, his first volume of poems, *Gypsy-Night,* appeared and before he graduated he was poetry-critic to the London *Saturday Westminster* and contributor to leading periodicals. He traveled extensively in Europe, North Africa, and America, often on foot, and has, he confesses, "a slight amateur knowledge of Balkan revolutions and seamanship."

Hughes began his career as a poet although his reputation was made by two dramas. The first of these has been mentioned; the other, composed in his twenties, was a comedy praised by Shaw and selected with works of Chekhov and Pirandello as "one of the three most important productions in London in seven years."

Gypsy-Night (1922) marked the début of a poet with acute sensibility, a precocious apprehension emphasized by the short stories in *A Moment of Time* (1925). After a silence of three years, Hughes published his first full-length novel, *The Innocent Voyage* (1929), published in England as *A High Wind in Jamaica.* This tale is an accomplishment in an untried genre. Upon a basis of traditional melodrama, including pirates and kidnaping, Hughes has constructed a story wholly unexpected, an unromantic romance, where the psychological reënforces the fantastic and where the union of cut-throats and children is convincing, delicate and, at the same time, horrible. Modern writing has produced several techniques for dealing fancifully with the commonplace; Hughes has developed a realistic way of handling the extraordinary.

This gift of familiarizing the unusual is of paramount service to his poetry. Chekhov counseled writers to cease being insincere about the moon and say what they really felt about a rain-puddle. But, Hughes implies, one can also be faithful to subject and self, when writing about the moon, or the mad immortal unicorn, or the elephant-swallowing roc, or inditing meditative and ecstatic odes to vision, or transfixing the windlike passing of Time. Such subjects brighten the pages of *Confessio Juvenis* (1926) which, as its title indicates, collects Hughes' early work. But if it is a poet's eye which rolls toward these strangenesses, it is his mind which carries them off in a fine frenzy.

Besides three privately printed volumes, Hughes is the author of some seven books. His collected *Plays* were issued in 1928 and his edition of John Skelton's poems appeared in 1924. *In Hazard* (1938) emphasizes his gift for fantastic fiction.

INVOCATION TO THE MUSE

Fair maiden, fair maiden,
  Come spin for me:
Come spin till you're laden
  Though hard it may be.

'Tis an honor and glory
  To be a king's maid,
Though (I'll not tell a story)
  You won't be well paid.

Aetat. 6

TRAMP

(*The Bath Road, June*)

When a brass sun staggers above the sky,
When feet cleave to boots, and the tongue's dry,
And sharp dust goads the rolling eye
Come thoughts of wine and dancing thoughts of girls:
They shiver their white arms, and the head whirls,
And noon light is hid in their dark curls;
Then noon feet stumble, and head swims,
Till out shines the sun, and the thought dims;
And death, for blood, runs in the weak limbs.

To fall on flints in the shade of tall nettles
Gives easy sleep as a bed of rose petals,
And dust drifting from the highway
As light a coverlet as down may.
The myriad feet of many-sized flies
May not open those tired eyes.

But the first wind of night
Twitches the coverlet away quite:
The first wind and large first rain,
Flickers the dry pulse to life again,
Flickers the lids burning on the eyes:
Come sudden flashes of the slipping skies:
Hunger, oldest visionary,
Hides a devil in a tree,
Hints a glory in the clouds,
Fills the crooked air with crowds
Of ivory sightless demons singing—
Eyes start: straightens back:
Limbs stagger and crack:
But brain flies, brain soars
Up, where the Sky roars
Upon the backs of cherubim:
Brain rockets up to Him.

Body gives another twist
To the slack waist-band;
In agony clenches fist
Till the nails bite the hand.
Body floats light as air,
With rain in its sparse hair.

Brain returns; and he would tell
The things he has seen well:

But Body will not stir his lips:
So Mind and Body come to grips
And deadly each hates the other
As his treacherous blood-brother.

Yet no sight, no sound shows
How the struggle goes.

I sink at last faint in the wet gutter;
So many words to speak that the tongue cannot utter.

LOVER'S REPLY TO GOOD ADVICE

Could you bid an acorn
When in earth it heaves
On Time's backward wing be borne
To forgotten leaves:
Could you quiet Noah's flood
To an essence rare,
Or bid the roaring wind
Confine in his lair:

Could round the iron shell
When the spark was in it
Hold gun-powder so well
That it never split:
Had you reins for the sun,
And curb and spur,
Held you God in a net
So He might not stir:

Then might you take this thing,
Then strangle it, kill:
By weighing, considering,
Conform it to will:
As man denied his Christ
Deny it, mock, betray—
But being Seed, Wind, God,
It bears all away.

ON TIME

Unhurried as a snake I saw Time glide
Out of the shape of his material frame:
I, who am part of Time's material name,
Saw that unhurried serpent quietly slide
Through a straight crack in his material side
Between a prince and a stone: flicker, and presently coil,
A small bright worm about a stalk of fennel;
While light stood still as spar, and smell
Spread like a fan, sound hung festooned, and toil
Rose balanced and patterned like a storied palace
Whose wild tons grapple in immovable grace;
While laughter sat on a rustic seat with tears
And watched the corn-sheaves lean across the plow:
Ah! then what wind across the nodding years!
What ecstasies upon the bough
Sang, like a fountain to its peers:
And in the meadows what deep-rooted men
Flowered their lovely faces in the grass,
Where death, like a butterfly of dark-colored glass,
Flitted and sipped, and sipped again!

BURIAL OF THE SPIRIT
OF A YOUNG POET

Dead hangs the fruit on that tall tree:
The lark in my cold hand is dead.
What meats his funeral stars decree
By their own light I've spread:
The bearded fog among the leaves
Too sad to move, excludes the air:
No bursting seed this stiff soil heaves,
Nor ever will again, when we have laid him there.

Then come, ye silent wheels of fire,
Ye birds among the tulip-trees,
And let your brilliancy conspire
In rings of visual threnodies:
And thou, heart-breaking nightingale
Who phoenix-like forever burnst
In thine own voice, oh Philomel
Let not thy tuneful flame now fail,
But burn in it this spirit pale
Which once was grand, but now to naught, to nothing-naught returns.

Roy Campbell

Roy Campbell was born October 2, 1901, in Durban, South Africa. A tempestuous figure, he was an editor discharged for his opinions, a professional steer-thrower and bull-fighter, a soldier under Franco, a Freethinker who became a Fascist and, subsequently, a Roman Catholic. He died in an automobile smashup in Portugal, April 24, 1957.

The Flaming Terrapin appeared in 1922. It was at once apparent that a poet of unusual vitality had come out of the Colonies. Campbell had chosen a huge theme and he had sufficient vigor to cope with it. The poem is a broad allegory: The ark of Noah plunges through terror and tempest carrying with it all of humanity. Unlike the Biblical vessel, this ark does not merely float; it is pulled along, swept to its goal by a tremendous saurian, blood brother to Leviathan, a Flaming Terrapin, which is the symbol of the all-suffering, all-surviving power of persistence. It is this monster, the life-force, which brings the ark to a richer Ararat.

So much for the theme. The reader, however, is scarcely aware of the philosophic content, for the lines sweep him on at such a pace that he is conscious of little except the momentum of the verse, the bright concatenation of figures, and a general sense of exuberance. The headlong speed may be accounted a vice, but Campbell's poetic vices and virtues are inseparable. Both proceed from prodigality; epithet and emotion rush forward in continual and creative excitement.

The Wayzgoose (1928) is a more local and less arousing work. Satirizing conditions in South Africa, it limits not only Campbell's audience but his own spirit, for this poet needs amplitude for his effects. The subsequent poetry is in the early, gustier vein with a new control. "Tristan Da Cunha" and "The Palm" display less alacrity and violence than *The Flaming Terrapin,* but contain much of its lavish energy. "The Palm" is particularly successful in its combinations of assonance and interior rhyming. In addition, the new poems have a condensed power which dignifies the sometimes too crashing effects in *Adamastor* (1930), the satirical "Charlotade," *The Georgiad* (1931), and *Flowering Reeds* (1933). They still suffer from the poet's uncertainty; undecided whether to be a satirist or a poet in the grand manner, Campbell fell back upon sonority and his own dynamic energy.

THE ZEBRAS

From the dark woods that breathe of fallen showers,
Harnessed with level rays in golden reins,
The zebras draw the dawn across the plains
Wading knee-deep among the scarlet flowers.
The sunlight, zithering their flanks with fire,
Flashes between the shadows as they pass
Barred with electric tremors through the grass
Like wind along the gold strings of a lyre.

Into the flushed air snorting rosy plumes
That smolder round their feet in drifting fumes,

With dove-like voices call the distant fillies,
While round the herds the stallion wheels his flight,
Engine of beauty volted with delight,
To roll his mare among the trampled lilies.

TRISTAN DA CUNHA

Snore in the foam: the night is vast and blind,
The blanket of the mist around your shoulders,
Sleep your old sleep of rock, snore in the wind,
Snore in the spray! The storm your slumber lulls,
His wings are folded on your nest of bowlders
As on their eggs the gray wings of your gulls.

No more as when, ten thousand years ago,
You hissed a giant cinder from the ocean—
Around your rocks you furl the shawling snow,
Half sunk in your own darkness, vast and grim,
And round you on the deep with surly motion
Pivot your league-long shadow as you swim.

Why should you haunt me thus but that I know
My surly heart is in your own displayed,
Round whom such wastes in endless circuit flow,
Whose hours in such a gloomy compass run—
A dial with its league-long arm of shade
Slowly revolving to the moon and sun.

My heart has sunk, like your gray fissured crags,
By its own strength o'ertoppled and betrayed:
I too have burned the wind with fiery flags,
Who now am but a roost for empty words—
An island of the sea whose only trade
Is in the voyages of its wandering birds.

Did you not, when your strength became your pyre,
Deposed and tumbled from your flaming tower,
Awake in gloom from whence you sank in fire
To find Antaeus-like, more vastly grown,
A throne in your own darkness, and a power
Sheathed in the very coldness of your stone?

Your strength is that you have no hope or fear,
You march before the world without a crown:
The nations call you back, you do not hear:
The cities of the earth grow gray behind you,
You will be there when their great flames go down
And still the morning in the van will find you.

You march before the continents: you scout
In front of all the earth: alone you scale
The masthead of the world, a lorn look-out,

Waving the snowy flutter of your spray
And gazing back in infinite farewell
To suns that sink, and shores that fade away.

From your gray tower what long regrets you fling
To where, along the low horizon burning,
The great swan-breasted seraphs soar and sing,
And suns go down, and trailing splendors dwindle,
And sails on lonely errands unreturning,
Glow with a gold no sunrise can rekindle.

Turn to the Night, these flames are not for you
Whose steeple for the thunder swings its bells:
Gray Memnon, to the tempest only true,
Turn to the night, turn to the shadowing foam,
And let your voice, the saddest of farewells,
With sullen curfew toll the gray wings home.

The wind your mournful syren haunts the gloom:
The rocks, spray-clouded, are your signal-guns
Whose stony niter, puffed with flying spume
Rolls forth in grim salute your broadside hollow,
Over the gorgeous burials of suns,
To sound the tocsin of the storms that follow.

Plunge forward; like a ship to battle hurled,
Slip the long cables of the failing light,
The level rays that moor you to the world:
Sheathed in your armor of eternal frost,
Plunge forward, in the thunder of the fight
To lose yourself as I would fain be lost.

Exiled, like you, and severed from my race
By the cold ocean of my own disdain,
Do I not freeze in such a wintry space,
Do I not travel through a storm as vast
And rise at times, victorious from the main,
To fly the sunrise at my shattered mast?

Your path is but a desert where you reap
Only the bitter knowledge of your soul,
You fish with nets of seaweed in the deep
As fruitlessly as I with nets of rhyme,
Yet forth you stride: yourself the way, the goal,
The surges are your strides, your path is time.

Hurled by what aim to what tremendous range!
A missile from the great sling of the past
Your passage leaves its track of death and change
And ruin on the world: you fly beyond,
Leaping the current of the ages vast
As lightly as a pebble skims a pond.

The years are undulations in your flight
Whose awful motion we can only guess:
Too swift for sense, too terrible for sight,
We only know how fast behind you darken
Our days like lonely beacons of distress:
We know that you stride on and will not hearken.

Now in the eastern sky the fairest planet
Pierces the dying wave with dangled spear,
And in the whirring hollows of your granite
That vaster Sea, to which you are a shell,
Sighs with a ghostly rumor like the drear
Moan of the nightwind in a hollow cell.

We shall not meet again: over the wave
Our ways divide, and yours is straight and endless—
But mine is short and crooked to the grave:
Yet what of these dark crowds, amid whose flow
I battle like a rock, aloof and friendless—
Are not their generations, vague and endless,
The waves, the strides, the feet on which I go?

FROM "THE FLAMING TERRAPIN"

Part I

Maternal Earth stirs redly from beneath
Her blue sea-blanket and her quilt of sky,
A giant Anadyomene from the sheath
And chrysalis of darkness; till we spy
Her vast barbaric haunches, furred with trees,
Stretched on the continents, and see her hair
Combed in a surf of fire along the breeze
To curl about the dim sierras, where
Faint snow-peaks catch the sun's far-swiveled beams:
And, tinder to his rays, the mountain-streams
Kindle, and volleying with a thunder-stroke
Out of their roaring gullies, burst in smoke
To shred themselves as fine as women's hair,
And hoop gay rainbows on the sunlit air.
Winnowed by radiant eagles, in whose quills
Sing the swift gales, and on whose waving plumes
Flashing sunbeams ignite—the towering hills
Yearn to the sun, rending the misty fumes
That clogged their peaks, and from each glistening spire
Fling to the winds their rosy fleece of fire.
Far out to sea the gales with savage sweep
Churning the water, waken drowsy fins
Huge fishes to propel from monstrous sleep,
That spout their pride as the red day begins,
"We are the great volcanoes of the deep!"

Now up from the intense creative Earth
Spring her strong sons: the thunder of their mirth
Vibrates upon the shining rocks and spills
In floods of rolling music on the hills.
Action and flesh cohere in one clean fusion
Of force with form: the very ethers breed
Wild harmonies of song: the frailest reed
Holds shackled thunder in its heart's seclusion.
And every stone that lines my lonely way,
Sad tongueless nightingale without a wing,
Seems on the point of rising up to sing
And donning scarlet for its dusty gray!

How often have I lost this fervent mood,
And gone down dingy thoroughfares to brood
On evils like my own from day to day;
"Life is a dusty corridor," I say,
"Shut at both ends." But far across the plain,
Old Ocean growls and tosses his gray mane,
Pawing the rocks in all his old unrest
Or lifting lazily on some white crest
His pale foam-feathers for the moon to burn—
Then to my veins I feel new sap return,
Strength tightens up my sinews long grown dull,
And in the old charred crater of the skull
Light strikes the slow somnambulistic mind
And sweeps her forth to ride the rushing wind,
And stamping on the hill-tops high in air,
To shake the golden bonfire of her hair.

This sudden strength that catches up men's souls
And rears them up like giants in the sky,
Giving them fins where the dark ocean rolls,
And wings of eagles when the whirlwinds fly,
Stands visible to me in its true self
(No spiritual essence of wing'd elf
Like Ariel on the empty winds to spin).
I see him as a mighty Terrapin,
Rafting whole islands on his stormy back,
Built of strong metals molten from the black
Roots of the inmost earth: a great machine,
Thoughtless and fearless, governing the clean
System of active things: the winds and currents
Are his primeval thoughts: the raging torrents
Are moods of his, and men who do great deeds
Are but the germs his awful fancy breeds.

For when the winds have ceased their ghostly speech
And the long waves roll moaning from the beach,
The Flaming Terrapin that towed the Ark
Rears up his hump of thunder on the dark,

And like a mountain, seamed with rocky scars,
Crinkles white rings, as from its ancient sleep
Into a foam of life he wakes the Deep.
His was the crest that from the angry sky
Tore down the hail: he made the bowlders fly
Like balls of paper, splintered icebergs, hurled
Lassoes of dismal smoke around the world,
And like a bunch of crisp and crackling straws,
Coughed the sharp lightning from his craggy jaws.
His was the eye that blinked beyond the hill
After the fury of the flood was done,
And breaching from the bottom, cold and still,
Leviathan reared up to greet the Sun.
Perched on the stars around him in the air,
White angels rinsed the moonlight from their hair,
And the drowned trees into new flowers unfurled
As it sank dreaming down upon the world.
As he rolled by, all evil things grew dim.
The Devil, who had scoffed, now slunk from him
And sat in Hell, dejected and alone,
Rasping starved teeth against an old dry bone.

Before the coral reared its sculptured fern
Or the pale shellfish, swinging in the waves
With pointed steeples, had begun to turn
The rocks to shadowy cities—from dark caves
The mixed and drowsy poisons of the sea
Mixed their corrosive strength with horny stones,
And coaxed new substances from them to be
The ponderous material of his bones.
The waves by slow erosion did their part
Shaping his heavy bonework from the mass,
And in that pillared temple grew a heart
That branched with mighty veins, through which to pass
His blood, that, filtering the tangled mesh,
Built walls of gristle, clogged each hollow gap
With concrete vigor, till through bone and flesh
Flowed the great currents of electric sap.
While thunder clanging from the cloudy rack
With elemental hammers fierce and red,
Tempered the heavy target of his back,
And forged the brazen anvil of his head.

Freed from the age-long agonies of birth
This living galleon oars himself along
And roars his triumph over all the earth
Until the sullen hills burst into song.
His beauty makes a summer through the land,
And where he crawls upon the solid ground,
Gigantic flowers, exploding from the sand,
Spread fans of blinding color all around.

His voice has roused the amorphous mud to life—
Dust thinks: and tired of spinning in the wind,
Stands up to be a man and feel the strife
Of brute-thoughts in the jungle of his mind.
Bellerophon, the primal cowboy, first
Heard that wild summons on the stillness burst,
As, from the dusty mesa leaping free,
He slewed his white-winged broncho out to sea,
And shaking loose his flaming coils of hair,
Shot whistling up the smooth blue roads of air:
As he rose up, the moon with slanted ray
Ruled for those rapid hoofs a shining way,
And streaming from their caves, the sirens came
Riding on seals to follow him: the flame
Of their moon-tinseled limbs had flushed the dim
Green depths, and as when winds in Autumn skim
Gold acres, rustling plume with fiery plume,
Their long hair flickered skyward in the gloom,
Tossed to the savage rhythms of their tune.
Till, far across the world, the rising moon
Heard, ghost-like, in the embered evening sky
Their singing fade into a husky sigh,
And splashed with stars and dashed with stinging spray
The dandy of the prairies rode away!

That voice on Samson's mighty sinews rang
As on a harp's tense chords: each fiber sang
In all his being: rippling their strings of fire,
His nerves and muscles, like a wondrous lyre,
Vibrated to that sound; and through his brain
Proud thoughts came surging in a georgeous train.
He rose to action, slew the grumbling bear,
Hauled forth the flustered lion from its lair
And swung him yelping skyward by the tail:
Tigers he mauled, with tooth and ripping nail
Rending their straps of fire, and from his track
Slithering like quicksilver, pouring their black
And liquid coils before his pounding feet,
He drove the livid mambas of deceit.
Oppression, like a starved hyena, sneaked
From his loud steps: Tyranny, vulture-beaked,
Rose clapping iron wings, and in a cloud
Of smoke and terror, wove its own dark shroud,
As he strode by and in his tossing hair,
Rippled with sunshine, sang the morning air.

Like a great bell clanged in the winds of Time,
Linking the names of heroes chime by chime
That voice rolled on, and as it filled the night
Strong men rose up, thrilled with the huge delight

Of their own energy. Upon the snows
Of Ararat gigantic Noah rose,
Stiffened for fierce exertion, like the thong
That strings a bow before its arrow strong
Sings on the wind; and from his great fists hurled
Red thunderbolts to purify the world.

THE PALM

Blistered and dry was the desert I trod
When out of the sky with the step of a god,
Victory-vanned with her feathers out-fanned,
The palm tree alighting my journey delayed
And spread me, inviting, her carpet of shade.
Vain were evasions, though urgent my quest,
And there as the guests of her lovely persuasions
To lie in the shade of her branches was best.
Like a fountain she played, spilling plume over plume in
A golden cascade for the winds to illumine,
Ascending in brilliance and falling in shade,
And spurning the ground with a tiptoe resilience
Danced to the sound of the music she made.
Her voice intervened on my shadowed seclusion
Like the whispered intrusion of seraph or fiend,
In its tone was the hiss of the serpent's wise tongue,
But soft as the kiss of a lover it stung—
"Unstrung is your lute? For despair are you silent?
Am I not an island in oceans as mute?
Around me the thorns of the desert take root;
Though I spring from the rock of a region accurst,
Yet fair is the daughter of hunger and thirst
Who sings like the water the valleys have nursed,
And rings her blue shadow as deep and as cool
As the heavens of azure that sleep on a pool.
And you, who so soon by the toil were undone,
Could you guess through what horrors my beauty had won
Ere I crested the noon as the bride of the sun?
The roots are my anchor struck fast in the hill,
The higher I hanker, the deeper they drill,
Through the red mortar their claws interlock
To ferret the water through warrens of rock.
Each inch of my glory was wrenched with a groan,
Corroded with fire from the base of my throne
And drawn like a wire from the heart of a stone:
Though I soar in the height with a shape of delight
Uplifting my stem like the string of a kite,
Yet still must each grade of my climbing be told
And still from the summit my measure I hold,
Sounding the azure with plummet of gold,
Partaking the strain of the heavenward pride
That soars me away from the earth I deride.

Though my stem be a rein that would tether me down
And fasten a chain on the height of my crown,
Yet through its tense nerve do I measure my might,
The strain of its curb is the strength of my flight:
And when by the hate of the hurricane blown
It doubles its forces with fibers that groan,
Exulting I ride in the tower of my pride
To feel that the strength of the blast is my own. . . .
Rest under my branches, breathe deep of my balm
From the hushed avalanches of fragrance and calm,
For suave is the silence that poises the palm.

The wings of the egrets are silken and fine,
But hushed with the secrets of Eden are mine:
Your spirit that grieves like the wind in my leaves
Shall be robbed of its care by those whispering thieves
To study my patience and hear, the day long,
The soft foliations of sand into song—
For bitter and cold though it rasp to my root,
Each atom of gold is the chance of a fruit,
The sap is the music, the stem is the flute,
And the leaves are the wings of the seraph I shape
Who dances, who springs in a golden escape,
Out of the dust and the drought of the plain,
To sing with the silver hosannahs of rain."

AUTUMN

I love to see, when leaves depart,
The clear anatomy arrive,
Winter, the paragon of art,
That kills all forms of life and feeling
Save what is pure and will survive.

Already now the clanging chains
Of geese are harnessed to the moon:
Stripped are the great sun-clouding planes:
And the dark pines, their own revealing,
Let in the needles of the noon.

Strained by the gale the olives whiten
Like hoary wrestlers bent with toil
And, with the vines, their branches lighten
To brim our vats where summer lingers
In the red froth and sun-gold oil.

Soon on our hearth's reviving pyre
Their rotted stems will crumble up:
And like a ruby, panting fire,
The grape will redden on your fingers
Through the lit crystal of the cup.

ON SOME SOUTH AFRICAN NOVELISTS

You praise the firm restraint with which they write—
  I'm with you there, of course.
They use the snaffle and the curb all right;
  But where's the bloody horse?

TOLEDO

July, 1936

Toledo, when I saw you die
And heard the roof of Carmel crash,
A spread-winged phoenix from its ash
The Cross remained against the sky!
With horns of flame and haggard eye
The mountain vomited with blood,
A thousand corpses down the flood
Were rolled gesticulating by.
And high above the roaring shells
I heard the silence of your bells
Who've left those broken stones behind
Above the years to make your home
And burn, with Athens and with Rome,
A sacred city of the mind.

FROM "THE GEORGIAD"

Hail, Mediocrity, beneath whose spell
Lion and fox as loving neighbors dwell:
For it is sweet with modesty to swell
When one has not a ghost of pride to quell.
Puffed up with modesty, the ambitious toad
May safely swell, and fear not to explode,
Until, ballooned with emptiness, he rise
To dwarf the ox he envies for his size.

THE SERF

His naked skin clothed in the torrid mist
That puffs in smoke around the patient hooves,
The ploughman drives, a slow somnambulist,
And through the green his crimson furrow grooves.
His heart, more deeply than he wounds the plain,
Long by the rasping share of insult torn,
Red clod, to which the war-cry once was rain
And tribal spears the fatal sheaves of corn,
Lies fallow now. But as the turf divides
I see in the slow progress of his strides
Over the toppled clods and falling flowers,
The timeless, surly patience of the serf
That moves the nearest to the naked earth
And ploughs down palaces, and thrones, and towers.

C. Day Lewis

⁂ C. (Cecil) Day Lewis was born April 27, 1904, at Ballintubber, Queens County, Ireland. He was educated at Sherbourne School and Wadham College, Oxford, where he became affiliated with Stephen Spender, W. H. Auden, and others of the post-war group. He taught at the Junior School of Cheltenham College and wrote with increasing rapidity and purpose.

There were two early publications (*Beechen Vigils* and *Country Comets*) which were derivative and received little attention. *Transitional Poem* (1929) is Day Lewis' first serious bid for notice. The early influences are not altogether discarded, but it is immediately evident that a new and indubitably lyric voice is being sounded. This is "nature poetry," but nature poetry sharply differentiated from the philosophic-meditative manner of Wordsworth and the tired detachment of the Georgians. Day Lewis is no mere onlooker, he is a passionate participant; there is courage as well as color in his lines, and even the awkward passages are redeemed by a challenging vision.

That vision is amplified, sometimes distorted, and finally explicated in *From Feathers to Iron* (1931) and *The Magnetic Mountain* (1933), both of which, with *Transitional Poem,* were assembled in *Poems 1929-1933,* published in America in 1935. Since the three young English poets were printed almost simultaneously in this country, Day Lewis was continually linked with Spender and Auden in the public press. Actually the so-called "triumvirate" was composed of three different types of poet. Auden is satirical, experimental, and often (except to those who understand his private parables) incomprehensible; Spender is rhapsodic, sometimes sentimental, and usually forthright; Lewis is almost continuously lyrical and candid. Although he, too, plays with internal rhyme and concealed assonance, he is less concerned than Auden with craftsmanship; although he shares Spender's political convictions, he does not lose himself, as Spender sometimes does, in emotion. Yet if he is the most dependable he is the least original of the three. He has not yet outgrown his influences; one does not have to read closely to recognize the accents of Gerard Manley Hopkins, Wilfred Owen, T. S. Eliot, most of all W. H. Auden, to all of whom C. Day Lewis pays credit. There are even moments (as in the poem "You'll be leaving soon and it's up to you boys") which sound strangely like Robert W. Service and Rudyard Kipling's "If" turned upside down. It should also be said that his social sentiments have little to do with the final effect of his poetry; it is, poetically speaking, unimportant that an author has chosen communism for his faith rather than a more popular conservatism. He knows that in the end a poet is measured by his poetry, not by his policies; that, although Southey was an ardent believer in the French Revolution, Southey means nothing to us, and readers of the *Ode on the Intimations of Immortality* do not care when or why Wordsworth ceased to be a liberal. But Day Lewis also knows that a poet must have a creed; and a belief in the dignity and possible brotherhood of man is certainly no more to be deplored than a belief in the sacredness of the Georgian Squirearchy and its incorporated nightingales. As a matter of record, the best of his poems are the least protesting ones.

Lewis continually fluctuates between a tradition which he distrusts, but in which he is quite at home, and a conviction which his mind applauds but his imagination has not yet fully accepted. From the conflict no less than half a dozen serene, illuminating, and indignant lyrics are born, lyrics which will find their way into even the most cautious anthologies. It is his certainties, coming after a generation of negativism, which matter, not his arbitrary symbols of "kestrel," "airman," and "magnetic mountain" (for imagination, poet, and the co-operative commonwealth). It is not the fighting figures and stretched metaphors, straining under the demands of their author, but the athletic belief, the alert spirit, which breaks through to music spontaneous and bitter-sweet.

A Time to Dance (1935) emphasizes this, although the title poem is something of a disappointment. It is ambitiously "symphonic," but it ends in a jumble of crude parodies, awkward as humor, ineffective as satire. Nevertheless, it apostrophizes the spirit—

> For those who had the power,
> Unhesitating whether to kill or cure:
> Those who were not afraid
> To dam the estuary or start the forest fire:
> Whose hearts were filled
> With enthusiasm as with a constant wind.

Short Is the Time (1944) and *Poems: 1933-1947* are often enthusiastic, sometimes exact, and occasionally electric—electricity being one of Lewis's favorite symbols. Lewis is always deft; his technique is almost as resourceful as Auden's, he employs the rhetorical flourish as roundly as Spender. The later poems extend his scope; they range all the way from mere exuberance to introspective autobiography. The lyrics are especially rewarding. If they frequently substitute energy for intensity, they are not without moral purpose and verbal power.

An unusually prolific author, Lewis has also written several serious novels, a penetrating book-length essay, *A Hope for Poetry* (1934), various textbooks and studies for young people, translations of Virgil's *Aeneid* and *Georgics,* part of an autobiography, *The Buried Day* (1960), and, under the pseudonym of Nicholas Blake, some sixteen skilfully plotted novels of crime and detection with such alluring titles as "A Penknife in My Heart," "The Widow's Cruise," "Malice in Wonderland," and "The Corpse in the Snowman."

NEARING AGAIN THE LEGENDARY ISLE

> Nearing again the legendary isle
> Where sirens sang and marines were skinned,
> We wonder now what was there to beguile
> That such stout fellows left their bones behind.

Those chorus-girls are surely past their prime,
Voices grow shrill and paint is wearing thin,
Lips that sealed up the sense from gnawing time
Now beg the favor with a graveyard grin.

We have no flesh to spare and they can't bite,
Hunger and sweat have stripped us to the bone;
A skeleton crew we toil upon the tide
And mock the theme-song meant to lure us on:

No need to stop the ears, avert the eyes
From purple rhetoric of evening skies.

REST FROM LOVING AND BE LIVING

Rest from loving and be living.
Fallen is fallen past retrieving
The unique flyer dawn's dove
Arrowing down feathered with fire.

Cease denying, begin knowing.
Comes peace this way, here comes renewing
With dower of bird and bud, knocks
Loud on winter wall on death's door.

Here's no meaning but of morning.
Naught soon of night but stars remaining,
Sink lower, fade, as dark womb
Recedes creation will step clear.

NOW SHE IS LIKE THE WHITE TREE-ROSE

Now she is like the white tree-rose
That takes a blessing from the sun:
Summer has filled her veins with light,
And her warm heart is washed with noon.

Or as a poplar, ceaselessly
Gives a soft answer to the wind:
Cool on the light her leaves lie sleeping,
Folding a column of sweet sound.

Powder the stars. Forbid the night
To wear those brilliants for a brooch
So soon, dark death, you may close down
The mines that made this beauty rich.

Her thoughts are pleiads, stooping low
O'er glades where nightingale has flown:
And like the luminous night around her
She has at heart a certain dawn.

DO NOT EXPECT AGAIN A PHOENIX HOUR

Do not expects again a phoenix hour,
The triple-towered sky, and dove complaining,
Sudden the rain of gold and heart's first ease
Tranced under trees by the eldritch light of sundown.

By a blazed trail our joy will be returning:
One burning hour throws light a thousand ways,
And hot blood stays into familiar gestures.
The best years wait, the body's plenitude.

Consider then, my lover, this is the end
Of the lark's ascending, the hawk's unearthly hover:
Spring season is over soon and first heatwave;
Grave-browed with cloud ponders the huge horizon.

Draw up the dew. Swell with pacific violence.
Take shape in silence. Grow as the clouds grew,
Beautiful brood the cornlands, and you are heavy;
Leafy the boughs—they also hide big fruit.

CHIEFLY TO MIND APPEARS

Chiefly to mind appears
That hour on Silverhowe
When evening's lid hung low
And the sky was about our ears.
Buoyed between fear and love
We watched in eastward form
The armadas of the storm
And sail superbly above;
So near, they'd split and founder
On the least jag of sense,
One false spark fire the immense
Broadside the confounding thunder.
They pass, give not a salvo,
And in their rainy wash
We hear the horizons crash
With monitors of woe.

Only at highest power
Can love and fear become
Their equilibrium,
And in that eminent hour
A virtue is made plain
Of passionate cleavage
Like the hills' cutting edge
When the sun sets to rain.
This is the single mind,
This is the star-solved equation
Of life with life's negation:
A deathless cell designed
To demonstrate death's act,
Which, the more surely it moves
To earth's influence, but proves
Itself the more intact.

TEMPT ME NO MORE

Tempt me no more; for I
Have known the lightning's hour,
The poet's inward pride,
The certainty of power.

Bayonets are closing round.
I shrink; yet I must wring
A living from despair
And out of steel a song

Though song, though breath be short,
I'll share not the disgrace
Of those that ran away
Or never left the base.

Comrades, my tongue can speak
No comfortable words;
Calls to a forlorn hope
Give work and not rewards.

Oh keep the sickle sharp
And follow still the plow:
Others may reap, though some
See not the winter through.

Father who endest all,
Pity our broken sleep;
For we lie down with tears
And waken but to weep.

And if our blood alone
Will melt this iron earth,
Take it. It is well spent
Easing a savior's birth.

THE CONFLICT

I sang as one
Who on a tilting deck sings
To keep their courage up, though the wave hangs
That shall cut off their sun.

As storm-cocks sing,
Flinging their natural answer in the wind's teeth,
And care not if it is waste of breath
Or birth-carol of spring.

As ocean-flyer clings
To height, to the last drop of spirit driving on
While yet ahead is land to be won
And work for wings.

Singing I was at peace,
Above the clouds, outside the ring:
For sorrow finds a swift release in song
And pride its poise.

Yet living here,
As one between two massing powers I live
Whom neutrality cannot save
Nor occupation cheer.

None such shall be left alive:
The innocent wing is soon shot down,
And private stars fade in the blood-red dawn
Where two worlds strive.

The red advance of life
Contracts pride, calls out the common blood,
Beats song into a single blade,
Makes a depth-charge of grief.

Move then with new desires,
For where we used to build and love
Is no man's land, and only ghosts can live
Between two fires.

WHEN THEY HAVE LOST

When they have lost the little that they looked for,
The poor allotment of ease, custom, fame:
When the consuming star their fathers worked for
Has guttered into death, a fatuous flame:
When love's a cripple, faith a bed-time story,
Hope eats her heart out and peace walks on knives,
And suffering men cry an end to this sorry
World of whose children want alone still thrives:
Then shall the mounting stages of oppression
Like mazed and makeshift scaffolding torn down
Reveal his unexampled, best creation—
The shape of man's necessity full-grown.
Built from their bone, I see a power-house stand
To warm men's hearts again and light the land.

NEWSREEL

Enter the dream-house, brothers and sisters, leaving
Your debts asleep, your history at the door:
This is the home for heroes, and this loving
Darkness a fur you can afford.

Fish in their tank electrically heated
Nose without envy the glass wall: for them
Clerk, spy, nurse, killer, prince, the great and the defeated,
Move in a mute day-dream.

Bathed in this common source, you gape incurious
At what your active hours have willed—
Sleep-walking on that silver wall, the furious
Sick shapes and pregnant fancies of your world.

There is the mayor opening the oyster season:
A society wedding: the autumn hats look well:
An old crock's race, and a politician
In fishing-waders to prove that all is well.

Oh, look at the warplanes! Screaming hysteric treble
In the long power-dive, like gannets they fall steep.
But what are they to trouble—
These silver shadows to trouble your watery, womb-deep sleep?

See the big guns, rising, groping, erected
To plant death in your world's soft womb,
Fire-bud, smoke-blossom, iron seed projected—
Are these exotics? They will grow nearer home:

Grow nearer home—and out of the dream-house stumbling
One night into a strangling air and the flung
Rags of children and thunder of stone niagaras tumbling,
You'll know you slept too long.

Peter Quennell

⁂ Peter Quennell was born March 5, 1905, in Kent. He was educated at Berkhamstead Grammar School and at Balliol College, Oxford, where he spent two years, and where he was co-editor of *Oxford Poetry.* He made "the customary pilgrimages" to Greece and the Balkans, and since 1927 has lived in London.

Poems (1926) appeared before Quennell was twenty-one years old, four of the poems being "very early"—"Procne," for example, having been written at the age of sixteen. Quennell's verse is wholly unlike that of his living compatriots, although American readers will detect a similarity to the verbal elegances of Wallace Stevens. It is as near the abstract as verse can come and still depend on words. Here language flowers of itself, feeding automatically on its own air; image suggests image, and associations grow freely on seemingly unrelated suggestions. In "The Divers" and "Leviathan," among others, the poetry wanders far from common experience or recognizable emotions or, for that matter, its own subject. But it is never less than poetry. Although the figures flowing into each other have the uncertain, fluid outlines of dream pictures, the musical progression is clear.

It is as music, first of all, that Quennell's poetry succeeds. His accomplishment is the greater since, without the aid of rhyme or definite rhythm, he achieves melodies intangible but more original than lightly summoned tunes. The actors in his verse are vague, the happenings remote and unreal, yet the intent is never false, and the effect is a set of nicely adjusted modulations and strange harmonics. It is, in essence, a poetry of shock, but shock without eccentricity, smoothed and almost without surprise.

As an essayist, Quennell has developed slowly but with increasing surety. His *Baudelaire and the Symbolists* (1930) contains five essays outlining the stream which sprang from Baudelaire and which swayed not only French literature but determined in no inconsiderable degree the course of English poetry during and after the Eighteen Nineties. *Sympathy* (1933) assembles his imaginative short stories.

Quennell made his most successful bid for popularity as biographer. Readers and reviewers united to praise the wit and vitality of his *Byron: The Years of Fame* (1935), the still more vivid *Byron in Italy* (1941), and *Four Portraits* (1945).

PROCNE

So she became a bird and bird-like danced
On a long sloe-bough, treading the silver blossom
With a bird's lovely feet,
And shaken blossoms fell into the hands
Of sunlight, and he held them for a moment
And let them drop.
And in the autumn Procne came again
And leapt upon the crooked sloe-bough singing
And the dark berries winked like earth-dimmed beads,
As the branch swung beneath her dancing feet.

THE DIVERS

Ah, look,
How sucking their last sweetness from the air
These divers run upon the pale sea verge;
An evening air so smooth my hand could round
And grope a circle of the hollow sky
Without a harshness or impediment.

Look now,
How they run cowering and each unknots
A rag, a girdle twisted on his loins,
Stands naked, quivered in the cool of night.

As boldest lovers will tire presently,
When dawn dries up a radiance on the limbs,
And lapse to common sleep,
To the deep tumult of habitual dreams,
Each sighing, with loosened limbs, as if regretfully,
Gives up his body to the foamless surge.

Water combs out his body, and he sinks
Beyond all form and sound.
Only the blood frets on,
Grown fearful, in a shallow dissonance.

Water strains on his hair and drums upon his flank,
Consumes his curious track
And straight or sinuous path
Dissolves as swift, impermanent as light.

Still his strange purpose drives him, like a beam,
Like the suspended shaft of cavern-piercing sun;
And, hardier still,
With wavering hands, divides the massive gloom,—
A vast caress through which he penetrates,
Or obscure death withdrawing
Veil upon veil,
Discovering new darkness and profounder terror.

"Consider you your loss,
For now what strength of foot or hand
Can take you by the narrow way you came
Through the clear darkness up again and up.
Watch a procession of the living days,
Where dawn and evening melt so soft together
As wine in water, or milk shed in water,
Filming and clouding into even dullness."

"Who weeps me now with pulse of noisy tears,
Who strikes the breast?
If I regret among the flowing weed,
My regret is
Not vocal, cannot pierce to hidden day,
Momentary, soon quenched, like a strangled flame."

LEVIATHAN

(Second Section)

A music met Leviathan returning,
While the still troubled waters of his passage
Danct every island like a lily head.
Through all the shadowed throats of the wide forest
His unnumbered monster children rode to greet him
On horses winged and dappled over like flowers.

Now huddled waves had lulled their bursting foam
And slight clouds laid their breasts upon the sea;
The sullen winds, head downward from the sky,
Solicited his movement on their viols.

And the palm trees, heat weary,
Chafing smooth limbs within a rinded shell,
Spoke of his coming with soft acclamation,
Like watchers long grown tired, languid and sorry:

"Look, how he comes"—as faint as whispering deer—
"What storm and state he brings." Then louder voices,
The unchaste turtles crying out with pleasure,
And badgers from the earth
Sprawled upon the rocks with animal laughter.

"The Cretan bull ferrying across the sea
Bore home no richer load;
In the reed forest of Eurotas' bank
That quivering swan, clapping strong wings together,
With harsh, sweet voice called out no keener marriage."

Then shrill response, as seeming from the air,
Invoking joy, summoning desire:

"Hither desires,
Coming as thick and hot as the press and hurry of blood
Striking the apse of the brain,
Ranging abroad, carrying your torches high,
Running as light and remote as a scattered cast of pearls."

Then antic spirits from the tulip trees:
"We must have tumblers like a wheel of fire.

We must have dancers moving their suave hands:
The tumblers strung backward like a hoop
Until they thrust vermilioned cheeks between their knees.
And the intricacy
Of sweet involving gayety,
And wine to warm our innocence,
Music to sooth the prickled sense,
Sounding like water or like ringing glass."

The mitered Queen of Heaven stirred on her broad, low throne,
Setting the lattice just so much ajar
That wandering airs from earth should cool the room,
Peered down on more-than-Leda and smoothed her wrinkled snood,
Crying to her Father-Spouse—"Dear Lord, how sweet she looks."
The clumsy hierarchies,
Wearied by their continual task of praise,
Rested wide heifer eyes upon her fallen lids.
Islanded in stars,
Even the keen Intelligences turned away
From the mathematic splendor of the spheres' incessant rolling chime.

Himself, the Father moved,
Traditional and vast,
Remembering fresher years,
Might have inclined his steeply pinnacled head,
But his more zealous son,
As neat as Thammuz, with smooth, pallid cheeks,
Sensing an evil, shut the casement fast.

*

But I, remembering Atlantis, wept,
Remembering her paths and unswept flowers,
Clean beaches, patterned by a light sea wrack,
And the ruined halcyon nests that came on shore.

Tears, in their freedom, cloud the eyes,
Drowsing the sense.
Honey and poppy equally mixed together,
They cannot drug away or curtain off with sleep
Such pitiless disharmony of shapes.

Patrick Kavanagh

⧫ Patrick Kavanagh, whom many consider the best Irish poet since Yeats, was born in 1905 in County Monaghan, Ireland. His schooling was brief. Educated at the National Elementary School until fourteen, he suffered from poverty and illness for a long time. He worked as a shoemaker (his father's trade) and as a small farmer until his mid-thirties, starved on free lance journalism through the Second World War, had cancer of the lung and recovered in his fiftieth year when the lung was removed. Among his other tribulations was a long lawsuit which he won in the end. Established as a writer, he became a lecturer at University College in Dublin, Joyce's university.

Besides his verse, Kavanagh is the author of *The Green Fool,* which he belittled as a "lying stage Irish autobiography," and *Tarry Flynn,* "a truthful work of fiction," which can be considered as his own story. It is, however, Kavanagh's poetry rather than his prose which gives him essential distinction. *A Soul for Sale* (1953) contains "Father Mat," "The Great Hunger," and other poems that display an original mind which, candid in expression, plays with humor and irony. *Come Dance with Kitty Strobling and Other Poems* (1960) is a richer and more rounded collection. Exuberant with a love for all the complexity and casualness of the actual world—"Nothing whatever is by love debarred"—he answers himself in "Question to Life":

> So be reposed and praise, praise praise
> The way it happened and the way it is.

Sometimes the spirit—"I will have love, have love / From anything"—recalls Hopkins', but Kavanagh has his own quiet, half-wild, half-whimsical voice. It is explicit in such poems as "The Self-Slaved," "Canal Bank Walk," "The One," "Question to Life," "Intimate Parnassus," and "Miss Universe," with its concluding high mockery:

> There are no recriminations in Heaven. O the sensual throb
> Of the explosive body, the tumultuous thighs!
> Adown a summer lane comes Miss Universe,
> She whom no lecher's art can rob,
> Though she is not a virgin who was wise.

No one can fail to detect the individual diction under what the London *Times Literary Supplement* characterized as "the mask of ease and diffidence, the digressive offhand manner, the poet murmuring to himself."

THE SELF-SLAVED

Me I will throw away.
Me sufficient for the day
The sticky self that clings
Adhesions on the wings.

To love and adventure,
To go on the grand tour
A man must be free
From self-necessity.

See over there
A created splendour
Made by one individual
From things residual
With all the various
Qualities hilarious
Of what
Hitherto was not:

A November mood
As by one man understood;
Familiar, an old custom
Leaves falling, a white frosting
Bringing a sanguine dream
A new beginning with an old theme.

Throw away thy sloth
Self, carry off my wrath
With its self-righteous
Satirising blotches.
No self, no self-exposure
The weakness of the proser
But undefeatable
By means of the beatable.

I will have love, have love
From anything made of
And a life with a shapely form
With gaiety and charm
And capable of receiving
With grace the grace of living
And wild moments too
Self when freed from you.
Prometheus calls me on.
Prometheus calls me: Son,
We'll both go off together
In this delightful weather.

CANAL BANK WALK

Leafy-with-love banks and the green waters of the canal
Pouring redemption for me, that I do
The will of God, wallow in the habitual, the banal,
Grow with nature again as before I grew.
The bright stick trapped, the breeze adding a third
Party to the couple kissing on an old seat,
And a bird gathering materials for the nest for the Word
Eloquently new and abandoned to its delirious beat.
O unworn world enrapture me, encapture me in a web
Of fabulous grass and eternal voices by a beech,
Feed the gaping need of my senses, give me ad lib
To pray unselfconsciously with overflowing speech
For this soul needs to be honoured with a new dress woven
From green and blue things and arguments that cannot be proven.

QUESTION TO LIFE

Surely you would not ask me to have known
Only the passion of primrose banks in May
Which are merely a point of departure for the play
And yearning poignancy when on their own.
Yet when all is said and done a considerable
Portion of living is found in inanimate
Nature, and a man need not feel miserable
If fate should have decided on this plan of it.
Then there is always the passing gift of affection
Tossed from the windows of high charity

In the office girl and civil servant section
And these are no despisable commodity.
So be reposed and praise, praise praise
The way it happened and the way it is.

THE ONE

Green, blue, yellow and red—
God is down in the swamps and marshes
Sensational as April and almost incredible the flowering of our catharsis.
A humble scene in a backward place
Where no one important ever looked
The raving flowers looked up in the face
Of the One and the Endless, the Mind that has baulked
The profoundest of mortals. A primrose, a violet,
A violent wild iris—but mostly anonymous performers
Yet an important occasion as the Muse at her toilet
Prepared to inform the local farmers
That beautiful, beautiful, beautiful God
Was breathing His love by a cut-away bog.

INTIMATE PARNASSUS

Men are what they are, and what they do
Is their own business. If they praise
The gods or jeer at them, the gods can not
Be moved, involved or hurt. Serenely
The citizens of Parnassus look on
As Homer tells us, and never laugh
When any mortal has joined the party.
What happens in the small towns—
Hate, love, envy—is not
The concern of the gods. The poet poor,
Or pushed around, or to be hanged, retains
His full reality; and his authority
Is bogus if the sonorous beat is broken
By disturbances in human hearts—his own
Is detached, experimental, subject matter
For ironic analysis, even for pity
As for some stranger's private problem.
It is not cold on the mountain, human women
Fall like ripe fruit while mere men
Are climbing out on dangerous branches
Of banking, insurance and shops; going
To the theatre; becoming
Acquainted with actors; unhappily
Pretending to a knowledge of art.
Poet, you have reason to be sympathetic—

Count them the beautiful unbroken
And then forget them
As things aside from the main purpose
Which is to be
Passive, observing with a steady eye.

William Empson

⁂ William Empson was born September 27, 1906, in Yorkshire and was educated at Winchester and Magdalene College, Cambridge. His first book—a book of criticism—*Seven Types of Ambiguity,* was published when he was twenty-four, after which he went to Tokyo and remained there three years as professor in English Literature. He returned to the East in 1937 to teach English literature, arrived at the start of a war, and spent two years with the refugee university at Changsha. Back in England, he joined the British Broadcasting Company, edited foreign broadcasts, and supervised programs in Chinese. After lecturing in the United States at the Kenyon Summer School, he was appointed professor of English literature at Sheffield University in 1953.

Seven Types of Ambiguity is a germinal book. Largely responsible for "The New Criticism," it explores not only the various possible meanings of a poem but the the multiple suggestions of individual words. It is, said Stanley Edgar Hyman, "the most elaborate and probably the finest close reading of poetry ever put down, the fantastic, wonderful, and almost endless spinning out of the implications and linguistic possibilities." On many writers its influence was excellent. It emphasized a studied approach instead of a vague wandering about the subject; it stressed the serious use of scientific as well as classical references rather than worn-out allusions and empty abstractions. On others, however, Empson's influence was harmful. He tended to place too great a value on erudition, on style instead of substance, on manner instead of content. *Seven Types of Ambiguity* was followed by *Some Versions of Pastoral* (1935) and *The Structure of Complex Words* (1951).

Empson's poetry has the same tone as his prose, intellectual and complex. *Collected Poems* (1935, 1940, corrected and amplified in 1955) is an involved and often witty display of virtuosity. The verse succeeds in spite of its almost total lack of music; Empson's tone-deaf ear permits him to commit such cacophonies as "soon boil fool's pots," "Law makes long spokes of the short stakes," and "Your spun farm's root still on that axis dwells." Many of the supplementary Notes (there are twenty-seven pages of them) point out—and gratuitously explain—Empson's double meanings and "ambiguous" puns. But if Empson is a riddling scholar he is also a valuable as well as an amusing instructor. He concludes one of his Notes by saying: "I suppose the reason I tried to defend my clotted kind of poetry was that I felt it was going a bit too far."

"Clotted" much of his poetry undoubtedly is, but it is never without discipline. "This Last Pain" is thickly philosophical but it has an intensity of feeling as well as organization; "Rolling the Lawn" is a half-metaphysical, half-playful sonnet;

"Homage to the British Museum" is a summation of incongruities; "Just a Smack at Auden" is a brilliantly rhymed parody of that poet's earlier tone and pyrotechnical mannerisms; "Missing Dates" is a paradox of form and feeling, a set of loose implications held within the tight confines of a villanelle, one of the strictest of old verse patterns. Even when Empson's poetry is most knotted (or "clotted") it is subtly concentrated, a concentration in which the reader must participate.

THIS LAST PAIN

This last pain for the damned the Fathers found:
"They knew the bliss with which they were not crowned."
  Such, but on earth, let me foretell,
  Is all, of heaven or of hell.

Man, as the prying housemaid of the soul,
May know her happiness by eye to hole:
  He's safe; the key is lost; he knows
  Door will not open, nor hole close.

"What is conceivable can happen too,"
Said Wittgenstein, who had not dreamt of you;
  But wisely; if we worked it long
  We should forget where it was wrong.

Those thorns are crowns which, woven into knots,
Crackle under and soon boil fools' pots;
  And no man's watching, wise and long,
  Would ever stare them into song.

Thorns burn to a consistent ash, like man;
A splendid cleanser for the frying-pan:
  And those who leap from pan to fire
  Should this brave opposite admire.

All those large dreams by which men long live well
Are magic-lanterned on the smoke of hell;
  This then is real, I have implied,
  A painted, small, transparent slide.

These the inventive can hand-paint at leisure,
Or most emporia would stock our measure;
  And feasting in their dappled shade
  We should forget how they were made.

Feign then what's by a decent tact believed
And act that state is only so conceived,
  And build an edifice of form
  For house where phantoms may keep warm.

Imagine, then, by miracle, with me,
(Ambiguous gifts, as what gods give must be)
  What could not possibly be there,
  And learn a style from a despair.

ROLLING THE LAWN

ɔu can't beat English lawns. Our final hope
flat despair. Each morning therefore ere
greet the office, through the weekday air,
ɔlding the Holy Roller at the slope
'he English fetish, not the Texas Pope)
ither and thither on my toes with care
oll ours flatter and flatter. Long, in prayer,
grub for daisies at whose roots I grope.

Roll not the abdominal wall; the walls of
Troy
Lead, since a plumb-line ordered, could
destroy.
Roll rather, where no mole dare sap, the
lawn,
And ne'er his tumuli shall tomb your brawn.
World, roll yourself; and bear your roller,
soul,
As martyrs gridirons, when God calls the roll.

HOMAGE TO THE BRITISH MUSEUM

There is a Supreme God in the ethnological section;
A hollow toad shape, faced with a blank shield.
He needs his belly to include the Pantheon,
Which is inserted through a hole behind.
At the navel, at the points formally stressed, at the organs of sense,
Lice glue themselves, dolls, local deities,
His smooth wood creeps with all the creeds of the world.

Attending there let us absorb the cultures of nations
And dissolve into our judgement all their codes.
Then, being clogged with a natural hesitation
(People are continually asking one the way out),
Let us stand here and admit that we have no road.
Being everything, let us admit that is to be something,
Or give ourselves the benefit of the doubt;
Let us offer our pinch of dust all to this God,
And grant his reign over the entire building.

JUST A SMACK AT AUDEN

Waiting for the end, boys, waiting for the end.
What is there to be or do?
What's become of me or you?
Are we kind or are we true?
Sitting two and two, boys, waiting for the end.

Shall I build a tower, boys, knowing it will rend
Crack upon the hour, boys, waiting for the end?
Shall I pluck a flower, boys, shall I save or spend?
All turns sour, boys, waiting for the end.

Shall I send a wire, boys? Where is there to send?
All are under fire, boys, waiting for the end.
Shall I turn a sire, boys? Shall I choose a friend?
The fat is in the pyre, boys, waiting for the end.

Shall I make it clear, boys, for all to apprehend,
Those that will not hear, boys, waiting for the end,
Knowing it is near, boys, trying to pretend,
Sitting in cold fear, boys, waiting for the end?

Shall we send a cable, boys, accurately penned,
Knowing we are able, boys, waiting for the end,
Via the Tower of Babel, boys? Christ will not ascend.
He's hiding in his stable, boys, waiting for the end.

Shall we blow a bubble, boys, glittering to distend,
Hiding from our trouble, boys, waiting for the end?
When you build on rubble, boys, Nature will append
Double and re-double, boys, waiting for the end.

Shall we make a tale, boys, that things are sure to mend,
Playing bluff and hale, boys, waiting for the end?
It will be born stale, boys, stinking to offend,
Dying ere it fail, boys, waiting for the end.

Shall we go all wild, boys, waste and make them lend,
Playing at the child, boys, waiting for the end?
It has all been filed, boys, history has a trend,
Each of us enisled, boys, waiting for the end.

What was said by Marx, boys, what did he perpend?
No good being sparks, boys, waiting for the end.
Treason of the clerks, boys, curtains that descend,
Lights becoming darks, boys, waiting for the end.

Waiting for the end, boys, waiting for the end.
Not a chance of blend, boys, things have got to tend.
Think of those who vend, boys, think of how we wend,
Waiting for the end, boys, waiting for the end.

MISSING DATES

Slowly the poison the whole blood stream
fills.
It is not the effort nor the failure tires.
The waste remains, the waste remains and
kills.

It is not your system or clear sight that mills
Down small to the consequence a life re-
quires;
Slowly the poison the whole blood stream
fills.

They bled an old dog dry yet the exchange
rills
Of young dog blood gave but a month's
desires
The waste remains, the waste remains and
kills.

It is the Chinese tombs and the slag hill
Usurp the soil, and not the soil retires.
Slowly the poison the whole blood stre
fills.

Not to have fire is to be a skin that shr
The complete fire is death. From partial f
The waste remains, the waste remains
kills.

It is the poems you have lost, the ills
From missing dates, at which the heart
pires.
Slowly the poison the whole blood str
fills.
The waste remains, the waste remains
kills.

John Betjeman

☙ John Betjeman, born in London in 1906, was educated at Marlborough and Oxford, where he was a contemporary of MacNeice and Auden. Earning his living as a teacher and journalist, he became an authority on English architecture, quaint villages, and unimportant but, to him, endearing places. *Mount Zion* (1933), *Continual Dew* (1937), *Old Bats in New Belfries* (1940), *Old Lights for New Chancels* (1945) are the titles of some of his volumes of verse; *Ghastly Good Taste* (1933), *Cornwall Shell Guide* (1936), *English, Scottish, and Welsh Landscape* (1944), *Berkshire* (1949), *Shell Guide to Shropshire* (1951) are some of his books of prose. Auden characterized his writing as "slick but not streamlined"; the phrase was adopted as the title of a selection of his poems (*Slick but Not Streamlined*) which appeared in 1947, and Auden supplied the introduction.

Nothing Betjeman had published before his fifty-second year prepared the public for the overwhelming success of his *Collected Poems* (1958). It sold a thousand copies a day for months, went into edition after edition, and won several awards, including the Duff Cooper Memorial Prize, which was presented to him by Princess Margaret. It appealed to all classes of readers, partly because of its mixture of wry cleverness and sentiment, partly because of its devotional and nostalgic tone, but chiefly because it was English to the core; it was merely accepted, pleasantly reviewed, but not vociferously acclaimed in America. Betjeman was hailed as a lyrical satirist, but he objected to the term. "I have," he wrote, "tried to catch the atmosphere of places and times in different parts of England and Eire. But when I do so I am not being satirical but topographical . . . I love suburbs and gas-lights and Pont Street and Gothic Revival churches and mineral railways, provincial towns and garden cities. They are, many of them, part of my background."

Only a lover of the ordinary and the seemingly prosaic could make poems with such titles as "Sudden Illness at the Bus Stop," "An Archaeological Picnic," "Invasion Exercise at the Poultry Farm," "Indoor Games Near Newbury," "Business Girls," "Monody on the Death of Aldersgate Station," "A Liverish Journey First Class," or address an athletic Olympic girl with a pseudo-love poem which ends ruefully:

> And when the match is over, I
> Would flop beside you, hear you sigh;
> And then, with what supreme caress,
> You'll tuck me up into my press.
> Fair tigress of the tennis courts,
> So short in sleeve and strong in shorts,
> Little, alas, to you I mean,
> For I am bald and old and green.

Humor and even hilarity are here—this footnote, for example: "The names in the last lines of these stanzas [T. S. Eliot, Edith Sitwell, Thomas Hardy, etc.] are put in not out of malice or satire but merely for their euphony." However, it is chiefly Betjeman's charm, a wistful piety, a tenderness for things past and present things overlooked, which has made him the celebrant of the commonplace and slightly outmoded, the unofficial laureate of the middle-class, the inglorious and often mute.

Summoned by Bells (1960) is Betjeman's partial biography which appeared in his mid-fifties. Written in blank verse, it is a sustained narrative of his bourgeois background, his unhappiness at the school where he was bullied, his lack of interest in the family manufacturing firm, his solace in nature and his escape via books, church architecture, and High Church religion. A few months after the publication of the book, Betjeman was awarded the Queen's Gold Medal for Poetry.

THE COTTAGE HOSPITAL

At the end of a long-walled garden
    in a red provincial town,
A brick path led to a mulberry—
    scanty grass at its feet.
I lay under blackening branches
    where the mulberry leaves hung down
Sheltering ruby fruit globes
    from a Sunday-tea-time heat.
Apple and plum espaliers
    basked upon bricks of brown;
The air was swimming with insects,
    and children played in the street.

Out of this bright intentness
    into the mulberry shade
Musca domestica (housefly)
    swung from the August light
Slap into slithery rigging
    by the waiting spider made
Which spun the lithe elastic
    till the fly was shrouded tight.
Down came the hairy talons
    and horrible poison blade
And none of the garden noticed
    that fizzing, hopeless fight.

Say in what Cottage Hospital
    whose pale green walls resound
With the tap upon polished parquet
    of inflexible nurses' feet
Shall I myself be lying
    when they range the screens around?
And say shall I groan in dying,
    as I twist the sweaty sheet?
Or gasp for breath uncrying,
    as I feel my senses drown'd
While the air is swimming with insects
    and children play in the street?

SLOUGH

Come, friendly bombs, and fall on Slough
It isn't fit for humans now,
There isn't grass to graze a cow
    Swarm over, Death!

Come, bombs, and blow to smithereens
Those air-conditioned, bright canteens,
Tinned fruit, tinned meat, tinned milk, tinned beans
    Tinned minds, tinned breath.

Mess up the mess they call a town—
A house for ninety-seven down
And once a week a half-a-crown
    For twenty years,

And get that man with double chin
Who'll always cheat and always win,
Who washes his repulsive skin
    In women's tears,

And smash his desk of polished oak
And smash his hands so used to stroke
And stop his boring dirty joke
    And make him yell.

But spare the bald young clerks who add
The profits of the stinking cad;
It's not their fault that they are mad,
    They've tasted Hell.

It's not their fault they do not know
The birdsong from the radio,
It's not their fault they often go
    To Maidenhead

And talk of sports and makes of cars
In various bogus Tudor bars
And daren't look up and see the stars
    But belch instead.

In labour-saving homes, with care
Their wives frizz out peroxide hair
And dry it in synthetic air
    And paint their nails.

Come, friendly bombs, and fall on Slough
To get it ready for the plough.
The cabbages are coming now:
    The earth exhales.

REMORSE

The lungs draw in the air and rattle it out again;
The eyes revolve in their sockets and upwards stare;
No more worry and waiting and troublesome doubt again—
She whom I loved and left is no longer there.

The nurse puts down her knitting and walks across to her,
With quick professional eye she surveys the dead.
Just one patient the less and little the loss to her,
Distantly tender she settles the shrunken head.

Protestant claims and Catholic, the wrong and the right of them,
Unimportant they seem in the face of death—
But my neglect and unkindness—to lose the sight of them
I would listen even again to that labouring breath.

INEVITABLE

First there was putting hot-water bottles to it,
Then there was seeing what an osteopath could do,
Then trying drugs to coax the thing and woo it,
Then came the time when he knew that he was through.

Now in his hospital bed I see him lying
Limp on the pillows like a cast-off Teddy bear.
Is he too ill to know that he is dying?
And, if he does know, does he really care?

Grey looks the ward with November's overcasting
But his large eyes seem to see beyond the day;
Speech becomes sacred near silence everlasting
Oh if I *must* speak, have I words to say?

In the past weeks we had talked about Variety,
Vesta Victoria, Lew Lake and Wilkie Bard,
Horse-buses, hansoms, crimes in High Society—
Although we knew his death was near, we fought against it hard.

THE ARREST OF OSCAR WILDE AT THE CADOGAN HOTEL

He sipped at a weak hock and seltzer
As he gazed at the London skies
Through the Nottingham lace of the curtains
Or was it his bees-winged eyes?

To the right and before him Pont Street
Did tower in her new built red,
As hard as the morning gaslight
That shone on his unmade bed,

"I want some more hock in my seltzer,
And Robbie, please give me your hand—
Is this the end or beginning?
How can I understand?

"So you've brought me the latest *Yellow Book*:
And Buchan has got in it now:
Approval of what is approved of
Is as false as a well-kept vow.

"More hock, Robbie—where is the seltzer?
Dear boy, pull again at the bell!
They are all little better than *cretins*,
Though this *is* the Cadogan Hotel.

"One astrakhan coat is at Willis's—
Another one's at the Savoy:
Do fetch my morocco portmanteau,
And bring them on later, dear boy."

A thump, and a murmur of voices—
("Oh why must they make such a din?")
As the door of the bedroom swung open
And TWO PLAIN CLOTHES POLICEMEN came in:

"Mr. Woilde, we 'ave come for tew take yew
Where felons and criminals dwell:
We must ask yew tew leave with us quoietly
For this *is* the Cadogan Hotel."

He rose, and he put down *The Yellow Book*.
He staggered—and, terrible-eyed,
He brushed past the palms on the staircase
And was helped to a hansom outside.

Louis MacNeice

Louis MacNeice was born September 12, 1907, in the North of Ireland. His family, however, came from the West of Ireland, so he is not to be designated an Orangeman. He was at Oxford, Merton College, from 1926 to 1930, when he married and moved to Birmingham, after which he lectured in Greek in London.

His first volume, *Blind Fireworks* (1929), is more than an exhibit of the usual juvenilia, but the author dismisses it with the assurance that none of it will survive. The influence of Edith Sitwell (obvious in "Cradle Song") is here, but an alert mind is fashioning an idiom of its own. In the succeeding *Poems* published in 1935, the imaginative power is apparent. Like his immediate contemporaries, MacNeice prefers to spice the piquant half-rhyme with the traditional full vowel; like Auden and Spender, he uses the strictly contemporary scene. Like them, also, he adapts, turns, and generally "heightens" the ordinary speech of the day. It is in such poems as "Sunday Morning," "Morning Sun" and "Birmingham" that MacNeice, in common with a few others, points to a revival of vitality, a reliance on contemporary life, however complicated and difficult it may be.

Poems: 1925-1940 is an odd mingling of the delicate lyrics which MacNeice wrote as a youth and the semi-jazz approximations which he composed in his thirties. In the later poems he often relies on a casual style and complacent finalities; he overuses the offhand tone and carries the natural order of words to the pitch of banality. The ideas suffer; the style becomes a loose set of statements dropped haphazardly into verse. This is, as Edwin Muir wrote in *The Present Age,* "the poetry of a man who will never go farther than he feels he can legitimately go, and who is never swept off his feet." *Springboard* (1945) and *Holes in the Sky* (1948) employ flat statement and the plodding manner to the point of weariness. Nevertheless, when MacNeice is not dispirited, he can sharpen his idiom and shoot a phrase which rankles but lodges firmly in the mind.

Besides his poetry, MacNeice wrote *Out of the Picture* (1937), a play in verse which is fantastic and satirical; collaborated with W. H. Auden in *Letters from Iceland* (1937); issued a sensible, if not inspired, examination of *Modern Poetry* (1938); and published a searching and highly readable summary of *The Poetry of W. B. Yeats* (1941).

THE BRITISH MUSEUM READING ROOM

Under the hive-like dome the stooping haunted readers
Go up and down the alleys, tap the cells of knowledge—
  Honey and wax, the accumulation of years—
Some on commission, some for the love of learning,
Some because they have nothing better to do
Or because they hope these walls of books will deaden
  The drumming of the demon in their ears.

Cranks, hacks, poverty-stricken scholars,
In pince-nez, period hats or romantic beards
  And cherishing their hobby or their doom.
Some are too much alive and some are asleep
Hanging like bats in a world of inverted values,
Folded up in themselves in a world which is safe and silent:
  This is the British Museum Reading Room.

Out on the steps in the sun the pigeons are courting,
Puffing their ruffs and sweeping their tails or taking
  A sun-bath at their ease
And under the totem poles—the ancient terror—
Between the enormous fluted Ionic columns
There seeps from heavily jowled or hawk-like foreign faces
  The guttural sorrow of the refugees.

AND LOVE HUNG STILL

And love hung still as crystal over the bed
  And filled the corners of the enormous room;
The boom of dawn that left her sleeping, showing
  The flowers mirrored in the mahogany table.

O my love, if only I were able
  To protract this hour of quiet after passion,
Not ration happiness but keep this door for ever
  Closed on the world, its own world closed within it.

But dawn's waves trouble with the bubbling minute,
  The names of books come clear upon their shelves,
The reason delves for duty and you will wake
  With a start and go on living on your own.

The first train passes and the windows groan,
  Voices will hector and your voice become
A drum in tune with theirs, which all last night
  Like sap that fingered through a hungry tree
Asserted our one night's identity.

CRADLE SONG

The clock's untiring fingers wind the wool of darkness
And we all lie alone, having long outgrown our cradles
(Sleep, sleep, Miriam)
And the flames like faded ladies always unheeded simper
And all is troubledness.

Soft the wool, dark the wool
Is gathered slowly, wholly up
Into a ball, all of it.

And yet in the back of the mind, lulled all else,
There is something unsleeping, un-tamperable-with,
Something that whines and scampers
And like the ladies in the grate will not sleep nor forget itself,
Clawing at the wool like a kitten.

The clock's fingers wind, wind the wool of Lethe,
(Sleep, sleep, Miriam)
It glides across the floor drawn by hidden fingers

And the beast droops his head
And the fire droops its flounces
And winks a final ogle out of the fading embers
But no one pays attention;

This is too much, the flames say, insulted,
We who were once the world's beauties and now
No one pays attention
No one remembers us.

Sleep, sleep, Miriam.
And as for this animal of yours
He must be cradled also.
That he may not unravel this handiwork of forgetfulness.
That he may not philander with the flames before they die.

The world like a cradle rises and falls
On a wave of confetti and funerals
And sordor and stinks and stupid faces
And the deity making bored grimaces.

Oh what a muddle he has made of the wool,
(God will tomorrow have his hands full),
You must muzzle your beast, you must fasten him
For the whole of life—the interim.

Through the interim we pass
Everyone under an alias
Till they gather the strands of us together
And wind us up for ever and ever.

SUNDAY MORNING

Down the road someone is practicing scales,
The notes like little fishes vanish with a wink of tails,
Man's heart expands to tinker with his car
For this is Sunday morning, Fate's great bazaar,
Regard these means as ends, concentrate on this Now,
And you may grow to music or drive beyond Hindhead anyhow,
Take corners on two wheels until you go so fast
That you can clutch a fringe or two of the windy past,
That you can abstract this day and make it to the week of time
A small eternity, a sonnet self-contained in rhyme.

But listen, up the road, something gulps, the church spire
Opens its eight bells out, skulls' mouths which will not tire
To tell how there is no music or movement which secures
Escape from the weekday time. Which deadens and endures.

MUSEUMS

Museums offer us, running from among the buses,
A centrally heated refuge, parquet floors and sarcophaguses,
Into whose tall fake porches we hurry without a sound

Like a beetle under a brick that lies, useless, on the ground.
Warmed and cajoled by the silence the cowed cypher revives,
Mirrors himself in the cases of pots, paces himself by marble lives,
Makes believe it was he that was the glory that was Rome,
Soft on his cheek the nimbus of other people's martyrdom,
And then returns to the street, his mind an arena where sprawls
Any number of consumptive Keatses and dying Gauls.

MORNING SUN

Shuttles of trains going north, going south, drawing threads of blue
The shining of the lines of trams like swords
Thousands of posters asserting a monopoly of the good, the beautiful, the true
Crowds of people all in the vocative, you and you,
The haze of the morning shot with words.

Yellow sun comes white off the wet streets but bright
Chromium yellows in the gay sun's light
Filleted sun streaks the purple mist,
Everything is kissed and reticulated with sun
Scooped-up and cupped in the open fronts of shops
And bouncing on the traffic which never stops.

And the street fountain blown across the square
Rainbow-trellises the air and sunlight blazons
The red butcher's and scrolls of fish on marble slabs
Whistled bars of music crossing silver sprays
And horns of cars, touché, touché, rapiers' retort, a moving cage,
A turning page of shine and sound, the day's maze.

But when the sun goes out, the streets go cold, the hanging meat
And tiers of fish are colorless and merely dead
And the hoots of cars neurotically repeat and the tiptoed feet
Of women hurry and falter whose faces are dead
And I see in the air but not belonging there
The blown gray powder of the fountain gray as the ash
That forming on a cigarette covers the red.

BIRMINGHAM

Smoke from the train-gulf hid by hoardings blunders upward, the brakes of cars
Pipe as the policeman pivoting round raises his flat hand, bars
With his figure of a monolith Pharaoh the queue of fidgety machines
(Chromium dogs on the bonnet, faces behind the triplex screens)
Behind him the streets run away between the proud glass of shops
Cubical scent-bottles artificial legs arctic foxes and electric mops
But beyond this center the slumward vista thins like a diagram:
There, unvisited, are Vulcan's forges who doesn't care a tinker's damn.

Splayed outwards through the suburbs houses, houses for rest
Seducingly rigged by the builder, half-timbered houses with lips pressed

So tightly and eyes staring at the traffic through bleary haws
And only a six-inch grip of the racing earth in their concrete claws;
In these houses men as in a dream pursue the Platonic Forms
With wireless and cairn terriers and gadgets approximating to the fickle norms
And endeavor to find God and score one over the neighbor
By climbing tentatively upward on jerry-built beauty and sweated labor.

The lunch hour: the shops empty, shopgirls' faces relax
Diaphanous as green glass empty as old almanacs
As incoherent with ticketed gewgaws tiered behind their heads
As the Burne-Jones windows in St. Philip's broken by crawling leads
Insipid color, patches of emotion, Saturday thrills—
(This theater is sprayed with "June")—the gutter take our old playbills,
Next week-end it is likely in the heart's funfair we shall pull
Strong enough on the handle to get back our money; or at any rate it is possible.

On shining lines the trams like vast sarcophagi move
Into the sky, plum after sunset, merging to duck's egg, barred with mauve
Zeppelin clouds, and pentecost-like the cars' headlights bud
Out from sideroads and the traffic signals, crême-de-menthe or bull's blood,
Tell one to stop, the engine gently breathing, or to go on
To where like black pipes of organs in the frayed and fading zone
Of the West the factory chimneys on sullen sentry will all night wait
To call, in the harsh morning, sleep-stupid faces through the daily gate.

NUTS IN MAY

May come up with bird-din
And May come up with sun-dint,
May come up with water-wheels
   And May come up with iris.

In the sun-peppered meadow the shepherds are old,
Their flutes are broken and their tales are told,
And their ears are deaf when the guns unfold
The new philosophy over the wold.

May come up with pollen of death,
May come up with cordite,
May come up with a chinagraph
   And May come up with a stopwatch.

In the high court of heaven Their tail-feathers shine
With cowspit and bullspit and spirits of wine
They know no pity, being divine,
And They give no quarter to thine or mine.

May come up with Very lights,
May come up with duty,
May come up with a bouncing cheque,
   An acid-drop and a bandage.

Yes, angels are frigid and shepherds are dumb,
There is no holy water when the enemy come,
The trees are askew and the skies are a-hum
And you have to keep mum and go to it and die for your life and keep mum.

May come up with fiddle-bows,
May come up with blossom,
May come up the same again,
The same again but different.

W. H. Auden

W(ystan) H(ugh) Auden was born in York, February 21, 1907. He was educated at Gresham's School, Holt, and Christ Church, Oxford. From 1930 to 1935 he taught school at Malvern. He was with the G. P. O. Film Unit from 1935 to 1936. In 1939 he came to America and took out citizenship papers.

By the time Auden was thirty he had already been the center of several controversies; an English magazine had brought out a special Auden number; an entire movement seems to have stemmed from his energy and versatility. At thirty-three he had written and compiled four books of poetry, three plays, a collection of prose fiction, two books of travel, and two anthologies. *Poems* (1930) and *The Orators* (1932) were published, together with the supplementary *Dance of Death,* in a one-volume American edition severely entitled *Poems* (1934). Printed in this country simultaneously with Stephen Spender, Auden was continually reviewed with Spender, and when it was learned that both poets had in common an Oxford education, poetic influences, and radical political policies, critics coupled them as though they were two parts of one poet, dangerous but distinguished Siamese twins. No understanding reader could have confused or coupled the two. Spender is a romantic and, in spite of a modern vocabulary, traditional poet; Auden is a satirical and restlessly experimental writer. But contrasts are as misleading as comparisons, and Spender's work is considered separately on page 468. Auden has entirely different claims upon the reader.

The outstanding feature of Auden's poetry is its combination of variety and originality. When Auden uses traditional forms, he imposes a new pattern upon them, from archaic ballads to street-corner "blues." No contemporary poet has a greater natural command of language; he makes rhetoric out of banal jargon, and summons eloquence without raising his voice. Even in the difficult long poems, parts break through which require no key or comment. "Paid on Both Sides" is typical; it is a thirty-page play (its author calls it a "charade") which has a collapsing civilization for its background and which, in its confusion of purpose and effects, baffles intelligences higher than the average. Yet every individual scene is dynamic; the sense of shock is communicated with a horror that is immediately comprehended.

It has been said with some justice that Auden's philosophy is self-divided. He is merciless in his mockery of "the old gang," yet he is not convincingly on the "other side." He speaks for those who are bullied into war and exploited in peace, but he is not really one of them. Nevertheless, Auden somehow manages to unite opposites, to combine the latest findings in science with the oldest dreams and visions. He reconciles incongruities with breathtaking daring and clothes abstractions in flesh and blood.

With *On This Island* (1937) Auden simplified his effects and clarified his idiom. He did not discard eloquence, but he frequently spoke in "plain" terms and easy measures, imitated popular songs, composed ballads reminiscent of folk tunes, and put purposely crude rhymes to "coarse" themes. The lines were more tightly organized, the form was strictly shaped. Auden somehow combined the fastidious scholar and the man-of-the-people. In *Another Time* (1940) the poetry alternates between nobility and rowdiness; cabaret songs, tender lyrics and tricky rhymes occur between poems as brilliant as "Law, say the gardeners, is the sun" and as uplifting as "In Memory of W. B. Yeats." In the midst of intricate experiments, there are love poems of the sharpest sensitivity. Auden is perhaps the only modern poet who can really express himself in a villanelle or a sestina—he uses the latter form to remarkable effect in the "Journal of an Airman" and in "Hearing of harvests rotting in the valleys."

The Double Man (1941) makes it more apparent than ever that Auden is the most provocative as well as the most unpredictable poet of his generation. In a poem of some seventeen hundred lines Auden speaks as the poet who has become the multiple man: the bravura performer and the careful craftsman, the lively iconoclast and the studious wit. *The Double Man* was immediately hailed as a phenomenon, a landmark, a Return to Order. The most experimental of contemporary poets had gone to school to Pope, and the result of his exercise in discipline seemed to be a turning-point for the 1940's, the long-awaited reply to the Wastelanders.

For the Time Being (1944) and the *Collected Poetry of W. H. Auden* (1945) defined an epoch; a book of critical essays acknowledged Auden's importance by its very title: *Auden and After*. Auden broke through the barriers between light verse and oratory, between high spirits and high seriousness. *For the Time Being* contains two long poems: "The Sea and the Mirror," which is an extraordinary commentary on Shakespeare's *The Tempest,* learned and illuminating; and the title poem, a Christmas cantata which, in its mixture of classic and colloquial speech, is a profound paradox. Auden's early work, like Eliot's, was written mainly out of revulsion. Disgust of a sick world overcame pity; fierce satire and coarse mockery ran the gamut from bitterness to burlesque; the tone was desperate and morose. An atmosphere of foreboding, of imminent catastrophe, hung over the work, an "immeasurable neurotic dread."

By the time he was forty Auden was recognized as the most influential poet after Eliot. It was observed that there was a geographical as well as a poetical justice in the fact. Auden, born in England, made his home in America; Eliot, born in Missouri, exchanged his American birthright for English citizenship. Like Eliot, Auden progressed from cynicism to mysticism, from a bewildered distrust of civilization to a doggedly religious hope for it. Going beyond Eliot,

Auden substituted exuberance for depression; to compressed constraint he added openness, flexibility, and an easy mastery of charm.

In the later and more solemn work, emphasized in the *Collected Poetry,* Auden did not relinquish his intransigence or his provocative wit. Those who complained of his preoccupation with metaphysics failed to see that Auden's attempts to find a fixed faith enlarged his gamut and altered a self-centered concern. Poems to Freud, Matthew Arnold, and Henry James, Yeats and Voltaire, Ernst Toller and Edward Lear speak for his catholicity as well as his convictions. That Auden has never lost his personal and pungent humor is proved again and again, notably by the brilliantly turned "Under Which Lyre," a Phi Beta Kappa poem ironically subtitled "A Reactionary Tract for the Times."

The Age of Anxiety (1947), which received the Pulitzer Prize in 1948, is another long stride in Auden's progress. Tcehnically it is a prime example of his virtuosity; using the language of the 1940's, it employs the severely stressed poetic form of the Anglo-Saxons, the tough, triply alliterative line of *Beowulf.* But the idiom is as modern as it is characteristic: a purposeful blend of casual horror and baleful *vers de société*—the patter which sometimes makes Auden seem the Freudians' Noel Coward—and the effect is that of a contemporary Purgatory. In this metropolitan baroque "eclogue," which opens in a New York bar, four people reenact the seven ages and seven stages of man, from a morass of reminiscence through the deserts of disillusion, including a dirge lamenting the lost leader (the "lost dad," the vanished God), to the final frustration which compels a hope of other values.

Thus Auden establishes himself as a protean poet, a capricious artist delighting in straight-face frivolities and a probing spirit torn between agnosticism and blind belief, a superb rhetorician rich in learning and a lover of extravagant oddities, a dramatic lyricist and a natural dialectician—in short, a poet who is equally adept at sheer fooling and pure enchantment.

In addition to the Pulitzer Prize, Auden received the King's Poetry Medal in 1937 and the Award of Merit Medal of the National Academy of Arts and Letters in 1945. Versatile enough in his own right, Auden has had to resort to collaborators in order to keep pace with his own energetic career. With John Garrett he compiled an anthology, *The Poet's Tongue* (1935); with Louis MacNeice he composed *Letters from Iceland* (1937); with Christopher Isherwood he wrote two plays, *The Dog Beneath the Skin* (1935), a satire, and *On the Frontier* (1938), a melodrama, and *Journey to a War* (1939), an account of a trip through war-torn China. The best analyses of Auden's varying sensibility appear in Stephen Spender's *The Destructive Element* (1935), David Daiches' *Poetry and the Modern World* (1940), and Francis Scarfe's *Auden and After* (1943).

Between his mid-forties and early fifties Auden completed three new volumes of varied and wide-ranging poetry: *Nones* (1951), *The Shield of Achilles* (1955), and *Homage to Clio* (1960). He was elected Professor of Poetry at Oxford in 1956.

CHORUS FROM A PLAY

Doom is dark and deeper than any sea-dingle:
Upon what man it fall
In spring, day-wishing flowers appearing,
Avalanche sliding, white snow from rock-face,
That he should leave his house;
No cloud-soft hands can hold him, restraint by women,
But ever that man goes
By place-keepers, by forest trees,
A stranger to strangers over undried sea,
Houses for fishes, suffocating water;
Or lonely on fell as chat,
By pot-holed becks
A bird stone-haunting, an unquiet bird.

There head falls forward, fatigued at evening,
And dreams of home:
Waving from window, spread of welcome,
Kissing of wife under single sheet;
But waking sees
Bird-flocks nameless to him, through doorway voices
Of new men making another love.

Save him from hostile capture
From sudden tiger's spring at corner:
Protect his house,
His anxious house where days are counted
Fom thunderbolt protect,
From gradual ruin spreading like a stain:
Converting number from vague to certain
Bring joy, bring day of his returning,
Lucky with day approaching, with leaning dawn.

WHO'S WHO

A shilling life will give you all the facts:
How Father beat him, how he ran away,
What were the struggles of his youth, what acts
Made him the greatest figure of his day:
Of how he fought, fished, hunted, worked all night;
Though giddy, climbed new mountains; named a sea:
Some of the last researches even write
Love made him weep his pints like you and me.

With all his honors on, he sighed for one
Who, say astonished critics, lived at home;
Did little jobs about the house with skill
And nothing else; could whistle; would sit still
Or potter round the garden; answered some
Of his long marvellous letters, but kept none.

ODE; TO MY PUPILS

Though aware of our rank and alert to obey orders,
Watching with binoculars the movement of the grass for an ambush,
The pistol cocked, the code-word committed to memory;
    The youngest drummer
Knows all the peace-time stories like the oldest soldier,
    Though frontier-conscious,

About the tall white gods who landed from their open boat,
Skilled in the working of copper, appointing our feast-days,
Before the islands were submerged, when the weather was calm,
    The maned lion common,
An open wishing-well in every garden;
    When love came easy.

Perfectly certain, all of us, but not from the records,
Not from the unshaven agent who returned to the camp;
The pillar dug from the desert recorded only
    The sack of a city,
The agent clutching his side collapsed at our feet,
    "Sorry! They got me!"

Yes, they were living here once but do not now,
Yes, they are living still but do not here;
Lying awake after Lights Out a recruit may speak up:
    "Who told you all this?"
The tent-talk pauses a little till a veteran answers
    "Go to sleep, Sonny!"

Turning over he closes his eyes, and then in a moment
Sees the sun at midnight bright over cornfield and pasture,
Our hope. . . . Someone jostles him, fumbling for boots,
    Time to change guard:
Boy, the quarrel was before your time, the aggressor
    No one you know.

Your childish moments of awareness were all of our world,
At five you sprang, already a tiger in the garden,
At night your mother taught you to pray for our Daddy
    Far away fighting,
One morning you fell off a horse and your brother mocked you:
    "Just like a girl!"

You've got their names to live up to and questions won't help,
You've a very full program, first aid, gunnery, tactics,
The technique to master of raids and hand-to-hand fighting;
    Are you in training?
Are you taking care of yourself? are you sure of passing
    The endurance test?

Now we're due to parade on the square in front of the Cathedral,
When the bishop has blessed us, to file in after the choir-boys,
To stand with the wine-dark conquerors in the roped-off pews,
Shout ourselves hoarse:
"They ran like hares: we have broken them up like fire-wood;
They fought against God."

While in a great rift in the limestone miles away
At the same hour they gather, tethering their horses beside them;
A scarecrow prophet from a bowlder foresees our judgment,
Their oppressors howling;
And the bitter psalm is caught by the gale from the rocks:
"How long shall they flourish?"

What have we all been doing to have made from Fear
That laconic war-bitten captain addressing them now?
"Heart and head shall be keener, mood the more
As our might lessens":
To have caused their shout "We will fight till we lie down beside
The Lord we have loved."

There's Wrath who has learnt every trick of guerilla war-fare,
The shamming dead, the night-raid, the feinted retreat;
Envy their brilliant pamphleteer, to lying
As husband true,
Expert Impersonator and linguist, proud of his power
To hoodwink sentries.

Gluttony living alone, austerer than us,
Big, simple Greed, Acedia famed with them all
For her stamina, keeping the outposts, and somewhere Lust
With his sapper's skill,
Muttering to his fuses in a tunnel "Could I meet here with Love,
I would hug her to death."

There are faces there for which for a very long time
We've been on the look-out, though often at home we imagined,
Catching sight of a back or hearing a voice through a doorway,
We had found them at last;
Put our arms round their necks and looked in their eyes and discovered
We were unlucky.

And some of them, surely, we seem to have seen before:
Why, that girl who rode off on her bicycle one fine summer evening
And never returned, she's there; and the banker we'd noticed
Worried for weeks;
Till he failed to arrive one morning and his room was empty,
Gone with a suitcase.

They speak of things done on the frontier we were never told,
The hidden path to their squat Pictish tower

They will never reveal though kept without sleep, for their code is
"Death to the squealer":
They are brave, yes, though our newspapers mention their bravery
In inverted commas.

But careful; back to our lines; it is unsafe there,
Passports are issued no longer; that area is closed;
There's no fire in the waiting-room now at the climbers' Junction,
And all this year
Work has been stopped on the power-house; the wind whistles under
The half-built culverts.

Do you think that because you have heard that on Christmas Eve
In a quiet sector they walked about on the skyline,
Exchanged cigarettes, both learning the words for "I love you"
In either language:
You can stroll across for a smoke and a chat any evening?
Try it and see.

That rifle-sight you're designing; is it ready yet?
You're holding us up; the office is getting impatient;
The square munition-works out on the old allotments
Needs stricter watching;
If you see any loiterers there you may shoot without warning,
We must stop that leakage.

All leave is cancelled tonight; we must say good-by.
We entrain at once for the North; we shall see in the morning
The headlands we're doomed to attack; snow down to the tide-line:
Though the bunting signals
"Indoors before it's too late; cut peat for your fires,"
We shall lie out there.

THE STRINGS' EXCITEMENT

he strings' excitement, the applauding drum
re but the initiating ceremony
hat out of cloud the ancestral face may
come.

nd never hear their subaltern mockery,
raphiti-writers, moss-grown with whimsies,
oquacious when the watercourse is dry.

is your face I see, and morning's praise
f you is ghost's approval of the choice,
iltered through roots of the effacing grass.

ear, taking me aside, would give advice
To conquer her, the visible enemy,
is enough to turn away the eyes."

Yet there's no peace in this assaulted city
But speeches at the corners, hope for news,
Outside the watchfires of a stronger army.

And all emotions to expression came,
Recovering the archaic imagery:
This longing for assurance takes the form

Of a hawk's vertical stooping from the sky;
These tears, salt for a disobedient dream,
The lunatic agitation of the sea;

While this despair with hardened eyeballs
cries
"A Golden Age, a Silver . . . rather this,
Massive and taciturn years, the Age of Ice."

THIS LUNAR BEAUTY

This lunar beauty
Has no history
Is complete and early;
If beauty later
Bear any feature
It had a lover
And is another.

This like a dream
Keeps other time
And daytime is
The loss of this;
For time is inches
And the heart's changes
Where ghost has haunted
Lost and wanted.

But this was never
A ghost's endeavor
Nor finished this,
Was ghost at ease;
And till it pass
Love shall not near
The sweetness here
Nor sorrow take
His endless look.

ALWAYS THE FOLLOWING WIND

Voice:

Always the following wind of history
Of others' wisdom makes a buoyant air
Till we come suddenly on pockets where
Is nothing loud but us; where voices seem
Abrupt, untrained, competing with no lie
Our fathers shouted once. They taught us war,
To scamper after darlings, to climb hills,
To emigrate from weakness, find ourselves
The easy conquerors of empty bays:
But never told us this, left each to learn,
Hear something of that soon-arriving day
When to gaze longer and delighted on
A face or idea be impossible.
Could I have been some simpleton that lived
Before disaster sent his runners here;
Younger than worms, worms have too much to bear.
Yes, mineral were best: could I but see
These woods, these fields of green, this lively world
Sterile as moon.

Chorus:

The Spring unsettles sleeping partnerships,
Foundries improve their casting process, shops
Open a further wing on credit till
The winter. In summer boys grow tall
With running races on the froth-wet sand,
War is declared there, here a treaty signed;
Here a scum breaks up like a bomb, there troops
Deploy like birds. But proudest into traps
Have fallen. These gears which ran in oil for week
By week, needing no look, now will not work;
Those manors mortgaged twice to pay for love
Go to another.

O how shall man live
Whose thought is born, child of one farcical night,
To find him old? The body warm but not
By choice, he dreams of folk in dancing bunches,
Of tart wine spilt on home-made benches,
Where learns, one drawn apart, a secret will
Restore the dead; but comes thence to a wall.
Outside on frozen soil lie armies killed
Who seem familiar, but they are cold.
Now the most solid wish he tries to keep
His hands show through; he never will look up,
Say "I am good." On him misfortune falls
More than enough. Better where no one feels,
The out-of-sight, buried too deep for shafts.

CHORUS

(*from "Paid on Both Sides"*)

To throw away the key and walk away
Not abrupt exile, the neighbors asking why,
But following a line with left and right
An altered gradient at another rate
Learns more than maps upon the whitewashed wall
The hand put up to ask; and makes us well
Without confession of the ill. All pasts
Are single old past now, although some posts
Are forwarded, held looking on a new view;
The future shall fulfill a surer vow
Not smiling at queen over the glass rim
Nor making gunpowder in the top room,
Not swooping at the surface still like gulls
But with prolonged drowning shall develop gills.

But there are still to tempt; areas not seen
Because of blizzards or an erring sign
Whose guessed-at wonders would be worth alleging,
And lies about the cost of a night's lodging.
Travelers may sleep at inns but not attach,
They sleep one night together, not asked to touch;
Receive no normal welcome, not the pressed lip,
Children to lift, not the assuaging lap.
Crossing the pass descend the growing stream
Too tired to hear except the pulses' strum,
Reach villages to ask for a bed in
Rock shutting out the sky, the old life done.

BALLAD

O what is that sound which so thrills the ear
Down in the valley drumming, drumming?

Only the scarlet soldiers, dear,
  The soldiers coming.

O what is that light I see flashing so clear
  Over the distance brightly, brightly?
Only the sun on their weapons, dear,
  As they step lightly.

O what are they doing with all that gear;
  What are they doing this morning, this morning?
Only the usual maneuvers, dear,
  Or perhaps a warning.

O why have they left the road down there;
  Why are they suddenly wheeling, wheeling?
Perhaps a change in the orders, dear;
  Why are you kneeling?

O haven't they stopped for the doctor's care;
  Haven't they reined their horses, their horses?
Why, they are none of them wounded, dear.
  None of these forces.

O is it the parson they want, with white hair;
  Is it the parson, is it, is it?
No, they are passing his gateway, dear,
  Without a visit.

O it must be the farmer who lives so near,
  It must be the farmer, so cunning, cunning;
They have passed the farm already, dear,
  And now they are running.

O where are you going? stay with me here.
  Were the vows you swore me deceiving, deceiving?
No, I promised to love you, my dear,
  But I must be leaving.

O it's broken the lock and splintered the door,
  O it's the gate where they're turning, turning;
Their feet are heavy on the floor
  And their eyes are burning.

VILLANELLE

Time can say nothing but I told you so,
Time only knows the price we have to pay;
If I could tell you, I would let you know.

If we should weep when clowns put on their show,
If we should stumble when musicians play,
Time can say nothing but I told you so.

There are no fortunes to be told, although
Because I love you more than I can say,
If I could tell you, I would let you know.

The winds must come from somewhere when they blow,
There must be reasons why the leaves decay;
Time can say nothing but I told you so.

Perhaps the roses really want to grow,
The vision seriously intends to stay;
If I could tell you, I would let you know.

Suppose the lions all get up and go,
And all the brooks and soldiers run away?
Time can say nothing but I told you so;
If I could tell you, I would let you know.

"LOOK, STRANGER"

Look, stranger, at this island now
The leaping light for your delight discovers,
Stand stable here
And silent be,
That through the channels of the ear
May wander like a river
The swaying sound of the sea.

Here at the small field's ending pause
Where the chalk wall falls to the foam, and its tall ledges.
Oppose the pluck
And knock of the tide,
And the shingle scrambles after the sucking surf, and the gull lodges
A moment on its sheer side.

Far off like floating seeds the ships
Diverge on urgent voluntary errands;
And the full view
Indeed may enter
And move in memory as now these clouds do,
That pass the harbor mirror
And all the summer through the water saunter.

HEARING OF HARVESTS ROTTING IN THE VALLEYS

Hearing of harvests rotting in the valleys,
Seeing at end of street the barren mountains,
Round corners coming suddenly on water,
Knowing them shipwrecked who were launched for islands,
We honor founders of these starving cities,
Whose honor is the image of our sorrow.

Which cannot see its likeness in their sorrow
That brought them desperate to the brink of valleys;
Dreaming of evening walks through learned cities,

They reined their violent horses on the mountains,
Those fields like ships to castaways on islands,
Visions of green to them that craved for water.

They built by rivers and at night the water
Running past windows comforted their sorrow;
Each in his little bed conceived of islands
Where every day was dancing in the valleys,
And all the year trees blossomed on the mountains,
Where love was innocent, being far from cities.

But dawn came back and they were still in cities;
No marvelous creature rose up from the water,
There was still gold and silver in the mountains,
And hunger was a more immediate sorrow;
Although to moping villagers in valleys
Some waving pilgrims were describing islands.

"The gods," they promised, "visit us from islands,
Are stalking head-up, lovely through the cities;
Now is the time to leave your wretched valleys
And sail with them across the lime-green water;
Sitting at their white sides, forget their sorrow,
The shadow cast across your lives by mountains."

So many, doubtful, perished in the mountains
Climbing up crags to get a view of islands;
So many, fearful, took with them their sorrow
Which stayed them when they reached unhappy cities;
So many, careless, dived and drowned in water;
So many, wretched, would not leave their valleys.

It is the sorrow; shall it melt? Ah, water
Would gush, flush, green these mountains and these valleys
And we rebuild our cities, not dream of islands.

LAW, SAY THE GARDENERS, IS THE SUN

Law, say the gardeners, is the sun,
Law is the one
All gardeners obey
Tomorrow, yesterday, today.

Law is the wisdom of the old
The impotent grandfathers shrilly scold;
The grandchildren put out a treble tongue,
Law is the senses of the young.

Law, says the priest with a priestly look,
Expounding to an unpriestly people,
Law is the words in my priestly book,
Law is my pulpit and my steeple.

Law, says the judge as he looks down his nose,
Speaking clearly and most severely,
Law is as I've told you before,
Law is as you know I suppose,
Law is but let me explain it once more,
Law is The Law.

Yet law-abiding scholars write;
Law is neither wrong nor right,
Law is only crimes
Punished by places and by times,
Law is the clothes men wear
Anytime, anywhere,
Law is Good-morning and Good-night.

Others say, Law is our Fate;
Others say, Law is our State;
Others say, others say
Law is no more,
Law is gone away.

And always the loud angry crowd
Very angry and very loud
Law is We,
And always the soft idiot softly Me.

If we, dear, know we know no more
Than they about the law,

f I no more than you
now what we should and should not do
xcept that all agree
ladly or miserably
hat the law is
nd that all know this,
f therefore thinking it absurd
o identify Law with some other word,
Jnlike so many men
cannot say Law is again,
lo more than they can we suppress
he universal wish to guess
)r slip out of our own position
nto an unconcerned condition.

lthough I can at least confine
our vanity and mine
o stating timidly
timid similarity,
Ve shall boast anyway:
ike love I say.

ike love we dont know where or why
ike love we cant compel or fly
ike love we often weep
ike love we seldom keep.

LAY YOUR SLEEPING HEAD, MY LOVE

Lay your sleeping head, my love,
Human on my faithless arm;
Time and fevers burn away
Individual beauty from
Thoughtful children, and the grave
Proves the child ephemeral:
But in my arms till break of day
Let the living creature lie,
Mortal, guilty, but to me
The entirely beautiful.

Soul and body have no bounds:
To lovers as they lie upon
Her tolerant enchanted slope
In their ordinary swoon,
Grave the vision Venus sends
Of supernatural sympathy,
Universal love and hope;
While an abstract insight wakes
Among the glaciers and the rocks
The hermit's sensual ecstasy.

Certainty, fidelity
On the stroke of midnight pass
Like vibrations of a bell,
And fashionable madmen raise
Their pedantic boring cry:
Every farthing of the cost,
All the dreaded cards foretell,
Shall be paid, but from this night
Not a whisper, not a thought,
Not a kiss nor look be lost.

Beauty, midnight, vision dies:
Let the winds of dawn that blow
Softly round your dreaming head
Such a day of sweetness show
Eye and knocking heart may bless,
Find the mortal world enough;
Noons of dryness see you fed
By the involuntary powers,
Nights of insult let you pass
Watched by every human love.

IN MEMORY OF W. B. YEATS

I

He disappeared in the dead of winter:
The brooks were frozen, the airports almost deserted,
And snow disfigured the public statues;
The mercury sank in the mouth of the dying day.
O all the instruments agree
The day of his death was a dark cold day.

Far from his illness
The wolves ran on through the everygreen forests,
The peasant river was untempted by the fashionable quays;

By mourning tongues
The death of the poet was kept from his poems.

But for him it was his last afternoon as himself,
An afternoon of nurses and rumors;
The provinces of his body revolted,
The squares of his mind were empty,
Silence invaded the suburbs,
The current of his feeling failed: he became his admirers.

Now he is scattered among a hundred cities
And wholly given over to unfamiliar affections;
To find his happiness in another kind of wood
And be punished under a foreign code of conscience.
The words of a dead man
Are modified in the guts of the living.

But in the importance and noise of tomorrow
When the brokers are roaring like beasts on the floor of the Bourse,
And the poor have the sufferings to which they are fairly accustomed,
And each in the cell of himself is almost convinced of his freedom;
A few thousand will think of this day
As one thinks of a day when one did something slightly unusual.

O all the instruments agree
The day of his death was a dark cold day.

2

You were silly like us: your gift survived it all;
The parish of rich women, physical decay,
Yourself; mad Ireland hurt you into poetry.
Now Ireland has her madness and her weather still,
For poetry makes nothing happen: it survives
In the valley of its saying where executives
Would never want to tamper; it flows south
From ranches of isolation and the busy griefs,
Raw towns that we believe and die in; it survives,
A way of happening, a mouth.

Earth, receive an honored guest;
William Yeats is laid to rest:
Let the Irish vessel lie
Emptied of its poetry.

Time that is intolerant
Of the brave and innocent,
And indifferent in a week
To a beautiful physique,

Worships language and forgives
Everyone by whom it lives;

Pardons cowardice, conceit,
Lays its honors at their feet.

Time that with this strange excuse
Pardoned Kipling and his views,
And will pardon Paul Claudel,
Pardons him for writing well.

In the nightmare of the dark
All the dogs of Europe bark,
And the living nations wait,
Each sequestered in its hate;

Intellectual disgrace
Stares from every human face,
And the seas of pity lie
Locked and frozen in each eye.

Follow, poet, follow right
To the bottom of the night,
With your unconstraining voice
Still persuade us to rejoice;

With the farming of a verse
Make a vineyard of the curse,
Sing of human unsuccess
In a rapture of distress;

In the deserts of the heart
Let the healing fountain start,
In the prison of his days
Teach the free man how to praise.

SEPTEMBER 1, 1939

I sit in one of the dives
On Fifty-Second Street
Uncertain and afraid
As the clever hopes expire
Of a low dishonest decade:
Waves of anger and fear
Circulate over the bright
And darkened lands of the earth,
Obsessing our private lives;
The unmentionable odour of death
Offends the September night.

Accurate scholarship can
Unearth the whole offence
From Luther until now
That has driven a culture mad,
Find what occurred at Linz,
What huge imago made
A psychopathic god:
I am the public know
What all schoolchildren learn,
Those to whom evil is done
Do evil in return.

Exiled Thucydides knew
All that a speech can say
About Democracy,
And what dictators do,
The elderly rubbish they talk
To an apathetic grave;
Analysed all in his book,
The enlightenment driven away,
The habit-forming pain,
Mismanagement and grief:
We must suffer them all again.

Into this neutral air
Where blind skyscrapers use
Their full height to proclaim
The strength of Collective Man,
Each language pours its vain
Competitive excuse:
But who can live for long
In an euphoric dream;
Out of the mirror they stare,
Imperialism's face
And the international wrong.

Faces along the bar
Cling to their average day:
The lights must never go out,
The music must always play,
All the conventions conspire
To make this fort assume
The furniture of home;
Lest we should see where we are,
Lost in a haunted wood,
Children afraid of the night
Who have never been happy or good.

The windiest militant trash
Important Persons shout
Is not so crude as our wish:
What mad Nijinsky wrote
About Diaghilev
Is true of the normal heart;
For the error bred in the bone
Of each woman and each man
Craves what it cannot have,
Not universal love
But to be loved alone.

From the conservative dark
Into the ethical life
The dense commuters come,
Repeating their morning vow;
"I *will* be true to the wife,
I'll concentrate more on my work,"
And helpless governors wake
To resume their compulsory game:
Who can release them now,
Who can reach the deaf,
Who can speak for the dumb?

All I have is a voice
To undo the folded lie,
The romantic lie in the brain
Of the sensual man-in-the-street
And the lie of Authority
Whose buildings grope the sky:
There is no such thing as the State
And no one exists alone;
Hunger allows no choice
To the citizen or the police;
We must love one another or die.

Defenceless under the night
Our world in stupor lies;
Yet, dotted everywhere,
Ironic points of light
Flash out wherever the Just
Exchange their messages:
May I, composed like them
Of Eros and of dust,
Beleaguered by the same
Negation and despair,
Show an affirming flame.

MUNDUS ET INFANS

Kicking his mother until she let go of his soul
Has given him a healthy appetite: clearly, her rôle
    In the New Order must be
To supply and deliver his raw materials free;
    Should there be any shortage
She will be held responsible; she also promises
To show him all such attention as befits his age.
    Having dictated peace,

With one fist clenched behind his head, heel drawn up to thigh,
The cocky little ogre dozes off, ready,
    Though, to take on the rest
Of the world at the drop of a hat or the mildest
    Nudge of the impossible,
Resolved, cost what it may, to seize supreme power, and
Sworn to resist tyranny to the death with all
    Forces at his command.

A pantheist not a solipsist, he cooperates
With a universe of large and noisy feeling states,
    Without troubling to place
Them anywhere special; for, to his eyes, Funny face
    Or Elephant as yet
Mean nothing. His distinction between Me and Us
Is a matter of taste; his seasons are Dry and Wet;
    He thinks as his mouth does.

Still, his loud iniquity is still what only the
Greatest of saints become—someone who does not lie:
    He because he cannot
Stop the vivid present to think; they by having got
    Past reflection into
A passionate obedience in time. We have our Boy-
Meets-Girl era of mirrors and muddle to work through
    Without rest, without joy.

Therefore we love him because his judgments are so
Frankly subjective that his abuse carries no
    Personal sting. We should
Never dare offer our helplessness as a good
    Bargain, without at least
Promising to overcome a misfortune we blame
History or Banks or the Weather for; but this beast
    Dares to exist without shame.

Let him praise his Creator with the top of his voice,
Then, and the motions of his bowels; let us rejoice
    That he lets us hope, for
He may never become a fashionable or
    Important personage.
However bad he may be, he has not yet gone mad;
Whoever we are now, we were no worse at his age:
    So of course we ought to be glad

When he bawls the house down. Has he not a perfect right
To remind us at any moment how we quite
    Rightly expect each other
To go upstairs or for a walk if we must cry over
    Spilt milk, such as our wish
That since, apparently, we shall never be above
Either or both, we had never learned to distinguish
    Between hunger and love?

SONG: AS I WALKED OUT ONE EVENING

As I walked out one evening,
  Walking down Bristol Street,
The crowds upon the pavement
  Were fields of harvest wheat.

And down by the brimming river
  I heard a lover sing
Under an arch of the railway:
  "Love has no ending.

I'll love you, dear, I'll love you
  Till China and Africa meet
And the river jumps over the mountain
  And the salmon sing in the street.

I'll love you till the ocean
  Is folded and hung up to dry
And the seven stars go squawking
  Like geese about the sky.

The years shall run like rabbits
  For in my arms I hold
The Flower of the Ages
  And the first love of the World."

But all the clocks in the city
  Began to whirr and chime:
"O let not Time deceive you,
  You cannot conquer Time.

In the burrows of the Nightmare
  Where Justice naked is,
Time watches from the shadow
  And coughs when you would kiss.

In headaches and in worry
  Vaguely life leaks away,
And Time will have his fancy
  To-morrow or to-day.

Into many a green valley
  Drifts the appalling snow;
Time breaks the threaded dances
  And the diver's brilliant bow.

O plunge your hands in water,
  Plunge them in up to the wrist;
Stare, stare in the basin
  And wonder what you've missed.

The glacier knocks in the cupboard,
  The desert sighs in the bed,
And the crack in the tea-cup opens
  A lane to the land of the dead.

Where the beggars raffle the banknotes
  And the Giant is enchanting to Jack,
And the Lily-white Boy is a Roarer
  And Jill goes down on her back.

O look, look in the mirror,
  O look in your distress;
Life remains a blessing
  Although you cannot bless.

O stand, stand at the window
  As the tears scald and start;
You shall love your crooked neighbour
  With your crooked heart."

It was late, late in the evening,
  The lovers they were gone;
The clocks had ceased their chiming
  And the deep river ran on.

SONG: FISH IN THE UNRUFFLED LAKES

Fish in the unruffled lake
The swarming colors wear,
Swans in the winter air
A white perfection have,
And the great lion walks
Through his innocent grove;
Lion, fish, and swan
Act, and are gone
Upon Time's toppling wave.

We till shadowed days are done,
We must weep and sing
Duty's conscious wrong,
The Devil in the clock,

The Goodness carefully worn
For atonement or for luck;
We must lose our loves;
On each beast and bird that moves
Turn an envious look.

Sighs for folly said and done
Twist our narrow days;

But I must bless, I must praise
That you, my swan, who have
All gifts that to the swan
Impulsive Nature gave,
The majesty and pride,
Last night should add
Your voluntary love.

SONG: STOP ALL THE CLOCKS

op all the clocks, cut off the telephone,
event the dog from barking with a juicy bone,
ence the pianos and with muffled drum
ing out the coffin, let the mourners come.

t aeroplanes circle moaning overhead
ribbling on the sky the message He Is Dead,
t crêpe bows round the white necks of the public doves,
t the traffic policemen wear black cotton gloves.

He was my North, my South, my East and West,
My working week and my Sunday rest,
My noon, my midnight, my talk, my song;
I thought that love would last for ever: I was wrong.

The stars are not wanted now; put out every one:
Pack up the moon and dismantle the sun;
Pour away the ocean and sweep up the woods:
For nothing now can ever come to any good.

UNDER WHICH LYRE

A Reactionary Tract for the Times

es at last has quit the field,
e bloodstains on the bushes yield
To seeping showers.
d in their convalescent state
e fractured towns associate
With summer flowers.

camped upon the college plain
w veterans already train
As freshman forces;
structors with sarcastic tongue
epherd the battle-weary young
Through basic courses.

nong bewildering appliances
r mastering the arts and sciences
They stroll or run,
d nerves that never flinched at slaughter
e shot to pieces by the shorter
Poems of Donne.

Professors back from secret missions
Resume their proper eruditions,
Though some regret it;
They liked their dictaphones a lot,
They met some big wheels and do not
Let you forget it.

But Zeus' inscrutable decree
Permits the will to disagree
To be pandemic,
Ordains that vaudeville shall preach,
And every commencement speech
Be a polemic.

Let Ares doze, that other war
Is instantly declared once more
'Twixt those who follow
Precocious Hermes all the way
And those who without qualms obey
Pompous Apollo.

Brutal like all Olympic games,
Though fought with smiles and Christian names
And less dramatic,
This dialectic strife between
The civil gods is just as mean,
And more fanatic.

What high immortals do in mirth
Is life and death on Middle Earth;
Their a-historic
Antipathy forever gripes
All ages and somatic types:
The sophomoric

Who face the future's darkest hints
With giggles or with prairie squints
As stout as Cortez,
And those who like myself turn pale
As we approach with ragged sail
The fattening forties.

The sons of Hermes love to play,
And only do their best when they
Are told they oughtn't;
Apollo's children never shrink
From boring jobs but have to think
Their work important.

Related by antithesis,
A compromise between them is
Impossible;
Respect perhaps, but friendship never:
Falstaff the fool confronts forever
The prig Prince Hal.

So, standing here, surrounded by
The eyes of Miltons and the high
Foreheads of Shaws,
A Hermes man, I call on you,
Phi-Beta-Kappa brethren, to
Defend his cause.

If he would leave the self alone,
Apollo's welcome to the throne,
Fasces and falcons;
He loves to rule, has always done it:
The earth would soon, did Hermes run it,
Be like the Balkans.

But, jealous of our god of dreams,
His common sense in secret schemes
To rule the heart;
Unable to invent the lyre,
Creates with simulated fire
Official art.

And when he occupies a college,
Truth is replaced by Useful Knowledge;
He pays particular
Attention to Commercial Thought,
Public Relations, Hygiene, Sport,
In his curricula.

Athletic, extrovert and crude,
For him, to work in solitude
Is the offense,
The goal a populous Nirvana:
His shield bears this device: *Mens sana*
Qui mal y pense.

Today his arms, we must confess,
From Right to Left have met success,
His banners wave
From Yale to Princeton, and the news
From Broadway to the Book Reviews
Is very grave.

His radio Homers all day long
In over-Whitmanated song
That does not scan,
With adjectives laid end to end,
Extol the doughnut and commend
The Common Man.

His too each homely lyric thing
On sport or spousal love or spring
Or dogs or dusters,
Invented by some courthouse bard
For recitation by the yard
In filibusters.

To him ascend the prize orations
And sets of fugal variations
On some folk ballad,
While dietitians sacrifice
A glass of prune juice or a nice
Marshmallow salad.

Charged with his compound of sensatio
Sex plus some undenominational
Religious matter,
Enormous novels by co-eds
Rain down on our defenseless heads
Till our teeth chatter.

ı fake Hermetic uniforms
·ehind our battle-line, in swarms
That keep alighting,
Iis existentialists declare
'hat they are in complete despair,
Yet go on writing.

Io matter. He shall be defied.
Ve have the ladies on our side.
What though his threat
'o organize us grow more critical?
eus willing, we, the unpolitical
Shall best him yet.

.one scholars, sniping from the walls
f learned periodicals,
Our facts defend,
ur intellectual marines,
anding in Little Magazines,
Capture a trend.

y night our student Underground
.t cocktail parties whisper round
From ear to ear;
at figures in the public eye
'ollapse next morning, ambushed by
Some witty sneer.

ı our morale must lie our strength:
o, that we may behold at length
Routed Apollo's

Battalions melt away like fog,
Keep well the Hermetic Decalogue,
Which runs as follows:

Thou shalt not do as the dean pleases,
Thou shalt not write thy doctor's thesis
On education,
Thou shalt not worship projects nor
Shalt thou or thine bow down before
Administration.

Thou shalt not answer questionnaires
Or quizzes upon World Affairs,
Nor with compliance
Take any test. Thou shalt not sit
With statisticians nor commit
A social science.

Thou shalt not be on friendly terms
With guys in advertising firms,
Nor speak with such
As read the Bible for its prose,
Nor, above all, make love to those
Who wash too much.

Thou shalt not live within thy means
Nor on plain water and raw greens.
If thou must choose
Between the chances, choose the odd;
Read the *New Yorker;* trust in God;
And take short views.

AFTER CHRISTMAS

(*From "For the Time Being"*)

Well, so that is that. Now we must dismantle the tree,
Putting the decorations back into their cardboard boxes—
Some have got broken—and carrying them up to the attic.
The holly and the mistletoe must be taken down and burnt,
And the children got ready for school. There are enough
Left-overs to do, warmed-up, for the rest of the week—
Not that we have much appetite, having drunk such a lot,
Stayed up so late, attempted—quite unsuccessfully—
To love all of our relatives, and in general
Grossly overestimated our powers. Once again
As in previous years we have seen the actual Vision and failed
To do more than entertain it as an agreeable
Possibility, once again we have sent Him away,
Begging though to remain His disobedient servant,
The promising child who cannot keep His word for long.
The Christmas Feast is already a fading memory,

And already the mind begins to be vaguely aware
Of an unpleasant whiff of apprehension at the thought
Of Lent and Good Friday which cannot, after all, now
Be very far off. But, for the time being, here we all are,
Back in the moderate Aristotelian city
Of darning and the Eight-Fifteen, where Euclid's geometry
And Newton's mechanics would account for our experience,
And the kitchen table exists because I scrub it.
It seems to have shrunk during the holidays. The streets
Are much narrower than we remembered; we had forgotten
The office was as depressing as this. To those who have seen
The Child, however dimly, however incredulously,
The Time Being is, in a sense, the most trying time of all.
For the innocent children who whispered so excitedly
Outside the locked door where they knew the presents to be
Grew up when it opened. Now, recollecting that moment
We can repress the joy, but the guilt remains conscious;
Remembering the stable where for once in our lives
Everything became a You and nothing was an It.
And craving the sensation but ignoring the cause,
We look round for something, no matter what, to inhibit
Our self-reflection, and the obvious thing for that purpose
Would be some great suffering. So, once we have met the Son,
We are tempted ever after to pray to the Father;
"Lead us into temptation and evil for our sake."
They will come, all right, don't worry; probably in a form
That we do not expect, and certainly with a force
More dreadful than we can imagine. In the meantime
There are bills to be paid, machines to keep in repair,
Irregular verbs to learn, the Time Being to redeem
From insignificance. The happy morning is over,
The night of agony still to come; the time is noon:
When the Spirit must practise his scales of rejoicing
Without even a hostile audience, and the Soul endure
A silence that is neither for nor against her faith
That God's Will will be done, that, in spite of her prayers,
God will cheat no one, not even the world of its triumph.

Stephen Spender

Stephen Spender was born near London February 28, 1909, of mixed German, Jewish and English origins; his mother was Violet Schuster, his father was Harold Spender, the well-known journalist. As a child he was especially interested in painting; at seventeen he supported himself by printing chemists' labels on his own press. At nineteen he attended University College, Oxford, but found university training alien to his temperament, and did not then complete his courses. After traveling abroad he returned to Oxford, and went down from University in 1931.

In his eighteenth year Spender himself set up and printed a paper-bound pamphlet of verse, *Nine Experiments* (1928), which is now unprocurable. Immature though much of it is, an individuality already declares itself. *Twenty Poems* (1930), printed while Spender was still an undergraduate, emphasizes his fecundity; it sounds, tentatively but distinctly, the note of passion so recognizable in the later verse. An imagination, and a fiery one, is at play in such early poems as "A Whim of Time," "Farewell in a Dream," "Winter Landscape," and "Epilogue."

Poems, published in England in 1933, reveals a complete poet. Maturity is suggested and a revolutionary fervor which caused the critics to compare Spender to Shelley. Some of the reviewers demurred at the unconcealed communism throughout, but the lyrical impulse was so great that Spender was hailed as one of the most significant voices of his day. Spender's subject matter is arresting—sometimes too arresting, for it directs too much attention on externals and leads to controversy about that which matters least in poetry. Spender himself is a little too conscious, even too belligerent, about his properties. Riding in a train, watching the world hasten away "like the quick spool of a film," he sees the grass, the cottage by the lake, the familiar symbols, "vivid but unreal."

> Real were iron lines, and, smashing the grass
> The cars in which we ride, and real our compelled time:
> Painted on enamel beneath the moving glass
> Unreal were cows, the wave-winged storks, the lime:
> These burned in a clear world from which we pass
> Like *rose* and *love* in a forgotten rhyme.

Oftener than not, Spender brings machinery over into poetry, accomplishing a fusion of modern imagery and traditional magic. He does not merely state the superficial aspects of the machine age, he assimilates and re-creates the daily symbols of his environment. As early as 1928, while a remnant of the Georgians were still invoking literary laverocks, lonely lambs, and dependable nightingales, Spender was writing, "Come let us praise the gasworks." A few years later, the same accent expressed itself in simple, transparent delight:

> More beautiful and soft than any moth
> With burring furred antennae feeling its huge path
> Through dusk, the air-liner with shut-off engines
> Glides over suburbs and the sleeves set trailing tall
> To point the wind. Gently, broadly, she falls,
> Scarcely disturbing charted currents of air.

Spender is not always as direct as this. Inclined to sentimentality he overcompensates by forcing himself to the other extreme; distrusting the appearance of his simplicities he disguises them in strained metaphors and involved images. The result is a blurring of vision and an ambiguity of communication. Too often the reader has to guess at the meaning of a line which begins clearly enough but ends in a verbal fog. There is, however, no uncertainty about Spender's emotion. The emotion is clear, warm, compelling. It is serious and straightforward, especially in such poems as "The Express," "What I Expected," reaching a powerful climax in "The Prisoners," "The Funeral" and the moving "An Elementary Classroom."

It is not Spender's choice of opinions which makes his work exciting; it is the integrity of his aim accompanied by charged and highly suggestive phrases, the thrust of his vision. The old images have gone down with the bombed buildings, as he tells us in "Not Palaces"; they are part of "beauty's filtered dusts." All our faculties must cooperate to appreciate the new values—the eye, that quickly darting, delicately wandering gazelle; the ear, which "suspends on a chord the spirit drinking timelessness"; touch, that intensifies all senses.

Vienna (1935) is Spender's least successful effort. *The Still Centre* (1939) is a return to Spender's power, an exploration of "the human conditions," personal in method, universal in implication. It was combined with new poems and republished as *Ruins and Visions* in 1942. A new note, resolute and increasingly confessional, is apparent here and in *Poems of Dedication* (1947) and *The Edge of Being* (1949). The limitations are obvious: the heavily burdened and sometimes inchoate line, the total lack of humor, the frequent failure of the baffled brain to win the approval of the badgered heart. But there is always the desperate sincerity, the intense voice of something dearly held and deeply felt. It is the voice that speaks up for "the palpable and obvious love of man," an utterance which, achieving the high level of the lines beginning "I think continually of those who were truly great," is exalted and often noble.

In addition to his poetry, Spender has been prolific in criticism, fiction, and drama. *Trial of a Judge* (1938) is a tragedy of the Nazi terror, a telescoping of the real and the incredible. *The Burning Cactus* (1936) is a volume of short stories, slightly reminiscent of D. H. Lawrence in its hurt sensibility. *The Destructive Element* (1935) is a critical appraisal of a civilization at once creative and corrupt, and a justification of his theory that "Poetry does not state truth; it states the condition within which something felt is true." An unusually candid autobiography, *World Within World* (1951), was followed by a winnowed *Collected Poems* (1955).

FAREWELL IN A DREAM

Now shout into my dream. These trumpets snored
Less golden by my side, when you were there . . .
It is no reason now to think me coward
That, being insulted by a gamekeeper,
I hung my head, or looked into the air:
Thrusting between the peaks without a word,
Buttressed against the winds, or like a sword,
Then you were undisputed conqueror.

But dragged into this nightmare symphony
Of drum and tempest surging in my head,
Faced by these symbols of reality
You showed as one most pitifully naked.
I hailed your earth. Salute my Hades too.
Since we must part, let's part as heroes do.

STATISTICS

Lady, you think too much of speeds,
   Pulleys and cranes swing in your mind;
   The Woolworth Tower has made you blind
To Egypt and the pyramids.

Too much impressed by motor-cars
   You have a false historic sense.
   But I, perplexed at God's expense
Of electricity on stars,

From Brighton pier shall weigh the seas,
   And count the sands along the shore:
   Despise all moderns, thinking more
Of Shakespeare and Praxiteles.

A WHIM OF TIME

A whim of time, the general arbiter,
Proclaims the love instead of death of friends.
Under the domed sky and athletic sun
The three stand naked, the new, bronzed German,
The young communist and myself, being English.
Yet to unwind the traveled sphere ten years
And two take arms, spring to a ghostly posture:
Or else roll on the thing a further ten
And the poor clerk with world-offended eyes
Builds with red hands his heaven; makes our bones
A necessary scaffolding to peace.

Now I suppose that the once-envious dead
Have learnt a strict philosophy of clay
After these centuries, to haunt us no longer
In the churchyard, or at the end of the lane,
Or howling at the edge of the city
Beyond the last bean-rows, near the new factory.
Our fathers enemies, yet lives no feud
Of prompting Hamlet on the kitchen stair,
There falls no shade across our blank of peace
Being together struck across the path
Or taper finger threatening solitude.

Our father's misery, the dead man's mercy,
The cynic's mystery, weaves a philosophy—
That history of man traced purely from dust
Is lipping skulls on the revolving rim
Or posture of slavery with the granite head bowed:
These, risen a moment, joined or separate,
Fall heavily, then are always separate.
A stratum scarce reckoned by geologers,
Sod lifted, turned, slapped back again with spade.

EPILOGUE

Time is a thing
That does not pass through boredom and the wishing,
But must be fought with, rushed at, over-awed,
And threatened with a sword:

For that prodigious voyager, the Mind,
Another self doth find
At each hour's stage, and riven, hewn and wrought
Cannot foretell its port.

Let heart be done, shut close the whining eyes,
And work, or drink, or sleep, till life defies
Minute, month, hour and day
Which are harrowed, and beaten, and scared away.

DISCOVERED IN MID-OCEAN

He will watch the hawk with an indifferent eye
Or pitifully;
Nor on those eagles that so feared him, now
Will strain his brow;
Weapons men use, stone, sling, and strong-thewed bow
He will not know.

This aristocrat, superb of all instinct,
With death close linked
Had paced the enormous cloud, almost had won
War on the sun;
Till now like Icarus mid-ocean-drowned,
Hands, wings, are found. . . .

WHAT I EXPECTED

What I expected was
Thunder, fighting,
Long struggles with men
And climbing.
After continual straining
I should grow strong;
Then the rocks would shake
And I should rest long.

What I had not foreseen
Was the gradual day
Weakening the will
Leaking the brightness away,
The lack of good to touch
The fading of body and soul
Like smoke before wind
Corrupt, unsubstantial.

The wearing of Time,
And the watching of cripples pass
With limbs shaped like questions
In their odd twist,
The pulverous grief
Melting the bones with pity,
The sick falling from earth—
These, I could not foresee.

For I had expected always
Some brightness to hold in trust,
Some final innocence
To save from dust;
That, hanging solid,
Would dangle through all
Like the created poem
Or the dazzling crystal.

THE PRISONERS

Far, far the least of all, in want,
Are these,
The prisoners
Turned massive with their vaults and dark with dark.

They raise no hands, which rest upon their knees,
But lean their solid eyes against the night,
Dimly they feel
Only the furniture they use in cells.

Their time is almost Death. The silted flow
Of years on years
Is marked by dawns
As faint as cracks on mud-flats of despair.

My pity moves amongst them like a breeze
On walls of stone
Fretting for summer leaves, or like a tune
On ears of stone.

Then, when I raise my hands to strike,
It is too late,
There are no chains that fall
Nor visionary liquid door
Melted with anger.

When have their lives been free from walls and dark
And airs that choke?
And where less prisoner to let my anger
Like a sun strike?

If I could follow them from room to womb
To plant some hope
Through the black silk of the big-bellied gown
There would I win.

No, no, no,
It is too late for anger,
Nothing prevails
But pity for the grief they cannot feel.

WINTER LANDSCAPE

Come home with white gulls waving across gray
Fields. Evening. A daffodil West.
Somewhere in clefts of rock the birds hide, breast to breast.

I warm with fire. Curtain shrouds dying day.
Alone. By the glowing ember
I shut out the bleak-tombed evenings of November.

And breast to breast, those swans. Sheep huddle and press
Close. Each to each. Oh,
Is there no herd of men like beasts where man may go?

Come home at last; come, end of loneliness.
Sea. Evening. Daffodil West.
And our thin dying souls against Eternity pressed.

THE FUNERAL

Death is another milestone on their way.
With laughter on their lips and with winds blowing round them
They record simply
How this one excelled all others in making driving-belts.

This is festivity, it is the time of statistics
When they record what one unit contributed:
They are glad as they lay him back in the earth
And thank him for what he gave them.

They walk home remembering the straining red flags,
And with pennons of song still fluttering through their blood
They speak of the world-state
With its towns like brain-centers and its pulsing arteries.

They think how one life hums, revolves and toils,
One cog in a golden and singing hive:
Like spark from fire, its task happily achieved,
It falls away quietly.

No more are they haunted by the individual grief
Nor the crocodile tears of European genius,
The decline of a culture
Mourned by scholars who dream of the ghosts of Greek boys.

THE EXPRESS

After the first powerful plain manifesto
The black statement of pistons, without more fuss
But gliding like a queen, she leaves the station.
Without bowing and with restrained unconcern
She passes the houses which humbly crowd outside,
The gasworks and at last the heavy page
Of death, printed by gravestones in the cemetery.
Beyond the town there lies the open country
Where, gathering speed, she acquires mystery,
The luminous self-possession of ships on ocean.
It is now she begins to sing—at first quite low
Then loud, and at last with a jazzy madness—
The song of her whistle screaming at curves,
Of deafening tunnels, brakes, innumerable bolts,

And always light, aerial, underneath
Goes the elate meter of her wheels.
Steaming through metal landscape on her lines
She plunges new eras of wild happiness
Where speed throws up strange shapes, broad curves
And parallels clean like the steel of guns.
At last, further than Edinburgh or Rome,
Beyond the crest of the world, she reaches night
Where only a low streamline brightness
Of phosphorus on the tossing hills is white.
Ah, like a comet through flames she moves entranced
Wrapt in her music no bird song, no, nor bough
Breaking with honey buds, shall ever equal.

THE LANDSCAPE NEAR AN AERODROME

More beautiful and soft than any moth
With burring furred antennae feeling its huge path
Through dusk, the air-liner with shut-off engines
Glides over suburbs and the sleeves set trailing tall
To point the wind. Gently, broadly, she falls,
Scarcely disturbing charted currents of air.

Lulled by descent, the travelers across sea
And across feminine land indulging its easy limbs
In miles of softness, now let their eyes trained by watching
Penetrate through dusk the outskirts of this town
Here where industry shows a fraying edge.
Here they may see what is being done.

Beyond the winking masthead light
And the landing-ground, they observe the outposts
Of work: chimneys like lank black fingers
Or figures frightening and mad: and squat buildings
With their strange air behind trees, like women's faces
Shattered by grief. Here where few houses
Moan with faint light behind their blinds
They remark the unhomely sense of complaint, like a dog
Shut out and shivering at the foreign moon.

In the last sweep of love, they pass over fields
Behind the aerodrome, where boys play all day
Hacking dead grass: whose cries, like wild birds,
Settle upon the nearest roofs
But soon are hid under the loud city.

Then, as they land, they hear the tolling bell
Reaching across the landscape of hysteria
To where, larger than all the charcoaled batteries
And imaged towers against that dying sky,
Religion stands, the church blocking the sun.

AN ELEMENTARY SCHOOL CLASSROOM IN A SLUM

Far far from gusty waves, these children's faces.
Like rootless weeds the torn hair round their paleness.
The tall girl with her weighed-down head. The paper-
seeming boy with rat's eyes. The stunted unlucky heir
Of twisted bones, reciting a father's gnarled disease,
His lesson from his desk. At back of the dim class
One unnoted, mild and young: his eyes live in a dream
Of squirrels' game, in tree room, other than this.

On sour cream walls, donations. Shakespeare's head
Cloudless at dawn, civilized dome riding all cities.
Belled, flowery, Tyrolese valley. Open-handed map
Awarding the world its world. And yet, for these
Children, these windows, not this world, are world,
Where all their future's painted with a fog,
A narrow street sealed in with a lead sky,
Far far from rivers, capes, and stars of words.

Surely Shakespeare is wicked, the map a bad example
With ships and sun and love tempting them to steal—
For lives that slyly turn in their cramped holes
From fog to endless night? On their slag heap, these children
Wear skins peeped through by bones, and spectacles of steel
With mended glass, like bottle bits in slag.
Tyrol is wicked; map's promising a fable:
All of their time and space are foggy slum,
So blot their maps with slums as big as doom.

Unless, governor, teacher, inspector, visitor,
This map becomes their window and these windows
That open on their lives like crouching tombs
Break, O break open, till they break the town
And show the children to the fields and all their world
Azure on their sands, to let their tongues
Run naked into books, the white and green leaves open
The history theirs whose language is the sun.

MASK

The face of the landscape is a mask
Of bone and iron lines where time
Has plowed its character.
I look and look to read a sign,
Through errors of light and eyes of water
Beneath the land's will, of a fear
And the memory of a struggle,
As man behind his mask still wears a child.

NOT PALACES

Not palaces, an era's crown
Where the mind dreams, intrigues, rests;
The architectural gold-leaved flower
From people ordered like a single mind,
I build. This only what I tell:
It is too late for rare accumulation,
For family pride, for beauty's filtered dusts;
I say, stamping the words with emphasis,
Drink from here energy and only energy,
As from the electric charge of a battery,
To will this time's change.
Eye, gazelle, delicate wanderer,
Drinker of horizon's fluid line;
Ear that suspends on a chord
The spirit drinking timelessness;
Touch, love—all senses—
Leave your gardens, your singing feasts,
Your dreams of suns circling before our sun,
Of heaven after our world.
Instead, watch images of flashing brass
That strike the outward sense, the polished will,
Flag of our purpose which the wind engraves.
No spirit seek here rest. But this: No man
Shall hunger; Man shall spend equally.
Our goal which we compel: Man shall be man.

The program of the antique Satan
Bristling with guns on the indented page,
With battleship towering from hilly waves:
For what? Drive of a running purpose,
Destroying all but its age-long exploiters.
Our program like this, yet opposite:
Death to the killers, bringing light to life.

I THINK CONTINUALLY OF THOSE

I think continually of those who were truly great.
Who, from the womb, remembered the soul's history
Through corridors of light where the hours are suns,
Endless and singing. Whose lovely ambition
Was that their lips, still touched with fire,
Should tell of the spirit clothed from head to foot in song.
And who hoarded from the spring branches
The desires falling across their bodies like blossoms.

What is precious is never to forget
The delight of the blood drawn from ageless springs
Breaking through rocks in worlds before our earth;

Never to deny its pleasure in the simple morning light,
Nor its grave evening demand for love;
Never to allow gradually the traffic to smother
With noise and fog the flowering of the spirit.

Near the snow, near the sun, in the highest fields
See how these names are fêted by the waving grass,
And by the streamers of white cloud,
And whispers of wind in the listening sky;
The names of those who in their lives fought for life,
Who wore at their hearts the fire's center.
Born of the sun they traveled a short while towards the sun,
And left the vivid air signed with their honor.

SONNET: "YOU WERE BORN; MUST DIE"

You were born; must die; were loved; must love;
Born naked; were clothed; still naked walk
Under your clothes. Under your skin you move
Naked; naked under acts and talk.
  The miles and hours upon you feed.
They eat your eyes out with their distance
They eat your heart out with devouring need
They eat your death out with lost significance.
  There is one fate beneath those ignorances
Those flesh and bone parcels in which you're split
O thing of skin and words hanging on breath:
Harlequin skeleton, it
Strums on your gut such songs and merry dances
Of love, of loneliness, of life being death.

JUDAS ISCARIOT

The eyes of twenty centuries
Pursue me along corridors to where
I am painted at their ends on many walls.
  Ever-revolving futures recognize
This red hair and red beard, where I am seated
Within the dark cave of the feast of light.
  Out of my heart-shaped shadow I stretch my hand
Across the white table into the dish
But not to dip the bread. It is as though
The cloth on each side of one dove-bright face
Spread dazzling wings on which the apostles ride
Uplifting them into the vision
Where their eyes watch themselves enthroned
  My russet hand across the dish
Plucks enviously against one feather
  —But still the rushing wings spurn me below!

    Saint Sebastian of wickedness
I stand: all eyes legitimate arrows piercing through

The darkness of my wickedness. They recognize
My halo hammered from thirty silver pieces
And the hemp rope around my neck
Soft as that spirit's hanging arms
When on my cheek he answered with the kiss
Which cuts for ever—
My strange stigmata,
All love and hate, all fire and ice!

But who betrayed whom? O you,
Whose light gaze forms the azure corridor
Through which those other pouring eyes
Arrow into me—answer! Who
Betrayed whom? Who had foreseen
All, from the first? Who read
In his mind's light from the first day
That the kingdom of heaven on earth must always
Reiterate the garden of Eden,
And each day's revolution be betrayed
Within man's heart each day?
Who wrapped
The whispering serpent round the tree
And hung between the leaves the glittering purse
And trapped the fangs with God-appointed poison?
Who knew
I must betray the truth, and made the lie
Betray its truth in me?

Those hypocrite eyes which aimed at you
Now aim at me. And yet, beyond this world
We are alone, eternal opposites,
Each turning on his pole of truth, your pole
Invisible light, and mine
Becoming what man is. We stare
Across two thousand years, and heaven, and hell,
Into each other's gaze.

THOUGHTS DURING AN AIR RAID

Of course, the entire effort is to put myself
Outside the ordinary range
Of what are called statistics. A hundred are killed
In the outer suburbs. Well, well, I carry on.
So long as the great "I" is propped upon
This girdered bed which seems more like a hearse,
In the hotel bedroom with flowering wallpaper
Which rings in wreathes above, I can ignore
The pressure of those names under my fingers
Heavy and black as I rustle the paper,
The wireless wail in the lounge margin.
Yet, supposing that a bomb should dive
Its nose right through this bed, with me upon it?

The thought is obscene. Still, there are many
To whom my death would only be a name,
One figure in a column. The essential is
That all the "I"s should remain separate
Propped up under flowers, and no one suffer
For his neighbour. Then horror is postponed
For everyone until it settles on him
And drags him to that incommunicable grief
Which is all mystery or nothing.

WINTER AND SUMMER

Within my head, aches the perpetual winter
Of this violent time, where pleasures freeze.
My inner eye anticipates for ever
Looking through naked trees and running wheels
Onto a blank transparent sky
Leading to nothing; as though, through iron aims,
It was stared back at by the filmy surface
Of a lid covering its own despair.
Thus, when the summer breaks upon my face
With the outward shock of a green wave
Crested with leaves and creamy foam of flowers,
I think the luxurious lazy meadows
Are a deceiving canvas covering
With a balmy paint of leafy billows,
The furious volleys of charioteering power
Behind the sun, racing to destroy.
   When under light lawns, heavy in their soil,
I hear the groaning of the wasted lives
Of those who revolve unreflecting wheels,
   Alas, I prove that I am right,
For if my shadowed mind affirmed the light
It would return to those green, foolish years
When to live seemed to stand knee-deep in flowers:
There, winter was an indoor accident,
Where, with head pressed against the glass, I watched
The garden, falsified by snow,
Waiting to melt, and become real again.

W. R. Rodgers

☙ W. R. Rodgers, an Ulsterman, was born in Belfast, Ireland, in 1909. During some twelve years he was an Irish country parson; subsequently he was connected with the British Broadcasting Corporation. His first book *Awake! And Other Wartime Poems,* was published in 1940, but the entire edition was destroyed in an enemy bombing raid. The book was reset and republished in 1942.

The prime quality of Rodgers's verse is its forthrightness. His is an energetic, free-speaking utterance which is honest and winning, vigorous to the point of occasional nonchalant noisiness. His liveliness is accompanied (and sometimes impeded) by a love of alliteration and assonance: "Now all our hurries that hung up on hooks," "whirling and wheeling and whorling," "juts and jets jumpily," etc. His breathless pace and hearty overemphasis recall Hopkins, especially in such lines as these from "Snow":

And soon the knock and hiss of cistern ceased as
Gradually with inklings and wrinkling strings
Of ice the thickening cold anchored the skin
And slow core of water, gluing and glossing
All leaks, niggling or great, naked or guarded.

But, in *New British Poets,* Kenneth Rexroth maintains that Rodgers's "labial, sibilant, and nasal music is a kind of counter-Hopkins. . . . The quality I associate most clearly with his work is a rugged, protestant magnanimity, courteous and polished enough superficially, but with, still underneath, a certain masculine gaucherie. The comparison that springs to mind is Andrew Marvell." In a review in *The Nation,* another poet, George Barker, concluded: "He has the gift of gab that in the long run makes Swinburne a greater poet than George Meredith; he has a green thumb for the verb with a nerve running along it; and he has simple but passionate convictions about the state of things generally." *Europa and the Bull* (1952) is, like his other work, uneven but stimulating.

Rodgers was elected to the Irish Academy of Letters in 1951.

THE RAIDER

There, wrapped in his own roars, the lone airman
Swims like a mote through the thousands of eyes
That look up at him ironing out the skies,
Frocked and fanged by fire, by nagging fingers
Of guns jagged and jogged, with shell-bursts tasselled.

Does ever the airman's eye, speeding on
To grim conclusion, alight and loiter
Curiously on the country below?
Or does his gaze easily dissolve
Upon the moving surfaces, and flow
Evenly away like rain on rivers?

Or, roaring back over our armoured rims
Does his mind take in only the bloom and boom
Of bomb beneath him, noting how neatly
It mopped up a map-point town or snouted out
This tip or else that tap-root of resistance?

Yet, pity him too, that navigator
Who now in archipelago of steel
Nears that place where, hooked upon barbed air, he'll
Halt, hang hump-backed, and look into his crater.

SING, BROTHERS, SING!

In cinemas we sought
The syrupy event,
In morning paper bought
Our cozy sentiment.

We eyed shop-windows packed
With leisure gun and rod
For the fastidious act
Of poking fun like God.

Each evening to amuse,
The radio-cage unveiled,
To speak the shocking news
The parrot never failed,

Its insulated tones
Reporting perfectly
Alarming war-zones,
The usual perfidy.

The bright and mirror voice
Reviewed the scrimmages,
Deleting heat and noise
From all its images.

Each evening it drew
A round-robin applause,
For it confirmed anew
Our own and Nature's laws.

At our back-door we failed to hear
War's dust-bin chariot drawing near.

WHITE CHRISTMAS

Punctually at Christmas the soft plush
Of sentiment snows down, enbosoms all
The sharp and pointed shapes of venom, shawls
The hills and hides the shocking holes of this
Uneven world of want and wealth, cushions
With cosy wish like cotton-wool the cool
Arm's-length interstices of caste and class,
And into obese folds subtracts from sight
All truculent acts, bleeding the world white.

Punctually that glib pair, Peace and Goodwill,
Emerges royally to take the air,
Collect the bows, assimilate the smiles,
Of waiting men. It is a genial time;

Angels, like stalactites, descend from heaven;
Bishops distribute their own weight in words,
Congratulate the poor on Christlike lack;
And the member for the constituency
Feeds the five thousand, and has plenty back.

Punctually, to-night, in old stone circles
Of set reunion, families stiffly sit
And listen: this is the night and this the happy time
When the tinned milk of human kindness is
Upheld and holed by radio-appeal:
Hushed are hurrying heels on hard roads,
And every parlour's a pink pond of light
To the cold and travelling man going by
In the dark, without a bark or a bite.

But punctually to-morrow you will see
All this silent and dissembling world
Of stilted sentiment suddenly melt
Into mush and watery welter of words
Beneath the warm and moving traffic of
Feet and actual fact. Over the stark plain
The stilted mill-chimneys once again spread
Their sackcloth and ashes, a flowing mane
Of repentance for the false day that's fled.

NEITHER HERE NOR THERE

In that land all Is and nothing's Ought;
No owners or notices, only birds;
No walls anywhere, only lean wire of words
Worming brokenly out from eaten thought;
No oats growing, only ankle-lace grass
Easing and not resenting the feet that pass;
No enormous beasts, only names of them;
No bones made, bans laid, or bones expected,
No contracts, entails, hereditaments,
Anything at all that might tie or hem.

In that land all's lackadaisical;
No lakes of coddled spawn, and no locked ponds
Of settled purpose, no netted fishes;
But only inkling streams and running fronds,
Fritillaried with dreams, weedy with wishes;
Nor arrogant talk is heard, haggling phrase,
But undertones, and hesitance, and haze;
On clear days mountains of meaning are seen
Humped high on the horizon; no one goes
To con their meaning, no one cares or knows.
In that land all's flat, indifferent; there
Is neither springing house nor hanging tent,

No aims are entertained, and nothing is meant,
For there are no ends and no trends, no roads,
Only follow your nose to anywhere.
No one is born there, no one stays or dies,
For it is a timeless land, it lies
Between the act and the attrition, it
Marks off bound from rebound, make from break, tit
From tat, also to-day from to-morrow.
No Cause there comes to term, but each departs
Elsewhere to whelp its deeds, expel its darts;
There are no homecomings, of course, no good-byes
In that land, neither yearning nor scorning,
Though at night there is the smell of morning.

Kathleen Raine

Kathleen J. Raine was born in 1909, daughter of a schoolmaster, and was educated at Girton College, Cambridge, where, later, she taught. She married the poet and professor, Charles Madge, by whom she had two children, but the marriage was dissolved.

Regarding her own work with critical detachment, Kathleen Raine did not publish a volume until she was in her mid-thirties, when *Stone and Flower* appeared in 1943. Three other books preceded her *Collected Poems* (1956), all of them disclosing a spontaneous lyric voice with a scrupulous examination of the sensibilities and the subconscious impulses which drive them. Nature and its impact on human nature are her constant preoccupation; hers is a severe seventeenth century mind confronting the confusion of the twentieth century.

"Love," she wrote in an introduction to her *Collected Poems,* "is important only in Plato's sense in so far as it gives wings to the imagination—whatever in love is personal and not imaginative matters not at all . . . The ever-recurring forms of nature mirror eternal reality; the never-recurring productions of human history reflect only fallen man."

Kathleen Raine is also the author of studies of Blake, Coleridge, and *Aspects of English Literature.* An American publication of her *Selected Poems* appeared in a limited printing in 1952.

QUESTION AND ANSWER

That which is, being the only answer
The question is its measure. Ask the flower
And the question unfolds in eloquent petals about the centre;
Ask fire, and the rose bursts into flame and terror.

Ask water, and the streams flow and dew falls;
Shell's minute spiral wisdom forms in pools.

Earth answers fields and gardens and the grave; birds rise
Into the singing air that opens boundless skies.

Womb knows the eternal union and its child,
Heart the blood-sacrifice of the wounded god.
Death charts the terrible negative infinity,
And with the sun rises perpetual day.

THE PYTHONESS

I am that serpent-haunted cave
Whose navel breeds the fates of men.
All wisdom issues from a hole in the earth:
The gods form in my darkness, and dissolve again.

From my blind womb all kingdoms come,
And from my grave seven sleepers prophesy.
No babe unborn but wakens to my dream,
No lover but at last entombed in me shall lie.

I am that feared and longed-for burning place
Where man and phoenix are consumed away,
And from my low polluted bed arise
New sons, new suns, new skies.

AIR

Element that utters doves, angels and cleft flames,
The bees of Helicon and the cloudy houses,
Impulse of music and the world's equipoise,

Dancer that never wearies of the dance
That prints in the blown dust eternal wisdom
Or carves its abstract sculpture in the snow,
The wind unhindered passes beyond its trace.

But from a high fell on a summer day
Sometimes below you may see the air like water,
The dazzle of the light upon its waves,
The flow unbroken to the end of the world.

The bird of god descends between two moments
Like silence into music, opening a way through time.

LOVE POEM

Yours is the face that the earth turns to me,
Continuous beyond its human features lie
The mountain forms that rest against the sky.
With your eyes, the reflecting rainbow, the sun's light

Sees me; forest and flowers, bird and beast
Know and hold me forever in the world's thought,
Creation's deep untroubled retrospect.

When your hand touches mine, it is the earth
That takes me—the deep grass,
And rocks and rivers; the green graves,
And children still unborn, and ancestors,
In love passed down from hand to hand from God.
Your love comes from the creation of the world,
From those paternal fingers, streaming through the clouds
That break with light the surface of the sea.

Here, where I trace your body with my hand,
Love's presence has no end;
For these, your arms that hold me, are the world's.
In us, the continents, clouds and oceans meet
Our arbitrary selves, extensive with the night,
Lost, in the heart's worship, and the body's sleep.

F. T. Prince

⁂ Frank Templeton Prince was born in 1912 at Kimberley, South Africa, and was educated in his native country and at Balliol College, Oxford. After serving as a captain in the Intelligence Corps during the Second World War he became a lecturer at the University of Southampton.

A fastidious scholar, Prince rejected most of his early *Poems* (1938) when he published *Soldiers Bathing and Other Poems* (1954), retaining only a few of the lyrics. The title-poem of his second volume elicited high praise from poets of every school; Stephen Spender considered it magnificent, and others called attention to its eloquent imagery. "Mr. Prince," wrote a reviewer in the London *Times Literary Supplement,* "has admirably extended the poetic conventions of our time to express without fear his own enthusiasm." "The Babiaantje," a poem in an entirely different key, is a colorful reflection of Prince's youthful background.

SOLDIERS BATHING

The sea at evening moves across the sand.
Under a reddening sky I watch the freedom of a band
Of soldiers who belong to me. Stripped bare
For bathing in the sea, they shout and run in the warm air;
Their flesh, worn by the trade of war, revives
And my mind towards the meaning of it strives.

All's pathos now. The body that was gross,
Rank, ravening, disgusting in the act or in repose,

All fever, filth and sweat, its bestial strength
And bestial decay, by pain and labor grows at length
Fragile and luminous. "Poor bare forked animal,"
Conscious of his desires and needs and flesh that rise and fall,
Stands in the soft air, tasting after toil
The sweetness of his nakedness: letting the sea-waves coil
Their frothy tongues about his feet, forgets
His hatred of the war, its terrible pressure that begets
A machinery of death and slavery,
Each being a slave and making slaves of others, finds that he
Remembers lovely freedom in a game,
Mocking himself, and comically mimics fear and shame.

He plays with death and animality.
And, reading in the shadows of his pallid flesh, I see
The idea of Michelangelo's cartoon
Of soldiers bathing, breaking off before they were half done
At some sortie of the enemy, an episode
Of the Pisan wars with Florence. I remember how he showed
Their muscular limbs that clamber from the water
And heads that turn across the shoulder, eager for the slaughter,
Forgetful of their bodies that are bare
And hot to buckle on and use the weapons lying there.
—And I think too of the theme another found
When, shadowing men's bodies on a sinister red ground,
Another Florentine, Pollaiuolo,
Painted a naked battle: warriors, straddled, hacked the foe,
Dug their bare toes into the soil and slew
The brother-naked man who lay between their feet and drew
His lips back from his teeth in a grimace.

They were Italians who knew war's sorrow and disgrace
And showed the thing suspended, stripped: a theme
Born out of the experience of war's horrible extreme
Beneath a sky where even the air flows
With *lachrimae Christi*. For that rage, that bitterness, those blows
That hatred of the slain, what could it be
But indirectly or directly a commentary
On the Crucifixion? And the picture burns
With indignation and pity and despair by turns,
Because it is the obverse of the scene
Where Christ hangs murdered, stripped, upon the Cross.
I mean,
That is the explanation of its rage.

And we too have our bitterness and pity that engage
Blood, spirit in this war. But night begins,
Night of the mind: who nowadays is conscious of our sins?
Though every human deed concerns our blood,
And even we must know what nobody has understood,
That some great love is over all we do,
And that is what has driven us to this fury, for so few

Can suffer all the terror of that love:
The terror of that love has set us spinning in this groove
Greased with our blood.
These dry themselves and dress,
Combing their hair, forget the fear and shame of nakedness.
Because to love is frightening, we prefer
The freedom of our crimes. Yet, as I drink the dusky air,
I feel a strange delight that fills me full,
Strange gratitude, as if evil itself were beautiful,
And kiss the wound in thought, while in the west
I watch a streak of red that might have issued from Christ's breast.

THE BABIAANTJE

Hither, where tangled thickets of the acacia
Wreathed with a golden powder, sigh
And when the boughs grow dark, the hoopoe
Doubles his bell-like cry,
Spreading his bright striped wings and brown crest
Under a softening spring sky,—
I have returned because I cannot rest,
And would not die.

Here it was as a boy that, I remember,
I wandered ceaselessly, and knew
Sweetness of spring was in the bird's cry,
And in the hidden dew
The unbelievably keen perfume
Of the Babiaantje, a pale blue
Wild hyacinth that between narrow grey leaves
On the ground grew.

The flower will be breathing there now, should I wish
To search the grass beneath those trees,
And having found it, should go down
To snuff it, on my knees.
But now, although the crested hoopoe
Calls like a bell, how barren these
Rough ways and dusty woodlands look to one
Who has lost youth's peace!

Lawrence Durrell

☙ Lawrence Durrell was born of Irish parentage, in the town of Jullundur in the Himalayas, February 27, 1912. He went to Indian schools until he was ten, at which time he was brought to St. Edmund's School in Canterbury, England. One of four children, while still young he was brought by his mother to the Mediterranean island of Corfu. In his forties he said that it tired him merely to think of all the journeys he had taken as a Foreign Service press officer, a British Council lecturer, and a private individual. "Backwards and forwards across the Balkans, round about among the islands of Greece . . . Egypt . . . Rhodes . . . Belgrade . . . the Argentine pampas."

Before he became a sensationally successful novelist, Durrell kept himself alive by being not only a journalist and a quasi-diplomat but also a lecturer, an instructor, a rent-collector, and a pianist in a nightclub. He bought himself a house in Cyprus, won the confidence of the natives by speaking Greek without a foreign accent, and taught English in the local gymnasium until the revolutionary situation elevated him to the status of a senior government official.

Energetically creative, in his late forties Durrell was the author of some twenty volumes ranging from poetry to the panoramic *Alexandria Quartet* (1957-1960), a major work of fiction; from the witty exposures of diplomatic procedure, *Esprit de Corps,* to a penetrating commentary of the crisis in Cyprus, *Bitter Lemons* (1958), an account which is both farcical and tragical; from the controversial novel, *The Black Book* (1938), with its implicit tribute to Henry Miller, to a translation of Royidis' scandalous *Pope Joan* (1961). For about twenty years, until he wrote the tetralogy which made him both famous and wealthy, Durrell had been making no more than a hundred pounds on each book and was seriously considering getting a job as a laborer or a sheepherder in the south of France, to which country he had emigrated.

Durrell's achievements in prose, feats of an ingenious but apparently effortless style, have obscured his accomplishment as a poet. Yet *Collected Poems* (1960) show many of the virtues if not the virtuosity of his prose. "Swans," "A Water-Colour of Venice," "In Arcadia," and "Visitations" are expressions of one who has been characterized as a poet who happened to stumble into prose. Most of his poems, when they are not downright mocking or bawdy, evoke not only the mood of a place but also the measure of a man, discriminating, meditative, sometimes mordant but always acutely responsive to the scene and its multiple suggestions.

Something is incomplete here,
Something in the story is unfinished,
A tale with no beginning,
The fragment of a voice that interrupts,
Like this unbroken coast,
Like this half-drawn landscape,
Like this broken torso of a poem.

Alternating simple and complex, sometimes plain and sometimes flashing with imagery, Durrell achieves continual sensuousness and, in the midst of confusion, an allusive elegance, a final serenity.

SWANS

Fraudulent perhaps in that they gave
No sense of muscle but a swollen languor
Though moved by webs: yet idly, idly

As soap-bubbles drift from a clay-pipe
They mowed the lake in tapestry,

Passing in regal exhaustion by us,
King, queen and cygnets, one by one,
Did one dare to remember other swans
In anecdotes of Gauguin or of Rabelais?
Some became bolsters for the Greeks,
Some rubber Lohengrins provided comedy.

The flapping of the wings excited Leda.
The procession is over and what is now
Alarming is more the mirror split
From end to end by the harsh clap
Of the wooden beaks, than the empty space
Which follows them about,
Stained by their whiteness when they pass.

We sit like drunkards and inhale the swans.

VISITATIONS

Left like an unknown's breath on mirrors,
The enchanters, the persuaders
Whom the seasons swallow up,
Only leave us ash in saucers,
Or to mice the last invaders
Open cupboard-doors or else
Lipstick-marks upon a cup.

Fingerprint the crook of time,
Ask him what he means by it,
Eyes and thoughts and lovely bodies,
David's singing, Daphne's wit
Like Eve's apple undigested
Rot within us bit by bit.

Experience in a humour ends,
Wrapped in its own dark metaphor,
And divining winter breaks:
Now one by one the Hungers creep
Up from the orchards of the mind
Here to trouble and confuse
Old men's after-dinner sleep.

IN ARCADIA

By divination came the Dorians,
Under a punishment composed an arch.
They invented this valley, they taught
The rock to flow with odourless water.

Fire and a brute art came among them.

Rain fell, tasting of the sky.
Trees grew, composing a grammar.
The river, the river you see was brought down
By force of prayer upon this fertile floor.

Now small skills: the fingers laid upon
The nostrils of flutes, the speech of women
Whose tutors were the birds; who singing
Now civilized their children with the kiss.

Lastly, the tripod sentenced them.

Ash closed on the surviving sons.
The brown bee memorized here, rehearsed
Migration from an inherited habit.
All travellers recorded an empty zone.

Between rocks 'O death', the survivors.
O world of bushes eaten like a moon,
Kissed by the awkward patience of the ant.
Within a concave blue and void of space.

Something died out by this river: but it seems
Less than a nightingale ago.

A WATER-COLOUR OF VENICE

Zarian was saying: Florence is youth,
And after it Ravenna, age,
Then Venice, second-childhood.

The pools of burning stone where time
And water, the old siege-masters,
Have run their saps beneath
A thousand saddle-bridges,
Puffed up by marble griffins drinking,

And all set free to float on loops
Of her canals like great intestines
Now snapped off like a berg to float,
Where now, like others, you have come alone,
To trap your sunset in a yellow glass,
And watch the silversmith at work
Chasing the famous salver of the bay . . .

Here sense dissolves, combines to print only
These bitten choirs of stone on water,
To the rumble of old cloth bells,
The cadging of confetti pigeons,
A boatman singing from his long black coffin . . .

To all that has been said before
You can add nothing, only that here,
Thick as a brushstroke sleep has laid
Its fleecy unconcern on every visage,

At the bottom of every soul a spoonful of sleep.

George Barker

George Barker was born February 26, 1913, in Loughton, Essex, attended school in Chelsea and the Regent Street Polytechnic, but had to leave at fourteen to go to work. He struggled to make a living at all sorts of work, including that of a garage mechanic, and was, at one time, so poor that he slept in parks with newspapers wrapped around him for warmth.

His first book, *Alanna Autumnal,* a novel, was published before he was twenty; *Thirty Preliminary Poems* appeared in the same year. At twenty-four he published *Calamiterror,* which, with its portmanteau Joyceian title, is a long, complex, apocalyptic poem. A year after *Lament and Triumph,* Barker achieved his first American publication with *Selected Poems* (1941). At twenty-six he taught English literature in Japan.

Barker's poetry is passionate, prolix, and often determinedly irrational. The pace is headlong, the pitch is high. Dudley Fitts, praising Barker's ingenuities ("I prefer the least controlled resonances of Mr. Barker to the sterile piddling of so many of the younger poets"), criticized his overquaint archness, his too surprising distortions, and "the violent hurling together of unpredictable images whose symbolic value seems often hopelessly private." In Barker, as in Dylan Thomas, there is great freedom of emotion matched by a freely flowing inventiveness. This emotional drive sometimes includes and sometimes ignores conventional standards of expression. Separating feeling from thinking, Barker and Thomas often lose themselves in a richly sensual but obscure rhetoric. Both poets delight in a loosely rolling language which, when they are not mastering the words, allows the words to master them. At their best, they are not only daring but distinguished. Barker's originality is not factitious; accomplishing desperate ascents he is willing to risk a plunge into absurdity. The juxtaposition of the sublime and the banal, of surging syllables and pounding energy, are apparent in *Sacred and Secular Elegies* (1943) and *Love Poems* (1947).

The heavy clusters of words, thick patches of sound used like impressionistic colors, are refined and clarified in the later work. The tone of the *Love Poems* is not only quieter but purer than anything Barker has written. Without losing its ability to communicate excitement, Barker's poetry has grown increasingly direct, tender, and deeply moving. *A Vision of Beasts and Gods* appeared in 1954.

"MY JOY, MY JOCKEY, MY GABRIEL"

(*First Cycle of Love Poems: V*)

My joy, my jockey, my Gabriel
Who bares his horns above my sleep
Is sleeping now. And I shall keep him
In valley and on pinnacle
And marvellous in my tabernacle.

My peace is where his shoulder holds
My clouds among his skies of face;
His plenty is my peace, my peace:
And like a serpent by a boulder
His shade I rest in glory coiled.

Time will divide us and the sea
Wring its sad hands all day between;
The autumn bring a change of scene.
But always and for ever he
At night will sleep and keep by me.

"O TENDER UNDER HER RIGHT BREAST"

(*Second Cycle of Love Poems: II*)

O tender under her right breast
  Sleep at the waterfall
My daughter, my daughter, and be at rest
  As I at her left shall.

At night the pigeon in the eaves
  Leaves open its bright eye;
Nor will the Seven Sisters cease
  To watch you where you lie.

The pine like a father over your bed
  Will bend down from above
To lay in duty at your head
  The candles of its love.

And in their mothering embrace,
  Sleep on the Rockies' bosom;
The Okanogan Valley shall grace
  Canada round your cradle.

The silver spoon and the one-eyed man,
  The rabbit's foot and the clover,
Be at your bed from morning till
  As now, the day is over.

"SHUT THE SEVEN SEAS AGAINST US"

(*Third Cycle of Love Poems: II*)

Shut the Seven Seas against us,
Close the five continents,
Set sepulchred the North Star
In a forsaken tense;
Lay every Sun and System
For ever away in bed,—
Nevertheless that day shall come
That resurects the dead.

When sleepless the wakes, weeping,
Mourn life on every leaf,
And the Moon covers her eye over
Rather than see our grief;
When in their dreams the liars and
The loveless regret life,—
The dove that stirs in every storm
Shall arrive bright with olive.

Step, Primavera, from your bed,
Dazzling with existence;
Put the Sun and the Moon and the Systems
  right;
Hang heaven on circumstance:
Lean from all windows like waterfalls,
Look, Love on us below:—
And so from their somnolence in sense
All things shall rise to you.

"SATAN IS ON YOUR TONGUE"

(*Secular Elegy: III*)

Satan is on your tongue, sweet singer, with
Your eye on the income and the encomium,
Angels rhapsodize for and from their faith.
And in the studios of chromium
Lucifer seduces Orpheus with a myth.

But the principle of evil is not autonomous.
Like the liberty horse with a plume at a circus
Under the whipmaster it steps proud in its circles.
When I let slip an instant the whip of the will
All hell's scot-free with fire at the nostril.

Thus if the crux and judgment never is
Left to our own to do with as we will,
But the decision, like a master key, lies
Entirely in the higher hands that holds all—
How can we be as innocent as this?

Everything that is profound loves the mask,
Said the Dionysian who never wore one.
Thus our damnation and our condemnation,
Wiser than Nietzsche, never taking a risk,
Wears the face of a necessary satisfaction.

Not, Love, when we kiss do the archangels weep
For we are naked then wherever we are
Like tigers in the night. But in our sleep
The masks go down and the beast is bare:
It is not Love but double damnation there.

Marooned on the islands of pride, lonely
And mad on the pyramids of achievement,
Disillusioned in cathedrals of doxology,
The sad man senses this continual bereavement:
God has just died, and now there is only

Us. The gold bull with its horns of finances
Over the sensual mountains goes gallivanting
In glory: all night and all day it dances
Absurd and happy because nothing is wanting.
The sad man hides his grief in his five senses.

Boy with the marvellous silver fish at thigh,
Whom two hundred million could call Little Father
Spawning all Russia in a night, go gather
Kisses and rosebuds under the German sky:
Tomorrow they'll find the mess of blood and the feather.

"O GOLDEN FLEECE"

(*Secular Elegy: VI*)

O Golden Fleece she is where she lies tonight
Trammelled in her sheets like midsummer on a bed,
Kisses like moths flitter over her bright
Mouth, and as she turns her head,
All space moves over to give her beauty room.

Where her hand, like a bird on the branches of her arm,
Droops its wings over the bedside as she sleeps,
There the air perpetually stays warm
Since, nested, her hand rested there. And she keeps
Under her green thumb life like a growing poem.

My nine-tiered tigress in the cage of sex
I feed with meat that you tear from my side
Crowning your nine months with the paradox:
The love that kisses with a homicide
In robes of red generation resurrects.

The bride who rides the hymeneal waterfall
Spawning all possibles in her pools of surplus,
Whom the train rapes going into a tunnel,
The imperial multiplicator nothing can nonplus:
My mother Nature is the origin of it all.

At Pharoah's Feast and in the family cupboard,
Gay corpse, bright skeleton, and the fly in amber,
She sits with her laws like antlers from her forehead
Enmeshing everyone, with flowers and thunder
Adorning the head that destiny never worried.

VERSES FOR A FIRST BIRTHDAY

Hang at my hand as I write now
My small one whom the dogs follow,
That, nuzzled in my stomach, dance
Like sea-lions with her innocence.

The roaring forties in the bed
Beat up disaster on her head,
And on the wall the calendar
Always enumerated War.

Thunder in the teacup and
Prognostications in the sand
Menaced her amusements with
The abracadabra of death.

She who kisses prettier than
Two breezes meeting round a fan
What shall she hold in her arms
But the catastrophes like lambs?

And when, among the temporal
Ruins of her landscape, shall
The giddygoat and Cupid chase
All but Disney from the place?

On the rag of a single summer
She dried all the tears of the future;
When the Winter made her grieve
The vernal equinox was up her sleeve

Happily the unhappy shall lie down
By her, and bounty be her own
Bubble. The hitherto inconsolable
Find solace at her first syllable.

The dove, in its code of coos,
Will carry abroad her good news:
That it was Love, and not
Law kept the ark afloat.

For the desire, and the daughter,
And the dog chasing its tail,
Renew all things in Nature,
And Nature renews it all.

Dylan Thomas

Dylan Thomas was born October 27, 1914, in Swansea, Wales, and was briefly educated at the local grammar school. A reporter for a year on the *South Wales Evening Post,* he became a reader and script-writer for radio and accepted other odd jobs and assignments. His vivid *Portrait of the Artist as a Young Dog* (1940) is largely autobiographical. At the age of twenty Thomas published his first volume, *18 Poems* (1934). Most of the poems in that volume and in *25 Poems* (1936), together with several from *The Map of Love* (1939), and eleven short stories were published in *The World I Breathe* (1939). *New Poems* appeared in 1943; *The Selected Writings of Dylan Thomas,* with an interpretive introduction by John L. Sweeney, in 1946.

At first glance Thomas's poems seem not only obscure but barbaric. The lines appear to be full of wild eldritch noises, with words, screams and shouts flung out in spectacular abandon. Upon re-reading, however, it is apparent that Thomas's poems, far from being disorganized, are curiously disciplined. The order imposed upon them does not stem from the strictures of traditional form but from a logic of emotion. The images blossom freely and profusely—there are obvious overtones of Hopkins and Hart Crane—but they are controlled by key phrases, central associations, and dominant ideas. Writing out of his own background and beliefs, Thomas plunges boldly into a new and dynamic language, a fierce vigor of speech remarkable even in a time of frantic experiment. Thomas is, as Stephen Spender wrote, "a poet obsessed with words, a linguistic genius, and with a mind filled with echoes of his Welsh Nonconformist religious upbringing and of childhood experiences which made a deep impression on him. His poems have a bardic primitive quality, and at the same time there is superimposed on this an awareness of the discoveries of modern psychology. But, above all, he impresses by his rich use of words and by his ability to write in free yet compelling meters."

Sensational and tempestuous, Thomas's poems are packed with brilliance, confusing in design but convincing in impact. They are composed of nightmare violence, sexual symbols, images of pain and the agonies of birth. Thomas identifies himself with the elemental powers of nature—"the force that through the green fuse drives the flower drives my green age; that blasts the roots of trees is my destroyer." The poet, irrepressibly spontaneous, becomes his own myth. "The more subjective a poem, the clearer the narrative line," wrote Thomas, and the remark is particularly true of his own poetry. It includes the "simple terrestrial gladness" (Peter Viereck's phrase) of "Fern Hill," that bright and joyful picture of summer on a Welsh farm, and the poignant evocation of "The Hunchback in the Park." Although profuse in imagery, "In Memory of Ann Jones" is one of Thomas's most luxuriant and yet one of his clearest poems. The gathering pictures of the burial, the feast, the home, and the spirit of the woman are logically and emotionally united. In *Auden and After* Francis Scarfe calls attention to the concentration of effects: "The typical furniture of her room, which appears early in the poem ('In a room with a stuffed fox and a stale fern') serves as a dominant tied image, reappearing brilliantly at the end to drive home the idea that her love might even bring the dead to life. . . . The poem is, in the poet's words, 'a monstrous thing blindly magnified out of praise.' "

Rhetoric is used so lavishly, allusiveness employed with such prodigality, that much of Thomas's verse seems to borrow the technique of surrealism. Actually Thomas has little kinship with the surrealists; he is desperately concerned with the frenzy of life, the struggle to be born and the agonized desire for peace, including the final peace of death. Even when the words seem to hurtle into incomprehensibility, the feeling emerges, almost explodes, from the poem. It communicates its thought darkly or jubilantly, but always powerfully, even before the full meaning of the poem is evident.

Beginning in his mid-thirties Thomas made several visits to the United States. His recitals of half-declaimed, half-chanted poetry were sensationally successful. Everywhere he went Thomas was acclaimed, adulated, and ruined. He drank too much, often having beer and brandy for breakfast. He alternately took his mission seriously and made fun of himself as well as his audiences by saying he was at work on such lectures as "A Bard's Eye View of New York by a Dollar-Mad Nightingale" and "A Typical Day in My Welsh Bog." He described himself as "old, small, dark, intelligent, and darting-doting-dotting-eyed, balding and toothlessing." He said he wanted to write only "poems of God's world by a man who doesn't believe in God"; at another time he declared: "My words are written for the love of man and the praise of God—and I'd be a damned fool if they weren't." During his third visit, he drank more recklessly than ever; his thirty-ninth birthday celebration in New York was followed by a complete collapse. Taken to the hospital, it was discovered that he was afflicted with encephalopathy, a virulent disease of the brain, and he died on November 9, 1953.

Thomas's death brought forth a spate of biographies, memoirs, tributes, and documented exposures of his excesses. Especially provocative are John Malcolm Brinnin's *Dylan Thomas in America* (1955), Caitlin Thomas's account of herself and her huband, *Leftover Life to Kill* (1957), and Henry Treece's revised *Dylan Thomas: Dog Among the Fairies* (1958).

Thomas's *Collected Poems,* appearing a year before his death, was followed by various posthumous books: *Quite Early One Morning* (1954), stories, sketches, and essays; *Under Milk Wood* (1954), a play which had been broadcast and in which he had taken part; *Adventures in the Skin Trade and Other Stories* (1955) and *A Prospect of the Sea* (1958), articles and vignettes from his notebooks. All of these are alive with Thomas's word-play, his love of alliterative sentences, Hopkins-like compound words, Joyceian fused puns, and, most of all, an exuberance which, in the best of his poetry, sometimes attains exaltation.

WHEN ALL MY FIVE AND COUNTRY SENSES SEE

When all my five and country senses see,
The fingers will forget green thumbs and mark
How, through the halfmoon's vegetable eye,
Husk of young stars and handful zodiac,
Love in the frost is pared and wintered by,
The whispering ears will watch love drummed away

Down breeze and shell to a discordant beach,
And, lashed to syllables, the lynx tongue cry
That her fond wounds are mended bitterly.
My nostrils see her breath burn like a bush.

My one and noble heart has witnesses
In all love's countries, that will grope awake;
And when blind sleep drops on the spying senses,
The heart is sensual, though five eyes break.

LIGHT BREAKS WHERE NO SUN SHINES

Light breaks where no sun shines;
Where no sea runs, the waters of the heart
Push in their tides;
And, broken ghosts with glowworms in their heads,
The things of light
File through the flesh where no flesh decks the bones.

A candle in the thighs
Warms youth and seed and burns the seeds of age;
Where no seed stirs,
The fruit of man unwrinkles in the stars,
Bright as a fig;
Where no wax is, the candle shows its hairs.

Dawn breaks behind the eyes;
From poles of skull and toe the windy blood
Slides like a sea;
Nor fenced, nor staked, the gushers of the sky
Spout to the rod
Divining in a smile the oil of tears.

Night in the sockets rounds,
Like some pitch moon, the limit of the globes;
Day lights the bone;
Where no cold is, the skinning gales unpin
The winter's robes;
The film of spring is hanging from the lids.

Light breaks on secret lots,
On tips of thought where thoughts smell in the rain;
When logics die,
The secret of the soil grows through the eye,
And blood jumps in the sun;
Above the waste allotments the dawn halts.

THE HAND THAT SIGNED THE PAPER FELLED A CITY

The hand that signed the paper felled a city;
Five sovereign fingers taxed the breath,
Doubled the globe of dead and halved a country;
These five kings did a king to death.

The mighty hand leads to a sloping shoulder,
The finger joints are cramped with chalk;
A goose's quill has put an end to murder
That put an end to talk.

The hand that signed the treaty bred a fever,
And famine grew, and locusts came;
Great is the hand that holds dominion over
Man by a scribbled name.

The five kings count the dead but do not soften
The crusted wound nor pat the brow;
A hand rules pity as a hand rules heaven;
Hands have no tears to flow.

THE FORCE THAT THROUGH THE GREEN FUSE DRIVES

The force that through the green fuse drives the flower
Drives my green age; that blasts the roots of trees
Is my destroyer.
And I am dumb to tell the crooked rose
My youth is bent by the same wintry fever.

The force that drives the water through the rocks
Drives my red blood; that dries the mouthing streams
Turns mine to wax.
And I am dumb to mouth unto my veins
How at the mountain spring the same mouth sucks.

The hand that whirls the water in the pool
Stirs the quicksand; that ropes the blowing wind
Hauls my shroud sail.
And I am dumb to tell the hanging man
How of my clay is made the hangman's lime.

The lips of time leech to the fountain head;
Love drips and gathers, but the fallen blood
Shall calm her sores.
And I am dumb to tell a weather's wind
How time has ticked a heaven round the stars.

And I am dumb to tell the lover's tomb
How at my sheet goes the same crooked worm.

THE HUNCHBACK IN THE PARK

The hunchback in the park
A solitary mister
Propped between trees and water
From the opening of the garden lock
That let the trees and water enter
Until the Sunday sombre bell at dark,

Eating bread from a newspaper
Drinking water from the chained cup
That the children filled with gravel
In the fountain basin where I sailed my ship
Slept at night in a dog kennel
But nobody chained him up.

Like the park birds he came early
Like the water he sat down
And Mister they called hey Mister
The truant boys from the town
Running when he had heard them clearly
On out of sound

Past lake and rockery
Laughing when he shook his paper
Hunchbacked in mockery
Through the loud zoo of the willow groves
Dodging the park keeper
With his stick that picked up leaves.

And the old dog sleeper
Alone between nurses and swans
While the boys among willows
Made the tiger jump out of their eyes
To roar on the rockery stones
And the groves were blue with sailors

Made all day until bell time
A woman figure without fault
Straight as a young elm
Straight and tall from his crooked bones
That she might stand in the night
After the lock and chains

All night in the unmade park
After the railings and shrubberies
The birds the grass the trees the lake
Had followed the hunchback
And the wild boys innocent as strawberries
To his kennel in the dark.

AND DEATH SHALL HAVE NO DOMINION

And death shall have no dominion.
Dead men naked they shall be one
With the man in the wind and the west
moon;
When their bones are picked clean and th
clean bones gone,
They shall have stars at elbow and foot;
Though they go mad they shall be sane,
Though they sink through the sea they shal
rise again;
Though lovers be lost love shall not;
And death shall have no dominion.

And death shall have no dominion.
Under the windings of the sea
They lying long shall not die windily;
Twisting on racks when sinews give way,
Strapped to a wheel, yet they shall not break
Faith in their hands shall snap in two,
And the unicorn evils run them through;
Split all ends up they shan't crack;
And death shall have no dominion.

And death shall have no dominion.
No more may gulls cry at their ears
Or waves break loud on the seashores;
Where blew a flower may a flower no mor
Lift its head to the blows of the rain;
Though they be mad and dead as nails,
Heads of the characters hammer through
daisies;
Break in the sun till the sun breaks down
And death shall have no dominion.

ESPECIALLY WHEN THE OCTOBER WIND

Especially when the October wind
With frosty fingers punishes my hair,
Caught by the crabbing sun I walk on fir
And cast a shadow crab upon the land,
By the sea's side, hearing the noise of birds
Hearing the raven cough in winter sticks,
My busy heart who shudders as she talks
Sheds the syllabic blood and drains her
words.
Shut, too, in a tower of words, I mark
On the horizon walking like the trees

The wordy shapes of women, and the rows
Of the star-gestured children in the park.
Some let me make you of the vowelled beeches,
Some of the oaken voices, from the roots
Of many a thorny shire tell you notes,
Some let me make you of the water's speeches.

Behind a pot of ferns the wagging clock
Tells me the hour's word, the neural meaning
Flies on the shafted disc, declaims the morning
And tells the windy weather in the cock.
Some let me make you of the meadow's signs;
The signal grass that tells me all I know
Breaks with the wormy winter through the eye.
Some let me tell you of the raven's sins.

Especially when the October wind
(Some let me make you of autumnal spells,
The spider-tongued, and the loud hill of Wales)
With fist of turnips punishes the land,
Some let me make you of the heartless words.
The heart is drained that, spelling in the scurry
Of chemic blood, warned of the coming fury.
By the sea's side hear the dark-vowelled birds.

IN MEMORY OF ANN JONES

After the funeral, mule praises, brays,
Windshake of sailshaped ears, muffle-toed tap
Tap happily of one peg in the thick
Grave's foot, blinds down the lids, the teeth in black,
The spittled eyes, the salt ponds in the sleeves,
Morning smack of the spade that wakes up sleep,
Shakes a desolate boy who slits his throat
In the dark of the coffin and shed dry leaves,
That breaks one bone to light with a judgment clout
After the feast of tear-stuffed time and thistles
In a room with a stuffed fox and a stale fern,
I stand, for this memorial's sake, alone
In the snivelling hours with dead, humped Ann
Whose hooded, fountain heart once fell in puddles
Round the parched worlds of Wales and drowned each sun
(Though this for her is a monstrous image blindly
Magnified out of praise; her death was a still drop;
She would not have me sinking in the holy
Flood of her heart's fame; she would lie dumb and deep
And need no druid of her broken body).
But I, Ann's bard on a raised hearth, call all
The seas to service that her wood-tongued virtue
Babble like a bellbuoy over the hymning heads,
Bow down the walls of the ferned and foxy woods
That her love sing and swing through a brown chapel,
Bless her bent spirit with four, crossing birds.
Her flesh was meek as milk, but this skyward statue
With the wild breast and blessed and giant skull
Is carved from her in a room with a wet window
In a fiercely mourning house in a crooked year.
I know her scrubbed and sour humble hands

Lie with religion in their cramp, her threadbare
Whisper in a damp word, her wits drilled hollow,
Her fist of a face died clenched on a round pain;
And sculptured Ann is seventy years of stone.
These cloud-sopped, marble hands, this monumental
Argument of the hewn voice, gesture and psalm
Storm me forever over her grave until
The stuffed lung of the fox twitch and cry Love
And the strutting fern lay seeds on the black sill.

FERN HILL

Now as I was young and easy under the apple boughs
About the lilting house and happy as the grass was green,
The night above the dingle starry,
Time let me hail and climb
Golden in the heydays of his eyes,
And honored among wagons I was prince of the apple towns
And once below a time I lordly had the trees and leaves
Trail with daisies and barley
Down the rivers of the windfall light.

And as I was green and carefree, famous among the barns
About the happy yard and singing as the farm was home,
In the sun that is young once only,
Time let me play and be
Golden in the mercy of his means,
And green and golden I was huntsman and herdsman, the calves
Sang to my horn, the foxes on the hills barked clear and cold,
And the sabbath rang slowly
In the pebbles of the holy streams.

All the sun long it was running, it was lovely, the hay-
Fields high as the house, the tunes from the chimneys, it was air
And playing, lovely and watery
And fire green as grass.
And nightly under the simple stars
As I rode to sleep the owls were bearing the farm away,
All the moon long I heard, blessed among stables, the nightjars
Flying with the ricks, and horses
Flashing into the dark

And then to awake, and the farm, like a wanderer white
With the dew, come back, the cock on his shoulder: it was all
Shining, it was Adam and maiden,
The sky gathered again
And the sun grew round that very day.
So it must have been after the birth of the simple light
In the first, spinning place, the spellbound horses walking warm
Out of the whinnying green stable
On to the fields of praise.

And honored among foxes and pheasants by the gay house
Under the new-made clouds and happy as the heart was long
In the sun born over and over,
I ran my heedless ways,
My wishes raced through the house-high hay
And nothing I cared, at my sky blue trades, that time allows
In all his tuneful turning so few and such morning songs
Before the children green and golden
Follow him out of grace.

Nothing I cared, in the lamb white days, that time would take me
Up to the swallow-thronged loft by the shadow of my hand,
In the moon that is always rising,
Nor that riding to sleep
I should hear him fly with the high fields
And wake to the farm forever fled from the childless land.
Oh as I was young and easy in the mercy of his means,
Time held me green and dying
Though I sang in my chains like the sea.

A REFUSAL TO MOURN THE DEATH, BY FIRE, OF A CHILD IN LONDON

Never until the mankind making
Bird beast and flower
Fathering and all humbling darkness
Tells with silence the last light breaking
And the still hour
Is come of the sea tumbling in harness

And I must enter again the round
Zion of the water bead
And the synagogue of the ear of corn
Shall I let pray the shadow of a sound
Or sow my salt seed
In the least valley of sackcloth to mourn

The majesty and burning of the child's death.
I shall not murder
The mankind of her going with a grave truth
Nor blaspheme down the stations of the breath
With any further
Elegy of innocence and youth.

Deep with the first dead lies London's daughter,
Robed in the long friends,
The grains beyond age, the dark veins of her mother,
Secret by the unmourning water
Of the riding Thames.
After the first death, there is no other.

DO NOT GO GENTLE INTO THAT GOOD NIGHT

Do not go gentle into that good night,
Old age should burn and rave at close of day;
Rage, rage against the dying of the light.

Though wise men at their end know dark is right,
Because their words had forked no lightning they
Do not go gentle into that good night.

Good men, the last wave by, crying how bright
Their frail deeds might have danced in a green bay,
Rage, rage against the dying of the light.

Wild men who caught and sang the sun in flight,
And learn, too late, they grieved it on its way,
Do not go gentle into that good night.

Grave men, near death, who see with blinding sight
Blind eyes could blaze like meteors and be gay,
Rage, rage against the dying of the light.

And you, my father, there on the sad height,
Curse, bless, me now with your fierce tears, I pray.
Do not go gentle into that good night.
Rage, rage against the dying of the light.

Norman Nicholson

⚘ Norman Nicholson was born January 8, 1914, in the small mining town of Millom, Cumberland, one of the loveliest counties in England, and his verse (to quote Kenneth Rexroth) "has the same peace, care, and mystical stillness that Wordworth sought, and sometimes found, in the same region." Son of a well-known tradesman in the town, Nicholson actively took part in the everyday life of the people. He was connected with the music festivals, the church work, the cricket club, and the youth movement; he lectured for the Workers' Educational Association. "All this is very different from the life of the literary world," he writes, "with which I have dealings only by correspondence. My home is at the mouth of the Duddon—Wordsworth's favorite river. Thus we have almost on top of one another the sea, industry, and the finest scenery in England."

Nicholson catches some of that juxtaposition in his poetry. The Wordsworthian bucolic note is there, but it is sharpened by a critical observation, hardened by an awareness of man's inhumanity to earth. Nicholson's first book of poems, *Five Rivers* (1945), owes its title to the five little rivers which flow from the western mountains of the English Lake District into the Irish Sea. The volume is almost wholly lyrical in tone, lucid and personal. But it never depends on mere fluidity and the reiterations of the stereotypes dear to the nature-lover's handbook. Nicholson's is genuine worship—"the Word shall shine on rock and beast and tree." Two other volumes of poetry, *Rock Face* (1948) and *The Pot Geranium* (1954), emphasize Nicholson's penetrating observation and vigorous imagination.

Five Rivers which won the first Royal Society of Literature Award, was preceded by *An Anthology of Religious Verse* (1942) and *Man and Literature* (1943). It was followed by *The Fire of the Lord* (1946), a novel concerned with the primitive feeling of awe and veneration for land breaking out in an urban population through a half-mad evangelist, and *The Old Man of the Mountains* (1946), a play in which the prophet Elijah is placed in modern Cumberland.

ROCKFERNS

On quarry walls the spleenwort spreads
Its green zipfasteners and black threads,
And pinches tight its unfurled purses
In every crevice with the cresses,
As if a blast of dynamite
Had spattered it upon the slate
That where the bluestone spine was broken
Spores might penetrate and quicken.
For in the fractures of the rock
Roots dig further than a pick,
As, though the sinews may not feel it,
The worm probes deeper than the bullet.
When this pen is dropped, my hand
May thrust up in a buckler frond,
And then my crushed and calcined bones
Prove better soil than arid stones.
Why need I fear the bursting bomb
Or whatsoever death shall come,
If brains and bowels be cast forth
Splintered to spleenwort on the earth?
And if a subtler part may cruise
Twice round the sun and Betelgeuse,
My soul shall detonate on high
And plant itself in cracks of sky.

THE BLACKBERRY

Between the railway and the mine,
Brambles are in fruit again.
  Their little nigger fists they clench,
  And hold the branches in a clinch.
Waggons of ore are shunted past,
And spray the berries with red dust,
  Which dulls the bright mahogany
But when the housewife, wind-and-rain,
Rubs the berry spick and span,
  Compound it gleams like a fly's eye,
  And every ball reflects the sky.
There the world's repeated like

Coupons in a ration book;
  There the tall curved chimneys spread
  Purple smoke on purple cloud.
Grant us to know that hours rushed by
Are photographed upon God's eye;
  That life and leaf are both preserved
  In gelatine of Jesus' blood.
And grant to us the sense to feel
The large condensed within the small;
  Wash clear our eyes that we may see
  The sky within the blackberry.

MICHAELMAS

Like a hound with nose to the trail
The 'bus follows the road;
The road leaps up the hill.
In the valley the railway line is carved like a groove in the wood,
The little towns smoke in the hollows;
The slagbanks are grey beneath the brown, bludgeoning fell.

This is the day the air has eyes,
And the Devil falls like hail
From the bright and thundering skies,
And soaks into soil and rock,
And the bad blood rises in nettle and dock,
And toadstools burst like boils between the toes of the trees.

The war that began in heaven still goes on.
Thorn trees twist like spears,
The owl haunts the grain,
The coursed rabbit weeps icicles of tears;
But the feathers of the clouds foretell
St. Michael's victory in the purged and praising rain.

Henry Reed

⁂ Henry Reed was born in 1914 in Birmingham, and educated there at schools and the University. Graduated M. A., he served in the Army and the Foreign Office, became a journalist and broadcaster—much of his verse was contained in plays for radio. One of these, *The Streets of Pompeii,* was awarded the Premio della Radio Italiana in 1953, and was subsequently broadcast in Canada and the United States. Besides his original writings, Reed has made notable translations from the French and Italian, in particular works by Pirandello, Betti and Montherlant.

A Map of Verona (1947) is a book in five sections, one of which, "Ishmael," consists of lyric interludes that were part of a radio version of *Moby Dick,* and which were extended into a full length work. A precisionist, Reed is equally at ease in compact lyrics and a flexible blank verse, in philosophical contemplation and styptic burlesque, as in "Chard Whitlow," a dry parody of Eliot's semi-arid, semi-sententious manner. The broad mockery of "Naming of Parts" (from a section ironically entitled "Lessons of the War") is sharply in contrast with the quiet tension of "Sailor's Harbor" and the straightforward but poignant narrative style of "The Auction Sale." Whatever the mood or subject matter, the style is distinctive, delicate but sure.

NAMING OF PARTS

Today we have naming of parts. Yesterday,
We had daily cleaning. And tomorrow morning,
We shall have what to do after firing. But today,
Today we have naming of parts. Japonica
Glistens like coral in all of the neighbouring gardens,
  And today we have naming of parts.

This is the lower sling swivel. And this
Is the upper sling swivel, whose use you will see,
When you are given your slings. And this is the piling swivel,
Which in your case you have not got. The branches
Hold in the gardens their silent, eloquent gestures,
  Which in our case we have not got.

This is the safety-catch, which is always released
With an easy flick of the thumb. And please do not let me
See anyone using his finger. You can do it quite easy
If you have any strength in your thumb. The blossoms
Are fragile and motionless, never letting anyone see
  Any of them using their finger.

And this you can see is the bolt. The purpose of this
Is to open the breech, as you see. We can slide it
Rapidly backwards and forwards; we call this
Easing the spring. And rapidly backwards and forwards
The early bees are assaulting and fumbling the flowers:
  They call it easing the Spring.

They call it easing the Spring. It is perfectly easy
If you have any strength in your thumb: like the bolt,
And the breech, and the cocking-piece, and the point of balance,
Which in our case we have not got; and the almond-blossom
Silent in all of the gardens and the bees going backwards and forwards,
  For today we have naming of parts.

SAILOR'S HARBOR

My thoughts, like sailors becalmed in Cape Town harbor,
Await your return, like a favorable wind, or like
New tackle for the voyage, without which it is useless starting.

We watch the sea daily, finish our daily tasks
By ten in the morning, and with the day to waste,
Wander through the suburbs, with quiet thoughts of the brothels,
And sometimes thoughts of the churches.

In the eating-houses we always contrive to get near to
The window, where we can keep an eye on the life-
Bearing sea. Suddenly a wind might blow, and we must not miss
First sight of the waves as they darken with promise for us.
We have been here too long. We know the quays,
And the streets near the quays, more than should ever be necessary.
When can we go on our way?

Certain we are of this, that when the wind comes,
It may be deceptive and sweet and finally blow
To shipwreck and ruin between here and the next port of call.
At all times we think of this. At last we have come to know
The marine charts can safely assure us of less and less
As we go farther south. So we cannot go out on the boulevards
Or climb Table Mountain,

Though if we had certainty, here there might be delight.
But all that is world in itself, the mountain, the streets,
The sand-dunes outside the town, we shyly and sadly return from.
They are too much to bear. And our curiosity
Lies alone in the over-scrubbed decks and the polished brasses
(For we have to look trim in the port) and in
The high-piled ambiguous cargo.

CHARD WHITLOW

(Mr. Eliot's Sunday Evening Postscript)

As we get older we do not get any younger.
Seasons return, and today I am fifty-five,
And this time last year I was fifty-four,
And this time next year I shall be sixty-two.
And I cannot say I should like (to speak for myself)
To see my time over again—if you can call it time:
Fidgeting uneasily under a draughty stair,
Or counting sleepless nights in the crowded Tube.

There are certain precautions—though none of them very reliable—
Against the blast from bombs and the flying splinter,
But not against the blast from heaven, *vento dei venti,*
The wind within a wind unable to speak for wind;
And the frigid burnings of purgatory will not be touched
By any emollient.
                    I think you will find this put,
Better than I could ever hope to express it,
In the words of Kharma: "It is, we believe,
Idle to hope that the simple stirrup-pump
Will extinguish hell."

Oh, listeners,
And you especially who have turned off the wireless,
And sit in Stoke or Basingstoke listening appreciatively to the silence,
(Which is also the silence of hell) pray not for your selves but your souls.

And pray for me also under the draughty stair.
As we get older we do not get any younger.

And pray for Kharma under the holy mountain.

THE AUCTION SALE

Within the great grey flapping tent
The damp crowd stood or stamped about;
And some came in, and some went out
To drink the moist November air;
None fainted, though a few looked spent
And eyed some empty unbought chair.
It was getting on. And all had meant
Not to go home with empty hands
But full of gain, at little cost,
Of mirror, vase, or vinaigrette.
Yet often, after certain sales,
Some looked relieved that they had lost,
Others, at having won, upset.
Two men from London sat apart,
Both from the rest and each from each,
One man in grey and one in brown.
And each ignored the other's face,
And both ignored the endless stream
Of bed and bedside cabinet,
Gazing intent upon the floor,
And they were strangers in that place.

Two other men, competing now,
Locals, whom everybody knew,
In shillings genially strove
For some small thing in ormolu.
Neither was eager; one looked down
Blankly at eighty-four, and then
Rallied again at eighty-eight,
And took it off at four pounds ten.
The loser grimly shook his fist,
But friendly, there was nothing meant.
Little gained was little missed,
And there was smiling in the tent.

The auctioneer paused to drink,
And wiped his lips and looked about,
Engaged in whispered colloquy
The clerk, who frowned and seemed to think,
And murmured: "Why not do it next?"
The auctioneer, though full of doubt,
Unacquiescent, rather vexed,
At last agreed, and at his sign
Two ministrants came softly forth
And lifted in an ashen shroud
Something extremely carefully packed,
Which might have been some sort of frame,
And was a picture-frame in fact.
They steadied it gently and with care,
And held it covered, standing there.

The auctioneer again looked round
And smiled uneasily at friends,
And said: "Well, friends, I have to say
Something I have not said to-day:
There's a reserve upon this number.
It is a picture which though unsigned
Is thought to be of the superior kind,
So I am sure you gentlemen will not mind
If I tell you at once before we start
That what I have been asked to say
Is, as I have said, to say:
There's a reserve upon this number."
There was a rustle in that place,
And some awoke as though from slumber.
Anxious disturbance fluttered there;
And as if summoned to begin,
Those who had stepped outside for air
Retrieved themselves and stepped back in.

The ministrants, two local boys,
Experienced in this sort of work,
And careful not to make too much noise,
Reached forward to unhook the shroud
Which slowly opening fell away
And on the public gaze released
The prospect of a great gold frame
That through the reluctant leaden air
Flashed a mature unsullied grace
Into the faces of the crowd.
And there was silence in that place.

Effulgent in the Paduan air,
Ardent to yield the Venus lay
Naked upon the sunwarmed earth.
Bronze and bright and crisp her hair,
By the right hand of Mars caressed,
Who sunk beside her on his knee,
His mouth towards her mouth inclined,
His left hand near her silken breast.
Flowers about them sprang and twined,
Accomplished Cupids leaped and sported,
And three, with dimpled arms enlaced
And brimming gaze of stifled mirth,
Looked wisely on at Mars's nape,
While others played with horns and pikes,
Or smaller objects of like shape.

And there was silence in the tent.
They gazed in silence; silently
The wind dropped down, no longer shook
The flapping sides and gaping holes.
And some moved back, and others went
Closer, to get a better look.

In ritual, amorous delay,
Venus deposed her sheltering hand
Where her bright belly's aureate day
Melted to dusk about her groin;
And, as from words that Mars had said
Into that hidden, subtle ear,
She turned away her shining head.

The auctioneer cleared his throat,
And said: "I am sure I'm right in feeling
You will not feel it at all unfair
For what when all is said and done
Is a work of very artistic painting
And not to be classed with common lumber
And anyway extremely rare,
You will not feel it at all unfair
If I mention again before proceeding,
There's a reserve on this number."
Someone was heard to say with meaning:
"What, did I hear him say *reserve*?"
(Meaning, of course, a different meaning.)
This was a man from Sturminster,
Renowned for a quiet sense of fun,
And there was laughter in that place,
Though, not, of course, from everyone.

A calm and gentle mile away,
Among the trees a river ran
Boated with blue and scarlet sails;
A towered auburn city stood
Beyond them on the burnished heights,
And afar off and over all
The azure day for mile on mile
Unrolled towards the Dolomites.

The auctioneer said:
"I very much fear I have to say
I'm afraid we cannot look all day.
The reserve is seven hundred pounds.
Will anyone offer me seven fifty?
Seven thirty? Twenty-five?
Thank you, sir. Seven twenty-five."
It was the man in brown who nodded,
Soon to be joined by him in grey.
The bidding started quietly.
No one from locally joined in.
Left to the men from London way,
The auctioneer took proper pride,
And knew the proper way to guide
By pause, by silence, and by tapping,
The bidding towards a proper price.
And each of the two with unmoved face
Would nod and pause and nod and wait.
And there was tension in that place.

And still within the Paduan field,
The silent summer scene stood by,
The sails, the hill-tops, and the sky,
And the bright warmth of Venus' glance
That had for centuries caught the eye
Of whosoever looked that way,
And now caught theirs, on this far day.

Two people only did not look.
They were the men so calmly nodding,
Intently staring at the floor;
Though one of them, the one in brown,
Would sometimes slowly lift his gaze
And stare up towards the canvas roof,
Whereat a few men standing near
Inquiring eyes would also raise
To try to see what he was seeing.
The bidding mounted steadily
With silent nod or murmured yes
And passed the fifteen hundred mark,
And well beyond, and far beyond,
A nodding strife without success,
Till suddenly, with one soft word,
Something unusual occurred.

The auctioneer had asked politely,
With querying look and quiet smile:

"Come then, may I saw two thousand?"
There was the customary pause,
When suddenly with one soft word,
Another voice was strangely heard
To join in, saying plainly: "Yes."
Not their voices, but a third.
Everyone turned in some surprise
To look, and see, and recognise
A young man who some time ago
Had taken a farm out Stalbridge way,
A very pleasant young man, but quiet,
Though always a friendly word to say,
Though no one in the dealing line,
But quiet and rather unsuccessful,
And often seen about the place
At outings or on market-day,
And very polite and inoffensive,
And quiet, as anyone would tell you,
But not from round here in any case.

The auctioneer, in some surprise,
Said: "Please, sir, did I hear you say
Yes to two thousand? Is that bid?
Twenty hundred am I bid?"
The two were silent, and the third,
The young man, answered plainly: "Yes.
Yes. Two thousand. Yes, I did."
Meaning that he had said that word.
"Ah, yes. Yes, thank you, sir," concurred
The auctioneer, surprised, but glad
To know that he had rightly heard,
And added: "Well, then, I may proceed.
I am bid two thousand for this picture.
Any advance upon that sum?
Any advance upon two thousand?
May I say two thousand twenty?
Twenty? Thirty? Thank you, sir.
May I say forty? Thank you, sir.
Fifty? You, sir? Thank you, sir."

And now instead of two, the three
Competed in the bargaining.
There was amazement in that place,
But still it gave, as someone said,
A sort of interest to the thing.
The young man nodded with the others,
And it was seen his nice young face,
Had lost its flush and now was white,
And those who stood quite near to him
Said (later, of course, they did not speak
While the bidding was going on)
That on his brow were beads of sweat,
Which as he nodded in acceptance
Would, one or two, fall down his cheek.

And in the tightening atmosphere
Naked upon the sunwarmed earth
Pauses were made and eyebrows raised,
Answered at last by further nods,
Ardent to yield the nods resumed
Venus upon the sunwarmed nods
Abandoned Cupids danced and nodded
His mouth towards her bid four thousand
Four thousand, any advance upon,
And still beyond four thousand fifty
Unrolled towards the nodding *sun.*
But it was seen, and very quickly,
That after four thousand twenty-five,
The man from over Stalbridge way
Did not respond, and from that point
He kept his silent gaze averted,
To show he would not speak again.
And it was seen his sweating face,
Which had been white, was glowing red,
And had a look almost of pain.

Oh hand of Venus, hand of Mars,
Oh ardent mouth, oh burnished height,
Oh blue and scarlet gentle sails,
Oh Cupids smiling in the dance,
Oh unforgotten, living glance,
Oh river, hill and flowering plain,
Oh ever-living dying light.

And had a look almost of pain.
The rest was quickly done. The bids
Advanced at slowly slackening pace
Up to four thousand sixty-five.
And at this point the man in grey
Declined his gaze upon the floor
And kept it there, as though to say
That he would bid no more that day
It was quite clear he had not won,
This man in grey, though anyone
Practised to read the human face
Might on his losing mouth descry
What could no doubt be termed a smile.
While on the face of him in brown
A like expertness might discern
Something that could be termed a frown.

There was a little faint applause.

The auctioneer sighed with joy,
The customary formalities

Were quickly over, and the strangers
Nodding a brief good-bye departed.
Venus and Mars were carefully veiled.
The auctioneer went on and proffered
Cupboard, table, chair and tray.
Bids of a modest kind were offered,
The traffic of a normal day.
A little later it was seen
The young man too had slipped away.
Which was, of course, to be expected.
Possibly there was nothing else
There at the sale to take his fancy.
Or possibly he even might
Be feeling ashamed at intervening,
Though possibly not, for after all,
He had certainly been within his right.

At all events, an hour later,
Along the Stalbridge Road a child
Saw the young man and told her mother,
Though not in fact till some days after,
That she had seen him in the dusk,
Not walking on the road at all,
But striding beneath the sodden trees;
And as she neared she saw that he
Had no covering on his head,
And did not seem to see her pass,
But went on, through the soaking grass,
Crying: that was what she said.

Bitterly, she later added.

Crying bitterly, she said.

John Manifold

☙ John Manifold was born in 1915, in Melbourne, Australia. Ranked as the first important Australian poet, Manifold modestly insists that there are at least four of his predecessors who merit the honor, but have not enjoyed much publicity overseas. "Down under," he writes, "we send soldiers and wool abroad, but keep poets and wine at home." After attending Geelong Grammar School, Manifold sailed from Australia to attend Jesus College, Cambridge. He stayed in England, working as a schoolmaster and a journalist, and went to Europe as translator for a German publisher. During the war he served in the Queen's Regiment, was commissioned into the Intelligence Corps in December, 1940, and was a captain in the Army of the Rhine. "The war," he said, "has confirmed more of my beliefs than it has destroyed. I still think that the human race is on the average rather likable, that nationality is no more important than class or occupation in making people likable or not, that authority is bad for the soul and responsibility good for it, and that once a thing has become official it's dead and damned."

Manifold's range is immediately apparent in *Selected Verse* (1946), from the macabre ballad of "The Griesly Wife" to the social consciousness of "Night Piece" and the tightness of his realistic sonnets. Manifold is both militant and lyrical; his position as poet is suggested by "A Hat in the Ring," with its satirically clinched couplets; of which the following are typical:

Verse is the chain of words in which to bind
The things we wish most often brought to mind.
Think of an ore new-fossicked, sparse, and crude,
Stamped out and minted it will buy your food,
Cajole a mistress, soften the police,
Raise a revolt or win ignoble peace,
Corrupt or strengthen, sunder or rejoin;
Words are the quartz, but poetry's the coin.

Whether narartive or lyric, his is the poetry of action. It is interesting to compare his sonnet, "The Sirens," with C. Day Lewis's "Nearing Again the Legendary Isle" on page 421.

THE GRIESLY WIFE

"Lie still, my newly married wife,
Lie easy as you can.
You're young and ill accustomed yet
To sleeping with a man."

The snow lay thick, the moon was full
And shone across the floor.
The young wife went with never a word
Barefooted to the door.

He up and followed sure and fast,
The moon shone clear and white.
But before his coat was on his back
His wife was out of sight.

He trod the trail wherever it turned
By many a mound and scree,
And still the barefoot track led on,
And an angry man was he.

He followed fast, he followed slow,
And still he called her name,
But only the dingoes[1] of the hills
Yowled back at him again.

His hair stood up along his neck,
His angry mind was gone,
For the track of the two bare feet gave out
And a four-foot track went on.

Her nightgown lay upon the snow
As it might upon the sheet,
But the track that led from where it lay
Was never of human feet.

His heart turned over in his chest,
He looked from side to side,
And he thought more of his gumwood fire
Than he did of his griesly[2] bride.

And first he started walking back
And then begun to run,
And his quarry wheeled at the end of her track
And hunted him in turn.

Oh, long the fire may burn for him
And open stand the door,
And long the bed may wait empty:
He'll not be back any more.

NIGHT PIECE

Three men came talking up the road
And still "tomorrow" was the word.

The night was clear with the lamp's glitter.
The first man spoke and his voice was bitter:

"Tomorrow like another day
I draw the dole and rust away."

The second one said scared and low,
"Tomorrow I may have to go."

And the two spoke never another word
But drew together and looked at the third.

[1] Dingoes: wild dogs.
[2] Griesly: uncanny

And the third man said, "If tomorrow exists,
It's a day of streets like rivers of fists,

"It's the end of crawling, the end of doles,
And men are treated as human souls."

I stood in the doorway and heard these things
As the three came past with the step of kings.

DEFENSIVE POSITION

Cupping her chin and lying there, the Bren[1]
Watches us make her bed the way a queen
Might watch her slaves. The eyes of a machine,
Like those of certain women, now and then

Put an unsettling influence on men,
Making them suddenly feel how they are seen:
Full of too many purposes, hung between
Impulse and impulse like a child of ten.

The careless challenge, issued so offhanded,
Seems like to go unanswered by default—
A strong position, small but not commanded
By other heights, compels direct assault.

The gunner twitches, and unreprimanded
Eases two tensions, running home the bolt.

THE SIRENS

Odysseus heard the sirens; they were singing
Music by Wolf and Weinberger and Morley
About a region where the swans go winging,
Vines are in color, girls are growing surely
Into nubility, and pylons bringing
Leisure and power to farms that live securely
Without a landlord. Still, his eyes were stinging
With salt and sea-blink, and the ropes hurt sorely.

Odysseus saw the sirens; they were charming,
Blonde, with snub breasts and little neat posteriors,
But could not take his mind off the alarming
Weather report, his mutineers in irons,
The radio failing: it was bloody serious.
In twenty minutes he forgot the sirens.

Judith Wright

Judith Wright was born in 1915 near Armidale, New South Wales, Australia. Descended from a pioneer family, she was in the countryside most of her girlhood and received her education by correspondence and from a local school before she attended Sydney University. She supported herself as a stenographer, private secretary, statistician, and agriculturist; at Tamborine, in southern Queensland, she specialized in fowls.

[1] Bren: a portable machine-gun

Her work has had a characteristic quality ever since her first book, *The Moving Image* (1946), a personal texture accentuated in *Woman to Man* (1949, reprinted in 1955) and *The Two Fires* (1955). She has been praised for "the richness and vitality of her images" and for her "marriage of passion and reason." The best of the poems in *The Two Fires* are a paradox of loveliness and terror; they are set against the menace of the bomb, the threat of destruction to a world begun in fire and seemingly doomed to die in it. They combine, moreover, a love of natural beauty with a dexterous wit. This is a poetry which is both spontaneous and controlled, often powerful and sometimes deeply moving.

Besides her creative work, Judith Wright edited *The Oxford Book of Australian Verse.*

THE TWO FIRES

Among green shades and flowering ghosts, the remembrances of love,
inventions of the holy unwearying seed,
bright falling fountains made of time, that bore
through time the holy seed that knew no time—
I tell you, ghosts in the ghosts of summer days,
you are dead as though you never had been.
For time has caught on fire, and you too burn:
leaf, stem, branch, calyx and the bright corolla
are now the insubstantial wavering fire
in which love dies: the final pyre
of the beloved, the bridegroom and the bride.
These two we have denied.

In the beginning was the fire;
Out of the death of fire, rock and the waters;
and out of water and rock, the single spark, the divine truth.
Far, far below, the millions of rock-years divide
to make a place for those who were born and died
to build the house that held the bridegroom and the bride.
Those two, who reigned in passion in the flower,
whom still the hollow seasons celebrate,
no ritual now can recreate.
Whirled separate in the man-created fire
their cycles end, with the cycle of the holy seed;
the cycle from the first to the last fire.
These too time can divide;
these too have died.

And walking here among the dying centuries—
the centuries of moss, of fern, of cycad,
of the towering tree—the centuries of the flower—
I pause where water falls from the face of the rock.

My father rock, do you forget the kingdom of the fire?
The aeons grind you into bread—
into the soil that feeds the living and transforms the dead;

and have we eaten in the heart of the yellow wheat
the sullen unforgetting seed of fire?

And now, set free by the climate of man's hate,
that seed sets time ablaze.
The leaves of fallen years, the forest of living days,
have caught like matchwood. Look, the whole world burns.
The ancient kingdom of the fire returns.
And the world, that flower that housed the bridegroom and the bride,
burns on the breast of night.
The world's denied.

AT COOLOOLAH

The blue crane fishing in Cooloolah's twilight
has fished there longer than our centuries.
He is the certain heir of lake and evening,
and he will wear their colour till he dies,

but I'm a stranger, come of a conquering people.
I cannot share his calm, who watch his lake,
being unloved by all my eyes delight in,
and made uneasy, for an old murder's sake.

Those dark-skinned people who once named Cooloolah
knew that no land is lost or won by wars,
for earth is spirit: the invader's feet will tangle
in nets there and his blood be thinned by fears.

Riding at noon and ninety years ago,
my grandfather was beckoned by a ghost—
a black accoutred warrior armed for fighting,
who sank into bare plain, as now into time past.

White shores of sand, plumed reed and paperbark,
clear heavenly levels frequented by crane and swan—
I know that we are justified only by love,
but oppressed by arrogant guilt, have room for none.

And walking on clean sand among the prints
of bird and animal, I am challenged by a driftwood spear
thrust from the water; and, like my grandfather,
must quiet a heart accused by its own fear.

. . . AND MR. FERRITT

But now Mr Ferritt
with his troublesome nose,
with his shaven chin
and his voice like a grief
that grates in dark corners,
moves in his house
and scrapes his dry skin
and sees it is morning.

O day, you sly thief,
now what have you taken
of all the small things

I tie on my life?
The radio serial
whines in the kitchen,
caught in a box,
and cannot get out.
The finch in his cage,
the border of phlox
as straight as a string
drawn up in my garden,
the potted geranium,
all are there.
But day from his cranium
twitches one hair;
and never again
will a hair grow there.
—O day, you sly thief,
how you pluck at my life,
frets Mr Ferritt;
but there, he must bear it.

Outside the fence
the wattle-tree grows.
It tosses; it shines;
it speaks its one word.
Beware, beware!
Mr Ferritt has heard.
—What are axes for?
What are fences for?
Who planted that wattle-tree
right at my door?
God only knows.
All over the garden
its dust is shaken.
No wonder I sneeze
as soon as I waken.

O world, you sly thief;
my youth you have taken,
and what have you given
who promised me heaven,
but a nagging wife
and a chronic catarrh,
and a blonde on the pictures
as far as a star?
And wild and gold
as a film-star's hair
that tree stands there,
blocking the view
from my twenty-perch block.
What are axes for,
what are fences for
but to keep this tree
away from my door?

And down came the tree.
But poor Mr Ferritt
still has hay-fever.
Nothing will cure it.

Alun Lewis

Alun Lewis was born July 1, 1915, in Wales, and taught in a Welsh secondary school. In 1942, during the Second World War, he was sent to India. Two years later, he was killed in Lower Burma, March 15, 1944.

Raiders' Dawn (1942), Lewis's first book of poems, appeared in the same year as a collection of his short stories, *The Last Inspection*. His second book of poetry, *Ha! Ha! Among the Trumpets* (1945) was published shortly after his death with the title he had chosen, "a sardonic title," he said "from *Job* 39." It carried an appreciative foreword by Robert Graves which quoted some of Lewis's characteristic correspondence. A posthumous book of letters and hitherto unpublished stories, *In the Green Tree* (1949), is a tragic commentary on his life and early death.

Lewis's poetry is often marred by a compulsion to register immediate impressions without sufficient consideration or imagination. But it is not without dignity and the power of simple but penetrating statements.

THE UNKNOWN SOLDIER

Everything has lasted till today.
He stares upon it like a velvet king.
Velasquez might have made this flaccid mask,
The silence round the languid mouth,
The weak and glassy eyes, the crumpled brow.
All things are out-distanced now.

All days are heaped in wrath upon today.
The senses sleep except one crazy spark
That leaps the lesion slashed between his eyes
And cries—not for a fertile century,
Nor for the secular ransom of the soul—
But for a sip of water from my flask.
What is the soul to him?
He has outlasted everything.

Joy's deceitful liturgy has ceased.
Tomorrow and tomorrow have no place
Among the seas of rain, the seas of peace
That are the elements of this poor face.
The mean humiliating self no more
Has access to him, nor the friends
Whose sensual persuasions first began
The brittle scattering that this day ends.
On pander, lord and jester slams the door.
An impotent in his kingdom the grey king
No longer clings to that which dies.

He has abandoned everything.
Velasquez, close those doglike dolorous eyes.

TO A COMRADE IN ARMS

Red fool, my laughing comrade,
Hiding your woman's love
And your man's madness,
Patrolling farther than nowhere
To gain what is nearer than here,
Your face will grow grey as Christ's garments
With the dust of ditches and trenches,
So endlessly faring.

Red fool, my laughing comrade,
Hiding your mystic symbols
Of bread broken for eating
And palm-leaves strewn for welcome,
What foe will you make your peace with
This summer that is more cruel
Than the ancient God of the Hebrews?

When bees swarm in your nostrils
And honey drips from the sockets
Of eyes that to-day are frantic
With love that is frustrate,

What vow shall we vow who love you
For the self you did not value?

Alex Comfort

⥈ Alex Comfort was born in London February 10, 1920, and was educated at Highgate School and Trinity College, Cambridge. His first volume, *A Wreath for the Living* (1942), appeared when he was twenty-two; five more books were published while he was still in his mid-twenties. Nevertheless, Comfort considers his literary output secondary to his real career, which is that of a practicing physician, a researcher, and lecturer in physiology at London Hospital.

A collection of poems, *The Song of Lazarus* (1945) was published in the same year as *The Power House,* a challenging novel of great strength, to which was added another novel, *On This Side Nothing* (1949), and three plays. Comfort's poetry is part of "the new romanticism," a movement which runs counter to the consciously intellectual manner cultivated by Eliot, extended by Auden, and incorporated by their imitators. Rebelling against the canons of the cerebralists, Comfort evolves his own personal philosophy. It centers, as Kenneth Rexroth has written, about "the personality at war with death—physical death, or the mechanization of the State, and all the other institutions of irresponsibility and spiritual sloth." The resulting work is a largeness of conception and a lyric poetry which richly express its author's pacifism and his sensuous enjoyment of life.

FEAR OF THE EARTH

In these cold evenings, when the rain
streams, and the leaves stand closer shuffling feet
the woods grow perilous. They are hungry, the trees,
eavesdropping, sending long shoots to tap the pane.

I can hear you, root, under my hearthstone moving;
white finger, longer since yesterday, nearer
the marrow. In these evenings
the earth leans closer: stones quietly jostle.

I can hear you, under my foot bending
your strange finger. I have heard
cold fruits of my flesh plotted, soft globes swaying—
have known of my skin a leaf foreshadowed.

The captive roses jostle under the hedge.
The celandine is innocent. Underneath
her finger fumbles eyeholes. Every petal
speaks man not hardy nor perennial.

The trees grow perilous. The patient dandelion
should not remain at large in our terrible garden.

EPITAPH

One whom I knew, a student and a poet,
makes his way shorewards tonight out of the sea
blown to a houseless coast near Bettystown
where along sleeping miles the sea is laying
printless meadows of sand, and beyond them to seaward
endless untrodden fields louder than corn. These nets
follow the long beaches. Tonight a guest
noses his way to shore. They wait for him
where the sand meets the grass—and one unmarried holds
her spine's long intricate necklace for his shoulders
pillows his broken face, his for another's
for she died waiting. He will learn much
of roots and the way of sand and the small stones,
and that the shoreward dead are friends to all
at whose heels yell the clock-faced citizens.
So like a ship the dead man comes to shore.

NOTES FOR MY SON

(*From "The Song of Lazarus": VI*)

Remember when you hear them beginning to say Freedom
Look carefully—see who it is that they want you to butcher.

Remember, when you say that the old trick would not have
fooled you for a moment,
That every time it is the trick which seems new.

Remember that you will have to put in irons
Your better nature, if it will desert to them.

Remember, remember their faces—watch them carefully:
For every step you take is on somebody's body

And every cherry you plant for them is a gibbet,
And every furrow you turn for them is a grave.

Remember, the smell of burning will not sicken you
If they persuade you that it will thaw the world

Beware. The blood of a child does not smell so bitter
If you have shed it with a high moral purpose.

So that because the woodcutter disobeyed
they will not burn her today or any day

So that for lack of a joiner's obedience
The crucifixion will not now take place

So that when they come to sell you their bloody corruption
You will gather the spit of your chest
And plant it in their faces.

SONG FOR THE HEROES

I wonder sometimes if the soldiers lying
Under the soil, wrapped in their coats like beggars
sleeping under an arch, their hands filled with leaves
could take vengeance for once on the men who sent them,
coming back like beggars, seeing the homes and fields
that their obedience lost to them, the men of all countries

whether they would have anything to say
as ghosts at frosty windows to sons or brothers
other than this—"Obedience is death."
If you are willing to die, then choose obedience.

"We who are here now, men of all nations,
our hands are full of twigs, stones on our eyes,
half-afraid of what we have done (but that is forgotten

a short wild dream, when we were other men
not ourselves—but now we are ourselves again
tradesmen, farmers, students—it is we who are telling you)

you must choose carefully, for your life, and not only your life
will depend on it, in years or days, between believing
like us, that by obedience you could help or profit

the land, the fields, the people; and saying "Death is obedience."

"Because we know now that every cause is just
and time does not discriminate between the aggressor
and the dead child, the Regrettable Necessity

And the foul atrocity—the grass is objective
And turns all citizens into green mounds—
we have had time, as soldiers always have time,

resting before Plataea or Dunkirk or Albuhera
to think about obedience—though we will still spring up
at the whistle; it is too late to withdraw—that someone must pay
for all this, and it will be the people.

"We have nothing to tell you but this: to choose carefully
and if you must still obey, we are ready,
your fathers, grandfathers, great-grandfathers, to find you

a place at our dry table, to greet you as soldiers
with a dry nod, and sit, elbow to elbow
silently for always under the sky of soil:

but know you are choosing. When they begin to appeal
to your better nature, your righteous indignation,
your pity for men like yourselves, stand still,

look down and see the lice upon your hide.

"It may be that you, or else your children, at last
will put down your hand and crush them. But if not
remember that we are waiting, good men as you,

not fools, but men who knew the price of obeying,
the lice for what they were, the Cause for a fraud,
hoped for no good and cherished no illusions;

and we will see your mounds spring up in clusters
beside our own, and welcome you with a nod,
crucified like us all, all fellow-ghosts together,
not fooled by the swine, but going with open eyes.

"You have only to speak once—they will melt like smoke,
you have only to meet their eyes—they will go
howling like devils into bottomless death

but if you choose to obey, we shall not blame you
for every lesson is new. We will make room for you
in this cold hall, where every cause is just.

Perhaps you will go with us to frosty windows
putting the same choice as the years go round
eavesdropping when the Gadarenes call our children

or sit debating—when will they disobey?

wrapped in our coats against the impartial cold."
All this I think the buried men would say
clutching their white ribs and their rusted helmets

nationless bones, under the still ground.

Sidney Keyes

Sidney Keyes was born May 27, 1922, in Dartford, Kent. His mother died of peritonitis a few weeks after her son was born, and his father, who had been in war service in India, entrusted the boy to his grandparents. His grandfather, a farmer who had become a famous miller, dominated the child who was sickly and so Keyes did not attend school until he was nine. At sixteen he began to write poems that were unusually perceptive. He was drawn to such visionaries as

Blake, Yeats, Hölderlin, and Rilke, but he was also attracted to the macabre suggestions of Donne, Webster, Beddoes, Rouault, and Klee.

At nineteen he prepared a volume of poems and gave it a title, *The Iron Laurel,* but as the manuscript was about to go to press, Keyes persuaded the publisher to postpone issuing the book. A few months later he entered the Army. He was in Africa less than two weeks when, during the Tunisian campaign he was sent forward with a dawn patrol. He was taken prisoner and died, according to the report, "of unknown causes" on April 29, 1943.

Like Charles Hamilton Sorley, another poet-victim of war who also died before he was twenty-one, Keyes had no use for the glib patriotics of wartime propaganda. "How can we account for the fact that a whole nation has gone stark mad with love of death?" he said in a letter. "The contemporary German attitude to death appears to be one of hopeless infatuation, mixed with fear and repulsion . . . Perhaps their task is to explore death, just as it has been that of the Jews to explore pain, and of the French (perhaps) to explore the possibilities of pleasure, whether of the intellect or the senses . . . It remains for someone to make an art of love, a much harder task."

It is the exploration of love which directs Keyes's lyrical impulses. Such poems as "Neutrality," "William Yeats in Limbo," and "The Gardener" are both intellectual and emotional. They share, as Harold Nicolson wrote, "with others of his age a dark resentment at the denial of opportunity; but with him resentment is no mere mood of irritation; it has about it a solemn tone of fate. It is not, therefore, his amazing poetic skill only which differentiates Sidney Keyes from so many of his contemporaries, but above all his grave acceptance of the tragedy to which his youth was destined."

NEUTRALITY

Here not the flags, the rhythmic
Feet of returning legions; nor at household shrines
The small tears' offering, the postcards
Treasured for years, nor the names cut in brass.
Here not the lowered voices.
Not the drum.

Only at suppertime, rain slanting
Among our orchards, printing its coded
But peaceful messages across our pavements.
Only the cryptic swift performing
His ordered evolutions through our sky.
Only the growing.

And in the night, the secret voices
Of summer, the progression
Of hours without suspense, without surprise.
Only the moon beholds us, even the hunting owl
May watch us without malice.
Without envy.

We are no cowards, we are pictures
Of ordinary people, as you once were.
Blame not nor pity us; we are the people
Who laugh in dreams before the ramping boar
Appears, before the loved one's death.
We are your hope.

THE GARDENER

If you will come on such a day
As this, between the pink and yellow lines
Of parrot-tulips, I will be your lover.
My boots flash as they beat the silly gravel.
O come, this is your day.

Were you to lay your hand like a veined leaf
Upon my square-cut hand, I would caress
The shape of it, and that would be enough.
I note the greenfly working on the rose.
Time slips between my fingers like a leaf.

Do you resemble the silent pale-eyed angels
That follow children? Is your face a flower?
The lovers and the beggars leave the park—
And still you will not come. The gates are closing.

O it is terrible to dream of angels.

GREENWICH OBSERVATORY

This onion-dome holds all intricacies
Of intellect and star-struck wisdom; so
Like Coleridge's head with multitudinous
Passages riddled, full of strange instruments
Unbalanced by a touch, this organism
From wires and dials spins introverted life.
It never looks, squat on its concrete shoulders,
Down at the river's swarming life, nor sees
Cranes' groping insect-like activity
Nor slow procession of funnels past the docks.
Turning its inner wheels, absorbed in problems
Of space and time, it never hears
Birds singing in the park or children's laughter
Alive, but in another way, it broods
On this its Highgate, hypnotized
In lunar reverie and calculation.
Yet night awakes it; blind lids open
Leaden to look upon the moon:
A single goggling telescopic eye
Enfolds the spheric wonder of the sky.

WILLIAM YEATS IN LIMBO

Where folds the central lotus
Flesh and soul could never seek?
Under what black-scar'd mountain
May Pallas with Adonis meet?

Spirit-bodies' loveliness
Cannot expiate my pain:
How should I learn wisdom
Being old and profane?

My thoughts have swarmed like bees
In an old ruined tower:
How should I go to drive them out
Lacking joy and power?

How could I learn youth again,
With figured symbols weaving
Truth so easily, now I
Am old and unbelieving?

By what chicanery of time
May sword and sheath be separated?
Silent be the singer who thinks of me
And how I was defeated.

EARLY SPRING

Now that the young buds are tipped with a falling sun—
Each twig a candle, a martyr, St. Julian's branched stag—
And the shadows are walking the cobbled square like soldiers
With their long legs creaking and their pointed hands
Reaching the railings and fingering the stones
Of what expended, unprojected graves:
The soil's a flirt, the lion Time is tamed,
And pain like a cat will come home to share your room.

Philip Larkin

⁂ Philip Larkin was born August 9, 1922, in Coventry, Warwickshire. He was educated at King Henry School in Coventry and St. John's College, Oxford. After leaving Oxford he presided over a small independent public library in Shropshire for nearly three years, then went as librarian to the University of Leicester, then to the Queen's University of Belfast, and then to the University of Hull. When asked why he chose to be a librarian, he replied, "A librarian is what you are when you have failed to do all the things you do want to do and have succeeded in avoiding all the things you don't want to do."

Before he was convinced that he was meant to be a poet he was sure that he was a novelist. Two novels, *Jill* (1946) and *A Girl in Winter* (1947), promised more than his first book of poems, *The North Ship* (1945). *A Girl in Winter* is an extraordinary evocation of sensibility and atmosphere, of unhappiness and tenderness, embodied in a language that is both plain and poetic. The combination of plainness and poetic subtlety marks the poetry in *The Less Deceived* (1955). Colloquial and, at first glance, commonplace, Larkin's verse is completely convincing; it is, wrote Walter Allen, "unemphatic, as unrhetorical as it is possible for poetry to be and yet remain poetry . . . It is unillusioned, skeptical, resolutely determined to claim nothing for itself that it has not experienced at its own nerve-ends."

Using the most unpretentions means, Larkin somehow distills the essence of the ordinary scene and the trivial moment while, at the same time, he suggests the importance of the inconsequential. He has the gift, rare in his times, of clarity, and a way of making things and events appear both "irrelevant and beautiful." The tone is casual and the touch is deceptively light, but the import is serious, immediate, and effectively communicated.

COMING

On longer evenings,
Light, chill and yellow,
Bathes the serene
Foreheads of houses.
A thrush sings,
Laurel-surrounded
In the deep bare garden,
Its fresh-peeled voice
Astonishing the brickwork.
It will be spring soon,
It will be spring soon—
And I, whose childhood
Is a forgotten boredom,
Feel like a child
Who comes on a scene
Of adult reconciling,
And can understand nothing
But the unusual laughter,
And starts to be happy.

NEXT, PLEASE

Always too eager for the future, we
Pick up bad habits of expectancy.
Something is always approaching; every day
Till then we say,

Watching from a bluff the tiny, clear,
Sparkling armada of promises draw near.
How slow they are! And how much time they waste,
Refusing to make haste!

Yet still they leave us holding wretched stalks
Of disappointment, for, though nothing balks
Each big approach, leaning with brasswork prinked,
Each rope distinct,

Flagged, and the figurehead with golden tits
Arching our way, it never anchors; it's
No sooner present than it turns to past.
Right to the last

We think each one will heave to and unload
All good into our lives, all we are owed
For waiting so devoutly and so long.
But we are wrong:

Only one ship is seeking us, a black-
Sailed unfamiliar, towing at her back
A huge and birdless silence. In her wake
No waters breed or break.

NO ROAD

Since we agreed to let the road between us
Fall to disuse,
And bricked our gates up, planted trees to screen us,
And turned all time's eroding agents loose,
Silence, and space, and strangers—our neglect
Has not had much effect.

Leaves drift unswept, perhaps; grass creeps unmown;
No other change.
So clear it stands, so little overgrown,
Walking that way tonight would not seem strange,
And still would be allowed. A little longer,
And time will be the stronger,

Drafting a world where no such road will run
From you to me;
To watch that world come up like a cold sun,
Rewarding others, is my liberty.
Not to prevent it is my will's fulfilment.
Willing it, my ailment.

SPRING

Green-shadowed people sit, or walk in rings,
Their children finger the awakened grass,
Calmly a cloud stands, calmly a bird sings,
And, flashing like a dangled looking-glass,
Sun lights the balls that bounce, the dogs that bark,
The branch-arrested mist of leaf, and me,
Threading my pursed-up way across the park,
An indigestible sterility.

Spring, of all seasons most gratuitous,
Is fold of untaught flower, is race of water,
Is earth's most multiple, excited daughter;

And those she has least use for see her best,
Their paths grown craven and circuitous,
Their visions mountain-clear, their needs immodest.

ARRIVALS, DEPARTURES

This town has docks where channel boats come sidling;
Tame water lanes, tall sheds, the traveller sees
(His bag of samples knocking at his knees),
And hears, still under slackened engines gliding,
His advent blurted to the morning shore.

And we, barely recalled from sleep there, sense
Arrivals lowing in a doleful distance—
Horny dilemmas at the gate once more.
Come and choose wrong, they cry, *come and choose wrong;*
And so we rise. At night again they sound,

Calling the traveller now, the outward bound:
O not for long, they cry, *O not for long—*

And we are nudged from comfort, never knowing
How safely we may disregard their blowing,
Or if, this night, happiness too is going.

CHURCH GOING

Once I am sure there's nothing going on
I step inside, letting the door thud shut.
Another church: matting, seats, and stone,
And little books; sprawlings of flowers, cut
For Sunday, brownish now; some brass and stuff
Up at the holy end; the small neat organ;
And a tense, musty, unignorable silence,
Brewed God knows how long. Hatless, I take off
My cycle-clips in awkward reverence,

Move forward, run my hand around the font.
From where I stand, the roof looks almost new—
Cleaned, or restored? Someone would know: I don't.
Mounting the lectern, I peruse a few
Hectoring large-scale verses, and pronounce
'Here endeth' much more loudly than I'd meant.
The echoes snigger briefly. Back at the door
I sign the book, donate an Irish sixpence,
Reflect the place was not worth stopping for.

Yet stop I did: in fact I often do,
And always end much at a loss like this,
Wondering what to look for; wondering, too,
When churches fall completely out of use
What we shall turn them into, if we shall keep
A few cathedrals chronically on show,
Their parchment, plate and pyx in locked cases,
And let the rest rent-free to rain and sheep.
Shall we avoid them as unlucky places?

Or, after dark, will dubious women come
To make their children touch a particular stone;
Pick simples for a cancer; or on some
Advised night see walking a dead one?
Power of some sort or other will go on
In games, in riddles, seemingly at random;
But superstition, like belief, must die,
And what remains when disbelief has gone?
Grass, weedy pavement, brambles, buttress, sky,

A shape less recognisable each week,
A purpose more obscure. I wonder who
Will be the last, the very last, to seek
This place for what it was; one of the crew
That tap and jot and know what rood-lofts were?

Some ruin-bibber, randy for antique,
Or Christmas-addict, counting on a whiff
Of gown-and-bands and organ-pipes and myrrh?
Or will he be my representative,

Bored, uninformed, knowing the ghostly silt
Dispersed, yet tending to this cross of ground
Through suburb scrub because it held unspilt
So long and equably what since is found
Only in separation—marriage, and birth,
And death, and thoughts of these—for whom was built
This special shell? For, though I've no idea
What this accoutred frowsty barn is worth,
It pleases me to stand in silence here;

A serious house on serious earth it is,
In whose blent air all our compulsions meet,
Are recognised, and robed as destinies.
And that much never can be obsolete,
Since someone will forever be surprising
A hunger in himself to be more serious,
And gravitating with it to this ground,
Which, he once heard, was proper to grow wise in,
If only that so many dead lie round.

Charles Tomlinson

Charles Tomlinson was born in 1927 in Staffordshire and attended Queen's College, Cambridge. After living in London and Northern Italy, he came to Somerset and taught at Bristol University. His first volume, *The Necklace,* was published in 1955, his second, *Seeing Is Believing,* in 1958.

Concerning his aims Tomlinson wrote: "The hardness of crystals, the facets of cut glass, but also the shifting of light, the energizing weather which is a result of the combination of sun and frost—these are the images for a certain mental climate, components for the moral landscape of my poetry in general." Such a description pronounces the limitations of Tomlinson's poetry which tends to be more visual than emotional or "moral." Praised by Richard Wilbur for its "kinetic imagination" as "the freshest, most exhilarating book of poems to come out of England in years," *Seeing Is Believing* owes something to Wilbur and more to another American poet, Wallace Stevens.

Tomlinson's world is a special one, one in which he seems to be a spectator rather than a participator. The craftsmanship is dazzling; the designs are clean, smooth, and highly polished; the results are cool, elegant, and eclectic. There is, however, an intellectual searching beneath the surface texture, and if the phrasing sometimes tends to be precious, it is never without the air of distinction and the charm of surprise.

THE CRANE

That insect, without antennae, over its
Cotton-spool lip, letting
An almost invisible tenuity
Of steel cable, drop
Some seventy feet, with the
Grappling hook hidden also
Behind a dense foreground
Among which it is fumbling, and
Over which, mantis-like
It is begging or threatening, gracile
From a clear sky—that paternal
Constructive insect, without antennae,
Would seem to assure us that
"The future is safe, because
It is in my hands." And we do not
Doubt this veracity, we can only
Fear it—as many of us
As pause here to remark
Such silent solicitude
For lifting intangible weights
Into real walls.

THE JAM TRAP

Wings filmed, the threads of knowledge thicken
Corded with mire. Bodies immerse
Slackly in sweetness. Sweetness is not satisfaction
Nor was the elation of the pursuit
The measure of its end. Aromas and inclinations
Delectable essences, and now
The inextricable gesture, sounds
Which communicate nothing, their sole speech
A scurrying murmur, each to himself his own
Monotone burden of discouragement. Preferring
The fed flock that, scattered, re-forms
Massed into echelon above copious fields,
The sky, their chosen element, has abandoned them.

IN DEFENSE OF METAPHYSICS

Place is the focus. What is the language
Of stones? I do not mean
As emblems of patience, philosophers' hopes
Or as the astrological tangents
One may assemble, draw out subjectively
From a lapidary inertia. Only we
Are inert. Stones act, like pictures, by remaining
Always the same, unmoving, waiting on presence
Unpredictable in absence, inhuman
In a human dependence, a physical
Point of contact, for a movement not physical
And on a track of force, the milestone
Between two infinities. Stones are like deaths.
They uncover limits.

Index of Authors and Titles

The names of authors and the page references to the sections devoted to their work are shown in italics. Titles of poems are shown in roman.

B 2
C 3
D 4
E 5
F 6
G 7
H 8
I 9
J 0
K 1